PAUL GUINNESS &
GARRETT NAGLE

REVISED EDITION

ADVANCED GEOGRAPHY
Concepts & Cases

Hodder Murray

A MEMBER OF THE HODDER HEADLINE GROUP

The authors would like to thank the Geography staff and pupils at King's College School, Wimbledon, and St. Edward's School, Oxford, for their comments on early drafts of the book; the librarians of the School of Geography, University of Oxford, for their help and support; Rory Reilly for assistance with the Great Langdale case study; Lucia Winn for help with research for the São Paulo case study; Sue Nicholas for her work on picture research.

On a personal note the authors would also like to acknowledge their appreciation of Mary, Courtenay and Christopher and Angela, Rosie, Patrick and Bethany, to whom the book is dedicated.

Orders: please contact Bookpoint Ltd, 130 Milton Park, Abingdon, Oxon OX14 4SB. Telephone: (44) 01235 827720, Fax: (44) 01235 400454. Lines are open from 9.00–6.00, Monday to Saturday, with a 24 hour message answering service. You can also order through our website www.hoddereducation.co.uk

British Library Cataloguing in Publication Data
A catalogue record for this is available from The British Library
A catalogue r

ISBN-10: 0 340 85826 5
ISBN-13: 978 0 340 85826 4

First published 1999
Impression number   10 9 8 7 6 5 4 3
Year   2006 2005

Typeset, design and production by Hart McLeod, Cambridge

Printed in Italy for Hodder Murray, an imprint of Hodder Education, a member of the Hodder Headline Group, 338 Euston Road, London NW1 3BH.

contents

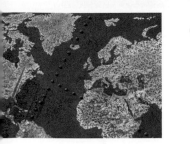

1 population *dynamics*

The numbers, densities and characteristics of human populations provide, at the very least, the background to the study of all other aspects of human geography. But in itself, population geography is a major dimension of the subject because of its spatial, socio-economic and political implications both within and between countries.

In 1998 it was estimated that the population of the world was increasing at a rate of 78.7 million a year, (Figure 1.1a). It had taken the entire evolution of humankind until 1960 to reach a global population of 3 billion but it would be less than another 40 years for this population to double (Figure 1.1b). In the same year the UN announced that 16 June 1999 would be observed as the 'Day of Six Billion'.

Early humankind

The first hominids appeared in Africa around 5 million years ago, on a planet which is generally accepted to be 4600 million years old. They differed from their predecessors, the apes, in the fact that they walked on two legs and did not use their hands for weight bearing. Other uses were soon found for these now liberated hands, with the acquisition of new skills charted in the evolutionary record as an increase in the size of the brain. After 2 million years cranial capacity had increased by 50 per cent from the 600 cm³ of the earliest hominid, *Australopithecus*, to the 900 cm³ of the primitive human named *Homo erectus*. The final increase to *Homo sapiens'* current average of 1450 cm³ took place about 100 000 years ago.

The evolution of humankind was matched by its geographical diffusion. Whereas the locational evidence for *Australopithecus* is confined to Africa (Figure 1.2),

Key Definitions

demography The scientific study of human populations.

crude birth rate (generally referred to as the 'birth rate') The number of births per thousand population in a given year. It is only a broad indicator as it does not take into account the age and sex distribution of the population.

crude death rate (generally referred to as the 'death rate') The number of deaths per thousand population in a given year. Again, only a broad indicator as it is heavily influenced by the age structure of the population.

rate of natural change The difference between the birth rate and the death rate.

infant mortality rate The number of deaths of infants under one year of age per thousand live births in a given year.

life expectancy (at birth) The average number of years a person may expect to live when born, assuming past trends continue.

demographic transition The historical shift of birth and death rates from high to low levels in a population.

census An official periodic count of a population including such information as age, sex, occupation and ethnic origin.

Figure 1.1a World vital events per time unit, 1998 (Figures may not add to totals due to rounding)

Time unit	Births	Deaths	Natural increase
Year	133 009 117	54 291 659	78 717 458
Month	11 084 093	4 524 305	6 559 788
Day	364 409	148 744	215 664
Hour	15 184	6 198	8 986
Minute	253	103	150
Second	4.2	1.7	2.5

Source: US Bureau of the Census, *International Data Base*

Figure 1.1b The increase in world population and the time taken to add another billion

1830	1 billion	
1930	2 billion	(100 years)
1960	3 billion	(30 years)
1975	4 billion	(15 years)
1987	5 billion	(12 years)
1999	6 billion	(12 years)

Figure 1.2 Reconstruction from skeletal remains of *Australopithecus robustus* found in southern Africa

remains of *Homo erectus* have been found over a wide area stretching from Europe to South East Asia. *Homo sapiens* roamed even further, making the first incursions into the cold environments of high latitudes.

During most of the period since *Homo sapiens* first appeared, global population was small, reaching perhaps some 125 000 people a million years ago, although there is not enough evidence to be precise about population in the distant past. It has been estimated that 10 000 years ago, when people first began to domesticate animals and cultivate crops, world population was no more than 5 million. Known as the Neolithic Revolution, this period of economic change significantly altered the relationship between people and their environments. But even then the average annual growth rate was less than 0.1 per cent per year, extremely low compared with contemporary trends.

However, as a result of technological advance the carrying capacity of the land improved and population increased. By 3500 BC global population reached 30 million and by the time of Christ this had risen to about 250 million (Figure 1.3).

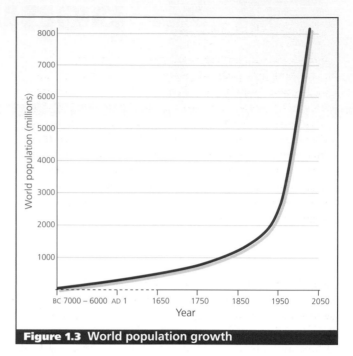

Figure 1.3 World population growth

Trends since early modern times: the model of demographic transition

Demographers estimate that world population reached 500 million by about 1650. From this time population grew at an increasing rate. By 1830 global population had doubled to reach 1 billion. Figure 1.1b shows the time taken for each subsequent billion to be reached.

Although the populations of no two countries have changed in exactly the same way, some broad generalisations can be made about population growth since the middle of the eighteenth century. These generalisations are illustrated by the model of demographic transition (Figure 1.4).

No country as a whole retains the characteristics of stage 1,

which applies only to the most remote societies on earth such as isolated tribes in New Guinea (Figure 1.5). All the developed countries of the world are now in stage 4, most having experienced all of the previous stages at different times. The poorest of the developing countries (e.g. Bangladesh, Niger, Bolivia) are in stage 2 but are joined in this stage by the oil-rich Middle East states where increasing affluence was not accompanied by a significant fall in fertility. Most developing

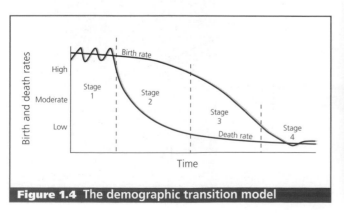

Figure 1.4 The demographic transition model

Figure 1.5 Primitive society with the characteristics of stage 1 of the demographic transition model

countries which have registered significant social and economic advances are in stage 3 (e.g. Brazil, China, Turkey) while some of the newly industrialised countries such as South Korea and Taiwan have just entered stage 4. With the passage of time there can be little doubt that more countries will attain the demographic characteristics of the final stage of the model. The basic characteristics of each stage are as follows:

The high fluctuating stage (stage 1): the birth rate is high and stable while the death rate is high and fluctuating due to the sporadic incidence of famine, disease and war. Population growth is very slow and there may be periods of considerable decline. Infant mortality is high and life expectancy low. A high proportion of the population is under the age of 15. Society is pre-industrial with most people living in rural areas, dependent on subsistence agriculture.

The early expanding stage (stage 2): the death rate declines to levels never before witnessed. The birth rate remains at its previous level as the social norms governing fertility take time to change. As the gap between the two vital rates widens, the rate of population growth increases to a peak at the end of this stage. Infant mortality falls and life expectancy increases. The proportion of the population under 15 increases. Although the reasons for the decline in mortality vary somewhat in intensity and sequence from one country to another, the essential causal factors are: better nutrition; improved public health particularly in terms of clean water supply and efficient sewage systems; and medical advance. Considerable rural to urban migration occurs during this stage. However, for developing countries in recent decades urbanisation has often not been accompanied by the industrialisation which was characteristic of the developed nations during the nineteenth century.

The late expanding stage (stage 3): after a period of time social norms adjust to the lower level of mortality and the birth rate begins to decline. Urbanisation generally slows while life expectancy continues to increase and infant mortality to decrease. Countries in this stage usually experience lower death rates than nations in the final stage due to their relatively young population structures.

The low fluctuating stage (stage 4): both birth and death rates are low. The former is generally slightly higher, fluctuating somewhat due to changing economic conditions. Population growth is slow and may even be negative if the birth rate dips below the death rate. Death rates rise slightly as the average age of the population increases. However, life expectancy still improves as age-specific mortality rates continue to fall. This stage completes the population cycle according to the model but will a further stage (stage 5), say significant and prolonged natural decrease, be evident in a few decades time?

Types of demographic transition

The Czech demographer Z. Pavlík has recognised three types of demographic transition. Apart from the 'classical or English type' described above, he also refers to the 'French' and 'Japanese–Mexican' types (Figure 1.6). In France the birth and death rates diminished at a similar pace and there was no intermediate period of high natural increase. In Japan and Mexico the birth rate actually increased in stage 2 due largely to the improved health of women in the reproductive age range.

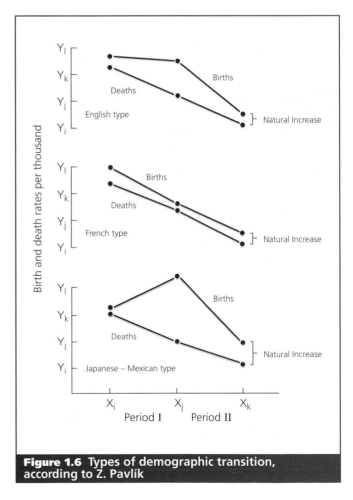

Figure 1.6 Types of demographic transition, according to Z. Pavlík

Demographic transition in England and Wales

North-west Europe was the first part of the world to undergo demographic transition as a result of the significant industrial and agrarian advances which occurred during the eighteenth and nineteenth centuries. In England and Wales in medieval times (stage 1) both the birth rate and the death rate hovered around 35 per 1000. The birth rate was generally a little higher, resulting in a slow rate of natural increase. While the birth rate tended to remain at a relatively stable level the death rate varied considerably at times. For example, the 1348–9 epidemic of bubonic plague, known as the Black Death, killed something like a third of the population. Also of great demographic consequence were the bubonic plagues of 1603, 1625 and 1665, the latter referred to as the Great Plague. The increase in mortality between 1720 and 1740 (Figure 1.7) has been attributed to the availability of cheap gin which took a considerable toll on the working class. These conditions of high fertility and high mortality persisted until about 1740.

Stage 2, which lasted until about 1875, witnessed a period of rapid urbanisation which alerted both public officials and factory owners to the urgent need for improvements in public health.

Factory owners soon realised that an unhealthy workforce had a huge impact on efficiency. The provision of clean piped water and the installation of sewage systems, allied to better personal and domestic cleanliness, saw the incidence of the diarrhoeal diseases and typhus fall rapidly.

Although in many ways life in the expanding towns was little better than in the countryside, there was a greater opportunity for employment and a larger disposable income so that more food and a wider range of food products could be purchased. Contemporary studies in developing countries show a strong relationship between infant nutrition and infant mortality. Infant mortality in England fell from 200 per 1000 in 1770 to just over 100 per 1000 in 1870. The weight of opinion seems to be that better nutrition played a substantial role in this decline.

The virulence of the common infectious diseases diminished markedly. For example, scarlet fever, which caused many deaths in the eighteenth century, had a much reduced impact in the following century. From about 1850 the mortality from tuberculosis (TB) also began to fall. A combination of better nutrition and the general improvements in health brought about by legislation such as the Public Health Acts of 1848 and 1869

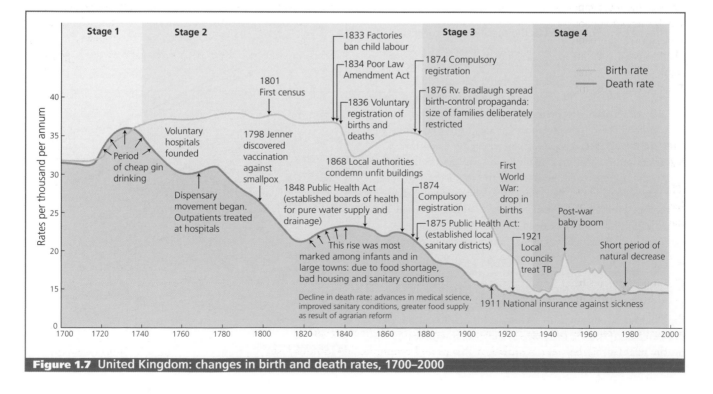

Figure 1.7 United Kingdom: changes in birth and death rates, 1700–2000

were the most likely causal factors. Public perception of the importance of cleanliness was also important and it is not coincidental that soap was one of the most advertised products of the century.

The final factor to be considered in stage 2 is the role of medicine. Although some important milestones were reached, such as Jenner's discovery of a vaccination against smallpox, there was no widespread diffusion of medical benefits. Of all the drugs available in 1850, fewer than ten had a specific action, so their impact on mortality was negligible. Surgery was no more advanced and anasthesia was unavailable until the last years of the century.

We can be much more sure about the accuracy of demographic data during this period. The first census of England and Wales was taken in 1801 (Figure 1.8) and every ten years thereafter, and from 1836 the registration of births and deaths was introduced on a voluntary basis, becoming compulsory in 1874.

After 1875 the continued decline of the death rate was accompanied by a marked downturn in the birth rate (stage 3). Medical science began to play an important role in controlling mortality and doctors were now able to offer potent, specifically effective drugs. From about 1906 increasing attention was paid to maternity and child welfare, and to school health. More measures to improve public health were introduced while there were further gains in nutrition. From the late 1870s onwards, cheap American corn began to arrive in Britain in large quantities, along with refrigerated meat and fruit from Australia and New Zealand.

The beginning of the decline in fertility coincided with, and was probably partly the result of, the widespread publicity which attended the trial of Charles Bradlaugh and Annie Besant. These two social reformers were prosecuted (and later acquitted) for publishing a book which gave contraceptive advice. However, perhaps the most important factor was the desire for smaller families now that people could be sure that the decline in mortality was permanent and because the monetary cost of children was higher in urban compared to rural areas. The term 'birth control' was coined just before the First World War, not in England but across the Atlantic.

Figure 1.8 Extract from the 1801 census of England and Wales

Family size varied by social group with the upper and professional middle classes leading the way in contraception. The birth rate which had been 30.5 per 1000 in 1890 fell to 25 per 1000 in 1910 and was down to 17 per 1000 by 1930 at which time it is reasonable to assert that England and Wales was entering the final stage of demographic transition.

By 1940 the birth rate had fallen further to 14.5 per 1000 but this was undoubtedly influenced by the outbreak of war the previous year. The higher figures in the three decades following the end of the Second World War are generally accounted for by the phenomenon known as the 'post-war baby boom'. However, by 1980 the birth rate was down again to 14 per 1000, remaining close to that figure ever since. The introduction of the oral contraceptive pill in 1960 and improvements in other forms of contraception meant that the relationship between desired family size and achieved family size had never been stronger.

Demographic transition in the Developing World

There are a number of important differences in the way that developing countries have undergone population change compared to the experiences of most developed nations before them. In the Developing World:

■ birth rates in stages 1 and 2 were generally higher

■ the death rate fell much more steeply and for different reasons

■ some countries had much larger base populations and thus the impact of high growth in stage 2 and the early part of stage 3 has been far greater

■ for those countries in stage 3 the fall in fertility has also been steeper

■ the relationship between population change and economic development has been much more tenuous.

Key Definitions

immigration rate The number of immigrants per thousand population in the receiving country in a given year.

emigration rate The number of emigrants per thousand population in the country of origin in a given year.

rate of net migration The difference between the rates of immigration and emigration.

population density The average number of people per km² in a country or region.

population distribution The way that the population is spread out over a given area, from a small region to the earth as a whole.

The components of population change

The relationship between births and deaths (natural change) is not the only factor in population change. The balance between immigration and emigration (net migration) must also be taken into account as the input–output model of population change shows (Figure 1.9). The corrugated divide on the diagram indicates that the relative contributions of natural change and net migration can vary over time within a particular country as well as varying between countries at any one point in time. The model is a simple graphical alternative to the population equation $P = (B - D) \pm M$, the letters standing for population, births, deaths and migration respectively.

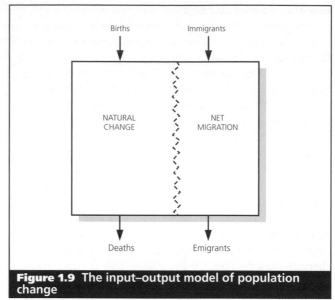

Figure 1.9 The input–output model of population change

Questions

1 State the differences between the first hominids (*Australopithecus*), *Homo erectus* and *Homo sapiens* in terms of (a) cranial capacity and (b) geographical diffusion.
2 Why are crude birth and death rates regarded as only broad indicators of fertility and mortality?
3 Why can we be more certain about demographic trends in England and Wales from the beginning of the nineteenth century than before this time?
4 Using atlas data sheets, or a comparable resource, plot the birth and death rates for the countries of South, Central and North America on a diagram of the model of demographic transition. Comment on your completed diagram.
5 Conduct demographic research to: (a) ascertain the reasons for the absence of a period of rapid population growth in France; (b) give a more detailed account of stages 2 and 3 of demographic transition in England and Wales.

Distribution and density

Figure 1.10 shows the distribution and density of population by world region. The huge contrast between the Developed and Developing Worlds is readily apparent. In mid-1998 the Developed World recorded only 19.9 per cent of world population and between 1990 and 1998 its population grew at only one quarter of the global rate. However, within the Developed World itself there is a considerable difference in natural change between Europe on the one hand, and North America and Oceania on the other.

There are also significant differences in the Developing World with Africa having by far the highest annual population growth rate; 28 times higher than Europe. It is interesting to note that there is now little difference between the rates for Asia and Oceania due largely to the falling growth rate of the former over the last decade or so. However, a high rate of immigration into Australia and New Zealand is also an

Figure 1.10 Demographic data by world region					
	Population mid-1998 (millions)	Population density km²	Natural increase (%)	Doubling time* (years)	Projected Population	
					2010	2025
World	5926	42	1.5	47	6894	8036
More developed	1178	22	0.1	564	1212	1226
Less developed	4748	54	1.8	38	5682	6810
Africa	763	23	2.6	26	990	1313
North America	301	13	0.6	117	331	372
Latin America and Caribbean	500	23	1.8	38	589	691
Asia	3604	107	1.6	44	4220	4914
Europe	728	32	−0.1	–	728	706
Oceania	30	3	1.1	63	34	39

*At current rate of growth

important contributory factor.

The global average for population density also covers a wide regional range. The overall difference between the Developed and Developing Worlds is largely accounted for by the extremely high figure for Asia. As for the other developing regions, Europe is about 50 per cent higher and North America 50 per cent lower in population density.

The average density figure for each region in turn masks considerable disparity. The most uniform distributions of population occur where there is little variation in the physical and human environments. Steep contrasts in these environments are sharply reflected in settlement patterns. People have always avoided hostile environments if a reasonable choice has been available. Visual correlation of an atlas map of the world illustrating population density with maps of relief, temperature, precipitation and vegetation shows the low densities associated with high altitudes, polar regions, deserts and rainforests. More detailed maps can show the influence of other physical factors such as soil fertility, natural water supply and mineral resources. At the physical/human interface the spatial incidence of disease and pests, particularly in developing countries, can seriously limit human settlement.

The more advanced a country is the more important the elements of human infrastructure become in influencing population density and distribution. While a combination of physical factors will have decided the initial location of the major urban areas, once such entities reach a certain size, economies of scale and the process of cumulative causation (Chapter 6) ensure further growth. As a country advances, the importance of agriculture decreases and employment relies more and more on the secondary and tertiary sectors which are largely urban based. The lines of communication and infrastructure between major urban centres provide opportunities for further urban and industrial location.

The most rapid changes in population density in human

Scale

Patterns and processes in human and physical geography can be examined at a range of scales from the global or macro scale, through the intermediate or meso scale, to the local or micro scale. When analysing data it is important to be clear about the scale to which it refers.

history have occurred in the Developing World in the latter half of the twentieth century. In Brazil (Figure 1.11) all regions have been affected, creating pressures on the physical environment and on human infrastructure. The sprawling cities of the Southeast and Northeast are an obvious indicator of increasing density and urban pressure. The changing landscapes of the Centre-West and the North are another consequence of population growth and increasing density. These latter regions were largely undeveloped prior to the 1950s, but significant changes since that time have brought them firmly into the national economy. The construction of Brasília, the new capital city since 1960, was the fundamental catalyst for significantly populating the Centre-West. However, in the North the resources of the Amazon rainforest have been exploited more to satisfy the demands of population pressures in other parts of Brazil and in the Developed World than in the region itself.

At the dawn of the nineteenth century, overall population density in Brazil was 2.0 per km^2; by 1940 it was 4.8 and by 1970 10.9. Even in 1970 the pattern of settlement still demonstrated the predominantly coastal distribution typical of colonial times. However, in spite of the considerable changes in density and distribution in the latter part of the twentieth century, the average population density for the country as a whole was only 19 per km^2 in 1996, compared with a global average of 39 per km^2.

Population density in North America

North America has a low population density compared with most other parts of the world. The United States has an average of 27 persons per km^2, while Canada has only 2 per km^2. In both countries population is highly concentrated in some areas while large expanses of land elsewhere are sparsely settled (Figure 1.12). Few people live in the cold, dry and mountainous regions. The influence of low temperature is clear in the north and largely explains why 75 per cent of Canadians live within 160 km of the main border with the United States. Life is extremely difficult in the permafrost environment of the northlands and, apart from the native Inuit and Indians, the few people living there are mainly involved in the exploitation of raw materials and in maintaining defence installations, although the role of tourism is expanding.

Figure 1.11 Population density in Brazil

Population per km²
- More than 100
- 50–100
- 10–49
- 1–9
- fewer than 1

The mountain ranges of the west form imposing landscapes but economic opportunities are scarce in this rugged environment. For example, Cheyenne (altitude 1850 m), the largest settlement in Wyoming, has a population of only 50 000. The Appalachian mountains in the east of the country are both lower in height and less extensive in area; nevertheless, the most isolated areas are very sparsely peopled.

Although much of the south-western United States is desert or semi-desert, no country in the world has been more successful in watering its drylands. Expensive irrigation schemes have opened up many parts of the region to farming, settlement and industry. Cities such as Phoenix, Tucson and Las Vegas, standing out like oases in the desert, are clear evidence of the high level of investment. Yet large parts of the South West still remain empty and may well do so in the future as the water supply problem in the region has now reached crisis point.

In the United States the greatest concentration of population is in the North East, the first region of substantial European settlement. By the end of the nineteenth century it had become the greatest manufacturing region in the world and by the 1960s the highly urbanised area between Boston and Washington had reached the level of a megalopolis. Although other parts of the country are growing at a faster rate, the intense concentration of job opportunities in the North East will ensure that it remains the most densely populated part of the continent in the foreseeable future.

The coastline and major lowland valleys are as attractive to settlement now as they have been in the past. More than half of all Americans live in the counties (sub-divisions of states) adjacent to the Atlantic and Pacific Oceans, the Gulf of Mexico and the Great Lakes.

Soil fertility is another influence, but the high level of mechanisation in modern agriculture means that this factor was more important in the past. The location of other natural resources such as coal, iron ore and oil has also been an attraction to settlement, but again such influence has lessened. Most North Americans are now employed in urban-based service or manufacturing jobs and the availability of employment in these sectors is the most important influence on the distribution and density of population today.

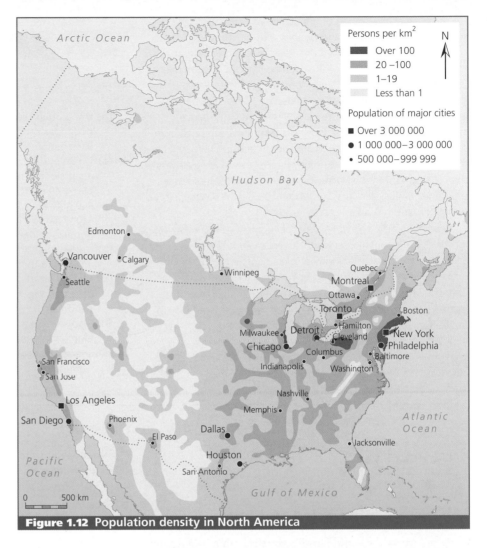

Figure 1.12 Population density in North America

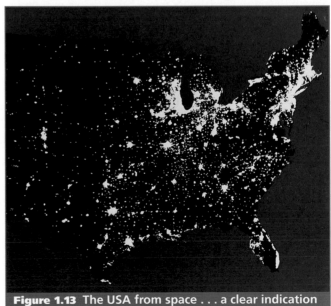

Figure 1.13 The USA from space . . . a clear indication of population centres

The main concentration of population in Canada is in the southern parts of Ontario and Quebec. This region has a combination of physical and human advantages greater than that found in most other parts of the country. Two of Canada's three 'million-size' cities, Toronto and Montreal, are located here. The third ranking city, Vancouver, is situated on the Pacific coast. A large area of low to moderate density is found in the cereal farming region of the Prairie Provinces (Manitoba, Saskatchewan, Alberta). In terms of political boundaries population density ranges from a high of 22.9 per km² on tiny Prince Edward Island to less than 0.1 per km² in the Northwest Territories. In comparison, in the United States, density varies from 410 per km² in New Jersey to 0.4 per km² in Alaska.

Population density is not a static phenomenon. The westward movement of population in North America which began within a century of the initial establishment of settlement has continued unabated in the twentieth century in both the United States and Canada, while the former has also experienced rapid growth in many southern states. In 1980 the mean centre of population in the United States crossed the Mississippi River for the first time and for the first time in US history more Americans lived in the South and West than in the North East and Midwest.

Questions

1 **(a)** Using Figure 1.11, describe the population distribution and density in each of Brazil's five regions.
 (b) Using other resources and the references to Brazil in this book assess the impact of rising population density in each region.

2 **(a)** On an outline map of North America, and with the aid of an atlas, carefully shade in different colours the areas: (i) above 400 m in height; (ii) with precipitation below 400 mm; (iii) with a mean January temperature below −20° C. At regular intervals on your map insert the population density of the areas you have shaded.
 (b) Under what circumstances might population density increase in the future in these areas?
 (c) Make a list of the regions with high population densities. What are the main reasons for such high densities?
 (d) Discuss the possible advantages and disadvantages of high population density.

Fertility

The factors influencing fertility

In most parts of the world fertility exceeds both mortality and migration and is thus the main determinant of population growth (Figure 1.14). Its importance has increased over time with the worldwide fall in mortality. According to the 1997 World Population Data Sheet, Niger has the highest crude birth rate at 53 per 1000 with Angola, Uganda, Malawi, Mali and Somalia all recording rates of 50 per 1000 or more. At the other end of the scale, the following nations had birth rates of only 9 per 1000: Belarus, Bulgaria, Czech Republic, Estonia, Italy, Latvia, Russia and Spain.

However, any meaningful analysis of fertility must look beyond the birth rate with the most detailed studies examining age-specific rates for each year of age. In terms of the total fertility rate (TFR) Niger again headed the list at 7.4, followed by Angola at 7.2 and Western Sahara and Somalia at 7.0. The lowest TFR of 1.2 was recorded for Bulgaria, Czech Republic, Italy, Latvia and Spain.

The factors affecting fertility levels can be grouped into four categories:

■ **Demographic** – other demographic factors, particularly mortality rates, influence the social norms regarding fertility. One study of sub-Saharan Africa, where the average infant mortality is over 100 per 1000, calculated that a woman must have an average of 10 children to be 95 per cent certain of a surviving adult son.

■ **Social/cultural** – in some societies, particularly in Africa, tradition demands high rates of reproduction. Here the opinion of women in the reproductive years will have little influence weighed against intense cultural expectations. Education, especially female literacy, is the key to lower fertility. With education comes a knowledge of birth control, greater social awareness, more opportunity for employment and a wider choice of action generally. Most countries exhibit different fertility levels according to social class with fertility decline occurring in the highest social classes first. In some countries religion is an important factor. For example, the Muslim and Roman Catholic religions oppose artificial birth control. However, the degree of adherence to religious doctrine tends to lessen with economic development.

■ **Economic** – in many of the least developed countries children are seen as an economic asset. They are viewed as producers rather than consumers. In the Developed World the general perception is reversed and the cost of the child dependency years is a major factor in the decision to begin or extend a family.

■ **Political** – there are many examples in the present century of governments attempting to change the rate of population growth for economic and strategic reasons. During the late 1930s Germany, Italy and Japan all

Key Definitions   3

fertility rate   The number of live births per 1000 women aged 15–49 years in a given year.

age-specific fertility rate   The fertility rate conventionally divided into seven age groups (15–19, 20–24, etc.) or for even more detail, into each year of age from 15 to 49 years.

total fertility rate (TFR)   The average number of children that would be born alive to a woman (or group of women) during her lifetime, if she were to pass through her child-bearing years conforming to the age-specific fertility rates of a given year.

replacement level fertility   The level at which each generation of women has just enough daughters to replace themselves in the population. Although the level varies for different populations, a total fertility rate of 2.12 children is usually considered as replacement level.

Figure 1.14 Fertility and contraception

	Birth rate	Total fertility rate	% of married* women using contraception (all methods)
World	24	3.0	56
More developed	11	1.6	66
Less developed	27	3.4	54
Africa	40	5.6	24
North America	14	1.9	71
Latin America and Caribbean	25	3.0	67
Asia	24	2.9	59
Europe	10	1.4	n/a
Oceania	19	2.4	n/a

Source: *1997 World Population Data Sheet* [For developed countries nearly all data refers to 1995 or 1996 and for less developed countries to some point in the early to mid-1990s.]
*married or 'in union'

offered inducements and concessions to those with large families. More recently Malaysia adopted a similar policy. However, today, most governments that are interventionist in terms of fertility want to reduce population growth.

The fertility issue: population explosion followed by implosion?

The world's population will peak at around 10.6 billion in 2080 and then decline, according to a report published in late 1996 by Earthscan entitled 'The Future Population of the World: What Can We Assume Today?'. This is in sharp contrast to warnings in earlier decades of population 'explosion'. The main reason for the slowdown in population growth is that fertility levels in most parts of the world are falling faster than previously expected. The report gathered predictions of fertility, mortality and migration and put them together in every possible combination, leading to 4000 different scenarios. Probability was calculated for each set of figures.

Two-thirds of the predictions show that the population will never go higher than 10.6 billion (Figure 1.15). Many of the predictions assume that there will be more migration than has previously been expected and the key point here is that people who move to the developed world tend to have fewer children once they get there.

In the second half of the 1960s, after a quarter century of increasing growth, the rate of world population growth began to slow down (Figure 1.16). Since then some developing countries have seen the speediest falls in fertility ever known and thus earlier population projections did not materialise. The UN predicted a global growth rate of 2.0 to 2.1 per cent for the 1970s but by 1975–80 growth was down to only 1.7 per cent.

Only since the Second World War has population growth in the poor countries overtaken that in the rich. However, the 1960s saw population growth in the Developing World peak at 2.4 per cent a year and by the late 1990s it was down to 1.8 per cent. But, even though the rate of growth has been falling for three decades, demographic momentum meant that the numbers being added each year did not peak until the late 1980s.

The demographic transformation, which took a century to complete in the Developed World, has occurred in a generation in some Developing countries. Fertility has dropped further and faster than most demographers foresaw 20 or 30 years ago. Except in Africa and the Middle East, where in almost 50 countries families of at least 6 children are the norm and population growth is still over 2.5 per cent per year, birth rates are now declining in virtually every country. In the poorest nations there is often a large gap between the private gains from having

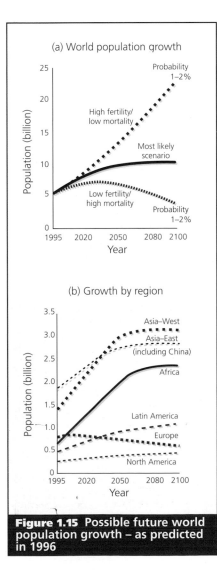

Figure 1.15 Possible future world population growth – as predicted in 1996

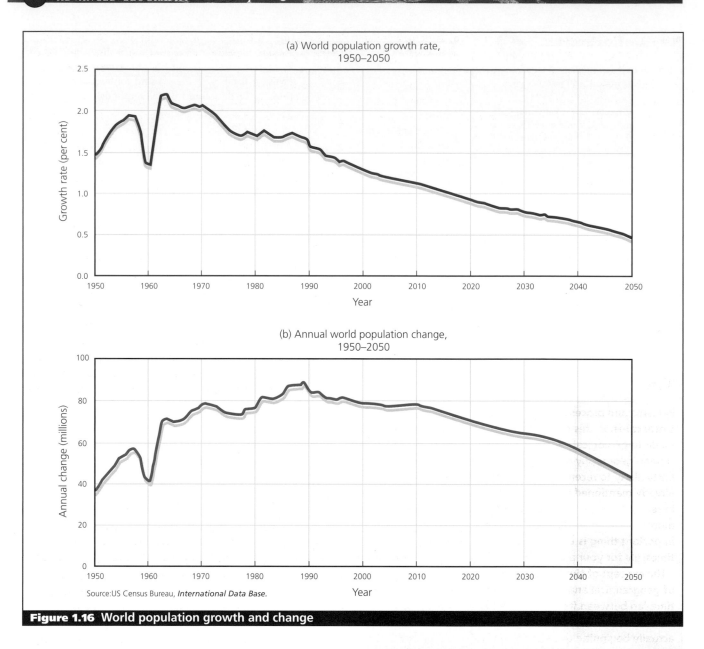

(a) World population growth rate,
1950–2050

(b) Annual world population change,
1950–2050

Source:US Census Bureau, *International Data Base.*

Figure 1.16 World population growth and change

many children and the social gains from reducing population growth.

India is on the way to catching China as the most populous country on earth. At the first census after independence, in 1951, India had a population of 361 million. It is now close to 1 billion and by 2050 it should overtake China (Figure 1.17). This assumes annual population growth of around 0.9 per cent for India, compared with only 0.4 per cent a year for China. In southern states such as Tamil Nadu and Kerala where literacy rates are high, fertility rates have fallen sharply. However, in the impoverished 'Hindi belt' in the north, traditional attitudes dominate, ensuring large numbers of children. Nevertheless, in India as a whole fertility has dropped more than 40 per cent in the past 25 years.

Modern contraceptive methods have played a key role in lowering global fertility. According to a recent paper on the

Figure 1.17 India: population exerting pressure

subject (*Scientific American*, September 1996) 'Among women of reproductive age who are married (or in nonmarital unions), half now depend on such methods as female sterilization (the most popular), male sterilization, hormonal implants, injectibles, intrauterine devices, birth control pills, condoms and diaphrams'. The first four methods are almost totally effective. Next are IUDs, followed by the pill and the male condom. Worldwide, 7 per cent of all women of reproductive age depend on traditional methods of birth control which are far less reliable than most current methods.

The 'Under 2.1 Club'

A fertility rate of 2.1 children per woman is the replacement level below which populations eventually start falling. There are already 51 nations with total fertility rates at or below 2.1. By 2016 the United Nations predicts there will be 88 nations in this category. China is in the 'Under 2.1 Club' but its population will not begin to decline until after 2045. The

UN's Population Division forecasts that by 2016 India and Indonesia, amongst many other countries, will have joined the club. For the world as a whole, because of the time-lag of up to 40 years between reaching replacement level fertility (as a result of falling fertility) and actual population decline, population will increase by almost as much in the twenty-first century as it has in the twentieth. The latest estimate from the British Government Actuary, published in December 1997, forecasts a slow increase from the current 59 million to a peak of just under 63 million in 2031, before starting a slow fall. In the past 20 years the number of British couples who have decided to have only one child has risen by 40 per cent to 2.9 million. The trend is particularly marked among professional and older parents.

In Italy, where the fertility rate is just 1.2 children per woman, population decline has already begun and the UN forecasts a fall in population of 4 million by 2020. Decline is also in progress in Russia, Ukraine, Georgia, Romania, Bulgaria, Belarus, Lithuania, Latvia, Estonia, Hungary, Czech Republic, Slovenia, Croatia and Portugal. This list is dominated by former Warsaw Pact countries where economic collapse and uncertainty following the end of communist rule has made many women postpone or abandon having children.

Time

Patterns and processes can be examined at different timescales. In this chapter reference has already been made to geological time, historical time and recent time. Human geography refers to the latter two and particularly to recent time. Each of the three timescales already mentioned can, of course, be subdivided. Trends in recent time may be examined on a daily, weekly, monthly, annual, or decade-by-decade basis. The important thing is to choose the most appropriate timescale for your analysis.

The concept of time-lag is important in various types of geographical analysis. For example, in this chapter the time-lag between fertility falling to population replacement level in a country and the total population actually beginning to decline is a significant factor in population change.

Population policies with regard to fertility

Figure 1.19 shows the officially stated position of governments on the level of the national birth rate. What is, perhaps, surprising is the number of countries that perceive their birth rate to be too low. However, there can be little doubt that more nations will come into this category in the future. Forming an opinion on demographic issues is one thing but establishing a policy to do something about it is much further along the line. Thus, not all nations stating an opinion on population have gone as far as establishing a formal policy.

Figure 1.18 Family planning poster in India

Figure 1.19 Government view on current birth rate*

	Too high	Satisfactory	Too low	No statement
Africa	41	11	1	2
North America	–	2	–	–
Latin America and Caribbean	18	14	1	5
Asia	19	21	6	4
Europe	1	24	15	–
Oceania	6	3	4	–
Total	85	75	27	11

Source: *1997 World Population Data Sheet*

*The officially stated position of country governments on the level of the national birth rate. Most indications are from the UN Population Division. 'Global Population Policy Data Base, 1995'.

The 1930s was a period of pronatalist policies in several European countries which saw population size as an important aspect of power. Even today there are nations conscious about population size in relation to their neighbours. However, in the post-war period most countries which have tried to control fertility have sought to curtail it. In 1952 India became the first developing country to introduce a policy designed to reduce fertility and it was not long before many other developing nations followed suit.

Population control in China

China, with a population in excess of 1.2 billion, operates the world's most severe family planning programme. Although it is the third largest country in the world in land area, 25 per cent of China is infertile desert or mountain and only 10 per cent of the total area can be used for arable farming. Most of the best land is in the east and south, reflected in the extremely high population densities found in these regions. Thus, the balance between population and resources has been a major cause of concern for much of the latter part of the twentieth century although debate about this issue can be traced as far back in Chinese history as Confucius (Chinese philosopher and teacher of ethics, 551–479 BC).

For people in the West it is often difficult to understand the all-pervading influence over society that a government can have in a centrally planned economy. In the aftermath of the communist revolution in 1949, population growth was encouraged for economic, military and strategic reasons. Sterilisation and abortion were banned and families received a benefit payment for every child. However, by 1954 China's population had reached 600 million and the government was now worried about the pressure on food supplies and other resources. Consequently, the country's first birth-control programme was introduced in 1956. This was to prove short lived, for in 1958 the 'Great Leap Forward' began. The objective was rapid industrialisation and modernisation. The government was now concerned that progress might be hindered by labour shortages and so births were again encouraged. But by 1962, the government had changed its mind, heavily influenced by a catastrophic famine due in large part to the relative neglect of agriculture during the pursuit of industrialisation. An estimated 20

million died during the famine. Thus, a new phase of birth control ensued in 1964. Just as the new programme was beginning to have some effect a new social upheaval, the Cultural Revolution, got underway. This period, during which the birth rate peaked at 45 per 1000, lasted from 1966 to 1971.

With order restored, a third family planning campaign was launched in the early 1970s with the slogan 'Late, sparse, few'. However, towards the end of the decade the government felt that the campaign's impact might falter and in 1979 the controversial 'One Child' policy was imposed. The Chinese demographer Liu Zeng calculated that China's optimum population was 700 million, and he looked for this figure to be achieved by 2080.

Figure 1.20 shows the changes in total population and vital rates since 1949. As fertility is illustrated here by the crude birth rate it does not give the full picture. The increases in the birth rate in the early and late 1980s are due mainly to earlier peaks in the 1960s with a large number of women initiating a family. China's population officially stood at 1224 million at the end of 1996, and the State Family Planning Commission forecasts a peak of around 1575 million in 2045.

Some organisations, including the UN Fund for Population Activities, have praised China's policy on birth control. Many others see it as a fundamental violation of civil liberties. This is official Chinese policy in practice:

'Any pregnant woman who is not married should be ordered to have an abortion ... Any woman who does not have an intra-uterine device inserted within four months after giving birth shall be fined 20 yuan per month. If a woman who has had one child fails at birth control, the pregnancy must be terminated and the

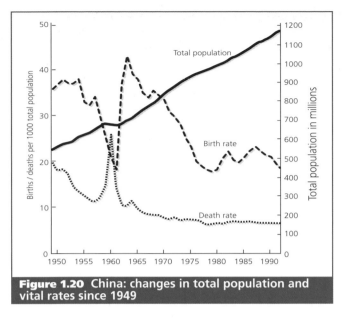

Figure 1.20 China: changes in total population and vital rates since 1949

woman sterilised ... If any unauthorised baby dies within three months of birth, the penalty will be [only] 300 yuan.'

Sunday Telegraph, 9 November 1997

The policy has had a considerable impact on the sex ratio which at birth in China is currently 118 boys to 100 girls. This compares with the natural rate of 106:100. This is already causing social problems which are likely to multiply in the future (Figure 1.21). Selective abortion after pre-natal screening is a major cause of the wide gap between the actual rate and the natural rate. But even if a female child is born her lifespan may be sharply curtailed by infanticide or deliberate neglect.

China's policy is based on a reward-and-penalty approach. Rural households which obey family planning rules get priority for loans, materials, technical assistance and social welfare. The slogan in China is, *shao sheng kuai fu* – 'fewer births, quickly richer'.

The one-child policy has been most effective in urban areas where the traditional bias of couples wanting a son has been significantly eroded. However, the story is different in rural areas where the strong desire for a male heir remains the norm. In most provincial rural areas, government policy has now relaxed so that couples can have two children without penalties.

1 Analyse the data presented in Figure 1.14.
2 **(a)** Explain the basis of the different scenarios of future world population growth illustrated in Figure 1.15(a).
 (b) Describe and explain the variations in predicted regional growth of global population (Figure 1.15b).
3 Explain the relationship between the data presented in Figures 1.16(a) and 1.16(b).
4 Suggest how the situation illustrated by Figure 1.19 might have changed in the previous 20 years.
5 **(a)** Using the spatial focus on China explain the population changes shown in Figure 1.20.
 (b) Discuss the short-term and possible long-term consequences of the one-child policy.

China child policy 'disaster'

FROM JONATHAN MIRSKY
IN HONG KONG

CHINA'S policy of one child per family is collapsing, with disastrous consequences, according to population experts.

Marcus Feldman, of Stanford University in California, says that because of traditional preference for boys and the pressures of the one-child policy, the abortion of female foetuses and the killing of infant girls will lead to 110 men of marriageable age for every 100 women within 25 years.

Writing in the Science Professor journal, he states that sonic imaging and amniocentesis are being used by Chinese to determine the gender of foetuses and to abort them if they are female. The Peking Government has recently banned the use of ultrasound machines for gender determination, but an estimated 10,000 have been introduced into the country since 1979, and peasants pay heavily to ensure they will have sons. It has been estimated that 97.5 per cent of abortions are performed on female foetuses.

Professor Feldman says the increasing shortage of women, which is already acute in many parts of China, will lead to more prostitution, much older marriages, and a decisive advantage for rich men who will be able to offer more money to prospective brides.

Chinese newspapers regularly report the abduction of women. Last December, 11 kidnappers were sentenced to be shot after they had taken 102 women, some of whom they raped before selling them in distant provinces to rich peasants. Two abducted women were recently imprisoned for attempting to murder their husbands. A newspaper recently published photographs of abandoned dead babies under the headline "Mothers, take back your daughters".

Figure 1.21 *The Times*, 11 February 1995

Figure 1.22 Mortality and life expectancy

	Death rate	Infant mortality rate	Maternal deaths per 100 000 live births	Life expectancy at birth
World	9	59	460	66
More developed	10	9	10	75
Less developed	9	64	500	63
Africa	14	89	880	53
North America	9	7	8	76
Latin America and Caribbean	7	39	180	69
Asia	8	58	410	65
Europe	12	10	10	73
Oceania	8	24	290	74

Source: 1997 *World Population Data Sheet* (For developed countries nearly all data refers to 1995 or 1996 and for less developed countries to some point in the early to mid-1990s.)

Mortality and life expectancy

From what has already been said about the influence of age structure, it is not surprising that the lowest crude death rates are in the developing nations (Figure 1.22). The 1997 Population Data Sheet recorded a rate of only 2 per 1000 for Kuwait and 3 per 1000 for Bahrain and the United Arab Emirates. Costa Rica and French Guiana were on 4 per 1000 with more countries including Mexico and Chile on 5 per 1000. However, the highest death rates were also in the Developing World – in the poverty belt of Sub-Saharan Africa. The following had death rates of 20 per 1000 or more: Gambia, Guinea-Bissau, Mali, Sierra Leone, Burundi, Malawi, Rwanda, Uganda and Zambia. Even the impact of very high fertility cannot mask high age-specific mortality resulting in

Figure 1.23 Famine, war, drought . . . they can all play a part in lowering life expectancy, as here in a refugee camp in Ethiopia

an average life expectancy in Africa as a whole of 53 years, well below any other world region. Indeed, life expectancy is the most common 'true' measure of mortality.

The infant mortality rate is generally regarded as a prime indicator of socio-economic progress. It is the most sensitive of the age-specific rates. Although it has fallen rapidly over recent time in most countries, wide spatial variations remain at the global scale. The gap between North America and Africa (Figure 1.22) is very telling indeed. The highest rates recorded by the 1997 World Population Data Sheet were as follows: Sierra Leone 195 per 1000, Afghanistan 163 per 1000 and Western Sahara 150 per 1000.

Over the world as a whole infant mortality has declined sharply since 1950. Between 1950 and 1955 the global average was 138 per 1000 but by 1975–80 it was down to 88 per 1000 and recently it has dipped below 60 per 1000.

Mortality can, of course, also vary significantly within individual countries. This holds true for both developed and developing countries. Regions benefiting from a higher level of medical infrastructure and a better quality of life generally will control mortality to a greater extent than worse-off regions. Figure 1.24 shows how infant mortality declined in Brazil from 1940 to 1995, illustrating also the differences between the richest (Southeast) and poorest (Northeast) regions of the country.

The decline in levels of mortality and the increase in life expectancy has been the most tangible reward of development. On a global scale, 75 per cent of the total improvement in longevity has been achieved in the twentieth century. In 1900 the world average for life expectancy is estimated to have been about 30 years but by 1950–5 it had risen to 46 years. By 1980–5 it had reached a fraction under 60 years and in 1997 was, according to the 1997 World Population Data Sheet, 66 years.

The twentieth-century fall in mortality was particularly marked after the Second World War which had provided a tremendous impetus for research into tropical diseases. It is, thus, not surprising that the pace of mortality reduction was

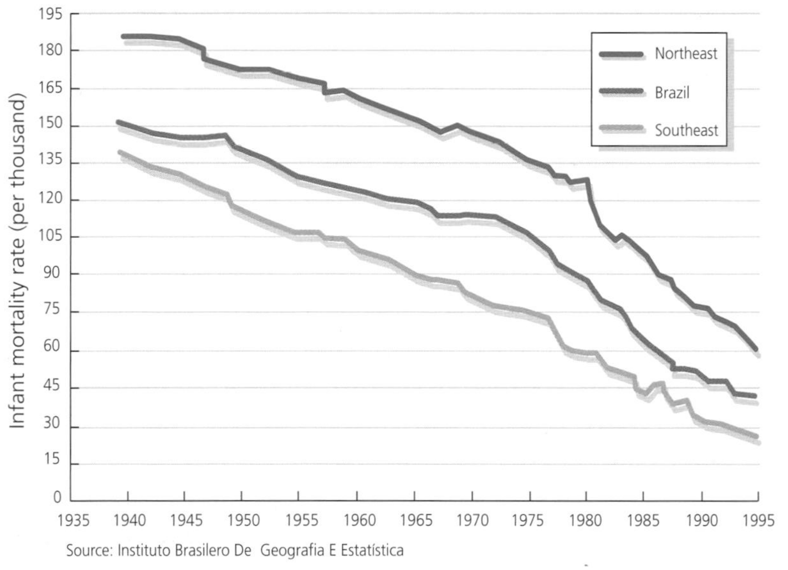

Figure 1.24 Infant mortality rates for Brazil, the Northeast and the Southeast 1940–95

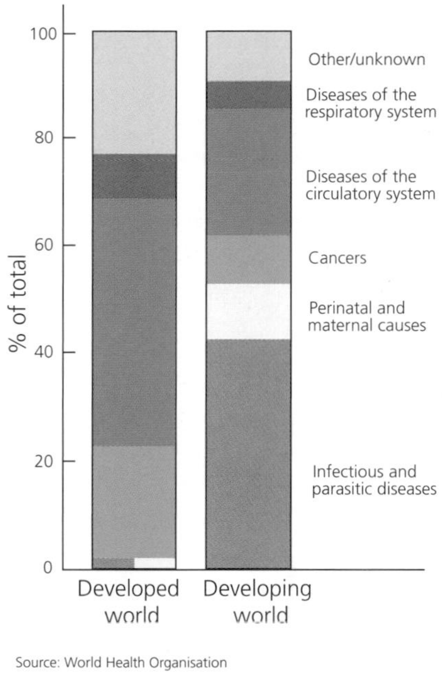

Source: Instituto Brasilero De Geografia E Estatística

Figure 1.25 Causes of death 1997

Source: World Health Organisation

especially rapid in the 1950s and 1960s. Mortality reduction slowed in the 1970s as large-scale disease eradication programmes reached their limits. Thereafter, the most obvious aspects of poverty, poor nutrition and lack of clean water and sanitation have slowed improvement in much of the Developing World.

Causes of death

The causes of death vary significantly between the Developed and Developing Worlds (Figure 1.25). The cause making the largest contribution to the general reduction in mortality is respiratory disease (influenza, pneumonia, bronchitis). Such diseases on average account for about 25 per cent of mortality change although, not surprisingly, the decline of these diseases is greater at higher mortality levels. Other infectious and parasitic diseases account for about 15 per cent of mortality change. Respiratory TB and diarrhoeal diseases are responsible for about 10 per cent of change each. Clearly, causes of death at any particular mortality level vary. Cancer and heart disease, which have a significant impact in the most developed nations, are much less influential in terms of mortality in poorer countries.

In the 1998 World Health Report, which included deaths below 50 years as a separate category for the first time, Britain came joint first in the world with Sweden. The figures show that 19 out of 20 people in Britain live to celebrate their half-century, a combination of good healthcare and a low accident rate. In Britain, average life expectancies for men and women are now 74 and 82 respectively.

By the late 1990s road accidents were killing half a million people a year, many more than are killed in wars and natural disasters. Over the twentieth century (the first recorded pedestrian death was in 1896), motor vehicles have claimed more than 30 million lives. The annual death toll will rise with increasing car ownership in the Developing World. The Federation of Red Cross and Red Crescent Societies calculate that road accidents cost developing countries about £32 billion a year, almost as much as all the aid they receive.

AIDS epidemic

The continual reduction in mortality cannot be taken for granted. For example, AIDS is taking a deadly toll in some countries as it tightens its grip on the Developing World. The number of people infected has risen dramatically (Figure 1.26). Of people worldwide currently infected; 63 per cent live in Sub-Saharan Africa. The Developing World will not be able to afford the expensive drugs to treat the disease, which appear to be cause for some optimism in the Developed World. By 1997 there had been 11.7 million AIDS deaths since the beginning of the epidemic. In an alarming report published in November 1997, the United Nations admitted that it had 'grossly underestimated' the scale of the global AIDS epidemic. The recent increase illustrated by Figure 1.26 partly reflects a more accurate method of collecting data. The epidemic is beginning to affect life expectancy in some southern African countries. In Zambia and Zimbabwe, the infant mortality rate is up 25 per cent and in Botswana, life expectancy has fallen to levels last seen in the 1960s.

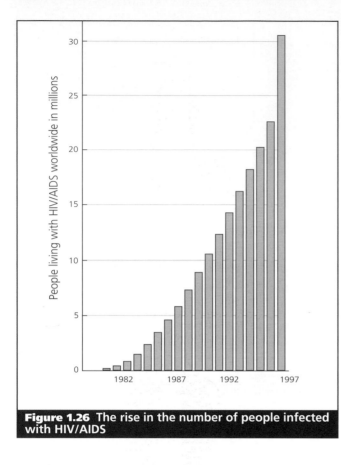

Figure 1.26 The rise in the number of people infected with HIV/AIDS

1 Analyse the data presented in Figure 1.22.
2 To what extent and why has infant mortality varied between the Southeast and Northeast of Brazil?
3 It is generally thought that mortality will continue to decline on both a global and regional scale. What might happen to frustrate such expectations?

Population composition

The composition or structure of a population is the product of the processes of demographic change (fertility, mortality, migration). It is not precisely defined but generally taken to include those characteristics for which data, particularly census data, are available. The most studied aspects of population composition are age and sex. The age, sex and life expectancy of a population has implications for a country's future economic and social development. Other structures that can be studied include race, language, religion and social/occupational groups.

Age structure

Age structure is conventionally illustrated by the use of population pyramids, as the diagrams in Figure 1.27 are known. Pyramids can be used to portray either absolute or relative data. The latter is most frequently used as it allows for easier comparison of countries of different population sizes. Each bar represents a five-year age group apart from the uppermost bar which usually illustrates the population 85 years old and over. The male population is represented to the left of the vertical axis with females to the right.

Population pyramids change significantly in shape as a country progresses through demographic transition. The wide

base in the Congo's pyramid reflects extremely high fertility. The marked decrease in width of each successive bar indicates high mortality and limited life expectancy. The base of the second pyramid (South Africa) is narrower reflecting a considerable fall in fertility in recent decades. Falling mortality and lengthening life expectancy is reflected in the slower decrease (compared to the Congo) from bar to bar with movement up the age groups.

In the pyramid for Argentina lower fertility still is illustrated by narrowing of the base. The reduced narrowing of each successive bar indicates a further decline in mortality and greater life expectancy. The final pyramid (Japan) has a distinctly inverted base reflecting the lowest fertility yet. The width of the rest of the pyramid is a consequence of the lowest mortality and highest life expectancy of all four countries.

South East Asia: the benefits of lower youth dependency

The rapid fall in fertility throughout the world in recent decades has resulted in a larger share of the population in the economically active age range. In South East Asia economists have matched the declining dependency ratio to rising rates of saving and investment. Before the early 1970s when the youth dependency burden was at its peak, saving rates were much lower. Only after dependency rates started to fall did saving rates start to rise. J. Williamson and M. Higgins (*Population and Development Review*, June 1997) take this relationship further and argue that changing population structure can also account for the patterns of both domestic and foreign capital investment in the region. They suggest that as the youth dependency ratio falls, people of working age will save a higher proportion of their incomes. As a consequence they expect more Asian countries to shift from importing capital to exporting it, just as Japan has done. If this happens the number of multinational companies from this region locating elsewhere in the world will rise sharply in the near future. For most Asian countries demographic ageing is some way off and demography is favourable for economic growth for about the next 30 years (Figure 1.28). This is one positive factor which should help the region overcome the economic crisis which began in late 1997.

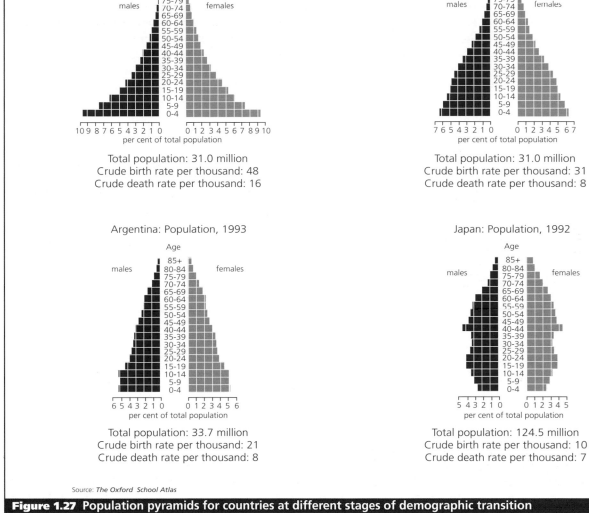

Figure 1.27 Population pyramids for countries at different stages of demographic transition

Congo (D.R.): Population, 1994

Total population: 31.0 million
Crude birth rate per thousand: 48
Crude death rate per thousand: 16

South Africa: Population, 1994

Total population: 31.0 million
Crude birth rate per thousand: 31
Crude death rate per thousand: 8

Argentina: Population, 1993

Total population: 33.7 million
Crude birth rate per thousand: 21
Crude death rate per thousand: 8

Japan: Population, 1992

Total population: 124.5 million
Crude birth rate per thousand: 10
Crude death rate per thousand: 7

Source: *The Oxford School Atlas*

Key Definitions   4

dependency ratio   The ratio of the number of people under 15 and over 64 years to those between 15 and 64 years of age.

median age   The age at which half the population is younger and half is older.

ageing of population   A rise in the median age of a population. It occurs when fertility declines while life expectancy remains constant or increases.

sex ratio   The number of males per 100 females in a population.

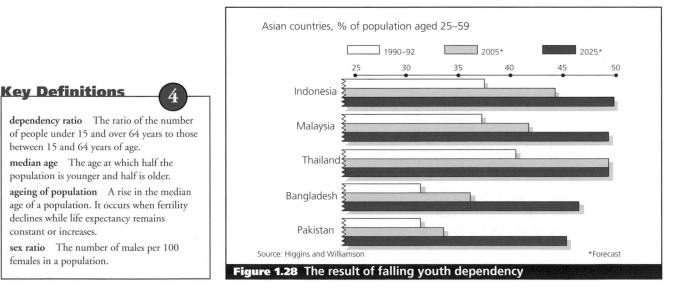

Asian countries, % of population aged 25–59

Source: Higgins and Williamson   *Forecast

Figure 1.28 The result of falling youth dependency

The problem of demographic ageing in the Developed World

The populations of the developed nations are ageing at a rapid rate and, in some countries, the total population will shrink as well. These developments will put healthcare systems and public pensions, and indeed government budgets in general, under increasing pressure. Four per cent of US population was 65 years of age and older in 1900. By 1995 this had risen to 12.8 per cent and by 2030 it is likely that one in five Americans will be senior citizens. The fastest growing segment of the population is the so-called 'oldest old': those who are 85 years or more. It is this age group which is most likely to need expensive residential care. The situation is similar in other developed countries.

The Organisation for Economic Co-operation and Development (OECD) has constructed long-term fiscal projections to examine the magnitude of this problem. Some countries such as the USA, Japan and Britain have made relatively good pension provision by investing wisely over a long period of time. However, others, for example France, Germany and Canada have more or less adopted a pay-as-you-go system, as the elderly dependent population rises. It is this latter group which will be faced with the biggest problems in the future.

Providing for the elderly is going to be an even more significant issue in the future. Few countries are generous in looking after their elderly at present. Poverty amongst the elderly is a considerable problem but technological advance might provide a solution by improving living standards for everyone. If not, other less popular solutions, such as increased taxation will have to be examined.

In Britain, the ratio of pensioners to working-age people is actually due to fall between 1994 and 2021, partly because the retirement age for women is to rise from 60 to 65 years between 2010 and 2020. After that, elderly dependency will rise sharply to 2061. However, over the whole period, increased elderly dependency will be partly offset by fewer young dependents. It is also, of course, possible that older people, who should be in better health in the future, will want to stay at work longer. Another way of reducing dependency is to allow more immigrants into the country. It will be interesting to see how far this option is exercised in the future.

1 Explain how the age structure of a country typically changes as it goes through the stages of demographic transition.
2 How will changing age structure in South East Asia over the next two to three decades provide opportunities for the countries in the region?

Sex composition

This is usually expressed as the number of males per 100 females in a population. Male births consistently exceed female births due to a combination of biological and social reasons. For example, in terms of the latter, more couples decide to complete their family on the birth of a boy than on the birth of a girl. In the United Kingdom in 1996, 105 boys were born for every 100 girls. However, after birth the gap generally begins to narrow until eventually females outnumber males, as at every age male mortality is the higher of the two. This happens most rapidly in the poorest countries where infant mortality is markedly higher among males than females. Here the gap may be closed in less than a year. In the United Kingdom it is not until the 45–59 age group that females outnumber males. In the age group 85 and over females make up 74 per cent of the population.

However, there are anomalies to the picture just presented. In countries where the position of women is markedly subordinate and deprived, the overall sex ratio may show an excess of males. Such countries often exhibit high mortality rates in childbirth. For example, in India in 1985 there were 107 males per 100 females.

Migration can have a substantial impact on sex composition. Historically, males have dominated the migration process causing imbalance in both the donor and receiving nations. In Australia there were 10 per cent more males than females at the beginning of the twentieth century.

Migration

Migration is more volatile than fertility and mortality, the other two basic demographic variables. It can react quickly to changing economic, political and social circumstances. However, the desire to migrate may not be achieved if the constraints imposed on it are too great. The desire to move within a country is generally inhibited only by economic and social factors. The desire to move to another country is now usually constrained by political factors in the form of strict immigration laws.

Migration typologies

Various attempts to classify migration (by duration, spatial extent and cause) have been made on the premise that classification is fundamental to the understanding of the phenomenon. L. Smith, after distinguishing between international migration and national migration, subdivided the latter into: rural to urban; urban to rural; state to state (region to region); and local movement. The Swedish demographer Hägerstrand arrived at a similar classification of: urban to rural; rural to urban; rural to rural; and urban to urban.

In 1958 W. Petersen noted the following five migratory types: primitive; forced; impelled; free; and mass.

- The nomadic pastoralism and shifting cultivation practised by the world's most traditional societies are examples of **primitive** migration.

- The abduction and transport of Africans to the Americas as slaves was the largest **forced** migration in history. In the seventeenth and eighteenth centuries 15 million people were shipped across the Atlantic Ocean as slaves. The expulsion of Asians from Uganda in the 1970s when the country was under the dictatorship of Idi Amin and the forcible movement of people from parts of the former Yugoslavia under the policy of 'ethnic cleansing' are much more recent examples. Migrations may also be forced by natural disasters (volcanic eruptions, floods, drought, etc.) or by environmental catastrophe such as nuclear contamination in Chernobyl.

- **Impelled** migrations take place under perceived threat, either human or physical, but an element of choice lacking in forced migration remains. Arguably the largest migration under duress in modern times occurred after the partition of India in 1947, when 7 million Muslims fled India for the new state of Pakistan and 7 million Hindus moved with equal speed in the opposite direction. Both groups were in fear of their lives but they were not forced to move by government, and small minority groups remained in each country. Perhaps the most significant recent example of impelled migration has been the movements within the borders of the former Soviet

Union. In 1996 the UN estimated that more than 9 million people had been on the move since the collapse of the communist system, many of them fleeing from fighting.

- The distinction between **free** and **mass** migration is one of magnitude only. The movement of Europeans to North America was the largest mass migration in history.

Within each category Petersen classed a particular migration as either innovating or conservative. In the former the objective of the move was to achieve improved living standards while in the latter the aim was just to maintain present standards.

International migration

International migration is a major global issue. In the past it has had a huge impact on both donor and receiving nations. In terms of the receiving countries the consequences have generally been beneficial. But today, few countries favour a large influx of outsiders for a variety of reasons.

A number of reasonably distinct periods can be recognised in terms of government attitudes to immigration:

- Prior to 1914 government controls on international migration were almost non-existent. For example, the United States allowed the entry of anybody who was not a prostitute, a convict, a lunatic and, after 1882, Chinese.

Key Definitions ⑤

migration The movement of people across a specified boundary, national or international, to establish a new permanent place of residence. The UN defines permanent as a change of residence lasting more than one year.

circulatory movements Movements with a timescale of less than a year. This includes seasonal movements which involve a semi-permanent change of residence. Daily commuting also comes into this category.

mobility An all-embracing term which includes both migration and circulation.

refugee A person who cannot return to his or her own country because of a well-founded fear of persecution for reasons of race, religion, nationality, political association or social grouping (UN definition).

push factors Negative conditions at the point or origin which encourage or force people to move.

pull factors Positive conditions at the point of destination which encourage people to move.

Figure 1.29 Returned boat people (from the USA), Port-au-Prince, Haiti

Thus, the obstacles to migration at the time were cost and any physical dangers that might be associated with the journey.

- Partly reflecting security concerns, migration was curtailed between 1914 and 1945. During this period many countries pursued immigration policies which would now be classed as overtly racist.

- After 1945 many European countries, facing labour shortages, encouraged migrants from abroad. In general, legislation was not repealed but interpreted liberally. The West Indies was a major source of labour for the United Kingdom during this period. The former West Germany attracted *Gastarbeiter* 'guest workers' from many countries but particularly from Turkey.

- In the 1970s slow economic growth and rising unemployment in developed countries led to a tightening of policy which, by and large, has remained in force. However, in some countries immigration did increase again in the 1980s and early 1990s, spurring the introduction of new restrictions.

A recent International Labour Organisation publication estimated that 80 million people live in countries they were not born in. Another 20 million are refugees in other countries, having fled from political oppression or natural disaster. About 1.5 million people currently emigrate each year while another million or so, on average, seek temporary asylum abroad. The United States takes as many immigrants each year as the rest of the world put together. Germany is the main receiving country in Europe.

Each receiving country has its own sources (Figure 1.30), the results of historical, economic and geographical relationships. Earlier generations of migrants form networks that help new ones to overcome legal and other obstacles. Today's tighter rules tend to confine immigration to family members of earlier 'primary' migrants.

The dynamic growth of the newly industrialised countries of Asia in recent decades has created an intricate network of labour migration flows of mutual benefit to both donor and receiving countries. However, the financial crisis that erupted in the latter part of 1997 has faced millions of foreign workers with despair (Figure 1.31). Nations that welcome foreign workers when times are good are keen to quickly see the back of them in periods of recession.

A recognisable recent trend has been the shift towards the migration of highly skilled workers. There are two main reasons for this. The first is that receiving countries prefer highly skilled immigrants and frequently set their immigration criteria accordingly. Another factor is the economic influence of multinational companies. These organisations, as they expand, develop their own internal markets for skilled migrants. Big companies want the freedom to shift employees from country to country as demand requires. If a truly global market for labour ever reappears (it can be argued that if it ever existed it did in the nineteenth century), it is likely to be for highly skilled workers only.

The costs and benefits of international migration

Much has been written by way of generalisation about the impact of international migration on donor and receiving nations and Figure 1.32 provides a useful framework for the debate. However, it must be remembered that each migration situation is unique. For donor countries a migration that might provide a vital safety valve by relieving pressure on food supply and other resources may for another country drastically reduce its future prospects by skimming off the skilled element of its labour supply. The impact on donor countries can also vary at the national and regional scales. Emigration from the Republic of Ireland has been perceived as generally beneficial to the public purse but its effect on the *Gaeltacht*, the isolated Irish-speaking regions of the west, has been devastating (Figure 1.33). One community that has

Figure 1.30 Melting pots. Country of origin of immigrants in 1995 (in thousands)					
Australia		**Britain**		**Canada**	
New Zealand	12.3	Pakistan	6.3	Hong Kong	31.7
Britain	11.3	India	4.9	India	16.2
China	11.2	United States	4.0	Philippines	15.1
Ex-Yugoslavia	7.7	Bangladesh	3.3	China	13.3
Hong Kong	4.4	Nigeria	3.3	Sri Lanka	8.9
India	3.7	Australia	2.0	Taiwan	7.7
France		**Japan**		**United States**	
Algeria	8.4	China	38.8	Mexico	89.9
Morocco	6.6	Philippines	30.3	Ex-Soviet Union	54.5
Turkey	3.6	United States	27.0	Philippines	51.0
United States	2.4	South Korea	18.8	Vietnam	41.8
Tunisia	1.9	Brazil	11.9	Dominican Rep.	38.5
Ex-Yugoslavia	1.6	Thailand	6.5	China	35.5

Source: *Economist,* 1 November 1997

Turmoil in Tiger nations as 3m foreign workers face forced return to poverty and despair

NICHOLAS CUMMING-BRUCE IN BANGKOK

THE South-east Asian financial crisis was last night threatening a new dimension in human misery as the governments of its battered Tiger economies planned to expel millions of foreign migrant workers.

Thailand and Malaysia aim to throw out at least 2.5 million labourers, while South Korea is likely to send back all its 270,000 guest workers.

The forced repatriation will cause unprecedented hardship for some of Asia's poorest countries, as well as threatening widespread political instability.

It represents a double blow, halting the flow of foreign earnings on which poor countries such as Indonesia, Burma and Bangladesh have relied heavily, and adding millions to the jobless total. Thailand will force tens of thousands of workers across the border into Burma, one of the world's most backward economies, crippled by decades of mismanagement and conflict and also suffering from the impact of the region's currency crisis.

Returnees will include many from ethnic minorities who fled bloody campaigns by the ruling military junta, which emptied entire villages, slaughtered livestock and forcibly relocated their populations to poorly prepared but easily controlled locations in an attempt to eradicate resistance by autonomy-seeking rebels.

The repercussions of the Malaysian move could prove even more drastic. Indonesia, the world's fourth most populous country, is already struggling to cope with up to 2 million people whom business leaders and military chiefs say have lost their jobs. And that is just the start. "This crisis is still in its early stage," said a political analyst, Dewi Fortuna Anwar.

Last year Indonesia was forced to take back thousands of workers from Saudia Arabia who had overstayed their permits. The much bigger repatriations that loom if Malaysia goes ahead with its plans would come as Indonesia grapples with the impact of severe drought as well as the regional crisis.

Source: *The Guardian, 7* January 1998

Figure 1.31 The insecurity of migrant workers

Figure 1.32 Migration: Short-term costs and benefits

	Benefits		Costs	
	Individual	Social	Individual	Social
Emigrant countries	1 Increased earning and employment opportunities 2* Training (human capital) 3* Exposure to new culture, etc.	1* Increased human capital with return migrants 2 Foreign exchange for investment via migrant remittances 3 Increased output per head due to outflow of unemployed and underemployed labour 4 Reduced pressure on public capital stock	1 Transport costs 2 Adjustment costs abroad 3 Separation from relatives and friends	1 Loss of social investment in education 2 Loss of 'cream' of domestic labour force 3* Social tensions due to raised expectations of return migrants 4* Remittances generate inflation by easing pressure on financing public sector deficits
Immigrant countries	1 (*) Cultural exposure, etc.	1 Permits growth with lower inflation 2 Increased labour force mobility and lower unit labour costs 3 Rise in output per head for indigenous workers	1 Greater labour market competition in certain sectors	1* Dependence on foreign labour in particular occupations 2 Increased demands on the public capital stock 3* Social tension with concentration of migrants in urban areas

*indicates uncertain effects

Source: *Economist,* 15 November 1988

Figure 1.33 Abandoned village on the west coast of Ireland

suffered severely from this trend is Lettermore, a group of islands off Galway. Most of the young people head abroad after completing their education. In the stony fields stand abandoned cottages, their windows boarded up. Villages lie almost deserted and the remaining population fear that the decline in public and private services caused by a reduced population will trigger a further outflow.

For receiving countries, previous immigration has almost universally been seen as beneficial but there has been a much higher level of debate about the overall impact of recent immigration. It appears that the economic benefits may take much longer to filter through than previously thought.

Theoretical aspects of migration

Although each individual or family decision to migrate is unique, analyses of migration dating from the latter part of the nineteenth century have identified general patterns and processes. Since then a large body of theory has accumulated of which only the briefest of reviews is given here.

In 1885 E. G. Ravenstein proposed the following laws of migration based on his study of movements within the United Kingdom:

1 Most migrants move only a short distance. As distance increases from a particular place the number of migrants from that place decreases.
2 Migration occurs in a series of waves or steps. For example, the 'space' left by people moving from a market town to a city will be filled by people moving into the market town from its rural hinterland.
3 The process of dispersion (emigration) is the inverse of that of absorption (immigration) and exhibits similar features.
4 Each significant migration stream (flow) produces, to a degree, a counterstream.
5 The longer the distance travelled the greater the likelihood of the destination being a major industrial and commercial centre.
6 Town dwellers are less migratory than those living in rural areas.
7 Females are more migratory over short distances while males are more likely to move further.

Later theoretical developments in some cases reinforced aspects of Ravenstein's work but in others, modified it.

G. K. Zipf, using the concept of distance decay, presented the Inverse Distance Law, stating that 'the volume of migration is inversely proportional to the distance travelled by migrants.' This is expressed mathematically as:

$$N_{ij} \ \alpha \ \frac{1}{D_{ij}}$$

Here N_{ij} is the number of migrants from town i to town j and D_{ij} is the distance between the two towns.

The gravity model went a stage further by linking distance to the relative attractiveness of two places of different population size:

$$N_{ij} = k \ \frac{P_i P_j}{D_{ij}^2}$$

Here N_{ij} and D_{ij} are as above while P_i and P_j are the populations of towns i and j respectively; k is a constant.

In 1940 S. A. Stouffer presented his Theory of Intervening Opportunities in which he stated 'the number of persons going a given distance is directly proportional to the number of opportunities at that distance and inversely proportional to the number of intervening opportunities.' The formula here is:

$$N_{ij} \ \alpha \ \frac{O_j}{O_{ij}}$$

N_{ij} is the number of migrants from town i to town j, O_j the number of opportunities at j, and O_{ij} the number of opportunities between i and j.

E. S. Lee in 1966 produced a series of Principles of Migration, bringing together all aspects of migration theory at that time. Of particular note was his origin–obstacles–destination model (Figure 1.34) which emphasised the role of push and pull factors.

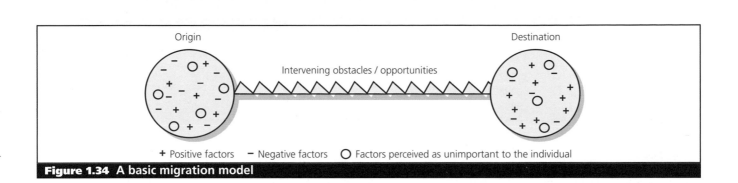

+ Positive factors   − Negative factors   ○ Factors perceived as unimportant to the individual

Figure 1.34 A basic migration model

Immigration: the United States

Immigration has arguably been the most dominant trend in the demographic history of North America. In the United States almost 60 million people have entered the country since 1820. However, during this time both the rate of entry and the origin of immigrants have changed considerably. The highest recorded rate for any decade was 10.4 per 1000 from 1901 to 1910, when 8.75 million newcomers arrived (Figure 1.35), although some decades in the nineteenth century were not far behind in proportional terms. The flood of immigrants continued until the outbreak of hostilities in Europe in 1914, whereupon it sharply abated from 12.3 per 1000 in 1914 to 3.2 per 1000 in 1915. It has rarely risen above the latter figure since, apart from a few exceptional years in the early 1920s and in recent years. The main reason for this was a growing concern about the numbers and origin of migrants.

In 1924 a system of 'national origins quotas' was introduced which operated with only slight modification until 1965. This legislation was designed to greatly reduce immigration and, in particular, to stem the influx of eastern and southern Europeans who poured into the United States at the turn of the twentieth century. Anti-Chinese restrictions had already been in force for

many years. The system aimed to preserve the ethnic balance which existed in the country at the 1920 census, offering the largest quotas of entry permits to British, Irish and German immigrants (70 per cent in total).

The racist overtones of this system, resulting in considerable internal and international opposition, led to its abolition in 1965. The 1965 Act, which became fully effective in July 1968, set an annual limit of 120 000 immigrants from the Western Hemisphere (the Americas) and 170 000 from the Eastern Hemisphere. People from every country within each hemisphere now had an equal chance of acceptance. However, immigration has exceeded this level considerably because relatives of US citizens are admitted without numerical limitation. The Immigration Act of 1990 raised immigration quotas by 40 per cent.

As the intervening obstacles were lowered for potential migrants from a number of world regions, so the ethnic composition of new arrivals changed significantly (Figure 1.36). Europe, the previous major source region, has been overtaken since 1970 by the rest of the Americas and by Asia, a trend that is likely to continue in the future.

The considerable increase in immigration in the 1990s, coinciding in the early part of the decade with a period of intense

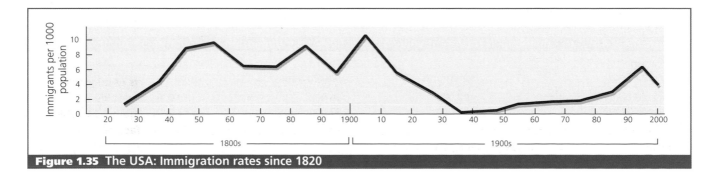

Figure 1.35 The USA: Immigration rates since 1820

Figure 1.36 Sources of immigration into the USA

	Immigrants (1000)			
	1820–1979[a]	1971–80[b]	1981–90[b]	1991–95[b]
Europe	36267	801	706	728
Asia	3038	1634	2817	1634
The Americas	9248	1929	3581	2682
Africa	142	92	192	160
Total (including others)	49124	4493	7338	5230

[a] by country of last permanent residence
[b] by country of birth

Figure 1.37 Border patrols, on mountain bikes, stop a suspected illegal immigrant on the US border in California

economic recession, reopened the immigration debate in the United States in a big way. More than 5 million immigrants arrived during 1991–6 alone. Some Americans argued that recent immigrants were taking scarce jobs that should be theirs, while others voiced concern about racial tension and the impact on the welfare system. A poll by Newsweek magazine in mid-1993 recorded a distinct hardening in attitudes to immigration with 60 per cent of Americans seeing current high levels of immigration as worrying.

Immigration into the United States is very spatially selective. In 1995, 55 per cent of all immigration was to just four states – California, New York, Florida and Texas. The main reasons for such concentrations are:

- the location of existing immigrant communities
- the availability of employment in the four most populous states
- the land border with Mexico for California and Texas and Florida's proximity to Caribbean countries.

Over a quarter of Californians in 1997 were born outside the United States. For Los Angeles the figure is almost 40 per cent. This compares with 16 per cent for New York, the next highest immigrant state, and 9.5 per cent for the United States as a whole.

Because of its very nature, it is difficult for the authorities to be precise about illegal immigration. Estimates vary from 2.5 to 4 million. In 1991 more than 1 million undocumented migrants were apprehended coming from Mexico (Figure 1.37). In 1996 Congress increased the number of guards on the border with Mexico, tightened asylum rules and made it harder for illegal immigrants to become legal; it also passed a Welfare Reform Act restricting the claims of legal immigrants on public assistance.

An OECD survey published in 1997 concluded that immigration is financially beneficial to the American economy in the long term (Figure 1.38). However, immigrants themselves take more out of the economy than they put in:

- Foreign-born residents are 35 per cent more likely to receive public assistance than natives
- Immigrants, on average, pay 32 per cent less in tax during their lifetimes than natives do.

The payback comes with the children of immigrants who, on average, pay far more to the state in taxes than they take from it. However, it takes 40 years after an immigrant enters the country, the OECD calculates, before the financial gain to the state outweighs the cost. For the public purse, the most lucrative immigrant is a 21 year old with a higher-level education.

Figure 1.38 America's dividend. Net present value of gains/losses per immigrant on government finances, $

Education level	Immigrants	Their descendants	Total
Educated below high school	−89 000	76 000	−13 000
Educated at high school	−31 000	82 000	51 000
Educated above high school	105 000	93 000	198 000
Average	−3 000	83 000	80 000

Source: *Economist*, 29 November 1997

China has more people chasing work than the whole US population. **Matt Frei** examines a desperate peasant migration

AS THE last fireworks of the Lunar New Year parties fizzled out last week, the Chinese government had little to celebrate. The country is facing a huge unemployment crisis and 1998 looks very bleak.

The figures are startling. Official statistics put the number of unemployed or "those waiting for work", as the state media euphemistically calls the swelling ranks of jobless, at a low 3.6 per cent in the cities – about 20 million workers. A more accurate estimate used by some candid officials in Beijing is closer to 40 million.

Zhou Lukuan, a director at the Labour and Personnel Bureau at the People's University in Beijing, has calculated that the unemployment rate could even be as high as 20 per cent.

Add to that an estimated 70 million "blind drifters", or peasants who have headed to the cities in search of casual labour. On top of that, rural China is believed to be saddled with 150 million "surplus labourers".

The total number of unemployed or underemployed Chinese thus amounts to a staggering 250 million people — slightly more than the entire population of the United States.

The drifting mass of newly destitute people has turned the pavements and parks around China's great railway stations into virtual dormitories. In Beijing hundreds of workers loiter around the central station every day advertising their skills by pinning a white piece of paper to their jackets, which bears their name and their profession.

Only 20 per cent of "drifters" are thought to have found regular employment. If they cannot produce papers that permit them to travel outside their home province, security officials try to send them back by train.

The capital's population hates the "blind drifters" for littering the streets and for allegedly fuelling the rising crime wave.

China's "miracle" economy, which Western businessmen swear by and over which Western politicians are happy to sacrifice their principles, resembles the worst of Europe at the time of the Industrial Revolution, multiplied by several million.

Figure 1.39 *Sunday Telegraph*, 1 February 1998

Internal migration

Migration flows occur to varying degrees within all countries. On a regional level movement is invariably from poorer peripheral to richer core regions. This holds for both developed and developing countries. However, this is as far as similarities go. Within developing countries, the strong rural–urban shift that began in the 1950s is still discernible, causing considerable problems in the rapidly growing urban areas and also, at times, impacting negatively on the rural donor regions. In contrast, the Developed World, which underwent its period of major rural–urban migration in the nineteenth century, now exhibits the process of counter-urbanisation.

The Developing World: rural–urban migration

The movement from rural to urban areas has been a major demographic trend in the second half of the twentieth century. In general, the intensity of such movements has been strongly related to the pace of change in both rural and urban regions. In rural areas mechanisation and other aspects of capital intensity have reduced the demand for farm labour. Although not a desirable trend from the individual employment point of view, the resultant increase in productivity benefits a country as a whole. However, movement from rural areas may also be induced by sudden natural disaster or by more gradual deterioration of the physical environment such as the spread of desertification. The urban areas with the greatest range or perceived range of employment and other opportunities will be the destinations of migrants from the countryside.

Recent economic change in China has unleashed a huge rural–urban migration (Figure 1.39), probably on a scale never reached anywhere in the world before. The full consequences of such a vast movement will become more apparent in the coming years (Figure 1.40).

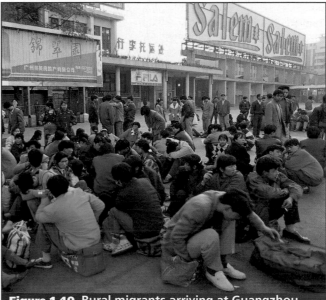

Figure 1.40 Rural migrants arriving at Guangzhou station in China

Population movements in Brazil

The Brazil of today is the result of population movements and resultant human activity over a long period of time. Following initial colonisation, the Northeast was the first area to experience significant Portuguese settlement. But after the demise of the sugar economy in this region, the focus of attention switched to the Southeast. The mineral, agricultural and other resources of the Southeast made it the focus of settlement and investment, and by the beginning of the twentieth century it was, without doubt, the economic core of Brazil and on its way to becoming the most important industrial region in Latin America.

Although earlier population movements provide a fascinating area for study the focus here is on recent movement. The 1991 census found that over 3 million people lived in a region different from 1986 (Figure 1.41). In terms of destination, the Southeast accounted for 46 per cent of in-migrants, followed by the Centre-West with 21 per cent. The Northeast was the region of origin for more than 53 per cent of migrants. Figure 1.41 does not, however, present the total migration picture as a certain number of people will have moved to another region but returned home within the limits of the period under consideration.

In the following five-year period, recorded internal migration fell to below 2.7 million (Figure 1.42). During this time, 57.4 per cent of migrants originated from the Northeast, relatively higher than in the preceding period. The most substantial change in out-migration occurred in the South. The state of Paraná was mainly responsible for this change in pattern, curtailing the trend established since the beginning of the 1970s, retaining people who formerly would have gone to agricultural areas in the North and Centre-West.

Despite a slight decline, north-eastern migration to the North and Centre-West regions continues to be expressive. Here, most migrants head for the state of Pará, the Tocantins river, and the outskirts of Brasília and Goiânia. The data also show a certain 'returning home' of 'Nordestinos'. Again, most in-migrants headed for the Southeast, with the state of São Paulo being the main focus within this region.

Within the Northeast movement from rural areas is greatest in the Sertão, the dry interior which suffers intensely from unreliability of precipitation. However, poor living standards and general lack of opportunity in the cities has also been a powerful incentive to move. Explaining the attraction of urban areas in the

Figure 1.41 Migrants per region of origin/destination, 1986–91

| Region of origin | Region of destination 1991 | | | | | |
1986	North	Northeast	Southeast	South	Centre-West	Total
North	–	72 913	73 280	29 176	95 364	270 733
Northeast	216 995	–	917 464	21 562	198 428	1 354 449
Southeast	78 931	218 206	–	170 416	203 018	670 571
South	41 428	9 410	310 580	–	148 294	509 712
Centre-West	71 162	36 304	125 607	64 110	–	297 183
TOTAL	408 516	336 833	1 426 931	285 264	645 104	3 102 648

Source: IBGE, *Censo Demográfico de 1991*

Figure 1.42 Migrants per region of origin/destination, 1991–6

| Region of origin | Region of destination 1996 | | | | | |
1991	North	Northeast	Southeast	South	Centre-West	Total
North	–	60 965	78 955	22 978	86 628	249 526
Northeast	182 999	–	835 562	24 914	194 097	1 237 572
Southeast	54 995	262 331	–	156 372	153 307	627 005
South	20 799	17 592	176 532	–	71 852	286 775
Centre-West	60 059	43 403	128 850	50 454	–	282 766
TOTAL	318 852	384 291	1 219 899	254 718	505 884	2 683 644

Source: IBGE, *Contagem da População de 1996*

Figure 1.43 Brasília, the capital of Brazil

Figure 1.44 Refugees on the move, Rwanda

Southeast demands more than the 'bright lights' scenario that is still sometimes bandied about. The Todaro model presents a more realistic conceptual framework. According to this model, migrants are all too well aware that they may not find employment by moving to, say, São Paulo. However, they calculate that the probability of employment, and other factors that are important to the quality of life of the individual and the family, is greater in the preferred destination than at their point of origin.

Refugees

Natural disasters, political upheaval and armed conflict have resulted in a huge number of refugees on the move in recent years. According to the United Nations Convention of 1951, refugees are people who have been forced to leave home and country because of 'a well-founded fear of persecution' on account of their race, religion, their social group or political opinions (Figure 1.44).

A report published by the United Nations High Commissioner for Refugees (UNHCR) in 1997 concluded that, although the refugee population worldwide was smaller than two years previously, the overall situation had got worse. This was primarily due to the way that conflicts were being pursued. Civilians are being targeted more than ever before, partly as the policy of 'ethnic cleansing' spreads from one zone of conflict to another. In certain areas, refugees have been pushed from one country to another, fleeing from the very camps they had headed to for sanctuary.

The most desperate conditions are often faced by 'internally displaced people' – those who are forced to abandon their homes, but who don't actually cross an international border. A newspaper report in January 1998 on the six-year Islamic insurgency in Algeria was entitled 'Massacre refugees flee to cities'. The report described how terrified villagers had fled their homes, flooding into public squares in the large urban areas, seeking a safe haven from attack.

The human suffering involved is all too apparent when the movement of large numbers is shown on global television. The impact on the human infrastructure of receiving regions can be overwhelming. But what is perhaps less evident at first is the environmental impact of refugees on the move. Refugees often concentrate in marginal and vulnerable environments where the potential for environmental degradation is high. Apart from immediate problems concerning sanitation and the disposal of waste, long-term environmental damage may result from deforestation associated with the need for firewood and building materials. Increased pressure on the land can result in serious soil degradation.

Questions

1 To what extent can periods of international migration be recognised in the twentieth century?
2 Has the construction of a body of theory relating to migration had any value beyond academic interest?
3 Why does the United States receive more immigrants than the rest of the world put together?
4 Describe and explain the pattern of internal migration in Brazil.
5 Discuss the main issues associated with the movement of refugees.

Bibliography

References

The Population of England and Wales in 1991: A Census Atlas by A. J. Fielding for the Geographical Association, 1993.

World Population Trends by Ray Hall, CUP, 1989.

1998 World Population Data Sheet (updated annually) published by the Population Reference Bureau and available from Population Concern, 178–202 Great Portland Street, London W1N 5TB.

Europe's Population: Towards the next century, edited by R. Hall and P. White, UCL Press, 1995.

Population movements and the Third World by M. Parnwell, Routledge, 1993.

Annual Abstract of Statistics 1998, HMSO, 1998.

North America: An Advanced Geography by B. Price and P. Guinness, Hodder & Stoughton, 1997.

An Introduction to Population Geography [2nd ed.] by W. Hornby and M. Jones, Cambridge, 1993.

The Population of Britain in the 1990s by Champion, A et al., OUP, 1996

'Migration' by P. Guinness, Hodder & Stoughton, 2002

Internet

Demography and Population Resources
http://pstc3.pstc.brown.edu/sites.html

PopNet: Global Population Information
http://www.popnet.org/

Population Studies Center, University of Michigan
http://www.psc.lsa.umich.edu/library/resources.shtml

US Census Bureau: World Population Information
http://www.census.gov/ipc/www/world.html

Summary of the World Health Organisation's World Health Report 1996
http://www.who.ch/whr/1996/exsume.htm

University of Leicester
http://www.geog.le.ac.uk/cti

2 resource management

Population and resources

Defining resources

Resources can be classed as either natural or human. Figure 2.1 provides a classification of natural resources, the focus of this chapter. The traditional distinction is between renewable or flow resources and non-renewable or stock resources. However, the importance of aesthetic resources is being recognised increasingly. Further subdivision of the non-renewable category is particularly relevant to both fuel and non-fuel minerals. Renewable resources can be viewed as either critical or non-critical. The former are sustainable if prudent resource management is employed while the latter can be seen as everlasting.

Ecological footprints

In the United States it takes 4.9 hectares (ha) to supply the average person's basic needs (Figure 2.2); in the Netherlands 3.2 ha; in India 0.4 ha. The Dutch ecological footprint covers 15 times the area of the Netherlands, whereas India's footprint exceeds its area by only about 35 per cent. Clearly, the Dutch can only realise such a high rate of resource use by substantial importing. Most alarmingly, if the entire planet lived like Americans, it would take three of planet earth to support the present global population.

Early views on the relationship between population and resources

The relationship between population and resources has concerned those with an understanding of the subject for thousands of years. However, the assumptions made by earlier writers were based on limited evidence as few statistical records existed more than two centuries ago. Below are just some of the views that have been expressed through time.

Key Definitions

resource Any aspect of the environment which can be used to meet human needs.

resource depletion The consumption of non-renewable, finite resources which will eventually lead to their exhaustion.

resource management The control of exploitation and use of resources in relation to economic and environmental costs.

sustainable development A carefully calculated system of resource management which ensures that the current level of exploitation does not compromise the ability of future generations to meet their own needs.

United States

The Netherlands

India

Figure 2.2 Ecological footprints

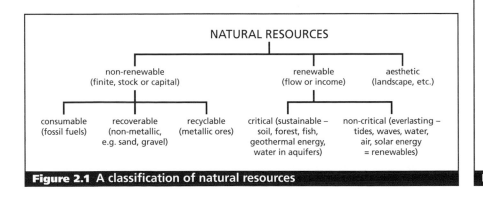

NATURAL RESOURCES

non-renewable (finite, stock or capital)

renewable (flow or income)

aesthetic (landscape, etc.)

consumable (fossil fuels)

recoverable (non-metallic, e.g. sand, gravel)

recyclable (metallic ores)

critical (sustainable – soil, forest, fish, geothermal energy, water in aquifers)

non-critical (everlasting – tides, waves, water, air, solar energy = renewables)

Figure 2.1 A classification of natural resources

- Confucius, the ancient Chinese philosopher, said that excessive population growth reduced output per worker, depressed the level of living and produced strife. He discussed the concept of optimum numbers, arguing that an ideal proportion between land and numbers existed and any major deviation from this created poverty. When imbalance occurred he believed the government should move people from overpopulated to underpopulated areas.

- Plato and Aristotle also considered the question of optimum size: on this depended human potentialities being fully developed and humans' 'highest good' being realised.

- Medieval writers generally favoured a high birth rate because of the constant threats of sudden depopulation through wars, famine and epidemics.

- The Mercantilist schools of political economy during the seventeenth and eighteenth centuries emphasised the economic, political and military advantages of a large and growing population.

- Thomas Malthus, who was concerned that population was rising too rapidly, wrote his first essay in 1798 entitled 'An essay on the principle of population as it affects the future improvement of society'.

- In the nineteenth century Karl Marx made the most powerful attack of any on the work of Malthus, stating 'an abstract law of population exists for plants and animals only'. Socialist and Marxist writers believed that any population problems would be solved through the reorganisation of society.

- Since the start of the twentieth century demographic debate has been based on the availability of increasingly sophisticated data in terms of both depth and breadth of coverage. Concern about the 'population explosion' developed in the 1960s.

The ideas of Thomas Malthus

The Reverend Malthus (1766–1834) said that the crux of the population problem was 'the existence of a tendency in mankind to increase, if unchecked, beyond the possibility of an adequate supply of food in a limited territory'. Malthus thought that an increased food supply was achieved mainly by bringing more land into arable production, and maintained that while the supply of food could, at best, be increased only by a constant amount in arithmetical progression (1 – 2 – 3 – 4 – 5 – 6), the human population tends to increase in geometrical progression (1 – 2 – 4 – 8 – 16 – 32), multiplying itself by a constant amount each time. In time, population would outstrip food supply until a catastrophe occurred in the form of famine, disease or war. The latter would occur as human groups fought over increasingly scarce resources. These limiting factors maintained a balance between population and resources in the long term. In a later paper Malthus placed significant emphasis on 'moral restraint' as an important factor in controlling population.

Clearly Malthus was influenced by events in and before the eighteenth century, and could not have foreseen the great advances that were to unfold in the following two centuries which have allowed population to grow at unprecedented rates alongside a huge rise in the production of resources.

Optimum population: theory and practice

The idea of optimum population has been understood mainly in an economic sense (Figure 2.3). At first, an increasing population allows for a fuller exploitation of a country's resource base causing living standards to rise. However, beyond a certain level rising numbers place increasing pressure on resources and living standards begin to decline.

In history, the power of the ruling elite or government has often had the edge over individual welfare as an aim. Here power represents a collective aim which may or may not take the form of armament (Figure 2.4). The power optimum is

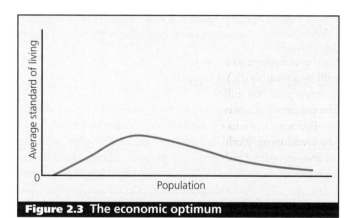

Figure 2.3 The economic optimum

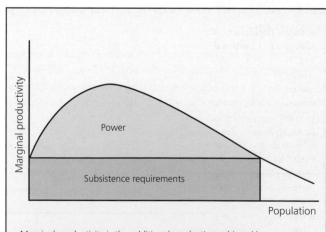

Marginal productivity is the additional production achieved by employing each extra worker. Such productivity is divided into two parts. One part is required by the worker to subsist at a basic level of well-being which will not impair his/her ability to work. All productivity above the subsistence level (power) may be taken from workers in the form of taxation and used by the government to achieve its aims. Such aims could be military, economic, social or cultural.

Figure 2.4 The power optimum

obviously smaller than the maximum population but is always higher than the economic optimum. Thus when a population increases and other factors are constant the following successive positions can be recognised:

- the minimum population
- **the population resulting in the maximum marginal productivity (fastest rate of growth in total output)**
- the economic optimum population
- the power optimum population
- the maximum population.

There is no historical example of a stationary population having achieved appreciable economic progress, although this may not be so in the future. In the past it is not coincidental that periods of rapid population growth have paralleled eras of technological advance which have increased the carrying capacity of countries and regions. Thus, we are led from the idea of optimum population as a static concept to the dynamic concept of optimum rhythm of growth (Figure 2.5) whereby population growth responds to substantial technological advances. For example, Abbé Raynal (*Revolution de l'Amerique*, 1781) said of the United States 'If ten million men ever manage to support themselves in these provinces it will be a great deal'. Yet today the population of the United States is over 260 million and hardly anyone would consider the country to be overpopulated.

The most obvious examples of population pressure are in the Developing World but the question here is: Are these cases of absolute overpopulation or the results of underdevelopment that can be rectified by adopting remedial strategies over time?

Questions

1 Explain the concept of ecological footprints.
2 How might socio-economic and political conditions differ between two countries, one pursuing the power optimum population and the other the economic optimum population as a matter of policy?
3 Study Figure 2.5.
   (a) Suggest why the population initially started to increase.
   (b) What could account for the increases in carrying capacity at times A and B?
   (c) Why can Figure 2.5 be described as a dynamic model while Figures 2.3 and 2.4 are static models?

Population and food supply

World food summits

Forecasts of famine tend to appear every few decades or so. In 1974 a world food summit held in Rome met against a background of rapidly rising food prices and a high rate of global population growth. The major concern was that the

Key Definitions 2

optimum population   The population that achieves a given aim in the most satisfactory way.

economic optimum   The level of population which, through the production of goods and services, provides the highest average standard of living.

power optimum   The population which achieves the greatest level of production above that which is required for its own subsistence.

underpopulation   When there are too few people in an area to use the resources available efficiently.

overpopulation   When there are too many people in an area relative to the resources and the level of technology available.

optimum rhythm of growth   The level of population growth that best utilises the resources and technology available. Improvements in the resource situation or/and technology are paralleled by more rapid population growth.

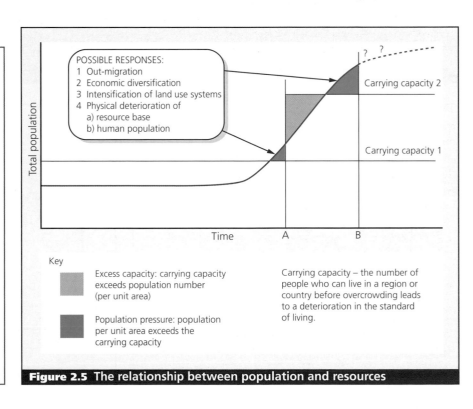

Figure 2.5 The relationship between population and resources

surge in population would overwhelm humankind's ability to produce food in the early twenty-first century. The possibility that the predictions of Thomas Malthus were going to come true was very real in the opinion of some experts. These neo-Malthusians began to issue dire warnings.

The next world food summit, again hosted by Rome, was held in 1996. It, too, met against a background of falling stocks and rising prices whereas the general trend in commodities is to show rising stock and falling prices (Figures 2.7 and 2.8). But new concerns, unknown in 1974 had appeared. Global warming threatened to reduce the productivity of substantial areas of land and many scientists were worried about the long-term consequences of genetic engineering. The errors of past strategies had also become all too apparent in many parts of the world. Across Asia vast areas

of irrigated land had become waterlogged and rendered almost totally unproductive. In many regions the intensive use of chemical fertilisers was taking a heavy toll in terms of both runoff into rivers and lakes and the re-emergence of crop diseases, such as the virulent fungus responsible for the Irish potato famine, having developed resistance to traditional farm chemicals.

Lester Brown, president of the environmental organisation the Worldwatch Institute and seen by some as the world's leading modern Malthusian, argued that the world was entering an era of food scarcity. He contended that growing demand for grain, from China in particular, could soon overwhelm the capacity of all the world's grain-producing countries. However, the modern anti-Malthusians counselled against panicking over short-term fluctuations, pointing in

Figure 2.6 Grain mountain

Key Definitions 3

Malthusians (or neo-Malthusians) The pessimistic lobby who fear that population growth will outstrip resources leading to the consequences predicted by Thomas Malthus.

Anti-Malthusians The optimists who argue that either population growth will slow well before the limits of resources are reached or that the ingenuity of humankind will solve resource problems when they arise.

Green Revolution The introduction of high-yielding seeds and modern agricultural techniques in developing countries.

perennial crops Crops that do not die off once harvested (annual crops), existing for years before reseeding may be required.

sustainable agriculture Agricultural systems, emphasising biological relationships and natural processes, that maintain soil fertility thus allowing current levels of farm production to continue indefinitely.

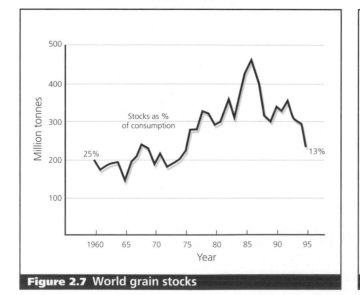

Figure 2.7 World grain stocks

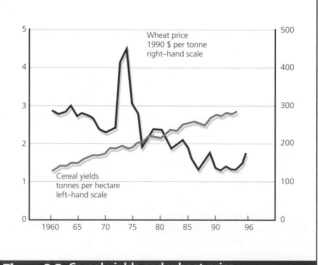

Figure 2.8 Cereal yields and wheat price

particular to the way in which food production has grown significantly faster than population in the second half of the twentieth century (Figure 2.9). Figure 2.10 summarises the opposing views of the neo-Malthusians and the resource optimists such as Boserup.

However, although it is true that the world grain harvest tripled between 1950 and 1990, it tapered off significantly in the 1990s. The neo-Malthusians stress the decline in the amount of grain area per person from a global average of 0.23 ha in 1950 to 0.13 ha in the mid-1990s. This is a consequence of (a) population growth and (b) loss of cropland due to urban expansion, soil degradation and a number of other factors. Population growth is concentrated in those developing countries least able to cope with the resource and food consequences of such growth.

Three agricultural worlds

In terms of agricultural production the nations of the world can be placed into three groups:

- **the haves** – Europe, North America, Australia and New Zealand – have sufficient cropland to meet most of their food needs and efficient farm production systems enabling the production of more food from the same amount of land;
- **the rich have-nots** – a mixed grouping of countries which includes land-short Japan and Singapore, along with rapidly developing countries such as Indonesia, China, Chile, Peru, Saudi Arabia and the other Gulf States – are unable to grow enough food for their populations but can afford to purchase imports to make up the deficit;
- **the poor have-nots** – consisting of the majority of the Developing World – have over 3 billion people and are unable to produce enough food for their populations but cannot afford the imports to make up the deficit.

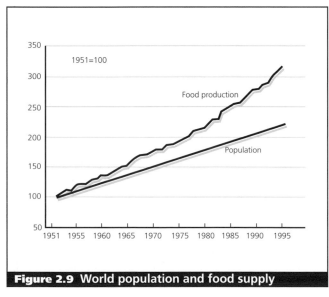

Figure 2.9 World population and food supply

The Green Revolution: a reassessment

The package of agricultural improvements generally known as the Green Revolution was seen as the answer to the food problem in many parts of the Developing World. India was one of the first countries to benefit when a high-yielding variety seed programme (HVP) commenced in 1966–7. In terms of production it was a turning point for Indian agriculture which had virtually reached stagnation. The HVP introduced new hybrid varieties of five cereals – wheat, rice, maize, sorghum and millet. All were drought resistant with the exception of rice, were responsive to the application of fertilisers and had a shorter growing season than the traditional varieties they replaced. Although the benefits of the Green Revolution are clear, serious criticisms have also been made. The two sides of the story can be summarised as follows:

Advantages

- **Yields are twice to four times greater than traditional varieties.**

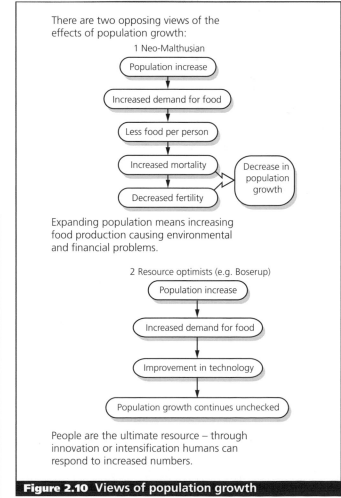

Figure 2.10 Views of population growth

- The shorter growing season has allowed the introduction of an extra crop in some areas.
- Farming incomes have increased allowing the purchase of machinery, better seeds, fertilisers and pesticides.
- The diet of rural communities is now more varied.
- Local infrastructure has been upgraded to accommodate a stronger market approach.
- Employment has been created in industries supplying farms with inputs.
- Higher returns have justified a significant increase in irrigation.

Disadvantages

- High inputs of fertiliser and pesticide are required to optimise production. This is costly in both economic and environmental terms. In some areas rural indebtedness has risen sharply.
- High-yielding varieties (HYVs) require more weed control and are often more susceptible to pests and disease.
- Middle and higher income farmers have often benefited much more than the majority on low incomes, thus widening the income gap in rural communities. Increased rural to urban migration has often been the result.
- Mechanisation has increased rural unemployment.
- Some HYVs have an inferior taste.
- The problem of salinisation has increased along with the expansion of the irrigated area.

The Green Revolution: the latest concern

In recent years a much greater concern has arisen about Green Revolution agriculture. In the early 1990s nutritionists

Figure 2.11 Topsoil is still vanishing; a tropical river with a heavy load

noticed that even in countries where average food intake had risen, incapacitating diseases associated with mineral and vitamin deficiencies remained commonplace and in some instances had actually increased. A 1992 UN report directly linked some of these deficiencies to the increased consumption of Green Revolution crops. The problem is that the HYVs introduced during the Green Revolution are usually low in minerals and vitamins. Because the new crops have displaced the local fruits, vegetables and legumes that traditionally supplied important vitamins and minerals, the diet of many people in the Developing World is now extremely low in zinc, iron, vitamin A and other micronutrients. This is threatening to lock parts of the Developing World into an endless cycle of ill-health, low productivity and underdevelopment. In some developing countries the majority of the population suffer this hidden starvation. People who are continually starved of micronutrients never fulfil their physical or intellectual potential. The World Bank has estimated that deficiencies of iron, iodine and vitamin A are responsible for reducing the GDP of the Developing World by as much as 5 per cent. The only real solution, according to a 1996 report by the International Food Policy Research Institute, is an international effort to breed new crop strains for the Developing World that are both high-yielding and rich in vitamins and minerals.

Perennial crops: the next agricultural revolution?

The answer to many of the world's current agricultural problems may lie in the development of perennial crops. Today's annual crops die off once harvested and new seeds have to be planted before the cycle of production can begin again. The soil is most vulnerable to erosion in the period between harvesting and the next planting. Perennial crops would protect the soil from erosion and also offer other advantages (Figure 2.12). Over the next few years, plant biologists hope to breed plants that closely resemble domestic crops but retain their perennial habit. Classical crossing methods have been proved to work in the search for perennial crop plants but the process is slow. Some plant breeders aim to speed up the process by using genetic engineering. The objective is to find the genes that are linked to domestication and then insert these into wild plants. The article from which Figure 2.12 is extracted concludes, 'In the meantime, farming is slowly approaching a crisis point. Topsoil is still vanishing, and what remains is becoming sterile and compacted. In this environment advocates of perennial agriculture are locked in a race against time. Sustaining topsoil is absolutely essential if viable agricultural systems are to be maintained'.

Among the other potential agricultural advances which have been discussed in the scientific journals recently are:

- The development of a variety of rice that can survive flooding because geneticists can now zero-in on the relevant gene. Farmers in flood-prone areas currently cope with high water levels by planting taller varieties of rice. However, these yield between 20 and 40 per cent less rice because the plants divert nutrients into vegetation growth rather than grain production.

■ The development of an enzyme that could one day allow plants to grow in climates that would otherwise be too dry to support them. The objective is to produce a kind of desert super-plant.

Sustainable agriculture

There has been a growing recognition that high technological input may not be the best way forward because in many areas such methods, if they can be afforded, are not sustainable indefinitely. Sustainable agricultural systems emphasise:

■ biological relationships and natural processes over chemically intensive methods

■ management over technology

■ the participation of farmers and rural people in problem solving and decision making.

The ultimate objective is a much higher level of self-reliance in farming communities. This does not involve a total rejection of modern methods but careful selection of those which are of indefinite benefit to the community. The need for sustainable agricultural systems is greatest in marginal, fragile environments where the shortcomings of Western high-input systems have been most exposed. For communities in such environments the sustainable production of food is the most important aspect of achieving food-secure livelihoods. These communities are often remote from the main lines of

Pastures new

The crops that feed us today give up their grain and die, leaving the soil exposed to wind and rain. But what if the plants lived on from one year to the next, asks *Meg Gordon*

A WIND whips across the bare fields. With the season's crop harvested, surface soil is swept up in spirals. It rises into the air, obscuring the Sun and turning the winter sky a paler shade of blue. Around the globe, from Australia to the Central Asian republics of Turkestan and Uzbeck-istan and California's Central Valley, dust storms are a seasonal certainty. Little by little, the world's fertile soil is vanishing.

Each year, farmers harvest their wheat, barley, maize and rice leaving the land exposed to the ravages of wind and rain. These forces erode agri-cultural soil at a rate of around 1 per cent a year, says ecologist Stuart Pimm of the University of Tennessee in Knoxville. The high-tech solution is to increase the productivity of remaining land by pumping the ground full of chemical fertilisers and using machines to plough up compacted soil. Such

methods, with fungicides and pesti-cides thrown in, have so far managed to feed most of the world's population, but not without enormous environ-mental and financial costs. No more than a quick fix that puts back nothing permanent into the soil, these cannot continue indefinitely.

But what if cereal crops only needed to be replanted once every few years instead of annually? Perennial crops would hold the soil in place with their extensive root systems. Roots also keep soil from compacting to the point where water and new roots can no longer penetrate. And the correct mixture of plants might even start the long process of soil regeneration. Plant geneticist Wes Jackson dared to think this more than 20 years ago. Today, his team at the Land Institute in Salina, Kansas, and a small band of researchers around the world are pursuing the idea in earnest.

If they succeed, a new agricultural revolution is on the cards. But the scale of the challenge is enormous. Today's domesticated cereals are all members of the grass family *Poaceae* and peren-nial species will need to come from their wild relatives. But no wild species of cereal grain has been domesticated since farming became established more than 6000 years ago.

Over the years, farmers have created cereals that behave in pre-dictable ways, so they can streamline planting and harvesting and prepare

accurate budgets. Their crops ripen uniformly, give large shatter-resistant seeds, and stay on the stem until harvest time. The seed's papery coat, or chaff, comes away easily when the crop is threshed, and the seeds can be kept for up to two years and still germinate uniformly when planted.

It has taken millennia to remove the ancient traits of individuality and lack of predictability that once increased the wild plant's chance of dodging predators, pests and competi-tors. Selection by farmers has also forced cereal plants to divert the energy previously expended on a strong root and vegetative system into the production of plump seeds.

Not only must plant breeders such as Jackson find a short cut that mimics these thousands of years of breeding, they must also create plants that can compensate for the loss of one great advantage of annual cereals—the ability of farmers to keep them one step ahead of pests by rotating them from field to field.

But the rewards are potentially huge. Perennials offer advantages beyond their ability to protect soil from erosion. They tend to retain more nutrients than annual crops, and so need fewer fertilisers. Also aeons of self-reliance have made them naturally more resistant to drought, disease and pests than cultivated plants.

Figure 2.12 *New Scientist*, **17 January 1998**

infrastructure and they commonly produce one-fifth to one-tenth as much food per hectare as farms in the most fertile Green Revolution areas. However, when yields increase as a consequence of the introduction of sustainable methods, farmers feel secure enough to diversify into new crops. A recent assessment of the global situation with regard to sustainable agriculture produced a ten-point plan to further the spread of sustainable systems (Figure 2.13).

The quest for sustainable agriculture: major problems

Over 100 sustainable programmes worldwide have illustrated that resource-conserving methods and farmer-centred approaches can dramatically raise food production and regenerate rural economies. However, with some encouraging exceptions most of the world is not moving significantly towards sustainable agriculture. The following problems make the quest for sustainable agriculture even more difficult.

- **Limited land**   The UN Food and Agriculture Organization (FAO) estimates that the amount of potentially arable land is 40 per cent more than currently cultivated. However, most of this is marginal requiring costly irrigation systems or large-scale soil fertility enhancement measures to bring it into efficient production.

- **Smaller farms**   In most developing countries the size of small family farms has been halved over the past four decades to provide for each new generation of male heirs. In India, three-fifths of all farms are less than 1 ha. At the same time the power of large-scale farmers has increased and in more and more countries the production of export crops has taken priority over food crops.

- **Degraded land**   Over the world as a whole nearly 2 billion ha of crop and grazing land is suffering from moderate to severe soil degradation. This is an area larger than the United States and Mexico combined. The main causal factor is soil erosion from wind and water. Every year 25 billion tonnes of topsoil are lost; 5 billion in China alone. Land degradation threatens the livelihoods of at least 1 billion people, mainly in the Developing World. Desertification, the process by which productive drylands become wasteland, now affects about 2.6 billion ha of range land, putting the livelihoods of over 800 million people at risk.

- **Irrigation troubles**   The 17 per cent of all cropland under irrigation produces one-third of the world's food supply. However, the yields on half of this irrigated land have fallen in recent years due to: (a) salinisation: in many dry regions, salts that occur naturally in the soil must be drained away with irrigation runoff, otherwise they accumulate in the soil. The salts gradually work their way to the surface, killing crops and poisoning the land; (b) waterlogging: if the drainage of irrigation water is

---

A ten-point plan for policy change

1   Establish national policies and strategies that support sustainable agriculture, such as redirecting subsidies and grants towards sustainable practices.

2   Reform agricultural teaching establishments to encourage the formal adoption of participatory approaches.

3   Develop farmer-centred research and extension by supporting farmer-to-farmer exchanges and schemes for farmer training in their own communities.

4   Create policies which encourage the retention of economic surpluses in rural areas gained from the production and marketing of agricultural products.

5   Enhance non-agricultural incomes and off-farm employment in rural areas.

6   Decentralise and devolve authority from governments and aid agencies, while developing the capacity of local organisations to demand the resources and services they need.

7   Support rural women as producers and innovators by increasing their access to productive resources (such as genetic material), savings and credit, agricultural information and formal education and training.

8   Secure property rights for peasant producers, especially through communal tenure systems, by protecting local access to and control of land and other productive resources.

9   Form or strengthen farmers' organisations to encourage persistent co-operative action in agricultural production and resource management.

10   Increase local access to capital for investment in agriculture and resource management by avoiding land-tied credit and supporting the establishment of local savings and credit schemes.

Figure 2.13 *People and the Planet*, Vol 7, No 1

---

impeded, the water table will rise and may eventually reach the root zone, drowning the crops. No more than half of the water withdrawn for irrigation purposes actually reaches crops due to losses into unlined irrigation canals, leakages from pipes and evaporation on its way to the targeted crops.

- **Water shortages**   Water is a finite resource and, already, most of Africa and the Middle East, much of the western United States and north-west Mexico, parts of Chile and Argentina, and nearly all of Australia endure water shortages. The problem is, however, not confined just to quantity as water quality is increasingly being compromised from a variety of pollution sources.

- **Genetic diversity**   Concern is growing about the continuing genetic erosion of the planet's wild strains of cereals and other cultivars. Although about 50 000 varieties of edible plant have been discovered since the beginning of settled agriculture, just 15 now provide 90 per cent of global food intake. Three – rice, wheat and maize – are the staple foods of 4 billion people. The FAO estimates that since 1900 about three-quarters of the genetic diversity of domestic agricultural crops has been lost. Rapid urbanisation, deforestation, the destruction of wetlands and the farming of drylands has destroyed innumerable habitats for wild progenitors of domestic crops. The two main concerns are (a) the spread of crop diseases, which can move rapidly through monocultural systems and (b) without constant infusions of new genes from the wild, geneticists cannot continue to improve domestic crops.

■ **Food security**   Huge global inequalities remain in people's ability to acquire food. Food is neither produced nor consumed equitably. Food security cannot be achieved if land and water continue to become increasingly degraded and polluted.

In a way it is perhaps not surprising that sustainable agricultural systems are few and far between. It was not until the 1930s that the web of relationships among organisms and their habitats began to be understood, and not until the late 1960s that ecology – the formal study of those relationships – exploded into public consciousness.

Figure 2.14 Water is critical to sustain agriculture

Food and sustainable farming in Africa

As Figure 2.15 shows the only world region to record falling food production is Africa. In Africa the downward trend has been continuous, decade by decade, since the 1960s. In 1990 the food consumption of the average Sub-Saharan African was 2053 kilocalories, just under three-quarters of the consumption of an average person in the Developed World. According to recent projections by the International Food Policy Research Institute (IFPRI), Africans can expect their food availability to increase only slightly in the next quarter-century. According to a 'baseline scenario' that incorporates future estimates of variables including income, population growth and agricultural productivity, average food availability in the continent will rise to only 2135 kilocalories per person by 2020 (Figure 2.16).

The farming and grazing lands which comprise Africa's arid, semi-arid and dry sub-humid zones cover about one-fifth of the continent and are inhabited by a quarter of its population. Although they may be considered marginal in one sense, they provide major crops such as cotton, groundnuts, millet and sorghum. These lands are also grazed by millions of livestock.

Dryland soils are low in humus, poor in nutrients and vulnerable to wind and water erosion, particularly at the start of the rains. To make the situation even worse, these parts of Africa have experienced reduced precipitation in recent decades. It is not clear how global warming will affect the drylands in the future. However, even though rainfall may well increase, it is likely to fall in fewer, more intense storms, with much lost through higher levels of evaporation and runoff.

In the 1960s and 1970s mechanisation, HYVs and capital improvements (such as irrigation schemes) were embraced in the push to significantly increase production. The poor performance of such capital investments, compounded by frequent droughts, necessitated a radical reassessment. Now the search is for more sustainable systems to assure a harvest rather than spectacular yields, utilising the knowledge of local farmers rather than relying on imported technologies. A recent article entitled 'Sustaining Africa's Soil' (*People and Planet*, Vol 7, No 1) quoted the following examples.

Figure 2.15 Index of regional food production per head (1979–81 = 100)

Region	Average for			
	1960s	1970s	1980s	early 1990s
World	92.8	97.4	102.6	105.0
Developing countries	91.2	95.8	106.4	115.4
Asia	86.2	93.8	109.2	122.6
Latin America	95.3	96.2	101.9	106.2
Africa	115.8	109.0	96.6	95.2

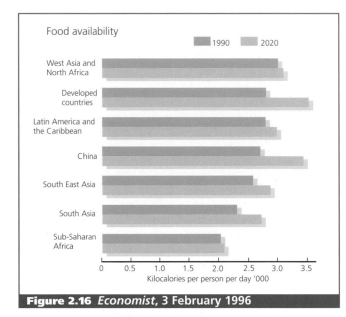

Food availability

Figure 2.16 *Economist*, 3 February 1996

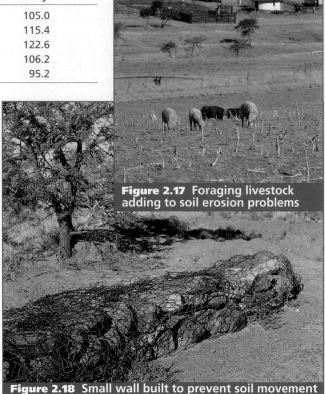

Figure 2.17 Foraging livestock adding to soil erosion problems

Figure 2.18 Small wall built to prevent soil movement

- In the north-west of Burkina Faso, Aly Ouedraogo from the village of Gourcy has reclaimed many hectares of barren land over a 15-year period, turning a hard pan, gravel surface into productive fields, able to produce dense stands of sorghum. The techniques employed were stone lines (Figure 2.18) reinforced by seeding of perennial grasses and fruit trees, while areas between the stone lines have been dug with planting pits. The pits trap runoff, drifting soil, dried leaves and other matter which termites break down. At harvest time, Aly leaves at least 20 cm of stubble to slow wind speeds and provide further material on which termites can feed. A compost and manure pit on the edge of his field provides a handful of fertiliser for each pit. A careful watch is kept for straying livestock. These techniques have been successfully copied in many other communities.

- In the highlands of northern Shewa, Ethiopia, farmers have traditionally used drainage ditches across their fields as a means of protecting land from being washed away when rains are heavy and to reduce surface runoff. This contrasts markedly with the huge terracing programmes carried out in the Ethiopian highlands, supported by government and donor agencies in the 1980s. However, having played no role in planning and designing these systems, local farmers felt no sense of ownership or interest in these structures which now lie abandoned.

Figure 2.19 Eroded, infertile lands (as seen here in Namibia) have affected Africa's food production capacity

Figure 2.20 Major famines and droughts in Africa since the late 1960s	
Years	Sub-regions and countries affected
1968–74	Djibouti, Nigeria (Biafra), Somalia, Sudano-Sahelian zone of West Africa and in particular Burkina Faso, Chad, Mali, Mauritania, Senegal
1972–4	Ethiopia, Nigeria (Hausaland)
1973–5	Niger
1974–6	Angola
1977–8	Zaire (Bas-Fleuve)
1980–2	Kenya (Turkana), Uganda (Karamoja)
1982–5	Angola, Burkina Faso, Ethiopia, Malawi, Mali, Mauritania, Mozambique, Niger, Tanzania, Uganda
1984–5	Chad, Mozambique, Sudan
1987	Ethiopia, Mozambique
1988	Somalia, Sudan
1991	Ethiopia, Liberia, Mozambique, Sudan
1992	Eritrea, Ethiopia, Liberia, Mauritania, Mozambique, Sierra Leone, Somalia, Zaire and Southern Africa sub-region
1993	Angola, Burundi, Chad, Liberia, Rwanda, Ethiopia, Eritrea, Kenya, Somalia, Sudan, Zaire and Southern Africa sub-region and in particular Angola, Mozambique, Tanzania
1994	Southern Africa sub-region

- The Dogon people of eastern Mali use a range of soil and water conservation techniques to produce high yields in a difficult environment. Every square centimetre of soil is used. The crops are carefully selected to make the most of each site. Drier fields grow the fine-grained grassy cereal fonio; damp spots grow rice; patches near water are for irrigated vegetables. On bare, baking rock ledges, crevices only 20 cm wide, as long as they have a little soil, are planted with millet and beans. Narrow hollows among huge boulders are planted with millet, thatching grass and gourds. When weeding occurs, the waste is raked into mounds 15 to 20 cm high in between the stalks, creating a trellis of mounds and hollows which slows runoff, allowing it to filter slowly without eroding the soil. The mounds, rich in humus from decaying weeds, are used to plant next year's seed. Along the downhill edge of fields, rocks are piled in long lines level with the contour.

The food situation in many parts of Africa is critical. The continent has been affected by famine and drought on a regular basis (Figure 2.20). However, the difficulties of the physical environment alone are far from fully responsible for the food problem. Human conflict and the host of pathologies that trail in its wake dogged the continent in the latter part of the twentieth century. Sustainability, therefore, is not just about an approach to natural resource exploitation. This cannot happen unless peaceful human interaction is sustained first.

Questions

1 Outline the contrasting attitudes of the Malthusians and neo-Malthusians to the current food supply situation.
2 To what extent is it realistic to recognise 'three agricultural worlds'?
3 Discuss the advantages and disadvantages of the Green Revolution.
4 **(a)** What is sustainable agriculture?
   (b) Why is it proving so difficult to put into practice on a significant scale?
5 Assess the extent of the food problem in Africa.

Overfishing: the tragedy of the commons

International trends

In 1946 world production of fish was approximately 20 million tonnes. By the late 1960s the total had risen to 70 million tonnes, a rate of increase of 6 per cent per annum. In contrast the 1970s was a decade of stagnation for world fish production, which totalled 72 million tonnes in 1980. However, in the 1980s global production again began to rise, boosted by the escalation of large-scale commercial fishing in deep waters, reaching just over 100 million tonnes in 1989 and topping 101 million tonnes in 1993 (Figures 2.21 and 2.22).

During the half century summarised above, there was a phenomenal increase in fishing capacity as more and more

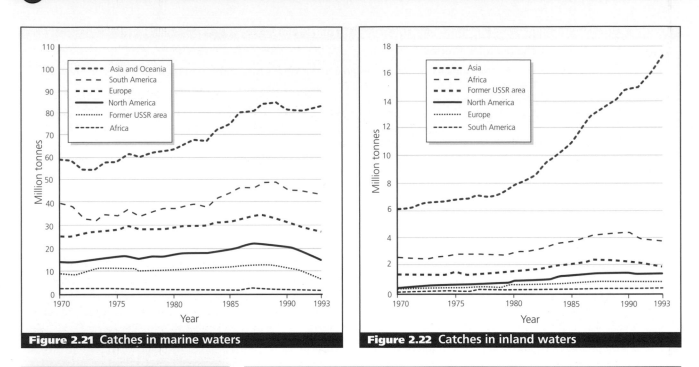

Figure 2.21 Catches in marine waters

Figure 2.22 Catches in inland waters

Figure 2.23 At work on a 'factory ship'

Key Definitions   4

tragedy of the commons The idea that common ownership of a resource leads to overexploitation as some nations will always want to take more than other nations see as their fair share.

overfishing A level of fishing resulting in the depletion of the fish stock.

bycatch Unwanted fish which are caught alongside the desired catch, but thrown overboard upon sorting.

quota A limit set on the total amount of fish allowed to be caught in a particular area over a given time, usually a year. The quota is usually divided among a number of different nations as a result of negotiation.

Regional takes of fish have fallen in most areas of the globe, having reached their peak values anywhere from 4 to 22 years ago. (The year of the peak catch is shown in parentheses.) Only in the Indian Ocean region, where modern mechanised fishing is just now taking hold, have marine catches been on the increase.
(Bars for the Indian Ocean show average annual growth since 1988.)

Atlantic Ocean
North West (1973)
North East (1976)
West Central (1984)
East Central (1990)
South West (1987)
South East (1973)

Mediterranean
and Black Seas (1988)

Pacific Ocean
North West (1988)
North East (1987)
West Central (1991)
East Central (1981)
South West (1991)
South East (1989)

Indian Ocean
Western (still rising)
Eastern (still rising)

-60   -50   -40   -30   -20   -10   0   10

Change in catch, peak year to 1992 (per cent)

Source: *Scientific American*, November 1995

Figure 2.24 Change in catch, peak year to 1992 (%)

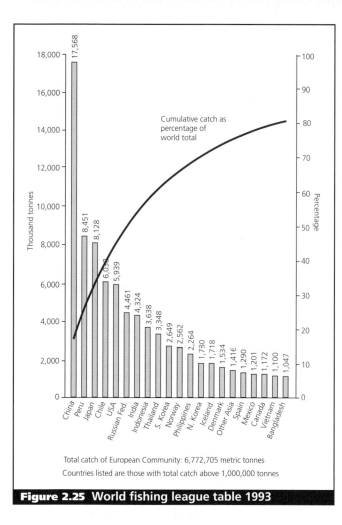

Figure 2.25 World fishing league table 1993

Total catch of European Community: 6,772,705 metric tonnes
Countries listed are those with total catch above 1,000,000 tonnes

(Figure 2.24). Recent FAO analyses have reiterated earlier reports that tonnage has been sustained only by 'fishing down the food chain' which involves catching smaller, younger and less palatable fish.

About 20 countries account for 80 per cent of global sea catch (Figure 2.25). China, Peru and Japan are the big three producers but all nations in the top 20 recorded catches of over 1 million tonnes in 1993. However, overall, fishing contributes only about 1 per cent to the global economy.

The 'strip miners of the sea'

The impact of the modern generation of huge, high-tech fishing vessels has been so great that environmentalists have labelled them 'the strip miners of the sea' (Figure 2.26). Electronic navigation aids such as LORAN (Long-Range Navigation) and GPS (satellite positioning systems) have turned the planet's water into a grid enabling vessels to return to within 10 m of a chosen location, namely sites where fish gather and breed. Ships can also receive satellite weather maps of water-temperature fronts, indicating where fish will be travelling. Aircraft are also sometimes used to track the movement of fish. Figure 2.27 provides at least part of the rationale for such a high level of investment in the industry in recent decades.

There is absolutely no comparison between this kind of fishing and that typical of an earlier age (prior to the 1950s). Then owner-skippers of boats no longer than 20 m, assisted by four or five crew, found fish using personal knowledge and instinct and caught them in nets no more than a hectare or two in size. Limited fuel and refrigeration along with the impact of weather conditions, kept boats relatively close to home.

Large-scale commercial fishing can be extremely wasteful. Many fish are thrown back into the sea because they are damaged, unsaleable, the wrong species or too small (Figure 2.28). In many cases fish are thrown back because regulations demand it. If a vessel has a licence to catch only haddock then any other species caught in the nets must be thrown back. The rejected fish – called bycatch – amount to an estimated 27 million tonnes a year, more than 25 per cent of the total caught worldwide. Bycatch has been a major factor in the depletion of North Sea herring. Its recent decline has been so steep that in July 1996 the EU reduced the annual catch quota from 313 000 tonnes to 156 000 tonnes. Unwanted young herring are caught by large industrial trawlers, mainly Danish, licensed to catch sprat for fish meal. However, young herring are regarded as a particular delicacy in the Netherlands, a country whose quota for herring is only one-third the amount thrown overboard by Danish vessels.

Many European fishermen operate so-called beam trawlers whereby heavy chains are dragged over the seabed to drive fish into the nets. Such action destroys shellfish, worms, sea urchins and other bottom-dwelling creatures. The vast dead biomass has led to a rise in the populations of scavengers

nations looked to the oceans to supplement agricultural production and to satisfy the ever-rising demand for protein. Worldwide, fish contributes 16 per cent of animal protein consumed by humans, the proportion varying from 7 per cent in North America to over 50 per cent in Indonesia, the Philippines and Japan. Fishery analyses have highlighted the fact that much of the growth in production was due to an enormous increase in industrial fish production for meal and oil with the industry moving to lower valued species in order to maintain aggregate total production. The new factory ships are highly sophisticated in terms of both fish hunting and fish processing, requiring high levels of throughput to justify their cost.

The increased catches of the 1980s set serious alarm bells ringing, with many experts fearing that the industry had reached the catastrophe stage. The capacity of the world's fishing industry was now far in excess of sustainable resources.

The FAO separates the oceans into 18 fishing areas for statistical purposes. The most important are the north-west Pacific, south-east Pacific and north-east Atlantic, which together account for 50 per cent of total catches. The FAO has reported that stocks in four of the world's major fishing areas are seriously depleted, with catches in nine others declining

The Grim Sweepers

Giant high-tech vessels roam the world's waters, scooping up their once bottomless bounty

By JAMES O. JACKSON

ENVIRONMENTAL ACTIVISTS CALL THE vessels the "strip miners of the sea." Oceanologists liken many of them to plows that rip open the sea bottom. When they sail into unauthorized areas, governments call them "pirates."

The targets of so much hate and hyperbole are the big, ocean-sweeping factory trawlers that are at the center of debate over the state of the world's fisheries. The ships, trailing nets at least a kilometer long capable of hauling up 400 tons of fish in a single gulp, are blamed for an assault on worldwide fish stocks that could do what once was thought impossible: wipe out whole species of marine wildlife. Thanks mainly to the trawlers and their high-tech gear, 70% of the world's fish stocks are being strained up to and beyond their ability to sustain commercial quantities of fish.

Worse, some kinds of sea life may face total obliteration. Alarmed scientists of the World Conservation Union have added more than 100 species of marine fishes to the group's Red List of Threatened Animals, including such familiar creatures as sharks, tuna, coral-reef fish and sea horses. "For the first time in this century, world marine fish catches are declining," warns a report by Greenpeace, the international environmental organization. "Many of the world's formerly productive fisheries are seriously depleted, and some have collapsed due to overfishing."

According to Greenpeace and a wide array of fisheries experts both in and out of government, the spread of large-scale factory trawling is the single most important cause of the pressure on fish stocks. Among the first big users of the ships was the former Soviet Union's state-run fishing industry, which operated 400 trawlers in the heydays of the 1960s and early 1970s. But the huge vessels are now operated by most of the world's major fishing countries. The U.S., which had no factory fleet at all before 1983, has about 60 large trawlers plowing the rich fishing grounds of the North Pacific. Spain operates a fishing fleet of more than 300,000 tons, including 85 freezer factory ships registered to the Galician port of Vigo alone.

The factory ships are marvels of modern fishing technology, behemoths ranging up to 100 m in length with crews of as many as 100. Sophisticated fish-finding sonar, spotting aircraft and precision satellite-based navigation leave little to luck. Once found, schools of fish numbering in the tens of thousands are swept into city-size nets and brought aboard for conveyer-belt sorting, gutting, filleting and freezing. Cruises can last for days or months, in all kinds of weather and in every corner of the ocean.

Figure 2.26 *Time*, 28 October 1996

ranging from seagulls to the dab. The latter is of little or no commercial value and known in the fishing industry as 'garbage fish'.

Management techniques

- **200-mile limits**   Until the 1970s most of the sea outside a narrow coastal strip 3 to 12 miles wide was regarded as international waters. In 1972, Iceland became the first country to claim an extended fisheries limit of 50 miles, which was increased to 200 miles in 1975. In the latter part of the 1970s the 200-mile fishing limit became accepted in global practice and thus in 1982 the UN Convention on the Law of the Sea established a 200-mile limit as the norm for all coastal countries. The contention that open access exploitation of a common property fish stock attracts excessive effort leading to depletion of stocks had become widely accepted. The objective of, and the main justification for, increased jurisdiction was that by limiting access and managing effort wisely, coastal nations could halt overexploitation and regenerate net economic benefits. The 200-mile limit encompasses most of the world's continental shelves and slopes so that the important demersal stocks that are tied to these shallower areas mostly come under coastal nation management. These 200-mile limits are often fished by foreign fleets which pay substantial licensing fees for the privilege. Nearly 90 per cent of the global marine catch takes place within these limits.

- **Quotas**   These are generally set to maintain a sustainable level of fishing. The problem is trying to ensure that all nations abide by them. For example, in EU waters each member country is given an upper limit to the amount of fish it can catch as well as restrictions on where it can fish.

- **Biological pauses**   Severe depletion of stocks may necessitate a moratorium (a complete cessation) of fishing for a certain time period. Fish scientists have observed that severely depleted populations can recover quickly if left alone. This technique has been employed by Canada in its north west Atlantic waters.

Export prices for fish have exceeded those for beef, chicken and pork by a substantial margin over the past two decades. To facilitate comparison, the price of each meat is scaled to 100 for 1975.

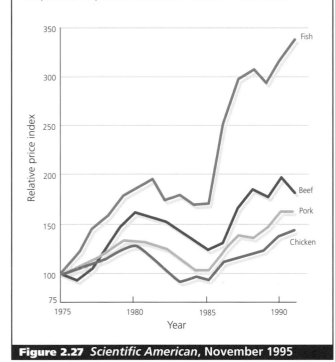

Figure 2.27 *Scientific American*, November 1995

Figure 2.28 Large-scale fishing leads to large-scale wastage

■ **Fleet restructuring programmes** Conservationists argue that without subsidies the profits of the fishing industry would be substantially less, making it less attractive to investors and leading to a considerable reduction in the number of fishing vessels worldwide. According to the Worldwatch Institute, fishing fleets receive some $54 billion annually in direct and indirect government aid. Now the EU is using subsidies to retire vessels and provide compensation for redundant fishers.

Figure 2.29 Traditional fishing in India

The impact on traditional fishing in the Developing World

The capital intensive nature of modern fishing has impacted considerably on fishing communities in both rich and poor nations. However, the impact has been much more severe in developing countries where opportunities for alternative employment are generally fewer and welfare and compensatory schemes usually non-existent. For almost three decades the Indian government has been criticised by the country's 8 million traditional fishers for the way it has encouraged large-scale modern fishing owned by both Indian and foreign companies. The traditional sector has seen its catches drop precipitously as a result of overfishing by large vessels. An additional criticism is that the bycatch from the foreign trawlers is nowadays ground down to feed farmed shrimp, poultry or pigs, for consumption in the Developed World. These 'garbage fish' used to be a primary source of protein for poor Indians. But because fishers bring home less of the no-name fish, prices have risen sharply, putting this essential food out of reach of the poor.

Pollution problems

The impact on fish stocks of dumping of all sorts of waste, both legally and illegally, is causing increasing concern in many parts of the world. In addition, accidents, particularly those involving oil tankers, can have a devastating immediate effect on the fish population of an area. However, only 12 per cent of marine pollution is due to oil spills and only 10 per cent is caused by ships dumping at sea. Runoff and discharges from land cause 44 per cent and airborne emissions 33 per cent of total sea pollution.

Although UN conventions have reduced such practices over the last decade or so, ships still tip rubbish overboard and empty oil waste into the sea. The dumping of high-level radioactive waste was banned by international agreement in the 1970s but many other types of toxic waste have been routinely 'buried at sea'. The impact on marine life, particularly on seabed life, remains imperfectly understood. It appears that the high seas still remain relatively clean, protected by their vast size. However, coastal seas have been seriously contaminated. For example, the Baltic Sea is polluted by more than 900 000 tonnes of nitrogen and 50 000 tonnes of phosphorus a year.

Pollution from factories, sewage and agriculture can bring toxic substances to the sea and can add excessive nutrients, causing phytoplankton to proliferate, thus reducing oxygen levels in the water. Deforestation can increase surface runoff, sometimes choking fragile river and coral habitats in sediment. In some areas coastal mangroves that could otherwise serve as nurseries for young marine fish have been cut down to accommodate aquaculture.

Poisons that find their way into the marine food chain can affect human health when seafood is consumed. Incidents have ranged from mercury poisoning by tuna fish in Japan to cholera-infected clams in the United States.

Problems and policies in North American waters

US commercial fishing is concentrated in three fishing areas but the Pacific North East is by far the most important, accounting for about 50 per cent of the total US catch. The only other fishing grounds of real significance for US fishing are the Atlantic North West and the Atlantic West Central. However, Canadian fishing is even more concentrated, with the Atlantic North West accounting for 71 per cent (1993) of the total catch. Inland waters, whilst locally significant, are of limited general importance, supplying 5.8 per cent of US and 3.1 per cent of Canadian production. Overall the United States and Canada rank fifth and nineteenth respectively in the world fishing league table (Figure 2.25).

The Canadian government in 1976 developed a comprehensive policy document concerning resource management and in the following year declared a 200-mile limit. The country's most extensive fisheries, in the Atlantic North West, had long been in a generally depressed state because of resource depletion resulting from a considerable increase in foreign fishing. Restrictions on foreign operations were partly balanced by quota concessions.

The United States adopted similar management policies in its Fishery Conservation Zone, although it must be noted that the United States and Canada have come into conflict in the delimitation of boundaries. The main dispute concerned where the line should be drawn off Maine, New Brunswick and Nova Scotia, with the rich Georges Bank at issue.

American fishery managers estimate that the US catch is almost half as valuable as it could be if fish stocks were allowed to recover. In 1975 the Alaskan fleet enjoyed a season for Pacific halibut lasting 120 days. The fleet can now take the year's entire catch in one or two 24–hour 'derbys'. If fishing went on longer there would be too few halibut to spawn future catches. The Alaskan herring-roe fishery is open for a mere 40 minutes a year. Boats queue to sell their catch to processors who gut and freeze the year's supply as quickly as possible. Overall, more than 40 per cent of the fish populations in US waters are considered overfished.

Conflict in the Atlantic North West

Since 200-mile limits were internationally recognised in 1982, every valuable fish that straddles or migrates across these borders has been hard hit by foreign fleets. Not surprisingly, the once-rich fishing grounds off Canada's Atlantic coast have become one of the focal points of such intense activity. Fierce competition has led to serious confrontations between fishing fleets here and in many other parts of the world.

Newfoundlanders have depended on the annual influx of cod for their livelihood for 400 years but recent decades have proved to be troublesome times for the numerous small fishing communities in the province. Until the mid-1950s only Canada, the United States and five or six western European countries fished off Canada's Atlantic coast. However, fishing intensified continuously from the late-1950s onwards. The groundfish catch more than doubled from 1.26 million tonnes in 1951 to a peak of 2.83 million tonnes in 1965, but by 1980 it was down to 1.21 million tonnes. In the latter year the cod catch alone, which accounted for 50 per cent by value of all Newfoundland landings, was down to less than a quarter of what it was in the early 1960s.

The decline was reversed for a while by the introduction of the 200-mile limit, but increased activity focusing on stocks straddling the limit has brought the industry to the edge of catastrophe in recent years. The cod stock declined to such an extent that in July 1992 Canada's Department of Fisheries and Oceans declared a two-year moratorium on its Newfoundland and Labrador cod industry, with the loss of 40 000 jobs, to prevent stocks of Atlantic cod from being totally fished out. EU fishing boats operating just beyond the 200-mile limit had contributed to a total haul of cod,

Canada takes firm line on EU overfishing

A Spanish trawler was arrested last week and taken to St John's, Newfoundland, where the captain will face charges under Canadian fisheries conservation laws. When the holds of the Estai were inspected 80% of the catch was found to contain under-sized fish.

A proposal put forward by Prime Minister Chrétien for a 60-day moratorium on turbot fishing has been ignored by the European Union. Their ships, mainly Spanish and Portuguese, continue to reject turbot quotas set by the North-west Atlantic Fisheries Organization and, after initially pulling back, some trawlers returned to the Grand Banks.

Fisheries Minister Brian Tobin says every time Europe ignores a quota, the type of fish being caught has been decimated. Mr Tobin says it's time for that to stop.

Mr Tobin also noted that 39 Spanish vessels just outside the 200-mile zone have already taken about seven thousand tonnes of turbot. That's almost double the quotas set earlier for the 15-country European Union.

Portugal condemned Canada's ultimatum to stop fishing for turbot just outside the 200-mile limit. Portugal's maritime affairs minister called Canada's actions 'deplorable' and a violation of international law.

Mr Tobin said patrol vessels are ready to make more arrests if necessary. Canada's chief negotiator at the United Nations talks to regulate international fishing, Paul Lapointe, said the dispute need never have reached a boiling point but, under the circumstances, most coastal nations would accept emergency action.

Figure 2.30 *Canada Focus*, **17 March 1995**

The result has been extremely costly, both for the province of Newfoundland and for Canada as a whole. Under a special scheme, 20 000 Newfoundlanders made jobless by the cod moratorium are drawing an average of C$335 a week from the government in compensation for their lost earnings. This is in the province with the lowest per capita income and the highest rate of unemployment in Canada. In some fishing communities unemployment has reached 80 per cent. Many villages may eventually die out, eliminating the island's traditional culture.

Concerned that the situation was continuing to deteriorate, the Canadian parliament in 1994 legislated to protect important fish stocks on the high seas that straddle Canada's 200-mile limit. However, it was clearly only a matter of time before this action would bring Canada into dispute with other fishing nations (Figure 2.30).

After tough negotiations Canada and the European Union reached a conservation agreement in April 1995 that was hailed in Ottawa as a model for saving endangered fish stocks around the world. The agreement was not just about providing immediate protection for turbot stocks, but also about rebuilding cod and flatfish stocks already under moratoria. Major components of the accord included:

- independent, full-time observers on board vessels at all times
- enhanced surveillance via satellite tracking
- increased inspections and quick reporting of infractions
- verification of gear and catch records
- significant penalties to deter violations
- new minimum fish-size limits
- improved dockside monitoring.

Fishing law is complex, confused and generally inadequate to meet the needs of world fishing in the 1990s and beyond. It is hoped that agreements such as that between Canada and the EU will set a model of 'best practice' to be followed on a global basis in the future.

redfish, flounder and plaice which was 16 times the quota recommended by the regulatory authorities. In September 1993 the ban was extended to the whole of eastern Canada and in spring 1994 all recreational fishing for cod was forbidden.

It is clear that the moratorium will have to stay in place for the forseeable future. No one knows for sure what caused the collapse but constant overfishing appears to be the most obvious factor. Canada blames EU vessels for this situation but the Europeans argue that Canada has also been guilty of overfishing. After declaring its 200-mile limit in 1977, the Canadian government subsidised new boats and fish processing plants against scientific advice. Other factors put forward as exacerbating the situation are the increasing seal population, colder water and higher salinity.

Questions

1 What is the evidence that the capacity of the world's fishing industry is now far in excess of sustainable resources?
2 Detail the ways in which technological advance has threatened fish stocks in terms of (a) locating schools of fish (b) fishing operations and (c) indirect action.
3 Why is it reasonable to assert that the fishing industry in North America is in crisis?
4 Research an international fishing dispute in the Developing World that has occurred in recent years.

Water resources

Increasing scarcity

The longest a person can survive without water is about ten days. All life and virtually every human activity needs water. It is the world's most essential resource. But for about 80 countries, with 40 per cent of the world's population, lack of water is a constant threat, and the situation is getting worse, with demand for water doubling every 20 years. In those parts of the world where there is enough water, it is being wasted, mismanaged and polluted on a grand scale. In the poorest nations it is not just a question of lack of water; the paltry supplies available are often polluted. The UN estimates that dirty water causes 80 per cent of disease in developing countries, resulting in the death of 10 million people each year. Every day 25 000 children die from diseases caused by unsafe water. At any given time, half the people in the Developing World are suffering from a water-related sickness. In 1995, 20 per cent of the world's people had no access to clean drinking water and 50 per cent lacked proper toilet facilities. Of the 25 countries the UN lists as having the least access to safe water, 19 are in Africa (Figure 2.31).

In June 1997, the UN Earth Summit II held in New York warned about the looming global water crisis. Water scarcity was presented as the 'sleeping tiger' of the world's environmental problems, threatening to put world food supplies in jeopardy, limit economic and social development and create serious conflicts between neighbouring drainage basin countries. In a recent report the UN estimates that two-thirds of world population will be affected by 'severe water stress' by 2025, noting that already a number of the world's great rivers such as the Colorado in the United States are running dry, and that groundwater is also being drained faster than it can be replenished.

Signs of stress

Figure 2.32 shows how demand for water, particularly from the agricultural sector, escalated in the twentieth century, increasing at more than twice the rate of population growth. Global water use tripled between 1950 and 1990 alone. In the past, increasing demand was largely satisfied by constructing new infrastructure. For example, the number of large dams rose from 5000 in 1950 to 38 000 in 1997. However, most of the best sites have now been utilised and environmental opposition now means that dam construction is more difficult than at any time in the past. With 1000 tonnes of water required to grow 1 tonne of grain, it is not obvious where the water to meet future food needs will come from on a sustainable basis. Worldwide, water tables are falling, underground aquifers are being depleted and lakes and wetlands are shrinking. Examples of the global stress on water supplies include:

- **In Central Asia, the diversion of water to irrigate cotton has caused the Aral Sea to shrink to less than half its original size.**
- **Mexico City is sinking by as much as 40 cm a year due to overdrawn aquifers.**
- **Water tables beneath a large area of irrigated farmland in north China are falling by about 1 m a year.**
- **In the Punjab, India's 'bread-basket', the water table is dropping by 20 cm a year.**
- **A 1996 report by China's National Environmental Protection Agency found that 78 per cent of the water in rivers flowing through Chinese cities was no longer drinkable.**
- **The Three Gorges Dam in China, which will be the world's largest, will displace over 1 million people.**
- **North Africa's non-recharging aquifers are being depleted by an estimated 10 billion m³ a year.**
- **Massive water overuse in the Arabian peninsula will exhaust groundwater reserves in 50 years.**

Sandra Postel, author of 'Last Oasis: Facing Water Scarcity' estimates that additional water supplies equivalent to 20 Nile rivers could be needed over the next 30 years just to grow food for the expected 2.6 billion population growth.

Water pollution in the Developing World

While rivers in more affluent countries have become steadily cleaner in recent decades, the reverse has been true in much of the Developing World. It has been estimated that 90 per cent of sewage in developing countries is discharged into rivers,

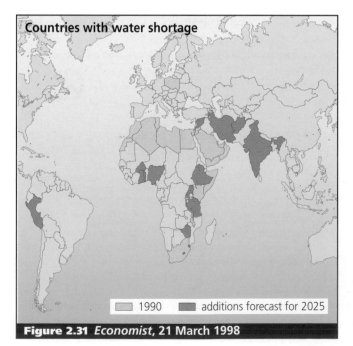

Countries with water shortage

1990   additions forecast for 2025

Figure 2.31 *Economist*, 21 March 1998

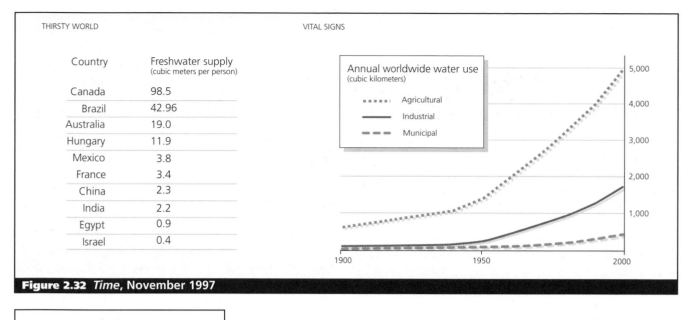

THIRSTY WORLD

Country	Freshwater supply (cubic meters per person)
Canada	98.5
Brazil	42.96
Australia	19.0
Hungary	11.9
Mexico	3.8
France	3.4
China	2.3
India	2.2
Egypt	0.9
Israel	0.4

VITAL SIGNS

Annual worldwide water use (cubic kilometers)

· · · · · Agricultural

———— Industrial

– – – – Municipal

Figure 2.32 *Time*, November 1997

Cost of urban water

Price ratio of water – private vendors: public utility water

Abijan (Côte d'Ivoire) 5:1

Dhaka (Bangladesh) 21.1 to 25.1

Istanbul (Turkey) 10:1

Kampala (Uganda) 4:1 to 9:1

Karachi (Pakistan) 28:1 to 83:1

Lagos (Nigeria) 4:1 to 10:1

Lima (Peru) 17:1

Lome (Togo) 7:1 to 10:1

Nairobi (Kenya) 7:1 to 11:1

Port-au-Prince (Haiti) 17:1 to 100.1

Surabaya (Indonesia) 20:1 to 60:1

Tegucigalpa (Honduras) 16:1 to 34:1

Figure 2.33 *Guardian Education*, 18 March 1997

Key Definitions ⑤

aquifer A permeable rock which will hold water and permit its passage.

groundwater Water found below the surface which is not combined chemically with any minerals present.

desalination The conversion of salt water into fresh water by the extraction of dissolved solids.

water table The top of the water-saturated part of a permeable rock. During periods of high rainfall the water table may extend into the soil and possibly reach the surface of the ground.

water management The organised collection and distribution of water, and the prevention of flooding.

lakes and seas without any treatment. The UN estimates that almost half the population in many Developing World cities does not have access to safe drinking water. For example, 200 million litres of sewage each day drains into the Yamuna river that flows through Delhi. For many people the only alternative to using this water for drinking and cooking is to turn to water vendors who sell tap water at greatly inflated prices (Figure 2.33).

However, the world's most serious water pollution problem has come from an almost totally unexpected source. In the Ganges delta at least 2 million people in West Bengal (India) and Bangladesh are being poisoned to death by drinking water. Millions more are at risk from arsenic that has been found in concentrations exceeding the 'safe' limit by more than 500 times. Although the scale of this tragedy is just emerging it has already been recognised as the world's largest outbreak of arsenic poisoning, with more than half of Bangladesh's 68 000 villages affected. Hundreds have already died since doctors identified the disease in 1984 and the death toll is sure to increase rapidly in the future.

Although as yet there is not unanimous agreement as to the cause, many experts believe that this crisis is the result of the Green Revolution when 3 million tube wells were sunk in Bangladesh alone. The problem is that the region's bedrock contains arsenic. By pumping up water on such a large scale, the rock dried out and oxidised, releasing arsenic in deadly amounts into the water table. The signs of arsenic poisoning can be seen in village after village. Gangrene and horrific skin cancers are the outward signs. Doctors in Calcutta have tried to neutralise the poison with chelating agents but so far the only cure for the disease is clean water and good food. The effects of the poison are exacerbated by the widespread incidence of malnutrition in the region.

To combat the crisis, three huge water-purifying plants are being built, two pipeline projects bringing water from the Ganges are planned and wells are being replaced with deeper tube wells with the objective of bypassing the arsenic-contaminated layer of rock.

The quantity *versus* quality debate

Since the mid-1980s it has become generally accepted that the quantity of water and the convenience of availability can be more important than improvements in quality (beyond a certain level). The rationale behind this view relates to the ways in which different infectious diseases are linked to water.

Figure 2.34 Water is vital for life – the village well, Rajasthan, India

Figure 2.35 Multiple uses of the same water can cause serious problems – The Ganges, India

■ **Faecal-oral diseases** are caused by micro-organisms present in the faeces of infected people. Most of them cause diarrhoea and kill over 3 million children a year. These diseases, including cholera and typhoid, are not only transmitted by water, but can also be passed on by contaminated food, fingers, utensils and even dirty clothes. Transmission of these diseases can be reduced by having more water available in the home to improve cleanliness.

■ **Water-washed skin and eye diseases**, for example trachoma, are most common in arid regions. These diseases have little to do with water quality and the best preventive measure is greater water availability for personal hygiene.

■ **Water-based diseases** such as schistosomiasis (bilharzia) are caused by parasitic worms which enter the body when people wade or swim in infected water. The avoidance of such areas by, for example, having piped-water washing areas, or their purification is the answer here. However, in many impoverished regions neither of these solutions might be an option.

■ **Water-related insect vector diseases** such as malaria and elephantiasis are spread by insects which breed in water. One type breeds in the water storage tanks on large buildings in Indian cities and transmits malaria.

Thus, the main public health benefit from improved water supplies (quality or quantity) is the reduction in faecal-oral diseases. It has been estimated that of the deaths in East Africa which can be prevented by improved water supplies, 90 per cent are in this category. Developing World water engineers, with limited funds, are therefore faced with deciding whether the faecal-oral infections are mainly water-borne, due to poor water quality or mainly transmitted by food, fingers and other such water-washed routes related to the lack of water. Should

Figure 2.36 Limited water supplies add to the problems – Egypt

money be spent on improving the quality of the existing supply or go on increasing that supply at the same quality?

An additional problem is that water authorities in developing countries are often bureaucratic and inefficient. In western Europe, water companies employ on average 2 to 3 people per 1000 connections. In most of Latin America the figure is between 10 and 20. Losses from leakages and theft are also well above those in the Developed World.

Hydropolitics and water terror

More than 300 major river basins as well as many groundwater aquifers cross national boundaries. However, as yet, there are no enforceable laws that govern the allocation and use of international waters.

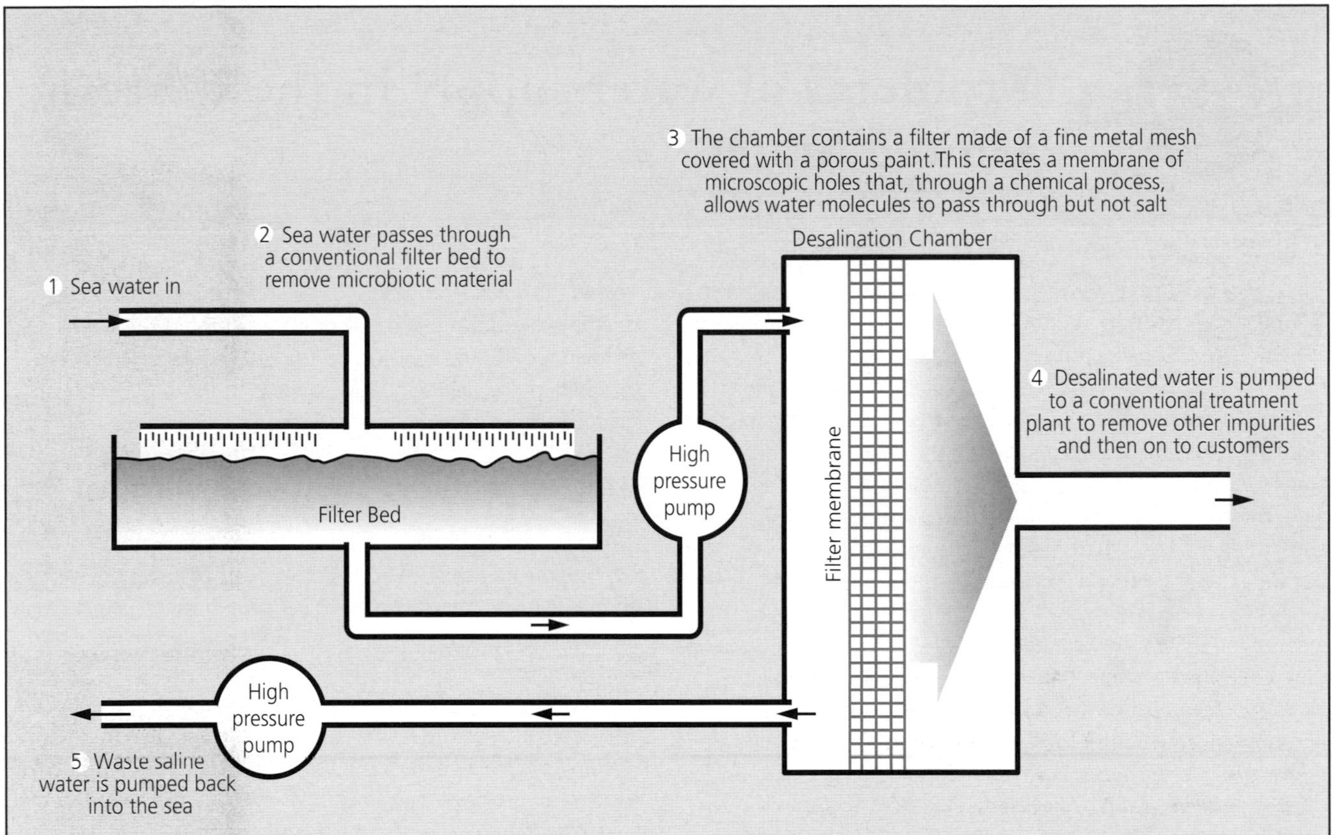

3 The chamber contains a filter made of a fine metal mesh covered with a porous paint. This creates a membrane of microscopic holes that, through a chemical process, allows water molecules to pass through but not salt

Desalination Chamber

2 Sea water passes through a conventional filter bed to remove microbiotic material

1 Sea water in

Filter Bed

High pressure pump

Filter membrane

4 Desalinated water is pumped to a conventional treatment plant to remove other impurities and then on to customers

High pressure pump

5 Waste saline water is pumped back into the sea

Source: *Sunday Telegraph*, 9 November 1997

Figure 2.37 Reverse Osmosis Desalination Plant

Denying access to water has become a familiar characteristic of conflict in recent years. In the Bosnian war of the early 1990s, one of the first acts of the Serbs, besieging Sarajevo, was to shut off the electricity and with it Sarajevo's water pumps. People then had no option but to gather at wells around the city, making them easy targets for Serb snipers and mortar shells. At about the same time water terror was also a potent weapon in the Somalian civil war. People retreating from the fighting filled wells with rocks and dismantled all water infrastructure. These two conflicts could be previews of 'water wars' that some environmentalists warn will eventually engulf the world. For example, in the Middle East, the late King Hussein of Jordan said that only a dispute over water could break the peace his country had established with Israel.

Desalination: the answer to water shortages?

Desalination plants are in widespread use in the Middle East where other forms of water supply are extremely scarce. Most of these plants distil water by boiling, generally using waste gases produced by oil wells. Without the availability of waste energy the process would be extremely expensive. This is the main reason why desalination plants are few and far between outside the Middle East.

However, another method of desalination does exist. Originally developed in California in the mid-1960s for industrial use, the 'reverse osmosis' technique (Figure 2.37) is now being applied to drinking water. In Britain, Anglian Water operated a reverse osmosis desalination pilot plant at Felixstowe in 1998. Although only a relatively small volume of water was extracted, the project engineers claimed to have cut the cost of desalination from ten times to just twice that of conventional supplies. However, the decision to build a full-scale plant remains to be made.

The sea water will still have to undergo conventional filter treatment to rid it of impurities such as microbes pumped into the sea from sewage plants. Thus it is likely that even when the technology has been highly refined, desalinated water will always be more expensive than obtaining water from conventional sources. However, desalination does have other advantages:

■ **it does not affect water level in rivers**

■ **it could mean that controversial plans for new reservoirs could be shelved.**

Problems of water supply in the western United States

The United States is a huge consumer of water and over the country as a whole there would not seem to be a problem (Figure 2.38). However, the western states of the United States, covering 60 per cent of the national land area with 40 per cent of the total population, receive only 25 per cent of the country's mean annual precipitation. Yet each day the west uses as much water as the east. The west has prospered this century. Agriculture, industry and settlement have flourished due to a huge investment in water transfer schemes. Hundreds of aqueducts take water from areas of surplus to areas of shortage. The federal government has paid most of the bill but now the demand for water is greater than the supply. If the west is to continue to expand, a solution to the water problem must be found.

Although much of the west is desert or semi-desert, large areas of dry land have been transformed into fertile farms and sprawling cities. It all began with the Reclamation Act of 1902 which allowed the building of canals, dams and hydro-electric power systems in the states that lie, all or in part, west of the 100th meridian. Water supply was to be the key to economic development in general, benefiting not only the west but the United States as a whole.

Bringing water to southern California

California has benefited most from this investment in water supply. A great imbalance exists between the distributions of precipitation and population as 70 per cent of runoff originates in the northern one-third of the state but 80 per cent of the demand for water is in the southern two-thirds. While irrigation is the prime water user, the sprawling urban areas have also greatly increased demand. The 3.5 million ha of irrigated land in California are situated mainly in the Imperial, Coachella, San Joaquin and the lower Sacramento valleys. Figure 2.39 shows the major component parts of water transfer and storage in the state which is based around two huge schemes.

The federally funded Central Valley Project was initiated by the State Water Plan of 1931. Water released by the Shasta Dam and other reservoirs flows down the Sacramento river, across the delta between the Sacramento and San Joaquin rivers, to Tracy where it is raised 60 m into the Delta-Mendota canal. The canal carries the water 160 km south to Mendota where it is transferred into the San Joaquin river to replace water drawn from the San Joaquin behind the Friant Dam. The latter stores water for diversion to the Bakersfield area via the Friant Kern canal. The Madiera canal irrigates an area north of Friant. The Central Valley Project, completed in 1951, has also played an important role in expanding the hydro-electric capacity of the state, controlling winter flooding in the lower Sacramento and San Joaquin, and improving navigation.

The other major scheme, the State Water Project, was designed primarily to supply water for non-agricultural use to the Los Angeles area. Completed in 1990, water flows the 965 km from behind Oroville Dam, the key storage reservoir, to the Perris reservoir south-east of Los Angeles. Water released from the Sacramento and Feather rivers flows into and through the delta into the California aqueduct, the main component of the scheme. After being lifted 366 m to the foot of the Tehachapi Mountains the water is then pumped 610 m over the mountains and from there flows into the Perris and Castaic reservoirs. The Castaic reservoir began to supply the Metropolitan Water District in 1971, followed by the Perris reservoir in 1975.

Concerned about eventual reductions in supply from the Colorado river, the state government in 1980 set in motion the

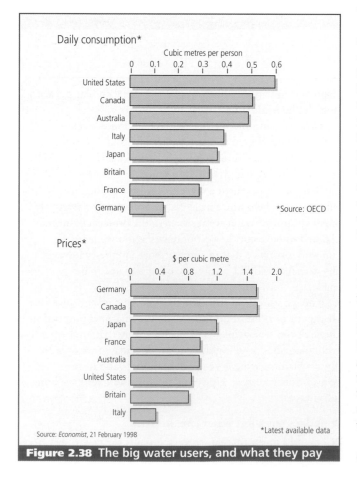

Daily consumption*

Cubic metres per person

Source: OECD

United States
Canada
Australia
Italy
Japan
Britain
France
Germany

Prices*

$ per cubic metre

Germany
Canada
Japan
France
Australia
United States
Britain
Italy

Source: *Economist*, 21 February 1998

*Latest available data

Figure 2.38 The big water users, and what they pay

long-proposed second phase of the State Water Project; the Peripheral canal. The 68-km long canal starts at the Sacramento river, cutting an arc southwards through the periphery of the delta, emptying into a collection point called Clifton Court Forebay and then feeding into the California Aqueduct. Although having separate origins, both projects are now subsumed, since 1957, under the California Water Plan.

Other water transfer schemes also play an essential role. The Colorado river aqueduct, 400 km long, carries water to the Metropolitan Water District from the Parker Dam. In the extreme south of the state the Imperial and Coachella aqueducts transport irrigation water impounded behind the Imperial Dam. The Owens Valley aqueduct, 400 km long, carries water from the Sierra Nevada mountains to the Metropolitan Water District.

Agriculture uses more than 80 per cent of the state's water, although it accounts for less than one-tenth of the economy. Water development, largely financed by the federal government, has been a huge subsidy to California in general and to big water users in particular. An interesting recent development is the proposed agreement between the Imperial Irrigation District, responsible for distributing water to the farms of the Imperial Valley and the San Diego County Water Authority. If approved farmers would be paid to conserve 246 400 million litres a year which would be sold to San Diego. This would be a start to bringing the price mechanism to bear on water resources.

The Colorado: a river under pressure

The 2333km long Colorado river is an important source of water in the south-west (Figure 2.40). The river rises 4250 m up in the Rocky Mountains of northern Colorado state and flows generally south-west through Colorado, Utah, Arizona and between Nevada and Arizona, and Arizona and California before crossing the border into Mexico. The river drains an area of about 632 000 km² which is larger than France. Centuries ago, Native Americans used the Colorado and other rivers to irrigate their fields. Ruins of their old canals are still found in some parts of the desert.

In 1912 Joseph Lippincott, seeking future water supplies for the growing city of Los Angeles, described the Colorado as 'an American Nile awaiting regulation'. The Colorado was the first river system in which the concept of multiple use of water was attempted by the US Bureau of Reclamation. In 1922 the Colorado River Compact divided the seven states of the basin into two groups: Upper Basin and Lower Basin. Each group was allocated 9.25 trillion litres of water annually, while a 1944 treaty guaranteed a further 1.85 trillion litres to Mexico. Completed in 1936, the Hoover Dam (Figure 2.41) and Lake Mead marked the beginning of the era of artificial control of the Colorado. Glen Canyon Dam and Lake Powell, and Parker Dam and Lake Havasu are among the most notable of several major units replicating the Hoover Dam's functions of irrigation, flood and silt control, power, domestic and industrial water supplies, and recreation. All these

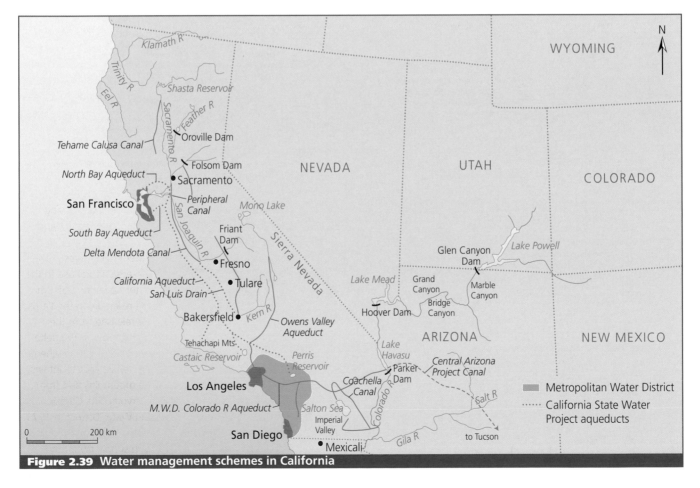

Figure 2.39 Water management schemes in California

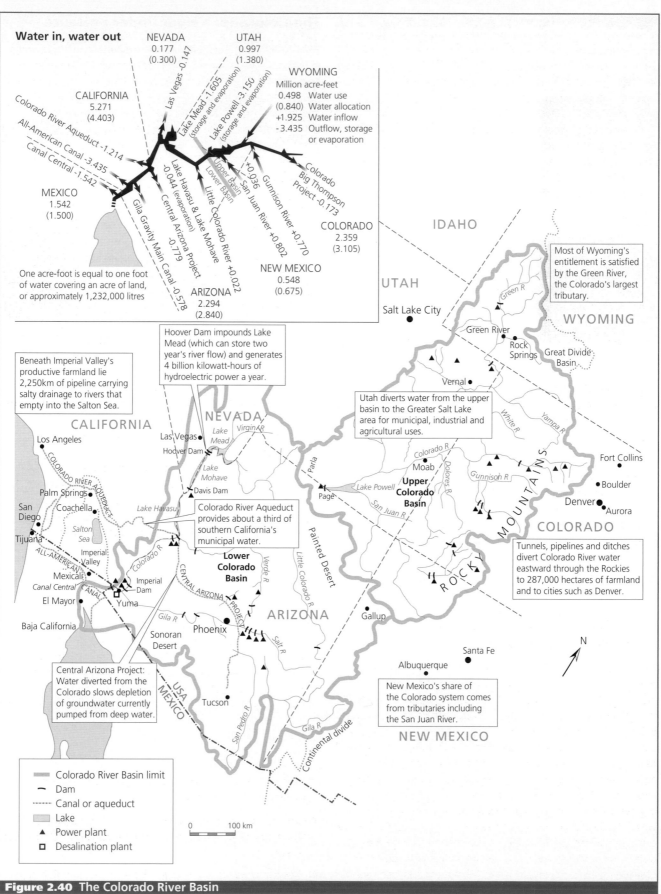

Water in, water out

NEVADA
0.177
(0.300)

UTAH
0.997
(1.380)

WYOMING
Million acre-feet
0.498 Water use
(0.840) Water allocation
+1.925 Water inflow
−3.435 Outflow, storage
or evaporation

CALIFORNIA
5.271
(4.403)

Colorado River Aqueduct −1.214

All-American Canal −3.435

Canal Central −1.542

Las Vegas −0.147

Lake Mead −1.605 (storage and evaporation)

Lake Powell −3.150 (storage and evaporation)

Upper Basin

Lower Basin

Little Colorado River +0.022

San Juan River +0.802

Gunnison River +0.770

+0.936

Colorado Big Thompson Project −0.173

MEXICO
1.542
(1.500)

Lake Havasu & Lake Mohave −0.044 (evaporation)

Central Arizona Project −0.779

Gila Gravity Main Canal −0.578

COLORADO
2.359
(3.105)

One acre-foot is equal to one foot of water covering an acre of land, or approximately 1,232,000 litres

NEW MEXICO
0.548
(0.675)

ARIZONA
2.294
(2.840)

Most of Wyoming's entitlement is satisfied by the Green River, the Colorado's largest tributary.

Beneath Imperial Valley's productive farmland lie 2,250km of pipeline carrying salty drainage to rivers that empty into the Salton Sea.

Hoover Dam impounds Lake Mead (which can store two year's river flow) and generates 4 billion kilowatt-hours of hydroelectric power a year.

Utah diverts water from the upper basin to the Greater Salt Lake area for municipal, industrial and agricultural uses.

Colorado River Aqueduct provides about a third of southern California's municipal water.

Tunnels, pipelines and ditches divert Colorado River water eastward through the Rockies to 287,000 hectares of farmland and to cities such as Denver.

Central Arizona Project: Water diverted from the Colorado slows depletion of groundwater currently pumped from deep water.

New Mexico's share of the Colorado system comes from tributaries including the San Juan River.

IDAHO

UTAH

WYOMING

Great Divide Basin

Salt Lake City

Green River

Rock Springs

Vernal

Fort Collins

Moab

Upper Colorado Basin

Boulder

Denver

Aurora

COLORADO

Los Angeles

Palm Springs

Coachella

San Diego

Tijuana

NEVADA

Las Vegas

Hoover Dam

Lake Mead

Virgin R

Davis Dam

Lake Mohave

Lake Havasu

Parla

Page

Lake Powell

Salton Sea

Imperial Valley

Mexicali

Canal Central

El Mayor

Imperial Dam

Yuma

Gila R

Lower Colorado Basin

Verde R

Little Colorado R

Painted Desert

Baja California

Sonoran Desert

Phoenix

Salt R

ARIZONA

Gallup

Tucson

San Pedro R

Gila R

Santa Fe

Albuquerque

USA
MEXICO

Continental divide

NEW MEXICO

N

Colorado River Basin limit

— **Dam**

········ **Canal or aqueduct**

▭ **Lake**

▲ **Power plant**

☐ **Desalination plant**

0   100 km

Figure 2.40 The Colorado River Basin

Figure 2.41 The Hoover Dam

Figure 2.42 Aqueduct providing water to Phoenix, Arizona

schemes together comprise the Bureau of Reclamation's Colorado River Storage Project.

Despite the interstate and international agreements major problems over the river's resources have arisen for the following reasons.

- Although the river was committed to deliver 20.35 trillion litres every year, its annual flow has averaged only 17.25 trillion litres since 1930. Evaporation from artificial lakes and reservoirs has removed 2.45 trillion litres, and in drought periods (e.g. late 1980s to early 1990s), this shortfall is accentuated.

- Demand has escalated. Between 1970 and 1990 the population of the seven Compact states increased from 22.8 million to 36.1 million. The river now sustains around 25 million people and 820 000 ha of irrigated farmland in the United States and Mexico.

The $4 billion Central Arizona Project (CAP) is the latest, and probably the last, big-money scheme to divert water from this great river (Figure 2.40). Before CAP, Arizona had taken much less than its legal entitlement from the Colorado; it could not afford to build a water transfer system from the Colorado to its main cities and, at the time, the federal government did not feel that national funding was justified. Most of the state's water came from aquifers but it was overdrawing this supply by about 2464 billion litres a year. If thirsty Phoenix and Tucson were to remain prosperous, something had to be done. The answer was CAP which the federal government agreed to part-fund. Since CAP was completed in 1992, 1.85 trillion litres of water a year has been distributed to farms, Indian reservations, industries and fast-growing towns and cities along its 570km route between Lake Havasu and Tucson. However, providing more water for Arizona

has meant that less is available for California. In 1997 the federal government told California that the state would have to learn to live with the 5421 billion litres of water from the Colorado it is entitled to under the 1922 Compact, instead of taking 6406 billion litres a year.

A proposal to allow exchanges of Colorado water between lower-basin states is under discussion. For example, Arizona which has been storing its unused portion of the Colorado's water in underground aquifers, would be able to gain much-needed revenue through water sales to Nevada and California.

Alternative sources and strategies for the future

The water situation in the region is critical. Of the ten US states that will grow fastest between 1995 and 2025, five are in the Colorado basin. A recent report on water supply in the region concluded, 'It may be fair to claim that the major period of settlement of the West did not occur in 1850: it is just now taking place', and substantial amounts of water will be needed to sustain it.

Reducing present waste

Implementation of the following strategies would conserve considerable quantities of water.

- Measures to reduce leakage and evaporation losses. Up to 25 per cent of all water moved is currently lost in these ways.

- Recycling water in industry where, for example, it takes 225 000 litres to make 1 tonne of steel.

- Recycling municipal sewage for watering lawns, gardens and golf courses could be implemented or extended, as Los Angeles has already shown.

- Introducing more efficient toilet systems which use only 6.5 litres for each flush instead of the conventional 26 litres.

- Charging more realistic prices for irrigation water. Many farmers pay only one-tenth of the true cost of water pumped to them; the rest is subsidised by the federal government. When long-term water contracts are eventually renewed, prices could be raised to more economic levels.

- Extending the use of drip irrigation systems which allocate specific quantities of water to individual plants, and which are 100 times more efficient than the open-ditch system still used by many farmers; or sprinkler systems, which are up to ten times more efficient than open-ditch irrigation.

- Changing from highly water-dependent crops such as rice and alfalfa to those needing less water.

- Changing the law to permit farmers to sell surplus water to the highest bidders. Since 1992, this has been allowed in California, where an emerging network of specialist brokers sells agricultural water to cities for less than they already pay but at a profit for the farmers.

- Requiring both cities and rural areas to identify the source of water to be used before new developments can commence. This proposal, first mooted in southern California in 1994, proved to be politically unacceptable.

Future options

- Developing new groundwater resources. Although groundwater has been heavily depleted in many areas, in regions of water surplus such as northern California they remain virtually untapped. However, the transfer of even more water from such areas would probably prove politically unacceptable.

- It has been claimed that various techniques of weather modification, especially cloud seeding, can provide water at reasonable cost. However, environmental and political considerations cannot be ignored here.

- In 1991, after several years of drought, the city of Santa Barbara approved the construction of a $37.4 million desalination plant. Although much too expensive for irrigation water, it is likely that more will be built for urban use.

- Exploiting the frozen reserves of Antarctic water. Serious proposals have been made to find a 100 million tonne iceberg (1.5 km long, 300 m wide, 270 m deep) off Antarctica, wrap it in sailcloth or thick plastic and tow it to southern California. The critical questions here are cost, evaporation loss and the environmental effects of anchoring such a huge block of ice off an arid coast.

There is now general agreement that planning for the future water supply of the south west should embrace all practicable options. Sensible management of this vital resource should rule out no feasible strategy if this important region is to sustain its economic viability and growing population.

Questions

1 Annotate a world outline map to illustrate the severity of the global water resource problem.
2 Although Britain appears to be relatively well off compared to many countries with regard to water, what is the evidence from the 1990s of a water supply problem?
3 Suggest why the term 'hydropolitics' has been increasingly used in magazines and journals in recent years.
4 Which is the main problem in the Developing World – poor water quality or insufficient quantity?
5 Exemplify the benefits of the Bureau of Reclamation's multipurpose dams along the Colorado river and its tributaries.
6 Suggest how a new 'demand-side' strategy might solve the problem of allocating the finite supply of Colorado water.

Population and energy resources

Recent trends

The *BP Statistical Review of World Energy* highlighted the following, in terms of the world energy market, for 1997:

- World consumption of energy grew by 1 per cent in 1997, below the average for the past 10 years.

- Continued rapid growth in emerging market economies (NICs) contrasted strongly with slow growth in the Developed World as a whole.

- India increased its consumption by 6.1 per cent, to become the world's sixth largest energy market, ahead of France, Canada and the United Kingdom.

- Hydro-electric power (HEP) and oil were the

fastest growing fuels, while gas and nuclear use decreased.

Global consumption of primary energy increased by 74 per cent between 1970 and 1997 (Figure 2.43). Although all five sources of energy illustrated contributed more in absolute terms, relative changes varied significantly. Consumption patterns differ considerably by region (Figure 2.44). South and Central America and the Middle East are the most heavily reliant on oil, while the countries of the former Soviet Union consume proportionately more gas than anywhere else. Coal has the largest share of the market in Asia and Australia.

The total global demand for energy has approximately increased in line with population with only relatively small changes in consumption per capita since the 1970s (Figure 2.45). North America's per capita consumption remains far higher than that of any other region.

Major energy issues

In the latter part of the twentieth century the dominant issues with regard to energy have been:

- fluctuating prices and concern about sufficient supplies of fossil fuels
- the environmental impact of the heavy use of fossil fuels
- the nuclear power dilemma

- the economic impact of either declining demand for, or the exhaustion of, a fossil fuel in a region or country
- recent concerns about the environmental impact of renewable resources, particularly HEP.

Oil: assured supplies or shortages ahead

The price of oil on the world market is usually taken as the most important indicator of the relationship between total energy demand and supply. At $13 a barrel in early 1998, its lowest point for almost a decade, it would seem that the world has energy a plenty. The reasons for such a low price are:

- Technological advances have driven down the cost of finding and producing oil.
- Many of the world's major economies are growing at only a very slow rate.
- The economic problems in Asia, which began in 1997, have cut demand in that region.
- Some OPEC countries were exceeding the quotas agreed amongst themselves. This has been a familiar scenario for OPEC since the cartel was founded in Baghdad in 1960. Because of such pressures the OPEC countries agreed to lift quotas by 10 per cent to 27.5 million barrels a day (Figure 2.46) from 1 January 1998.

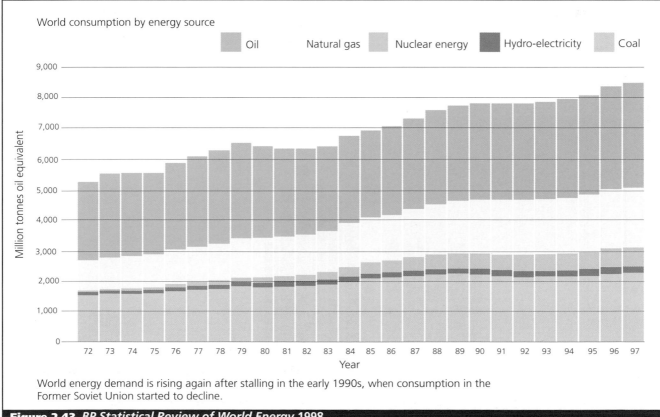

World energy demand is rising again after stalling in the early 1990s, when consumption in the Former Soviet Union started to decline.

Figure 2.43 *BP Statistical Review of World Energy* **1998**

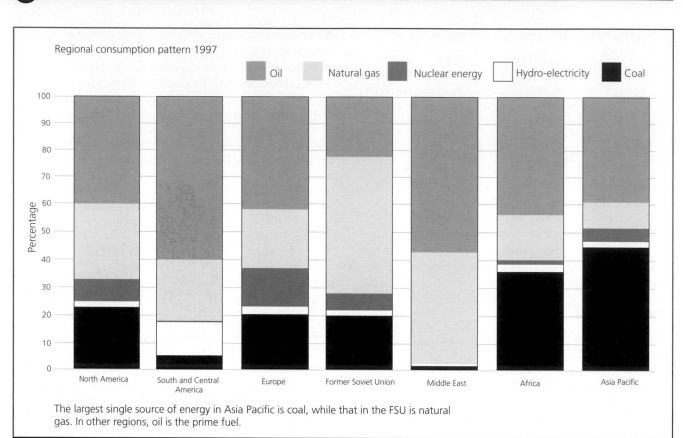

Regional consumption pattern 1997

The largest single source of energy in Asia Pacific is coal, while that in the FSU is natural gas. In other regions, oil is the prime fuel.

Figure 2.44 *BP Statistical Review of World Energy* **1998**

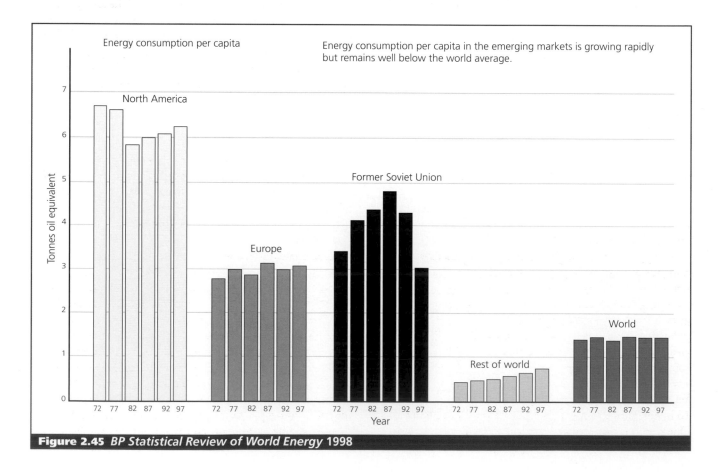

Energy consumption per capita

Energy consumption per capita in the emerging markets is growing rapidly but remains well below the world average.

Figure 2.45 *BP Statistical Review of World Energy* **1998**

Figure 2.46 OPEC's quotas (million barrels per day) from 1st January 1998

Saudi Arabia	8.76
Iran	3.94
Venezuela	2.58
United Arab Emirates	2.37
Kuwait	2.19
Nigeria	2.04
Libya	1.52
Indonesia	1.46
Iraq	1.31
Algeria	0.91
Qatar	0.41
	Total: 27.50

Thus it would seem that there is, and will be, no problem with the supply of oil. As an article in the *Sunday Times*, 29 March 1998 concluded:

In short, in one way or another, the world's capacity to produce oil will continue to rise. And the cost of finding and producing oil will continue to fall – to as low as $5 a barrel if my Middle Eastern sources are correct, and so far they have been. The temptation to step up output will prove irresistible, increasing the supply coming to market. Meanwhile, worldwide oil demand will fail to keep pace with supply as the Asian recession continues, environmentalists force drivers into more fuel-efficient cars, and revenue-hungry governments in industrialised countries dampen demand by raising taxes and concocting new levies on the use of oil and other carbon-based fuels.

The thrust of this article is in line with others in a variety of journals and with some television documentaries at that time. The now common argument is that there has never been a real shortage of energy. The problem was that politicians, environmentalists and others did not fully understand the basis of the reserves to production ratios produced by the energy industry. The fact that the energy companies would spend enough money at any point in time only to confirm reserves for the next decade or two did not mean that lots more oil did not exist.

However, some energy analysts argue that there is indeed cause for concern (Figure 2.47). Campbell and Laherrère, writing in the journal *Scientific American*, say that although according to most accounts oil reserves have increased, such growth is an illusion. About 80 per cent of the oil produced today flows from fields that were found before 1973, and the great majority of them are declining. In the 1990s oil companies have discovered an average of 7 billion barrels of oil a year; but in 1997 extracted more than three times as much. Yet official data indicated that proved reserves did not fall by 16 billion barrels – rather they expanded by 11 billion barrels. One reason is that several dozen governments opted not to report declines in their reserves, perhaps to enhance their

political cachet and their ability to obtain loans. A more important cause for the expansion lies in revisions: oil companies replaced earlier estimates of the reserves left in many fields with higher figures which are difficult to justify.

Coal: decline in Britain but growth in China and India

Peak output of coal in Britain was in 1913 when 290 million tonnes were hewn from coal faces. The tale thereafter was one of lost export and domestic markets. The decline in employment has been dramatic. The peak year for employment was 1920 when 1.25 million worked in the mines. This fell to 700 000 in 1955, 235 000 in 1979 and 17 000 in 1997. Although environmentalists have welcomed the reduction in the use of coal, the worst polluter of all the fossil fuels, the impact on many mining communities has been devastating, particularly where alternative employment opportunities have been lacking. Figure 2.49 illustrates the decline of coal in Britain in recent decades. A significant proportion of regional development funding in Britain in the post-war period has been directed at mining communities.

However, while coal production in Britain fell by 47 per cent between 1989 and 1995, production in China and India rose by 24 per cent and 26 per cent respectively. China is the world's largest producer, with India in third place (the United States is second in global coal production). The essential issue here is that as the world's two most populous nations strive to expand their economies they will use more and more coal, the major energy resource in both countries. The impact of such an increase on the atmosphere has been well documented. Already the use of coal is responsible for more than 30 per cent of carbon dioxide emissions (Figure 2.51).

The nuclear dilemma

Figure 2.52 shows the distribution of nuclear power by world region since 1972. Despite the nuclear accidents at Three Mile Island in the United States (1979) and Chernobyl in the Ukraine (1986) the production of nuclear energy continues to rise, although at a slower pace than that forecast in the 1960s and 1970s.

Chernobyl was, without doubt, the worst technogenic environmental disaster in history. The destroyed reactor released hundreds of times more radiation than was produced by the atomic bombs dropped on Hiroshima and Nagasaki. Well over 260 000 km² in Ukraine, Russia and Belarus still have more than one curie per km² of contamination with caesium 137. At this level annual health checks for radiation are advised. Some 30 000 people have fallen ill among the 400 000 workers who toiled as 'liquidators', burying the most dangerous wastes and constructing a special building around the ruined reactor. Of these, about 5000 are now too ill to work. It is difficult to know how many people have died as a result of this nuclear accident. Greenpeace Ukraine has

The End of Cheap Oil

Global production of conventional oil will begin to decline sooner than most people think, probably within 10 years

BY COLIN J. CAMPBELL AND JEAN H. LAHERRÈRE

In 1973 and 1979 a pair of sudden price increases rudely awakened the industrial world to its dependence on cheap crude oil. Prices first tripled in response to an Arab embargo and then nearly doubled again when Iran dethroned its Shah, sending the major economies sputtering into recession. Many analysts warned that these crises proved that the world would soon run out of oil. Yet they were wrong.

Their dire predictions were emotional and political reactions; even at the time, oil experts knew that they had no scientific basis. Just a few years earlier oil explorers had discovered enormous new oil provinces on the north slope of Alaska and below the North Sea off the coast of Europe. By 1973 the world had consumed, according to many experts' best estimates, only about one eighth of its endowment of readily accessible crude oil (so-called conventional oil). The five Middle Eastern members of the Organization of Petroleum Exporting Countries (OPEC) were able to hike prices not because oil was growing scarce but because they had managed to corner 36 percent of the market. Later, when demand sagged, and the flow of fresh Alaskan and North Sea oil weakened OPEC's economic stranglehold, prices collapsed.

The next oil crunch will not be so temporary. Our analysis of the discovery and production of oil fields around the world suggests that within the next decade, the supply of con-ventional oil will be unable to keep up with demand. This conclusion con-tradicts the picture one gets from oil industry reports, which boasted of 1,020 billion barrels of oil (Gbo) in "proved" reserves at the start of 1998. Dividing that figure by the current production rate of about 23.6 Gbo a year might suggest that crude oil could remain plentiful and cheap for 43 more years—probably longer, because official charts show reserves growing.

Unfortunately, this appraisal makes three critical errors. First, it relies on distorted estimates of reserves. A second mistake is to pretend that production will remain constant. Third and most important, conventional wisdom erroneously assumes that the last bucket of oil can be pumped from the ground just as quickly as the barrels of oil gushing from wells today. In fact, the rate at which any well—or any country—can produce oil always rises to a maximum and then, when about half the oil is gone, begins falling gradually back to zero.

From an economic perspective, when the world runs completely out of oil is thus not directly relevant: what matters is when production begins to taper off. Beyond that point, prices will rise unless demand declines commensurately. Using several different techniques to estimate the current reserves of con-ventional oil and the amount still left to be discovered, we conclude that the decline will begin before 2010.

Figure 2.47 *Scientific American*, **March 1998**

Figure 2.48 Oil prices are affected by economic trends, production methods, available reserves and other factors

estimated a total of 32 000 deaths by comparing mortality rates before and after the accident. Ukraine's rate of thyroid cancer among children has increased about tenfold from pre-accident levels. One in every three liquidators has been plagued by sexual or reproductive disorders. Among children evacuated from the reactor zone, there has been a 10- to 15-fold increase in the incidence of neuropsychiatric disorders. More than 30 million people are at risk of being contaminated by radioactivity when flood water sweeps downstream from Chernobyl.

Two reactors, generating 5 per cent of Ukraine's power, are still in operation at Chernobyl. In December 1995 Ukraine and the Group of Seven industrial nations signed an agreement to shut down the whole Chernobyl plant by the year 2000. However, the impact of the disaster will linger much longer than this.

The disposal of nuclear waste is a major issue confronting the nuclear industry worldwide. In the United States the long search for a permanent site for high-level nuclear waste has been narrowed down to one location – Yucca Mountain in Nevada. However, opposition to the plan has been intense, not least because of strong seismic activity in the region. A more detailed study of the location is being conducted before a final decision is made.

(a) Production of energy in the United Kingdom

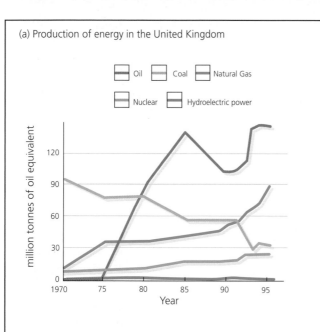

(b) Decline in coal production in the United Kingdom

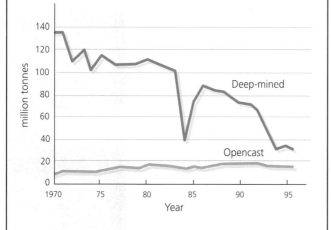

(c) Decline in coal mining employment in the United Kingdom

Thousands, 1983–96

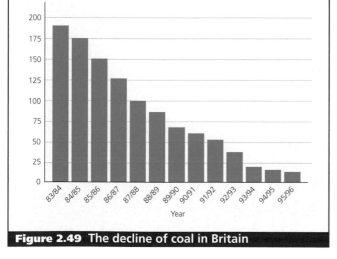

Figure 2.49 The decline of coal in Britain

Figure 2.50 Coal mining; coal is still a major power source in the Developing World

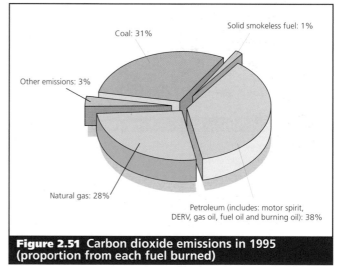

Figure 2.51 Carbon dioxide emissions in 1995 (proportion from each fuel burned)

Hydropower threat to global warming

A recent study carried out by the Brazilian National Institute for Research in Amazonia, published in the journal *Environmental Conservation*, claims that HEP dams with reservoirs in tropical forests can contribute far more to global warming than fossil fuel plants. Philip Fearnside, the research team leader, has calculated that in 1990 emissions of CO_2 and methane from water and rotting vegetation in the Balbina reservoir had 26 times more impact on global warming than emissions from coal-fired plants generating the same amount

Consumption by area

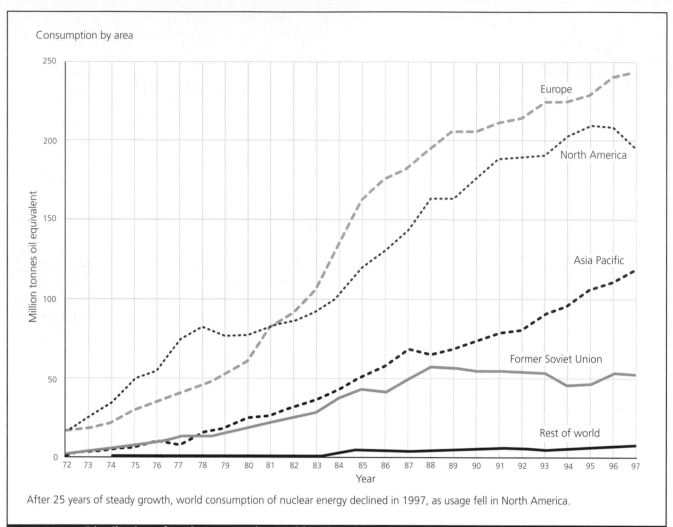

After 25 years of steady growth, world consumption of nuclear energy declined in 1997, as usage fell in North America.

Figure 2.52 Distribution of nuclear power by world region since 1972

of electricity. While the gases released from Balbina will slowly fall as the vegetation decays, they will always be higher than those from equivalent fossil fuel generation. In contrast, emissions from the Tucurui dam's reservoir had only 60 per cent as much impact on global warming in 1990 as an equivalent coal-fired plant because it floods far less land per unit of electricity generated. The study notes that the total area of reservoirs planned in the region is about 20 times the area existing in 1990, an expansion that will contribute significantly to global greenhouse gas emissions.

Dr Fearnside's calculations have been seized upon by the International Rivers Network (IRN), the US-based lobby group which led criticism of the World Bank's now abandoned plans to build run-of-river dams in Nepal. The pro-dam lobby has been shifting its arguments over the years. At one time, large dams were advocated because they provided cheap power, despite the social and surface environmental damage caused. More recently large dams have been promoted as 'carbon free', a claim that is now under intense pressure.

Figure 2.53 Tucurui dam . . . much less impact on global warming than an equivalent coal-fired plant

North America: energy alternatives for the future

 Although the United States can justifiably be criticised for the impact of its use of energy on the global environment, it has invested more in absolute terms in alternative energy sources than any other nation.

The first major wave of interest in new energy sources resulted from the energy crisis of the early 1970s. However, the fall in the price of oil in the 1980s and the withdrawal of tax advantages sent this sector of the energy industry into depression and many renewable energy firms folded. As a result, the projected contributions of such energy sources have not lived up to earlier expectations. Solar electricity accounts for less than 0.5 per cent of the power generated in the United States today, instead of the 2 to 5 per cent envisaged in the late 1950s. The tentative rebirth of the renewable energy industry in the 1900s was due to:

■ the 1990 Clean Air Act amendments which provide a financial incentive to electricity utilities to purchase renewable energy

■ the 1992 Energy Policy Act which reinstated a modest tax credit for renewable energy

■ technological advances within the sector.

A recent report from the World Energy Council (WEC) predicted slow growth for the alternative energy industry unless governments take a more active role. The most important policy envisaged by the WEC would be pricing fossil fuels to include their full environmental costs. Financial assistance for research and development is also important. The renewable energy industry in the United States has long argued that it receives too little in government funding (Figure 2.54).

Solar power

Although the United States is the world leader in this field, solar power contributed only 0.2 per cent to total generation in 1993. Two types of system are currently in operation. The most significant at present are solar furnaces. The principle here is to

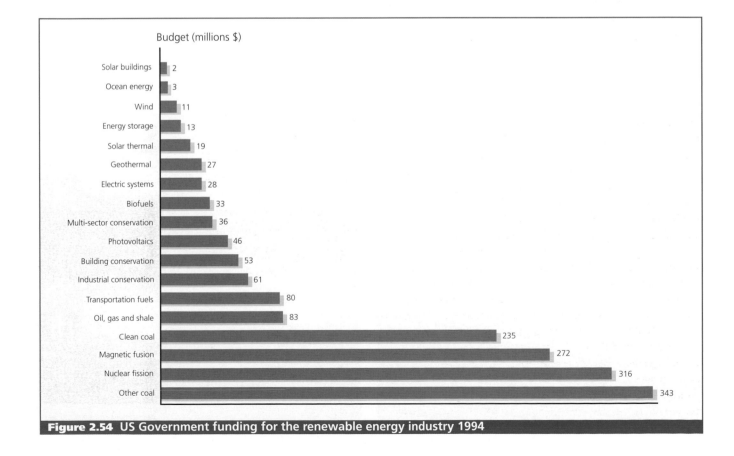

Figure 2.54 US Government funding for the renewable energy industry 1994

focus the sun's rays on a target. A fluid is pumped inside the target where it is heated. Nine power plants of this nature are located in the Mojave desert of southern California, covering a total area of 7.8 km² (Figure 2.55). Long parallel lines of troughs, each about 100 m in length are computer controlled to rotate and follow the sun during the course of the day. Each trough is made up of 224 glass mirrors. The parabolic shape ensures that the light from all the mirrors reflects on to a receiver, a horizontal pipe containing oil that runs above the trough. Generating a total of 354 megawatts (MW), they account for about 50 per cent of world production of solar electricity. The rest is largely supplied by hundreds of small photovoltaic systems generating less than 1 MW. Photovoltaic cells consist of thin slices of semiconductor material, made mainly of silicon. When the sun shines on a photovoltaic cell, electric current flows from one side of the cell to the other.

The solar furnaces of the Mojave desert produce power at over twice the cost of coal power. Photovoltaic power is more expensive still. But, as solar proponents argue, the environmental effects of solar generation are confined mainly to the size of the land area required and the visual impact of these facilities.

Wind power

The United States had more than 1700 MW of installed wind capacity in early 1995. Most of the 19 000 turbines are located along a few mountain passes in California. However, 16 states have wind energy potential equal to or greater than California's, according to the Department of Energy. Most recent development has centred on the concept of the 'wind farm', where many turbines operate at a single site and feed power into the local grid (Figure 2.56). Altamont Pass near San Francisco boasts over 7000 turbines operated by the Kenetech Corporation. Power produced here costs 75 per cent more than in fossil fuel plants but the local electric utility is required by state law to purchase all the wind power produced within its catchment area.

The environmental concerns about wind power centre around the visual impact, the 'hum' of the turbines and the deaths of birds flying into the turbines.

Biomass

Biomass is organic material from which energy can be produced. Some developing countries get over 90 per cent of their energy from biomass, mainly by burning firewood. In the United States wood accounts for 84% of biomass energy production. This is mainly in the paper and forest products industries which use the technology to meet more than half of their own energy needs. But biomass is also used to generate electricity and to mix with petrol to produce the petrol substitute, gasohol, for motor vehicles. There are already about 1000 biomass-fuelled power plants in the United States, although all have capacities of less than 25 MW.

Worldwide, Brazil is the largest producer of liquid biofuels, mainly in the form of ethanol from sugar cane. In the United States ethanol made from surplus maize replaces about 0.5 per cent of national petrol consumption. Here a mixture of 10 per cent ethanol and 90 per cent gasoline is sold as 'gasohol' in several Midwestern states. A combination of state and federal subsidies as well as tax exemptions supports the production of ethanol. When added to petrol, ethanol reduces emissions of carbon monoxide and hydrocarbons. However, critics point to the pollution caused by the burning of coal within the ethanol distilleries and in the power stations that supply them with electricity.

In 1993 the Department of Energy announced encouragement for energy crops and energy conversion systems tailored to the resources and needs of specific US regions. Crops to be tested include elephant grass, eucalyptus, bagasse, sorghum and sugar cane. Farmers could be producing for the energy market rather than the food market in future.

Geothermal energy

Geothermal energy is the natural heat found in the earth's crust in the form of steam, hot water and hot rock. At present, virtually all the geothermal power plants in the world operate on steam resources (Figure 2.57). The United States is the world leader in the use of geothermal heat to generate electricity. In 1993 this source contributed 0.3 per cent to the national power supply, enough for 3 million households. This amounted to over

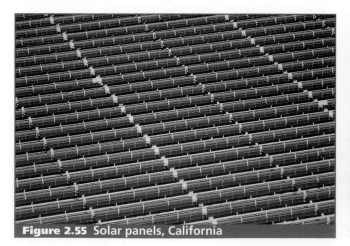
Figure 2.55 Solar panels, California

Figure 2.56 Wind farm: Altamont Pass, California

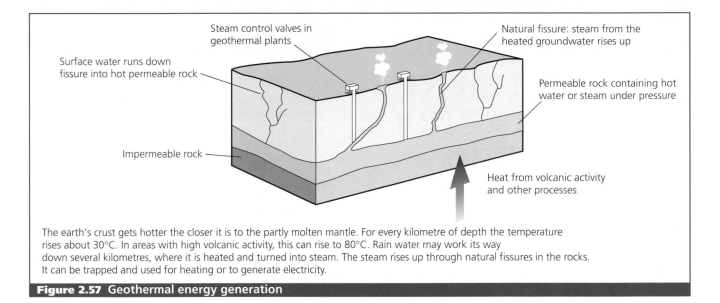

Steam control valves in geothermal plants

Natural fissure: steam from the heated groundwater rises up

Surface water runs down fissure into hot permeable rock

Permeable rock containing hot water or steam under pressure

Impermeable rock

Heat from volcanic activity and other processes

The earth's crust gets hotter the closer it is to the partly molten mantle. For every kilometre of depth the temperature rises about 30°C. In areas with high volcanic activity, this can rise to 80°C. Rain water may work its way down several kilometres, where it is heated and turned into steam. The steam rises up through natural fissures in the rocks. It can be trapped and used for heating or to generate electricity.

Figure 2.57 Geothermal energy generation

2800 MW, mostly located in California. There is some degree of pollution involved because the steam contains impurities such as hydrogen sulphide.

Research into the use of hot-water reservoirs is in progress. However, the hot water below the Imperial Valley facility in California is briny. For every litre brought to the surface, up to a quarter may be salts and solid particles that corrode and clog piping. In addition, there is the task of disposing of the waste.

It is more difficult still, at present, to use the heat of hot rocks at depth below the surface. Energy companies are experimenting by pumping water several kilometres underground and then bringing it back to the surface after it has been heated. But it may be some time before such technology is fully developed.

Another possibility under consideration by the Department of Energy is magma energy extraction. This would involve drilling a hole through the earth's crust to the molten rock below. A heat exchanger would be installed at the bottom. Energy could be extracted by water or another fluid that is brought to the surface. Sites must be found where molten magma is not much more than 5 km below the surface to keep costs at a reasonable level.

The Interior Department estimates that a staggering 1.2 million quads (quadrillion British Thermal Units) of geothermal energy underlie 1.4 million ha of land in the western United States. However, much of this potential resource is in National Parks or other protected areas, or is too deep for current technology.

Tidal power

Annapolis Royal is home to the first and only modern tidal plant in North America. Located by the Bay of Fundy, Nova Scotia, Canada, it employs the largest straight-flow turbine in the world. This is one of only 40 sites identified worldwide which are suitable for large-scale electricity generation from the tides. Opened in 1984, the plant generates power from 95 per cent of all tides and each year produces 30 million kW hours, enough to power 4500 homes. At peak output it can generate up to 20 MW.

More ambitious projects at other sites along the Bay of Fundy are under consideration, but before these projects begin, more information about the possible environmental impact has to be gathered. The main concerns are potential effects on fish populations, levels of sedimentation building up behind facilities and the possible impact on tides along the coast.

Ocean thermal energy conversion (OTEC)

OTEC uses the temperature difference between the ocean's warm surface water and the cold deep waters to generate electricity. The system can work only in the tropics where the temperature difference between surface and deep water is at least 20° C. The United States has developed the world's first at-sea power plant, located off the coast of Hawaii. Here the warm surface water vaporises ammonia which is used to drive a turbine. The ammonia is then condensed by deep cold water and the cycle begins all over again.

Unlike some other renewable energy sources, OTEC provides 'base load' power (a continuous electricity flow). However, at present the costs of OTEC are high and the amount of electricity produced is small.

Conservation and demand-side management

In 1992 electric utilities in the United States spent 1.3 per cent of their total revenues on demand-side management (DSM) programmes (Figure 2.58). In return, these programmes cut annual electricity sales by 1.2 per cent and peak demand by 6 per cent. Relative to economic growth the United States has reduced energy consumption significantly. In 1970 the country used 23 400 BTU per dollar of GDP; by 1994 this was down to 16 200. It is clear to the electric utilities that much more new energy can be obtained through efficiency compared to new alternative sources of energy.

DEMAND-SIDE MANAGEMENT BY U.S. ELECTRIC UTILITIES

Electric utilities in the United States have been world leaders in taking the initiative to improve the efficiency of electricity use by consumers because so often an investment in efficiency improvement shows a better payoff than an investment in additional supply capabilities. From among a great many, illustrative examples include the following:

- The Smart Light program of the Burlington, Vermont, Electric Department provides energy-efficient compact fluorescent light bulbs to customers who pay a small leasing fee as part of their monthly electric bills. This program is part of the more general Neighbor $ave program, which has an estimated lifetime savings of more than 45 gigawatt-hours of electricity supply.

- The Peak Corps Air Conditioner Load Management program of the Sacramento, California, Municipal Utility District (SMUD) allows the utility to reduce peak power supply requirements by cycling customers' air conditioners. SMUD also offers rebates and financing to encourage the purchase of more efficient end-use equipment, and it offers incentives to builders to make new construction more energy efficient.

- The Good Cents New and Improved Homes program of Waverly, Iowa, Light and Power offers reductions of 10 percent for 10 years in the energy portion of the electricity bill for homes that qualify for "Good Cents" designation for being energy-efficient. The program includes financing programs to make efficiency improvements more accessible to customers. The utility also provides appliance rebates, free energy audits, and innovative rate structures.

Figure 2.58 *Environment*, 36(9), November 1994

1 Outline the changes in, and spatial distribution of, world energy consumption shown by Figures 2.43, 2.44 and 2.45.
2 Discuss the alternative views concerning the supply of oil in the future.
3 Research the economic impact of the decline of coal in one region of the United Kingdom.
4 **(a)** Account for the global distribution of nuclear power.
 (b) Examine the major concerns about the generation of nuclear power.
5 Why has the development of hydro-electric resources become a more controversial issue in recent years?
6 Discuss the advantages and disadvantages of the different forms of renewable energy.
7 Examine the merits of demand-side management of energy.

Bibliography

References

People and Planet, published quarterly by Planet 21, 1 Woburn Walk, London WC1H 0JJ. Tel: 0171 383 4388. Internet site: http://www.oneworld.org/patp/
BP Statistical Review of World Energy, published annually and available from The British Petroleum Company plc, Britannic House, 1 Finsbury Circus, London EC2M 7BA. Internet site: http://www.bp.com/bpstats
North America: An Advanced Geography by B. Price and P. Guinness, Hodder & Stoughton, 1997.
The Last Oasis: Facing Water Scarcity by Sandra Postel, Earthscan, 1993.

Internet

FAO Women and Population Division: Linkages between population, natural resources and environment http://www.fao.org/waicent/faoinfo/sustdev/Wpdirect/Wpan0004.htm
Global Resources: Understanding the Population/Environment Connection http://ucsusa.org/resources/population.html

3 the rural environment

Urban and rural: the problem of definition

A number of criteria have been used to distinguish between urban and rural environments (Figure 3.1), of which the following are the most important:

- **Population size** There are no standard international definitions of urban and rural: the official minimum population size of an urban area varies considerably from country to country. In Norway it is 'localities of 200 or more', while in Malaysia it is 'areas with a population of 10 000 or more'. The rural-urban divide for most countries falls between 1500 and 5000. In England the population ranges shown in Figure 3.3 provide a reasonable classification.

- **Land use** The density of buildings in rural settlements is low and they are rarely above two floors in height. Urban areas have much higher residential densities and exhibit a much greater variety of land use.

- **Employment** Traditionally, rural settlements have been dominated by farmers, farm workers and those in other primary occupations. While this is still generally true of the developing world, many villages in the developed world now contain very few people associated with primary activities. Instead they commute to work in urban areas.

- **Functions** Rural settlement is characterised by its small number and low level of services. In developed nations the decline of service provision in rural areas is a major issue.

- **Social characteristics** In general, rural communities have a longer history than their urban counterparts and are more close-knit. However, in remote rural areas depopulation has resulted in a high level of aged dependency.

Key Definitions

rural Belonging to or relating to life in the countryside in contrast to an urban lifestyle.

rural landscape A mental or visual picture of countryside scenery which is difficult to define as rural areas are constantly changing and vary from place to place.

rural settlement/rural population People living in the countryside in farms, isolated houses, hamlets and villages. Under some definitions small market towns are classed as rural.

site The characteristics of the actual point at which the settlement is located and its immediate surroundings.

situation The location of a settlement in relation to its wider surroundings.

rural-urban continuum The notion that movement along a scale from a single isolated farm to a megalopolis does not reveal clear cut boundries between the categories of settlement (eg. hamlets, villages, towns). Instead the change is viewed as a continuum.

palimpsest The idea that, to some degree, each new wave of settlement and economic activity erases the imprints of previous human development on the landscape.

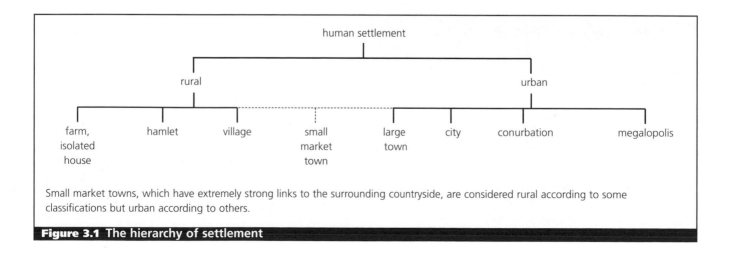

Small market towns, which have extremely strong links to the surrounding countryside, are considered rural according to some classifications but urban according to others.

Figure 3.1 The hierarchy of settlement

Figure 3.2 Photographs illustrating the hierarchy of settlement

Farmhouse and adjacent buildings in County Kerry, Ireland

Hamlet in the Cotswolds

Small market town in the Cotswolds

Figure 3.3 A possible classification of settlements in Britain by population size

Hamlet	2–50 in more than one household
Village	50–2000
Small town	2000–10 000
Large town	10 000–100 000
City	100 000–1 000 000
Conurbation	1 000 000–10 000 000

In some countries definitions incorporate two measures of rurality. For example, in the Netherlands rural settlements are municipalities with a population of less than 2000 but with more than 20% of their economically active population engaged in agriculture.

Rural settlements form an essential part of the human landscape. In the past, rural society was perceived to be distinctly different from urban society. The characteristics upon which this idea was based are shown in Figure 3.5. However, rapid rural change over the past 40 years or so in Britain and other developed countries has seen the idea of a rural-urban divide superseded by the notion of a rural-urban continuum. The latter is a wide spectrum which runs from the most remote type of rural settlement to the most highly urbanised. A number of the intermediate positions exhibit both rural and urban characteristics. Paul Cloke (1979) used 16 variables (including population density, land use and remoteness) to produce an 'index of rurality' for England and Wales (Figure 3.6). Urban areas now make substantial demands on the countryside, the evidence of which can be found in even the remotest of areas.

Figure 3.4 Cave dwellings: primitive rural settlement in Tunisia

Figure 3.5 Principal characteristics of traditional rural society

1. Close-knit community with everybody knowing and interacting with everyone else.
2. Considerable homogeneity in social traits: language, beliefs, opinions, mores, and patterns of behaviour.
3. Family ties, particularly those of the extended family, are much stronger than in urban society.
4. Religion is given more importance than in urban society.
5. Class differences are less pronounced than in urban society. Although occupational differentiation does exist, it is not as pronounced as in towns and cities. Also, the small settlement size results in much greater mixing, which in turn weakens the effects of social differentiation.
6. There is less mobility than in urban society, both in a spatial sense (people do not move house so frequently) and in a social sense (it is more difficult for a farm labourer to become a farmer or farm manager than for a factory worker to become a manager).

Source: *The Geography of Rural Resources* by C. Bull, P. Daniel and M. Hopkinson, Oliver & Boyd, 1984

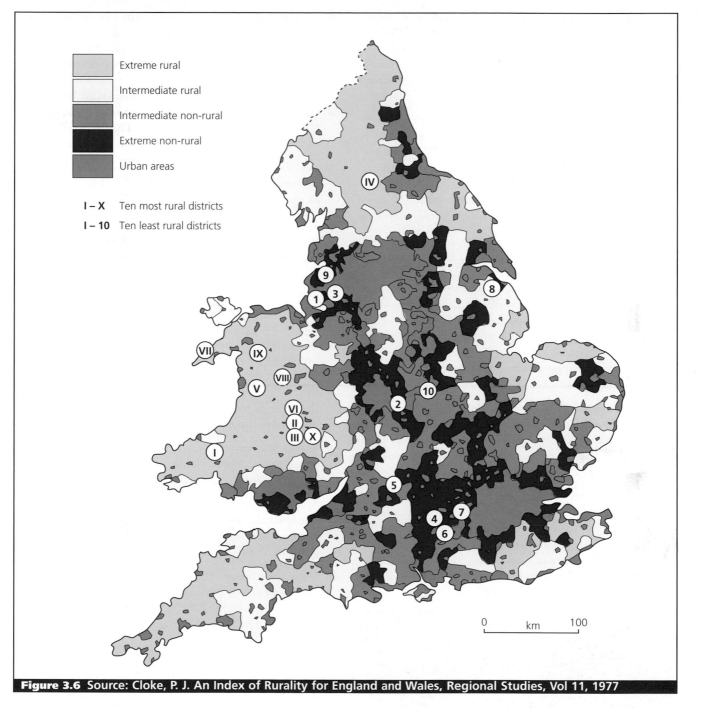

Figure 3.6 Source: Cloke, P. J. An Index of Rurality for England and Wales, Regional Studies, Vol 11, 1977

Legend:
- Extreme rural
- Intermediate rural
- Intermediate non-rural
- Extreme non-rural
- Urban areas

I – X   Ten most rural districts
I – 10 Ten least rural districts

Site and situation

The site of a settlement describes the characteristics of the actual point at which the settlement is located and its immediate surroundings. These characteristics would have been of major importance in the initial establishment of the settlement and its subsequent growth. When trying to identify site characteristics from Ordnance Survey maps, consider the land covered by the built environment and a zone about three to four kilometres around it. The latter would be the reasonable daily walking distance to grow crops, tend cattle, collect wood and so on when the settlement was first established.

The term 'situation' refers to the location of a settlement in relation to its wider surroundings. Relevant factors are other settlements, rivers, relief, major roads and railways.

The original decision to locate a settlement at a particular point would have involved the consideration of a range of factors. It is unlikely that all of the characteristics of the site selected were ideal, but that it was the best of all the realistic alternatives. The following are the main factors which have influenced the location of settlements:

■ **Relief** Flat, low-lying land with fertile soils such as the clay vales of southern England was preferable to the steeper Chalk downlands for a number of obvious reasons. However, hazards such as flooding and potential hostility from other human groups sometimes persuaded early settlers to opt for sites on higher land.

■ **Defence** Many early settlements in Britain were on hill-tops, along recognised trade routes and in commanding positions, providing defence from attack. Of the larger settlements in Britain, Edinburgh occupies the most commanding hill-top site. Another classic defensive site was to be surrounded by water on three sides. The site of Durham, on high ground in the neck of a meander of the River Wear, is a prime example.

■ **Water supply** In pre-Industrial times Britain's rivers provided a clean and safe water supply. This was the main reason why so many settlements developed on river systems. Water transport was often an added bonus. Spring-line settlement along the foot of chalk escarpments is a clear example of the importance of water supply in settlement location. Sites located in immediate proximity to a supply of water are known as wet-point sites. (Figure 3.7)

■ **Flood avoidance** Where the likelihood of flooding was significant, settlements were usually built above the level of the perceived threat. Good examples of such dry-point (or water-avoiding) sites are the Fenland settlements, such as Ely, which were built on mounds of land forming natural islands above the surrounding marsh.

■ **Bridging points** Wherever routes could ford, or later bridge, a river (e.g. Oxford, Guildford), a settlement often developed. Of particular importance was the lowest bridging point. Downstream of this crossing point the tidal waters of an estuary would have been too wide and turbulent for bridge construction.

■ **Food supply** Because all food was locally produced, sites were sought which were suitable for both arable and pastoral farming. Spring-line settlement at the foot of chalk escarpments in South East England grazed sheep on the higher and steeper chalk and utilised the fertile clay vales for arable farming and for raising cattle. In upland landscapes, such as the Pennines and Lake District, agricultural land use also changed from flat-valley floors to steeper windswept slopes.

■ **Building materials** Locally available wood, stone and clay were major influences on site selection. Wood was, of course, more commonly available than it is today.

■ **Fuel supply** For early settlement in Britain, firewood was the dominant source of fuel, as it is in much of the developing world today.

■ **Accessibility** Settlements frequently developed where natural routeways converged. Confluence settlements developed where two or three rivers met and the valley routes converged. Good examples are Monmouth, Salisbury and Reading. Gap towns command key routeways through hills or mountains. For example, Dorking controls the scarp slope end of the gap through the North Downs cut by the River Mole, a tributary of the River Thames, while Leatherhead is at the dip slope entrance to the gap.

■ **Aspect** Where possible, early settlers selected south-facing slopes to benefit from maximum insolation and protection from cold northerly airstreams.

■ **Mineral resources** The distribution of coalfields has had a considerable influence on the location of settlement in Britain. Other minerals such as iron ore, salt and tin have also contributed to site selection in certain areas.

■ **Natural harbours** The combination of flat land and a sheltered harbour provided the ideal location for fishing communities (Figure 3.8). Many larger coastal settlements eventually developed important trade functions.

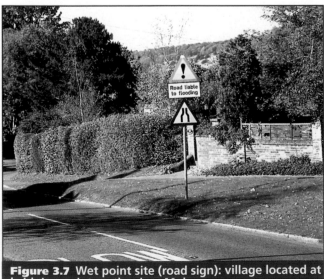

Figure 3.7 Wet point site (road sign): village located at bridging point on the river Mole

Figure 3.8 Small harbour in South Devon

The evolution of settlement in South East England: a summary

The human landscape may be viewed as a palimpsest, consisting of the legacy of layer upon layer of human occupation, with each successive human imprint obscuring, at least partially, the evidence of earlier periods of settlement and economic activity.

The following are significant periods in the settlement of South East England. The grid references refer to the 1:50 000 Dorking, Crawley and Reigate Ordnance Survey map. Analysis of OS maps can confirm a considerable amount about the evolution of settlement in an area, but examination of other sources is also required to obtain a fuller picture.

■ Between 4000 and 2000 BC woodland was being cleared for grazing and cultivation as more permanent settlements than had existed beforehand were established. By the late Bronze Age, some enclosed hilltop sites, such as that now covered by Queen Mary's hospital, Carshalton (280625) were occupied. Iron implements began to appear about 800 BC. These have been found at the sites of earthen-rampart forts crowning St George's Hill in the Thames Valley (085615) and Cardinal's Gap on the downs south of Caterham (328533). However, it is uncertain whether any of these hill-forts were occupied on a long-term basis.

■ The Roman invasion found a fairly densely populated countryside of agricultural villages interspersed with a few larger centres, largely established by the Belgae who arrived in Britain early in the first century BC. The influence of the Belgae extended over most of South East England.

■ The most important Roman town in England was London [Londinium] with a population of 25 000. In regional terms the South East had the greatest concentration of Roman towns. Associated with the towns were the roads (i.e. 357475) which linked the towns to their hinterlands. Outside the towns, and developed later, was a scattering of villas – large farmsteads belonging to Romanised folk. One of the best known examples is the Roman palace at Fishbourne, Sussex. Others were located along the gault clay vale in Sussex (i.e. 410545) and further south at Ewhurst (083417). However, much of the countryside was little affected by Romanisation.

■ Recognisable towns all but vanished during the post-Roman period and a resurgence did not occur until the 8th and 9th centuries. Again, the South East was at the forefront. There is only limited evidence of the Germanic settlers who penetrated lowland England during the 5th and 6th centuries (Angles, Saxons and Jutes). Much of our understanding of this colonisation is through place name study. Map evidence can be seen in the tumuli (burial grounds) at Banstead (248608) and Coulsdon (300582), both of which probably date from the mid-seventh century. Other pagan cemeteries have been found at Tattenham Corner (227582), Leatherhead and Guildford.

■ By the time of Alfred, the settlement pattern that was to prevail until comparatively modern times was probably established. Villages thrived in the Thames valley and along the dip-slope spring line of the North Downs. Smaller settlements were sited at favourable places on the chalk downs themselves. On the gault clay to the south, a limited area of fertile soils was farmed by a long line of closely spaced settlements.

■ The Normans built strong castles at strategic places like Guildford, and manor houses at fertile and accessible locations. The parks which usually accompanied Norman castles and manor houses were generally broken up for farmland in the Tudor period. In some cases, such as that of the former park at Lagham in south Godstone (370474), the distinctive curved outline of their boundaries can still be traced among the modern fields.

■ The settlement pattern was consolidated during the Middle Ages with only limited change. Only Southwark, Guildford, Kingston and to a lesser extent Farnham could really be called towns in medieval Surrey. Here, the proximity of London appears to have inhibited the growth of urban centres. Henry VIII was an enthusiastic builder and built Nonsuch (230630) and Oatlands Palaces in Surrey. Industries appeared in some towns, including the spinning and weaving of wool (Guildford), leather-working (Leatherhead) and metal-working.

■ The construction of turnpikes and then railways brought suburban London to the north-eastern part of Surrey, followed by the expansion of Croydon, Guildford and Horley, and the creation of 'railway towns' at New Woking, Redhill and Surbiton. Between the two world wars, motor cars and electric trains brought a further exodus out of London into Surrey. Meanwhile, the destructive ugliness of the speculative builder was threatening some of the finest scenery in the county. This process was to continue, checked only by philanthropy and the National Trust, until the Green Belt Act was passed.

■ In spite of increasing legislation to protect the landscape, post-war development has had a significant impact. Crawley (270364) is one of eight New Towns built around London following the New Towns Act of 1946. To the north of Crawley, the construction and subsequent expansion of Gatwick airport has had a considerable effect on the demand for housing in the surrounding area.

■ The villages and towns of the region have increasingly become the preserve of commuters, changing considerably the socio-economic character of these settlements. The South East exhibits the most advanced landscape of counter-urbanisation in Britain.

Questions

1 Discuss the criteria that can be used to distinguish between urban and rural.
2 Outline the principal characteristics of traditional rural society.
3 Describe the regional differences illustrated by Figure 3.6.
4 Using Ordnance Survey maps, describe and explain the site and situation of three contrasting villages.
5 What is the evidence to suggest that your home region can be viewed as a palimpsest?

Classifying rural settlement

At the beginning of this chapter, reference was made to classification by size. However, rural settlement is also classified by its general pattern over the landscape and by the morphology of individual settlements.

Settlement patterns

The settlement pattern in most areas is the result of the interaction of physical, economic and social factors over a long period of time (Figure 3.9). The basic types of settlement pattern recognised by geographers are:

■ **nucleated; and**

■ **dispersed.**

A dispersed settlement pattern occurs where isolated farms and houses are widely scattered throughout the countryside. Such a pattern is common in sparsely populated areas such as central Wales and the west of Ireland. In such a landscape the

clustering of dwellings is very limited and is characterised by hamlets and small villages rather than by larger settlements.

Dispersed settlement has tended to develop where:

■ natural resources such as fertile land were limited at any one place and sufficient only to support a very small number of people

■ the 'agricultural revolution' of the 18th century resulted in the enclosure of land previously farmed under the traditional open field system which had the village as its nucleus. With enclosure, many farmers left villages to build isolated farmhouses on their new blocks of land

■ the system of land tenure resulted in farms being divided upon inheritance

■ land has been settled relatively recently, as in the Dutch polders and the Canadian Prairies.

A nucleated settlement pattern occurs where most dwellings are clustered around a central feature such as a village green, a crossroads or church. There are few dwellings in the surrounding fields. Thus, hamlets and villages are much larger than in areas with a dispersed pattern of settlement.

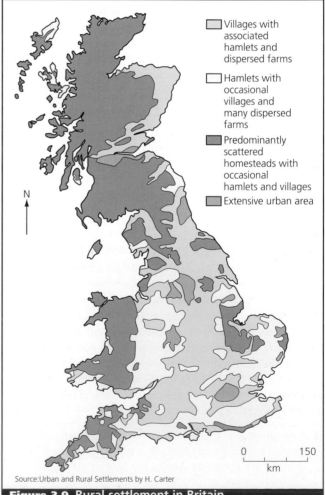

Villages with associated hamlets and dispersed farms

Hamlets with occasional villages and many dispersed farms

Predominantly scattered homesteads with occasional hamlets and villages

Extensive urban area

N

0   150
km

Source: Urban and Rural Settlements by H. Carter

Figure 3.9 Rural settlement in Britain

A nucleated pattern of settlement has tended to develop where:

- **cooperative styles of farming** operate, such as the open field system discussed above

- **defense** has been a concern and appropriate sites, within a meander, or on a hilltop, have been available

- significant supplies of **water** have been available, such as along spring lines

- **islands of dry ground** were found within poorly drained areas

- very fertile land has led to **intensive farming**, so a large number of rural service centres developed to serve a high rural population density.

Shape

The morphology (form) of a settlement refers to its shape or pattern. The main types of village morphology recognised are:

- **Nucleated:** Exhibiting a stong concentration of buildings around a focal point.

- **Linear/ribbon:** Buildings are spread out in a line because of physical constraints or because development over time has taken place along a road.

- **Cruciform:** A village has developed at a road junction and expanded outwards in all directions.

- **Fragmented/loose-knit:** Building density is low with no original nucleus to the village.

- **Green:** Nucleated around a central green or common which may include a church and/or pond.

- **Planned:** The shape of the village was determined from the beginning, rather than evolving over time.

> ### Key Definitions 2
>
> **settlement pattern** The nature of the distribution of settlements over a landscape.
>
> **settlement morphology** Refers to the shape or internal pattern of a settlement.
>
> **rural depopulation** The decrease in population of rural areas, whether by migration or by falling birth rates as young people move away, usually to urban areas.
>
> **rural development** The encouragement and assistance given to economic growth in countryside areas, usually in an attempt to halt rural depopulation. The Rural Development Commission is the government agency responsible for the well-being of rural England.
>
> **key village** A village designated to be developed in terms of the goods and services available to its own population and the population of a designated surrounding area.

Changing rural environments

Rural areas are dynamic spatial entities. They constantly change in response to a range of economic, social, political and environmental factors. In recent years the pace of change has been more rapid than ever before.

The economy of rural areas is no longer dominated by farmers and landowners. As agricultural jobs have been lost, new employers have actively sought to locate in the countryside. Manufacturing, high technology and the service sector have led this trend. Most of these firms are classed as SMEs – small and medium-sized enterprises. In fact, in recent decades, employment has been growing faster in rural than in urban areas. Other significant new users of rural space are recreation, tourism and environmental conservation. The rural landscape has evolved into a complex multiple-use resource.

These economic changes have fuelled social change in the countryside with the in-migration of particular groups of people. To quote Brian Ilbery, a leading authority on rural geography, 'The countryside has been repopulated, especially by middle-class groups … who took advantage of relatively cheap housing in the 1960s and 1970s to colonize the countryside'. Once they are significant in number, the affluent newcomers exert a strong influence over the social and physical nature of rural space. In many areas newcomers have

dominated the housing market to the detriment of the established population in the locality. Increased demand has pushed up house prices to a level beyond the means of the children of many original families who then have no option but to move elsewhere.

Gentrification is every bit as evident in the countryside as it is in selected inner-city areas. However, the increasing mobility of people, goods and information has eroded local communities. A transformation that has been good for newcomers has been deeply resented by much of the established population.

In the post-war period the government has attempted to contain expansion into the countryside by creating green belts and by the allocation of housing to urban areas or to large key villages. Rural England has witnessed rising owner-occupation and low levels of local authority housing. The low level of new housing development in smaller rural communities has been reflected in higher house prices and greater social exclusivity.

Such social and economic changes have increased the pressure on rural resources so that government has had to re-evaluate policies for the countryside. Regulation has become an important element in some areas, notably in relation to sustainability and environmental conservation.

Murdoch and Marsden (1994) recognise four current types of rural area:

- The **preserved countryside** which is highly accessible from urban areas. The middle-class population, many of whom are newcomers, lobby strongly against most new development proposals.

- The **contested countryside** which lies outside the main commuter zones. Here, farmers and development interests remain dominant and thus a high proportion of development proposals are pushed through. However, newcomers are increasing in number and adopting attitudes similar to those in the preserved countryside.

- The **paternalistic countryside** dominated by large private estates and farms. Here development is controlled by established landowners who take a long-term-management view of their property. Development is largely related to the economic diversification needed to raise incomes.

- The **clientist countryside** of remote rural areas where agriculture is dominant but dependent on government subsidy.

Changing agriculture

The countryside in Britain and other developed nations has been affected by major structural changes in agricultural production. Although agricultural land forms 73% of the total land area of the UK only 2.1% of the total workforce were employed in agriculture in 1994. This was down from 6.1% in 1950 and 2.9% in 1970. In absolute terms nearly a million people were employed in farm work in 1938. By 1998 it was less than 500 000. Even in the most rural of areas, agriculture and related industries rarely account for more than 15% of the employed population.

At the same time the size of farms has steadily increased. 33% of farms in the UK were over 50 ha in 1995, up from 27% in 1970. Such changes have resulted in a significant loss of hedgerows which provide important ecological networks.

In 1996 an average farm-worker earned £91 a week less than the average for manufacturing work. As a result farmers are among the poorest of the working poor. A quarter of the 11 million people who live in rural England are on or below the margin of poverty. However, this fact has not been reflected in government funding. In 1996-97, £346 million was allocated to alleviate inner-city deprivation while just over £20 million was set aside to help the rural poor. This disparity is puzzling, considering the overlap of urban and rural deprivation (Figure 3.10).

As many farmers have struggled to make a living from traditional agricultural activities, a growing number have sought to diversify both within and outside agriculture (Figure 3.11). However, while diversification may initially halt job losses, if too many farmers in an area opt for the same type of diversification, a situation of over-supply can result in a further round of rural decline.

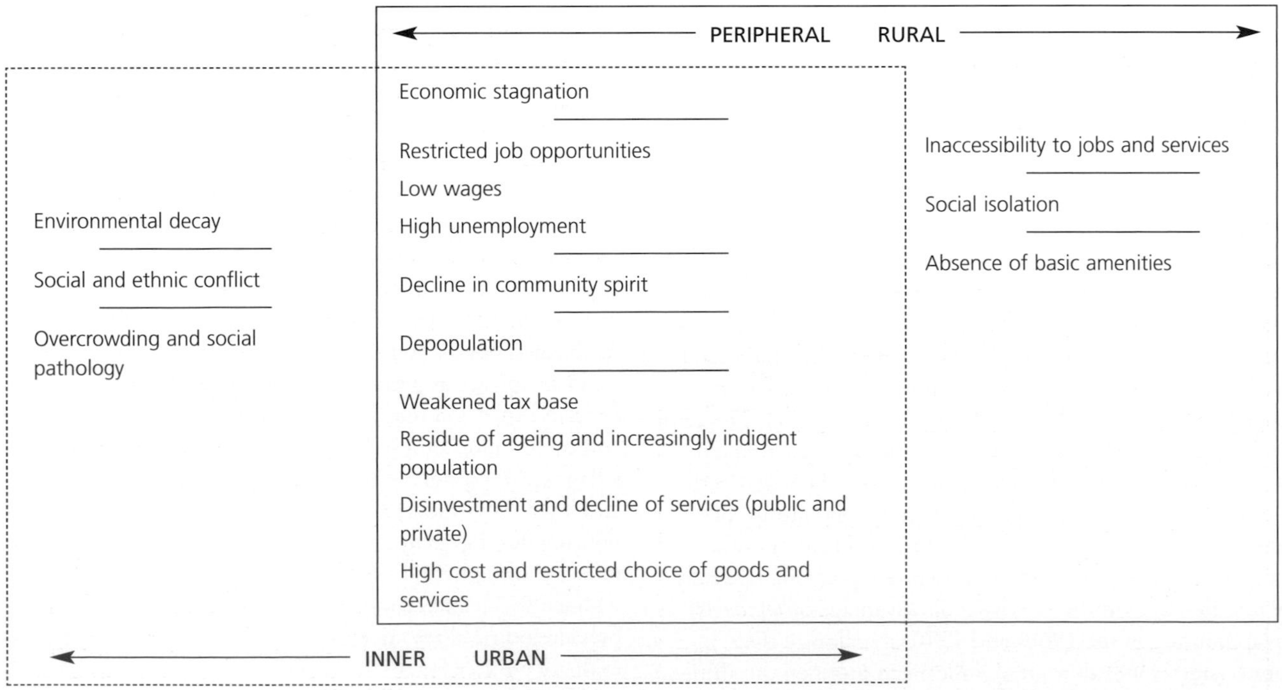

PERIPHERAL   RURAL

Economic stagnation

Restricted job opportunities

Low wages

High unemployment

Decline in community spirit

Depopulation

Weakened tax base

Residue of ageing and increasingly indigent population

Disinvestment and decline of services (public and private)

High cost and restricted choice of goods and services

Inaccessibility to jobs and services

Social isolation

Absence of basic amenities

Environmental decay

Social and ethnic conflict

Overcrowding and social pathology

INNER   URBAN

Source: Knox and Cottam (1981a)

Figure 3.10 The overlap of urban and rural deprivation

TOURIST AND RECREATION	VALUE-ADDED
Tourism	**By marketing**
Self-catering	Pick your own
Serviced accommodation	Home delivered products
Activity holidays	Farm-gate sales
Recreation	**By processing**
Farm visitor centre	Meat products – patés, etc.
Farm museum	Horticultural products to
Restaurant/tea room	jam
	Farmhouse cider
UNCONVENTIONAL	Farmhouse cheese
PRODUCTS	
	ANCILLARY RESOURCES
Livestock	
Sheep for milk	**Buildings**
Goats	For craft units
Snails	For homes
	For tourist accommodation
Crops	
Borage	**Woodlands**
Evening primrose	For timber
Organic crops	For game
	Wetlands
Source: Slee, 1987.	For lakes
	For game

Figure 3.11 Areas of potential farm diversification

Counter-urbanisation and the rural landscape

In recent decades counter-urbanisation has replaced urbanisation as the dominant force shaping settlement patterns. It is a complex and multifaceted process which has resulted in a 'rural population turnaround' in many areas where depopulation had been in progress. Green belt restrictions have limited the impact of counter-urbanisation in many areas adjacent to cities. But, not surprisingly, the greatest impact of counter-urbanisation has been just beyond green belts, where commuting is clearly viable. Here rural settlements have grown substantially and been considerably altered in character .

Figure 3.12 shows the changing morphology of metropolitan villages identified by Hudson (1977). Stage 1 is characterised by the conversion of working buildings into houses with new building mainly in the form of in-fill. However, some new building might occur at the edge of the village. The major morphological change in Stage 2 is ribbon development along roads leading out of the village. Stage 3 of the model shows planned additions on a much larger scale, of either council or private housing estates, at the edge of villages. As time passes, the early morphology of the village becomes less apparent. Clearly, not all metropolitan villages will have evolved in the same way as the model, particularly those where green belt restrictions are in place. Nevertheless, the model provides a useful framework for reference.

Studies of metropolitan villages in the post-1950 period have charted the gradual disappearance in such settlements of the former integrated community structure and its replacement by a system of two co-existing groups; long-established residents, and newcomers. Figure 3.13 shows, at its most extreme, the differences that may exist between the two groups. However, in the last decade or so there is evidence of a reduction in socio-economic differences between long-established residents and newcomers. This has been due to the movement of relatively high-paid manual workers to rural areas because of:

■ **the urban-rural shift of manufacturing industry**

■ **the broadening appeal of rural life across the socio-economic groups.**

In addition, a growing number of long-established residents are commuting to work in urban areas as a result of the decline in rural employment opportunities. The term 'inertia commuters' has been applied to this group of travellers to distinguish them from commuting newcomers, the so-called 'voluntary commuters'.

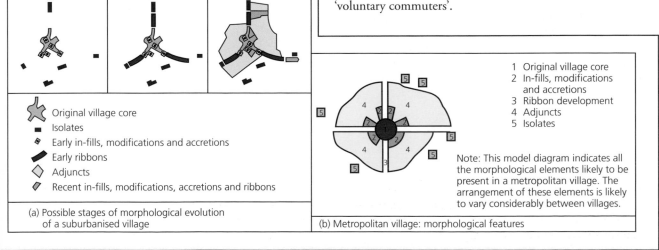

Stage 1   Stage 2   Stage 3

Original village core
Isolates
Early in-fills, modifications and accretions
Early ribbons
Adjuncts
Recent in-fills, modifications, accretions and ribbons

(a) Possible stages of morphological evolution of a suburbanised village

1 Original village core
2 In-fills, modifications and accretions
3 Ribbon development
4 Adjuncts
5 Isolates

Note: This model diagram indicates all the morphological elements likely to be present in a metropolitan village. The arrangement of these elements is likely to vary considerably between villages.

(b) Metropolitan village: morphological features

Figure 3.12 Morphology of metropolitan villages

Figure 3.13 Comparison of long-established residents and newcomers to metropolitan villages

Long-established residents	Newcomers
■ Born in village or local area.	■ Born elsewhere, often in another part of the country.
■ Live in council property and tied property.	■ Live in owner-occupied property.
■ Predominantly in socio-economic groups 9, 10, 11, 15.*ᵃ	■ Predominantly in socio-economic groups 1, 2, 3, 4.*ᵇ
■ Work locally.	■ Work in nearby towns and cities.
■ Travel to work on foot, by bike, by bus.	■ Travel to work by car and train.
■ Earnings below the national average.	■ Earnings above the national average.
■ Average age higher than that of total village population.	■ Average age lower than that of total village population.*ᶜ
■ Composite families not uncommon.	■ Simple nuclear families.
■ Relatives live in village and/or surrounding rural area.	■ Relatives unlikely to be found in village or surrounding area.
■ Much use made of village shops and community organisations.	■ Shopping and recreation trips over wide area, especially to surrounding towns and cities.

*ᵃ Skilled manual workers, semi-skilled manual workers, unskilled manual workers and agricultural workers respectively. There have always been exceptions to this generalisation; for example, farmers, doctors, parsons and school teachers are examples of long-established village residents who belong to socio-economic groups 1 to 4.

*ᵇ Various kinds of employers, managers and professional workers.

*ᶜ Some settlements, especially in coastal areas, contain large numbers of retired newcomers.

Areas of tranquillity in the English countryside have shrunk by more than a fifth since 1965. Studies for the Protection of rural England and the Countryside Commission show that nearly 19 000 km² of tranquil countryside have become blighted by noise and other adverse human impact. These analyses concluded that only three large areas of England are now left untouched by urbanisation and industry; the Marches of Shropshire and Herefordshire, the north Pennines, and north Devon. Areas of tranquillity, defined as peaceful and unspoilt places, typically between one and three kilometres from roads, four kilometres from a power station, beyond large settlements and the noise of military or industrial activity, remain in all of England's counties. However, they are smaller and more fragmented than they were three decades ago, with large swathes under pressure from development. The greatest change has occurred in the South East. In the 1960s, 58% of the region was considered tranquil. By 1995 this was down to 38%. In contrast, the North East was the least changed since the 1960s, losing only 9% of its tranquil area.

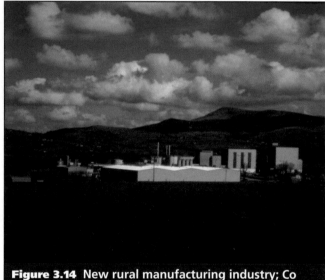

Figure 3.14 New rural manufacturing industry; Co Tipperary, Ireland

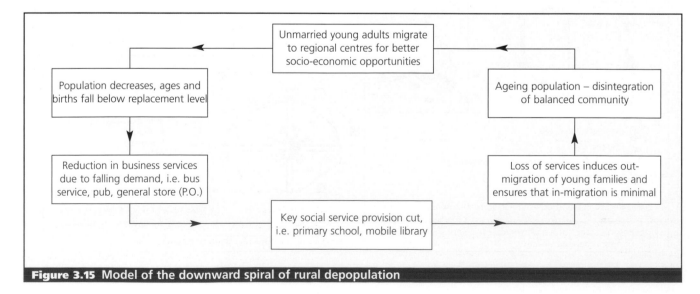

Unmarried young adults migrate to regional centres for better socio-economic opportunities

Population decreases, ages and births fall below replacement level

Ageing population – disintegration of balanced community

Reduction in business services due to falling demand, i.e. bus service, pub, general store (P.O.)

Loss of services induces out-migration of young families and ensures that in-migration is minimal

Key social service provision cut, i.e. primary school, mobile library

Figure 3.15 Model of the downward spiral of rural depopulation

Rural depopulation

In more remote rural areas the pattern of population decline that had begun in the 19th century continued into the second half of the 20th century, with the 1971 census showing that almost a third of all rural districts were still losing population. However, because of the geographical spread of counter-urbanisation since the 1960s, the areas affected by rural depopulation have diminished. Depopulation is now generally confined to the most isolated areas of the country, but exceptions can be found in other areas where economic conditions are particularly dire. Figure 3.15 is a simple model of the depopulation process.

Significant parts of the Gaeltacht, the Irish-speaking districts in the west of Ireland, have suffered depopulation. One community which has been very badly affected is Lettermore, a group of islands off Galway, connected with the mainland by bridges. After a lull in the 1970s, emigration rose sharply with the economic problems of the 1980s. Most of those who left were young, and their departure made it impossible for local football and hurling clubs to assemble teams on a regular basis. The evidence of long-term depopulation can clearly be seen in the landscape. In the stony fields stand abandoned cottages with boarded-up windows. Some villages lie almost deserted. Although the rate of emigration slowed in the 1990s due to the buoyant Irish economy, the very limited employment opportunities in the Gaeltacht gives many communities a very uncertain future.

Questions

1 Explain the pattern of rural settlement illustrated by Figure 3.9.
2 To what extent, and why, is there an overlap between rural and urban deprivation (Figure 3.10)?
3 What impact has agricultural change in Britain had on the rural landscape?
4 Why does the potential for farm diversification vary from region to region?
5 Explain the morphological changes in metropolitan villages illustrated by Figure 3.12.
6 Discuss the differences between newcomers and long-established residents in metropolitan villages (Figure 3.13).
7 Examine the causes and consequences of rural depopulation.
8 Why are fewer areas of Britain experiencing rural population today compared with fifty years ago?

The issue of rural services

The 1997 Survey of Rural Services was the third in a unique series, providing information about the availability of services in the 9 677 rural parishes in England. Earlier surveys were held in 1991 and 1994 (Figure 3.17). Rural parishes are defined as those with a population under 10 000. It should be

Figure 3.16 Deserted village: Léon, Spain

Figure 3.17 Rural services in England

Percentage of rural parishes without key services

	1991	1994	1997
permanent shop (of any kind)	41	42	42
general store	71	72	70
post office	42	43	43
village hall/community centre	30	29	28
public house	n/a	30	29
daily bus service	72	71	75
school (for any age)	50*	52*	49
school (for 6 year olds)	53*	52*	50

Note: * there may have been a slight undercount of schools in these surveys.

Percentage of rural parishes without other important services

	1991	1994	1997
petrol station or garage	n/a	58	56
bank or building society	89	90	91
public nursery	96	95	93
private nursery	93	90	86
day-care group for elderly	93	92	91
GP (based in the parish)	84	83	83
dentist	91	91	91
pharmacy (of any kind)	81	81	79
Benefit Agency office	n/a	n/a	99
Job Centre	n/a	n/a	99
library (permanent or mobile)	12	16#	12
community minibus or social car scheme	82	79	79
police station	89	91	92

Note: # this is probably a rogue figure and is considered unreliable.

Source: *The 1997 Survey of Rural Services*

noted that this is not a village survey, since parishes may contain more than one village. The 10 000 population threshold means that the survey also covered larger rural settlements, including small market towns.

The most recent survey showed that the proportion of rural parishes without key services remained high, although there

Our dying villages

The villagers of Mollington in Oxfordshire have watched with sadness as many of the things that once made it a community, not just a collection of houses, have vanished.

The primary school, a modern building which had only been in use for 20 years, was shut two years ago due to falling numbers.

Mollington's village shop had already gone the same way, taking the sub-post office with it.

Elderly residents must now struggle into Banbury, five miles away, to collect their pensions, and the sprawling out-of-town Tesco store is now the favoured shopping destination.

At the supermarket check-outs, of course, no village news or gossip is exchanged, and cars are the only practical way to get there.

Sheila Bywaters, 57, president of Mollington's WI branch, said: 'We do have a small pub left in the village, which is thriving, but there's almost nothing else going on, now. My husband hardly knows any men in the village.

'When the school was open there were always open days, barn dances and concerts and everyone got to know each other. When it closed the whole focus of the village disappeared. The

Scout group shut four years ago because numbers were down and the Cubs had to combine with another village.'

Mrs Bywaters has personal experience of the common problem of rising house prices, often pushed up by demand from commuters, forcing young people to leave the villages where they grew up.

'My children couldn't afford to buy houses in the village,' she said. 'Even quite ordinary cottages now sell for well over £100,000. As a result, there are virtually no young families in the village. There's not much to attract them anyway. The playgroup is closing this year, and so the village hall won't get used as much and may struggle financially. The only employment in the village is a handful of jobs on farms. Most people commute miles.

'It's becoming just a dormitory village with no vitality or sense of belonging to a community. We've watched all these changes over the years, and it's very sad. The future doesn't seem bright.

'If I could change one thing, it would be to open the school again, but the young families to support it have been forced out.'   *Daily Mail*, Monday, July 5 1999

Figure 3.18 Our dying villages

had been no significant decline in most services over the period 1991 to 1997. The sharpest decline was in bus services. However, some services had increased, including childcare and village halls. The main findings of the 1997 survey were:

- 75% of parishes had no daily bus service

- 49% of parishes had no school

- 43% of parishes had no post office

- 42% of parishes had no permanent shop of any kind.

The survey, not unsurprisingly, found a strong relationship between population size and service provision. For example, 59% of parishes with under 1000 population were without a permanent shop of any kind, compared with 1% for parishes with a population between 3000 and 9999. Similarly, 67% of parishes with under 1000 population were without a school, compared with 1% for parishes with a population between 3000 and 9999. Service decline can have a huge impact on rural populations (Figure 3.18).

Key villages

Between the 1950s and 1970s the concept of key settlements was central to rural settlement policy in many parts of Britain, particularly where depopulation was occurring. The concept relates to central place theory and assumes that focussing services, facilities and employment in one selected settlement will satisfy the essential needs of the surrounding villages and

Figure 3.19 A specialised service in a thriving mid-Surrey village

hamlets (Figure 3.20). The argument was that, with falling demand, dispersed services would rapidly decline in vulnerable areas. The only way to maintain a reasonable level of service provision in such an area was to focus on those locations with the greatest accessibility and the best combination of other advantages. In this way, threshold populations could be assured, and hopefully the downward spiral of service decline would be halted. Thus, in remote areas, the main role of key settlements was to act as 'stabilising centres' in a sea of decline, whereas in pressurised areas they acted as 'control centres' to which economic and population overspill could be channelled.

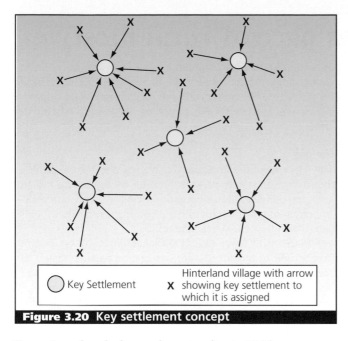

Figure 3.20 Key settlement concept

Key Settlement ○

X Hinterland village with arrow showing key settlement to which it is assigned

Devon introduced a key settlement policy in 1964 to counter the impact of:

- rural depopulation
- the changing function of the village in relation to urban centres
- the decline in agricultural employment
- the contraction of public transport.

The selection of key settlements in Devon was part of a wider settlement policy involving sub-regional centres, sub-urban towns and coastal resorts. The criteria used for selecting key settlements were as follows:

- existing services
- existing employment other than agriculture in or near the village
- accessibility by road
- location in relation to current bus (and possibly rail) services
- location in relation to other villages which would rely on them for some services
- the availability of public utilities capable of extension for new development
- the availability and agricultural value of land capable of development
- proximity to urban centres (key settlements would not flourish too close to competing urban areas).

Sixty-eight key settlements were initially selected, then reduced to sixty-five in 1970. Although it has been difficult to measure the effectiveness of the policy with precision, depopulation in north- and mid-Devon did fall considerably after the introduction of the policy, and in many areas the decline in service provision was slower than the predictions before the policy was implemented. In recent decades the concept has received less attention, both in Devon and in the country as a whole, due to:

- local authority spending cuts resulting in the closure of many public services that local people and councils would have liked to maintain
- the relentless domination of private sector services by large companies based in or just outside urban areas.

In a recent publication by Devon County Council (Devon Structure Plan, First Review 1995–2011, February 1999) the term 'key settlement' is not even used. Policy S2 states:

Particular rural settlements should be identified in Local Plans as Local Centres. These will form the focal points for a modest scale of development, supporting services and the economic well-being of the hinterland. They should therefore:

- be accessible to the community they serve and well related to public transport and the highway network; and
- be defined to ensure that the local needs of all rural areas can be met, taking into account their location, relative to other designated Centres, including those in adjoining Districts.

The 1995 White Paper for Rural England

A White Paper is an official government report which sets out the government's policy on a matter that is, or will come, before Parliament. This was the first attempt for over 50 years to address rural issues in a strategy document. Figure 3.21 is a summary of the most important aspects of the White Paper. Although a new White Paper is likely as a result of the change of government in 1997, the key issues have not changed.

The rural transport problem

The considerable increase in car ownership in recent decades has had a devastating effect on public transport. While this has not disadvantaged rural car owners very much, it has considerably increased the isolation of the poor, the elderly and the young. The lack of public transport puts intense pressure on low income households to own a car, a large additional expense that many could do without. Recent increases in the price of fuel have exacerbated this problem.

- There is concern that Britain's rural railway lines are under threat in a repeat of the 'Beeching cuts' of the 1960s. The new fears about government intentions towards rural rail closures were first awakened in 1998 when the transport minister said that branch lines in

White Paper plots faster pace of rural lifestyle

Business

Small business development in the countryside is seen as a vital source of job creation. The paper proposes to relax planning controls on the conversion of redundant farm and other rural buildings for business use, with particular emphasis on light industry, exploiting new information technology and 'teleworking'. Approval of such conversions would depend on road traffic forecasts to prevent 'uncontrolled expansion' of such business from damaging the countryside.

Schools

Rural schools are seen as the focus of family life. About 4000 of England's 19 000 primary schools are in rural areas, but 52 per cent of parishes now have no school. The rate of closure is slowing: 350 small rural schools closed over the past 12 years but only 80 since 1990. The paper says one way to stop further closures is to integrate schools more into village life.

Transport

Although 87 per cent of parishes have some kind of bus service, only 29 per cent have a daily service. But the paper sees little hope of reducing reliance on the private car in the countryside. Frequent bus services for all rural communities, no matter how remote or sparsely populated, are not a practical option. The paper would like to see more community bus services, run by volunteers and subsidised if necessary by the relevant county council. The paper says there should be fewer new trunk roads in the countryside and more spending on improving existing motorways and providing bypasses to relieve villages.

Housing

The paper identifies an acute shortage of cheap rural homes. Increasing the supply of such housing is seen as the key to keeping young people working and living in the countryside. At present only 12 per cent of rural housing is subsidised, compared to 25 per cent in urban areas.

Villages with fewer than 3000 inhabitants will be exempt from a right-to-buy for housing association tenants. That is to prevent such housing disappearing on to the open market and being bought up at prices local people cannot afford.

The Government will also speed the disposal of surplus Ministry of Defence housing. There are an estimated 13 000 empty MoD homes in Britain, many of them in rural areas. Rural households will be encouraged to take in lodgers through the rent-a-room scheme.

More private-sector bodies and charities will be encouraged to bid for funding to provide cheap rural housing.

The Times, 18 October 1995

Figure 3.21 The 1995 White Paper for Rural England

Figure 3.22 Preparing the bonfire for Guy Fawkes' night on the 'Green' of a Surrey village

sparsely populated areas might be replaced by coaches. It would be possible to convert track beds into guided busways, and then for buses to divert into towns and villages. However, one study of replacing trains with buses found that at most only half of former rail passengers used the bus replacements. With one in five rural households lacking a car and a low level of bus service in many country areas, the train is essential for many.

Figure 3.23(a) Positive aspects of second home development

Advantages

1. Bring new employment opportunities to areas previously dependent upon a contracting agricultural economy (e.g. building trade, gardening and domestic staff).
2. Local restaurants, shops and garages derive new business and additional profits (which may be essential to year-round economic survival).
3. Specialized shops opened to cater for second home owners also benefit local residents.
4. Property taxes imposed on second homes increase the finances of the local community.
5. Second home owners make fewer demands on local services since education and other community facilities are not required.
6. Renovation of old buildings improves the appearance of the rural area.
7. Rural residents have the opportunity to sell-off surplus land and buildings at a high price.
8. Contacts with urban-based second home owners can benefit local residents by exposing them to national values and information, broadening outlooks or stimulating self-advancement via migration.

Figure 3.23(b) Negative aspects of second home development

Disadvantages

1. Concentrations of second homes may require installation of costly sewerage schemes, extension of water and electricity lines to meet peak season demand, and more frequent maintenance of rural roads, with the costs being partly borne by locals.
2. Demand for second homes by urbanites pushes up house prices to the disadvantage of locals.
3. Future schemes for farm enlargement or agricultural restructuring may be hindered by inflated land prices.
4. Fragmentation of agricultural land.
5. Destruction of the 'natural' environment (e.g. soil erosion and stream pollution).
6. Visual degradation may result from poorly constructed or inappropriately located second homes.
7. Second home construction may distract the local workforce from ordinary house building and maintenance.
8. The different values and attitudes of second home families disrupt local community life.

The rural housing problem

The lack of affordable housing in village communities has resulted in a large number of young people having to move to market towns or larger urban centres. Only 12% of rural housing is subsidised, compared to 25% in urban areas. The 1995 White Paper on Rural Development sought to improve the rural housing situation by exempting villages with fewer than 3000 inhabitants from the right-to-buy for housing association tenents. This is to prevent such housing disappearing on to the open market and being bought up at prices local people cannot afford. The Government also announced plans to speed up the disposal of Ministry of Defence housing. It estimated that there were 13 000 empty MoD homes in Britain, many of them in rural areas. Rural households would also be encouraged to take in lodgers through the rent-a-room scheme.

The isue of second homes has become increasingly contentious. Figure 3.23, from a book published in the mid-1980s, indicates that some advantages might accrue from second home development. However, recent debate on the issue has centred firmly on the problems created.

The village of Urchfont, Wiltshire

Figure 3.24 Urchfont from the air

A recent article in the Guardian newspaper used the village of Urchfont in Wiltshire to exemplify the problems facing rural communities (Figure 3.24). The village has a population of 1100. The opening paragraph of the article reads as follows: 'Rural life is in crisis. Farmers are crying "ruin", shops are closing, and wages low. To top it all, city folk escaping from the urban sprawl are causing house prices to soar'.

- **The village bus** After deregulation, Urchfont looked likely to lose most of its bus services. Now dozens of villagers depend on the community bus, run by a team of volunteers, and the Wiggly Bus, which is subsidised by the district council and comes out when you call it. In 1997 75% of rural parishes had no daily bus. Traffic on rural roads is forecast to increase by 50% over the next 25 years.

- **The new development** High-speed trains from Pewsey station, a 20-minute drive away, have made it possible for commuters to move into the village, bringing with them London prices (the train to the capital takes 70 minutes). An executive home in a recent development is for sale at £235 000. Each week, 1 700 people leave our major cities.

- **The new arrivals' home** A couple moved to Urchfont six years ago because they couldn't afford the prices around Newbury. They bought a house for £135 000 and it has just been revalued at £225 000. They came to the village for the quality of life and sense of community.

- **Manor Farm House** The farmhouse is rented out for £1 800 a month to a couple who have just left London. They find prices comparatively cheap, and have found a period house to buy in the area for £400 000. For farmers, income from residential property can be as important as that from the land. Another local has rented out her farmhouse for £1 200 a month and moved into a house in Urchfont for £390 a month.

- **Knights Leaze Farm** Once predominantly a dairy farm, its owners, the Bodmans, say they can no longer live on what they get for milk. Now, 90% of their income comes from contract work – farm construction, fencing, hedging, straw-baling. They employ 13 people, but have met some opposition in the village to their heavy lorries and machinery.

- **The last shop** Until it closed recently, the butcher's was Urchfont's last shop; it also sold a few groceries. It has now been converted into a house and is on the market for £152 000. It has no garden. Seventy per cent of rural parishes are now without a general store; 49% of villages have no school.

- **The weekenders' cottage** About 7% of houses in Urchfont are weekend homes. Small two-bedroomed cottages would have been suitable for first-time buyers five years ago; now they fetch as much as £150 000. Local people can no longer afford the villages and have to look in nearby towns, according to estate agents. 'A one-bedroomed house will be over £50 000 and £10 000 might be a typical wage.'

- **Manor Farm** Situated in the centre of the village its site is unsuitable for the size of today's agricultural machinery, according to its owner, John Snook. The noise and mess of a farm is also thought unacceptable in a conservation area. One use for it would be as a site for new homes, but planning permission is unlikely on a 'zone for employment' and many villagers oppose new housing.

- **Rookery Farm** Farmer John Snook has decided that he will have to sell his dairy herd, although there have been cows here for over a century and his herdsman will lose his job. 'We've stopped investing. We are lucky we don't have any borrowing – we can get by – but small farms will be packing up in droves. 'Farm incomes have collapsed by more than two-thirds in two years.'

- **The council estate** Some houses on the Foxley Fields estate are rented out by a housing association; others have been sold with a covenant on them enabling the council to nominate future buyers. The aim is to ensure that the village retains some affordable housing. Of 15 people on the district council's housing waiting list, eight have been on it for more than four years.

The *Guardian* 18 October 1999

The future of rural areas

The Rural Development Commission is the government agency responsible for the well-being of rural England. The stated objectives of the RDC are that the English countryside should be a place where:

- people both live and work and villages and small towns provide for the varied needs of people in a wide range of circumstances

- the economy of all rural areas provides a broad range of job opportunities and makes the most effective contribution to the national economy

- residents are not unduly disadvantaged as a result of living in rural areas, and rural communities have reasonable and affordable access to services

- development respects and, where possible, enhances the environment.

To achieve these objectives the RDC has designated parts of rural England as RDAs. In these rural areas there is clear evidence of relative economic and social disadvantage. Funding is available for the following types of projects: social, community, environment, transport, housing, training, economic, tourism.

RDC funding, with a maximum of 50% of total cost, is normally directed at providing an initial capital contribution to launch a particular project. Projects should aim for self-sufficiency within three years at the most.

Questions

1 Explain the chain of causation illustrated by Figure 3.15.
2 (a) Analyse the data presented in Figure 3.17.
   (b) Why is the level of service provision such a key issue in rural areas?
3 Discuss the validity of the key village concept.
4 Examine the balance between the positive and negative aspects of second home development (Figure 3.23).
5 Discuss the key issues confronting the village of Urchfont.

In the 1990s the world's population became more urban than rural. It seems likely that the watershed year was 1996 but national variations in the quality of data and the way in which urban areas are defined make it difficult to be precise. It has taken about 8000 years for half of the world's population to become urban but it is predicted that it will take less than 80 years for urbanisation to encompass most of the remainder. The patterns that make up urban areas and the processes that formed, and are changing them, are amongst the most important spatial entities on our planet. It is not surprising that the study of urban areas is one of the foremost branches of geographical investigation.

The history of urbanisation

The first cities

Gordon Childe used the term *Urban Revolution* to describe the change in society marked by the emergence of the first cities some 5500 years ago. The areas which first witnessed this profound socio-economic change were (a) Mesopotamia – the valleys of the Tigris and Euphrates rivers, (b) the lower Nile valley and (c) the plains of the River Indus. Later, urban civilisations developed around the Mediterranean, in the Yellow River valley of China, in South East Asia and in the Americas. These early urban communities appeared when the material foundations of life were such as to yield a surplus of food in excess of the consuming needs of the food producers and when the means were also available to concentrate this surplus at particular locations. In each case the volume of surplus production imposed a ceiling on urban development. The most talented in society were freed to perform specialised functions which the newly acquired agricultural techniques, based on irrigation, not only made possible but even demanded for their full application. Such people gathered in clusters to organise and discharge these special services. Compared with anything that had gone before these new settlements were distinctive in size, function and appearance. However, the basis of these earliest urban centres was relatively local. For example, the population of Sumerian cities ranged from 7000 to 20 000.

The catalyst for this period of rapid change was the Neolithic Revolution which occurred about 8000 BC. This was when sedentary agriculture, based on the domestication of animals and cereal farming, steadily replaced a nomadic way of life. As farming advanced irrigation techniques were developed. Other major advances which followed were the ox-drawn plough, the wheeled cart, the sailing boat and metallurgy. However, arguably the most important development was the invention of writing about 4000 BC; for it was in the millennium after this that some of the villages on the alluvial plains between the Tigris and Euphrates rivers increased in size and changed in function so as to merit the classification of urban. Childe and others also stress the importance of social processes. A level of social development had been achieved that allowed large communities to be socially viable and stable. In this context religious activity, centred around the construction of temples, was undoubtedly an important force in the process of urbanisation.

Considerably later than the first cities, trading centres began to develop. The Minoan civilisation cities of Knossos and Phaistos which flourished in Crete during the first half of the second millennium BC derived their wealth from maritime trade. Next it was the turn of the Greeks and then the Romans to develop urban and trading systems on a scale larger than ever before. For example, the population of Athens in the fifth century BC has been estimated at a minimum of 100 000. The fall of the Roman Empire in the fifth century AD

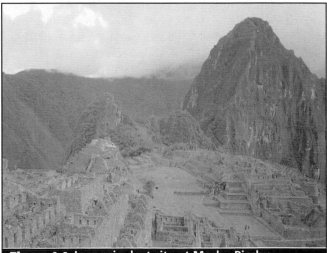

Figure 4.1 Inca ruin: lost city at Machu Picchu

Figure 4.2 Excavated Roman remains

Figure 4.3 Paris in the Medieval period

Figure 4.4 Principal stages in global urban development

	1780–1880	1880–1950	1950–
Mode of accumulation			
Economic formation	Industrial capitalism	Monopoly capitalism	Corporate capitalism
Source of wealth	Manufacturing	Manufacturing	Manufacturing and services
Representative unit of production	Factory	Multinational corporation	Transnational corporation, global factory
World-system characteristics			
Space relations	Atlantic basin	International	Global
System of supply	Colonialism/imperialism	State imperialism	Corporate imperialism
Hegemonic powers	Britain	Britain, USA	USA
Urban consequences			
Level of urbanisation at start of period (%)	3	5	27
Areas of urbanisation during period	Britain	North-western Europe, the Americas, coasts of Empires	Africa and Asia
Dominant cities	London	London, New York	New York, London, Tokyo

Source: *The Geographical Journal* Vol 164, No 1, March 1998

led to a major recession in urban life in Europe which did not really revive until medieval times.

The medieval revival was the product of population growth and the resurgence of trade with the main urban settlements of this period located at points of greatest accessibility. While there were many interesting developments in urban life during the medieval period it required another major technological advance to set in train the next urban revolution.

The urban industrial revolution

The second 'Urban Revolution' based on the introduction of mass production in factories commenced in Britain in the late eighteenth century (Figure 4.4). This was the era of the industrial revolution when industrialisation and urbanisation proceeded hand in hand. The key invention, among many, was the steam engine, which in Britain was applied to industry first and only later to transport. The huge demand for labour in the rapidly growing coalfield towns and cities was satisfied

by the freeing of labour in agriculture through a series of major advances. The so-called 'Agricultural Revolution' had in fact begun in the early seventeenth century.

By 1801 nearly one-tenth of the population of England and Wales was living in cities of over 100 000 people. This proportion doubled in 40 years and doubled again in another 60 years. The 1801 census recorded London's population at one million, the first city in the world to reach this figure. By 1851 London's population had doubled to two million. However, at the global scale fewer than 3 per cent of the population lived in urban places at the beginning of the nineteenth century.

As the processes of the industrial revolution spread to other countries the pace of urbanisation quickened. The change from a population of 10 per cent to 30 per cent living in urban areas of 100 000 people and more took about 80 years in England and Wales; 66 years in the United States; 48 years in Germany; 36 years in Japan and 26 years in Australia.

The transition from industrial capitalism to monopoly

Figure 4.5 The industrial revolution: cotton mills in Bolton

Key Definitions

urbanisation   The process whereby an increasing proportion of the population in a geographical area lives in urban settlements.

urban growth   The absolute increase in physical size and total population of urban areas.

urbanism   The tendency for people to lead increasingly urban ways of life.

counterurbanisation   The process of population decentralisation as people move from large urban areas to smaller urban settlements and rural areas.

reurbanisation   When, after a clear period of decline, the population of a city, in particular the inner area, begins to increase again.

cycle of urbanisation   The stages of urban change from the growth of a city to counterurbanisation through to reurbanisation.

Percentage of population urban in 1950

- 0–19.9
- 20–39.9
- 40–59.9
- 60–79.9
- 80–100

Source: *The Geographical Journal*, March 1998

Figure 4.6 The percentage of the world's population that was urban in 1950

capitalism (Figure 4.4) marked the next of the principal stages in urbanisation in recent history. This transition was characterised by:

- a much greater scale of economic activity
- the consolidation of firms into multinational corporations
- the domination of newly created international markets by a small number of producers in each sector
- the mass production of a very much wider range of goods and services than previously
- the ruthless exploitation of peripheral areas.

The initial urbanisation of much of the Developing World was restricted to concentrations of population around points of supply of raw materials for the affluent developed countries. For example the growth of São Paulo was firmly based on coffee, Buenos Aires on mutton, wool and cereals, and Calcutta on jute.

By the beginning of the most recent stage of urban development in 1950, 27 per cent of people lived in towns and cities (Figure 4.6), with the vast majority of urbanites still living in the Developed World. In fact in the latter the cycle of urbanisation was nearing completion.

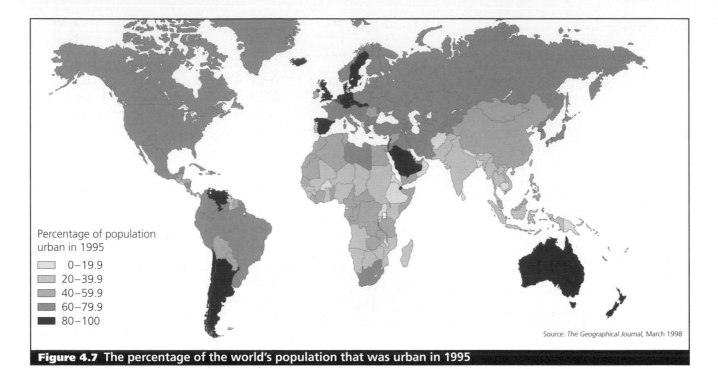

Percentage of population
urban in 1995

- 0–19.9
- 20–39.9
- 40–59.9
- 60–79.9
- 80–100

Source: *The Geographical Journal*, March 1998

Figure 4.7 The percentage of the world's population that was urban in 1995

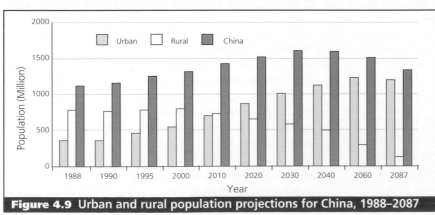

Number of people, m

Source:*Economist*, November 1997

*Cities and immediate metropolitan surroundings

Figure 4.8 The largest urban agglomerations in the world, 1996

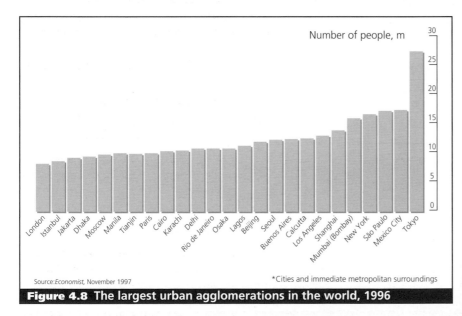

Figure 4.9 Urban and rural population projections for China, 1988–2087

Figure 4.10 Urban poverty: Jakarta, Indonesia

Current patterns

Current levels of urbanisation, as in the past, vary considerably across the globe (Figure 4.7). South America, perhaps surprisingly, is the most urbanised continent with only one of its 13 countries, Guyana, having more rural than urban dwellers. North America, most of Europe, Australia and New Zealand, parts of the Middle East and Japan and Korea in north east Asia are all highly urbanised. In Britain, 89 per cent of people live in towns and cities. In contrast, levels of urbanisation are low through most of Africa, and South and East Asia. The country credited with the lowest urban population of all is Bhutan (6 per cent).

In the Developed World around 75 per cent of people live in urban areas compared to only 38 per cent in the developing nations as a whole. Tokyo remains the world's most heavily populated city with 27.2 million people (Figure 4.8), followed by Mexico city with 16.9 million. Of the world's ten largest cities, seven are in less developed countries.

The UN expects that between 1990 and 2025 the number of people living in urban areas will double to more than five billion, and that 90 per cent of that growth will be in developing countries. In Asia and Africa more than half the population remains in the countryside, compared with only a fifth in North America and Europe. In most developed nations the proportion of people living in large urban areas is actually declining, a process known as 'counterurbanisation'.

The post-1950 urban 'explosion' in the Developing World

Throughout history urbanisation and significant economic progress have tended to occur together. In contrast, the rapid urban growth of the Developing World in the latter part of the twentieth century has in general far outpaced economic development, creating huge problems for planners and politicians. Because urban areas in the Developing World have been growing much more quickly than the cities of the Developed World did in the nineteenth century the term 'urban explosion' has been used to describe contemporary trends. Between 1990 and 1995, the world's urban population grew by nearly 60 million, with four-fifths of this increase in the Developing World. Singapore tops the world urbanisation league as everyone in this small city-state is classed as an urban resident. However, the clear distinction between urbanisation and urban growth should be kept in mind as some of the least urbanised countries, such as China and India contain many of the world's largest cities. China's urban population at 37 per cent in 1995 is predicted to rise to 70 per cent by 2040 and 89 per cent by 2087 (Figure 4.9).

An approach known as dependency theory has been used by a number of writers to explain the urbanisation of the Developing World, particularly the most recent post-1950 phase. According to this approach, urbanisation in the Developing World has been a response to the absorption of

countries and regions into the global economy. The capitalist global economy induces urbanisation by concentrating production and consumption in locations that:

- **offer the best economies of scale and agglomeration**
- **provide the greatest opportunities for industrial linkage**
- **give maximum effectiveness and least cost in terms of control over sources of supply.**

Thus urban development is one of the spatial outcomes of the capitalist system. TNCs are the major players in this economic process which enables and encourages people to cluster in geographical space. The actions of TNCs encourage urbanisation directly in response to localised investment. However, TNCs also influence urbanisation indirectly through their impact on traditional patterns of production and employment. For example, the advance of export-oriented agriculture at the expense of traditional food production has reduced employment opportunities in the countryside and encouraged rural to urban migration.

Other factors which have encouraged urbanisation in the Developing World include:

- **the investment policies of central governments which have generally favoured urban over rural areas, often in an attempt to enhance their prestige on the international stage**
- **the higher wage rates and better employment protection in cities**
- **greater access to health care and education**
- **the decline in the demand for locally produced food as consumers increasingly favour imported food.**

The combined result of these factors has been 'backwash urbanisation', destroying the vitality of rural areas and placing enormous pressure on cities.

Counterurbanisation

Urban deconcentration is the most consistent and dominant feature of population movement in Britain today, in which each level of the settlement hierarchy is gaining people from the more urban tiers above it but losing population to those below it. However, it must be remembered that the net figures hide the fact that there are reasonable numbers of people moving in the opposite direction. Figure 4.11 shows the consistent loss of population for metropolitan England in terms of net within-UK migration for the period 1981–94. It does not, however, mean an overall population decline of this magnitude, because population change is also affected by natural change and international migration. London is the prime example of the counterbalancing effect of the latter two processes.

Figure 4.12, based on the 1991 census, is a summary of change of addresses within Great Britain during the year preceding census night. It focuses on migration between local authority districts grouped according to their degree of 'urbanness' and their distance from the main metropolitan centres. The top six most urban areas all averaged net migration losses while the other seven district types were all net gainers. The trend from most urban to least urban is highly regular. The data presented in Figure 4.13 also shows a distinct 'down-the-urban-hierarchy', or counterurbanisation, cascade.

Around London, where central rents are particularly high, back offices have diffused very widely across South East England. Between 20 and 30 decentralisation centres can be identified in the Outer Metropolitan Area, between 20 and 80 km from central London, especially along the major road and rail corridors. Examples include Dorking, Guildford and Reigate.

Liverpool's population has been falling since 1931 (Figure 4.14) with a current outflow of about 2500 a year. Population loss accelerated in the 1960s when the port of Liverpool and its associated industries went into steep decline. Many people left for new towns such as Runcorn and Skelmersdale, lured by the promise of better housing and new jobs. However, over the past decade the decline has slowed. The population of Glasgow shrank from more than one million in 1960 to 623 000 in the mid-1990s. Manchester has lost up to a third of its population in the last thirty years. There is clear evidence of counter-urbanisation in most developed countries.

Figure 4.11 Net within-UK migration, 1981–94 for metropolitan England

	All metropolitan England	Greater London	Six metropolitan counties
	thousands		
1981	−82.6	−32.2	−50.4
1982	−78.2	−33.5	−44.7
1983	−88.3	−33.3	−55.0
1984	−89.2	−33.1	−56.1
1985	−111.1	−55.2	−55.9
1986	−113.7	−49.2	−64.5
1987	−125.1	−72.9	−52.2
1988	−118.8	−74.4	−44.5
1989	−64.8	−36.9	−27.8
1990	−64.9	−37.4	−27.5
1991	−80.6	−52.7	−27.9
1992	−81.3	−51.7	−29.6
1993	−87.4	−52.9	−34.6
1994	−89.9	−45.9	−44.0

Source: NHSCR data. Reproduced from *Population Trends 83*, Spring 1996

Figure 4.12 Net within-Britain migration, 1990–91, by district types

District type	Population 1991	Net migration 1990–91	%
Inner London	2 504 451	−31 009	−1.24
Outer London	4 175 248	−21 159	−0.51
Principal metropolitan cities	3 992 670	−26 311	−0.67
Other metropolitan districts	8 427 861	−6 900	−0.08
Large non-metropolitan cities	3 493 284	−14 040	−0.40
Small non-metropolitan cities	1 861 351	−7 812	−0.42
Industrial districts	7 475 515	7 194	0.10
Districts with new towns	2 838 258	2 627	0.09
Resorts, ports and retirement districts	3 591 972	17 637	0.49
Urban-rural mixed	7 918 701	19 537	0.25
Remote urban-rural	2 302 925	13 665	0.59
Remote rural	1 645 330	10 022	0.61
Most remote rural	4 731 278	36 450	0.77

Note:
Metropolitan cities and districts includes the Central Clydeside conurbation area
Source: Calculated from the 1991 Census SMS and LBS/SAA (ESRC/JISC purchase) Reproduced from *Population Trends 83*, Spring 1996

Reurbanisation

In very recent years British cities have, to a limited extent so far, reversed the population decline that has dominated the post-war period (Figure 4.15). In fact Merseyside was the only urban region whose population fell between 1991 and 1996. Central government finance, for example the millions of pounds of subsidies poured into London's docklands, Manchester's Hulme wastelands and Sheffield's light railway, has been an important factor in the revival. New urban design is also playing a role. The rebuilding of part of Manchester's city centre after a massive IRA bomb has allowed the planners to add new pedestrian areas, green spaces and residential accommodation.

In London the City's so-called 'ring of steel' security measures against terrorism have proved so successful in deterring traffic that they are being extended over a much wider area to do just that. Road traffic in the City has been cut by 25 per cent, with pollution down 25 per cent and road accidents reduced by more than a third. Peak period bus journey times have been reduced by as much as 70 per cent. The popularity of the City's scheme suggests that the advantages of urban traffic restriction measures of this kind may have been underestimated in the past.

The reduction in urban street crime due to the installation of automated closed-circuit surveillance cameras has significantly improved public perception of central areas. In Newcastle police claim that crime in areas covered by cameras was cut by nearly half between 1991 and 1997. Rather than

Figure 4.13 Net migration between 13 district types, 1990–91

From \ To	IL	OL	PMC	OMD	LNC	SNC	DIA	NT	RPR	MUR	RMUR	RMR	RRMR
IL	XXX	17 442	−240	175	−128	−657	1 866	1 281	2 461	5 162	1 081	557	2 009
OL		XXX	−661	517	24	70	3 213	2 863	5 741	18 329	2 493	1 395	4 617
PMC			XXX	11 652	−23	17	2 710	1 640	1 116	4 486	542	1 215	2 055
OMD				XXX	−2	109	4 056	1 538	1 889	5 068	679	2 116	3 791
LNC					XXX	57	2 267	637	617	2 725	3 717	378	3 513
SNC						XXX	906	416	1 100	2 318	1 117	−7	1 498
DIA							XXX	−387	1 423	−337	264	2 054	4 807
NT								XXX	911	765	788	413	2 484
RPR									XXX	−3 980	613	−58	947
MUR										XXX	2 765	3 169	9 065
RMUR											XXX	−131	585
RMR												XXX	1 079
RRMR													XXX

Key to district types: IL Inner London Boroughs; OL Outer London boroughs; PMC Principal metropolitan cities; OMD Other metropolitan districts; LNC Large non-metropolitan cities; SNC Small non-metropolitan cities; DIA Districts with industrial areas; NT Districts with new towns; RPR Resorts, ports and retirement districts; MUR Mixed urban-rural; RMUR Remote mixed urban-rural; RMR Remote mainly rural; RRMR Most remote rural

How to read the table: Positive figure indicates net shift from row to column (i.e. first entry: 17,442 from Inner to Outer London); negative figure indicates net shift the other way (i.e. second entry: −240 net shift from principal metropolitan cities to inner London)

Source: T. Champion and D. Atkins: *The Counterurbanisation Cascade: An Analysis of the 1991 Census Special Migration Statistics for Great Britain.* Department of Geography Seminar Paper 66, University of Newcastle upon Tyne, Nov. 1996

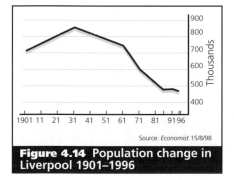

Source: *Economist* 15/8/98

Figure 4.14 Population change in Liverpool 1901–1996

displacing crime to nearby areas as some critics have claimed, a recent Home Office study found that, on the contrary, the installation of cameras had a halo effect, causing reductions in crime in surrounding areas.

Is the recent reurbanisation just a short-term blip or the beginning of a significant trend at least in the medium-term? Perhaps the most important factor favouring the latter is the government's prediction of the formation of 4.4 million extra households over the next two decades. Sixty per cent of these new households will have to be housed in existing urban areas because there is such fierce opposition to the relaxation of planning restrictions in the countryside.

Britain's cities are booming thanks to a reviving economy and changed attitudes to urban living.

IT WASN'T supposed to happen this way. In the 1980s Britain's cities looked fated to a long slow decline as the middle class succumbed to the lure of green countryside, or a suburban pastiche of it. Telecommunications and computers were making the hard slog into work unnecessary for growing numbers. Retailers were following, as they did years ago in America, to out-of-town shopping malls. Those left behind were mostly the rich and the poor. The future of cities looked bleak. But that is not the way things have turned out. Instead, all these trends look as if they may have gone into reverse. Rather than declining, Britain's cities are booming.

London is once again humming (or "swinging"—take your pick). Its economy is growing twice as fast as the nation's as a whole. A range of London-based industries, from finance to theatre to fashion, are booming. Elsewhere, city centres have become huge construction sites as their economies, and populations, revive. Newcastle is embarking on a £120m ($195m) reconstruction of its city centre, Sunderland is building a new £70m city-centre shopping complex. Bristol is rebuilding its docklands. Birmingham is tearing up its infamously ugly Bull Ring inner-city shopping centre. From Coventry to Glasgow the shops are full; restaurants and cafes are crowded; house prices are rising and jobs are on offer.

Much of this activity is, of course, the direct result of Britain's long economic expansion. But wider trends also seem to be contributing to the urban revival. It is not just greater numbers of young people who wish to live in cities, but people of all ages, including the old. The population of inner London has begun once again to increase. The Office for National Statistics predicts that six inner-London boroughs will be among the 11 fastest-growing local authority areas in the country in the next ten years.

Figure 4.15 *Economist*, 2 August 1997

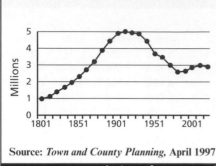

The influx of young migrants to London has brought with it a whole host of new industries and services, not only because of their connections back to their country of origin, but also because migrants tend to be the more imaginative and enterprising of their peers.

London is now a recognised world leader in design, arts, fashion, food, entertainment, music, computer software development, multi-media programming and in a whole range of other new industries. This generates billions of pounds of new revenue for the country.

Source: *Town and County Planning*, April 1997

Figure 4.16 Population of Inner London

Also, as many of the new households will be single person, the existing urban areas may well be where most would prefer to live.

The rejuvenation of inner London

For the first time in about 30 years London stopped losing population in the mid-1980s and has been gaining people ever since, due to net immigration from overseas and natural increase. Perhaps the most surprising aspect of this trend is the rejuvenation of Inner London where the population peaked at 5 million in 1900 (Figure 4.16), but then steadily dropped to a low of 2.5 million by 1983. The subsequent rise, forecast by the Department of the Environment to reach 3 million by 2011, will subside thereafter. Young adults now form the predominant population group in Inner London, whereas in the 1960s all the Inner London Boroughs exhibited a mature population structure.

1 Outline the reasons for the development of the first cities in terms of both space and time.
2 Discuss the principal stages in the modern period of global urban development illustrated by Figure 4.4.
3 Describe and explain the spatial development of urbanisation between 1950 and 1995 (Figures 4.6 and 4.7).
4 (a) What are the reasons for counterurbanisation?
 (b) Analyse the data provided in Figures 4.11, 4.12 and 4.13.
5 (a) What is reurbanisation?
 (b) Why is it regarded by many planners as a vital urban process?
6 What is the evidence on the OS map covering the region in which you live that settlement has evolved over time?

The location, spacing and size of urban settlements

The analysis of any landscape of at least a regional scale will reveal settlements of varying sizes (the vertical component) along with some degree of order and logic in their location and spacing (the horizontal component). The two components are, of course, mutually interrelated, with the largest settlements being fewer in number and spaced farther apart than settlements of a lesser size. Not surprisingly geographers and those of other related disciplines have tried to explain the reasons behind such regularity.

Settlements above a certain minimum size act as central places. Small central places tend only to provide a narrow range of convenience (low order) services which have a limited range and a low threshold. With ascent of the hierarchy of settlement the range of services on offer increases, in particular the supply of comparison (high order) services. The latter have more extensive ranges and higher thresholds. Settlements

provide services on the basis of the threshold population available to utilise them. The range of a service is controlled at the lower level by the minimum threshold population necessary to sustain it. In the regional landscape the largest settlements have wide market or catchment areas within which can be found the more limited market areas of the smaller settlements. The well established relationship between settlement size and function is shown in Figure 4.17.

Walter Christaller's central place theory

One of the earliest attempts to seek an understanding of the order underlying settlement spacing was that of Walter Christaller. Christaller's work entitled '*Die zentralen Orte in Süddeutschland*' (Central places in southern Germany) was published in 1933. He asserted that the numbers, sizes and spatial patterns of central places can be explained by the operation of the forces of supply and demand. But first, as with all theories, certain assumptions had to be made:

■ **unbounded flat land with an even distribution of resources**

Key Definitions   2

central place   A settlement which provides goods and services not only for its own population but also for those living in a surrounding area.

hierarchy of settlement   The grouping together of central places into distinctive levels of functional importance. Settlements at the top of the hierarchy have larger populations, a wider range of functions and more extensive market areas than settlements lower down the hierarchy.

range   The maximum distance people are willing to travel to obtain a good or a service.

threshold   The minimum number of customers necessary to support the profitable sale of a good or a service.

market area   The spatial area in which the consumers of an enterprise's goods or services are located.

sphere of influence   The area around a settlement that comes under its economic, social and political influence.

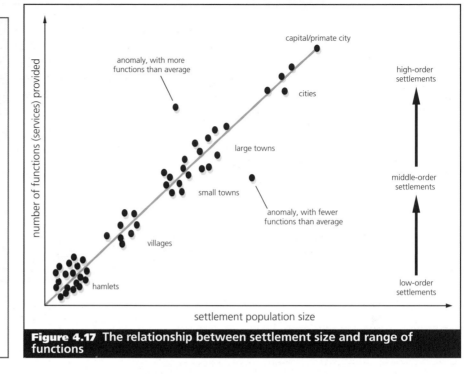

Figure 4.17 The relationship between settlement size and range of functions

- **equal ease and opportunity of movement in all directions with only one form of transport and with transport costs proportional to distance**

- **an evenly distributed population**

- **consumers with identical needs, tastes and purchasing power whose objective was to minimise the distances they travelled to obtain goods and services. This was done by using the nearest central place**

- **different orders of central place in the landscape with higher order central places providing both high and low order goods**

- **no excess profit made by any central place with all central places located as far away as possible from each other in order to maximise profits**

- **hexagonal market areas, the hexagon being the shape nearest to the circle which will pack tightly together without leaving gaps or overlapping.**

The term isotropic surface has been applied to the uniform landscape assumed. Christaller proposed that settlements with the lowest order of specialisation would be equally spaced and surrounded by hexagonal-shaped market areas. For every six lowest order settlements there would be a larger and more specialised settlement which in turn would be situated at an equal distance from other settlements of the same order. These higher order settlements would also be surrounded by hexagonal market areas. Progressively more specialised settlements would be similarly located at an equal distance from each other, with, at each stage, the hexagonal market area becoming larger (Figure 4.18). The six to one relationship is

maintained between every pair of levels in the hierarchy. Each level in the settlement hierarchy would provide all the services of lower order settlements as well as a range of high order services which could not be offered on a profitable basis lower down the hierarchy. Christaller referred to this regular progression as the K = 3 hierarchy. His logic was that each lowest order settlement was situated at the corners of the hexagonal market areas and was thus equidistant from three settlements of the next level up the hierarchy. The purchasing power of the smaller settlements for the goods and services of the larger settlements would be split on this basis (Figure 4.19). Thus a larger settlement would benefit from one-third of the custom of each of the six smaller settlements on its hexagonal boundary, equivalent to the full purchasing power of two lower order settlements. Added to this would be the purchasing power of its own population to give a total of 3.

In spatial terms each settlement would serve three times the market area of the next order settlement down the hierarchy. For every settlement of the largest size, there would be three of the second level, nine of the third level, twenty-seven of the fourth level and so on. According to Christaller's study of southern Germany the smallest settlements would be spaced 7 km apart. Centres at the next level up, serving three times the area and population, would be located 12 km apart (sq root 3 times 7). This relationship would continue throughout the hierarchy. The K = 3 network was based on the 'marketing principle' which placed lower order settlements as close as possible to higher order settlements.

Christaller recognised that different hierarchical arrangements would be formed if other factors were more important than the demand for and supply of goods in a

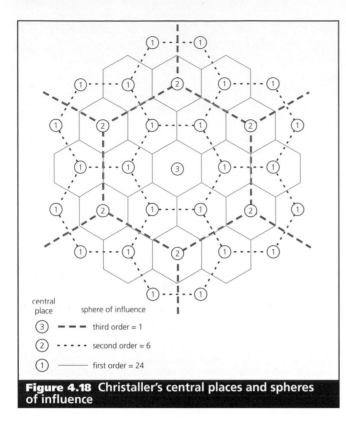

Figure 4.18 Christaller's central places and spheres of influence

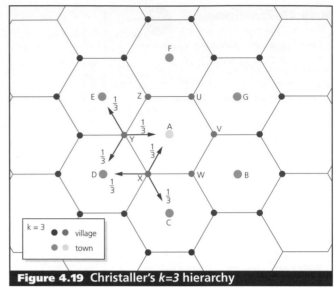

Figure 4.19 Christaller's *k=3* hierarchy

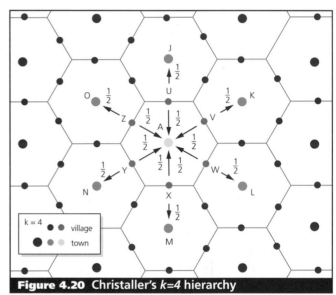

Figure 4.20 Christaller's *k=4* hierarchy

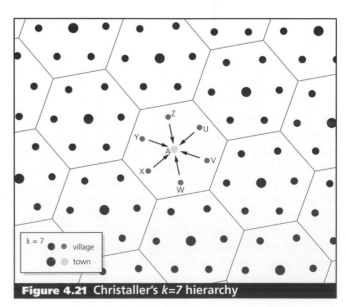

Figure 4.21 Christaller's *k=7* hierarchy

region. Thus he also devised networks based on the 'traffic principle' (K = 4) and the 'administrative principle' (K = 7). He postulated that a K = 4 hierarchy (Figure 4.20) would develop in regions where transport costs were particularly important since such an arrangement maximises the number of central places on straight-line routes. In regions with a highly developed system of central administration a K = 7 hierarchy (Figure 4.21) would tend to evolve, maximising the number of central places dependent on any one higher order central place and eliminating the shared allegiances of the other K value systems.

Criticisms of central place theory

Nowhere in the world does the settlement pattern exactly match that set out in central place theory. Thus it is not surprising that the model has been criticised. Equally unsurprising is the fact that most criticism is linked to the assumptions on which the theory is based. So:

■ perfectly uniform physical landscapes rarely exist in reality

■ there is usually competition within and between different modes of transport, and transport costs are not generally proportional to distance

■ the distribution of population and purchasing power is not uniform

■ for a variety of reasons people do not always use the same central place

- the main function of some settlements is not as a central place, for example industrial towns
- the level of profit tends to vary between businesses and places, thus perfect competition exists only in theory
- as the century has progressed government has played an increasingly important role in the location of settlement.

However, despite the criticisms, Christaller's central place theory has provided a starting point for planners and others interested in the arrangement of the human landscape. Of later works perhaps the most famous is that of the economist August Losch, to whom reference is made in Chapter 5 in relation to industrial location theory. Following Christaller, Losch used hexagonal market areas but allowed various hexagonal systems to co-exist. Each system operated at a different level and is superimposed on the other. This more variable and complex system produces a continuum of settlement sizes which more closely relates to reality, rather than the stepped distribution in the Christaller model.

The hierarchical arrangement of settlement

The vertical component in the organisation of settlements has also led to the formulation of a body of theory. Although earlier writers had pointed to a certain regularity in the size of cities when ranked from the largest downward, G. K. Zipf expressed this relationship precisely when he proposed the rank-size rule in 1949. He stated that 'if all the urban settlements in an area are ranked in descending order of population, the population of the nth town will be 1/nth that of the largest town. Thus, according to the rank-size rule the fifth urban settlement in a country would be expected to have a population one-fifth the size of the largest settlement. Plotted on a logarithmic graph a perfect rank-size relationship produces a straight line. The hierarchy of cities in some countries fits this pattern to a reasonable degree but even then significant changes can occur over time. For example, when the rank-size rule was proposed the United States provided quite a good fit but the relationship is not so good today. Near the top of the hierarchy the rapid growth of Los Angeles in the latter part of the twentieth century to just overtake Chicago as the second ranking city means that after New York at the top the next two cities are very similar in population size. Alternative patterns to the rank-size rule are (Figure 4.22):

- a stepped order pattern where there are distinct levels but where a number of settlements occur at each level
- a binary pattern where a couple of cities of similar size dominate the upper end of the hierarchy, as is the case in Canada with Toronto and Montreal, and in Spain with Madrid and Barcelona
- a primate pattern where the largest city, usually the capital, is many times the size of the next ranking city. The Law of the Primate City proposed by M. Jefferson in 1939 suggested that once a major city had become larger than its competitors a combination of economic, social and political factors will tend to create a much faster rate of growth in that city compared to its rivals. Clear examples of urban primacy are London, Paris, Montevideo and Lima.

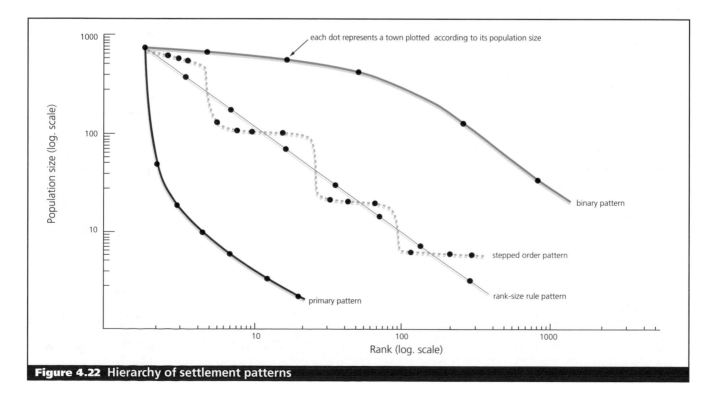

Figure 4.22 Hierarchy of settlement patterns

Interaction between settlements

Reilly's gravity model

W. J. Reilly's retail gravitation model (1931) attempts to predict the degree of interaction between two places. The model states that two centres attract trade from intermediate places in direct proportion to the size of the centres and in inverse proportion to the distance between them. Thus the 'breaking-point' between two settlements can be calculated by using the following formula:

$$\text{Breaking point AB} = \frac{\text{Distance from A to B}}{1 + \sqrt{\dfrac{\text{Population A}}{\text{Population B}}}}$$

(The breaking point will be given in terms of distance from the smaller of the two centres.)

The basic assumption that the larger the settlement the greater will be its trade area may not always be true because:

- **the level of services in a place is not always related to population size. For example tourist resorts have more services than expected in relation to their resident populations**
- **the accessibility of different places can vary significantly**
- **consumer perceptions, negative or positive, of a place may override logical considerations.**

Testing of the model has shown that it suits agricultural areas where towns are of limited size and fairly evenly spaced better than closely packed urban areas.

Huff's behavioural model

D. L. Huff (1962) was responsible for restating the gravity model in probabalistic terms on the basis that the likelihood of a consumer going to any centre is based on the relative attractiveness of different centres and the distance that would have to be travelled in each case. The attraction of towns can be measured in various ways but perhaps the best is the total number of shops in each centre. Thus the formula would be:

$$P_1 = \frac{\dfrac{\text{Number of shops in centre 1}}{\text{Distance or time to reach them}}}{\dfrac{\text{Total number of shops in study area}}{\text{Total distance and time to reach them}}}$$

If P is calculated for a series of points of origin then isopleths, or equiprobability contours can be drawn for each of the centres in an area.

Urban structure

The patterns evident and the processes at work in large urban areas are complex but by the beginning of the twentieth century geographers and others interested in urban form were beginning to see more clearly than before the similarities between cities as opposed to laying stress on the uniqueness of each urban entity. The first generalisation about urban land use to gain widespread recognition emanated from the so-called 'Chicago School'.

The concentric zone model

Published in 1925, and based on American Mid-Western cities, particularly Chicago, E. W. Burgess's model (Figure 4.23) has survived much longer than perhaps its attributes merit as it has only limited applicability to modern cities. However, it did serve as a theoretical foundation for others to investigate further. The main assumptions upon which the model was based are:

- **a uniform land surface**
- **free competition for space**
- **universal access to a single-centred city**
- **continuing in-migration to the city, with development taking place outward from the central core.**

Burgess concluded that the city would tend to form a series of concentric zones. The model's basic concepts were drawn from ecology, with the physical expansion of the city occurring by invasion and succession, with each of the concentric zones expanding at the expense of the one beyond.

Business activities agglomerated in the central business district (CBD) which was the point of maximum accessibility for the urban area as a whole. Surrounding the CBD was the 'zone in transition' where older private houses were being subdivided into flats and bed-sitters or converted for offices and light industry. Newcomers to the city were attracted to this zone because of the concentration of relatively cheap, low quality rented accommodation. Immigrants tended to group in ethnic ghettos and areas of vice could be recognised. However as an ethnic group assimilated into the wider

Questions

1 Describe and explain the relationship between settlement size and function shown in Figure 4.17.
2 Carefully explain the distinction between Christaller's K = 3, K = 4, and K = 7 networks.
3 Assess the merits and limitations of central place theory.
4 Consult a geographical data book which contains figures for the largest half a dozen or so settlements in countries. Try to find examples which (a) conform to the rank-size rule (b) conform to the alternatives shown in Figure 4.22.
5 Use the Reilly model to calculate the breaking-point between two towns with 80 000 and 50 000 people respectively which are 30 km apart.

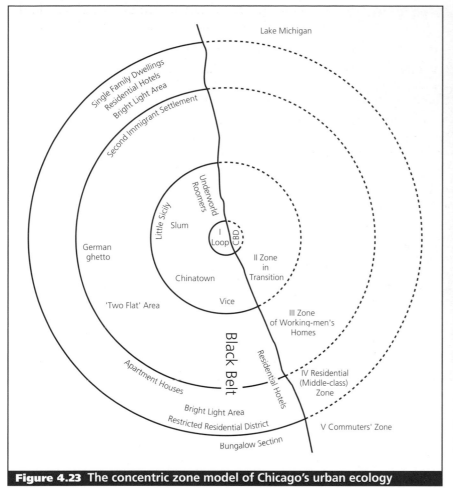

Figure 4.23 The concentric zone model of Chicago's urban ecology

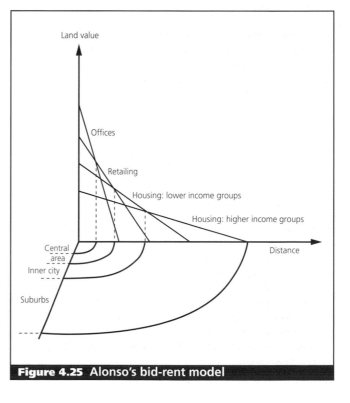

Figure 4.24 Chicago's central business district and lake front

community, economically, socially and politically its members would steadily move out to zones of better housing, to be replaced by the most recent arrivals. Beyond the zone in transition came the 'zone of working-men's homes' characterised by some of the oldest housing in the city and stable social groups. Next came the 'residential zone' occupied by the middle classes with its newer and larger houses. Finally, the commuters' zone extended beyond the built-up area.

Burgess observed in his paper that 'neither Chicago nor any other city fits perfectly into this ideal scheme. Complications are introduced by the lake front, the Chicago river, railroad lines, historical factors in the location of industry, the relative degree of the resistance of communities to invasion, etc.'

Bid-rent theory

Alonso's theory of urban land rent (1964) also produces a concentric zone formation, determined by the respective ability of land uses to pay the higher costs of a central location (Figure 4.25). The high accessibility of land at the centre, which is in short supply, results in intense competition among potential land users. The prospective land use willing and able

Figure 4.25 Alonso's bid-rent model

Figure 4.26 Inner city redevelopment in Chicago

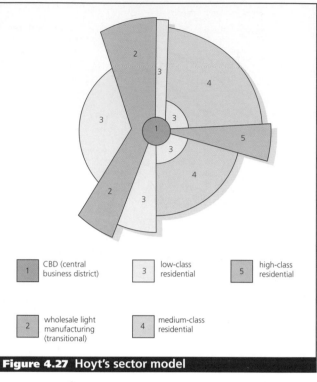

1	CBD (central business district)	3	low-class residential	5	high-class residential
2	wholesale light manufacturing (transitional)	4	medium-class residential		

Figure 4.27 Hoyt's sector model

to bid the most money will gain the most central location. The land use able to bid the least will be relegated to the most peripheral location. He explained the paradox of poorer people living on expensive land in inner areas and more affluent people living on cheaper land further out as follows:

- With poor personal mobility low income groups prefer to reside in inner locations. They overcome the problem of land costs by living at high densities, each household buying or renting only a small amount of space.
- The more affluent, desiring a large house and garden, seek out cheaper land in the low density suburbs where they can realise their 'dreams'. Being highly mobile they trade off space against accessibility to the CBD.

The assumptions upon which the theory is based and the criticisms of it are similar to the Burgess model.

The sector model

Homer Hoyt's sector model (1939) was based on the study of 142 cities in the United States (Figure 4.27). Following Burgess, Hoyt placed the business district in a central location for the same reason – maximum accessibility. However, he observed that once variations arose in land uses near to the centre, they tended to persist as the city expanded. High income housing usually developed where there were distinct physical or social attractions with low income housing confined to the most unfavourable locations. Middle income groups occupied intermediate positions. Major transport

routes often played a key role in influencing sectoral growth, particularly with regard to industry. As new land was required by each sector it was developed at the periphery of that sector. However, medium and high class housing near the centre, the oldest housing in each case, was subject to suburban relocation by its residents, leading to deterioration, subdivision and occupation by incoming low income groups.

The mutiple nuclei model

C. D. Harris and E. Ullman (1945) argued that the pattern of urban land use does not develop around a single centre but around a number of discrete nuclei (Figure 4.28). Some nuclei may be long established, for example old villages which have been incorporated into the city by urban expansion. Others, such as industrial estates for light manufacturing, are much newer. Similar activities group together, benefiting from agglomeration while some land uses repel others. Middle and high income house buyers can afford to avoid residing close to industrial areas which become the preserve of the poor. A very rapid rate of urban expansion may result in some activities being dispersed to new nuclei, such as a new out-of-town shopping centre.

A British urban land use model

P. Mann based his land use model for a typical British city on the theories of both Burgess and Hoyt (Figure 4.29) which he tried to apply to Sheffield, Nottingham and Huddersfield. The outcome was very much a compromise between the two

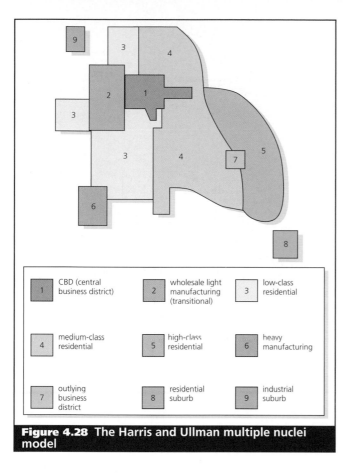

Figure 4.28 The Harris and Ullman multiple nuclei model

1 CBD (central business district)	**2** wholesale light manufacturing (transitional)	**3** low-class residential
4 medium-class residential	**5** high-class residential	**6** heavy manufacturing
7 outlying business district	**8** residential suburb	**9** industrial suburb

models which he regarded as being complimentary. Identifying four residential sectors from middle class to lower working class he noted the influence of prevailing winds on the location of industry and the most expensive housing. He also allowed for local authority house building, particularly towards the periphery of the urban area, and for commuter villages.

A model of the modern North American city

Another model which incorporates aspects of both Burgess and Hoyt was produced by David Clark (Figure 4.31) in his book *Post-Industrial America*, although similar diagrams have also been produced by others. Here the CBD is subdivided into core and frame. Outside the low income inner city are three suburban rings divided into sectors of lower middle, middle and high income. Important elements in the commercial hierarchy are included along with industrial and office parks. Thus, decentralisation is a key element of this model. The central city boundary shows the legal limits of the main city which once contained the whole urban area. In the twentieth century the city has sprawled way beyond its legal limits to incorporate other legal entities. The Standard Metropolitan Statistical Area (SMSA) also includes the rural sections of counties which form part of the wider urban area.

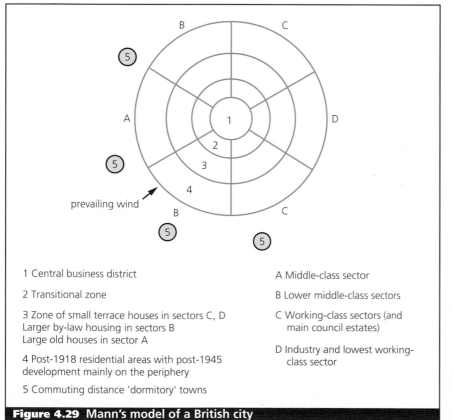

1 Central business district

2 Transitional zone

3 Zone of small terrace houses in sectors C, D
Larger by-law housing in sectors B
Large old houses in sector A

4 Post-1918 residential areas with post-1945 development mainly on the periphery

5 Commuting distance 'dormitory' towns

A Middle-class sector

B Lower middle-class sectors

C Working-class sectors (and main council estates)

D Industry and lowest working-class sector

Figure 4.29 Mann's model of a British city

Key Definitions

concentric zone   A region of an urban area, circular in shape, surrounding the CBD and possibly other regions of a similar shape, that has common land use/socio-economic characteristics.

zone in transition (twilight zone)   The area just beyond the CBD which is characterised by a mixture of residential, industrial and commercial land use, tending towards deterioration and blight. The poor quality and relatively cheap cost of accommodation makes this part of the urban area a focus for immigrants, resulting in a rate of population change higher than in other parts of the urban area.

sector   A section of an urban area in the shape of a wedge, beginning at the edge of the CBD and gradually widening to the periphery.

bid-rent   Decreasing accessibility from the centre of an urban area, with corresponding declining land values, allows (in theory) an ordering of land uses related to rent affordability.

keno capitalism   A synoptic term adopted to describe the spatial manifestation of the postmodern urban condition.

Figure 4.30 A British 1960's council estate

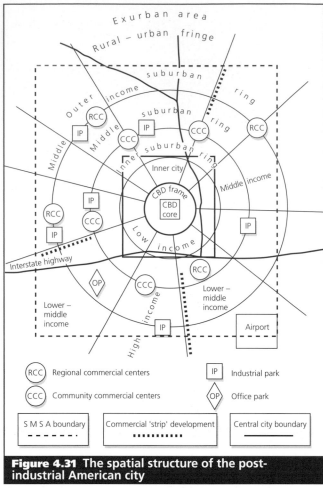

Figure 4.31 The spatial structure of the post-industrial American city

The Los Angeles school: an alternative model of urban structure

In the debate on the processes moulding postmodern urbanisation some writers assert that all that has changed is the pace at which traditional processes operate. However, others argue that we have arrived at a radical break in the way that cities are developing; the process is most advanced in American cities with Los Angeles leading the way. Global processes are exerting a considerable influence on the form of major cities creating a new time-space fabric.

The views encapsulated in this new approach have evolved since the 1980s in a period when a group of loosely-associated urban analysts based in southern California began to examine the notion that the processes at work in the Los Angeles region were somehow symptomatic of a broader socio-geographic transformation taking place within the US as a whole. There is general agreement that the fastest growing American cities are developing in a manner similar to Los Angeles, characterised by an acute fragmentation of the urban landscape – a landscape not unlike that formed by a keno gamecard (an American game of chance similar to bingo). The card itself appears as a numbered grid, with some squares being marked during the course of the game and others not, according to a random draw. The assertion of the 'Los Angeles School' of urban analysts is that the apparent random development and redevelopment of urban land may be regarded as the outcome of exogenous investment processes inherent to flexism, thus creating the landscape of keno capitalism (Figure 4.32) where:

- capital is attracted to a particular parcel of land as if by chance, sparking the development process here but ignoring the opportunities in other places in the urban region
- the relationship between development of one parcel and nondevelopment of another is a disjointed, seemingly unrelated affair
- the urban periphery, characterised by edge cities, organises the centre within the context of global capitalism
- social polarisation has reached a stage more extreme than ever before with intervening (interdictory) spaces designed to exclude interaction across social groups.

Models of developing cities

Although the development of urban land use models has favoured Western cities some interesting contributions relating to developing cities and socialist cities have appeared at various points in time.

Griffin and Ford's model (Figure 4.34) summarises many of the characteristics they noted in modern Latin American cities:

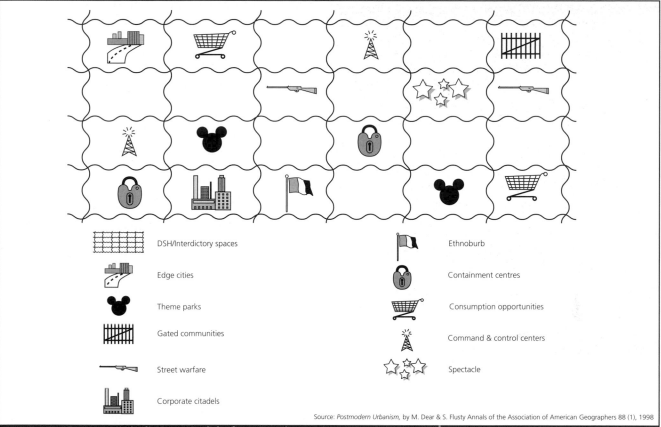

DSH/Interdictory spaces

Edge cities

Theme parks

Gated communities

Street warfare

Corporate citadels

Ethnoburb

Containment centres

Consumption opportunities

Command & control centers

Spectacle

Source: *Postmodern Urbanism*, by M. Dear & S. Flusty Annals of the Association of American Geographers 88 (1), 1998

Figure 4.32 Keno capitalism: a model of postmodern urban structure

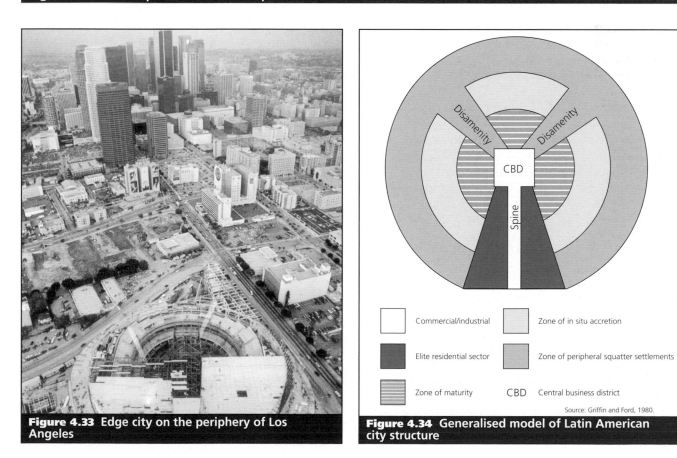

Commercial/industrial

Elite residential sector

Zone of maturity

Zone of in situ accretion

Zone of peripheral squatter settlements

CBD Central business district

Source: Griffin and Ford, 1980.

Figure 4.33 Edge city on the periphery of Los Angeles

Figure 4.34 Generalised model of Latin American city structure

- central areas which had changed radically from the colonial period to now exhibit most of the characteristics of modern Western CBDs

- the development of a commercial spine, extending outwards from the CBD, enveloped by an elite residential sector

- the tendency for industries with their need for urban services such as power and water to be near the central area

- a 'zone of maturity' with a full range of services containing both older, traditional style housing and more recent residential development. The traditional housing, once occupied by higher income families who now reside in the elite sector, has generally undergone subdivision and deterioration. A significant proportion of recent housing is self-built of permanent materials and of reasonable quality

- a zone of 'in situ accretion' with a wide variety of housing types and quality but with much still in the process of extension or improvement. Urban services tend to be patchy in this zone with typically only the main streets having a good surface. Government housing projects are often a feature of this zone

- a zone of squatter settlements which is the place of residence of most recent in-migrants. Services in this zone are at their most sparse with open trenches serving as sewers and communal taps providing water. Most housing is of the 'shanty' type, constructed of wood, flattened oil cans, polythene and any other materials available at the time of construction. The situation is dynamic and there is evidence of housing at various stages of improvement.

Of perhaps greater familiarity is Waugh's model based on Brazilian cities. The annotations on Figure 4.35 make the model largely self-explanatory.

The arrangement of land use in the large colonial port cities of South-East Asia (Figure 4.36) shows both similarities and contrasts with Latin American cities. In addition to European colonists and indigenous people, most of these cities also housed a large 'alien' group from India or China who dominated the commercial activities of the city. The Asian commercial areas are characterised by shophouses, combining commercial and residential functions. The high-class residential area, once the preserve of Europeans only, often occupied high land, if it was available at not too great a distance from the centre. As so many of the Europeans worked in government administration at the upper and middle levels it was logical that their houses adjoined the area of government buildings. On the periphery McGee noted the intermixture of squatter areas and purpose-built suburban housing, the former generally filling gaps left by the latter.

Socialist cities

Although communism as a political ideology appears to be in its death throes, the impact of decades of central planning is still very clear in the urban and rural landscapes of the countries of the old Soviet Union, its eastern European satellites and other countries such as China and Cuba, where such a system of government has operated. Evidence of the pre-communism era is most widespread in the historic core. Beyond this the communist or socialist city shows a greater degree of uniformity by urban region than other cities because of the absolutely dominant role of central planning and the absence of private enterprise.

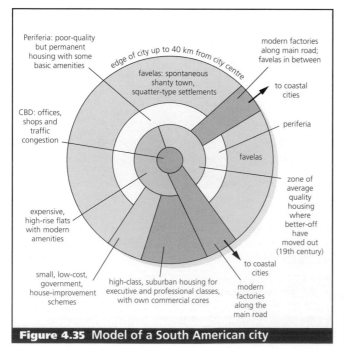

Figure 4.35 Model of a South American city

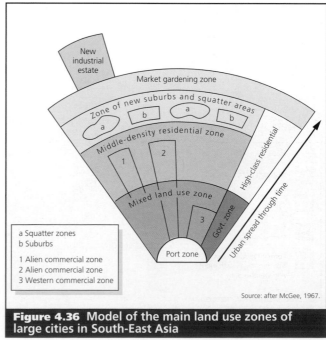

Source: after McGee, 1967.

Figure 4.36 Model of the main land use zones of large cities in South-East Asia

F. E. Hamilton's study of East European socialist cities (Figure 4.37) identified the following characteristics:

- the historic core, generally conserved for the purposes of cultural heritage
- the CBD where public buildings are much more dominant than in Western cities
- areas of 1950s housing, mainly in the form of high-rise apartment blocks
- integrated neighbourhoods and residential districts constructed in the 1970s and 1980s. A reaction to the unpopularity of high-rise, neighbourhoods were planned to contain all necessary services to minimise population movement
- open or planted 'isolation belts' to contain the expansion of the built-up area
- industrial zones located at the periphery of the urban area and separated from residential areas by isolation belts to minimise the impact of pollution and other externalities.

Questions

1 Discuss the similarities and differences between the concentric zone, sector and multiple nuclei models.
2 Explain bid-rent theory. Which, if any, urban model does bid-rent theory support?
3 Critically analyse Mann's model for a typical British city and David Clark's model of the modern North American city.
4 Examine the recent contribution of the Los Angeles school of urban analysis to urban model building.
5 To what extent does urban form differ in developing countries and countries with a socialist history compared to western cities?

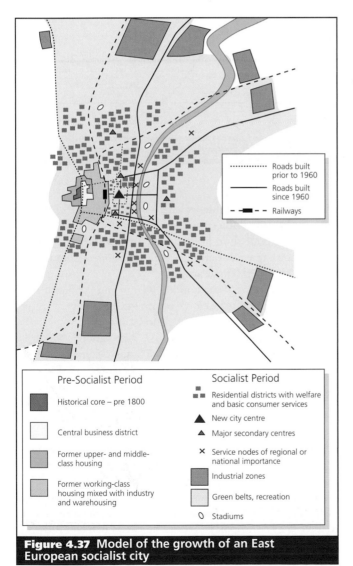

Pre-Socialist Period	Socialist Period
Historical core – pre 1800	Residential districts with welfare and basic consumer services
Central business district	▲ New city centre
Former upper- and middle-class housing	▲ Major secondary centres
Former working-class housing mixed with industry and warehousing	✕ Service nodes of regional or national importance
	Industrial zones
	Green belts, recreation
	○ Stadiums

Roads built prior to 1960
Roads built since 1960
Railways

Figure 4.37 Model of the growth of an East European socialist city

Urban density gradients

Contrasting functional zones within urban areas characteristically vary in residential population density. Examination of population density gradients, termed gradient analysis, shows that for most cities densities fall with increasing distance from the centre. Gradient analysis of developed cities over time (Figure 4.38) shows the following trends:

- the initial rise and later decline in density of the central area
- the outward spread of population and the consequent reduction in overall density gradient over time.

In contrast, analysis of density gradients in developing countries shows:

- a continuing increase in central area densities
- the consequent maintenance of fairly stable density gradients as the urban area expands.

In developing cities both personal mobility and the sophistication of the transport infrastructure operate at a considerably lower level. Also, central areas tend to retain an important residential function. Both of these factors result in a more compact central area and the transport factor in particular has restricted urban sprawl to levels below that of developed cities. The presence of extensive areas of informal settlement in the outer areas also results in higher suburban densities. However, in the more advanced of the developing nations where car ownership is rising rapidly, significant sprawl is now occurring.

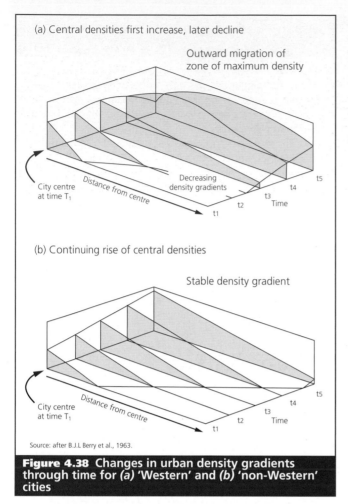

(a) Central densities first increase, later decline

Outward migration of zone of maximum density

City centre at time T₁

Distance from centre

Decreasing density gradients

Time

(b) Continuing rise of central densities

Stable density gradient

City centre at time T₁

Distance from centre

Time

Source: after B.J.L Berry et al., 1963.

Figure 4.38 Changes in urban density gradients through time for *(a)* 'Western' and *(b)* 'non-Western' cities

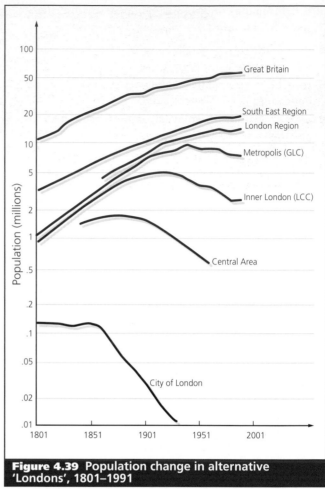

Figure 4.39 Population change in alternative 'Londons', 1801–1991

Changing population densities in London

Towards the end of the eighteenth century the population of the London metropolis was growing rapidly at a geometric rate of 1.9 per cent annually. Such growth was sustained until 1901, after which the rate of increase slowed until the peak population was reached in 1939. After that population decreased at a geometric rate of around 10 per cent per decade, although this rate fell to virtually zero between 1981 and 1991 (Figure 4.39).

The demographic decline of London began in the City. As a wave of building spread outward it resulted in population decline; first the City, then the Victorian inner city and finally some suburbs. In the City, residences were replaced by more profitable activities. In the late seventeenth century the City had a population of over 200 000. This fell to 129 000 in 1801, 27 000 in 1901, 5000 in 1951 and 3300 in 1991. The population of the central area peaked around 1871 while Inner London peaked in 1911. After significant decline in the following 70 years the population of Inner London stabilised after 1981. In large part the decline in Inner London reflected a general

rejection of inner city life as large numbers moved to the suburbs. However other factors which played a part were (1) the demolition of slum housing to be replaced by new lower density housing estates and (2) the expansion of commercial functions into residential areas.

The populations of the London Region and the South East Region have continued to grow except for the slight downturns during the 1971–81 period caused by an exceptionally rapid decline of the GLC population.

The impact on density of the population decline of successively larger 'Londons' is shown in Figure 3.41. The mean distance of population from the centre of London has increased continuously, except for the year 1841 (Figure 4.42). Figure 4.43 shows a distance–density plot for 1991 out to a distance of 75 km, the approximate extent of the London region. Beyond a distance of 25 km there is a greater variation of density with distance than within the metropolis. Outside the metropolis the peak at around 50 km from the centre reflects the existence of a ring of non-metropolitan centres, including certain New Towns. It is also due to the post-war restriction of development within the Green Belt and the resulting leap-frogging of development to land outside the restricted area.

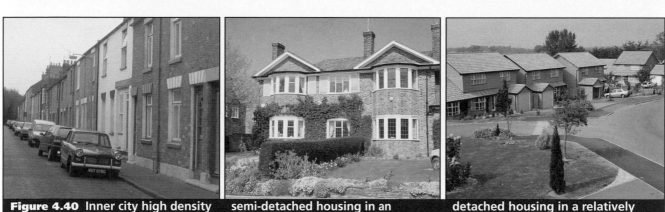

Figure 4.40 Inner city high density terraced housing;

semi-detached housing in an older inner suburb;

detached housing in a relatively new outer suburb

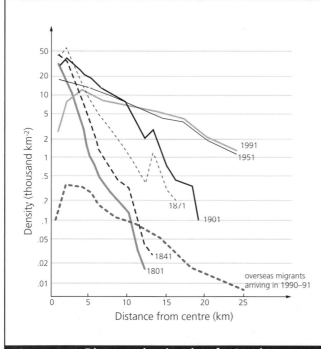

Figure 4.41 Distance–density plots for London metropolis in selected years, 1801–1991

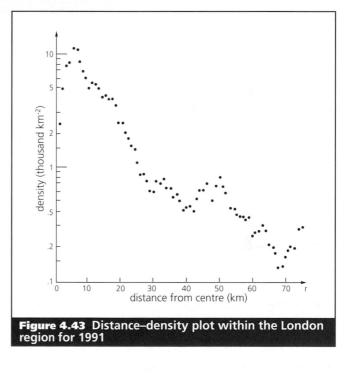

Figure 4.43 Distance–density plot within the London region for 1991

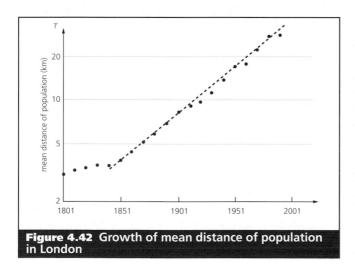

Figure 4.42 Growth of mean distance of population in London

The family life-cycle

Demographic analysis shows that movements of population within cities are closely related to stages in the life-cycle, with the available housing stock being a major determinant of where people live at different stages in their life. Studies in Toronto show a broad concentric zone pattern (Figure 4.44). Young adults frequently choose housing close to the CBD while older families occupy the next ring out. Middle-aged families are more likely to reside at a greater distance from the central area and farther out still, in the newest suburban areas, young families dominate. This simplified model applies particularly well to a rapidly growing metropolis like Toronto where an invasion and succession process evolves over time.

Toronto's inner city contains a much higher percentage of rented and small unit accommodation than the outer regions which, along with the stimulus of employment and the social

Key Definitions ④

urban density gradient The rate at which population density and/or the intensity of land use falls off with increasing distance from the centre of the city.

family life-cycle Families with children pass through various stages over time (pre-child stage, family building, dispersal, post-child stage) with corresponding changes in housing needs.

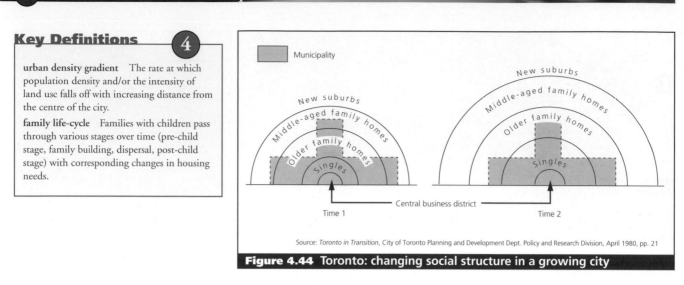

Source: *Toronto in Transition*, City of Toronto Planning and Development Dept. Policy and Research Division, April 1980, pp. 21

Figure 4.44 Toronto: changing social structure in a growing city

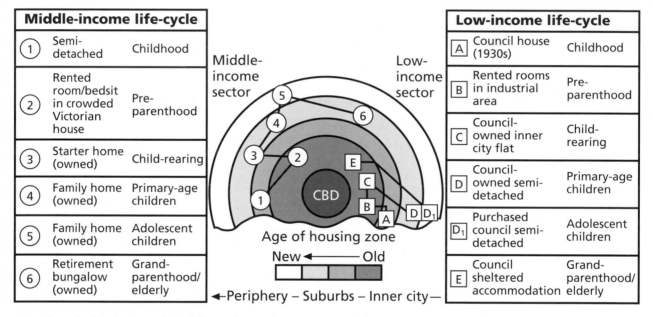

Middle-income life-cycle			Low-income life-cycle		
①	Semi-detached	Childhood	Ⓐ	Council house (1930s)	Childhood
②	Rented room/bedsit in crowded Victorian house	Pre-parenthood	Ⓑ	Rented rooms in industrial area	Pre-parenthood
③	Starter home (owned)	Child-rearing	Ⓒ	Council-owned inner city flat	Child-rearing
④	Family home (owned)	Primary-age children	Ⓓ	Council-owned semi-detached	Primary-age children
⑤	Family home (owned)	Adolescent children	Ⓓ₁	Purchased council semi-detached	Adolescent children
⑥	Retirement bungalow (owned)	Grand-parenthood/ elderly	Ⓔ	Council sheltered accommodation	Grand-parenthood/ elderly

Housing choice is based on life-cycle and income. Residential patterns are influenced by building societies, landowners, local authorities/housing associations, and free choice.

Figure 4.45 Middle income and low income models of the family life-cycle

attractions of the central area, has attracted young adults. Most housing units built in the inner area in recent decades have been in the form of apartments.

Studies in Britain have highlighted the spatial contrasts in life-cycle between middle- and low-income groups (Figure 4.45). With life-cycle and income being the major determinants of where people live, residential patterns are also influenced by a range of organisations foremost of which are local authorities, housing associations, building societies and landowners. On top of this is the range of choice available to the household. For those on low income this is frequently very restricted indeed. As income rises the range of choice in terms of housing type and location increases.

Questions

1 Outline the reasons for contrasting urban density gradients in the Developed and Developing Worlds.
2 Analyse the data provided in Figures 4.39 to 4.43.
3 Explain the locational implications of the different stages in the family life-cycle.

American Cities

Urban sprawl

Cities in the United States have spread upwards and outwards more than anywhere else in the world. The clusters of steel-framed skyscrapers, first built in Chicago in the late 1800s, now mark the centre of all large cities. However, it is the outward spread of cities that has had the greatest effect on people and the landscape (Figure 4.46). Cities have sprawled over such vast areas because:

- the United States is an extremely large country and until recently land was perceived as being in plentiful supply

- planning regulations have been weak compared with Europe giving land speculators and property developers in the United States a much freer hand

- high average incomes meant that people could afford large homes

- a high level of personal mobility allied to massive investment in the transport infrastructure allows people to commute long distances to work.

By the early part of the twentieth century some neighbouring urban areas had merged to form conurbations. In the north-eastern United States in particular the conurbations came closer together as urban sprawl continued. Here the intervening countryside was much reduced and its character changed. Criss-crossed by freeways, the density of rural settlement is high. A high proportion of these rural dwellers commute to work in the nearby towns and cities. In the early 1960s the term 'megalopolis' was applied by Jean Gottman to this heavily urbanised area between Boston and Washington. With over 40 million people this coastal zone is sometimes known as 'Boswash'. Its other major cities are New York, Philadelphia and Baltimore.

The term megalopolis has also been used for two other areas in the United States, although not all geographers agree that this is correct. The areas are:

- 'Chipitts', the major industrial area between Chicago and Pittsburgh

- 'Sansan', the west coast region in California between San Francisco and San Diego.

In 1970 America's suburbs housed 25 per cent more families than its central cities; by the late 1990s they contained 75 per cent more. Middle-class families, 'the bedrock of a stable community', according to the Department of Housing and Urban Development, associate central cities with poverty and crime. The demise of the inner cities has resulted in such urban sprawl that the environmental group the Sierra Club termed it 'the dark side of the American dream' in a report published in September 1998. It highlighted:

- traffic congestion, with each 1 per cent increase in new lane-miles generating a 0.9 per cent increase in traffic within five years

- commuting journeys that 'steal time from family and work', with petrol that costs about half as much as in Europe

- lost farmland and recreational space. In the 1980s the loss of prime farmland equalled the combined area of the states of Connecticut and Rhode Island

- more taxation to pay for the full range of suburban infrastructure

- the under-utilisation of inner city infrastructure leading to dereliction and closure.

Robert Geddes talks of a new form of human settlement, the 'city-region', with relatively fewer people spread over a relatively larger area. For example between 1970 and 1990:

- the New York region grew by 8 per cent in population but by 65 per cent in built-up land

- Chicago increased by 4 per cent in population and 46 per cent in urban area.

As suburbs expand, tax bases in inner cities shrink, resulting in a downward cycle of higher taxes, lower corporate profits, higher unemployment and reduced property values. Between 1970 and 1990 in the twin cities of Minneapolis-St Paul, 162 schools were

Source: *Economist*, 12 September 1998

Figure 4.46 Suburbs unlimited: ten most sprawl-threatened large cities in the USA

closed in the inner areas while 78 new schools were constructed in the outer suburbs.

What can be done to limit urban sprawl?

- In parts of Maryland and Michigan communities are being encouraged to buy farmland or environmentally sensitive land to prevent its development.

- In Washington and Oregon 'urban growth boundaries' and green belts have been established.

- Some cities like Portland, Oregon are looking inward rather than outward for new sites for development. Almost every city has a considerable number of brownfield sites – disused warehouses and industrial sites, and other abandoned land uses – which can be redeveloped.

- Another idea is to offer tax inducements to communities that forgo development rights.

The CBD

The CBD is now distant from the affluent suburbs and has suffered through vigorous competition from outer suburban and out-of-town shopping centres in the latter half of the twentieth century. 'Downtown', the term frequently applied to the major retail area, declined significantly as a consequence. Small-scale labour intensive manufacturing has all but ebbed away from the CBD. However, the administrative function of the CBD has been strengthened and the area has become more and more the preserve of the white-collar worker. Frequently, large areas have been cleared and rebuilt under ambitious urban renewal schemes which have given birth to new administrative, educational, cultural and to a lesser extent, residential areas.

In the 1990s Downtown areas in a number of large cities have shown spectacular signs of revival in their retail function (Figure 4.48). This upturn has been due to a number of factors, the most important of which have been:

- a sustained period of national economic growth in the 1990s

Figure 4.47 Denver, Colorado: one of the fastest growing cities in the USA

THE STATE OF THE CITIES

Downtown is up

IT WAS a typical story of urban woe. In 1983, Sears Roebuck closed the doors of its State Street store in Chicago after 51 years in business. Two neighbouring retailers had gone bankrupt; pedestrians had all but abandoned the street, End of the story? No. Sears is coming back. The retailer has announced plans to open a five-storey, 237,000-square-foot store on State Street by the spring of 2000. In a revival matched by the downtown areas of many other American cities, Chicago's State Street is once again a place for doing business.

All Chicagoans can hum "State Street, that great street." Alas, they have not always meant it. State Street was the heart of Chicago's retail world in the early 1900s. The second half of the century was not so kind. Shoppers flocked to new suburban malls. Some Chicago retailers went bust; others migrated to trendier Michigan Avenue. Then, in 1979, the city made bad worse by converting State Street into a "transit mall". It was closed to all vehicles except public transport; the pavements were widened to make it feel like a suburban mall.

Far from attracting more shoppers, this repelled them. As the planners have since learned, some spaces can be too open. The wide, grey pavements were empty and uninviting. The increased bus traffic, belching exhaust, made things still bleaker. By the time State Street hit bottom, seven department stores with a total of 2.5m square feet of retail space had closed.

Nearly two decades later, the city has taken another crack at redeveloping State Street, and this time it has done a better job. To begin with, the transit mall was scrapped and traffic was re-introduced in 1996. The pavements were narrowed from 36 feet to 26 feet, providing "a pleasant sense of bustle". The street got a $25m facelift designed to recall its greatness in the early 1900s: old-fashioned subway entrances, landscaped flower beds, decorative newspaper kiosks. The designers even found the company that made the first street lamps in 1926, and ordered replicas. All this not only drew sightseers, it won the American Institute of Architects' honour award for urban design.

And business followed the award. The total available retail space in the State Street area increased by 8% between 1990 and 1997, and vacancy rates fell from 6.4% to 1.8%. The Palmer House Hilton, a smart hotel just off State Street, is enjoying its highest occupancy rate since it opened in 1924.

Figure 4.48 *Economist,* 22 August 1998

Figure 4.49 State Street in Chicago

- young people starting families later and thus remaining in cities longer with at the same time 'empty-nesters', couples whose children have left home, moving back to the city because it is more practical than a large empty house in the suburbs

- the importance of 'people-friendly' street design being recognised and acted upon

- various incentive schemes to encourage redevelopment proving successful.

Inner Cities

The inner city is in the main the residence of minority groups living at high densities in deteriorating low-cost housing. Persons of the same nationality or ethnic origin tend to congregate together to form ethnic ghettos which exhibit a high degree of social deprivation. Figure 4.50 illustrates the chain of causation of inner city problems. The large-scale out-migration to the suburbs of the white population has created a disturbing duality in American cities. In virtually all inner cities the proportion of the population that is white is still falling and ageing. However, this out-migration must not be exaggerated as the white population more often than not still accounts for more than 50 per cent of the population contained within official city boundaries. Nevertheless ethnic segregation is generally intense. Virtually every city has its black area such as Chicago's 'South Side', Detroit's 'Paradise Valley', New York's Harlem, Los Angeles 'Watts' and San Francisco's 'Fillmore'. Black out-migration from some of these areas has resulted in the abandonment of inner city housing.

Unlike successive groups of immigrants from Europe in the nineteenth and the early part of the twentieth century, black Americans have found it extremely difficult to 'break out' to higher quality housing areas elsewhere in the city. The decline of inner city manufacturing has resulted in very heavy black, and other minority, unemployment. Hemmed into ghetto areas by social immobility the black population frequently lacks the physical mobility to gain sufficient access to suburban employment.

However, a high degree of segregation has been maintained as many whites remain reluctant to share social space with blacks

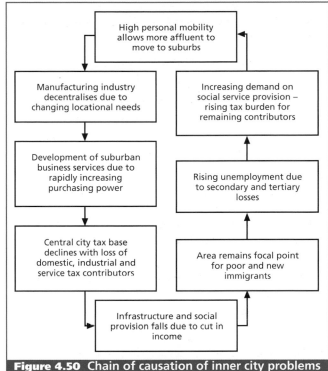

Figure 4.50 Chain of causation of inner city problems

Figure 4.51 A ghetto scene

and other minorities. Such attitudes go a long way to explain the 'tipping process' by which the ghetto expands (Figure 4.52).

In the 1950s and 1960s urban renewal schemes, often huge in scale, began to alter the face of many US cities. They were usually attempts at comprehensive redevelopment involving a mixture of different land uses and invariably incorporating substantial high-rise construction. This process of 'Manhattanization' was encouraged by substantial federal grants towards clearance. Renewal agencies were given the power of eminent domain to condemn and clear slum neighbourhoods and resell the cleared land to private developers at below market price. The twin original aims of renewal were to improve the housing stock and upgrade

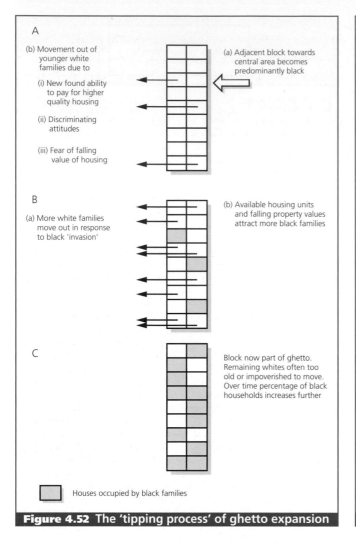

Figure 4.52 The 'tipping process' of ghetto expansion

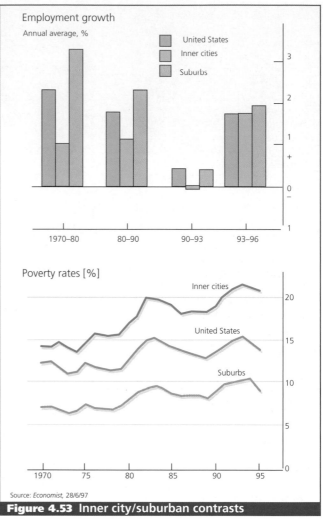

Source: *Economist*, 28/6/97

Figure 4.53 Inner city/suburban contrasts

the tax base of the central area. This led to widespread demolition of low-cost housing, factories and declining retail centres to make way for quite different functions. The loss of low-income housing frequently resulted in greater overcrowding elsewhere in the inner city while the demolition of factories and shops caused unemployment to rise. At their very worst, renewal schemes were tagged 'negro clearance' projects.

From the 1970s renovation, as opposed to clearance and renewal, has been the priority but a very low level of funding has limited its impact. Reductions in federal funding in the 1980s hit the inner cities badly, as the poverty rate figures show (Figure 4.53): in 1970 the poverty rate in inner cities was 14 per cent, by 1995 it was over 20 per cent. Most new jobs, even the low-skilled ones, are being created in the suburbs. An example of central city/suburban contrast is Detroit and neighbouring Oakland County, both with a population of about one million people. In 1996:

- 86 building permits were issued in Detroit compared with 7197 in Oakland

- Detroit's rate of unemployment at over 8 per cent was almost three times higher than Oakland's

- Median household income was $21 000 in Detroit and $47 000 in Oakland.

However, with a strong national economy in the 1990s there have been some signs of hope for the inner cities (Figure 4.54).

Spreading suburbs

The expansion of the suburbs has been the most consistent feature of American urban geography in the twentieth century. The first suburbs had developed in the late nineteenth century along the new railroads which radiated from city centres and also with electric streetcar development from the 1890s onwards. As suburban communities were established along the new lines of communication many cities began to annex their adjacent areas in order to exert political and financial control. Movement to the new suburbs was almost totally confined to the middle and upper income groups. Early zoning regulations often ensured that suburban areas would remain the preserve of the well-to-do. Industrial decentralisation from central cities occurred as companies fled from the union control that was being established in close-knit communities.

Key Definitions 5

urban sprawl The physical pattern of low density expansion of urban areas under market conditions into surrounding agricultural areas. The rate and nature of urban sprawl is related to a number of factors, the most important of which is the strength of planning controls.

conurbation A large continuous urban area resulting from (a) the engulfment of expanding smaller centres by the physical extension of a major city or (b) the coalescence of two or more urban areas of roughly similar size through urban sprawl.

megalopolis A highly urbanised region which encompasses a number of large conurbations and many smaller urban centres where urban decentralisation and coalescence are at an advanced stage. There is a high level of interaction between the individual urban areas. The non-urban areas have a dense rural population dominated by commuter villages.

downtown American term used to describe the heart of the city, or the central business district.

edge city A significant recent concentration of retailing, offices and high technology industry at the periphery of a large urban area. Characterised by a cluster of high-rise building and usually located where a major circumferential freeway intersects with an arterial highway, the employment centre is enveloped by recently built private housing estates.

rural-urban fringe An indeterminate transition zone around a town or city where urban functions and activities impinge on those that are agricultural and rural.

The contrast between America's rich suburbs and benighted inner cities could hardly be more stark. Yet, against all expectation, urban life in America is showing signs of revival

THE immaculate homes of Bethesda, in Maryland, almost caricature the American dream. Two cars stand in the driveway; a manicured front lawn stretches to a gleaming sidewalk; overfed white children throw footballs across the smoothly surfaced road. Less than ten miles (16km) away, in the heart of Washington, DC, is the American nightmare. Unemployed blacks sit on the grimy front-steps of crumbling houses that were once grand; old sedans skirt the potholes. The contrast between outer suburbs and inner cities is bleak.

Yet America also has its urban optimists. They point out that the picture is better than it was. Unemployment in the 50 biggest cities has fallen by a third over the past four years, to around 6%. Rates for serious crime have declined to their lowest in a generation. Cities such as New York—which 20 years ago nearly went bankrupt—and Los Angeles, victim of race riots and earthquake within the past six years, are growing in both population and confidence. Even Detroit, a metaphor for urban decline, trots out promising figures for new investment. Cleveland, for heaven's sake, has rebuilt itself as a cultural centre. The question is not whether America's cities have improved—they have—but whether the improvement can be continued.

Lately in America a prosperous economy has helped cities and suburbs alike; but cities are probably the more vulnerable to the next downturn, when it comes. By the standards of Europe and Japan, they still suffer appalling crime, yawning social disparities and remarkable underachievement in education. Despite a fall of two-thirds in New York's murder rate during the past seven years, there were still 767 murders in 1997; in London (which is about the same size), there were 129 in the year to March 1997. As for education, in New Orleans some 28% of adult blacks and Latinos—groups which together make up 64% of the city's population—have failed to complete high school.

True, such figures are bad even by American city standards, but virtually all big cities have suffered blight at their centres which will take time to reverse. The causes are complex. The mostly white middle classes began to move to the suburbs after the second world war, but most cities remained vigorous enough until the 1960s, when court-mandated desegregation of the schools turned the white exodus into a full-scale stampede. Jobs, businesses and services left, too; the tax base narrowed; taxes rose, pushing still more employers out, as well as the black middle class. What remained was a huddle of people without means or motivation to leave, most of them black, most of them unemployed, and all of them a prey to rising crime and rapidly deteriorating schools.

Figure 4.54 *Economist*, **10 January 1998**

In the 1920s there was an important new phase of suburban building. This continued earlier trends but on a larger scale and was carried out largely by the construction of small housing estates near public transport lines. This phase came to an end in the 1930s due to the depression, and suburban growth remained limited during the 1940s due to the war. However, after the war there was a tremendous demand for new housing and in the following decade a major phase of suburban construction ensued, greatly encouraged by federal government guarantees for low-interest mortgages with low deposits, income tax concessions for house buyers and further finance to extend the road system. During these years the interstitial areas were progressively infilled and then construction spread gradually outwards. There was little resistance by many local jurisdictions since new housing increased the tax base.

By the mid-1950s vast numbers of Americans were living far from their workplaces and from retail centres, resulting in long journeys to work, to shop and to entertainment. In response to this spatial imbalance the mid-1950s witnessed a substantial construction phase of new shopping centres, industrial estates and administrative complexes being established in peripheral locations. Such development was not entirely new but had generally been very small scale beforehand.

The decentralisation of manufacturing had two important effects. It now meant that many more of those who lived in the new suburbs could also find employment in these areas but conversely this process took many irreplaceable jobs from the inner city to locations difficult to reach by the less affluent.

The extension of urban areas has generally continued unabated in recent decades with planning regulations that are relatively weak compared to Western Europe. The selective use of zoning powers remains an important influence on suburban development today. R. J. Johnson (1981) noted two basis types of suburb, the **exclusive** suburb and the **mixed land use** suburb, which he classified according to the use of such powers. The exclusiveness of the former is preserved primarily by using density controls where minimum building lots may be set at say two acres, thus allowing entry to only the very affluent. The mixed land use suburbs tend to be the preserve of those in the middle income range where commercial and industrial use is frequently encouraged to increase the local tax base. The overall effect of zoning in both types of areas is to restrict population growth in outer urban regions while acting as a barrier to those of low income.

Suburban freeway corridors and edge cities

The suburban freeways that encircle the large cities of the United States have become new focal points for commercial and industrial development in the 1980s and 1990s, often to the detriment of the CBD. Circumferential freeways have generally experienced the most intensive corridor development because they contain a wide variety of sites of approximately equal accessibility from elsewhere in the metropolitan area.

The classic location for contemporary edge cities is at the intersection of a circumferential freeway and a hub-and-spoke lateral road. However in more recent years some edge cities have emerged on greenfield sites. The edge city phenomenon is most developed in Los Angeles where up to two dozen have been identified by some writers. One of the better examples is the Warner Center-Woodland Hills complex located 50 km from the centre of Los Angeles. Many of the offices in this complex have decentralised from downtown Los Angeles. Here many people live close to their place of work whereas previously they commuted into the centre of Los Angeles.

The residential form that characterises edge cities is private housing schemes based on common-interest developments (CIDs) and administered by homeowners' associations. The number of such associations increased from fewer than 500 in 1964 to 150 000 (covering 32 million Americans) in 1992. Critics have used the term 'privatopia' to describe this type of housing which they argue induces a culture of non-participation, creating even greater social division.

The rural-urban fringe

The rural-urban fringe is the boundary zone where urban and non-urban land meet and is an area of transition from agriculture and other rural activities to urban use. The exact size and nature of the area undergoing such transition has been the subject of much research, the more conclusive observations of which are illustrated by Figure 4.56. In general the size of the fringe area is dependent on the size of the overall metropolitan area and the effect of nearby and competing metropolitan areas.

As land values can change so rapidly in fringe areas speculators frequently hold much of the undeveloped land with the ownership and character of land frequently beginning to change more than 20 years before the area is actually built over. Investors and property developers own a higher proportion of fringe land where development pressures are strong compared to areas where such pressures are moderate or weak.

A marked change in the size of land ownership with distance from the built-up area is apparent as is the rate at which land ownership changes.

Figure 4.55 Increasing congestion within Los Angeles has encouraged the growth of edge cities

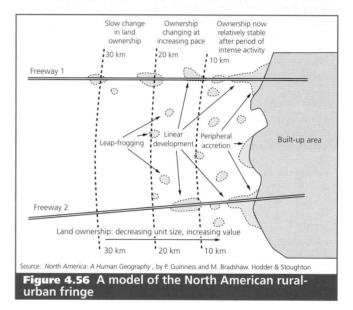

Source: *North America: A Human Geography*, by P. Guinness and M. Bradshaw. Hodder & Stoughton

Figure 4.56 A model of the North American rural-urban fringe

Questions

1. Examine the reasons for, and the extent of, urban sprawl in the United States.
2. Discuss the measures which have been introduced to try to limit urban sprawl.
3. (a) Explain the decline of many downtown areas in the United States.
   (b) What are the reasons behind the recent revitalisation of some downtown areas?
4. Why is the inner city/suburban contrast much greater in the United States than in European countries?
5. Conduct your own research into edge cities in Los Angeles. Is this really a new urban phenomenon or simply a new term for very large outer suburban centres?
6. Identify the patterns and processes at work in the rural-urban fringe.

The quality of life in cities

The quality of life usually varies considerably both between and within cities in the same country. Over time a wide range of different socio-economic indicators have been used to identify such variation. It is not surprising that each indicator, at least to some extent, produces a different pattern as every individual measure has its merits and limitations. Thus most recent attempts to measure spatial variations in the quality of life have combined a range of indicators to form a composite quality of life index.

The Department of the Environment used 1991 census data and other information to compile an Index of Deprivation for the 366 local authority districts (including London Boroughs) of England. The index gave equal weight to each of the following 13 indicators:

- **level of unemployment**
- **proportion of long-term unemployed**
- **proportion of adults receiving income support**
- children in low earning households
- children in unsuitable accommodation
- proportion of households without a car
- standardised mortality rate
- low educational achievement (GCSE)
- educational participation of 17 year-olds
- house contents premiums, as a proxy for crime
- proportion of housing which is overcrowded
- households lacking basic amenities
- amount of derelict land.

The results of this analysis for London are shown in Figure 4.57. The average for the country has been set at zero. Positive scores indicate above average levels of deprivation, negative scores below average levels. Fourteen of the twenty most deprived districts in England are in London (Figure 4.58), with Newham, Southwark, Hackney and Islington being the most deprived boroughs in the country in that order. The most affluent London boroughs are Bromley (208th), Harrow (207th), Sutton (183rd), and Bexley (181st).

The same study also looked at the incidence of deprivation down to the enumeration district (ED) level, of which there

England = 0

- ■ 35.0 or over
- ■ 17.5 to 34.9
- ▨ 0 to 17.4
- ▢ -17.5 to -0.1
- ▢ under -17.5

High scores = more deprived

Source: Department of the Environment

Figure 4.57 London: index of deprivation by borough 1991

Key Definitions   6

deprivation   Defined by the Department of the Environment as when 'an individual's well-being falls below a level generally regarded as a reasonable minimum for Britain today'.

standard mortality ratio   The ratio expresses the number of deaths in an area as a percentage of the hypothetical number that would have occurred if the area's population had experienced the sex/age specific rates of England and Wales in that year.

gentrification   A process in which wealthier people move into, renovate and restore run-down housing in an inner city or other neglected area. Such housing was formerly inhabited by low-income groups, the tenure shifting from private-rented to owner-occupation.

residential mosaic   The complex pattern of different residential areas within a city reflecting variations in socio-economic status which are mainly attributable to income.

Figure 4.58 Most severely deprived districts in England 1991

Ranking[1]	Districts	Ranking[1]	Districts
1	Newham	16	Hammersmith and Fulham
2	Southwark	17	Newcastle-upon-Tyne
3	Hackney	18	Barking and Dagenham
4	Islington	19	Kensington and Chelsea
5	Birmingham	20	Waltham Forest
6	Liverpool	21	Wandsworth
7	Tower Hamlets	22	South Tyneside
8	Lambeth	23	Bradford
9	Sandwell	24	Middlesbrough
10	Haringey	25	Nottingham
11	Lewisham	26	City of Westminster
12	Knowsley	27	Wolverhampton
13	Manchester	28	Salford
14	Greenwich	29	Brent
15	Camden	30	Blackpool

[1]Based on the Index of Deprivation
Source: Department of the Environment

are about 250 within each London borough. EDs within the bottom 7 per cent of the national ranking are regarded as deprived and the proportion of a borough's EDs which fall into this category is a measure of the internal spread of its deprivation. On this measure the ten most deprived districts in England are all in London.

According to this analysis and to others that have been conducted, the contrast between inner and outer London is striking with the most intense deprivation in inner London being concentrated towards the east. However, significant contrasts exist within virtually all boroughs so that the better off wards in some inner London boroughs often record a higher quality of life than the least affluent wards in outer London boroughs. The pattern found within boroughs is often quite intricate, forming the 'residential mosaic' that social geographers frequently talk about. Even within wards considerable contrasts can be found as fieldwork and examination of ED data will confirm. The government identifies deprivation not as an academic exercise but as a means of targeting resources on areas most in need (Figure 4.61).

In terms of individual measures perhaps the standard mortality ratio conveys the contrast within London at its most bleak (Figure 4.62). Mortality is to a significant extent the product of all the other indicators of relative deprivation/affluence. Figure 4.63 presents two indicators on a ward-by-ward basis to illustrate in greater detail the contrast between the most and least deprived boroughs. The percentage of households without a car is a good measure of economic status. The percentage of houses which are detached is not a factor usually incorporated into indexes of deprivation as people of affluence may choose to live in other types of

Figure 4.59 High-rise council housing in Wandsworth, London

housing. However, it does convey a good image of the respective residential environments.

Detailed analysis down to ED level shows quite clearly that there are small areas of striking affluence in Inner London, and to a lesser extent in inner areas of other large cities. There are two main reasons for clusters of high socio-economic status in the inner city:

■ **Some areas have always been fashionable for those with money. Areas such as St John's Wood and Chelsea are both only a short journey to the City and West End, and pleasantly laid out with a good measure of open space. The original high quality of housing has been maintained to a very good standard.**

Figure 4.60 Council flats on Blackwall Tunnel approach road: residents' views

■ Other fashionable areas have become so in recent decades through the process of gentrification which in the areas where it takes place reverses the filter-down process of older property (Figure 4.64). Gentrification is marked by the occupation of more space per person than the original occupants from lower socio-economic groups.

The inner city problem: a sequence of explanations

The nature of and linkage between inner city problems is reasonably illustrated by the web of decline, deprivation and despair (Figure 4.66). Inner city decline is the counterpart of suburbanisation. Over the years a number of different explanations of the inner city problem have appeared (Figure 4.67). For over two decades after the Second World War inner

Government zones in on deprivation

Multi-pronged attack answers critics of New Labour Policy towards poor, **Simon Buckby** reports

Roy Hattersley, former deputy leader of the Labour party, frequently claims that New Labour does not care sufficiently about the poor. Yet rarely can the socially deprived have received so much attention from a government.

Its work-centred welfare policy is aimed at people living on benefits. The Social Exclusion Unit, due to report next month, has developed plans to tackle homelessness and improve run-down housing estates. And combination punches from a first wave of 12 education action zones, five employment action zones and 11 health action zones are designed to deal a knock-out blow to many of the ill effects of poverty.

The health action zones, the most developed of the three, will receive priority access to capital funding, including money from the private finance initiative, and to National Lottery support.

The zones' priority is to be tough on the causes of poor health. They will "promote local partnerships to tackle pollution, homelessness, unemployment, and poverty", says Frank Dobson, the health secretary. As further evidence of the government's desire to encourage a multiplicity of agents working to prevent deprivation, the health authorities selected from the 41 applications reflect joint proposals with social services departments, GPs and the voluntary and private sectors.

One health action zone is in the Lambeth, Southwark and Lewisham health authority in south London, where the hospitals, social services departments, police and probation services discovered they were all dealing with problems from the same families.

"Those who complained to the council about poor housing were often the same people who regularly visit their GP or turn up in the accident and emergency department at the hospital, report drug problems, are in conflict with the schools over truancy, or suffer family breakdown," says Matthew Swindells, general manager for women and children's services at Guys Hospital. "We are trying to co-ordinate our response to them, rather than treating each of their problems separately."

The health authority has the highest rate of under-age pregnancies in the country, and 38 per cent of local children are raised in households with no earned income. One of the central projects of the zone is to co-ordinate education campaigns to reduce the number of pregnancies among the young and encourage parental responsibility.

The programme has the support of Simon Hughes, MP for Southwark North and Bermondsey and Liberal Democrat health spokesman.

"An urgent move away from early sex, early children and early single parenting as a result will be one of the best legacies we could leave, both to this generation and the next," he says.

Beating the blackspots

1 Northumberland: to tackle pockets of severe deprivation in an environment scarred by industrial decline
2 Tyne and Wear: to tackle transport and housing problems
3 N Cumbria: to deal with acute deprivation on west coast
4 Bradford: community-based diabetes service being set up
5 Manchester: to provide employment and training opportunities to people with marital problems
6 S Yorks: to tackle problems of the young in communities ravaged by pit closures
7 Sandwell, West Midlands: to develop community-focused health service
8 Luton: to tackle health needs of Asian women
9 Hackney, Newham and Tower Hamlets: to address greatest concentration of poverty in the country
10 Lambeth, Southwark and Lewisham: area with country's highest rate of teenage pregnancies
11 Plymouth: some of the most deprived neighbourhoods in Britain

Figure 4.61 *Financial Times,* July 1998

England and Wales = 100

- 110 or over
- 100 to 109
- 90 to 99
- Less than 90

Source: Office for National Statistics

Figure 4.62 London: standard mortality ratios 1995

Lower-income migrants move into deteriorated housing (previously owned by middle-income groups)

Lower-income groups gradually move up the housing scale

CBD

Gentrification: upper-middle-income groups move to old housing

Older housing occupied by lower-income groups

Better housing occupied by middle-income groups

Best housing occupied by upper-middle-income groups

Expansion: new houses built for upper-middle-income groups

Filtering occurs as housing deteriorates and it moves downwards through the social groups.

Gentrification reverses this process as middle-income groups upgrade older city properties by renovating them.

Source: *Advanced Geography Revision Handbook*, by G. Nagle & K. Spencer, OUP

Figure 4.64 The process of filtering and gentrification

Figure 4.65 Chelsea – a fashionable area of London

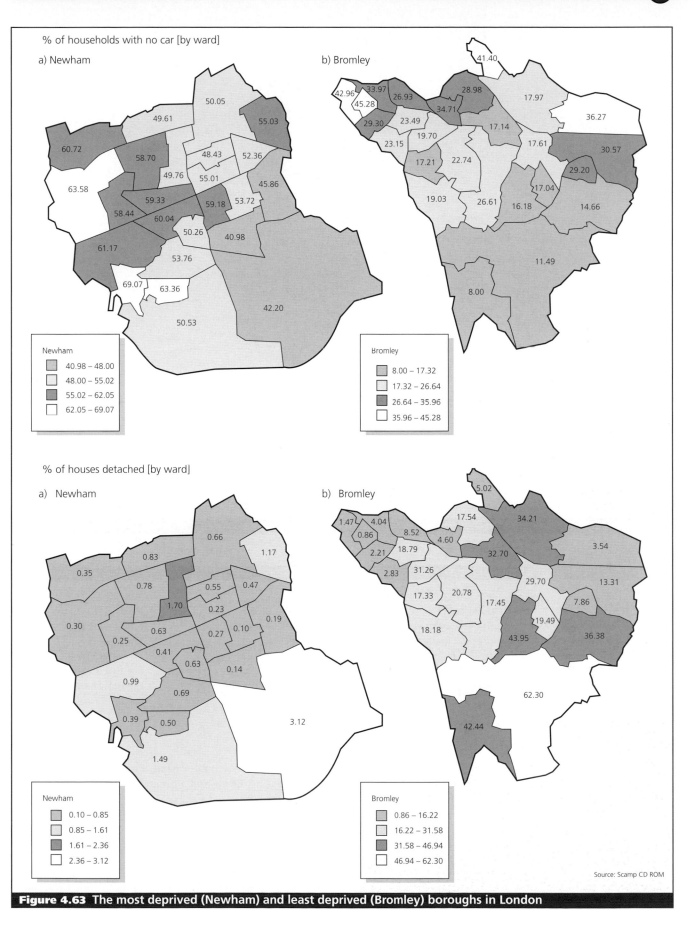

% of households with no car [by ward]

a) Newham

b) Bromley

Newham
	40.98 – 48.00
	48.00 – 55.02
	55.02 – 62.05
	62.05 – 69.07

Bromley
	8.00 – 17.32
	17.32 – 26.64
	26.64 – 35.96
	35.96 – 45.28

% of houses detached [by ward]

a) Newham

b) Bromley

Newham
	0.10 – 0.85
	0.85 – 1.61
	1.61 – 2.36
	2.36 – 3.12

Bromley
	0.86 – 16.22
	16.22 – 31.58
	31.58 – 46.94
	46.94 – 62.30

Source: Scamp CD ROM

Figure 4.63 The most deprived (Newham) and least deprived (Bromley) boroughs in London

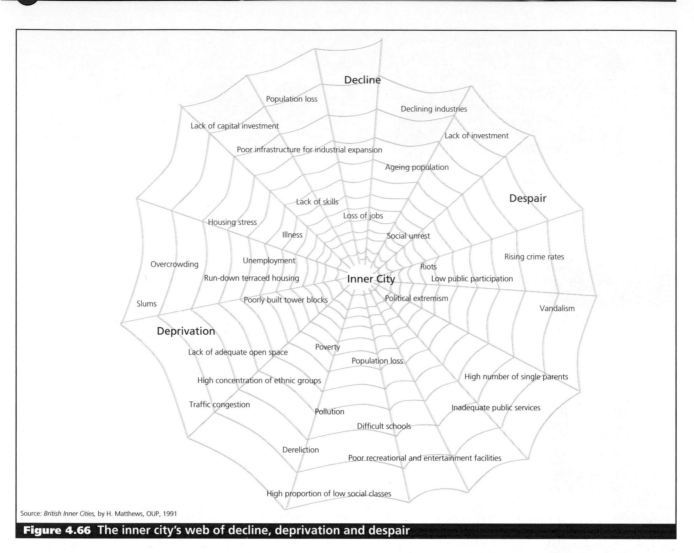

Source: *British Inner Cities*, by H. Matthews, OUP, 1991

Figure 4.66 The inner city's web of decline, deprivation and despair

Figure 4.67 Different explanations of the inner city problem

Perspective	Perceived problem	Goal	Means
Physical decay	Obsolescence	Better built environment	Physical planning
Culture of poverty	Pathology of deviant groups	Better social adjustment	Social education
Cycle of deprivation	Individual inadequacy	Better families	Social work
Institutional malfunction	Planning failure	Better planning	Co-ordinated planning
Resource maldistribution	Inequality	Reallocation of resources	Positive discrimination
Structural conflict	Underdevelopment	Redistribution of power	Political change

city problems were attributed primarily to poor housing and other aspects of the run-down built environment. The solutions were clearance and redevelopment.

From the late 1960s to the mid-1970s the focus of attention shifted to issues of social deprivation. Within this broad area three alternative explanations emerged:

■ a culture of poverty in which families of a certain kind pass on an anti-social life style from one generation to the next. Social norms in certain areas encouraged

vandalism, early school-leaving, early marriage, early child-rearing, crime and a general disrespect for authority

■ the cycle of deprivation (Figure 4.70) which was seen as preventing the poor from improving the quality of their lives

■ institutional malfunctioning characterised by poor links between social and welfare services on the one hand and populations most in need on the other.

Figure 4.68 Houses secured prior to demolition, Newcastle, 1959

Figure 4.69 Renovating terraced housing in the 1980s

From the mid-1970s two additional explanations emerged which focused on the structural (economic) fabric of the inner city:

■ resource maldistribution as a result of the decentralisation of population, industry and commerce to the suburbs and beyond. The massive decline of inner city manufacturing was seen as the most important deprivation factor

■ structural conflict whereby large companies benefit from keeping the inner city underdeveloped, viewing it as an area providing a pool of expendable, unskilled labour, and cheap land, which can be taken up or abandoned according to fluctuations in the economy. This

Figure 4.70 The cycle of deprivation

POVERTY
low wages or unemployment

POOR SKILLS
poor occupational skills

POOR LIVING CONDITIONS
poor accommodation
overcrowding
run-down area

POOR EDUCATION
old schools

ILL HEALTH
stress and strain

Source: *British Inner Cities* by Hugh Matthews, OUP, 1991

Questions

1 **(a)** Discuss the merits of the indicators used by the Department of the Environment to compile the Index of Deprivation.
  (b) State and justify four other indicators that you feel are also good measures of deprivation.
2 Describe and attempt to explain the variations in deprivation within London.
3 Examine the evolution of explanation with regard to inner city problems.
4 Why are local authority housing estates more marginalised in a socio-economic sense than ever before?

explanation sees the need for capitalism to be replaced by a socialist system of production.

Although not all local authority housing estates are in inner cities, a significant proportion are. As a recent study confirmed such estates are increasingly becoming the focal points of deprivation (Figure 4.71). This is in effect the spatial marginalisation of those who are already socially marginalised. If these trends continue the successful metropolis, according to Siebel (1984) is likely to be divided into three different cities:

■ the most visible city is the 'international' city

■ hidden behind the international city is the 'normal' city or middle-class city

■ in the shadow remains the 'marginalised' city.

The processes of reurbanisation and gentrification are likely to accelerate this division. Where gentrification expands the 'international' city, the poor are further pushed out into the worst segment of the housing market.

Estates 'dumping grounds for the poor'

HALF of all men in council homes are now unemployed as estates become dumping grounds for the poor, unemployed and benefit-dependent, a report by the Institute for Fiscal Studies said yesterday.

Government subsidies to reduce rents in council and housing association properties would be the best way to reverse a trend that had seen such housing take only the most marginalised in society.

In the 1960s, 90 per cent of men of working age on such estates were employed. Now, tenants of councils or housing associations were more than twice as likely to be unemployed as people in other tenures and one in five families were headed by a single parent.

Even among men working, half earned less than £6 an hour and half the women earned less than £4 an hour.

The report, Living with the State, surveyed the steady decline of social housing tenants as policies stressing the importance of home ownership and the private rented sector have taken hold.

Half of all council tenants were now in the poorest fifth of the population and those entering such homes were far poorer than those moving out. Average income of council tenants in 1993 was a fifth lower than 20 years before while average income across the population as a whole had risen by 30 per cent.

Rents, about £50 a week in London, and £30 in Yorkshire and Humberside, had also doubled in real terms since 1979 as state aid switched from direct rent subsidy to means-tested housing benefit.

Paul Johnson, one of the authors, said the concentration of the poorest families on council and housing association estates was one of the biggest social changes of the last 20 years.

"The better off have moved out, many who remained have not done well in the recent economic climate and only the very needy have been able to move in."

Figure 4.71 *Guardian*, 24 May 1996

Urban planning and management

Although urban planning can be said to be as old as urban settlement it was not until the 1940s that the modern era of urban planning began in Britain. What started as a gradual shift towards government involvement in town planning in the first forty years of the century, climaxed in a radical transformation in official attitudes towards state intervention from the late 1930s to 1945. The passage through parliament of the Green Belt Act in 1944, the New Towns Act in 1946 and the Town and Country Planning Act in 1947 were milestones in spatial organisation, having evolved from a series of reports on major urban areas which appeared a few years earlier (Figure 4.72). There can be little doubt that Britain would be a much worse place without the level of organisation imposed by planning measures, but as Figure 4.72 explains the urban landscape of today does not reflect the optimistic forecasts of fifty years ago.

The Town and Country Planning Act of 1947

This was the first comprehensive piece of planning legislation in England and Wales. The planning measures of the inter-war period had been piecemeal in nature, attempting to solve particular problems rather than treating the urban system as a whole, and as a result it was largely ineffectual. Under the Town and Country Planning Act local authorities were placed under a statutory obligation to prepare Development Plans which were to state the general use to which each plot of land and building was to be put. Developers had to submit proposals to local authority planning committees which had the power to refuse applications deemed undesirable. Previously a local authority could only do this by purchasing the land on which the development was planned. The inter-war years had witnessed a huge expansion of suburbia as the general absence of planning controls gave developers a virtual free hand to take over thousands of acres of countryside. The Town and Country Planning Act has been amended on a number of occasions since 1947 to take account of emerging trends.

Garden Cities and New Towns

Town planning as we know it today began in the eighteenth century. James Craig laid out Edinburgh's granite grey New Town while in England the fashion for taking the waters led to the development of Buxton and Bath. The next step in the evolution of town planning came with the industrial revolution. In 1817 the utopian socialist Robert Owen created New Lanark around the Clydesdale woollen mills built by his father-in-law. Cadbury's (cocoa) and Levers (soap) followed suit and used some of their profits to build the towns of Bourneville and Port Sunlight. The objective of these

The written plans that ushered in the planning era in the 1940s — Lock on Middlesbrough, Abercrombie on London, Nicholas on Manchester — were full of idealism, certainty and a grand missionary spirit. They captured the flavour of excitement and conviction out of which the 1947 Act emerged.

There was a template for a better life and it was one that could be delivered through the physical redesign of the urban environment. Green belts, new towns, land use zoning and the separation of uses, neighbourhood design, integrated transport; all were important parts of the prescription. Many of those written plans formed the inputs into the rebuilding and redesign of our towns and cities in the 1950s and 1960s and well beyond. They epitomised the dreams of an exhausted but hopeful nation which thought that it could indeed build a new Jerusalem.

But the flame of idealism grew dim as reality returned. So much of what was achieved was so much less than what had been planned: financial constraints, selfish interests, pressures from a changing world economy, misplaced and sometimes corrupt political partisanship were all conducive to a less than ideal outcome.

PERHAPS WE were never bold enough — or the economy was never sufficiently expansive — to wipe away the urban detritus which industrialisation and war had wrought. Perhaps Corbusian ideas were fundamentally implausible as a way of tackling the patching and re-making of an established urban landscape, as opposed to their use in the green-field contexts of a Brasília.

1   **Perhaps the restructuring of the economy since the 1970s — which worked so much to undermine the economic roles of towns and cities — simply exposed the inadequacies of a planning system whose mechanism was based fundamentally on the control, not the attraction of development.**
2   **Perhaps the unforeseen speed of growth of private cars produced a leviathan which planning ideas could not contain.**
3   **Perhaps the underlying assumption of a physical determinism was too strongly embedded in planning's ideology.**
4   **Perhaps planners, as with so many other experts, suffered the inevitable reversal of esteem which came with a more informed and powerful public.**
5   **Perhaps it was that the bulldozers of the 1950s and 1960s, which had started to clear areas about which few could have had regrets, did not know when to stop.**
6   **Perhaps the gestation period of implementing grand designs is simply so long that events inevitably leave them looking like tired responses to yesterday's problems.**

Whatever the causes, there is no doubt that much of the planning of the post-war years (and the architecture with which planners are inevitably, if unfairly, linked) is now widely condemned.

However, in the present-day climate of infinite regret for the 'little terraces' and the 'neighbourhood' it is so easy to forget that what was needed was better-quality housing fast, and that the lumbering giants of Victorian public buildings were not then as admired as they are today.

Figure 4.72 *Town and Country Planning,* **May 1997**

philanthropists and others was to provide good housing and pleasant environmental conditions for their workers.

Of enormous significance was the publication in 1898 of *Tomorrow, A Peaceful Path to Real Reform* by Ebenezer Howard, which was republished four years later as *Garden Cities of Tomorrow.* Howard was appalled by the squalor of urban Britain and was sure that there was a better way. In 1899 the Garden City Association (GCA) was founded and it drew up plans for Letchworth in Hertfordshire which was started in 1903. Not just a visionary writer, Howard had persuaded a number of rich and influential people to invest in a real garden city. In 1918 the GCA published *New Towns after the War* in which a hundred new towns were proposed. Between 1919 and 1939 four and a half million houses were built, but only one New Town, Welwyn Garden City, begun in 1920, was constructed (Figure 4.73).

Howard's ideas were to provide inspiration for like minds in a number of other countries (Figure 4.74). Howard died in 1928 but his followers continued to campaign and after the Second World War the government accepted their arguments, largely because of the strong recommendation of the Barlow Report published in 1940. In 1948 Welwyn Garden City became one of London's New Towns and the town thus provides visible continuity between the aims of Howard and the objectives of post-World War II planners.

When in 1976 it was decided not to undertake for the time being any more New Town projects, 32 such towns had already been designated in the United Kingdom. Fourteen were designated between the passage of the New Towns Act in 1946 and 1950 with only one, Cumbernauld in Scotland, added in the 1950s. These are regarded as the first generation New Towns which were largely mechanisms for replacing bomb-damaged houses and reducing the extremely high population densities in the inner areas of London and Glasgow. However a few such as Cwmbran in South Wales were intended to act primarily as small growth poles in the commercially depressed Development Areas. Most were designed for a maximum of 60 000 people, although for some the target was later raised to over 100 000. At the time the proportion of housing that was rented was, at an average of 80 per cent, above the national norm.

Later New Towns, the so-called second generation, such as Washington on Tyneside and Livingston in Scotland were seen primarily as new economic growth poles which would bring prosperity to traditional industrial areas. Their projected populations were higher than the earlier New Towns and some were already quite sizeable towns such as Northampton, Peterborough and Warrington.

Last of all came the 'New Cities' or third generation New Towns of Milton Keynes, Telford and Central Lancashire which were planned to be larger than their earlier counterparts and act as 'counter magnets' to people who might otherwise have moved to London. All three include within their areas a number of established settlements. Central Lancashire already had a population of 235 000. Milton Keynes was seen as a

Living and working in the smoke

Living in the Suburbs-Working in the smoke

Living & Working in the Sun at Welwyn Garden City

Houses for immediate occupation have been built and are now for sale. Sites for Factories and Industrial purposes are also available. Apply to Estate Office: Welwyn Garden City, Herts. and at 3 Gray's Inn Place, Gray's Inn WCI

Source: Original advert taken from *The Express* 9/10/98

Figure 4.73 Advertising the benefits of Welwyn Garden City in the 1920s

For 50 years, Britain's 32 new towns have provided international role models for urban dispersal and planned development. "We lead the world," says Professor David Lock, chief planning officer at the Environment Department, "because we were the first country to experience an industrial revolution and urbanise our population, and the first to have to tackle the resulting dysfunctions of overcrowding and congestion."

Long before the 1946 Act, Ebenezer Howard's 1898 proposal for privately funded garden cities inspired parallel movements in France, Germany, Italy, the Netherlands, Russia and the USA. But the successful UK experiments at Letchworth and Welwyn Garden City remained lonely beacons until massive reconstruction after the Second World War brought government funding.

Early European post-war programmes drew heavily on British experience. The Paris Ring followed the model of the London Ring, which was inaugurated by the 1946 designation of Stevenage; while the Dutch new town of Almere, built on reclaimed land, owes much to Peterborough. Developing countries have also looked to Britain. Milton Keynes, for example, played a key role in planning the Nigerian federal capital of Abuja.

More recently it is in Asia, with exploding populations and booming economies creating intense pressures for urban dispersal and regional development, where Britain's integrated communities are proving relevant. The Thai Government has reacted to the rapid urbanisation of Bangkok by tasking the National Housing Authority (NHA) to ring the capital with six new towns to accommodate 1.8 million people. To help plan these effectively, the NHA has commissioned an appraisal of UK experience from De Montfort University Centre for New Town Development Studies.

Figure 4.74 *The Times '50 Years of New Towns'*, 11 October 1996

Figure 4.76 Harlow: putting people's needs first

Figure 4.75 Harlow New Town: housing

new growth pole midway between London and Birmingham, while taking overspill from London and other parts of the South East. The M1 motorway forms its north-eastern boundary and it is on the main railway line from London to the Midlands.

The objectives of the New Towns were:

- to strike a balance between the needs of living and working
- to provide good quality housing with all amenities for people across the income range
- to give a green and open quality to the towns – the boundaries of new towns were generously drawn giving architects space to experiment in contrast to the high-rise blocks that were mushrooming in the large cities.

New Towns were designed to be 'self-contained and balanced communities for work and living'. They exhibited many new ideas in urban planning:

- houses grouped in self-contained neighbourhoods, each with its own local service centre – the 'neighbourhood principle'
- through-traffic routed away from housing areas
- pedestrianised shopping centres
- factories grouped into industrial estates
- cycle path networks
- large areas of planned open space.

NEW TOWN PROFILES

1st GENERATION

• BRACKNELL

Designated: 1949
Current Population: 51,000
Since the 1960s employment has changed from manufacturing to distribution, research and service industry, with particular emphasis on the computer industry. Major companies in the area include Honeywell, BMW, Panasonic and ICL. Bracknell in the 1990s claims to be the "Leisure Centre of the South-East" with a Countryside and Heritage Centre, a Water World, 10-screen cinema, arts centre and theatre.

• CRAWLEY

Designated: 1947
Current Population: 87,000
Crawley is 30 miles south of London and close to the M25 and the M23 which has excellent international links via Gatwick Airport. The town's business profile has changed from heavy manufacturing to greater emphasis on electronics, electrical engineering, pharmaceuticals and computers. Major companies include KPMG Peat Marwick, Smithkline Beecham and Schlumberger Geco Prakla.

2nd GENERATION

• WASHINGTON

Designated: 1964
Current Population: 62,000
Located six miles from Newcastle, Washington is linked to the UK's national motorway network by the A1(M). It is close to the east coast ports and to Newcastle's international airport, and also has good rail links. The town is the European base for a number of overseas companies, Nissan being the most prominent. Apart from automotive, other key industries are pharmaceuticals, electronics, engineering, plastics and data processing, and major names include Littelfuse and ASDA.

• REDDITCH

Designated: 1964
Current Population: 80,000
Redditch is 15 miles south of Birmingham, between the M5, M40, M42. A large number of overseas firms have located to the town, which is also the centre of the country's needle-making industry. Main employment is in production engineering and machine tool manufacture, both automotive and aerospace; medical equipment, electronics, computing, food, plastics, printing and distribution. Major employers include AT&T Istel, GKN, Ross Young, Hymatic, The Law Society and Halfords.

3rd GENERATION

• MILTON KEYNES

Designated: 1967
Current Population: 161,500
Dubbed "the fastest growing city in Britain", Milton Keynes is the business base for more than 3,500 companies, including around 300 from overseas. It also has the country's largest number of Japanese companies outside of London. Main industries in the area include electronics, computing, financial services, food processing, distribution and business services. A large number of high profile international companies have been attracted to the town, including Mercedes Benz, Hitachi, Minolta, Ericsson, Alps Electric, PolyGram and Mobil.

• TELFORD

Designated: 1968
Current Population: 123,000
All types of industry are represented in the area, including plastics, automotive, computing, robotics, electronics and financial services. The town has been extremely successful in attracting overseas investment. There are 140 non-UK companies from 18 countries, creating the highest concentration of both Japanese and Taiwanese manufacturers in the UK. Companies include Ricoh, Epson, Hoechst, Tatung, Samsung and NEC.

Figure 4.77 *The Times '50 Years of New Towns'*, 11 October 1996

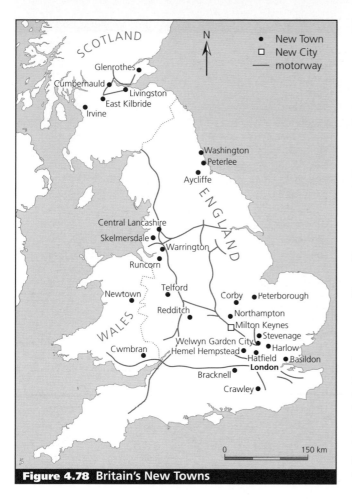

Figure 4.78 Britain's New Towns

The New Towns have generally been perceived as successful because:

- they have been a key element in the protection of the countryside from sprawl and spasmodic development
- the quality of housing was far better than most residents could have hoped for within the conurbations
- they have produced a superior economic performance compared with the national average
- they have attracted much foreign investment. For example Telford has the highest concentration of Japanese and Taiwanese manufacturing companies in Britain
- they have a strong record of spawning small businesses – the small-scale industrial estate with workshops and low-rent 'nursery' units is essentially a new town concept
- New Towns have been pioneers in energy conservation and other environmental matters.

Criticisms of New Towns

- people living at or close to areas where New Towns were planned were some of the first to exhibit the now well-known 'not-in-my-back-yard' (NIMBY) syndrome

- in the early years at least the New Towns were perceived by many as boring and lacking in character. The media frequently ran stories about "New Town Blues" and the general social problems caused by what was felt to be a 'lack of community' compared with places of origin such as London's East End
- the London New Towns did not become as self-contained as at first hoped and commuting has been at a higher level than originally envisaged
- New Towns found it difficult to insulate themselves from the characteristics of the regions in which they were located. High unemployment in the wider region was usually reflected by unemployment above the national average in the New Town
- the difficulty of attracting the middle class which was necessary to achieve a good social mix
- the success of the New Towns in creating half a million new homes in 50 years has to be measured against the huge numbers of demolished terraced houses which were structurally sound and simply in need of renovation.

The New Town adventure came to an end when the concept fell out of favour with the two main political parties. To the Conservatives, particularly under the leadership of Margaret Thatcher, they were part of a burgeoning welfare state that needed to be reduced in scope. In contrast, the Labour Party was concerned at the way New Towns attracted employment, skilled workers and investment from the inner cities which were invariably dominated politically by Labour.

The development corporations that set up the New Towns have all been wound up. What remains of their publicly-owned land is being gradually sold off by the Commission for New Towns (CNT), established in 1961, when it receives what it deems to be appropriate offers. Its job is to manage and dispose of an estate encompassing some 3 million square feet of mainly office buildings and factories, and over 11 000 acres of development land. Through the disposals programme of the CNT the government should eventually recoup the entire historic cost of the New Towns along with a reasonable 'profit'.

Expanded Towns

A number of existing well-established settlements also took overspill population from London and some other conurbations as a result of the Town Development Act of 1952. Industrial areas and new housing estates were constructed with both central and local government money. London entered into house-building agreements with a number of towns such as Andover, Swindon and King's Lynn, which were prepared to take population from London. The expansion schemes had two big advantages:

- Londoners got better homes and working conditions
- new life was brought to declining or static towns. Some expanded towns grew to three or four times their original size and in most services grew correspondingly.

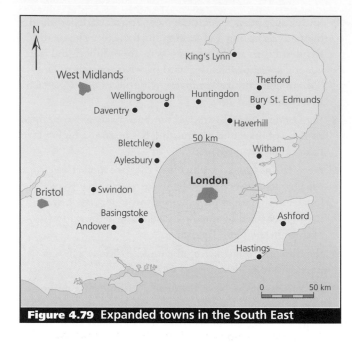

Figure 4.79 Expanded towns in the South East

Figure 4.80 Green belts in England

Area	Size (hectares)
Tyne and Wear	200 000
Lancaster and Fylde Coast	5 750
York	50 000
South and West Yorkshire	800 000
Greater Manchester, Central Lancs, Merseyside and Wirral	750 000
Stoke on Trent	125 000
Nottingham, Derby	200 000
Burton-Swadlincote	2 000
West Midlands	26 500
Cambridge	26 500
Gloucester, Cheltenham	20 000
Oxford	100 000
London	1 200 000
Avon	220 000
Total in England	4 495 300

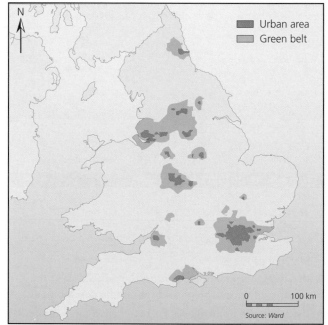

Source: *Ward* (1994)

The expanded towns were in general too far from London for a significant level of commuting and because of their longer history of development, many newcomers saw them as having more character than the New Towns. Figure 4.79 shows the location of expanded towns in the South East.

Green belts

The idea of the green belt dates back, according to some writers, to Ebenezer Howard, although others attribute the concept to earlier thinkers, including Robert Owen. The concept was formalised in 1938 when the then London County Council promoted the Green Belt (London and Home Counties) Act, which set out powers for local councils to acquire land to ensure it could not be built on. One of the wartime planners, Sir Patrick Abercrombie, proposed that restrictions on development could be extended to privately-owned land and these powers were given to local councils by the 1947 Town and Country Planning Act.

The first green belt was established around London in 1947. Since then green belts have been set around a number of other conurbations and cities (Figure 4.80). They have always enjoyed a very high level of public support. Green belts serve the following purpose:

■ limiting urban sprawl
■ preventing neighbouring towns from merging
■ preserving the special character of historically or architecturally important towns
■ protecting farmland from urban development
■ providing recreational areas for city dwellers.

However, while they contain development within their boundaries there is often intense growth just beyond their outer limits. In order to limit such development London's Green Belt was extended outwards in several areas in the early 1980s.

Green belt restraint has never stopped landowners submitting planning applications for development, and although success in obtaining planning permission is low, the huge financial rewards for those who do succeed has always encouraged land speculation in the rural-urban fringe. The most spectacular breaching of London's Green Belt was the construction of the M25. Despite intense opposition from environmentalists and others, the perceived need to reduce the traffic burden on London was given precedence. Not surprisingly the M25 has increased other pressures on the

Green Belt. It has been estimated that between 5 per cent and 10 per cent of the land statutorily approved as green belt in the 1950s has been developed. Land use change has taken place unevenly with considerably more land being developed on the western edge of London than elsewhere, and much of this development has been the direct result of public sector investment. Anyone who wants to build on green belt land must demonstrate 'exceptional circumstances' to be allowed to do so.

Examples of development that has been granted include:

- the building of science parks on poorly reclaimed gravel land with employment and environmental gains offsetting the loss of green belt
- the construction of housing estates in the extensive grounds of large mental hospitals which have been closed. Development has often been deemed to be more desirable than dereliction
- building on pieces of land cut off by new roads which are too small to be farmed effectively.

Criticisms of the green belt

- they restrict the supply of development land, thus raising its price and that of houses constructed upon it. One consequence of this is higher housing densities
- they do not serve the recreational needs of urban areas as a whole, being used largely by local residents
- they are usually managed in an unimaginative way with some areas which could be described as being derelict
- they result in increased commuting distances and greater traffic-related pollution.

New pressures on the green belts and beyond

The latest pressure on the green belts and other parts of the countryside arises from a report published in 1995 which

Figure 4.81 New housing development in green belt land

projected that the number of households in Britain would rise by 4.4 million between 1991 and 2016. On that basis counties have been told to find space for given numbers of new homes. A number of organisations have however questioned the line that successive governments have taken on this issue:

- the figure of 4.4 million merely projects past trends and thus should not be seen as a forecast
- no account is taken of income or price, just that every household must have 'access to decent housing' including 'those who would not otherwise be able to afford it'
- making more homes available may itself cause more households to be formed
- the government could act to encourage subdivision of existing large properties. For example, at present, building conversions attract VAT at 17½ per cent, while building new homes is VAT-free.

Britain is currently losing countryside at the rate of an area of new development the size of Bristol each year. Every part of the country is under pressure which is at its most intense in the South East. Between 1945 and 1990 development has eaten up an area of land larger than Greater London. The equivalent of a city one and a half times the size of Manchester could be built in the South East outside Greater London between 2006 and 2016. This would follow the equivalent of a city the size of Birmingham which will have to be built in the same counties between 1991 and 2006. The new strategy for the South East threatens dozens of areas of countryside previously considered out-of-bounds to house builders. Figure 4.82 shows the favoured option drawn up by Serplan, the regional planning conference of county councils for the South-East. It is a midway figure between the 1 104 000 households it is estimated will be formed in the South East between 1991 and 2016 and the 847 000 homes that planners calculate could be built on land in cities and on already-allocated greenfield sites by 2006. Land in south-east England which commands around £2500 an acre for farming is worth as much as £500 000 when released for housing around booming towns. However, rather than piecemeal development, some writers favour the resurrection of New Towns (Figure 4.83).

Inner cities

It is reasonable to view the development of inner city planning in five phases.

Phase 1 (1946–67)

In 1947 the concept of Comprehensive Development Areas was introduced, launching a massive programme of slum clearance. During this period, when physical planning was seen as the solution to the problems of the inner city, one and a half million properties were knocked down. However, apart

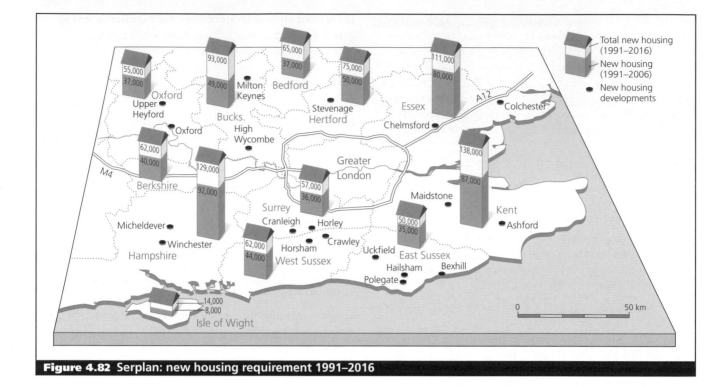

Figure 4.82 Serplan: new housing requirement 1991–2016

Back in fashion

LIKE flared trousers, the concept of the "new town" goes in and out of fashion. Two eye-catching proposals launched this week, one for a town outside Cambridge, the other for three new towns in the south of England, suggest that more of the countryside may give way to bricks and mortar.

This year marks the centenary of the publication of Ebenezer Howard's "Garden Cities of Tomorrow", which set out a revolutionary vision of a modern new town. This led to the founding, at the turn of the century, of garden cities at Letchworth and Welwyn. In celebration, *Sir Peter Hall, chairman of the Town and Country Planning Association, has written a book, published this week, chronicling* the rise of the new town *and setting out proposals for the building of further new towns in Kent, East Anglia and the Midlands.* This week, too, **Peter Dawe, a millionaire entrepreneur, has launched a scheme to build a new town for 50,000 people, five miles outside Cambridge.**

These proposals are a response to projections of the need for new housing. The government reckons that England will need 4.4m new dwellings by 2016, largely because of changing family structures. That represents a 22% increase in the present number of homes over the next 17 years. The government has stipulated that 60% of all new housing should be built on "brownfield" sites—derelict land, preferably in cities. But that implies the other 40% will be on greenfield sites in rural areas.

Mr Dawe, who chairs the Cambridge New Town Corporation, says his approach is entrepreneurial. Towns will be built on the basis of market research rather than architectural whimsy. In this respect the new plans mark a return to Howard's original conception: of garden cities built by private developers, not the government. But environmentalists argue that no matter how pleasant the new towns are, they are still going to be built on greenfield sites. There may, however, be no choice.

But what about objections to paving over more of the already overcrowded south-east of England? A clever solution may have been found by the Cambridge New Town Corporation. Their preferred location is a disused air base, five miles outside the city, which is classified as a brownfield site. If they get the go-ahead to build on this land, it may act as a precedent for the development of other rural brownfield sites, such as disused quarries, military bases and industrial estates. They may constitute a happy half-way house for both developers and government.

Source: *Economist*, 17/10/98

Figure 4.83 *Economist*, 17 October 1998

Figure 4.84 Slum clearance project in the 1950s

from physical reconstruction inner city policy lacked further direction, with little thought given to the social consequences of redevelopment. By the end of the period a number of issues were provoking debate:

- in many instances redevelopment did not keep pace with slum clearance, leaving large areas of derelict land
- clearance often dissected communities leaving a mood of despondency hanging over those who remained
- the tower blocks into which so many were rehoused soon came to be loathed by the majority of their residents. They proved to be particularly unsuitable environments for the old and the young
- the economic decline and social problems of inner cities were largely ignored
- redevelopment was failing to match the pace of decay.

Phase 2 (1967–77)

During this phase two new strands to inner city policy were developed; environmental improvement, and social and economic welfare.

Environmental improvement

- The 1969 Housing Act enabled Local Authorities to set up General Improvement Areas (GIAs) for which grants would be available to improve both housing and the surrounding environment. This was the first move towards renovation as opposed to clearance.
- This trend was strengthened by the 1974 Housing Act which allowed for the establishment of Housing Action Areas (HAAs) in areas of greatest housing and social stress. Successful HAAs could be upgraded into GIAs.

Although the principle of area-based renewal had been firmly established two significant concerns were voiced by critics: (a) the overall scale of improvement was limited by underfunding

(b) in some areas the better off saw their chance of buying cheap rented accommodation for improvement and owner-occupation – the beginnings of gentrification.

Social and economic welfare

The Urban Programme launched in 1968 was a major effort to assist areas of multiple deprivation, many of which were experiencing high rates of immigration. Local authorities and voluntary agencies bid for grants to fund projects such as pre-school provision, child care and community work. From 1967 Education Priority Areas were established to improve the resourcing of schools in difficult areas. Between 1974 and 1979 Comprehensive Community Programmes were introduced to improve the delivery and coordination of welfare services. However, this initiative was limited in scope and in time because of lack of funding. Two major investigative projects, under the titles of Community Development Projects and Inner Areas Studies, were undertaken during this phase with the objective of gaining a better understanding of inner city decline.

Phase 3 (1977–1979)

The publication of the White Paper, 'Policy for the Inner Cities' in 1977 marked the beginning of this phase. At last the inner city was viewed as a problem region requiring broad-based action. The Inner Urban Areas Act of 1978 created Partnership and Programme Areas involving action plans to improve social, economic and environmental conditions in seven metropolitan authorities. A key aim of this new urban policy was to retain existing jobs and hopefully attract new jobs.

Phase 4 (1979–1997)

The new Conservative government continued most of the initiatives begun by Labour in the late 1970s but added a new emphasis. The objective now was for the public and private sectors to work as partners with economic regeneration being the most important aim with environmental and social issues following. Of particular significance were:

- the Enhanced Urban Programme with assistance extended to cover more areas. Greater emphasis was placed on funding projects with an economic focus
- Urban Development Corporations (UDCs), introduced in 1981 with the objective of regenerating large tracts of derelict land in inner cities. Thirteen UDCs were established between 1981 and 1993. The first were set up in London's Docklands and on Merseyside
- Enterprise Zones (EZs) introduced in 1981 to attract growth industries to relatively small (50 to 450 ha) areas of inner city land. For example the EZ in London Docklands covered only about one-tenth of this UDC area run by the London Docklands Development

Figure 4.85 Renovated housing in the 1980s

Corporation. EZs had a ten-year life span during which time the main benefits were exemption from rates, tax allowances for capital expenditure on industrial and commercial property, and a simplified planning regime. 23 were created with no more designated after 1983

■ City Action Teams (CATs) set up in nine cities between 1985 and 1987. These teams of civil servants encouraged joint action between regional government departments to encourage new private sector investment

■ the Inner Cities Initiative (ICI) launched in 1986 created Task Forces in unemployment black spots to 'unlock development opportunities'

■ City Grants which replaced and combined a number of earlier schemes to encourage the private sector to develop run-down inner city areas

■ Land Registers which identified vacant land held by local authorities so that it could be offered for sale to private developers

■ City Challenge announced in 1991. Local authorities were challenged to devise imaginative redevelopment projects and bid against each other for the funding available.

Phase 5 (1997–)

With Labour returning to power in 1997 it was almost inevitable that new inner city policy would be developed. Regional Development Agencies (for England) will commence operation in April 1999 although the London Development Agency will not start up until a year later. A major role of the RDAs will be to manage the Single Regeneration Budget which replaces the previously fragmented nature of the Urban Programme funding. Local authorities have to bid against each other for SRB project funding. The Social Exclusion Unit is examining all aspects of deprivation and has already set up 12 education action zones, 5 employment action zones and 11 health action zones.

Town centres

Town centres have been generally neglected in recent decades as new retail forms have dominated the planning agenda. Five waves of out-of-town retailing have been recognised since the early 1970s (Figure 4.86) as retailers have continued to create new ways to shop in order to boost turnover and increase market share. This has put town centres under intense competition from other locations for the patronage of retailers and developers. Despite central government intervention in the form of PPG 6, it is likely that only the more dynamic town centres will be successful in the future. The worst scenario is that Britain will follow the example of so many American cities to the point where, because of extreme decentralisation, the settlement becomes a 'doughnut' with a hole in the middle.

The centres of many market towns are now in danger of losing the food shopping which brings most people into town. The loss of vitality caused by a decline in pedestrian flow leads in time to a loss of viability as retailers fail to reinvest. As a recent article on the subject stated (*Built Environment* Vol 24, No 1) 'The centre is then left to those with time but no money, thus intensifying the pressures towards suburbanisation and spatial segregation that have bedevilled English towns'.

A recent study of shopping centres in inner London found that most serve only a local, limited catchment area with spending power shifting away to some 30 out-of-town centres. In addition there is competition from superstores and new regional centres like Lakeside, Thurrock and Bluewater. The use of a car for shopping trips in London rose from 23% in 1981 to 41% in 1991. In comparison to the newer peripheral centres shoppers found it difficult to park and unpleasant to walk in traditional centres.

Recently, government policy in the form of PPG 6 (Department of Environment, 1996) has tightened up planning control over off-centre developments, although government views on out-of-town developments had begun to harden from 1993. It seems that central government now regards the availability of a town centre site as sufficient reason for refusing off-centre retail park proposals. Local authorities are increasingly imposing conditions on planning consents for retail parks, usually to restrict retailing to bulky household and electrical goods.

In 1997 the Urban and Environmental Development Group (URBED) published a Department of the Environment sponsored report entitled 'Town Centre Partnerships: Their Organisation and Resourcing'. The report recommended the following:

■ town improvement zones in larger centres loosely modelled on North American business improvement districts

Figure 4.86 Off-centre retail development in the UK

Period	Retail Offer	Store Type	Centre Type
Early 1970s	Food and household goods	Hypermarket	District centre
Mid-1970s	Food	Superstore	District centre
Late 1970s	Household goods	Retail warehouse	
Mid-1980s	Personal goods and fashion	Retail warehouse	Retail park
Late 1980s	All shopping		Regional shopping centre
Early 1990s	Low prices: (food)	Limited line discounter	
	(mixed goods)	Club warehouse	
	(personal and fashion)	Factory outlet	Factory outlet centre

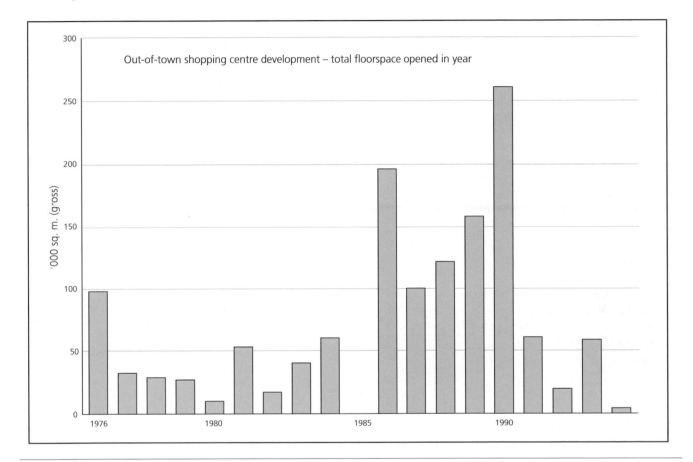

Out-of-town shopping centre development – total floorspace opened in year

Source: Trading Places: The Future of the Town Centre, *Built Environment* Vol 24, No 1

- investment priority areas using incentives such as rate relief to reduce the cost of occupying property in areas of high vacancy, incentives for refurbishment, and penalties on allowing buildings to decay

- a restructuring of the business rate to allow local authorities more flexibility. Planners argue that the current operation of the business rate penalises small businesses and increases the likelihood of properties remaining vacant

- the government should ensure that all the different spending regimes should have a town centre dimension.

Figure 4.87 A declining town centre

Many local authorities have undertaken so-called 'health checks' on town centres and have appointed town centre managers. It is now generally acknowledged that the design of urban space is vital to the success of a town centre. The good practice guide 'Managing Urban Spaces in Town Centres' (DoE/ATCM, 1997) highlights all the elements of good urban design including functional, social, perceptual, spatial, contextual, visual and morphological aspects.

Questions

1 Discuss the development of the New Town concept.
2 Conduct your own research to examine the economic, social and environmental characteristics of one New Town to ascertain to what extent it has fulfilled its original objectives.
3 What are the reasons for and against maintaining a strong Green Belt Policy?
4 How has the direction and emphasis of inner city policy changed in the post-war period?
5 Identify the main issues relating to the planning and management of town centres.

Figure 4.88 Lakeside: a major out-of-town shopping centre

São Paulo: World City

Background: Urbanisation in Brazil

Brazil, like most other countries in South America is highly urbanised. Figure 4.89 shows the speed at which Brazil has changed from a rural to an urban society. Between 1970 and 1995 some 30 million Brazilians moved to urban areas, either 'pushed' from their rural environments by adverse factors or 'pulled' by aspirations of a better life in the cities.

The main push factors responsible for rural to urban migration have been:

■ the mechanisation of agriculture which has reduced the demand for farm labour in most parts of the country

■ the amalgamation of farms and estates, particularly by agricultural production companies

■ the generally poor conditions of rural employment. Employers often ignore laws relating to minimum wages and other employee rights

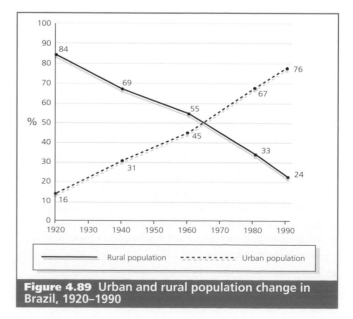

Figure 4.89 Urban and rural population change in Brazil, 1920–1990

- desertification in the Northeast and deforestation in the North
- unemployment and underemployment
- poor social conditions particularly in terms of housing, health and education.

People were attracted to the urban areas because they perceived life there would provide at least some of the following: a greater variety of employment opportunities; higher wages; a higher standard of accommodation; a better education for their children; improved medical facilities; the conditions of infrastructure often lacking in rural areas, and a wider range of consumer services. The diffusion of information from previous migrants was usually such that most potential new migrants realised fully that there was no guarantee of achieving all or even most of the above but most rationalised that their quality of life would hardly decrease overall. Employment was the key. The most fortunate found jobs in the formal sector. A regular wage then gave some access to the other advantages of urban life. However, because the demand for jobs greatly outstripped supply, many could do no better than the uncertainty of the informal sector.

Location and early development

São Paulo was established as a mission station by Jesuit priests in 1554 near the confluence of the Rio Tietê and a southern tributary, the Tamanduatei. It was located 70 km inland at an altitude of 730 m, on the undulating plateau beyond the Serra do Mar. The cool, healthy climate attracted settlers from the coast while the Paraná river system facilitated movement into the interior.

In 1681, São Paulo, as the settlement became known, became a seat of regional government and in 1711 it was constituted as a municipality. Coffee was the catalyst for the rapid growth in the latter part of the nineteenth century that transformed the city into a bustling regional centre. It became the focus of roads and railways and its prosperity was assured by a rail link with the port of Santos, completed in 1867. This was the only major routeway scaling the great escarpment of the Serra do Mar. The profits from coffee were invested in industry and by the end of the century São Paulo had become the financial and industrial centre of Brazil. The wealth of the coffee barons was lavished on sumptuous town houses, and prestigious public buildings mushroomed in the business district, the Triângulo.

Twentieth-century growth

São Paulo's population growth was relatively slow until the late 19th century. In 1874 its population was only about 25 000. However the rapidly increasing demand for labour encouraged immigration and the city's population soared to almost 70 000 by 1890 and reached 239 000 in 1910. The city reached 'millionaire' status in 1934. By 1950 the population had grown to 2.2 million and São Paulo had clearly established its dominant role in the urbanisation of Brazil. Thereafter the population of both the city and the metropolitan area grew rapidly (Figure 4.90) with the

latter reaching 16.5 million in 1995, making it the fifth largest city in the world. The annual growth in population is currently 200 000 in the city and 340 000 in the metropolitan area (Figure 4.91). However, a marked change occurred between 1980 and 1991 (Figure 4.92) with negative net migration recorded for both the City of São Paulo and Greater São Paulo. This appears to be the start of the process of decentralisation that has affected most developed countries over the last half a century.

Original mono-nuclear form

In the early part of the century São Paulo retained its mono-nuclear structure around the Triângulo, its CBD. From here emanated radial highways which were connected by a concentric sub-system which often acted as 'barriers' between different socio-economic areas. In general, residential areas became progressively poorer with distance from the centre, reflecting limited intra-urban mobility and economic concentration in the central area.

Metropolitanisation and industrialisation

The 'metropolitanisation' of the city occurred between 1915 and 1940 due to high rates of both natural increase and immigration. During this period industrialisation had a marked impact on urban structure. The first industrial districts had been located on the south bank flood plain and terraces of the Tietê, but in the 1930s new industrial satellites emerged in the south-east. These areas were to grow rapidly in the following decades and now form the most important industrial region in metropolitan São Paulo, known as the 'ABCD' complex after its constituent districts of Santo André, São Bernardo, São Caetano and Diadema. This is the focal point of Brazil's motor vehicle industry and also the location of a wide variety of other industries.

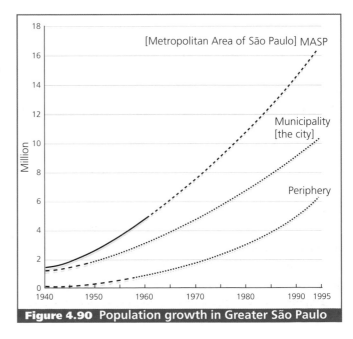

Figure 4.90 Population growth in Greater São Paulo

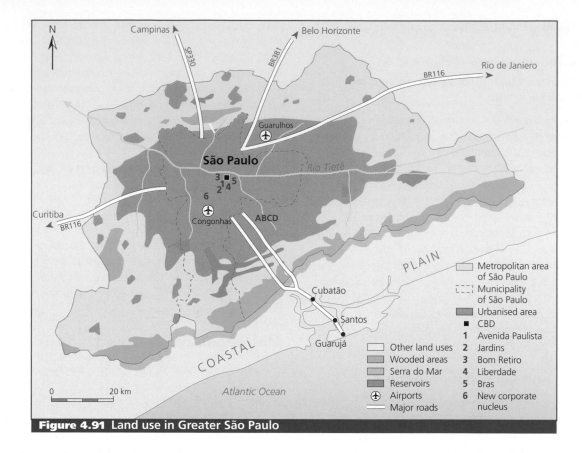

Figure 4.91 Land use in Greater São Paulo

Figure 4.92 Population change: natural change and migration, 1970–91			
	Greater São Paulo	**City of São Paulo**	**State of São Paulo**
Population			
1970	8 139 730	5 924 615	17 771 948
1980	12 588 725	8 493 226	25 040 712
1991	15 416 416	9 626 894	31 546 473
Absolute increase 1970/80	4 448 995	2 568 611	7 268 764
1970/80 Contribution to change			
Natural change (%)	+ 26.45	+ 24.05	+ 6.28
Net migration (%)	+ 28.20	+ 19.31	+ 17.35
Absolute increase 1980/91	2 827 691	1 133 668	6 505 761
1980/91			
Natural change (%)	+ 24.64	+ 22.25	+ 23.64
Net migration (%)	− 2.18	− 8.90	+ 2.34

Until the late 1960s the city largely grew unplanned. The Triângulo had developed all the characteristics which make it indistinguishable from any other central business district, and the 1970s, particularly, saw a huge increase in the construction of high rise apartments for the growing middle class in the inner area. The ravines of the River Tietê had become sites for numerous favelas (many now removed to make way for inner city parklands), and some of the old mansions near the centre had deteriorated into run-down multi-family dwellings.

Low-grade apartment blocks were built for the workers in the industrial suburbs, but demand far exceeded supply and the authorities were obliged to resort to site-and-service schemes. These too, were insufficient, and large areas of unplanned favelas developed. Meanwhile, the very rich had begun to move out to estates within commuting distance of the Triângulo via the new motorways. Here they live in luxurious villas set in extensive gardens, often with swimming pools and staff quarters. Security men stand guard at the entrance.

Figure 4.93 CBD of São Paulo

Property speculation has resulted in large undeveloped areas within the conurbation, which could accommodate a two-thirds increase in population without any further expansion if undeveloped land was put to use. According to official data 25 per cent of the city's 1500 square kilometres remains unoccupied. However, the forested water catchments of the uplands to the south and to the north are now protected by the 1975 Water Resources Protection Law. However, the two main rivers are said to be dead – most residential sewage and industrial effluent flows directly into rivers and reservoirs; only 10 per cent of the solid waste is collected and treated.

The rapid and generally unplanned growth of São Paulo means that the functional differentiation of different parts of the city is less clearly defined than in most Developed World cities. In some cases, squatter settlements are large swathes of urban territory housing hundreds of thousands of people. But more often they are islands of shanty housing, located on vacant land along railway tracks, under flyovers, and in other areas unattractive to the more affluent.

From horizontal to vertical development

In the last 30 years São Paulo has lost its characteristic of being a predominantly horizontal city. As competition for land increased it became more important to take full advantage of inner locations and São Paulo embarked on a period of intense vertical development, a phenomenon in Brazil that first appeared in Rio de Janeiro, a city squeezed between the mountains and the sea. A contributory factor to the high-rise boom has been the increasing concern over crime which reduced single-family residential security to the point where many affluent home-owners began to opt for well protected apartments.

The establishment of the metropolitan region

It was not until 1968 that the first attempts to formulate a comprehensive planning strategy were made, resulting in the establishment of the metropolitan region in 1973. The fundamental objective was to coordinate administration and planning at the various levels of government and in 1974 the Metropolitan Planning and Administration System began to develop the necessary operational tools. The original mono-nuclear city had developed into a poly-nuclear conurbation, a fundamental fact recognised by the Metropolitan Planning Corporation (EMPLASA) when it set out its objectives.

Redevelopment of the central area

The Anhangabaú Valley is the historic heart of the city and for decades was the centre of the economic and cultural activities of São Paulo. However the old nucleus gradually lost its significance with increasing suburbanisation and the huge rise in traffic volume which saturated the valley with over 12 000 vehicles per hour. But in December 1991, the old centre recovered its vitality. After a five year reconstruction, the 77 000 square metre area (one-seventh green space) was reopened to the 1.5 million people who daily cross the centre of the city. Traffic now runs underground in 570 metre-long tunnels that connect the northern and southern sections of the city. Much of the area is now pedestrianised and the most important historic buildings have been renovated.

The Jardins – inner city affluence

No more than a few kilometres southwest of the central area are the most elegant residential areas, comparable to European and North American suburbs. In this area, known as the Jardins, there are 50 m² of greenery per capita; houses average 60 m² per dweller, and the standard of living is that of the upper middle class in most developed countries. The area was laid out in 1915, following the British idea of a garden suburb. It is now dominated by expensive apartment buildings protected by high railings and comprehensive security systems. These exclusive residential neighbourhoods have long since taken over from the city centre as the location of most of the city's best restaurants and shopping streets.

Avenida Paulista – São Paulo's financial centre

To the south-west of the centre and separating it from the Jardins is the 3 km-long Avenida Paulista, the most important financial centre in the city. It is the address of many of the largest banks in the country, two business federations and hundreds of corporations. Mansions once lined this fashionable routeway, but most were replaced in the late 1960s and in the 1970s by skyscrapers. Real estate along the avenue alone is worth $7 billion. The Museu de Arte de São Paulo (MASP) is also located on the avenue.

The southwest – the new corporate nucleus

The corporate addresses in large cities like São Paulo are often related to major road foci. First it was the Anhangabaú Valley, then Avenida Paulista and most recently the road alongside the Pinheiros river. A privileged rectangular area served by four of the most important avenues in the city: Juscelino Kubistchek, Morumbi, Luis Carlos Berrini and Nacoes Unidas has become the favoured location for corporate headquarters. It is not only easy access that favours this location. Modern concepts of integrated management require large areas – often over 1000 m² per floor, impossible to find in other already crowded commercial areas of the city.

From 1986 to 1991, nearly 100 large corporations moved their head offices to modern buildings in this area. Residents include Philips, Dow Chemical, Johnson and Johnson, Hoescht, Autolatina, Fuji and Nestlé. Finance conglomerates like Chase Manhattan and Deutsche Bank also have their offices there. The impressive World Trade Center complex which opened in 1995 acts as the focal point of this office region. Between 1990 and 1993 the area accounted for almost 70 per cent of all new office building in the city.

Shopping malls

Service industry occupies 54.4 million m³ of built area, while manufacturing facilities take up 29.5 million m³. The city has 55 000 shops and 11 shopping malls. The largest shopping mall, Center Norte, is located on the north bank of the River Tietê, about four kilometres north of the CBD. It contains 483 shops on one floor and the parking area can accommodate 17 000 cars.

Transportation

It has been estimated that a quarter of all vehicles in Brazil circulate in São Paulo. Car ownership in the city is rising fast and much has been spent on roads to accommodate this trend. Over 35 per cent of households in the municipality own a car. The noise of traffic on the main roads into and out of the city is incessant twenty-four hours a day. The answer to at least part of the problem is to invest more in public transport which in 1991 was used by 3.4 million passengers daily.

The environment

São Paulo has done much to improve the air quality of the region in recent years with regard to sulphur dioxide and lead. However, levels of other pollutants such as ozone, carbon monoxide and suspended particulate matter are still of concern. Traffic is the greatest emission source in São Paulo.

The City of São Paulo spends $1 million a day on rubbish collection. The cost has risen sharply over the last decade because of (1) a lack of strategic planning (2) a growing population and (3) the rising amount of rubbish per person because of increased consumption. Cost is only one aspect of this problem. The other is

physical disposal; at present the city has only two landfills for rubbish. In an effort to resolve the latter, two enormous waste incinerators, burning 7500 tonnes a day, are expected to begin operation in São Paulo in 1999. São Paulo is now involved in a major project to clean up the Tietê river.

'Sub normal' housing

Brazil's large urban areas could not cope with the large influx of rural migrants. In the early 1970s around 150 migrants arrived in São Paulo every hour. With no prospect of accommodation in the city itself they put up makeshift shelters (*barracos*) on the outskirts of the city. With such a high rate of inmigration these makeshift settlements or '*favelas*' rapidly expanded in size and number. Favelas are found both within the City of São Paulo, which is now basically the inner part of the wider urban area, and of course at the periphery of the wider urban area itself. In the city of São Paulo in 1991 it is estimated that 8.9 per cent of the population lived in favelas. However as many again were classed as living in 'corticos', overcrowded and decaying building in the city itself. Figure 4.94 shows the number of people living in 'sub normal' or inadequate housing in the Municipality of São Paulo, according to the City authorities. These figures include those living in both favelas and corticos. Some favelas are found in close proximity to very affluent areas, a situation known as urban dualism.

The corticos are essentially nineteenth-century large houses in former affluent areas which have been subdivided into a number of one-room dwellings where four or more people live and sleep. Many people live in corticos to be close to their place of work and thus avoid spending money on transportation. For those living at the margin this can make all the difference.

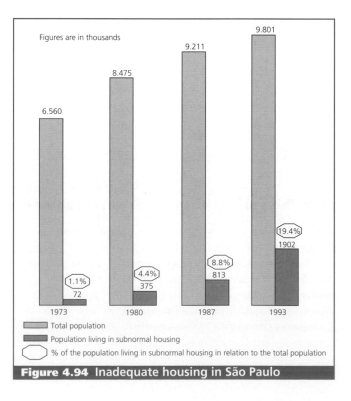

Figure 4.94 Inadequate housing in São Paulo

The Cingapura project

This recently announced project has been named after Singapore's huge slum clearance programme. It aims to replace hundreds of favelas and derelict areas with low-rise blocks of flats. The inhabitants – the *favelados*, are removed to army-like barracks while construction proceeds. Residents will pay for their new homes with low interest 20 year mortgages. The Cingapura project is massive: the initial target is to resettle 92 000 families (about 500 000 people) from 243 favelas. In targeted areas the project provides:

- new housing
- water supply
- modern sewerage systems
- electricity supply for housing and public areas
- building of new streets and ways of access
- garbage collection
- construction of essential community and social facilities
- extensive support for families through its own Social Division.

The fundamental aim of the Cingapura project is to keep those families who are the main target of the project residing in the same geographic area instead of relocating them to other areas. A section of the project is being developed for senior citizens. This is part of a pilot project the Department of Housing and Urban Development is implementing. Aimed initially at the favela problem the City authorities are now looking at the Cingapura project as a model for replacing the derelict corticos. Because it is so esential for people in such dwellings to live within walking distance of employment in the central area, building peripheral estates is clearly not the answer.

1 Summarise the data presented in Figures 4.90, 4.91 and 4.92.
2 How important has industrialisation been to the growth of São Paulo?
3 To what extent and why have large commercial organisations decentralised from the historic heart of the city?
4 Discuss the problems of, and possible solutions for, inadequate housing in São Paulo.

Bibliography

References

Postmodern Urbanism by M.Dear and S.Flusty. *Annals of the Association of American Geographers*, 88(1), 1998, pp.50–72.
Cities in Competition, edited by J. Brotchie et al., Longman, 1995.
Focus on London 97, The Stationery Office, 1996.
Trading Places: The Future of the Town Centre, *Built Environment* 1998, Vol. 24, No1.
British Inner Cities by Hugh Matthews, OUP, 1991.
Interdependent Urbanization in an Urban World: A Historical Overview by David Clarke, *The Geographical Journal*, Vol 164 No 1, March 1998.
Changing settlements by G. Nagle, Nelson, 1998.
World Cities in a World System by P. Knox and T. Taylor, Cambridge, 1995.
The Third World City by D. Drakakis-Smith, Routledge, 1987.
Brazil: Advanced Case Studies by P. Guinness, Hodder & Stoughton, 1998.
North America: An Advanced Geography by B. Price and P. Guinness, Hodder & Stoughton, 1997.

Internet

The Commission for New Towns
http://www.cnt.org.uk/
CTI Centre for Geography
http://www.geog.le.ac.uk/cti/index.html
UK Government Index
http://www.open.gov.uk/index/findex/html

5 economic activity: *the impact of change*

Key Definitions (1)

gross domestic product (GDP) The total value of goods and services produced by a country in a given time period, usually a year.

GDP at purchasing power parity (PPP$) The GDP of a country converted into US dollars on the basis of the purchasing power parity of the country's currency. It is assessed by calculating the number of units of a currency required to purchase the same representative basket of goods and services that a US dollar would buy in the United States. Data is provided on both an absolute and a per capita basis.

World Bank (International Bank for Reconstruction and Development) Established in 1947 to provide aid to developing countries in the form of loans and technical assistance. Originally restricted to supplying loans for capital projects, particularly with regard to infrastructure, from 1980 onwards it was allowed to assist with balance of payment difficulties, subject to the recipient agreeing conditions.

International Monetary Fund (IMF) An international financial organisation established in 1944 with the objective of encouraging international trade by assisting countries with short-term liquidity problems.

General Agreement on Tariffs and Trade (GATT) An international agreement to reduce barriers to trade such as tariffs, quotas and subsidies.

globalisation The increasing integration of national economies through international flows of trade, investment and financial capital.

The global economy

Measurement

Figure 5.1 shows the relative size of the top ten global economies according to the traditional measure, gross domestic product (GDP). However, more and more organisations such as the UN and the International Monetary Fund are publishing GDP data at purchasing power parity (PPP). Once differences in the local purchasing power of currencies are taken into account, China's economy is just over half the size of the United States' (Figure 5.2).

According to the World Bank's 1997 annual report on global economic prospects, developing countries are set to double their share of global output over the next 25 years, taking their importance in the world economy to levels last seen in the early nineteenth century (Figure 5.3). The prediction that developing economies would grow by 5–6 per cent a year between the late 1990s and 2020 would raise their share of world output from around one-sixth to almost a third, a figure last recorded in the 1820s. The growing importance of the developing countries as a whole will be driven by the 'Big Five' – Brazil, China, India, Indonesia and Russia (which in the post-communist era is classed by many analysts as a developing rather than a developed country). They account for 8–10 per cent of world output and trade, a figure that could double by 2020 given continued policy reforms. However, all the big five, to varying degrees, have suffered significant economic problems since late 1997 so that earlier predictions of growth rates are likely to be revised downwards.

World trade: from GATT to the WTO

Trade is the most vital element in the growth of the global economy. In 1948 a group of 23 nations agreed to reduce tariffs on each other's exports under the General Agreement on Tariffs and Trade (GATT). This was the first multilateral accord to lower trade barriers since Napoleonic times. Since the GATT was established there have been eight 'rounds' of global trade talks, of which the most recent, the Uruguay round, was completed in 1993 (Figure 5.4). The most important recent development has been the creation of the World Trade Organisation (WTO). Unlike the loosely organised GATT, the WTO was set up as a permanent organisation with far greater powers to arbitrate trade disputes.

Although agreements have been difficult to broker at times, the overall success of GATT/WTO is undeniable: today average tariffs are only a tenth of what they were when GATT came into force and world trade has been increasing at a much faster rate than GDP (Figure 5.5). However, in some areas protectionism is still alive and well, particularly in clothing, textiles and agriculture. For example, the United States still charges a tariff of 14.6 per cent on imports of clothing, five

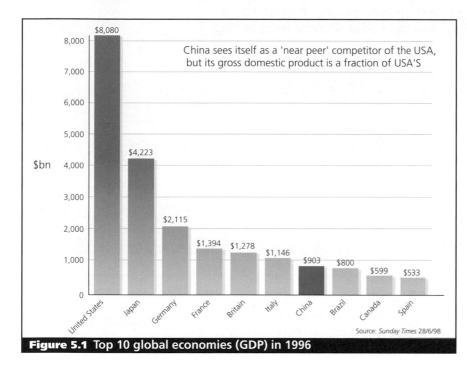

China sees itself as a 'near peer' competitor of the USA, but its gross domestic product is a fraction of USA'S

Source: *Sunday Times* 28/6/98

Figure 5.1 Top 10 global economies (GDP) in 1996

Figure 5.4 A GATT/WTO chronology

1947 Birth of the GATT, signed by 23 countries on October 30th at the Palais des Nations in Geneva.

1948 The GATT comes into force. First meeting of its members in Havana, Cuba.

1949 Second round of talks at Annecy, France. Some 5000 tariff cuts agreed to; ten new countries admitted.

1950–51 Third round at Torquay, England. Members exchange 8700 trade concessions and welcome four new countries.

1956 Fourth round at Geneva. Tariff cuts worth $1.3 trillion at today's prices.

1960–62 The Dillon round, named after US Under-Secretary of State Douglas Dillon, who proposed the talks. A further 4400 tariff cuts.

1964–67 The Kennedy round. Many industrial tariffs halved. Signed by 50 countries. Code on dumping agreed to separately.

1973–79 The Tokyo round, involving 99 countries. First serious discussion of non-tariff trade barriers, such as subsidies and licensing requirements. Average tariff on manufactured goods in the nine biggest markets cut from 7% to 4.7%.

1986–93 The Uruguay round. Further cuts in industrial tariffs, export subsidies, licensing and customs valuation. First agreements on trade in services and intellectual property.

1995 Formation of World Trade Organisation with power to settle disputes between members.

1997 Agreements concluded on telecommunications services, information technology and financial services.

1998 The WTO now has 132 members. More than 30 others are waiting to join.

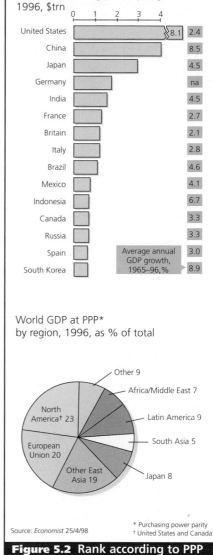

World GDP at PPP* by region, 1996, as % of total

Source: *Economist* 25/4/98
* Purchasing power parity
† United States and Canada

Figure 5.2 Rank according to PPP

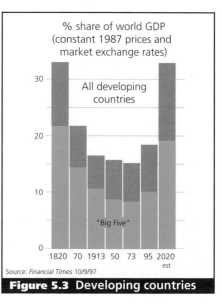

Source: *Financial Times* 10/9/97

Figure 5.3 Developing countries

times higher than its average levy. Tariffs and other barriers on farm products average 40 per cent worldwide, a major challenge to the next set of global farm talks due to begin in 1999. Another big contemporary challenge is to assist trade in services, which is growing faster than trade in goods. The next round of service talks is planned to commence in 2000. However, the most difficult issues currently facing the WTO concern labour standards and the environment where the gap in

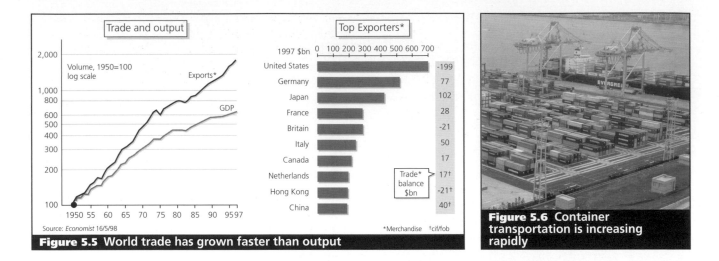

Figure 5.5 World trade has grown faster than output

Figure 5.6 Container transportation is increasing rapidly

Figure 5.7 World competitiveness index, 1998

perception between rich and poor countries is extremely wide.

In 1996 Europe accounted for 47.9 per cent of world merchandise exports, followed by Asia (25.6 per cent), North America (16.2 per cent), Latin America (4.9 per cent), the Middle East (3.2 per cent) and Africa (2.3 per cent). In terms of the composition of merchandise exports, agricultural products accounted for 11.4 per cent, mining products for 11.2 per cent, and manufactures for 73.3 per cent. In total, global merchandise exports were valued at $5127 billion in 1996. In the same year global exports of commercial services totalled $1257 billion.

Regional trade agreements

Regional trade agreements have proliferated in the last decade. In 1990 there were less than 25; by 1998 there were more than 90. The most notable of these are the European Union, NAFTA in North America, ASEAN in Asia, and Mercosur in Latin America. The United Nations (1990) refer to such organisations as 'geographically discriminatory trading arrangements'. All but three of the WTO's 132 members (the exceptions are Japan, South Korea and Hong Kong) belong to at least one regional pact. All such arrangements have one unifying characteristic: the preferential terms of trade participants have over non-participating countries. Although no regional group has as yet adopted rules contrary to those of the WTO, there are some concerns:

- **regional agreements can divert trade, inducing a country to import from a member of its trading bloc rather than from a cheaper supplier elsewhere**
- **regional groups might raise barriers against each other, creating protectionist blocks**

- **regional trade rules may complicate the establishment of new global regulations.**

Competitiveness

A major factor contributing to a country's economic strength is the ability to compete in the global market place. Although the concept of 'competitiveness' is difficult to define, a few attempts have been made in recent years to rank countries according to this attribute. One of the better-known analyses is produced annually by the Institute for Management Development in Lausanne, Switzerland (Figure 5.7). The index is based on 223 criteria, intended to capture a country's ability to help firms compete. Positive factors include an efficient banking system, low budget deficits and a high level of research and development. Protectionism, high labour costs and low skill levels are examples of negative factors in competitiveness terms. Analysis of Figure 5.7 and other data published on this subject reveals reasonably clear geographical patterns.

The causes of growth

There has been much debate about the cause of economic growth. The Harvard Institute for International Development (HIID) analysing global patterns of growth during 1965–90, concluded that variations between countries were due to:

- initial conditions: if other factors are equal poorer countries tend to grow faster than richer ones as the potential for growth from a low base point is much greater
- physical geography: (a) landlocked countries grew more slowly than coastal ones with entirely landlocked countries suffering a deficit of 0.7 per cent in terms of annual growth. (b) tropical countries grew more slowly (1.3 per cent per year) than those in temperate latitudes reflecting the cost of poor health and unproductive farming. However, richer non-agricultural tropical countries such as Singapore do not suffer a geographical deficit of this kind. (c) a generous allocation of natural resources spurred economic growth
- economic policies: (a) open economies grew 1.2 per cent faster per year than closed economies. (b) fast-growing countries tend to have high rates of saving and low spending relative to GDP. (c) institutional quality in terms of law and order, efficiency of public administration, lack of corruption etc. delivers a high rate of growth
- demography: progress through demographic transition was a significant factor with the highest rates of growth experienced by those nations where the birth rate had fallen the most.

Figure 4.8 shows to what extent and why South Asia, Sub-Saharan Africa, and Latin America had slower growth rates than East and South East Asia between 1965 and 1990 according to the HIID analysis.

Globalisation and the communications revolution

The transformation towards a knowledge-based global economy is being driven by a number of forces at the forefront of which are:

- the growing role of information and communication technologies (ICT). The world market for information technology grew twice as fast as GDP between 1987 and 1995
- the increasing importance of services
- the globalisation of markets and societies.

The term globalisation has been applied to the increased integration of national economies in the 1990s through cross-border flows of trade, investment and financial capital. However, this is not the first time that such a surge in international economic integration has taken place. The fifty years or so before the First World War saw large cross-border flows of goods, capital and people. That period of integration, like the present one, was driven by reductions in trade barriers and by sharp falls in transport costs, thanks to the development of railways and steamships. In contrast, today's globalisation is being driven by plunging communication costs, creating new ways to organise firms at a global level.

The global telephone network has grown nearly tenfold in the past 40 years and will reach almost a billion lines by 2000

Figure 5.8 Contribution of selected factors to the difference between growth (per person, per year) in the regions shown and growth in East and South East Asia, 1965–90 %

	South Asia	Sub-Saharan Africa	Latin America
Initial conditions	**0.3**	**0.7**	**−1.2**
Initial GDP per person	0.5	1.0	−1.2
Schooling	−0.2	−0.4	−0.1
Policy variables	**−2.1**	**−1.7**	**−1.8**
Government saving rate	−0.4	−0.1	−0.3
Openness	−1.2	−1.2	−1.0
Institutional quality	−0.5	−0.4	−0.5
Demography	**−0.9**	**−1.9**	**−0.2**
Life expectancy	−0.5	−1.3	0.1
Growth in working-age population	−0.3	0.1	−0.2
Growth in total population	−0.2	−0.7	−0.1
Resources and geography	**0.2**	**−1.0**	**−0.6**
Natural resources	0.1	−0.2	−0.2
Landlocked	0.0	−0.3	−0.1
Tropics	0.5	−0.2	0.0
Ratios of coastline distance to land area	−0.3	−0.3	−0.3
Predicted difference in growth	**−2.5**	**−3.9**	**−3.8**
Actual difference	**−2.9**	**−4.0**	**−3.9**

Source: *Economist* 14/6/97

(Figure 5.9a). Teledensity, the number of lines per 100 people, has quadrupled since 1960, although a quarter of the world's nations still have a teledensity below one. As Figure 5.9b shows, the speed of network growth is increasing.

Of enormous significance are the new information pipelines linking the players of greatest importance in the global economy. The transoceanic copper wires that made communications possible in the pre-satellite era are being replaced by arrays of sophisticated fibre optics capable of carrying huge amounts of data. Where these prime conduits for the technological revolution are routed is of great significance for change in the future. The most important of the recently constructed links are:

- **The FLAG (Fiberoptic Link Around the Globe) project, a $1.5 billion, 28 000 km underwater cable snaking its way across the ocean floor from Britain to Japan. It offers uninterrupted data traffic between Europe and Asia, traffic that was previously routed through the US. The magazine *Time* stated in 1997 'It is akin to opening a new navigation route that will link 75 per cent of the world's population. Its 5 gigabits of information a second will allow for a huge increase in electronic traffic'.**
- **The SEA-ME-WE 3 cable, approved in January 1997 by the 70 countries involved in its construction. The $1.73 billion project stretches 38 000 km and connects Western Europe, the Middle East and South East Asia with fibre-optic technology capable of carrying 120 000 simultaneous phone conversations.**

Fibre-optic cables have a number of advantages over satellite transmission. Voice and data traffic is faster, cheaper, more reliable and subject to less interference. However, the submarine pipelines are vulnerable to both physical and human attack. The cable routes pass through some of the planet's major troublespots.

The cost of computer processing power has been falling by an average of 30 per cent a year in real terms over the past couple of decades (Figure 5.9c). With the costs of communication and computing falling rapidly, the natural barriers of time and space that separate national markets have been tumbling too.

The twenty-first century economy

The economic crisis which began in Asia in 1997 and spread to other parts of the world produced many gloomy predictions for the global economy moving into the new millennium. In September 1998 the International Labour Office put worldwide measured unemployment at 150 million, an increase of 10 million as a result of the Asian crisis, with further rises expected. In addition, the ILO calculates that between 750 and 900 million people are underemployed. However, some of the business and financial journals are very upbeat about the global economy in the medium and long term (Figure 5.11).

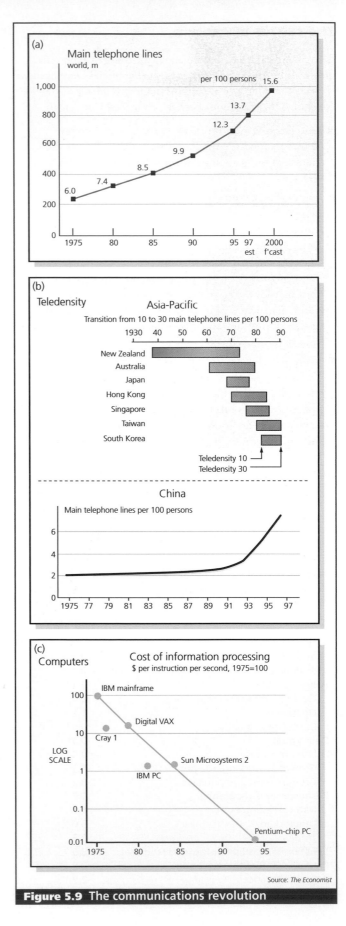

Source: *The Economist*

Figure 5.9 The communications revolution

Figure 5.10 Telecommunications: backbone of the new century?

THE 21st CENTURY ECONOMY

Despite Asia's woes, all the ingredients are in place for a surge of innovation that could rival any in history. Over the next decade or so, the New Economy [of the 1990s]—so far propelled mainly by information technology—may turn out to be only the initial stage of a much broader flowering of technological, business, and financial creativity that will sweep across the world.

Call it the 21st Century Economy—an economy that, driven by technological progress, can grow at 3% pace for years to come. The innovation pipeline is fuller than it has been in decades. With the advent of the Internet, the information revolution seems to be spreading and accelerating rather than slowing down. Biotechnology is on the verge of having a major economic impact, and in labs, scientists are testing the frontiers of nanotechnology, with the goal of creating new devices that can transform entire industries.

What's more, the U.S. economy seems to be undergoing a wholesale rejuvenation. Businesses, financial services firms, and universities are reinventing themselves. Even politicians and policymakers are starting to grasp the new technological and economic realities.

To be sure, the path from the New Economy to the 21st Century Economy will likely be a bumpy one. Each innovative surge creates economic and social ills, from recessions to stock-market crashes to widespread job losses—and this one won't be different. But that's the price a nation must pay to achieve the benefits of dynamic change.

Figure 5.11 *Business Week*, 31 August 1998

While the 1980s was the Japanese decade, according to most indicators the 1990s has turned out to be a decade of unexpected prosperity for the United States – what some of the American journals have called 'the New Economy'. The assertion is that the New Economy is the beginning of a major new wave of innovation. Historically, periods of major innovation have brought substantial increases in living standards. The view is that the latest wave could make it much easier to address some of the vexing social and environmental problems that affect individual countries and global society in general.

Questions

1 Why do some economists prefer to make international comparisons of GDP on the basis of purchasing power parity (PPP) rather than on the use of crude rates?
2 Assess the importance of GATT/ WTO to the global economy.
3 How might the development of regional trade agreements hinder the future liberalisation of world trade?
4 Analyse the data presented in Figure 5.8.
5 Examine the role of communications in the global economy.
6 With reference to Figure 5.11 explain the term 'The twenty-first century economy'.

Sectors and systems

Sectors of employment

In all modern economies of a significant size people do hundreds, and in some cases thousands, of different jobs, all of which can be placed into four broad economic sectors:

■ the primary sector exploits raw materials from land, water and air. Farming, fishing, forestry, mining and quarrying make up most of the jobs in this sector. Some primary products are sold directly to the consumer but most go to secondary industries for processing

■ the secondary sector manufactures primary materials into finished products. Activities in this sector include the production of processed food, furniture and motor vehicles. Secondary products are classed either as

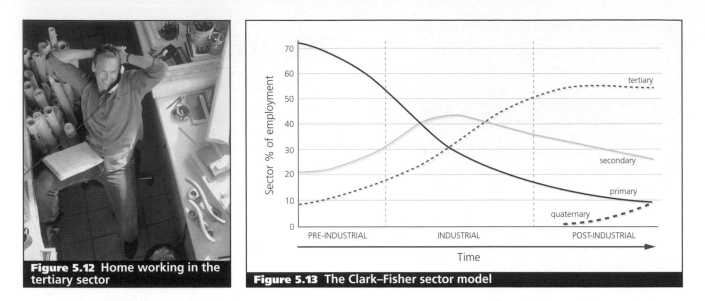

Figure 5.12 Home working in the tertiary sector

Figure 5.13 The Clark–Fisher sector model

consumer goods (produced for sale to the public) or capital goods (produced for sale to other industries)

■ the tertiary sector provides services to businesses and to people. Retail employees, drivers, architects and nurses are examples of occupations in this sector

■ the quaternary sector uses high technology to provide information and expertise. Research and development is an important part of this sector. Quaternary industries have only been recognised as a separate group since the late 1960s. Before then, jobs now classed as quaternary were placed in either the secondary or tertiary sectors depending on whether a tangible product was produced or not. However, even today much of the available information on employment does not consider the quaternary sector.

As an economy advances the proportion of people employed in each sector changes (Figure 5.13). Countries such as the United States, Japan and the UK are 'post-industrial societies' where the majority of people are employed in the tertiary sector with the quaternary sector growing rapidly. Yet in 1900 forty per cent of employment in the United States was in the primary sector. However, the mechanisation of farming, mining, forestry and fishing drastically reduced the demand for labour in these industries. As these jobs disappeared people moved to urban areas where most secondary, tertiary and quaternary employment is located. Less than 4 per cent of employment in the United States is now in the primary sector.

Human labour is steadily being replaced in manufacturing too. In more and more factories, robots and other advanced machinery handle assembly line jobs which once employed large numbers of people. Automation is expensive to install but in the long term it reduces wage bills considerably. In 1950 the same number of Americans were employed in manufacturing as in services. By 1980 two-thirds were working in services.

The tertiary and quaternary sectors are also changing. In banking, insurance and many other types of business, computer networks have reduced the number of people required. But elsewhere service employment is rising such as in health, education and tourism. The employment structure of a country or region is an important influence on spatial patterns and processes.

Economic systems

The economic system of a country describes the relationship that exists between consumers, producers and the state. Economists recognise the following types of economic system:

■ traditional – a non-monetary system based largely on subsistence with limited exchange conducted through bartering. Only the most isolated societies in the world remain in this category

■ free market – a system run entirely by private enterprise with no public ownership. This is a theoretical concept as no national economy has ever reached this extreme, but the United States is generally recognised as the nearest country to a free market economy

■ centrally planned – a system where the state decides what is to be produced, where production will be located, and what can be consumed. Such a system, denying private ownership, is associated with communist states. Although another theoretical extreme, many countries, the former Soviet Union in particular before the fall of communism, came very close to it

■ mixed – where some sectors of an economy are in public ownership and others in private. The nations of western Europe are classic examples of this type of system.

The geography of economic systems is dynamic, being particularly so over the last two decades. Clearly, traditional systems, which are largely rural based, were once more prevalent than they are today. Since the early 1980s many countries which had a reasonable balance between public and private ownership, the classic mixed economies, have privatised most of their publicly-owned industries on the premise that private ownership is more efficient. This has had a major impact on spatial decision making. For example, the privatisation of electricity in Britain hastened the decline of coal as a source of power resulting in a significant drop in the proportion of power stations which are coal-fired and closure of many coal mines. In the mid-1980s the concepts of 'glasnost' and 'perestroika' introduced into the Soviet Union by President Gorbachev began the demise of central planning and the introduction of the concept of private ownership in communist countries. This change is having an important influence on geographical patterns in all the countries it is embracing.

Manufacturing industry

Classification and importance

In an advanced economy manufacturing industry covers a wide range of processes and products. In the UK's Standard Industrial Classification, manufacturing occupies three of the ten employment divisions. Some industries such as textiles and shipbuilding, which were of major importance during the industrial revolution, have shed employment consistently over much of the twentieth century. Production has in general been lost to competitors benefiting from cheaper labour and other advantages. However, even for industries with stable or rising production, employment has generally declined as increasing investment in capital has replaced labour.

For developed countries the share of GDP accounted for by manufacturing industry has been in decline in recent decades (Figure 5.14). This has occurred more recently in some developing nations (Figure 5.15).

Industries are also described or classified by the use of opposing terms. The most frequently used are:

- large scale and small scale – depending on the size of plant and machinery, and the numbers employed
- heavy and light – depending on the nature of processes and products in terms of unit weight
- market oriented and raw material oriented – where the location of the industry or firm is drawn either towards the market or the inputs required, usually because of transportation costs
- processing and assembly – the former involving the direct processing of raw materials with the latter putting together parts and components

1 Account for the declining importance of first agriculture and then manufacturing industry to the economies of developed countries.
2 Suggest how the change from a centrally planned to a market economy might affect geographical patterns within a country.

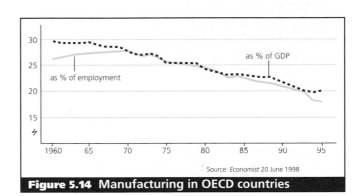

Source: *Economist* 20 June 1998

Figure 5.14 **Manufacturing in OECD countries**

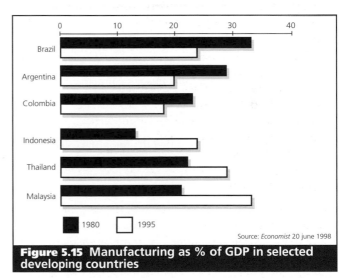

1980   1995

Source: *Economist* 20 june 1998

Figure 5.15 **Manufacturing as % of GDP in selected developing countries**

- capital intensive and labour intensive – depending on the ratio of investment on plant and machinery to the number of employees
- Fordist and flexible – Fordist industries, named after the assembly line methods used in the early automobile industry mass produce standardised products. Flexible industries make a range of specialised products using high technology to respond quickly to changes in demand
- national and transnational – many firms in the small to medium size range manufacture in only one country. Transnationals, which are usually extremely large companies, produce in at least two countries but may manufacture in dozens of nations.

Location, scale and change

Significant spatial variations are apparent in the location of manufacturing industry from the global to the intra-urban scales. At the global scale the Developed World still retains the lion's share of industrial production although there have been significant changes in the last thirty or forty years led by the rapid development of the Newly Industrialised Countries (NICs). Some of these, led by South Korea and Taiwan, have recently invested considerable sums of money in manufacturing facilities in the Developed World. The share of manufacturing accounted for by the Developing World will take another major step forward as the largest countries in this global sector, led by China and India, extend their industrial capabilities. This 'global shift' has been resourced in two ways: by transnationals based in developed countries seeking lower cost locations elsewhere; and by indigenous investment within the Developing World.

Within each country, rich or poor, there are areas where manufacturing is highly concentrated and other regions where it is largely absent. In the United States the Northeast 'manufacturing belt', which covers only one-eighth of the country, has over 40 per cent of all manufacturing jobs although at the turn of the twentieth century the figure was around 70 per cent. In the latter part of the century in particular, industry in the United States has been drawn towards the 'sunbelt' states of the south and the west for a number of important locational reasons. Similar concentrations can be recognised in other countries as well as changes in location over time. Everywhere the most significant locational change has been from traditional manufacturing regions, more often than not on coalfields, to higher quality of life regions offering the hard and soft infrastructural requirements of modern industry.

Within individual regions, such as in the standard economic regions of the UK, manufacturing has historically concentrated in and around the largest urban agglomerations. However, in recent decades there been a significant shift of industry towards 'greenfield' rural locations. This movement has been so great that it is generally recognised as the most important locational change in the Developed World in the latter part of the twentieth century.

At the urban scale the relative shift from inner city to suburbs has increased as the century has progressed, impacting clearly on both of these urban regions. Although there has been much debate about the demise of the inner city many would agree that the loss of employment, much of it in manufacturing, was the initiating factor in the cycle of decline. The dereliction and social pathologies of inner cities have presented major problems to the different levels of government. In the suburbs the location of both large individual firms and the construction of major industrial estates have contributed to urban sprawl and intensified the competition for land use.

Questions

1 Suggest reasons for the different trends experienced by the two groups of developed countries referred to in Figure 5.15.
2 Find examples to illustrate the opposing terms that can be used to classify industry.
3 Briefly discuss the major changes that have occurred in the location of industry in the twentieth century.

Industrial location: influential factors

Every day decisions are made about where to locate industrial premises, ranging from small workshops to huge industrial complexes. In general, the larger the company the greater the number of real alternative locations available. For each possible location a wide range of factors can impact on total costs and thus influence the decision making process. The factors affecting location will differ from industry to industry and their relative importance is subject to change over time.

Raw materials

Industries which use raw materials directly, such as oil refining and metal smelting, are known as processing industries. Once the dominant type of manufacturing, processing industries are in a minority today as most industries now use components and parts made by other firms.

The processes involved in turning a raw material into a manufactured product usually result in weight loss so that the transport costs incurred in bringing the raw materials to the factory will be greater than the cost of transporting the finished product to market. If weight loss is substantial the location of the factory will be drawn towards its most costly to transport raw material(s). The clearest examples of this influence are where one raw material only is used. In Britain, sugar beet refineries are centrally located in crop growing areas because there is a 90 per cent weight loss in manufacture.

In many processing industries technological advance has reduced the amount of raw material required per finished product and in some cases less bulky and cheaper substitutes have been found. Thus, across the industrial board the raw material requirement per unit of finished product has been reduced.

Tidewater locations are particularly popular with industries using significant quantities of imported raw materials. Examples include flour milling, food processing, chemicals and oil refining. Tidewater locations are break-of-bulk points where cargo is unloaded from bulk carriers and transferred to

Key Definitions ②

break of bulk   A location, such as a seaport, where freight has to be transferred from one mode of transport (usually an ocean-going bulk carrier) to another (usually rail or road).

hard infrastructure   The basic utilities (road, rail, air links; water, sewage and telephone systems etc.) which provide a network that benefits business and the community.

soft infrastructure   Other services such as health, education, banking and retailing that are important to business and the community.

industrial inertia   The continued presence of an industry in an area even though the factors which caused it to locate there originally no longer apply.

industrial revolution   The transformation in the late eighteenth and the nineteenth centuries of first Britain and then other European countries and the United States from agricultural into industrial nations.

sectoral spatial division of labour   The concentration of specific industrial skills in particular regions or countries.

Figure 5.16 Heavy industry: iron and steel production

Figure 5.17 Small workshop manufacturing

smaller units of transport for further movement. However, if raw materials are processed at the break-of-bulk point, significant savings in transport costs can be made.

Energy

The industrial revolution in Britain and many other countries was based on the use of coal as a fuel which was usually much more costly to transport than the raw materials required for processing. It is therefore not surprising that outside of London most of Britain's industrial towns and cities developed on coalfields or at ports nearby. The coalfields became focal points for the developing transport networks, first canals, then rail, and finally road. The investment in both hard and soft infrastructure was massive so that even when new forms of energy were substituted for coal, many industries remained at their coalfield locations, a phenomenon known as industrial inertia. Apart from the advantages of the infrastructure in place the cost of relocating might be prohibitive. Also, a certain number of new industries have been attracted to urban areas on coalfields because of the acquired advantages available such as a pool of skilled labour and the existing network of linkages between firms. However overall, the coalfields have suffered considerable economic distress due to the decline of coal and the traditional industries associated with it. So much so that they constitute the main problem regions in many developed countries.

During the twentieth century the construction of national electricity grids and gas pipeline systems has made energy virtually a ubiquitous resource in the Developed World. As a

Figure 5.18 Eidfjord: HEP providing cheap energy to Bergen, Norway

result most modern industry is described as footloose in that it is not tied to certain areas because of its energy requirement or other factors. However, there are some industries that are constrained in terms of location because of an extremely high energy requirement. For example, the lure of low cost hydroelectric power has resulted in a huge concentration of electrometallurgical and electrochemical industries in southern Norway.

Transport

Although once a major locational factor the share of industry's total costs accounted for by transportation has fallen steadily over time. For most manufacturing firms in the UK, transportation now accounts for less than 4 per cent of total costs. The main reasons for this reduction are:

- major advances in all modes of transport
- great improvements in the efficiency of transport networks
- technological developments moving industry to the increasing production of higher value/lower bulk goods.

The cost of transport has two components: fixed (terminal) costs and line-haul costs. Fixed costs are accrued by the equipment used to handle and store goods, and the costs of providing the transport system. Line-haul costs refer to the cost of actually moving the goods and are largely composed of fuel costs and wages. In Figure 5.19 the costs of the main methods of freight transport are compared. While water and pipeline transport have higher fixed costs than rail and road their line-haul costs are significantly lower. Air transport, which suffers from both high fixed and line-haul costs, is only used for high value freight or for goods such as flowers which are extremely perishable. Other factors affecting the cost of transport are:

- the type of load carried – perishable and breakable commodities which require careful handling are more costly to move than robust goods such as iron ore and coal
- journeys that involve transferring cargo from one mode of transport to another are more costly than those using the same mode of transport throughout
- the degree of competition within and between the competing modes of transport.

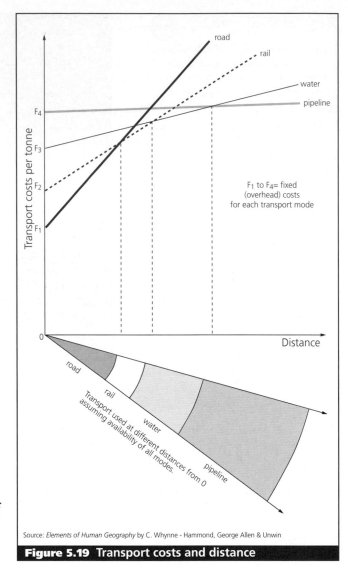

Source: *Elements of Human Geography* by C. Whynne - Hammond, George Allen & Unwin

Figure 5.19 Transport costs and distance

Land

The space requirements of different industries, and also of firms within the same industry, vary enormously. Technological advance has made modern industry much more space-efficient than in the past. However, the other side of the coin is that modern industry is horizontally structured (on one floor) as opposed to, for example, the textile mills of the nineteenth century with four or five floors. In the modern factory transportation takes up much more space than it used to. Consider, for example, the area required to park cars for a firm employing 300 people.

During the industrial revolution entrepreneurs had a relatively free choice of where to locate, providing of course they could afford to purchase the site desired. However with the passage of time more and more areas have been placed off limits to industry, mainly in an effort to conserve the environment. Areas such as National Parks, Country Parks and Areas of Special Scientific Interest now occupy a significant part of Britain. In urban areas, land use zoning considerably restricts where industry may locate and green belts often prohibit location at the edge of urban areas.

Capital

Capital represents the finance invested to start up a business and to keep it in production. That part of capital invested in plant and machinery is known as fixed capital as it is not mobile compared with working capital (money). Capital is obtained either from shareholders (share capital) or from banks or other lenders (loan capital). Some geographers also use the term 'social capital' which is the investment in housing, schools, hospitals and other amenities valued by the community, which may attract a firm to a particular location.

In the early days of the industrial revolution in the present-day developed countries, the availability of capital was geographically constrained by the location of the major capital-raising centres and by limited knowledge, and therefore confidence, about untested locations. It was thus one of the factors that led to the clustering of industry. In the modern world the rapid diffusion of information and the ability to raise and move capital quickly within and across international borders means that this factor has a minimal constraining influence in the Developed World today. However, in less developed economies the constraints of capital are usually greater depending on the level of economic development. It is the perceived risk that is the vital factor. The political unrest that has dogged so many African countries in recent decades has made it very difficult for these nations to raise the amount of capital desired.

Virtually all industries have over time substituted capital for labour in an attempt to reduce costs and improve quality, so, in a competitive environment capital has become a more important factor in industry. In some industries the level of capital required to enter the market with a reasonable chance of success is so high that only a few companies monopolise the market. This has a major influence on the geography of manufacturing.

Labour

The interlinked attributes of labour that influence locational decision making are cost, quality, availability and reputation.

Although all industries have become more capital intensive over time, labour still accounts for over 20 per cent of total costs in manufacturing industry across the board. The cost of labour can be measured in two ways; as wage rates and as unit costs (Figure 5.20). The former is simply the hourly or weekly amount paid to employees while the latter is a measure of

productivity, relating wage rates to output. Industrialists are mainly influenced by unit costs which explains why industry often clusters where wages are higher rather than in areas where wage rates are low. It is frequently, although not always, the high quality and productivity of labour that pushes up wages in an area. In such an area unit costs may well be considerably lower than in an economically depressed area with poor quality labour and lower wage rates. Certain skills sometimes become concentrated in particular areas, a phenomenon known as the sectoral spatial division of labour. As the reputation of a region for a particular skill or set of skills grows, more firms in that particular economic sector will be attracted to the area.

Variation in wage rates can be identified at different scales. By far the greatest disparity is at the global scale. The low wages paid to semi-skilled labour has been a major reason for transnational investment in regions such as South East Asia and Latin America. A filter-down of industry to lower and lower wage economies can be recognised in particular in Asia.

At the continental scale wage differentials can still be substantial. Within the EU there is a large gap between Germany and Greece. At the national scale wage variation is usually of a lesser magnitude, particularly where trade union membership is strong. In the UK, a history of national pay bargaining has resulted in a narrow regional wage range with most differences between regions accounted for by industry mix.

Recent analyses of labour costs in manufacturing have highlighted the wide variations in non-wage labour costs which include employer social security contributions, payroll taxes, holiday pay, sick leave and other benefits. Figure 5.21 shows the range for the EU in 1996. In Italy, Austria, France, Belgium, Spain, Germany and Portugal non-wage labour costs were more than double the rate in Britain.

The availability of labour as measured by high rates of unemployment is not an important location factor for most industries. The regions of the UK that have struggled most to attract new industry are the traditional industrial areas which

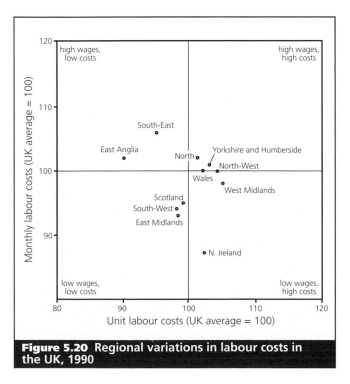

Figure 5.20 Regional variations in labour costs in the UK, 1990

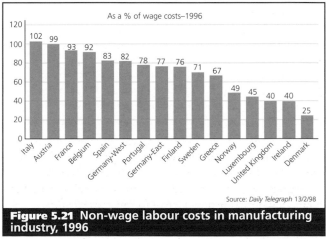

Figure 5.21 Non-wage labour costs in manufacturing industry, 1996

have consistently recorded the highest unemployment rates. In such regions, although there are many people available for work, they frequently lack the skills required by modern industry. The physical dereliction and the social problems generated by unemployment also act to deter new investment. Where availability really has an impact is in sparsely populated areas because large prospective employers know that they will struggle to assemble enough workers with the required skills. Thus, such regions are often ruled out at the beginning of the locational search.

The fact that there have always been considerable regional differences in unemployment in the UK, a relatively small country, indicates that the geographical mobility of labour is limited. A major factor impeding the movement of labour from region to region is the huge differential in the cost of housing between the South East and the traditional industrial areas. In general the degree of geographical mobility increases with skill levels and qualifications. It is the most able and financially secure that can best overcome the obstacles to mobility.

People can of course move from one type of job to another within the same town or region. Such movement is referred to as occupational mobility. However, like geographical mobility it is limited in extent. People who have been employed in heavy industry, in particular, often find it very difficult to adjust to working environments that are less physically demanding but require much more in terms of concentration.

The reputation of a region's labour force can influence inward investment. Regions with militant trade unions and a record of work stoppages are frequently avoided in the locational search. In the United States, manufacturing firms often avoid states in the Northeast where trade union membership is high, favouring instead the South and the West where union influence is minimal. Trade union membership in the UK and most other countries has weakened in recent decades for two main reasons:
(a) many governments have passed legislation to restrict the power of unions and
(b) the decline in employment in manufacturing, the historic nucleus of trade unionism, has had severe implications for membership.

Markets

Where a firm sells its products may considerably influence where a factory is located. Where the cost of distributing the finished product is a significant part of total cost and the greater part of total transport costs a market location is logical. However, there are other reasons for market location; at both national and international scales, industries where fashion and taste are variable need to be able to react quickly to changes demanded by their customers. For example, one of the reasons why the global car giants spread themselves around the world is to ensure that they can produce vehicles which customers will buy in the different world regions.

Agglomeration economies

These are the benefits that accrue to a firm by locating in an established industrial area. Agglomeration economies, known as external economies of scale by economists, can be subdivided into:

- **urbanisation economies, which are the cost savings resulting from urban location due to factors such as the range of producer services available and the investment in infrastructure already in place, and**
- **localisation economies which occur when a firm locates close to suppliers (backward linkages) or firms which it supplies (forward linkages). This reduces transport costs, allows for faster delivery, and facilitates a high level of personal communication between firms.**

However, when an urban-industrial area reaches a certain size urbanisation diseconomies may come into play. High levels of traffic congestion may push up transport costs. Intense competition for land will increase land prices and rents. If the demand for labour exceeds the supply wages will rise. Thus, locating in such a region may no longer be advantageous with fewer new firms arriving and some existing firms relocating elsewhere. In the United States such a process has occurred in the Santa Clara valley (Silicon Valley) with entrepreneurs looking in particular at the less crowded Mountain states such as Arizona and Colorado.

Government policy

Clearly, in the old-style centrally planned economies of the communist countries the influence of government on industry was absolute. In other countries the significance of government intervention has depended on:

- **the degree of public ownership**
- **the strength of regional policy in terms of restrictions and incentives.**

Governments influence industrial location for economic, social and political reasons. Regional policy largely developed after the Second World War although examples of legislation with a regional element can be found before this time. There is a high level of competition both between countries and between regions in the same country to attract foreign direct investment.

Currency exchange rates

When the value of the pound rises compared to other currencies it is good news for Britons going on holiday abroad but it creates problems for British companies that sell to other countries. The price of British products increases in foreign markets and potential customers may well opt for lower priced products from elsewhere. In 1998 Harris Tweed, a hallmark of quality British clothing abroad, was at crisis point because of

1 Why does industry still tend to concentrate on coalfields?

2 Account for the substantial decline of transportation as a proportion of overall industrial costs in the twentieth century.

3 Why, over time, have more and more parts of Britain been placed off limits for industrial location?

4 Examine the importance of the cost, quality, availability and reputation of labour in locational decision making.

5 Discuss the significance of exchange rates in industrial location.

6 Explain how Toyota chose Valenciennes as the location for its new European car plant (Figure 5.23).

7 Explain the phenomenon of phantom factories.

the strength of sterling and the resultant plunge in foreign sales. For the first time since the Second World War, annual production on the isles of Harris and Lewis in the Outer Hebrides dipped to under a million yards of cloth, one-seventh of its peak figure. Here the existence of a whole industry in an area with few alternative job opportunities has been put into question by exchange rates. However, this important economic factor also arises when initial location decisions are made, particularly by transnational companies. If a North American or Asian transnational is looking to expand production in Europe, selling to the continent as a whole, its decision about where to site may well be influenced by the relative values of European currencies, particularly if there is little difference in other factors.

Phantom factories

A not insignificant number of new factory building announcements fail to materialise. This seems to have happened more in the 1990s than in any previous decade. 'Phantom factories' fail to make the journey from site selection

Figure 5.22 Things that can spirit that plant away

- Boycotts or sanctions in your preferred site location
- Changes in government policy or simply government
- Company lies to keep competition guessing
- More detailed feasibility study shows project is not viable
- Cash flow difficulties
- Changes in corporate strategy
- Industry trends – eg: falling semiconductor prices
- Internal wranglings – particularly in the case of joint venture plants
- Opposition from firms already in your target market
- Corruption – executives getting locked up
- Changes in tariff regimes
- Phantom searches used to gain political leverage at home
- Environmental opposition
- Wars and civil conflict

Source: *Corporate Location*, March/April 1998

to construction for a variety of reasons (Figure 5.22). For example, brewing rivals Carlsberg and Heineken were both poised to establish breweries in Myanmar (Burma) in 1997. However, both succumbed to human rights pressure against the Rangoon military regime and announced their withdrawals in July 1997. Phantom site searches are also used by some companies as a bargaining tool to negotiate better deals for the expansion of an existing plant.

Industrial location theory

Theories concerning industrial location can be placed in four broad groups where the emphasis is on: **a) cost factors** (*Weber*), **b) locational interdependence** (*Hotelling*), **c) demand** (*Losch*), **d) profit and human behaviour** (*Smith, Pred*).

Weber: cost factors

Alfred Weber published his *Theory of the Location of Industries* in 1909. At the turn of the century transportation was for many industries the major cost. Thus transportation is central to Weber's theory. However, he did recognise that other elements of total cost could also vary, particularly labour and the savings associated with agglomeration.

Along with other location theorists Weber assumed perfect competition. This means that individual firms cannot influence the price of the product which is the same everywhere. At the prevailing price there is unlimited demand and all sellers have unlimited access to the market. Therefore, the firm which secures the location where lowest costs are incurred will achieve the greatest profit.

Weber used the 'location triangle' to illustrate the basis of his approach. In this simplified example just two raw materials are required to make the product which is sold in only one market. Logically, the firm will locate somewhere in the triangle joining the two individual points where the raw materials are exploited and the point where the market is situated. Each point has a pull on the location of the firm, depending upon its influence on total transport costs. Figure 5.24 is an adaptation of the locational triangle where three possible sites have been selected for a factory.

Industries for which the finished product is lighter than the weight of the raw materials required to manufacture it are said to be 'weight loss' industries. As such they are raw material oriented. In general, the heavier the nature of the industry the higher the weight loss and the greater the degree of raw material orientation.

How Toyota parked in Europe

On December 9, Toyota, Japan's biggest car maker announced plans to build a $660 million car plant in Valenciennes, 60km from Lille.

Toyota had started the search in late 1996 by looking at the whole of western and eastern Europe for the 2,000-job project. At this stage, the company was only weighing up the national traits of each country. Belgium, the Czech Republic, France, Germany, Poland and the UK all seemed to fit the bill.

But the list was quickly whittled down. Germany was struck off for being too expensive. Belgium was too apathetic. In the Czech Republic, Toyota's search focused on an existing plant near the capital, Prague, formerly used by local car maker Skoda. But the company was put off by the age of the factory and the country's poor labour climate.

So Poland became the east European favourite, a low-cost alternative to the more mature western markets and with a sizeable market of its own. But Toyota was uneasy about the uncertainty surrounding the country's prospects for EU membership and how this might affect future exports. The feeling was that it would be too risky to build a car plant there so soon.

This left a head-to-head battle between two of Europe's oldest foreign investment rivals – France and the UK. On the face of it, the UK seemed the obvious choice.

Toyota has its only European car assembly plant at Burnaston, in the UK's Midlands, where much managerial experience has been gained and a skilled workforce amassed. The company built 117,000 Carina E cars there in 1996. And a further $330 million, creating 1,000 new jobs, is being invested for a second model, the Corolla, to enter production alongside its larger cousin this year. This will raise Burnaston's capacity to 200,000 units.

All this means Burnaston has had time to develop a well-established automotive infrastructure and cluster of related firms.

The UK site also had the spare land to accommodate the new project to build a third small car. All three models could be integrated into a single site to gain considerable economies.

France, on the other hand, was notorious for difficult labour relations and high wages. And the French language and culture can be a problem for Japanese firms used to speaking English when working overseas. One Toyota spokesman admitted France was "a difficult market". The company has had less success selling there due to what a Toyota director termed "a greater degree of nationalism".

So, at the start of 1997, the UK looked set to bag another of Europe's most prestigious greenfield investments.

But alarm bells soon started to ring for the UK's development agencies. At the end of January, company president Hiroshi Okuda voiced doubts over the UK for investment because of its changeable attitude to European monetary integration: "If we were to make fresh investments, we would prefer to make them in continental Europe rather than Britain."

In March, the *Financial Times* newspaper said it had been tipped off that France had won the contest.

It was true. Toyota had decided to site the plant in France. Burnaston's past success in attracting projects had caused its downfall. The company did not want to place all of its production at one site on the edge of Europe, the same consideration that scored against Poland. And making cars in France, it was felt, would help Toyota crack the nationalist sentiment.

Once France was chosen, the Toyota team started to consider different sites in more detail. Alsace Lorraine, Bordeaux, Lyon, Marseilles and Nord-Pas de Calais all received visits. Nord-Pas de Calais, in north-west France, soon became the preferred choice. Toyota might not want to locate in the UK, but it wanted to be close enough to ship engines over from its north Wales plant cheaply. And the area is a short distance from Brussels, home to Toyota's European headquarters.

The winner was Valenciennes, near Lille, a joint decision between the company's people in Japan and Europe. The physical location was almost ideal. Paris is two hours away by road or rail. The Belgian Border is just 6km from the site. Nearby Lille offers rapid freight and passenger access to the UK through the Channel Tunnel. And connections to the rest of mainland Europe, where the company wants to sell its cars, are good.

Northern France and neighbouring Belgium also have the skills base. The region is home to several car manufacturers that have created a large pool of suitable workers. And high unemployment should help keep a lid on wage inflation. Not to mention the scope for fatter grants.

Though the level of sweeteners has not been disclosed the package is likely to be generous. The north-east is a government priority zone, with 20% unemployment, so Toyota was offered aid for training. A waiving of social security contributions was included in the package too. Valenciennes' authorities may also cut the annual property tax on the site while helping to set up Japanese-French schooling. France's *tax professionelle* rule meant Toyota was able to buy its 100ha site cheaply because it belonged to the local chamber of commerce.

So what does Valenciennes get for its $60 million-odd sweetener? The plant, due to open in 2001, will initially create around 1,000 jobs, and have an annual capacity of 100,000 vehicles. A second phase may double capacity by 2005. The factory will make a small car tailor-made for the European market, to compete head-on with Renault's Twingo and the Ford Ka.

Figure 5.23 *Corporate Location*, January/February 1998

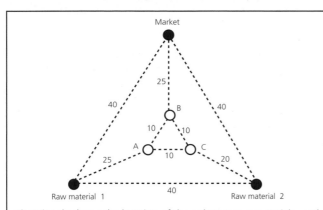

The triangle shows the location of the only two raw materials used to manufacture a product and the single market in which the product is sold. The road network and the distance in km between road junctions is also shown.

There are three possible locations for the factory, A, B, or C.

Two tonnes of raw material 1 and one tonne of raw material 2 are required to manufacture one tonne of the finished product.

Transport costs are £1 per tonne km.

Figure 5.24 The location triangle

Using the information provided in Figure 5.24, calculate the least transport cost location.

A small number of industries, including soft drinks and brewing are 'weight gaining' and are thus market oriented in terms of location. The heavy weight gain for both of these industries comes from the addition of water, a ubiquitous resource. The baking industry is also cited frequently as an example of weight gain but here it is largely a case of increase in volume rather than weight, although the impact on transport costs is similar.

Weber designed a simple 'Material Index' to show the relationship between the relative weights involved in transportation:

$$\text{Material Index} = \frac{\text{Weight of Raw Materials}}{\text{Weight of Finished Product}}$$

Building on the concept of the locational triangle, the variation of transport costs in a region can be more clearly illustrated by the use of isotims and isodapanes (Figure 5.25). Isotims are lines of equal cost, showing the increasing cost with distance relating to one factor such as the movement of one raw material to the factory. Isodapanes show variations in total costs and are thus the product of isotims.

In Figure 5.26a, M is clearly the least transport cost location [£10] with total transport cost isodapanes increasing from it. Let us now assume that there is an alternative location where a saving of £4 per tonne of finished product can be made in the cost of labour. Clearly, if this location (D) is on the £14 isodapane the savings in the cost of labour would exactly balance the extra transport costs incurred. In this case the £14 isodapane would be the 'critical isodapane'. If the point of cheap labour lies outside the critical isodapane (A,C and E), the optimum location would remain at M.

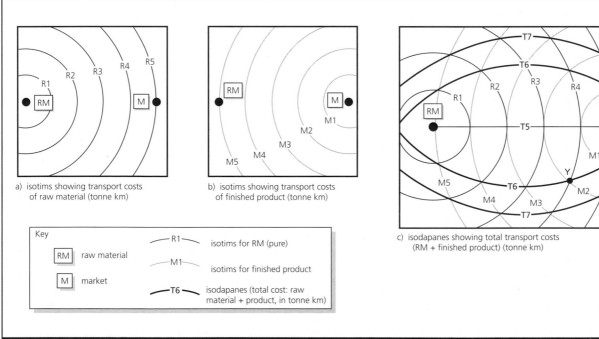

Figure 5.25 Isotims and isodapanes

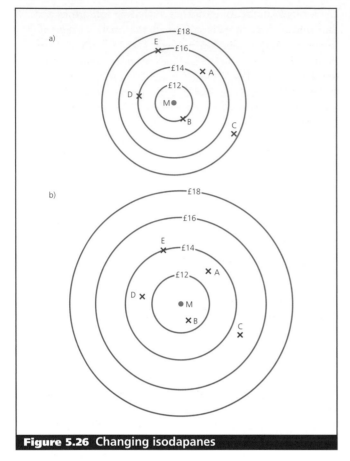

Figure 5.26 Changing isodapanes

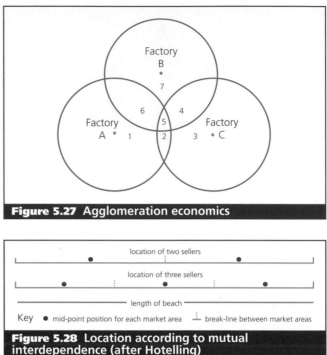

Figure 5.27 Agglomeration economics

location of two sellers

location of three sellers

length of beach

Key ● mid-point position for each market area ⊥ break-line between market areas

Figure 5.28 Location according to mutual interdependence (after Hotelling)

Alternatively, if it lies within it (B), it would be logical for the factory to locate at this point since the savings in labour costs more than compensate for the extra transport costs incurred. Weber described such a shift as a deviation from the least transport cost location.

Weber also recognised that the pull of low cost labour was becoming stronger over time as improvements in transport were increasing the distance over which goods could be moved for a given cost. In terms of Figure 5.26b, the distance between isodapanes has increased so more cheap labour locations would be likely to fall within the critical isodapane.

Weber referred to the savings that could be made when firms located together as 'agglomeration economies' (Figure 5.27). Here least transport cost location and the critical isodapanes for agglomeration for three factories are shown. Only in area 5 will all three factories benefit from siting together.

Hotelling: locational interdependence

The locational interdependence approach, which introduced a new element into the field of industrial location theory, is concerned with:

■ the impact of demand upon location, and
■ the interaction of entrepreneurial decisions.

The best known model adopting this approach was proposed by Harold Hotelling in 1929 and illustrated in terms of two ice-cream sellers on a beach. As with all models Hotelling made certain assumptons;

■ **an evenly distributed population**
■ **a market served by two competing entrepreneurs (a duopoly) each with equal production costs and capable of supplying the entire market, producing two identical products**
■ **infinitely elastic demand**
■ **costs of production the same everywhere**
■ **entrepreneurs able to relocate without cost.**

The basis of Hotelling's theory is illustrated in Figure 5.28. For a period of time each seller would attempt to out-manoeuvre his competitor by cutting his price or by changing his position on the beach in order to gain a larger share of the market. Eventually, after failing to oust each other, since they are equally able to compete, they would agree to compromise: they would charge the same price and locate in positions that would give each 50 per cent of market share. For their own convenience, and for that of their customers, they would position themselves at the centre of the two market areas. If another ice-cream seller entered the market a similar process would operate.

As with all theories, Hotelling's approach attracted criticism, mainly because his initial assumptons are rarely, if ever, replicated in reality. Nevertheless, the recognition that entrepreneurial decisions cannot be made without considering competing organisations was an important theoretical advance.

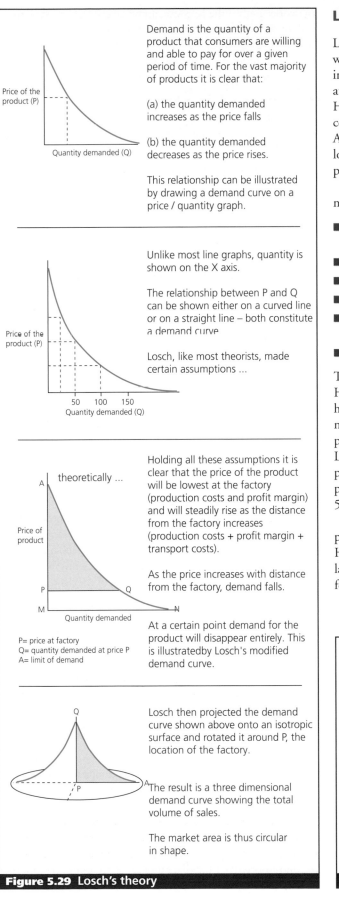

Demand is the quantity of a product that consumers are willing and able to pay for over a given period of time. For the vast majority of products it is clear that:

(a) the quantity demanded increases as the price falls

(b) the quantity demanded decreases as the price rises.

This relationship can be illustrated by drawing a demand curve on a price / quantity graph.

Unlike most line graphs, quantity is shown on the X axis.

The relationship between P and Q can be shown either on a curved line or on a straight line – both constitute a demand curve

Losch, like most theorists, made certain assumptions ...

Holding all these assumptions it is clear that the price of the product will be lowest at the factory (production costs and profit margin) and will steadily rise as the distance from the factory increases (production costs + profit margin + transport costs).

As the price increases with distance from the factory, demand falls.

At a certain point demand for the product will disappear entirely. This is illustrated by Losch's modified demand curve.

Losch then projected the demand curve shown above onto an isotropic surface and rotated it around P, the location of the factory.

The result is a three dimensional demand curve showing the total volume of sales.

The market area is thus circular in shape.

Figure 5.29 Losch's theory

Losch: demand

Losch's theory is contained in *The Economics of Location* which was originally published in German in 1939 and translated into English in 1954. It is widely recognised as the first attempt to construct a comprehensive general location theory. He argued that the optimum location was one which commanded the largest market area and maximised revenue. Assuming that the costs of production are uniform spatially, a location which maximised demand would also maximise profit.

Losch, like most theorists, made certain assumptions, the most important of which were:

- **a surface exhibiting the same physical properties in all directions**
- **an evenly distributed population**
- **transport costs proportional to distance**
- **uniform production costs**
- **uniform levels of production for all firms in the same industry**
- **uniform purchasing power.**

The basis of Losch's theory is a modified demand curve. However, for those unfamiliar with such diagrams it might be helpful to consider a simple demand curve first, before moving on to Losch's modification (Figure 5.29). After proving that theoretically the market area is circular in shape, Losch looked for the nearest shape to the circle that will pack (neither overlapping nor leaving gaps). Elementary packing theory confirms his choice of the hexagon (Figure 5.30).

In the first of the series of diagrams in Figure 5.31 a basic pattern of hexagonal market areas for one product is shown. However, because demand for different products will vary, the landscape will have a complex network of market areas, one for each product. Losch rotated each of the many hexagonal

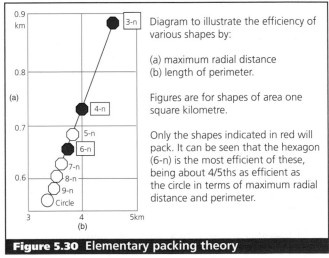

Diagram to illustrate the efficiency of various shapes by:

(a) maximum radial distance
(b) length of perimeter.

Figures are for shapes of area one square kilometre.

Only the shapes indicated in red will pack. It can be seen that the hexagon (6-n) is the most efficient of these, being about 4/5ths as efficient as the circle in terms of maximum radial distance and perimeter.

Figure 5.30 Elementary packing theory

a)

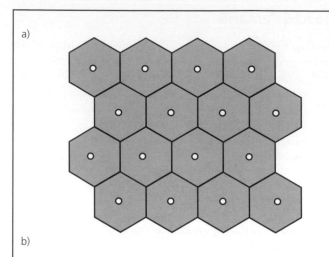

b)

Although Losch superimposed a large number of hexagonal arrangements, the principle can be demonstrated by using the smallest hexagonal patterns known as the k = 3 and k = 4 networks.

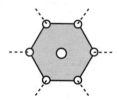

k = 3 network with a high order central place at the centre of the hexagon and six central places of a lower order on the periphery.

For simplicity the trade areas of the lower order central places are not shown.

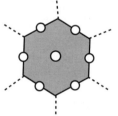

k = 4 network.

Here the position of lower order central places on the periphery of the hexagon is different.

c)

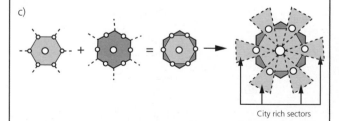

City rich sectors

By superimposing the two hexagons all the central places coincide so that the six city rich sectors can be clearly identified. With only two hexagons superimposed there are no central places in the city poor sectors. However some central places will gradually appear in these sectors as larger hexagons are added.

Figure 5.31 Losch's economic landscape

networks around the largest central place which acted as the hub of the settlement system, dominating the economy of the region. The networks were rotated until as many as possible of the higher order services coincided in the same central places. Such an arrangement ensures that:

- **the aggregate distance between all settlements is minimised**
- **the maximum number of goods can be supplied locally**
- **transport routes and movement along them are minimised.**

This pattern of central places, called an 'economic landscape' by Losch has twelve sectors. The six 'city rich' sectors contain many central places. In contrast the six 'city poor' sectors are sparsely populated, have few central places and offer a much narrower range of goods and services.

Smith and Pred: Profit and human behaviour

The theories examined so far have assumed that locational decisions are taken by economic man. In reality, such enlightened decision makers rarely exist and locations are selected by individuals or groups with less than perfect knowledge or ability. Nevertheless it is still necessary for such decision makers to choose locations where total costs are less than total revenue, so that a profit can be achieved.

David Smith (1971) developed a model to show the relationship between costs and revenue over space. Like earlier theorists, Smith used isodapanes to identify the optimum location and decreasing levels of profitability from that point (Figure 5.32a). The 'Space Cost Curve' as the model is generally termed is a cross-section through an isodapane map. In the simplest version of the model the space revenue curve is held constant. This means that the price of the product is the same everywhere. Costs are made up of two elements, production costs and transport costs. Here production costs are taken to be the same everywhere while transport costs increase with distance from a certain point. The most profitable location is where the greatest gap between revenue and costs occurs. In Figure 5.32a this point is also the least-cost location. The spatial margins of profitability are where the space-cost curve and the space-revenue curve intersect. At these points a firm would break even, incurring neither a loss nor a profit.

Figure 5.32b shows a more complicated cost environment with zones of high and low cost production resulting in three sets of spatial margins of profitability. Going a stage further, Figure 5.32c illustrates a situation closer to reality. Here both revenue and costs vary over space and the relationship between revenue and costs is such that different locations can be identified for minimum cost, maximum revenue, and maximum profit. In the diagram costs have not been subdivided for purposes of graphical clarity.

Key Definitions 3

economic man The decision-maker in classical economic theory who has perfect knowledge and the absolute ability to obtain the maximum benefit from such knowledge. As a result the optimum location will always be selected.

sub-optimal location A location which is profitable but not the best in terms of the primary aim of the entrepreneur or firm (minimum cost, maximum profit etc.).

psychic income The non-monetary reward or satisfaction an entrepreneur obtains from setting up a firm in a particular location.

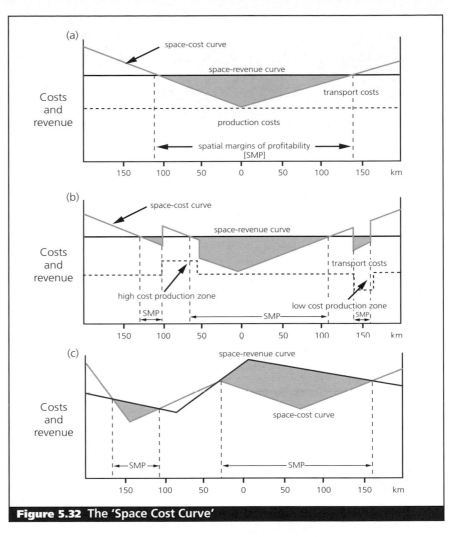

Figure 5.32 The 'Space Cost Curve'

Some industries have wide spatial margins while others are more spatially restricted. However, skilled entrepreneurs may be able to expand their spatial margins. This is generally achieved by reducing the costs of production. However, it is possible to achieve the same result by improving the product or the image of the product so that the price can be increased.

Whereas economic man is an optimiser, many decision makers are satisficers. As such they are satisfied to make a reasonable profit which may be considerably less than the maximum that could be achieved. Satisficing behaviour takes account of non-material goals, with entrepreneurs often placing substantial value on factors such as an attractive environment which can be viewed as 'psychic income'.

Alan Pred's behavioural matrix summarises the behavioural approach to decision making (Figure 5.33). The spatial margins of a particular industry have been mapped, showing two optimum locations. In addition the location decisions of industrialists have been plotted on the matrix. A firm placed in the top left-hand corner with little information and limited ability to use such information would probably make a poor locational decision. Conversely, a firm positioned near the bottom right-hand corner would probably select a profitable location close to the optimum. Of the three firms in the upper left-hand corner, two, not surprisingly, have made decisions which put them outside the spatial margins of profitability.

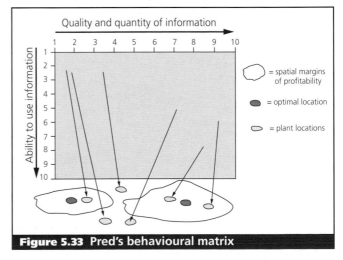

Figure 5.33 Pred's behavioural matrix

However, because of the chance element in decision making, one has located inside. This is clearly a case of luck rather than judgement. However, with the passage of time, decision makers should obtain more/better information and should become more skilled in its use.

Essay Question

Discuss the evolution of industrial location theory.

The US manufacturing belt: the challenge of change

The regions of New England, Middle Atlantic and East North Central cover only one-eighth of the United States, yet, along with a few extensions in neighbouring regions, they contained over 42 per cent of all manufacturing jobs in the country in 1995 (Figure 5.34). It had even more in the past. In 1910, 68 per cent of manufacturing employment was here. Because of this the region became known as the 'manufacturing belt', the world's most important industrial region in the twentieth century. Industry developed here on such a large scale because:

■ this was the first major centre of population. Immigrants brought industrial and business skills with them and the rapidly rising population provided both a market and a source of labour

■ major raw materials were available locally. The development of the Appalachian and Illinois coalfields and the iron ore fields of the Lake Superior region were of immense importance

■ the Great Lakes, major rivers and the coast provided relatively cheap water transport for the movement of bulky goods

■ easy access to Europe across the North Atlantic, the world's busiest shipping route, encouraged trade

■ firms benefited from the wide variety of manufacturers in the region by using each other's products and skills

■ substantial investment in research meant that most of the United States's new products were developed in the region. Successful innovation encouraged even more investment

■ transportation arteries rapidly developed to all parts of the continent to 'import' raw materials and export manufactured goods

■ the sophistication of the region's infrastructure compared with possible alternative locations meant that decentralisation only occurred due to very strong competitive factors in other regions.

Yet the dominance of the core region was not to last as industry was increasingly attracted to other regions in the second half of the twentieth century. For example in 1995, California had more employees in the manufacturing sector, 1.9 million more than any other state. The reasons for decentralisation from the manufacturing belt were:

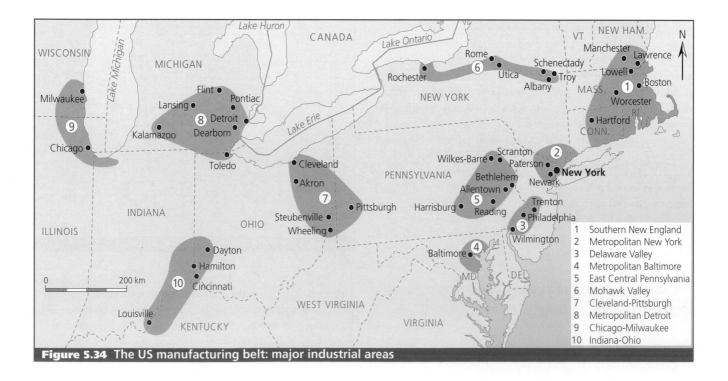

Figure 5.34 The US manufacturing belt: major industrial areas

1 Southern New England
2 Metropolitan New York
3 Delaware Valley
4 Metropolitan Baltimore
5 East Central Pennsylvania
6 Mohawk Valley
7 Cleveland-Pittsburgh
8 Metropolitan Detroit
9 Chicago-Milwaukee
10 Indiana-Ohio

Figure 5.35 Average hourly earnings of production workers in manufacturing industries [selected States] 1996

States	$
The manufacturing belt	
Michigan	16.01
Ohio	14.69
Connecticut	14.01
The South	
Florida	10.54
South Carolina	10.26
Mississippi	10.19

Source: US Statistical Abstract 1997

Figure 5.36 Traditional iron and steel industry still operating in the manufacturing belt

- the movement of population both to the south and west significantly increased the market potential of these regions

- the location and exploitation of important raw materials, particularly energy sources, encouraged investment in associated industries and strengthened the independence of these regions. California and Texas are prime examples of the way in which raw material endowment has had a cumulative effect on industrial development

- the attraction of lower general costs particularly in terms of lower real estate prices, tax and labour rates (Figure 5.35) along with the continuing availability of undeveloped land

- the climate of the sunbelt states from Florida in the east to California in the west provided specific advantages to some industries such as aerospace, reduced space-heating costs for all, and added positively to the perceived high quality of life

- the construction of the Interstate Highway System and other major aspects of infrastructure considerably upgraded the accessibility of the south and west

- federal spending per capita has favoured the regions outside of the manufacturing belt

- the development of innovation centres in the south and west acted as seedbeds for new manufacturing industry.

As traditional industries declined in the core, and new industries frequently looked to locate elsewhere, the region acquired the undesired name of 'the rustbelt'. Of the ten major industrial areas in the manufacturing belt some regions, such as East Central Pennsylvania, have struggled badly in the attempt to attract new industry. In contrast Southern New England has attracted a wide range of new industry.

East Central Pennsylvania

Iron and steel became the basis of manufacturing here in the nineteenth century because of the local deposits of coal, iron ore and limestone. A range of other metal-working activities grew up around iron and steel and other industries such as textiles, clothing, silk, lace and shoes also developed.

Today the region's traditional industrial base is only a shadow of its former self. Demand for these products has either fallen or they are being produced more cheaply elsewhere. Local government has tried to attract new enterprise by offering a range of incentives and new roads have improved accessibility. However most new firms were small in size and some did not remain in the region for very long.

The region has over one million people with most living in a line of towns stretching from Scranton to Harrisburg (Figure 5.34). Unemployment is high and wages are well below the national average. The situation could get even worse in the future: some iron and steel production remains because of industrial inertia but as competition among steelmakers gets even sharper it is likely that only the lowest cost producers will survive. A major problem for the region is that it lacks a central urban core.

Southern New England

This is the oldest industrial area in the United States (Figure 5.34). Many traditional activities such as textiles, leather goods, clothing, small metal goods and jewellery are still of some importance. However, the region has been successful in attracting new fast-growing industry. High technology industry has developed at a rapid rate. Its main location is alongside Route 128 which arcs around Boston. The quality of the region's universities, including the Massachusetts Institute of Technology, Harvard and Yale has been a major stimulus to development. The Boston-Cambridge area has the United States' largest concentration of educational institutions which employ nearly 10 per cent of the labour force.

Figure 5.37 Harvard University, Cambridge, Massachusetts

The region also has other attractions for high-tech firms. These include:

- the heavy concentration of industry in the Northeast which provides a large market for high-tech products

- the high quality of life

- excellent transport, communications and general infrastructure

- local government which is keen for high-tech industry to expand.

Questions

1 Account for the initial concentration of industry in the manufacturing belt.
2 What are the reasons for the decentralisation of industry to other regions?
3 Why have some parts of the manufacturing belt found it more difficult than others to readjust after the decline of traditional manufacturing?

Deindustrialisation and the filter-down process

The declining importance of manufacturing in the Developed World

In the United States and Britain the proportion of workers employed in manufacturing has fallen from around 40 per cent at the beginning of the twentieth century to barely half that now. Even in Japan and Germany, where so much industry was rebuilt after 1945, manufacturing's share of total employment has dropped below 30 per cent. Not a single developed country has bucked this trend (Figure 5.38) known as deindustrialisation, the causal factors of which are:

- the filter-down of manufacturing industry from developed countries to lower wage economies, such as those of South East Asia
- the increasing importance of the service sector in the developed economies.

There can be little surprise in the decline of manufacturing employment for it has mirrored the previous decline in employment in agriculture in the Developed World. So, if the decline of manufacturing in the Developed World is part of an expected cycle, the consequence of technological improvement

and rising affluence, why is so much concern expressed about this trend? The main reasons would appear to be:

- the traditional industries of the industrial revolution were highly concentrated, thus the impact of manufacturing decline has had severe implications in terms of unemployment and other social pathologies in a number of regions
- the rapid pace of contraction of manufacturing has often made adjustment difficult
- there are defence concerns if the production of some industries falls below a certain level
- some economists argue that over-reliance on services makes an economy unnecessarily vulnerable.

Rather than being a smooth transition, manufacturing decline tends to concentrate during periods of economic recession. As Figure 5.39 indicates the recession of the early 1980s was particularly severe on the manufacturing sector in the UK. The economic crisis that began in Asia in 1997 was beginning to have a significant impact on British industry a year later.

In general high-technology manufacturing, such as computers, aerospace, pharmaceuticals and electronics, has been able to hold its share in the economy. However, medium and low technology manufacturing, such as chemicals, food products and textiles has declined markedly. These trends have been reflected clearly in the composition of trade of the richer economies.

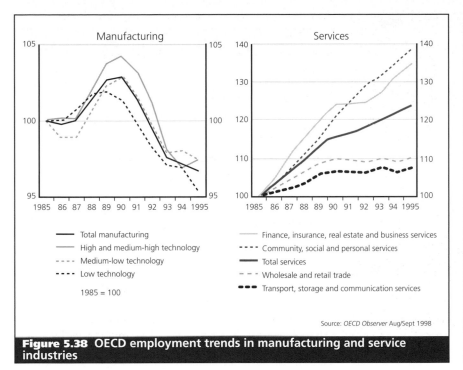

Figure 5.38 OECD employment trends in manufacturing and service industries

Key Definitions

4

deindustrialisation The long-term absolute decline of employment in manufacturing.

reindustrialisation The establishment of new industries in a country or region which has experienced considerable decline of traditional industries.

economies of scale A situation in which an increase in the scale at which a business operates will lead to a reduction in unit costs.

product life-cycle The pattern of sales in the life of a product usually divided into four stages: early, growth, maturity and decline.

industry mix The industrial structure of a country or region. A positive industry mix denotes a bias towards industries which are growing at rates above the national or international average. A negative industry mix is the reverse of this situation.

From Shell, the oil giant, to Fujitsu, the Japanese chip maker, the fallout from Asia's slump is cutting deep into Britain's industrial heartland, write **John Waples** and **David Parsley**

THERE is now little doubt that the battle to protect Britain's shrinking manufacturing employment base will become one of the dominant issues for the government. One element at stake is the country's reputation as an industrial magnet capable of attracting big multinationals to use Britain as the springboard for their European expansion plans.

Opinion is split as to whether the current spate of foreign-owned plant closures and cutbacks are a series of significant but isolated events or the start of a damaging, widespread trend.

Britain is particularly exposed to the world semi-conductor recession because inward-investment chiefs specifically targeted the sector for development and proved highly successful — at least initially — in winning microchip projects.

Some economists fear that Britain is facing a repetition of the wave of branch factory closures that caused such havoc in Scotland and northern England during the 1980–82 recession. As the pound soared, factories like the Linwood car plant near Glasgow, the Speke factory on Merseyside, the British Steel plant at Consett, and the RCA record plant near Durham were axed in what became a manufacturing jobs massacre.

Figure 5.39 *The Sunday Times*, 20 September 1998

The filter-down process of industrial relocation

This process, detailed by W. R. Thompson and others, operates at both a global and a national scale. It is based on the notion that corporate organisations respond to changing critical input requirements by altering the geographical location of production to minimise costs and thereby ensure competitiveness in a tightening market.

The economic core (at a national and global level) has monopolised invention and innovation, and has continually benefited from the rapid growth rates characteristic of the early stages of an industry's life-cycle (the product life-cycle), one of exploitation of a new market. Production is likely to occur where the firm's main plants and corporate headquarters are located. Figure 5.40, illustrating the product life-cycle, indicates that in the early phase scientific-engineering skills at a high level and external economies are the prime location factors.

In the growth phase, methods of mass production are gradually introduced and the number of firms involved in production generally expands as product information spreads. In this stage management skills are the critical human inputs. Production technology tends to stabilise in the mature phase. Capital investment remains high and the availability of unskilled and semiskilled labour becomes a major locating factor. As the industry matures into a replacement market the production process becomes rationalised and often routine. The high wages of the innovating area, quite consistent with the high level skills required in the formative stages of the learning process, become excessive when the skill requirements

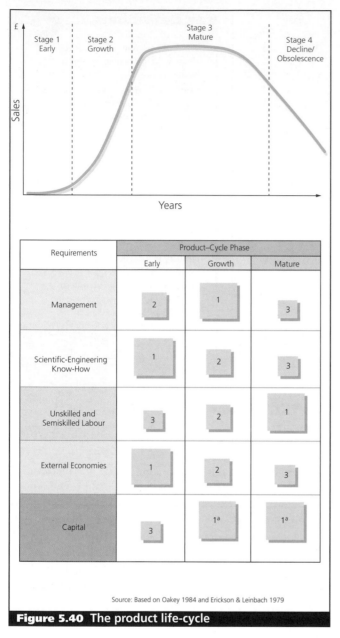

Source: Based on Oakey 1984 and Erickson & Leinbach 1979

Figure 5.40 The product life-cycle

Questions

1 What is the evidence that deindustrialisation has taken place in the Developed World?
2 Explain the filter-down process of industrial relocation.
3 Compare the industry mix of the region you live in with one other region in terms of the product life-cycle.

competition from the Developing World rather than from the corporate strategy of huge North American, European, and Japanese transnationals.

Although the theory of the product life-cycle was developed in the discipline of business studies to explain how the sales of individual products evolve, it can usefully be applied at higher scales. A firm with a range of ten products, half in stage three and half in stage four, would have no long-term future. A healthy multi-product firm will have a strong R&D department ensuring a steady movement of successful products on to the market to give a positive distribution across the four stages of the model. Likewise, the industry mix of a region or a country can be plotted on the product life-cycle diagram. Regions with significant socio-economic problems are invariably over-represented in stages three and four. In contrast, regions with dynamic economies will have a more even spread across the model with particularly good representation in the first two stages.

New techniques and trends

Organisational innovation

'Lean' manufacturing techniques were first developed in the 1950s in Japan, by a Toyota manager called Taiichi Ohno. Lean production involves:

- **carrying minimal stocks**
- **having parts delivered direct to the assembly line 'just in time' (JIT)**
- **'right-first-time' quality management**
- **continuously seeking small improvements to gain greater efficiency**
- **seeing the factory as part of a supply chain with its suppliers upstream and its customers downstream.**

Lean manufacturing seeks to combine the best of both craftwork and mass production. It seeks to use less of each

decline and the industry, or a section of it, 'filters-down' to smaller, less industrially sophisticated areas where cheaper labour is available, but which can now handle the lower skills required in the manufacture of the product.

On a global scale, large transnational companies have increasingly operated in this way by moving routine operations to the Developing World since the 1950s. It has been the revolution in transport and communications that has made such substantial filter-down of manufacturing to the Developing World possible. However, the role of indigenous companies in developing countries should not be ignored. Important examples are the '*chaebols*' of South Korea, such as Samsung and Hyundai and Taiwanese firms such as Acer. Here the process of filter-down has come about by direct

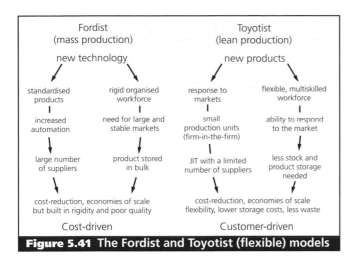

Figure 5.41 The Fordist and Toyotist (flexible) models

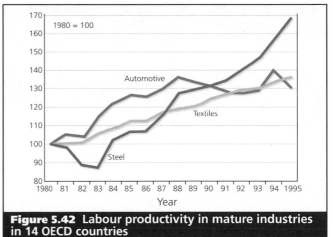

Figure 5.42 Labour productivity in mature industries in 14 OECD countries

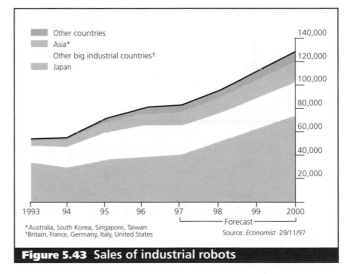

Figure 5.43 Sales of industrial robots

input and to eliminate defects – if a fault is spotted the production line is halted immediately and remedial action taken. The process eliminates waste by making only as much as is wanted at any given time. Advances in manufacturing software programs have allowed companies to integrate the various aspects of their work to a higher degree than ever before. Figure 5.41 compares the Fordist and Toyotist (flexible) models of manufacturing.

At first JIT transferred the burden of storing parts to the suppliers of assembly plants but at its most advanced it extends all the way along the supply chain. JIT encourages suppliers to concentrate around assembly plants to ensure rapid delivery. In fact some assembly plants insist on suppliers being no more than a certain distance away. Ideally the number of suppliers should not be too extensive and long-term contracts should be agreed. Increasingly production plants and suppliers are collaborating on research. As supply interruptions would prove disastrous, agreements are often signed between employers and employees to avoid such an occurrence. Single union agreements are an important part of this process.

It was not until the mid-1970s that US firms began to employ lean manufacturing, as Japanese goods were making considerable inroads into US markets. Once it was proved that such techniques could work outside Japan, large European companies followed suit in an effort to bridge the productivity gap. However Japanese companies still lead in the productivity stakes. It is thus not surprising that Japanese car production soared from 1 million in 1989 to 2.5 million in 1998. Although lean manufacturing developed in the car industry, similar strategies are now employed in a wide range of industries.

The adoption of the lean system paved the way for further increases in productivity and manufacturing flexibility through the integration of IT-based AMT (Advanced Manufacturing Techniques). This replaced simple automating devices with numerically-controlled tools, industrial robots and flexible-transfer machines, and eventually computer-integrated manufacturing systems. These new techniques have been largely responsible for significant advances in productivity in a number of large mature industries (Figure 5.42).

Robots

Increasing worldwide sales of industrial robots will bring the global robot population to more than one million by the end of 2000 (Figure 5.43), according to forecasts by the UN. More than half of this total will be in Japan which leads the current world ranking by a wide margin, ahead of the United States, Germany and South Korea.

The car industry is the largest user of robots. In 1997, Japan had over 830 robots for every 10 000 car workers compared to 370 in the United States. As one robot generally performs the tasks of at least two persons it has been estimated that robots in the Japanese car industry correspond to about 20 per cent of the labour force. Unlike other countries, Japan also makes widespread use of robots in the engineering and electrical machinery industries. Compared with wages, robot prices have fallen significantly in the 1990s.

Figure 5.44 Advanced robotics in a German car factory

Questions

1 Discuss the attributes of lean manufacturing techniques.
2 Why is the use of robots in manufacturing increasing so rapidly?
3 Explain the terms
   (a) reindustrialisation
   (b) rationalisation
   (c) restructuring.

Reindustrialisation, rationalisation and restructuring

The development of new industries has to a limited extent offset the decline of traditional manufacturing. The sector at the forefront of reindustrialisation is high technology. In terms of the process as a whole small firms have led the way.

The increasing level of global competition has driven all industries to improve their productivity. The consequences have generally been:

■ **rationalisation or 'downsizing' of the workforce with the expectation that a smaller number of workers will maintain the same level of production**
■ **closure of inefficient plants**
■ **restructuring by**
   (a) introducing more efficient production methods
   (b) merging with another company in the same sector.

Large TNCs continuously compare all aspects of production in their plants in different countries and can move quickly to rationalise either when the market becomes more crowded as a result of increasing competition or during a recession when demand in general declines.

Newly industrialised countries

Three generations

The term Newly Industrialised Country (NIC) is generally applied to nations that have undergone rapid and successful industrialisation since the 1960s. In South East Asia three generations of NIC can be recognised (Figure 5.45) each with different economic characteristics. Within this region, only Japan is at a higher economic level than the NICs but there are a number of countries at much lower levels of economic development. The latter form the least developed countries in the region and most, if not all, also merit this label in global terms.

Nowhere else in the world is the filter-down concept of industrial relocation better illustrated. When Japanese companies first decided to locate abroad in the quest for cheap labour, they looked to the most developed of their neighbouring countries, particularly South Korea and Taiwan. Most other countries in the region lacked the physical infrastructure and skill levels required by Japanese companies. Companies from elsewhere in the Developed World, especially the United States also recognised the advantages of locating branch plants in such countries. As the economies of the first generation NICs developed, the level of wages increased resulting in:

■ **Japanese and Western TNCs seeking locations in second generation NICs where the physical and human infrastructures now satisfied their demands but where wages were still low**
■ **indigenous companies from the first generation NICs also moving routine tasks to their cheaper labour neighbours such as Malaysia and Thailand.**

With time, the process also included the third generation NICs, being at least partly responsible for the very high growth rates in China and India in the 1980s and 1990s. The least developed countries in the region, nearly all hindered by conflict of one sort or another at some time in recent decades, are now beginning to be drawn into the system. It should not be too long before the financial journals recognise a fourth generation of NICs in Asia.

First generation NICs

What were the reasons for the phenomenal rates of economic growth recorded in South Korea, Taiwan, Kong Hong and Singapore from the 1960s? What was it that set this group of 'Asian Tigers' apart from so many others? From the vast literature that has appeared on the subject the following factors are usually given prominence:

Figure 5.45 Comparison between the OECD and NICS

	Average annual growth (GNP per capita)	GDP per capita (1993)*	Manufacturing hourly wage (US$ 1992)	Average annual growth in investment	Average annual growth in exports
	(1980–93)	(US = 100)		(1980–93)	(1980–93)
OECD					
United States	1.7	100.0	11.45	2.5	5.1
Japan	3.4	84.3	18.96	5.5	4.2
France	1.6	76.8	7.88	2.1	4.5
Italy	2.1	72.1	–	1.5	4.3
United Kingdom	2.3	69.6	10.56	4.0	4.0
Germany	2.1	68.1	14.41	2.4	4.2
First generation Asian NICs					
Hong Kong	5.4	87.1	3.28	5.0	15.8
Taiwan	–	–	5.31	–	10.0
Republic of Korea	8.2	38.9	5.25	11.8	12.3
Singapore	6.1	78.9	5.31	5.7	12.7
Second generation Asian NICs					
Thailand	6.4	25.3	0.67[91]	11.4	15.5
Indonesia	4.2	12.7	–	7.1	6.7
Malaysia	3.5	32.1	1.41[90]	6.3	12.6
Third generation Asian NICs					
Philippines	−0.6	10.8	0.48[91]	−0.1	3.4
India	3.0	4.9	0.34[89]	5.7	7.0
China	8.2	9.4	0.26	11.1	11.5
Latin American NICs					
Argentina	−0.5	33.3	–	−1.3	3.2
Brazil	0.3	21.7	1.82[88]	−0.3	5.2
Mexico	−0.5	27.5	2.11	0.1	5.4
Eastern European NICs					
Hungary	1.2	24.5	1.66	−1.6	2.3
Poland	0.4	20.2	1.12[91]	−1.1	2.8

* Based on purchasing power parity

Source: *Bank of England Quarterly Bulletin*, February 1996

Key Definitions 5

newly industrialised country (NIC) Countries which since the 1960s have experienced very rapid growth in manufacturing industry.

transnational corporation (TNC) A company operating in more than one country. The largest TNCs have worldwide manufacturing capability.

the informal sector That part of the economy operating outside official recognition without formal systems of control and remuneration.

Figure 5.46 The CBD of Singapore at night

- a good initial level of hard and soft infrastructure providing the preconditions for structural economic change

- as in Japan previously, the land-poor NICs stressed people as their greatest resource, particularly through the expansion of primary and secondary education but also through specialised programmes to develop scientific, engineering and technical skills

- cultural traditions that revere education and achievement

- the Asian NICs became globally integrated at a 'moment of opportunity' in the structure of the world system, distinguished by the geostrategic and economic interests of core capitalist countries (especially the United States and Japan) in extending their influence in East and South East Asia

- all four countries had distinct advantages in terms of geographical location. Singapore is strategically situated to funnel trade flows between the Indian and Pacific oceans and its central location in the region has facilitated its development as a major financial, commercial and administrative-managerial centre. Hong Kong has benefited from its position astride the trade routes between North East and South East Asia, as well as acting as the main link to the outside world for southeast China. South Korea and Taiwan were ideally located to expand trade and other ties with Japan

- the ready availability of bank loans, often extended at government behest and at attractive interest rates, allowed the chaebols (huge business conglomerates) in particular to pursue market share and to expand into new fields.

As their industrialisation processes have matured, the NICs have occupied a more intermediate position in the regional division of labour between Japan and other less developed Asian countries.

Recent economic problems

After decades of impressive growth a major economic crisis hit the economies of East and South Asia in 1997/98 which has had a ripple effect around the world. The detail of this crisis is considered in the Spatial Focus on South Korea. The main concerns of the Developed World during this crisis have been:

- Japan, South Korea and others might cut the price of exports to 'jump-start' their economies and set off a trade war

- banking collapses could pull back large amounts of capital from the United States and the EU

- the potential fall in demand for the Developed World's exports.

The economist Patrick Minford observes that the emerging economies have flooded the world market with manufactured products in wave after wave for several decades, which has produced a considerable decline in the relative price of their goods on the world market (Figure 5.47). Minford muses 'Could it be that we are observing the latest lurch in the price chart, as these countries unload their rapidly rising productive capacity on to the world market? If so, it means that, cheap as these countries are, the goods in which their capacity has been built up are in over-supply.' If this assertion is correct it will lead to falling relative wages for unskilled workers everywhere and further deindustrialisation, with manufacturing contracting everywhere in the West.

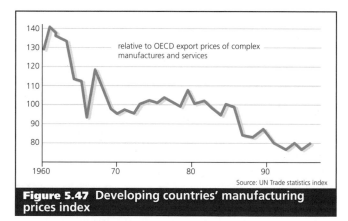

relative to OECD export prices of complex manufactures and services

Source: UN Trade statistics index

Figure 5.47 Developing countries' manufacturing prices index

South Korea: the economic miracle

Few countries have grown so rich in such a short time as South Korea, and much has been written about the reasons for its success. A recent article in the *Economist* (29 November 1997) summed up the most important factors: 'A mixture of hard work, rigorous schooling, state-enforced austerity and imported technology transformed the economy. State-directed bank loans at negative real rates of interest allowed "strategic" industries to invest and expand at a sizzling pace'.

Figure 5.48 World positions of Korean industry, 1994

	Market share %	World rank
Electronics	6.4	5
Semiconductors	11.5	3
Cars	4.6	6
Shipbuilding	22.2	2
Iron and steel	4.7	6
Petrochemicals	4.6	5
Textiles	7.6	5

A prime objective was to be keenly competitive on the world market and to achieve and maintain a high volume of exports which grew from $33 million in 1960 to $130 billion in 1996. Figure 5.48 shows the world ranking and market share of South Korea's most important industries in 1994. Growth was so impressive that in December 1996 the country joined the Organisation for Economic Cooperation and Development (OECD), the club of the world's richest 29 nations.

Huge business conglomerates, known as chaebols, came to dominate the economy. In 1997 the top four (Hyundai, Daewoo, LG and Samsung) accounted for over half of the country's exports. The exporting success of the chaebol encouraged them to diversify. Those named above are in an average of 140 different businesses apiece. When growth rates were high such diversification was seen as a sign of strength. The army-run governments of the 1960s and 1970s held the growth of wages well below that of productivity by banning most trade union activities. In return workers were afforded excellent job security by law. A system of subcontractors, similar to Japan's, developed as an integral part of the economic system. The maxim was to invest heavily and copy the Developed World's technology.

The 1997–98 crisis

The economic crisis of 1997 and 1998 affected all the significant Pacific Rim economies to varying degrees. The South Korean economy was particularly badly hit because of the following reasons according to the financial journals:

■ In late 1995 and early 1996 there was a considerable downturn in the semiconductor, metals and petrochemical businesses. At the same time the value of the yen fell, increasing the relative price of South Korea's products compared with Japan. Profits slumped and company borrowing rose. South Korea's foreign debt doubled between 1995 and 1997.

■ The emergence of low-cost competitors in the region, particularly China, undercut a range of South Korean products in overseas markets.

■ Manufacturing wages in 1997 were 30 per cent higher than in Britain and because of the country's employment protection laws the industrial workforce, according to one estimate, was almost 10 per cent larger than necessary.

■ The extremely high rate of borrowing by chaebols could be serviced when profits were high but became an enormous burden as the country's manufacturing competitiveness was eroded. As growth slowed, South Korea, under international trading pressure was forced to open its economy to a greater extent to foreign competition, which further eroded profits.

■ Profligate lending by the banks tempted the chaebols to diversify into areas where they had little expertise.

■ The banking system collapsed under a mountain of bad debt. One estimate in late 1997 was that

   (a) 18 per cent of the banks' outstanding loans could never be repaid

   (b) 25 of the top 30 chaebols had debt-to-equity ratios of more than three-to-one.

■ The heavy control of the economy by government stifled the emergence of high quality business talent in key sectors of the economy.

■ The chaebols have crowded out small firms leaving the country with few innovative start-ups.

The future

Because so many variables are involved it is difficult to estimate how long the restructuring of the economy will take and what the total cost will be. Whether South Korea likes it or not the chaebols will be exposed to more competition from abroad in the future. Although painful in the short term they will be forced to improve efficiency and productivity to survive if they are to fend off the challenge from countries with cheaper labour such as Thailand and China, and from those with better technology and greater

Figure 5.49 Bank workers demonstrating in Seoul in 1998 during the financial crisis

economies of scale such as the United States and Japan. However, South Korea's strong reliance on heavy industry could make its problems harder to resolve compared to economies based more firmly on light manufacturing and services. Then there is the unpredictability of neighbouring North Korea. There is always the risk of war but many observers think that North Korea will collapse, as East Germany did and then demand to be reconstructed with South Korean help. If this were to be the case the financial burden would be immense.

1 Examine the reasons for South Korea's rapid economic advance since the 1960s.
2 Why was South Korea so badly affected by the recent global economic crisis?

The informal sector in developing countries

An International Labour Office Mission to Kenya in the early 1970s was the first official recognition of what later became known as the informal sector. In developing countries many immigrants to cities along with locally born urban dwellers find that the only possibility of employment is in the informal sector. This 'unofficial' sector of the economy has characteristics that set it apart from the formal or officially documented part of the economy.

■ 'firms' in the informal sector tend to be small labour intensive organisations, usually employing only their owner plus some family labour. However, many people such as street vendors just work on their own
■ there is very little in the way of fixed capital
■ wages are relatively low although it must be recognised that there are many jobs in the formal sector which are poorly paid as well.

Research suggests that about 75 per cent of those working in the informal sector are employed in services. Typical jobs are as messengers, shoe-shiners, roadside food stalls, repair shops, drivers and market traders. Informal sector manufacturing tends to include both the workshop sector making for example cheap furniture, hardware and clothing, and the traditional craft sector. Many of these goods are sold in bazaars and street markets.

In the last decade or so the socio-economic importance of the informal sector in developing countries has gained increasing recognition:

■ it provides much employment and in some trades important skills are learned and passed on
■ many informal activities recycle scarce materials such as plastic containers, oil drums and tyres
■ it produces goods and services which low income households can afford to buy
■ traditional crafts, which may be an important source of foreign exchange, are kept alive
■ domestic savings are mobilised at a level which would be unlikely to occur in the absence of the informal sector

Figure 5.50 Informal industry in the Philippines

1 Why did Hong Kong, Singapore, South Korea and Taiwan become the first generation of Asian NICs?
2 Study Figure 5.45. How do first generation NICs compare in economic terms to the UK and other OECD countries? To what extent are there distinct economic gaps between the three generations of Asian NIC?
3 Discuss the advantages and disadvantages of a significant informal sector in a developing country.

■ there are important linkages between the formal and informal sectors, for example sub-contracting and outworking.

Transnational corporations

Large companies often reach the stage when they want to produce outside of their home country and take the decision to become transnational. The benefits of such a move include:

- **cheaper labour, particularly in developing countries**
- **circumventing trade barriers**
- **tapping market potential in other world regions**
- **avoidance of strict domestic environmental regulations**
- **exchange rate advantages.**

With increased size, greater economies of scale can be achieved, sharpening the company's competitiveness in international markets.

TNCs have a substantial influence on the global economy in general and in the countries in which they choose to locate in particular. They play a major role in world trade in terms of what and where they buy and sell. A not inconsiderable proportion of world trade is intra-firm, taking place within TNCs. The organisation of the car giants exemplifies intra-firm trade with engines, gearboxes and other key components produced in one country and exported for assembly elsewhere.

Large TNCs often exhibit three organisational levels – headquarters, research and development and branch plants. The headquarters of a TNC will generally be in the Developed World city where the company was established. Research and development will most likely be located here too or in other areas within this country. It is the branch plants that are the first to be located overseas. However, some of the largest and most successful TNCs have divided their industrial empires into world regions, each with research and development facilities and a high level of decision making (Figure 5.51).

The world's largest corporations, all of them transnational, boast annual revenues that are greater than the GDPs of many developing nations. In terms of both individual corporations (Figure 5.52a) and industry totals (Figure 5.52b) the list of the top twenty contains services as well as manufacturing businesses. Nine of the world's 20 biggest companies are Japanese; six are American; but 12 of the 20 biggest profit makers are American and none is Japanese.

The combined stock market capitalisation of the world's top 100 companies is now an enormous $4.5 trillion. However, time can take its toll on large companies – research by Leslie Hannah at the LSE showed that of the 100 biggest firms in the world in 1912, nearly half had disappeared by 1995. Thus a reasonable conclusion is that small firms matter as much as big ones.

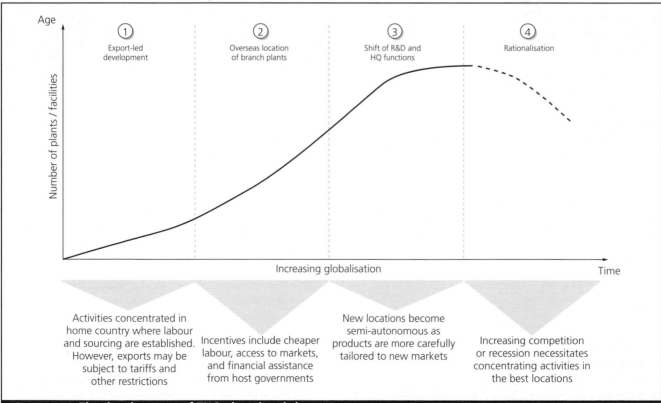

Figure 5.51 The development of TNCs: locational changes

Figure 5.52(a) The world's largest corporations: the top twenty in Fortune's Global 500

Rank 1997	1996			Revenues $ mil.	Profits $ mil.	Rank	Assets $ mil.	Rank	Stockholders' equity $ mil.	Rank	Employees Number	Rank
1	1	GENERAL MOTORS	U.S.	178 174.0	6 698.0	6	228 888.0	46	17 506.0	42	608 000	3
2	2	FORD MOTOR	U.S.	153 627.0	6 920.0	5	279 097.0	34	30 734.0	12	363 892	5
3	3	MITSUI	JAPAN	142 688.3	268.7	336	55.070.5	143	5 272.1	252	40 000	292
4	4	MITSUBISHI	JAPAN	128 922.3	388.1	287	71 407.8	123	7 569.4	177	36 000	314
5	6	ROYAL DUTCH/SHELL GROUP	BRIT./NETH.	128 141.7	7 758.2	3	113.781.4	87	59 981.8	2	105 000	105
6	5	ITOCHU	JAPAN	126 631.9	(773.9)	484	56 307.9	136	2 956.6	353	6 6752	473
7	8	EXXON	U.S.	122 379.0	8 460.0	1	96 064.0	102	43 660.0	4	80 000	149
8	11	WALL-MART STORES	U.S.	119 299.0	3 526.0	25	45 525.0	162	18 502.0	36	825 000	2
9	7	MARUBENI	JAPAN	111 121.2	140.4	388	55 403.4	140	3 563.9	323	64 000	187
10	9	SUMITOMO	JAPAN	102 395.2	209.8	360	42 866.1	171	4 318.6	296	29 500	346
11	10	TOYOTA MOTOR	JAPAN	95 137.0	3.701.3	21	103 893.8	93	45 158.2	3	159 035	48
12	12	GENERAL ELECTRIC	U.S.	90 840.0	8 203.0	2	304 012.0	29	34 438.0	10	276 000	15
13	13	NISSHO IWAI	JAPAN	81 893.8	24.7	443	40.799.3	180	2 019.6	403	18 158	408
14	15	INTL. BUSINESS MACHINES	U.S.	78 508.0	6 093.0	8	81 499.0	117	19 816.0	29	269 465	17
15	14	NIPPON TELEGRAPH & TELEPHONE	JAPAN	76 983.7	2 361.3	56	113 409.5	88	35 989.7	6	226 000	27
16	78	AXA	FRANCE	76 874.4	1 357.0	109	401.206.0	13	13 075.0	69	80 613	146
17	20	DAIMLER-BENZ	GERMANY	71 561.4	4 639.2	12	76 190.7	121	19 510.8	32	300 068	9
18	24	DAEWOO	SOUTH KOREA	71 525.8	526.9	253	44 860.6	165	6 325.3	212	265 044	20
19	18	NIPPON LIFE INSURANCE	JAPAN	71 388.2	2 118.3	62	316 530.4	24	5 575.3	241	75 851	163
20	21	BRITISH PETROLEUM	BRITAIN	71 193.5	4 046.2	16	54.009.1	144	23 221.3	19	56 450	222

Source: *Fortune*, 3 August 1998

Figure 5.52(b) Industry totals: the top twenty in Fortune's Global 500

Rank		Number of companies	1997 revenues $ millions	Profits $ millions	Rank	Assets $ millions	Rank	Stockholders' equity $ millions	Rank	Employees Number	Rank
1	BANKS: COMMERCIAL AND SAVINGS	68	1 243 155	49 353	2	17 372 718	1	686 105	1	2 879 083	3
2	MOTOR VEHICLES AND PARTS	25	1 150 812	33 564	4	1 257 833	5	234 318	5	3 659 169	1
3	TRADING	19	1 013 106	2 714	34	486 545	12	51 074	18	580 090	18
4	PETROLEUM REFINING	31	945 174	54 928	1	864 312	9	363 941	2	1 077 912	9
5	ELECTRONICS, ELECTRICAL EQUIPMENT	25	782 434	21 458	6	969 969	7	234 695	4	3 656 120	2
6	TELECOMMUNICATIONS	22	534 222	40 371	3	869 711	8	291 179	3	2 384 667	5
7	FOOD AND DRUG STORES	28	486 405	8 809	17	233 172	15	72 208	14	2 782 912	4
8	INSURANCE: LIFE, HEALTH (STOCK)	19	425 851	13 132	10	2 375 456	2	134 686	8	570 553	19
9	INSURANCE: LIFE, HEALTH (MUTUAL)	17	410 825	11 933	12	1 782 715	3	36 739	24	415 298	26
10	GENERAL MERCHANDISERS	13	373 322	9 696	13	227 227	18	68 128	15	2 380 587	6
11	INSURANCE: P&C (STOCK)	16	351 062	19 241	7	1 476 487	4	171 081	6	518 891	23
12	UTILITIES, GAS AND ELECTRIC	16	307 208	8 967	16	674 152	11	150 078	7	645 450	16
13	CHEMICALS	16	294 472	11 981	11	329 295	13	99 120	9	968 841	10
14	COMPUTERS, OFFICE EQUIPMENT	9	264 385	14 877	8	242 453	15	76 830	12	913 196	11
15	FOOD	13	258 779	13 354	9	204 938	20	75 959	13	1 146 006	8
16	METALS	13	168 947	3 144	31	191 216	23	46 970	20	566 384	20
17	MAIL, PACKAGE, AND FREIGHT DELIVERY	8	168 743	3 953	29	197 248	21	49 344	19	2 287 173	7
18	PHARMACEUTICALS	10	161 822	24 463	5	211 391	19	90 166	11	608 893	17
19	AEROSPACE	8	154 422	4 836	25	150 708	26	35 727	25	859 673	12
20	ENGINEERING, CONSTRUCTION	10	150 331	(1 099)	45	174 001	24	29 166	31	460 675	25

Source: *Fortune*, 3 August 1998

The United Nations Conference on Trade and Industry constructs an Index of Transnationality (Figure 5.53) by calculating company averages for the following three ratios:

■ foreign assets to total assets

■ foreign sales to total sales

■ foreign employment to total employment.

According to this measure, Nestlé, the Swiss food company was the world's most foreign-oriented company in 1995 with 87 per cent of its assets, 98 per cent of its sales and 97 per cent of its workforce outside Switzerland. However, it is not surprising that several of the most transnational companies are from small developed countries with limited home markets. In contrast Coca-Cola and McDonalds, makers of arguably the best-known global brands, ranked only 31st and 42nd respectively, reflecting the huge size of the US domestic market.

Foreign direct investment

The phenomenal growth in foreign direct investment (FDI) is the most obvious sign of the increasing integration of the world's economies (Figure 5.54) and much of this investment is by transnational corporations. Most FDI is in the Developed World but investment in developing economies has also risen substantially in the 1980s and 1990s. Of the emerging economies, the big five in order of importance, all with an FDI stock of over $50 billion, are China, Brazil, Mexico, Singapore and Indonesia. The UN expects the growth in FDI to continue as more governments are liberalising their investment rules to attract FDI in the quest for capital and growth.

In 1997 the stock of FDI in Britain stood at $345 billion (Figure 5.55), the highest for any economy outside the United States. The inflow has been high in recent years, reaching £16 billion in 1996 and taking the total for the five year period, 1992–96, to more than £53 billion. The figure for 1997 was

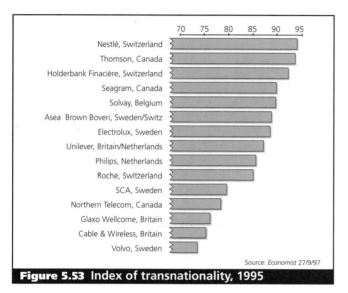

Source: *Economist* 27/9/97

Figure 5.53 Index of transnationality, 1995

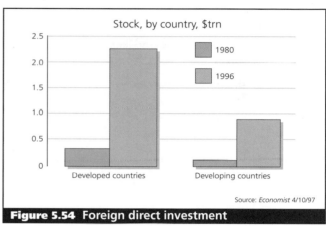

Source: *Economist* 4/10/97

Figure 5.54 Foreign direct investment

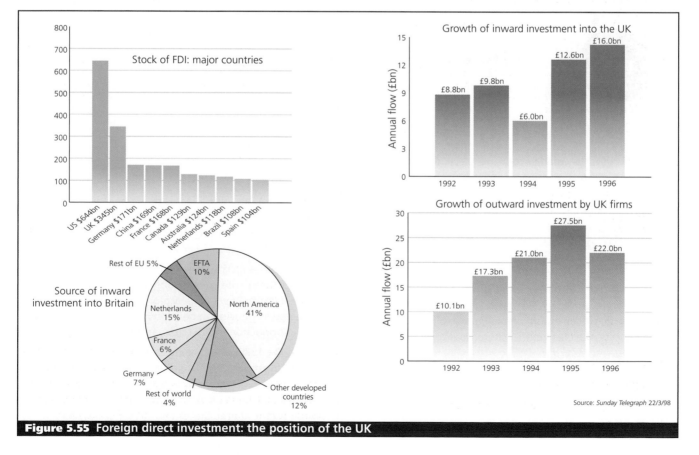

Source: *Sunday Telegraph* 22/3/98

Figure 5.55 Foreign direct investment: the position of the UK

even higher at £23 billion. There are now in excess of 2400 foreign-owned manufacturing firms in the UK, representing 26 per cent of net output and 17 per cent of the manufacturing workforce. The attractions of a UK location as cited by foreign companies are:

- relatively low levels of corporate and personal taxation
- labour flexibility
- access to the EU market
- a less oppressive regulatory climate than in many other countries
- a stable economy with low inflation
- welcoming national, regional and local agencies involved in economic regeneration
- an attractive quality of life
- the English language, the second language for so many foreign executives.

The nature of FDI in Britain has changed over the years. Initially branch plants carrying out routine tasks dominated foreign investment but increasingly research and development has located here. By 1997 there were 150 Japanese R&D centres in Britain. Microsoft, the computer giant, has chosen Cambridge for its first high-tech plant outside the United States. The UK has also become the favoured location for

Questions

1 Why do many large companies decide to manufacture on a transnational basis?
2 Assess the importance of TNCs in the global economy.
3 Discuss the reasons for the popularity of Britain as a recipient of FDI.
4 Why is outward investment of benefit to the UK economy?

international companies to site their pan-European call centres and headquarters.

However, by the latter part of 1998 evidence was growing that Britain was probably no longer the magnet for foreign investment that it once was with a number of foreign companies announcing plant closures or abandoning plans for expansion.

Britain is the world's second largest outward investor with a total outflow of almost £98 billion in the period 1992–96. Such outward investment strengthens the global reach of UK companies, bringing in substantial flows of money from profits made overseas.

SPATIAL FOCUS

The car industry

The car industry is the world's largest manufacturing industry. In 1997 those companies producing motor vehicles and parts in *Fortune* magazine's list of the world's 500 largest companies recorded revenues of $1 150 812 million. General Motors and Ford occupied the top two places in the global listing with Mitsubishi, Toyota, Daimler-Benz and Daewoo also in the world's top 20. Production is still dominated by developed countries but a number of developing nations, such as Brazil and South Korea have moved rapidly up the global league table in the last decade. The three largest producers are Japan, the United States and Germany with the latter leading in the export of automotive products, amounting to 18.5 per cent of global exports of vehicles and parts in 1996 (Figure 5.56).

Although the first motor car was built in 1885 by Karl Benz, a German, it was the United States that established early dominance in the industry by being the first to introduce mass production based on the assembly line principle. The industry became multinational when, in 1911, Ford chose Manchester as the

location for its first assembly plant outside the United States. The following stages can be recognised in terms of global location:

- before 1950 the United States dominated production with Western Europe well behind in second place. During this period an increasing number of assembly plants were established in Western Europe by US manufacturers
- in the 1950s and 1960s the market share of European manufacturers rose considerably (VW, Fiat, Renault, Citroen, BMW, Rover etc.). Major US and European firms were now producing in developing countries such as Brazil. Production in Japan began to increase significantly
- during the 1970s and beyond Japanese market share rose rapidly, overtaking the United States as the world's leading producer in the late 1980s. In the 1980s and 1990s Japanese car firms invested heavily in both the Developed World (in the United States and UK especially) and in developing countries. Other leading car manufacturers

also extended their spread around the globe during this period.

The industry is dominated by firms of great size because of the importance of achieving economies of scale and because of the high cost barrier to entry into the market. In 1991 just ten companies produced three-quarters of the world's cars. The recent merger between Daimler and Chrysler and Volkswagen's brand buying spree could see the number of independent car makers shrink from 22 today to less than 10 within a decade. In an effort to maintain and preferably increase their market share most have invested heavily in key developing countries, clear evidence that on a global scale the industry is market oriented.

The large car producers are using advanced information technology to link their worldwide operations and control costs. In the 1990s they have been making the transition from internationalisation to globalisation. The former is based very much on diverse locations, the latter implies firm, real time linkage between all production facilities.

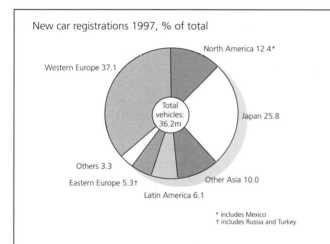

New car registrations 1997, % of total

Western Europe 37.1
North America 12.4*
Total vehicles: 36.2m
Japan 25.8
Others 3.3
Eastern Europe 5.3†
Latin America 6.1
Other Asia 10.0

* includes Mexico
† includes Russia and Turkey

Exports of automotive products $bn, 1996

	% of world exports
Germany	18.5
Japan	15.9
United States	11.7
Canada	9.5
France	7.3
Spain	5.4
Belgium-Luxembourg	5.3
Britain	5.1
Italy	4.1
Mexico*	3.2
South Korea	2.5
Sweden	2.1
Netherlands	1.6
Austria	1.5
Brazil	0.7

Source: *Economist* 20/12/97   * 1995 (includes significant shipments through processing zones)

Figure 5.56 Global car industry

Brazil's car industry

In 1995 Brazil produced 1.6 million motor vehicles (Figure 5.58) making it the seventh largest car manufacturer in the world. Total vehicle sales in the country accounted for 65 per cent of the South American market. By the turn of the century Brazil is expected to replace Italy as the fifth biggest producer with a capacity of 2.6 million cars a year. Strong domestic demand, the advantages of Mercosul and export markets are all contributing to the industry's rapid growth. The industry, with the inclusion of parts, is expected to invest $20 billion in Brazil between 1995 and 2000. Figure 5.59 shows the estimated investment by car manufacturers by region during this period.

Volkswagen is the biggest car manufacturer in Brazil producing 35 per cent of total output, with Fiat coming in second with 27 per cent. The Brazilian automotive parts industry is the largest and most advanced in the Developing World.

The car industry has been the most important single element of the Brazilian economy since its introduction in the 1950s. Much of the investment in Brazil announced by transnational companies goes to the automotive sector. With a ratio of one car for every 11.3 people the growth potential is substantial and much higher than in mature markets like Europe and the United States. Also,

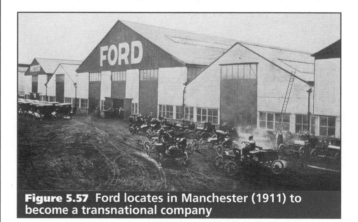

Figure 5.57 Ford locates in Manchester (1911) to become a transnational company

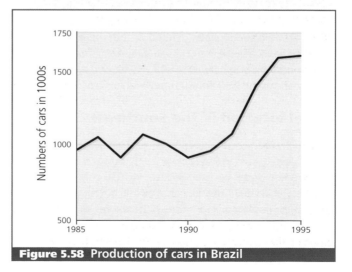

Numbers of cars in 1000s

Figure 5.58 Production of cars in Brazil

Figure 5.59 Estimated investment 1995–2000, in the assembly of cars, trucks and jeeps ($ billions)

Southeast

Fiat	Minas Gerais	3.0
Ford	São Paulo	2.5
General Motors	São Paulo	2.4
Volkswagen	São Paulo and Rio de Janeiro	2.3
Mercedes	Minas Gerais and São Paulo	0.8
Toyota	São Paulo	0.6
Honda	São Paulo	0.3
Scania	São Paulo	0.16
BMW	Undecided	0.15

South

General Motors	Rio Grande do Sul and Santa Catarina	1.1
Renault	Paraná	1.0
Audi	Paraná	0.5
Chrysler	Paraná	0.3
Volvo	Paraná	0.15

Northeast

Asia	Bahia	0.72
Inpavel	Pernambuco	0.3
Hyundai	Bahia	0.29
General Motors	Undecided	0.16
Subaru	Ceará	0.15
Skoda	Bahia	0.1
Troller	Ceará	0.016

North

Zam	Acre	0.014
Nanjing	Tocantins	0.009

Centre-West

Mitsubishi	Goiás	0.035

Brazil's current vehicle fleet, with an average age of fifteen years for buses and eleven years for cars promises a booming replacement market. The sales volume that can be achieved in Brazil is only possible in countries of continental proportions and a rapidly growing middle class – which rules out China, India and Eastern Europe, at least in the near future. Annual vehicle sales in Brazil almost doubled between 1992 and 1996 making the country one of the world's fastest-growing domestic car markets.

Initial location in the Southeast

The first Brazilian car was a Model 'T' Ford which was assembled from imported parts in São Paulo in 1919. However, before Juscelino Kubitschek became President in 1956 only a few cars were assembled in Brazil and there was one government-owned factory manufacturing trucks. Foreign companies were invited by the Kubitschek government to establish branch plants and then pressed to manufacture more and more of the parts for their vehicles in Brazil. Motor vehicles were seen as a key industry which

would stimulate the development of other industries because of the great variety of components required for the finished product.

It is not surprising that foreign car manufacturers first located in and around São Paulo. The largest metropolitan area in South America offered the following advantages:

- a good regional raw material base
- the largest pool of skilled labour in South America
- proximity to Santos, now one of the largest port complexes in the world
- a mature web of industrial linkages
- the largest market by far in the country
- the hub of road, rail and air transport, and telecommunications
- welcoming federal and state governments.

Once the industry had become established in São Paulo it was only a matter of time before other locations in the Southeast region became attractive, namely Rio de Janeiro and Belo Horizonte. For example in 1978 Fiat opened a large plant in Belo Horizonte employing over 10 000 people and producing 130 000 cars a year. However, it must be noted that the first motor vehicle plant outside the state of São Paulo opened in 1966 at Jaboatão, near Recife. Here Willys-Overland do Brasil produced jeeps and pick-up trucks.

Although car makers are now looking beyond the Southeast in terms of location the region is still attracting substantial inward investment. For example Mercedes-Benz is building a $460 million plant in Minas Gerais state (Figure 5.60). This is only the company's second fully fledged car plant outside Germany, the first being in Alabama, United States. High labour costs in Germany are a major reason for the company's decision to extend manufacturing overseas.

The spread to the South

Among the new manufacturers to locate in Brazil, the most ambitious project belongs to the French company Renault which has invested $1 billion in a huge plant producing the 'Megane'. The site selection process promoted what the press termed a 'fiscal war' among a number of states anxious to benefit from such substantial inward investment. For Renault, locating in Brazil is a matter of survival. Ranked eight in the world with a production of 1.8 million vehicles per year, the newly privatised company lacks space to grow in Europe where competition is intense. The selection of Curitiba in the state of Paraná, as the location for the new Renault plant marked an important stage in the development of the industry – the beginning of its spread outwards from the Southeast. Major factors in Renault's choice of location were:

- the high quality of life in Curitiba
- improvements in the port of Paranaguá (Curitiba's outport) where handling charges are considerably below those of Santos

Newcomers flood auto market

In 1997, Brazil ranked eighth in the world vehicle industry, with an output of 2,067,452 units, excluding motorcycles. In theory, it is one of the most promising markets in the world. The country is huge (8.5 million square kilometers). The population is large (165 million inhabitants). And its economy is the ninth-ranked worldwide (a $760 billion Gross Domestic Product), though the per capita income is relatively low (around $4,600).

It's no wonder that several car makers have disclosed plans to settle here, partially encouraged by heavy fiscal breaks. Last October, Honda began production of its first car in Brazil, the Civic sedan. The Japanese automaker has publicly announced a goal of getting a humble stake of the market in the coming years, near 8%. Volkswagen has been the main producer for decades — its market share nears 33%, followed by Fiat, General Motors and Ford. So far, Toyota has had a modest participation, by producing a single utilitarian vehicle since the 1960s. But this year, it will kick off production of the Corolla sedan at a new plant in the state of São Paulo.

There are many expansion plans. In the second half of this year, Volkswagen will inaugurate a new plant in the southern state of Paraná to produce the Audi A3, Santana and Golf models. In 1999, General Motors should open a plant in Rio Grande do Sul to make the Astra sedan and a subcompact car. Ford is to begin construction of a plant in the same state, and Fiat is upscaling its factory in Minas Gerais to produce light trucks and vans. In the same state, Mercedes Benz — which has locally produced trucks and buses since the 1960s — will manufacture the compact car Classe A as of this year.

Meanwhile, French group Peugeot-Citroen will set up a plant in the state of Rio de Janeiro to assemble compact and mid-sized automobiles by the end of 1999. Renault, for its turn, is slated to open a plant in Paraná to assemble sedan and van models, in the coming year. BMW, in a joint venture with Chrysler, will set up an engine plant in Paraná (the motors will be exported to Great Britain and the United States). Still in Paraná, BMW will produce, in association with its British subsidiary Rover, the utilitarian vehicle Defender. Chrysler alone will assemble the Dakota pick-up model. Korean automakers Asia Motors and Hyundai, reported plans of settling here too, but the Asian financial crisis is likely to postpone their projects.

If all projects reported by local producers and newcomers are put into practice, the aggregate investment in the automotive sector will reach $20 billion by the year 2000, and total output would increase by 40% or 50%.

Figure 5.60 *Gazeta Mercantil*, 9 March 1998

■ the success of existing multinational companies in Curitiba such as Phillip Morris, Bosch and Volvo (tractors)

■ proximity to the large markets in the Southeast

■ Paraná borders Argentina and Paraguay; both viewed as expanding markets.

More recently the state of Rio Grande do Sul has been criticised by competing states for offering an over-generous package of incentives to General Motors. GM was given R$253 million before plant construction had even started. Opponents argue that:

Figure 5.61 New car plant in Northeast Brazil

1. Foreign transnationals assembling components mainly produced in developed countries for the Brazilian market.
2. Foreign transnationals assembling components mainly produced in Brazil for the Brazilian market.
3. Foreign transnationals assembling components mainly produced in Brazil for the South American market in general.
4. Foreign transnationals exporting parts and some cars to developed countries.

Future
5. Foreign transnationals exporting cars to developed countries in significant volumes.
6. Brazilian car manufacturer(s) compete for the domestic market with foreign transnationals.

Figure 5.62 The Brazilian car industry: stages of development

■ the state is failing to collect taxes from those who can afford them

■ the capital intensive nature of the modern car industry brings only limited new employment.

New plants planned in the Northeast

Foreign vehicle manufacturers have also targeted the Northeast in terms of car plant location. This has been due mainly to government incentives aimed at encouraging the industry to spread out beyond the Southeast and South. Asia Motors should be the first car manufacturer to benefit from the incentives included in the new Provisional Measure (MP). Planning to build either in the state of Bahia or in Ceará an investment of $500 million should realise production of 60 000 cars by 1999.

While labour availability is high in the region, levels of education and industrial skill are low compared to the Southeast and South. Thus low productivity appears to be the major obstacle for the car industry to overcome in this problem region.

Stages in development

Figure 5.62 can reasonably be seen as the life-cycle of the Brazilian car industry. The country has recently moved into stage four as exemplified by GM's São José dos Campos plant near São Paulo which exports engines to the United States. The eventual aim shared by the government and leading manufacturers is that cars produced in Brazil will be shipped in large numbers to the Developed World, a purpose for which the Northeast is strategically located. At present such export is very limited. When stage five is fully achieved Brazil will really have come into her own as a global player in the industry.

Questions

1 Examine the stages in the locational history of the car industry in Brazil.
2 Why is the market for cars growing more rapidly in Brazil than in other large developing countries such as India and China?
3 Explain the following statement: 'The car industry has a considerable multiplier effect leading to the growth of other industries'.

Urban and rural manufacturing

The urban-rural shift

The relatively compact nature of towns and cities during the industrial revolution years of the nineteenth century resulted in a concentration of manufacturing industry in the inner cities of the twentieth century as the era of the motor vehicle allowed cities to sprawl far beyond their previous limits. However, as the decades evolved the disadvantages of inner city location became more and more obvious. The first reaction to the constraints of inner city sites was to select new suburban locations but increasingly, from the 1960s in particular, manufacturing industry has been attracted to rural areas. This latter movement has been generally recognised as the most important trend in the location of manufacturing industry in Britain in the second half of the twentieth century.

The explanation for the inner city decline of manufacturing industry lies largely in constrained location theory which identifies the problems encountered by manufacturing firms in congested cities, particularly in the inner areas:

■ the industrial buildings of the nineteenth and early twentieth century, mostly multi-storey, are generally unsuitable for modern manufacturing with a preference for single-storey layout
■ the intensive nature of land use usually results in manufacturing sites being hemmed in by other land users preventing on-site expansion
■ the size of most sites is limited by historical choice and frequently deemed to be too small by modern standards, making change of use to housing, recreation or other uses likely. Old sites can rarely accommodate industrial estates,

Figure 5.63 Example of new rural manufacturing; Northants

the preferred form of industrial location in most local authority areas

■ where larger sites are available the lack of environmental regulations in earlier times has often resulted in high levels of contamination. In such situations reclamation is very costly indeed
■ the high level of competition for land in urban areas has continuously pushed up prices to prohibitive levels for manufacturing industry in many towns and cities.

Other factors specific to inner cities which have contributed to manufacturing loss are:

■ urban planning policies in the form of the huge slum clearance schemes of the 1950s, 1960s and 1970s meant that factories located in slum housing areas were frequently demolished as well
■ regional economic planning also had an impact in some areas, London in particular. The availability of incentives in Development Areas provided the stimulus that some firms needed to abandon the inner city
■ before the era of decline, important inter-firm linkages had been built up in inner city areas. As these links were steadily broken, the locational 'raison d'etre' of many of the remaining inner city firms gradually evaporated.

In contrast rural areas have offered plenty of available land at relatively low prices. This has allowed firms to purchase generous allocations of space for single-storey development and for future expansion. With agriculture being the previous use in most cases, pre-construction costs have been minimal.

Other reasons for the urban-rural shift which have been debated in the literature include:

- residential preference in terms of the high perceived quality of life in rural areas. This tends to be truer for small to medium-sized enterprises than for large firms. For the latter it is likely that the decision makers will live near company HQ rather than near the new site in question
- the cost and turnover of labour: both tend to be lower in rural compared to urban areas
- the lack of traffic congestion in rural areas may reduce transport costs
- green belt policies preventing development at the edges of cities have encouraged 'leapfrogging' into rural areas proper.

Intra-urban changes in manufacturing

Although manufacturing employment has declined in cities as a whole in recent decades, job loss has been much more severe in inner cities compared with suburban areas. Thus there has been a marked relative shift of manufacturing employment within urban areas in favour of the suburbs and, in a few instances, manufacturing employment in the suburbs has shown an absolute increase.

The reasons for the decline in inner city manufacturing have been largely covered above. For industries wishing to remain within urban areas the suburbs offered the following attractions compared to the older, crowded inner areas:

- the movement of population from inner to suburban areas increased the relative strength of the latter in terms of labour supply. For some industries population movement also meant a locational shift of their markets
- investment in new roads, particularly motorways, dual carriageways and ring roads has given many suburban areas a very high level of accessibility
- industrial estates in suburban areas are usually much larger than those in inner areas because of contrasts in building density and competition for land
- land prices and rents are, in general, considerably lower in suburban locations
- the quality of life is perceived to be significantly higher in the suburbs.

Centrally located manufacturing

Despite substantial decline some industries remain within the inner parts of urban areas. Where applicable, waterfront locations remain attractive for some industries such as sugar cane refining, flour milling and timber, which have benefited from break-of-bulk and immediate access to a large market. However, many factories which were centrally located along waterfronts have left for reasons covered above. A comparison of industrial location along the River Thames decade by decade since the

Figure 5.64 Inner city industry in East London

1960s shows a continuous and huge overall loss. For example, the north bank stretch between Hammersmith Bridge and Fulham football ground was still dominated by manufacturing and the storage of river transported products in 1960. Now all that remains is one oil storage depot, although a large building once occupied by Duckhams oil has been converted into small workshops. Elsewhere housing, at first local authority but later private development, has taken up the vacant land.

Other industries have historically located just outside the CBD which has provided the markets for the goods they produce. Examples include furniture, clothing, printing and jewellery, all of which have traditionally had a strong presence in London's East End. Such industries generally operate in small units that have important linkages between them. Premises are often small and run-down and therefore low in rent. Location in the so-called zone in transition means that an abundant labour supply is available locally. Another type of inner city industry is one whose market is all of the city and its close surroundings. Major examples are breweries, bakeries and newspapers.

Questions

1 Discuss the assertion that 'the urban-rural shift' has been the most important change in the location of manufacturing industry in Britain over the past fifty years.
2 Account for the decline of manufacturing in inner cities. Which type of industries still tend to remain in inner cities? Explain why.

Economic activity and the environment

Externalities

Virtually all forms of economic activity impact adversely on the environment but the greatest problems are usually attributable to manufacturing industry. The latter generates clearly defined externalities, which are the costs and benefits of manufacturing which are felt beyond the factory gates. The positive externalities (benefits) are primarily in the form of employment and the prosperity this generates. The negative externalities (costs) include the various forms of pollution caused by the manufacturing processes, congestion due to increased traffic flows, and parking problems if the site is restricted in size.

In general, externalities decline with increasing distance from the source and it should be possible to plot externality gradients, positive and negative, on a graph. The points where these cease to have an impact marks the limit of the respective 'externality fields'.

The most serious polluters are the large-scale processing industries which tend to form agglomerations as they have similar locational requirements. The impact of a large industrial agglomeration may spread well beyond the locality and region to cross international borders. For example, prevailing winds in Europe generally carry pollution from west to east. Thus the problems caused by acid rain in Scandinavia have been due partly to industrial activity in Britain. In the mid-1980s the environmental pressure group Friends of the Earth produced a 'dirty' picture postcard supposedly sent to Britain from its European neighbours, with the caption 'We love your country but not your pollution'. Dry and wet deposition can be carried for considerable distances. For example, pollution found in Alaska was traced back to the Ruhr industrial area in Germany.

Pollution control in the Developed World

Considering the intense use of energy and materials, levels of pollution are relatively low in the Developed World because:

■ in recent decades increasingly strict environmental legislation has been passed in developed countries. This is the beginning of a process to make polluters pay for the cost of their actions themselves rather than expecting society as a whole to pay the costs

■ industry has spent increasing amounts on research and development to reduce pollution – the so-called 'greening of industry'

■ the relocation of the most polluting activities, such as commodity processing and heavy manufacturing to the emerging market economies.

Thus the expectation is that after a certain stage of economic development in a country the level of pollution will decline (Figure 5.65). The 1990s have witnessed the first signs of 'product stewardship'. For example in Germany the 1990 'take-back' law required auto manufacturers to take responsibility for their vehicles at the end of their useful lives. Japanese manufacturers are also beginning to improve their environmental credentials although much remains to be done (Figure 5.66).

Dumpers and dustbins

As environmental legislation has tightened in the Developed World many poorer countries have become dustbins for unwanted waste. In 1990 the UN estimated that one-tenth of the waste produced worldwide each year was being shipped from the Developed World to the Developing World, with Asia the main recipient. For example in 1996 an American freighter sat in Hong Kong harbour for four months before it

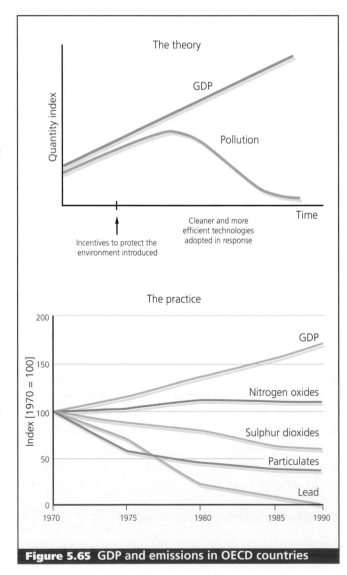

Figure 5.65 GDP and emissions in OECD countries

Toxic waste in Japan
THE BURNING ISSUE

A PENCHANT for wrapping everything in plastic and then burning the rubbish indiscriminately has turned Japan into the dioxin centre of the world. Dioxins, a highly toxic group of chemicals that are known to cause birth defects, skin disease and cancer, are produced when polyvinyl chloride (PVC) and other plastic waste is burned at temperatures below 700 degrees celsius. So toxic is dioxin that a dose no bigger than a single grain of salt can kill a man.

A recent study by Nicholas Smith, from the Tokyo office of Jardine Fleming, a stockbroking firm, found that more than 100 of the 1,500 or so incinerators in Japan failed to meet the country's (already lax) dioxin emissions criteria. Japanese law allows 80 billionths of a gram of dioxin per cubic metre of air—800 times greater than typical standards in Western Europe and North America. Only eight incinerators in Japan actually meet the international norm. And one, in Hyogo, continues to spew out dioxin at 10,000 times the concentration allowed elsewhere.

All that poison floating around in the air may pass unnoticed. But when it falls to earth and contaminates the soil and groundwater, it becomes harder to ignore. A wake-up call for Japanese industry—on the scale of the Love Canal incident in America in 1980—came in April when the soil surrounding an incinerator in Nosecho, a residential suburb north of Osaka, was found to contain a staggering 8,500 picograms of dioxin per gram of soil. This has given Nosecho the unpleasant distinction of having the highest concentration in the world.

The outcry over the toxic waste that contaminated the soil at Love Canal in New York state prodded the American Congress into establishing a trust fund (the "Superfund")—financed by a levy on the oil and chemical industries—to clean up such sites. In the same way, Nosecho has focused public anger on industrial polluters in Japan. Rather than

being hauled over the coals, sensible firms have started to publish ugly details about the frightening condition of some of their sites.

First to come clean was Toshiba. In early June, the electrical group reported illegally high levels of a carcinogen, trichlorethylene—an industrial cleaning agent that is believed to cause kidney and liver damage as well as cancer—in the groundwater beneath four of its domestic factories. The company carried out on-site inspections of all its 25 plants in Japan after detecting trichlorethylene levels at 15,600 times the permitted level at a factory in Nagoya last October. Having found similar levels of the toxic waste outside the plant, the local government is checking the health of residents in the neighbourhood.

Next a consumer-electronics giant, Matsushita, reported harmful carcinogen levels in the groundwater beneath four of its factories in the Osaka area. The level of the cancer agent tetrachlorethylene—used for cleaning semiconductors—at one of the plants was 9,400 times the permissible limit. At another plant, in Hokkaido, the groundwater contamination was 5,200 times the maximum. The company suspects that the groundwater beneath 80 of its 112 plants in Japan may be contaminated with harmful compounds.

Such findings have come to light more than a year after Japan's amended Water Pollution Prevention Act came into effect. But the recent rush to reveal all has been prompted as much by the "Nosecho effect" as by the retroactive nature of the legislation, which forces the original polluter to clean up an affected site.

But the remedial work is not just required at big manufacturers. The Environment Agency of Japan points to the plethora of small plating shops as the country's worst offender in terms of toxic waste, followed (surprisingly) by dry-cleaners, hairdressers and public bath-houses. Big industries such as chemicals and electronics follow close behind. So far, only a fraction of the small backstreet offenders have had their land surveyed. There is still a lot of nasty stuff out there in the Japanese soil. And an awful lot of work will be needed to clean it up.

Figure 5.66 *Economist*, 25 July 1998

Key Definitions

externality The side-effects, positive and negative, of an economic activity that are experienced beyond its site.

product stewardship A system of environmental responsibility whereby producers take back a product, recycling it as far as possible, after the customer has finished with it.

subsidy Financial aid supplied by government to an industry for reasons of public welfare, the balance of payments etc.

was refused entry and sent back to the United States with its 200-ton cargo of 'renewable plastic' mixed with rotten food and metal. In the same year Lebanon was trying to force Germany to take back a 750-ton shipment of contaminated plastics which had been exported for recycling. The load was found to contain pesticides, fertilisers and other potent chemicals. Greenpeace has branded the shipment of waste to the Developing World as immoral.

Race and environment

According to the journal *Environment* (May 1994) in a review of the relationship between race/social status and environmental quality in the United States. 'The geographic distribution of both minorities and the poor has been found to be highly correlated to the distribution of air pollution, municipal landfills and incinerators,

Figure 5.67 Urban 'pollution' in the US

1 Describe and explain the graphs presented in Figure 4.65.
2 With reference to Figure 4.66 examine the extent to which Japanese industry has reduced its environmental impact.
3 Discuss the relationship between race/social class and the environment.
4 Why can government subsidies to various economic activities be counterproductive in environmental terms?

abandoned toxic waste dumps, and lead poisoning in children. The race correlation is even stronger than the class correlation.' The article in question asserted that unequal environmental protection undermined three basic types of equity which were:

- **procedural equity which refers to the extent that planning procedures, rules, regulations are applied in a non-discriminatory way**
- **geographic equity which refers to the proximity of communities to environmental hazards and locally unwanted land uses such as smelters, refineries, sewage treatment plants and incinerators**
- **social equity which refers to the role of race and class in environmental decision making.**

Ironically some government actions have created and exacerbated environmental inequity. More stringent environmental regulations have driven noxious facilities to follow the path of least resistance toward poor, overburdened communities where protesters lack the financial clout and professional skills of affluent areas. However, the prospects of bringing in much needed jobs justifies the risks in the eyes of some residents in poor areas.

Perverse subsidies

A 1998 report entitled 'Perverse Subsidies', published by the International Institute for Sustainable Development highlighted the huge amounts that taxpayers worldwide fork out to subsidise industry, energy, transport, farming, water and fishing. But taxpayers then have to spend almost as much again to help repair the damaging effects subsidies can have on the environment and the economy. The report concluded that 'by removing perverse subsidies we find that economies become more efficient and productive, at the same time as being more conserving of our natural resources'.

The pressure builds

Large European and Asian insurance companies have recently entered the industrial pollution debate. These companies,

which are among the world's biggest stockowners, have warned environment damaging companies that they will unload their shares if appropriate remedial action isn't taken. The insurance industry is concerned that unchecked pollution will eventually cause major economic problems.

A much more detailed discussion of the impact of economic activity on the environment can be found in Chapter 14.

The service sector

The service sector is by far the most dominant employer in developed economies and it is also of considerable significance in most developing countries. As an economy becomes more sophisticated the contribution of the service sector increases in terms of employment, GDP and all other standard measures. It can be argued that a service sector can be recognised historically at all levels of development but it was not until the industrial revolution that it really came to maturity. Its economic influence increased steadily to attain a prominent role in the second half of the twentieth century. As Figure 5.52 (page 168) shows, in terms of the industry totals for the world's 500 largest corporations, major service industries are very well represented. However, this data does not include smaller companies. For example, insurance is a giant industry with a $2 trillion turnover, several times more than the entire oil industry. It controls £10 000 billion in equities, a third of the value of global stockmarkets.

The service sector encompasses a wide range of industries, occupations and products, and it can be classified in a number of different ways (Figure 5.68). Perhaps the most important distinction is between producer services and consumer services. Producer services are supplied to other firms or organisations, helping them to deliver their product or service to the final consumer. Many producer services are 'high order', including market research, management consultancy, advertising and legal services. In contrast, many consumer or household services are 'low order' and provided generally on a

Figure 5.68 Summary of alternative classifications for service industries

Dichotomous classifications

A Producer (or intermediate) services
   Consumer (or final) services

B Local (population-serving, industry-serving) services
   Non-local services (serving regional, national or
   international markets)

C Market services (funded from private resources)
   Non-market services (funded from public resources)

D Footloose services   stresses influence
   Tied services   of location on operation

E Office services   based on relative importance
   Non-office services   of office occupations

Other classifications

A Complementary services
   Old services
   New services

B Productive services
   Individual consumption services
   Collective consumption services

C Distributive services
   Producer services
   Social services
   Personal services

Source: *Service Industries: Growth and Location* by P. Daniels, CUP,
1986

personal basis. Examples include retailing, refuse collection, hairdressing and dry cleaning. Generally speaking, services are grouped together in 'central places' which are hierarchically arranged in terms of the services offered: places with larger populations offer a wider variety of services than smaller places.

The variety of services has increased over time in response to:

- the adoption of new technology
- increases in personal disposable income
- greater leisure time
- demographic changes
- new social values.

It is not difficult to think of a considerable number of services available today which were not around thirty or forty years ago.

The aspect of service provision which is of greatest interest to the geographer is location. Important locational factors affecting service provision include:

- the distribution and density of population
- variations in purchasing power
- availability of labour with appropriate skills
- proximity to other service activities
- demographic factors such as age and gender.

The distribution of services in a region can be to a considerable extent explained by reference to OS maps at various scales and census data, and by conducting judicious field research.

In the UK service industries employ about 17 million people, accounting for two-thirds of GDP. The South East has the highest concentration of service employment with the lowest rates found in the East Midlands and the West Midlands.

Business and financial services

The increasing concentration of high level services

As a result of a combination of globalisation and informationalisation, the production of services has become increasingly detached from the production of goods. Although producer services do depend to a certain extent on production, the financial services sector has no direct relationship to manufacturing. In locational terms contrasting trends have been at work. As manufacturing has dispersed worldwide, high level services have increasingly concentrated and have been doing so in places different from the old centres of manufacturing.

At the top of the urban service hierarchy are the global cities of London, New York and Tokyo. These cities are the major nuclei of global industrial and financial command functions. The economic strength of these cities has become more and more detached from the local economies in which they are located and they have become embedded in a truly global set of economic relations. The prominence of the global cities is now less as centres of corporate headquarters and more as leaders in financial markets and financial innovation. In an era of hypermobility of financial capital the volume of activity conducted in these centres is absolutely crucial to their success, as margins on transactions have become increasingly slight as a result of intense competition. However, the knowledge structures and institutions which comprise the growth engines of the global cities are difficult for other cities lower down the hierarchy to capture.

Below the three global cities is a second level of about 20 cities, including Paris, Brussels, Milan, Chicago and Los Angeles, which also have significant global connections. All the cities in the two top rungs of the global hierarchy offer a wide range of highly specialised services. There is a production process in these services which benefits from proximity to other specialised services. For example the production of a financial instrument requires inputs from accounting, advertising, legal expertise, economic consulting, designers, public relations and printers. Time replaces weight in this process as a force for agglomeration.

The City of London

London is the world's leading financial centre with the largest share of many world markets. With a resident population of less than 3000 its workforce is just under 300 000, 75 per cent of which work in banking, finance, insurance and business services. Office floor space in the City amounts to 7.2 million square metres. The net overseas earnings of UK financial institutions, predominantly based in the City of London, totalled over £22.7 billion in 1996. More trading in the dollar and the Deutschmark takes place in London than in either the United States or in Germany. The following facts help to underline London's importance to the global financial system:

■ the London foreign exchange market is the largest in the world. Its daily turnover of $464 billion accounts for 30 per cent of global business

■ London is the world's largest international insurance market, with net premium income of £14 billion in 1996

■ the London Stock Exchange, with 60 per cent of global turnover in 1996, is the world's largest centre for the trading of foreign equities. More foreign companies are listed on the LSE than on any other exchange

■ there are approximately 570 foreign banks in London, more than in any other city

■ London is the world's second largest fund management centre, after Tokyo, with over $1.8 trillion in equities under management

■ London is the largest centre in the world for maritime service with net overseas earnings of £2 billion

■ banks based in the City of London invest more capital abroad than those of any other country, amounting to 18 per cent of external bank lending globally

■ London is the global clearing centre for gold forward trading and financing

■ London is second in the world, after Chicago, in exchange traded derivatives.

To remain in such a formidable position continuing investment is vital. Thirty per cent of high-tech City office buildings were constructed since the late 1980s. Information technology expenditure in the City in 1996 amounted to £2.2 billion. The Corporation of London's Economic Development Unit is responsible for maintaining London's prime global position. Using the Corporation's statutory powers to invest in economic development, the Unit's objectives are:

■ to ensure that all the leading entities in global finance and commerce are in the City and that they have the professional support to function efficiently

■ to enhance the quality of the working and living environment within the City

■ to ensure the provision of an efficient infrastructure and a high quality workforce by working closely with the property and training sectors

■ to market the attributes of the City and of London as a whole on a worldwide basis

■ to achieve an orderly property market by using its influence as both planning authority and landowner.

The Unit has specialist teams such as:

■ the City Property Advisory Team which helps business occupiers, developers, owners and investors, and

■ a European Office to help promote dialogue between the City and Europe.

A survey of office rents in the world's major commercial centres for June 1998 found the City of London to be the second highest, after Hong Kong, with an average of $1173 a square metre (including service charges and taxes). During the initial phase of a substantial foreign company's presence in London, there is a marked preference for location within the City. However, following an initial period of settling into the London market many foreign firms expand and become more locationally footloose, usually requiring larger premises at more economic rents in areas such as the South Bank and West End.

The decentralisation of 'back office' functions

In the 1980s and 1990s in particular routine 'back office' functions have been moved away from core locations to less expensive sites as companies have sought to reduce costs in order to remain competitive. Back office functions process large volumes of paper, electronic transactions and telephone enquiries. They include international call centres and customer services such as direct banking and computer support. These routine functions have relocated to:

- **elsewhere in metropolitan areas**
- **peripheral locations at the edge of urban areas**
- **more distant locations in peripheral regions**
- **developing countries with pools of labour able to handle such tasks.**

In Britain the recent wave of private sector relocations has mirrored the decentralisation of public sector back offices, such as the Inland Revenue, from London to the regions in the 1960s. The North East in particular has benefited from recent decentralisation. Examples include British Airways which opened its ticket telesales operation on the Newcastle Business Park in 1991, Abbey National (Teesside), Orange (Darlington) and Ladbroke (Peterlee).

Although relocation can reduce costs in a number of ways the main savings are in terms of labour and office space costs. Labour accounts for about 70 per cent of total costs in back office functions and thus considerable savings can be made by moving from London to lower wage regions within Britain. Labour availability is also important as turnover rates are high, often exceeding 15 per cent. This reflects the moderate salaries and the routine, unchallenging nature of many of the tasks involved.

Some companies have really sought to slash labour costs by moving back office functions to the Developing World. For example, India and Russia have become major centres for subcontracting computer programming.

Key Definitions

global city Major world city supplying financial, business, and other significant services to all parts of the world. The world's major stock markets and the headquarters of large TNCs are located in global cities.

back offices Offices of a company handling high volume communications by telephone, electronic transaction or letter. Such low to medium level functions are relatively footloose and have been increasingly decentralised to locations where space, labour and other costs are relatively low.

Dublin's International Financial Services Centre (IFSC)

Dublin's IFSC was established in 1987 as a spatially discrete 'offshore financial centre'. After overcoming early problems the IFSC has emerged as an important financial centre in Europe and in terms of offshore funds it is in competition with Luxembourg and the Channel Islands. A recent article on the subject (Area (1998) 30.2) states that 'the IFSC represents an important attempt to reposition Ireland in the international divison of labour'. By 1996, the eleven hectare site constructed on a disused dockland area;

- contained over 400 companies
- employed over 2300 people
- contributed £200 million in corporate taxes.

Although many of the companies represented are essentially back offices the Irish government has made every effort to attract more sophisticated financial and business services.

The IFSC has benefited from a low tax regulatory environment set up by the Irish government but sanctioned by the European Commission (Figure 5.69a). The justification for EU approval was Ireland's high unemployment rate, and to benefit from the incentives on offer firms were required to make firm job commitments. Dublin's position in the EU and the package available proved particularly attractive to insurance, reinsurance, back office banking functions and corporate treasury activities. For the latter the major firms represented include IBM, Hewlett-Packard, General Electric and Heinz.

The back offices pay relatively low wages but the IFSC is also about graduate employment opportunities and emerging institutional thickness. The Irish government has been particularly anxious to encourage the latter and upgrade the nature of investment. Dublin is becoming an important centre of US corporate treasury operations and banking activities for the whole of Europe (Figure 5.69b). In 1997, *Fortune* magazine ranked Dublin as the best city in Europe in which to do business. This corresponds very much with the image of Ireland in the 1990s as the 'Celtic Tiger Economy'.

The IFSC has had a significant multiplier effect in the Dublin region. Local financial services outside the boundary of the IFSC, such as tax consultants, accountants and law firms have benefited in particular.

Figure 5.69(a) Dublin's IFSC tax benefits

10% corporate tax rate on trading income
- Guaranteed to 31 December 2005
- Time limit on approvals 31 December 2000

A range of double taxation treaties
- 24 countries covered, including USA, Canada, Japan, Korea, Germany

No withholding tax on dividends and interest

Availability of tax-based financing

Zero tax on certain fund-management entities owned exclusively by non-Irish residents

Figure 5.69(b) Banking operations based at the IFSC

ABN Amro	Heleba
AIB Bank	ICC
Ansbacher	ING
Bacob	Investors Bank & Trust
Banco San Paolo	Kredietbank
Bank in Liechtenstein	MeesPierson
Bank of America	Mellon Bank
Bank of Bermuda	Merrill Lynch
Bank of Ireland	Midland Bank
Bankinter	Mitsubishi Trust & Bank
Baring Brothers	Morgan Grenfell
BCI	National Irish Bank
BNP	NatWest
Brown Brothers	Paribas
Chase Manhattan	PNC
Chemical Bank	Rabobank
Citibank	Royal Bank of Scotland
Clydesdale Bank	Sanwa
Commerzbank	Scotiabank
Credito Italiano	Sumitomo
Daiwa	Ulster Bank
Dresdner Bank	West LB
Deutsche Bank	Wuerttembuergische
Generale Bank	

Retailing

The retailing of goods and services is a major source of employment in all towns and cities. It has a significant impact on land use and is a considerable influence on the daily lives of most people. Traditionally, urban retail organisation has been in the form of a hierarchy with the central business district at the top with subsequent layers, the number depending on the overall size of the urban area, down to the corner shop. The lowest levels of the retail hierarchy mainly provide convenience or low order goods. With ascent of the hierarchy comparison or high order goods become increasingly dominant, although a full range of convenience goods can usually be found at the top of the hierarchy alongside the goods and services for which consumers want to compare price and quality.

The concept of threshold, explained in the previous chapter, is central to the understanding of this hierarchical organisation. Low order centres which require small threshold populations to survive will be spread throughout the urban area with most customers living within walking distance, although they will still probably use their cars to shop. In contrast, the large threshold populations required by the highest order goods ensures that these will only be found in the CBD.

Retailing has been affected by a number of important organisational trends in recent decades:

- the number of independent traders has declined sharply in the face of severe competition from the multiples which compete amongst themselves for market share
- big retailers like Marks & Spencer have gone transnational by opening stores in a number of other countries, and foreign retailers such as Carrefour are having an increasing presence in Britain
- new technology has facilitated developments such as teleshopping.

Figure 5.70 is evidence of the decline of independent grocery stores and the growing dominance of the large supermarkets. For example, in 1950, Sainsbury's had 244 stores in Britain, each with an average of just 2000 sq ft of floorspace, stocking 550 different products. In 1996 Sainbury's had 355 supermarkets with the average store now covering 30 000 sq ft. This retailing giant stocks 19 000 different products. As stores have increased in size they have extended their product range, thus affecting more and more shops in traditional centres. In recent years the large retailers have moved into services, particularly in the financial sector.

The most startling growth has been in superstores which are frequently sited in accessible out-of-town locations. The big chains are keen to open more but they have faced increasing opposition in recent years because:

- they take customers away from rural shops and traditional shopping areas in towns and cities
- they are often built on greenfield sites which local people would like to be kept in the original land use
- they have huge parking areas and generate large volumes of traffic.

In terms of location, decentralisation has been the main trend which has resulted in the partial decline of many central business districts. New planned shopping centres and retail parks have sprung up in both suburban and out-of-town locations. Accessibility has been the main factor in site selection. The planned shopping centres of the modern era originated in North America in the 1950s before arriving in Europe a decade later. Initially most planned shopping centres in Britain were of limited size; located in town centres and allied to new pedestrian precincts. It wasn't until the 1970s that larger schemes, often in New Towns, were constructed. At this

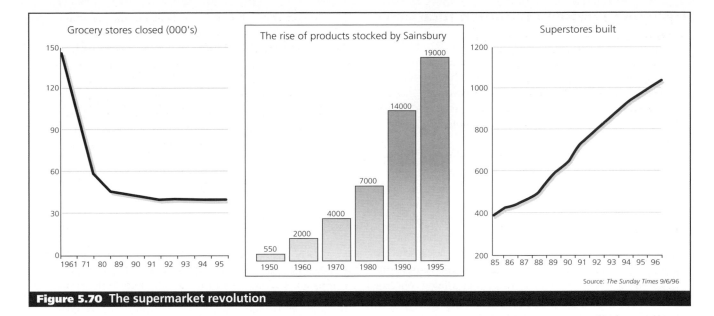

Grocery stores closed (000's)

The rise of products stocked by Sainsbury

Superstores built

Source: *The Sunday Times* 9/6/96

Figure 5.70 The supermarket revolution

time only Brent Cross, near the start of the M1 in north London, could be considered as an out-of-town centre serving a regional market. However, it was not long before other centres of a similar size appeared elsewhere.

The next significant advance in size was the construction of MetroCentre at Gateshead, following the 'multi-purpose mega-mall' concept from North America. For a while it was the largest shopping centre in Western Europe, occupying 160 000 m². There is free parking for 10 000 cars and new bus and rail stations were built for non-motorists. There are 100 buses an hour and 69 trains daily. Other shopping centres of this magnitude include Lakeside at Thurrock and Meadowhall in Sheffield. The overall objective of this new size of shopping centre was to create an extended shopping experience which

would encourage families to think of a visit as a day out. Not only are a full range of goods and services on offer but there are numerous eating places and many leisure opportunities.

The popularity of supermarkets and superstores is evident from the profits made by the retail giants. However, not all sections of society have benefited from the trends in retailing in recent decades. Rural areas have suffered from shop closures, a process which will be discussed below. The government is also concerned that the lack of shops selling reasonably priced goods on many urban estates forces people on low incomes to travel long distances and often pay inflated prices. Under the government's scheme to tackle social exclusion, it is trying to encourage the large retailers to open more shops in deprived urban areas which have been identified as 'food deserts'.

Some large central shopping centres are now beginning to fight back to maintain their market share. In Cardiff a retail partnership has been formed to coordinate action.

Figure 5.71 Meadowhall, Sheffield

Figure 5.72 Local shops have closed because of heavy competition from large stores

Declining service provision in rural areas

A large number of rural communities in Britain have lost shops, pubs, banks and many other services highly valued by the people who used to use them. This has created inconvenience for most rural dwellers but a crisis for those who lack personal mobility – the poor, the old and the young.

Village shops suffered first from the development of large supermarkets in urban areas because the growth in car ownership allowed an increasing number of rural inhabitants to use the new urban services. The second major blow was the widespread development of very accessible out-of-town supermarkets and superstores. It has been impossible for rural outlets to compete on price, quality and range because of the huge economies of scale that the large stores can achieve. In the 1990s the government has become increasingly concerned about service decline in rural areas (Figure 5.73). A Rural Development Commission survey in 1994 found that 41 per cent of rural parishes in England had no permanent shop of any kind.

Questions

1 Briefly discuss the various classifications of service industries presented in Figure 5.68.
2 Explain the attraction of the City of London to major financial institutions and business organisations.
3 Why is it so difficult for other large cities to attain the status of London, New York and Tokyo?
4 What are the reasons for the decentralisation of back office functions?
5 Why was Dublin's IFSC established? How successful has it been?
6 Why has service provision in rural areas declined?

Rural areas 'are losing essential services'

RURAL life is becoming increasingly hard, according to a report published yesterday. Services once taken for granted are absent, a conference organised in London by the Rural Development Commission was told.

Many of England's 10 million rural population find it increasingly hard to get to the nearest shop, Post Office, doctor's surgery, day centre, Job Centre or benefits office.

Miles Middleton, chairman of the commission, called for rural communities to be given the same priority as deprived urban areas.

Referring to last week's report by the Social Exclusion Units, *Bringing Britain Together*, he said: "Rural people need choice too. This isn't about rural versus urban. This is about ensuring that disadvantaged people throughout England have access to good quality, affordable services.

"Many small market towns and country areas lack the basic public and private services which others take for granted. The Government has recognised that there should not be any further decline in rural services.

"I welcome their strategy for tackling the problems of services in the nation's poorest neighbourhoods, but policy-makers must recognise that poverty and social exclusion are not just urban problems.

"Current funding mechanisms mitigate against rural areas because they focus on accepted notions of urban poverty," said Mr Middleton.

Last year, the commission said that half of England's rural shops selling food only had closed since 1991. More than eight out of 10 parishes with fewer than 10,000 people do not have a food-only shop and seven out of 10 do not have a general store.

There is no post office in 43 per cent of the parishes, 92 per cent do not have a police station and 93 per cent lack a public nursery.

More than 90 per cent do not have day care for the elderly, a bank or a building society. More than 60 per cent do not have parent-toddler groups and 59 per cent lack a playgroup.

Source: *Daily Telegraph* 7 October 1998

Figure 5.73 The decline of rural services

Bibliography

References

Global Shift by P. Dickens, Paul Chapman Publishing, 1992.
North America: An Advanced Geography by B. Price and P. Guinness, Hodder & Stoughton, 1997.
Brazil: Advanced Case Studies by P. Guinness, Hodder & Stoughton, 1998.
Manufacturing Industry: the Impact of Change by M. Raw, Collins, 1993.
Service Industries: Growth and Location by P. Daniels, Cambridge University Press, 1986.

Internet

University of Leicester
http://www.geog.le.ac.uk/cti
International development exchange
http://www.index.org/
Financial Times
http://www.ft.com

6 global and regional *disparity and development*

The global development gap

Measuring disparity

In recent decades development economists have increasingly stressed the distinction between economic growth and development. The former denotes an increase in the productive capacity and output of a country or region while the latter is a much more far-reaching concept, encompassing the social, cultural, environmental and political factors that affect the quality of life, as well as the economic conditions that influence a person's well-being. Thus, composite indexes like the Physical Quality of Life Index (PQLI) and the Human Development Index (HDI) are now generally recognised as better indicators of a country's position in the global development spectrum than the traditional measure, GDP per capita. The HDI, devised in 1990 by the UN, contains three variables:

- life expectancy
- educational attainment (adult literacy and combined primary, secondary and tertiary enrolment)
- real GDP per capita (PPP$).

The process of widening people's choices and the level of well-being they achieve are at the core of the notion of human development. As Figure 6.2 shows, all regions of the world are significantly better off now than in 1960. However, the rate of progress has varied widely and the development gap remains extensive. The 1997 Human Development Report (HDR) ranks 175 countries according to the HDI. Figure 6.1 is a selected sample from this development table showing the top and bottom five for the three major groupings of high, medium and low human development countries. The final column in Figure 6.1 compares each country's HDI position with its ranking according to GDP per capita.

Progress and problems

Over the years the concept of poverty has been defined in different ways (Figure 6.3). In assessing the progress made in

reducing global poverty, the Human Development Report notes that:

- in the past 50 years poverty has fallen more than in the previous 500 years
- poverty has been reduced in some respects in almost all countries
- child death rates in developing countries have been cut by more than half since 1960
- malnutrition rates have declined by almost a third since 1960
- the proportion of children not in primary education has fallen from more than half to less than a quarter since 1960
- the share of rural families without access to safe water has been cut from nine-tenths to about a quarter since 1960.

Key Definitions 1

Human Development Index A measure of development which combines three important aspects of human well-being (life expectancy, education and income).

real GDP per capita (PPP$) The GDP per capita of a country converted into US dollars on the basis of the purchasing power parity of the country's currency. It is assessed by calculating the number of units of a currency required to purchase the same representative basket of goods and services that a US dollar would buy in the United States.

absolute poverty A person is absolutely poor if his/her income is less than the defined income poverty line. This will vary from country to country and from region to region depending on the cost of living.

relative poverty Refers to falling behind most others in the community, determined by inclusion in a bottom income group, such as the poorest 10 per cent.

Figure 6.1 Human Development Index: selected countries

HDI rank	Life expectancy at birth (years) 1994	Adult literacy rate (%) 1994	Combined first-, second- and third-level gross enrolment ratio (%) 1994	Real GDP per capita (PPP$) 1994	Adjusted real GDP per capita (PPP$) 1994	Life expectancy index	Education index	GDP index	Human development index (HDI) value 1994	Real GDP per capita (PPP$) rank minus HDI rank
High human development	74.6	97.0	80	17 052	6 040	0.83	0.91	0.98	0.907	–
1 Canada	79.0	99.0	100	21 459	6 073	0.90	0.99	0.99	0.960	7
2 France	78.7	99.0	89	20 510	6 071	0.89	0.96	0.99	0.946	13
3 Norway	77.5	99.0	92	21 346	6 073	0.88	0.97	0.99	0.943	6
4 USA	76.2	99.0	96	26 397	6 101	0.85	0.98	0.99	0.942	1
5 Iceland	79.1	99.0	83	20 566	6 071	0.90	0.94	0.99	0.942	9
60 Malaysia	71.2	83.0	62	8 865	5 945	0.77	0.76	0.97	0.832	–13
61 Mauritius	70.7	82.4	61	13 172	6 022	0.76	0.75	0.98	0.831	–30
62 Belarus	69.2	97.9	80	4 713	4 713	0.74	0.92	0.76	0.806	13
63 Belize	74.0	70.0	68	5 590	5 590	0.82	0.69	0.91	0.806	1
64 Libyan Arab Jamahiriya	63.8	75.0	91	6 125	5 869	0.65	0.80	0.95	0.801	–8
Medium human development	67.1	82.6	64	3 352	3 352	0.70	0.76	0.54	0.667	–
65 Lebanon	69.0	92.0	75	4 863	4 863	0.73	0.86	0.79	0.794	8
66 Suriname	70.7	92.7	71	4 711	4 711	0.76	0.85	0.76	0.792	10
67 Russian Federation	65.7	98.7	78	4 828	4 828	0.68	0.92	0.78	0.792	7
68 Brazil	66.4	82.7	72	5 362	5 362	0.69	0.79	0.87	0.783	0
69 Bulgaria	71.1	93.0	66	4 533	4 533	0.77	0.84	0.73	0.780	9
126 Iraq	57.0	56.8	53	3 159	3 159	0.53	0.56	0.51	0.531	–24
127 Nicaragua	67.3	65.3	62	1 580	1 580	0.70	0.64	0.24	0.530	10
128 Papua New Guinea	56.4	71.2	38	2 821	2 821	0.52	0.60	0.45	0.525	–24
129 Zimbabwe	49.0	84.7	68	2 196	2 196	0.40	0.79	0.35	0.513	–10
130 Congo	51.3	73.9	56	2 410	2 410	0.44	0.68	0.38	0.500	–14
Low human development	56.1	49.9	47	1 308	1 308	0.52	0.49	0.20	0.403	–
131 Myanmar	58.4	82.7	48	1 051	1 051	0.56	0.71	0.16	0.475	25
132 Ghana	56.6	63.4	44	1 960	1 960	0.53	0.57	0.31	0.468	–8
133 Cameroon	55.1	62.1	46	2 120	2 120	0.50	0.57	0.33	0.468	–12
134 Kenya	53.6	77.0	55	1 404	1 404	0.48	0.70	0.22	0.463	5
135 Equatorial Guinea	48.6	77.8	64	1 673	1 673	0.39	0.73	0.26	0.462	–5
171 Mali	46.6	29.3	17	543	543	0.36	0.25	0.07	0.229	1
172 Burkina Faso	46.4	18.7	20	796	796	0.36	0.19	0.11	0.221	–9
173 Niger	47.1	13.1	15	787	787	0.37	0.14	0.11	0.206	–8
174 Rwanda	22.6	59.2	37	352	352	0.00	0.52	0.04	0.187	1
175 Sierra Leone	33.6	30.3	28	643	643	0.14	0.30	0.09	0.176	–4
All developing countries	61.8	69.7	56	2 904	2 904	0.61	0.65	0.46	0.576	–
Least developed countries	50.4	48.1	36	965	965	0.42	0.44	0.14	0.336	–
Sub-Saharan Africa	50.0	55.9	42	1 377	1 377	0.42	0.51	0.21	0.380	–
Industrial countries	74.1	98.5	83	15 986	6 037	0.82	0.93	0.98	0.911	–
World	63.2	77.1	60	5 798	5 798	0.64	0.71	0.94	0.764	–

Source: Human Development Report 1997

Figure 6.2 Changes in global and regional human development 1960–93

Region or country group	HDI 1960	HDI 1970	HDI 1980	HDI 1993
World	0.392	0.459	0.518	0.746
Industrial countries	0.798	0.859	0.889	0.909
OECD	0.802	0.862	0.890	0.910
Eastern Europe and the CIS	0.625	0.705	0.838	0.773
Developing countries	0.260	0.347	0.428	0.563
Arab States	0.228	0.295	0.410	0.633
East Asia	0.255	0.379	0.484	0.633
Latin America and the Caribbean	0.465	0.566	0.679	0.824
South Asia	0.206	0.254	0.298	0.444
South East Asia and the Pacific	0.284	0.372	0.469	0.646
Sub-Saharan Africa	0.201	0.257	0.312	0.379
Least developed countries	0.161	0.205	0.245	0.331

Source: *Human Development Report 1996*

These are just some of the achievements made during what the HDR calls the 'second Great Ascent from poverty', which started in the 1950s in the Developing World, Eastern Europe and the former Soviet Union. The first Great Ascent from poverty began in Europe and North America in the late nineteenth century in the wake of the industrial revolution.

On the negative side the HDR details the substantial problems still remaining:

- more than a quarter of all people living in the Developing World still live in poverty with more than 1.3 billion living on less than $1 a day. 'In a global economy of $25 trillion, this is a scandal – reflecting shameful inequalities and inexcusable failures of national and international policy'
- for a significant number of countries per capita incomes are actually lower now than in previous decades (Figure 6.4)
- nearly a billion people are illiterate
- some 840 million go hungry or face food insecurity
- more than 1.2 billion people lack access to safe water
- nearly a third of the population in the least developed countries, most of which are in Sub-Saharan Africa, are not expected to survive to the age of forty
- women are disproportionately poor. Half a million women in developing countries die each year in childbirth.

The HDR also notes that the face of poverty has changed considerably in recent decades (Figure 6.5).

The North/South divide

Although the global development picture is complex a general distinction can be made between the developed 'North' and the developing 'South' (Figure 6.6). These terms were first

- *Income perspective.* A person is poor if, and only if, her income level is below the defined poverty line. Many countries have adopted income poverty lines to monitor progress in reducing poverty incidence. Often the cut-off poverty line is defined in terms of having enough income for a specified amount of food.
- *Basic needs perspective.* Poverty is deprivation of material requirements for minimally acceptable fulfilment of human needs, including food. This concept of deprivation goes well beyond the lack of private income: it includes the need for basic health and education and essential services that have to be provided by the community to prevent people from falling into poverty. It also recognizes the need for employment and participation.
- *Capability perspective.* Poverty represents the absence of some basic capabilities to function—a person lacking the opportunity to achieve some minimally acceptable levels of these functionings. The functionings relevant to this analysis can vary from such physical ones as being well nourished, being adequately clothed and sheltered and avoiding preventable morbidity, to more complex social achievements such as partaking in the life of the community. The capability approach reconciles the notions of absolute and relative poverty, since relative deprivation in incomes and commodities can lead to an absolute deprivation in minimum capabilities.

Source: *Human Development Report 1997*

Figure 6.3 Perspectives on poverty

used in *North-South: A Programme for Survival* published in 1980, a significant exercise in international diplomacy oriented towards global reform. This publication was produced by a distinguished international commission and is generally known as the 'Brandt Report' after its chairperson Willy Brandt, former chancellor of the then West Germany. Other terms used to distinguish between the richer and poorer nations are:

- developed and developing
- more economically developed and less economically developed
- the First, Second and Third Worlds – labels first used in the 1950s by French academics to distinguish between the advanced capitalist world (First), the communist bloc of the Soviet Union and its eastern European satellites (Second) and the poor nations of the world (Third), located in Africa, Latin America and Asia.

The main objectives of the Brandt Report were to provide the most accurate assessment to date of the global development situation and to produce detailed recommendations for closing the development gap. Its main suggestions were:

- an emergency programme to aid the world's least developed nations in the poverty belts of Africa and Asia

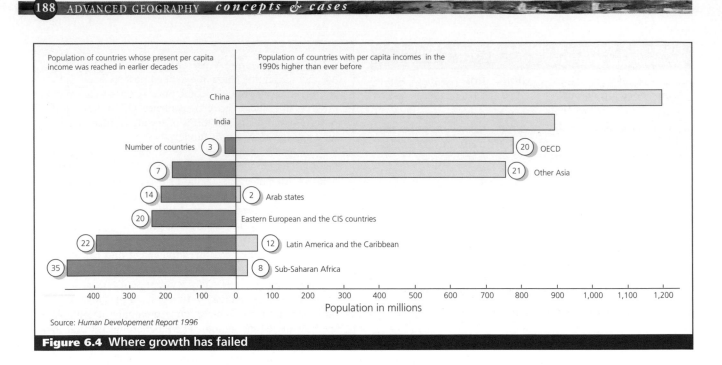

Source: *Human Developement Report 1996*

Figure 6.4 Where growth has failed

- major investment and reform to end mass hunger and malnutrition
- increased international support for family planning programmes
- redirecting investment and labour used for arms production into peaceful needs
- reorganising world trade to encourage developing countries to play a greater role in the processing, marketing and distribution of their own commodities
- developing international codes to improve the sharing of technology and to control the activities of TNCs
- reforming the international monetary system to make it fairer to the South
- establishing a timetable for the richer countries to increase their official development assistance, rising to 1 per cent of GNP before the year 2000
- setting an international 'income tax' to spread wealth from the rich to the poor
- creating an international energy strategy to lessen dependence on non-renewable sources
- expanding and improving lending through financial institutions such as the World Bank
- taking significant measures to reduce the debt burden on developing countries.

A follow-up report entitled *Common Cause* was published in 1983. Alarmingly, it noted that, rather than improving, the international development situation had actually deteriorated, to a large extent due to the debt crisis which broke in 1981/82. In terms of income, the gap has continued to widen. In 1965, average income per head in the richest quintile of countries was 31 times the income of the poorest quintile; in 1990 it was 60 times and in 1996, 78 times greater. It is ironic that there was such a large increase in the first half of the 1990s, the so-called 'golden era' of globalisation. The widening gap reflects the growing marginalisation of many of the world's poorest countries.

Development decades

In 1959 the UN declared that the 1960s would be the Development Decade. During these optimistic times the modernisation theorists and others saw the development of the Developing World as achievable in twenty or thirty years. However, as hopes faded, the UN declared a Second Development Decade in the 1970s and a Third in the 1980s.

The 1990s began with a renewed surge of optimism. The end of the Cold War provided the opportunity for the world to channel new resources into human development. A number of major international conferences emphasised the urgency of eradicating poverty and almost all countries committed themselves to this goal at the World Summit for Social Development in 1995. The costs of eradicating poverty are less than most people imagine – about 1 per cent of global income and no more than 2–3 per cent of national income in all but the poorest countries. In 1997 the president of the World Bank, James Wolfensohn, used his keynote speech at the annual meeting of the World Bank and the International Monetary Fund to stress that without more equality there would be neither peace nor global stability: 'What we are seeing in the world today is the tragedy of exclusion. Whether you broach it from the social or the economic or the moral perspective, this is a challenge we cannot afford to ignore.' Critics of the World Bank, however, argue that while it is strong on rhetoric its real impact on poverty has been very limited because of the way in which it operates.

Figure 6.5 The changing face of income poverty

In 1993 more than 500 million of the Developing World's 1.3 billion income-poor people – those subsisting on less than $1 a day – lived in South Asia, a majority of them in rural areas. But the face of poverty is constantly changing. Compared with 1970, an income-poor person today is:

Less likely to be	More likely to be	And likely to be poor as a result of
Asian	African or Latin American	• Economic stagnation and slow employment growth • Increasing disparity • Lack of pro-poor growth • Increased marginalisation from global trade and financial flows • Higher fertility and the spread of HIV/AIDS • Accelerated degradation of natural resources • Increased displacement from home and country
An adult male	A child, a woman or elderly (in some countries)	• Increased cuts in social welfare • Greater disintegration of the family • Higher unemployment, particularly chronic unemployment and involuntary part-time work • High costs of social and economic transition • Increased time burdens
A small farmer	An unskilled, low-wage worker	• Continuing globalisation and trade liberalisation • Increased liberalisation of labour markets
Rural	Urban	• Rapid demographic change and migration to urban areas • Growth of the low-productivity informal sector • Worsening access to productive resources • Inadequate development of urban housing and physical infrastructure
Settled	A refugee or internally displaced	• Increasing wars and conflicts • Deepening economic and environmental crises

Source: Lipton and Maxwell and Human Development Report Office
Human Development Report 1997

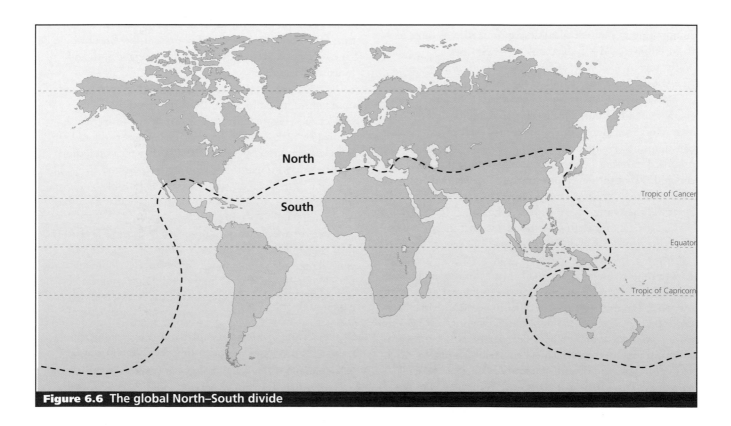

Figure 6.6 The global North–South divide

Questions

1 (a) Comment on the measures used in the compilation of the HDI.

(b) Select and justify two more indicators which could be incorporated into the index to give an even more comprehensive picture of contrasts in development.

2 Discuss the trends illustrated by Figure 6.2.

3 Outline the distinction between the different perspectives on poverty (Figure 6.3).

4 In what ways and why has the face of income poverty changed since the 1970s (Figure 6.5)?

5 Discuss the assertion that 'the development gap has widened rather than narrowed'.

Models of global development

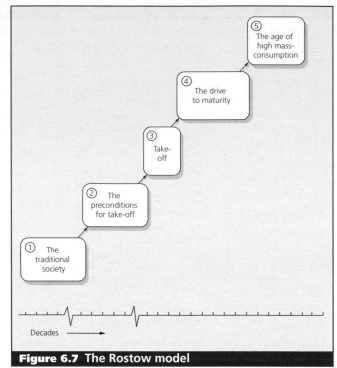

Figure 6.7 The Rostow model

Modernisation theory: W. W. Rostow

Early theories described a typical sequence of stages through which nations move in the course of their economic development. Such ideas originated in the late nineteenth century with the German economists Hildebrand and List, culminating in more detailed descriptions such as those of E. M. Hoover and J. Fisher, and W. W. Rostow.

Rostow in *The Stages of Economic Growth: A Non-Communist Manifesto* (1960), recognised five stages of economic development from the traditional society, characterised by limited technology and a static and hierarchical social structure, to an age of high mass consumption (Figure 6.7). Although Rostow's model was proposed in terms of the national economic unit, he concluded that the development gap was explained by the fact that countries were at different stages of the model. Following Rostow, other writers have also used the model to this effect.

The crucial part of Rostow's model is the third or 'take-off' stage, the decade or two when economy and society are transformed in such a way that thereafter a steady rate of growth can be sustained. Take-off is launched by an initial stimulus and characterised by a rise in the rate of productive investment to over 10 per cent of national income, the development of one or more substantial manufacturing sectors with a high rate of growth and the emergence of administrative systems which encourage development. After take-off follows the 'drive to maturity' when the impact of growth is transmitted to all parts of the economy with the transition to the age of high mass consumption following in a

relatively short time. The model was based on the economic history of over a dozen European countries, all of which are now firmly in the final stage.

Rostow suggested that countries further down the development path would learn from the experience of more developed nations so that the number of years taken for countries to progress through the stages would decrease over time. Thus the 'learning curve' of present-day Brazil would be much shorter than that of the UK in the eighteenth and nineteenth centuries.

Rostow noted the US reaching take-off, maturity and high mass consumption in 1860, 1910 and the early 1920s respectively (Figure 6.8). He saw Canada and Australia as anomalies, with Canada showing the characteristics of high mass consumption by the mid-1920s after take-off a short time before, with maturity following later around 1950. The inversion of the last two stages was made possible by the profitable export of staple commodities in demand on the world market.

Modernisation theory, as proposed by Rostow and others, held sway in the 1950s and early 1960s, when there was general optimism about the prospects for development in the Developing World. But as the painfully slow progress became more and more obvious, criticism of modernisation theory grew:

■ there was a low level of explanation concerning the specific mechanisms which link the different stages

■ the model was analogy-based – it was too simplistic to expect that developing nations could easily follow the economic history of the Developed World

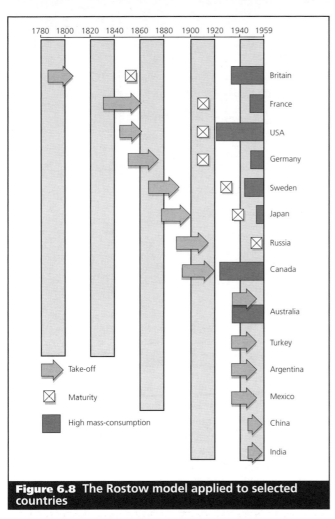

1780 1800 1820 1840 1860 1880 1900 1920 1940 1959

Britain
France
USA
Germany
Sweden
Japan
Russia
Canada
Australia
Turkey
Argentina
Mexico
China
India

➡ Take-off

⊠ Maturity

■ High mass-consumption

Figure 6.8 The Rostow model applied to selected countries

- not all countries, which according to Rostow were ready for take-off, could manage the final jump
- the perspective was endogenic, concentrating on internal factors within individual countries and largely ignoring the importance of external economic relationships
- some writers argued that Rostow's approach was compromised by his political views (very conservative and strongly anti-communist).

Dependency theory: A. G. Frank

By the late 1960s an increasing number of writers were challenging the views of modernisation theorists such as Rostow. The apparent failure of the capitalist model resulted, for a while, in the ascendency of Marxist and neo-Marxist interpretations of underdevelopment. Andre Gunder Frank, a Chicago-trained economist, popularised many of these ideas throughout the English-speaking world with his 'development of underdevelopment theory' (1966). Frank used an historical approach arguing that:

- poverty in the Developing World was not an original condition but has arisen through the spread of world capitalism; many countries had been prosperous before the arrival of European colonists
- the process of absorption into the capitalist system, at first dominated by the European powers, sowed the seeds of underdevelopment. The development of the First World was accomplished by surplus extraction from the Developing World
- the First World powers installed in the colonies a class of 'comprador bourgeoisie' (collaborators) to help administer the system of exploitation
- Developing World economies became even more dependent on the West by substituting the production of export goods where once local food crops prevailed
- the stronger the links to the Developed World the worse the level of development
- the Developing World could not develop so long as it remained a part of the world economy dominated by the rich developed countries.

Frank used a simple model (Figure 6.9) to explain how the 'metropolis' (the Developed World) exploited the 'periphery' (the Developing World). The model shows a chain of exploitation which begins with small towns in the periphery expropriating surplus from their surrounding rural areas. This process of exploitation works its way up the urban hierarchy in the periphery until, finally, the largest settlements are exploited by cities in the metropolis. The intensity of poverty increases with the number of stages down the chain of exploitation. To support his arguments Frank referred to South America, stating that:

- the process of underdevelopment, which has continued to the present, began with Portuguese and Spanish conquest
- flourishing civilisations such as the Inca had been prosperous before conquest
- in Brazil, the Northeast, the poorest region of the country, was most closely linked to the Portuguese economy in the seventeenth and eighteenth centuries
- industrial development intensified during the world depression of the 1930s and the Second World War when Latin American countries were unable to import sufficient manufactured products. Under such conditions a number of important import substitution industries developed.

It is not surprising that such strident views attracted criticism. The main arguments against dependency theory are:

- many parts of the Developing World were impoverished before the arrival of European colonists
- some countries, such as the United States and Australia, undoubtedly developed at a faster rate as a result of colonisation (but what of the fate of the indigenous peoples?)
- Frank's explanation of the process of exploitation related to unfair trade and ignored other factors such as labour exploitation and taxes imposed by the colonial powers which stimulated the outflow of resources

Key Definitions 2

modernisation theory A deterministic approach based on the economic history of a number of developed countries. Countries pass through a number of stages on the path to development (five in the Rostow model). Distinct economic and social changes are required within the country to move from one stage to another.

dependency theory An approach which blames the relative underdevelopment of the Developing World on exploitation by the Developed World. This has been achieved by making the Developing World dependent on the Developed World, first through colonialism and then by the various elements of neocolonialism.

world system theory An approach based on the history of the capitalist world economy since its formation in the sixteenth century. Countries fall into three economic levels: core, semi-periphery and periphery, and can move from one level to another if their contribution to the world economy changes.

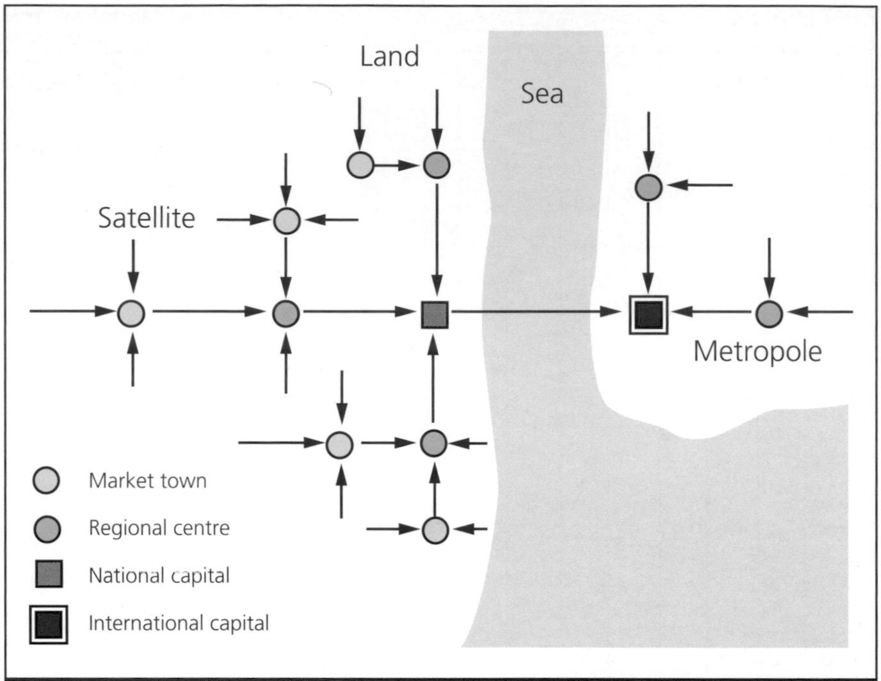

Land

Sea

Satellite

Metropole

○ Market town
● Regional centre
■ National capital
■ International capital

Figure 6.9 Frank's model of surplus extraction

- capitalism did not permeate most developing countries to the degree implied by Frank
- some of the poorest nations today are those which have been historically isolated from the world trading system
- development and underdevelopment are connected but not in the direct way suggested by Frank.

Although far from perfect, Frank's explanation considerably advanced thinking on the subject. Undoubtedly the pattern of development in the Developing World has been greatly influenced by the Developed World. The historical imprint is too strong to deny this, but its impact has been highly variable. A. Gilbert (1985), a leading authority on the subject, makes the following observations:

- **Most of the areas colonised that became relatively prosperous had small initial populations with European settlers quickly becoming the majority. Such was the case in North America, the temperate zone of Latin America, and Australia and New Zealand. In contrast, most of Asia and Africa were already well settled when the Europeans arrived and the latter were always in a small minority. The key point was the level of resources available per settler, particularly in terms of land, which was high in areas like North America.**
- **The methods of production used were important to the pace of development. Areas where smallholder agriculture developed (eg, southern Brazil, South Africa) have usually experienced more rapid development. Other less equitable methods of production, such as the latifundias and haciendas of Latin America, resulted in rural stagnation.**

- Of crucial importance was the nature of the raw material exploited, as the production and export of some products generates considerably more socio-economic development than others. The greatest benefits are from those products which employ more people initially, involve some degree of processing in the country of origin, and require the construction of an extensive transport network. For example, research has shown that temperate agricultural products and coffee have fared significantly better in these respects than tropical products.

World system theory: I. G. Wallerstein

New approaches are often stimulated by the shortcomings of previous theorising. The breakthrough of world system theory in the mid-1970s, popularised by Immanuel Wallerstein and others, was at least partly a response to the deficiencies of earlier approaches, although some elements of earlier analysis (particularly Frank) can be discerned.

The world system approach asserts that a capitalist world economy has been in existence since the sixteenth century. Before this, global interdependence did not exist. Instead the world was made up of a number of relatively independent mini-systems. From then on capitalism incorporated a growing number of previously more or less isolated and self-sufficient societies into a complex system of functional relationships. A small number of core states transformed a much larger external area into a periphery. In between core and periphery, semi-peripheries existed which played a key role in the functioning of the global system. The semi-periphery is an economic condition to which parts of the periphery may rise or parts of the core may fall.

Within the system a division of labour operated with the core countries as industrial producers and the peripheral areas as agricultural and other raw material producers. The terms of trade were heavily skewed in favour of the core, particularly with regard to the periphery but also to a lesser extent in relation to the semi-periphery. The process of underdevelopment started with the incorporation of a particular external area into the world system. As the system expanded, first Eastern Europe, then Latin America, Asia and Africa, in that order were peripherised.

The semi-peripheral countries/regions form the most dynamic part of the system, characterised by an increase in the relative importance of industrial production. The rising semi-peripheries of the present, the NICs, are ambitious, competing to varying degrees for core status. Thus the world system approach has a degree of optimism lacking in dependency theory, recognising that some countries can break out of the state of underdevelopment. However, Wallerstein (1979) acknowledges that rapid change is not easy and that there are indeed 'limited possibilities of transformation within the capitalist world economy'.

The rise and fall of major economic powers forms part of the cyclical movements of the world system, movements which are basically influenced by economic long waves. Thus the world system has periods of expansion, contraction, crisis and structural change, paving the way to renewed expansion.

The criticisms of Wallerstein's approach include:

- **too high a level of eurocentricity by underrating the sophistication of other early trading systems, particularly with regard to China, Japan and elsewhere in Asia**
- **too great a degree of simplicity in assuming a universal one-way flow of resources from the periphery to the core**
- **failing to recognise the high level of competition between core nations by suggesting that they organise the world economy in order to maintain a clearly defined core club.**

Differentiation, inequality and aid

Differentiation in the Developing World

Some of the more advanced Developing World nations base their status on strategic natural resources, others on successful experiments with industrialisation, while a third category combines one or both of these criteria with geopolitical power in the context of their own region (Figure 6.10). Any future economic superpower is likely to emerge in the shaded area of the diagram, but how many serious candidates are there? At the other end of the scale (Figure 6.11) are those nations, the world's poorest, sometimes termed the Fourth World. In this

Questions

1 **(a)** Outline the merits and limitations of the Rostow model.
  (b) Although the Rostow model has at times been used to explain the development gap, why is it essentially a national rather a global model of development?
2 Examine the merits and limitations of dependency theory.
3 To what extent is world system theory an improvement on earlier theories?

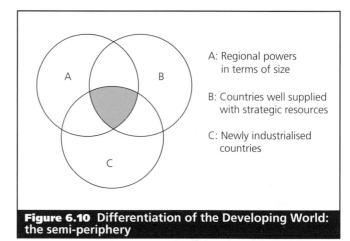

A: Regional powers in terms of size

B: Countries well supplied with strategic resources

C: Newly industrialised countries

Figure 6.10 Differentiation of the Developing World: the semi-periphery

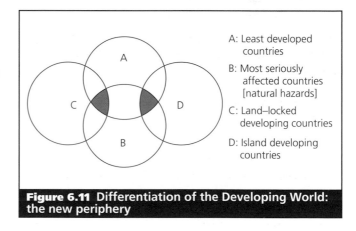

A: Least developed countries

B: Most seriously affected countries [natural hazards]

C: Land–locked developing countries

D: Island developing countries

Figure 6.11 Differentiation of the Developing World: the new periphery

case the shaded areas of the diagram indicate the most problematic situations. In the latter part of the twentieth century a much more distinctive hierarchy of development has arisen in the Developing World which is strongly linked to the concepts of interdependence and globalisation.

Inequality and development

The Gini coefficient, with a range between zero and one, is the most frequently used measure of income inequality. Zero

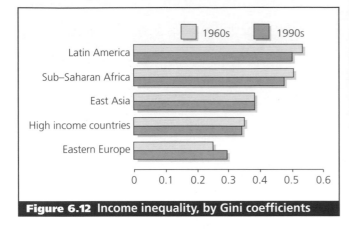

Figure 6.12 Income inequality, by Gini coefficients

Figure 6.13 Emergency food aid for flood victims in Bangladesh

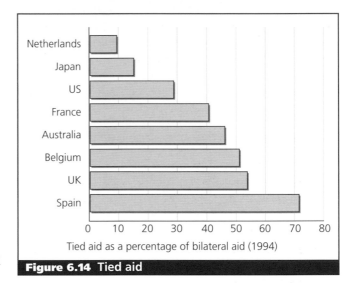

Figure 6.14 Tied aid

indicates perfect equality while a score of one implies absolute inequality. Figure 6.12 shows the average Gini coefficients of different world regions in the 1960s and 1990s. Latin America, with a Gini coefficient of around 0.5 is the world's most unequal region.

In the 1950s the economist Simon Kuznets suggested that in poor countries growth would initially increase the gap between rich and poor and only as economies became richer would the gap close. His hypothesis was based on the economic history of Britain, Germany and the United States. However, the conclusion of recent research is that growth in developing countries does not necessarily increase inequality. Different regions of the world have had remarkably varied growth rates since the 1960s but the Gini coefficients have been extremely stable. The World Bank's economists concluded that in 88 cases where a country's GDP per head grew for a decade, income inequality decreased in 45 cases and increased in 43.

Recent work has also asked the question, 'might great inequality itself damage the prospects for development?'. Latin America, for example, has generally grown more slowly than East Asia where income is more evenly spread. It seems that the link between high inequality and low growth lies largely in the inability of many poor people to borrow, which hinders their ability to both produce and consume.

The role of aid in development

The origins of foreign aid can be traced back to the Marshall Plan of the late 1940s when the United States set out to reconstruct the war-torn economies of Western Europe and Japan as a means of containing the international spread of communism. By the mid-1950s the battle for influence between East and West in the Developing World began to strongly affect the geography of aid. Even today bilateral aid is dictated primarily by ties of colonialism and neocolonialism and by strategic considerations. However, it would be wrong to deny that aid is also given for humanitarian and economic reasons. The willingness of Developing World countries to accept foreign aid is based on three deficiencies:

- the 'foreign exchange gap' whereby many developing countries lack the hard currency to pay for imports which are vital to development
- the 'savings gap' where population pressures and other drains on expenditure prevent the accumulation of sufficient capital to invest in industry and infrastructure
- the 'technical gap' caused by a shortage of skilled personnel.

But why do richer nations give aid – is it down to altruism or self-interest? Much of the evidence suggests the latter. Contrary to popular belief, most foreign aid is not in the form of a grant, nor is famine relief a major component. In addition a significant proportion of foreign aid is 'tied' to the purchase of goods and services from the donor country and often given for use only on jointly agreed projects. Aid that is tied accounts for around 40 per cent of donations from OECD countries (Figure 6.14). The overall effect has been that foreign aid is linked to strong reverse flows of goods and money, with trade following aid as a result of the creation of

Figure 6.15 The Pergau Dam under construction in Malaysia . . . part of a controversial 'arms for aid' deal with the UK government

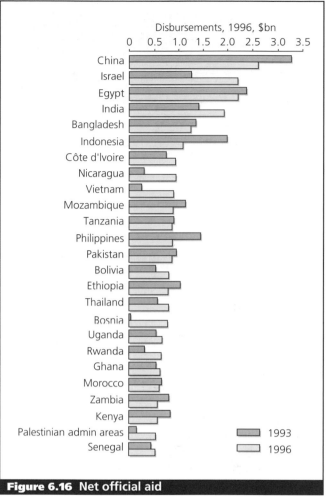

Figure 6.16 Net official aid

new dependency linkages. The OECD estimates that tying aid increases a developing country's costs by an average of 15 per cent. With tied aid worth $15 billion in 1994, the extra cost to the Developing World during that year amounted to some $2 billion. The OECD has tried to reduce this burden with its 1992 Helsinki Agreement, so far with limited success.

According to some left-wing economists aid is an obstacle to development because:

- the tied nature of much aid benefits the donor more than the recipient in economic terms
- the frequently inappropriate use of aid on large capital-intensive projects may actually worsen the conditions of the poorest people
- the strengthening of political ties as a result of bilateral aid may increase dependency and hinder democracy in the recipient country
- aid may delay the introduction of reforms, for example the substitution of food aid for land reform.

Arguments put forward by the political Right against aid are as follows:

- aid encourages the growth of a larger than necessary public sector
- the private sector is 'crowded out' by aid funds
- aid distorts the structure of prices and incentives
- aid is often wasted on grandiose projects to raise the profile of political regimes which seem to have little concern for the poorest in their societies
- the West did not need aid to develop.

There has been a general decline in official aid flows to poor nations in the 1990s, largely because of financial pressures in the Developed World. Between 1992 and 1996 net official aid to developing countries from developed nations and multilateral institutions fell by 16 per cent in real terms. China remains the biggest recipient of official aid (Figure 6.16). Of the countries included in Figure 6.16, Mozambique

relies most heavily on foreign aid accounting for 72 per cent of GDP in 1996. In contrast, in China, foreign aid flows amount to less than 0.5 per cent of GDP. At about $400 each, Israelis receive the most foreign aid per person. In the Palestinian administrative area per capita aid amounts to almost $300. Some commentators see it as ironic that just as the West seems to have learned important lessons about the misuse of aid such funds are declining.

In its best form there can be little doubt that aid can combat poverty but all too often it fails to reach the very poorest people and when it does the benefits are frequently short-lived. Non Governmental Organisations (NGOs) such as Oxfam and CAFOD have often been much better at directing aid towards sustainable development. The selective nature of such aid has targeted the poorest communities using appropriate technology and involving local people in decision making. Many development economists argue that there are two issues more important to Developing World development than aid: changing the terms of trade so that developing nations get a fairer share of the benefits and writing off Developing World debt.

Questions

1 Explain how Figures 6.10 and 6.11 illustrate differentiation in the Developing World.

2 With reference to Figure 6.12 discuss the relationship between growth and income inequality in developing countries.

3 Assess the effectiveness of international aid in the development process.

Figure 6.17 Resettlement scheme: example of NGO aid – CAFOD

Figure 6.18 Balance sheet of human development in Sub-Saharan Africa

Progress	Deprivation

HEALTH

Progress
- Between 1960 and 1993 life expectancy at birth increased from 40 to 51 years.
- In the past decade the proportion of the population with access to safe water nearly doubled – from 25 per cent to 43 per cent.

Deprivation
- There is only one doctor for every 18 000 people, compared with 6000 in the Developing World as a whole and 390 in the industrial countries.
- More than ten million people are infected with HIV, two-thirds of all those infected in the world.

EDUCATION

Progress
- During the past two decades adult literacy more than doubled – from 27 per cent to 55 per cent.
- Between 1960 and 1991 the net enrolment ratio at the primary level increased from 25 per cent to 50 per cent, and at the secondary level from 13 per cent to 38 per cent.

Deprivation
- Only about half the entrants to grade 1 finish grade 5.
- At the primary and secondary levels more than 80 million boys and girls are still out of school.

INCOME AND POVERTY

Progress
- Over the period 1980–92 five countries – Botswana, Cape Verde, Lesotho, Mauritius and Swaziland – had an annual GDP growth rate of more than 5 per cent.

Deprivation
- About 170 million people (nearly a third of the region's population) do not get enough to eat.
- During the past three decades the ratio of military to social spending increased, from 27 per cent in 1960 to 43 per cent in 1991.

WOMEN

Progress
- Between 1960 and 1991 the female enrolment ratio at the secondary level quadrupled – from 8 per cent to 32 per cent.
- Women hold 8 per cent of parliamentary seats, nearly double their 5 per cent share in South Asia.

Deprivation
- The region has the world's highest maternal mortality rate – 929 per 100 000 live births (compared with 33 in the OECD countries).
- There are six HIV-infected women for every four infected men.

CHILDREN

Progress
- Over the past three decades the infant mortality rate dropped from 167 per thousand live births to 97.

Deprivation
- About 23 million children in the region are malnourished, and 16 per cent of babies are underweight.

ENVIRONMENT

Progress
- Combined logging in primary and secondary forests is the lowest in the Developing World; less than 40% of the yearly rate in Asia and Latin America.

Deprivation
- During the past 50 years desertification has claimed an average 1.3 million hectares of productive land a year.

POLITICS AND CONFLICTS

Progress
- Since 1990, 27 multiparty presidential elections have been held – in 21 cases for the first time.
- Since 1980 opposition parties have been legalised in 31 countries.

Deprivation
- In 1994 there were still 16 governments representing a single-party system or a military regime.
- At the end of 1994 nearly six million people – 1 per cent of the population – were refugees.

Source: *Human Development Report 1996*

Sub-Saharan Africa: global problem region

Most of the least developed countries of the world are in Sub-Saharan Africa. This region faces the biggest challenge in eradicating poverty in the future. Here are found the countries in greatest economic difficulty and those most often in conflict. Human poverty is growing faster here than anywhere else in the world. Yet important progress has nevertheless been made as the balance sheet of human development indicates (Figure 6.18). Nevertheless, nearly 32 per cent of people in the region are not expected to survive to age 40, compared with 9 per cent in East Asia. In 1992 about 45 per cent of Sub-Saharan Africa's population was income-poor according to national poverty lines. The growth of income in the region has been dismal in recent decades. Between 1970 and 1992 per capita GDP (PPP$) grew by only $73, compared with $420 in South Asia and $900 in East Asia, regions with incomes comparable to those of Sub-Saharan Africa in 1970. Between 1981 and 1989 the region experienced a cumulative fall of 21 per cent in real GDP per capita with the most serious declines in Gabon (58 per cent) and Nigeria (50 per cent).

With 12 per cent of the world's population, Sub-Saharan Africa has seen its share of world trade and investment fall by half over the past two decades. It is now slightly over 1 per cent of the total. According to one commentator, 'In effect, the region's citizens have been decoupled from the engine of growth in the world economy. The consequence is a vicious circle of rising poverty and social tensions, culminating in the collapse of states.' (Kevin Watkins, *The Guardian*, 1 December 1997).

In Sub-Saharan Africa 65 million hectares of productive land have become desert in the past 50 years. In the region overall the highest incidence of poverty occurs in arid zones. Here the growing claims on common property resources are making the poor even less secure, and population pressure is adding to the demands. Such resources – not just water, fuel and grazing areas but also nuts, berries and medicinal herbs – are particularly important in the most arid zones, providing livelihoods for many of the very poor. With traditional social structures weakened by social change, traditional rights are not always upheld and protected as exemplified by the increasing conflicts between farmers and herders in the region. Population growth has been greater than the increase in agricultural production. Between 1974 and 1990 food imports increased by 185 per cent while food aid rose by 295 per cent.

The region suffers heavily from the unequal terms of world trade. The industrialised nations collectively impose tariffs which are some 30 per cent higher on imports from the poorest countries than on goods traded between themselves. In November 1997 the EU and the United States set aside their own trade

Figure 6.19 Poor transport infrastructure in Mozambique – hampering development ambitions

differences to sink a World Trade Organisation plan for the elimination of all trade barriers for the 48 least developed countries, which collectively account for 0.5 per cent of their imports. The reasons given for this action were a concern to maintain agricultural subsidies and to limit textile imports.

Unsustainable debt is a huge obstacle to progress in many countries. Zaire is embarking on a reconstruction programme saddled with a $14 billion debt (three times its GDP) incurred by the discredited Mobutu regime. Most of this money is owed to the World Bank, the IMF and Western governments who refuse to integrate debt cancellation into a reconstruction programme.

Another obstacle to fuller integration into the world economy is the cost of transport. In 1991 Sub-Saharan Africa's net freight and insurance payments were around 15 per cent of the value of total exports, compared with 5.8 per cent for developing countries as a whole. The high level of costs in this region are due to (a) efforts to promote national shipping fleets resulting in restrictive practices (b) the generally poor condition of roads and railways and (c) the considerable distance of the average movement.

1 Discuss the assertion that Sub-Saharan Africa is undoubtedly the world's major problem region.

Models of regional development

A full understanding of the factors generating regional economic development is vital if funds from the different levels of government are to be used in the most efficient manner. The development of appropriate models is an important part of this process. However, in comparison to models of national economic development the art of regional growth theorising is still relatively primitive.

G. Myrdal and A. Hirschman

The Swedish economist, Gunnar Myrdal, originally framed his cumulative causation theory (1957) in the context of developing countries but it can also be applied reasonably to more advanced nations. According to the theory a three-stage sequence can be recognised:

- the pre-industrial stage when regional differences are minimal
- a period of rapid economic growth characterised by increasing regional economic divergence
- a stage of regional economic convergence when the significant wealth generated in the most affluent region(s) spreads to other parts of the country.

In Myrdal's model, economic growth begins with the location of new manufacturing industry in a region with a combination of advantages greater than elsewhere in the country. Once growth has been initiated in a dominant region spatial flows of labour, capital and raw materials develop to support it and the growth region undergoes further expansion by the cumulative causation process (Figure 6.20). A detrimental 'backwash effect' is transmitted to the less developed regions as skilled labour and locally generated capital is attracted away. Manufactured goods and services produced and operating under the scale economies of the economic 'heartland' flood the market of the relatively underdeveloped 'hinterland' undercutting smaller scale enterprises in such areas.

However, increasing demand for raw materials from resource-rich parts of the hinterland may stimulate growth in

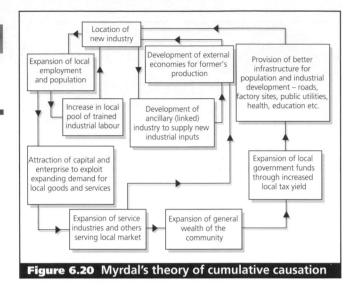

Figure 6.20 Myrdal's theory of cumulative causation

other sectors of the economies of such regions. If the impact is strong enough to overcome local backwash effects a process of cumulative causation may begin leading to the development of new centres of self-sustained economic growth. Such 'spread effects' are spatially selective and will only benefit those parts of the hinterland with valuable raw materials or other significant advantages.

The American economist Albert Hirschman (1958) produced similar conclusions to Myrdal although he adopted a different terminology. Hirschman labelled the growth of the 'core' (heartland) as 'polarisation', which benefited from 'virtuous circles' or upward spirals of development whereas peripheral areas (the hinterland) were impeded by 'vicious circles' or downward spirals. The term 'trickle-down' was used to describe the spread of growth from core to periphery. The major difference between Myrdal and Hirschman was that the latter stressed to a far greater extent the effect of counterbalancing forces overcoming polarisation (backwash), eventually leading to economic equilibrium being established. The subsequent literature has favoured the terms core and periphery rather than Myrdal's alternatives.

Figure 6.21 is an application of core-periphery theory to North America. The economic core, the manufacturing belt of the United States and Canada, developed rapidly throughout the nineteenth and early twentieth centuries at the expense of peripheral areas. National flows into the core were dominated by raw materials with much labour and capital coming from Europe. In both countries the major sub-cores, California and the Vancouver city region respectively, developed at significant distances from the core region itself. Apart from the location of important raw materials, transport costs clearly insulated these regions to a certain extent against competition from the economic core of the continent. In addition, Pacific coastal location ensured increasing volumes of trade as the North American economy developed a more significant Asian outlook.

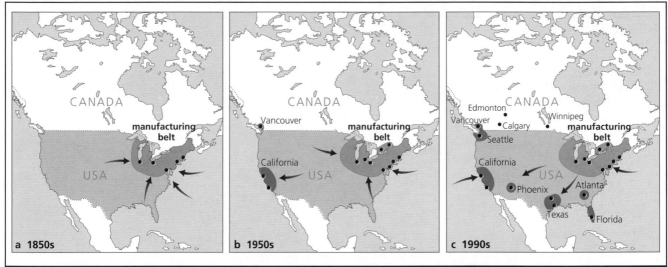

Figure 6.21 Core and periphery in North America

Figure 6.22 US: per capita income by division, 1900–1995

Division	Percentage of US average					
	1900	1940	1970	1980	1990	1995
New England	135	127	108	106	118	116
Middle Atlantic	143	132	114	108	116	115
East North Central	107	112	105	101	98	101
West North Central	98	81	94	94	94	95
South Atlantic	51	77	90	93	98	98
East South Central	50	49	74	78	79	83
West South Central	61	64	85	94	85	87
Mountain	140	87	90	95	89	92
Pacific	163	135	111	115	103	103
Mean deviation (%)	37	28	12	8	11	9

Key Definitions ③

core A region of concentrated economic development with advanced systems of infrastructure, resulting in high average income and low unemployment.

periphery A region of low or declining economic development characterised by low incomes, high unemployment, selective out-migration and poor infrastructure.

cumulative causation The process whereby impulses to economic growth or economic decline within regions (or countries) are, via the operation of market forces, self-reinforcing. This is a consequence of multiplier and scale economy effects.

Minor sub-cores such as Seattle, Houston, Dallas-Fort Worth, New Orleans and Atlanta-Birmingham in the United States and Edmonton, Calgary and Winnipeg in Canada also developed due to various factors including local resource endowment, key transportation functions and regional administrative importance.

Regional income patterns in the United States and Canada indicate a clear pattern of convergence. Figure 6.22 shows the shifting per capita income balance between the nine census divisions of the US. The recent resurgence of New England and the Middle Atlantic contrasts markedly with the third region in the traditional 'manufacturing belt', the East North Central, which recently dipped below the national average for the first time. In this economic core region New England and the Middle Atlantic have enjoyed greater success in attracting new growth industries to replace the large number of jobs lost in traditional manufacturing. Per capita incomes in the Pacific region have fallen in a relative sense in recent years while the

East South Central remains the poorest region in the nation. Throughout the whole time period all three divisions of the South have recorded per capita incomes below the national average but have steadily moved towards the norm, with the exception of the West South Central between 1980 and 1995. Figure 6.23 shows in greater detail the clear patterns of relative poverty and wealth across the US. The state with the highest per capita income is Connecticut ($36 263) while Mississippi is at the bottom of the fifty-state list ($18 272).

J. R. Friedmann

Friedmann (1964) has related the work of Myrdal and Hirschman to a general theory of urbanisation (Figure 6.26) linking regional income differences to the stage of development of city systems. In the North American context the economic dominance of the core region (the North East) has been dependent on the intense urbanisation and

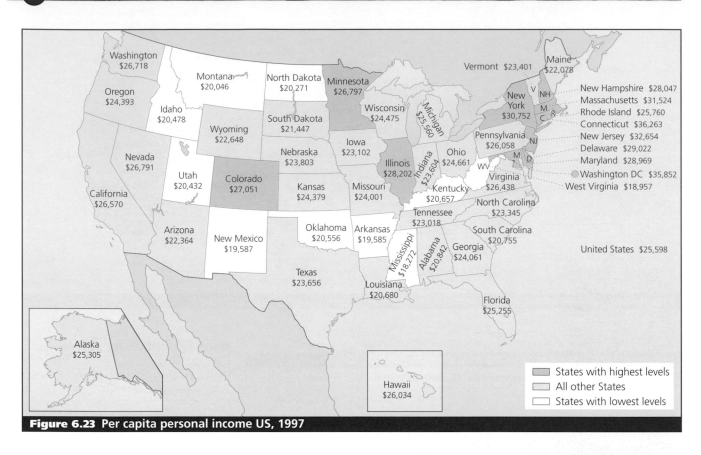

Figure 6.23 Per capita personal income US, 1997

industrialisation of this area relative to the rest of the continent. The operation of agglomeration economies and economies of scale in the core region heightened regional contrasts in the nineteenth and early twentieth centuries.

According to Friedmann the process of convergence is only initiated when urbanisation has progressed enough to generate self-sustained growth. The rapid development of urbanisation in California paralleled the emergence of the state as the major sub-core in the US while the relatively low level of urbanisation in the South has been cited by many authorities as a major factor in explaining the persistence of low incomes in this region. In national terms, the situation in the US and Canada approximates the third stage of the Friedmann model with the US leading the way to the final stage.

A basic assumption of Myrdal's model is government non-intervention but he does suggest that in advanced economies spread effects may be induced by government policies aimed at assisting problem regions and that such action can be interpreted as only another aspect of cumulative causation. While Myrdal was rather sceptical of government ability to promote significant spread effects, Hirschman attached much more importance to this factor. Friedmann also saw government action as crucial in helping to establish peripheral growth centres.

In the US the west and south have in general been in receipt of a surplus of federal funds while the northeastern states have frequently complained that economic activity has been 'drained' from their region as a result of such action.

Figure 6.24 Affluent suburb in Connecticut (decorated for Halloween!)

However, there does seem to be general agreement that in the US spread effects were already operable before effective federal regional policies were underway and that the strong post-war development of the sunbelt would still have occurred in the absence of federal action although regional shifts would have proceeded more slowly.

Figure 6.25 Rural poverty – Alabama, USA

Questions

1 With reference to Figure 6.20 explain the processes of upward and downward cumulative causation.
2 Compare the theories of Myrdal and Hirschman.
3 To what extent did Friedmann advance the work of Myrdal and Hirschmann?
4 Describe the changing relationship between core and periphery in North America.

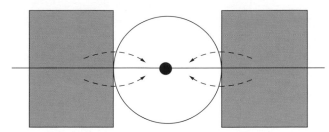

Stage 1. Relatively independent local centres; no hierarchy. Typical pre–industrial structure; each city lies at the centre of a small regional enclave.

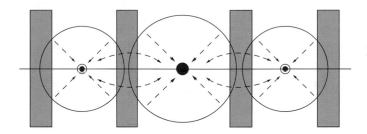

Stage 2. A single strong core. Typical of period of incipient industrialisation; a periphery emerges; potential entrepreneurs and labour move to the core, national economy is virtually reduced to a single metropolitan region.

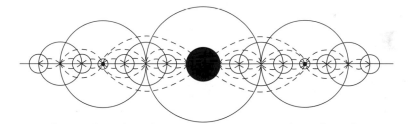

Stage 3. A single national core, strong peripheral sub-cores. During the period of industrial maturity, secondary cores form, thereby reducing the periphery on a national scale to smaller inter-metropolitan peripheries.

Stage 4. A functional interdependent system of cities. Organised complexity characterised by national integration, efficiency in location, and maximum growth potential.

Figure 6.26 Friedman's development model

Regional policy

The post-war period since 1945 has witnessed a growing awareness of inter-regional contrasts by governments, due primarily to the heightened perception of economic variations by the general population and a new realisation of political power by disadvantaged areas or ethnic groups. This trend has been to a significant extent a consequence of the spread of advanced systems of transport and communications intensifying both the quality and quantity of information diffusion. Even the most capitalistic societies, epitomised by the United States, have come generally to recognise intense regional differences as being socially and politically unacceptable.

The era of regional planning developed first in western Europe, later spreading to the rest of the developed world. In recent decades a number of developing countries have activated important and far-reaching regional policies. Within the Developed World, North America reacted slowly to its problem regions. Although previous policies can be recognised as having specific regional benefits it was not until the 1960s that both the United States and Canada introduced comprehensive systems of regional planning.

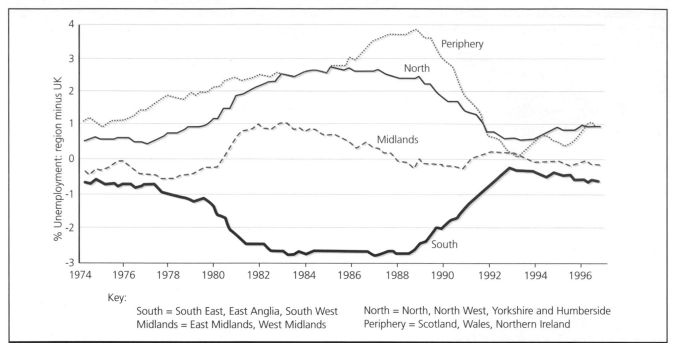

Figure 6.27 Unemployment rates in the UK

Regional policy in the UK: the equity and efficiency arguments

Regional policy in the UK can be said to have begun in 1928 when the Industrial Transference Board was established to retrain men from declining industries and by the use of grants to enable them to move and find employment in expanding industries. Since that time a wide range of policy measures have been used to create or maintain jobs in the areas with persistently high unemployment. Although the unemployment gap within the UK (Figure 6.27) widens and narrows as economic conditions change the regional ranking remains very consistent. The most recent narrowing occurred during the recession of the early 1990s which hit the southern regions severely. Figure 6.28 shows that the pattern of unemployment at county level has remained remarkably stable. It is this persistence of high unemployment by area that is the main justification for spatially discriminating policies such as regional policy.

In a recent paper Taylor and Wren state the main arguments in favour of a strong and effective regional policy in the UK:

■ **Reducing unemployment in depressed areas has direct economic and social benefits.** The increased income of the previously unemployed benefits others through the multiplier effect. The national economy also gains through reduced transfer payments and increased tax revenues. Improved prospects within depressed regions increases motivation with positive outcomes such as higher educational attainment. The range of social ills associated with unemployment decreases in intensity.

Figure 6.28 County unemployment rates over time

	Correlation coefficient between unemployment rates across all GB counties in each pair of years			
Year	**1982**	**1986**	**1990**	**1995**
1982	1			
1986	0.91	1		
1990	0.84	0.92	1	
1995	0.70	0.82	0.82	1

■ Reducing spatial unemployment disparities will lessen inflationary pressure in the national economy. When general economic conditions are favourable labour shortages tend to arise in the affluent south. The result is a sharp increase in wage inflation which is transmitted to other parts of the country through (a) national industry-wide wage agreements (b) inter-plant wage setting arrangements in multi-plant firms and (c) wage-setting based on relatives between workers in related occupations. A more even regional playing field with regard to unemployment would reduce wage inflation during periods of substantial growth.

■ Unbalanced regional growth leads to the persistence and intensification of regional problems through the process of cumulative causation. Selective migration from depressed areas can in the longer term be harmful to both the origin and destination regions. The depressed regions lose their most highly skilled workers and it has been shown that the occupational mix of a locality is an important determinant of the quality of school outputs and hence the formation of human capital. In contrast, the more affluent destination regions may suffer because of the increased pressure on available resources.

■ Reducing unemployment in areas of high unemployment is politically necessary. The evidence for this assertion is in the sharp differences in regional voting patterns.

Thus, according to Taylor and Wren regional policy is desirable not only for reasons of equity or fairness but also in terms of efficiency as real benefits will accrue to the national economy as a whole. Not surprisingly some regional economists and politicians hold alternative views. The onset of Thatcherism resulted in the run-down of regional policy during the 1980s on the grounds that regional policy could be defended only on social grounds (the equity argument). The

assertion was that there were no efficiency gains (the economic argument) to the economy as a whole as one region's gain in terms of jobs created was simply another region's loss. In general, in the post-war period Labour governments have been more supportive of regional policy, stressing the efficiency as well as the equity reasons for such action.

However Conservative government attitudes to regional policy changed significantly during the early 1990s, with the 1995 White Paper on 'Regional Industrial Policy' stating that:

■ 'the Government recognises the importance of enhancing the competitiveness of the Assisted Areas. There has been a refocusing of regional industrial policy to reflect its role in achieving both economic and social objectives'

■ regional financial incentives 'enabled the UK to compete effectively for internationally mobile investment'.

The European Union's Structural Funds have become an increasingly important source of development funding to the UK's disadvantaged regions (Figures 6.29 and 6.30). Regions may be eligible for funding in one of three categories:

■ 'Objective 1' funds promote the development of regions lagging well behind the rest of the EU. Eligible regions must have a per capita GDP of 75 per cent or less of the EU average, although there are some exceptions to this. In assisted areas emphasis is placed on creating a sound

Figure 6.29 UK Government spending on regions and EU structural funds to UK assisted areas

Year	Expenditure on regional preferential assistance to industry (£m at current prices)	Year	EU structural funds (£m at current prices)
1989/90	666	1989	565
1990/91	629	1990	659
1991/92	566	1991	687
1992/93	470	1992	712
1993/94	512	1993	747
1994/95	502	1994	857
1995/96	474	1995	922

Figure 6.30 Allocation of EC structural funds

	Million ECUs[1]								
	Objective 1			Objective 2			Objective 5b		
	1995	1996	1997	1995	1996	1997[2]	1995	1996	1997
United Kingdom	350	375	402	714	736	–	127	147	148
North	–	–	–	111	115	–	7	8	8
Yorkshire & Humberside	–	–	–	105	108	–	9	10	10
East Midlands	–	–	–	26	27	–	9	11	11
East Anglia	–	–	–	–	–	–	9	11	11
South East	–	–	–	29	30	–	–	–	–
Greater London	–	–	–	25	26	–	–	–	–
Rest of South East	–	–	–	5	5	–	–	–	–
South West	–	–	–	10	10	–	34	39	40
West Midlands	–	–	–	124	128	–	7	8	8
North West	121	130	139	110	113	–	1	2	2
England	121	130	130	515	531	–	77	89	89
Wales	–	–	–	63	65	–	29	33	33
Scotland	46	49	53	136	140	–	22	25	26
Northern Ireland	183	196	210	–	–	–	–	–	–

[1]The average sterling value of the ECU in 1995 was 1.2211

[2]Objective 2 allocations for 1997 had not been agreed at the time of going to press

infrastructure, encouraging research and development, providing training and helping small businesses.

- ■ 'Objective 2' funding benefits areas suffering industrial decline which need to adjust their economies towards new activities. Grants may be provided to create jobs, encourage new businesses, renovate land and buildings, promote Research and Development, and foster links between higher education and industry.

- ■ 'Objective 5b' funds are for rural areas where economic development needs to be encouraged. In such areas the focus is on developing jobs outside agriculture in small businesses and tourism, and improvements to transport and basic services are promoted to prevent rural depopulation.

The other objectives under which grants are allocated (3, 4, 5a) are not defined geographically.

In the UK only London merits status as one of the EU's richest areas (Figure 6.31). The term 'hot banana' has been used for a number of years to describe the economic core of the EU with Greater Paris being the only major economic region outside of it. Clearly it is in the areas outside the core where development assistance is concentrated.

Regional policy: changing dimensions

The times when economic growth was taken for granted, and when regional policy was concerned simply with where to direct it are over. Regional policies designed for the 1990s and the early twenty-first century in most developed and in a growing number of developing countries are much more sophisticated than their earlier counterparts (Figure 6.34, page 206). Given the thrust of today's policies it is perhaps not surprising that the regional initiatives developed in the

---

Hot banana splits Europe

Richest regions	GDP billion francs
Greater Paris	2178.1
Lombardy	1415.9
London	1206.5
N. Rhine Westphalia	765.5
Hesse	753.5
Bavaria	748.1
Lazio	719.4
Denmark	609.9
Catalonia	682.8
Rhône-Alps	682.2

Poorest regions		
Ahvenanmaa-Aaland	Finland	3.6
Voreio Aigaio	Greece	10.9
Ionia Nisia	Greece	14.1
Ipeiros	Greece	18.4
Vallée d'Aoste	Italy	18.9
Dytiki Makedonia	Greece	21.3
Notio Aigaio	Greece	23.1
Burgenland	Austria	24.0
Flevoland	Holland	24.3
Corsica	France	25.5

Source: *The Guardian*, Friday 14 August 1998

GREATER London is the European Union's third most productive economic area, according to a French study of Europe's 196 officially registered geographical units. Paris and its suburbs are at the top of an international league of gross domestic product (GDP), and Lombardy, north Italy, is second.

The study, the first of its kind to produce a map of the disparity in EU production capacity, reinforces the "hot banana" theory devised by the geographer Roger Brunet 10 years ago that prosperity is concentrated in a curve running through London, Brussels, Munich and Milan.

The exception is Paris-Ile de France, a region of nearly 12 million people well to the west of the "banana". Even using a EU standard buying power factor, Parisians were still rated much richer than Londoners or Milanese.

Paris-Ile de France produces 5 per cent of European GDP with only 3 per cent of the 350 million community population. Greater London contributes about 2 per cent.

Yesterday Michel Hannoun and Christine Lalong, who drew up the report for the government statistics department, Insee, said it was a valuable indicator of the differences in productivity and income across Europe.

"This is the only comparable basis available in Europe and will be used as the criteria for [European] Commission experts to distribute funds," an Insee official said.

The study is also a geography lesson, showing how Brussels looks at the 15 EU countries when considering aid. The UK is split into 30 regional units while Ireland and Denmark are considered as single areas. One of the smallest units, the Finnish Aland Islands, is also the poorest, while Luxembourg, whose population is not much bigger, is one of the richest.

The Rhineland is the fourth most powerful unit in GDP terms but the richest in average capacity per head using weighed EU criteria on purchasing power.

France, with 22 regions, provides some striking internal comparisons. While two areas are in the top 10 — Ile de France and Lyon-Rhone-Alps — Corsica is 186th.

Ireland is only 126th in prosperity. Only 12 of the UK regions are in the top half of the league. South Yorkshire, Essex, Clwyd, Cornwall, Derbyshire and Nottinghamshire, Dorset and Somerset, and Merseyside are fairly low down. Greater London, Greater Manchester and Grampian are in the top 20.

Eight countries produced above average GDP: Luxembourg, Belgium, Austria, Denmark, Germany, France, the Netherlands and Italy, in that order. The below-average states were Sweden, the UK, Finland, Ireland, Spain, Portugal and Greece. Some of the poorest regions, like the Vallée d'Aoste high up in the Alps, fall within the banana curve.

Figure 6.31 The richest and poorest areas of Europe

aftermath of the Second World War generally achieved only limited success. Regional analysis is now a much more detailed affair concerning a wide range of attributes. Policy development and implementation is no longer dominated by remote central government but now hinges on the active involvement of successive layers of government. The French government, for instance, considers that regional administration is the most appropriate institution to bring together local forces and to determine the specific place of each region in both national and European contexts, in terms, for example, of product mix. The Australian government favours a 'bottom-up' approach, in which states and cities help themselves to develop. Figure 6.32 compares the main characteristics of the newer and traditional approaches.

Private sector involvement has steadily become a more and more important component of regional development but with a notable shift away from large-scale businesses towards small and medium-sized enterprises. The stress is on entrepreneurship and the dissemination of good practice through a range of private sector organisations such as

chambers of commerce. Many of the countries of central and eastern Europe, in particular, where such institutions have been scarce, are especially eager to see them appear.

Figure 6.32 Key characteristics of regional policy

	Traditional top-down	New-model bottom-up
Level of operation	national	regional
Economic objectives	interregional equality	regional competitiveness
Development strategy	imported growth	indigenous growth
Policy instruments	bureaucratic regulation	venture capital
	international promotion	advisory services
	grants	technical infrastructure
	advance factories	training
Implementation	segregated	integrated

Regional development in Canada

Although many criteria have been used to identify area distress, most analyses focus on per capita income and levels of unemployment, as both factors have been reported consistently over a long period of time.

Figure 6.33 shows the regional convergence of income in Canada since 1950. The most noticeable development has been the income improvement in both the Atlantic provinces and Quebec. Taking into account both per capita income and provincial populations, the nuclei of wealth in the country are in Ontario and the western provinces of British Columbia and Alberta. Unemployment trends in recent decades (Figure 6.35) show that the Atlantic provinces and Quebec have consistently recorded jobless rates above the rest of the country. However, the relatively low unemployment rates of the Prairie provinces, the most important agricultural area in the country, is partly explained in terms of disguised unemployment on the land. Figure 6.36 shows how the provinces compare over a range of other criteria.

Prior to the 1950s no explicit federal regional policy had been pursued in Canada, although certain programmes such as the Prairie Farm Rehabilitation Act had firm regional implications. The first direct effort to compensate for regional disparities was the Equalisation Programme established in 1957.

Figure 6.33 Regional convergence of income, Canada

	Per capita income as a percentage of Canadian average				
Province	1950	1960	1970	1980	1990
Newfoundland	51	56	63	64	79
Prince Edward Island	55	57	67	71	77
Nova Scotia	74	76	78	79	86
New Brunswick	70	68	72	72	82
Quebec	86	87	89	95	91
Ontario	121	118	118	107	110
Manitoba	101	99	93	90	91
Saskatchewan	83	89	72	91	86
Alberta	101	100	99	112	101
British Columbia	125	115	109	111	105
Yukon and N.W. Territories	n.a.	106	95	103	n.a.
Mean deviation (%)	23	19	18	16	12

1990 data = Average Family Income

Phase one: the equalisation programme

Equalisation is based on the concept that the federal system should enable every province to provide services of average Canadian standards to its population without having to impose

New Goals for Regional Policy

RÉMY PRUD'HOMME

For many OECD countries, the reduction of regional disparities in output, unemployment and income is a major political goal, a contribution to – or a condition of – national cohesion. In no one country, though, is the reduction of interregional disparities seen as the only or even the primary objective of regional policies. Regional policy is now expected to promote growth throughout the entire country by encouraging competitiveness and regional self-sufficiency.

The concept of 'interregional disparities' must now be given a wider meaning. They exist not merely in income or unemployment between regions, since new types of imbalance are appearing – in the quality of the environment, in infrastructural endowment, in educational opportunity, in the availability of capital or in access to expertise. These are, so to speak, 'upstream' disparities, affecting the context in which enterprises and local governments operate. Reducing them will thus make it possible for businesses and local administrations to compete on a fairer basis. That also offers a way of eliminating potential conflict between the reduction of disparities and the promotion of growth: the reduction of disparities in development potential (not in development) is itself likely to contribute to growth.

The new disparities are also within regions, not only between them. The suggestion that there are well-off regions which can be neglected and problem regions which require help is a clumsy simplification. In reality, there are problem areas in most well-off regions, and well-off areas in many problem regions. Indeed, the most dramatic differences are often to be found within single areas, particularly in large cities. Regional policy must therefore often become sub-regional, and cannot be divorced from urban policy.

Another objective of regional policy is to ease sectoral and structural adjustment. Increased globalisation, rapid technological progress, and major geopolitical changes all lead to the disappearance of entire lines of activities (textiles, say) – which, fortunately, is often associated with the appearance of new lines of activities (such as electronics). This process – the working of Schumpeter's 'gales of creative destruction' – has often a marked regional dimension. The enterprises that have to disappear, or to shrink,

tend to be located in the same areas (shipbuilding and mining are examples); and there is no reason that the enterprises that will develop should appear in the same place. Even when the restructuring benefits an economy as a whole, it can hit some regions particularly hard. The problem is especially acute for the reduction of defence activities, which in most countries are disproportionately located in a small number of areas.

Devolving Responsibility

Until recently regional policy was the responsibility of central government. Nowadays, very few, if any, of the goals of regional policy can be reached without the close co-operation of lower tiers of government, of enterprises and of other countries.

Private enterprise is equally important in regional policy, particularly in the form of small and medium-sized enterprises (SMEs). There was a time, around twenty years ago, when regional policy was focused on large, often international, enterprises – frequently car-building companies – and on attracting them to designated areas. This sort of 'exogenous' policy is on the wane. Instead, 'endogenous' policies now focus on the role that must be played by the creation and the development of local SMEs. Enterpreneurship, rather than heavy-handed government, has become the key to regional development.

Increasing attention is being paid to the role of intermediate or co-operative private bodies – chambers of commerce, local banks, centres for the exchange of information (both private and public), institutions supplying venture capital, commodity markets, trade fairs and exhibitions.

Central governments nonetheless still have an important, if new, role to play, to facilitate and co-ordinate the action of others. They used to be soloists; they have to become conductors. This role is reflected in the new tools of regional policy.

New Tools

There is widespread disappointment with some (or most) of the traditional tools of regional policy. In

Figure 6.34 The *OECD Observer*, No. 193 April/May 1995

particular, grants and subsidies to enterprises, once one of the main tools of action, now stand accused of inefficiency, even of being counter-productive, since they can reduce motivation and create a culture of dependency. The new approach to regional policies obviously calls for new instruments.

The first of these is co-ordination. Vertical co-ordination – between central and lower tiers of government, between the European Union and its member states or their regions, between government and business – can take many forms.

There is also horizontal co-ordination of the activities of different regions, or of different municipalities in a given urban area, or more generally of other local institutions and organisations.

Third, there is horizontal co-ordination nationally. Many national policies established for good sectoral reasons fail to take into account their regional impact and thus may not be in line with the objectives of regional policy.

But, whatever the extent of policy co-ordination, the decisions of private enterprises and local governments will be taken, and bear fruit only if business operates in a supportive environment – of which the most important element is infrastructure. Infrastructure cannot be provided by enterprises themselves, because its benefits are dispersed. In many cases, too, as with roads, it cannot be entirely provided by local and regional governments alone, because of its network effects, and also because local governments in poor areas usually have little spare cash. Yet there are differences as to the types of infrastructure that central government should provide.

The 'traditional', basic type of infrastructure, roads, say, are still necessary in many countries, particularly central and eastern Europe. But interest is strong also in soft infrastructure, in information and education or training. The relative importance of 'hard' infrastructure probably declines with the extent of development, although the less advanced countries cannot afford to ignore the softer forms, nor can the more advanced ones neglect their harder infrastructure.

A further instrument in the new approach to regional policy involves the provision of advice and information. Enterprises, particularly when located in problem areas, are often short on information and ideas, about, say, technologies or markets. This problem is especially serious for SMEs, which are precisely the type of enterprises required for regional development. Markets can provide some of this infor-

mation. But in practice, the market for information is not very efficient; it can usefully be supplemented by government intervention, by providing free or subsidised advice, at least at the beginning of a period of development.

Labour-market assistance falls in the same category. In practice, local labour markets are not always efficient, since the supply of skills is often ill-adapted to demand. Government action in retraining the workers of declining industries can smooth the transition. In both cases, these new policies are aimed not at supporting declining or threatened old activities but at favouring the development of promising, often high-tech, new ones.

The shift in emphasis from action by central government to involving local and regional governments has financial implications. The development of a system of transfers through the national budget to the weaker local and regional governments is a necessary corollary of the increased independence of sub-national governments. Yet it is a delicate issue. Sufficiently large transfers are necessary to compensate differences in tax bases. But excessive transfers are dangerous because they decrease local and regional incentives and encourage inefficiency.

The fifth instrument of the new regional policy is pricing. People and enterprises should pay, inasmuch as possible, the full costs of the goods and services they consume; by the same token, local consumption should be paid for locally. That condition is particularly important for large cities, where the benefits accruing to companies and households are usually higher, as are costs, particularly of transport, environmental services and welfare. These urban costs should not be borne by weaker regions outside the cities.

A 'new model' of regional policy is thus emerging. It now has a variety of objectives – competitiveness and employment as much as the reduction of disparities. It has a range of targets – urban as well as border areas, not now only marginal parts of countries. It involves a number of institutions – local and regional governments and business, not only central government. It uses a large number of policy instruments. Not least, regional policy will rely more on the economic and social potential of every area of OECD countries, though it often will have to be stimulated, facilitated, co-ordinated, and otherwise aided. This will be the new role of central government – a more modest one, but it is also more complex, and certainly no less important, than in the past.

Figure 6.34 *cont.*

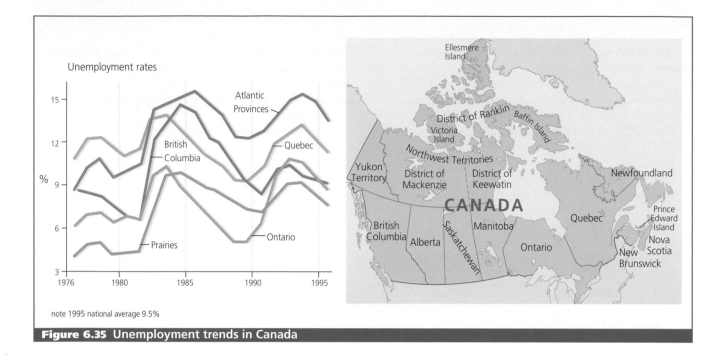

Figure 6.35 Unemployment trends in Canada

note 1995 national average 9.5%

Figure 6.36 Comparisons between Canadian provinces using a variety of criteria

	Infant mortality rates 1993	% of labour force with university degree 1995	Per capita health expenditures C$ 1994	Average weekly earnings for all employees Oct 1995 C$	Inmates in provincial custody per 1000 pop. 1994	Net inter-provincial migration 1994/95
Newfoundland	7.79	7.9	2259	538.55	0.68	−8410
Prince Edward Island	9.12	11.4	2299	482.88	0.70	875
Nova Scotia	7.09	11.9	2231	486.88	0.47	−2817
New Brunswick	7.18	9.9	2389	508.42	0.56	−833
Quebec	5.73	12.4	2263	551.93	0.48	−15284
Ontario	6.24	14.9	2614	611.09	0.66	4602
Manitoba	7.06	11.4	2546	509.61	0.83	−2162
Saskatchewan	8.06	9.6	2352	495.88	1.22	−4167
Alberta	6.65	13.6	2400	553.55	0.99	−4078
British Columbia	5.74	13.4	2631	600.40	0.63	32412
Yukon Territory	7.87	n.a. ⎫		719.73	2.30	94
NWT	9.62	n.a. ⎬	4418	713.86	6.36	−232
Canada	6.30	13.3	2478	–	0.67	–

heavier than average tax burdens. Although equalisation remains an integral part of the federal system, it is not a regional development programme in the true sense, in that payments are not conditional on development use of the funds. Since 1957, the annual equalisation transfers to low-income provinces have risen from C$138 million to over C$8 billion.

In 1992–3 Ontario, Alberta and British Columbia received no equalisation payments, the other seven provinces were allocated varying amounts, ranging from C$450 per person in Saskatchewan to C$1500 in Newfoundland. While the introduction of the Equalisation Programme eased the financial

burden on the poorer provinces, it did nothing directly to tackle the structural weaknesses which cause regional imbalance.

Phase two: the introduction of regional incentives

This second phase of policy was initiated by a New Products Programme for surplus manpower areas which commenced in 1960 to help areas of high unemployment and slow economic growth. The scheme permitted firms to obtain double the normal rate of capital cost allowances on most of the assets acquired to

Figure 6.37 Small farm in the Atlantic Provinces

manufacture products which were new to designated areas. This use of tax incentives mirrored existing schemes in Britain and other European countries.

The Agriculture and Rural Development Act (ARDA) of 1961 was designed to alleviate the high incidence of low incomes in rural areas through federal-provincial programmes to increase small farmers' output and productivity. In 1966 a Fund for Rural Economic Development was set up to provide comprehensive rural development schemes in areas characterised by widespread low incomes and major problems of adjustment, but considered to have development potential. The areas assisted were: the interlake region of Manitoba, the Gaspé region in Quebec, the Mactaquac and northeast areas of New Brunswick, and all of Prince Edward Island.

A totally area-specific scheme was established by the Atlantic Development Board (ADB) which was set up in 1962 to improve the economic structure of the Atlantic provinces. A similar agency was established in Quebec in the form of the Eastern Quebec Development Board.

The Area Development Incentives Act, 1963, aimed to help areas of chronic high unemployment, using accelerated capital cost allowances, income tax exemptions and cash grants as an inducement to manufacturing industry to locate in worst affected areas. The scheme, although achieving certain successes, was generally criticised for lack of co-ordination and long-term planning.

Phase three: the Department of Regional Economic Expansion (DREE)

DREE was established in 1969 to assist the various regions realise their economic and social potential and to provide the national co-

ordination frequently missing from earlier schemes. While earlier efforts had generally concentrated on worst affected regions, DREE proposed to focus activity on areas which had the potential for significant economic growth. As well as continuing the work of earlier schemes DREE embarked on two new projects: the 'Special Areas' programme and a new package of industrial incentives under the Regional Development Incentives Act (RDIA). The Special Areas scheme helped to upgrade existing and potential growth centres, rendering them more attractive locations while RDIA provided a direct inducement to industry to locate in designated regions, particularly in the Special Areas.

The Special Areas programme, which was seen as experimental, lasted for only three years and a major policy review in 1972 witnessed the emergence of a new level of federal-provincial co-operation with the introduction of General Development Agreements (GDAs) and their subsidiary agreements. These ten-year programmes covered a wide range of development projects from construction of industrial and social infrastructure to financial assistance for resource development, secondary industry and tourist projects.

Phase four: the Department of Regional Industrial Expansion (DRIE)

During the 1970s DREE's regional development approach was increasingly considered to be too restricted in scope and in 1982 a new strategic approach was announced. DRIE was set up merging the regional programmes of the existing DREE with the industry, small firms and tourist components of the Department of Industry, Trade and Commerce. The revised federal-provincial agreements became known as 'Economic and Regional Development Agreements'. Reflecting the severe cyclical problems affecting the economy in the early 1980s, the new approach shifted away from the disadvantaged regions for a time to place greater emphasis on nation wide assistance. Incentives ranged from investment grants for new plants and plant modernisation to financial and technical assistance for product development, research and marketing. The eligibility of a region for assistance was determined by its 'Development Index' which was based on a variety of socio-economic characteristics. Counterparts to DRIE were also created at provincial level.

Phase five: new policy directions

There was growing recognition that, despite a variety of efforts over the previous 25 years, unacceptable levels of regional disparity continued to exist. These concerns led to a fundamental restructuring of regional development policy announced in 1986, which laid the foundation for the current structure of regional development in Canada. Significantly, there was a decentralisation away from Ottawa to give regional agencies the primary responsibility for development within their local area. Greater flexibility in terms of support and wider consultation and participation at the local level were also promoted.

In 1987, the new policy resulted in the creation of two major regional development agencies: the Atlantic Canada Opportunities

Figure 6.38 One of the major seaports in the Atlantic Provinces

Agency (ACOA), to develop and implement programmes contributing to the long-term economic development of the Atlantic provinces; and Western Economic Diversification (WD), to develop and diversify the Western economy to make it less vulnerable to international economic developments and fluctuating commodity prices.

A new 'flagship' economic development department – the Department of Industry, Science and Technology – was also created to promote the effective integration of advanced technology and competitive industrial capacity. The Department took responsibility for regional development in Northern Ontario and for Eastern Quebec. Subsequently in 1991, regional development in Quebec as a whole was decentralised to a new agency, the Federal Office of Regional Development-Quebec.

The Atlantic Provinces: Canada's main problem region

The four provinces of New Brunswick, Newfoundland, Nova Scotia and Prince Edward Island make up the region of Atlantic Canada. Just over 2.3 million people live in an area covering half a million km². Long regarded as the major problem region in Canada, the provinces are characterised by slow economic growth, heavy reliance on primary industries, low per capita incomes and persistently high unemployment rates. In an attempt to rectify such relative deprivation the region has figured prominently in Canadian regional development programmes. Although this injection of federal funding has resulted in significant improvements covering many aspects of the regional economy, the Atlantic Provinces still lag behind the rest of the nation according to most socio-economic indicators.

Development in the provinces has been hindered by a number of factors, particularly the paucity of natural resources, the low level of manufacturing industry and capital investment, and the scattered nature of rural settlement. Although the provinces are

the most rural of Canada's regions, the generally infertile soils and cool summers have restricted agricultural improvement. A consequence of such a lack of agricultural potential is the highest percentage of rural non-farm population in the country.

The principal urban nuclei of the region are the seaports of St John in New Brunswick, Halifax in Nova Scotia and St John's in Newfoundland. However, these urban areas had 1995 populations of only 129 000, 343 000, and 177 000 respectively. These urban nuclei account for the lowest percentage of population for any region in the country. Such a small and dispersed population provides a very limited attraction for industries attempting to achieve economies of scale. Low capital intensity in the private sector and poor public services have often been cited as disincentives to new industry.

The four provinces have benefited from a range of region-specific programmes and the highest levels of assistance under centrally administered policies. With the introduction of a decentralised approach in 1987, the Atlantic Canada Opportunities Agency (ACOA) was the first of the regional agencies to be created, with a funding allocation of C$1.05 billion over a five-year period. ACOA's overall objective is to foster the long-term economic renewal of Atlantic Canada through:

- a self-sustaining entrepreneurial climate
- a greater number of successful small and medium-sized businesses
- more lasting employment opportunities
- increased earned income
- an expanding competitive economy
- national policies and programmes that reflect the aspirations and opportunities of Atlantic Canada.

To further these aims ACOA operates two main programmes: Action and Co-operation and Advocacy and Co-ordination. The former comprises a package of assistance (grants, loans, interest-rate subsidies, loan insurance and equity support) for small and medium-sized enterprises, as well as the provision of information, advice and consultancy, and access to technology. Action programme assistance may provide up to 50 per cent of investment costs. Eligible projects encompass both commercial and non-commercial operations involving activities such as innovation, business studies, capital investment, supplier development, market development and business support.

Under the Co-operation Programme, ACOA and each of the provincial governments enter into a series of cost-shared, federal-provincial co-operation agreements which fund infrastructure initiatives targeting the business environment for entrepreneurship, market and trade development, innovation and technology transfer, human resource development and a sustainable environment. Agreements are also signed between ACOA and non-governmental organisations. Between June 1987 and August 1992, agreements worth almost $600 million were signed for projects ranging from agricultural development, forestry and fisheries, minerals, energy and industrial development projects to transport, tourism and cultural initiatives (Figure 6.39).

Figure 6.39 The Atlantic Provinces co-operation programme initiatives, June 1987–August 1992

	Number of initiatives	Federal share $ million	Provincial share $ million	Total cost $ million
Newfoundland	18	265.1	125.2	390.3
Prince Edward Island	13	95.2	59.8	155.0
Nova Scotia	18	333.4	365.8	699.2
New Brunswick	20	367.4	202.3	569.7
Pan-Atlantic	3	10.0	4.0	14.0
Total	72	1071.1	757.1	1828.2

The Advocacy and Co-ordination functions involve advocating the region's interests and co-ordinating federal economic programmes in Atlantic Canada to ensure maximum impact. Activities targeted by ACOA include fisheries, offshore mining, tourism, transportation, trade policy, environment and shipbuilding.

Questions

1 (a) Using the data in Figures 6.33, 6.35 and 6.36 draw up a composite quality of life index for the provinces of Canada.
(b) How strong is the correlation between the various indicators?
(c) What other information would you require for a more comprehensive picture of regional disparity in Canada?
2 To what extent are the five phases of regional policy proposed above distinctive stages in the development of policy?
3 (a) 'The Atlantic Provinces are without doubt Canada's number one problem region'. Discuss.
(b) How has regional policy attempted to improve socio-economic conditions in the region?

Bibliography

References

Human Development Report 1997, published annually for the United Nations Development Programme by OUP, 1997.
Development Theory and the Three Worlds by B. Hettne, Longman, 1990.
An Unequal World by A. Gilbert, Nelson, 1992.
'UK Regional Policy: An Evaluation' by J. Taylor and C. Wren, *Regional Studies*, 1997 Vol. 31.9, pp.835–948.
Brazil: Advanced Case Studies by P. Guinness, Hodder & Stoughton, 1998.
Regional Problems and Policies in Canada, OECD Publications, 1994.
North America: An Advanced Geography by B. Price and P. Guiness, Hodder & Stoughton, 1997.
Geography of the Third World by J. Dickenson et al., Routledge, 1996.
Development and underdevelopment by G. Nagle, Nelson, 1998.

Internet

Millennium Institute: State of the world Indicators – http://www.igc.apc.org/millenium/inds/
Africa online
http://www.africaonline.com/
Oxfam
http://www.heinemann.co.uk/oxfam
World health Organisation
http://www.who.ch/

7 tourism and *recreation*

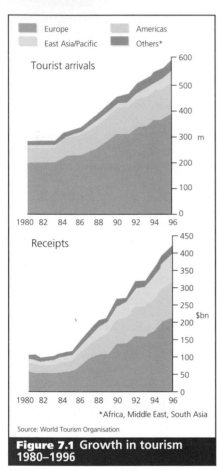

Figure 7.1 Growth in tourism 1980–1996

Europe
East Asia/Pacific
Americas
Others*

Tourist arrivals

600
500
400
300 m
200
100
0

1980 82 84 86 88 90 92 94 96

Receipts

450
400
350
300
250
200 $bn
150
100
50
0

1980 82 84 86 88 90 92 94 96

*Africa, Middle East, South Asia

Source: World Tourism Organisation

Key Definitions ①

tourism A recreational or leisure time activity which involves an overnight absence from the normal place of residence.

spa A resort based around a mineral spring.

package holiday (tour) The most popular form of foreign holiday whereby travel, accommodation and predetermined meals are all included in the price and are booked in advance, usually through a travel agent. Optional extras such as car hire and special visits may also be booked at the same time. A wide range of such holidays are advertised in the brochures published by the major tour operators.

ecotourism A specialised form of tourism where people experience relatively untouched natural environments such as coral reefs, tropical forests and remote mountain areas.

Tourism

The tourism juggernaut

The World Tourism Organisation calculated that in 1996 travellers took 595 million trips abroad (Figure 7.1), 77 per cent more than ten years earlier. It predicts that by 2010 the number will reach 937 million. Receipts from international travel, excluding airfares, totalled $423 billion in 1996. Figure 7.2 shows the top twenty countries in terms of arrivals and receipts. On most counts, travel and tourism is the largest industry in the world. The World Travel and Tourism Council (WTTC) estimates that tourism sustains more than one in ten jobs around the world, employing 255 million people. The rapid expansion of the industry in recent decades has, however, brought the economic, environmental and social/cultural issues surrounding it to the fore. Tourism is arguably the most contentious aspect of the trend towards globalisation. As a recent publication states (*People and the Planet*, Vol. 6, No. 4) 'Evidence of the downside of tourism – culturally, environmentally and economically – is now such that tourism has become a dirty word among many communities, environmental groups, and human rights campaigners.'

The industry has a huge appetite for basic resources which often impinge heavily on the needs of local people. A long-term protest against tourism in Goa has highlighted the fact that one five-star hotel consumes as much water as five local villages with the average hotel resident using 28 times more electricity per day than a local person.

Apart from its voracious appetite for resources, tourism has also been criticised for:

- denying local people access to beaches
- violation of environmental regulations by hotels and other aspects of the industry
- unscrupulous tactics by local authorities to free-up beach areas for hotel use
- destruction of traditional lifestyles
- commercialisation of culture
- abuse of human rights.

The development of tourism

Humankind has had a fascination for travel since the very earliest historical period. There has always been an urge to discover the unknown and experience new environments. Thus, travel to achieve these ends is not new, but tourism, as the term is understood today, is of relatively modern origin. Tourism is distinguished by its mass character from the travel undertaken in the past.

Figure 7.2 Top 20 tourism destinations and top 20 tourism earners

Top 20 tourism destinations

Rank			International tourist arrivals in millions			Market share % of world total	
1990	1997	Country	1990	1997	1990	1997
1	1	France	52 497	66 800	11.52	10.83
2	2	US	39 363	48 977	8.64	7.94
3	3	Spain	34 085	43 403	7.48	7.04
4	4	Italy	26 679	34 087	5.86	5.53
7	5	UK	18 013	26 052	3.95	4.22
12	6	China	10 484	23 770	2.30	3.85
8	7	Mexico	17 176	22 700	3.77	3.68
27	8	Poland	3400	19 560	0.75	3.17
5	9	Hungary	20 510	19 478	4.50	3.16
10	10	Canada	15 209	17 556	3.34	2.85
16	11	Czech Rep.	7278	17 400	1.60	2.82
6	12	Austria	19 011	16 575	4.17	2.69
9	13	Germany	17 045	15 828	3.74	2.57
–	14	Russian Fed.	–	15 000	–	2.43
11	15	Switzerland	13 200	11 077	2.90	1.80
19	16	Hong Kong (China)	6581	10 534	1.44	1.71
13	17	Greece	8873	10 126	1.95	1.64
14	18	Portugal	8020	10 100	1.76	1.64
24	19	Turkey	4799	9040	1.05	1.47
21	20	Thailand	5299	7263	1.16	1.18
		Total 1–20	327 522	445 326	71.90	72.22
		World total	445 547	616 635	100.00	100.00

Top 20 tourism earners

Rank			International tourism receipts $bn			Market share % of world total	
1990	1997	Country	1990	1997	1990	1997
1	1	US	43 007	75 056	15.99	16.74
3	2	Italy	20 016	30 000	7.44	6.69
4	3	Spain	18 593	28 147	6.91	6.28
2	4	France	20 184	27 947	7.50	6.23
5	5	UK	14 940	19 875	5.55	4.43
6	6	Germany	14 288	18 989	5.31	4.24
7	7	Austria	13 417	12 393	4.99	2.76
25	8	China	2218	12 074	0.82	2.69
11	9	Hong Kong (China)	5032	9635	1.87	2.15
8	10	Switzerland	7411	9015	2.75	2.01
65	11	Poland	358	9000	0.13	2.01
14	12	Australia	4088	8900	1.52	1.99
9	13	Canada	6339	8825	2.36	1.97
13	14	Thailand	4326	8700	1.61	1.94
12	15	Singapore	4596	7950	1.71	1.77
–	16	Russian Fed.	–	7318	–	1.63
10	17	Mexico	5467	7307	2.03	1.63
21	18	Turkey	3225	7000	1.20	1.56
16	19	Netherlands	3636	6597	1.35	1.47
15	20	Belgium	3721	5997	1.38	1.34
		Total 1–20	194 862	320 725	72.43	71.55
		World total	269 032	448 265	100.00	100.00

Source: World Tourism Organisation

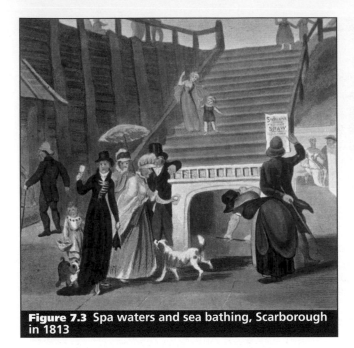

Figure 7.3 Spa waters and sea bathing, Scarborough in 1813

Figure 7.4 An 1860s Thomas Cook tour to the Nile

The medical profession was largely responsible for the growth of taking holidays away from home. During the seventeenth century doctors began increasingly to recommend the medicinal properties of mineral waters and by the end of the eighteenth century there were hundreds of spas in existence in Britain. Bath, Tunbridge Wells, Epsom, Buxton and Malvern were among the most famous. The second stage in the development of holiday centres was the emergence of the seaside resort. Sea bathing is usually said to have begun at Scarborough about 1730.

The annual holiday for the masses was essentially a product of the Industrial Revolution, which brought substantial social and economic changes. However, until the latter part of the nineteenth century, only the very affluent could afford to take a holiday away from home. At the time the majority of resorts were small and functioned largely as centres of fashion and privilege, as well as therapeutic centres.

The first package tours were arranged by Thomas Cook in 1841. These took travellers from Leicester to Loughborough, 19 km away, to attend temperance meetings. At the time it was the newly laid railway network that provided the transport infrastructure for Cook to expand his tour operations. Of equal importance was the emergence of a significant middle class with time and money to spare for extended recreation. Thus, the traditional week or fortnight by the sea and the design of resorts, centred around promenade, main street and railway station, reflects the habits of the nineteenth century.

By far the greatest developments have occurred since the end of the Second World War, arising from the substantial growth in leisure time, affluence and mobility. In Britain, in 1950, 25 million people took a holiday away from home, with 1.25 million of these travelling abroad. By 1970 these figures had risen to 34.5 and 5.75 million respectively.

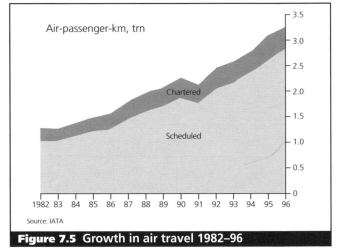

Figure 7.5 Growth in air travel 1982–96

However, it took the jet plane to herald the era of international mass tourism. In 1970 when Pan Am flew the first Boeing 747 from New York to London, scheduled planes carried 307 million passengers. By 1995 the figure had increased to 1.15 billion. Figure 7.5 illustrates the expansion of air travel since the early 1980s while Figure 7.6 shows the correlation between income and air travel.

Wealth is the main determinant of demand for tourism. Most of the world's tourists originate from the Developed World but their numbers will not rise much further in the future because of demographic trends. However, as the population of the Developed World ages further, the nature of demand will change. The tourist industry is increasingly turning its attention to the Developing World where the growing middle classes in a significant number of countries want to experience regular foreign travel.

In the western economies there has been a rapid growth in the number of people taking second (or more) holidays. In the UK over 30 per cent of people now fall into this category. This is a consequence of:

■ **steadily rising real incomes**

■ **an increase in the average number of days of paid leave**

■ **the decreasing real costs of holidays**

■ **the widening range of destinations within the middle-income range**

■ **the heavy marketing of shorter foreign holidays aimed at those who have the time and disposable income to take an additional break**

■ **'air miles' and other retail reward schemes aimed at travel and tourism.**

Another important trend is the growing popularity of specialised holidays. Ecotourism is a major case in point. Although generally perceived as an acceptable form of tourism and a form of sustainable development, much that passes for ecotourism is merely an expensive package holiday cleverly marketed with the 'eco' label.

The economic impact

There has been much debate about the extent of the economic benefits of tourism at the local, regional and national scales. Precise calculation is very difficult indeed because of the considerable indirect economic consequences that result from direct spending. Average tourist spending in 1996, according to the industry consultancy Euromonitor, was $559 per head. However, to calculate the knock-on effects of this direct spending the WTTC uses a 'satellite accounting system' shown by the flow chart in Figure 7.7. Taking into account all the indirect inputs, the WTTC puts the total economic value of goods and services attributable to tourism in 1996 at $3.6 trillion, or 10.6 per cent of gross global product. The WTTC argues that a full economic analysis of this kind is required to persuade governments that spending money on tourism, particularly on infrastructure, is a profitable investment.

Canada introduced a satellite accounting system for tourism in 1994 and increased its spending on tourism ninefold over the next three years, reaching $200 million in 1997. Over the same period receipts from tourism increased by around 25 per cent to $18.5 billion. Canada has determined that air travel accounts for 20 per cent of the total tourism expenditure while travel by car follows closely behind at 17 per cent. Mexico is planning to launch a tourism satellite accounting system in 1999 while several other countries including the UK and the United States have undertaken assessment programmes.

Some economists have argued that the UK has not taken tourism seriously enough in the past. In July 1998 the UK's travel deficit surged to £1.7 billion, the highest on record, with a strong pound making foreign travel cheaper for British people but expensive for overseas visitors coming to Britain. The British Tourist Authority receives a grant-in-aid that is modest compared with the amounts spent by many other countries. A larger investment is required to market Britain abroad and to persuade more British people to holiday in their own country. Unless this happens the travel deficit may increase further, placing a considerable strain on the economy.

While those parts of Britain attractive to foreign tourists have done well from the industry in recent years, many regional seaside resorts are in deep trouble. Of little appeal to foreigners they have been abandoned in large numbers by British holidaymakers who head for places like the Mediterranean and Florida for guaranteed sunshine. Generally, the support given to communities of declining

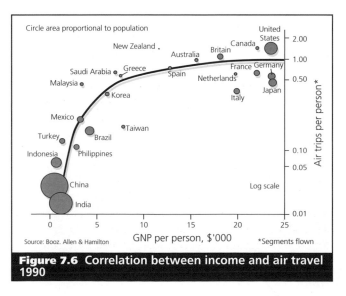

Figure 7.6 Correlation between income and air travel 1990

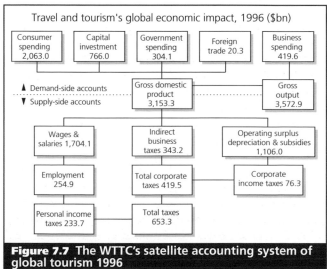

Figure 7.7 The WTTC's satellite accounting system of global tourism 1996

Models relating to tourism

The core-periphery enclave model of tourism (Figure 7.8) proposed by Britton in 1981 stresses that in many developing countries the benefits/impact of tourism are very limited geographically. Most tourists come from the developed or core nations. In many developing countries (the periphery) tourists frequently stay in specially designated enclaves with all the required facilities immediately on hand. Outside of the resort enclaves there are a number of attractions (scenic, historic, cultural) at locations that can usually be reached and returned from within a day. At such locations the expected infrastructure is usually provided. Thus the majority of the country is unaffected by tourism. As a result most tourists have little or no contact with local people and fail to experience the reality of life in the country they have chosen to visit.

Butler's model of the evolution of tourist areas (Figure 7.9) illustrates how tourism develops and changes over time. In the first stage the location is explored independently by a small number of visitors. If visitor impressions are good and local people perceive that real benefits are to be gained then the number of visitors will increase as the local community becomes actively involved in the promotion of tourism. In the development stage, holiday companies from the developed nations take control of organisation and management with package holidays becoming the norm. Eventually growth ceases as the location loses some of its former attraction. At this stage local people have become all too aware of the problems created by tourism. Finally, decline sets in, but because of the perceived economic importance of the industry efforts will be made to re-package the location which, if successful, may either stabilise the situation or result in renewed growth (rejuvenation).

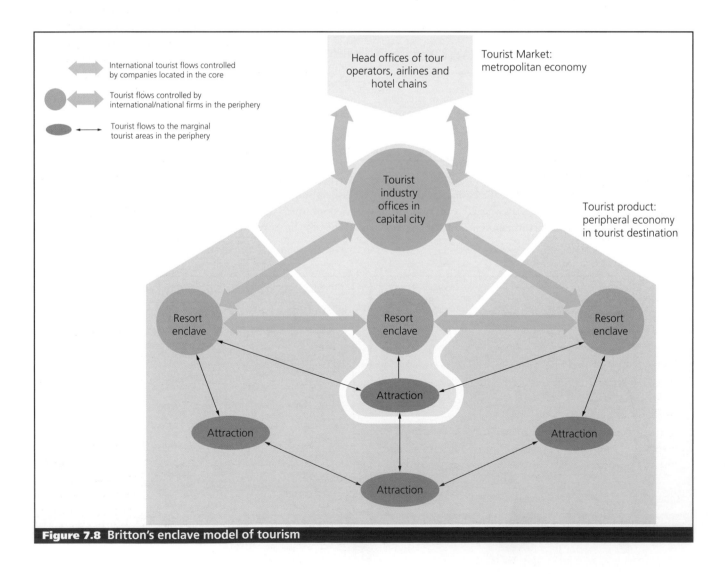

Figure 7.8 Britton's enclave model of tourism

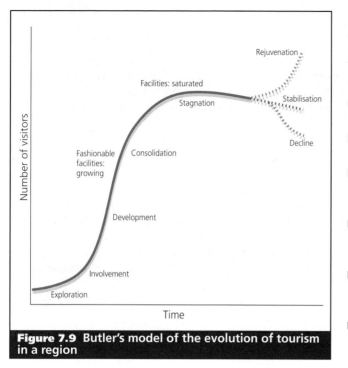

Figure 7.9 Butler's model of the evolution of tourism in a region

industries such as coalmining and shipbuilding has not materialised for tourism decline.

How great are the economic benefits for developing countries?

Tourism undoubtedly brings valuable foreign currency to developing countries and a range of other obvious benefits but critics argue that its value is often overrated because:

■ foreign exchange leakages from developing to developed countries run at a rate of between 60 per cent and 75 per cent. With cheap package holidays, by far the greater part of the money paid stays in the country where the holiday was purchased

■ most local jobs created are menial, low paid and seasonal. Overseas labour may be brought in to fill middle and senior management positions

■ money borrowed to invest in the necessary infrastructure for tourism increases the national debt

■ at some destinations tourists spend most of their money in their hotels with minimum benefit to the wider community

■ tourism might not be the best use for local resources which could in the future create a larger multiplier effect if used by a different economic sector.

External shocks and local catastrophes

Unfortunately, more than many other industries, tourism is vulnerable to 'external shocks'. Periods of economic recession

characterised by high unemployment, modest wage rises, and high interest rates, affect the demand for tourism in most parts of the world. As a big-ticket discretionary purchase, it suffers when times are hard. However, particular places are often exposed to risks of their own:

■ the attacks on British and German tourists in Miami in 1992 and 1993 put off many foreign visitors to Florida

■ tourists have avoided Egypt since the terrorist massacre of 58 tourists at Luxor in November 1997 (**Figure 7.10**)

■ the tropical smogs that engulfed parts of Indonesia and Malaysia in 1997 resulted in mass cancellations of holidays

■ large spillages from oil tankers have devastated beaches in various parts of the world at different times including the Middle East, Alaska and Southwest England

■ the holiday infrastructure on various Caribbean islands has been destroyed by hurricanes, often taking years to replace

■ the destruction of beaches by natural forces can have a devastating effect on tourism. Over the winter of 1997–8 it is estimated that storm waves powered by El Niño stripped 5 million cubic yards of sand off California's beaches. The waves have lowered many beaches by as much as 15 feet; some are now bare rock. The damage matters as southern California's beaches are worth an estimated $10 billion to the state's economy.

Social and cultural impact

Many communities in the Developing World have suffered through the imposition of the worst of western values, resulting in varying degrees in the development of some or all of the following problems (Figure 7.11):

■ the loss of locally owned land
■ the abandonment of traditional values and practices
■ displacement
■ alcoholism
■ prostitution, sometimes involving children
■ drug abuse
■ crime.

At best there is usually some degree of irritation caused by tourism (Figure 7.12), at its very worst the impact of tourism amounts to gross abuse of human rights. For example, the military junta in Burma has forcibly moved millions of people from their homes to make room for tourist development, and used hundreds of thousands of people as forced labour on tourism-related projects.

Welcome to the Nile's ghost town

SINCE the massacre of 58 tourists at the Temple of Hatshepsut on Nov 17 1997, Luxor has become a ghost town.

Most of the hotels have closed and laid off staff. The horse-drawn *caleches* circle aimlessly, almost all empty, the drivers apparently in a state of shock.

The only bright side is that they still have the spirit to try to get twice their proper fare.

At Aswan, I counted 50 large Nile cruise boats at anchor yesterday. At Luxor, there were at least twice that many.

Yet the tourist centres of Upper Egypt must now be among the safest places in the world. Soldiers and police are everywhere. The Temple of Kom Ombo, near Aswan, has sharp-shooters stationed all around the outer walls. The Valley of the Kings and the Luxor temples are under equally close guard.

If you long for the days before mass tourism, with its yelling guides and trampling hordes, it is the best possible time to visit Egypt.

Tourists are a precious commodity, sincerely welcomed. In the Valley of the Kings, I counted about 50 people. In the Valley of the Queens, there were 20, and in the Valley of the Nobles, none. At the Hatshepsut Temple itself, there were five visitors.

Early in the morning, I had the magnificent Karnak Temple entirely to myself. I was the only person in the Tomb of Queen Nefertari, which has some of the freshest and most beautiful wall paintings in Egypt.

In the Egyptian Museum in Cairo, I was alone with the treasures of Tutunkhamun for 25 minutes.

The blow to the Egyptian tourist industry — in which the Mubarak presidency has invested heavily and which brings in £3 billion a year to the economy — is obviously catastrophic.

What has not yet been sufficiently stressed is how much the disaster was due to a level of police incompetence that is almost impossible to credit. The police simply did not arrive for nearly two hours, during which time the six terrorists roamed the temple massacring at will, and then mutilating the bodies.

Scenes like this discourage tourism

Figure 7.10 *Daily Telegraph*, 9 January 1998

WHAT'S THE PROBLEM?

FAR TOO OFTEN, DISPLACEMENT IS THE REAL PRICE OF TOURISM, AND IT IS PAID BY LOCAL PEOPLE. YOUR LIVELIHOOD, TRADITIONS AND CULTURE MAY COUNT FOR NOTHING IF YOUR HOME IS ON AN IDYLLIC COASTLINE, OR BY A COOL HILL, OR AMONG ANCIENT TEMPLES....

IF YOU LIVE IN A COUNTRY WITH PLENTY OF SUNSHINE AND A GROWING TOURISM INDUSTRY, AND IF YOUR LAND WOULD SUIT A NEW BEACH COMPLEX, A GOLF COURSE, A SAFARI PARK OR A CULTURE AND HERITAGE SITE, YOU COULD BE 'IN THE WAY' OF PROFITABLE DEVELOPMENT. YOU MIGHT AS WELL PACK YOUR BAGS AND LEAVE - OR ELSE YOU MAY WELL BE FORCED OFF YOUR OWN LAND.

'How could any money compare with what they have taken from us, to the grazing we have lost, to the human lives we have lost by being kept out of the Amboseli?'
(METOE OLE LOMBAA MAASAI PASTORALIST)

THE TOURISM INDUSTRY IS BIG. IF IT WAS A COUNTRY IT WOULD BE THE THIRD RICHEST IN THE WORLD. AND IT'S GROWING - FIVE YEARS FROM NOW IT WILL BE THE WORLD'S BIGGEST INDUSTRY. THERE ARE TIMES WHEN IT SEEMS THAT ABSOLUTELY NOTHING CAN STAND IN ITS WAY....

DISPLACEMENT: WHAT IT REALLY MEANS TO PEOPLE

Displacement isn't a simple matter of persuasion, compulsory purchase and compensation. It's a matter of force. People just HAVE to leave.

1996 - BURMA'S YEAR OF THE TOURIST. Among Burma's (Myanmar's) many attractions is the Royal Palace at Mandalay, where the moat has been cleared - by forced 'voluntary' labour - and homes demolished. And there is Pagan, where 5,200 people who lived in villages among the ancient pagodas were given two weeks to pack up and leave. Now Pagan and its pagodas welcome tourists in peace and quiet, while Pagan's people have been moved to a site of bare, parched earth with little shelter.

ISLAND PARADISE? The lovely tropical island of Lombok is increasingly popular with visitors to Indonesia. According to witnesses, the Government is tearing down homes to make way for development, and the tourism frontier is moving so fast that communities have no time to prepare and adjust....

FAIR GAME? In Kenya, the Maasai have been forced off their ancestral lands. These places have become National Parks, where tourists are free to roam and observe big game. But the Maasai are banned. Many have migrated to urban slums. Many of those that have stayed sell souvenirs, or beg money for posing for photos.

DISPLACEMENT: WHAT TOURISM CONCERN IS DOING

You may be asking: "Well, what on earth can I do about it?" Just like displaced people around the world, those of us who travel with a conscience can't help but feel helpless.

But the cause isn't altogether lost. Tourism Concern is trying to make tourism fairer, to make it possible for us to travel and take holidays without costing local people their homes and livelihoods. Tourism Concern campaigns - all over the world - on behalf of people displaced by the tourism industry.

Tourism Concern CAMPAIGNS WORLDWIDE FOR JUST AND SUSTAINABLE TOURISM • HELPS DEVELOP PROJECTS WORLDWIDE FOR JUST AND SUSTAINABLE TOURISM • WORKS TO HELP TOURISTS AND TRAVELLERS UNDERSTAND THE ISSUES • FORGES LINKS WITH PEOPLE IN TRAVEL AND TOURISM DESTINATION AREAS • LOBBIES THE TOURISM INDUSTRY TO TAKE LOCAL PEOPLE INTO ACCOUNT.

If you have a conscience about your travel and holidays, and if you want to help the process of making the tourism industry more responsible, more sensitive and more just, please help us with our work.

EVERY PENNY YOU DONATE HELPS US WORK FOR A FAIRER DEAL FOR THE PEOPLE WHO HAVE TO PAY THE GREATEST PRICE FOR TOURISM.

YOU CAN MAKE A DIFFERENCE

Figure 7.11 The negative impact of tourism according to the pressure group Tourism Concern

In India the 32 000 hunter-gatherer Adivasis have had their access to the forest they lived in for centuries severely curtailed because it forms part of Nagarahole National Park. They are now not allowed to hunt or cultivate, keep livestock or collect forest produce, and visit sacred sites and burial grounds. The Adivasis, for their part, went to court to prevent the construction of a hotel in the national park. Apart from the denial of their historic rights the Adivasis are concerned about the erosion of their tribal culture.

---

1. Euphoria
- Enthusiasm for tourist development
- Mutual feeling of satisfaction
- Opportunities for local participation
- Flows of money and interesting contacts

2. Apathy
- Industry expands
- Tourists taken for granted
- More interest in profit making
- Personal contact becomes more formal

3. Irritation
- Industry nearing saturation point
- Expansion of facilities required
- Encroachment into local way of life

4. Antagonism
- Irritations become more overt
- The tourist is seen as the harbinger of all that is bad
- Mutual politeness gives way to antagonism

5. Final level
- Environment has changed irreversibly
- The resource base has changed and the type of tourist has also changed
- If the destination is large enough to cope with mass tourism it will continue to thrive

Figure 7.12 Doxey's index of irritation caused by tourism

Key Definitions   2

satellite accounting system   A comprehensive system of accounting that includes not only direct expenditure and receipts but also all the indirect knock-on effects.

external shock   An economic, political or other trend or event in a major market that significantly reduces the demand for tourism at a particular destination or a range of destinations.

sustainable tourism   Tourism organised in such a way that its level can be sustained in the future without creating irreparable environmental, social and economic damage to the receiving area.

In Hawaii, traditional burial grounds have been razed to make way for new resorts while in Bali devout Hindus are angry that their temples are overshadowed by recently constructed large-scale tourist developments.

In some areas the social behaviour of foreign tourists has become a major issue. In August 1998 the Costa Brava banned the sale of alcohol from all-night stores in response to a sharp increase in incidents of riotous behaviour by tourists – many of them British. Residents claim that the drunken excesses of tourists is ruining the region's reputation. The resort of Lloret de Mar which promotes itself as 'the most exciting spot in Europe' has experienced some of the worst problems.

The creation of Kruger National Park resulted in the total denial of resources to local people (Figure 7.14). The advent of democracy in South Africa now means that this situation may change as the government looks towards a sharing arrangement which it hopes will balance local, national and international interests. The development of this process will be closely watched by a number of other developing countries.

Environmental impact

Tourism that does not destroy what it sets out to explore has come to be known as 'sustainable'. The term comes from the 1987 UN Report on the Environment which advocated the kind of development that meets present needs without compromising the prospects of future generations. Following the 1992 Earth Summit in Rio de Janeiro, the WTTC and the Earth Council drew up an environmental checklist for tourist development which included waste minimisation, re-use and recycling, energy efficiency, and water management. The WTTC has since established a more detailed programme called 'Green Globe', designed to act as an environmental blueprint for its members.

Figure 7.13 British tourists in Spain...what kind of impact?

Sharing deal may hold key to future of Kruger Park

By Christopher Munnion in Skukuza

SOUTH Africa's Kruger National Park celebrates its centenary today under pressures and uncertainties that could change the face of one of the world's great wildlife sanctuaries.

For most of its existence, the park has been regarded by blacks as an Afrikaner-dominated institution reserved for whites.

Poverty-stricken tribesmen living on its borders would gaze resentfully as the relatively affluent drove around looking at the game they craved for food, the trees they wanted for firewood and building material and water they needed for survival.

Worse, many of them had been dispossessed of ancestral land as the authorities expanded the boundaries of the reserve to create the vast wilderness, the size of Wales, the Kruger Park now occupies.

The park had a curious provenance. Paul Kruger, the president of the old Transvaal Republic and a strict Calvinist not noted for his far-sightedness, proclaimed the vast tract of land on the Mozambique border a conservation area in an age when most people thought all wild animals should be slaughtered for sport and food. His vision was translated into reality by a Scottish soldier, Major James Stephenson-Hamilton.

The reserve is now home to more than 8,000 elephants, 2,200 rhinos, 19,000 buffalo, 2,000 lions and some 600 species of birds as well as myriad other creatures. It has a dramatic array of plants too in its nearly five million acres.

But the Kruger Park has never had such a challenge as those posed by the economic, social and cultural realities of the new South Africa. There are now more than two million people living in villages, townships and squatter camps on its boundaries, most of them on or below the poverty line.

The Mandela government, while recognising the Kruger's value as a prime attraction for foreign tourists, is insisting that these once hostile neighbours should share in the economic benefits generated by the reserve.

Yvonne Dladla, head of the Kruger's social ecology unit, points out that while some 500 water holes have been created for wild animals, women on the other side of the fence have to walk for miles to find potable water for their families.

Several black communities have made legal claims for restitution of substantial portions of the park, saying their people were forcibly removed during the apartheid years. Some of these claims have official backing.

One — by the Makuleke community for 70,000 acres near the Zimbabwean border in the north — has succeeded but has been accompanied by a heartening compromise that will benefit both the Kruger Park and the local people.

The community and the park authorities will jointly manage the region as a tourist attraction with wilderness trails and tented camps.

Lamson Makuleke, the community spokesman, is delighted with the arrangement. "Our dream to have our ancestral land returned has come true and we will now be able to get involved in nature conservation and eco-tourism," he said.

The new head of South African National Parks, Mavuso Msimang, the first black to hold the post, hailed the Makuleke example as "a conservation breakthrough". It ensured the protection of the ecological integrity of Kruger "while rights to land restitution are accommodated".

Figure 7.14 *Daily Telegraph*, **26 March 1998**

The pressure group Tourist Concern defines sustainable tourism as 'Tourism and associated infrastructures that: operate within capacities for the regeneration and future productivity of natural resources, recognise the contribution of local people and their cultures, accept that these people must have an equitable share in the economic benefits of tourism, and are guided by the wishes of local people and communities in the destination areas.' This definition emphasises the important issues of equity and local control which are difficult to achieve for a number of reasons:

■ **governments are reluctant to limit the number of tourist arrivals because of the often desperate need for foreign currency**

■ **local people cannot compete with foreign multinationals on price and marketing**
■ **it is difficult to force developers to consult local people.**

In so many developing countries newly laid golf courses have taken land away from local communities while consuming large amounts of scarce freshwater. It has been estimated that the water required by a new golf course can supply a village of 5000 people. In both Belize and Costa Rica coral reefs have been blasted to allow for unhindered watersports. Like fishing and grazing rights, access to such common goods as beach front and scenically desirable locations does not naturally limit itself. As with overfishing and overgrazing the solution to over-touristing will often be to establish ownership and charge for use. The optimists argue that because environmental goods such as clean water and beautiful scenery are fundamental to the tourist experience, both tourists and the industry have a vested interest in their preservation. The fact that 'ecotourism' is a rapidly growing sector of the industry supports this viewpoint, at least to a certain extent.

Education about the environment visited is clearly the key. Scuba divers in the Ras Mohammad National Park in the Red Sea, who were made to attend a lecture on the ecology of the local reefs, were found to be eight times less likely to bump into coral (the cause of two-thirds of all damage to the reef), let alone deliberately pick a piece.

A new form of ecotourism in which volunteers help in cultural and environmental conservation and research is developing. An example is the Earthwatch scientific research projects which invite members of the general public to join the experts as fully-fledged expedition members, on a paying basis of course. Several Earthwatch projects in Australia have helped Aboriginal people to locate and document their prehistoric rock art and to preserve ancient rituals directly.

In some resorts coastal erosion has diminished beaches so much that expensive replenishment schemes have been undertaken. In 1994, a multi million pound scheme to replenish Skegness's dunes and beach with eight million tonnes of sand from the North Sea was begun and now the beach resembles its former fulsome state. However, the dredging has had a catastrophic effect on the shrimp catch in nearby coastal waters. Also, such replenishment is only a short-term solution because the dredging offshore eventually increases erosion on the coast, creating a vicious circle. As a result, it is predicted that the coast at Skegness will again become denuded in about 40 years' time. In Morocco, sand dunes have been removed to create artificial beaches on rocky shores in the Canary Islands.

Tourists face no-go zones

In March 1998 the issue of no-go zones for tourists was debated at the Royal Geographical Society in London. The move comes amid concern that tourism is damaging many environments and social cultures. Environmentalists and an increasing number of people in the tourist industry itself believe that tourists should be banned from some wildlife sites to prevent their degradation, and from remote areas where indigenous tribes could be affected adversely by exposure to foreigners. Other partial bans could be introduced to curb the impact of traffic on historic towns and cities. The idea of imposing access restrictions is not of course completely new but the scale of restriction currently being discussed is.

Nearly all the world's most valuable coral reefs have been damaged by tourism (as well as by shipping and destructive fishing technologies). It is likely that dive tourism will be increasingly restricted and replaced by viewing from glass-bottomed boats instead. The Victoria Falls on the Zimbabwean-Zambian border is suffering from an increasing number of visitors undertaking a growing range of activities. This World Heritage Site has become a magnet for bungee-jumpers, whitewater rafters, sky-divers and kayakers. The rainforest in the surrounding area is suffering from trampled vegetation, soil erosion, litter and the threat of fires. The wild game is being squeezed out and local people are finding it more and more difficult to practise traditional activities. The pressure for imposing restrictions is growing.

Examples of restrictions currently in place are:

- **visitors can no longer wander among the ruins of Stonehenge, but are confined to a perimeter walkway**
- **the National Trust refused to provide a car park when it reopened Prior Park, an eighteenth-century garden near Bath, relying instead on public transport**
- **Bologna (Italy) has closed much of its centre to private cars to end congestion and pollution damaging historic buildings.**

The North American Solution

A huge new wilderness area has recently been created in British Columbia (Figure 7.16) with a considerable buffer zone around it where exploitation will only be allowed to occur at a sustainable rate. Called the 'North American Solution' by conservationists, the idea is expected to become a model for other regions in North America and possibly other regions of the world.

Figure 7.15 Stonehenge: 'protecting the past'

Industry and conservationists create Canadian Yellowstone

BY CHARLES LAURENCE IN NEW YORK

A HUGE wilderness area in British Columbia has been hailed as a "Canadian Yellowstone" after a deal between mining and logging companies, provincial officials and environmental groups.

It involves the creation of a vast buffer zone around the 2.5 million acres of the Rocky Mountains to be known as Muskwa-Kechika, after its two main rivers.

The wilderness in the Canadian Rockies to the south of the Yukon is a spectacular combination of mountain peaks and Alpine valleys, thick with bear, caribou and wolf. It is wilder than anything left in the United States.

But the significance of the deal lies in the buffer zone, another eight million acres in which Indian tribes, oil companies, loggers and environmentalists have all agreed to a controlled, balanced development plan.

Prince Philip, the former head of the World Wildlife Fund, sent a message of congratulation to the province's government, saying: "This is a triumph of good sense."

Companies will be able to tap the vast reserves of natural gas in the buffer zone, but only at a pace and in a way that does nothing to disrupt the ecosystem. More than 1,000 jobs will be protected.

The idea is to link six existing British Columbia wilderness parks with the remaining virgin territory. The buffer zone will protect the migration routes of the wildlife, updating the concept that produced America's Yellowstone Park more than 100 years ago. The national park is only part of a full ecosystem, with the result that this year's winter led to the slaughter of half the buffalo herd as the animals left the park along the ancient routes in search of food.

"This is a decision on the scale of Yellowstone in terms of its significance for conservation in North America," said Mary Granskou of the Canadian Parks and Wilderness Society. "We have unprecedented co-operation here to preserve wildlife values as a whole."

Oil and gas drilling will be banned in the "core area" of 2.5 million acres, in exchange for limited, carefully planned exploitation in the buffer zone.

Conservationists have called the scheme the North American Solution, and now hope to stretch the core and buffer zone idea along the Rocky Mountains from Yellowstone to the Yukon.

"This will preserve wildlife for all time. Wildlife does not recognise boundaries, and the essential need is to enable species to move safely from one protected area to the next," Ms Granskou said.

Canada expects an eventual tourist windfall from what should become the best stretch of wildlife and wilderness in North America.

Figure 7.16 *Daily Telegraph*, 11 October 1997

Changes in the organisation of the tourist industry

The rapid growth rates experienced by the tourist industry, particularly in recent decades, have resulted in considerable changes in its organisation:

■ Following the example of retailing, independent hotel businesses are decreasing in number as the multiples or 'chains' expand rapidly. The latter employ computer reservation systems, compiling information about their customers which is used as a database for direct marketing. In the United States, three-quarters of all hotels are part of a chain. In the rest of the world the proportion, although less than a quarter, is rapidly increasing. Large economies of scale can be achieved by linking hotels together in a chain.

1 Analyse the data presented in Figures 7.1 and 7.2. Produce a time chart to show key periods in the development of tourism.
2 Discuss the value of using a satellite accounting system as opposed to traditional methods for assessing the economic impact of tourism.
3 Research the reasons for declining demand in a tourist destination that you have studied.
4 How important is the role of organisations like Tourism Concern (Figure 7.11)?
5 To what extent will the proposals for the future use of Kruger National Park rectify a long time injustice?
6 Examine the 'North American Solution' (Figure 7.16) in terms of providing a global model.
7 Explain the sequence of changes illustrated in Doxey's index (Figure 7.12).

Figure 7.17 Euro Disney: Mickey comes to Europe

■ The latest information technology, using computer reservation and global distribution systems, allows travel agents to rapidly match availability to the demands of individual customers. The growing use of debit and credit cards (as well as cash and cheques) allows immediate purchase.

■ Customers are increasingly buying direct from airlines, a trend the latter are keen to encourage. As a result airlines

are putting the squeeze on the commission they pay travel agents, reducing it from 10 per cent to 8 per cent between 1995 and 1997. The use of the Internet to purchase tickets is increasing rapidly.

■ Once disparate and fragmented, the industry has developed a more professional identity. An important part of this process has been the establishment of organisations such as the WTTC which concentrates on making the case for tourism's economic value to host countries.

■ The WTTC is looking at technology such as face-recognition that might replace scrutiny by officials at border-control points.

Distinctive types of tourism

Theme parks: the purpose-built experience

Theme parks create artificial destinations from scratch. The largest are located close to Tokyo, Paris, Los Angeles and Orlando. These four Disney theme parks are the world's biggest tourist draws. Attendance at the most popular theme park in the world, Tokyo Disneyland, topped 15.5 million in 1995. Disney operations accounted for two-thirds of all trips by Britons to foreign parks and the growth of Disneyland Paris, launched in 1992 as Euro Disney, means that by the end of 1997 European parks may finally have more UK visitors than parks in the United States. In 1996 the number of Britons visiting theme parks abroad reached 3.7 million, up 68 per cent from 1992.

One of Disney's advantages is that the company started out in entertainment, the business that tourism is coming increasingly to resemble. It has also moved into retailing, selling vast quantities of souvenirs and branded goods. A vital element of the Disney empire is its research centre in Glendale, California where the very latest technology is used to produce even more exciting novelties and experiences for visitors. It researches what audiences want and then strives to create it.

The biggest rivals to Disney's 24 per cent of the global theme park market, which totalled 320 million admissions in 1996, were Six Flags (8 per cent) with ten parks across the United States; Anheuser Busch (6 per cent) with six attractions including Sea Worlds at Orlando and San Diego; and Universal and Paramount, both attracting 4 per cent. The expanding markets in Europe and the rest of the world as well as steady performance in the core North American businesses meant that parks outside Britain increased business by 30 per cent between 1992 and 1997. In the UK, Alton Towers in

Staffordshire remains the most popular charging tourist attraction with 2.7 million customers in 1996. Only one other theme park, Chessington World of Adventures, attracts more Britons than Disneyland Paris.

Gambling destinations: diversification and change

Las Vegas, Nevada, is the largest gambling destination in the world. In 1997 it attracted 32 million visitors and earned gambling revenues of over $6 billion. Las Vegas developed as a stop-over for travellers heading for southern California. It then became a service centre for local ranches and mines. The gambling industry developed here because of:

- Nevada's liberal gambling regulations
- electricity generated at the Boulder Dam
- the attractive climate and landscapes of the region
- accessibility: regular air services to all large cities in the United States; only 420 km along Interstate Highway 15 from Los Angeles
- large investors willing to back the entertainment potential of the city.

However, it has long since lost its monopoly on gambling in the United States. Atlantic City which legalised the activity in 1971, quickly emerged as a serious competitor with its central location in the eastern seaboard megalopolis. And in the early 1990s a succession of new casinos opened up in a range of locations including Indian reservations and Mississippi riverboats. However, Las Vegas has maintained its number one position because of its ability to reinvent itself:

- initially the hotels were no more than two storey dormitories for gamblers
- in 1966 the huge Caesars Palace opened, with the theme of ancient Rome running through the whole complex. While shows had long been an important part of the attraction of Las Vegas, with Caesars Palace the hotel itself was the show
- in 1989 the $700 million Mirage with 3000 rooms opened, promising good times to non-gamblers and gamblers alike. Its lagoon and waterfalls are a major attraction
- in 1991 the same developer opened Treasure Island, where the Hispaniola goes down twice a night to the blazing guns of HMS Britannia and the restaurants are set as pirates' taverns. Other developers quickly followed suit with Excalibur (Arthurian pageantry), Luxor (pyramid), and New York New York where a roller coaster whips through a succession of famous skyscrapers
- the city has become one of America's top convention centres attracting 3.3 million conference participants in 1996

- in 1997, 11 per cent of visitors brought children with them, double the share a decade before. Apart from New York New York's, there are four other roller coasters along Sunset Strip and there is an entire theme park in the MGM Grand complex.

Cruising: rapid growth and larger scale

Cruising really took off with the death of the passenger shipping industry, killed in the 1960s by the long-haul passenger jet. Redundant liners were converted to offer entertainment rather than transport. In the early days marketing was firmly directed towards the elderly rich and although this group still make up a large slice of the market the appeal of this sector of the industry has spread across the age and income spectrum.

Cruising is growing faster than any other type of holiday. North Americans take more cruises than anybody else – 4.86 million in 1997, an increase of 8.6 per cent on the previous year. The growth of this sector of the market has attracted companies such as Disney, Thomson Holidays and Airtours, while established operators are adding to the size of their fleets with ever-larger vessels. A new record will be set in 1999 when Royal Caribbean Cruise Line launch a 130 000-ton vessel. This construction boom is not surprising given the fact that studies of the North American cruise sector put the potential size of the market at 35 to 50 million passengers. However, there are problems with increasing the size of cruise ships:

- the largest cruise liners are unable to pass through the Panama Canal
- the number of destinations capable of providing shore facilities for thousands of passengers is also limited.

Innovation is the name of the game in most significant sectors of the tourism market and cruising is no exception. One designer has put forward a proposal for a 500 000-ton,

Figure 7.18 Floating resorts: a cruise ship in port

Package-tour facelifts in Poland

Surgeon warns 'stupid' Britons of medical risks

BY NANETTE VAN DER LAAN IN WROCLAW

BRITONS are flocking to Poland on package tours which offer cut-price plastic surgery, despite warnings from doctors here that they face serious health risks.

The tours offer "a comprehensive range of corrective procedures for both men and women, including eyelid surgery, collagen and fat transfer treatment and tummy tucks", away from the prying eyes of family and friends.

But Professor David Sharpe, of the British Association of Aesthetic Plastic Surgeons, described the "holiday-makers" as needing brain transplants not cosmetic surgery.

"These people are stupid to go to someone they have never seen before for cosmetic surgery which can have complications, either minor or major," Prof Sharpe said.

"It is like buying a second-hand car without seeing it. They're laying themselves open to all sorts of risks. Do they know, for instance, whether the blood used in the operation is free of infection? Who do they go to if the operation goes wrong?"

Yet these fears do not deter the Britons intent on new noses, larger breasts and tighter faces.

After the surgery, the patients are promised daily trips back to the clinic for aftercare and free hairdressing to cover up the scars behind the ears.

The second week is devoted to the usual holiday activities of shopping, sight-seeing, a trip to the mountains or visit to the opera.

Patients are usually afraid that there might be gossip about their bandages and scars, so they spend at least 10 days in Poland after the surgery in the hope that the worst bruising and swelling is over before they arrive back in Britain.

Alina Deeble, who runs the tours through her Cheshire-based Euromedica company, takes her patients to Wroclaw, in western Poland. Because prices are roughly half that of similar surgery in Britain, people are willing to take the risk of having an operation done in a country where most expats would not dream of using the medical system.

Figure 7.19 *Sunday Telegraph*, **14 June 1998**

12 deck ship costing $1.5 billion. This vessel, known as the Cruise Bowl, would comprise a mothership of 240 000 tons with two detachable satellites of 130 000 tons each. The mothership would house a 12 000-seat arena to stage concerts and sporting events, while the satellites would provide cabins, shops and poolside areas.

Cosmetic surgery tourism

More and more people from western Europe are looking to the east of the continent for cosmetic surgery which is much cheaper than in their own countries (Figure 7.19). They undergo surgery shortly after arrival and spend the rest of the two weeks or so on aftercare and tourism. Hopefully the worst of the tell-tale marks will have gone by the time they return home.

'Conflict tourism'

Tourism has reached the Falls Road, Belfast, one of the world's most troubled streets. For 30 years, the Falls Road has been the focus of some of the worst tensions in the bitter Northern Ireland conflict. However, the infamous street has recently undergone a cultural renaissance. In August 1997, a West

Figure 7.20 The 'Peace Line' in Belfast, a suitable destination for tourists?

Belfast community festival attracted more than 80 000 people. Now residents are being encouraged to open bed and breakfast facilities to cope with the growing number of visitors. There is already a bus tour around the city's 'trouble spots'. A favourite with many tourists is to have their photographs taken in front of the dramatic murals commemorating the violent past. The Northern Ireland Tourist Board sees such 'cultural tourism' as a distinct growth area. However, it all depends on peace lasting in this troubled part of the UK.

Antarctica: tourism's last global frontier

Although the number of people visiting Antarctica (Figure 7.21) is currently no more than about 10 000 each year, the annual rate of growth over the last decade has been significant and environmentalists have become increasingly concerned about the future of this southern wilderness.

Very few tourists actually stay a night on the continent. The vast majority are cruise passengers brought to shore for only three or four hours to gain a better sense of the unique scenery, wildlife and remoteness of Antarctica. Only the smallest minority venture beyond the edge of the continent. Seaborne tourism began in the late 1950s at a very modest level but increased considerably in the 1980s with improvements in polar transport and a growing interest in 'adventure tourism'. The Antarctic Peninsula receives most visitors because of its relative proximity to the ports of Punta

Arenas and Ushuaia at the tip of South America. From here it takes only 48 hours to cross the Drake Passage to the peninsula. A smaller number of cruises originate in Australia and New Zealand, heading for the Ross Ice Shelf and McMurdo Sound.

The alternative option is to view Antarctica from the air. The first such visit took place in 1956 from Chile. However, after a New Zealand DC-10 crashed into Mount Erebus in 1979 killing all 257 passengers and crew, overflights of this nature virtually ceased.

So why such concern over a relatively small number of visitors?

■ **the Antarctic ecosystem is extremely fragile. In its permafrost environment disturbances leave their imprint for a long time (footprints on moss can remain for decades). Waste disposal presents particular problems**

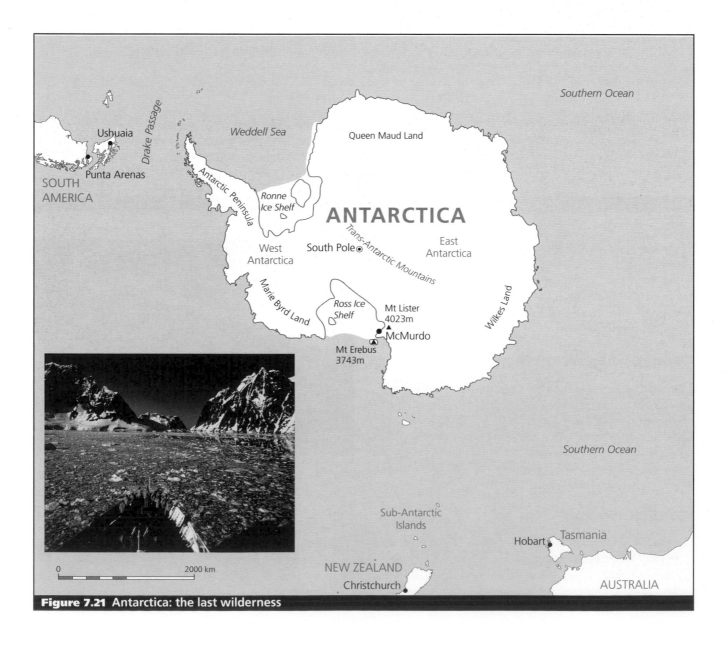

Figure 7.21 Antarctica: the last wilderness

- the ecosystem dynamics on the continent are unique and are of great scientific interest
- the summer tourist season coincides with peak wildlife breeding periods
- both land-based installations and wildlife agglomerate in the few ice-free locations on the continent

- the demand for fresh water is not easy to satisfy
- visitor pressure is being felt on cultural heritage sites such as old whaling and sealing stations and early exploration bases
- the unique legal status of Antarctica makes enforcement of any code of tourist behaviour difficult.

Tourism is certainly not the only aspect of development confronting Antarctica. Like the other pressure points (potential exploitation of minerals, depletion of marine resources, impact of bases) demand will undoubtedly increase. What is required is a research-based management strategy that is truly sustainable.

The moon and beyond?

The intensity and nature of tourism will undoubtedly evolve through even more stages in the future. However, some of the largest operators are beginning to look beyond planet Earth. Hilton International want to be first to build a hotel on the moon. Called the Lunar Hilton, the massive complex would be more than twice the size of the Millennium Dome and would have 5000 rooms (Figure 7.23). Powered by two huge

Figure 7.22 The Moon: a holiday destination for you in the future?

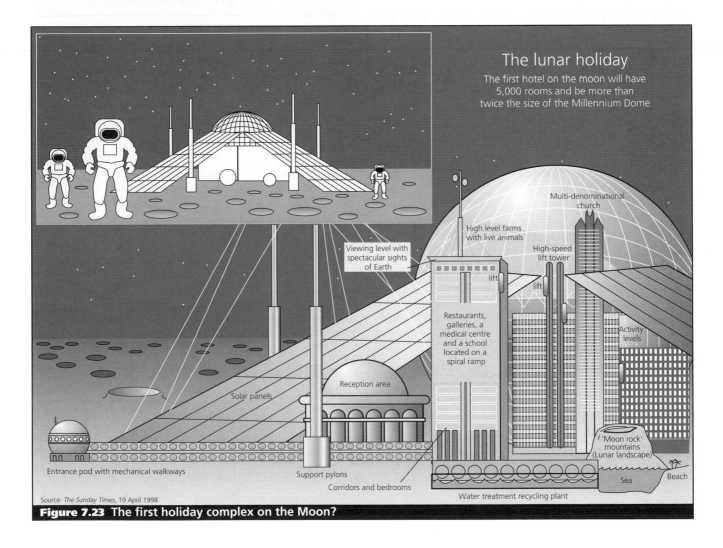

The lunar holiday
The first hotel on the moon will have 5,000 rooms and be more than twice the size of the Millennium Dome

Multi-denominational church

High level farms with live animals

High-speed lift tower

lift

lift

Activity levels

Viewing level with spectacular sights of Earth

Restaurants, galleries, a medical centre and a school located on a spiral ramp

'Moon rock' mountains (Lunar landscape)

Reception area

Solar panels

Sea

Beach

Entrance pod with mechanical walkways

Support pylons

Corridors and bedrooms

Water treatment recycling plant

Source: *The Sunday Times*, 19 April 1998

Figure 7.23 The first holiday complex on the Moon?

solar panels, the blueprint shows areas of beach, sea, and a working farm. Hilton hopes to form a partnership with NASA, which would ferry guests to the complex. The 325-metre-high structure would rival the world's biggest hotel, the MGM Grand in Las Vegas. Drinking water would be pumped up from the newly discovered ice reserves and would also be used to fill the sea. However, Hilton has spent little more than £100 000 on the project so far compared with the £25 million that three Japanese companies have already invested in their own moon projects.

Questions

1 Outline the ways in which the organisation of the tourist industry is changing.

2 **(a)** Why have theme parks become so popular in recent decades?

   (b) Research the development and growth of a major theme park.

3 Assess the advantages and disadvantages of large-scale gambling to the residents of settlements such as Las Vegas and Atlantic City.

4 Explain why the market for cruising has expanded so rapidly.

5 Describe and explain the policies you would advocate for Antarctica with regard to tourism.

6 Lunar tourism – future fact or fantasy? Discuss.

Tourism in Brazil: developing a modern strategy

A developing industry

Although Brazil now counts on services for half its GDP, tourism is one part of this sector which is relatively undeveloped, thus offering considerable scope for expansion. Nevertheless, tourism does currently represent as much as 7.8 per cent of GDP, and employs, directly and indirectly, about six million people.

The late 1980s was a gloomy period for international tourism in Brazil as the number of foreign visitors fell from 1.7 million in 1988 to little over 1 million in 1990 (Figure 7.24). However, since then the situation has steadily improved, with 1.85 million foreigners arriving in 1994 and spending a total of $1.8 billion. Not surprisingly, Brazil trails the major European countries such as Spain (43 million visitors, spending $21 billion), but it is also some way behind Latin American rivals such as Mexico (16.4 million

visitors, spending $16.8 billion) and Argentina (4 million visitors and $4 billion). Although rising prosperity is encouraging more Brazilians to take holidays both at home and abroad, the industry's chief hope lies with foreign visitors who account for about a quarter of all the country's holidaymakers.

A tourism strategy

With the strong backing of the WTTC, a major overhaul of Brazil's tourism industry is underway. Embratur, the organisation responsible for tourist policy has identified three major objectives:

■ improvement in basic infrastructure in the regions that are designated for tourism

Figure 7.24 International tourists in Brazil 1970–1995							
Year	**Tourists**	**Year**	**Tourists**	**Year**	**Tourists**	**Year**	**Tourists**
1970	249.900	1977	634.595	1984	1.595.726	1991	1.228.178
1971	287.926	1978	784.316	1985	1.735.982	1992	1.692.078
1972	342.961	1979	1.081.799	1986	1.934.091	1993	1.641.138
1973	399.127	1980	1.625.422	1987	1.929.053	1994	1.853.301
1974	480.267	1981	1.357.879	1988	1.742.939	1995	1.991.416
1975	517.967	1982	1.146.681	1989	1.402.897		
1976	555.967	1983	1.420.481	1990	1.091.067		

Source: Forte Coordenação de informatica/DPF – EMBRATUR

- the need to improve the quality of service, so as to become competitive in an international market

- the need to invest in marketing and promotion to change Brazil's image abroad.

Embratur aims to double the number of foreign visitors to Brazil by 1999 (from 1996). That will entail increasing employment in the tourist sector by about a fifth. European tourists in particular are being targeted: for example only about 30 000 British tourists visit Brazil each year (Figure 7.25). At the same time, the stabilisation of the Brazilian currency and increasing purchasing power have led to a sudden growth in internal tourism in Brazil. The number of Brazilians travelling abroad has also risen markedly, which makes it all the more necessary to raise the number of incoming tourists.

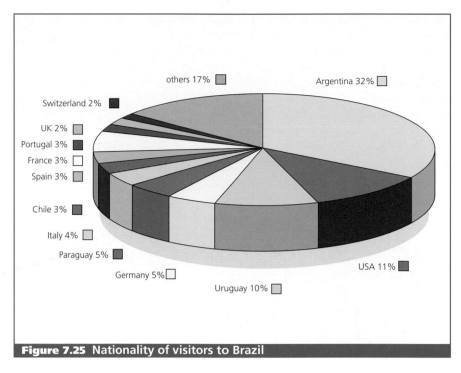

Figure 7.25 Nationality of visitors to Brazil

Iguaçu: an inland multiple attraction destination

One of the most popular inland tourist destinations in Brazil is the Iguaçu region at the western extremity of Paraná State (Figure 7.26). The main attractions are (1) the Iguaçu Falls (2) the flora and fauna of the National Park (3) the Itaipu hydroelectric plant and reservoir (4) the developing tourist facilities in the city of Foz do Iguaçu (5) cheap shopping and the casinos across the border in Ciudad del Este (6) observing the local Indians and (7) fishing on the Paraná River.

The economic benefits of an expanding tourist industry are clearly evident but the potential pitfalls have also become increasingly obvious. As a relatively new tourist destination of significance, the region's tourist managers have the opportunity to avoid many of the mistakes made in similar destinations elsewhere in the world.

The falls

Iguaçu's 275 falls are higher than Niagara, wider than Victoria, and without doubt one of the world's most spectacular natural phenomena. In 1986 the falls and the sub-tropical forest park surrounding them was declared a World Heritage Site by UNESCO. Although most of the falls lie in Argentina, the best views of the falls and the greater area (170 000 ha) of the national park are in Brazil.

The falls are formed by the Iguaçu river, which has its source to the east near Curitiba. Beginning at an altitude of 1300 m, the Iguaçu snakes westward, developing in size and power as tributaries join it along its 1200-km course. Approximately 15 km west of its confluence with the Paraná River, the Iguaçu broadens out before plunging over an 80-metre-high cliff, the centre of the 275 inter-linking cataracts that extend nearly 3 km across the river. The volume of water is at its greatest in the winter months of April to July (Figure 7.28). By the end of the summer dry season the volume of water is reduced by about a third. Only once in recorded history, in 1977, did the falls dry up altogether.

The majority of visitors to the falls come across the open border with Argentina (Figure 7.29). However international tourists from further afield, particularly from the United States, Japan and Germany, are increasing in number. Walkways have been built into the 'Garganta do Diablo' (Devil's Throat) at the edge of the biggest fall, but during the flood season (March–May) waters often cover them.

Figure 7.26 The Iguaçu region

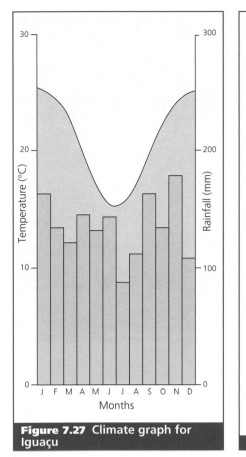

Figure 7.27 Climate graph for Iguaçu

Power of the water

The waters of Iguaçu can generate electricity as well as rainbows

FOZ DO IGUAÇU, A medium-sized town on Brazil's borders with Argentina and Paraguay, is the third most popular tourist destination in the country, after Rio and São Paulo – and the reason is not hard to find.

Just outside the town there is a mammoth series of waterfalls that send water plunging over a precipice three kilometres wide, filling the air of a large area around with clouds of spray. At the centre of the spectacle is what's called the Devil's Throat, where fourteen separate falls come together, cascading thunderously down a 110 metre drop.

This is one of the natural wonders of the world, which perhaps justifies the rather extravagant claim by Embratur's president Caio Luiz de Carvalho that "Niagara Falls is a shower compared with Iguaçu!" Visitors who do not mind getting drenched can follow a cat-walk round the base of the first level of the falls, to savour the unforgettable sensation of being surrounded by churning and falling water on all sides, while through the spray they glimpse a colossal and perfect rainbow.

The falls are set within a large protected park that straddles the Brazil-Argentine border. Visitors often pop across to the Argentinean side for a few hours, to catch the falls at a different angle and in a different light, as well as to get a brief taste of another culture.

Tourism is not the only reason for the economic boom affecting the superficially unremarkable town of Foz de Iguaçu. Nearby, one can find the world's largest hydro-electric plant, at Itaipu, where the dam has itself become an important tourist attraction.

Figure 7.28 Brazil [*The Times* supplement], 9 December 1996

Figure 7.29 Monthly visitors to the Iguaçu National Park by nationality 1995

Months	Total visitors	Brazilian	Foreign	Main nationalities visiting		
Jan.	118 595	86 107	32 488	Argentina 16 336	Paraguay 3 433	Chile 2 076
Feb.	83 535	54 139	29 396	Argentina 12 854	Chile 3 200	Paraguay 2 621
Mar.	56 735	31 727	25 008	Argentina 10 173	Germany 2 859	USA 1 661
Apr.	78 746	50 095	28 651	Argentina 13 628	Uruguay 2 478	Paraguay 2 455
May	44 309	26 874	17 435	Argentina 7 867	Paraguay 1 972	France 1 293
June	41 467	27 243	14 224	Argentina 6 883	Paraguay 1 804	Germany 730
July	91 134	63 144	27 990	Argentina 17 096	Paraguay 2 369	Uruguay 1 764
Aug.	62 456	32 657	29 799	Argentina 14 996	Paraguay 2 578	Spain 2 073
Sept.	69 808	41 873	27 935	Argentina 12 211	Paraguay 3 467	Chile 3 407
Oct.	82 911	46 130	36 781	Argentina 18 797	Paraguay 4 311	Germany 2 116
Nov.	81 051	51 019	30 032	Argentina 12 249	Germany 3 117	Paraguay 2 835
Dec.	73 588	53 036	20 555	Argentina 6 784	Paraguay 3 940	Germany 1 399
Total	884 335	564 044	320 291			

Figure 7.30 The waterfalls of Iguaçu

Figure 7.31 Rio and the Botafogo Beach

Iguaçu National Park

The National Park covers an area of dense tropical forest. In an effort to increase tourism in the area the price of a ticket to enter the park has been kept very low. There are a number of signposted trails with well organised information centres at entry points. Visitors can walk or travel by jeep with a guide. A popular option is then to join a boat tour from the banks of the Iguaçu to the base of the larger falls. Due to the number of visitors and the noise of the numerous helicopter rides viewing the falls and other attractions, it is rare for visitors to see the full range of wildlife. The forest contains over 2000 plant varieties, 400 bird species including toucans, parakeets and hummingbirds, dozens of types of mammals and innumerable insects and reptiles. There are 50 species of deer and 200 species of butterfly. Jaguars and mountain lions have occasionally been seen and tapirs are sometimes found around the water's edge. Much more common is the coatimundi, the size of a domestic cat but related to the racoon, and the capuchin monkey. The latter often travel the forest canopy in large groups and emit strange bird-like cries. Expert guides are available to lead serious birdwatchers, botanists and photographers into the forest. The elegant, regency-style Hotel das Cataratas, located just out of sight of the falls, offers the only accommodation to be found actually within the National Park.

Adjacent to the National Park and the river is the 16-hectare Foz Tropicana, a bird park that doubles as a tourist attraction and a conservation and research centre. Only a quarter of the area is taken up with aviaries and other buildings. The remaining area is unspoilt sub-tropical forest where the birds live freely. Most of the birds are from Brazil, including some from the Pantanal and the Amazon. A successful breeding programme has been established.

Fishing

One of the world's greatest freshwater game fish, the dourado, inhabits the upper reaches of the Paraná River. Known as the 'Golden Salmon' because of their size and colouring, these powerful fish are popular with both South American and European anglers. The largest fish are most likely to be caught in the fast-flowing stretch of the Paraná river around Iguaçu. Here the dourado weigh between 13 and 18 kg and are caught from boats positioned side on and allowed to drift with the current. The dourado season is from October to March but the best fishing is experienced between November and January.

Frontier urban attractions

Large-scale human activity is a relatively recent phenomenon in this part of South America. The administrative district was created in 1914, shortly before development actively began in the region when military villages were constructed because of the area's strategic position. As commerce developed a programme of road and bridge building was undertaken. However it has only been in the last twenty years that really significant development has taken place due to a combination of the expansion of tourism and the construction of the Itaipu power complex.

Foz do Iguaçu, about 20 km north west of the entrance to the National Park, is now a bustling city of over a quarter of a million people, boasting an international airport and a large convention centre. The airport is served by flights from throughout Brazil, Ascunción and Buenos Aires. Foz is by far the largest urban entity in the frontier region. Part of its tourist strategy has been to host sporting events to draw in more visitors, particularly from south and south-eastern Brazil as well as from Argentina and Paraguay.

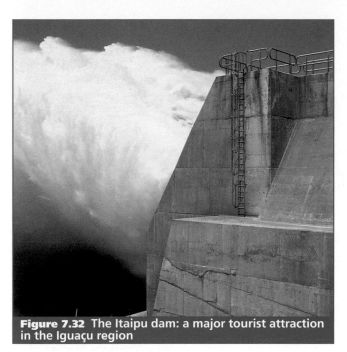

Figure 7.32 The Itaipu dam: a major tourist attraction in the Iguaçu region

1 Is it justifiable to refer to the falls as one of the world's great natural phenomena? Give reasons for your answer.
2 **(a)** Why, until relatively recently, did the great majority of tourists visiting the region come from Brazil, Argentina, and Paraguay?
   (b) Suggest why the number of visitors from elsewhere has increased significantly in the 1990's.
3 To what extent can the area genuinely claim to be a multiple attraction destination?
4 In which order would you rank the attractions of the area? Give reasons for your rank order.
5 **(a)** Suggest why visitors stay an average of only two days in Foz de Iguaçu.
   (b) What strategies could Foztur use to try to extend the average length of stay?
6 How might the number of visitors be allowed to significantly increase without damaging the environment?

Foz has become an important pole for Latin American integration, as have, to a lesser extent, the nearby towns of Puerto Iguazu (Argentina) and Ciudad del Este (Paraguay). The latter is reached by the Amizade (Friendship) bridge across the Paraná river. The attraction for Brazilians is that taxes on imported goods are much lower in Paraguay and thus there are regular queues of traffic on the bridge as Brazilians from a wide area seek to buy electronic equipment, perfume, clothes, footware, cigarettes and alcohol. Ciudad del Este also boasts a number of casinos which encourage cross-border movement. To a lesser extent people cross the

Tancredo Neves bridge to visit the town of Puerto Iguazu. From here there are daily flights to and from Buenos Aires, Cordoba and elsewhere in Argentina.

A priority for Foztur, the city's tourist organisation, is increasing the average length of stay which at present is two days. Recently it has improved tours of the Itaipu dam (Figure 7.32), upgraded the facilities there, and promoted a range of smaller attractions such as the Three Frontiers, where the Paraná and Iguaçu rivers meet.

Expanding tourism in the Northeast

New investment

 The Northeast has gained more than any other region from the government's recent push to expand tourism. The National Economic and Social Development Bank has launched a $3 billion plan to boost the region, including subsidised financing for hotels. A separate project, backed by the Inter-American Development Bank, will put $800 million into infrastructure, ranging from sewerage systems to airport development. Both SUDENE, the

regional development agency for the Northeast, and the private sector are keen to develop the potential of what could possibly become the premier international tourist destination in South America.

First-class beaches and colonial heritage

The coastline is over 2000 km of practically unbroken beach, much of it just what most people imagine tropical beaches to be – palm trees, white sands and warm, blue sea (Figures 7.33 and

Where the beach is Brazil

Whether a passing tourist or local worker, Brazil's beaches are the place to hang out

WITH NEARLY 8,000 kilometres of extremely varied coastline, Brazil boasts many of the best beaches in Latin America. There's a beach to suit every taste. If it's people-watching you are into, then Copacabana in Rio still draws the crowds and the ratio of beautiful bodies per square metre beats even California hands down. Body-builders strut, while girls of every conceivable racial combination bare all but a token symbol of modesty in mini-bikinis aptly named 'dental floss'.

But if it is the celebrity that you are after, then you need to get away from the big cities, to the expensive up-market resorts like Buzios in Rio de Janeiro state, which was 'discovered' by Brigitte Bardot thirty years ago. It's the nearest you will get to the chic bohemianism of the French Cote d'Azur – but with a far bigger hinterland.

The jet-set may still favour the better-known resorts, many of which get unbearably busy during the high-season (December to February), but the more adventurous beach-bums have been pushing ever further north, through Bahia, with its endless succession of palm-fringed, deserted shores, up into Natal and Ceará, in search of the perfect place to get away from it all.

Over the past two decades, a whole series of former fishing villages in Ceará, in particular, have become 'paradise' for a few seasons. For a while, Canoa Quebrada, cut off by dunes and cliffs from the nearby town of Aracati, was the haunt of all that was hip. The local fishermen were welcoming; the food was fresh, if basic. And all one had to do for lodgings was to hang up one's hammock. But in the new communication age, the secret was soon out, and a situation developed that has become the pattern for so many of the formerly isolated communities along the North East coast.

Roads were built, buses arrived. The villages were put on tourist itineraries. The beach groupies turned their back on Canoa Quebrada when the 'respectable' tourists arrived, and moved on to Jericoquara – even more remote, even more unspoilt – for a brief while. But now that too is firmly on the tourist map. The local men, who used to take their little boats out to fish, are getting more adept at running simple guest houses or managing the ubiquitous little drinks stalls on wheels that seem to sprout on every beach in Brazil whenever any swimmer, foreign or local, has arrived.

Purists deplore the loss of the centuries-old simplicity among the coastal peoples. But, for many of the locals concerned, change has brought a prosperity that their fore-fathers could never have dreamed of. And, by European standards, it is still picturesquely primitive and very tropical. The Brazilian tourist authorities know the beaches are their strongest selling point.

Source: Brazil, [*The Times* supplement], 9 December 1996

Figure 7.33 The development of new beach locations

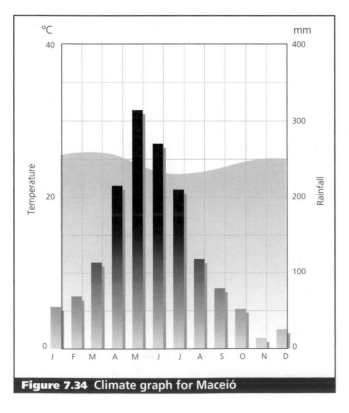

Figure 7.34 Climate graph for Maceió

7.34). The sunshine is virtually guaranteed. Visitors are also attracted by the region's colonial heritage which survives in the Baroque churches and cobbled streets of Salvador, Olinda and São Luis, often side by side with the modern Brazilian mix of skyscrapers and shanty towns. In Salvador and Recife, the Northeast has two of Brazil's great cities. Salvador, the capital of Bahia was, until 1763, also the capital of Brazil. It is said that Salvador has 365 churches, one for each day of the year. The carnival in Salvador is a major attraction for tourists – a fancy dress revelry that lasts four days without interruption. Recife is known as the 'Brazilian Venice' because of its many canals and waterways and the innumerable bridges that span them. The name 'Recife' comes from the barrier reef ('arrecife' in Portuguese) that protects the city's beaches. Recife is the major gateway to the Northeast with regular flights to all major cities in Brazil as well as to international destinations, particularly Lisbon, London, Frankfurt and Paris.

The interior

Inland of the flat coastal strip, the 'zona da mata', is an intermediate area, the 'agreste', where hills rear up into rocky mountain ranges and the lush, tropical vegetation of the coast is gradually replaced by highland scrub and cactus. Then comes the 'sertão', the vast semi-arid interior that covers more than three-quarters of the Northeast. In the sertão, Portuguese and Indian influences predominate while in the coastal area African influences become very obvious. Brazil's colonisation began in the Northeast, ensuring that the region is rich in folklore and tradition. However, to date the bulk of the investment in tourism has gone to the coast. Not until the industry 'matures' will the interior command more attention. Thus at present the interior is the preserve of the more adventurous, personally organised tourist (Figure 6.37).

Marketing strategies

Marketing has played an important role in the development of tourism. For example:

■ visitors can take out a 'sun insurance' policy, guaranteeing an extra day with no charge for every rainy day during their stay

Figure 7.35 Beach at Recife in the Northeast

Figure 7.36 Brazil's interior and its colonial past has great tourist potential

Into the sertão

Travelling in the sertão requires some preparation, as the interior is not geared to tourism. Hotels are fewer and dirtier; buses are less frequent, and you often have to rely on country services which leave very early in the morning and seem to stop every few hundred yards. A **hammock** is essential, as it's the coolest and most comfortable way to sleep, much better than the grimy beds in inland hotels, all of which have hammock hooks set into the walls as a standard fitting. The towns are much smaller than on the coast, and in most places there's little to do in the evening, as the population turns in early to be up for work at dawn. Far more people carry arms than on the coast, but in fact the *sertão* is one of the safest areas of Brazil for travellers – the guns are mainly used on animals, especially small birds, which are massacred on an enormous scale. Avoid tap water, by sticking to mineral water or soft drinks: dysentery is common, and although not dangerous these days it's extremely unpleasant.

But don't let these considerations put you off. People in the *sertão* are intrigued by gringos and are invariably very friendly. And while few *sertão* towns may have much to offer in terms of excitement or entertainment, the landscape in which they are set is spectacular. The Pernambucan *sertão* is hilly and the main highway, which runs through it like a spinal column, winds through scenery unlike any you'll have seen before – an apparently endless expanse of cactus and scrub so thick in places that cowboys have to wear leather armour to protect themselves. If you travel in the rainy season here – March to June, although rain can never be relied upon in the interior – you may be lucky enough to catch it bursting with green, punctuated by the whites, reds and purples of flowering trees and cacti. Massive electrical storms are common at this time of year, and at night the horizon can flicker with sheet lightning for hours at a stretch.

Source: *Brazil: The Rough Guide*

Figure 7.37 Travelling into the interior

- Samba dancers in Rio's world famous carnival were recently paid to sing about the positive environment for tourism in Ceará

- a former governor of Ceará state has been the major backer of a TV soap opera filmed on Ceará's beaches.

The major players in the industry are only too well aware of how intense competition is in the tourist market both nationally and internationally.

International hotel groups move in

The Northeast received one million visitors in 1994, who spent $497 million, a tenfold increase from 1990. The region's total receipts from tourism doubled to $1 billion between 1991 and 1994. Beach Park, an $18 million aquatic park, handled 1.2 million visitors and $22 million in sales in 1995, almost three times the 1994 figures. International hotel groups such as Sheraton, Ramada, Westin, and Best Western have ventured into the region, but generally to manage rather than build hotels. If this 'testing the water' exercise proves successful there is little doubt that these big players will develop in a significant manner. However the high interest rates required to protect the economy against the traditional problem of inflation make hotel construction expensive and result in high prices for foreign visitors. But if the government's economic reforms are successful, interest rates should fall, attracting more foreign visitors and Brazil's own increasingly rich middle class.

Water parks

Apart from hotels, most other elements of tourist infrastructure are also planned. For example, Canadian WhiteWater West Industries has formed a joint venture with Brazilian Transversal Marketing to plan five new water parks in Brazil, two in the Northeast. The newly formed company, White Water Brazil is working on projects in Recife, Salvador, Gioânia, Rio de Janeiro and Brasília. Recife's Acquamundi project will require a total investment of $25 million but should begin repaying capital investment within three to five years. It has been estimated that for every person employed within the water park, five indirect jobs will also be created outside the park.

The Golden Coast project

With over 60 per cent of tourists to the Northeast demanding beach holidays, the state of Pernambuco is well placed to increase its tourist revenue. A project of considerable significance is the 'Costa Dourada' (Golden Coast), located 65 km south from Recife's international airport. Here lie the best beaches in the state. Jesus Camara Zapata, Pernambuco's director of special projects is convinced that this development will soon be on the European tourist trail.

The Golden Coast, with an average sea temperature of 28°C, provides more than 15 km of coastline, alternating wide open sea with sheltered reef beaches, coconut groves, mangroves and forests. It has been based on the best aspects of international tourism in Cancun, the Dominican Republic and Polynesia. The project has strict development rules, being determined to avoid the mistakes of mass tourism, exemplified perhaps at their worst in Spain and Florida. For example;

- no more than 2 per cent of the 10 000 hectares can be built on

- there is a two-storey maximum building height and construction has to be in a traditional style

- the environmental considerations extend to a Mangrove Research Centre sited along the estuary.

Apart from illustrating the beautiful and varied environment, marketing will stress:

- that Northeast Brazil is closer to Europe than Cancun (Mexico) or California

- that the Northeast isn't a one-stop destination as many Caribbean islands are

- for tourists from southern Brazil, Argentina, and Chile, this is the closest tropical destination.

However tourists will be shielded from the deprivation that is clearly evident in the nearby towns. The entrances to the beaches will have security controls and like many Caribbean resorts, visitors will not be encouraged to leave the reserve. While the neighbouring areas will not benefit directly from profits generated by the project, jobs will be created and there will be considerable improvements in roads, sewage and water supply.

The first hotels opened in mid-1997. The federal and state governments who have provided half of the $70 million infrastructure costs, estimate that the project will attract a million visitors a year, generating more than $500 million in receipts. If successful, the Golden Coast project will provide a model for many more developments in the region.

Questions

1 Why has the Brazilian government identified the Northeast as the region with the greatest potential for tourist development?

2 Assess the scale and significance of the Golden Coast project.

3 What else does the Northeast have to offer the tourist apart from beach holidays?

4 What are the disadvantages of expanding the tourist industry in the Northeast?

Recreation

Classification

Recreational activities may be classified in the following ways:

- **active/passive** – depending on the amount of physical exercise involved
- **formal/informal** – depending upon the level to which participation is organised
- **resource-based/user-oriented** – depending upon the degree of reliance on the natural environment, purpose-built facilities and special equipment.

While some passive recreational activities, such as watching television and reading involve minimal physical effort and are undertaken mainly in the home, more active pursuits usually take place away from the participant's home. Strictly speaking, however, if the activity involves a stay away from home of at least one night, then recreation becomes tourism.

Growth

In developed countries and to an emerging extent in the more affluent of the developing nations, recreation has become an increasingly important aspect of people's lives for several reasons:

- **household disposable incomes are higher than ever before**
- **annual holiday entitlements have risen. For example, in North America an increasing number of people work a four day week**
- **more and more people possess the mobility to visit recreational areas and facilities that were previously remote and inaccessible**
- **health education has made the population at large more aware of the importance of relaxation and regular exercise.**

Impact

The steadily rising demand for recreation impacts on society in the following ways:

- **spatial** – more space is required as demand for facilities in both urban and rural areas increases. Land use competition is intense in many areas
- **environmental** – some activities and the traffic generated by them can do considerable harm to the environment. This is often greatest in rural areas, reaching a maximum at honeypot locations
- **economic** – recreation is a significant sector of many national economies. The industry is a big employer but much of the work is seasonal
- **social** – some activities cost little or nothing while others are only open to people on high incomes. Public facilities are often worst in poor areas while those on low incomes can't afford the membership fees of private clubs
- **political** – as the industry expands it can exert more political pressure at a range of scales.

Urban stadia: an increasingly contentious issue

The impact of recreation generates most conflict when large numbers of people congregate at one particular point. In urban areas this usually occurs at major stadia whose use has increasingly become multipurpose. In Britain, the rise in the number of people wanting to watch Premiership football has resulted in a number of clubs wanting either to redevelop their existing grounds or to move to new locations. Almost every proposal has met with considerable opposition from those people likely to be affected the most. Newcastle United were forced to abandon plans to construct a new 60 000-seater stadium in the city while Arsenal endured a long battle and even threatened to move out of the London borough of Islington, before getting permission to increase the capacity of Highbury stadium. The negative

Figure 7.38 Highbury stadium in the heart of North London

Key Definitions ③

recreation The use of leisure time for relaxation and enjoyment.

user-oriented recreation Activities generated primarily by the energy and imagination of the user, with limited reliance on the physical and human environment.

resource-based recreation Activities depending heavily on purpose-built facilities or on specific natural attractions.

honeypot An area of attractive scenery or of historic interest to which tourists swarm in large numbers. Careful management is particularly crucial at such locations.

externalities imposed on local communities on match days include:

- extra parking restrictions
- saturation of public transport and other local services
- huge pedestrian flows converging on the stadium
- considerable increase in the volume of litter
- noise and floodlight 'pollution' while the match is in progress
- rowdy behaviour and at times property damage and the threat of violence from 'supporters'.

However, major stadia can provide some benefits or positive externalities to local communities, including:

- some permanent jobs and a significant number of occasional jobs in restaurants, bars, at turnstiles, stewarding, clearing litter and so on
- opening facilities to the wider community
- forging educational links, with players acting as positive role models
- using small local firms for maintenance and supply, thus boosting the local economy
- increased trade experienced by local businesses on match days
- investment in local infrastructure required to accommodate the influx of a large number of people on an occasional basis benefits the locality on a permanent basis.

Rural pop concerts: straining local relationships

Most recreational visits to rural areas are to 'permanent' destinations. However, there are notable exceptions, the most contentious of which are probably large rock music festivals. Some of these, such as Glastonbury, have become annual events attracting hundreds of thousands of people. Although better managed than when they were first promoted such large-scale events can impact considerably on the physical and human environment:

- narrow rural roads can become heavily congested with extensive tailbacks disrupting movement and the economy in the locality
- local services may be completely overwhelmed

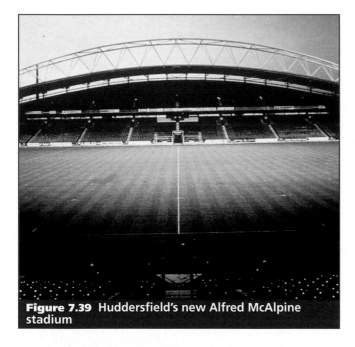

Figure 7.39 Huddersfield's new Alfred McAlpine stadium

A recreation model

Figure 7.40, after M. Dower (1970), shows the theoretical pattern of recreational activities around a large urban area. Clearly the geographical extent of the zones will vary according to time and place. For example, the development of the road network will improve personal mobility and push zones one and two outward. Visits to national parks are now made mainly on a 'day out' basis, whereas three or four decades ago many more people would have stayed over for at least one night.

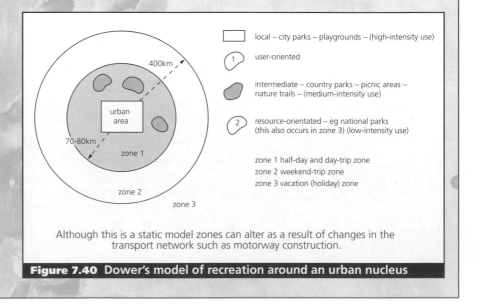

local – city parks – playgrounds – (high-intensity use)

1   user-oriented

intermediate – country parks – picnic areas – nature trails – (medium-intensity use)

2   resource-orientated – eg national parks (this also occurs in zone 3) (low-intensity use)

zone 1 half-day and day-trip zone
zone 2 weekend-trip zone
zone 3 vacation (holiday) zone

Although this is a static model zones can alter as a result of changes in the transport network such as motorway construction.

Figure 7.40 Dower's model of recreation around an urban nucleus

- the noise over such a long period of time may disturb local people
- local people may find the behaviour of concert-goers anti-social and threatening
- depending on weather conditions, erosion of the ground may be significant
- disturbance to wildlife may be considerable.

Questions

1 For a city or region show how recreational activities have demanded more space in the last 50 years or so.
2 Investigate the development of a proposal to redevelop or to build from new a major urban stadium.
3 Choose a major rural recreational activity (other than pop concerts) and draw up a cost-benefit analysis for it.

Recreation in the United States

Recreation is big business in the United States where spending reached almost $370 billion in 1994 (Figure 7.41), an increase of 294 per cent from 1970 in constant dollar terms. During this period recreation's share of all personal consumption expenditure rose from 4.3 per cent to 8.3 per cent. With around one billion visits a year, cinema-going is by far the most popular spectator activity in the United States. Interest in most of the major spectator sports has increased substantially while active pastimes have become increasingly popular (Figure 7.42). In addition in 1991, 35.6 million anglers fished on 511 million days, spending $24 billion on their pastime. Equivalent figures for American hunters (mostly for big game) were 14.1 million, 236 million days and $12 billion.

A recent investigation of Americans' recreational habits over the past century concluded that people of all income levels have steadily increased the amount of time and money they devote to leisure pursuits. Although by almost any measure, incomes in the United States are distributed less equally than two or three decades ago, leisure is more evenly spread than ever. This research by Dora Costa, an economist at the Massachusetts Institute of Technology, was based on consumption surveys dating back to 1888. Over time, leisure has steadily become less of a luxury. An interesting trend is that the share of the family budget spent on leisure now rises much less sharply with income than it used to. At the beginning of the twentieth century a family's recreational spending tended to rise by 20 per cent for every 10 per cent rise in income. By 1972–3, a 10 per cent income gain resulted in roughly a 15 per cent rise in recreational spending, falling to only 13 per cent in 1991. This implies that people of all income levels are now able to spend much more of their money on leisure.

However, rising incomes are responsible for at most only half of the changing structure of leisure spending. Much of the rest is due to the fact that lower income Americans have more time off than they used to. The population has also had an increasing number of recreational possibilities to choose from. At a time when technology is often blamed for the widening wage gap between skilled and unskilled workers, Costa's research gives it a much more egalitarian face. By lowering the price of entertainment, technology has improved the standard of living of those at the lower end of the income scale. However, at the same time, technology has created new leisure activities that people on lower incomes may desire but cannot afford.

The locations of most key recreation points and zones are clearly understandable but as in any area of study there are exceptions. A prime example is Branson, Missouri, the busiest coach tour destination in the United States. Its population is only 3700 but its 37 theatres offer more seats for live entertainment than Broadway. Yet as recently as two decades ago its visitors were retreating to a backwater for some good bass fishing and a

Figure 7.41 USA: recreational expenditures, 1970 and 1994		
Category	1970 ($ billions)	1994 ($ billions)
Books and maps	12.8	19.1
Magazines, newspapers and sheet music	16.7	22.5
Toys, sports & photographic supplies and equipment	22.5	77.5
Video and audio products, computer equipment and musical instruments	6.2	89.0
Spectator and commercial amusements	18.6	51.2
Other	17.0	110.6
Total	93.8	369.9
Percentage of total personal consumption expenditure	4.3	8.3

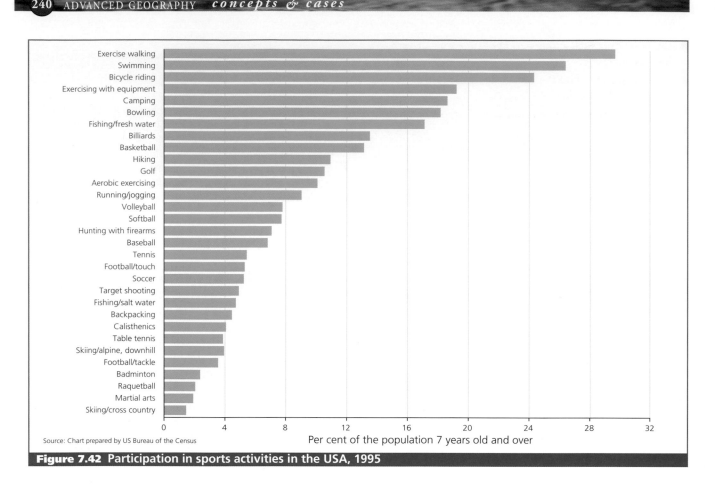

Figure 7.42 Participation in sports activities in the USA, 1995

spot of golf. By the early 1980s, the town's huge silver dollar theme park was drawing a million visitors a year, and a local nightclub owner saw a potential audience for the biggest names in entertainment. Celebrities such as Boxcar Willie and Andy Williams found themselves selling out weeks at a time and soon opened their own venues.

National parks and national forests

These are the jewels in the crown of recreational facilities in the United States. The world's first national park was Yellowstone (Figure 7.43), located mainly in the state of Wyoming. Yellowstone was designated in 1872 when members of a scientific expedition brought back photographs and persuaded the federal government to preserve this great wilderness in its unspoilt natural condition. The park boasts numerous spectacular thermal features including the famous Old Faithful geyser along with mountains, rivers, waterfalls, forests and a wide range of wildlife. The protection of such a huge area was at the time contrary to the 'growth ethic' that was dominating the American psyche. However, the idea was to spread quickly and most countries now have several national parks within their boundaries.

The National Park Service (NPS) was set up in 1916. It takes responsibility for a range of other protected areas as well (Figure 7.44). In total the United States' national parks account for an area 1.4 times larger than England. The popularity of the parks has risen steadily, causing a number of problems:

■ the most popular park sites regularly have their full quota of visitors at peak holiday times

■ traffic on access routes and on roads within the parks has risen substantially, adding to environmental pollution

■ footpath erosion is severe in some of the most attractive areas

■ vegetation has been destroyed and wildlife adversely affected due to off-trail hiking, trail-biking, camping and parking. General carelessness by visitors adds to the impact

■ the volume of litter and the level of graffiti has increased

■ there is pressure to increase building to provide more and better facilities for tourists. Also, more people want to live in those parks which are not too far from the cities

■ the risk of fires being started by carelessness is growing.

The considerable rise in the number of visits to national parks is in part due to the establishment of a series of new parks since 1971. Human impact on the individual parks is generally related to their popularity. Just eight parks accounted for 54 per cent of all visits in 1994. The Great Smokey Mountains National Park with 8.6 million visitors recorded twice as many visitors as the next most popular park, Grand Canyon. Other parks, in order of popularity, which recorded more than two and a half million visitors were Yosemite, Yellowstone, Acadia, Rocky Mountain, Grand Teton,

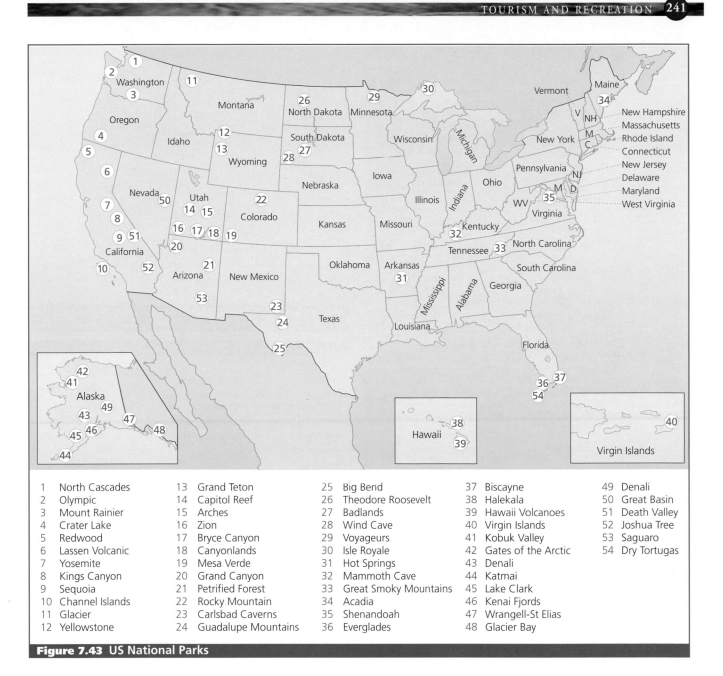

1	North Cascades	13	Grand Teton	25	Big Bend	37	Biscayne	49	Denali
2	Olympic	14	Capitol Reef	26	Theodore Roosevelt	38	Halekala	50	Great Basin
3	Mount Rainier	15	Arches	27	Badlands	39	Hawaii Volcanoes	51	Death Valley
4	Crater Lake	16	Zion	28	Wind Cave	40	Virgin Islands	52	Joshua Tree
5	Redwood	17	Bryce Canyon	29	Voyageurs	41	Kobuk Valley	53	Saguaro
6	Lassen Volcanic	18	Canyonlands	30	Isle Royale	42	Gates of the Arctic	54	Dry Tortugas
7	Yosemite	19	Mesa Verde	31	Hot Springs	43	Denali		
8	Kings Canyon	20	Grand Canyon	32	Mammoth Cave	44	Katmai		
9	Sequoia	21	Petrified Forest	33	Great Smoky Mountains	45	Lake Clark		
10	Channel Islands	22	Rocky Mountain	34	Acadia	46	Kenai Fjords		
11	Glacier	23	Carlsbad Caverns	35	Shenandoah	47	Wrangell-St Elias		
12	Yellowstone	24	Guadalupe Mountains	36	Everglades	48	Glacier Bay		

Figure 7.43 US National Parks

and Zion. Although winter use is rising sharply in some parks, visits reach a peak in July and August (Figure 7.46).

The United States' National Forest system was started in 1891 when the Shoshone National Forest was established in Wyoming. The system now incorporates 155 national forests which are managed for the purposes of timber, livestock grazing, watershed control, wildlife preservation and outdoor recreation. The forest service has the difficult job of maintaining a reasonable balance between the needs and impacts of these different land uses.

Like other federal lands, such as the national parks, much of the national forest is in the west. So, while most people live in the east, the greatest opportunities for outdoor recreation are elsewhere. Alaska, Idaho and California have the largest forest areas, although all the western states have substantial areas of

Figure 7.44 US National Park Service areas: recreation visits

	1960*	1994*
National parks	26.6	60.1
National monuments	10.7	26.5
National historic, archaeological and commemorative areas	21.8	59.5
National parkways	9.0	29.3
National recreation areas	3.7	52.3
National seashores and lakeshores	0.5	24.0
National capital parks	6.9	5.4
Other areas	n.a.	10.5
Totals	79.2	267.6

* Figures in millions

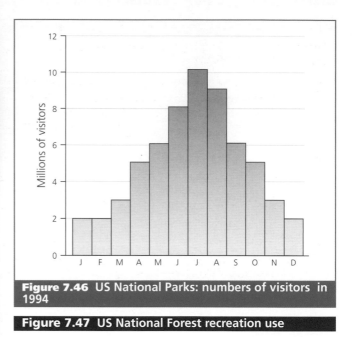

Figure 7.46 US National Parks: numbers of visitors in 1994

Figure 7.45 Hot springs in the Yellowstone National Park

Figure 7.47 US National Forest recreation use

	1981	1993
	(% visitor-days)	
Mechanised travel and viewing scenery	27.0	33.7
Camping, picnicking and swimming	31.7	26.8
Hiking, riding and water travel	8.5	9.0
Winter sports	4.8	6.5
Hunting	7.0	5.8
Resorts, cabins and organisation camps	6.3	5.8
Fishing	7.2	5.5
Nature studies	0.9	0.9
Other (team sports, attending talks and programmes, gathering forest products, etc.)	6.6	6.0
Total	100.0%	100.0%
Recreation visitor-days (1000)	235 709	295 473

forest land. In the east, large national forests are in the Green, White, Allegheny and Blue Ridge mountains. Although the forests provide less spectacular landscapes than the parks they are very popular, partly because there are fewer restrictions than in the parks and partly because campgrounds and other facilities in many parks have reached capacity. In 1993 recreation use in national forests totalled 295 million visitor-days, a 26 per cent increase over 1981 levels (Figure 7.47).

Figure 7.48 is a profile of three contrasting national forests. Each is unique in its own way with plenty to see and do. Both the White Mountain and Bridger-Teton forests have Wilderness areas. These are isolated virgin forest lands where the protection of the environment is all-important and there are strict regulations about access. The 1964 Wilderness Act specifically prohibits permanent or temporary roads, motor boats or vehicles, and mechanised equipment or transport, including bicycles, trail bikes, all-terrain vehicles, snowmobiles, hang gliders, parasails and parachutes. Seventeen per cent of all National Forest land is classed as Wilderness but environmental groups would like it to be much more. However, commercial interests, particularly the forest industry, are against this, arguing that the regulations are already too strict.

Much of the United States' timber and mineral resources are in national forest and other federal lands. Therefore the government has considerable control over the rate of exploitation. For example, the Forest Service carefully calculates how much timber it will allow to be cut on its land each year.

The Forest Service is very aware of the environmental problems it faces. To manage the impact of recreation properly it studies the

Questions

1 Analyse the data in Figures 7.41 and 7.42.
2 Explain the relationship between income and spending on leisure in the United States over the last century.
3 Describe and explain the distribution of national parks in the United States.
4 What are the main problems facing park managers?
5 Compare the wildlife and special attractions in the three national forests profiled (Figure 7.48).

carrying capacity of camps and trails to assess the amount of use an area can take without causing real damage. The balance between the number of visitors and the impact they cause varies from place to place. Visitor impact is greatest in mountain areas where the ecosystem is fragile.

Figure 7.48 A profile of three national forests in the US

Forest, size, location	Facilities and services	Activities	Special attractions	Wildlife
OCALA 382 000 acres in central Florida	Campgrounds, picnic areas, boat ramps, canoe rentals, visitors' centre	Camping, picnicking, hiking hunting, fishing, boating, canoeing, swimming, snorkelling, scuba diving	Only entirely sub-tropical forest in USA; the Oklawaha wild and scenic river; freshwater springs; more than 600 lakes	Threatened red-cockaded woodpecker, bald eagle and American alligator; black bear; bobcat; great variety of birds
WHITE MOUNTAIN 687 000 acres in New Hampshire and Maine	Campgrounds, picnic areas, visitors' centre, backpacking shelters	Camping, picnicking, hiking, backpacking, hunting, fishing, snowshoeing, cross-country skiing, snowmobiling	Mount Washington; alpine habitats with unusual plant life; virgin stands of red spruce; unmatched autumn foliage; two wilderness areas	Endangered American peregrine falcon; moose and black bear; several birds usually found in far northern regions
BRIDGER-TETON 3 440 000 acres in western Wyoming	Campgrounds, picnic areas, boat ramps, swimming beaches, horse corral	Camping, picnicking, hiking, backpacking, hunting, fishing, boating, swimming, horseback riding, nature study, winter sports	Bridger Wilderness (glaciers, over 1000 lakes); Kendall Warm Springs; Periodic Springs; Gros Ventre Slide Area; Teton Wilderness 20 peaks over 12 000 ft	Endangered or threatened bald eagle, rare trumpeter swan, grizzly bear and Kendall Warm Springs dam; moose, elk, Rocky Mountain bighorn sheep, mountain lion, bobcat

Bibliography

References

'US National Parks' by D. Flint, *Geography Review*, May 1998.
North America: An Advanced Geography by B. Price and P. Guinness, by Hodder & Stoughton, 1997.
'Sustainable Tourism', *People and Planet*, Vol. 6, No. 4.
'Antarctica: Tourism's Last Frontier' by J. Dove, *Geography Review*, March 1997.
'A Survey of Travel and Tourism', *The Economist*, 10 January 1998.
Business Traveller, Oct. 1997 [published monthly].
'World Tourism', *Financial Times* Survey, 18 June 1998.
Tourism, leisure and recreation by G. Nagle, Nelson, 1999.
Managing Wilderness Regions by J. Chaffey, Hodder & Stoughton, 1996.
Global Tourist Development by A. Kenward and J. Whittington, Hodder & Stoughton, 1999.
Leisure, Recreation and Tourism by R. Prosser, Collins, 1997.
Brazil: Advanced Case Studies by P. Guinness, Hodder & Stoughton, 1998.

Internet

The Virtual Tourist
http://www.vtourist/com/uk/
Brazilinfo
http://www.brazilinfo.com
Brazilian Tourist Board
http://www.embratur.gov.br
US National Parks Service
http://www.nps.gov
English Tourist Board
http://www.travelengland.org.uk

8 hydrological systems and *fluvial processes*

The hydrological cycle refers to the cycle of water between atmosphere, lithosphere and biosphere (Figure 8.1). It governs the availability of fresh water for human use. The difference between precipitation over land and evaporation is about 40 000 km³ of which only some 9000 km³ is reliably available over inhabited land and therefore suitable for human use. At a local scale the cycle has a single input, precipitation (PPT), and two major losses (outputs), evapotranspiration (EVT) and runoff. A third output, leakage, may also occur from the deeper subsurface to other basins.

Throughput refers to the transfer of water through the system. Water can be stored at a number of stages or levels within the cycle. These stores include vegetation, surface, soil moisture, groundwater and water channels. Quantities of fresh water are also locked up in snow and ice. The global hydrological cycle also includes the oceans and the atmosphere.

Human modifications are made at every scale. Good examples include large-scale changes of channel flow and storage, irrigation and land drainage, and large-scale abstraction of groundwater and surface water for domestic and industrial use.

The hydrological cycle

Precipitation

Precipitation is considered in detail in Chapter 12. Here it is important to mention the main characteristics that affect local hydrology. These are the amount of precipitation, the seasonality, intensity, type (snow, rain, etc.), geographic distribution and variability.

Interception

Interception refers to water that is stored by vegetation. There are three main components:

- **interception loss** – water which is retained by plant surfaces and which is later evaporated away or absorbed by the plant
- **throughfall** – water which either falls through gaps in the vegetation or which drops from leaves, twigs or stems
- **stemflow** – water which trickles along twigs and branches and finally down the main trunk.

Interception loss from vegetation is usually greatest at the start of a storm following a dry period. This is due to a number of reasons:

- **the interception capacity of the vegetation cover is high when leaves and twigs are dry – as leaves become wetter the weight of water reduces surface tension and causes throughfall**
- **meteorological conditions, especially windspeed, may also decrease interception loss as intercepted rain is dislodged**
- **rainfall amount is not important but relative importance of interception losses will decrease as the amount increases**
- **the more frequent the storm events the less interception loss.**

Interception loss varies with different types of vegetation (Figure 8.2). Interception is less from grasses than from deciduous woodland. Interception losses are high from coniferous forests because:

- **pine needles allow individual accumulation**
- **freer air circulation allows more evapotranspiration.**

From agricultural crops, and from cereals in particular, interception increases with crop density.

Key Definitions

1

hydrology The study of water.

water cycle The movement of water between air, land and sea. It varies from place to place and over time.

precipitation This includes all forms of rainfall, snow, frost, hail and dew. It is the conversion and transfer of moisture in the atmosphere to the land.

interception The precipitation that is collected and stored by vegetation.

overland runoff Water that flows over the land's surface.

infiltration Water that seeps into the ground.

evaporation Water from the ground or a lake that changes into a gas.

transpiration Water loss from vegetation to the atmosphere.

evapotranspiration The combined losses of evapotranspiration and evaporation.

hydrological cycle The movement of water between air, land and sea. It varies from place to place and over time.

river regime The annual variation in the flow of a river.

storm hydrograph This shows how a river changes over a short period, such as a day or a couple of days.

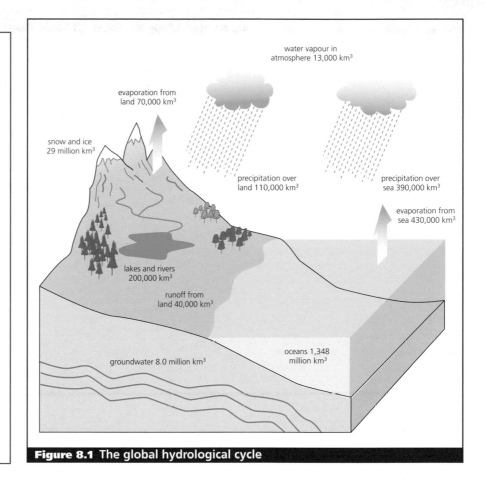

Figure 8.1 The global hydrological cycle

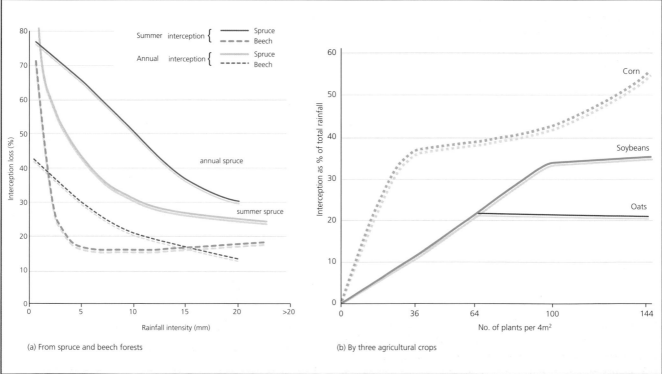

(a) From spruce and beech forests

(b) By three agricultural crops

Figure 8.2 Interception losses

Evaporation

Evaporation is the process by which a liquid or a solid is changed into a gas. It is the conversion of solid and liquid precipitation (snow, ice and water) to water vapour in the atmosphere. It is most important from oceans and seas. Evaporation increases under warm, dry conditions and decreases under cold, calm conditions. When the air is warm the **saturation vapour pressure** (E) of water is high. By contrast, when the air is dry, the **actual vapour pressure** (e) of water in the air is low. Therefore, the **saturation deficit** (E − e) is large. Increased saturation deficit leads to an increased evaporation rate.

Factors affecting evaporation include meteorological factors such as temperature, humidity, and windspeed (Figure 8.3). Of these, temperature is the most important factor. Other

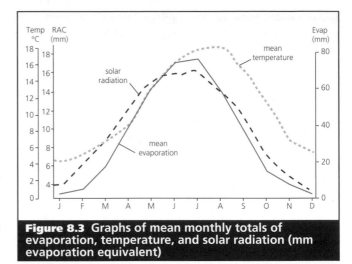

Figure 8.3 Graphs of mean monthly totals of evaporation, temperature, and solar radiation (mm evaporation equivalent)

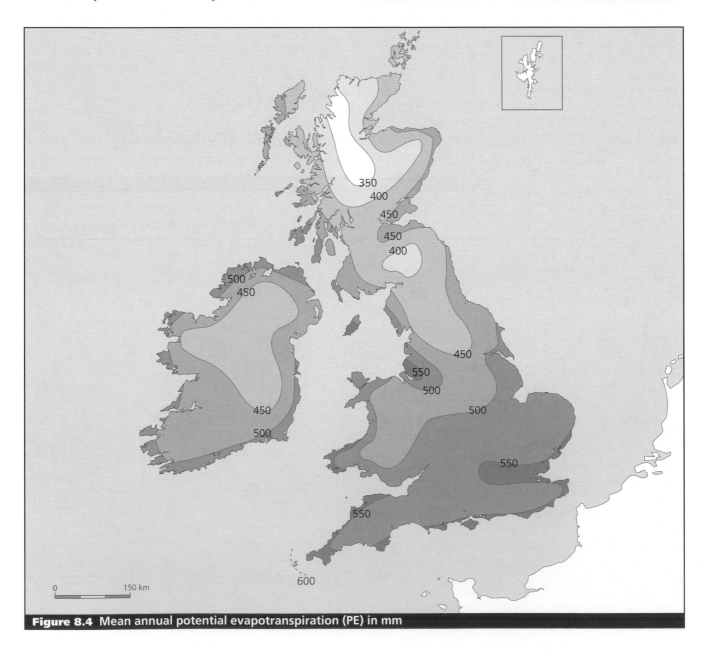

Figure 8.4 Mean annual potential evapotranspiration (PE) in mm

factors include water quality, depth of water, size of water body, vegetation cover and colour of the surface (albedo or reflectivity of the surface).

Evapotranspiration

Transpiration is 'the process by which water vapour escapes from the living plant, principally the leaves and enters the atmosphere'. The combined effects of evaporation and transpiration are normally referred to as evapotranspiration (EVT). EVT represents the most important aspect of water loss, accounting for the disposal of nearly 100 per cent of the annual precipitation in arid areas and 75 per cent in humid areas. Only over ice and snow fields, bare rock slopes, desert areas, water surfaces and bare soil do purely evaporative losses occur.

Potential evapotranspiration (PEVT)

The distinction between actual EVT and PEVT lies in the concept of moisture availability. Potential evapotranspiration is the water loss that would occur if there was an unlimited supply of water in the soil for use by the vegetation. Rates of potential evapotranspiration for Britain are shown in Figure 8.4. The factors affecting evapotranspiration include all those which affect evaporation. In addition, some plants have physiological and behavioural adaptations to help them reduce moisture loss.

Infiltration

Infiltration is the process by which water soaks into or is absorbed by the soil. It is distinguished from percolation which is the downward flow of water through the zone of aeration towards the water table. The two are closely related. The **infiltration capacity** is the maximum rate at which rain can be absorbed by a soil in a given condition.

Infiltration capacity decreases with time through a period of rainfall until a more or less constant value is reached (Figure 8.5). The main factors affecting infiltration are soil surface, surface cover and flow conditions. Infiltration rates of 0 to 4 mm^{-1} h^{-1} are common on clays whereas 3 to 12 mm^{-1} h^{-1} are common on sands. Vegetation also increases infiltration. On bare soils where rainsplash impact occurs infiltration rates may reach 10 mm^{-1} h^{-1}. On similar soils covered by vegetation rates of between 50 and 100 mm^{-1} h^{-1} have been recorded. Infiltrated water is chemically rich as it picks up minerals and organic acids from vegetation and soil.

Infiltration is inversely related to overland runoff and is influenced by a variety of factors such as duration of rainfall, antecedent soil moisture (pre-existing levels of soil moisture), soil porosity, vegetation cover, raindrop size and slope angle (Figure 8.6).

Soil moisture

Soil moisture refers to the subsurface water in the zone of aeration (vadose zone). This is the unsaturated soil and subsurface layers above the water table, and it marks the upper zone of the zone of saturation. In the zone of aeration water may undergo a number of processes. It may be:

- absorbed
- held
- **transmitted downwards towards the water table, or**
- **transmitted upwards towards the soil surface and the atmosphere.**

In coarser textured soils much of the water is held in fairly large pores at fairly low suctions, while little is held in small pores. In the finer textured clayey soils the range of pore sizes is much greater and, in particular, there is a higher proportion of small pores in which water is held at high suctions.

Field capacity refers to the amount of water held in the soil after excess water drains away (i.e. saturation or near saturation). The largest pores (macropores) contain air, while the smaller pores (micropores) contain some water. By contrast, wilting point refers to the range of moisture content in which permanent wilting of plants occurs. Together they define the approximate limits to plant growth.

Groundwater

Groundwater refers to subsurface water. The permanently saturated zone within solid rocks and sediments is known as the **phreatic zone**, and here nearly all the pore spaces are filled

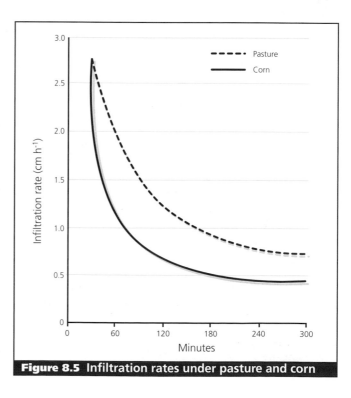

Figure 8.5 Infiltration rates under pasture and corn

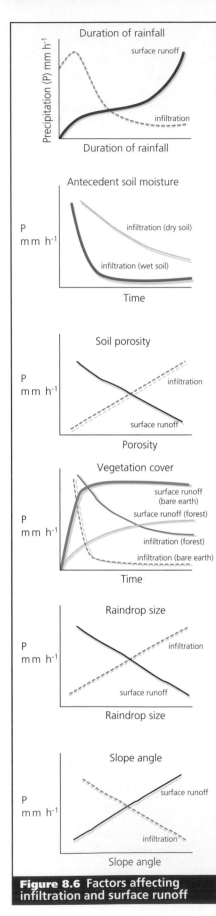

Figure 8.6 Factors affecting infiltration and surface runoff

with water. The upper layer of this is known as the water table. The water table varies seasonally. It is higher in winter following increased levels of precipitation. The zone that is seasonally wetted and seasonally dries out is known as the aeration zone or the **vadose** zone. Most groundwater is found within a few hundred metres of the surface but has been found at depths of up to 4 km beneath the surface (Figure 8.7).

Groundwater is important. It accounts for 96.5 per cent of all fresh water on the earth. However, while some soil water may be recycled by evaporation into atmospheric moisture within a matter of days or weeks, groundwater may not be recycled for as long as 20 000 years. Hence, in some places, where recharge is not taking place, groundwater is considered a **non-renewable resource**.

Aquifers (rocks which contain significant quantities of water) provide a great reservoir of water. Aquifers are permeable rocks such as sandstones and limestones. This water moves slowly and acts as a natural regulator in the hydrological cycle by absorbing rainfall which otherwise would reach streams rapidly. In addition, aquifers maintain stream flow during long dry periods. A rock which will not hold water is known as an **aquiclude** or **aquifuge**. These are impermeable rocks which prevent large-scale storage and transmission of water.

The groundwater balance is shown by the formula:

$$\Delta S = Qr - Qd$$

where ΔS is the change in storage ($+$ or $-$),
Qr is recharge to groundwater and
Qd is discharge from groundwater.

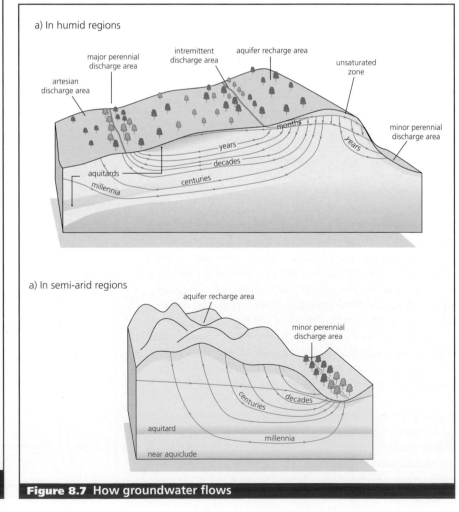

Figure 8.7 How groundwater flows

Groundwater recharge occurs as a result of:

- **infiltration of part of the total precipitation at the ground surface**
- **seepage through the banks and bed of surface water bodies such as ditches, rivers, lakes and oceans**
- **groundwater leakage and inflow through adjacent aquicludes and from aquifers**
- **artificial recharge from irrigation, reservoirs, etc.**

Losses of groundwater result from:

- **evapotranspiration particularly in low-lying areas where the water table is close to the ground surface**
- **natural discharge by means of spring flow and seepage into surface water bodies**
- **groundwater leakage and outflow through aquicludes and into adjacent aquifers**
- **artificial abstraction, for example the London Basin.**

The influence of human activity

Human activities and rivers

River landforms may be changed quite considerably by human activity. Such activity can increase or decrease flow, build dams and reservoirs, modify channels, build bridges and upset the natural dynamic equilibrium of rivers. Many of the changes caused are accelerations of natural processes. The effect is to compress such changes in time and, effectively, intensify them.

In some cases, human activity can create new landforms, such as the Norfolk Broads, a group of over 20 fresh water lakes. The Broads are the result of peat cutting in the Middle Ages. Over 25.5 million m³ of peat was excavated, thereby forming the depressions in which the lakes are formed.

Large features such as dams can have many unforeseen consequences. The Hoover Dam, for example, built in 1935, created a number of mild earthquakes. The case study later in this chapter of the Three Gorges Dam in China illustrates many of the advantages and disadvantages of large-scale engineering projects. On the other hand, human activity can improve the environment. This may be a case of making good what has first gone wrong. The examples of **river restoration** and the Edwards Dam in Maine are good illustrations.

The human impact on precipitation

There are a number of ways in which human activity affects precipitation. Cloud seeding has probably been one of the more successful. Rain requires either ice particles or large water droplets. Seeding introduces silver iodide, solid CO_2

(dry ice) or ammonium nitrate to attract water droplets. The results are unclear; partly it might be related to chance, some of it may be natural, some may be coincidental. In Australia and the United States seeding has increased precipitation by 10 to 30 per cent on a small scale and on a short-term basis, but the increase in precipitation in one place might decrease precipitation elsewhere and it might also lead to an increase in hail. In urban and industrial areas precipitation is often increased by up to as much as 10 per cent due to increased cloud frequency and amount, and because of the addition of pollutants, the heat island effect and turbulence.

The human impact on evaporation and evapotranspiration is relatively small in relation to the rest of the hydrological cycle but is nevertheless important. There are a number of reasons:

- **Land use changes** Pine trees, for example, intercept more than deciduous trees. Tropical afforestation leads to increased transpiration.
- **Dams** Evaporation increases locally following the construction of large dams. For example Lake Nasser behind the Aswan Dam loses up to a third of its water due to evaporation. Water loss can be reduced by chemical sprays, by building sand-fill dams and by covering the dams.
- **Urbanisation** This leads to a huge reduction in evapotranspiration due to the lack of vegetation. There may be a slight increase in evaporation because of higher temperatures and increased surface storage. The main physical controls include heat, wind and humidity.

Figure 8.8 The construction of dams is one of the most obvious of human impacts on the hydrological cycle

Human impact on interception

Interception is determined by vegetation, density and type. Most vegetation is not natural but represents some disturbance by human activity. In farmland areas cereals intercept less than broad leaves. Row crops leave a lot of soil bare. For example, in the Mississippi valley sediment yields in woodland areas produce 1 unit of soil erosion, pasture produces 30 units, and corn leaves 350 units. Deforestation leads to a reduction in evapotranspiration, an increase in surface runoff, a decline of surface storage and a decline in time-lag. Afforestation has the opposite effect, although the evidence does not necessarily support it. For example, in parts of the Severn catchment sediment loads increased four times after afforestation. Why was this? The result is explained by a combination of an increase in overland runoff, little ground vegetation, young trees, access routes for tractors and fire breaks and windbreaks. All of these resulted in extensive areas of bare ground. However, figures for five years later showed that the amount of erosion had decreased.

Human impact on infiltration and soil water

Human activity has a great impact on infiltration and soil water. Land use changes are important. Urbanisation creates an impermeable surface with compacted soil. This reduces infiltration. Infiltration is up to five times greater under forests compared with grassland. This is because trees channel water down their roots and stems. With deforestation there is reduced interception, increased soil compaction and more overland flow. Land use practices are also important. Grazing leads to a decline in infiltration due to compaction and ponding of the soil. By contrast, ploughing increases infiltration because it loosens soils. Waterlogging and salinisation are common if there is poor drainage. When the water table is close to the surface evaporation of water leaves salts behind and may form an impermeable duricrust. (This is a hardened, impermeable layer within a soil and may consist of silica, calcium or iron.) Human activity also has an increasing impact on surface storage which is increased due to the building of large-scale dams. These dams are larger in size and in greater volume and number. This leads to a number of effects:

- increased storage of water
- decreased flood peaks (a decline of 71 per cent in the Cheviots)
- low flows in rivers, for example the River Hodder in Lancashire, where the flow declined 10 per cent in winter, but 62 per cent in summer
- decreased sediment yields (clear water erosion)
- decreased losses due to evaporation and seepage leading to changes in temperature and salinity of the water
- increased flooding of the land

- triggering of earthquakes
- salinisation, for example in the Indus Valley, Pakistan, 1.9 million ha are severely saline and up to 0.4 million ha are lost per annum to salinity
- large dams can cause local changes in climate.

In other areas there is a decline in the surface storage – for example, in urban areas water is channelled rapidly away over impermeable surfaces into drains and gutters.

Changing groundwater

Human activity has seriously reduced the long-term viability of irrigated agriculture in the High Plains of Texas. Before irrigation development started in the 1930s, the High Plains' groundwater system was stable (i.e. in a state of dynamic equilibrium), with long-term recharge equal to long-term discharge. However, groundwater is now being used at a rapid rate to supply **centre-pivot irrigation schemes**. In less than 50 years, the water level has declined by 30 to 50 m in a large area to the north of Lubbock, Texas. The aquifer has narrowed by more than 50 per cent in large parts of certain counties, and the area irrigated by each well is contracting as well yields are falling.

By contrast, in some industrial areas, recent reductions in industrial activity have led to less groundwater being taken out of the ground. As a result, groundwater levels in such areas have begun to rise, adding to the problem caused by leakage from ancient, deteriorating pipe and sewer systems. This is happening in many British cities including London, Liverpool and Birmingham. In London, due to a 46 per cent reduction in groundwater abstraction, the water table in the Chalk and Tertiary beds has risen by as much as 20 m. Such a rise has numerous implications including:

- **increase in spring and river flows**
- **re-emergence of flow from 'dry springs'**
- **surface water flooding**
- **pollution of surface waters and spread of underground pollution**
- **flooding of basements**

Dynamic equilibrium

The concept of dynamic equilibrium states that all features are the result of the relative strength of factors and processes that operate. For example, a stream's load depends on local geology, gradient, vegetation cover and climate. However, if any one factor changes, e.g. deforestation, the balance is upset. As a result, the processes respond and change. This changing balance is known as dynamic equilibrium – in which the environment adjusts to change.

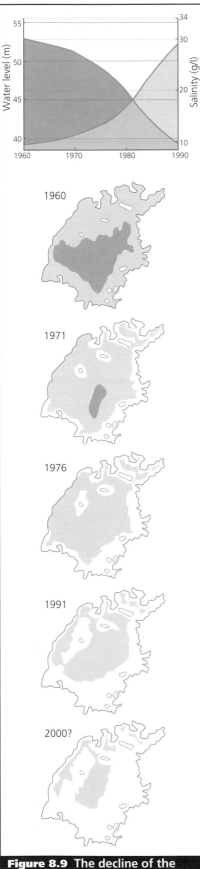

- increased leakage into tunnels
- reduction in stability of slopes and retaining walls
- reduction in bearing capacity of foundations and piles
- increased **hydrostatic uplift** and swelling pressures on foundations and structures
- swelling of clays as they absorb water
- chemical attack on building foundations.

There are various methods of recharging groundwater resources, providing sufficient surface water is available. Where the materials containing the aquifer are permeable (as in some alluvial fans, coastal sand dunes or glacial deposits) water spreading is used. This is similar to irrigation and allows water to seep into the ground. By contrast, in sediments with impermeable layers, such water-spreading techniques are not effective, and the appropriate method may then be to pump water into deep pits or into wells. This method is used extensively on the heavily settled coastal plain of Israel, both to replenish the groundwater reservoirs when surplus irrigation water is available and to attempt to diminish the problems associated with salt-water intrusions from the Mediterranean.

Changing hydrology of the Aral Sea

The Aral Sea began shrinking in the 1960s when Soviet irrigation schemes took water from the Syr Darya and the Amu Darya. This greatly reduced the amount of water reaching the Aral Sea. By 1994, the shorelines had fallen by 16 m, the surface area had declined by 50 per cent and the volume had been reduced by 75 per cent (Figure 8.9). By contrast, salinity levels had increased by 300 per cent.

Increased salinity levels killed off the fishing industry. Moreover, ports such as Muynak are now tens of kilometres from the shore (Figure 8.10). Salt from the dry seabed has reduced soil fertility and frequent dust storms are ruining the region's cotton production. Drinking water has been polluted by pesticides and fertilisers and the air has been affected by dust and salt. There has been a noticeable rise in respiratory and stomach disorders and the region has one of the highest infant mortality rates in the former Soviet Union.

Figure 8.9 The decline of the Aral Sea

Figure 8.10 Boats stranded by the former edge of the Aral Sea

SPATIAL FOCUS

The Three Gorges Dam

When the Three Gorges Dam has been built on the Yangtze, only two of the world's great rivers will not be dammed, the Amazon and the Zaire. While governments, developers and constructors are overjoyed at the prospect of such a major investment and engineering project there are serious concerns about the impact of the dam.

The facts

- The Three Gorges Dam will be over 2 km long and 100 m high (Figure 8.11).

- The lake will be over 600 km long.

- The dam will generate up to 18 000 MW, eight times more than the Aswan Dam and 50 per cent more than

the world's largest existing HEP dam, the Itaipu on the Brazil/Paraguay border.

- It will enable China to reduce its dependency on coal.

- It will supply Shanghai (population over 13 million), one of the world's largest cities, and Chongqing (population 3 million), an area earmarked for economic development.

- It will take between 15 and 20 years to build and could cost as much as $70 billion.

- It will protect 10 million people from flooding (since 1860 over 5 million people in China have died as a result of flooding).

- It will allow shipping above the Three Gorges: the dams will raise water levels by 90 m, and turn the rapids in the gorge into a lake.

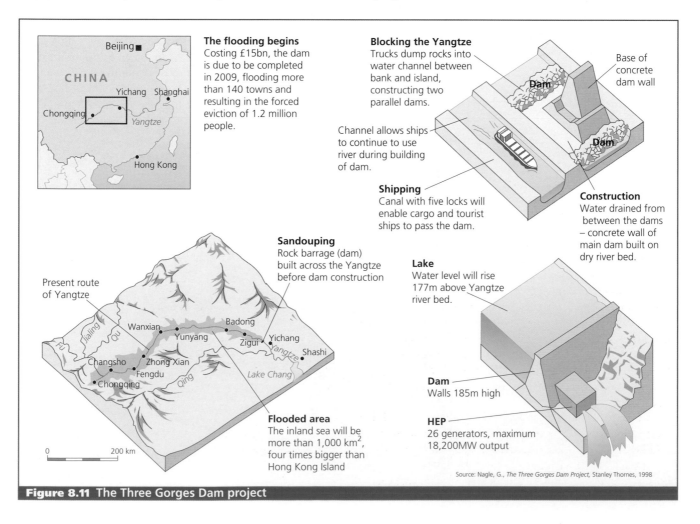

The flooding begins
Costing £15bn, the dam is due to be completed in 2009, flooding more than 140 towns and resulting in the forced eviction of 1.2 million people.

Blocking the Yangtze
Trucks dump rocks into water channel between bank and island, constructing two parallel dams.

Channel allows ships to continue to use river during building of dam.

Base of concrete dam wall

Shipping
Canal with five locks will enable cargo and tourist ships to pass the dam.

Construction
Water drained from between the dams – concrete wall of main dam built on dry river bed.

Sandouping
Rock barrage (dam) built across the Yangtze before dam construction

Lake
Water level will rise 177m above Yangtze river bed.

Present route of Yangtze

Flooded area
The inland sea will be more than 1,000 km², four times bigger than Hong Kong Island

Dam
Walls 185m high

HEP
26 generators, maximum 18,200MW output

Source: Nagle, G., *The Three Gorges Dam Project*, Stanley Thornes, 1998

Figure 8.11 The Three Gorges Dam project

- The Yangtze provides 66 per cent of China's rice and its catchment area contains 400 million people.

- The Yangtze drains 1.8 million km² and discharges 700 km³ of water annually.

The protesters' case

- Most floods in recent years have come from rivers which join the Yangtze below the Three Gorges Dam.

- The region is seismically active and landslides are frequent (Figure 8.12).

- The port at the head of the lake may become silted up as a result of increased deposition and the development of a delta at the head of the lake.

- Up to 1.2 million people will have to be moved to make way for the dam.

- Much of the land available for resettlement is over 800 m above sea level, and is colder with infertile thin soils and on relatively steep slopes.

- Dozens of towns, for example Wanxian and Fuling with 140 000 and 80 000 people respectively, will be flooded.

- Up to 530 million tonnes of silt are carried through the Gorge annually: the first dam on the river lost its capacity within seven years and one on the Yellow River filled with silt within four years.

Figure 8.12 The Three Gorges prior to drowning

- To reduce the silt load, afforestation is needed but resettlement of people will cause greater pressure on the slopes above the dam.

- The dam will interfere with aquatic life – the Siberian Crane and the White Flag Dolphin are threatened with extinction.

- Archaeological treasures will be drowned, including the Zhang Fei temple.

Edwards Dam, Maine

In 1997, for the first time in its history, the United States government ordered the removal of a working hydro-electric dam. The dam was located on the Kennebec river, Maine, near the state capital, Augusta (Figure 8.13). For over 160 years, the dam had prevented migratory fish such as sturgeon and salmon from reaching their old spawning grounds. But in 1997 the Federal Energy Regulatory Commission (FERC) gave the owners of the Edwards Dam one year to develop a plan for demolishing it at their own expense.

The decision was a victory for environmentalists and a big upset for the dam's owners, Edwards Manufacturing. Although this was a private dam, one of around 70 000 on America's rivers, it had to be licensed by the Federal Government because it produced electricity for the Central Maine Power Company.

In 1997, in a preliminary study, the FERC concluded that the dam could stay if the company added fish-lifts to help millions of spawning fish over the obstacle. But the agency changed its mind after studies showed that adding lifts would cost $10 million – almost double the cost of removing the dam and purchasing replacement power. Moreover, the fish-

Figure 8.13 Location of the Edwards Dam, Maine

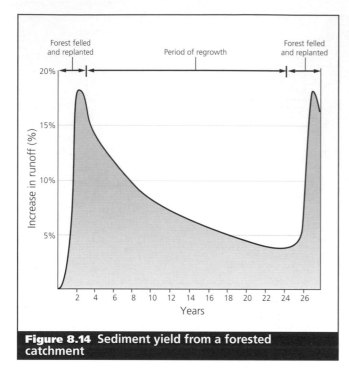

Figure 8.14 Sediment yield from a forested catchment

Questions

Hydrology

1 **(a)** Define the following hydrological characteristics:
   (i) interception;
   (ii) evaporation;
   (iii) infiltration.
   (b) Discuss the significance of the above hydrological characteristics to the production of:
   (i) surface runoff in a drainage basin;
   (ii) throughflow in a drainage basin.
   (c) Explain, illustrating your answer with specific examples, how human activity may modify the hydrological characteristics listed in (a) and (b).

2 Study Figure 8.6 which shows factors influencing infiltration and overland runoff. Write a paragraph on each of the factors, describing and explaining the effect it has on infiltration and overland runoff.

3 Figure 8.14 shows a graph of the sediment yield from a small forested catchment during and after the felling and replanting of trees.
   (a) Explain why sediment yields are high in the period of felling and replanting.
   (b) Explain why sediment yields decline in subsequent years.
   (c) How would you expect the hydrological response of the catchment to have changed during the 25-year period?
   (d) Suggest ways in which forestry practices might be designed to reduce sediment yield during felling and replanting.

Human impact

4 **(a)** What should the normal operating level of the Three Gorges Dam be: as full as possible to maximise HEP or as low as possible to capture flood waters? Justify your answer.
   (b) How can the dam be prevented from filling with silt?
   (c) How will the dam have an effect on the greenhouse effect?
   (d) What do you think the terms 'clear water erosion' and 'red water famine' mean? What changes are likely to occur to the river downstream of the dam? Explain your answer.

5 **(a)** Why did the former Soviet Union embark on a programme of large-scale irrigation? Use an atlas to produce detailed information.
   (b) Why have salinity levels in the Aral Sea increased so much?
   (c) What problems does the shrinking of the Aral Sea cause for towns such as Aralsk and Muynak?
   (d) What is the likely effect of the irrigation scheme on rivers Syr Darya and Amu Darya in terms of velocity, erosion, sediment transport and deposition?

lifts would not help all the fish. The agency also concluded that Maine's economy would not be harmed by losing the dam.

The dam is not large by any standards. It is just 6 m high and 300 m wide, and is made of a mixture of concrete, rocks and logs. It produces 3.5 MW of electricity, less than one-tenth of 1 per cent of the state's annual energy use.

Since 1920, the FERC has ordered the demolition of just seven of the more than 1600 private power-producing dams under its control, all for safety reasons after the owners had abandoned them. Only in 1994 did the agency decide it has the right to deny new licences to operators of working dams. The agency is considering removal requests for at least six other dams, which have bottled up once-productive salmon rivers in the Pacific Northwest.

Flood hydrographs

A flood hydrograph shows how the discharge of a river varies over a short time (Figure 8.15). Normally it refers to an individual storm or group of storms of not more than a few days in length. Before the storm starts the main supply of water to the stream is through groundwater flow or **baseflow** which is the main supplier of water to rivers. During the storm some water infiltrates into the soil while some flows over the surface as overland flow or runoff. This reaches the river quickly as **quickflow** which causes the rapid rise in the level of the river.

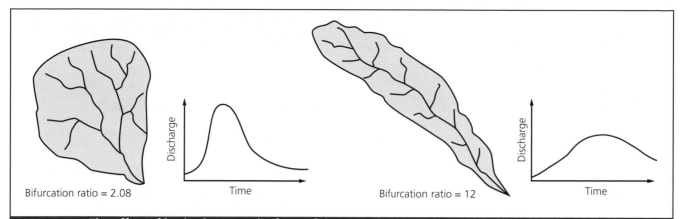

Figure 8.15 The effect of basin shape on the form of the storm hydrograph

Figure 8.16 Potential hydrological effects of urbanisation

Urbanising influence	Potential hydrological response
Removal of trees and vegetation	Decreased evapotranspiration and interception; increased stream sedimentation
Initial construction of houses, streets and culverts	Decreased infiltration and lowered groundwater table; increased stormflows and decreased baseflows during dry periods
Complete development of residential, commercial and industrial areas	Decreased porosity, reducing time of runoff concentration, thereby increasing peak discharges and compressing the time distribution of the flow; greatly increased volume of runoff and flood damage potential
Construction of storm drains and channel improvements	Local relief from flooding; concentration of flood waters may aggravate flood problems downstream

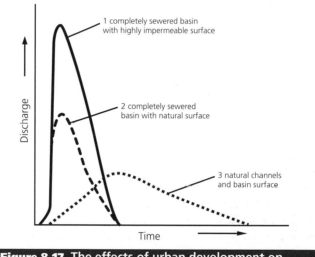

Figure 8.17 The effects of urban development on flood hydrographs

Figure 8.18 Precipitation and runoff data for a storm on the Delaware River, New York

Date	Time	Duration of rainfall	Total (cm)
29 Sept.	6 a.m.	12 hours	0.1
29 Sept.	6 p.m.	12 hours	0.9
30 Sept.	6 p.m.	24 hours	3.7
30 Sept.	12 p.m.	6 hours	0.1
			Total 4.8

Date	Stream runoff (m³ s⁻¹)

Date	Stream runoff ($m^3 \ s^{-1}$)
28 Sept.	28.3 (baseflow)
29 Sept.	28.3 (baseflow)
30 Sept.	339.2
1 Oct.	2094.2
2 Oct.	1330.1
3 Oct.	594.3
4 Oct.	367.9
5 Oct.	254.2
6 Oct.	198.1
7 Oct.	176.0
8 Oct.	170.0
9 Oct.	165.2 (baseflow)

Key Definitions ②

rising limb This shows us how quickly the flood waters begin to rise.

peak flow The maximum discharge of the river as a result of the storm.

time-lag The time between the height of the storm (not the start or the end) and the maximum flow in the river.

recessional limb The speed with which the water level in the river declines after the peak.

baseflow The normal level of the river, which is fed by groundwater.

quickflow or **stormflow** The water which gets into the river as a result of overland runoff.

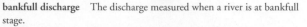

1 Study Figure 8.16 and Figure 8.17 which show the impact of urbanisation on flood hydrographs. Describe and explain the differences in the relationship between discharge and time.

2 The data in Figure 8.18 show precipitation and runoff data for a storm on the Delaware River, New York. Plot the storm hydrograph for this storm.

Flood hazard

Floods are one of the most common of all environmental hazards. This is because so many people live in fertile river valleys and in low-lying coastal areas. The nature and scale of flooding varies greatly. Less than 2 per cent of the population of England and Wales and in Australia live in areas exposed to flooding, compared to 10 per cent of the US population who live on a flood plain at risk of flood. The worst problems occur in Asia where floods damage about 4 million ha of land each year and affect the lives of over 17 million people. Worst of all is China where over 5 million people have been killed in floods since 1860.

Some environments are more at risk than others. The most vulnerable include the following:

■ **Low-lying parts of active flood plains and river estuaries, for example in the lower Thames in London. In Bangladesh, 110 million people live relatively unprotected on the flood plain of the Ganges, Brahmaputra and Meghna. Floods caused by the monsoon regularly cover 20 to 30 per cent of the flat delta. In high floods up to half of the country may be flooded. In 1988 46 per cent of the land was flooded and over 1500 people were killed.**

■ **Small basins subject to flash floods. These are especially common in arid and semi-arid areas. In tropical areas some 90 per cent of lives lost through drowning are the result of intense rainfall on steep slopes.**

■ **Areas below unsafe or inadequate dams. In the United States there are about 30 000 sizeable dams and 2000 communities are at risk from dams breaching. One of the most well-known spectacular failures was that of the Vaiont dam in Italy in 1963.**

■ **Low-lying inland shorelines such as along the Great Lakes and the Great Salt Lake in the United States.**

■ **Alluvial fans in semi-arid areas are prone to flash floods.**

In most developed countries the number of deaths from floods is declining although the number of deaths from flash floods is changing little. By contrast the average national figure for

Key Definitions ③

bankfull discharge The discharge measured when a river is at bankfull stage.

bankfull stage A condition in which a river's channel fills completely, so that any further increase in discharge results in water overflowing the banks.

channel The passageway in which the river flows.

channelisation Modifications to river channels, consisting of some combination of straightening, deepening, widening, clearing or lining of the natural channel.

discharge The quantity of water that passes a given point on the bank of a river within a given interval of time.

drainage basin The total area that contributes water to a river.

flash flood A flood in which the lag time is exceptionally short – hours or minutes.

flood A discharge great enough to cause a body of water to overflow its channel and submerge surrounding land.

flood-frequency curve Flood magnitudes with respect to the recurrence interval calculated for a flood of that magnitude at a given location.

flood plain The part of any stream valley that is inundated during floods.

hazard assessment The process of determining when and where hazards have occurred in the past, the severity of the physical effects of past events of a given magnitude, the frequency of events that are strong enough to generate physical effects, and what a particular event would be like if it were to occur now; and portraying all this information in a form that can be used by planners and decision makers.

load The particles of sediment and dissolved matter that are carried along by a river.

natural hazards The wide range of natural circumstances, materials, processes and events that are hazardous to humans, such as locust infestations, wildfires, or tornadoes, in addition to strictly geologic hazards.

risk assessment The process of establishing the probability that a hazardous event of a particular magnitude will occur within a given period and estimating its impact, taking into account the locations of buildings, facilities and emergency systems in the community, the potential exposure to the physical effects of the hazardous situation or event and the community's vulnerability when subjected to those physical effects.

flood damage has been increasing. The death rate in developing countries is much greater, partly because warning systems and evacuation plans are inadequate. It is likely that the hazard in developing countries will increase over time rather than decrease as more people migrate and settle in low-lying areas and river basins. Often newer migrants are forced into the more hazardous zones.

Since the Second World War there has been a change in the understanding of the flood hazard, in the attitude towards floods and policy towards reducing the flood hazard. The focus of attention has shifted away from physical control (engineering structures) towards reducing vulnerability through non-structural approaches. Three overlapping stages have been identified.

1 The structural era of the 1930s to 1960s (reservoirs, levées, channel improvements).

2 The unified flood plain management era of the 1960s to 1980s (flood warning, land use planning, insurance).

3 Post-flood hazard mitigation era of the 1980s onwards (property acquisition and land use control).

Natural causes of floods

A flood is a high flow of water which overtops the banks of a river. The primary causes of floods are mainly the result of external climatic forces whereas the secondary causes tend to be drainage-basin specific. Most floods in Britain are associated with deep depressions (low-pressure systems) in autumn and winter which are both long in duration and wide in areal coverage. By contrast in India, up to 70 per cent of the annual rainfall occurs in 100 days during the summer south west monsoon. Elsewhere, melting snow is also responsible for widespread flooding.

Flood-intensifying conditions cover a range of factors which alter the drainage basin response to a given storm. These factors include topography, vegetation, soil type, rock type, characteristics of the drainage basin and so on.

The potential for damage by flood waters increases exponentially with velocity and speeds above 3 ms^{-1} can undermine the foundations of buildings. The physical stresses on buildings are increased even more, probably by hundreds of times, when rapidly flowing water contains debris such as rock, sediment and trees.

Other conditions which intensify floods include changes in land use. Urbanisation, for example, increases the magnitude and frequency of floods in at least four ways:

■ **creation of highly impermeable surfaces, such as roads, roofs, pavements**

■ **smooth surfaces served with a dense network of drains, gutters and underground sewers increase drainage density**

■ **natural river channels are often constricted by bridge supports or riverside facilities reducing their carrying capacity**

■ **due to increased storm runoff many sewerage systems cannot cope with the resulting peak flow without investment in greater capacity (Figure 8.19).**

Deforestation is also a cause of increased flood runoff and a decrease in channel capacity. This occurs because of higher levels of deposition within the channel. However, there is little evidence to support any direct relationship between deforestation in the Himalayas and changes in flooding and increased deposition of silt in parts of the lower Ganges–Brahmaputra. Critics say that flooding occurs whether there is deforestation or not. It is due to the combination of high monsoon rains in the Himalayas, steep slopes and the seismically unstable terrain, which ensure that runoff is rapid and sedimentation is high, irrespective of the vegetation cover.

Human causes of floods

Economic growth and population movements throughout the twentieth century have caused many flood plains to be built on. However, in order for people to live on flood plains there needs to be flood protection. This can take many forms such as loss-sharing adjustments and event modifications.

Loss-sharing adjustments include disaster aid and insurance. Disaster aid refers to any aid, such as money, equipment, staff and technical assistance, that is given to a community following a disaster. However, there are many taxpayers who argue that taxpayers cannot be expected to fund losses which should have been insured.

In developed countries insurance is an important loss-sharing strategy. However not all flood-prone households have insurance and many of those who are insured may be underinsured. In the floods of central England in 1998 (Figure 8.20) many of the affected households were not insured against losses from flooding because the residents did not believe that they lived in an area that was likely to flood.

Event-modification adjustments include environmental control and hazard-resistant design. Physical control of floods depend on two measures – flood abatement and flood diversion. Flood abatement involves decreasing the amount of runoff, thereby reducing the flood peak in a drainage basin. This can be achieved by weather modification and/or watershed treatment, for example, to reduce flood peak over a drainage basin. There are a number of strategies including:

■ **reforestation**

■ **reseeding of sparsely vegetated areas to increase evaporative losses**

■ **mechanical land treatment of slopes such as contour ploughing or terracing to reduce the runoff coefficient**

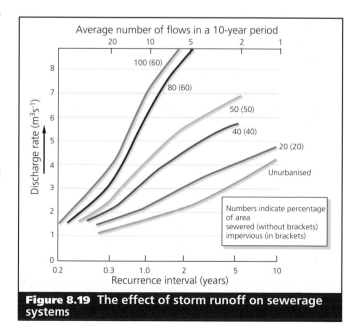

Figure 8.19 The effect of storm runoff on sewerage systems

- comprehensive protection of vegetation from wild fires, overgrazing, clear cutting of forests, land or any other practices likely to increase flood discharge and sediment load
- clearance of sediment and other debris from headwater streams
- construction of small water and sediment holding areas
- preservation of natural water detention zones.

Flood diversion measures, by contrast, include the construction of levées (Figure 8.21), reservoirs, and the modification of river channels. Levées are the most common form of river engineering. They can also be used to divert and restrict water to low-value land on the flood plain. For example, over 4500 km of the Mississippi River has levées. Channel improvements include measures such as enlargement to increase the carrying capacity of the river.

Reservoirs store excess rain water in the upper drainage basin. Large dams are expensive and may cause earthquakes and siltation. It has been estimated that some 66 billion m³ of storage will be needed to make any significant impact on major floods in Bangladesh!

Hazard-resistant design

Flood proofing includes any adjustments to buildings and their contents, which help reduce losses. Some methods are temporary such as blocking up vulnerable entrances, use of shields to seal doors and windows, removal of damageable goods to higher levels, and the use of sandbags. By contrast, long-term measures include moving the living spaces above the likely level of the flood plain. This normally means building above the flood level, but could also include building homes on stilts (Figure 8.22).

Forecasting and warning

During the 1970s and 1980s flood forecasting and flood warning had both become more accurate and is now among the most widely used measures to reduce the problems caused by flooding. Despite advances in weather satellites and the use of radar for forecasting, over 50 per cent of all of unprotected dwellings in England and Wales have less than six hours of flood warning time. In developed countries flood warnings and forecasts reduce economic losses by as much as 40 per cent. In most developing countries there is much less effective flood forecasting. An exception is Bangladesh. Most floods in Bangladesh originate in the Himalayas, so authorities have about 72 hours' warning.

Land use planning

Most land use zoning and land use planning has come into being in the last 30 to 40 years. Land use management has been effective in protecting new housing developments in the

Figure 8.20 Flooded Leicestershire, 1998

Figure 8.21 Engineered levée alongside the River Tees, near Darlington

Figure 8.22 Stilted flood shelter in Bangladesh

United States from losses up to the 1:100 year flood. In England and Wales flood plain development has been controlled by the Town and Country Planning Acts since 1947. In Britain there has been less encroachment on to the flood plain than there has been in the United States. Partly this is due to population growth; for example, between 1952 and 1982 the population of England and Wales grew by 12 per cent compared to 50 per cent in the United States, 73 per cent in Canada and 78 per cent in Australia, therefore in Britain fewer new buildings have been required, whereas in the United States and Australia more buildings have been required, hence more encroachment on to flood plains. The older age of settlement in Britain also explains why less new settlement occurs in the flood plains in the twentieth century.

One example where partial urban relocation has occurred is at Soldier's Grove on the Kickapoo river in south-western Wisconsin. The town experienced a series of floods in the 1970s, and the US Army Corps of Engineers proposed to build two levées and to move part of the urban area. Following floods in 1978 they decided that relocation of the entire business district would be better than just flood-damage reduction. Although levées would have protected the village from most floods, they would not have provided other opportunities. Relocation allowed energy conservation and an increase in commercial activity in the area.

Floods in China and Bangladesh

China

Floods are a natural feature of all rivers. For most of the time a river is contained in its channel but occasionally it may burst its bank and a flood occurs. Floods bring advantages such as water and fertile **alluvium** (river deposits or silt) which allow farmers to grow crops. But the problem is that they may bring too much water and too much silt. The results can be devastating as the experience of China shows.

The Hwang He river (the Yellow River) flows over 4000 km and drains an area of 1 250 000 km² (Figure 8.23). It is said to have killed more people than any other natural feature and for this reason it is called the 'river of sorrow'. The worst flood occurred in 1332 – over 7 million people drowned and a further 10 million died as a result of the famine that followed.

Attempts to control the river go back at least as far as 2356 BC and there have been levées on the river for at least 2500 years! Despite this long history of engineering the Hwang He has shifted its course on at least ten occasions. When the river shifts its course it can change where it enters the sea by as much as 1100 km.

Why does the river shift? When a river deposits its load it builds up its flood plain and also the base of the river channel. As more material is deposited in the river channel, the base of the river channel may become higher than the level of the flood plain (Figure 8.24). The levées stop the river from flooding.

For example, in 1887 the Hwang He overtopped its bank and flooded an area of 22 000 km² to a depth of 8 m. Over 1 million people were killed by the floods and the famine that happened as a result. It is ironic that famine should follow floods but the silt carried by the river destroys the crops that it is deposited on. During normal flow conditions the river contains a large amount of silt. In fact, 40 per cent of the river flow is sediment. An 8 m consistency flood might be expected to dump over 3 m of material on the ground.

Now the river is 20 m higher than the flood plain and the risk of flooding is great. As China's population continues to grow, more and more people are living on the fertile flood plains. This makes the risk of a disaster even greater. To prevent flooding, the Chinese authorities have built levées to contain the water. How long these will last is a real problem for the people living on the flood plain.

Flooding and flood management in Bangladesh

Much of Bangladesh has been formed by deposition from three main rivers – the Brahmaputra, the Ganges and the Meghna. The sediment from these and more than 50 other rivers forms one of the largest deltas in the world, and up to 80 per cent of the country is located on the delta (Figure 8.25). As a result much of the country is less than 1 m above sea level and is under threat from flooding and rising sea levels (see also Chapter 15, pages 513–4). To make matters worse, Bangladesh is a densely populated country (over 900 people per km²) and is experiencing rapid population growth (nearly 2.7 per cent per annum). It contains nearly twice as many people as the United Kingdom, but

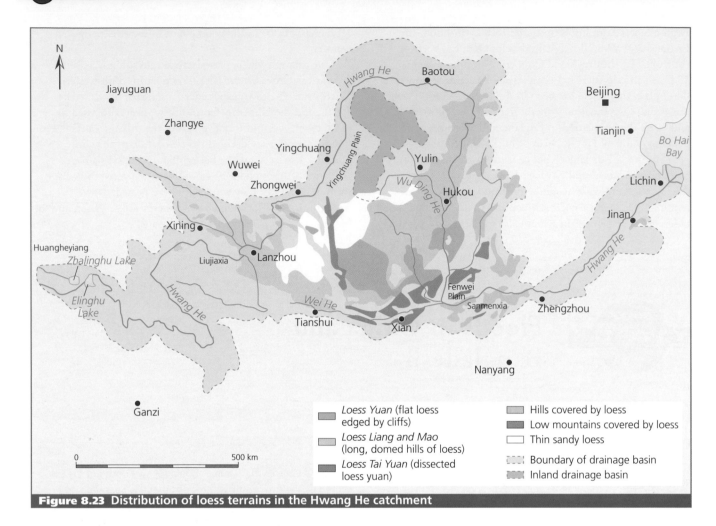

Loess Yuan (flat loess edged by cliffs)

Loess Liang and Mao (long, domed hills of loess)

Loess Tai Yuan (dissected loess yuan)

Hills covered by loess

Low mountains covered by loess

Thin sandy loess

Boundary of drainage basin

Inland drainage basin

Figure 8.23 Distribution of loess terrains in the Hwang He catchment

Figure 8.24 India's Ganges flood plain has always been important to the life of the nation

30 million people in Bangladesh depend on river for livelihood

Increasing percentage of monsoon rains

Deforestation in the Himalayas increases runoff, soil erosion

80% of Ganges annual flow takes place in 4 months (July – Oct)

Water carries topsoil into rivers, raises bed

Too much rain in rainy season (June–Oct), too little in dry (Nov–May)

Source: Broadley, E. & Cunningham, R., *Core themes in geography*, Oliver & Boyd, 1991

Figure 8.25 Causes of flooding in Bangladesh

is only about half its size. Hence, the flat, low-lying delta is vital as a place to live as well as a place to grow food.

Almost all of Bangladesh's rivers have their source outside the country. For example, the drainage basin of the Ganges and Brahmaputra covers 1.75 million km² and includes the Himalayas, the Tibetan Plateau and much of northern India. Total rainfall within the Brahmaputra–Ganges–Meghna catchment is high and seasonal – 75 per cent of annual rainfall occurs in the monsoon between June and September. Cherrapungi, high in the Himalayas, has an average annual rainfall of over 10 000 mm, and this can rise as high as 20 000 mm in a 'wet' year. Moreover, the Ganges and Brahmaputra carry snow-melt waters from the Himalayas. This normally reaches the delta in June and July. Peak discharges of the rivers are immense – up to 100 000 m³ per second (i.e. 100 000 cumecs) in the Brahmaputra, for example. In addition to water, the rivers carry vast quantities of sediment. This is deposited annually to form temporary islands and sand banks.

The advantages of flooding

During the monsoon between 30 per cent and 50 per cent of the entire country is flooded (Figure 8.26). The flood waters

- replenish groundwater reserves
- provide nutrient-rich sediment for agriculture in the dry season
- provide fish – fish supply 75 per cent of dietary protein and more than 10 per cent of annual export earnings
- reduce the need for artificial fertilisers
- flush pollutants and pathogens away from domestic areas.

Figure 8.26 Flooding in Bangladesh

The causes of flooding

There are five main causes of flooding in Bangladesh – river floods, overland runoff, flash floods, 'back-flooding' and storm surges. Snow-melt in the Himalayas combined with heavy monsoonal rain causes peak discharges in all the major rivers during June and July. This leads to flooding and destruction of agricultural land. Outside the monsoon season, heavy rainfall causes extensive flooding which may be advantageous to agricultural production, since it is a source of new nutrients. In addition, the effects of flash floods, caused by heavy rainfall in northern India, have been intensified by the destruction of forest which reduces interception, decreases water retention and increases the rate of surface runoff. Human activity in Bangladesh has also exacerbated the problem. Attempts to reduce flooding by building embankments and dikes have prevented the backflow of flood water into the river. This leads to a ponding of water (also known as 'drainage congestion') and back-flooding. In this way, embankments have sometimes led to an increase in deposition in drainage channels, and this can cause large-scale deep flooding. Bangladesh is also subject to coastal flooding (see pages 312–4). Storm surges caused by intense low-pressure systems are funnelled up the Bay of Bengal.

The Flood Action Plan

It is impossible to prevent flooding in Bangladesh. The Flood Action Plan attempts to minimise the damage of flooding and maximise the benefits of flooding. The plan relies upon huge embankments which run along the length of the main rivers. However, they are not able to withstand the most severe floods, for example those of 1987 and 1988, but provide some control of flooding. The embankments contain sluices which can be opened to reduce river flow and to control the damage caused by flood waters.

The embankments are set back from the rivers. This protects them from the erosive power of the river and has the added advantage of being cheap both to install and to maintain. In addition, the area between the river and embankment can be used for cereal production.

Nevertheless, the Flood Action Plan is not without its critics. There are a number of negative impacts of the scheme:

- Increased time of flooding, since embankments prevent backflow into the river.

- An insufficient number of sluices have been built to control the levels of the flood waters in the rivers – this means that there may be increased damage by flooding if the embankments are breached, since the rapid nature of the breach is more harmful than gradual flooding.

- Sudden breaches of the embankments may also deposit deep layers of infertile sand thereby reducing soil fertility.

- Compartmentalisation may reduce the flushing effect of the flood waters, increasing the concentration of pollutants from domestic effluents and agrochemicals.

■ By preventing backflow to the river, areas of stagnant water will be created which may increase the likelihood of diseases such as cholera and malaria.

■ Embankments may cause some wetlands to dry out, leading to a loss of biodiversity.

■ Decreased flooding will reduce the input of fish, which is a major source of protein, especially among the poor.

The rivers of Bangladesh are, in part, controlled by factors beyond the country. There is a delicate balance between the disadvantages that the rivers create, such as death and destruction, and the advantages that the rivers bestow, such as a basis for agriculture and export earnings. To date there has been little agreement as to how to control the peak discharges of the rivers. The Flood Action Plan uses embankments to control the distribution and speed of flooding, although the embankments have, in turn, led to serious social, economic and environmental problems.

1 Study Figure 8.19 which shows the effect of urban development on flooding. Describe and explain the changes in flood frequency and flood magnitude that occur as urbanisation increases.
2 Describe the physical and human factors which have made flooding a problem in Bangladesh and China.
3 Briefly explain the ways in which hazards can be managed.

Stream flow

Stream flow occurs as a result of overland runoff, groundwater springs, from lakes and from meltwater in mountainous or sub-polar environments. The character or **regime** of the resulting stream or river is influenced by several variable factors:

■ the amount and nature of precipitation
■ the local rocks, especially porosity and permeability
■ the shape or morphology of the drainage basin, its area and slope
■ the amount and type of vegetation cover
■ the amount and type of soil cover.

On an annual basis the most important factor determining stream regime is climate. Figure 8.27a shows a simple regime, based upon a single river with one major peak flow. By contrast, Figure 8.27b shows a complex regime for the River Rhine. It has a number of large tributaries which flow in a variety of environments, including alpine, Mediterranean and temperate. By the time the Rhine has travelled downstream it is influenced by many, at times contrasting, regimes.

Stream flow and associated features of erosion are complex. The velocity and energy of a stream are controlled by:

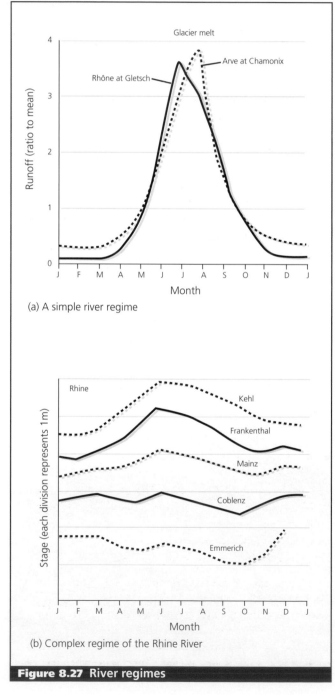

(a) A simple river regime

(b) Complex regime of the Rhine River

Figure 8.27 River regimes

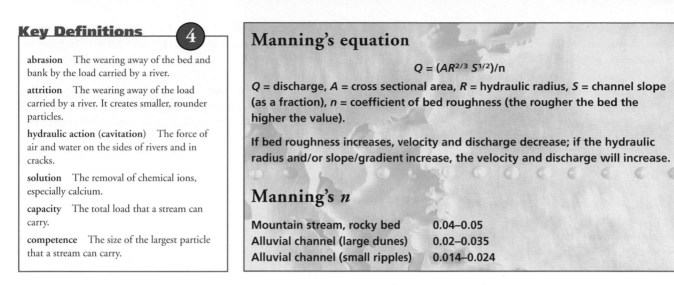

Key Definitions — (4)

abrasion The wearing away of the bed and bank by the load carried by a river.

attrition The wearing away of the load carried by a river. It creates smaller, rounder particles.

hydraulic action (cavitation) The force of air and water on the sides of rivers and in cracks.

solution The removal of chemical ions, especially calcium.

capacity The total load that a stream can carry.

competence The size of the largest particle that a stream can carry.

Manning's equation

$$Q = (AR^{2/3} S^{1/2})/n$$

Q = discharge, A = cross sectional area, R = hydraulic radius, S = channel slope (as a fraction), n = coefficient of bed roughness (the rougher the bed the higher the value).

If bed roughness increases, velocity and discharge decrease; if the hydraulic radius and/or slope/gradient increase, the velocity and discharge will increase.

Manning's n

Mountain stream, rocky bed	0.04–0.05
Alluvial channel (large dunes)	0.02–0.035
Alluvial channel (small ripples)	0.014–0.024

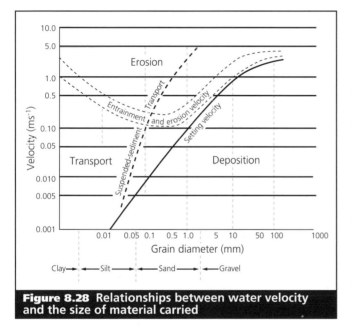

Figure 8.28 Relationships between water velocity and the size of material carried

- the gradient of the channel bed
- the volume of water within the channel, which is controlled largely by precipitation in the drainage basin (e.g. 'bankfull' gives rapid flow whereas low levels give lower flows);
- the shape of the channel
- channel roughness, including friction.

There are two main types of flow: laminar and turbulent. For **laminar** flow a smooth, straight channel with a low velocity is required. This allows water to flow in sheets or laminae parallel to the channel bed. It is rare in reality and most commonly occurs in the lower reaches. However, it is more common in groundwater and in glaciers when one layer of ice moves over another.

Turbulent flow occurs where there are higher velocities and complex channel morphology such as a meandering channel with alternating pools and riffles. Turbulence causes marked variations in pressure within the water. As the turbulent water swirls (eddies) against the bed or bank of the river, air is trapped in pores, cracks and crevices and put under great pressure. As the eddy swirls away, pressure is released, the air expands suddenly, creating a small explosion which weakens the bed or bank material. Thus turbulence is associated with hydraulic action (cavitation).

Vertical turbulence creates hollows in the channel bed. Hollows may trap pebbles which are then swirled by eddying, grinding at the bed. This is a form of vertical corrasion or abrasion and given time may create potholes. Cavitation and vertical abrasion may help to deepen the channel, allowing the river to downcut its valley. If the downcutting is dominant over the other forms of erosion (i.e. vertical erosion exceeds lateral erosion) then a gulley or gorge will develop.

Factors affecting erosion

- **Load** The heavier and sharper the load the greater the potential for erosion.
- **Velocity** The greater the velocity the greater the potential for erosion (Figure 8.28).
- **Gradient** Increased gradient increases the rate of erosion.
- **Geology** Soft, unconsolidated rocks such as sand and gravel are easily eroded.
- **pH** Rates of solution are increased when the water is more acidic.
- **Human impact** Deforestation, dams and bridges interfere with the natural flow of a river and frequently end up increasing the rate of erosion.

It is possible to convert a value of mean annual sediment and solute load to an estimate of the rate of lowering of land surfaces by fluvial denudation. This gives a combined sediment and solute load of 250 tonnes per km² per year (i.e. an annual rate of lowering of the order of 0.1 mm per year). There is a great deal of variation in sediment yields. These range from 10 tonnes per km² per year in such areas as northern Europe and parts of Australia to in excess of 10 000 tonnes per km² per year in certain areas where conditions are especially conducive to high rates of erosion (Figure 8.29). These include Taiwan, South Island New Zealand and the Middle Hwang He Basin in China. In the two former cases steep slopes, high rainfall and tectonic instability are major influences whilst in the latter case the deep loess deposits and the almost complete lack of natural vegetation cover are important. Rates of land surface lowering associated with this component of fluvial transport can be seen as varying over more than three orders of magnitude from less than 0.004 mm per year to in excess of 4 mm per year. The broad pattern of global suspended sediment is shown in the diagram and it reflects the influence of a wide range of factors including climate, relief, geology, vegetation cover and land use.

Information on the dissolved loads of rivers at the global scale is less complete than that available for suspended sediment. Existing knowledge suggests loads ranging from less than 1 tonne per km² per year to approximately 500 tonnes per km² per year. These values are somewhat lower than those associated with suspended sediment transport and, if total material transport from the land surface of the earth to the oceans is considered, the value for suspended sediment, which is in the order of 15×10^9 tonnes per year, exceeds that for dissolved material (see 4×10^9 tonnes per year) by nearly four times. As a global generalisation the relative efficiency of mechanical and chemical fluvial denudation could, therefore, be seen as being in the ratio of 4 to 1.

Gorge development is common, for example, where the local rocks are resistant to weathering but more susceptible to the more powerful river erosion. Similarly, in arid areas where the water necessary for weathering is scarce, gorges are formed by episodes of fluvial erosion. A rapid acceleration in downcutting also occurs when a river is rejuvenated, again creating a gorge-like landscape. Gorges may also be formed as a result of:

- **antecedent drainage (Rhine Gorge)**
- **glacial overflow channelling (Newtondale)**
- **collapse of underground caverns in carboniferous limestone areas (River Axe at Wookey Hole)**
- **periglacial runoff (Cheddar)**
- **retreat of waterfalls (Niagara)**.

Plunge flow occurs where the river spills over a sudden change in gradient, undercutting rocks by hydraulic impact and abrasion, thereby creating a waterfall (Figure 8.30). There are many reasons for this sudden change in gradient along the river:

- **a band of resistant strata (the resistant limestones at Niagara Falls)**
- **a plateau edge (Livingstone Falls)**
- **a fault scarp (Gordale)**
- **a hanging valley (Glencoyne, Cumbria)**
- **coastal cliffs (Kimmeridge Bay, Dorset)**.

The undercutting at the base of the waterfall creates a precarious overhang which will ultimately collapse. Thus a waterfall may migrate upstream, leaving a gorge of recession downstream. The Niagara Gorge is 11 km long due to the retreat of Niagara Falls.

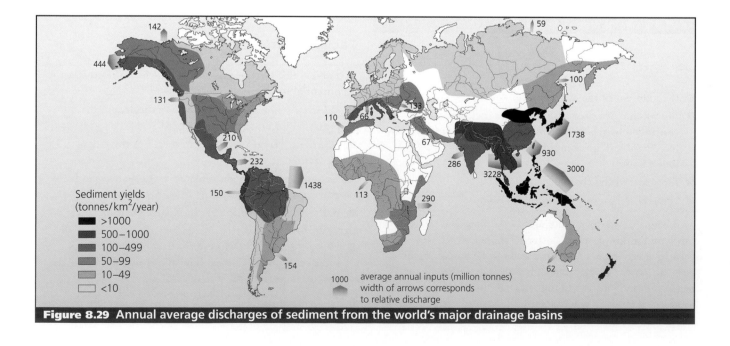

Figure 8.29 Annual average discharges of sediment from the world's major drainage basins

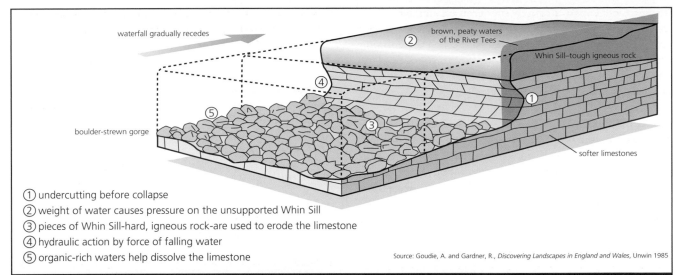

① undercutting before collapse
② weight of water causes pressure on the unsupported Whin Sill
③ pieces of Whin Sill-hard, igneous rock-are used to erode the limestone
④ hydraulic action by force of falling water
⑤ organic-rich waters help dissolve the limestone

Source: Goudie, A. and Gardner, R., *Discovering Landscapes in England and Wales*, Unwin 1985

Figure 8.30 Waterfall formation, Teesdale

Figure 8.31 The Victoria Falls

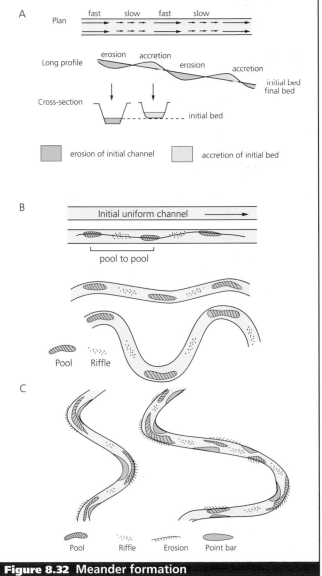

Figure 8.32 Meander formation

Horizontal turbulence often takes the form of **helicoidal flow**, a 'corkscrewing' motion. This is associated with the presence of alternating pools and riffles in the channel bed, and where the river is carrying large amounts of material. The erosion and deposition by helicoidal flow creates meanders (Figure 8.32).

Traditionally the study of meanders focused upon their shape and their role in the evolution of a river valley. The processes involved received little attention. Initial process measurements focused on the rates of development as a surrogate for the processes, but increasing concern for mechanics and models has now generated a greatly improved understanding of the hydraulics of meanders, even if the factors ultimately responsible for them remain unclear.

Meanders occur as the top current impinges against the channel bank, undercutting it and causing bank caving. This leaves river cliffs at the channel edge. As the water heaps up against this bank area, a bottom or subsidiary current develops carrying energy and material to the opposite bank but slightly downstream. Thus a corkscrew motion is established. Immediately opposite the area of bank caving there will be an area of slow-moving water where deposition occurs, forming a slip-off slope. Hence, as one bank area is being eroded, the opposite bank area is being built out – thus a meander is allowed to develop, with a characteristic asymmetric cross-section.

Once established, a meandering pattern is self-perpetuating. As a result, the meanders become accentuated (i.e. the amplitude of the bends is increased) sometimes to such an extent that the meander swings round almost to meet itself, leaving only a 'swan neck' of land between. The flow round this accentuated meander becomes increasingly tortuous and only a slight increase in volume or velocity will cause the water to flood the swan's neck, eroding a new, straighter channel, and abandoning the meander as an ox-bow lake (cutoff). Eventually, this ox-bow lake will silt up and be colonised by marshland vegetation.

As well as the change in amplitude, there is a change over time, in the wavelength of the meander. This increase in wavelength will cause (a) the trimming of the intervening spurs and bluffs lying alongside the channel; (b) the erosion and reworking of the slip-off slope and other deposited material and (c) the apparent shift or migration of the meander downstream.

These changes in the dimensions of the meanders allow the river to cut a trough-like area, with the meanders swinging from side to side, filling the flood plain. Gradually this trough will be enlarged by meander development, while the bluffs at the sides of the flood plain will be degraded by weathering and

other surface processes of erosion. Thus gradually, the river will meander freely over the extensive plain.

Transport

Erosion by the river will provide loose material. This eroded material (plus other weathered material that has moved downslope from the upper valley sides) is carried by the river as its load. The load is transported downstream in a number of ways (Figure 8.33):

■ the smallest particles (silts and clays) are carried in suspension as the **suspended load**

■ larger particles (sands, gravels, small stones) are transported in a series of 'hops' as the **saltated load**

■ pebbles are shunted along the bed as the **bed or tracted load**

■ in areas of calcareous rock, material is carried in solution as the **dissolved load**.

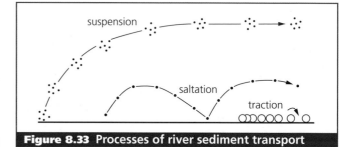

Figure 8.33 Processes of river sediment transport

The Yellow River

The Hwang He (Yellow River) is one of the world's greatest rivers. The river drains an area of over 750 000 km², in which a population of 84 million people live, farming 13 million ha of land (Figure 8.34a). It is called the Yellow River because of the large amount of yellow wind-blown sediment (known as loess) that it erodes and deposits (Figure 8.34b). The combination of this easily eroded material and the seasonal flow of the river cause great problems for the people who live in the lower parts of the catchment.

The Hwang He varies greatly on its course from its source in Guzunglie Basin in the Qinghai province. The area is a cold plateau at an altitude of 5000 m. It produces a stream which is clear and a valley that is narrow and shallow. As it flows over solid rock

(bedrock) it carves a meandering channel, sometimes with deep gorges.

In its middle stages the river flows across yellow loess deposits rather than solid rock. In some places the loess deposits are over 300 m thick. The combination of the seasonal flow of the river and the highly erodable nature of the loess give rise to the extremely high rates of erosion and transport by the river. As the river flows through the loess plateau rates of erosion increase dramatically.

The Hwang He then flows north through desert. As a result, discharge and rates of erosion decrease. Here the river is said to be braided and consists of wide channels separated by islands in the river.

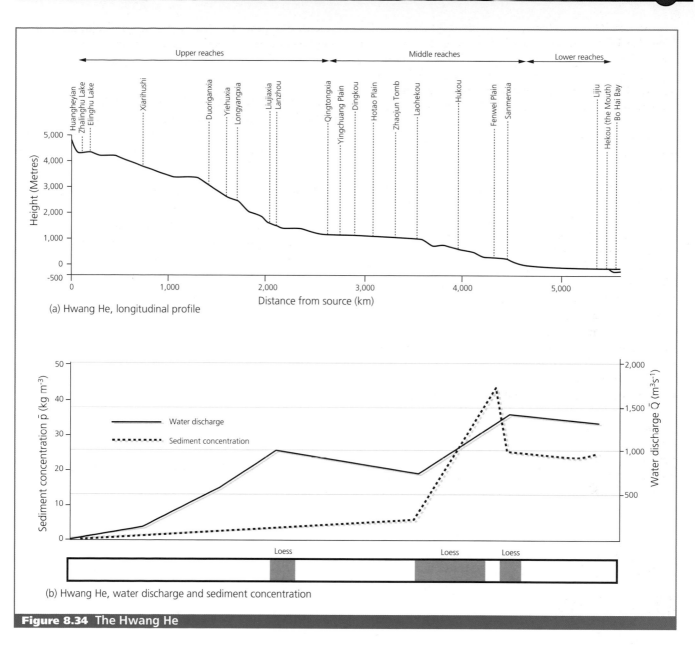

(a) Hwang He, longitudinal profile

(b) Hwang He, water discharge and sediment concentration

Figure 8.34 The Hwang He

As the river flows south into a wetter region it again flows across thick beds of loess. Rates of erosion increase dramatically. In some parts, such as near Yulin close to the Great Wall of China, up to 25 000 tonnes of loess are eroded per km²!

The sediment that the river carries has its advantages. First, much of it is fertile soil and can be used for farming. Second, where the deposits have been dropped on the coastal plains they have formed a large alluvial fan, with a delta at the sea. The area houses over 10 million people, with population density of over 500 per km². It also contains a dense network of communications systems and many towns, forming the industrial base of northern China.

The river has been used extensively by humans. There is a huge potential for hydro-electric power, much of which is in the upper part of the river where sediment loads are low. By the mid-1980s over 150 reservoirs had been built and power stations were added to 80 of these.

Questions

1 Why is the Hwang He also called the Yellow River?
2 Study Figure 8.34 which shows rates of erosion. How do rates of erosion vary with (a) geology and (b) the amount of water in the river?

Deposition

There are a number of causes of deposition such as:

- a shallowing of gradient which decreases velocity and energy
- a decrease in the volume of water in the channel
- an increase in the friction between the water and the channel.

Many types of deposition are found along the course of a river. **Piedmont alluvial fans and cones** (Figure 8.35) are found in semi-arid areas where swiftly flowing mountain streams enter a main valley or plain at the foot of the mountains. There is a sudden decrease in velocity causing deposition. Fine material is spread out as an alluvial fan with a nearly flat surface, under 1° gradient. By contrast, coarse material forms a relatively small, steep-sided alluvial cone, with a slope angle of up to

15°. These features are also common in glaciated areas at the edges of major troughs, particularly at the base of hanging valleys. However, they are much smaller than their semi-arid counterparts.

Piedmont alluvial plains are formed in semi-arid and glaciated areas when streams emerging from mountains are closely spaced. Each stream may deposit a cone or fan. These features may enlarge and join up to form an alluvial plain, such as in the Central Valley of California. In semi-arid areas this type of deposit is known as a **bajada** deposit.

Riffles are small ridges of material deposited where the river velocity is reduced midstream, in between pools (the deep parts of a meander). If many such ridges are deposited, the river is said to be 'braided'. On the inner bends of meanders, water flow is slack and **slip-off slopes** are deposited.

Levées and **flood plain deposits** are formed when a river bursts its banks over a long period of time. Water quickly loses velocity, leading to the rapid deposition of coarse material (heavy and difficult to move a great distance) near the channel edge. These coarse deposits build up to form embankments (**levées**). The finer material is carried further away to be dropped on the **flood plain**, sometimes creating **backswamps**.

In estuaries, there is a constant mixing of fresh river water and saline sea water. When the tide is flowing in, the river flow is slowed down, losing energy. The mixing of the waters results in a chemical reaction that causes the salts and clays (the suspended load) to clot together (a process known as **flocculation**) and become too heavy for further transport. Thus the flocculated material is deposited as **mud-flats** or **mudbanks**, uncovered at low tide and dissected by many creeks. If the mud-flats are built up, they may become colonised by marshland plants to create salt marsh (see pages 305–9). The non-clay load is carried a little further seaward to the outer estuary and then deposited as sandbanks.

Deltas

Deltas are river sediments deposited when a river enters a standing body of water such as a lake, a lagoon, a sea or an ocean (Figure 8.36). They are the result of the interaction of fluvial and marine processes. For a delta to form there must be a heavily laden river, such as the Nile or the Mississippi, and a

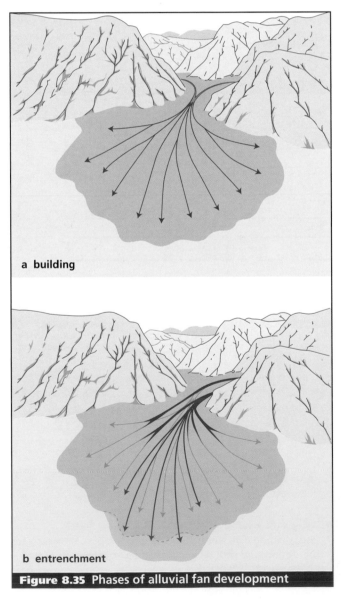

a building

b entrenchment

Figure 8.35 Phases of alluvial fan development

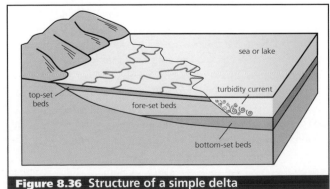

Figure 8.36 Structure of a simple delta

standing body of water with negligible currents, such as the Mediterranean or the Gulf of Mexico. Deposition is enhanced if the water is saline: since salty water causes small clay particles to flocculate. Other factors include the type of sediment, local geology, sea level changes, plant growth and human impact.

The material deposited as a delta can be divided into three types:

1 **Bottom-set beds**   The lower parts of the delta are built outwards along the sea floor by turbidity currents (currents of water loaded with material). These beds are composed of fine material.

2 **Fore-set beds**   Inclined layers of coarse material are deposited over the bottom-set beds. Each bed is deposited above and in front of the previous one, the material moving by rolling and saltation. Thus the delta is built seaward.

3 **Top-set beds**   Composed of fine material, they are really part of the continuation of the river's flood plain. These top-set beds are extended and built up by the work of numerous distributaries (the main river has split into several smaller channels).

The character of any delta is influenced by the complex interaction of several variables:

■ the rate of river deposition
■ the rate of stabilisation by vegetation growth
■ tidal currents
■ the presence or absence of longshore drift
■ human activity (deltas often form prime farmland when drained).

There are many delta types, but the three 'classics' are (Figure 8.37):

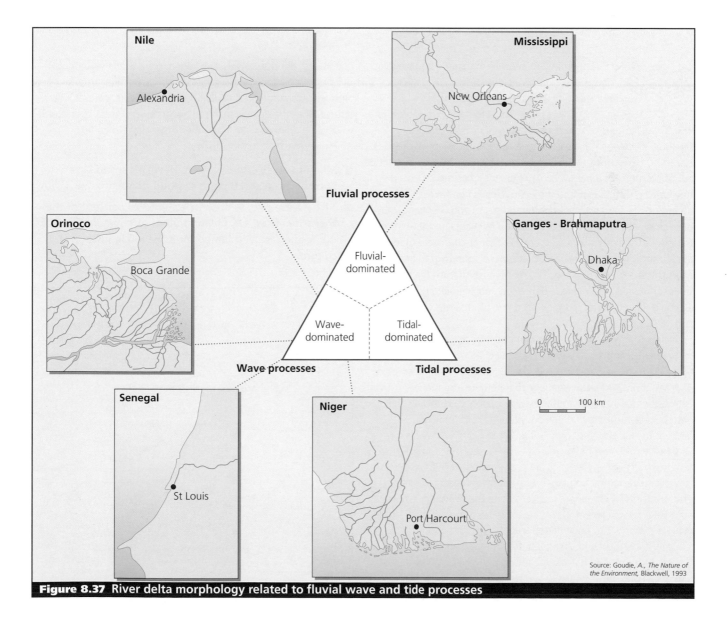

Source: Goudie, A., *The Nature of the Environment*, Blackwell, 1993

Figure 8.37 River delta morphology related to fluvial wave and tide processes

- **arcuate** Fan-shaped; these are found in the areas where regular longshore drift of other currents keep the seaward edge of the delta trimmed and relatively smooth in shape, such as the Nile and Rhone deltas.

- **cuspate** Pointed like a tooth or cusp, for example the Ebro and Tiber deltas, shaped by regular but opposing, gentle water movement.

- **bird's foot** Where the river brings down enormous amounts of fine silt, deposition can occur in a still sea area, along the edges of the distributaries for a vast distance offshore such as the Mississippi delta.

Deltas can also be formed inland. When a river enters a lake it will deposit some or all of its load, so forming a **lacustrine delta**. As the delta builds up and out, it may ultimately fill the lake basin. The largest lacustrine deltas are those which are being built out into the Caspian Sea by the Volga, Ural, Kura and other rivers.

Managing the changing Mississippi Delta

 Deltas are difficult areas to manage. The Mississippi (Figure 8.38) illustrates this clearly. The delta covers an area of 26 000 km², drains an area of 3 220 000 km² and carries 520 km³ of water and 450 million tonnes of sediment into the Gulf of Mexico every year. Much of the sediment is carried in suspension, 210 million tonnes. About 40 per cent of the load is silt and 50 per cent clay. The silt is deposited to form a bar up to 7 m high whereas the clay is transported further out into the delta. Deposition takes place during floods forming levées and flood plains and is enhanced by biological activities, notably colonisation by plants and the trapping of sediment by vegetation. Sediment-charged waters break through the natural levées (**crevasse splaying**) to find shorter steeper routes, a process known as **avulsion**, the channel splits (bifurcates), sediment is deposited and the delta grows; for example, distributaries in West Bay grew 16 km between 1839 and 1875.

Deltas follow a cycle of development. This may take anything between 100 and 1000 years. First, new channels are created due to crevasse splays. Sediment is deposited and new land is created. As a result of changes in gradient channels are abandoned, deposition declines and a new area is developed. However, this pattern is disrupted by human activities. According to some geographers, if the Mississippi were left to her own devices a new channel would have been created by the mid-1970s, so much so that the ports at New Orleans and Baton Rouge would be defunct. However, river protection schemes have prevented this. For example, at New Orleans 7-m levées flank the river and 3-m levées abut Lake Pontchartrain. New Orleans is 1.5 m below the average river level and 5.5 m below flood level!

The Mississippi Delta is retreating at rates of up to 25 m per annum (Figure 8.39). It accounts for 40 per cent of US wetlands, and over 100 km² of wetlands are being lost each year. The cause of the delta's decline is a mixture of natural and artificial conditions: rising sea levels, subsidence (due to the weight of the delta on the earth's crust), groundwater abstraction, tropical storms and changes in the location of deposition. Increasingly, it appears that the delta is trying to abandon its current course and to develop a new course along the Atchafalaya Channel.

Flood relief measures include:

- Bonnet Carre Waterway from New Orleans to Lake Pontchartrain and then to the Gulf of Mexico.

- Atchafalaya river which carries up to 25 per cent of the Mississippi flow, 135 million tonnes of sediment (but this is a fertile area and famed for its bayou landscape and culture).

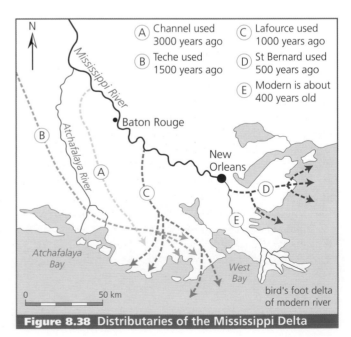

Figure 8.38 Distributaries of the Mississippi Delta

■ Dredging of the Atchafalaya and Mississippi rivers.

■ Morganza floodway between Mississippi and Atchafalaya.

Figure 8.39 The Mississipi Delta

The river course – long and cross profiles

The long profile of a river is the gradient of the channel bed from source to mouth (Figure 8.40 and Figure 8.34). From an intensive study of long profiles in rivers, W. M. Davis proposed that the long profile is attained after a long period of time, during which the river's activities change (in time and place), creating a slope/profile and an associated velocity that allows erosion and deposition to be exactly balanced, that is **equilibrium** is reached and the profile is **graded** to the lowest level (base level), which is usually sea level. Near the source of the river (the upper course) erosion is limited because the volume of water in the channel and the load are small. Erosion is also limited near the mouth (the lower course) because the river is heavily laden and much energy is expanded on transport. In a relative sense, therefore, erosion is at a maximum in the middle course. Thus, the graded profile of a river is typically concave.

In recent years, considerable criticism has been made of this concept of 'grade'. Such a graded profile may never be achieved by some rivers for a number of reasons. These include:

■ the presence of local base levels
■ changes in the general activity of the river by rejuvenation.

Waterfalls and lake basins form important local base levels. However, many of these are only temporary interruptions in the long profile. For example, waterfalls may retreat and lakes

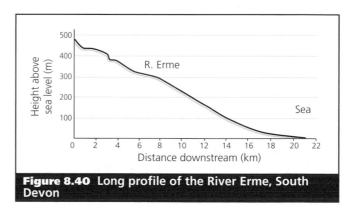

Figure 8.40 Long profile of the River Erme, South Devon

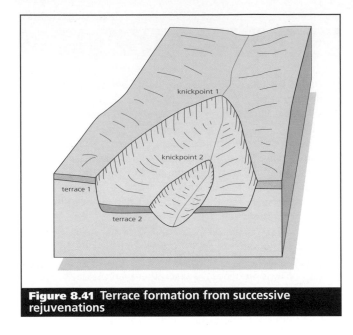

Figure 8.41 Terrace formation from successive rejuvenations

may fill. Sediment is deposited in the lake as a lacustrine delta which gradually enlarges to fill the lake. Meanwhile, the outflowing water will accelerate down the steeper slope downstream of the basin, causing headward erosion at the outlet. Both processes will cause the lake and local base level to disappear.

Rejuvenation can seriously interrupt the attainment of a graded profile (Figure 8.41). It causes the river to increase its downcutting activity. Rejuvenation is caused by:

■ **tectonic activity (folding, faulting, uplift, subsidence, tilting) causing dynamic rejuvenation**

■ **an increase in the volume of water in the drainage system, due to**

   (a) an increase in precipitation in the catchment area due to climatic change, or

   (b) the result of river capture

■ **changes in base level (either sea level falls or the land rises) due to**

   (a) eustatic fall in sea level (a worldwide fall in sea level) as in the Pleistocene Ice Age when water was 'locked up' as ice on the land; or

   (b) an isostatic change in the level of the land (the local uplift of the land, in late and post-glacial times as a result of the ice melting, relieving pressure on the land).

Rejuvenation has affected the vast majority of rivers throughout the world. As the last major period of rejuvenation has occurred in recent geological time, its effects can still be clearly seen in fluvial landscapes. Indeed, some areas that were heavily glaciated are still experiencing rejuvenation and landscape change.

Features associated with rejuvenation include knick points,

river terraces and incised meanders. With the fall in base level, the seaward end of the river will fall over a sharp change in gradient, creating a waterfall. The sudden change in gradient is called a **knickpoint**. As with ordinary waterfalls, the plunging water will cause the river to retreat upstream. If stability continues for a long time, the knickpoint may retreat to the river source, creating a profile 'graded' to the new lower base level.

Rejuvenation causes the river to cut down, leaving portions of the former flood plain untouched and upstanding as **terraces**. These paired terraces will converge at the associated knickpoint. In one period of rejuvenation, one knickpoint and one pair of terraces will be created. However, there are often cycles of rejuvenation, creating a series of knickpoints and terraces. This is known as polycyclic relief (i.e. many cycles of rejuvenation).

Incised meanders are formed where the meander pattern of the river is maintained as the river increases its downcutting. There are two types of incised meander, ingrown and entrenched. In an ingrown meander downcutting is slow. As the incision of the river continues, there is time for the ordinary processes of meander development and migration to operate. Hence, greatly enlarged river cliffs (bluffs) and slip-off slopes are created, and the meander has an asymmetric cross-section as with normal meanders. By contrast, entrenched meanders occur where downcutting is so rapid that meander migration is not allowed. Thus the river cuts more of a winding gorge with a symmetric cross-section. Incised meanders are well developed along the course of the River Wye (Figure 8.42).

As the long profile changes, so does the cross profile. The general characteristics of this cross profile are controlled by:

■ **the type and rate of river activity**

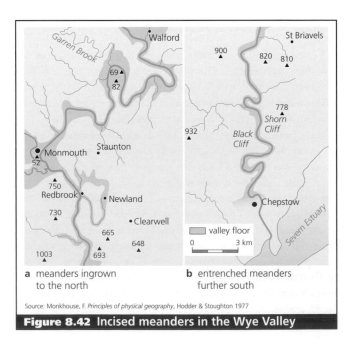

a meanders ingrown to the north   **b** entrenched meanders further south

Source: Monkhouse, F. *Principles of physical geography*, Hodder & Stoughton 1977

Figure 8.42 Incised meanders in the Wye Valley

Figure 8.43 Data response: downstream changes in a river

Site	1	2	3	4	5
Gradient	1:8	1:14	1:26	1:45	1:85
Width (m)	1.3	1.6	2.4	4.1	8.3
Depth (m)	0.7	1.1	1.4	1.9	2.6
Velocity (cm/sec)	13	16	21	28	34
Discharge	...	...	...	...	...
Bedload size (cm)	25	21	12	7	2
and shape	Angular	Angular	Subangular	Rounded	Rounded
Cross-sectional area	...	...	...	...	...

Questions

1 Study figure 8.43. Describe how the ratio of width/depth varies with distance from the source of the river.
2 Work out (a) the cross-sectional area and (b) the discharge of the stream for each site. How and why do these change downstream?
3 Describe the changes in bedload size and shape as you proceed downstream. What processes cause these changes to take place?
4 If the channel between sites 4 and 5 were straightened, what effect would it have on (a) the velocity of the river (b) the load and (c) the work of the river?

- the type and rate of weathering and downslope transport of this weathered material
- local geology.

Davis's Cycle of Erosion

In his *Cycle of Erosion*, W. M. Davis stated that a river's activity would change over time. In the early stages the river would be 'youthful' engaged primarily in cutting narrow, V-shaped valleys into the general land level. In the middle part of the time cycle, the river begins to 'mature', eroding and depositing material, while the action of weathering etc. has begun to open up the valley sides, generally subduing the relief. In the last stage of the cycle, the river becomes more sluggish ('senile'), flowing over the land that has become degraded by other agents of weathering and erosion. These three stages are, according to Davis, reflected in the long and cross profiles of many rivers: the upper reaches reflect the 'youthful' stage, the middle reaches the 'mature' stage, while the lower reaches reflect the 'senile' stage.

The terms upper, middle and lower course are generally preferred to Davis's terms youthful, mature and senile.

There are a number of reasons for this preference:

- erosion occurs in the lower course as well as the upper course of a river
- deposition occurs in the upper course as well as the lower course of a river
- the river is the same 'age' in the upper and lower courses.

Drainage patterns in drainage basins

Each river/drainage system is contained within a **drainage basin** or catchment area. Neighbouring systems are separated by a drainage divide or **watershed**. Some watersheds are major such as the Western Cordillera in North America and the continuation into South America as the Andes, while others are much smaller in scale. These smaller divides are often modified by the erosional activity of the headwaters of the streams within the catchment areas. In some places, active headward erosion may even breach the divide leading to river capture (Figure 8.44).

River capture

Since both systems on either side of a divide are constantly at work modifying the divide by headward erosion, the divide may migrate towards one or the other, eventually leading to breaching. The possibility of river capture will depend upon a number of factors:

- the relative power of erosion of the two systems
- the relative amount of precipitation in each of the basins (more precipitation leads to more energy)
- the geological structure of each basin and the resistance of the local rocks
- human activity such as deforestation in one catchment.

Some form of river capture is almost certain to occur anywhere, since it is highly unlikely that two adjacent systems will experience identical conditions. For one reason or another, one system will dominate the other. River capture is common in Wales, for example the capture of the upper Teifi by first the Ystwyth and then the Rheidol.

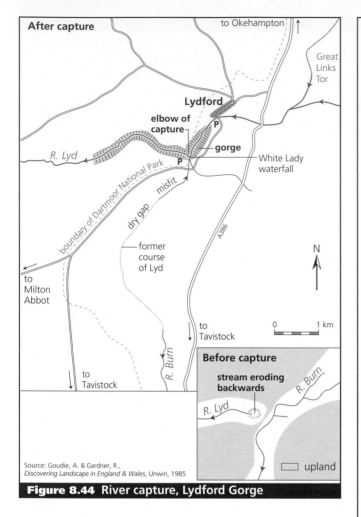

After capture

to Okehampton

Great Links Tor

Lydford

elbow of capture P

R. Lyd

P

gorge

White Lady waterfall

boundary of Dartmoor National Park

misfit

dry gap

A386

— former course of Lyd

to Milton Abbot

N

to Tavistock

0   1 km

R. Burn

to Tavistock

Before capture

stream eroding backwards

R. Burn

R. Lyd

☐ upland

Source: Goudie, A. & Gardner, R.,
Discovering Landscape in England & Wales, Unwin, 1985

Figure 8.44 River capture, Lydford Gorge

Classification of drainage patterns

There are various ways of classifying drainage patterns. The most common are by shape of river networks, accordancy with geological and topographic structures, and morphometry (order and plan).

River networks are often described as being dendritic, radial, trellised or centrapetal drainage systems (Figure 8.45). In a **dendritic** system a number of main streams flow directly down the slope of the original land surface. These are known as consequent streams. In a basin of similar geology, each consequent stream will receive a number of tributaries flowing in at an oblique angle. These are, in turn, fed by smaller tributaries, and so on. The resulting pattern is described as 'dendritic' (from the Greek *Dendros* – a tree).

By contrast, if the basin is composed of a variety of rocks (heterogeneous geology), then the rocks and their structure will control the development of the drainage system. For example, the land is tilted seaward creating a gentle slope. The local rocks, though, are varied and alternating bands of hard and soft rock lie at right angles to the general slope. The consequent slope will develop, flowing down the

Dendritic
Irregular branching of channels ("treelike") in many directions. Common in massive rock and in flat-lying strata. In such situations, differences in rock resistance are so slight that their control of the directions in which valleys grow headward is negligible.

Parallel
Parallel or subparallel channels that have formed on sloping surfaces underlain by homogenous rocks. Parellel rills, gullies, or channels are often seen on freshly exposed highway cuts or excavations having gentle slopes.

Radial
Channels radiate out, like spokes of a wheel, from a topologically high area, such as a dome or a volcanic cone.

Rectangular
Channel system marked by right-angle bends. Generally results from the presence of joints and fractures in massive rocks or foliation in metamorphic rocks. Such structures, with their cross-cutting patterns, have guided the directions of valleys.

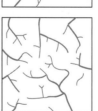

Trellised
Rectangular arrangement of channels in which principal tributary streams are parallel and very long, like vines trained on a trellis. This pattern is common in areas where the outcropping edges of folded sedimentary rocks, both weak and resistant, form long, nearly parallel belts.

Annular
Streams follow nearly circular or concentric paths along belts of weak rock that ring a dissected dome or basin where erosion has exposed successive belts of rock of varying degrees of erodibility.

Centripetal
Streams converge toward a central depression, such as a volcanic crater or caldera, a structural basin, a breached dome, or a basin created by dissolution of carbonate rock.

Deranged
Streams show complete lack of adjustment to underlying structural or lithologic control. Characteristic of recently deglaciated terrain whose preglacial features have been remodelled by glacial processes.

Source: Skinner, J. & Porter, S., *The dynamic earth*, Wiley 1989

Figure 8.45 Stream patterns related to rock type and structure

general slope of the land. Flowing over more resistant beds, this river will cut a narrow, steep-sided reach, while over the softer beds, the valley will be broader. At a later stage, tributary streams will develop in the softer beds, creating wide vales; these later streams are called subsequent streams.

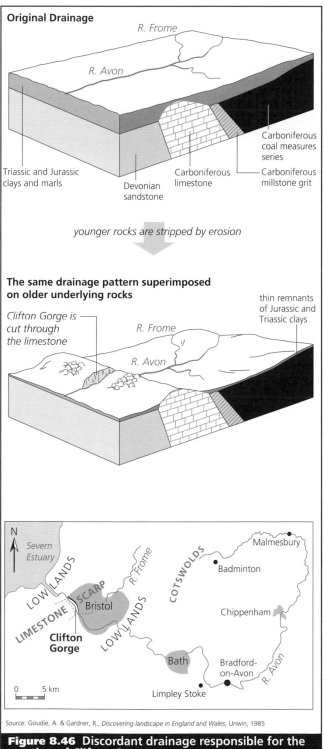

Original Drainage

R. Frome

R. Avon

Carboniferous coal measures series

Triassic and Jurassic clays and marls

Devonian sandstone

Carboniferous limestone

Carboniferous millstone grit

younger rocks are stripped by erosion

The same drainage pattern superimposed on older underlying rocks

Clifton Gorge is cut through the limestone

thin remnants of Jurassic and Triassic clays

R. Frome

R. Avon

N

Severn Estuary

LOWLANDS

LIMESTONE SCARP

Bristol

Clifton Gorge

LOWLANDS

R. Frome

COTSWOLDS

Malmesbury

Badminton

Chippenham

Bath

Bradford-on-Avon

R. Avon

Limpley Stoke

0   5 km

Source: Goudie, A. & Gardner, R., *Discovering landscape in England and Wales*, Unwin, 1985

Figure 8.46 Discordant drainage responsible for the creation of Clifton Gorge

Even later, other smaller tributaries will flow into the subsequents, as secondary subsequents. Thus, a more rectangular drainage pattern emerges. The scarpland landscape of the chalklands of South East England exhibits **trellised** drainage. This type of pattern is closely associated with river capture.

Radial drainage is associated with dome structures, where the consequent streams flow down from the dome centre, radiating outwards. Rivers that flow out from the English Lake District and from the European Alps are good examples of radial drainage. By contrast, **centripetal** drainage occurs where a large number of streams converge from all directions into one main stream.

Drainage networks can also be described in relation to the underlying geology and topography. **Accordant** patterns are rivers which appear to flow with respect to geology and topography. By contrast, **discordant** patterns pay little attention to geology or topography.

Accordant drainage commonly occurs on folded structures, domed structures and faulted structures. The trellis and radial patterns described above are good examples. Discordant patterns show no systematic relationship to the local rocks and their structures (Figure 8.46). Two main types exist – antecedent patterns and superimposed patterns. **Antecedent** patterns are river systems which developed before a period of earth uplift. If the rate of uplift was slow enough, the river could maintain its course. Thus the River Colorado has maintained its course through a series of canyons through the plateaus of the south west United States. **Superimposed** drainage refers to river patterns developed on rock strata which have since been eroded away. For example, the rivers of East Glamorgan in Wales cross the Devonian and Carboniferous rocks at right angles. Similarly, rivers in Hampshire flow south across the east–west folds of the tertiary sediments.

An increasingly popular method of classification is by the rank of the stream or river. Horton's **stream order analysis** defines streams without tributaries (the 'finger-tip' tributaries) as 'first order' streams. Where two first order streams meet, they create a second order and so on (Figure 8.48a). (If a lower order stream meets a high-order stream, the order of the latter remains the same.) The major river of the basin is always of the highest order in the basin. The basin is named after this major river (e.g. a fourth order basin).

Figure 8.48b shows the statistical relationships between stream order and various drainage basin properties. These relationships are often referred to as 'laws' of drainage basin morphology, although it must be emphasised that they are only general trends around which there may be significant variability.

The bifurcation ratio refers to the number of streams of one order relative to the order above e.g. the number of first order streams compared to second order streams, or third order streams relative to fourth order streams. Usually the ratio is between 3 and 5.

Semi-log graphs

Semi-log graph paper has a 'normal' scale on one axis – usually the horizontal axis – and a logarithmic scale on the other axis – usually the vertical axis (Figure 8.50). Semi-log graphs are used to show data which has a wide range of values. For example, it allows us to compare small-scale features with large features. This could not be done in a meaningful way on ordinary graph paper.

The logarithmic scale compresses the range of values. It gives more space to the smaller values and reduces the amount of space for the larger values. Thus it shows relative growth values clearly.

On a semi-log graph, there are 'cycles' of values. Each cycle increases by a larger amount, usually to the power of 10. Thus on Figure 1, the first cycle increases by 1 each time – 1, 2, 3, 4, 5, 6 and so on. The second cycle increases by 10 – 10, 20, 30, 40, 50 and so on. The third cycle increases by 100 and so on.

The vertical axis on a semi-log graph begins at 1 (or some other 1, such as 0.1, 10, 100, 1000). The horizontal axis, however, has a regular scale. Each unit increases by a standard value.

Hints
- If there is more than one feature use different colours for each one.
- Label the axes clearly.
- Label the lines clearly.

In some cases double-log graph paper is used. This means that both scales are logarithmic. The use of double-log graph paper allows us to plot data which contains large and small values.

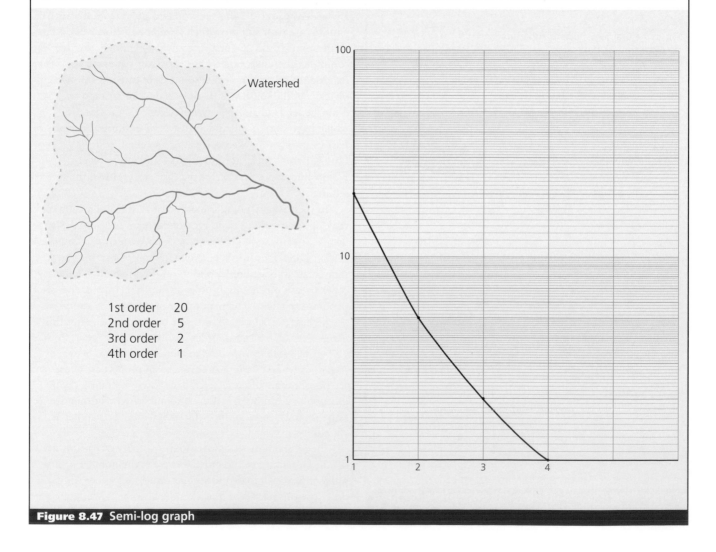

1st order	20
2nd order	5
3rd order	2
4th order	1

Figure 8.47 Semi-log graph

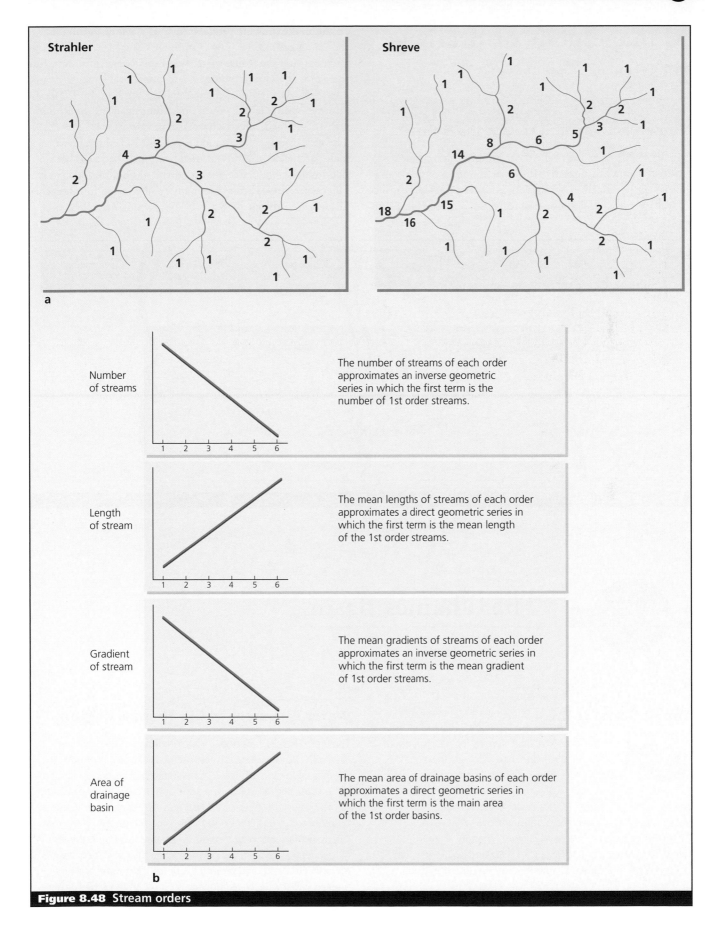

Figure 8.48 Stream orders

Management of drainage basins

Human activity and rivers: the Rhine

The River Rhine is one of the most important rivers in Europe. It flows through five different countries and acts as a line of communication, a reservoir, a source of power, a source of waste removal and a source of recreation and tourism.

Pollution is a growing problem for the 'sewer of Europe' as thousands of factories, power stations, sewage treatment plants and boats use the Rhine to get rid of their waste products. But the Rhine is also developing an additional problem – increased flood risk. As a result of channel modification in the 1950s (to improve hydro-electric power and aid navigation) the Rhine was straightened, effectively creating a new river (Figure 8.49). The new river was faster and deeper, but lacked the flood plains and water meadows which previously had held back flood waters. The result: increased risk of flooding, such as in 1997 when floods across Germany resulted in serious breaches of preventive dykes.

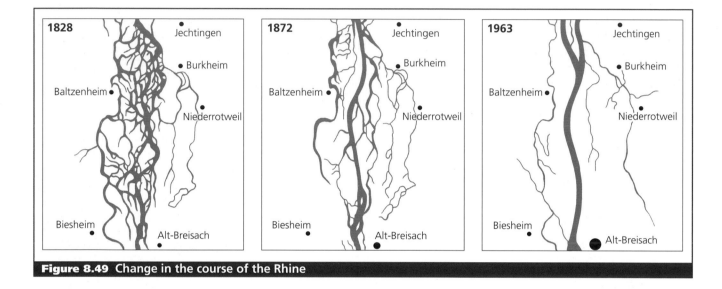

Figure 8.49 Change in the course of the Rhine

The Thames Basin

The national scene

In the UK there is a surplus or over-supply of water in the north and west of the country and a shortage of water in the south and east, especially in the Thames Region which serves almost one-fifth of the nation's population. This pattern is likely to become intensified over the next 20 to 30 years as a result of climatic change. It will become increasingly important to maintain a balance between the needs of the water environment, the demands for water and the supply and development of new water resources.

Water resources in the Thames Region

The River Thames rises near Cirencester and flows eastwards towards Oxford, then south to Reading and east to London. The Thames Basin consists of two main geological sections – an upper basin consisting of Oolitic limestone and a lower basin consisting of mainly tertiary rocks, sands and gravels (Figure 8.50). These two sections join at the Goring Gap, a gap through the Chiltern Hills, where the outcrop of chalk was breached during the last glacial period. Ice from the north blocked the river from flowing towards the Wash, and projections of ice filled some of the preglacial valleys (such as the Vale of St Albans and the Finchley Depression) thereby preventing the Thames from flowing in these routes. As a result the river cut a new route through the solid chalk. Geologically, the area contains much chalk, limestone, sand and gravel, which creates pressure for mineral extraction.

The Thames Region comprises the main drainage basins of the Thames and its tributaries. It is the most developed part of the United Kingdom, with a population of about 12 million. It covers an area of over 13 000 km², and includes 14 counties, 58 district councils and 33 local planning authorities. The Region comprises the main drainage basin of the River Thames and its tributaries such as the Colne, Lee, Kennet, Wey and Loddon, and covers an area of over 12 900 km². Much of the region, particularly in the west is rural in character, where the dominant land use is agriculture. The River Thames and its tributaries are a vital feature of the physical and human landscape: they are important commercial channels, water supply systems, recreation facilities and support high levels of ecological diversity (Figure 8.51).

There are considerable development pressures in the region, and these are likely to increase in the future. Of 25 areas identified as likely to boom before the end of the twentieth century, 9 are in the Thames Region whereas only 1 out of 20 areas was identified as likely to decline in the region. Growth in housing and infrastructure creates additional pressures on the water environment and water resources. For example, in the Thames Region there is a need for more new housing, for development of derelict sites, for mineral extraction, flood defences, a supply of safe drinking water and sustained agricultural yields.

The Thames Region is one of the most intensively managed catchments in the world. Every day approximately 4700 million litres are abstracted from the region's rivers and groundwater. Water falling in the Cotswolds can be used up to eight times before it reaches the Thames Estuary. Overuse of water has had a disastrous effect on some rivers. For example, of the 20 low-flow rivers which have been nationally identified as top priority, 5 are within the Thames Region and another, the River Darent, is closely linked with the London supply system. In addition, the region has seen continued growth in housing and commercial development and mineral extraction increasing pressure on land use, water resources and the water environment generally.

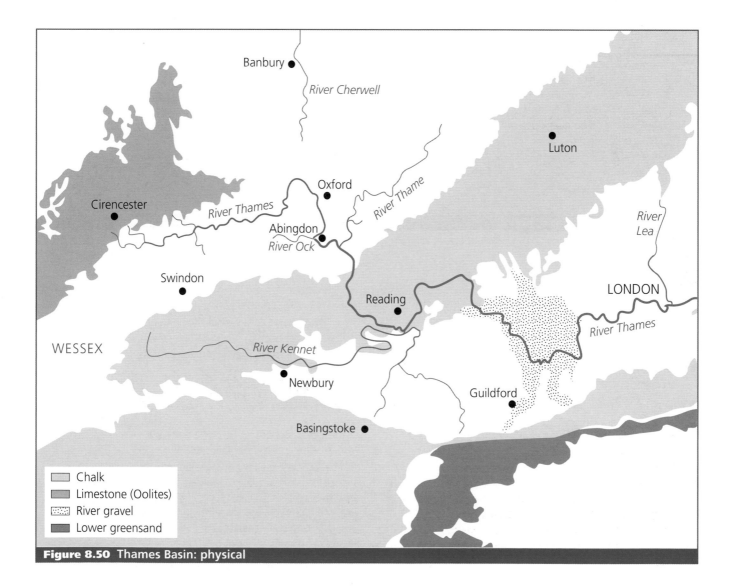

Figure 8.50 Thames Basin: physical

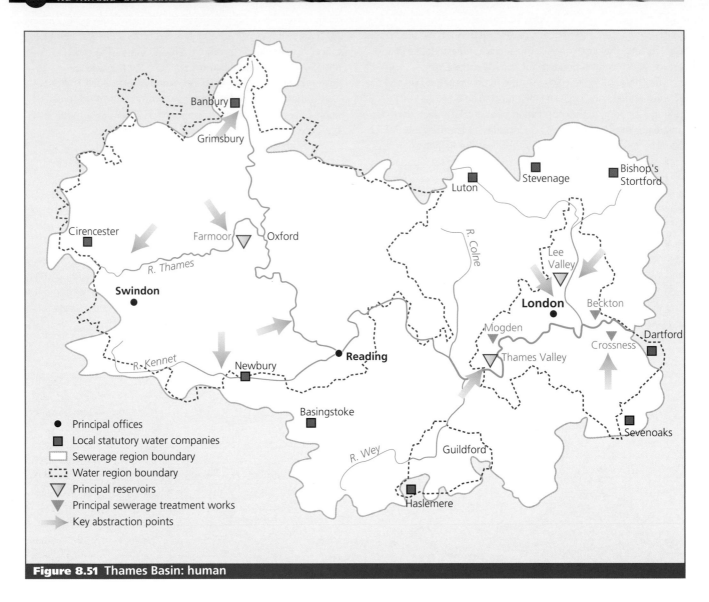

Figure 8.51 Thames Basin: human

The key strategic issues with which the Environment Agency is concerned in the Thames region are:

- the impact of major developments on the water environment and water resources
- the impact of major infrastructure proposals on the water environment
- the effects of discharges on water quality
- the effects of pollution on groundwater
- the impact of mineral extraction on the water environment
- the impact of waste disposal on the water environment.

The Thames hydrological cycle

The Thames Basin has amongst the lowest rainfall in Britain but some of the highest temperatures. This means that

evapotranspiration rates are high and therefore there is a potential deficiency of moisture in summer. Rainfall varies from about 900 mm in the western part of the basin to below 600 mm near London. By contrast, evaporation figures are higher in the east (over 600 mm per annum) compared with the west (about 500 mm per annum).

Water balance

The water balance of a drainage basin is the result of the inputs (precipitation) – the outputs (evapotranspiration). There may also be short-term and long-term changes in the storage capacity of the basin. The water balance can be shown by a simple line graph. Figure 8.52 shows the seasonal patterns of precipitation and evapotranspiration. It is clear that precipitation is higher in winter whereas evapotranspiration is higher in summer. What are the hydrological implications of this pattern?

Figure 8.53 shows annual variations in soil moisture status.

Figure 8.52 Rainfall and evaporation in the Thames Basin

Month	Average rainfall (mm)	Potential evaporation (mm)
January	69.4	5.5
February	48.4	12.7
March	48.3	33.3
April	48.7	55.4
May	59.3	83.9
June	55.2	100.6
July	57.2	97.8
August	71.9	80.0
September	64.6	48.9
October	67.2	22.2
November	78.5	6.5
December	71.6	3.2

Source: Thames Water

Figure 8.54 Rainfall and runoff for the River Thames near Abingdon

	Rainfall (mm) (1938–94 average)	Runoff (mm) (1938–94 average)
January	67	44
February	47	40
March	53	35
April	47	23
May	58	16
June	55	11
July	54	7
August	65	6
September	61	7
October	65	12
November	70	23
December	72	35
Year	714	259

Source: Institute of Hydrology, 1996

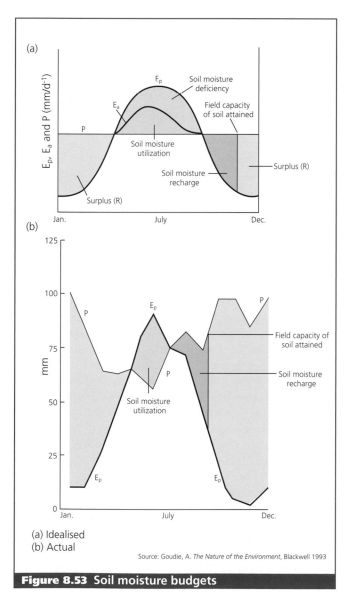

(a) Idealised
(b) Actual

Source: Goudie, A. *The Nature of the Environment*, Blackwell 1993

Figure 8.53 Soil moisture budgets

In January there is a positive water balance. Precipitation exceeds potential evapotranspiration and there is a plentiful store of water supplying groundwater recharge, runoff and plant use. By July potential evapotranspiration exceeds precipitation. The store of water in the soil is being taken up by plants or being evaporated. This stage is known as soil moisture utilisation. Eventually all of the soil moisture has been used up. Any rainfall is likely, therefore, to be absorbed by the soil, although in some cases dry soils may generate flash floods. Then there is still a deficiency of soil moisture. Farm crops will need to be irrigated whereas wild plants will need mechanisms to survive dry conditions. Towards the end of the year precipitation exceeds potential evapotranspiration and there is a net excess of water again. Consequently, the soil is recharged with moisture. Once the soil store is full (field capacity) water will percolate down to the water table.

Runoff from a basin also varies throughout the year. During winter runoff as a percentage of rainfall is high, whereas during the summer months it is low. The figures in Figure 8.54 show the annual variation in runoff and rainfall for the River Thames near Abingdon.

The pattern of flow in the Thames and its tributaries is quite similar. All show a maximum flow in winter and a lower flow in summer. However, there are important variations between the hydrographs (Figure 8.55). This reflects important differences in the characteristics of the streams measured, and whereabouts they are measured. For example, the River Ock, a small tributary of the Thames, flows mainly over impermeable clays through the Vale of the White Horse. Runoff is influenced by groundwater abstractions and return of effluents. By contrast, the River Kennet drains an area four times larger than the Ock. Much of it is on tertiary rocks, sands and gravels. Although there is some abstraction of groundwater, and use of the water for agriculture and industry, the net impact of these is limited. In contrast to both

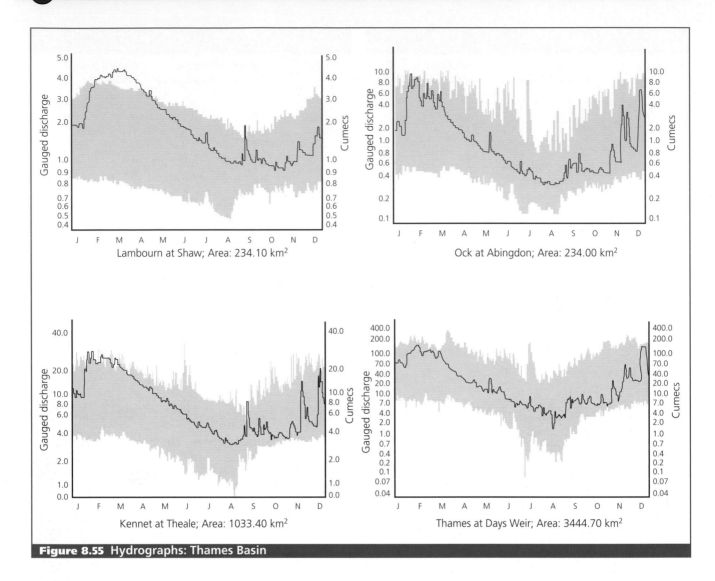

Figure 8.55 Hydrographs: Thames Basin

of these rivers is the Lambourn. This flows mostly over chalk, and consequently has a much lower discharge. The river is maintained by groundwater, as rain water soaks into the porous chalk rather than flowing over its surface.

Changing hydrology of the Thames

The Thames Basin is one of the most intensively managed basins in the world due to the large number of people who live in the Basin and the importance of the river.

There is little doubt that the climate of the Thames is changing. The droughts of 1976 and the 1988–92 droughts are the lowest on record.

The aquifer below London is one of the most important in the country (Figure 8.56). About 25 per cent of the water falling on the permeable chalk of the North and South Downs makes its way to the aquifer below London. This water supplies most of the domestic, industrial and commercial demand. However, demand is changing. Increased demand for water during the nineteenth and

early twentieth centuries caused the water table to drop by as much as 0.7 m per year. In some places the aquifer declined as much as 90 m causing subsidence. In addition, the suburban growth of London led to an increase in the amount of impermeable surfaces and a decline in the infiltration of water into the soil. Hence soil moisture replenishment declined. However, since the 1960s there has been a reduced demand for water. Manufacturing industries have declined or relocated causing groundwater levels to rise. In places the levels have risen by as much as 35 m, and London now has to pump water out to keep the Underground tunnels dry (Figure 8.57).

The effects of rising groundwater include:

■ flooding of basements

■ since 1994 London Underground have spent £18 million on tunnel repairs

■ increased chemical weathering of steel and concrete.

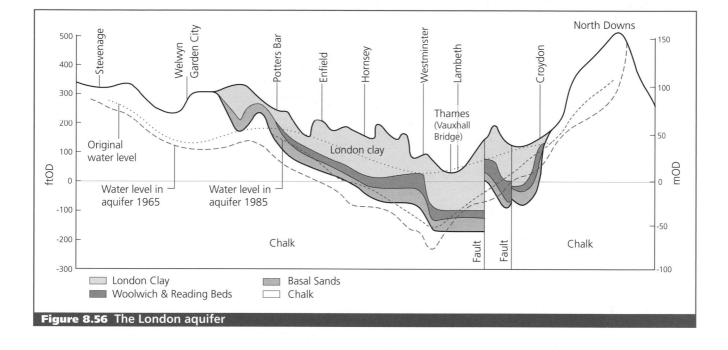

Figure 8.56 The London aquifer

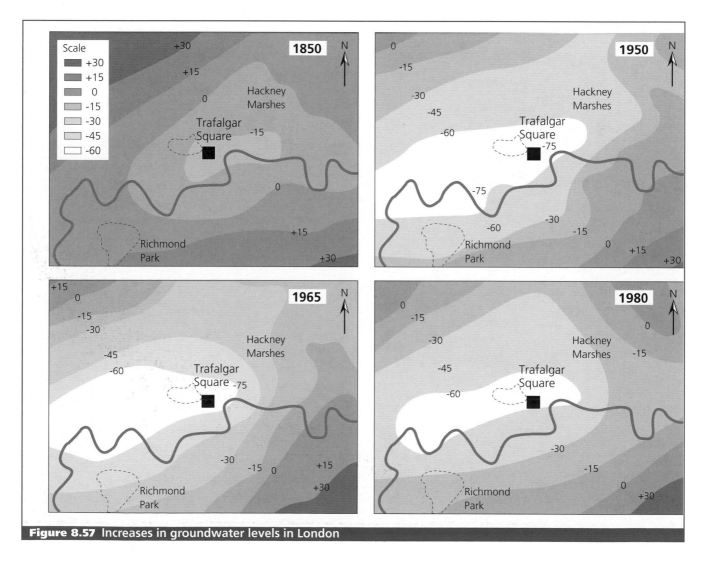

Figure 8.57 Increases in groundwater levels in London

In addition, the South East of Britain is sinking at a rate of about 3 mm per annum or 30 cm per century. Another threat is related to the greenhouse effect. With increased amounts of atmospheric energy the possibility of storm surges increases. Hence the Thames valley is threatened with prospects of an increase in tidal flooding. The Thames Barrier was built to protect London from tidal flooding – between 1982 and 1996 it was closed 26 times.

The succession of hot summers in the 1980s and early 1990s heightened the awareness of water resources in the United Kingdom. Since the Middle Ages there have only been four droughts that have lasted as long as the four-year drought of 1989–92. There have, however, been shorter, more intensive droughts such as those in 1921–2, 1933–4, 1943–4 and 1975–6. Nevertheless, there should be sufficient water to meet the planned level of growth in most areas across the region in the foreseeable future. However, there remain a number of uncertainties in forecasting demand over the next 20 to 30 years.

Groundwater resources

The importance of groundwater in the Thames Region cannot be underestimated. There are hundreds of private, domestic and commercial boreholes and springs in daily use. The total volume of groundwater licensed for abstraction amounts to over 2305 million litres per day of which about 85 per cent is used for potable supply. Water companies in the region operate over 300 public supply sources from groundwater. Groundwater also provides a considerable baseflow component to many rivers, especially in the upper reaches of the catchment.

Approximately two-thirds of the catchment is permeable and thus subject to direct recharge from rainfall. Polluting discharges may also infiltrate into the ground in these areas. Rainfall varies from 850 mm per year in western parts of the catchment to less than 650 mm per year in eastern parts. Rates of recharge to groundwater vary considerably from 524 mm per year in the north-west to 124 mm per year in the east.

In much of the catchment a situation has been reached where there is no remaining capacity for abstraction because of the need to protect streamflows and the valley environment. In some areas over-abstraction has led to reduced flows and the drying up of some groundwater-fed rivers, particularly on the chalk aquifer. Abstraction in proximity to the Thames estuary has resulted in the ingress of saline waters several kilometres inland (Ghyben-Herzburg principle). A notable exception to the above trend is the

Figure 8.58 The Upper Thames

chalk aquifer in the London Basin. The considerable reduction in abstractions since 1970 has resulted in rising groundwater levels. Particular groundwater problems occur.

- Flows in several rivers have been depleted as a result of large groundwater abstractions close to the headwaters or along the river valleys. Worst affected are the rivers Misbourne, Wey, Pang and Letcombe Brook.

- Groundwater has been affected by saline intrusions along the River Thames.

- Most sites which have been considered suitable for waste disposal, landfill and quarries are located on aquifers, for example sand and gravel quarried overlying the chalk aquifer in south Hertfordshire.

- There is continued pressure for redevelopment of former industrial sites many of which occupy prime locations in urban areas. The land is frequently contaminated and there is often associated groundwater pollution with, possibly, considerable pollution potential remaining, especially in areas such as the Thames Gateway.

- Rising nitrate concentrations are evident in other parts of the catchment. In July 1996 the EU criticised the United Kingdom for failing to comply with a 1980 Drinking Water Directive. The country had allowed the level of pesticides in tap water to exceed 0.1 mg/l. Certain parts of the country, especially London and the South East, were affected.

- Other chemicals, such as pesticides, are in widespread usage across the catchment and the frequency of detection in groundwater has risen.

- Groundwater in some urban areas has been contaminated by leakage from sewers and through widespread usage of chemicals such as solvents.

- The EU Groundwater Action Programme aims to improve the integration of water planning into agricultural, industrial and regional planning. Over-exploitation and pollution are widespread. Member states are expected to prepare national programmes to identify, map and protect groundwater resources by the year 2000. In the EU more than 65 per cent of drinking water supplies come from groundwater. Between 1970 and 1985 demand increased by 35 per cent.

Trends in water use

The vast majority of water abstracted in the Region is for drinking water supply. Almost 60 per cent of the water for public consumption comes from surface water supplies, mainly from the Thames and the Lee in association with the major surface storage reservoirs around London. An average of 150 litres are used per person per day in the home, the majority of which is used to flush toilets, take baths and showers and in washing machines.

Water use in the home accounts for 45 per cent of the total public water supply demand. A further 27 per cent of the public water supply is used by industry and commerce. The remainder, 28 per cent across the region, is lost through leakage from distribution and trunk mains systems, and supply pipes on customer premises.

Since the 1970s demand for public water supplies has increased by approximately 1.7 per cent each year. The key factors which have influenced demand are:

- the use of water in the home and garden

- losses through leakage from distribution systems and consumers' plumbing

Figure 8.59 The urban Thames

- population growth and household size

- development pressure and economic activity.

In addition, the main areas of uncertainty regarding water demand and supply are:

- climatic change

- uptake of household appliances and levels of ownership

- the methods of charging for water and the price level adopted

- the effectiveness of demand management measures, particularly control of losses through leakage

- agricultural change.

The trend in growth of demand has been significantly reduced in recent years owing to improvements by water companies in controlling losses, a decline in economic activity within the region and increased awareness and publicity over drought-related issues.

A national strategy for water resources needs must include the following issues:

- Sustainable development – there should be no long-term systematic deterioration of the water environment owing to water resources development or water use.

- Precautionary principle – where significant environmental change may occur but understanding of the issues is incomplete, decisions made or measures implemented should err on the side of caution.

- Managing demand – demand on water resources can be managed by measures to minimise losses, for example through distribution systems and by improved efficiency in water use.

- New schemes – redistribution of water, such as the transfer of Severn/Anglian water to the Thames Region.

For example, in the Thames Region the strategy for future planning and sustainable management of water resources by the Environment Agency (EA) was initially set out by the National Rivers Authority (NRA) in *Future water resources in the Thames Region*. The strategy aims to:

- sustain the natural resource for future use

- provide a flexible framework for the management and development of water resources in the region

- secure proper safeguards for the water environment

- identify opportunities to enhance the water environment, particularly in association with new schemes but also to address existing problems such as low-flow rivers

- respond to reasonable expectations of social and economic development.

The EA has to manage surface water, mineral extractions, sewage capacity, water efficiency and demand, waste disposal, habitat

enhancement and restoration, and research and development. The EA is concerned with the overall policies on water resources, water quality and surface water management, which includes flood defence issues. This is achieved through the licensing of water abstraction, control over discharges and negotiation over granting land drainage consents. The EA has a duty to conserve and enhance the water environment when carrying out any of its functions, and a further duty to promote conservation and enhancement more widely. Increasingly, the way to achieve this is through catchment management plans (CMPs).

The role of catchment management plans

The EA has a nationwide programme for the completion of the first round of CMPs by the end of 1998. CMPs allow integrated planning of the water environment. They identify appropriate threshold levels for acceptable limits to growth at the location in question. CMPs can be achieved only through a partnership between a number of key agencies and organisations. The CMP is a locally based document developed from the discussions of national, regional and local organisations. CMPs are closely connected with local sustainable development plans, Agenda 21s.

Agenda 21 gives a high priority to fresh water, reflecting the management crisis facing the world's fresh water resources. By the year 2000 all states should have national action programmes for water management, based on catchments, and efficient water-use programmes.

For the EA Agenda 21 offers:

- the opportunity to place greater weight on environmental considerations when assessing planning applications

- the opportunity to increase community involvement in water issues

- help to implement CMPs

- the opportunity for integration of land use and water-related issues, leading to full-scale integrated catchment management planning

- additional opportunities to protect the water environment

- increased public awareness of the water environment

- help to identify appropriate environmental indicators.

Managing future demands

Managing the growth in demand will require a combination of methods such as leakage control, selective metering and improvements in water efficiency. Many water-efficient appliances are now available such as low-water-use washing machines, low-flush toilet cisterns and water-wise gardening products. There is also likely to be a change in the demand for water. Demand from the manufacturing industry is likely to decline since the patterns of manufacturing are changing but companies are becoming more efficient at using water. Future agricultural demands depend mainly on changes in agricultural policy. The growth in tourism and recreation will increase the demand for water; for example, the restoration of disused canals may become a pressure on water resources. There are a number of restoration projects currently being considered in the Thames Region.

Recent experience of the promotion of major new water-resource schemes indicates that it can take up to 15 to 20 years from starting feasibility studies to commissioning for a new scheme. The planning of schemes required by the year 2017 should have begun in 1997.

Water resource development options in the Thames Region

A number of options have been considered but rejected, at least for the present, because of financial and/or environmental costs (Figure 8.60):

- use of gravel workings for storage
- redevelopment of existing resources
- fresh water storage in the tidal Thames Estuary
- inter-regional transfers from Wales via the River Wye, Northumbria (Kielder Water) and Scotland
- desalinisation of water.

Options which are carried forward for further evaluation (Figure 8.61) include:

- London basin groundwater including artificial recharge
- inter-regional transfer form the River Severn and the Anglian region.
- reservoir storage in south west Oxfordshire
- re-use of effluents presently discharged into the tidal Thames Estuary
- (riverside) groundwater development opportunities
- reallocation of under-utilised resources.

Figures 8.62 and 8.64 indicate the environmental and cost implications of some of these proposals.

1 London Basin groundwater
The confined chalk aquifer of the London Basin provides an extensive natural storage body which has limited connection with the river systems. During the early part of the twentieth century, water levels in the aquifer in North and Central London fell owing to over-abstraction leaving a large volume of empty aquifer. Since the 1940s abstractions have decreased so that in most parts of London, but especially the central area, water levels are now rising. Artificial recharges during times of surplus, largely in winter, are almost complete in North London and a similar scheme is being investigated for South and Central London. Rising groundwater levels may pose a threat to foundations and tunnels constructed while levels were depressed.

2 Transfers from the River Severn and Anglian Water
There are a number of questions still to be answered. What would be:

- the physical, chemical and ecological implication of transferring and mixing water from the River Severn into the River Thames;
- the security of supplies during periods of naturally low flows;
- the infrastructure and water treatment implications, costs and feasibility of an inter-basin transfer of different river water qualities;
- the potential need for additional reservoir storage in Wales and regulation of the River Severn, and the associated environmental implications?

Development in conjunction with the restoration of the Thames and Severn canal has been ruled out on engineering feasibility and cost grounds.

3 A new reservoir
The NRA proposed a new reservoir for south west Oxfordshire. The plan was for the reservoir to store water from the Thames during high flows and supply the Upper Thames area during low flow. However, changes in demand and the more efficient conservation of water have meant that the project has been deferred, at least for the present. There are a number of issues that need to be considered.

(a) On-site

- pollution risks during construction
- effect of the reservoir on flood risk and drainage
- diversion of water courses
- effect on groundwater levels (leakage from reservoir).

(b) Operational effects

- the physical, chemical and ecological implications of abstraction from the Thames
- maintaining reservoir water quality in terms of oxygen, algal and temperature characteristics
- low flow effects.

(c) Benefits

- security of water resources
- restoration of the Wiltshire–Berkshire canal.

4 Re-use of water
A number of possibilities exist:

- recycling by industry and power generation
- possible 'grey-water' uses (water which may be recycled or treated to a lower level than drinking water); for example, use for flushing toilets or outside uses (car washes, gardens, sports grounds and irrigation)

Figure 8.60 Rejected water resource development options

Option	Yield	Cost	Environmental impact	Reasons for rejection
Fresh water storage in the tidal Thames estuary i.e. Thames Barrier as a barrage	up to 200 Ml/d	MOD–HIGH	HIGH	■ rise in groundwater levels could affect stability of buildings and underground services ■ restrictions to navigation through barriers ■ changes in siltation patterns ■ increase in flooding risks ■ significant ecological impacts, e.g. Syon Park SSSI ■ pollution risk from sewage treatment works and storm outfalls ■ change in tidal character of the river ■ significant legal implications, i.e. amendment of Barrier Act required to allow change of use
Transfer from River Wye to Upper Thames – transfers supported by regulating storage – run of river transfer from Lower Wye without further flow augmentation	–	MOD	MOD–HIGH	■ reservoir in Wye valley required to supply the Thames Region ■ unreliable without regulating storage. River Wye low flows are not well maintained ■ engineering feasibility in question ■ longer periods when transfer unavailable ■ smaller transfer volume than Severn–Thames transfer ■ longer, more costly transfer route with greater environmental impact
Imports from Northumbria (Kielder Reservoir) by river/aqueduct	?	HIGH	LOW	■ high transmission costs ■ high capital and operating costs – uncompetitive compared to river transfers
Kielder–London submarine pipeline	200 Ml/d	HIGH	LOW–MOD	■ cost makes it only viable in absence of the regional options ■ not yet fully investigated
Imports from Northumbria/ Scotland by sea – towing storage tanks behind ocean-going tugs	100–200? Ml/d	HIGH	LOW	■ more expensive compared to other resource options with few compensating advantages
Redevelopment of existing reservoirs	70–150 Ml/d	HIGH	HIGH	■ would require a major new resource substitute during redevelopment ■ temporary loss of SSSI ■ significant local disturbance
Desalination	?	HIGH	HIGH	■ consistent source water quality required and low pollution risk ■ land availability dictates sites away from Thames estuary ■ energy intensive ■ abstraction of seawater and discharge of brine could create significant environmental impacts ■ to produce potable quality water requires blending and chemical dosing, increasing production costs ■ high transmission, operation, power and production costs make the option uncompetitive

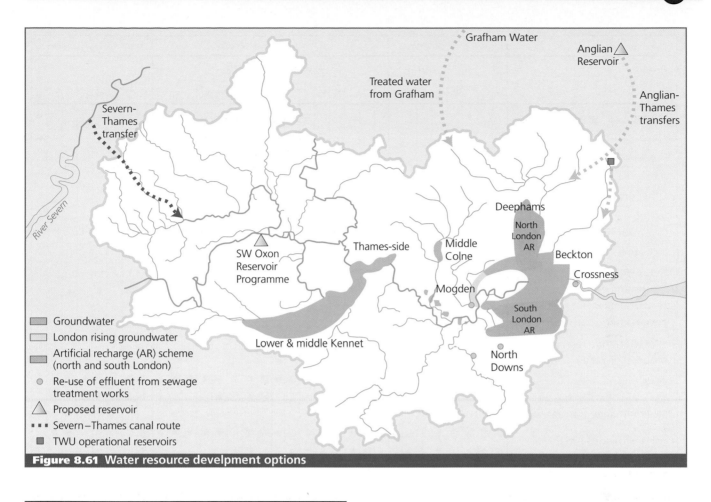

Figure 8.61 Water resource develpment options

Legend:
- Groundwater
- London rising groundwater
- Artificial recharge (AR) scheme (north and south London)
- Re-use of effluent from sewage treatment works
- △ Proposed reservoir
- ••• Severn–Thames canal route
- ■ TWU operational reservoirs

Map labels: Grafham Water, Anglian Reservoir, Treated water from Grafham, Anglian-Thames transfers, Severn-Thames transfer, River Severn, SW Oxon Reservoir Programme, Thames-side, Middle Colne, Deephams, North London AR, Beckton, Crossness, Mogden, South London AR, Lower & middle Kennet, North Downs

Figure 8.62 Cost of each option

Option	Yield (Ml/d) expenditure (£ million)	Indicative capital
London Basin groundwater:		
North London Artificial Recharge	90	11
South London Artificial Recharge	90	16
Rising groundwater	30	*
Other groundwater:		
Thames-side	50	1
Lower and Middle Kennet	20–50	4
North Downs	5	*
Lower Greensand	*	*
Effluent Re-use	100	25
South west Oxfordshire	2350	450
Reservoir proposal		
Severn–Thames transfer:		
to Buscot (200 Ml/d)	120	52
to SW Oxfordshire Reservoir (200 Ml/d)	145	62
to London (pipeline)	200?	160
Anglian–Thames transfer:		
via River Thame (with storage)		190
via Grafham	up to	150
via Stort	100	125
via Roding		125

- the use of high-grade treated effluent to supplement existing water resources available to London which would otherwise be discharged to tidal waters.

The feasibility of further re-use depends upon a number of factors, principally the achievement standards to meet drinking water and public health requirements, and the provision of adequate environmental protection to rivers.

Figure 8.63 Water storage at Farmoor reservoir, Farmoor

Engineering options	Sensitivity to change								Potential environmental risks																Environmental opportunities							
									Construction								Operation																
	🐟	🌳	〰	⛵	🐑	🚶	🏰	🌊	🐟	🌳	〰	⛵	🐑	🚶	🏰	🌊	🐟	🌳	〰	⛵	🐑	🚶	🏰	🌊	🐟	🌳	〰	⛵	🐑	🚶	🏰	🌊
London basin groundwater		●													●			●							●	●						●
North London artificial recharge		●													●		⊘	⊘	●						●	●						●
South London artificial recharge		●																●														
Rising groundwater																																
Other groundwater																																
Thames-side	●	●			●		●		●	●		●		●	●		●	●		●												
Lower & Middle Kennet	●	●			●		●		●	●		●		●	●		●	●		●												
North Downs	●	●							●	●							●	●	●						●	●						
Lower Greensand	●	●	●						●	●		●					●	●		●					●	●						
Opportunities for re-allocation																									●	●			●		●	
Effluent re-use	●	●	●	●										●			●		●		●								●			
SW Oxfordshire reservoir proposal (SWORP)														●		●																
On-site	●	●	●	●	●		●		●	●	⊘	⊘	⊘	●	●	●	●	●	⊘	●	●	●	●	●	●	⊘	●	●	⊘	●	●	●	●
River Thames & River Corridor	●	●	●	●					⊘	⊘	⊘	●							⊘	⊘	⊘	●			●	●	●	●	●			
Severn–Thames transfer																																
To Buscot	●	●	●	●	●		●	●	●	⊘	⊘	⊘	⊘	●	●	●	●	●	●	●	●	●	●	●	●			●		●	●	
To SWORP (pipeline)	●	●	●		●	●	●		●	●	●			●	●			●							●							
To London (pipeline)	●										●			●	●	●		●														
Anglian–Thames transfer																																
Via Grafham										●				●	●	●																
Via rivers: Thames, Sort, Roding	●	●	●	●	●	●	●	●	●	●	●	●	●	●	●	●	●	●	●	●	●	●	●	●								

Key

Aquatic ecology 🐟	Agriculture 🐑	Low ●
Terrestrial ecology 🌳	Community impacts 🚶	Medium ●
Water quality 〰	Archaeology and heritage 🏰	High ●
Recreation and navigation ⛵	Planning and general landscape including built environment 🌊	Impact might be mitigated /

Figure 8.64 Environmental impacts of each option

Question

1 Using as much evidence as possible, outline a case for the development of water resources in the Thames Region. You may choose up to three of the options mentioned above to form an integrated approach to sustainable development. You must reject at least one of the options.

River restoration – the River Cole

River restoration schemes are becoming more and more common as the advantages of natural rivers and their flood plains are realised.

The aims of the River Restoration Project (RRP) are:

- to recreate natural conditions in damaged river corridors

- to improve understanding of the effects of restoration work on nature conservation value, water quality, recreation and public opinion

- to encourage other groups to restore streams and rivers.

The RRP is an independent organisation backed by scientific and technical advisers. These are drawn mainly from organisations connected with rivers and river environments. Its aims are to restore and enhance damaged rivers for conservation, recreation and economic use, returning them as closely as possible to their natural condition.

The River Cole is one of three river restoration sites in Europe. The others are the River Skerne in Darlington and the River Brede in Denmark. The aim of the RRP for the River Cole near Swindon is to change the water course, improve water quality and manage the bankside vegetation.

Why restore rivers?

Over the last fifty years rivers have been seriously affected by urban and agricultural flood defences, land drainage and flood plain urbanisation. The result has been:

- extensive straightening and deepening of river channels, which has damaged wildlife habitats, reduced the value of fisheries and reduced much of the natural appeal of river landscapes

- a major loss of flood plains and wetlands to intensive agriculture and urbanisation, which has destroyed flood plain habitats and reduced the ability of flood plains to function as areas of flood control

- rivers are used intensively as transport routes, carriers of waste disposal, for industrial purposes, water abstraction, recreation etc.

There are two main ways in restoring rivers, natural and artificial. Natural ways can take hundreds of years, consequently artificial restoration needs to take place. The benefits are greatest when natural river shapes, flows and loads are copied.

Improving the River Cole

- **Stretch 1** It is planned to raise the river bed below Coleshill Bridge to bring it back in line with its flood plain and to make it an important feature in the local landscape. This will involve the introduction of more gravel riffles (fast-flowing water over midstream ridges) and, possibly, some small weirs.

- **Stretch 2** The new river bed will run at the higher level at this length to fit in with the mill channel just upstream of the bridge. Rather than filling in part of the straightened river, a new meandering course will be cut. Parts of the old course can then be retained as backwaters which will provide shelter for fish, birds and insects during high flows. This also means that neighbouring fields will flood more frequently and help to recreate a water meadow.

- **Stretch 3** The restoration of the ancient course of the Cole appears to be possible at this site. Flood waters will restore the flood meadows along the western side of the mill.

- **Stretch 4** The RRP hopes to restore the Cole Mill for occasional operation. The water levels in the Mill stream need to be raised for this to happen. The feeder stream (known locally as the Leat) is to be developed as a long lake with wet pasture and reed beds along its side.

Reed, willow and alder tree beds are very useful in cleansing streams which have been polluted by silt, fertiliser and treated sewage. A few carefully located beds of these plants are very effective at removing unwanted debris and pollutants.

Management

The overall aim of the proposals is to increase the extent to which the river and its flood plain interact, to sustain a landscape that is rich in riverine and wetland wildlife. The key to success is the management of the flood plain, worked out in conjunction with local land managers. The main road at Coleshill Bridge and nearby buildings and sports fields will have to be protected from the increased risk of erosion and flooding.

Evaluation of the scheme

Rivers and their flood plains are complex physical systems. However, they also have economic, social and political consequences. Balancing the physical demands of rivers with the economic and political demands that are based on the human use of the rivers and their flood plains is difficult. The impact of human activity on natural systems is often very negative and it is impossible to imagine rivers and flood plains without wide-scale human activity.

In practice most restoration schemes will only partially restore or rehabilitate the river due to the large number of human-related uses in the flood plains (buildings, farmland, transport, for example).

Benefits of restoration

■ Greater nature conservation of wetland wildlife in the river and on the flood plain

■ increased diversity and numbers of fish

■ improved water quality due to increased interception of pollutants by vegetation and natural settling of sediments on flood plain and river bed

■ increased flood defence – additional flood storage provided by the enlarged flood plain

■ more opportunities for recreation – there is a strong public perception in favour of natural landscapes.

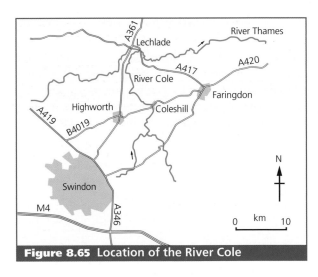

Figure 8.65 Location of the River Cole

Review Questions

1 Figure 8.28 shows the relationship between water velocity and the size of material carried. Using this diagram, describe the sequence of processes and their likely consequences in a stream channel with a wide range of sediment sizes, as discharge changes during a flood event from a low-flow velocity of 0.05 ms⁻¹, to 0.5 ms⁻¹, then to peak velocity of 1.5 ms⁻¹.

2 **(a)** Outline the processes by which a river may erode its channel.
(b) Describe the methods by which a river may transport material.
(c) Explain the meaning of the following terms:
 (i) the competence of a river;
 (ii) the capacity of a river.
 Discuss how competence and capacity are related to the flow of a river.
(d) Describe how you would measure the discharge of a small river.

Bibliography

References

Horizons in Physical Geography by M. J. Clark et al, Macmillan, 1987.
Thames 21 – A planning perspective and a sustainable strategy for the Thames region, National Rivers Authority, 1995.
Environmental Hazards by K. Smith, Routledge, 1992
Hydrological and Fluvial Processes: Revolution and Evolution by D. Walling, 1987.

Internet

River Severn river link
http://mail.bris.ac.uk/0/6/7Extss/river/.html
US flood insurance data
http://www.insure.com/home/flood/stats.html

9 coastal environments

Marine geomorphology

Coasts are very varied landscapes (Figure 9.1) and there are a number of factors controlling coastal evolution. These include

- the work of waves and currents, including longshore drift
- the degree of exposure to wave action – i.e. the 'trend' of the coast
- variations in local geology such as rock type and structure
- long- and short-term changes in relative levels of land and sea
- 'special' factors, such as volcanic activity and glaciation
- the effect of vegetation and animals
- human activities, particularly since the Coast Protection Act of 1949 and the use of improved marine engineering, and land reclamation.

Waves

Waves result from friction between wind and the sea surface (Figure 9.2). Waves in the open, deep sea (waves of oscillation) are different from those breaking onshore. Waves of oscillation are forward surges of energy. Although the surface wave shape appears to move, in fact the water particles move in a roughly circular orbit within the wave.

Wave height is an indication of wave energy. It is controlled by wind strength, fetch, and the depth of the sea. Waves of up to 12–15 m are formed in open sea and can travel vast distances away from the generation area, reaching distant shores as **swell waves**, characterised by a lower height and a longer wavelength.

Key Definitions

wavelength The distance between two successive crests or troughs (Figure 9.2).

wave frequency The number of waves per minute.

wave height or **amplitude** The distance between the trough and the crest.

fetch The amount of open water over which a wave has passed.

velocity The speed a wave travels at, influenced by wind, fetch and depth of water.

swash The movement of water up the beach.

backwash The movement of water down the beach.

wave orbit The shape of the wave. It varies between circular and elliptical. The orbit diameter decreases with depth, to a depth roughly equal to wavelength (which is the distance between neighbouring crests or troughs) when no further movement occurs as related to wind energy (this point is called the **wave base**).

longshore drift The irregular movement of particles along a beach as they travel obliquely up the slope of a beach with the swash and directly down this slope with the backwash.

Figure 9.1 The Gower coast, west of Port Eynon

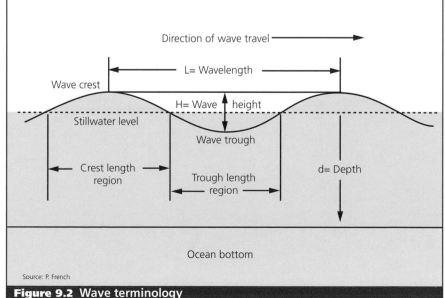

Source: P. French

Figure 9.2 Wave terminology

Waves reaching shore are known as **waves of translation**. As waves move more onshore, the wave base comes in contact with the sea bed. Friction slows down the wave advance, causing the wave fronts to crowd together. Wavelengths are reduced and the wave height increases. Thus a **breaker** is formed. Once the breaker has collapsed, the wave energy is transmitted onshore as a 'wave of translation'. The swash will surge up the beach with its speed gradually lessened by friction and the uphill gradient. Gravity will draw the water back as the backwash. There are two basic types of wave translation – constructive and destructive waves.

Constructive waves tend to occur when wave frequency is low (6–8 arriving onshore per minute), particularly when these waves advance over a gently shelving sea floor (formed, for example, of fine material such as sand) (Figure 9.3). These waves have been generated far offshore. The gentle offshore slope will create a gradual increase in friction, which will cause a gradual steepening of the wave front. Thus, a **spilling** breaker will be formed, where water movement is elliptical. As this breaker collapses, the powerful/constructive swash will surge up the gentle gradient. Because of the low frequency, the backwash of each wave will be allowed to return to the sea, before the next wave breaks, i.e. the swash of each wave is not impeded and retains maximum energy.

Destructive waves are the result of locally generated winds, which create waves of high frequency (12–14 per minute) (Figure 9.4). This rapid approach of the waves, particularly if moving onshore up a steeply shelving coastline (formed from coarse material such as gravel or shingle), will create a rapid

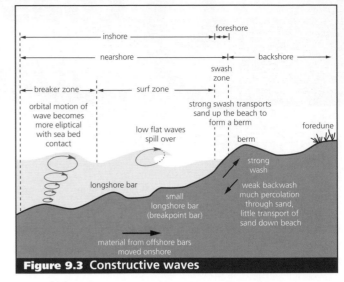

Figure 9.3 Constructive waves

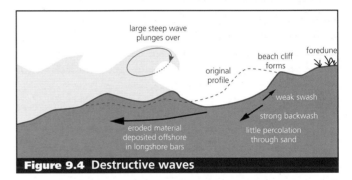

Figure 9.4 Destructive waves

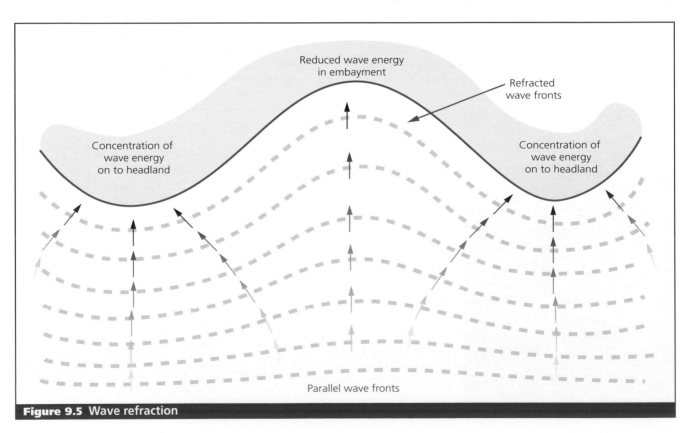

Figure 9.5 Wave refraction

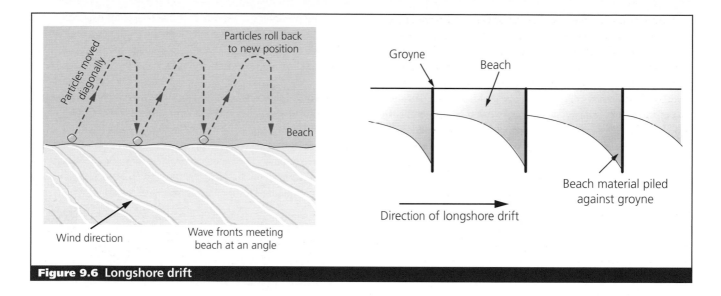

Figure 9.6 Longshore drift

increase in friction and thus a very steep, **plunging** breaker where water movement is circular. Due to the rapid steepening and curling of the wave breaker, the energy of the wave is transmitted down the beach (on breaker collapse), accelerated by the steeper gradient and so the wave becomes destructive, combing down the beach material.

Wave refraction

As wave fronts approach the shore, their speed of approach will be reduced as the waves 'feel bottom'. Usually, due to the interaction between onshore wind direction (and therefore direction of wave advance) and the trend of the coast, the wave fronts will approach the shore obliquely. This causes the wave fronts to bend and swing round in an attempt to break parallel to the shore. The change in speed and distortion of the wave fronts is called **wave refraction** (Figure 9.5). If refraction is completed, the fronts will break parallel to the shore. However, due primarily to the complexities of coastline shape, refraction is not always totally achieved.

Wave refraction also distributes wave energy along a stretch of coast. Along a complex transverse coast with alternating headlands and bays, wave refraction will concentrate erosional activity on the headlands, while deposition will tend to occur in the bays.

If refraction is not complete longshore drift occurs (Figure 9.6). This leads to a gradual movement of sediment along the shore, as the backswash moves in the direction of the prevailing wind whereas the swash moves straight down the beach following the steepest gradient.

Human activity and longshore drift in West Africa

Ocean currents along the coast of West Africa have removed huge amounts of coastline between Ghana and Nigeria. The removal of the beach material has affected settlements, tourism and industry. The increase in coastal retreat has been blamed on the construction of the Akosombo Dam on the Volta River in Ghana. The Guinea Current is among the strongest in the world, and is removing approximately 1.5 million m³ of sand each year, between the Ivory Coast and Nigeria (Figure 9.7). The effect upon Ghana, Benin and Togo is especially catastrophic.

Figure 9.7 Human activity and longshore drift along the coast of West Africa

The cause of the coastal retreat is traced to the building of the Akosombo Dam in 1961. It is just 110 km from the coast and disrupts the flow of sediment from the River Volta and stops it from reaching the shore. Thus there is less sand to replace that which has already been washed away and so the coastline retreats due to erosion by the Guinea Current. Towns, such as Keta, 30 km east of the Volta estuary, have been destroyed as their protective beaches have been removed. Other towns in neighbouring Togo, Kpeme and Tropicana, are threatened with destruction.

In Togo the problem has been intensified by the use of artificial breakwaters. In the mid-1960s a deepwater port was opened at Lome, the country's capital, to improve trade with landlocked neighbouring countries, such as Mali, Niger and Burkina Faso. Lome is protected by a 1300 m breakwater, which obstructs the natural flow of the Guinea Current from west to east. Sand carried by the current collects on the westward (updrift) side of the breakwater. Thus the east side (downdrift) is open to erosion. The result has been the erosion of beach and infrastructure. In 1984 a 100-metre stretch of the main Ghana-Benin highway was destroyed in just twenty-four hours. Erosion near the holiday resort of Tropicana caused the sea to advance 100 m towards the holiday complex. Ironically, the erosion uncovered a bed of resistant sandstone, which now protects the resort, but is not as attractive for the tourist trade as the sandy beach that existed before. At Kpeme, 18 km from Tropicana, most of Togo's

processed phosphate is exported. This accounts for over half of Togo's foreign exchange. The jetty from which the exports take place was threatened with erosion. To manage the risk of erosion, engineers have reinforced the foundations of the jetty with boulders. In doing so they have trapped sand and stopped it from moving down the coastline. As a result, towns further east, such as Aneho, are now even more at risk from erosion. At a cost of between £1 million and £2 million to protect every kilometre of coastline it is hard to imagine how the coast can be protected. If Togo were to protect its coastline by preventing the movement of sand eastwards, it might lead to an increase in erosion in Benin, where the foundations of oil wells may be threatened.

Questions

1 Define the following terms: (a) wave refraction (b) long-shore drift.
2 Describe how human activity can affect longshore drift.
3 Distinguish between constructive waves and destructive waves.

Erosion

Waves perform a number of complex and interacting processes of erosion (Figure 9.8). **Hydraulic action** is an important process as waves break on to cliffs. As the wave breaks against the cliff face any air trapped in cracks, joints and bedding planes will be momentarily placed under very great pressure. As the wave retreats this pressure will be released with explosive force. Stresses will weaken the coherence of the rock, aiding erosion (comparable to cavitation in rivers). This is particularly obvious in well-bedded and well-jointed rocks such as limestones, sandstones, granite and chalk, as well as in rocks that are poorly consolidated such as clays, and glacial deposits. Hydraulic action is also notable during times of storm wave activity – for example, the average pressure of Atlantic storm waves is 11 000 kg/m³.

Corrasion is the process whereby a breaking wave can hurl pebbles and shingle against a coast, thereby abrading it. **Attrition** takes place as other forms of erosion continue. The eroded material will itself be worn down by attrition, partly explaining the variety of sizes of beach material. **Solution** is a form of chemical erosion. In areas of calcareous (lime rich) rock, waves remove material by acidic water.

As wave activity is constantly at work between high water mark (HWM) and low water mark (LWM) it causes undercutting of a cliff face, forming a notch and overhang.

Breaking waves, especially during storms and spring tides, can erode the coast higher than HWM. As the undercutting continues, the notch becomes deeper and the overhang more pronounced. Ultimately the overhang will collapse, causing the cliff line to retreat. The base of the cliff will be left behind as a broadening **platform**, often covered with deposited material, with the coarsest near the cliff base, gradually becoming smaller towards the open sea.

Cliffs and erosion

Cliff profiles are very variable and depend on a number of controlling factors. One major factor is the influence of bedding and jointing. The well-developed jointing and bedding of certain harder limestones creates a very geometric cliff profile – with angular, steeped cliff faces and flat top (bedding plane). Wave erosion will open up these lines of weakness causing complete blocks to fall away and the creation of angular overhangs and cave shapes. This is well exemplified at Tresilian Bay near Llantwit Major (Figure 9.9). In other well-jointed and bedded rocks, a whole variety of features will be created by wave erosion, such as caves, geos (inlets), arches, stacks and stumps.

The dip of the bedding alone will create varying cliff profiles. For example if the beds dip vertically, then a sheer cliff face will be found e.g. the old red sandstone cliffs

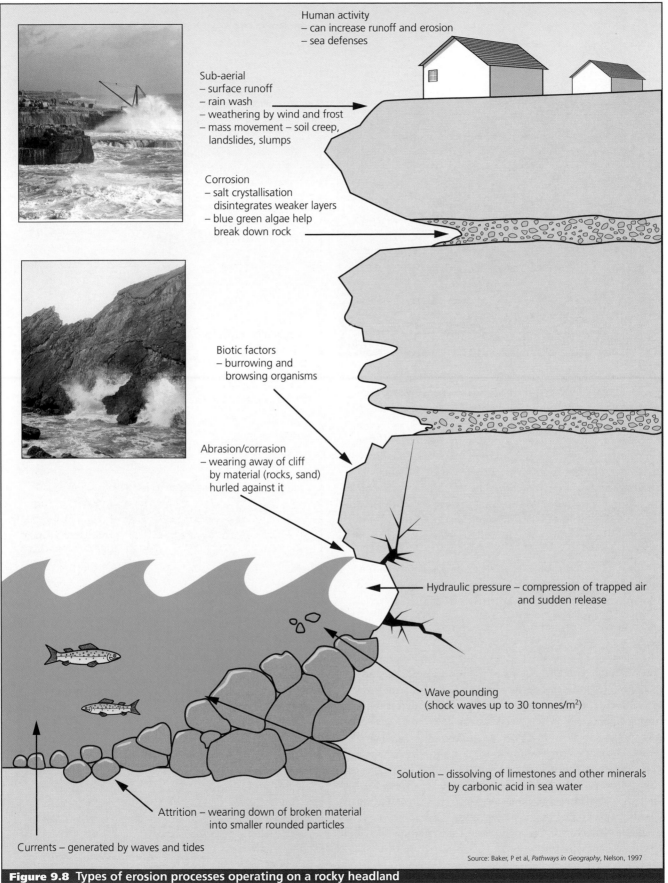

Human activity
– can increase runoff and erosion
– sea defenses

Sub-aerial
– surface runoff
– rain wash
– weathering by wind and frost
– mass movement – soil creep,
  landslides, slumps

Corrosion
– salt crystallisation
  disintegrates weaker layers
– blue green algae help
  break down rock

Biotic factors
– burrowing and
  browsing organisms

Abrasion/corrasion
– wearing away of cliff
  by material (rocks, sand)
  hurled against it

Hydraulic pressure – compression of trapped air
and sudden release

Wave pounding
(shock waves up to 30 tonnes/m^2)

Solution – dissolving of limestones and other minerals
by carbonic acid in sea water

Attrition – wearing down of broken material
into smaller rounded particles

Currents – generated by waves and tides

Source: Baker, P et al, *Pathways in Geography*, Nelson, 1997

Figure 9.8 Types of erosion processes operating on a rocky headland

Figure 9.9 Llantwit Cliffs, South Wales

in Dyfed. By contrast, if the beds dip steeply seaward, then steep, shelving cliffs with landslips will be found e.g. the cliffs at Tenby.

Rates of cliff retreat are quite rapid in chalk, over 100 m per century. This is due to rapid undercutting by all forms of erosion and by the common occurrence of landslipping. This creates sheer faces to chalk cliffs. The cliff tops will take on an undulating appearance if the coastal dry valleys are eaten into. For example, in the Seven Sisters on the south coast of England, the mouths of the dry valley are as much as 15–30 m above the cliff base.

Thus, each cliff profile, to some extent, is unique, but a model of cliff evolution or modification has been produced to take into account not only wave activity, but also sub aerial weathering processes.

The Seven Sisters

The Seven Sisters cliffs are one of the most impressive and recognisable landforms of the south coast. During the last glacial period, river systems would have flowed across the then impermeable chalk. These rivers flowed down to a sea level that was much lower than now. At the end of the glacial period, as temperatures warmed, sea levels rose again and the chalk became permeable once more. The rising sea drowned river valleys forming indented coastlines such as along Devon and Cornwall. However, the chalk was less resistant and the coastline was eroded by the waves, attacking first the headlands (due to wave refraction) and then planing the whole cliff line (Figure 9.10).

The dry valleys are short – the longest, Gap Bottom, is only 1.8 km and the shortest just 400 m. The cliffs are

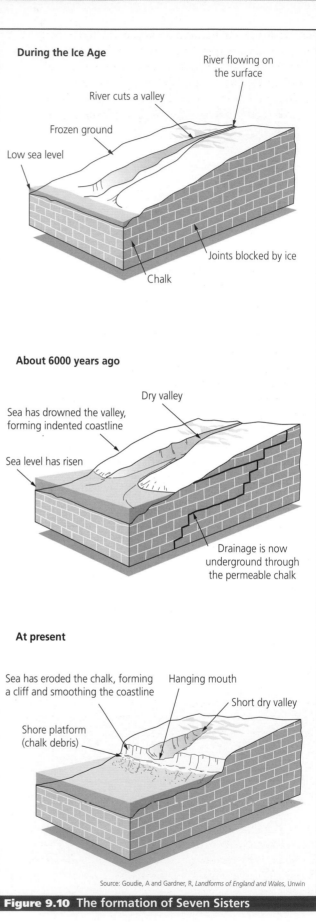

During the Ice Age

River flowing on the surface

River cuts a valley

Frozen ground

Low sea level

Joints blocked by ice

Chalk

About 6000 years ago

Dry valley

Sea has drowned the valley, forming indented coastline

Sea level has risen

Drainage is now underground through the permeable chalk

At present

Sea has eroded the chalk, forming a cliff and smoothing the coastline

Hanging mouth

Short dry valley

Shore platform (chalk debris)

Source: Goudie, A and Gardner, R, *Landforms of England and Wales*, Unwin

Figure 9.10 The formation of Seven Sisters

eroding at a rate of between 50 m and 125 m per century. Most retreat takes place in occasional pulses, such as in the early 1950s. Erosion and mass movement of the chalk is helped by the chalk beds dipping gently towards the sea. Erosion at the base of the cliff de-stabilises the cliff above. As the cliffs retreat they leave behind a lengthening shore platform.

Coastal platforms

As a result of cliff retreat, a platform along the coast is normally created (Figure 9.11). Traditionally, this feature was described as a **wave cut platform**, because it was believed that it was created entirely by wave action. However, there is some controversy over the importance of other agents of weathering and erosion in the production of the coastal platform, especially the larger ones.

In post-glacial times, sea level has not remained sufficiently constant to erode such platforms. However, some marine geomorphologists believe that these platforms could be **relict** or ancient features, originally cut long ago when sea level was constant and that the contemporary sea level is at about the same height and is just 'trimming up' the ancient platform.

Secondly, in high latitudes, **frost action** could be important in supporting wave activity, particularly as these areas are now rising as a result of isostatic recovery (after intense glaciation). In other areas, **solution weathering**, **salt crystallisation** and **slaking** could also support wave activity, particularly in the tidal zone and splash zone. **Marine organisms**, especially algae, can accelerate weathering at low tide and in the area just above HWM. At night carbon dioxide is released by algae because photosynthesis does not occur. This carbon dioxide combines with the cool sea water to create an acidic environment, causing 'rotting'.

Other organisms, such as limpets, secrete organic acids which can slowly rot the rock. Certain marine worms (polychaetes and annelids), molluscs and sea urchins can actually 'bore' into rock surfaces, particularly chalk and limestone.

Coast erosion

Coast erosion rates vary greatly around the UK and depend on the geology of the coast and its exposure to wind, wave and current action. Rapid erosion is found along parts of the coast of southern and eastern England where relatively soft geological formations are being eroded (Figure 9.12). At the same time, however, parts of the same coast may be moving seawards as sediments build up.

Coast erosion is also a cause of landslides and rock fall. Of about 8500 landslides in Britain, about 15 per cent were in the coastal zone. These latter include many of the largest landslide complexes such as The Undercliff on the Isle of Wight, Folkestone Warren and Black Ven in Dorset. On the Isle of Wight it is almost impossible to obtain insurance with a post code of PO38, The Undercliff (Figure 9.12).

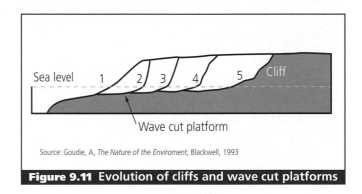

Source: Goudie, A, *The Nature of the Enviroment*, Blackwell, 1993

Figure 9.11 Evolution of cliffs and wave cut platforms

At Covehithe, in Suffolk, 6 m of coastline are eroded each year. This has carried on for a number of decades. A 40 km stretch of coast around Holderness is eroded by about 2 m/year, depositing about 1.5 million m³ of sediment into the North Sea. Indeed, since Roman times the coast has moved inland by over 3 km, and over 30 villages have been lost to the sea. Rapid erosion is thus localised occurring most readily on soft rocks exposed to storm waves with a large fetch.

Questions

1 What are the main types of marine erosion to affect costal environments?
2 Briefly explain the factors which affect rates of coastal erosion.
3 Why is the term 'wave cut platform' considered to be 'misleading'?
4 Why are mass movements important in coastal areas?

Deposition

Beaches

A whole variety of materials can be drifted along the coast by waves, fed by longshore drift. The coarse material is found deposited (and fallen from the backing cliffs) in the **backshore** and **foreshore** zones as **littoral deposits**. The finer material, worn down largely by attrition, is usually found in the **offshore** zone as **neritic** deposits (Figure 9.14).

The term **beach** refers to the accumulation of material deposited between LWM spring tides and the highest point reached by storm waves at HWM spring tides. A typical beach will have three zones: backshore, foreshore and offshore. The backshore is cliffed or marked by a line of dunes. Above and at

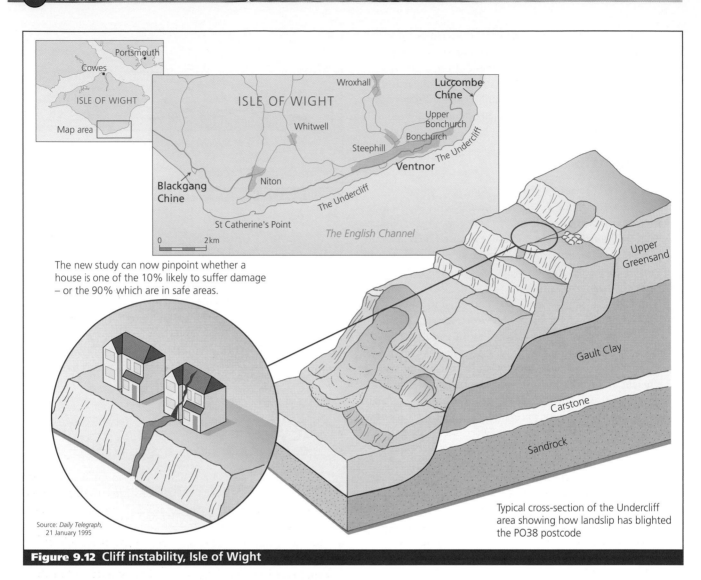

The new study can now pinpoint whether a house is one of the 10% likely to suffer damage – or the 90% which are in safe areas.

Source: *Daily Telegraph*, 21 January 1995

Typical cross-section of the Undercliff area showing how landslip has blighted the PO38 postcode

Figure 9.12 **Cliff instability, Isle of Wight**

Figure 9.13 Shingle ridge offering some protection to the cliff, Dorset coast

HWM there may be a berm or shingle ridge. This is coarse material pushed up the beach by spring tides and aided by storm waves flinging material well above the level of the waves themselves. These are often referred to as storm beaches. The seaward edge of the berm is often scalloped and irregular due to the creation of beach **cusps**. Their origin is still controversial – they could be due to the edge of the swash itself often scalloped or due to the action of two sets of wave fronts approaching the shore obliquely from opposite directions. Once initiated, the cusps are self-perpetuating – the swash is broken up by the cusp projection, concentrating energy onto the cusp (compare with refraction onto headlands) bulldozing up material.

The foreshore is exposed at low tide. The beach material may be undulating due to the creation of ridges, called **fulls**, running parallel to the water line, pushed up by constructive waves at varying heights of the tide. These are separated by troughs, called **swales**. Great stretches of sand too, may comprise the foreshore. In areas of complex coast sand beaches may only be exposed as small **bayhead beaches** in bays.

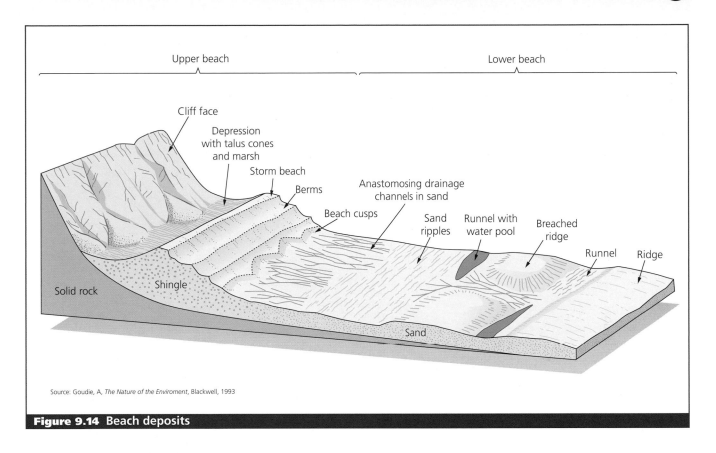

Source: Goudie, A, *The Nature of the Enviroment*, Blackwell, 1993

Figure 9.14 Beach deposits

Offshore the first material is deposited. In this zone, the waves touch the sea bed and so the material is usually disturbed, sometimes being pushed up as **offshore bars**, when the offshore gradient is very shallow.

Excellent beach development occurs on a lowland coast (constructive waves) with a sheltered aspect/trend composed of 'soft' rocks, which provides a good supply of material, or where longshore drift supplies abundant material.

Bars and spits

These more localised features will develop where:

■ **abundant material is available, particularly shingle and sand**

■ **the coastline is irregular due to, for example, local geological variety (transverse coast)**

■ **where there are estuaries and major rivers.**

Offshore bars are usually composed of coarse sand or shingle. They develop as bars offshore on a gently shelving sea bed (Figure 9.15). Waves feel bottom far offshore. This causes disturbance in the water which leads to deposition. Between the bar and shore, lagoons (often called **sounds**) develop. If the lagoonal water is calm and fed by rivers, marshes and mud-flats can be found. Bars can be driven onshore by storm winds and waves. A classic area is off the coast of the Carolinas in the south east of the United States.

Spits are common along an indented coast. For example along a transverse coast where bays are common or near river mouths (estuaries and rias), wave energy is reduced. The long, narrow ridges of sand and shingle which form spits are always joined at one end to the mainland. There are many classic examples of simple, straight spits in Britain, such as Orford Ness. This spit has been deposited where the north-south longshore drift of the North Sea has been interrupted by the flow of the Rivers Alde and Butley. The spit, well fed by the longshore drift, has grown rapidly – as recently as the seventeenth century, the town of Orford was a small port next to the open sea.

Spits often become curved as waves undergo refraction. Cross currents or occasional storm waves may assist this hooked formation. A good example is Hurst Castle spit on the Dorset coast. The main body of the spit is curved but has additional, smaller hooks or **recurves**, and is 2 km long. On the seaward side, the slope to deeper water is very steep. Within the curve of the spit, the water is shallow and a considerable area of mud-flat and salt marsh (**salting**) is exposed at low water. These salt marshes are continuing to grow as mud is being trapped by the marsh vegetation. The whole area of salt marsh is intersected by a complex network of channels and **creeks**, which contain water even at low tide.

A major factor in the development of the spit is the eastward flowing longshore drift which cannot adapt to the abrupt change of angle of the coast. Occasional storm waves come from the north-east down the Solent, building up the recurves.

Figure 9.15 Depositional features

Managing a spit – the case of Dawlish Warren

The Dawlish Warren spit is located at the mouth of the Exe estuary (Figure 9.16). The sand spit receives its materials from a number of sources.

The main source is the red sandstone and breccia cliffs at Langstone Rock headland. Eroded material is drifted eastwards to Dawlish. Constructive waves and swell waves move material on to Dawlish from offshore bars. In addition, at low tide wind erosion blows sand from the beach onto the dunes where it is trapped by marram grass. Finally, the River Exe carries material down in suspension and solution. Much of this is deposited in the low energy environment behind the dunes. In addition the mixing of fresh water and sea water causes clay particles to stick together and, owing to their increased weight, they are deposited.

Dawlish Warren has been mapped for over 200 years (Figure 9.17). Over 200 m of the sand spit have been eroded since 1787, an annual average of 1 m. In addition, there has been sand lost from the dunes as a result of recreational trampling on the dunes. Moreover, the presence of a large breakwater at Langstone Rock

has prevented sand from being drifted onto the spit and replenishing some of the sand lost by erosion. Hence the spit is getting narrower and there is a real danger that it could be breached in a major storm.

In 1989–90 Dawlish Warren experienced severe storms. Initially, storm waves from the south built up sand and shingle against the breakwater at Langstone Rock, while removing sand from the western end of Dawlish. Later, storm winds from the south east caused considerable damage to the rock armour. Boulders were dislodged, and unprotected sand was washed away, undermining the promenade. Other problems included:

■ boulders in the rock armour had moved position and were no longer interlocking

■ rocks which should have reduced the impact of backwash had been eroded

■ limestone boulders had been weathered and eroded

Figure 9.16 Dawlish Warren (from the air)

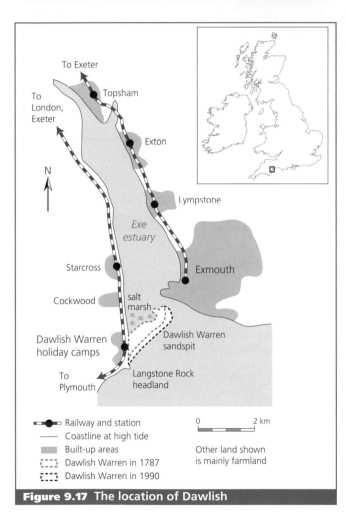

Figure 9.17 The location of Dawlish

Railway and station
Coastline at high tide
Built-up areas
Dawlish Warren in 1787
Dawlish Warren in 1990

0   2 km

Other land shown
is mainly farmland

Figure 9.18 Dawlish showing the vulnerability of the site and the size of the problem

- it is an internationally valuable habitat for plants and birds, and is managed as a nature reserve

- it is an important holiday destination – over 20 000 people use the spit at peak times and the revenue from the car parks is a major source of income for Teignbridge District Council

- there are over 50 businesses on the spit and the adjoining village providing services and employment for visitors and local residents

- the spit is a natural flood defence, protecting the low-lying Exe estuary.

The new defences at Dawlish were built in 1992, costing £1.5 million. The main features were a new rock armour revetment with a curved sea wall. Rocks for the armour were imported from Norway, although local materials were used to 'face' the wall (Figure 9.18). Sea defences are not cheap:

- large interlocked boulders cost £3500 per metre (all 1992 prices)
- sloping concrete walls cost £2000 per metre
- gabions (stones in wire baskets) cost £100 per metre
- offshore breakwaters cost £5000 per metre
- beach nourishment costs £3 per cubic metre
- stone walls cost £6000 per metre
- groynes cost £10 000 each.

It is easy to see why some planning authorities are keen to allow nature to take its course, and why others have fallen behind in the maintenance of their defences. It is also clear that there has to be a good reason to protect land. So far, the sea defences have protected Dawlish Warren.

- boulders had become more rounded making them liable to be rolled away during severe storms
- boulders were now small enough to be lifted by storm waves.

There are a number of reasons why Dawlish deserves to be protected:

Bars and barrier beaches

If a spit continues to grow lengthwise, it may ultimately link two headlands to form a **bay bar**. These are composed either of shingle, as in the case of the Low Bar in Cornwall, or of sand, such as the 'Nehrung' of the Baltic coast, with pond back lagoons called the 'Haff'.

Tombolo

If a ridge of material links an island with the mainland, this ridge is called a **tombolo**. The Llandudno tombolo consists of clays and sands supplied by the River Conwy (Conway) and glacial deposits left in Conwy Bay. The sheltered, shallow waters behind Great Orme Head are ideal for deposition. Winds are weak, wave energy is low, hence deposition occurs. The tombolo links the carboniferous limestone of Great Orme Head to the mainland (Figure 9.19).

The other 'classic' example is Chesil Beach. Chesil Beach is 25 km long, connecting the Isle of Portland with the mainland Dorset coast at Burton Bradstock, near Abbotsbury. At its eastern end at Portland, the ridge is 13 m above sea level and composed of flinty pebbles about the size of a potato. At its western end near Abbotsbury the ridge is lower, only 7 m above sea level and built of smaller flinty material about the size of a pea.

The height of the ridge and the sizing of material would suggest that dominant wave action occurred from east to west – the largest material is piled up at the eastern end, being the heaviest and most difficult to transport. Smaller, lighter material is carried further west before being deposited. However, the dominant wave action comes from the south west, up the Channel from the Atlantic Ocean. In other words, the morphology of the ridge should be completely opposite to what it is.

Thus, the origin of Chesil Beach remains a problem. One theory to explain this situation is that Chesil is a very youthful feature and so is unstable in the present environment. During the Pleistocene (18 000–20 000 years BP) sea level fell at least 100 m below present sea level. As a result, much of the present Channel lay dry. During the Ice Age, vast amounts of debris were produced on the nearby land surface by glacial and periglacial action. This debris could have been carried into the dry Channel area by meltwater at the close of the Ice Age. As sea level rose in early post-glacial times, this material could have been pushed onshore and trapped by the Isle of Portland and Lyme Bay. Present-day wave action is gradually sorting this material.

Cuspate forelands

Cuspate forelands consist of shingle ridges deposited in a triangular shape and are the result of two separate spits joining or the combined effects of two distinct sets of regular storm waves. The best example is at Dungeness, near Dover, where the foreland forms the seaward edge of Romney Marsh. This

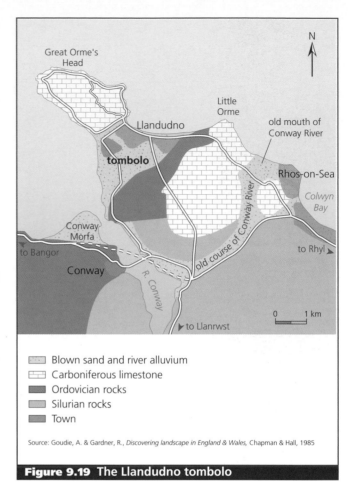

Blown sand and river alluvium

Carboniferous limestone

Ordovician rocks

Silurian rocks

Town

Source: Goudie, A. & Gardner, R., *Discovering landscape in England & Wales*, Chapman & Hall, 1985

Figure 9.19 The Llandudno tombolo

marsh used to be a bay as recently as AD 900. Within the last 1000 years this bay has silted up with mud-flats and marshes as a direct result of the growth of the cuspate foreland. The shingle was deposited by longshore drift curling west from the North Sea and by the longshore drift flowing eastwards up the Channel.

Sand dunes

Extensive sandy beaches are almost always backed by sand dunes because strong onshore winds can easily transport inland the sand which has dried out and is exposed at low water. The sand grains are trapped and deposited against any obstacle on land to form dunes. Dunes can be blown inland and can therefore threaten coastal farmland and even villages. There are methods to slow down the migration of dunes:

- special grasses, such as marram, with long and complex tap root systems bind the soil
- brushwood fencing reduces sand movement
- planting of conifers which can stand the saline environment and poor soils such as Scots and Corsican Pine.

Figure 9.20 Formby sand dunes

youngest ones are closest to the shore. On the shore, conditions are windy, arid and salty. The soil contains few nutrients and is mostly sand – hence the foredunes are referred to as yellow dunes. Few plants can survive, although sea couch and marram can tolerate these conditions. Once the vegetation is established it reduces wind speed close to ground level. The belt of no wind may increase to a height of 10 mm. As grasses such as sea couch and marram need to be buried by fresh sand in order to grow, they keep pace with deposition. As the marram grows it traps more sand. This is known as **bioconstruction**. As it is covered it grows more and so on. Once established the dunes should continue to grow, as long as there is a supply of sand. However, once another younger dune, a foredune, becomes established the supply of sand, and so the growth of the dune, is reduced.

As the dune gets higher the supply of fresh sand is reduced to dunes further back. Thus marram dies out. In addition, as wind speeds are reduced, evapotranspiration losses are less, and the soil is moister. The decaying marram adds some nutrients to the soil, which in turn becomes more acidic. In the slacks, the low points between the dunes, conditions are noticeably moister and marsh vegetation may occur.

Towards the rear of the dune system 'grey' dunes are formed, grey due to the presence of humus in the soil. The climax vegetation found depends largely upon the nature of the sand. If there is a high proportion of shells (providing calcium) grasslands are found. By contrast, acid dunes are found on old dunes where the calcium has been leached out and on dunes based upon outwash sands and gravels. Acid-loving plants such as heather and ling dominate. Pine trees favour acid soils, whereas oak can be found on more neutral soils. Thus the vegetation at the rear of the sand dune complex is quite variable (Figure 9.21)

Mud-flats and salt marshes

The **intertidal zone**, the zone between high tide and low tide, experiences severe environmental changes in salinity, tidal inundation and sediment composition. **Halophytic** (salt tolerant) plants have adapted to the unstable, rapidly changing conditions (Figure 9.22).

Salt marshes are typically found in three locations: low energy coastlines such as the Norfolk coast; behind spits and barrier islands, such as Scolt Head Island; and in estuaries and harbours, such as Poole Harbour.

Silt accumulates in these situations and, on reaching sea level, form mud-banks. With the appearance of vegetation a salt marsh is formed. The mud-banks are often intersected by creeks. Reclamation is often possible when mud-banks and salt marsh are extensive – for example, Romney Marsh behind Dungeness and the Dovey Marshes lying behind Borth Spit along the Cardigan Bay coast of Wales. Examples of marshes found within estuaries and bays include the original Fens (now been reclaimed), the marshes in Morecambe Bay (Lancashire) and those in Southampton Water.

Sand dunes are young features. Sea levels around the British Isles only reached their current position about 6000 years ago, so sand dunes have been formed since then. (There are fossil beaches and fossil dunes but live dunes are less than 600 years old.) Dunes are common around many parts of Britain but especially so in north east Scotland, north east Norfolk and Cardigan Bay. Other good examples of sand dunes and their associated plant succession can be found at Formby, Lancashire (Figure 9.20), Studland Beach, Dorset, and Braunton Burrows, Devon.

Sand dune succession

Initially, sand is moved by the wind. However, wind speed varies with height above a surface. The belt of no wind is only 1 mm above the surface. As most grains protrude above this height they are moved by saltation. The strength of the wind and the nature of the surface are important. Irregularities cause increased wind speed and eddying, and more material is moved. On the leeward side of irregularities, wind speed is lower, transport decreases and deposition increases.

For stable dunes to occur vegetation is required. Plant succession and vegetation succession can be interpreted by the fact that the oldest dunes are furthest from the sea and the

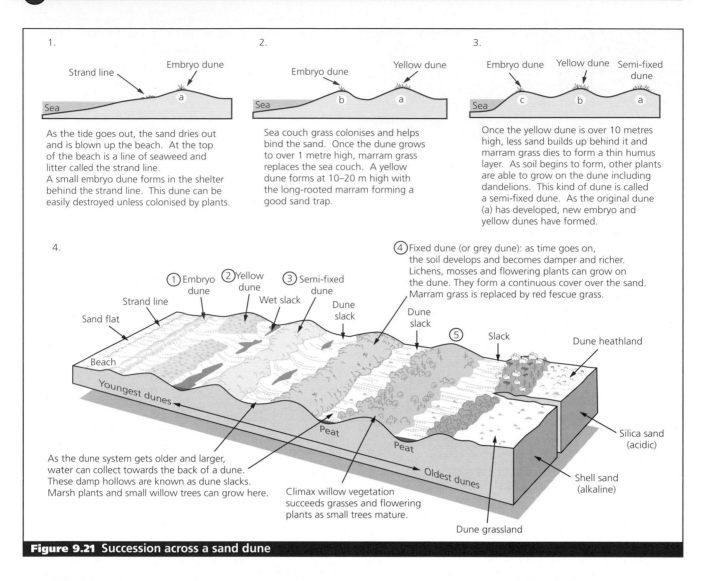

1.

Strand line → Embryo dune →

Sea
a

As the tide goes out, the sand dries out and is blown up the beach. At the top of the beach is a line of seaweed and litter called the strand line.
A small embryo dune forms in the shelter behind the strand line. This dune can be easily destroyed unless colonised by plants.

2.

Embryo dune → Yellow dune →

Sea
b   a

Sea couch grass colonises and helps bind the sand. Once the dune grows to over 1 metre high, marram grass replaces the sea couch. A yellow dune forms at 10–20 m high with the long-rooted marram forming a good sand trap.

3.

Embryo dune → Yellow dune → Semi-fixed dune →

Sea
c   b   a

Once the yellow dune is over 10 metres high, less sand builds up behind it and marram grass dies to form a thin humus layer. As soil begins to form, other plants are able to grow on the dune including dandelions. This kind of dune is called a semi-fixed dune. As the original dune (a) has developed, new embryo and yellow dunes have formed.

4.

① Embryo dune   ② Yellow dune   ③ Semi-fixed dune

Strand line   Wet slack   Dune slack

Sand flat

Beach

Youngest dunes

④ Fixed dune (or grey dune): as time goes on, the soil develops and becomes damper and richer. Lichens, mosses and flowering plants can grow on the dune. They form a continuous cover over the sand. Marram grass is replaced by red fescue grass.

Dune slack

⑤ Slack   Dune heathland

Silica sand (acidic)

Shell sand (alkaline)

Dune grassland

Peat   Peat   Oldest dunes

As the dune system gets older and larger, water can collect towards the back of a dune. These damp hollows are known as dune slacks. Marsh plants and small willow trees can grow here.

Climax willow vegetation succeeds grasses and flowering plants as small trees mature.

Figure 9.21 Succession across a sand dune

Figure 9.22 Grasses and artificial barriers used to stabilise coastal sand dunes

Salt marsh succession at Scolt Head Island

Scolt Head Island is located on the north Norfolk coast, and is exposed to cold winds from the east (Figure 9.23). At high tide it is cut off by the sea, while at low tide it is joined to the mainland. The island developed from an extensive sand and shingle foreshore. Wave action during storms sorted the shingle from the sand forming shingle ridges near the high water mark. The early ridges were unstable and mobile. However, as they became more stable, dunes developed and gradually moved the island westwards, in a series of stages. Most of the shingle came from offshore glacial deposits, while other shingle was drifted along the shore. Each of the former ends of the island are marked by curving lateral ridges of shingle, some with high and well developed dunes.

The marshes change in age and height from east to west. The older marshes are higher with more developed creek patterns. However, in some cases human activity has disrupted the pattern. Drainage may lead to settling and subsidence, hence the oldest marshes may not always be the highest.

The marshes include small basins called pans. These can result from creeks being dammed by bank collapse. This impedes drainage, the water in the pan slowly evaporates, leaving very salty water in the pan. High salinity will inhibit vegetation growth, and so the floor of the pan remains bare.

On Scolt Head Island the vegetation is varied and natural. By contrast, many other marshes in southern England are dominated by the recently introduced cord grass (Spartina anglica). Once the bare marsh-flat is formed the first plants, such as green algae (enteromorpha), colonise the mud-flat (Figure 9.24). The algae trap sediment from the sea and provide ideal conditions for the seeds of the salt-tolerant marsh samphire (Salicornia), and eel grass (Zostera) which then colonises the marsh. These plants increase the rate of deposition by slowing down the water as it passes over the vegetation. This is known as **bioconstruction**. In addition, when clay particles enter into sea water they stick together, become heavier and are deposited. This is known as **flocculation**. Gradually, the clumps of vegetation become larger and the flow of tidal waters is restricted to specific channels, namely the creeks. The slightly increased height of the surface around plants leads to more favourable conditions. Here plants are covered by seawater for shorter periods of time and this

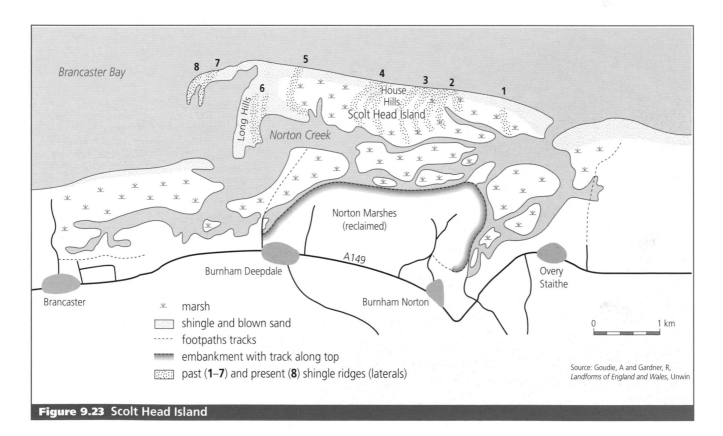

Figure 9.23 Scolt Head Island

Source: Goudie, A and Gardner, R, *Landforms of England and Wales*, Unwin

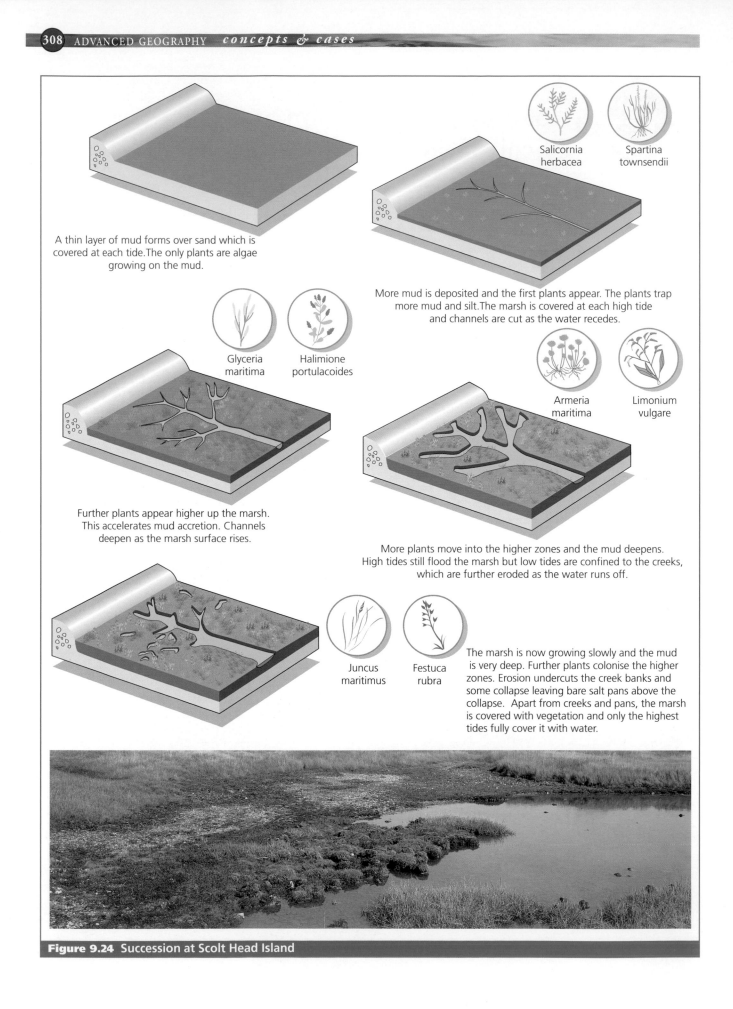

A thin layer of mud forms over sand which is covered at each tide. The only plants are algae growing on the mud.

Salicornia herbacea

Spartina townsendii

More mud is deposited and the first plants appear. The plants trap more mud and silt. The marsh is covered at each high tide and channels are cut as the water recedes.

Glyceria maritima

Halimione portulacoides

Further plants appear higher up the marsh. This accelerates mud accretion. Channels deepen as the marsh surface rises.

Armeria maritima

Limonium vulgare

More plants move into the higher zones and the mud deepens. High tides still flood the marsh but low tides are confined to the creeks, which are further eroded as the water runs off.

Juncus maritimus

Festuca rubra

The marsh is now growing slowly and the mud is very deep. Further plants colonise the higher zones. Erosion undercuts the creek banks and some collapse leaving bare salt pans above the collapse. Apart from creeks and pans, the marsh is covered with vegetation and only the highest tides fully cover it with water.

Figure 9.24 Succession at Scolt Head Island

encourages other plants to colonise, such as sea aster, sea poa and sea blite. These are even more efficient at trapping sediment and the height of the salt marsh increases. New plants colonise as the marsh grows, including sea lavender, sea pink and sea purslane. As the height increases, tidal inundation of marsh become less frequent and the rate of growth slows down. Sea rush (Juncus) and black saltwart become the most common type of plants. It takes about 200 years on Scolt Head to progress from the marsh samphire (Salicornia) stage to the sea rush (Juncus) stage.

Coastal morphology

Each stretch of coast will be, in its way, unique, dependent upon local geological differences (rock type and structures), exposure to wave action and types of wave action. However, it is possible to draw up certain classifications of coasts.

Coastal morphology due to differential erosion

Transverse coasts will develop where the rock strata run at right angle to the shoreline. The harder rocks will tend to form headlands and the softer rocks, bays. A clear example of this type of coast is found in the Tenby area of South Wales (Figure 9.25). Here, the headlands, such as St Catherine's Head, Giltar Point and Old Castle Head, are composed of carboniferous limestone or old red sandstone which are relatively harder than the millstone grit and alluvium that form the bays or **havens**. A similar situation occurs on the Dorset coast near Swanage – the local chalk and limestone form the headlands, while the bays are found in the clay belts.

Longitudinal coasts occur where the rock strata run parallel to the coast (Figure 9.26). This is seen in the Lulworth area of Dorset. The local rocks in the Lulworth area were folded and tilted up to 70° during the Alpine mountain

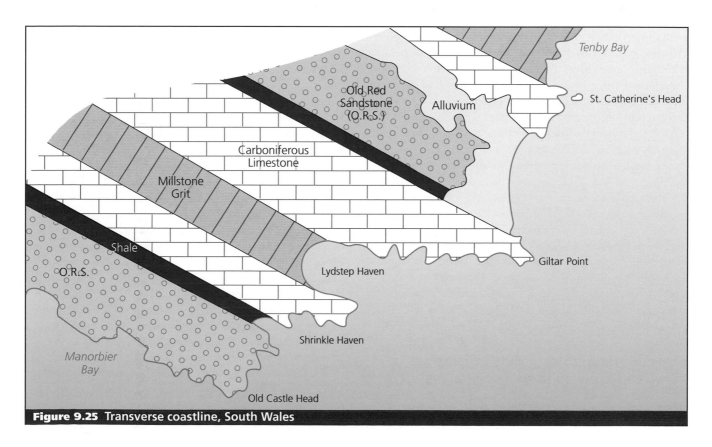

Figure 9.25 Transverse coastline, South Wales

Figure 9.26 Longitudinal coastline, Dorset

building period (30 million years BP). The rock forming the coastline is the relatively resistant Portland limestone, behind which lies the relatively resistant, but weakened, Purbeck limestone. Further inland lie the clays and sands of the Wealden Beds and then the Upper Greensand. At Stair Hole wave action has attacked joints in the Portland stone forming a narrow cleft and two arches. The sea is now able to erode the Purbeck Beds and the Wealden Beds (at high water) to form a cove inland. Mass wasting of the cove sides has occurred, making the cove larger.

This same process has occurred at Lulworth Cove, though to a greater degree. A weak point (major joint) was opened in the Portland stone by two streams during a periglacial period and as sea level rose it flooded in through this low point and eroded the relatively softer rocks to form a large cove whose back wall is formed of the local chalk. Erosion by the sea is now limited (due to the size of the cove and the relative resistance of the chalk) but wasting of the chalk is still proceeding.

Coastal morphology due to changes in relative levels of land and sea

These changes have occurred throughout geological time. The most recent changes (which are still affecting our present

coastlines) have occurred in the last 20 000 years since the Ice Age of the Pleistocene in the Quaternary Era (Figure 9.27). Sea level fell as water was locked up in the great ice sheets and glaciers that developed. During these cold phases, water did not return to the oceans in the normal way. At the end of the Ice Age, the sea level rose worldwide as the ice melted. These worldwide changes in sea level are known as **eustatic changes**.

An additional result of intense glaciation was that under the weight of ice the local earth's crust 'sagged' causing local rises in sea level. When these areas were relieved of the weight of ice at the end of glaciation, there was a period of time of inactivity and then the crust began to 'rebound' upwards, creating a local rise in the level of the land (and so a fall in sea level) and the creation of certain 'raised' coastal landforms. These more localised changes, which are still occurring today, are called **isostatic changes**.

These fluctuations of sea level due to the Ice Age are being superimposed on a present worldwide (eustatic) fall in sea level. It is thought that this eustatic fall may be due to the creation of very deep ocean trenches by plate tectonics.

It is possible to classify coasts according to whether they have 'emerged' from the sea (by way of a fall in sea level or a rise in land level) or have been 'submerged' (by a rise in sea level or a drop in land level).

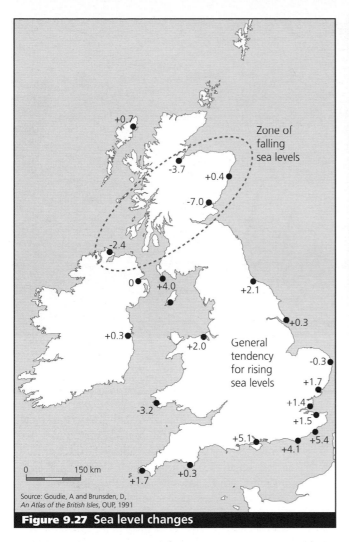

Source: Goudie, A and Brunsden, D,
An Atlas of the British Isles, OUP, 1991

Figure 9.27 Sea level changes

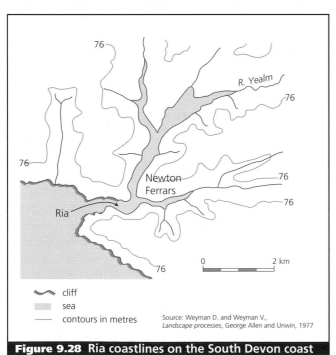

Source: Weyman D. and Weyman V.,
Landscape processes, George Allen and Unwin, 1977

Figure 9.28 Ria coastlines on the South Devon coast

Figure 9.29 Geiranger Fjord, Norway

Submergence – drowned coasts

Drowned coasts are very common as a result of the post-glacial sea level rise of up to 100 m in Britain (known as the Flandrian Transgression). Submergence on all but the flattest coastlines will cause some degree of **indentation**.

Rias are drowned river valleys found in an upland area, where the river valleys are deep and narrow, and surrounded by undulating high ground (Figure 9.28). Two good examples are the Fowey Estuary in Cornwall and Milford Haven in Dyfed. The Fowey is 300 m wide at its mouth and extends inland for almost 8 km, varying in width from 300 m to 200 m. The surrounding land rises steeply from sea level to 100 m. At Milford Haven, the main valley of the Cleddau river and its tributaries have been drowned. The calm water of the ria has allowed deposition to occur in the form of mud-flats exposed at low water. Some of the coastal headlands are being attacked and the material is now beginning to be deposited and fashioned as bay head beaches and spits across the mouth of the ria. By contrast, fjords are drowned glaciated U-shaped valleys (Figure 9.29).

Emergence – raised coasts

Emerged coasts are common in areas that were glaciated during the last Ice Age – they are very well developed in Scandinavia around the Gulf of Bothnia; here many ports functioning during the Middle Ages now lie several kilometres inland and new 'out-ports' have had to be built as a result. Britain too has its emerged or raised coastlines, seen very well in Scotland and Northern England (the most intensely glaciated areas) as the pre-glacial beach, the 30 m beach and the youngest 8 m raised beach.

The most typical raised coastlines are lowlands or former coastal plains that emerged. As a result of emergence, a gently shelving, smooth and wide **coastal plain** develops. This consists of the area of former offshore shallows, backed by the former beach (now raised) and/or cliff line. Coastal plains form rich farming land as a result of the thick marine deposits that cover it. Offshore, in the shallow water, lagoons and offshore bars may be common. An excellent example is the south eastern coast of the USA.

Managing the coastline

In England and Wales protection is given to scenic coasts under the Heritage Coast protection scheme. There are 44 Heritage Coasts covering one third of the coastline and one third of the total length of Heritage Coast owned by the National Trust. Nearly 80 per cent of Scotland's coast is designated as preferred Coastal Conservation Zones through the National Planning Guidelines.

The main concern of coast protection is to protect coastal areas by halting or reducing coast erosion and thereby saving homes, farmland, coastal paths etc. However, other considerations need to be taken into account such as the possible adverse effects of remedial measures on the natural environment.

Flooding

Storm surges present the major flooding threat to low lying coastal areas. They are caused by a combination of low atmospheric pressure and wind stress on the sea surface. A storm surge gets stronger in shallowing water and converging coastlines, for example the North Sea from the north and the Bristol Channel from the south west. The risk of flooding is greater in winter, with the most dangerous period about the fortnightly high waters (spring tides). In estuaries and tidal rivers the problem is worse after prolonged heavy rain. Although storm surges present the major threat, coastal defences may be overtopped or breached by wave action resulting in flood and recent notable examples are Portland (1979) and Towyn (1989) where this was the primary cause.

Major surges in the North Sea result from depressions tracking north-eastwards across northern Scotland. These are exacerbated when the depression reaches the northern North Sea when the winds become northerly, helping the surge on its way, whilst the Coriolis force (the force generated by the earth's rotation) confines the surge to the east coast of Britain. Such conditions were responsible for the east coast floods of 1953 affecting areas from the Humber estuary to the Thames. Following these floods, a national network of tide gauges and the Storm Tide Warning System (STWS) were established to get tidal information and to warn of possible recurrence.

Figure 9.30 The Thames Barrier

The Thames Barrier

The Thames Barrier was completed in 1982 to protect London from flooding which might otherwise result from exceptionally high surges and tides. High levels in central London have been rising for a number of reasons: a rise in the sea level, the gradual subsidence in the south east due to downwarping of the margins of the North Sea basin, and local subsidence which may be due to water abstraction and clay shrinkage. The threat of flooding may be compounded by peak river flows. An early warning system operates which can predict exceptional levels from surge, tide and river flows several hours in advance, giving time for the barrier to be closed.

Rising sea levels

As a result of increasing concentrations of greenhouse gases resulting from emissions due to human activities, the earth's surface and lower atmosphere are expected to warm (see also Chapters 13 and 14). This warming is likely to continue, even if emissions of greenhouse gases were to cease, because of past increases in greenhouse gases and lags in the climate system. One of the major consequences of this warming will be a rise in the mean sea level globally. In addition there may be an increase in the frequency and intensity of coastal storms.

Changes in sea level are the result of two effects: increases in the volume of the ocean and subsidence of the coast. Global heating increases the volume of the ocean as glaciers and ice caps melt and causes thermal expansion of water near the surface of the ocean.

Over the past century the mean sea level is estimated to have risen by around 10 to 15 cm and the rate of rise is thought likely to increase over the next hundred years or so. (This figure is less than local rising and subsidence of land in

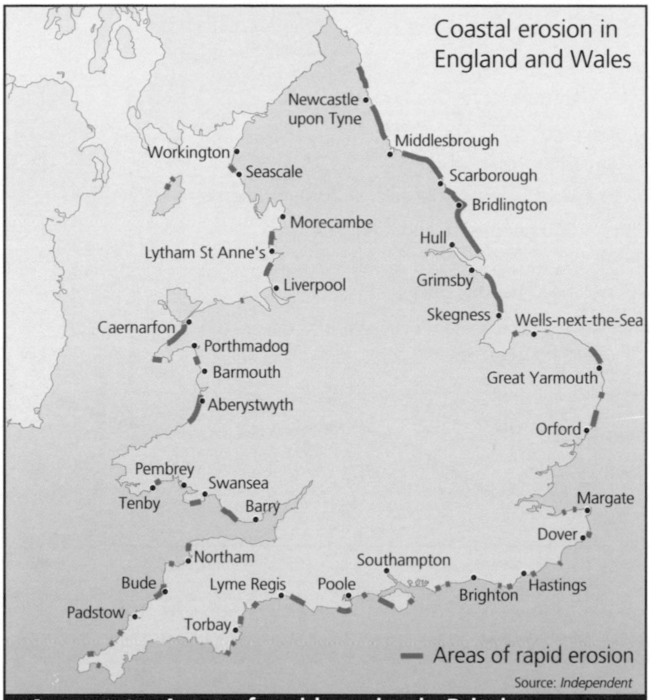

Coastal erosion in
England and Wales

— Areas of rapid erosion

Source: *Independent*

Figure 9.31 Areas of rapid erosion in Britain

many areas, hence different areas show different effects.) Estimates of the likely effects of global warming suggest additional rises in the sea level of perhaps 20 cm by 2030, with a likely range of 10 to 30 cm. Rising sea levels could have adverse effects, particularly coastal flooding and erosion, unless action is taken. In certain parts of the country (notably the South East) the rise in the sea relative to the land may be greater than this owing to subsidence. Since the last Ice Age, the British Isles has been readjusting in the north and west following glacier load removal, which has resulted in a gradual uplift. However, gradual subsidence has occurred on the margins of the North Sea basin in the east and south east. Estimates vary but it may be of the order of 1 mm per year and such subsidence has caused the loss of numerous villages from low-lying east coast areas since the compilation of the Domesday Book. In particular regions other geological processes may occur which need to be monitored in the long term.

Figure 9.31 shows the areas of Britain where a sea level rise could have a significant effect (shaded areas indicate land which is less than 5 m above sea level) and where erosion will be rapid. Many of these include major conurbations or high grade agricultural land. Major road and rail links situated near the coast would also be at risk. Several power stations are also situated on low lying land. In Northern Ireland, such areas are confined to narrow coastal strips and no significant areas exist inland.

The effects of sea level rise may be exacerbated by possible increases in the incidence of storms and thus wave activity, the greatest impact being likely on the exposed western coasts facing the Atlantic. A recent report has suggested that the

north east Atlantic has become notably rougher over the last 25 years.

As well as direct effects such as coastal erosion or the flooding of coastal areas, higher mean sea levels could also have an impact on underground water resources. The zone of mixing of sea water with freshwater in rivers is dynamic and a rise in sea level can cause it to move upstream. A similar effect can occur between freshwater contained in rocks under the land and salt water in sea floor sediments, causing intrusion of salt water beneath the land. This would adversely affect some abstractions along the lower reaches of rivers for domestic and irrigation purposes. These abstraction points would have to be moved upstream or become intermittent to avoid abstracting saline water. See also Chapter 8 on water resources and abstraction.

Rising sea level could also affect coastal habitats, particularly coastal wetlands and salt marshes. The extent to which ecosystems are likely to be affected would depend on the rate of the sea level rise and the ability of ecosystems to adjust, and the extent to which habitats are prevented from migrating inland by coastal defences.

Much of the east coast of Britain is at serious risk of flooding due to inadequate sea defences and the willingness of planning authorities to allow development along low lying areas. Many of Britain's sea walls need substantial amounts of investment if they are to be effective. Many were constructed in the 1950s following the storm surge of 1953 which killed over 300 people. Indeed, the amount of money spent on sea defences has fallen (Figure 9.32).

In addition, natural flood defences, such as salt marshes, have been reclaimed for agricultural and leisure development. Existing sea defences were designed for certain return periods. However, changes in sea levels, a sinking land mass and increased atmospheric storminess means that these return periods are over optimistic. Most of the risk is along the east coast between the River Humber and the Thames estuary. This stretch of coast has a history of flooding and tidal surges measured at London Bridge have been steadily increasing. This is in part due to global warming. In addition, as water heats up it expands – this is known as the **steric effect**.

The increased concentration of housing and other developments on land at risk of flooding is likely to have a negative effect on insurance costs. On the other hand, high insurance premiums are a good way of dissuading people from moving into areas at risk from sea level rises.

Although Britain has not had a storm surge inundation since 1953 the cost of wind damage in coastal areas has been rising. The Great Gale of 1987 caused over £1.6 billion of damage and the gales which swept across Britain in 1998 over £300 million.

In 1994 the government introduced the Habitat Scheme in an attempt to get farmers to enhance the landscape and create natural habitats for plants and animals. In coastal areas this meant allowing farmland to become salt marsh again. For nearly 2000 years parts of the Wash have been defended from the sea, and enclosed salt marsh converted into quality

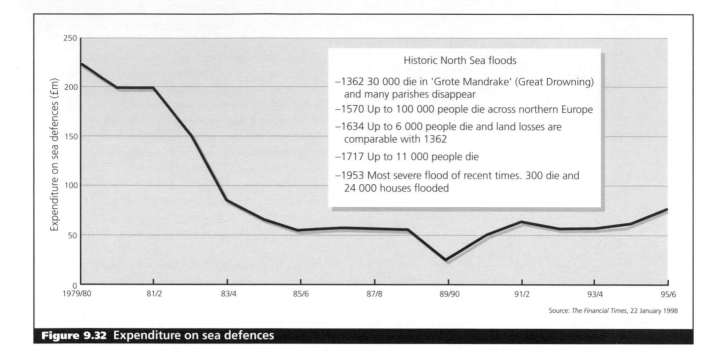

Historic North Sea floods

–1362 30 000 die in 'Grote Mandrake' (Great Drowning) and many parishes disappear

–1570 Up to 100 000 people die across northern Europe

–1634 Up to 6 000 people die and land losses are comparable with 1362

–1717 Up to 11 000 people die

–1953 Most severe flood of recent times. 300 die and 24 000 houses flooded

Source: *The Financial Times*, 22 January 1998

Figure 9.32 Expenditure on sea defences

St Mark's Square in Venice could be flooded every day by 2050. Flooding of the Square has increased from seven days per year at the start of the century to between 40 and 60 days annually at the end of the century, and will become a daily occurrence by the middle of the twenty-first century because of world-wide rises in sea levels. Rising sea levels brought about by man-made global warming are likely to equal the 30 cm of extra tide height it takes at present to send water pouring into the Doge's palace and St Mark's Cathedral. In addition to sea-level rise, Venice's position at the top of the Adriatic makes it particularly vulnerable to storm surges.

British experts have made a direct call for the Italian government to scrap its preferred solution to Venice's threat from the sea – a £3.6 billion system of concrete flap gates fixed on the sea bed at three entrances to the Venetian lagoon

and able to be raised to counter high tides and lowered again to let ships pass.

The likely savings in flood damage will in no way justify the cost of the system and with the sea level rise expected by 2050, the gates will probably have to be closed every day, thus in effect sealing off the lagoon from the sea. Far better, they say, to plan over the next 50 years to seal off the lagoon by natural means, while tackling its formidable pollution problems caused by industrial and agricultural wastes, and build an interim series of small scale local flood defence works.

The Italian government had recently put back for a further nine months the long-awaited decision to proceed with its system of massive sea gates to control tidal surges into the city, which was first proposed in 1973. Over thirty years years on from the devastating tidal flood of November 1966 nothing has yet been created and Venice is still as vulnerable.

Figure 9.33 Flooding in Venice

farmland. However, due to the rising cost of sea defences and the impact of sea defences on other parts of the coast (i.e. the transfer of the erosion problem elsewhere), sea defences have been re-evaluated. Farmers are paid up to £525 for each hectare of land that reverts to salt marsh. Britain is not alone with the problem of rising sea levels. Low lying areas from Bangladesh to Cairo, Miami to Venice (Figure 9.33) are also threatened.

Questions

1 Distinguish between Atlantic (transverse) coastlines and Pacific (longitudinal) coastlines.
2 Describe and explain the features associated with: (a) submerged coastlines (b) emerged coastlines.
3 With reference to specific examples, describe and explain how changes in sea level are likely to affect coastlines over the next 50 years.

Coastal features in Wales

 The Welsh coastline shows many characteristics of submergence. For example, there is the ria of Milford Haven and the indented coast of Cardigan Bay (Figure 9.34). This submergence occurred after the ice retreated from the land, i.e. the post-glacial sea level rise. In addition substantial submergence occurred in the Cardigan Bay area before the Bronze Age, in Neolithic times.

However, in the Tertiary Era, Wales experienced a series of 'emergent' adjustments in base level, which created a series of **uplifted peneplains** or **platforms** in the interior. Moreover, around the coast a series of marine platforms at heights varying from 60–120 m above today's sea level have been identified.

Shape-wise, therefore, the coast seems to point to submergence, but this submergence was recent and relatively minor, occurring in a number of small movements of sea level. The dominant process is emergence, even though the associated features are found inland.

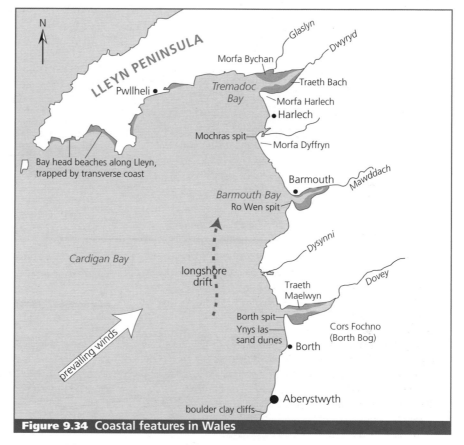

Figure 9.34 Coastal features in Wales

Features due to submergence

The initial stage in the **cycle of submergent coasts** is well illustrated by Milford Haven. This ria represents an early stage in the cycle. Calm waters in the Haven caused sediment to be deposited by the main river and its tributaries, particularly the Pembroke, Cresswell and the East and West Cleddau. This sediment is exposed at low water as **mud-flats**. These flats have not extended into the deeper waters of the Haven because the water here is more turbulent.

The Cardigan Bay coast, north of Aberystwyth, shows three very good examples of the 'mature' stage of the cycle in the estuaries of the Dovey, Mawddach and Dwyryd rivers. Each of these estuaries must originally have been a broad ria formed immediately after submergence. Wave attack upon the exposed headlands on either side of these rias released enormous quantities of eroded material. This was moved northwards by longshore drift. There are also substantial deposits of boulder clay.

This boulder clay was banked up against the cliffs of Cardigan Bay by Irish Sea ice as it moved eastward during the Pleistocene. This unconsolidated boulder clay has given rise to great quantities of pebbles and boulders which can be carried by longshore drift.

In the Mawddach estuary, longshore drift deposited the pebbles and finer material in the calm water across the ria mouth, forming the Ro Wen Spit. The continuing action of longshore drift is seen at Barmouth, where groynes built this century have been virtually covered by drifted material. Behind the spit, deposition of alluvial material has built up mud-flats exposed at low water and poorly drained coastal areas. Similarly Borth Bog (Cors Fochno in Welsh) has been formed behind the boulder and pebble spit at Borth. The spit is covered with sand dunes and curves at the tip, developing several laterals.

Further north, a complex system of ria, mud-flats and poorly drained 'morfa' is developing in the estuaries of the Glaslyn and Dwyryd rivers near Harlech. Here a 5 km dune-covered spit runs north from Harlech sealing off the estuaries of these two rivers.

The extensive stretch of water which formerly existed behind Portmadoc was reclaimed in 1811 by the construction of an embankment.

Milford Haven has not yet developed beyond the youthful stage in the Cycle of Submergence mainly because its mouth faces the direction of the prevailing winds and, therefore, wave approach. Consequently there is no pronounced longshore drift. Moreover, the water at its mouth is more turbulent since it faces a long fetch from across the Atlantic. Thus, spit development is unlikely.

Features due to emergence

Many of these features may have been formed during the Tertiary. The coastal 'plains' of Wales in Anglesey, Lleyn, Dyfed, Gower and the Vale of Glamorgan are mainly composed of a series of uplifted marine platforms at heights ranging from 60–210 m above present sea level. These platforms are young in age and have not been very modified by sub-aerial erosion. The platforms have been eroded across varying rock outcrops and structural lines in a way uncharacteristic of sub-aerial erosion. These platforms are most extensively developed in South West Wales – this is consistent with the direction of maximum fetch of the Atlantic waves and therefore maximum erosion. In addition, many of these platforms, particularly the highest (which lies at 198–210 m) seem to end landward in a marked break of slope. This could be taken to be a degraded cliff line. This old coastline can be followed virtually everywhere near the Welsh coast. Below this old coastline lie a series of other levels at approximately 60 m and 120 m. For example, in the Vale of Glamorgan, Cardiff Airport uses the 60 m platform while the A48 trunk road between Cowbridge and Cardiff follows the 120 m platform.

Around Gower are a number of raised beaches probably formed during the interglacial periods of the Pleistocene (Figure 9.35). The earliest raised beach is called the Patella beach (due to the abundance of Patella/limpets found on the beach) and can be seen around the edges of Port Eynon and Oxwich Bays. The beach is 3 m above present sea level and can be related to similar features elsewhere in the Bristol and English Channels. Opening on this beach are a number of caves (excavated by the sea along planes of weakness). The most famous of these caves is that at Paviland. These are thought to have been inhabited by man and animals during the Old Stone Age.

1 To what extent is there a cycle of evolution with regard to coastal features in Wales?
2 How are raised beaches formed? Use examples to support your answer.
3 Study Figure 9.35. What features of erosion and deposition are shown on the map? Explain why dunes are located on 5087.

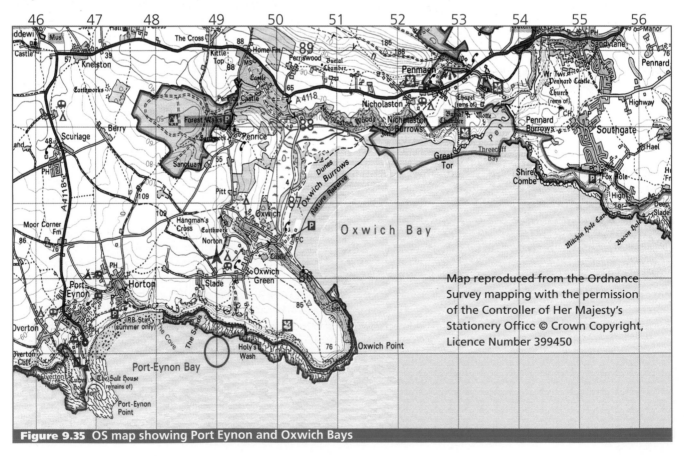

Figure 9.35 OS map showing Port Eynon and Oxwich Bays

Map reproduced from the Ordnance Survey mapping with the permission of the Controller of Her Majesty's Stationery Office © Crown Copyright, Licence Number 399450

The United States' eastern seaboard

Along many parts of the United States' eastern seaboard coast seawalls have protected buildings, but not beaches. Many beaches along the east coast have disappeared this century, such as Marshfield, Massachusetts and Monmouth Beach, New Jersey. As sea level rises, the beaches and barrier islands (barrier beaches), that line the coasts of the Atlantic Ocean and Gulf of Mexico from New York to the Mexican border, are in retreat. This natural retreat does not destroy the beaches or barrier islands, it just moves them inland.

Barrier islands

Barrier islands are natural sandy breakwaters that form parallel to flat coastlines. By far the world's longest series is that of roughly 300 islands along the east and southern coasts of the US (Figure 9.37). The distance between barrier islands and shore is variable. The islands are generally 200 to 400 m wide but some are wider. Some Florida islands are so close to the shore that residents do not even realise they are on an island. By contrast, parts of Hatteras Island in North Carolina, are 20 km offshore.

Barrier islands form only under certain conditions and America's eastern seaboard provides the ideal conditions for barrier islands (Figure 9.37). First, a gently sloping and low-lying coast unprotected by cliffs faces an ocean. Over the last 15 000 years, the sea level has risen by 120 m as glaciers and ice caps have melted. Wind and waves have formed sand dunes at the edge of the continental shelf. As the rising sea breaks over the dunes they form lagoons behind the sandy ridge of islands. Waves washed sand from the islands, depositing it further inland, forming new islands. Currents, flowing parallel to the coast scour sand from barrier islands and deposit it further up or down the coast to form new islands. The island in Chatham Harbour appears to migrate south over 140 years.

Problems protecting the coastline

The problem is that much of the shore cannot retreat naturally because of industries and properties worth billions of dollars . Many important cities and tourist centres, such as Miami, Atlantic City and Galveston (Texas), are sited on barrier islands. Consequently, many shoreline communities have built sea-walls and other protective structures to protect them from the power of destructive waves. Such fortifications, which can cost millions of dollars for a single kilometre, protect structures at least for the short term, but they accelerate erosion elsewhere. The first great sea-wall was built at Galveston after a hurricane devastated the

| Skagway, Alaska (+19.5) |
| Juneau, Alaska (+13.8) |
| San Diego (+0.4) Los Angeles (+0.4) |
| 0 |
| New York (-1.5) Boston (-1.0) Miami Beach (-1.1) |
| Atlantic City (-2.9) |
| Galveston, Texas (-5.1) |
| Grand Isle, Louisiana (-8.9) |
| Sabine Pass, Texas (-12.0) |

Source: *New Scientist*

Figure 9.36 Relative sea level change in the US

city and killed more than 6000 people in 1900. The city survived a later hurricane, but lost its beach. Now the rising sea level is making the sea-wall's protection less effective. Much of the city is less than 3 m above sea level.

Three factors put the east coast of the US at particularly high risk from changing sea levels. First, the flat topography of the coastal plains from New Jersey southward means that a small rise in sea level can make the ocean advance a long way inland. A rise of just a few millimetres each year in sea level could push the ocean a metre inland, while a rise of a few metres could threaten large areas such as southern Florida. Miami, in particular, faces severe problems as it is the lowest lying US city facing the open ocean. Few places in metropolitan Miami are more than 3 m above sea level.

Second, much of the North American coast is sinking relative to the ocean, so local sea levels are rising faster than global averages. The level of tides along the coasts shows that subsidence varies between 0.5 and 19.5 mm a year. By contrast, the west coast, in particular Alaska, is rising (Figure 9.36).

Third, extensive coastal development has accelerated erosion. While sea level rises, apartment blocks, resorts and second homes have developed rapidly along the shoreline. By 1990 75 per cent of Americans lived within 100 km of a coast (including the Great Lakes).

Until the late 1970s most Americans assumed they could successfully protect their coastline against the rising sea. Now they are considering an alternative: strategic retreat – barriers against invasion of the sea. The term retreat does not mean abandoning

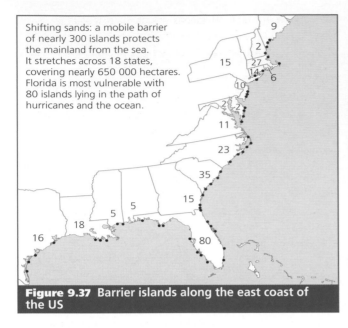

Shifting sands: a mobile barrier of nearly 300 islands protects the mainland from the sea. It stretches across 18 states, covering nearly 650 000 hectares. Florida is most vulnerable with 80 islands lying in the path of hurricanes and the ocean.

Figure 9.37 Barrier islands along the east coast of the US

Figure 9.38 Low lying Miami Beach, Florida

the shore, but moving back from it. Instead of protecting the coast with sea-walls, buildings are moved away from the rising sea, and new buildings are prevented too close to the sea. Hence engineers have stopped challenging nature and have begun to work with natural coastal processes.

In the long term this makes the most economic sense. While it is impossible and impractical to abandon coastal cities such as Boston and New York, state and federal governments are discouraging some new coastal development, especially in areas presently undeveloped.

The nature of erosion further complicates the issue. It is far from a uniform process. Most erosion occurs during coastal storms, especially at high tide. Wind-driven waves create storm surges that flood low-lying areas causing severe damage. In addition, annual storm intensities are very variable, so coastal geologists try to plan for 'hundred year' storms, i.e. an intensity likely only once every century. This often makes their plans seem excessively cautious to coastal residents, especially in areas which have not experienced a severe storm for many years.

Erosion is a dynamic process that varies from storm to storm and from point to point along the shore. Nevertheless, in many places there are observable cycles of erosion and deposition. During calm conditions, moderate currents often redeposit large quantities of sediment removed during a severe storm. This natural compensation reduces total erosion, but it can also disguise the real hazards of storms.

For example, storm damage at Chatham, a town on Cape Cod in Massachusetts, illustrates the dynamics of erosion. In 1987, winter storms broke through a barrier beach separating Chatham Harbour from the Atlantic. This dramatically increased erosion in areas exposed to the full strength of ocean waves. By 1988, more than 20 m had eroded from the shore.

The events at Chatham are part of a 140 year cycle of erosion and deposition. The ocean moves sand along the eastern shore of

Cape Cod, forming and then eroding a barrier island that protects Chatham Harbour. Once the ocean breaks through, currents deposit sand on the north side of the inlet, building the island southward. The inlet moves south, as the ocean erodes the southern island. Eventually, the northern island builds far enough south that the ocean again breaks through during a storm.

Some ocean currents passing through the inlet erode the mainland. As the inlet moves south, currents in the harbour deposit sand in areas eroded earlier. Many homes now threatened were built over 50 years ago on sand dunes that had been deposited during the last cycle of erosion and beach building.

In other parts of Cape Cod, and elsewhere along the American coast, erosion is changing the shoreline permanently. The sea is eroding about a metre a year from the glacial banks (which now form sandy cliffs) on the east side of Cape Cod. These cliffs and Cape Cod were formed 15 000 years ago at the end of the Ice Age. The Cape is less than 2 km wide at its narrowest point: if nature takes its course, the northern end will be left an island within a few thousand years. Human interference, such as building sea-walls, could accelerate this.

Further south, erosion has isolated the Cape Hatteras lighthouse, located on a barrier island off the coast of North Carolina. The lighthouse was built in 1870 about 460 m from the ocean, but by the 1930s the ocean had eroded all but about 30 m. Except for a small promontory around the lighthouse itself the shore has receded nearly 500 m since 1870.

Erosion is evident at many other places along the coast of the Atlantic and the Gulf of Mexico. Major resorts such as Miami Beach and Atlantic City have pumped in dredged sand to replenish eroded beaches. Erosion threatens islands to the north and south of Cape Canaveral, although the cape itself appears safe. Resorts built on barrier beaches in Virginia, Maryland, and New Jersey have also suffered major erosion (Figure 9.39).

Overall losses are not well known. Massachusetts loses about 26 ha a year to rising seas. Nearly 10 per cent of that loss is from the island of Nantucket, south of Cape Cod. However, these losses pale into insignificance when compared with Louisiana, which is losing 40 ha of wetlands a day – about 15 500 ha a year.

Florida's extreme measures to combat erosion are well known. Intense development of Miami Beach in the 1920s started the widespread exploitation of coastal areas exposed to major storms and erosion. At the same time coastal towns in New Jersey, such as Sea Bright and Monmouth Beach, began building sea-walls and groynes to prevent erosion. Since 1945 there have been many developments in coastal areas near large cities, especially for holiday homes and retirement communities.

Hard defences can cost millions of dollars a kilometre and they require maintenance. Despite their cost, sea-walls have failed at several places, including Texas, South Carolina and California. This is usually due to flaws in construction or poor maintenance.

Many US coastal geologists believe that the best compromise between building defences and leaving the shore to be eroded is pumping sand from other locations, usually offshore, to replace eroded sand. The main limitations include the cost and the possible loss of the new sand. For example, between 1976 and 1980 the US Army Corps of Engineers spent $64 million on beach replenishment and flood prevention at Miami Beach. Erosion quickly removed 30 m of the new sand, but then the beach stabilised at 60 m wide. Other coastal resorts, including Atlantic City and Virginia Beach, Virginia, have chosen to add sand rather than build structures to keep out the sea.

Elsewhere, land use management has been introduced. Regulations vary widely. North Carolina, Maine and Massachusetts are in the forefront of restricting development. In Massachusetts, for example, there are restrictions on new developments of natural areas, although it is neither practical nor possible to abandon Boston's downtown or the international airport, both are built on low-lying land facing the harbour. The Massachusetts Wetlands Protection Act limits building on coastal land. The regulations ban sea-walls or permanent structures to control erosion on coastal dunes, as these are dynamic areas that supply the sand to beaches. Similarly, North Carolina was one of the first coastal states to legislate that land be left between the shore and new

Figure 9.39 Barrier islands along the east coast of Florida, US

buildings to allow for erosion. Since 1979, small buildings have had to be built at least 30 times the annual rate of erosion from the shore. In 1983, the state doubled the distance from the sea for large buildings. In addition, in 1986 the state banned the construction of hard defences, such as bulkheads and groynes. Although this was a controversial decision, people and developers have adjusted, in part because the state's beaches are a major economic asset. Moreover, few people want huge sea-walls and tiny beaches.

Other states, such as South Carolina and Texas, impose few limitations, and even encourage coastal development. For example, developers have built high-rise condominiums close to the shoreline at Myrtle Beach, South Carolina. Similarly, at Galveston, Texas, a new beach-front apartment block was built at the west end of the Galveston sea-wall, where the rate of erosion is 5 m a year.

Rising sea levels and retreating coasts could pose continuing tough economic and environmental issues for Americans in the next century. The

- competition for space
- over-confidence in new building techniques
- subsidised insurance
- absence of great Atlantic storms for 25 years
- ignorance, and
- the temptation of great profits

have erased the lessons of experience and history.

Thus some forms of protective 'hard engineering' are justified for major coastal cities, such as New York. However, it might not be justified for less developed areas such as Carolina Beach, North Carolina. Deciding where to draw the line between fortification and retreat will be the tricky issue.

Questions

1 How are barrier islands formed?
2 In what ways have human activities interfered with the natural development of barrier islands along the eastern seaboard of the USA?
3 Comment on the effectiveness of methods used to prevent erosion on the eastern seaboard of the USA.

Bibliography

References

Coasts by E. Bird, Blackwell, 1984.
Classic coastal landforms of Dorset by D. Brunsden and A. Goudie, Geographical Association, 1981.
Coastal and estuarine management by P. French, Routledge, 1997.
An introduction to coastal geomorphology by J. Pethick, published by Arnold, 1984.
Coastal problems: geomorphology, ecology and society at the coast by H. Viles and T. Spencer, Arnold, 1995.

Internet

Ministry of Agriculture, Fisheries and Food
http://www.open.gov.uk.maff.maffhome.html
Sea Empress oil spill
http://www.swan.ac.uk.biosci/empress/empress.htm
World wave heights
http://www.oceanweather.com/date/data/htm

10 geology and tectonic hazards

Classification of rock by formation

There are three main types of rock: igneous, sedimentary and metamorphic. **Igneous** rocks (from the Latin meaning fire) are formed by the cooling of magma. **Sedimentary** rocks are formed by the compression and cementing of sediments including soluble material, loose particles (e.g. gravel, sand and clay) and organic material. **Metamorphic** rocks are those which are changed as a result of intense heat and/or pressure.

The earth's crust consists of about 95% igneous rock or metamorphic rock derived from igneous. However, at the earth's surface 75% of the rock is sedimentary and 25% of the rock is igneous (Figure 10.1).

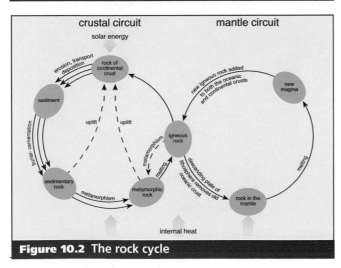

Figure 10.1 Relative amounts of sedimentary and igneous rock

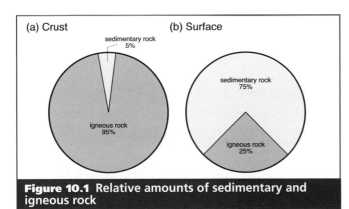

Figure 10.2 The rock cycle

Just as there is a hydrological cycle, there is a **rock cycle** too. New rock is formed by the cooling of molten magma. When igneous rock is eroded it provides sediments which in time are cemented to form new rock types. In places where the sedimentary rock is formed at great depth, the rock may be changed into a metamorphic rock. If deep enough, the metamorphic rock may form magma, which can rise to the surface to form new igneous rock. Thus, there is a rock cycle of igneous, sedimentary and metamorphic rock.

The rock cycle involves continental crust and oceanic crust. The ways in which rocks may be changed into other types of rock are shown in Figure 10.2. The continental crust is continuously being recycled, but at a very slow speed. The average age of continental crust is 650 million years, thus recycling is slow. By contrast, oceanic crust is recycled faster. Nowhere is the ocean crust older than 180 million years, and the average age of crust is 60 million years. Recycling of oceanic crust occurs at subduction zones, where dense slabs of crust sink back down into the mantle. The slab is melted to form magma, which in turn rises to form new material. The rising magma may absorb seawater, and chemicals in it, to form new rocks.

The speed of the rock cycle has varied over time. Because the driving force for the convection of magma is radioactive decay in the core, it is likely that there were more radioactive particles in the past. Hence more heat was produced and rates of movement were therefore faster than at present.

Igneous rocks

Extrusive igneous rocks are formed by the cooling lava, while **intrusive** igneous rocks are formed when magma cools and solidifies in the crust or mantle. Intrusive rocks tend to be coarse-grained since the magma cools slowly and has sufficient time to form large crystals. By contrast, extrusive igneous rocks cool rapidly at the earth's surface producing fine-grained or glassy rocks. Basalt is fine-grained because it cools very rapidly (Figure 10.3) whereas gabbro and granite (Figure 10.4) are coarse-grained because they have cooled slowly.

All common igneous rocks contain one or more of six minerals - quartz and feldspar (potassium feldspar and plagioclase) mica (both muscovite and biotite) amphibole, pyroxene, and olivine (Figure 10.5). The colour of a rock provides clues to its mineral composition: quartz, muscovite and feldspar are light; whereas biotite, amphibole, pyroxene and olivine are dark.

Figure 10.3 Basalt at Vik, Iceland

Figure 10.4 Granite tor, Dartmoor

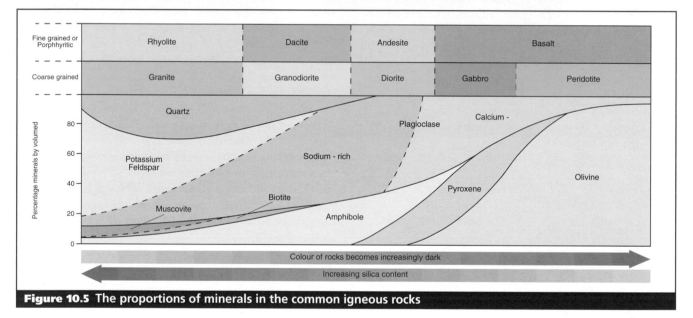

Fine grained or Porphhyritic	Rhyolite	Dacite	Andesite	Basalt	
Coarse grained	Granite	Granodiorite	Diorite	Gabbro	Peridotite

Colour of rocks becomes increasingly dark

Increasing silica content

Figure 10.5 The proportions of minerals in the common igneous rocks

Granite is an igneous rock containing feldspar, quartz and, usually, mica. All granites contain quartz and potassium feldspar. By contrast, grandiorite refers to similar rocks in which plagioclase is the main feldspar. Basalt is the main rock of the ocean crust. This is a fine-grained rock, generally black or grey in colour. It is the most common type of extrusive igneous rock.

Plutons

Any intrusive igneous rock is called a **pluton**. Major plutons include **batholiths** and **stocks** (Figure 10.6). By contrast, minor plutons include dikes, sills and laccoliths. A **dike** is a shaft of igneous rocks that cuts across the geological layers, whereas a **sill** runs parallel to the geological strata. A **laccolith** forms a larger intrusion which causes rocks above to be domes. The landforms produced by plutons depend on the size of the intrusion and its strength relative to surrounding rocks. If it is more resistant it forms uplands or elevated areas; if it is weaker it may form topographic depressions.

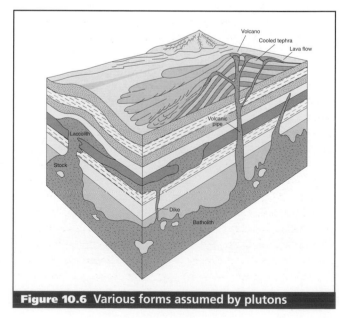

Figure 10.6 Various forms assumed by plutons

Intensity of metamorphism			
	Not metamorphosed	Low grade	Intermediate grade	High grade
Rock name	Shale ⟶	Slate ⟶	Phyllite ⟨	Schist / Gneiss
Foliation	None	Subtle, salty cleavage	Distinct, schistosity apparent	Conspicuous; schistosity and compositional layering
Size of mica grains	Microscopic	Microscopic	Just visible with hand lens	Large and obvious
Typical mineral assemblage	Quartz, clays, calcite	Quartz chlorite, muscovite, plagioclase	Quartz biotite, garnet, kyanite, plagioclase	Quartz, biotite, garnet, sillimanite, plagioclase

Intensity of metamorphism			
	Not metamorphosed	Low grade	Intermediate grade	High grade
Rock name	Basalt $\xrightarrow{+H_2O}$	Greenschist ⟶	Amphibolite ⟶	Granulite Indistinct because of absence of micas
Foliation	None	Distinct schistosity	Indistinct, when present due to parallel grains of amphibole	
Size of mica grains	Visible with hand lens	Visible with hand lens	Obvious by eye	Large and obvious
Typical mineral assemblage	Olivine, pyroxene, plagioclase	Chlorite, epidote, plagioclase, calcite	Amphibole, plagioclase, epidote, quartz	Pyroxene, plagioclase, garnet

Figure 10.7 Progressive metamorphism of shale and basalt

Metamorphic rocks

Slate is a metamorphic rock formed from shale or mudstone. The minerals in shale and mudstone generally include quartz, calcite and feldspar. By contrast, basalt contains olivine, pyroxene and plagioclase. As metamorphism progresses, the olivine disappears and is replaced by other minerals (Figure 10.7). During metamorphism limestone and sandstone are converted to marble and quartzite. Marble consists of coarsely crystalline, interlocking grains of calcite. Pure marble consists purely of calcite grains and is hard and snow-white in colour. Quartzite occurs when the pore spaces in sandstone are filled in by silica, and then the whole rock mass is recrystallised.

There are a number of types of metamorphism. **Contact metamorphism** (Figure 10.8) occurs in areas adjacent to bodies of hot magma intruded into the cold crust. The increase in temperature produces large-scale chemical recrystallisation. **Burial metamorphism**, by contrast, occurs when sediments are buried deep beneath the earth's surface. Temperatures may reach in excess of 300°C causing changes to the rocks. **Regional metamorphism** occurs when rocks are placed under tremendous stress. For example, at a collision plate boundary, such as the Alps or Himalayas, as sediments are compressed and folded, the base of the thickened mass is pushed deeper into the mantle where temperatures are higher (Figure 10.9). Rocks at the base of the continental crust are subject to greater heat and pressure, hence new minerals are formed.

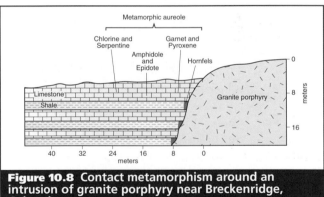

Figure 10.8 Contact metamorphism around an intrusion of granite porphyry near Breckenridge, Colorado

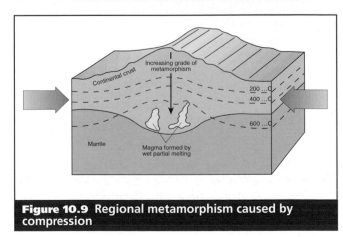

Figure 10.9 Regional metamorphism caused by compression

Sedimentary rocks

Sedimentary rocks are formed from the remains of former rocks or organic material. These have been weathered, eroded, and the remains have been transported and deposited elsewhere. The remains are then cemented, in a number of ways, to form sedimentary rocks. Consequently, this is a large group, characterised by a whole variety of colour, texture and composition.

The loose material is usually deposited in layers (or strata) on land or in water. The material is then consolidated in various ways, a process called **lithification** or **diagenesis**. The surface dividing one stratum (layer) from another is called a **bedding plane**. In some sedimentary rocks, jointing may develop at 90° to the bedding planes to form lines of weakness (such as in some types of limestone and sandstone). After lithification, earth movements may affect the rocks.

The sedimentary group may itself be further classified according to manner of formation:

- **mechanical**

- **organic**

- **chemical.**

Mechanically formed sedimentary rocks occur where individual grains/remnants of former rock have been compacted and then cemented together. For example, sandstone (a medium-grained rock) develops when grains have been cemented by silica, calcite or iron oxide. Those with a high silica content are tough, those with a low content are weaker. Gritstone contains longer particles including quartz or even small pebbles which are cemented strongly. Conglomerate is formed of rounded pebbles, cemented strongly, whereas breccia contains angular fragments cemented together. Shale (also called 'mudstone') is a form of clayey mud deposited in deep, still-water environments forming a fine-grained, thinly-bedded, impermeable rock.

Organically formed rocks occur when the remains of plants and animals, accumulated over a long period of time, are consolidated. Common examples include limestones, consisting essentially of calcium carbonate. There is a great variety of limestone ranging from almost unconsolidated masses of shells, **shelly limestone**; to hard, resistant masses, such as **Carboniferous Limestone**. Chalk is the purest form of limestone. Coal is the accumulations of carbon rich material derived from rotting vegetation. The hardest and purest type of coal is anthracite.

Chemically formed sedimentary rocks develop when the rocks have been precipitated or evaporated from salt solutions. Examples include **calcite** (deposited as stalactites and stalagmites in caverns), **gypsum** (from evaporation of water in inland seas) and **iron ores**.

Limestone is the most widespread and important of organic sedimentary rocks, formed mostly of calcite. Oil shale is a clastic sedimentary rock, having a high organic content, and of great economic value.

Weathering processes

Many rocks are formed deep in the earth under conditions of high temperature, high pressure, and in the absence of large amounts of water or air. When these rocks are exposed at ground level, they come into an alien environment and are 'unstable'. To become 'stable' in the conditions of lower temperatures, lower pressures and abundant water or air, they have to alter by 'weathering'.

There are two major types of weathering:

- **mechanical weathering or disintegration** – this breaks down the rocks into smaller and smaller fragments;

- **chemical weathering or decomposition** – this alters the original rock minerals into different materials, so weakening the rock.

The new products of weathering may remain 'in situ' (in place) as **regolith** or soil, or may be transported away by, for example, running water, wind, or ice. Most weathering is accompanied by erosion and **mass movements**, which is the removal of weathered products. If weathering is to continue, erosion and mass movement must be active: these take away the weathered material, revealing fresh rock surfaces that can be weathered.

Mechanical weathering/disintegration

The major processes involved in mechanical weathering are:

- **frost action**

- **thermal expansion and contraction of rock minerals**

- **disintegration of whole rocks due to temperature changes**

- **salt crystallisation**

- **biological action.**

In general, these processes tend to be more common

- **in Tundra or Alpine / mountainous environments**

- **in arid environments**

- **on steep slopes.**

Frost action

This form of disintegration becomes obvious in areas having temperatures that fluctuate around freezing point (0°C), causing freeze-thaw cycles. This occurs with great regularity in cool and cold temperate lands in winter, in mountainous areas and in tundra zones of the world.

As water freezes, changing into ice, there is an increase in volume (about 10%) which can exert (under ideal conditions) stresses of about 2100 kg/cm². During periods of thaw, meltwater will trickle into joints, cracks, and/or along bedding planes. On freezing, the ice will prise open these lines of weakness, causing the shattering of the rock. Hence the alternative descriptions of **ice wedging** or **frost shattering**. During the subsequent thaw, the moving meltwater will remove some of the weathered material, exposing fresh rock for weathering.

Where flat or undulating rock, or gently sloping areas are covered with angular, frost-shattered blocks, this is described as a **blockfield**. Where this material lies concentrated on the lower slopes of hillsides and mountains, it is called **scree** or **talus**.

Thermal expansion and contraction

Minerals make up rocks. Each mineral will have its own rate and volume expansion when heated, and contraction when cooled. If a rock is composed of a number of different minerals (that is, it has a heterogeneous composition) stresses will be created by this **differential expansion/contraction** and these stresses will cause the minerals to become separated into different minerals. This is also known as **granular disintegration**.

Temperature variations will also cause the rock to expand and contract. This is called **insolation weathering**. The temperature variations can be frequent, on a daily or diurnal basis, or seasonal.

If rock is weakened by jointing, it can disintegrate into smaller blocks (**block disintegration**). As the rock successively expands and contracts, the joints widen and small weathered particles fall inside. On contracting, the joints no longer close because of the wedging and this sets up stresses within the rock. The stresses further widen the joints until the rock cracks up. This process currently helps to break up granite tors.

Exfoliation is the development of layers of weathered rock, due to temperature changes in the rocks. Sheets of material break away from the main body of the rock, owing to differential expansion and contraction between the surface of the rock, which expands and contracts, and the core of the rock, which is unaffected.

If the layers of weathered rock peel off as curved sheets (due to minute structure within the rock) like giant onion skins, it is called **sheeting**.

Exfoliation can also be caused by the process of **pressure release** or **unloading**. For example, granite is formed deep underground under conditions of high temperature and pressure. If the granite is exposed at ground level, the pressure suddenly decreases. It expands, causing cracks to develop parallel to the rock surface. Similar load release can be seen along the floors of glacial valleys after melting removes the weight of ice.

Salt crystal growth

This is common in coastal environments (and desert environments). When salty water evaporates, salts will crystallise out (or be precipitated). As the salt crystals grow, they can prise open cracks in the rock, causing it to break up

(similar to freeze thaw). This salt weathering is most powerful where wetting and drying occur most.

A related form of weathering in coastal areas is **slaking**. Here, the rocks that are rich in clay minerals quickly disintegrate when wetted because the clay minerals take up water and expand, creating stress. On drying, the minerals contract and again create stress. This slaking is therefore common in the tidal zone.

Biological weathering

Animals and plants affect physical weathering in a number of ways:

- **growing roots prise apart cracks and joints in rock**
- **burrowing animals loosen and mix residual deposits, making it easier for them to be removed, thus exposing fresh surface for weathering**
- **agricultural and industrial activities can greatly assist natural disintegration.**

In addition, biological action can enhance chemical weathering as:

- **plants abstract certain elements from rocks, weakening them**
- **decaying organisms give off organic acids that help 'rot' the rock**
- **living organisms (such as fungi, lichen and algae) give off similar acids.**

Vegetation can, however, form a protective 'mat', so reducing weathering and, more particularly, erosion.

Chemical weathering or decomposition

This is more common in areas of warm wet conditions. Chemical weathering is largely due to the action of water, which carries oxygen and carbon dioxide (CO_2) together with various acids and organic products. Even in arid environments, water is available in sufficient amounts for decomposition to occur, as dew.

The main types of chemical weathering include:

- **carbonation**
- **oxidation**
- **hydrolysis**
- **hydration.**

Carbonation

Limestone shows most clearly the effect of carbonation (or carbonation-solution). Here slightly acidic groundwater (CO_2 is dissolved in rainwater forming a weak carbonic acid), dissolves the calcium carbonate ($CaCO_3$) of the rock, removing this material in solution as $Ca(HCO_3)_2$.

In 'massive' limestones, such as Carboniferous limestone, the solution is confined to joints and bedding planes, causing the joints to widen and form **grikes**, **swallow-holes** and **dolines**. Surface solution may create irregularities which enlarge to form solution grooves or **lapies**.

Underground, solution weathering can aid the development of caves, caverns (with redeposited/precipitated $CaCO_3$ as stalagmites and stalactites) and underground drainage systems.

Oxidation

Oxidation involves the addition of O_2 to minerals, often through the action of water being added to minerals (during hydration). Where a rock is rich in iron minerals, the chemical reaction will create a yellow, brown or red crust on the surface of the weathered rock.

Hydrolysis

Weak carbonic acid will quickly and easily break down feldspar minerals, to create clayey minerals. In the rotting of granite, the feldspar breaks down into **kaolin** or **china clay**. Other residues include potassium hydroxyl and silicic acid and these are removed in solution.

Hydration

This is the chemical reaction of minerals with water, where susceptible minerals absorb water, swell and cause stress and disintegration of the rock. This results in rusty-coloured flakes appearing on the rock. Repeated flaking (**spalling**) helps to round off boulders and deepen hollows.

Chemical weathering (Figure 10.10), therefore contributes to the disintegration of rocks by:

- generally weakening the bond between minerals (granular disintegration)

- the formation of solutions which flow away, so that the parent rock becomes porous and ready to crumble (e.g. some sandstones may crumble if the cement/matrix is dissolved)

- the creation of altered minerals which are often greater in volume than the originals, creating stress within the rock, and final breakup.

Factors affecting weathering

Rock type and structure influence the rate of weathering. Resistant minerals such as quartz, muscovite and feldspar resist weathering. Hence granite typically forms uplands. Finely jointed rocks are also more prone to weathering than those with few joints.

Joints exert a major influence on weathering (Figure 10.11).

1 Production of carbonic acid by solution of carbon dioxide:

$$H_2O \;+\; CO_2 \;\rightleftarrows\; H_2CO_3 \;\rightleftarrows\; H^{1+} \;+\; HCO_3^{1-}$$

Water   Carbon   Carbonic   Hydrogen   Bicarbonate
     dioxide   acid   ion   ion

2 Hydrolysis of potassium feldspar:

$$4KalSi_3O_8 \;+\; 4H^{1+} \;+\; 2H_2O \;\rightarrow\; 4K^{1+} \;+$$

Potassium   Hydrogen   Water   Potassium
feldspar   ions   ions

$$Al_4Si_4O_{10}(OH)_8 \;+\; 8SiO_2$$

Kaolinite   Silica

3 Oxidation of iron (Fe^{2+}) oxide to form goethite:

$$4FeO \;+\; 2H_2O \;+\; O_2 \;\rightarrow\; 4FeO.OH$$

Iron oxide   Water   Oxygen   Goethite

4 Dehydration of goethite to form hematite:

$$2FeO.OH \;\rightarrow\; Fe_2O_3 \;+\; H_2O$$

Goethite   Hematite   Water

5 Dissolution of carbonate minerals by carbonic acid:

$$CaCO_3 \;+\; H_2CO_3 \;\rightarrow\; Ca^{2+} \;+\; 2(HCO_3)^{1-}$$

Calcium   Carbonic   Calcium   Bicarbonate
carbonate   acid   ion   ions

Figure 10.10 **Common chemical weathering reactions**

Figure 10.11 **Limestone pavement, Burren, Ireland**

Figure 10.12 **The effects of freeze-thaw weathering at the summit of Snowdon's Glyder Fawr**

Rocks formed deep underground are confined by great pressure. As erosion removes overlying rocks, the pressure is reduced and the rock adjusts by expanding upwards. This produces joints, fractures in a rock along which no observable movement has occurred. Joints are lines of weakness and act as routeways for water to enter the rock.

Climate is an important determinant of weathering (Figure 10.12). Evaporating ground water leaves salts behind causing crystal growth. Temperature controls freeze-thaw action: this is most important at a temperature between -5°C and -15°C. Heat is also a prerequisite for thermal expansion and contraction (exfoliation). Intense heat in the form of fire causes rock to spall (loose its outer layer).

Plants are important in wedging away bedrock (Figure 10.13). They also help to weather walls, pavements, drives and roads.

Figure 10.13 Biological weathering, Cheddar Gorge

Mass Movement

Mass movement is the movement of regolith (weathered material), soil and/or bedrock under the pull of gravity (Figure 10.14). Due to gravity, loose material will tend to move downslope. There are two opposing forces acting on a slope: **shear stress** and **shear strength**. Shear stress is the force acting to cause movement downslope while shear strength is the resistance of a body to such movement. If shear strength is greater than shear stress, the slope remains intact. As slope angle increases shear stress increases and shear strength decreases.

Slumps

A slump is a downward and outward rotational movement along a curved surface (Figure 10.15). The top of the displaced block is usually tilted backward, producing a reverse slope. Slumps are assaulted with heavy rainfalls, and/or sudden shocks such as earthquakes. Slumping may be seasonal, related to rainfall characteristics.

Falls, slides

A fall is a free fall of bedrock from a cliff or steep slope. It may be a single boulder, or , a huge mass of rock. Slides are also rapid displacements of bedrock or debris along an inclined surface, such as a bedding plane. They are common on steep slopes.

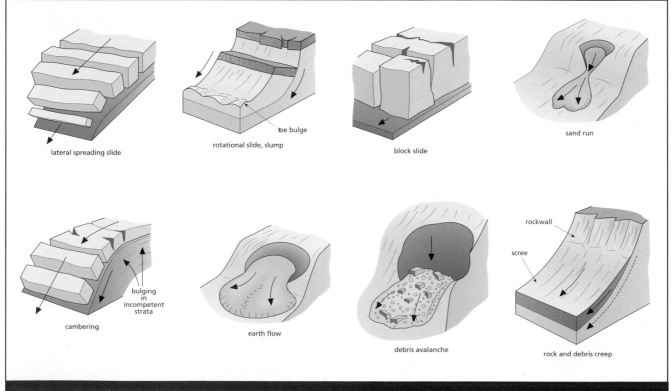

lateral spreading slide

rotational slide, slump
toe bulge

block slide

sand run

cambering
bulging in incompetent strata

earth flow

debris avalanche

rock and debris creep
rockwall
scree

Figure 10.14 Failure modes in unconsolidated earth materials

Flows

A debris flow is the downward movement of unconsolidated material, typically spreading out from a river channel to form an alluvial fan. Flows range from just 1m/year to over 100 km/hour!

Mud flows are highly mobile and travel at great speeds along valley floors. They have a higher water content than debris flows, hence they generally travel faster too.

Creep

Creep is the gradual movement of regolith downslope. (Soil creep refers to the movement of soil downslope.) Evidence of creep includes tilted trees, fences, and telegraph poles. A number of factors contribute to creep (Figure 10.15).

Figure 10.15 Factors affecting soil creep

Frost heaving	Freezing and thawing, without necessarily saturating the regolith, causing lifting and subsidence of particles
Wetting and drying	Causes expansion and contraction of clay minerals
Heating and cooling without freezing	Causes volume changes in mineral particles
Growth and decay of plants	Causes wedging, moving particles downslope; cavities formed when roots decay are filled from upslope
Activities of animals	Worms, insects, and other burrowing animals displace particles, as do animals trampling the surface
Dissolution	Mineral matter taken into solution creates voids in bedrock that tend to be filled from upslope
Activity of snow	A seasonal snow cover tends to creep downslope and drag with it particles from the underlying ground surface.

Research in Colorado, USA, suggests rates of 9.5 mm/year on slopes of 39°, but just 1.5 mm on a 19° slope. Rates increase as soil moisture increases. However, in wet climates vegetation density increases and the roots bind the soil, thereby reducing movement. Rates in the UK for slopes as steep as 33° are as low as 0.2 mm/year.

Earthflow

An earthflow is a rapid movement of earth and water (Figure 10.16). Earthflows vary in speed from 1metre/day to several hundred metres/hour. Most of the material is silt or clay sized, and flows occur on slopes of between 2° and 35°. They are associated with high rainfall and saturated ground.

Debris avalanche

Debris avalanches are mass movements involving large volumes of falling rock and debris that break up on impact, but continue to travel downslope. They have their greatest impact in populated mountainous areas. For example, in September 1717 a large volume of rock and ice fell from the Triolet Glacier near Mount Blanc. The debris moved rapidly downslope, travelling 7 km in 2 minutes and falling over 1850 m (Figure 10.17). It reached a velocity estimated to be 320 km/hour. As the debris hit the valley floor and travelled 60 m up the other side. There it overwhelmed two entire villages.

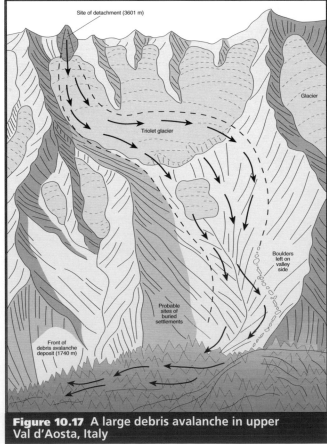

Figure 10.17 A large debris avalanche in upper Val d'Aosta, Italy

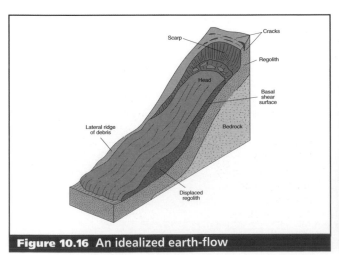

Figure 10.16 An idealized earth-flow

Classification of natural hazards

A natural hazard is defined as an extreme event or condition in the natural environment causing harm to people or property (Figure 10.18). Current thinking separates extreme events in nature (the purely physical geography) from the hazard or risk aspect affecting people. The root cause therefore of natural hazards and any associated disasters, is people living in hazardous areas. Hence natural processes are labelled 'hazardous' only when they present a threat to human life, health, or interests, either directly or indirectly. Thus there is an **anthropocentric** approach to the study and management of natural and geologic hazards, i.e. without humans natural hazards would not exist. Another approach focuses on increased understanding of natural **processes** and their triggering mechanisms in order to provide a foundation for better management.

Figure 10.19 shows a classification of natural hazards. Geomorphological hazards include earthquakes, volcanic eruptions, floods, landslides, and other processes and occurrences. They are included in the broader concept of natural hazards, which encompasses processes or events such as locust infestations, wildfires, and tornadoes in addition to tectonic hazards. These hazards may cause death, injury and damage or loss of physical property through the disruption of economic activities. The amount of loss is affected by the type of society (developed or developing), the methods used to deal with hazards, and the strength, frequency and duration of the hazard itself. For example blizzards and heavy snowfalls cause much more damage and disruption in relatively mild winters of Britain than in the more severe conditions in the Arctic tundra. Earthquakes of similar magnitude on the Richter scale cause more severe damage and loss of life where buildings

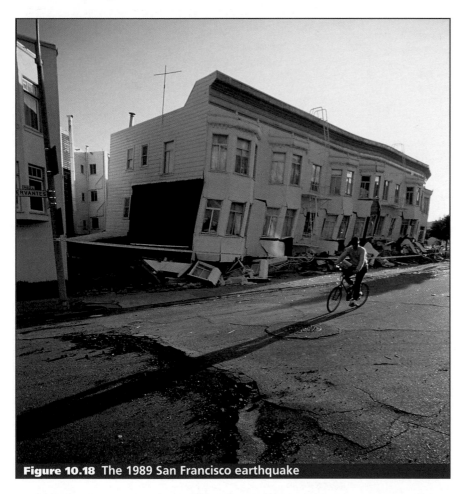

Figure 10.18 The 1989 San Francisco earthquake

Figure 10.19 A classification of natural hazards by principal causal agent

Geophysical		Biological	
Climatic and meteorological	Geological and geomorphological	Floral	Faunal
Snow and ice	Avalanches	Fungal diseases, e.g.	Bacterial and viral
Droughts	Earthquakes	athlete's foot, Dutch	diseases, e.g.
Floods	Erosion	elm disease, wheat	influenza, malaria,
Frosts	(including soil	stem rust	smallpox, rabies
Hail	erosion and shore	Infestations, e.g.	Infestations, e.g.
Heatwaves	and beach erosion)	weeds, phreatophytes,	rabbits, termites
Tropical cyclones	Landslides	water hyacinth	Venomous animal
Lightning strikes	Shifting sand	Hay fever	bites
and tornadoes	Tsunami	Poisonous plants	Locusts
Fires	Volcanic eruptions		

Source: Burton and Kates, 1964

are poorly constructed as shown by recent examples in Turkey and Afghanistan, compared with areas prepared for earthquakes such as Tokyo or California.

Some natural hazards are catastrophic events, striking quickly with devastating consequences. Events that strike quickly and with little warning, such as earthquakes or flash floods are called **rapid onset hazards**. Other hazardous processes operate more slowly. Droughts, for instance, can last 10 years or more, and are called **creeping hazards**.

Geographers often refer to hazards as having primary, secondary and tertiary effects. **Primary effects** result from the event itself, such as the collapse of a building as a result of ground motion during an earthquake. **Secondary effects** result from hazardous processes that are associated with, but not directly caused by, the main event. For example forest fires caused by lava flows, or house fires caused by gas lines breaking during an earthquake are secondary hazards. **Tertiary effects** are long-term or even permanent. These might include regional or global climatic changes and resulting crop losses after a major volcanic eruption; or changes in landscape as a result of an earthquake (Figure 10.20).

Increasingly, efforts are made to control extreme events wherever technology permits. Examples include flood control dams, avalanche and rockfall barriers, sea-walls and groynes, as well as building **aseismic** (earthquake-proof) buildings. Despite these efforts, there is evidence that the toll of death and damage from natural hazards is rising (Figure 10.21). This may be attributed in large part to the growth of human population and the world economy. There is also evidence to suggest that new development is occurring disproportionately in areas of higher risk such as floodplains, earthquake zones, low-lying coastal areas, drought-prone regions, and steep slopes, hence the number of reported disasters is increasing (Figure 10.22).

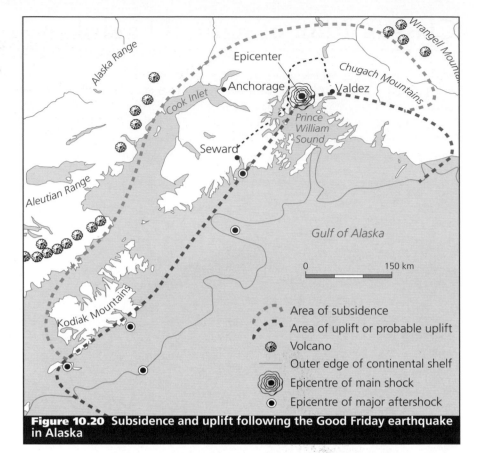

Figure 10.20 **Subsidence and uplift following the Good Friday earthquake in Alaska**

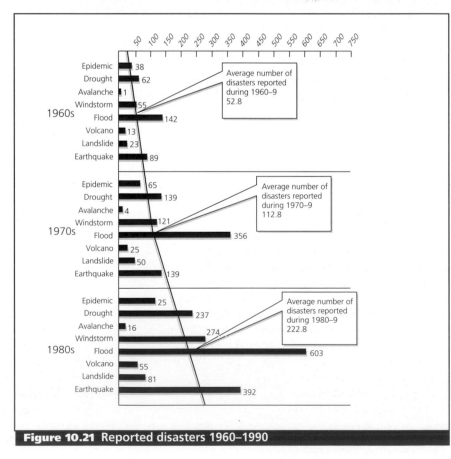

Figure 10.21 **Reported disasters 1960–1990**

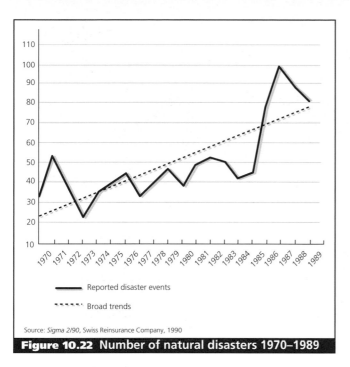

Source: *Sigma 2/90*, Swiss Reinsurance Company, 1990

Figure 10.22 Number of natural disasters 1970–1989

1 Distinguish between the terms 'natural hazards', 'extreme events' and 'natural disasters'.
2 Study Figure 10.19 which gives a classification of hazards. Make a similar table showing the hazards present in the area you live.

Tectonic hazards

Tectonic processes that are termed 'hazardous' have existed throughout the earth's history, and even the most destructive events are part of the normal functioning of the earth. To a large extent they make the planet habitable. Earthquakes and volcanic eruptions, for example, are among the processes that have formed the continents and have provided mineral deposits upon which economic development has occurred.

The earth's interior

The earth is made up of a number of layers (Figure 10.23). On the outside there is a very thin crust, and underneath is a mantle which makes up 82 per cent of the volume of the earth. Deeper still is a very dense and very hot core. In general these concentric layers become increasingly dense towards the centre. The density of these layers is controlled by temperature and pressure. Temperature softens or melts rocks. At the centre of the earth the temperature is about 3000°C whereas it is only 375°C at the mantle-crust boundary. With increased depth there is increased pressure and rocks become solidified. However, close to the surface rocks are mainly solid and brittle. This upper surface layer is known as the **lithosphere** and includes the **crust** and the upper **mantle**, and is about 70 km deep. The earth's crust is commonly divided up into two main types – **continental crust** and **oceanic crust** (Figure 10.24). In continental areas silica and aluminium are very common. When combined with oxygen they make up the most common rock, granite. By contrast, below the oceans the

crust consists mainly of basaltic rock in which silica, iron, and magnesium are most common.

Below the crust and mantle, in the **asthenosphere**, there is a change in density. The asthenosphere extends for about 200 km and is a zone of melted rocks capable of flowing. Below the asthenosphere is the **mesosphere** which extends for about 2500 km. Despite the heat, the effects of pressure are so great that rock and material become very rigid and can only creep at a very slow rate. Finally, the **core** consists of two parts, a liquid **outer core** about 2200 km deep and a solid **inner core** extending for about 1300 km.

The evidence for plate tectonics

The evidence of plate tectonics includes the past and present distribution of earthquakes (Figure 10.25), changes in the earth's magnetic field, meteorites, chains of islands and volcanoes. Increasingly, geologists study plate tectonics with the use of satellite laser ranging techniques and rock magnetism (Figure 10.26) as well as echo-sounders and small explosions to detect shock waves in the earth's interior (Figure 10.27). The study of seismic waves also enables geologists to examine the theory of plate tectonics. By determining the speed and the path of these shock waves through the earth geologists are able to identify the density and thickness of rocks that lie thousands of kilometres within the earth's interior.

In the seventeenth century Frances Bacon noted that the coastline of the eastern side of the Americas was very similar to the coastline of the western side of Africa and could fit together like pieces in a jigsaw. In addition settlers in the New World found that huge coal deposits in the American continent were similar in location to their European counterparts. In 1857 the Irish civil engineer Robert Mallet produced the first scientific investigation of earthquakes. He produced a map which included land earthquakes as well as submarine earthquakes. Many of the seaquakes, as they were called, were found around the centre of the Atlantic Ocean. In the late nineteenth century and early twentieth century it was realised that many earthquakes were caused by rocks suddenly breaking along faults such as the 1906 San Francisco earthquake along the San Andreas fault.

In the early twentieth century an American, Harry Hess, suggested that convection currents would force molten rock

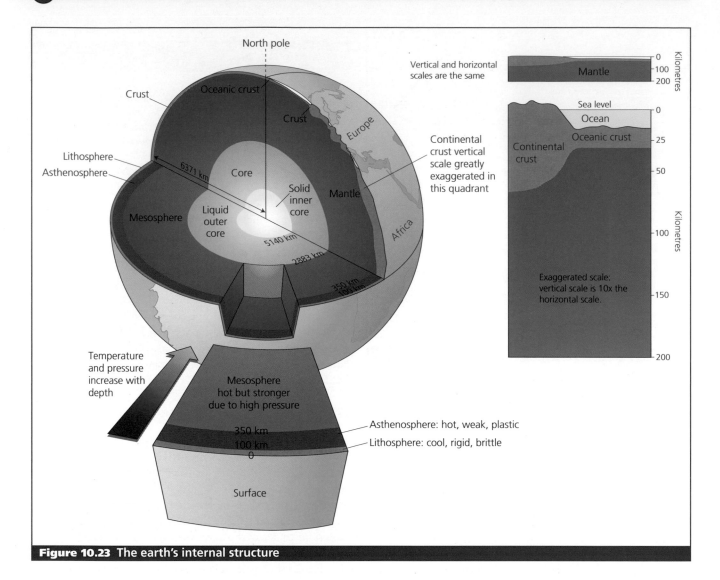

Figure 10.23 The earth's internal structure

Figure 10.24 A comparison of oceanic crust and continental crust

Examples	Continental crust	Oceanic crust
Thickness	35 km to 70 km on average	6 km to 10 km on average
Age of rocks	very old, mainly over 1500 million years	very young, mainly under 200 million years
Sight of rocks	lighter with an average density of 2.6; light in colour	heavier with an average density of 3.0; dark in colour
Nature of rocks	numerous types, many contain silica and oxygen, granite is the most common	few types, mainly basalt

(magma) to well up in the interior and to crack the crust above and force it apart. In the 1960s research on rock magnetism supported Hess. The rocks of the Mid-Atlantic Ridge were magnetised in alternate directions in a series of identical bands on both sides of the ridge. This suggested that fresh magma had come up through the centre and forced the rocks apart. In addition with increasing distance from the

ridge the rocks were older. This supported the idea that new rocks were being created at the centre of the ridge and the older rocks were being pushed apart.

In 1965 a Canadian geologist J Wilson linked together the ideas of continental drift and sea floor spreading into a concept of mobile belts and rigid plates, which formed the basis of plate tectonics. He argued that the earth consists of an

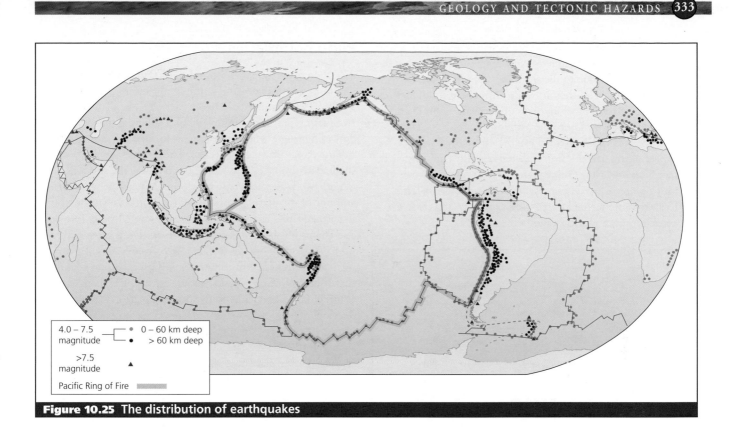

4.0 – 7.5 magnitude
0 – 60 km deep
> 60 km deep
>7.5 magnitude
Pacific Ring of Fire

Figure 10.25 The distribution of earthquakes

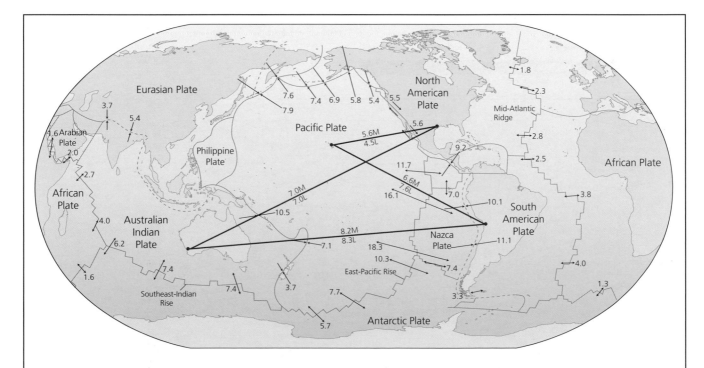

Present-day plate velocities in centimetres per year, determined in two ways. Numbers along the mid-ocean ridges are mean velocities indicated by magnetic measurements. A velocity of 16.1, as shown for the East Pacific Rise, means that the distance between a point on the Nazca Plate and a point on the Pacific Plate increases, on the average, by 16.1 cm each year in the direction of the arrows. The long red lines connect stations used to determine plate motions by means of satellite laser ranging (L) techniques. The measured velocities between stations are very close to the average velocities estimated from the magnetic measurements (M).

Figure 10.26 Velocities of plate movement as detected by satellite imagery

outer layer of six or more major plates which move over a hot partially molten asthenosphere. New material is formed at the mid-ocean ridges. Due to the sea floor spreading continents move relative to each other. In some areas there is subduction whereby one crustal block of dives underneath another and is melted and taken back into the asthenosphere.

In some areas geologists believe they have discovered rocks from part of the mantle. In North Italy, South East Turkey, the Persian Gulf and New Guinea dark heavy rocks known as **peridotites** are composed of olivine and pyroxene silicate minerals that are formed only at high pressure and these are very rich in iron and magnesium.

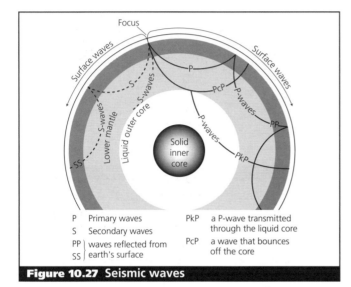

P	Primary waves	PkP	a P-wave transmitted through the liquid core
S	Secondary waves		
PP	waves reflected from	PcP	a wave that bounces off the core
SS	earth's surface		

Figure 10.27 Seismic waves

Plate boundaries

The zone of earthquakes around the world has helped to define six major plates and a number of minor plates (Figure 10.28). The boundaries between plates can be divided into two main types: spreading plates and colliding plates. Spreading ridges where new crust is formed are mostly in the middle of oceans (Figure 10.29). These ridges are zones of shallow earthquakes (less than 50 km below the surface). Where two plates converge the deep sea trench may be formed and one of the plates is **subducted** (deflected downwards) into the asthenosphere. In these areas fold mountains are formed and chains of island arcs may be formed. Deep earthquakes, up to 700 km below the surface, are common. Good examples include the trenches off the Andes and the Aleutian Islands that stretch out from Alaska (Figure 10.29). If a thick continental plate collides with an ocean plate a deep trench develops. The partial melting of the descending ocean plate causes volcanoes to form in an arc-shaped chain of islands, such as in the Caribbean.

Along some plate boundaries plates slide past one another to create a **transform fault** (fault zone) without colliding or separating (Figure 10.29). Again these are associated with shallow earthquakes, such as the San Andreas fault in California. Where continents embedded in the plates collide with each other there is no subduction but **crushing and folding** may create young fold mountains such as the Himalayas and the Andes (Figure 10.29).

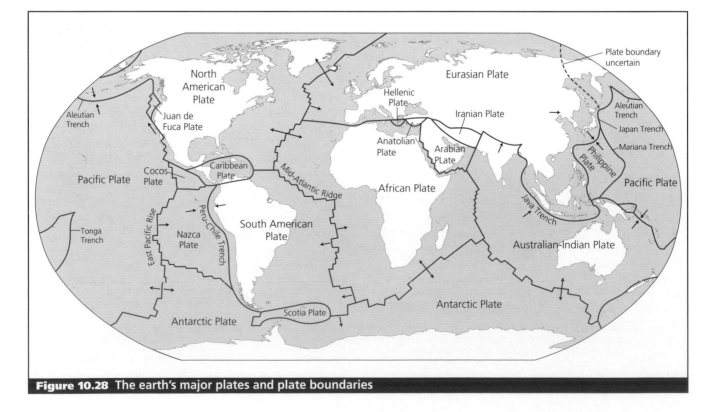

Figure 10.28 The earth's major plates and plate boundaries

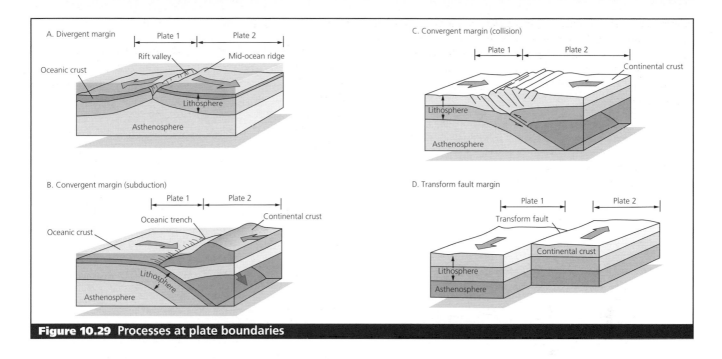

Figure 10.29 Processes at plate boundaries

1 Briefly outline the evidence for plate tectonics.
2 What is a convection current? How does it help explain the theory of plate tectonics?
3 What happens at (a) a mid-ocean ridge and (b) a subduction zone?

Earthquakes

Earthquakes occur in the outermost layer of the earth's crust, where rocks are strong and brittle, and about 95 per cent of earthquakes take place along plate boundaries. Rock temperatures increase with depth – on average this is between 25°C and 40°C per kilometre. At depths greater than 20 km the rocks become hot and tend to bend rather than break. Thus there are few deep focus earthquakes. However, in the subduction zones the movement of cold rocks from the sea floor down into the mantle causes earthquakes to occur at depths of up to 700 km. The size of the earthquakes depends upon the thickness of the descending slab and the rate of movement. Along mid-ocean ridges earthquakes are small because the crust is very hot, and brittle faults cannot extend more than a few kilometres.

The movement of oceanic crust into the subduction zone creates some of the deepest earthquakes recorded from 700 km below the ground. When the oceanic crust slides into the hotter fluid mantle it takes time to warm up; as the slab descends it distorts and cracks and eventually creates earthquakes. However, subduction is relatively fast so by the time the crust has cracked it has slid several hundred kilometres down into the mantle.

In areas of active earthquake activity the chances of an earthquake increase with increasing time since the last earthquake. Plates move at a rate of between 1.5 cm and 7.5 cm a year (the rate at which fingernails grow). However, a large earthquake could involve a movement of a few metres which could occur every couple of hundred years rather than movements of a few centimetres each year. Many earthquakes are caused by the pressure created by moving plates. This increases the stress on rocks and they deform somewhat and eventually give way and snap. The snapping is the release of energy, namely the earthquake. The strength of an earthquake is measured by the Richter scale and the Mercalli scale.

The Richter and Mercalli scales

In 1935 Charles Richter of the California Institute of Technology developed the Richter scale to measure the magnitude of earthquakes. By contrast the Modified Mercalli Intensity scale (Figure 10.30) relates ground movement to commonplace observations around light bulbs and bookcases. It has an advantage in that it allows ordinary eyewitnesses to provide information for how strong the earthquake was.

Earthquakes and seismic waves

An earthquake is a violent shock within the earth that releases huge amounts of energy as shockwaves or seismic waves. These seismic waves radiate from the source or **focus** of the

1 Rarely felt.

2 Felt by people who were not moving, especially on upper floors of buildings, hanging objects may swing.

3 The effects are notable indoors, especially upstairs. The vibration is like that experienced when a truck passes.

4 Many people feel it indoors, a few outside. Some are awakened at night. Crockery and doors are disturbed and standing cars rock.

5 Felt by nearly everyone, most people are awakened. Some windows are broken, plaster becomes cracked and unstable objects topple. Trees may sway and pendulum clocks stop.

6 Felt by everyone, many are frightened. Some heavy furniture moves, plaster falls. Structural damage is usually quite slight.

7 Everyone runs outdoors. Noticed by people driving cars. Poorly designed buildings are appreciably damaged.

8 Considerable amount of damage to ordinary buildings, many collapse. Well-designed ones survive but slight damage. Heavy furniture is overturned and chimneys fall. Some sand is fluidised.

9 Considerable damage occurs to even buildings that have been well designed. Many are moved from their foundations. Ground cracks and pipes break.

10 Most masonry structures become destroyed, some wooden ones survive. Railway tracks bend and water slops over banks. Landslides and sand movements occur.

11 No masonry structure remains standing, bridges are destroyed. Broad fissures occur in the ground.

12 Total damage. Waves are seen on the surface of the ground, objects are thrown into the air.

Figure 10.30 The Modified Mercalli Intensity scale

earthquake (Figure 10.27). The **epicentre** marks the point on the surface of the earth immediately above the focus of the earthquake. A large earthquake can be preceded by smaller tremors known as **foreshocks** and followed by numerous **aftershocks**. Aftershocks can be particularly devastating because they damage, perhaps demolish, buildings that have already been damaged by the first main shock. Seismic waves are able to travel along the surface of the earth and also through the body of the earth.

Following an earthquake two types of **body waves** (waves within the earth's interior) occur. The first are P-waves (primary waves or pressure waves) and the second are the transverse S-waves (secondary waves or shear waves). These are a series of oscillations at right angles to the direction of movement.

P-waves travel by compression and expansion, and are able to pass through rocks, gases and liquids. S-waves travel with a side to side motion, and are able to pass through solids but not liquids and gases, since they have no rigidity to support sideways motion. In 1909 Andrija Mohorovicic, a Yugoslavian

geophysicist who was studying earthquakes in Croatia, detected four kinds of seismic wave, two of them pressure waves and two of them shear waves. Seismographs close to the earthquake epicentre showed slow travelling P-waves and S-waves. By contrast those further away from the shock showed faster moving S-waves and P-waves. These shock waves are reflected or refracted when they meet rock with different densities. If the shock waves pass through denser rocks they speed up. If they pass through less dense rocks they slow down. Mohorovicic deduced that the slower waves had travelled from the focus of the earthquake through the upper layer of the crust. By contrast the faster waves must have passed through the denser material in the earth's core, this denser material speeded up the waves and deflected them. He suggested that a change in density from 2.9 g/cm³ to 3.3 g/cm³ marked the boundary between the earth's crust and the mantle below. This boundary is known as the **Mohorovicic Discontinuity** or quite simply the **Moho**.

Later geologists found a shadow zone, an area between 105° and 142° from the source of the earthquake within which they could not detect shock waves. The explanation was that the shock waves had passed from a solid to a liquid. Thus S-waves would stop and P-waves would be refracted. The geologists concluded that there was a change in density from 5.5 g/cm³ at 2900 km to a density of 10 g/cm³. This was effectively the boundary between the mantle and the core. Within the earth there is an inner core of very dense solid material, the density of the inner core goes up to as much as 13.6 g/cm³ at the centre of the earth.

The nature of rock and sediment beneath the ground influences the pattern of shocks and vibrations during an earthquake. Unconsolidated sediments such as sand shake in a less predictable way than solid rock. Hence the damage is far greater to foundations of buildings. P-waves from earthquakes can turn solid sediments into fluids like quicksand by disrupting sub-surface water conditions. This is known as **fluidisation** or **liquefaction** and can wreck foundations of large buildings and other structures.

Earthquake damage

Most earthquakes occur with little if any advance warning. Some places, such as California and Tokyo, with a history of coping with earthquakes have developed 'earthquake action plans' and information programmes to increase public awareness about what to do in an earthquake.

Most problems are associated with damage to buildings, structures and transport systems. The collapse of building structures is the direct cause of many injuries and deaths, but it also reduces the effectiveness of the emergency services. In some cases more damage is caused by the aftershocks that follow the main earthquake, as they shake the already weakened structures. Aftershocks are more subdued but longer lasting and more frequent than the main tremor. Buildings partly damaged during the earthquake may be completely destroyed by the aftershocks.

Some earthquakes involve surface displacement, generally along fault lines. This may lead to the fracture of gas pipes, as well as causing damage to lines of communication. The costs of repairing such fractures is considerable.

Earthquakes may cause other geomorphological hazards such as landslides, liquefaction (the conversion of unconsolidated sediments into materials that act like liquids) and tsunamis. For example, the Good Friday earthquake (magnitude 8.5) which shook Anchorage in Alaska in March 1964 released twice as much energy as the 1906 San Francisco earthquake, and was felt over an area of nearly 1.3 million km². Over 130 people were killed and over $500 million of damage was caused. It triggered large avalanches and landslides which caused much damage. It also caused a series of tsunamis through the Pacific as far as California, Hawaii and Japan.

The amount of damage and loss of life associated with earthquakes depends largely on six factors:

- population density
- the nature of buildings
- the size of the earthquake
- the nature of the bedrock
- building density
- the accessibility or isolation of a region (Figure 10.31).

The relative importance of these factors varies a great deal. For example, the Kobe earthquake of January 1995 had a magnitude 7.2 and caused over 5000 deaths. By contrast, the Northridge earthquake which affected parts of Los Angeles in January 1994 was 6.6 on the Richter scale but caused only 57 deaths. Yet an earthquake of force 6.6 at Maharashtra in India, in September 1993, killed over 22 000 people. So why did these three earthquakes have such differing effects? Kobe and Los Angeles are on known earthquake zones and buildings are built to withstand earthquakes. In addition, local people have been prepared to cope with earthquakes. By contrast Maharashtra has little experience of earthquakes. Houses were unstable and quickly destroyed, and people had little idea of how to cope with an earthquake.

Another earthquake in an area not noted for seismic activity shows that damage is often most serious where buildings are not designed to withstand shaking or ground movement. In the 1992 Cairo earthquake many poor people in villages and the inner city slums of Cairo were killed or injured when their old, mud-walled homes collapsed. By contrast, many wealthy people were killed or injured when modern high-rise concrete blocks collapsed. Indeed, some of these had been built without planning permission.

Earthquakes and human activity

Human activities can trigger earthquakes, or alter the magnitude and frequency of earthquakes, in three main ways:

- underground disposal of liquid wastes
- underground nuclear testing and explosions
- increased crustal loading.

Disposal of liquid waste

In the Rocky Mountain Arsenal in Denver, Colorado, waste water was injected into underlying rocks during the 1960s (Figure 10.32). Water was contaminated by chemical warfare agents, and the toxic wastes were too costly to transport off-site for disposal. Thus it was decided to dispose of it down a disposal well over 3500 m deep. Disposal began in March 1962 and was followed soon afterwards by a series of minor earthquakes, in an area previously free of earthquake activity. None of the earthquakes caused any real damage, but they caused alarm. Between 1962 and 1965 over 700 minor earthquakes were monitored in the area.

The injection of the liquid waste into the bedrock lubricated and reactivated a series of deep underground faults which had been inactive for a long time. The more waste water was put down the well, the larger the number of minor earthquakes. When the link was discovered, disposal stopped. The well was filled in 1966 and the number of minor earthquake events detected in the area fell sharply.

Underground nuclear testing

Underground nuclear testing has triggered earthquakes in a number of places. In 1968 underground testing of a series of 1200-tonne bombs in Nevada set off over 30 minor earthquakes in the area over the following three days. Since 1966 the Polynesian island of Mororua has been the site of over 80 underground nuclear explosion tests by France. More than 120 000 people live on the island. In 1966 a 120 000-tonne nuclear device was detonated, producing radioactive fallout which was measured over 3000 km downwind.

Figure 10.31 Afghan earthquake in February 1998; inaccessibility made the problem worse

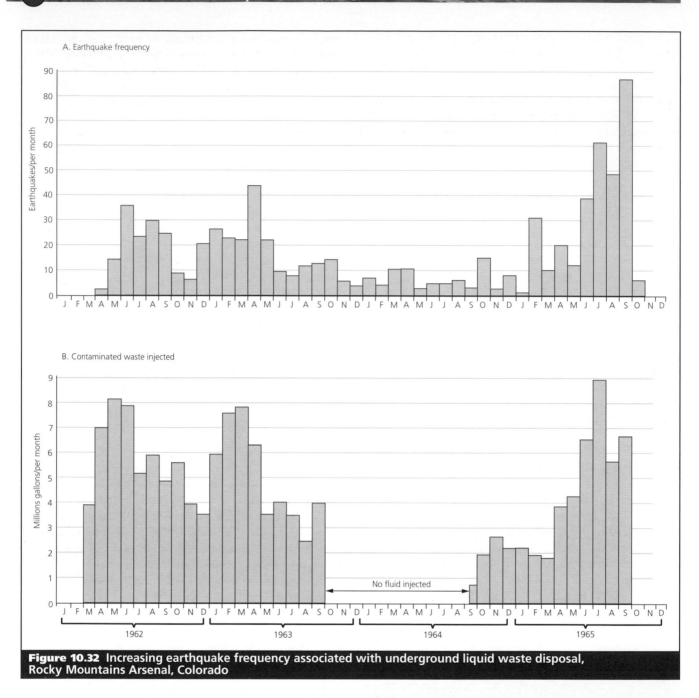

Figure 10.32 Increasing earthquake frequency associated with underground liquid waste disposal, Rocky Mountains Arsenal, Colorado

Increased crustal loading

Earthquakes can be caused by adding increased loads on previously stable land surfaces. For example, the weight of water behind large reservoirs can trigger earthquakes. In 1935 the Colorado river was dammed by the Hoover Dam to form Lake Mead. As the lake filled and the underlying rocks adjusted to the new increased load of over 40 km³ of water, long-dormant faults in the area were reactivated, causing over 6000 minor earthquakes within the ten years. Over 10 000 events had been recorded up to 1973, about 10 per cent of which were strong enough to be felt by residents. None caused damage.

Questions

1 Account for the location of (a) shallow focus earthquakes and (b) deep focus earthquakes.
2 Study Figure 10.32 which shows the relationship between earthquake frequency and underground liquid waste disposal. Describe the relationship between the two variables. Suggest reasons to explain the relationship.

Volcanoes

Volcanoes are found among the boundaries of the earth's major plates. Although the deeper levels of the earth are much hotter than the surface, the rocks are usually not molten because the pressure is so high. However, along the plate boundaries there is molten rock, magma, which supplies the volcanoes.

Most of the world's volcanoes are found in the Pacific Rim or Ring of Fire. These are related to the subduction beneath either oceanic or continental crust. Subduction in the oceans provides chains of volcanic islands known as island arcs, such as the Aleutian Islands. Where the subduction of an oceanic crust occurs beneath the continental crust young fold mountains are formed such as the Andes.

Not all volcanoes are formed at plate boundaries. Those in Hawaii for example are found in the middle of the ocean (Figure 10.33). The Hawaiian Islands are a line of increasingly older volcanic islands which stretch north west across the Pacific Ocean. These volcanoes can be related to the movement of plates above a hot part of the fluid mantle. A mantle **plume** or **hot spot** (a jet of hot material rising from the deep within the mantle) is responsible for the volcanoes. Hot spots can also be found beneath continents and can produce isolated volcanoes. These hot spots can also play a part in the break up of continents and the formation of new oceans.

At subduction zones volcanoes produce more viscous lava, tend to erupt explosively and produce much ash. By contrast volcanoes that are found at mid-ocean ridges, or hot spots, tend to produce relatively fluid basaltic lava as in the case of Iceland and Hawaii. At mid-ocean ridges hot fluid rocks from deep in the mantle rise up due to convection currents. The upper parts of the mantle begin to melt and basaltic lava

erupts forming new oceanic crusts. By contrast at subduction zones the slap of cold ocean floor slides down the subduction zone warming up slowly. Volatile compounds such as water and carbon dioxide leave the slab and move upwards into the mantle so that it melts. The hot magma is able to rise.

Huge explosions occur wherever water meets hot rock. Water vaporises increasing the pressure until the rock explodes. Gases from within the molten rock can also build up high pressures. However, the likelihood of a big explosive eruption depends largely on the viscosity of a magma and hence its composition. Gases dissolve quite easily in molten rock deep underground due to the very high pressures. As magma rises to the surface the pressure drops and some of the gas may become insoluble and form bubbles. In relatively fluid magma the bubbles rise to the surface. By contrast viscous magma can trap enough gas so that it builds up enough pressure to create a volcanic eruption.

The style of eruption is greatly influenced by the processes operating at different plate boundaries which produce magma of different, but predictable, composition. Some minerals melt before others in a process called **partial melting**. This alters the composition of molten rock produced. Partial melting of the earth's mantle produces basalt. At subduction zones the older and deeper slabs experience greater partial melting and this produces a silica rich magma.

Volcanic hazards

Ash and debris falls steadily from the volcanic cloud blanketing the ground with a deposit known as a **pyroclastic fall**. These can be very dangerous, especially as the fine ash particles can damage people's lungs. Also ash is fairly heavy – a small layer only a few centimetres thick can be enough to cause a building to collapse. Dust and aerosol also cause havoc with global climatic patterns. Pyroclastic falls are powerful enough to knock down trees and to leave a trail of destruction.

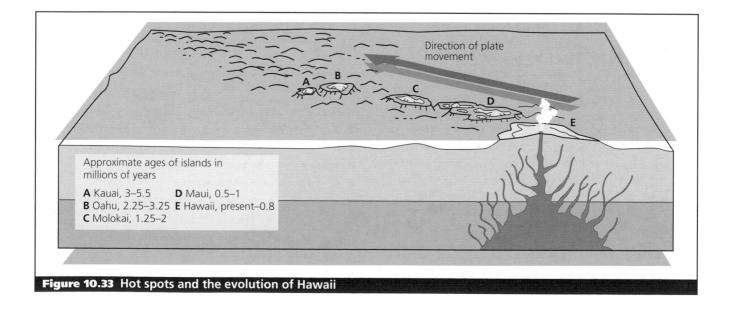

Direction of plate movement

Approximate ages of islands in millions of years

A Kauai, 3–5.5   **D** Maui, 0.5–1
B Oahu, 2.25–3.25 **E** Hawaii, present–0.8
C Molokai, 1.25–2

Figure 10.33 Hot spots and the evolution of Hawaii

Figure 10.34 Volcanic disasters since 1800 in which more than one thousand people lost their lives

Volcano	Country	Year	Primary Cause of Fatalities			
			Pyroclastic Eruption	Mud flow	Tsunami	Famine
Mayon	Philippines	1814	1200			
Tambora	Indonesia	1815	12 000			80 000
Galunggung	Indonesia	1822	1500	4000		
Mayon	Philippines	1825		1500		
Awu	Indonesia	1826		3000		
Cotopaxi	Ecuador	1877		1000		
Krakatau	Indonesia	1883			36 417	
Awu	Indonesia	1892		1532		
Soufrière	St Vincent	1902	1565			
Mt Pelée	Martinique	1902	29 000			
Santa Maria	Guatemala	1902	6000			
Taal	Philippines	1911	1332			
Kelud	Indonesia	1919		5110		
Merapi	Indonesia	1930	1300			
Lamington	Papua-New Guinea	1951	2942			
Agung	Indonesia	1963	1900			
El Chichón	Mexico	1982	1700			
Nevado del Ruiz	Colombia	1985		23 000		

Lahars or volcanic mud flows are another hazard associated with volcanoes. A combination of heavy rain and unstable ash increase the hazard of lahars. The hazards associated with volcanic eruption vary spatially. Close to the volcano people are at risk of large fragments of debris, ash falls and poisonous gases. Further away pyroclastic flows may prove hazardous and further still mud and debris flows may have an impact on more distant settlements. In addition, volcanoes can lead to tsunami and to famine. Although there is good evidence for the spatial distribution of volcanoes, there is little pattern in their temporal distribution (Figure 10.34).

Vulnerability and susceptibility

Since 1975 over 3 million lives have been lost as a direct result of hazardous events, and at least 800 million people have suffered adverse effects such as loss of property or health. In addition, the average number of reported disasters is rising. A United Nations estimate for the 1990s suggests there will be tens of thousands of landslides and earthquakes; 1 million thunderstorms; 100 000 floods; and many thousands of tropical cyclones and hurricanes, tsunamis, droughts and volcanic eruptions. Natural disasters cause about $40 billion each year in physical damage; windstorms, floods and earthquakes alone cost about $18.8 million per day!

The concept of vulnerability encompasses not only the physical effects of a natural hazard but also the status of people

Questions

1 What are the main hazards associated with volcanoes?
2 Study Figure 10.34 which shows volcanic disasters since 1800. Describe the location of these disasters. How do you account for this pattern?

and property in the area. Many factors can increase one's vulnerability to natural hazards (Figure 10.35), especially catastrophic events. Aside from the simple fact of living in a hazardous area, vulnerability depends on:

■ **population density – a large number of rapidly growing cities occur in hazardous areas (Figure 10.36)**
■ **understanding of the area**
■ **public education**
■ **awareness of hazards**
■ **the existence of an early-warning system**
■ **effective lines of communication**
■ **availability and readiness of emergency personnel**
■ **insurance cover (Figure 10.37)**
■ **construction styles and building codes**
■ **the nature of society**
■ **cultural factors that influence public response to warnings.**

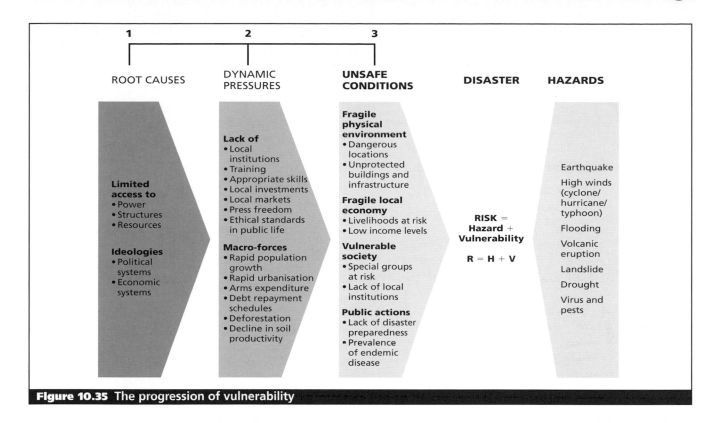

Figure 10.35 The progression of vulnerability

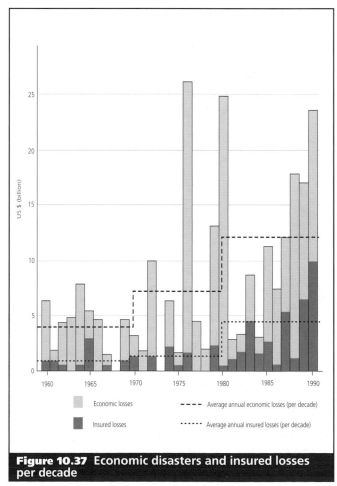

Figure 10.36 Major urban areas and the risk to natural hazards

City/ conurbation	Population 1980 (millions)	Projected population 2000 (millions)	Hazard(s) to which exposed
Mexico City	14.5	25.8	earthquake
Tokyo-Yokohama	17.7	20.0	earthquake
Calcutta	9.5	16.5	cyclone; flood
Tehran	5.4	11.3	earthquake
Jakarta	6.6	13.3	earthquake; volcano
Rio de Janeiro	9.2	13.2	landslide
Shanghai	11.7	13.2	flood; typhoon
Delhi	5.8	13.2	flood
Dhaka	3.4	11.2	flood; cyclone
Manila	5.9	11.1	flood; cyclone
Cairo-Giza	6.9	11.1	flood; earthquake
Los Angeles	9.5	11.0	earthquake; landslide
Beijing	9.0	10.4	earthquake

Figure 10.37 Economic disasters and insured losses per decade

Many of these factors help explain the fact that less developed countries are much more vulnerable to natural hazards than are industrialised countries.

Hazard management

The Guatemala earthquake, 4 February 1976

The Guatemala earthquake of 1976 was a milestone for many aid agencies involved in disaster assistance. Some major 'mistakes' were committed, and some innovative ideas in the construction of earthquake-resistant (aseismic) houses were developed.

The earthquake killed 22 000 people living in unsafe houses in the rural highlands of Guatemala as well as within dangerous squatter settlements in Guatemala City (Figure 10.38). In this well-known fault zone most of the poorest housing was in the ravines or gorges which were highly susceptible to landslides whenever earth movements occurred (Figure 10.39). By contrast, the upper and middle classes were virtually unharmed as their houses were built to costly anti-earthquake specifications.

This was the first major earthquake widely recognised as having such a markedly selective class impact. The disaster focused attention on the urban and rural poor people's vulnerability to exploitation by the landlords of Guatemala. Vulnerability variations can be clearly detected in the Guatemalan case.

First, there was a strong ethnic as well as class factor that operated. The highland rural people who died were not only poor, but were indigenous Mayan Indians. The dead in Guatemala City (some 1200 people) and the 90 000 homeless were almost exclusively from the city's slums. Secondly, it was exceedingly difficult for either Indians or urban squatters to obtain post-disaster assistance from the government. The city received proportionately little aid largely because it is governed by the most radical opposition tolerated in Guatemala, the Frente Unido de la Revolucion, a social democratic coalition. Thus the socio-economic conditions that led to so many people living in unsafe conditions, and the political forces that controlled post-disaster aid, were a mirror of the society at large.

A survey in 1989 re-examined the vulnerability of the urban poor. While there were still houses on the steep slopes, they were certainly not as congested or precarious. Many of the urban poor who lost their homes immediately left the most dangerous slopes for flat or gently sloping sites a short distance away. This illegal 'invasion' took place from the day of the earthquake onwards. Ever since, the shanty town or barrio has been known as 4th of February. When survivors first moved into the safer sites, there were a large number of visiting newsmen in the city to report on the disaster and the authorities turned a blind eye to the 'invasion'. Eventually, perhaps due to the sheer force of numbers linked to sustained political pressure, the occupiers were granted legal titles to the land by the government.

However, there is little evidence that the new homes had

earthquake-resistant design. So although the sites are safer from earthquake-induced landslides, flash-floods and eviction orders, the homes remain dangerous. In fact the risk of houses collapsing may have increased. When they were illegally sited they were generally built out of lightweight materials, including corrugated iron sheet roofing. However, when the buildings were legalised many families began to build in heavy materials such as reinforced concrete which is likely to cause greater damage than structures built of lighter materials.

By contrast to the progress in Guatemala City, there was political repression in the rural highlands of Guatemala. In the early 1980s, tens of thousands of highland Indians were killed by the military in disputes over expropriation of Indian land.

Figure 10.38 People huddle in the street after a major earthquake struck Guatemala City

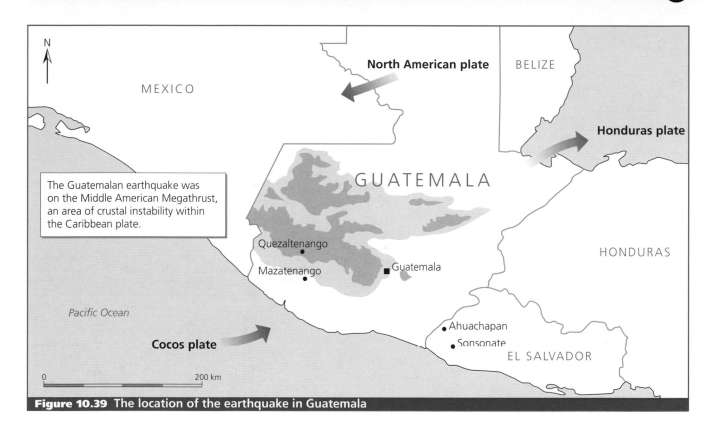

North American plate

BELIZE

MEXICO

Honduras plate

GUATEMALA

The Guatemalan earthquake was on the Middle American Megathrust, an area of crustal instability within the Caribbean plate.

Quezaltenango

Mazatenango

■ Guatemala

HONDURAS

Pacific Ocean

Cocos plate

● Ahuachapan

● Sonsonate

EL SALVADOR

N

0   200 km

Figure 10.39 The location of the earthquake in Guatemala

Post-disaster response after the Nevado del Ruiz volcanic eruption

SPATIAL FOCUS

Another example is the effects of the eruption at Nevado del Ruiz, on the town of Armero in Colombia on 13 November 1985 (Figure 10.40). The volcano had been inactive since 1845 and resumed activity over a century later. A series of minor eruptions and earth tremors caused a cloud of hot pumice and ash. As a result, part of the ice cap of the 5400-metre (17 700-feet) volcano exploded and caused the Guali river to overflow. This in turn caused a natural dam to burst, releasing a torrent that travelled at speeds of about 70 km (45 miles) per hour and a massive mud flow (10.41) which enveloped the town of Armero, population 29 000. As a result of the volcano's inactivity there had been limited evacuation drills, and the volcano had not been perceived as a threat to human life.

In 1988, three years after the disaster, a group of lawyers inserted a notice in the local press of Manizales and in the small towns close to Armero. They invited anyone who had suffered injury or the loss of relatives or property to sue the government of Colombia for gross negligence in not warning or evacuating them in time to avoid injury or property losses. Over 1000 claims were lodged amounting to a total claim about £40 million. The claim against the government was their alleged negligence in failing to

develop effective preparedness planning (including evacuation procedures) to enable the population to escape falling debris and mudslides. It was expected that government lawyers would argue that the residents were aware of the risks in choosing to occupy a hazardous yet highly fertile area. Three expert vulcanologists were questioned as to whether the scale, location and timing of the mud flow could have been accurately forecast. They gave a negative answer and on this basis the government was cleared of responsibility.

Following the legal challenge, the government created the Governmental Preparedness System at central and provincial level, which includes detailed warning and evacuation systems. However, while evacuation exists on paper, economic priorities may outweigh the needs for safety. For example, in 1993 the Galeras volcano erupted putting the nearby town of Pasto at risk. Although the government Disaster Preparedness Agency had repeatedly attempted to issue warnings to the public, the local authorities refused to authorise them, following an economic crash years earlier, when a volcano warning caused a financial crisis.

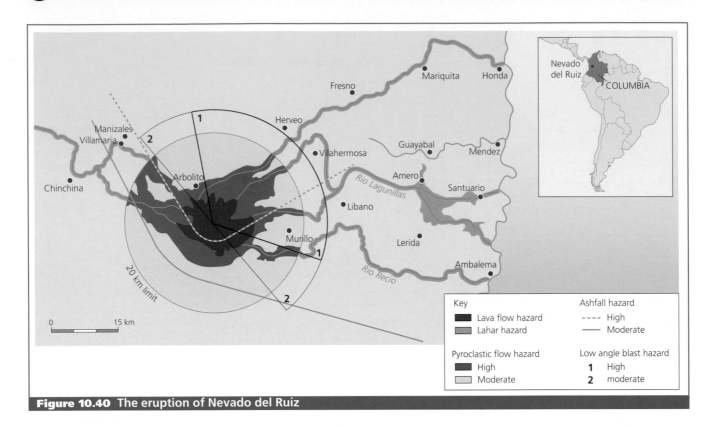

Figure 10.40 The eruption of Nevado del Ruiz

Figure 10.41 Landscape devastated by the aftermath of the Nevado del Ruiz eruption

Pre-disaster planning, Taal volcano, the Philippines

An example of the conflicting demands of economic prosperity versus safety is illustrated by the example of Taal volcano in the Philippines (Figure 10.43). This is one of the world's deadliest volcanoes and is located on an island in Lake Taal, about 60 km south of Manila (Figure 10.42). Taal has erupted 33 times since its earliest recorded explosion in 1572. The 1911 eruption resulted in 1334 deaths and covered an area of 2000 km² with ash and volcanic debris which fell as far away as Manila.

The island is small and the population is less than 4000 people. However, they are relatively prosperous. The economy is based on fishing, fish-farming, agriculture, mining for scoria, and tourism. The location of settlements on the island is closely related to the rich fertile soils suitable for sweet potatoes and corn. Alarmingly, population growth is rapid, growing at 9.6 per cent per year, more than three times the national average. Moreover, the island could not cope with a major eruption. It has only 215 boats which could transport less than 2000 people. Hence, in the event of a very sudden eruption with limited warning, only about half of the population would be able to escape.

A Disaster Management Training Workshop in 1988 found that there was very little anxiety on the part of the population over the risks they faced. This was true even among survivors of the 1965 Taal eruption. The lack of escape boats was also of

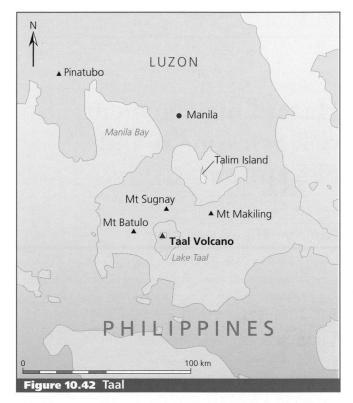

Figure 10.42 Taal

Figure 10.43 Taal volcano, a disaster waiting to happen?

minimal concern. Islanders referred to a building set up by the Philippine Institute of Volcanology (PIV), as a form of 'volcanic eruption insurance policy'. They assumed that the PIV would look after them in the event of a disaster. The very presence of a warning station made some feel that the island was therefore safe for them to live on.

Thus the local resident population took a view in which the Taal volcano was just one of many perceived risks that influenced their decision on where to live and work. By contrast, members of the Disaster Management Training Workshop sought to prevent residential occupation of the island. They adopted a narrow view of risk and vulnerability based on physical processes and failed to acknowledge the advantages that the area offered. Each side has an entirely legitimate and logical response to the same hazard. However, their views differ on account of their different needs, priorities, perceptions and values.

Hazard management, risk assessment and perception

Coping with earthquakes

Most places with a history of earthquakes have developed plans for coping with them. The aim is to reduce the effect of the earthquakes and thus save lives, buildings and money. The ways of reducing earthquake impact include earthquake prediction, building design, flood prevention and public information.

Preparation

Earthquakes have killed about 1.5 million people in the twentieth century and the number of earthquakes appears to be rising (Figure 10.44). Most of the deaths were caused by the collapse of unsuitable and poorly designed buildings. More than a third of the world's largest and fastest growing cities are located in regions of high earthquake risk, hence the problems are likely to intensify (Figure 10.36 on page 341).

It is difficult to stop an earthquake from happening, thus prevention normally involves minimising the prospect of death, injury or damage by minimising building in high-risk areas, and using aseismic designs (Figure 10.45). In addition, warning systems can be used to warn people of an imminent earthquake and what to do when it does happen. Insurance schemes are another form of preparation, by sharing the costs between a wide group of people.

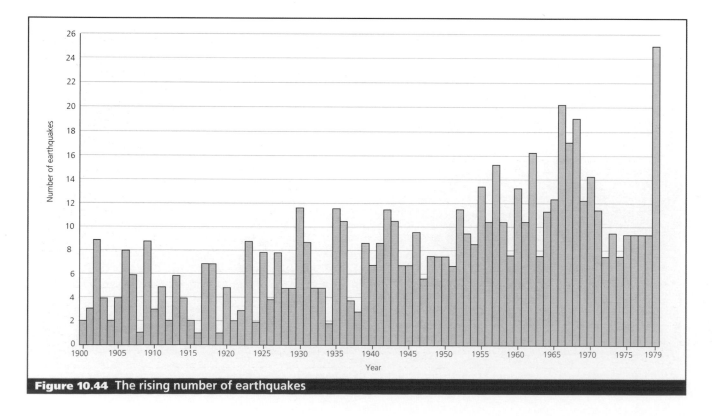

Figure 10.44 The rising number of earthquakes

Building design

Increasingly, as the availability of building land is reduced, more and more people are living in seismic areas. This increases the potential impact of an earthquake. However, buildings can be designed to withstand the ground-shaking that occurs in an earthquake (Figure 10.45). Single-storey buildings are more suitable than multi-storey structures, because this reduces the size of the population at risk, and threat of collapse over roads and evacuation routes. Some tall buildings are built with a 'soft storey' at the bottom, such as a car park raised on pillars. This collapses in an earthquake, so that the upper floors sink down onto it and it cushions the impact. Basement isolation, i.e. mounting the foundations of a building on rubber mounts which allow the ground to move under the building, is widely used. This isolates the building from the tremors.

Building reinforcement strategies include building on foundations built deep into underlying bedrock and the use of steel constructed frames that can withstand shaking. Land use planning is another important way of reducing earthquake risk (Figure 10.46).

Controlling earthquakes

In theory, by altering the fluid pressure deep underground at the point of greatest stress in the fault line, a series of small and less damaging earthquake events may be triggered. This could release the energy that would otherwise build up to create a major event. Additionally, a series of controlled underground nuclear explosions might relieve stress before it reached critical levels.

Prediction and risk assessment

There are a number of methods of detecting earthquakes – distortion of fences, roads and buildings are some examples, changing levels of water in bore-holes is another. As strain can change the water-holding capacity or porosity of rocks by closing and opening its tiny cracks then water levels in bore-holes will fluctuate with increased earthquake activity. In addition satellites can now be used to measure the position of points on the surface of the earth to within a few centimetres. However, predicting earthquakes is not simple. Some earthquakes are very irregular in time and may only occur less than once every one hundred years. By contrast other earthquakes may continually slip and produce a large number of very small earthquakes. In addition different parts of the fault line may behave differently. Areas which do not move are referred to as seismic gaps whereas areas which move and have lots of mini earthquakes may be far less hazardous.

Earthquake prediction is only partly successful although it offers a potentially valuable way of reducing the impact of earthquakes. Some elements of prediction are relatively easy. For example, the location of earthquakes is closely linked to the distribution of fault lines. However, the timing of earthquakes is difficult to predict, although previous patterns and frequencies of earthquake events can offer some clues as to what is likely to happen in the future. Similarly the size of an earthquake event is difficult to predict.

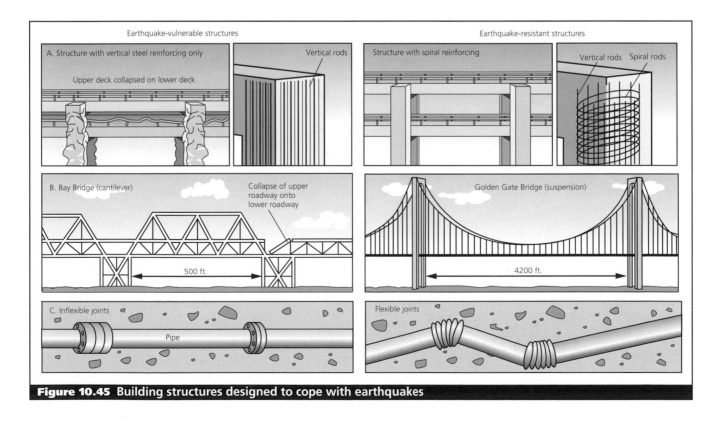

Figure 10.45 Building structures designed to cope with earthquakes

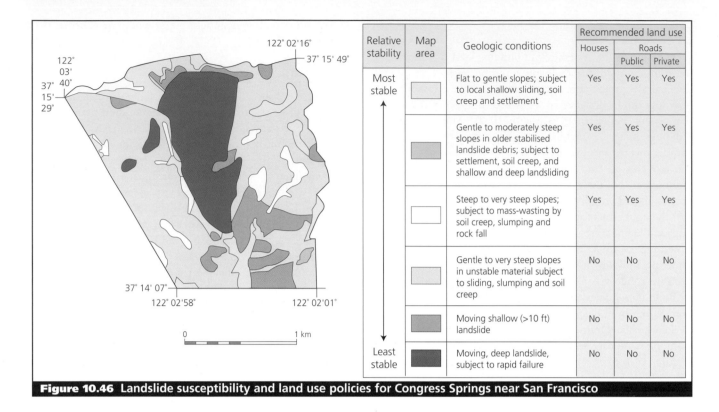

Relative stability	Map area	Geologic conditions	Recommended land use		
			Houses	Roads	
				Public	Private
Most stable ↑		Flat to gentle slopes; subject to local shallow sliding, soil creep and settlement	Yes	Yes	Yes
		Gentle to moderately steep slopes in older stabilised landslide debris; subject to settlement, soil creep, and shallow and deep landsliding	Yes	Yes	Yes
		Steep to very steep slopes; subject to mass-wasting by soil creep, slumping and rock fall	Yes	Yes	Yes
		Gentle to very steep slopes in unstable material subject to sliding, slumping and soil creep	No	No	No
		Moving shallow (>10 ft) landslide	No	No	No
↓ Least stable		Moving, deep landslide, subject to rapid failure	No	No	No

Figure 10.46 Landslide susceptibility and land use policies for Congress Springs near San Francisco

The most reliable predictions focus on:

- **measurement of small-scale ground surface changes**
- **small-scale uplift or subsidence**
- **ground tilt**
- **changes in rock stress**
- **micro-earthquake activity (clusters of small quakes)**
- **anomalies in the earth's magnetic field**
- **changes in radon gas concentration**
- **changes in electrical resistivity of rocks.**

One particularly intensively studied site is Parkfield in California, on the San Andreas fault (Figure 10.47). Parkfield, with a population of less than 50 people, claims to be the earthquake capital of the world. Parkfield is heavily instrumented: strain meters measure deformation at a single point; two-colour laser geodimeters measure the slightest movement between tectonic plates; and magnetometers detect alterations in the earth's magnetic field, caused by stress changes in the crust.

Predicting volcanoes

The rise of magma beneath a volcano may fill a magma chamber and distort the shape of a volcano. This was certainly the case at Mount St Helen's in 1980. Seismometers monitoring earthquakes often pick up large clusters of earthquakes before a volcano and immediately after the eruption. Gases may seep from fissures in the surface known as vents or fumaroles.

Managing volcanic eruptions

It is impossible to prevent volcanoes from erupting. In addition, it is virtually impossible to monitor all active volcanoes. However, there are a number of measures that can be taken to limit their effect. Hazard zonation maps can be used to guide decisions regarding evacuation and other responses. Land use planning is also important. Monitoring of active volcanoes provides early warning of likely eruptions. The most reliable forecasts depend on detailed monitoring of micro-earthquake activity in the vicinity of the volcanic cone, which indicates that magma is working its way upwards. Recent years have seen significant improvements in hazard assessment, volcano monitoring and eruption forecasting, particularly for less explosive eruptions, and lessons from disasters like Mount St Helens (1980) are helping to improve volcanic hazard management and reduce risk. Other measures (including preparation of contingency plans) can be used to reduce the effects when vulnerable areas cannot be avoided.

In the 1991 Mount Pinatubo eruption over 320 people died in the eruption, mostly due to collapse of ash-covered roofs. Many more lives were saved because early warnings were issued and at least 58 000 people were evacuated from the high-risk areas. Management of the 1991 eruption seems to have been well coordinated and effective because:

- **state-of-the-art volcano monitoring techniques and instruments were applied**
- **the eruption was accurately predicted**

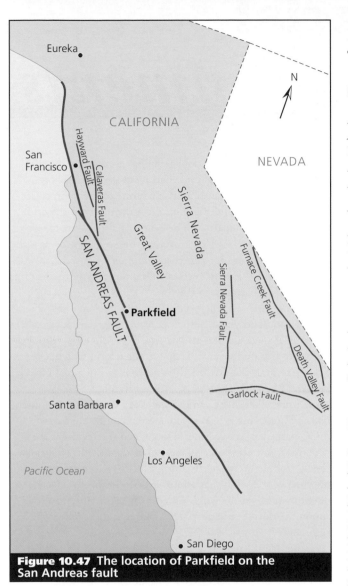

Figure 10.47 The location of Parkfield on the San Andreas fault

- hazard zonation maps were prepared and circulated a month before the violent explosions
- an alert and warning system was designed and implemented
- the disaster response machinery was mobilised on time.

Questions

1 Discuss the ways in which earthquakes can be managed. Use examples to support your answer.
2 Explain why the risk of damage from volcanos and earthquakes is increasing.
3 How can volcanic hazards be managed? Use examples to support your answer.

Bibliography

References

Natural disasters by P. Abbott, W. C. Brown, 1996.
At risk: natural hazards, people's vulnerability, and disasters by P. Blaikie et al, Routledge, 1994.
Earthquakes and Volcanoes by S. Bowler, New Scientist, 1993.
Natural hazards by E. Bryant, CUP, 1991.
The environment as hazard by I. Burton, R. Kates and G. White, Guildford Press, 1993.
Regions of risk: a geographical introduction to disasters by K. Hewitt, Longman, 1997.
Hazards by G. Nagle, Nelson, 1998.
Volcanoes by C. Ollier, Blackwell, 1988.
The environment by C. Park, Routledge, 1997.
The dynamic earth by B. Skinner and S. Porter, Wiley, 1995.
Environmental hazards by K. Smith, Routledge, 1992.
Disasters by J. Whittow, Pelican, 1980.
Natural disasters: Acts of God or Acts of Man by A. Wijkman and L. Timberlake, Earthscan, 1984.

Internet

Global assessment of active volcanoes
http://www.geo.mtu.edu/eos/
Alaska volcanoes
http://www.avo.alaska.edu/
Hawaii volcanoes
http://www.soest.hawaii.edu/hvo
Internet Resources in the Earth Sciences
http://www.lib.berkeley.edu/EART/EarthLinks.htmlArtwork summary
Volcano World
 http://volcano.und.nodak.edu/
MTU Volcanoes Page
http://www.geo.mtu.edu/volcanoes/
World earthquakes
http://gldfs.cr.usgs.gov/
World quakes
http://www.civeng.carleton.ca/cgi-bin/quakes/

Timescale and causes

From Precambrian to Quaternary

The Quaternary Ice Age is the most recent such event to have occurred in geological time. There is evidence for at least four ice ages in the Precambrian Period (prior to 600 million years ago) and two more between that time and the Quaternary Period. Of the more recent ice ages, evidence of the Ordovician (*c.* 450 million years ago) is mainly found in North Africa while the Permo-Carboniferous (*c.* 280 million years ago) is represented in all the southern continents.

The Quaternary Ice Age

Global temperature declined long before the start of the Quaternary Period. It seems likely that a major ice sheet had developed on Antarctica by at least 20 million years ago but the large-scale incursion of ice into other areas required temperature decline below the 'Quaternary glacial threshold' (Figure 11.1). On a number of occasions during the Quaternary, temperature increased again to roughly present-day levels. These periods, known as interglacials, separated the main cold periods, referred to as glacials.

Prior to the 1970s it was thought that there were four main glacials in the Quaternary Ice Age, but recent research, particularly the analysis of ocean floor cores, presents a more complex picture. This evidence suggests as many as 20 glacials. Figure 11.2, showing the extent of ice cover at the Quaternary maximum, clearly indicates that the major areas of ice expansion were in North America and northern Europe. The relatively small increases in the Antarctic and Greenland ice sheets were due mainly to the island nature of these land masses where increasing ice accumulation fuelled iceberg production at the edges.

The causes of ice ages

There is, as yet, no complete and totally accepted explanation of the causes of ice ages, although it is clear that climatic fluctuations occur on a variety of timescales from the spacing of ice ages (10^{-8} years) to minor fluctuations within the instrument record ($10^{-1} - 10^{-2}$ years). Most progress has been made in explaining changes in the middle range (i.e. $10^{-4} - 10^{-5}$ years).

The analysis of ocean floor cores has established that the major glacial/interglacial cycle had a wavelength of about 100 000 years. This corresponds with one of the main cycles of the earth's orbit around the sun, the eccentricity of the orbit (degree of non-circularity). The evidence also points to two further cycles of a lesser magnitude. This seems to confirm the earlier work of the Yugoslavian astronomer Milankovitch who first calculated the earth's orbital variations and their effect on incoming insolation from the sun.

Milankovitch established cycles with wavelengths of 95, 42 and 21 thousand years. In the major cycle glacials occur when the orbit is most circular and interglacials when it is elliptical in shape. The middle cycle is due to the way in which, over time, the tilt of the earth's axis varies from its plane of orbit by between 21.5° and 24.5°, not by a constant 23.5° as is sometimes believed. When the angle of tilt increases summers become hotter but winters colder. Such conditions favour interglacials with glacials occurring when the reverse is true. The third or precession cycle relates to the fact that the earth slowly wobbles in space. As a result its axis describes a circle once in every 21 000 years. The best conditions for glacials to develop are when the wobble places the earth closest to the sun in the northern hemisphere's winter and furthest away in summer.

Other factors that may also have a significant impact on climatic change are plate movement, changes in the paths of jet streams and ocean currents, variations in atmospheric carbon dioxide, major volcanic eruptions and sunspot activity.

From snow to ice

When the climate deteriorates an increasing amount of precipitation will fall as snow, while shorter and less intense summers will reduce the degree of melting. Snow will begin to lie throughout the year in areas which were previously only fleetingly snow-covered, forming a permanent (in the short term) snow line. Gradually the snow line, which is always lowest near to the poles and highest at the equator, will become lower in altitude and also affect lower latitudes.

The delicate, feathery crystals of freshly fallen snow trap much air between them giving a density that may be as little as one-twentieth that of water. However, the fragile crystals break on settling as they are compressed by the weight of additional snow on top. They also break down when they become wet. Gradually, the snowflakes become rounded and granular. Air is forced out to the surface as the snow becomes harder and denser. At a specific gravity (the ratio of a density of a

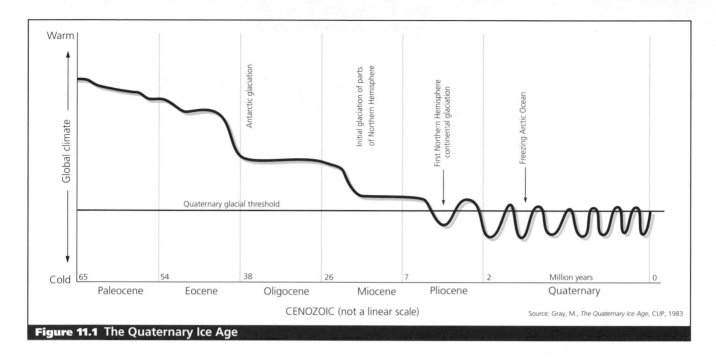

Figure 11.1 The Quaternary Ice Age

Source: Gray, M., *The Quaternary Ice Age*, CUP, 1983

Figure 11.2 Ice cover today and the Quaternary maximum

Region	Present area (km²)	Maximum Quaternary area (km²)	% Expansion
Antarctica	12 535 000	13 800 000	10
Greenland	1 726 400	2 295 300	33
Laurentide complex	147 248	13 386 964	8 991
Fennoscandia	3 810	6 666 708 (includes ice in UK)	174 879
Rocky Mtns N America (includes Alaska south)	76 880	2 610 127	3 295
Alps	115 021	3 951 000	3 335
Asia	3 600	37 000	928
South America	26 500	870 000	3 183
Australasia	1 015	30 000	2 856
TOTAL	14 898 320*	44 383 436*	198

* These totals include other small complexes

Source: *The Quaternary Ice Age*, M. Gray

Key Definitions ①

Quaternary Period The latest period in geological time spanning the last 2 million years. It is sub-divided into the Pleistocene epoch (the most recent ice age) and the Holocene epoch (the post-glacial period of the last 10 000 years).

a glacial A period of time when masses of ice develop and advance into lower altitudes due to a sustained decline in temperature. Extensive continental ice sheets form during such periods.

an interglacial A period of time, such as the present day, when ice still covers part of the earth's surface, but has retreated to the polar regions.

1 When did the Quaternary Ice Age occur?
2 What is the significance of the 'Quaternary glacial threshold'?
3 Briefly discuss the suggested causes of ice ages.
4 How is snow transformed to ice?

substance to that of water) of 0.55 snow becomes 'firn', a stage generally reached after one complete winter–summer cycle. Further compaction causes the round grains of firn to begin to recrystallise creating larger crystals of ice. Air is now present only as bubbles trapped inside the growing crystals. The change from firn to ice is said to occur at a specific gravity of 0.8. The transformation from firn to ice may take five years in temperate glacial environments but much longer in polar areas where there is little or no surface melting and relatively light snowfall. These changes are aided by the flow of the glacier, as ice crystals deform in a manner similar to plastic substances. After the year-by-year accumulation of snow and its subsequent change into firn, then ice, a layered structure called sedimentary stratification develops.

Classification, systems and movement

Classification by size and shape

Ice mass classifications can vary in detail. The following is a standard list from smallest upwards:

- **Niche glaciers** Small patches of glacier ice found on an upland slope. They are most prevalent on north-facing slopes in the northern hemisphere. They differ from cirque glaciers in that their ice has little effect upon topography.
- **Cirque (corrie) glaciers** Small ice masses which accumulate on mountain slopes, gradually eroding armchair-shaped hollows. They may be contained by the hollow or if sufficiently large, spill over the lip of the hollow to feed a valley glacier.
- **Valley glaciers** Larger tongues of moving ice that usually follow pre-glacial river valleys. The ice may originate from (a) an icefield (b) a cirque (c) at the head of the valley in the form of a trough end.
- **Piedmont glaciers** Large lobes of ice formed when glaciers spread out and merge after extending beyond their valleys on to lowland areas.
- **Ice caps** Flattened dome-shaped masses of ice, similar to an ice sheet, but under 50 000 km² in area. They tend to develop on high plateaus and may, in fact, cover only a few square kilometres.
- **Ice sheets** Areas of ice spreading over more than 50 000 km². The Antarctic ice sheet contains 91 per cent of the world's fresh water ice and 85 per cent of its fresh water. It attains a thickness of over 4000 m in places (Figure 11.3).
- **Ice shelves** In Antarctica the net accumulation of ice close to sea level encourages glacier ice to extend out to sea. These slabs of floating ice generally range in thickness from over 1000 m close to land to 500 m at the periphery where icebergs calve and float away.

Classification by temperature

Glacier ice temperatures are similar to the mean annual temperature of the air in the areas of ice accumulation. In polar regions the temperature of the snowfall is well below freezing point and as the snow is compacted into ice, the temperature throughout the glacier remains substantially below freezing point. The result is that the glacier is frozen to the bedrock and this has a major effect on glacier movement. Glaciers in such an environment are termed polar or cold-based.

In lower latitudes the temperature in a glacier, except for the upper surface layer, is near to the pressure melting point. At atmospheric pressure, the pressure melting point is 0°C but it falls below this figure with increasing depth of ice. Thus water can exist in liquid form below 0°C. The existence of a thin film of meltwater at the base of such glaciers, where the temperature may be −3°C or −4°C (much warmer than polar glaciers), acts as a lubricant which facilitates movement. Glaciers in this kind of environment are called temperate or warm-based.

The glacier as a system

A glacier is a mass of ice (and debris) which is continually changing, although at a pace that is much too slow for direct

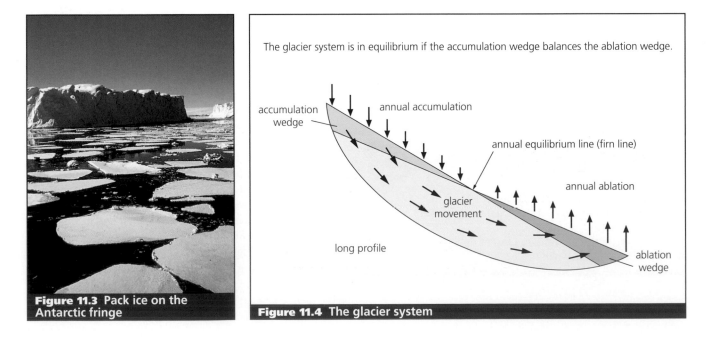

Figure 11.3 Pack ice on the Antarctic fringe

The glacier system is in equilibrium if the accumulation wedge balances the ablation wedge.

accumulation wedge

annual accumulation

annual equilibrium line (firn line)

annual ablation

glacier movement

long profile

ablation wedge

Figure 11.4 The glacier system

human observation. It can be viewed as a system with inputs which add to the mass and outputs which decrease the mass. Inputs generally exceed outputs near the source of a glacier because:

■ **high-altitude terrain receives more precipitation than lower areas (the orographic effect)**

■ **much of the precipitation is in the form of snow**

■ **new snow is highly reflective so that it absorbs less heat and therefore melts more slowly**

■ **the rugged topography of high-altitude areas causes a thin snow cover to be blown away from some areas and concentrated in other areas as deep accumulations in hollows and basins**

■ **sublimation and other losses are low**

■ **meltwater is likely to refreeze.**

Near the snout of the glacier precipitation will generally be lower with less in the form of snow, while temperatures will be higher. Outputs are in the form of melting (surface, basal and within the glacier), sublimation (the change in state from solid to vapour), evaporation and calving.

The section of the glacier, beginning at the source, where inputs exceed outputs is known as the zone of accumulation (Figure 11.4). Conversely, in the lower part of the glacier towards the snout outputs generally exceed inputs. This is the zone of ablation. The dividing line between the two zones is called the firn (or equilibrium) line. Ice moves continually across the equilibrium line (under the influence of gravity) to maintain a balance between the volumes of ice on both sides. This is the most important process in the glacier system. At the firn line the direction of flow is parallel to the surface of the glacier. In the accumulation zone ice flow is angled downwards with respect to the surface, and in the ablation zone it is angled upwards.

In the lower part of a typical Alpine glacier the melting of ice may exceed 10 m a year which is normally replenished by ice flowing from above. The difference between the total accumulation and total ablation for the whole of the glacier over one year is called its mass balance or net balance. This is calculated for the balance year which runs from autumn to autumn, when summer ablation will have reduced the total ice mass to a minimum. Clearly there will be a positive winter balance and a negative summer balance (Figure 11.5).

When the amounts of accumulation and ablation are equal the glacier is said to be in a steady state. If a glacier loses more than it gains, it will either recede or waste downward. Conversely, if the glacier gains more than it loses it will either advance or increase in depth. It may take a number of years of constant gain or consistent loss before a glacier advances or retreats. In general, the larger the glacier the longer the time lag. The main exceptions to this rule occur in areas where the snowfall is exceptionally heavy. In such an event the glacier may react quickly and surge forwards. Retreating glaciers have a gently graded, flat snout while an advancing glacier snout usually has a steep, convex front.

Rates of movement of flowing glaciers are extremely variable. The fastest parts of most reasonably sized glaciers flow anything between 50 and 400 m a year; even faster if they end in the sea. Large ice streams in Antarctica and outlet glaciers in Greenland flow steadily at 1000 m a year or more.

How glaciers move

The movement of ice has two main components (Figure 11.6):

■ **Internal flow** Movements within the glacier ice resulting from the stresses applied by the force of gravity. Such movements often result in the formation of crevasses within and at the surface of the ice.

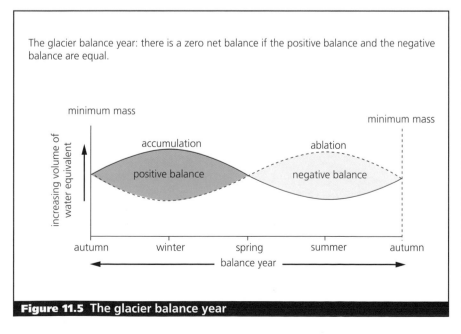

The glacier balance year: there is a zero net balance if the positive balance and the negative balance are equal.

Figure 11.5 The glacier balance year

Key Definitions ②

pressure melting point The temperature at which ice under pressure will melt.

a steady state When the amounts of accumulation and ablation are equal over the course of a year. As a result, the snout of the glacier will remain stationary.

ablation The process of wastage of snow or ice, especially by melting.

accumulation The net gain in an ice mass. The sources of accumulation are direct snowfall and avalanching from higher slopes.

surge A short-lived phase of accelerated glacier flow.

extending flow The extension and related thinning of glacier ice in those zones where velocity increases.

compressing flow The type of glacier flow whereby a reduction in velocity leads to an increase in thickness of a glacier.

■ **Basal slippage** The sliding effect of a glacier over the bedrock surface which may be achieved by either regelation slip or creep. Regelation slip operates most effectively with smaller obstacles while creep is the process which mainly overcomes larger protuberances. Figure 11.7 shows how, on the up-glacier side of an obstacle the increasing pressure in the lower ice causes pressure melting locally. The water formed aids the movement of the ice over the obstacle but then refreezes in the lower pressure conditions on the down-glacier side of the obstacle. The layer of ice (usually a few centimetres thick) affected by this process is called the regelation layer. When large obstacles appear in the path of moving ice the considerable increase in stress in the ice causes it to become more plastic in nature, enabling it to flow or 'creep' around the obstacle.

Because the temperature at the base of polar glaciers is usually well below the pressure melting point, basal slippage does not generally occur. The exception is where the ice is thick enough to be warmed to melting point by geothermal heat. Polar glaciers can thus usually move only through internal flow. In contrast, temperate glaciers move through a combination of both internal flow and basal slippage. Warm ice also deforms more easily than cold ice, further contributing to the difference in behaviour. Thin glaciers on steep slopes may move largely by basal slippage, and thick glaciers on gentle slopes usually exhibit a greater proportion of internal flow.

Influences on the rate of movement

■ Mass is important; snow and ice accumulating on a mountainside do not generally move until the thickness exceeds 60 m.

■ Steep glaciers flow faster than gently graded ones and, as a result, are usually thinner.

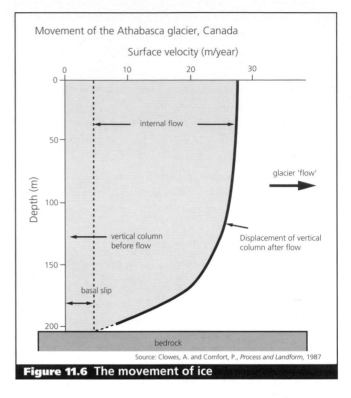

Figure 11.6 The movement of ice

Source: Clowes, A. and Comfort, P., *Process and Landform*, 1987

Questions

1 Explain the difference between (a) cirque and valley glaciers and (b) ice caps and ice sheets.
2 Why are ice masses classified by temperature?
3 How does a glacier operate as a system?
4 How do glaciers move?
5 Examine the factors that affect the rate of glacier movement.

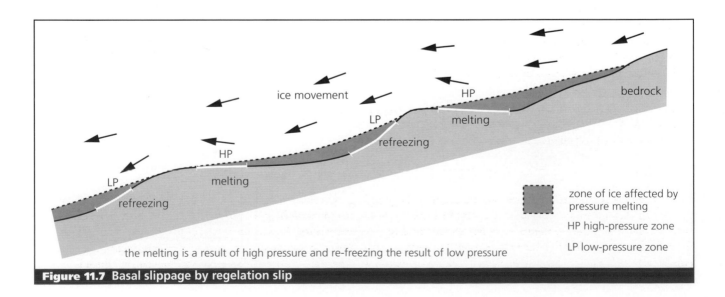

Figure 11.7 Basal slippage by regelation slip

the melting is a result of high pressure and re-freezing the result of low pressure

zone of ice affected by pressure melting
HP high-pressure zone
LP low-pressure zone

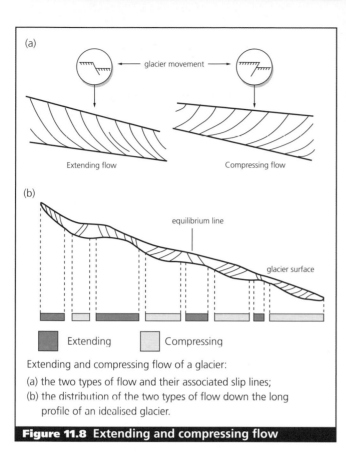

(a)

glacier movement

Extending flow

Compressing flow

(b)

equilibrium line

glacier surface

■ Extending ☐ Compressing

Extending and compressing flow of a glacier:

(a) the two types of flow and their associated slip lines;

(b) the distribution of the two types of flow down the long profile of an idealised glacier.

Figure 11.8 Extending and compressing flow

Figure 11.9 Seracs at icefall, Casement Glacier, Alaska

■ Movement is faster over an impermeable surface compared to a permeable surface. In the latter, meltwater will percolate into joints, reducing the amount available to 'lubricate' the flow of ice at the ice/bedrock interface.

■ Since sliding velocities are related to the availability of meltwater, glaciers flow faster in summer than in winter, and faster in daytime than at night. Exceptional speeds may be induced by heavy rain.

■ If a glacier has a channel of reasonably uniform shape and size and if the down-valley slope is uniform, the greatest velocity is at the firn line, as velocity is directly related to thickness. It is quite common for the snouts of otherwise sliding glaciers to be frozen to the bedrock because the ice is thinner there and thus is affected more by the low mean annual air temperature.

■ The centre of the glacier, where the ice is thickest, moves more rapidly than the margins where friction plays a considerable role in reducing speed.

Extending and compressing flow

The concept of differential ice movement throughout the length of a glacier was introduced by J. F. Nye in 1952. In theory, velocities in the accumulation zone increase steadily from the head to the firn line because down-valley ice is consistently pulling away from up-valley ice. Such a condition is called 'extending flow'. Conversely, below the firn line,

velocities reduce as up-valley ice is continually pushing against down-valley ice, causing 'compressing flow'. However, irregularities in the pre-glacial valley also influence the extension and compression of ice, and in most valleys of a significant size evidence of alternating extending and compressing flow can be found (Figure 11.8). Where the slope steepens, velocity increases and extending flow operates. Where the gradient reduces, velocity decreases and compressing flow occurs. Extreme extending flow occurs at icefalls, causing both transverse and longitudinal crevasses to form, creating a landscape of sharp-crested angular blocks called seracs (Figure 11.9). The plunge pool at the base of an icefall is characterised by intense compressing flow.

Erosion

The processes of erosion

It is important to distinguish clearly between the processes of erosion and those of weathering and ice movement. Frost shattering (also known as freeze-thaw), which is of considerable importance in glacial environments, is a weathering process. The rotational movement which is fundamental to the formation of cirques is a process of ice movement, as are, of course, extending flow and compressing flow.

It is generally accepted that there are four processes of glacial erosion: abrasion, plucking, dilatation and sub-glacial fluvial action.

Abrasion

Abrasion is the 'sandpaper' effect of a glacier moving over bedrock in which the latter is gradually ground down over a long period of time. The best proof of the impact of abrasion is in areas of recent glacier retreat, which exhibit the scratching and polishing of rock surfaces and the smoothing and rounding of protuberances.

The effectiveness of abrasion depends largely on the relationship between the characteristics of the load embedded at the base of the glacier and the nature of the bedrock. Abrasion is particularly effective when the load is dominated by angular fragments of hard minerals such as quartz. Striations and grooves are the evidence of such action. Clay,

on the other hand, while a good polishing agent, has little effect in reducing the thickness of rock strata. In terms of the bedrock, quartzite (7 on the hardness scale of 10) is much less easily abraded than an exposure of marble composed of the mineral calcite (hardness of 3). Permeability is another important factor: an impermeable rock is more difficult to abrade because water is concentrated at the rock/ice interface rather than percolating into the rock.

As a warm-based glacier becomes thicker the rate of abrasion increases until a critical point is reached (Figure 11.10). As pressure melting increases, firm contact between the base of the glacier and the bedrock lessens. At the same time the grip of the ice on its load at the rock/ice interface is reduced. As Figure 11.10 shows the glacier eventually stops eroding and starts to deposit.

Plucking

Plucking is a process by which glaciers loosen, pick up and remove masses of rock varying in size from relatively small

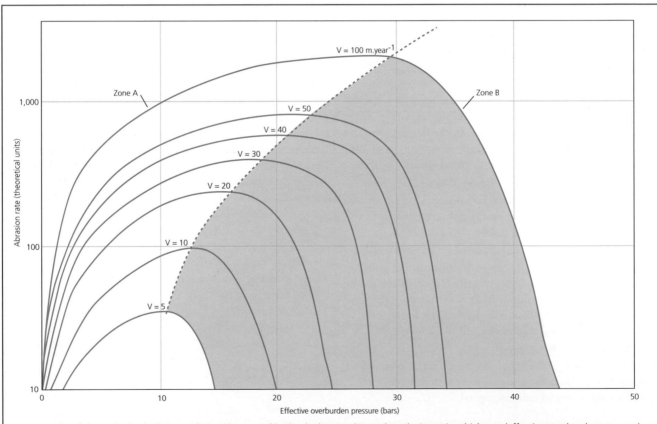

The results of theoretical calculations relating the rate of bedrock abrasion beneath a glacier to ice thickness (effective overburden pressure) and the velocity (V) of glacier flow. Figures on the vertical axis represent the abrasion rate in theoretical units; the effective overburden pressure, plotted along the horizontal axis, is measured in bars (1 bar is the equivalent of 1 atmosphere); and the velocity curves are expressed in metres per year. The dashed line connects the peak of each curve and separates Zone A from Zone B (shaded). Abrasion increases with both pressure and velocity within Zone A, but decreases with increasing pressure and velocity within Zone B. Abrasion ceases altogether at those points where a velocity curve intersects the horizontal base of the plot in Zone B. Indeed, abrasion changes to deposition when a velocity line extends below the horizontal base.

Source: Sharp, R. P., *Living Ice: Understanding Glaciers and Glaciation*, CUP, 1988

Figure 11.10 The relationship between abrasion and ice thickness

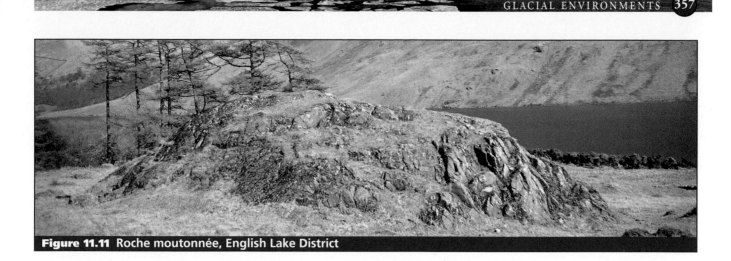

Figure 11.11 Roche moutonnée, English Lake District

fragments to substantial blocks. Plucking is most effective in (a) bedrock areas of at least moderate relief and (b) zones of well-jointed rock. Plucking can take different forms:

- **Significant protuberances in the path of a glacier often exhibit a gentle, smooth up-glacier side as a result of abrasion and a steeper, rugged down-glacier side due to plucking. Such a feature is known as a roche moutonnée. As the ice moves over the up-glacier side, pressure increases and melting is induced. As the ice moves over the down-glacier side, water percolates into the joints, refreezes and, as the ice moves on, the now continuous bond between ice and rock tears at the latter and from time to time pieces of rock of various sizes are ripped away from the bedrock.**
- **In permeable bedrock, water produced by pressure melting percolates into cracks and upon refreezing shatters the rock. The broken fragments are then picked up and carried away by the glacier.**
- **Bedrock material loosened by dilatation (see below) may be picked up by the moving ice.**

Dilatation

Dilatation (pressure release) occurs when a certain thickness of bedrock is eroded. The replacement of this rock by ice, which is approximately one-third the density of rock, may cause the uppermost layers of bedrock to separate along sheet joints. Such weakening of the upper bedrock allows other erosive processes to operate rapidly.

Sub-glacial fluvial action

Sub-glacial fluvial action is particularly effective near the snout of a glacier where melting is at a relatively high intensity. The degree of erosion is determined partly by the size and nature of the load but also by the characteristics of the bedrock.

Abrasion and plucking are the most important forms of ice erosion and there has been much discussion as to which is the most effective. The weight of opinion favours plucking – you might like to suggest why!

The landforms of erosion

Erosion has been most effective in highland areas but its impact on lowlands should not be underestimated. It can be useful to divide the landforms of glacial erosion into (a) higher-altitude, (b) middle-altitude and (c) lowland. The actual altitudinal limits for each category will, of course, vary from region to region. For example, the highest cirques in Britain are at around 800 m whereas in really mountainous areas such as the Alps, valley floors may be well above this height.

Higher-altitude features

At this level the classic landforms are, in their sequence of formation: cirques, arêtes and pyramidal peaks.

Cirques

Cirques (also known as corries and cwms) are large, rounded basins with three steep, frost-shattered walls and a smooth over-deepened floor bounded on its open, downslope side by a small rock lip. They form at the highest significant collecting points for snow which cascades down from the highest slopes where gradients are too steep for it to settle. Initially, a nivation hollow is formed due to solifluction (the moving of soil downslope in periglacial areas caused by the summer melting of the surface layer) and freeze-thaw action beneath the snow patch, which cause the underlying rocks to disintegrate. A possible role for chemical weathering has also been hypothesised. During warmer periods meltwater from beneath the patch flows out and washes away the weathered material. In time the hollow may enlarge so that it contains sufficient snow to last through summer. At this stage the hollow has become an embryo cirque.

The absence of complete summer melting facilitates the compaction process and the snow is steadily transformed, first to firn and then to ice. When the ice mass attains a certain thickness it starts to move by internal deformation and by sliding over its bed. At this point it has become a small glacier. With movement, erosion increases significantly and the small glacier excavates a basin in the side of the mountain peak.

Several processes operate to form a fully developed cirque and, as Figure 11.12 shows, it is possible to recognise a sequence of processes from back wall to lip. Essential to the effectiveness of these processes is the rotational movement of the ice which was first proposed by W. V. Lewis. This is initiated by the steepness of the back wall and the great depth of winter snow accumulation against it. In contrast, the outer and lowest part of the cirque experiences most losses by summer ablation. The surface of the cirque glacier is thus

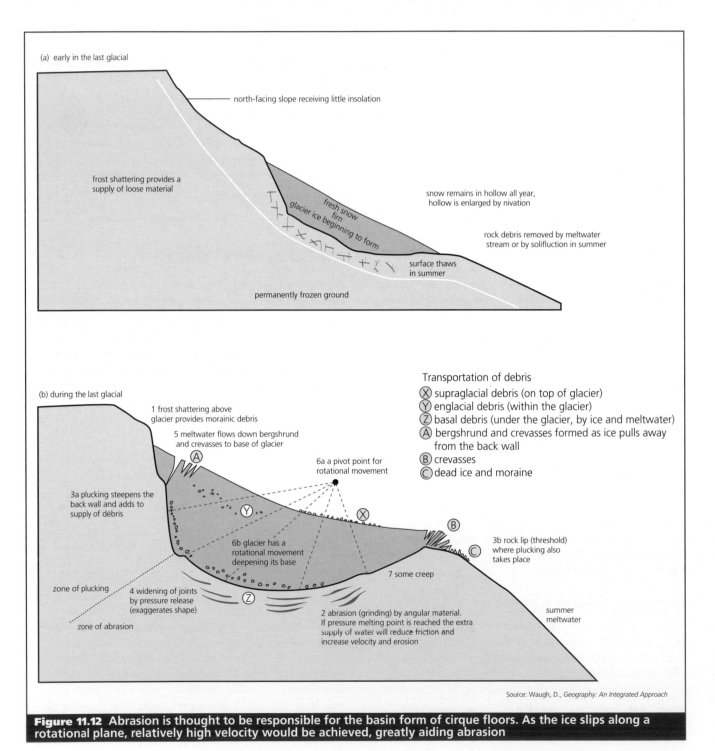

(a) early in the last glacial

north-facing slope receiving little insolation

frost shattering provides a supply of loose material

fresh snow
firn
glacier ice beginning to form

snow remains in hollow all year, hollow is enlarged by nivation

rock debris removed by meltwater stream or by solifluction in summer

surface thaws in summer

permanently frozen ground

(b) during the last glacial

1 frost shattering above glacier provides morainic debris

5 meltwater flows down bergshrund and crevasses to base of glacier

6a a pivot point for rotational movement

3a plucking steepens the back wall and adds to supply of débris

6b glacier has a rotational movement deepening its base

3b rock lip (threshold) where plucking also takes place

7 some creep

zone of plucking

4 widening of joints by pressure release (exaggerates shape)

zone of abrasion

2 abrasion (grinding) by angular material. If pressure melting point is reached the extra supply of water will reduce friction and increase velocity and erosion

summer meltwater

Transportation of debris

(X) supraglacial debris (on top of glacier)
(Y) englacial debris (within the glacier)
(Z) basal debris (under the glacier, by ice and meltwater)
(A) bergshrund and crevasses formed as ice pulls away from the back wall
(B) crevasses
(C) dead ice and moraine

Source: Waugh, D., *Geography: An Integrated Approach*

Figure 11.12 Abrasion is thought to be responsible for the basin form of cirque floors. As the ice slips along a rotational plane, relatively high velocity would be achieved, greatly aiding abrasion

Figure 11.13 Red Tarn: Striding Edge on the left-hand skyline

Figure 11.14 Striding Edge, a classic arête

Figure 11.15 The Matterhorn: one of the best examples of a pyramidal peak in the Alps

steepened and rotation occurs to restore the balance. The importance of rotational movement is supported by the considerable depth of cirques in relation to their overall size. A rock lip develops where the rate of erosion falls significantly. The lip may exhibit a thin veneer of moraine, making it the highest place in a glaciated landscape where deposition occurs. The factors influencing the extent of cirque development are:

- **pre-glacial relief**
- **rock structure**
- **duration of glaciation.**

Well-developed cirques tend to have regular characteristics in terms of height, length and orientation. A length to height ratio of between 2.8:1 and 3.2:1 has been found for many examples in Britain and Scandinavia. In Europe and North America most cirques are orientated (face outwards) between north west and south east. North-facing slopes receive less insolation than those facing south and thus patches of snow and ice are much more likely to be preserved. Also, the main snow-bearing winds are from the west, and eddies would ensure that snow banks were preserved on the lee slopes. In some places two or more adjacent basins have merged into a compound cirque, with scalloped headwall and outline. An impressive example in the Lake District is Red Tarn to the east of Helvellyn.

A cirque glacier steadily erodes backwards into the slope behind it, a headward process known as sapping. If two cirques are sapping headwards towards each other on opposite sides of a divide they will, in time, convert it to a narrow, knife-edged ridge called an **arête**. An arête with a smooth profile indicates rock which is homogeneous. However, if the rock is heterogeneous and irregular in structure, particularly if it is jointed, the arête will be in the form of a jagged sawtoothed ridge. Besides being narrowed, the divide between two opposing cirques may be lowered, forming a saddle-shaped gap, or col.

Pyramidal peaks

Pyramidal peaks (or horns) are formed when three or even four cirques on the flanks of a high peak erode back towards the summit. Eventually the summit will become a steep-sided pyramid-like spire. The alternative name of 'horn' is taken from the Matterhorn on the Swiss–Italian border. Good examples of pyramidal peaks are generally found only in very high-altitude areas and thus a classic example does not exist in the British Isles.

Middle-altitude landforms

Glacial trough

The most important landform at middle altitudes is the **glacial trough** (U-shaped valley) and all the other features in this category relate to it. Ice flowing from high to lowland areas followed the easiest paths, largely under the influence of gravity. These paths were, in general, pre-existing river valleys. The ice which modified these valleys had three possible source areas:

■ **a highland icefield from which tongues of ice spilled out to follow valley routeways**

■ **a cirque at a higher level – ice flowing over the lip of the cirque flowed down steep slopes until it entered a valley**

■ **ice accumulated at the head of the valley itself and the process of general enlargement and steepening of the back wall formed a trough end.**

The great glacial troughs, such as those of the Alps and the Norwegian mountains, are carved out to depths of hundreds or even thousands of metres. Erosion was most intense when thick, well-nourished glaciers were flowing rapidly down a steep slope towards a free outlet. Conditions were like this on the windward slopes of highland regions in temperate latitudes, in areas such as western Norway, north west Britain, British Columbia, southern Chile and south west New Zealand.

The action of ice deepened, widened and straightened pre-existing river valleys to create significant changes in both long and cross profiles. At this scale all four processes of erosion would operate, although perhaps not all in every part of the valley.

Figure 11.16 shows the typical changes to the cross profile of a river valley after a prolonged period of glaciation. Although the greatest agent of change is erosion, there will generally be evidence of glacial and fluvioglacial deposition as well, providing a generally fertile carpet over the flat floor of the glacial trough. The scree slopes are the result of weathering in the post-glacial period. Valleys are straightened by the removal of interlocking spurs as glaciers are less able than rivers to negotiate bends in their course and consequently grind back obstacles in their path. The **truncated spurs** of the post-glacial valley are clear evidence of the erosive power of ice. The smooth sides of truncated spurs may contrast sharply with the more jagged appearance of the upper parts of valleys which may generally have been above the level of the glacier. Deepening was aided by the effects of weathering during the periglacial period preceding the ice advance. Valley floors were particularly subject to frost action because of the presence there of water draining down from the valley sides.

Ice action also has a considerable impact on the long profile. In Figure 11.18 the accumulation of first snow and later ice has formed a distinct trough end. However, the most striking characteristic is the series of basins and steps. Glaciated valleys are much more irregular than the river valleys that preceded them.

The ice in a glacier flows in two different ways, extending flow and compressing flow (Figure 11.8). The basins in a glacial trough are associated with the much greater degree of erosion caused by compressing flow. The steps (often marking the position of bands of more resistant rock) are zones where extending flow operated.

Elongated **ribbon lakes** (Figure 11.19) often occupy areas of extensive overdeepening which must have been the result of compressing flow. But what encouraged the ice to thicken in such a zone? The following factors are all possibilities and overdeepening will have been greatest where the largest number of factors coincided:

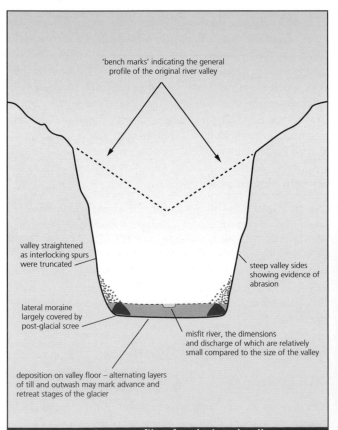

'bench marks' indicating the general profile of the original river valley

valley straightened as interlocking spurs were truncated

steep valley sides showing evidence of abrasion

lateral moraine largely covered by post-glacial scree

misfit river, the dimensions and discharge of which are relatively small compared to the size of the valley

deposition on valley floor – alternating layers of till and outwash may mark advance and retreat stages of the glacier

Figure 11.16 Cross profile of a glaciated valley

Figure 11.17 The classic glaciated valley profile, English Lake District

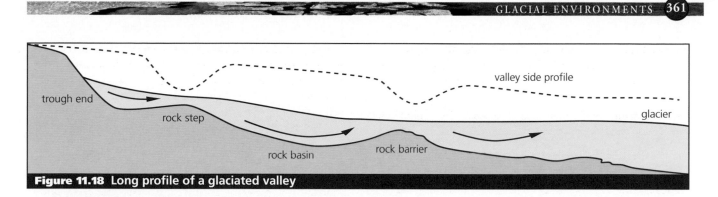

trough end

rock step

valley side profile

glacier

rock basin

rock barrier

Figure 11.18 Long profile of a glaciated valley

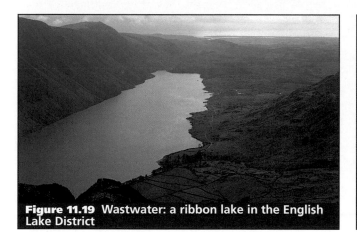

Figure 11.19 Wastwater: a ribbon lake in the English Lake District

Figure 11.20 Hanging valley above Wasdale, English Lake District

- the confluence of the main and a tributary glacier
- a band of less-resistant rock
- an area where the rock was deeply weathered prior to glaciation
- a zone of particularly well-jointed rock
- constriction of the valley walls.

To summarise, there will be changes in the long profile wherever there are changes in the thickness and velocity of the ice.

Perhaps the most spectacular landform of glacial environments is the **hanging valley**. These occur at confluence points where tributaries join the main valley. Prior to glaciation a person would have been able to walk from one valley into the other because at the confluence both valleys were at the same level. With the onset of glaciation the much greater mass of ice in the main valley eroded much more deeply than the smaller tributary glacier.

Say, for example, that the main valley was deepened by 150 m and the tributary valley was deepened by 50 m; then with the retreat of ice from both valleys, the tributary valley would be left 'hanging' 100 m above the main valley. The tributary river would now reach the main river by way of a waterfall. Immediately after glaciation such falls were generally steep but fluvial erosion and weathering over the past 10 000 years or so has reduced the angles of these slopes. Excellent examples can be found above the sides of lakes such as Thirlmere, Wastwater and Ullswater in the Lake District.

The best examples of all these landforms in the British Isles are in the North West Highlands of Scotland, the Lake District and Snowdonia. These were the regions of most intense erosion during the Quaternary (Figure 11.21).

Glaciated coastlines

The classic feature in such environments is the **fjord** which is a glaciated trough drowned by the sea. Fjords originate when the deepening of a trough continues below the former sea level, which is made possible because of the fall in sea level during the ice age. During deglaciation, with its subsequent rise in sea level, the trough is submerged to form a fjord. These long, narrow sea inlets are often marked at their entrance by small islands (the skerryguard) and a partly submerged platform (strandflat). **Hidden hanging valleys** may enter the main channel from the sides as arms of the fjord, where the discordant junctions have been drowned with the rise in sea level.

Lowland landforms

Erosion in lowland areas is related largely to the movement of ice sheets. A number of small-scale features, the result of glacial erosion, may be found in lowland areas although it must be made clear that most also occur in higher areas as well. Areas of bare rock, from which soil and vegetation has been removed, often exhibit the impact of abrasion. If the abrading material was particularly fine the rock will be

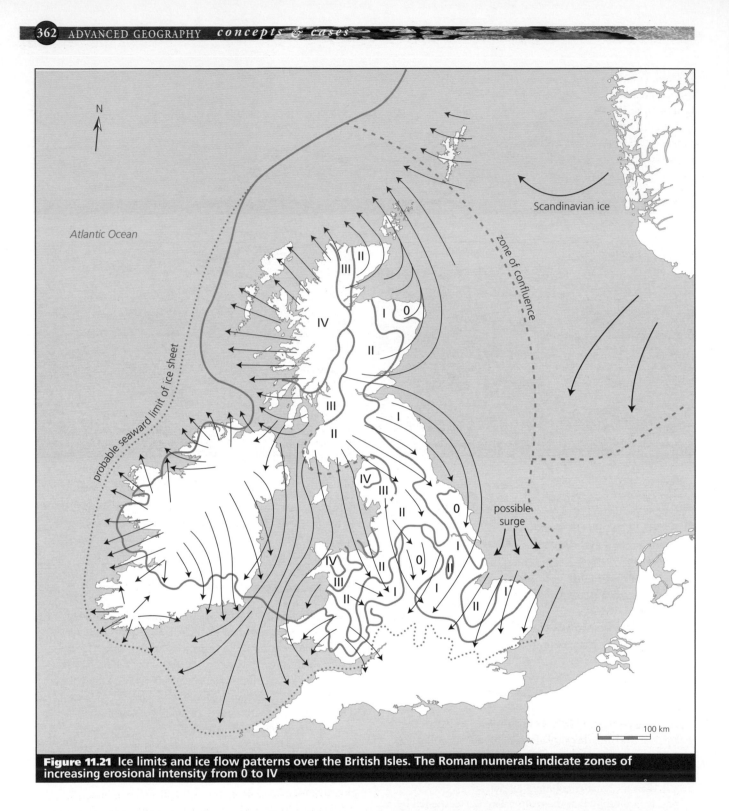

Figure 11.21 Ice limits and ice flow patterns over the British Isles. The Roman numerals indicate zones of increasing erosional intensity from 0 to IV

polished. Slightly larger and harder particles of rock embedded in the ice may cause a series of fine, parallel scratches known as **striations** (or striae). These can vary in length from a few centimetres to a couple of metres. Where the abrasive action is carried out by larger, angular pieces of rock, deeper furrows called **grooves** are formed. A typical groove is a few to 10 or 20 cm deep, twice as wide, and up to several tens of metres long but dimensions can be much larger. Grooves form along weak zones in rock, but may also cut

directly across rock structures. Sometimes striations or grooves are discontinuous but rhythmic in occurrence and are known as **chatter-marks**. Apart from the evidence of abrasion on bedrock the fine eroded material forms the 'rock flour' which gives the characteristic milky appearance to glacial streams.

Roches moutonnées are a familiar glacial feature in lowlands as well as being common at the bottom and along the flanks of glacial troughs. The name derives from a wavy French wig popular in the eighteenth century. Another lowland landform is the **crag and tail** which features evidence of both erosion and deposition. The rock outcrop forming the crag may be polished and striated, and in the lee of the crag deposition will have formed a tapered tail. This landform will be examined in more detail later in this chapter.

Whalebacks are bedrock features that can occur individually or in schools. They have a smooth, somewhat elongated, gently curved form resembling the back of a whale. Typically they are 5 to 10 m long, 3 to 4 m wide, and a metre or two high. The upstream (stoss) end is blunter and steeper than the downstream end. Whalebacks usually carry the smaller-scale markings discussed above.

Rock drumlins are bedrock hillocks eroded into a streamlined drumlinoidal form by moving ice. They are much larger than whalebacks with lengths from tens to hundreds of metres, and their asymmetry is more marked.

Glacial basins are a characteristic lowland glaciation feature. Ice sheets can excavate rapidly, particularly in well-jointed bedrock, but usually in places not too close to their margins where deposition is more likely. Southern Sweden, Finland and the Canadian Shield are all areas where excavation has taken place on a grand scale. The evidence is the vast number of lakes in each region.

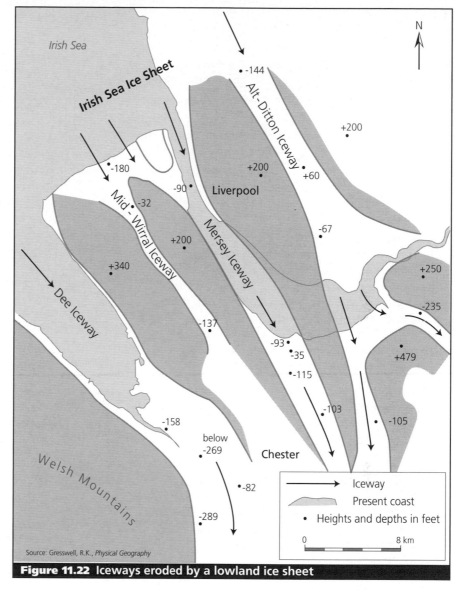

Figure 11.22 Iceways eroded by a lowland ice sheet

Source: Gresswell, R.K., *Physical Geography*

1 What evidence of the process of abrasion might you expect to find in a landscape that has been glaciated?
2 Explain the process of plucking. What is the landscape evidence for this process?
3 Explain how a sequence of processes operated to form cirques and roche moutonnées.
4 Detail the ways in which the long and cross profiles of a river valley may be changed by glaciation.
5 Why do rates of erosion vary within the same valley glacier?
6 Briefly summarise the impact of glacial erosion on lowlands.

Iceways

Frequently, areas of intense lowland erosion have been covered by subsequent glacial deposition. An example is the iceways of south west Lancashire. Here the Irish Sea ice sheet found its southerly route impeded by the North Wales mountains. While some ice moved west and then south, a significant proportion flowed in the opposite direction between East Wales and the Pennines, where the Mersey and Dee estuaries are today. The ice was compressed in this area, became thicker, and eroded deeply, forming a series of hollows or iceways in the solid rock (Figure 11.22). These iceways are between 2 and 5 km in width and the deepest parts of their floors are nearly 150 m lower than the rock ridges that lie between them. They are characterised by irregular long profiles comparable to those of glaciated valleys.

Deposition

The collective name for all material deposited under glacial conditions is drift (Figure 11.23). This is subdivided into:

■ **Till**   Unsorted and unstratified angular material directly deposited by ice. It comprises rock of all shapes and sizes, hence it is sometimes referred to as boulder clay.

■ **Ice-contact stratified drift**   (eskers, kames and kame terraces) Deposited in the vicinity of melting ice. Here debris is partly sorted by water action and roughly stratified.

■ **Outwash deposits**   Material deposited over a wide area by streams and rivers emanating from glaciers and ice sheets. Outwash deposits are rounded and well sorted according to particle size with the heaviest deposits dropped nearest the ice front and the lightest deposits carried well away. The rounding is due to the process of attrition in meltwater streams. Deposits are also stratified (layered vertically), with each layer representing the material deposited during one season's ice melt.

As till is deposited directly under ice it is referred to as glacial deposition. Ice-contact stratified drift and outwash are classed as fluvioglacial deposition.

Till

In the early stages of deposition with the ice deforming quickly, melting near its bed and sliding rapidly, debris is actively plastered on to the surface to form 'lodgement till'. However, towards the snout of a glacier or ice sheet direct melting out of debris from the ice takes place producing 'meltout till' (Figure 11.24).

Till sheets

The **till sheet** or **till plain** is the most widespread depositional feature, completely covering the undulations of the ice-eroded topography beneath. However, in places the surface may be streamlined, reflecting either deposition on the lee side of rock obstructions (Figure 11.25) or the variations in stress at the base of the ice sheet. The most frequently occurring of this family of streamlined features are **flutes** or areas of **fluted ground moraines**. These streamlined undulations occur either as individuals or in large groups.

Till sheets may be composed of a single till type or comprise several tills separated by meltwater sands and gravels. Much of East Anglia is covered by an extensive till sheet, producing a subdued landscape. It is made up of a variety of different tills deposited by separate ice advances during each of the major glaciations. The average thickness of the till is about 30 m, but in the north the thickness exceeds 70 m. Cromer Ridge, the most distinctive relief feature, rising to a height of 90 m, is composed almost entirely of glacial till (Figure 11.26). On mainland Europe classic examples of till plains are located in southern Sweden, eastern Jutland and the Danish islands.

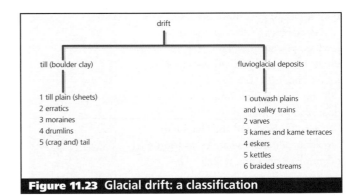

Figure 11.23 Glacial drift: a classification

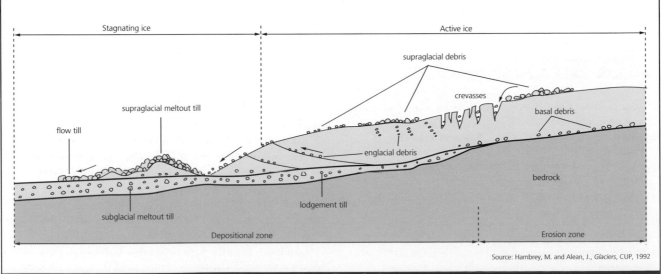

Source: Hambrey, M. and Alean, J., *Glaciers*, CUP, 1992

Figure 11.24 Longitudinal profile through a retreating valley glacier

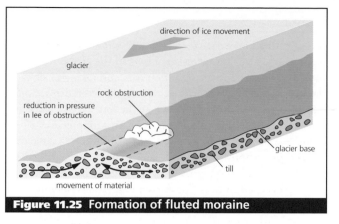

Figure 11.25 Formation of fluted moraine

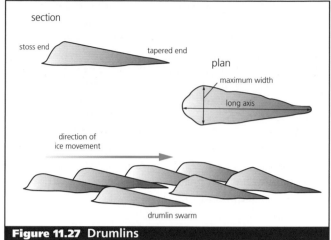

Figure 11.27 Drumlins

Figure 11.26 The Cromer Ridge, East Anglia

Drumlins

Drumlins are the most extreme form of streamlined ice-moulded topography found on till plains. These elongated, rounded hills are asymmetrical in form. They may occur in isolation but are usually found in 'swarms' (Figure 11.27). A great belt of drumlins extends across nearly all of the northern half of Ireland, and in Finland an area of some 25 000 km² contains 14 500 drumlins.

The long axes of drumlins are parallel to the direction of ice movement. They may exceed 50 m in height, over 1 km in length and measure almost 500 m in width. The steep stoss end faces the direction from which the ice came. The elongation ratio is used to describe the shape of individual drumlins. This is the length of the drumlin divided by its maximum width.

The origin of drumlins is not completely clear, although it is agreed that they form beneath an ice mass. The most widely accepted view is that they were formed when the ice became overloaded with material and so the competence of the ice sheet or glacier was reduced. The latter may have been due to the melting of the ice mass or to changes in velocity related to

the pattern of extending and compressing flow. Once deposited the material may then have been moulded and streamlined by later ice movement. To quote Embleton and King: 'Drumlins remain an intriguing and enigmatic feature of many areas of glacial deposition.'

Moraines

Moraines are distinctive ridges or mounds of debris laid down directly by an ice mass or pushed up by it. The material is mainly till, but fluvial, lake or marine sediments may also be involved. Moraines can be active or inactive according to whether or not they are in contact with active ice. The following are the most common types:

■ **Lateral moraine** is debris derived from frost shattering on high valley sides and carried along the edges of a glacier. An embankment of material is left along the sides of the valley when the glacier melts. Such moraines may soon become indistinct as a result of the downslope movement of material in the post-glacial period.

■ **Medial moraine** results from the merging of two lateral moraines at the confluence of two glaciers. However, after glaciation, the medial moraine, since it is located at or near the centre of a valley, may be quickly destroyed by fluvial action.

■ **Ground moraine** is featureless till deposited over a valley floor. It can be up to 30 m deep and may include large boulders called erratics (see below).

■ **Terminal moraines** are high mounds of material extending across a valley, marking the maximum advance of the glacier or ice sheet. Terminal moraines can only form effectively when a glacier is advancing or stationary and when the ice is active. An advancing glacier often has a fairly steep, high front against which a bank of material accumulates, pushed ahead as the ice advances. In addition, till not deposited beneath the ice may be carried by streams in the ice to the snout of the glacier where it adds to the terminal moraine. Terminal moraines usually have steeper ice-contact slopes and gentler distal slopes. In the east of Denmark the ice sheet remained stationary long enough to build up morainic hills reaching an altitude of over 170 m. Terminal moraines are not always high or continuous, having been eroded by subsequent fluvioglacial meltwater activity, or having their lower part buried beneath the rising mass of outwash material. Temperature also plays a part. Warmer glaciers move faster and thus build up larger moraines than colder glaciers. However, they also produce more meltwater to remove the moraine. The coarser the till the larger the moraine as removal by meltwater becomes less effective.

- **Recessional moraines** are parallel to and found behind terminal moraines. Usually smaller in size, they mark interruptions in the retreat of the ice when the glacier or ice sheet remained stationary long enough for a mound of material to build up.

- **Push moraines** may develop if the climate deteriorates sufficiently for the ice temporarily to advance again. Previously deposited moraine (usually ground moraine) may be shunted up into a mound.

Erratics

The occurrence of erratics provides a significant clue to the nature and extent of ice movement. Erratics are large blocks of rock that have been transported from their source to be left perched on a different rock type. The location of erratics at high altitudes demonstrates the ability of ice sheets to override watersheds. If an erratic is so distinctive in character that its source can be unequivocally identified, it is known as an **indicator** (Figure 11.28). Some indicator sources are so localised that their stones are spread over a fan-shaped area downstream, forming a **boulder train** or **indicator fan**. A good example is the boulder trains of Shap granite indicating that ice once moved from the Shap area of the Lake District across the Pennines into Yorkshire.

Crag and tail

A crag and tail may develop where a rock outcrop obstructs the flow of a glacier. The resistant rock of the crag is ice moulded with extensive deposition (the tail) taking place to the lee, tapering downstream of the crag. Curved depressions may be eroded in the bedrock where the lower ice layers were forced to diverge around the crag. The most impressive example in Britain is the crag on which Edinburgh Castle was built with its gently sloping tail, along which the Royal Mile runs, tapering off to the east (Figure 11.29). The crag is an outcrop of igneous rock. The curved depressions on either side of Castle Rock have been partly infilled in post-glacial times.

Till fabric analysis

Till fabric analysis is the standard technique used to ascertain the direction of ice movement. This involves the study of pebble orientation because the long axis of each pebble is usually parallel to the direction of ice movement and angled down towards the origin. The results of till fabric analysis are usually recorded on a star or rose diagram.

Ice-contact stratified drift

The following features (Figure 11.30) are formed in tunnels or at the end of tunnels in glaciers or ice sheets. They may be classed as ice-contact stratified drift, forming in the late stages of glaciation when the ice mass is stagnant or retreating.

Esker

An esker is a sinuous ridge of material deposited by meltwater flowing in subglacial channels or through tunnels within the ice (Figure 11.31). The fact that meltwater streams can flow uphill under hydrostatic pressure accounts for the fact that some eskers do, in fact, run uphill. Consisting of silt, sand and gravel eskers form at right angles to the ice front. The deposits

Figure 11.28 Partly submerged erratic

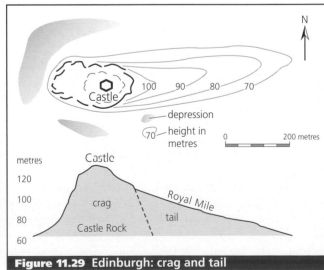

Figure 11.29 Edinburgh: crag and tail

often exhibit some degree of sorting both in a downstream direction and from the centre of the ridge outwards. However, this may be disrupted by the slumping which occurs when the ice which forms the channel side eventually melts. Some of the largest eskers occur in central Sweden, where they may be hundreds of kilometres long, 400 to 700 m wide and 40 to 50 m high. Smaller eskers may be only a few hundred metres long, 40 to 50 m wide and 10 to 20 m high. Eskers rarely develop in isolation and often occur as a complex network of ridges. In Finland, eskers provide convenient flat-topped ridges on which roads are often built through lake-studded country. The Galtrim eskers north west of Dublin, extending over about 100 km² are among the best preserved examples in the British Isles. In places, eskers are beaded (broadening out like beads in a chain), almost certainly the result of stationary phases during ice retreat.

Kame

A kame is a mound of sand and gravel deposited by meltwater. Kames generally form along the front of a stationary or slowly receding glacier or ice sheet, when streams flowing off the ice build up a small delta in the static water of an ice marginal lake. Where englacial streams emerged some height above lake level, the resultant kames built up to that height providing the ice margin remained stationary for long enough. Alternatively, kames may originate in large crevasses. Debris washed into such crevasses is stranded there until the ice melts. The debris is then dropped down as a kame on the valley floor. Thus kames vary in shape, dimension and stratification. The latter is usually disturbed to a significant extent by ice melt.

Kame terraces may form at the sides of a glacier where supraglacial and englacial meltwater streams deposit material which, after retreat of the ice, forms terraces. Slumping of the ice-contact side of the terrace frequently occurs after the ice has retreated.

Outwash deposits

Outwash is the material deposited beyond the snout of a glacier by the meltwater streams which issue from it. Gently sloping **outwash plains** (also known by the Icelandic term *sandur*), which may stretch for hundreds of kilometres from the ice front, are composed of sands and gravels. The largest particles are found nearest the ice front. Fertile clay particles are largely absent from such deposits, being so light they are carried far away, often out to sea. The deposits in an outwash plain also exhibit vertical gradation. In summer, the high discharge of the meltwater streams can transport particles of all sizes across the plain. But in winter discharge is much lower and the ability to transport is reduced, with larger particles generally absent from deposition during this part of the year. Consequently, a vertical stratification can be found with alternating layers of coarse and fine particles. This is frequently best exemplified in lake floor deposits where the evidence of annual deposition consists of a layer of silt lying on top of one

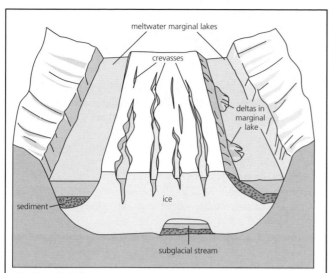

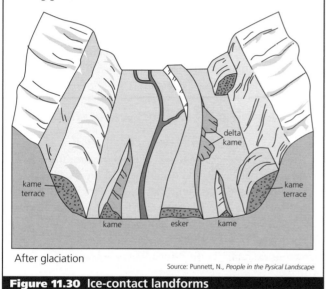

Source: Punnett, N., *People in the Pysical Landscape*

Figure 11.30 Ice-contact landforms

Figure 11.31 Esker landscape in glaciated valley floor

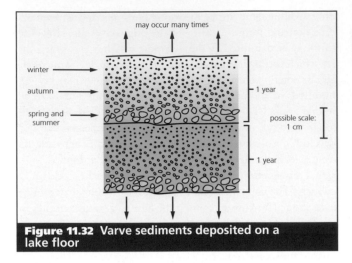

Figure 11.32 Varve sediments deposited on a lake floor

Questions

1 How are the different types of moraine formed?
2 Distinguish between the formation and characteristics of (a) a drumlin and a crag and tail, and (b) an esker and a kame.
3 Explain the differences between till, ice-contact stratified drift and outwash deposits.
4 Explain the stratification of varves.
5 In a glaciated area what evidence, in terms of both erosion and deposition, might indicate past directions of ice movement?

of sand. The latter was deposited during spring and summer melt, while the silt represents the period of decreasing discharge towards the autumn when the finer material settled. Such deposits are known as **varves** (Figure 11.32).

Outwash deposits are rounder and smaller than glacial deposits due to attrition in meltwater streams. Outwash plains are characterised by multi-thread river channels, a formation known as **braiding**. Small ponds, called **kettle holes** may also be present. These formed where blocks of dead ice melted slowly, leaving depressions in the outwash.

If the ice mass is confined within steep valley walls, the outwash deposit is also confined and builds up a feature known as a **valley train**.

The impact of glaciation on drainage patterns

In many areas the pattern of drainage was substantially altered by the passage of ice. Four major effects can be recognised: the disintegration of pre-glacial drainage in lowlands, the breaching of upland watersheds, glacial lakes and overflow channels, and the displacement of drainage around ice fronts.

The disintegration of pre-glacial drainage in lowlands

Extensive erosion or deposition by ice sheets in lowlands can almost totally change the original pattern of drainage. Classic examples of scoured and eroded landscapes of shallow lake basins, peat-filled depressions, low hills and roches moutonnées are the Central Lakes plateau of Finland and the Canadian Shield. On a smaller scale is the 'knock and lochan' landscape of low-lying areas in the Highlands and Islands of

western Scotland. In these areas drainage is frequently indeterminate, rivers and lakes are not fully integrated and there is a general lack of adjustment to structure. Similar patterns of drainage can be found in areas with thick deposits of glacial and fluvioglacial material.

The breaching of upland watersheds

The process of **glacial diffluence** has modified the drainage pattern in many glacial environments. Diffluence frequently occurs when the normal flow of a glacier is blocked by a larger mass of ice. With its outlet blocked the glacier will increase in depth until it may eventually be able to flow over the lowest point available. This overflow of ice gradually erodes a gap or **diffluence col** through the pre-glacial watershed. There are numerous examples in the North West Highlands of Scotland.

Glacial lakes and overflow channels

During periods of rapid melting pro-glacial lakes formed at ice margins when the flow of meltwater away from the ice was impeded by relief or another ice mass. In such instances the water level rose until it reached and flowed through the lowest point in the surrounding landscape. The intense discharge quickly eroded a distinctive overflow channel. The end product of an impressive example of this process can be found in the North York Moors (Figure 11.33).

The valley of the eastward flowing River Esk was blocked by the southward movement of North Sea ice, resulting in the formation of a large pro-glacial lake (Lake Eskdale). The water level in the lake rose and eventually overflowed across the North Yorkshire Moors through Newtondale into Lake Pickering, another pro-glacial lake which had formed for the same reason to the south (Figure 11.34). The larger Lake Pickering also rose in level until it, too, finally overflowed through Kirkham Abbey Gorge. Evidence of the existence of the lakes and subsequent overflow includes: the remains of old

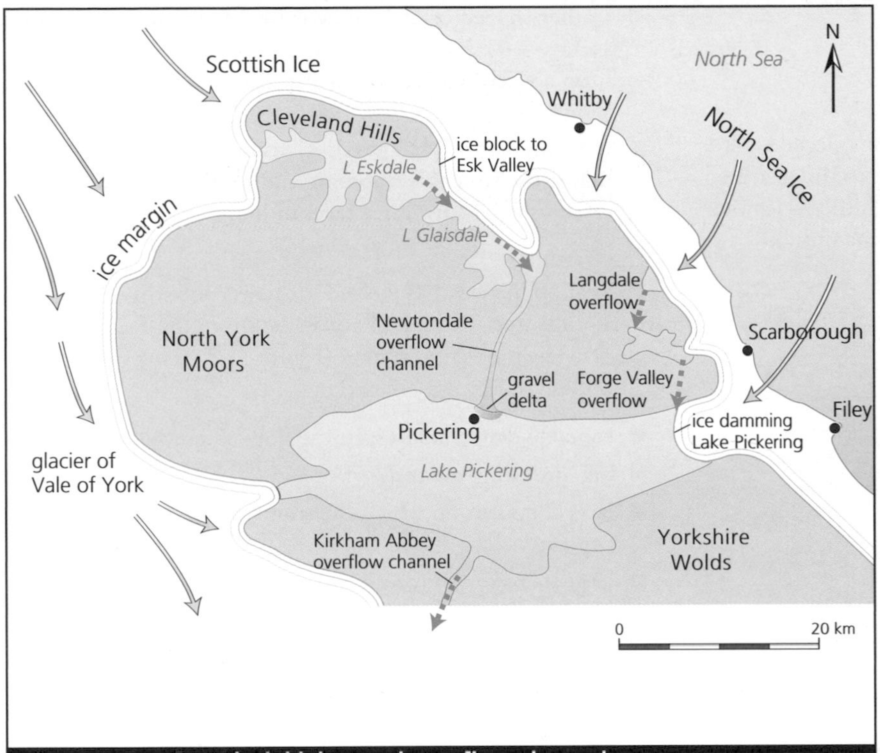

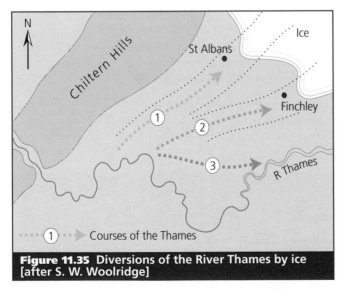

Figure 11.33 Pro-glacial lakes and overflow channels

Figure 11.34 Newtondale Gorge

and thus continued to flow inland through Kirkham Abbey Gorge, before eventually reaching the sea more than 120 km from its source. The steep-sided and flat-floored Newtondale is today essentially a dry valley while the fertile Vale of Pickering marks the location of Lake Pickering.

The displacement of drainage around ice fronts

The diversion of pre-glacial rivers by ice did not always involve the creation and overflow of pro-glacial lakes, as exemplified by the River Thames (Figure 11.35). Ice advancing from the north east first diverted the Thames from its original course in the Vale of St Albans into the Finchley Depression. Further advance of the ice resulted in another displacement into the river's present course.

Figure 11.35 Diversions of the River Thames by ice [after S. W. Woolridge]

strand-lines marking the former lake margins; deltaic deposits where streams entered the former lake; lacustrine deposits marking the extent of the former lake floor; and the distinctive nature of the overflow channels.

After glaciation the River Esk reverted to its original course, entering the North Sea south of Whitby. However, the River Derwent, rising just a few kilometres from the coast near Scarborough, had its eastward exit blocked by glacial deposits

Questions

1 Explain why a gravel delta would develop at the edge of Lake Pickering.
2 What types of processes are likely to occur on the North Yorkshire Moors during the formation of the overflow channel and the pro-glacial lakes?

Glacial hazards

Human populations are more at risk from glacial hazards today than at any time in the past due to the increased penetration of economic development into hitherto remote mountain regions and the great increase in the number of people involved in sports such as skiing and mountaineering.

Hazard 1: Avalanches

Avalanches are the most serious hazard both in terms of regularity and potential devastation. Upwards of a million avalanches occur around the world each year with an average annual death toll of more than 200 people.

Avalanches can be classified in the following ways:

- **type of breakaway – loose snow or slab avalanche**
- **position of sliding surface – surface or full-depth avalanche**
- **humidity of snow – wet or dry**
- **form of track – unconfined or channelled**
- **form of movement – airborne powder or ground flow.**

The ideal slope angle for an avalanche is anything between 30° and 45°. Loose snow or 'wet avalanches' are the most destructive, usually occurring in spring when melting snow produces large amounts of water which are initially absorbed by the snow cover. The entire snowpack loses its cohesion, turning into a thick slush that trickles down the mountain at only 3 to 5 km per hour. Although slow it is unstoppable, blanketing everything in its path. An airborne powder-snow avalanche is also hazardous because of the powerful shock waves which precede it, strong enough to cause buildings to explode because of the sudden change of air pressure.

Avalanches happen because of differences in strength between layers of snow settling on a slope. Temperature, wind and sunlight can change the constitution of these layers, as well as further overlying accumulation. If a strong slab layer develops on a weak one and the latter crumbles under the weight of it an avalanche begins. Just the weight of a passing skier may be enough to start a crack under the surface which spreads out in the weak layer until the slab detaches. The average slab weighs 1500 tonnes and travels at around 80 km per hour. However, the slab may become airborne, gliding on a cushion of air and reaching speeds of 240 km per hour.

The surface gives no clue that this might happen. For prior warning it is necessary to dig down into the snowpack to examine its layered profile, to see how well it is banded and to attempt to estimate what sort of force will be required to shear. Weak layers can form when:

- feather-shaped crystals of hoar frost freeze on to the snow surface – the hoar frost crystals are extremely fragile and form a weak layer inside the snowpack if buried by a fresh snowfall
- the temperature changes deep inside the snowpack, which may cause water to evaporate and recrystallise into new crystal shapes forming a layer of loose, gravelly 'sugar snow'.

Population increase has pushed the newer suburbs of Chamonix into the path of avalanches from the Tacona glacier. The protection system (Figure 11.36) constructed cost 25 million francs and is based on:

- concrete deflectors to split the flow of an avalanche
- big 'breaking' mounds
- large flat areas on which the snow is supposed to deposit
- large dams of reinforced earth to prevent snow flowing outside the expected paths.

In the Chamonix region and in other avalanche-risk areas buildings are increasingly being designed and built to withstand avalanches.

On the higher slopes avalanches can be triggered deliberately before the mass of snow becomes too large and dangerous. This can be done by:

- **ski-cutting, when a ski patrol skis just above an unstable slab in order to dislodge it under controlled conditions**
- **using artillery; in the United States more than 100 000 rounds of ammunition are fired every year in avalanche-risk areas to dislodge unstable slabs.**

A more permanent solution is to prevent the snowpack from developing in the first place. In some areas fences have been built on mountain ridges to control the location of snow

Figure 11.36 Avalanche prevention, Switzerland

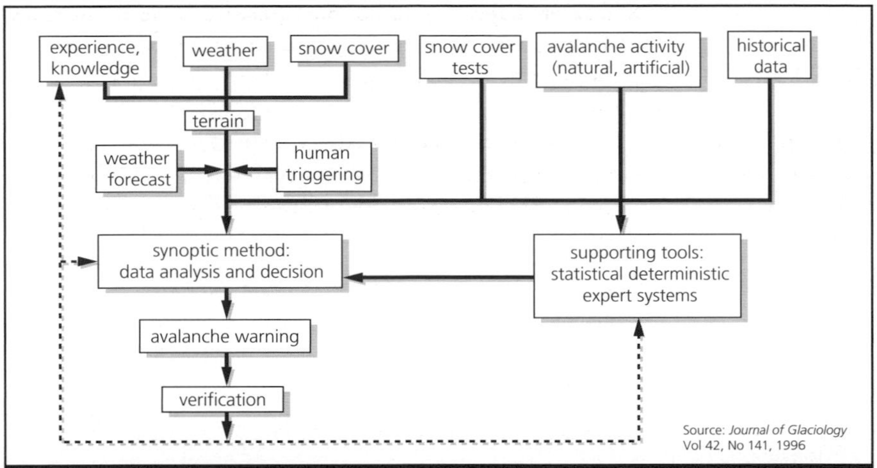

Figure 11.37 The classical conventional method supplemented with different supporting tools to forecast the avalanche hazard on the regional scale

Source: *Journal of Glaciology* Vol 42, No 141, 1996

Key Definitions (4)

avalanche A rapid gravitational movement of snow and ice *en masse* down steep slopes, generally in mountainous terrain.

jokulhlaup A flood which occurs when volcanic activity beneath glaciers or icecaps causes melting.

alluvione A stream of liquid mud formed either by the bursting of morainic dammed pro-glacial lakes or by ice-rock avalanches, usually in high tropical areas.

surge A relatively short-lived episode of greatly accelerated flow within a glacier.

iceberg A massive chunk of glacier ice floating in a water body or stranded on its shore.

accumulation. Steel barriers have also been sunk into bare rock to stop slabs from sliding if their formation cannot be prevented.

Trees form the best natural protection. They can break up and slow avalanches and also hold snow in place. But so many have been lost as people have pushed further and further into glacial environments.

The Alps account for more than half of all avalanche deaths worldwide each year – 120 on average compared to just 20 in North America. Almost half the people caught in avalanches are buried. The chance of surviving a burial of more than 30 minutes is just 50 per cent; only 10 per cent survive more than 3 hours. Training rescuers to react quickly is vital. The chances of survival improve considerably if the skier is carrying a safety beacon. Air bags which the skier can inflate with a rip-cord are now available – the idea is that the airbag floats the victim to the top of the snow preventing full burial. The ideal, of course, is to close off areas at significant risk but in ski resorts this is often a fine balancing act. Closed resorts do not generate the flow of money that the local economy relies on. Decisions are made in two ways (Figure 11.37):

■ using software models to analyse a range of data
■ the observations and experience of ski patrols.

Hazard 2: Jokulhlaups

The most dramatic and serious floods associated with glaciation occur where volcanic activity beneath ice caps or glaciers causes melting. In Iceland, floods of this nature, known as *jokulhlaups*, have been responsible for the build-up of the outwash deposits fringing the big ice caps of Vatnajokull and Myrdalsjokull. The amount of sediment carried by jokulhlaups is so great that the coastline can be changed within a few days.

Floods from the Grimsvotn caldera under Vatnajokull (Figure 11.38) are due to geothermal heating which heats the ice from below, the water accumulating until it reaches a critical level at which it bursts out in a *hlaup* lasting for several days to a few weeks. There have been about 20 such floods in the twentieth century. Jokulhlaups are reported annually in Iceland and a careful watch is kept for signs of increasing volcanism.

Hazard 3: Alluviones

This hazard relates primarily to tropical glaciers, for example those high in the Peruvian Andes. Recession of these glaciers in the last 70 years or so, has sometimes caused the formation of pools of water which united and enlarged to form superglacial lakes. The lakes expanded until they reached the terminal moraines formed during the Little Ice Age. In the Andes Laguna de Safuma Alta, little more than a pool in 1950, enlarged swiftly to hold nearly 5 million m³ of water in 1969. Continued glacier retreat and the formation of pro-glacial lakes insecurely held back by unstable moraine, caused a great increase in sudden floods which, as they moved down the steep slopes below, became streams of liquid mud (alluviones). The danger was quickly recognised and a commission set up in 1941 to control the lakes of the Cordillera Blanca organised the gradual lowering of the 35 lakes considered to be the most dangerous.

However, the most destructive of the alluviones in the Cordillera Blanca were caused not by the breaching of pro-glacial lakes but were triggered by huge ice-rock avalanches. In 1962, such an avalanche from Huascaran descended 4000 m to overwhelm the town of Ranrahiva, drowning 4000 people. In 1970, a huge landslide involving a large amount of ice triggered by an earthquake, killed over 15 000 people, most of them in the town of Yungay.

Volcano adds to glacier drama in flood-hit Iceland

FROM HILDUR HELGA SIGURDARDOTTIR IN REYKJAVIK

A VIOLENT eruption from an Icelandic volcano yesterday sent clouds of ash and smoke soaring up to 14,000ft as the nation was taking stock of the damage caused by the flood of the century.

The new eruption started in a huge fissure in the Icelandic glacier Vatnajokull, just south of the crater left by last month's spectacular outburst, which lasted two weeks and brought on Tuesday's flood.

The fresh eruption in Europe's largest glacier spewed a 12,000ft to 14,000ft-high column of ash in the air and was first spotted yesterday afternoon by pilots sightseeing over the flooded area on the south coast.

Two great explosions shot ashes into the sky, but last night meteorologists said that the eruption seemed to be quietening.

There are still considerable seismic activity and tremors originating in the area. But according to Ragnar Stefansson, head of the geophysics department at Iceland's Meteorological Institute, because of the intense and dramatic geological activity originating in the glacier lately, scientists are finding it difficult to tell if the present earth tremors are an indication of increasing volcanic activity or a result of the flood from under the glacial lake Grimsvotn.

The water level of the lake has gone down dramatically since the flood burst through the ice-cap on Tuesday morning. Magnus Tumi Gudmundsson, a glacier expert, is inclined to believe that the new eruption is a last release of gas from the glacier after the torrent was released from the nearby lake.

The glacial torrent demolished three of the country's largest bridges as well as several miles of the important ring road along the south coast. Several power lines have also collapsed.

House-size blocks of ice and millions of tonnes of black sulphurous water are pouring on to uninhabited regions of Iceland.

This disaster will weigh heavily on the Icelandic economy, already burdened by two recent avalanches in which two villages were swept to sea and almost 40 lives lost.

One immediate result is that the country's transport system will be transformed, with all traffic on land between the east coast fishing towns and the capital, Reykjavik, on the southwest coast, now having to go through the rough terrain of the north coast.

David Oddsson, the Prime Minister, said after the latest eruption: "This is going to put us back to the time when we did not have the great bridges on the south coast. Our financial losses are certainly great, but at least there is no loss of human life."

Figure 11.38 *The Times*, 7 November 1996

Hazard 4: Surging glaciers

The distribution of surging glaciers has limited their human impact. They are concentrated in the Karakoram, Pamir, Tien Shan and Alaska-Yukon, and also occur in the Caucasus, Iceland and parts of the Andes. In the Karakoram irrigation systems have been destroyed by surging. However, the greatest danger from surging glaciers is associated with the bursting of ice-dammed lakes. This situation is most likely to occur when the meltwater exit from a tributary glacier is blocked by the glacier in the main valley surging past the confluence. If the ice barrier is thin, the pressure of water may become so great that a breach is created, flooding the valley below.

Hazard 5: Icebergs

Floating ice tongues are extremely unstable and subject to sudden advance and retreat. Most belong to tidewater glaciers, which occur numerously along the coasts of Greenland, Alaska, Chile and Antarctica. Retreat of such a glacier in deep water causes iceberg calving. The flow of icebergs in busy sea lanes is a significant hazard, illustrated by the sinking of the *Titanic* which went down on its maiden voyage in April 1912 with the loss of 1513 lives.

In late 1998 passenger cruise ships in the South Atlantic were warned about a mammoth iceberg, originating in Antarctica, named Atlantic (A) 22B which was 56 km long and 19 km wide. This and other icebergs are tracked by satellite from the National Ice Centre in Washington.

Questions

1   Discuss the causes and consequences of avalanches.
2   Examine the different ways of reducing the avalanche risk.
3   How significant are the following hazards: (a) alluviones (b) surging glaciers (c) icebergs (d) jokulhlaups?

Valley Glaciation in the English Lake District

 The Lake District was one of the main areas of both ice accumulation and erosional intensity in the British Isles. Although, at times, the whole region was covered by ice there were substantial periods when the higher landscapes were not ice covered and valley glaciers were the main agents of erosion (Figure 11.39).

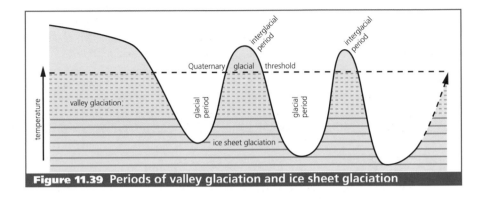

Figure 11.39 Periods of valley glaciation and ice sheet glaciation

The effect of rock type on the variety of glacial landforms

The main rock groups cross the region from north east to south west (Figure 11.40):

■ The Skiddaw slates (metamorphic) to the north are the oldest rocks, dating from the Cambrian period. The landscape is dominated by smooth slopes (Figure 11.41) due, in part, to the relatively uniform resistance to erosion of these rocks. However, in addition, although not as hard as the igneous rocks immediately to the south, the poor jointing of the Skiddaw slates has limited the impact of plucking.

■ The Borrowdale volcanic group (igneous) was formed about 500 million years ago when volcanic eruptions threw up lavas and **tuffs** (volcanic ash) to constitute the central core of the Lake District. The classic landforms of highland glaciation characterise this region. The variety of rock type within this geological grouping gives rise to a rugged stepped topography. Plucking has been an effective erosional process on these generally well-jointed rocks.

■ The Silurian rocks (sedimentary) to the south are considerably less resistant than the above two groups, resulting in a lower landscape with much more evidence of glacial deposition. However, it must be noted that most of the lowland fringes of the Lake District were heavily eroded during the Ice Age, more so in fact than the upland areas. Thus, the action of ice accentuated the differences in relief between the Silurian rocks and the Borrowdale volcanics.

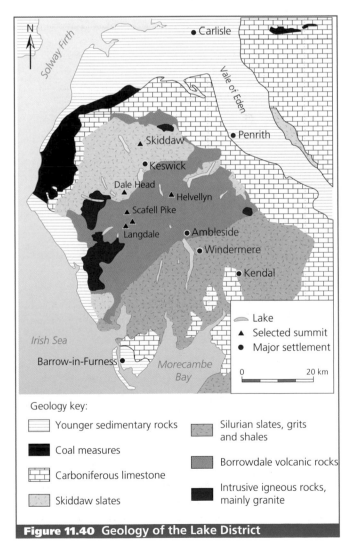

Geology key:

Younger sedimentary rocks

Coal measures

Carboniferous limestone

Skiddaw slates

Silurian slates, grits and shales

Borrowdale volcanic rocks

Intrusive igneous rocks, mainly granite

Figure 11.40 Geology of the Lake District

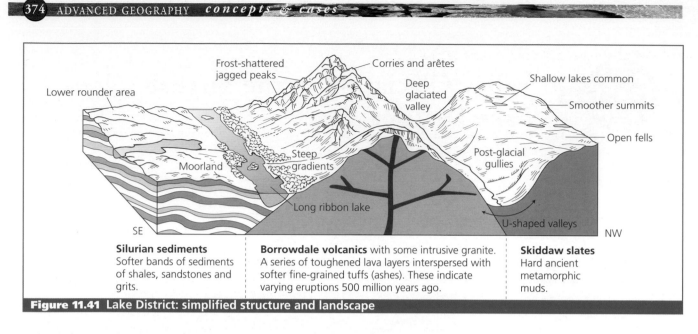

Frost-shattered jagged peaks
Corries and arêtes
Deep glaciated valley
Shallow lakes common
Smoother summits
Lower rounder area
Open fells
Steep gradients
Moorland
Post-glacial gullies
Long ribbon lake
U-shaped valleys
SE
NW

Silurian sediments
Softer bands of sediments of shales, sandstones and grits.

Borrowdale volcanics with some intrusive granite. A series of toughened lava layers interspersed with softer fine-grained tuffs (ashes). These indicate varying eruptions 500 million years ago.

Skiddaw slates
Hard ancient metamorphic muds.

Figure 11.41 Lake District: simplified structure and landscape

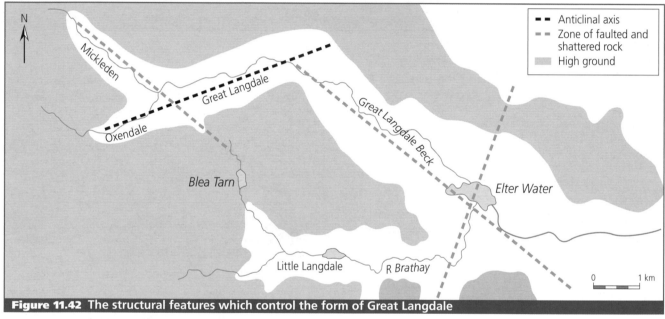

N

- Anticlinal axis
- Zone of faulted and shattered rock
- High ground

Mickleden
Great Langdale
Oxendale
Great Langdale Beck
Blea Tarn
Elter Water
Little Langdale
R Brathay

0   1 km

Figure 11.42 The structural features which control the form of Great Langdale

- Layers of carboniferous limestone, coal measures and red sandstone which built up on top of the existing rocks are now found on the outskirts of the area.

The relative resistance of rocks seems to have influenced the location of lakes. Only three of the major lakes, Thirlmere, Wastwater and Haweswater, lie on the Borrowdale volcanic group. Most lakes are located to the north or south on softer rocks. Deep ribbon lakes are particularly common on the fringes of the Borrowdale volcanics.

Earth movements during the Caledonian orogeny (mountain building period) and later during the Alpine orogeny, combined to fold the area into a giant dome. A radial drainage pattern, discordant in nature was superimposed on the landscape and the overlying layers of sediment were gradually eroded, exposing the older rocks at the centre of the area. Faulting appears to have had

a considerable effect on later erosional events, particularly on the location of some of the lakes and the direction of valleys. For example, a prominent fault runs from Coniston through Grasmere, Dunmail Raise, Thirlmere and the Vale of St John's. Thus, a combination of faulting and the radial drainage pattern gives us the pattern of river valleys running across the major rock bands, which then formed the basis for the pattern of ice movement.

The glaciated landforms of the Great Langdale area

Great Langdale is one of many valleys that radiate outwards from the central dome of the Lake District (Figure 11.43). However, it is unique among lakeland valleys in that it has a distinctive twisting form as a result of the fault lines that cross it (Figure 11.42). Lying in the lee of the highest peaks, such as Great Gable, the valley head was assured of heavy snowfall. The area also felt the full force of outwardly moving ice streams when the whole central region was covered by an ice cap.

Ice accumulated at the head of the Mickleden and Oxendale valleys. Here the glacier began largely as a self-contained unit but also received ice from Langdale Combe, a niche corrie. The top of Rossett Crag can be identified as a modest arête where the trough end of Mickleden backs on to the corrie of Angle Tarn from which ice flowed to the north.

The ice thickened at the confluence of Oxendale and Mickleden and eroded deeply as a result of its increased mass. Further ice was added from Stickle Tarn, a corrie sited below Pavey Ark. A smearing of morainic material is evident at the lip of the corrie. The glacier emanating from Stickle Tarn eroded a shallower trough than the main valley floor which, after glaciation, was left as a hanging valley. Today Stickle Beck flows rapidly over waterfalls and rapids before it joins Great Langdale Beck (Figure 11.44). As the post-glacial period has progressed Stickle Beck has incised more and more deeply into the landscape. Erosion of the valley sides has exposed masses of resistant rock, for example Gimmer Crag. As the glacier moved eastwards it left truncated spurs with clear evidence of striations in places.

Figure 11.44 Great Langdale as seen from above Stickle Tarn

Diffluence cols

As the depth of ice increased, particularly after the confluence of Mickleden and Oxendale, it reached the level of a col marking the position of a zone of faulted and shattered rock. A tongue of ice flowed south over the col into the valley now occupied by Blea Tarn, and then on to the Little Langdale Valley. Once over the col the ice probably accumulated at the first marked change in gradient and compressing flow excavated Blea Tarn. However, it is possible that the depression was first formed as an independent corrie. Not all lakeland corries have steep and craggy back walls. There is a prominent roche moutonnée just south of Blea Tarn.

Another diffluence col is evident at Red Bank where a tongue of ice from the Easedale glacier picked out a dip in the horizon marking another geological line of weakness.

Basins and steps

The long profile of Great Langdale exhibits a number of different levels (Figure 11.45), which are due in part to the rock barriers of Chapelstile and Skelwith Force. Along with other factors they set the scene for the phases of extending and compressing flow which left the valley with its basin-and-step profile. Both rock bars mark the position of beds of toughened volcanic ash, and at one time both barriers held back lakes. The long ribbon lake that existed behind Chapelstile was completely drained in the post-glacial period when its outlet was lowered sufficiently. The flat lacustrine sediments provide clear evidence of what once was. Elterwater is what remains of a larger water body once held back by the Skelwith Force rock barrier. The ice, by plucking at the well-cleaved slates and jointed lava beds on either side of the two rock bars, tended to accentuate these features. Great Langdale Beck has cut mini-gorges through these obstacles – that at Skelwith Force is particularly impressive.

Not far beyond Elterwater, the ice of Great Langdale merged with that of Little Langdale. The latter valley also exhibits over-deepened basins and steps. This larger ice mass was joined at Ambleside by a glacier moving from the north which was also the product of merging ice streams. Most ice originated in Easedale but this was joined by diffluent ice from Thirlmere which, on finding its natural exit to the north blocked by a much larger mass

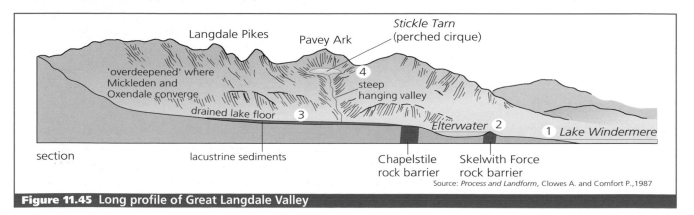

Source: *Process and Landform*, Clowes A. and Comfort P., 1987

Figure 11.45 Long profile of Great Langdale Valley

Figure 11.43 Source: Ordnance Survey Touring Map and Guide 3: The Lake District 1":1 mile (scale slightly enlarged for clarity)

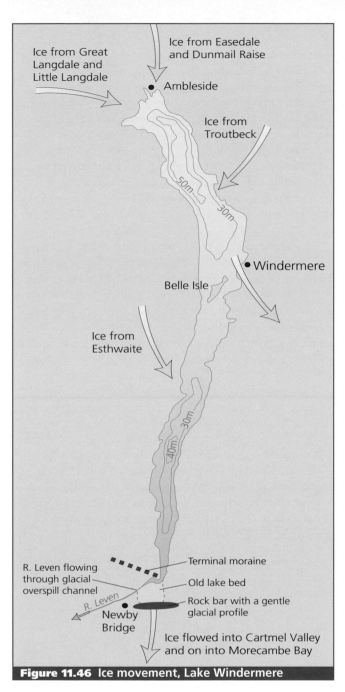

Ice from Great Langdale and Little Langdale

Ice from Easedale and Dunmail Raise

● Ambleside

Ice from Troutbeck

50m

30m

● Windermere

Belle Isle

Ice from Esthwaite

30m

40m

R. Leven flowing through glacial overspill channel

R. Leven

● Newby Bridge

Terminal moraine

Old lake bed

Rock bar with a gentle glacial profile

Ice flowed into Cartmel Valley and on into Morecambe Bay

Figure 11.46 Ice movement, Lake Windermere

of ice, was forced up over the col at Dunmail Raise, lowering it significantly in the process. This now formidable body of ice moved southwards eroding what was to become Lake Windermere, the longest lake in England. Compressing flow gouged out two distinct troughs while Belle Isle and the shallow water around it mark a phase of extending flow (Figure 11.46).The lake at one time was much more extensive, retained by a large terminal moraine which has been partly cut through by the River Leven near Newby Bridge.

Deposition

Evidence of deposition can be found at a number of locations. Near the head of Great Langdale is an impressive series of hummocky moraines, possibly formed by a minor renewal of glacial conditions at the end of the Pleistocene Period. A few drumlins of a modest size can be found between Elterwater and Windermere. There is little evidence of lateral moraines because of the considerable scree slopes formed in the post-glacial period. The limited medial moraines that were probably evident immediately after the retreat of ice were most likely removed by fluvial action. However, the terminal moraine at the southern end of Windermere is impressive.

The braiding which is evident at various places along Great Langdale Beck is due to fluvioglacial deposition, and the interleaving of till and outwash is evidence of a number of advances and retreats of the ice. The most widespread fluvioglacial deposits are found beyond the terminal moraine.

Questions

1 Using the OS map extract (Figure 11.43) draw a large, fully labelled sketch map of the Great Langdale valley and its surroundings to show all the glacial features identified in the case study.
2 Account for the irregularities in the long profile of Great Langdale.
3 Identify and explain the examples of glacial diffluence in this area.

Periglaciation

In certain high latitude and/or high altitude environments, the temperature remains so low that the ground remains frozen for all or part of the year. Repeated freezing and thawing at the surface provides a distinctive set of landforms, which are termed periglacial (literally meaning at the edge of glaciers).

Periglacial areas now account for about one-quarter of the world's surface, but they amounted for a much larger area during cold phases (glacial) of the Pleistocene. Consequently many temperate areas contain evidence of relict periglacial

processes and landforms. Some of these areas have important economic resources and political boundaries.

Most periglacial areas are underlain by permafrost (permanently frozen subsoil). They are also characterised by intense freeze-thaw action, and a seasonally snow-free ground.

The upper climatic limit for periglacial environments is generally between -1°C and -3°C , with annual precipitation less than 1000 mm. Nevertheless, there is a variety of periglacial climates (Figure 11.47) including cold and arid (such as Greenland) to warmer and wetter (such as Iceland, Figure 11.48). In addition there are mountainous (alpine) periglacial areas.

Figure 11.47 Periglacial typology

Polar lowlands
Mean temperature of coldest month <-3°C. Zone is characterised by ice caps, bare rock surfaces and tundra vegetation.

Subpolar lowlands
Mean temperature of coldest month <-3°C and of warmest month >10°C Taiga type of vegetation. The 10°C isotherm for warmest month roughly coincides with tree-line in northern hemisphere.

Mid-latitude lowlands
Mean temperature of coldest month is <-3°C but mean temperature is >10°C for at least four months per year.

Highlands
Climate influenced by altitude as well as latitude. Considerable variability over short distance depending on aspect. Diurnal temperature ranges tend to be large.

Figure 11.48 Periglacial landscape, Thingvellir, Iceland

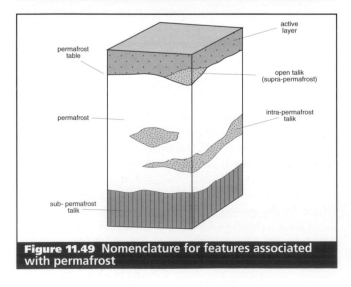

Figure 11.49 Nomenclature for features associated with permafrost

Permafrost

Permafrost has been defined as a thickness of soil, sediment or rock below ground which has been frozen for at least two years. The mean annual temperature required to keep permafrost frozen may be less than 0°C as soluble salts and clay can affect the freezing point of subsurface water. The **active layer** is the layer above the permafrost which freezes and thaws annually (Figure 11.49). The boundary between permafrost and the active layer is known as the **permafrost table**. **Taliks** and pockets of unfrozen water occur above the permafrost. Due to different rates of freezing in winter, water may be trapped between the frozen surface and the permafrost table.

Permafrost covers over one-quarter of the earth's surface. (this includes permafrost under ice sheets.) Most occurs in the Northern Hemisphere in Russia, Canada and Alaska (Figure 11.50). In the coldest regions permafrost is continuous, but as the mean annual temperature approaches 0°C the permafrost is broken and sporadic. At low latitude permafrost may be found at high altitude. For example, in Hawaii, permafrost is found beneath the slopes of Mauna Kea at a height of over 4170 m.

Most permafrost occurs in areas where the mean annual temperature is less than -1°C. Most areas with permafrost have daily temperatures of < 0°C for at least nine months, and < -10°C for at least six months. Precipitation is low: less than 100 mm in winter, and less than 300 mm in summer.

Permafrost grows slowly – usually only a few cm a year. Hence thick layers of permafrost must take many thousands of years to form. Nevertheless, permafrost is vulnerable to change – and there are a wide variety of factors that may cause it to grow or decline (Figure 11.51).

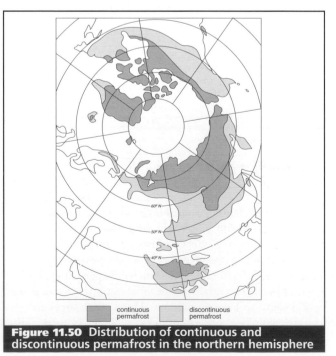

Figure 11.50 Distribution of continuous and discontinuous permafrost in the northern hemisphere

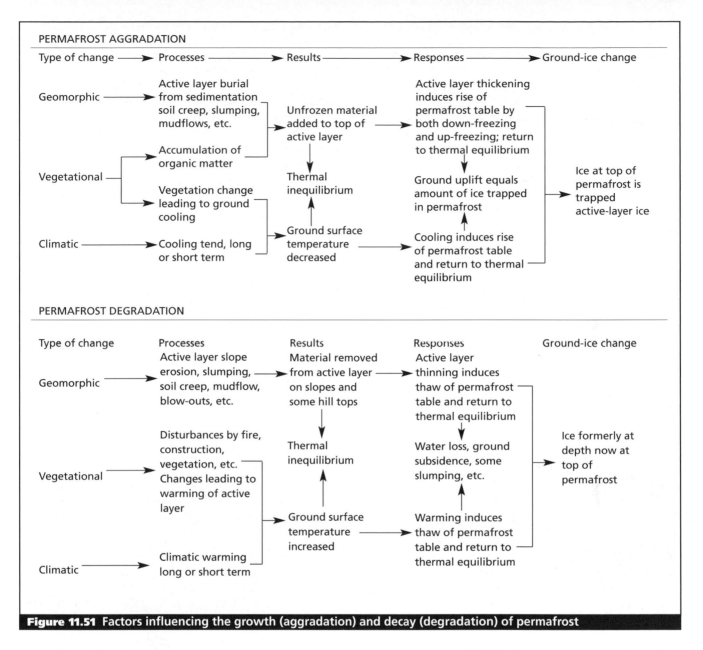

PERMAFROST AGGRADATION

Type of change ⟶ Processes ⟶ Results ⟶ Responses ⟶ Ground-ice change

Geomorphic ⟶ Active layer burial from sedimentation soil creep, slumping, mudflows, etc.

Vegetational ⟶ Accumulation of organic matter

Vegetation change leading to ground cooling

Climatic ⟶ Cooling tend, long or short term

Unfrozen material added to top of active layer

Thermal inequilibrium

Ground surface temperature decreased

Active layer thickening induces rise of permafrost table by both down-freezing and up-freezing; return to thermal equilibrium

Ground uplift equals amount of ice trapped in permafrost

Cooling induces rise of permafrost table and return to thermal equilibrium

Ice at top of permafrost is trapped active-layer ice

PERMAFROST DEGRADATION

Type of change | Processes | Results | Responses | Ground-ice change

Geomorphic — Active layer slope erosion, slumping, soil creep, mudflow, blow-outs, etc.

Vegetational — Disturbances by fire, construction, vegetation, etc. Changes leading to warming of active layer

Climatic — Climatic warming long or short term

Material removed from active layer on slopes and some hill tops

Thermal inequilibrium

Ground surface temperature increased

Active layer thinning induces thaw of permafrost table and return to thermal equilibrium

Water loss, ground subsidence, some slumping, etc.

Warming induces thaw of permafrost table and return to thermal equilibrium

Ice formerly at depth now at top of permafrost

Figure 11.51 Factors influencing the growth (aggradation) and decay (degradation) of permafrost

Periglacial processes

Frost action

Frost action is arguably the most distinctive process of periglacial areas. Although it occurs in other climatic regions, the frequency and intensity of frost action in periglacial areas is such that it creates a distinctive set of landforms (Figure 11.52). This relationship between climatic process and landform is known as climatic geomorphology.

Frost action has greatest impact on silt-sized materials. Coarse materials, such as gravel, are highly permeable, but have a low suction potential (i.e. the ability of water to move to the point where freezing is taking place) whereas fine-grained clays have low permeability but high suction potential. Medium-sized silts have both high permeability and suction potential, hence frost action is intensified.

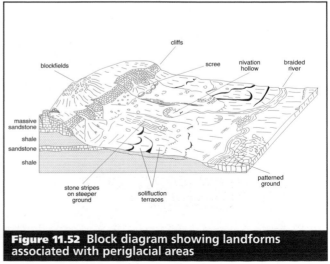

Figure 11.52 Block diagram showing landforms associated with periglacial areas

Frost action also varies with depth from the surface. A survey in Kergevlen, Antarctica recorded 441 freeze-thaw cycles at the surface over a two year period, but no frost at a depth of just 50 mm.

Frost action is responsible for the angular rock debris that is characteristic of periglacial environments (Figure 11.53). However, studies in the Rockies of Colorado, USA, have shown that due to the insulating effect of snow, temperatures at a depth of 10 mm rarely fell below -5°C. Hence, despite abundant moisture and frequent fluctuations of temperature around freezing point, frost weathering was minimal.

It is now believed that **hydration** and **salt weathering** may also be important in periglacial areas.

Frost heave

Frost heave refers to the vertical movement of material due to ice forming, while **frost thrust** refers to the horizontal movement of material as a result of frost formation. Frost heave has a number of effects:

- **the growth of ice lenses down from the surface as freezing continues**

- **the growth of ice lenses at the top of the permafrost**

- **freezing of water in the active layer.**

The upward movement of stones through the soil in periglacial areas has been explained by frost push-and-pull theories. The push theory explains why stones close to the surface are pushed upwards. Soil water flowing around the soil collects under the stone. When it freezes it pushes the stone upwards. When the ice melts, fine-grained material falls into the gap left by the ice. These support the stone in its new elevated position.

The pull theory states that rocks are raised when soil water freezes. Ice under the fine material melts first, and the finer

grains slip back downwards. The ice under the stones melts later (rock is a poor conductor of heat, so larger stones protect the ice immediately below them). Hence the larger stone is subsequently supported by finer material.

Frost cracking

Frost cracking occurs at temperatures below 0°C. The rate of cracking is believed to be related to the rate of temperature decrease.

Chemical weathering

From studies in Sweden, A. Rapp has calculated that chemical weathering accounts for up to 50% of material removed by denudation. The absence of thick residues of chemical weathering may be due to the efficiency of transport processes, or the removal of such material by glacial erosion in the Pleistocene.

Figure 11.53 The effects of frost action, Glyder range, North wales

Figure 11.54 Braided river, glacial outwash plain, Myrdalsjokull, Iceland

Mass movement

Solifluction and **frost creep** are especially important in periglacial areas, although it may be difficult to differentiate between the two. Rates of movement for solifluction are dependent on moisture content. Studies in North East Greenland showed that less steep, more vegetated slopes retained more moisture and had higher rates of solifluction than steeper less vegetated drier slopes.

Solifluction is most effective on silt-sized material. Maximum velocities may reach 200 mm/year, although 50-100 mm/year is more common. Rates decrease with depth, and below 1m hardly any movement occurs.

Nivation

Nivation refers to frost action beneath a blanket of snow. The frost action may include solifluction, freeze-thaw weathering, and melt water. The main landform produced is a **nivation hollow**, which may, given the right conditions, develop into a **cirque**.

Snow provides meltwater, but also acts as an insulator. Nivation appears to be controlled by the thickness of snow, and the presence or absence of permafrost. If permafrost is present, freeze-thaw is limited to the edge of the snow path. Where permafrost is absent, frost action is more widespread (beneath the snow as well as at the edges). Hollows 500 m long and a metre wide have been produced in one season.

River action

Rivers in periglacial areas are highly seasonal and are usually braided (Figure 11.54). Discharges are very high but last only a few days. Such rivers have great potential for erosion and transport. Thus, despite low rainfall totals and relatively low discharge rates, erosion is high. For example, the River Mechen in Canada has an annual precipitation of just 135 mm. About half of this falls as snow. Up to 90% of the annual discharge is concentrated in just ten days and velocities of up to 4m/second occur.

Figure 11.55 Outwash plain, The Myrdalsjokull glacier, Iceland

Circles	Occur singly or in groups. Typical dimensions 0.5-3 m. Non-sorted type characteristically rimmed by vegetation. Sorted type bordered by stones, which tend to increase in size with size of circle. Found in both polar and alpine environments but not restricted to areas of permafrost. Unsorted circles also recorded from non-periglacial environments.
Polygons	Occur in groups. Non-sorted polygons range from small features (<1m across) to much larger forms up to 100 m or more in diameter. Sorted polygons attain maximum dimensions of only 10 m. Stones delimit polygon border and surround finer material. Non-sorted forms are delineated by furrows or cracks. Some types of polygon occur in hot desert environments but most are best developed in areas subject to frost. Ice-wedge polygons only form in the presence of permafrost.
Nets	A transitional form between circles and polygons. Usually fairly small (<2 m across). Earth hummocks, comprising a core of mineral soil surmounted by vegetation, are a common form of unsorted net.
Steps	Found on relatively steep slopes. They develop either parallel to slope contours or become elongated downslope into lobate forms. In non-sorted forms the rise of the step is well vegetated and the tread is bare. In the sorted type the step is bordered by larger stones. Lobate forms are known as stone garlands. Neither type are confined to permafrost environments.
Stripes	Tend to form on steeper slopes than steps. Sorted stripes are composed of alternating stripes of coarse and fine material elongated downslope. Non-sorted variety delineated by vegetation in slight troughs. Not confined to periglacial environments.

Figure 11.56 Patterned ground

Figure 11.57 Low lying periglacial areas are characterised by numerous depressions filled with water

Wind activity

Wind action is important in periglacial areas for a number of reasons, including:

- **strong winds**
- **dry sediments**
- **low rainfall**
- **low temperatures**
- **minimal vegetation cover.**

Major deposits include the vast **loess sheets** of North America, Europe and China. Although these may form in warm desert areas, most are thought to have formed in periglacial environments. Glacial erosion, salt weathering and frost action are able to produce a large volume of fine-grained material which the wind can easily pick up and transport. **Glacial outwash plains** (Figure 11.55) are an important source of material.

Patterned ground

Patterned ground varies from a few centimetres in size to over a hundred metres. It includes a variety of shapes such as circles, polygons and stripes (Figure 11.56). Some patterned ground is sorted, while some is not. Circles and polygons are more common on flat ground, while stripes are more common

on slopes of between 5° and 30°. (On slopes of over 30° rapid mass movement limits patterned ground formation).

Frost heaving is a major cause of patterned ground. As discussed above, it helps move larger stones to the surface, where they form the edges of the pattern, leaving the fine-grained material to form the raised core. **Surface wash** is important for the formation of stripes.

Ice wedges are downward tapering bodies of ice, up to 10 m deep, and a metre wide at the top. Frost cracking is important in the development of ice wedges. Extreme cooling leads to the cracking of the surface and allows an ice wedge to develop.

Pingos

Pingos (from the Inuit word for a hill) are large ice-cored mounds. They are up to 70 m high and about 600 m in diameter. The ice core which forms the pingo grows as a result of two mechanisms. In **closed-system pingos** freezing occurs from the surface, the permafrost and the sides, causing a sub-surface body of water to be surrounded by ice. As this water finally freezes, it expands, causing a blistering at the surface (Figure 11.58). In the Mackenzie Delta of Canada, 98% of the 1380 pingos are located close to lakes basins. **Open system pingos**, by contrast, involve the freezing of water flowing under hydrostatic pressure beneath a thin layer of permafrost (Figure 11.59).

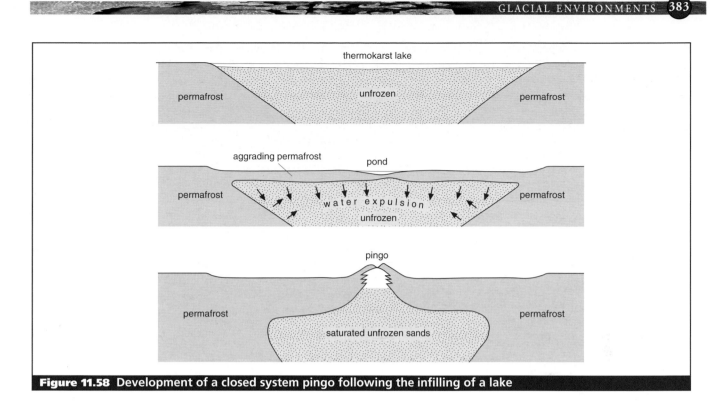

Figure 11.58 Development of a closed system pingo following the infilling of a lake

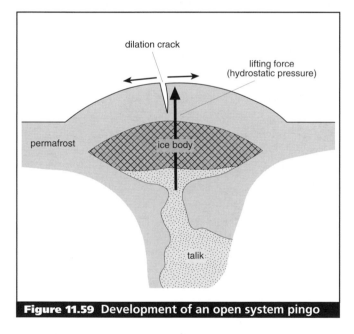

Figure 11.59 Development of an open system pingo

Palsas

Palsas are mounds, and elongated mounds occurring in bogs. They contain a large amount of peat and have ice lenses rather than a single core of ice.

Thermokarst

Thermokarst refers to depressions formed by the thawing of ice (Figure 11.57). It is called karst as it resembles the depressions in true karst (limestone). **Thaw lakes** are shallow depressions filled with water. Most are less than 2 km wide and less than 5 m

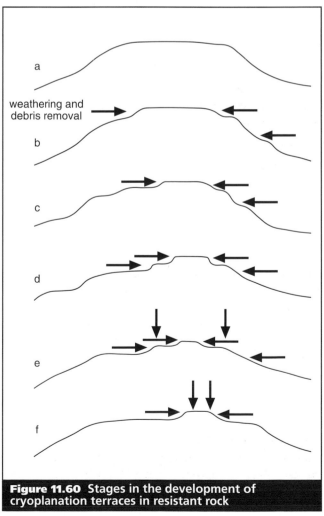

Figure 11.60 Stages in the development of cryoplanation terraces in resistant rock

deep. They are formed in poorly drained regions by the melting of ice. **Alases** are major depressions up to 15 km wide and 40 m deep. They result from the degradation of permafrost and can be related to climate change and fire.

Depositional features

There are a variety of depositional features associated with periglacial environments such as solifluction lobes, blockfields and block streams. **Solifluction sheets** are smooth, gently sloping surfaces whereas **solifluction lobes** are longer, tongue-shaped features. **Block slopes** are covered with angular boulders, while **block streams** have sharp angular blocks concentrated in valleys.

Asymmetric valleys

Asymmetric valleys are valleys in which one slope is much steeper than the other. The main reason for the difference is aspect. In the northern hemisphere, south-facing slopes have a much greater frequency of mass movement, and transport. By contrast, north-facing slopes are colder, less thawing occurs, hence less activity takes place. South-facing slopes are therefore likely to be less steep than their north-facing counterparts.

Cryoplanation terrace

Cryoplanation terraces are gently sloping surfaces cut into bedrock or upper hill summits. They may be up to 10 km long and 2 km wide, and the terrace rise (edge of terrace) may be 70 m high. The terraces are formed by the denudation of the bedrock in conjunction with slope retreat. Development begins with a nivation hollow. The rear of the hollow is over-deepened to form a cliff which retreats due to weathering and debris removal. Retreat on two or more sides of a summit produces a pair of summit terraces with a rock mass in the centre (Figure 11.60).

Periglacial features in the north of England and Scotland

North of England

Much of the north of England, in particular the upland areas, have had a periglacial climate for at least the last 10 000 years, and there is much evidence of periglacial processes and landforms. For example, Tufnell has surveyed frost-shattered bedrock in the limestone and sandstone of the Alson block and in the Cheviots. There are many nivation terraces in North Yorkshire. Also head deposits, consisting of angular debris, in the Cheviots (Howgill Fell), the Lake District and the Pennines. In the Lake District, scree slopes are moving at rates of up to 30 cm/year.

Smaller features, such as stone polygons, are found on Cross Fell and Little Dun Fell in the northern Pennines, but most are to be found in the Lake District. Currently they are forming in areas above 600 m. **Thufurs**, small hummocks less than one metre high, occur on Great Dun Fell, and in other high areas. Their formation is linked to the freezing and blistering of subsurface water in winter, which pushes the surface upwards.
In the northern Pennines the accumulation of snow is associated with high ground, slopes on the leeward side of summits, and shaded sites. **Altiplanation terraces** and nivation hollows are formed as a result of freeze-thaw weathering and removal of

material by snowmelt. In the higher altitudes, snow may remain for up to 100 days each year. Current nivation in the Cheviots occurs on altitudes above 700 m. During the exceptionally long winter of 1963, snow remained on the Cheviots for 260 days of the year.

The remains of pingos have been observed on the Isle of Man. Fossil open-system pingos, consisting of depressions with ramparts at their edges are all that remain. In many places, they have been obscured by modern farming practices. They are mostly found in the valleys that drain towards the western lowlands of the northern part of the island, areas like Glens Mooar, Wylling, Dhoo, Sulby and Auddyn. The largest of the ponds is 130 m by 90 m but many of the ramparts have been removed by ploughing which has occurred right up to the edge of the pond. Some geographers have, however, questioned whether these ponds are relict pingos or dead ice features (such as kettle holes).

The higher parts of the Lake District have many of the best modern features of periglaciation. That these features can be found on mine debris, such as at Glenridding, provides evidence that they are currently forming. Mining took place until 300 years ago, therefore the features located on the mine waste must be more recent.

On the summit of Hellvelyn there are examples of small, poorly sorted patterned ground. These generally contain a ring of coarser material and a centre of finer material. Where the slope angle increases the circles become elongated into stripes. Given the small-scale of these features, stripes are about 30 cm wide and circles less than a metre in diametre, they can be formed within a year. Patterned ground is confined to areas above 900 m.

Turf-banked terraces caused by freezing and thawing of water during winter consist of a long bare tread (terrace) and a rise (mini-cliff) of turf. These are becoming more widespread in the Lake District as grazing by sheep reduces the vegetation cover.

Scotland

Periglacial features are found on many of the higher parts of Scottish mountains. There is a mix of active and relict landforms. During the height of the glacial advances, periglacial processes extended over most of the country and operated as low as sea-level. The lower limit of periglacial activity is currently about 500 m. However, much of the evidence of periglaciation has been removed by glacial action, so there are few extensive deposits to be found.

Stone polygons, stripes and solifluction terraces are currently active. Stripes on Tinto Hill, Lanarkshire have been destroyed and reformed in as little as two years. On exposed mountains, solifluction terraces are common. Typically these are up to 10 m long, with a tread of up to one metre. Solifluction sheets are widespread on high ground with gentle to moderate slopes. Wind action is very important in northwest Scotland, and many areas have extensive covering of sand, often metres thick.

There are a large number of fossil periglacial features. Most of the fossil ice wedges that exist occur in **kames, sandur** and **raised beaches**. They must, therefore, have been formed since glaciers covered the land. Relict solifluction terraces have been located as low as 150 m in Banffshire and Dumfrieshire.

Many of cols and gaps of high mountains are covered with frost-shattered debris. Excellent examples include the blockfields of western Rhum, Schiehallion in the central Grampians, and on the Cairngorms. Quartzite is especially prone to frost action and hence scree slopes. The screes of Rhum are still active whereas others, such as in the Southern Upland, are relict and are mantled by a cover of soil and vegetation.

Fossil nivation hollows occur in the Red Hills of Skye. These were last active during the Loch Lomond re-advance about 10 000 years ago. Similarly, there is evidence for numerous landslides on Skye, and the Highlands and Islands.

Tors occur on a number of mountains in Scotland. Excellent examples include Morven, Smean and Maiden Pap in Caithness (formed of conglomerate), Ben Loyal in Sutherland (formed of syenite), and in the Cairngorms (formed of granite). The Cairngorms arguably has the best tors in Scotland. Some are up to 25 m high. Their distribution is related in part to glacial activity. In the intensely glaciated areas of western Scotland they are largely absent, whereas in the east of Scotland, where the land was sheltered from glacial erosion, tors are more numerous.

Bibliography

References

Living Ice: Understanding Glaciers and Glaciation by R. P. Sharp, CUP, 1988.
Glaciers by M. Hambrey and J. Alean, CUP, 1992.
The Quaternary Ice Age by Murray Gray, CUP, 1983.
Glacial Geomorphology by C. E. Embleton and C. A. M. King, Edward Arnold, 1975.

Glaciers and Glaciation by D. I. Benn and D. J. A. Evans, Edward Arnold, 1997.
Cold Environments by G. Nagle and M. Witherick, Nelson Thornes, 2002.

Internet

British Antarctic Survey
http://www.nerc-bas.ac.uk
British Geological Survey
http://www.bgs

12 people, weather and climate

Climate and weather

The term **climate** refers to the state of the atmosphere over a period of not less than 30 years. It includes variables such as temperature, precipitation, winds, humidity, cloud cover and pressure. It refers not only to the averages of these variables but also to the extremes. By contrast, **weather** refers to the state of the atmosphere at any particular moment in time. However, we usually look at the weather over a period of between a few days and a week. The same variables are considered as for climate. Climate and weather are affected by a number of factors such as atmospheric composition, latitude, altitude, distance from the sea, prevailing winds, aspect, cloud cover and, increasingly, human activities.

The energy that drives all weather systems and climates comes from the sun. Most of this energy is absorbed by the earth in the tropical regions whereas there is a loss of energy from more polar areas. To compensate for this there is also a redistribution of energy to higher latitudes from lower latitudes, caused by the circulation of winds and ocean currents.

Figure 12.1 1998 floods in Bangladesh – the result of extreme rains

The atmosphere

Atmospheric composition

The atmosphere contains a mix of gases, liquids and solids. Atmospheric gases are held close to the earth by gravity. Close to the earth these gases are relatively constant in the lower atmosphere. Nevertheless, there are important spatial and temporal variations in atmospheric composition, and this causes variations in temperature, humidity and pressure over time and between places. The normal components of dry air include nitrogen (78 per cent), oxygen (21 per cent), argon (0.96 per cent), and carbon dioxide (0.03 per cent). In addition, there are other important gases such as helium, ozone, hydrogen and methane. These gases are crucial. For example, changes in the amount of carbon dioxide in the atmosphere are having an effect on global warming (see Chapter 15, pages 510–5) and the destruction of ozone is having an important effect on the quality of radiation reaching the earth's surface (see pages 515–6).

The atmosphere also contains moisture. Most water vapour is held in the lower 10 to 15 km of atmosphere. Above this it is too cold and there is not enough turbulence to carry vapour upwards. In addition, there are solids such as dust, ash, soot and salt. These allow condensation to occur which can cause cloud formation and precipitation. On a local scale, large concentrations of solid particles cause an increase in fog, smog, haze and/or precipitation.

Figure 12.2 Hot, dry summers affect human activity

Variations in composition with altitude

Turbulence and mixing in the lower 15 km of the atmosphere produces fairly similar 'air'. At high altitudes, by contrast, marked concentrations of certain gases occur. For example, between 15 km and 35 km there is a concentration of ozone. Although this forms only a small percentage of the atmospheric gas, it is significant enough to lead to an increase in atmospheric temperature in this region and has an important screening function.

Key Definitions ①

adiabatic processes   The change in temperature of a parcel of air caused by its ascent or descent (i.e. there is no external source of heating or cooling). All changes are internal.

air mass   A large body of air with relatively similar temperature and humidity characteristics.

albedo   The reflectivity of the earth's surfaces.

anticyclone   A high pressure system.

atmosphere   The mixture of gases, predominantly nitrogen, oxygen, argon, carbon dioxide, and water vapour, that surrounds the earth.

climate   The average weather conditions of a place or an area over a period of 30 years or more.

coriolis effect   An effect which causes any body that moves freely with respect to the rotating earth to veer to the right in the northern hemisphere and to the left in the southern hemisphere.

cyclone   An atmospheric low-pressure system that gives rise to roughly circular, inward-spiraling wind motion, called vorticity.

El Niño   An anomalous warming of surface waters in the eastern equatorial Pacific Ocean linked with climatic disturbances throughout the world.

environmental lapse rate (ELR)   The normal decline of temperature with altitude – usually about 6°C/1000 m.

evapotranspiration   The combined losses of transpiration and evaporation.

front   A boundary between a warm air mass and a cold air mass, resulting in frontal (depressional or cyclonic) rainfall.

general circulation models (GCMs)   Climate models that show interconnected processes in the atmosphere over the whole world.

humidity   A measure of the amount of moisture in the air. Absolute humidity tells us how much moisture is in the air (g/m³) whereas relative humidity expresses this amount as a percentage of the maximum that air of a certain temperature could hold.

hurricane   A tropical cyclonic storm having winds that exceed 120 km/h.

instability   Unstable atmospheric conditions (rising air) likely to cause cloud formation and precipitation.

jet stream   An intense thermal wind, found in the upper troposphere.

meteorology   The study of the earth's atmosphere and weather processes.

precipitation   A term including all forms of rainfall, snow, frost, hail and dew. It is the conversion and transfer of moisture in the atmosphere to the land.

stability   Balanced pressure conditions; air is unable to rise above a low level; calm, dry conditions, limited cloud formation.

tornado   A cyclonic storm with a very intense low-pressure centre.

troposphere   One of the four thermal layers of the atmosphere, which extends from the surface of the earth to an altitude of 10 to 16 km.

weather   The state of the atmosphere at a given time and place.

The most significant concentrations of gases at altitude include:

- **nitrogen between 100 and 200 km**
- **oxygen between 200 and 1100 km**
- **helium between 1100 km and 3500 km**
- **hydrogen above 3500 km.**

The concentrations of gases have an important effect on changes in temperature through the atmosphere (Figure 12.3). At the tropopause there is a reversal in the temperature gradient. This acts as the ceiling to weather systems. Its height varies seasonally and latitudinally: it is higher in summer and towards the equator. In the stratosphere the increase in temperature at between 30 and 50 km is related to the presence of ozone. Temperatures then fall in the mesosphere but increase again in the thermosphere.

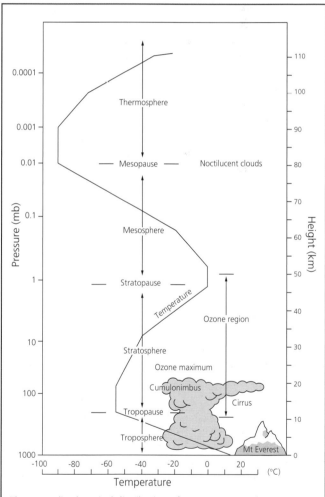

The generalised vertical distribution of temperature and pressure up to about 110 km. Note particularly the tropopause and the zone of maximum ozone concentration with the warm layer above.

Source: Barry, R. and Chorley, R., *Atmosphere, Weather and Climate*. Routledge, 1998

Figure 12.3 Changes in temperature through the atmosphere

Increasing lightness and decreasing density occur with increasing altitude. As air is compressible, air at ground level will be denser than that at altitude, since there is more air above it.

Atmospheric energy

The atmosphere is an open energy system receiving energy from both the sun and the earth. Although the energy from the latter is small, it has an important local effect, as in the case of urban climates. Incoming solar radiation is referred to as **insolation**.

Atmospheric energy budget

The atmosphere constantly receives solar energy yet, until recently, the atmosphere was not getting any hotter. This recent heating – known as global warming – has been linked with human activities and is discussed in depth in Chapter 15. Therefore, there has been a balance between inputs (insolation) and outputs (re-radiation) (Figure 12.4). Under 'natural' conditions the balance is achieved in three main ways:

- **radiation – the emission of electromagnetic waves such as X-ray, shortwave and longwave; as the sun is a very hot body, radiating at a temperature of about 5700°C most of its radiation is in the form of very short wavelengths such as ultraviolet and visible light**
- **convection – the transfer of heat by the movement of a gas or liquid; warm air rises while cold air sinks because it is dense**
- **conduction – the transfer of heat by contact.**

Of incoming radiation 17 per cent is absorbed by atmospheric gases, especially oxygen and ozone at high altitudes, and carbon dioxide and water vapour at low altitudes. Scattering accounts for a net loss of 6 per cent, and clouds and water droplets reflect 23 (19+4) per cent. In fact, clouds can reflect up to 80 per cent of total insolation. Reflection from the earth's surface (known as the **planetary albedo** – Figure 12.5) is generally about 4 per cent. Hence, only about 47 per cent of the insolation at the top of the atmosphere actually gets through to the earth's surface.

Energy received by the earth is re-radiated at long wavelength. (Very hot bodies, such as the sun, emit shortwave radiation, whereas cold bodies, such as the earth, emit longwave radiation.) Of this, 8 per cent is lost to space. Some energy is absorbed by clouds and re-radiated back to earth. Evaporation and condensation account for a loss of heat of 23 per cent. The heat gained by the atmosphere from the ground amounts to 39 units.

The atmosphere is largely heated from below. Most of the incoming shortwave radiation is let through, but the outgoing longwave radiation is trapped by carbon dioxide. This is known as the greenhouse principle.

Annual temperature patterns

There are important large-scale east–west temperature zones (Figure 12.6). For example, in January highest temperatures over land (above 30°C) are found in Australia and Southern Africa. By contrast, the coldest temperatures (less than −40°C) are found over parts of Siberia, Greenland and the Canadian Arctic. In general there is a decline in temperatures northwards from the Tropic of Capricorn,

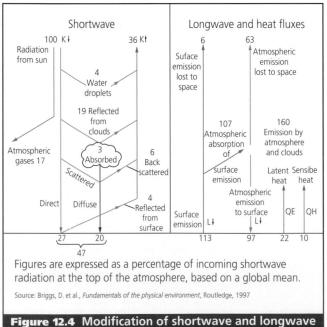

Figures are expressed as a percentage of incoming shortwave radiation at the top of the atmosphere, based on a global mean.

Source: Briggs, D. et al., *Fundamentals of the physical environment*, Routledge, 1997

Figure 12.4 Modification of shortwave and longwave radiation by the atmosphere and the surface

Figure 12.5 Albedos for the shortwave part of the spectrum

Surface	Albedo (%)
Water (zenith angles above 40°)	2–4
Water (angles less than 40°)	6–80
Fresh snow	75–90
Old snow	40–70
Dry sand	35–45
Dark, wet soil	5–15
Dry concrete	17–27
Black road surface	5–10
Grass	20–30
Deciduous forest	10–20
Coniferous forest	5–15
Crops	15–25
Tundra	15–20

Source: Briggs, D et al, *Fundamentals of the physical environment*, Routledge, 1997

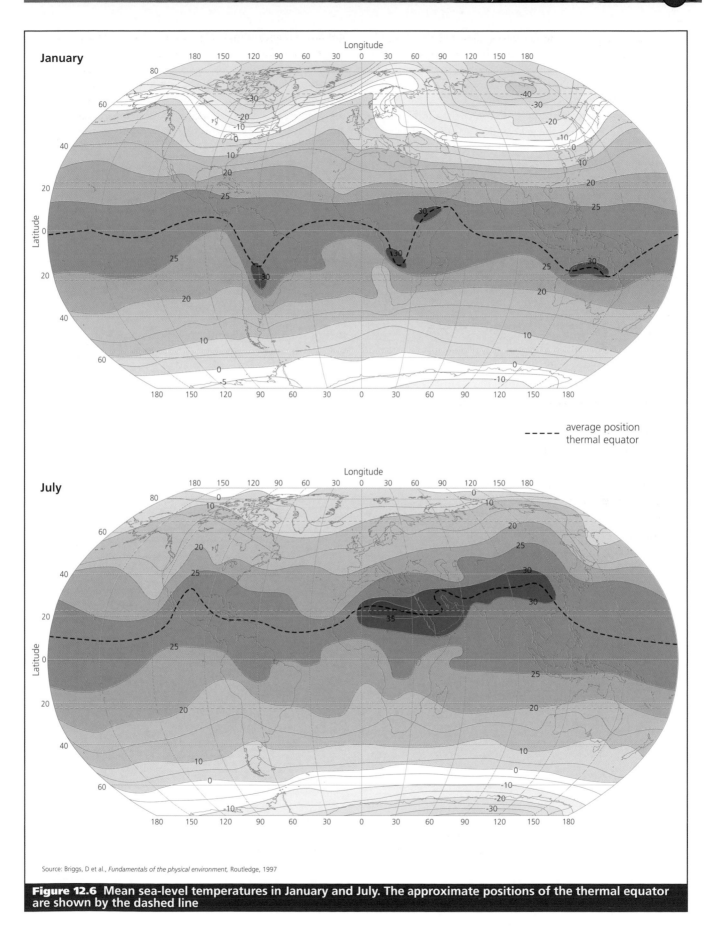

average position thermal equator

Source: Briggs, D et al., *Fundamentals of the physical environment*, Routledge, 1997

Figure 12.6 Mean sea-level temperatures in January and July. The approximate positions of the thermal equator are shown by the dashed line

although there are important anomalies, such as the effect of the Andes in South America and the effect of the cold current off the coast of Namibia. By contrast, in July maximum temperatures are found over the Sahara, Near East, northern India and parts of southern United States and Mexico, while areas in the southern hemisphere are cooler than in January.

These patterns reflect the general decrease of insolation from the equator to the poles and the changes in the length of the day. There is little seasonal variation at the equator, but in mid or high latitudes large seasonal differences occur. There is also a time-lag between the overhead sun and the period of maximum insolation, up to two months in some places, largely because the air is heated from below not above. The coolest period is after the **winter solstice** (the shortest day), since the ground continues to lose heat even after insolation has resumed. Over oceans the time-lag is greater than over the land, due to differences in their specific heat capacities.

Diurnal variations in temperature

Changes in temperature between day and night are known as **diurnal** changes. On a calm, cloudless day, minimum temperature is just before dawn since the ground is losing heat all night. After dawn, insolation increases, the temperature of the ground rises, and air temperature rises. This is known as a **positive energy budget**. Maximum insolation is at midday when the sun is highest in the sky. However, as it takes a few hours for the ground to heat the air above it, maximum temperature is sometime around 2 p.m. By mid-afternoon convection currents mix warm air with cold air and the temperature begins to drop. After dusk, temperature falls, although the air stays warm for a short while, due to outgoing longwave radiation.

Specific heat capacity

The specific heat capacity is the amount of heat needed to raise the temperature of a body by 1°C. There are important differences between the heating and cooling of land and water. Land heats and cools more quickly than water. It takes five times as much heat to raise the temperature of water by 2°C as it does to raise land temperatures.

Water heats more slowly because:

■ it is clear, hence the sun's rays penetrate to great depth (**distributing energy over a wider area**)

■ **tides and currents cause the heat to be further distributed.**

Thus a larger volume of water is heated for every unit of energy than land, hence water takes longer to heat up.

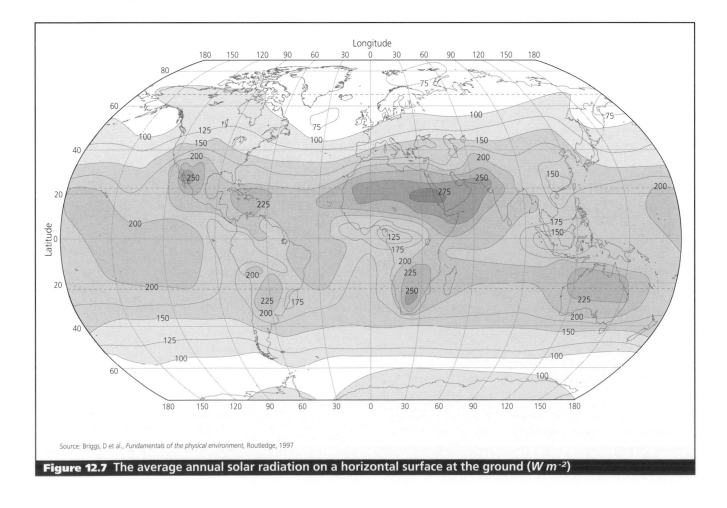

Source: Briggs, D et al., *Fundamentals of the physical environment*, Routledge, 1997

Figure 12.7 The average annual solar radiation on a horizontal surface at the ground (*W m⁻²*)

Factors affecting temperature

There are many factors which affect the temperature of a place. These include latitude, length of day, altitude, aspect, distance from the sea, the nature of nearby ocean currents, dominant winds, cloud cover, amount of dust in the atmosphere and human impact.

Latitude

On a global scale **latitude** is the most important factor determining temperature (Figure 12.7), due to the angle of the overhead sun and the thickness of the atmosphere (Figure 12.8). At the equator, the overhead sun is high in the sky, hence the insolation received is of a great quality or intensity. At the poles, the overhead sun is low in the sky, hence the quality of energy received is poor. Energy has more atmosphere to pass through nearer the poles, so more energy is lost, scattered or reflected by the atmosphere than at the equator, therefore temperatures are lower nearer the poles than at the equator. In addition, the **albedo** (reflectivity) is higher in polar regions. This is because snow and ice are very reflective and low-angle sunlight is easily reflected from water surfaces. However, variations in length of day and season partly offset the lack of intensity in polar and Arctic regions.

The longer the sun shines the greater the amount of insolation received, which may overcome, in part, the lack of intensity of insolation in polar regions. (Alternatively, the long polar nights in winter cause vast amounts of energy to be lost.)

The result is an imbalance: a positive budget in the tropics, a negative budget at the poles (Figure 12.9). However, neither region is getting progressively hotter or colder due to the horizontal transfer of energy from the equator to the poles by winds and ocean currents. Thus the imbalance is in the heating of the earth's atmosphere. This gives rise to an important second energy budget in the atmosphere – the horizontal transfer between low latitudes and high latitudes to compensate for differences in global insolation.

The earth is roughly spherical and orbits the sun in an elliptical trajectory at an average distance of 150 million km. However, it is slightly closer to the sun in January (only 147 million km), but slightly further from the sun (153 million km) in July (Figure 12.10). This affects the amount of insolation (incoming solar radiation) that the earth receives from the sun, so there is a difference in the seasonal heating of the planet. Because of the earth's axial tilt the planet's surface slopes away from the sun, this means that the incoming solar energy is concentrated in equatorial areas but is dispersed over polar areas, so higher latitudes are much colder than lower latitudes.

Incoming solar radiation is mostly in the **visible wavelengths** (Figure 12.11). These are not absorbed by the earth's atmosphere; instead these wavelengths heat the earth which, in turn, emits longwave radiation. This longwave radiation is largely trapped by the various greenhouse gases (carbon dioxide, methane and water vapour) and this heats the planet by some 25°C.

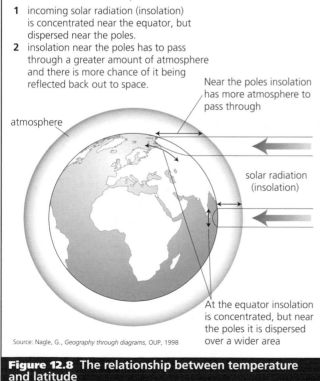

Latitude

Areas that are close to the equator receive more heat than areas that are close to the poles. This is due to two reasons:

1 incoming solar radiation (insolation) is concentrated near the equator, but dispersed near the poles.

2 insolation near the poles has to pass through a greater amount of atmosphere and there is more chance of it being reflected back out to space.

Near the poles insolation has more atmosphere to pass through

atmosphere

solar radiation (insolation)

At the equator insolation is concentrated, but near the poles it is dispersed over a wider area

Source: Nagle, G., *Geography through diagrams*, OUP, 1998

Figure 12.8 The relationship between temperature and latitude

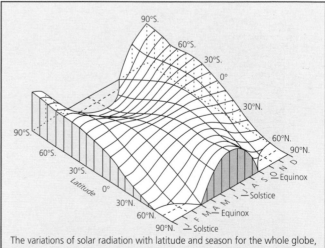

The variations of solar radiation with latitude and season for the whole globe, assuming no atmosphere. This assumption explains the abnormally high amounts of radiation received at the poles in summer, when daylight lasts for 24 hours each day.

Source: Barry, R. and Chorley, R., *Atmosphere, Weather and Climate*, Routledge, 1998

Figure 12.9 Solar radiation variations

Length of day and season

Variations in the length of day and seasons have a dramatic effect on the temperature of an area. They are caused by the earth's revolution and rotation. The earth revolves around the sun every 365.25 days. It also rotates around its own axis every 24 hours. The earth's axis is inclined at an angle of 23.5°, thus the overhead sun appears to migrate from the Tropic of Cancer (23.5°N) on 21 June to Tropic of Capricorn (23.5°S) on 22 December. The higher the overhead sun the greater the amount of heat energy received. Midsummer in the northern hemisphere is June, whereas in the southern hemisphere it is in December. The intermediate positions, 21 March and 23 September, are called the **equinoxes**.

Length of daylight varies with the overhead sun. On the equinoxes, the sun is overhead at the equator and all places receive 12 hours day and 12 hours night. On 21 June, the **summer solstice**, the sun is overhead at the Tropic of Cancer. Hence the northern hemisphere has its longest day and shortest night. By contrast, 22 December is the **winter**

solstice. The sun is overhead at the Tropic of Capricorn, and the northern hemisphere has its longest night and shortest day. By contrast, places north of the Arctic Circle (66.5°N) receive 24 hours of darkness on 22 December, while places south of the Antarctic Circle (66.5°S) receive 24 hours of daylight.

Altitude

In general, temperatures decrease with altitude. At low altitudes heat escapes from the surface slowly because the dense air contains dust and water vapour which trap the heat. By contrast, heat escapes rapidly from high altitudes because the thin air contains little water vapour and dust. Temperatures vary with height because at altitude air is less dense and unable to absorb heat. The normal decrease of temperature with height is known as the normal or environmental lapse rate, on average 6.4°C per km. If temperatures increase with height then a **temperature inversion** is formed.

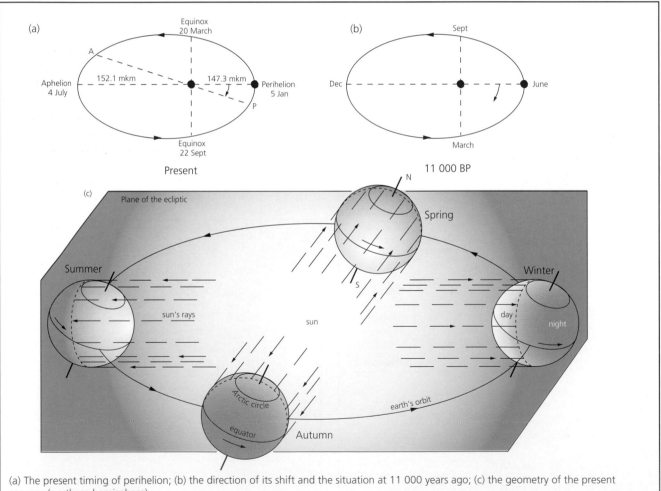

(a) The present timing of perihelion; (b) the direction of its shift and the situation at 11 000 years ago; (c) the geometry of the present seasons (northern hemisphere).

Source: Barry, R. and Chorley, R., *Atmosphere, Weather and Climate*, Routledge, 1998

Figure 12.10 Perihelion shifts

Aspect

Aspect is noticeable only in temperate latitudes. It refers to whether a slope faces south or north. In the northern hemisphere, south-facing slopes (adret slopes) are warmer than the north-facing slopes (ubac slopes). The reverse is true in the southern hemisphere.

Ocean currents

Surface ocean currents are caused by the influence of prevailing winds blowing steadily across the sea. The dominant pattern of surface ocean currents (known as a **gyre**) is a roughly circular flow, clockwise in the northern hemisphere and anticlockwise in the southern hemisphere

(Figure 12.12). The main exception is the circumpolar current that flows around Antarctica from west to east. There is no equivalent current in the northern hemisphere because of the distribution of land and sea. Within the circulation of the gyres water piles up into a dome. The effect of the rotation of the earth is to cause water in the oceans to push westward; this piles up water on the western edge of ocean basins rather like water slopping in a bucket. The return flow is often narrow, fast-flowing currents such as the Gulf Stream. The Gulf Stream in particular, transports heat northwards and then eastwards across the North Atlantic; the Gulf Stream is the main reason why the British Isles have mild winters and relatively cool summers (Figure 12.13).

The effect of ocean currents on temperatures depends upon whether the current is cold or warm. Warm currents from equatorial regions raise the temperatures of polar areas (with the aid of prevailing westerly winds). However, the effect is noticeable only in winter; for example, the North Atlantic Drift raises the winter temperatures of north west Europe. By contrast, there are other areas which are cooled by ocean currents. Cold currents such as the Labrador Current off the north east coast of North America may reduce summer temperatures, but only if the wind blows from the sea to the land.

Distance from the sea has an important influence on temperature. Water takes up heat and gives it back much more slowly than the land. In winter, in mid latitudes sea air is much warmer than the land air, therefore onshore winds bring heat to the coastal lands. By contrast, during the summer coastal areas remain much cooler than inland sites. Areas with a coastal influence are termed **maritime** or **oceanic** whereas inland areas are called **continental**.

In the Pacific Ocean two main atmospheric states exist – the first is warm surface water in the west with cold surface water in the east; the other is warm surface water in the east with cold in the west. In whichever case, the warm surface causes low pressure. As air blows from high pressure to low pressure there is a movement of water from the colder area to the warmer area. These winds push warm surface water into the warm region exposing colder deep water behind them maintaining the pattern. The reversal of this is known as the El Niño phenomenon, discussed on pages 413–4.

The ocean conveyor belt

In addition to the transfer of energy by wind and the transfer of energy by ocean currents there is also a transfer of energy by deep sea currents. Oceanic convection occurs from polar regions where cold salty water sinks into the depths and makes its way towards the equator (Figure 12.12). The densest water is found in the Antarctic area; here sea water freezes to form ice at a temperature of around about −2°C. The ice is fresh water, hence the sea water left behind is much saltier and therefore denser. This cold dense water sweeps round

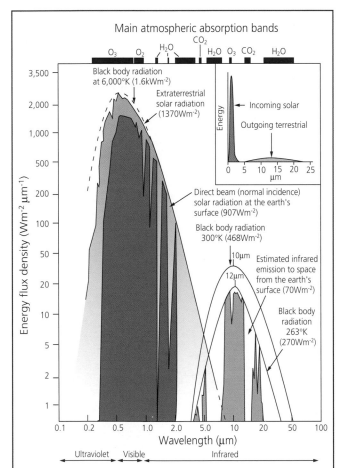

Spectral distribution of solar and terrestrial radiation, plotted logarithmically, together with the main atmospheric absorption bands. The blue areas in the infrared spectrum indicate the 'atmospheric windows' where radiation escapes to space. The black-body radiation at 6,000 K is that proportion of the flux which would be incident on the top of the atmosphere. The inset shows the same curves for incoming and outgoing radiation with the wavelength plotted arithmetically on an arbitrary vertical scale.

Source: Barry, R., and Chorley, R., *Atmosphere, Weather and Climate*, Routledge, 1998

Figure 12.11 Incoming solar radiation

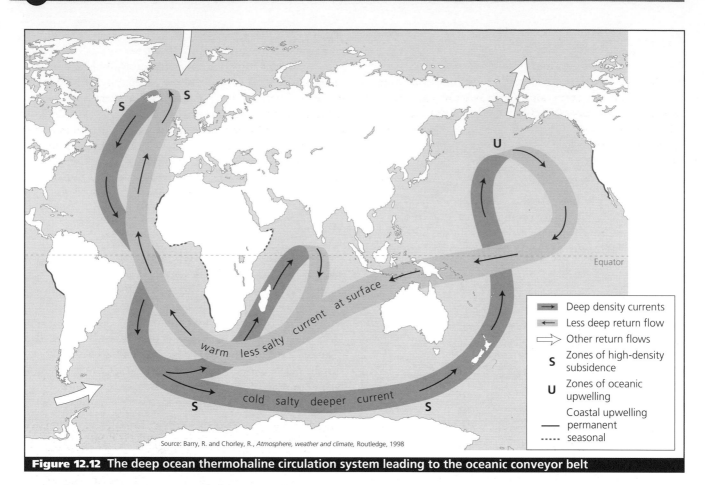

Source: Barry, R. and Chorley, R., *Atmosphere, weather and climate*, Routledge, 1998

Figure 12.12 The deep ocean thermohaline circulation system leading to the oceanic conveyor belt

Antarctica at a depth of about 4 km. It then spreads into the deep basins of the Atlantic, the Pacific and the Indian Oceans. In the oceanic conveyor belt model, surface currents bring warm water to the North Atlantic from the Indian and Pacific Oceans, and these waters give up their heat to cold winds which blow from Canada across the North Atlantic. This water then sinks and starts the reverse convection of the deep ocean current. The amount of heat given up is about a third of the energy that is received from the sun. The conveyor belt pattern is maintained by salt. The North Atlantic is warmer than the North Pacific so there is proportionally more evaporation in the North Atlantic. The water left behind by evaporation has a higher salt content and therefore is much denser which causes it to sink. Eventually, the dense water is transported into the Pacific where it picks up more water and its density is reduced.

Winds

In temperate latitudes prevailing (most frequent) winds from the land lower the winter temperatures, but raise the summer temperatures. Prevailing winds from the sea do the opposite – lower the summer temperatures, raise the winter temperatures. Much depends upon the original characteristics of the air, whether it is warm or cold, moist or dry (see pages 415–9 on air masses). Local winds are also of importance.

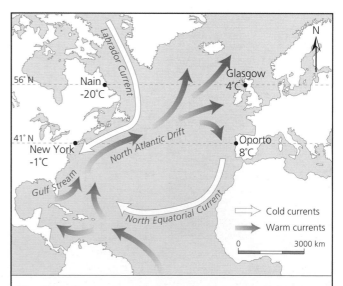

The effect of an ocean current depends upon whether it is a warm current or a cold current. Warm currents move away from the equator, whereas cold currents move towards it. The cold Labrador Current reduces the temperatures of the western side of the Atlantic, while the warm North Atlantic Drift raises temperatures on the eastern side.

Source: Nagle, G., *Geography through diagrams*, OUP, 1998

Figure 12.13 Ocean currents

Cloud cover

Cloud cover decreases the amount of insolation reaching the earth's surface and the amount leaving it. If there is no cloud then incoming shortwave radiation and outgoing longwave radiation are at a maximum. For example, rainforest areas with thick cloud cover experience days of about 30°C and nights of about 20°C, whereas in deserts without much cloud cover days might reach 38 to 40°C, whereas nights drop to around freezing. This is because humid air absorbs heat by day and retains it at night.

Aerosols and human activity

Dust and other impurities such as volcanic fallout may block insolation from getting to the earth and keep temperatures low. In addition, human impact may affect temperatures by agriculture, forestry and urban lifestyle (see pages 429–30). Deforestation releases carbon which allows insolation in, but does not allow outgoing longwave radiation out, and therefore may lead to an increase in temperatures. Aerosols destroy ozone which prevents harmful ultraviolet light from getting to the earth's surface (both factors ars discussed in Chapter 15).

The climatic effect of the Pinatubo eruption

The volcanic plume from the 1991 eruption of Mount Pinatubo in the Philippines reached an altitude of more than 30 km (Figure 12.14). In addition to particulate matter, the eruption also injected gaseous sulphur dioxide (SO_2) into the stratosphere. The total load ejected into the atmosphere was estimated to be 30×10^{12} G (30 Tg), the largest aerosol disturbance to the stratosphere in the twentieth century. Nevertheless, it is still smaller than the eruption of Tambora in 1815 (over 100 Tg) and Krakatoa in 1883 (some 50 Tg). However, Pinatubo is the most intensively observed eruption on record.

The material erupted from volcanoes may remain in the atmosphere for many years. The injected material may include ash which typically does not remain for more than a few months, and gaseous components including water vapour, sulphur dioxide and hydrochloric acid. Most hydrochloric acid is dissolved into condensing water vapour and rains out of the original cloud. Aerosols are produced when the sulphur dioxide (SO_2) is chemically transformed into sulphuric acid (H_2SO_4) which rapidly condenses into aerosols. The new aerosol increases the earth's albedo by reflecting solar radiation back into space and so can warm the stratosphere by absorbing upwelling infrared radiation. Substantial heating in the stratosphere was observed immediately after the eruption of Pinatubo. Fallout and atmospheric circulation eventually transports the aerosol into the troposphere where it may modify cloud properties, especially cirrus clouds and may further modify the earth's energy budget. This effect, coupled with increasing stratospheric chlorine levels (as a result of human activity), leads to ozone destruction by modifying the chemistry of reactive chlorine and nitrogen (see also Chapter 15 on ozone depletion).

Figure 12.14 Volcanic plume from the Pinatubo eruption, 1991

Questions

1 Make copies of the grid provided (Figure 12.16). Using the data in Figure 12.15 show the variations in day-time and night-time temperatures between the four stations.

2 Using a map of Europe locate each of the stations. How do they vary in terms of continentality?
Work out (a) the average annual rainfall for each station; (b) the average annual temperature for each station; and (c) the number of days in which it rains.

3 Define the term 'diurnal range of temperature'. How does the diurnal range vary over the course of a year in Moscow? How can this be explained?

4 Describe how (a) day-time and (b) night-time temperature varies annually between the four stations.

5 Using an atlas, account for the annual variations in day-time and night-time temperature for each station in terms of (a) proximity to the sea; (b) altitude; (c) latitude; (d) ocean currents; (e) cloud cover.

6 How does rainfall vary between the four stations in terms of (a) total and (b) seasonality. Give examples to support your answer.

Figure 12.15 Selected data for European sites

Shannon

	Jan	Feb	Mar	Apr	May	Jun	Jul	Aug	Sep	Oct	Nov	Dec
Daily max°C	8	9	11	13	16	19	19	20	17	14	11	9
Daily min°C	2	2	4	5	7	10	12	12	10	7	5	3
Monthly ppt	94	67	56	53	61	57	77	79	86	86	96	117
No. of rain days	15	11	11	11	11	11	14	14	14	14	15	18

London

	Jan	Feb	Mar	Apr	May	Jun	Jul	Aug	Sep	Oct	Nov	Dec
Daily max°C	6	7	10	13	17	20	22	21	19	14	10	7
Daily min°C	2	2	3	5	8	11	13	13	11	8	5	3
Monthly ppt	52	47	40	48	48	44	56	54	50	52	56	53
No. of rain days	11	9	8	8	8	8	9	9	9	9	10	9

Berlin

	Jan	Feb	Mar	Apr	May	Jun	Jul	Aug	Sep	Oct	Nov	Dec
Daily max°C	2	3	8	13	19	22	24	23	19	13	7	3
Daily min°C	−3	−3	0	4	8	12	14	13	10	6	2	−1
Monthly ppt	43	40	31	41	46	62	70	68	46	47	46	41
No. of rain days	11	9	8	9	9	9	11	9	8	9	10	9

Moscow

	Jan	Feb	Mar	Apr	May	Jun	Jul	Aug	Sep	Oct	Nov	Dec
Daily max°C	−7	−6	0	9	17	22	24	22	16	8	0	−5
Daily min°C	−14	−13	−8	0	6	11	13	12	7	1	−4	−10
Monthly ppt	31	28	35	35	52	67	74	74	58	51	36	36
No. of rain days	8	7	8	7	8	9	11	11	10	9	9	8

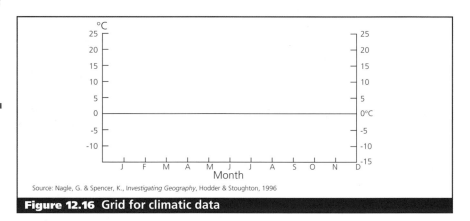

Source: Nagle, G. & Spencer, K., *Investigating Geography*, Hodder & Stoughton, 1996

Figure 12.16 Grid for climatic data

Moisture in the atmosphere

Chapter 8 examined the processes of evaporation and condensation in depth. Evaporation is the process by which a liquid is transformed into a gas. The main points to recall are that evaporation depends on three major factors:

■ the supply of heat – the hotter the air the more evaporation that takes place

■ wind strength – in windy conditions saturated air is removed, whereas under calm conditions the air becomes saturated rapidly but is not removed

■ the initial humidity of the air – if air is dry then strong evaporation occurs, whereas if it is saturated then little occurs.

Most condensation occurs when the temperature drops so that dew point (the temperature at which air is saturated) is reached. Alternatively, it can occur when water vapour is evaporated into an air mass for it to become saturated. The decrease in temperature occurs in three main ways:

■ radiation cooling of the air

■ cooling by contact when the air rests over a cold surface

■ adiabatic (expansive) cooling when air rises.

For condensation to occur there must be a tiny particle or nucleus on to which the vapour can condense. In the lower atmosphere these particles are quite common and include sulphur dioxide, nitrous oxides, dust and pollution particles. Some of these particles are hygroscopic (i.e. they attract water), hence condensation may occur when the relative humidity is as low as 80 per cent.

Precipitation

For precipitation to occur, three factors must be satisfied:

- **air is saturated (i.e. it has a relative humidity of 100 per cent)**
- **particles of soot, dust, ash, ice etc. are present in the air**
- **air temperature is below dew point (i.e. the temperature at which the relative humidity is 100 per cent, saturation is complete and clouds form).**

There are two main ways in which air is cooled. It can be chilled by contact with a cold surface such as warm air blowing over a cold current or land mass. This normally gives rise to mist and fog. Secondly air may be forced to rise. There are three main types of uplift: cyclonic (depressional or frontal), orographic and convectional (Figure 12.17).

- **Cyclonic** Convergence and uplift of air within a low-pressure area (warm air rises over cold air): it normally brings low to moderate intensity rain which may last for a few days.
- **Orographic** A deep layer of moist air is forced to rise over a range of hills or mountains (Figure 12.18): the intensity of precipitation varies with the depth of the air mass (deep air gives heavy rain, shallow air gives light rain).
- **Convectional** Instability is due to surface heating which causes the ascent of pockets of air that cool adiabatically (internally) to below the dew point of that air (see above).

Temporal variations in precipitation

Three main time periods can be identified:

- **secular (long-term climatic change)**
- **periodic (to do with astronomical cycles, diurnal or seasonal variations)**
- **stochastic (to do with the random nature of precipitation).**

Secular changes may be cyclic or non-cyclic. They are difficult to categorise because the timescale is too large. Ice ages and the greenhouse effect come into this category. Periodic changes are easily observed. These include time intervals of one year or less (i.e. seasonal, monthly, daily, hourly). By contrast, stochastic or random variations obscure any cyclical periodicity.

Rainfall variability and intensity

The reliability of rainfall increases with the time interval (i.e. more reliable annually than for individual months or seasons),

and with the amount of precipitation (i.e. higher annual totals are more reliable than low ones). There are close links between rainfall intensity, precipitation and flooding (Figure 12.19). High-intensity events are rare, but they do the most damage.

World precipitation

Isohyets are lines on a map joining places of equal precipitation. The pattern of world precipitation is a much more complex pattern than that of annual temperatures. Only a broad world pattern exists (Figure 12.20). In addition, there are important variations in evaporation and in precipitation minus evaporation (i.e. effective precipitation) (Figure 12.21).

Equatorial areas have most precipitation. This is due to high temperatures and therefore a large moisture-holding capacity. The oceans are the source of water. Most precipitation is convectional. Annual precipitation also has a marked seasonal contrast such as monsoonal areas in South East Asia. By contrast, in polar areas there is a small absolute precipitation, partly caused by the low temperature and therefore the low holding capacity of the air.

In the mid latitudes the pattern is complicated. Controls include the general circulation of the atmosphere. High precipitation occurs in the path of the mid-latitude westerlies and cyclone tracks where low pressure prevails, while the lowest precipitation is found where there is subsiding (sinking) air. Such air is warmed adiabatically and made dry especially in the subtropics and eastern side of oceans such as the Sahara.

Mountain ranges affect rainfall. The Rockies and the Andes have high rainfall on windward sides and rain shadows on the leeward side. Altitude is important especially on a local scale. In general, there is an increase of precipitation up to about 2 km. Above this the precipitation decreases because air temperature is low.

Fog

Fog is caused by clouds occurring at ground level. In fog, visibility is less than 1 km, whereas in mist it is above 1 km. Fog is common in many areas, for example the North Sea coast of Britain in summer, the Grand Banks of Newfoundland and coastal Peru. Fog is basically a suspension of small water droplets in the lower atmosphere. It occurs when moist air cools below its dew point and condenses or when more moisture is added to the air. The most common types are radiation fog and advection fog (Figure 12.22).

The cooling of air is quite common (orographic, frontal and convectional uplift). By contrast, the addition of moisture to the atmosphere is relatively rare. However, it does occur over relatively warm surfaces such as the Great Lakes in North America or over the Arctic Ocean. Water evaporates from the warm surface and condenses into the cold air above to form fog. Calm high-pressure conditions are required to avoid the saturated air being mixed with drier air above. In addition, contact cooling at a cold ground surface may produce saturation. As warm, moist air passes over a cold surface it is

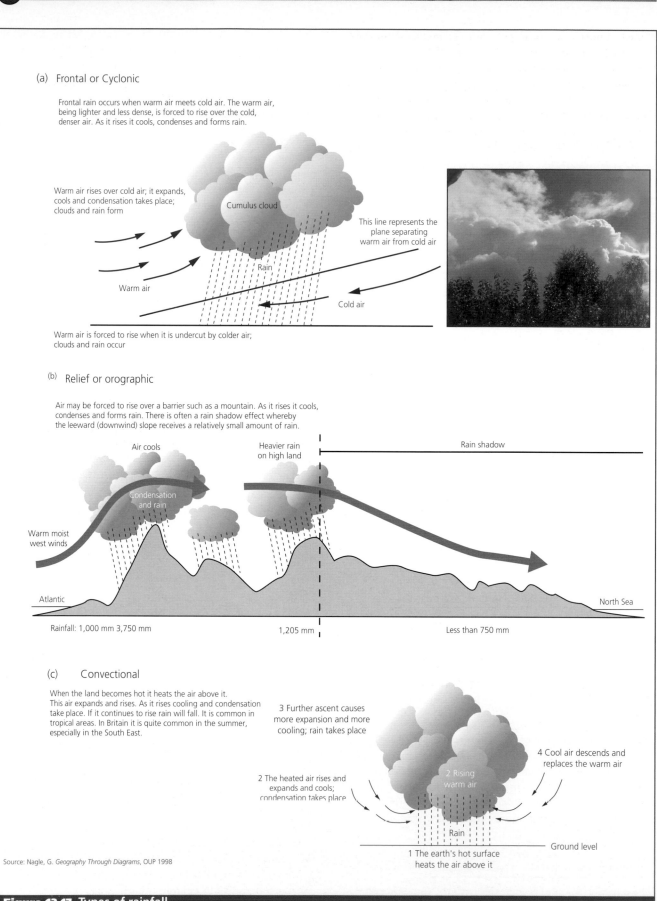

(a) Frontal or Cyclonic

Frontal rain occurs when warm air meets cold air. The warm air, being lighter and less dense, is forced to rise over the cold, denser air. As it rises it cools, condenses and forms rain.

Warm air rises over cold air; it expands, cools and condensation takes place; clouds and rain form

Cumulus cloud

This line represents the plane separating warm air from cold air

Rain

Warm air

Cold air

Warm air is forced to rise when it is undercut by colder air; clouds and rain occur

(b) Relief or orographic

Air may be forced to rise over a barrier such as a mountain. As it rises it cools, condenses and forms rain. There is often a rain shadow effect whereby the leeward (downwind) slope receives a relatively small amount of rain.

Air cools

Heavier rain on high land

Rain shadow

Condensation and rain

Warm moist west winds

Atlantic

North Sea

Rainfall: 1,000 mm 3,750 mm

1,205 mm

Less than 750 mm

(c) Convectional

When the land becomes hot it heats the air above it. This air expands and rises. As it rises cooling and condensation take place. If it continues to rise rain will fall. It is common in tropical areas. In Britain it is quite common in the summer, especially in the South East.

3 Further ascent causes more expansion and more cooling; rain takes place

4 Cool air descends and replaces the warm air

2 The heated air rises and expands and cools; condensation takes place

2 Rising warm air

Rain

Ground level

1 The earth's hot surface heats the air above it

Source: Nagle, G. *Geography Through Diagrams*, OUP 1998

Figure 12.17 Types of rainfall

chilled, condensation takes place as the temperature of the air is reduced and the air reaches dew point. When warm air flows over a cold surface **advection fog** is formed; for example, air from the North Atlantic Drift blowing over cold surfaces in Devon and Cornwall will often form a fog. Similarly, near the Grand Banks off Newfoundland warm air from the Gulf Stream passes over the waters of the Labrador Current. This is between 8 and 11°C cooler, since it brings with it meltwater from the disintegrating pack ice further north. Dense fog is

Figure 12.18 Orographic uplift rainfall over the west coast of Ireland

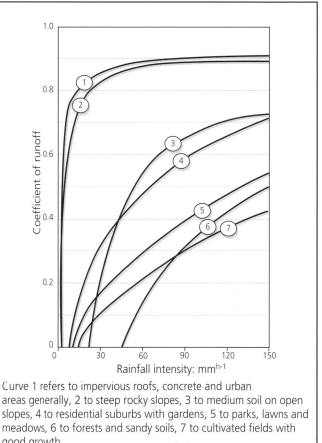

Curve 1 refers to impervious roofs, concrete and urban areas generally, 2 to steep rocky slopes, 3 to medium soil on open slopes, 4 to residential suburbs with gardens, 5 to parks, lawns and meadows, 6 to forests and sandy soils, 7 to cultivated fields with good growth. Source: Linacre, E and Geerts, B., *Climates and weather explained*, Routledge, 1997

Figure 12.19 Effect of rainfall intensity and kind of surface on the runoff coefficient

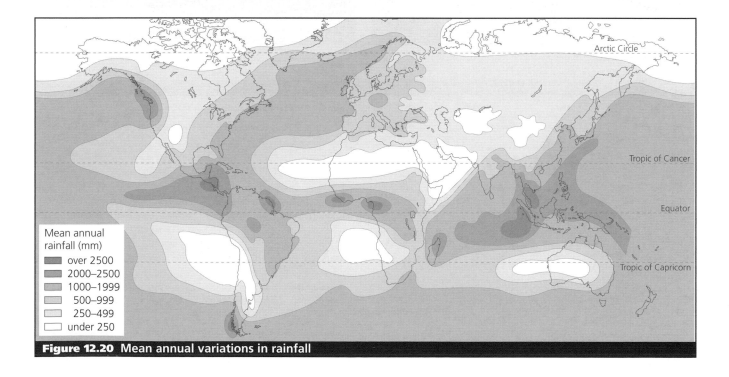

Mean annual rainfall (mm)

- over 2500
- 2000–2500
- 1000–1999
- 500–999
- 250–499
- under 250

Figure 12.20 Mean annual variations in rainfall

formed on 70 to 100 days per year. This type of fog also occurs on an average 40 days a year around the Golden Gate Bridge, at the mouth of San Francisco Bay, because warm air blows onshore over the cold offshore currents. With fairly light winds, the fog forms close to the water surface, but with stronger turbulence the condensed layer may be uplifted to form a low stratus sheet.

Radiation fog occurs when the ground loses heat at night by longwave radiation. This occurs during high-

pressure conditions associated with clear skies (Figure 12.22).

Fog is a major environmental hazard – airports may be closed for many days and road driving conditions are difficult and slow. Freezing fog is particularly problematic. Large economic losses result from fog but the ability to do anything about it is limited. This is because it would require too much energy (and hence cost) to warm up the air or to dry out the air to prevent condensation.

Source: Linacre, E and Geerts, B., *Climates and Weather Explained*, Routledge, 1997

Figure 12.21 Variation with latitude of the annual-mean, zonal-average precipitation (P), evaporation (E), the difference between the two (P – E), and the ocean's surface salinity

Figure 12.22 Radiation fog in the Usk Valley, South Wales

Figure 12.23 Characteristics of fog in the British Isles

Type of fog	Season	Areas affected	Mode of formation	Mode of dispersal
radiation fog	October to March	inland areas, especially low-lying, moist ground	cooling due to radiation from the ground on clear nights when the wind is light	dispersed by the sun's radiation or by increased wind
advection fog (a) over land	winter or spring	often widespread inland	cooling of warm air by passage over cold ground	dispersed by a change in air mass or by gradual warming of the ground
(b) over sea and coastline	spring and early summer	sea and coasts, may penetrate a few miles	cooling of warm air by passage over cold sea	dispersed by a change in air mass and may be cleared on coast by the sun's heating
frontal fog	all seasons	high ground	lowering of the cloud base along the line of the front	dispersed as the front moves and brings a change of air mass
smoke fog (smog)	winter	near industrial areas and large conurbations	similar to radiation fog	dispersed by wind increase or by convection

Formation of raindrops

Clouds are tiny droplets of water suspended in air, whereas raindrops are comparatively much larger. Therefore, to fall as rain, cloud droplets must get much larger, although not necessarily by normal condensation processes. There are a number of theories to suggest how raindrops are formed.

Bergeron–Findeisen theory

According to the Bergeron–Findeisen theory the formation of rain requires water and ice to exist in clouds at temperatures below 0°C. Cloud temperatures are often as low as –40°C, and they contain supercooled water droplets. This is due to the absence of freezing nuclei required to form ice crystals. In a cloud where water droplets and ice droplets co-exist, air is oversaturated with water in respect to ice. Condensation occurs on ice to decrease vapour pressure, though at the same time condensation occurs from water droplets to restore vapour pressure. Ice crystals therefore grow at the expense of water droplets. As they become large enough to overcome atmospheric turbulence, they fall. As they fall, crystals will grow to form larger snow flakes, although as they pass into the warm air layers near the ground they melt and become rain. Thus, rain comes from clouds which exist well below freezing level, where co-existence of water and ice is possible.

However, other mechanisms must also exist because rain comes from clouds where there is not any great vertical development. These mechanisms include:

- condensation on extra large hygroscopic nuclei
- coalescence by sweeping, whereby a falling droplet sweeps up others in its path
- the growth of droplets by electrical attraction.

Coalescence theory

The most important of other theories is probably the coalescence theory. When minute droplets of water are condensed from water vapour, they float in the atmosphere as clouds. If droplets coalesce they form large droplets which, when heavy enough to overcome an ascending current by gravity, fall as rain.

Types of precipitation

The Bergeron theory relates mostly to the formation of ice. Rain and drizzle are found when the temperature exceeds 0°C (drizzle has a diameter of <0.5 mm). Sleet is partly melted snow and hail is alternate concentric rings of clear and opaque ice, formed by being carried up and down in vertical air currents in large cumulonimbus clouds. Freezing and partial melting may occur several times before the pellet is large enough to escape from the cloud.

Lapse rates

The heating and cooling of air causes changes in its relative humidity and buoyancy, which may lead to condensation and evaporation which, in turn, can cause cloud formation.

Air is heated from below. When the ground is heated, air that is in contact with it will be heated. As the temperature of the air rises it expands. As the air expands its density falls. Consequently, the volume of the air is much larger. As air density falls it becomes lighter than the surrounding air and begins to rise. By contrast when air is cooled it contracts, its density increases and the air sinks. This heating and cooling therefore causes vertical movements within a body of air. In addition, as air becomes cooler its ability to hold moisture is reduced. For example, if air is cooled to the point where it can no longer hold any more moisture in the form of vapour, condensation takes place and water droplets form. If the air is heated the droplets evaporate and become vapour again. Hence the heating and cooling of air are linked with the processes of evaporation, condensation and the formation of precipitation.

The rising of warm air is a common process. Local heating occurs for a variety of reasons. These include variations in the colour and moisture content of a surface. Air above dark-coloured or dry surfaces heats up more rapidly than above light-coloured or wet surfaces.

The **environmental lapse rate** (ELR) is the vertical change in air temperature away from the ground. Normally temperature falls with height. This is because incoming solar radiation heats the ground through absorption. Some of this energy is transmitted downwards into the soil but most of it is returned as longwave radiation into the atmosphere. Hence, heating is greatest closest to the ground surface and declines with altitude. The average rate at which temperature drops with altitude is 6.4°C per 1000 m.

Consider the heating of air above an island. The island converts sunlight to heat much more effectively than the surrounding water (due to the specific heat capacity). Above the island the air will be warmed, density decreases, pressure falls and the air will rise. If air is warmer than the surrounding ELR it will continue to rise, if it is cooler it will sink. As air moves away from the ground surface air pressure decreases. As the parcel of air rises it encounters surrounding air of lower density. The pressure confining the parcel of air is reduced and the parcel of air therefore expands. As the air expands, heat is released from it and it becomes cooler. The rate at which air cools with height as a result of this expansion is about 9.8°C per 1000 m. This is known as the **dry adiabatic lapse rate** (DALR). Adiabatic means there is no heat exchange between the parcel of air and the surrounding air, the air is referred to as dry because it is unsaturated hence condensation does not take place. Thus, air rises at the DALR as long as no condensation takes place. By contrast, surrounding air will cool at the ELR. The parcel of air therefore rises until its temperature and its density are equal to that of the ELR. Once the air becomes colder and denser than the ELR it will sink. This is known as **stability.**

In most cases, however, air contains moisture. Even relatively cold air contains some moisture. If the air is cooled enough, to its dew-point temperature, condensation will take place. Once this happens the rate of cooling is reduced. In general, as air temperature rises so too does its ability to hold moisture. Consequently, warm air can hold much more moisture than cold air. The amount of moisture that is held in the air is expressed in a number of ways. **Absolute humidity** refers to the amount of moisture in grams per cubic metre (g/m³) that is held in the air; by contrast **relative humidity** expresses this amount as a percentage of the maximum that air of a given temperature can hold. However, it is misleading to compare relative humidity of air of different temperatures. For example, air of 30°C with a relative humidity of 50 per cent may contain about 16 g of moisture. By contrast air of 4°C, with a relative humidity of 50 per cent, may contain only 2 g of moisture. Thus, relative humidity is temperature dependent. An alternative way, and a better way, is to look at the **saturation vapour pressure curve** (Figure 12.24). As a rising parcel of air cools it approaches the temperature at which condensation takes place. When the parcel reaches that temperature it becomes saturated and condensation occurs.

As water changes from a vapour to a liquid it releases latent heat. This release of latent heat counteracts the cooling process by warming the air. Thus, air in which condensation has taken place (saturated air) cools more slowly than the DALR. This rate is known as the **saturated adiabatic lapse rate** (SALR) and its rate depends on the amount of heat released by condensation. This depends on the temperature of the air and the amount of moisture it contains. Hence, warm air which holds a lot of moisture releases a lot of latent heat. This may cool at a rate of 5°C per 1000 m. By contrast cold air, which contains limited amounts of moisture, will cool at a rate closer to the DALR because less latent heat is released during condensation.

If the ELR is greater than the DALR there is **absolute instability** (i.e. as parcels of air rise they cool at their maximum rate). They remain warmer than the surrounding air and, therefore, being less dense will continue to rise (Figure 12.25 section c). By contrast, if the ELR is less than the SALR **absolute stability** exists. The rising pocket of air remains colder and denser than the ELR and therefore sinks (Figure 12.25 section a). If, on the other hand, the ELR is between the DALR and the SALR there is **conditional instability** (i.e. instability depends on the air reaching its saturation point)

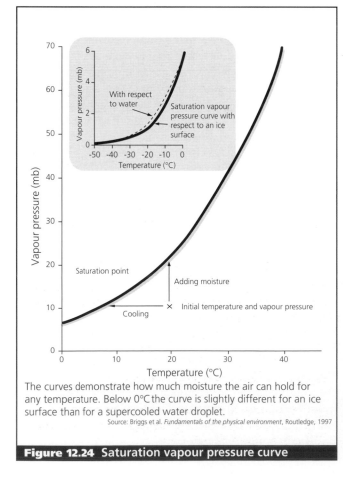

The curves demonstrate how much moisture the air can hold for any temperature. Below 0°C the curve is slightly different for an ice surface than for a supercooled water droplet.

Source: Briggs et al. *Fundamentals of the physical environment*, Routledge, 1997

Figure 12.24 Saturation vapour pressure curve

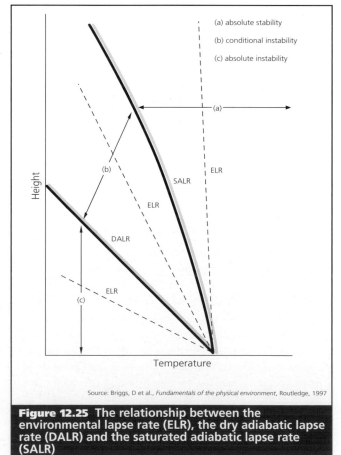

Source: Briggs, D et al., *Fundamentals of the physical environment*, Routledge, 1997

Figure 12.25 The relationship between the environmental lapse rate (ELR), the dry adiabatic lapse rate (DALR) and the saturated adiabatic lapse rate (SALR)

(Figure 12.25 section b). Stability and instability are important concepts in terms of cloud formation and rising air. Unstable air rises and produces clouds. In stable air uplift and cloud formation are limited, hence precipitation is reduced.

In most cases the ELR lies somewhere between the DALR and the SALR. In this case (i.e. conditional instability), the atmosphere is stable for air which has not reached saturation point (i.e. dry air), but is unstable for saturated air. If the air can be forced to reach condensation level, for example by being forced over mountains or by being forced to rise at a front, it becomes unstable and uplift of air is common.

Questions

1 Define the terms: adiabatic; environmental lapse rate; stability; instability; saturated adiabatic lapse rate and dry adiabatic lapse rate.
2 Using some of the terms defined above, briefly explain why air on the leeward (downwind) side of a mountain may be warmer and drier than air on the windward (upwind) side of a mountain.

Statistics

There are many types of statistics, some of them extremely easy and some complex. At the most basic there are simple **descriptive** statistics. These include the **mean** or **average**, the **maximum, minimum, range** (maximum minus minimum), the **mode** (the most frequently occurring number, group or class) and the **median** (the middle value when all the numbers are placed in ascending or descending rank order). In any project or inquiry it is important to use these statistics as they provide invaluable summaries of the data, and are often the only statistics that are appropriate.

Summarising data

There are many types of average. One of the most commonly used statistics is the **arithmetic mean**. This is found by totalling the values for all observations (Σx) and then dividing by the total number of observations (n)

$$\frac{\Sigma x}{n}$$

For example, the number of wet days (over 0.2 mm of rain) per month over the course of a year was 22, 18, 19, 21, 18, 7, 9, 14, 14, 16, 15, 19

The mean is

$$\frac{22 + 18 + 19 + 21 + 18 + 7 + 9 + 14 + 14 + 16 + 15 + 19}{12}$$

$$= \frac{192}{12} = 16$$

The **mode** is another type of average. It refers to the group or class which occurs most often. In the above case 14, 18 and 19 occur twice – these are the **modal groups**. A pattern which has two peaks is called **bimodal**. (One clear peak is known as **unimodal**.)

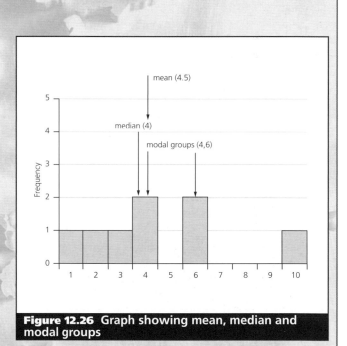

Figure 12.26 Graph showing mean, median and modal groups

Another method is to use the **median**. This is the middle value when all the data are placed in ascending or descending order. Thus,

22, 21, 19, 19, 18, 18, 16, 15, 14, 14, 9, 7

In this case, because there are two middle values we take the average of these two. So the 6th and 7th values are 18 and 16. Hence the median is

$$\frac{18 + 16}{2} = 17$$

Summarising groups of data

In some cases data is collected in the form of a group (e.g. daily rainfall, slope angles or ages may be recorded as 0–4, 5–9, 10–14, 15–19 etc.).

The data below show daily rainfall in an area of rainforest. To make recording simpler groups of 5 mm have been used. Finding an average is slightly more difficult. The mid-point of the group is used and multiplied by the frequency.

Figure 12.27 Daily rainfall for an area of typical rainforest

Daily rainfall (mm)	Mid-point	Frequency	Mid-point × frequency
0–4	2	20	40
5–9	7	42	294
10–14	12	24	288
15–19	17	12	204
20–24	22	2	44
Total		$n = 100$	$\Sigma x = 870$

Mean = $\Sigma x/n$ = 870/100   = 8.7

The **modal group** is the one which occurs with the most frequency (i.e. 5–9 mm). The **median** or middle value will be the average of the 50th and 51st values when ranked: these are both in the 5–9 mm group.

Measures of dispersion

Ways of summarising the data by showing some sort of 'average' are called **measures of central tendency**. They give one figure to describe a complete data set. Sometimes, however, it is just as useful to show how far figures differ from the average as it is to show how close they are to the average. This is known as **dispersion**, and there are a number of ways of showing this.

The simplest is to use the **range** – the difference between the **maximum** (largest) and the **minimum** (smallest) values. This has its limits and is not good for data where there is considerable variation between the

records, as in the case of rainfall figures, for example. An alternative measure is the **inter-quartile range**. This is similar to the range but gives only the range of the middle half of the results – by this, the extremes are omitted, the importance of which is clearly illustrated in Figure 12.29.

Figure 12.28 Rainfall figures for Oxford (mm) 1976–97

Year	Rainfall (mm)	Year	Rainfall (mm)
1976	509	1987	593
1977	710	1988	571
1978	577	1989	598
1979	752	1990	473
1980	634	1991	528
1981	683	1992	597
1982	654	1993	731
1983	578	1994	702
1984	608	1995	609
1985	662	1996	471
1986	704	1997	591

Listing these figures in order we get:

471, 473, 509, 528, 571, 577, 578, 591, 593, 597, 598, 608, 609, 634, 654, 662, 683, 702, 704, 710, 731, 752

The **maximum** is 752 mm, the **minimum** is 471 mm and the **range** is thus from 752 to 471 mm (i.e. 752 – 471 = 281 mm).

The **inter–quartile range** is found by removing the top and bottom **quartiles** (quarters) and stating the range that remains. The top quartile is is found by taking the 25 per cent highest values and finding the mid-point between the lowest of these and the next lowest point. The lower quartile is found by taking the 25 per cent

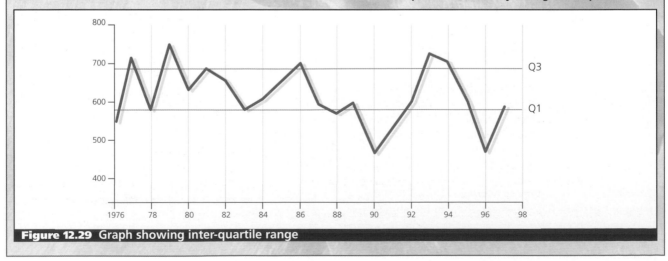

Figure 12.29 Graph showing inter-quartile range

lowest values and finding the mid-point between the highest of these and the next highest value. The first quartile is termed *Q1*, and the third quartile *Q3*.

In the example above there are 22 values. The method for working out the inter-quartile range when the number of values is not directly divisible by 4 is more complex, so, in the first instance it is better to focus on the data for the last 20 years which are, in ascending order:

471, 473, 528, 571, 577, 578, 591, 593, 597, 598, 608, 609, 634, 654, 662, 683, 702, 704, 731, 752

In this case to find *Q3* first find the mid-point between 683 and 662, (i.e. 672.5). *Q1* is the mid-point of 578 and 577, (i.e. 577.5). The inter-quartile range is *Q3 – Q1*. Thus the inter-quartile range is 672.5 – 577.5 = 95.

Not every case is as easy! In situations where the number of observations is not divisible by 4 the boundaries of the quartile require an informed guess.

In the case of 21 observations (i.e. with rainfall for 1977 (710 mm) added) the principle is the same as before. Find the values which represent 25 per cent and 75 per cent of the values. Then, find half the difference between the bottom of the top 25 per cent and the next value below. Then find half the difference between the top of the lowest 25 per cent and the next value above.

The 25 per cent value is found one-quarter way between 577 and 578 (i.e. 5¼ values along the scale as there are now 21 values), while the 75 per cent value (16¾) lies three-quarters of the way between 683 and 702 (i.e. 16¾ values along the scale). Thus the first quartile is found by adding one-quarter of the difference of 578 and 577 to 577.

$$577 + \frac{(578-577)}{4} = 577.25$$

Q1 is halfway between 577.25 and 578 (i.e. 577.625).

The 75 per cent value is found by adding three-quarters of the difference of 702 and 683 to 683.

$$683 + 3\frac{(702-683)}{4} = 697.25$$

Q3 is found halfway between the 75 per cent value and the value immediately below (i.e. midway between 697.25 and 683) at 690.125.

Thus, the inter-quartile range is 690.125 – 577.625 = 112.5.

In the original case there are 22 observations.

The 25 per cent and 75 per cent values now are found at 5½ and 16½ (as each quartile is 5½ values in size, i.e. 2⅔). Thus the 25 per cent is found halfway between the 5th and 6th figures, 577 and 578 (i.e. 577.5) and the 75 per cent is found halfway between the 16th and 17th values, 683 and 702 (i.e. 692.5). Hence *Q1* is found halfway between the 25 per cent value and the next value above, or midway between 577.5 and 578, namely 577.75. *Q3* is found halfway between the 75 per cent value and the next value below, or the mid-point between 692.5 and 683 namely 687.75.

Thus the inter-quartile range in this case is 687.75 – 577.75 = 110.

Standard deviation

Another way of showing grouping around a central value is by using the standard deviation. This is one of the most important descriptive statistics because:

■ it takes into account all the values in a distribution

■ it is necessary for calculating probability and for more complex inferential, explanatory statistics. It measures dispersal of figures around the mean, and is calculated by first measuring the mean and then comparing the difference of each value from the mean.

It is based on concept of probability. If a number of observations is made then we would expect most to be quite close to the average, few much larger or smaller, and equal proportions that are above and below the mean. If we were to plot such a distribution on a graph (either in the form of a histogram or a continuous line graph) it would look something like Figure 12.30.

This graph shows quite clearly all of the above points. The **standard deviation** is found by measuring the dispersion or variation around the mean. The formula is:

$$\text{standard deviation } (\sigma \text{ or } s) = \sqrt{\frac{\Sigma(x_1-x_2)^2}{n}}$$

where x_1 refers to each observation, x_2 to the mean, n the number of points, and $(x_1-x_2)^2$ tells us to take the mean from each observation, and then to square the result. The following example shows the working out.

Rainfall figures for Oxford, 1976–97

509, 710, 577, 752, 634, 683, 654, 578, 608, 662, 704, 593, 571, 598, 473, 528, 597, 731, 702, 609, 471, 591

First calculate the mean $\frac{(\Sigma x)}{n} = \frac{13\,535}{22} = 615.2$

Then construct a table as follows (although laborious it is the way to make sure that you get it right).

x_1	x_2	$(x_1 - x_2)$	$(x_1 - x_2)^2$
509	615.2	−106.2	11 278.44
710	615.2	94.8	8987.04
577	615.2	−38.2	1459.24
752	615.2	136.8	1 8714.24
634	615.2	18.8	353.44
683	615.2	67.8	4596.84
654	615.2	38.8	1505.44
578	615.2	−37.2	1383.84
608	615.2	−7.2	51.84
662	615.2	46.8	2190.24
704	615.2	88.8	7885.44
593	615.2	−22.2	492.84
571	615.2	−44.2	1953.64
598	615.2	−17.2	295.84
473	615.2	−142.2	20 220.84
528	615.2	−87.2	7603.84
597	615.2	−18.2	331.24
731	615.2	115.8	13 409.64
702	615.2	86.8	7534.24
609	615.2	−6.2	38.44
471	615.2	−144.2	20 793.64
591	615.2	−24.2	585.64
$\Sigma = 13\,535$			$\Sigma = 131\,665.88$
$\Sigma x/n = 615.2$			

Thus, the standard deviation is found by putting the figures into the formula:

$$\sigma\,(s) = \sqrt{\frac{131\,665.88}{22}} = \sqrt{5984.81} = 77.36$$

Thus the average deviation of all values around the mean (615.2 mm) is 77.36 mm. This gives a much more accurate figure than the range or the inter-quartile range, as it takes into account all values and is not as

affected by extreme values. Given normal probability we would expect that approximately 68 per cent of the observations would fall within 1 standard deviation of the mean, about 95 per cent within 2 standard deviations of the mean, and about 99 per cent within 3 standard deviations.

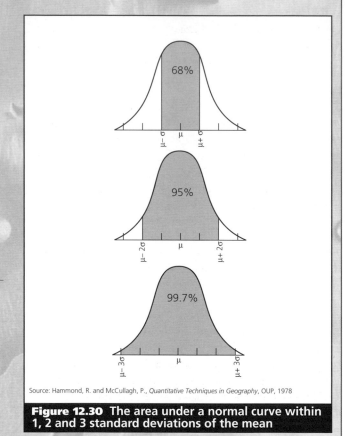

Source: Hammond, R. and McCullagh, P., *Quantitative Techniques in Geography*, OUP, 1978

Figure 12.30 The area under a normal curve within 1, 2 and 3 standard deviations of the mean

Questions

1 The following monthly rainfall measurements (in mm) were recorded at Oxford over one year.
81.2, 62.4, 41.9, 52.0, 84.5, 13.5, 54.2, 52.5, 62.6, 67.4, 55.7, 74.6
  (a) Plot the data on a graph similar to Figure 12.26. (Use groups of 0.0–9.9, 10.0–19.9, 20.0–29.9 and so on.)
  (b) Work out the mean, the mode and the median.
  (c) Which of these statistics best summarises the data for these figures? Which method is least satisfactory? Justify your choice.
2 Use the data in Figure 12.27 for daily rainfall in the rainforest.
  (a) Plot the data in the form of a bar graph.
  (b) Which measure out of the mean, modal group and

median rainfall is (i) most and (ii) least satisfactory? Explain your choice.
3 The data below are annual rainfall records from 1965 to 1984 for Niamey, Niger (part of the Sahel).
570, 705, 582, 807, 432, 630, 552, 567, 407, 379, 650, 641, 558, 748, 413, 621, 599, 296, 392, 384
(Data adapted from Agnew, C., in Binns, T., *People and environment in Africa*, Wiley, 1995)
  (a) Illustrate the data by means of (i) a line graph and (ii) a dispersion diagram.
  (b) State (i) the maximum (ii) minimum (iii) range and (iv) the inter-quartile range of the rainfall for the 20-year period.
  (c) Which of these descriptive statistics is the best in your opinion? Explain your answer.

Air motion

Vertical air motion is important on a local scale whereas horizontal motion (wind) is important at many scales from small-scale eddies to global wind systems. The basic cause of air motion is the unequal heating of the earth's surface. The major equalising factor is the transfer of heat by air movement. Variable heating of the earth causes variations in pressure and this, in turn, sets the air in motion. There is thus a basic correlation between winds and pressure.

Pressure variations

Pressure is measured in millibars (mb) and is represented on a map by isobars, lines joining places of equal pressure. On maps pressure is adjusted to mean sea level (MSL), therefore eliminating elevation as a factor. Global MSL pressure is 1013 mb, although the mean range is from 1060 mb in the Siberian winter high-pressure system to 940 mb (although some intense low-pressure storms may be much lower). The trend of pressure change is of more importance than the actual reading itself. Decline in pressure indicates poorer weather and rising pressure indicates better weather.

Surface pressure belts

Sea level pressure conditions show marked differences between the hemispheres. In the northern hemisphere there are greater seasonal contrasts whereas in the southern hemisphere much simpler average conditions exist (Figure 12.31). The differences are largely related to unequal distribution of land and sea, because ocean areas are much more equable in terms of temperature and pressure variations.

One of the most permanent features is the subtropical high pressure belts (STHP), especially over oceanic areas. In the southern hemisphere these are almost continuous at about 30° latitude, although in summer over South Africa and Australia they are somewhat broken. Generally, pressure is about 1026 mb. In the northern hemisphere, by contrast, at 30° the belt is much more discontinuous because of the land. High pressure occurs only over the ocean as discrete cells such as the Azores and Pacific highs. Over continental areas such as south west United States, southern Asia and the Sahara, major fluctuations occur: highs in winter and summer lows because of overheating.

Over the equatorial trough pressure is low, 1008 to 1010 mb. The trough coincides with the zone of maximum insolation. In the northern hemisphere (July) it is well north of the equator (25°C over India), whereas in the southern hemisphere (January) it is just south of the equator because land masses are not of sufficient size to displace it further southwards. The Doldrums refers to the equatorial trough over sea areas; slack pressure gradients have a becalming effect on sailing ships.

In temperate latitudes pressure is generally less than in subtropical areas. The most unique feature is the large number of depressions (low pressure) and anticyclones (high pressure) which do not show up on a map of mean pressure. In the northern hemisphere there are strong winter low-pressure zones over Icelandic and oceanic areas, but over Canada and Siberia there is high pressure, due to the coldness of the land. In summer, high pressure is reduced.

In polar areas pressure is relatively high throughout the year, especially over Antarctica, owing to the coldness of the land mass.

Factors affecting air movement

The driving force is the **pressure gradient**, the difference in pressure between any two points. Air blows from high pressure to low pressure. Globally areas of intense high pressure exist over Asia in winter due to the low temperatures. Cold air contracts, leaving room for adjacent air to converge at high altitude, adding to the weight and pressure of the air. By contrast, the MSL pressure is low over continents in summer. High surface temperatures produce atmospheric expansion and therefore a reduction in air pressure. High pressure dominates at around 25 to 30° latitude. The highs are centred over the oceans in summer and over the continents in winter, whichever is cooler.

The **Coriolis effect** is the deflection of moving objects caused by the easterly rotation of the earth (Figure 12.32). Air flowing from high pressure to low pressure is deflected to the right of its path in the northern hemisphere and to the left of its path in the southern hemisphere. The Coriolis force is at right angles to wind direction.

The balance of forces between the pressure gradient and the Coriolis effect is known as the **geostrophic balance** and the resulting wind is known as a **geostrophic wind**. The geostrophic wind in the northern hemisphere blows anticlockwise around the centre of low pressure and clockwise around the centre of high pressure.

This **centrifugal force** is the force experienced when you drive around a corner – objects travelling round a corner are forced outwards. The centrifugal force acts at right angles to the wind, pulling objects outwards. Thus for a given pressure air flow is faster around high pressure (because the Coriolis and centrifugal forces work together rather than in opposite directions) (Figure 12.33).

The drag exerted by the earth's rough surface is also important. **Friction** decreases wind speed, therefore it decreases the Coriolis effect, hence air is more likely to flow towards low pressure.

Upper air motion

Upper air patterns have been studied extensively since the Second World War. The causes of weather at ground level are closely related to events at high altitude, especially

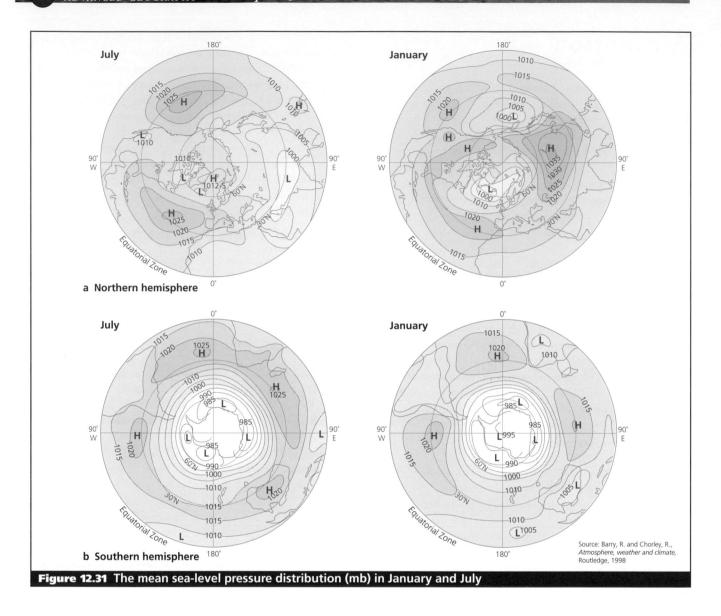

Source: Barry, R. and Chorley, R.,
Atmosphere, weather and climate,
Routledge, 1998

Figure 12.31 The mean sea-level pressure distribution (mb) in January and July

depressions and the general circulation. In general, wind speeds increase with altitude due to lower densities and less friction. This can be seen by the fact that different cloud layers may move at different speeds and in different directions.

Strong westerly winds exist over much of the tropopause. These are thermal winds found just above the polar front where temperatures contrast most. The strongest winds are known as the jet streams. Jet streams do not flow steadily eastwards but meander in a wave-like pattern, known as the Rossby wave pattern (Figure 12.37). Generally between 3 and 6 waves occur in each hemisphere and these are important in the explanation of surface depressions. The initial deflection of the upper winds could be a mountain range or differences found in coastal areas, for example the relative warmth over a peninsula causes air to rise, which may deflect the upper air around it. As the upper winds are geostrophic they flow clockwise around the high pressure (at altitude) and

anticlockwise around the low pressure (at altitude).

The polar front jet stream lies at about 30 to 50° of latitude with wind speeds of 200 km per hour in summer and up to 400 km per hour in winter. In tropical and subtropical areas easterly flowing winds produce the subtropical jet stream at about 20 to 30° of latitude.

If an air stream flowing west to east approaches a large mountain barrier, such as the Rockies, it is forced to rise over the mountain range and is squeezed between the mountain peaks and the tropopause. As the air flows beyond the mountains, it stretches out and begins to spin. In the northern hemisphere this creates anticlockwise turning. The result is a cyclonic trough (low-pressure system) in the westerlies in the lee of the mountains. This explains the anchoring of a pronounced wave trough in the westerlies over eastern North America. Once such a large wave has been initiated it generally persists for some time.

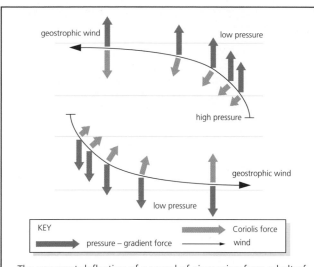

KEY

pressure – gradient force ⟶ wind

Coriolis force

The apparent deflection of a parcel of air moving from a belt of high pressure in the southern hemisphere, (e.g. from the band of subtropical high pressures). The parcel is assumed stationary initially. As soon as it starts to move, it suffers a sideways Coriolis force, increasing in proportion to its acceleration. The force deflects the parcel until it is travelling along an isobar, with a constant speed such that the Coriolis force balances the pressure–gradient force.

Source: Linacre, E and Geerts, B., *Climates and Weather Explained*, Routledge, 1997

Figure 12.32 The Coriolis effect

The general circulation

Surface wind belts

Winds between the tropics converge on a line known as the **intertropical convergence zone** (ITCZ) or equatorial trough. This convergence zone is a few hundred kilometres wide, into which winds blow and subsequently rise (thereby forming an area of low pressure). The rising air releases vast quantities of latent heat which, in turn, stimulates convection.

Latitudinal variations in the ITCZ occur as a result of the movement of the overhead sun. In June the ITCZ lies further north whereas in December it lies in the southern hemisphere. The seasonal variation in the ITCZ is greatest over Asia – owing to the large land mass present. By contrast over the Atlantic and Pacific Oceans its movement is far less. Winds at the ITCZ are generally light – the Doldrums, these are broken by occasional strong westerlies, generally in the summer months.

Low-latitude winds between 10° and 30° are mostly easterlies (i.e. they flow towards the west). These are the reliable trade winds, which blow over 30 per cent of the world's surface. The weather in this zone is fairly predictable – warm, dry mornings and showery afternoons, caused by the continuous evaporation from tropical seas. Showers are heavier and more frequent in the warmer summer season.

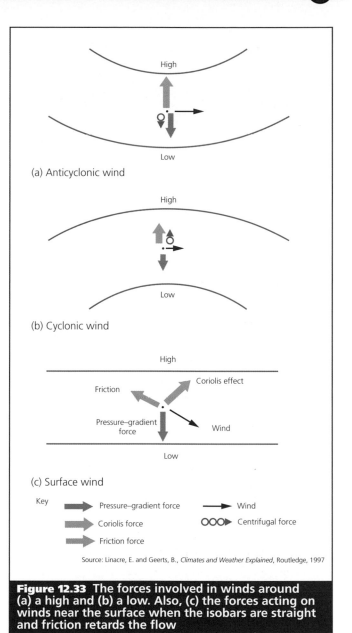

(a) Anticyclonic wind

(b) Cyclonic wind

(c) Surface wind

Key

Pressure–gradient force — Wind

Coriolis force OOO▶ Centrifugal force

Friction force

Source: Linacre, E. and Geerts, B., *Climates and Weather Explained*, Routledge, 1997

Figure 12.33 The forces involved in winds around (a) a high and (b) a low. Also, (c) the forces acting on winds near the surface when the isobars are straight and friction retards the flow

Occasionally there are disruptions to the pattern; easterly waves are small-scale systems in the easterly flow of air. The flow is greatest not at ground level but at the 700 mb level. Ahead of the easterly wave air is subsiding, hence there is surface divergence. At the easterly wave there is convergence of air, and descent – as in a typical low-pressure system. Easterly waves are important for the development of tropical cyclones (pages 420–3).

Westerly winds dominate between 35° and 60° of latitude, this accounts for about a quarter of the world's surface. However, unlike the steady trade winds these contain rapidly evolving and decaying depressions (pages 419–20).

The word 'monsoon' means reverse. The monsoon is a reversing of wind systems. For example, the south-east trades from the southern hemisphere cross the equator in July.

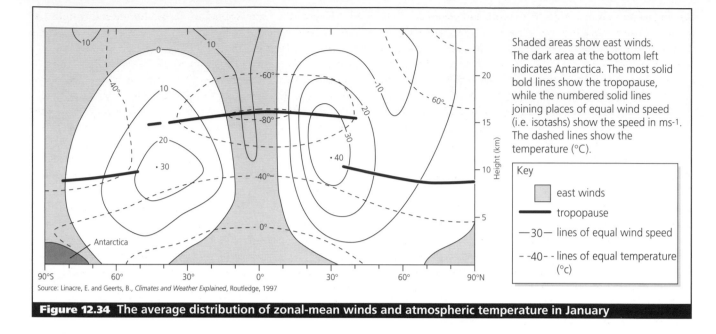

Shaded areas show east winds. The dark area at the bottom left indicates Antarctica. The most solid bold lines show the tropopause, while the numbered solid lines joining places of equal wind speed (i.e. isotashs) show the speed in ms-1. The dashed lines show the temperature (°C).

Key

▨ east winds

━━ tropopause

—30— lines of equal wind speed

- -40- - lines of equal temperature (°c)

Antarctica

Source: Linacre, E. and Geerts, B., *Climates and Weather Explained*, Routledge, 1997

Figure 12.34 The average distribution of zonal-mean winds and atmospheric temperature in January

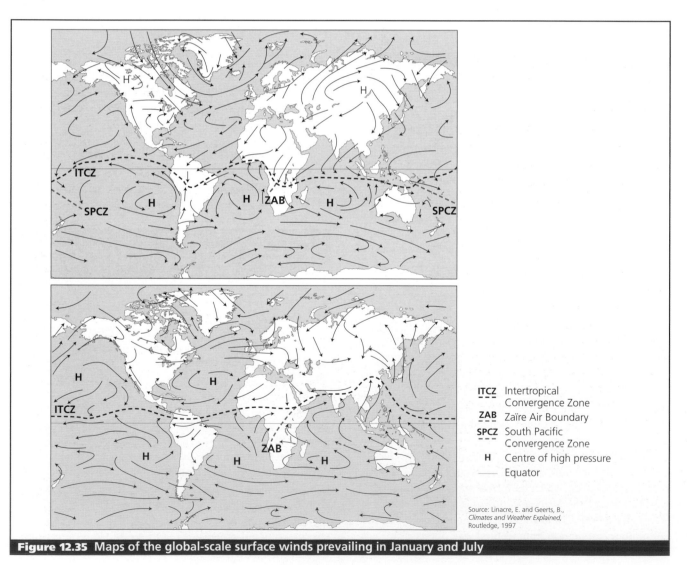

ITCZ Intertropical Convergence Zone

ZAB Zaïre Air Boundary

SPCZ South Pacific Convergence Zone

H Centre of high pressure

—— Equator

Source: Linacre, E. and Geerts, B., *Climates and Weather Explained*, Routledge, 1997

Figure 12.35 Maps of the global-scale surface winds prevailing in January and July

Owing to the Coriolis effect these south-east trades are deflected to the right into the northern hemisphere and become south-west winds. The monsoon is induced by Asia – the world's largest continent – which causes winds to blow outwards from high pressure in winter but pulls the southern trades into low pressure in the summer.

The monsoon is therefore influenced by the reversal of land and sea temperatures between Asia and the Pacific and Indian Oceans during the summer and winter. In winter surface temperatures in Asia may be as low as –20°C. The surrounding oceans have temperatures of 20°C . During the summer the land heats up quickly and may reach 40°C. The sea remains cooler at about 27°C. This initiates a land sea breeze blowing from the cooler sea (high pressure) in summer to the warmer land (low pressure), whereas in winter air flows out of the cold land mass (high pressure) to the warm water (low pressure). In addition, the presence of the Himalayan Plateau disrupts the strong winds of the upper atmosphere, which forces winds either to the north or south and results in a deflection of surface winds.

Figure 12.34 shows zonal winds by altitude and latitude. At the surface there is a belt of surface equatorial easterlies, then a belt of mid-latitude westerlies and finally a belt of surface easterlies. At higher altitudes there are also belts of easterlies over the equator, but at about 30° north and south there are rapid winds (over 30 ms⁻¹ or 180 km an hour) at an altitude of between 10 and 15 km. These strong winds result from the steep temperature contrast between polar and equatorial air – note the position of the tropopause and how it varies from equatorial to polar areas. This is the region of the polar front, the warmer area of the lower latitudes raises the height of the tropopause.

The uneven pattern in Figure 12.35 is the result of seasonal variations in the overhead sun. Summer in the southern hemisphere means that there is a cooling in the northern hemisphere, thereby increasing the differences between polar and equatorial air. Consequently high-level westerlies are stronger in the northern hemisphere in winter.

General circulation model

In general:

- warm air is transferred polewards and is replaced by cold air moving towards the equator
- air that rises is associated with low pressure whereas air that sinks is associated with high pressure
- low pressure produces rain, high pressure produces dry conditions.

Any circulation model must take into account the meridional transfer of heat, latitudinal variations in rainfall and winds. (Any model will be descriptive and static, unlike the atmosphere.) In 1735 George Hadley described the operation of the Hadley cell, produced by the direct heating of air over the equator. The air is forced to rise by convection, travels polewards then sinks at the subtropical anticyclone belt. Hadley suggested that similar cells might exist in mid latitudes and high latitudes. William Ferrel suggested that Hadley cells interlink with a mid-latitude cell, rotating it in reverse direction and these cells, in turn, rotate the polar cell.

There are very strong differences between surface and upper winds in tropical latitudes. Easterly winds at the surface are replaced by westerly winds above, especially in winter. At the ITCZ, convectional storms lift air into the atmosphere. This increases air pressure near the tropopause, which causes winds to diverge at high altitude. They move out of equatorial regions towards the poles, gradually losing heat by radiation and, as they contract, more air moves in, and the weight of the air increases the air pressure at the subtropical high pressure zone (Figure 12.36). The denser air sinks causing subsidence (stability). The north–south component of the Hadley cell is known as a **meridional flow**.

The **zonal flow** over the Pacific was discovered by Gilbert Walker in the 1920s. The Southern Oscillation Index (SOI) is a measure of how far temperatures vary from 'average'. A high SOI is associated with strong westward trades (because winds near the equator blow from high pressure to low pressure and are unaffected by the Coriolis effect). Tropical cyclones are more common in the South Pacific when there is an El Niño Southern Oscillation (ENSO) warm episode.

The polar cell is found in high latitudes (Figure 12.37). Winds at highest latitudes are generally easterly. Air over the North Pole continually cools and being cold it is dense, therefore it subsides creating high pressure. Air above the polar front flows back to the North Pole creating a polar cell. In between the Hadley cell and the polar cell is an indirect cell, the Ferrel cell, driven by the movement of the other two cells, rather like a cog in a chain.

In the early twentieth century research investigated patterns and mechanisms of upper winds and clouds at an altitude of between 3 and 12 km. These identified large-scale, fast-moving belts of westerly winds, which

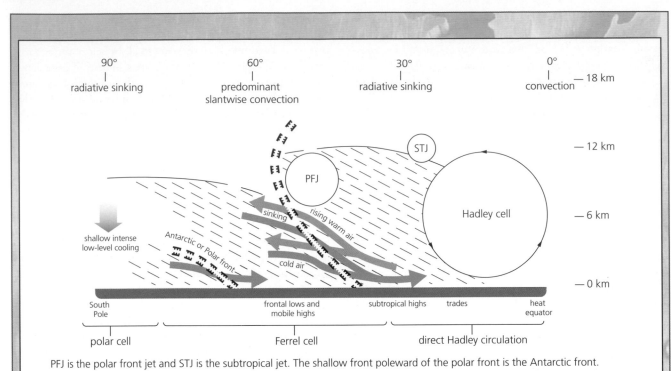

PFJ is the polar front jet and STJ is the subtropical jet. The shallow front poleward of the polar front is the Antarctic front.

Source: Linacre, E. and Geerts, B., *Climates and Weather Explained*, Routledge, 1997

Figure 12.36 The Palmen–Newton model of the meridional winds of the general circulation

follow a ridge and trough wave-like pattern known as Rossby waves or planetary waves.

The presence of these winds led to Rossby's 1941 model of the atmosphere. This suggested a three-cell north–south (meridional) circulation with two thermally direct cells and one thermally indirect cell. The thermally direct cell is driven by the heating at the equator (the Hadley cell) and by the sinking of cold air at the Poles (the polar cell). Between them lies the thermally indirect cell whose energy is obtained from the cells to either side by the mixing of the atmosphere at upper levels. The jet streams are, therefore, key locations in the transfer of energy through the atmosphere. Further modification of Rossby's models were made by Palmen in 1951 (Figure 12.36).

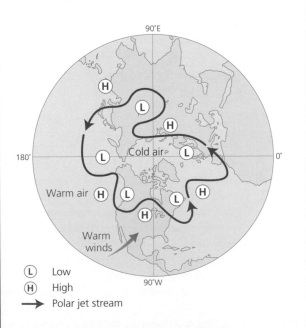

Source: Park, C., *The environment: principles and applications*, Routledge, 1997

Figure 12.37 Impact of the polar jet stream on air masses in the northern hemisphere

The El Niño Southern Oscillation

El Niño, which means Christ Child, is an irregular occurence of warm surface water in the Pacific off the coast of South America that affects global wind and rainfall patterns. In July 1997 the sea surface temperature in the Eastern tropical Pacific was 2.0 to 2.5°C above normal, breaking all previous climate records. The El Niño's peak continued into early 1998 before weather conditions returned to normal.

In the 1920s Sir Gilbert Walker identified a characteristic of the southern hemisphere which became known as the Southern Oscillation. This consisted of a sequence of surface pressure changes within a regular time period of three to seven years, and was most easily observed in the Pacific Ocean and around Indonesia. When eastern Pacific pressures are high and Indonesian pressures are low relative to the long-term average the situation is described as having a high Southern Oscillation Index (SOI). By contrast, when Pacific pressures are low and Indonesian pressures

are high the SOI is described as low. In 1972, J. N. Walker identified a cell-like circulation in the tropics that operates from an east to west (intrazonal) direction rather than a north to south (meridional) direction. The cell works by convection of air to high altitudes caused by intense heating, followed by movement within the subtropical easterly jet stream and its subsequent descent (Figure 12.38).

El Niño is a phase of the Southern Oscillation when the trade winds are weak and the sea surface temperatures in the equatorial Pacific increase by between 1° and 4°C. The impacts of ENSO, which is the most prominent signal in year-to-year natural climate variability, are felt worldwide. During the 1982–3 ENSO the most destructive event of this century, damages amounted to about $13 billion; the event has been blamed for droughts in countries from India to Australia, floods from Ecuador to New Zealand and fires in West Africa and Brazil. Scientists are capable of forecasting

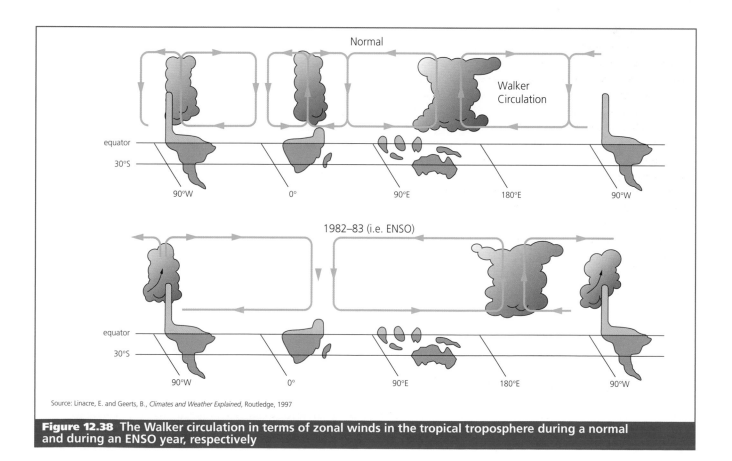

Source: Linacre, E. and Geerts, B., *Climates and Weather Explained*, Routledge, 1997

Figure 12.38 The Walker circulation in terms of zonal winds in the tropical troposphere during a normal and during an ENSO year, respectively

Figure 12.39 Drought: a possible effect of El Niño

the onset of El Niño up to one year in advance through sea surface temperature signals. El Niño has been studied since the early 1900s. In 1904 Sir Gilbert Walker investigated annual variability of the monsoon. He discovered a correlation in the patterns of atmospheric pressure at sea level in the tropics, the ocean temperature and rainfall fluctuations across the Pacific Ocean. He showed that the primary characteristic of the Southern Oscillation is a seesaw in the atmospheric pressure at sea level between the south-eastern subtropical Pacific and the Indian Ocean. During normal conditions dry air sinks over the cold waters of the eastern tropical Pacific and flows westwards along the equator as part of the trade winds. The air is moistened as it moves towards the warm waters of the western tropical Pacific. The sea surface temperature gradients (the cold waters along the Peruvian coast and the warm waters in the western tropical Pacific) are necessary for the atmospheric gradients that drive circulation.

Climatic anomalies induced by El Niño have been responsible for severe worldwide socioeconomic damage (Figure 12.39). Among the effects of the 1997–8 El Niño were:

- a stormy winter in California (the 1982–3 event took 160 lives and caused $2 billion damage in floods and mudslides)
- worsening drought in Australia, Indonesia, the Philippines, Southern Africa and north east Brazil

- drought and floods in China
- increased risk of malaria in South America
- lower rainfall in northern Europe
- higher rainfall in southern Europe.

Perception of the El Niño hazard has developed in a series of stages. Until the 1972–3 event it was perceived as affecting local communities and industries along the eastern Pacific coast near Peru, then from 1972–3 to 1982–3 El Niño was recognised as a cause of natural disasters worldwide. However, since 1982–3 countries have begun to realise that there is a need for national programmes that will use scientific information in policy planning and that an integrated approach from a number of countries is required to reduce the effect of El Niño.

Current research includes the Global Atmospheric Research Programme (GARP) which is aiming to determine to what extent the climate can be predicted and the extent of human influence on climate on a variety of timescales from weeks to decades.

The role of oceans in global climate

The central role of oceans in influencing global climates has been recognised for many years. For example, the link between Pacific Ocean temperatures and recent worldwide weather extremes (El Niño events) is well noted. The oceans have two important roles:

- providing water for the land-based hydrological cycle
- absorbing solar energy, distributing it round the globe and transferring it to the atmosphere.

About 80 per cent of the energy received at the earth's surface from the sun is absorbed by the oceans, so the oceans are the main receivers of energy entering the global climate system. Since almost all of this energy is absorbed by the top 100 m of the ocean, it is clear that sea surface temperatures are of considerable significance. Variations in sea surface temperature or sea surface temperature anomalies (SSTAs) will influence variations of weather on a variety of scales, but in the mid latitudes studies have shown that there is little statistical correlation between SSTAs and weather unless simulated SSTAs far exceed those observed in reality. This is probably because a large-scale natural variation in weather in mid latitudes masks the influence of SSTAs. However, when the SSTAs are placed in the tropics they produce large, local and remote responses.

Questions

1 What is meant by the term 'El Niño'? Why is it called this?
2 What were the possible effects of the 1997–8 El Niño season?

Weather

The term 'weather' refers to daily changes on a small scale, rather than anything global. One of the main factors which influences the weather is the nature and type of air mass affecting an area.

Air masses

The original concept of air masses was that they were bodies of air whose physical properties, especially temperature and humidity, were uniform over a large area. By contrast, they are now redefined as large bodies of air where the horizontal gradients (variation) of the main physical properties are fairly slack, i.e. they vary slightly over long distances. It is generally applied only to the lower layers of the atmosphere, although air masses can cover areas of tens of thousands of square kilometres (Figure 12.40a).

Air masses derive their temperature and humidity from the regions over which they lie. These regions are known as source regions. The principal regions are:

- areas of relative calm such as semi-permanent high-pressure areas
- where the surface is relatively uniform including deserts, oceans and icefields.

Air masses can be modified when they leave their sources as (Figures 11.40b and c) on the modification of lapse rate (temperature profiles) in an air mass illustrate.

Principal air masses

The main air masses to affect the United Kingdom are polar (P) and tropical (T) air masses which meet at the polar front (Figure 12.41). Some polar air masses may originate in cool temperate or sub-Arctic areas. Others include equatorial (E) and Arctic (A) air masses. These are then generally divided into maritime (m) or continental (c) depending upon the humidity characteristics of the air, i.e. whether it originated over the ocean and so is moist (m) or over the land and thus dry (c).

Polar continental (Pc) air masses originate over Siberia, which can be extremely cold. The air is cold, dry and cloud free giving extremely cold weather in the United Kingdom. Pollution, fog and frost are common. The air mass is initially stable, but is warmed as it crosses the North Sea where it picks up moisture and may become unstable in lower layers. This produces heavy snow in eastern Britain and bright, clear conditions on the west coast. Pc air often lasts for several days and may be associated with blocking anticyclones. If it occurs in summer, it brings warm, cloudy weather. Heating at the base of the air mass makes it less stable and cloudier.

Polar maritime (Pm) air comes from the high latitudes over the Pacific and Atlantic oceans and is essentially cool, moist and relatively unstable in the lower layers. It gives dull, wet weather with winds from the north west or west. It is the most common air mass to affect the British Isles. It warms slightly as it crosses the Atlantic, hence it is unstable in lower layers. Pm air masses are associated with cumulus clouds and strong winds, especially after the passing of a cold front.

Tropical maritime (Tm) air masses are also common. Tm air comes from the oceans of the lower latitudes. It is warm, moist and unstable, especially in summer when convectional heating causes cooling of the air. Tm air masses produce mild and wet weather in winter with thick cloud cover, while in summer they are warm rather than hot. The lower air is stable but, if forced to rise over hills, upper layers can become conditionally unstable to give thunder showers. Tm air masses often produce stratus cloud giving hill and coastal fog. They are also associated with the warm sector of a depression. Winds are from the south west and are usually moderate to fresh.

Tropical continental (Tc) air masses occur only in summer when sub tropical high pressure moves northwards. Tc air masses come from over the hot deserts. They are characterised by southerly winds from North Africa or southern Europe bringing hot, dry air. They produce heatwave conditions such as in 1976 and 1989. Tc air masses are stable in lower layers, producing gentle winds and a dusty haze. Associated with high pressure, prolonged spells may cause drought whereas short episodes are associated with pollution and high pollen counts. Their effect varies over the United Kingdom, South East England may suffer drought conditions whereas the north and west might be less affected.

Arctic maritime (Am) air produces northerly winds from Norway and Greenland with very cold, dry, 'biting' air during the winter months. As it travels over oceans it slowly heats up, picks up water and becomes unstable. Am produces snow in winter in Scotland, hail in spring, and heavy showers at other times. Am air masses last several days.

When two contrasting air masses meet, they form a **front**. As warm air is lighter than dense, cold air, the warm air begins to rise over the cold air, condensing as it rises to form cloud and rain.

Modification of air masses

As air masses move from their source regions they may be modified due to:

- internal changes
- the effects of the surface over which they move.

These changes create **secondary air masses**. For example, a warm air mass which travels over a cold surface is cooled and becomes more stable. Hence, it may form low cloud or fog but is unlikely to produce much rain. By contrast, a cold air mass which passes over a warm surface is warmed and becomes less stable. The rising air is likely to produce more

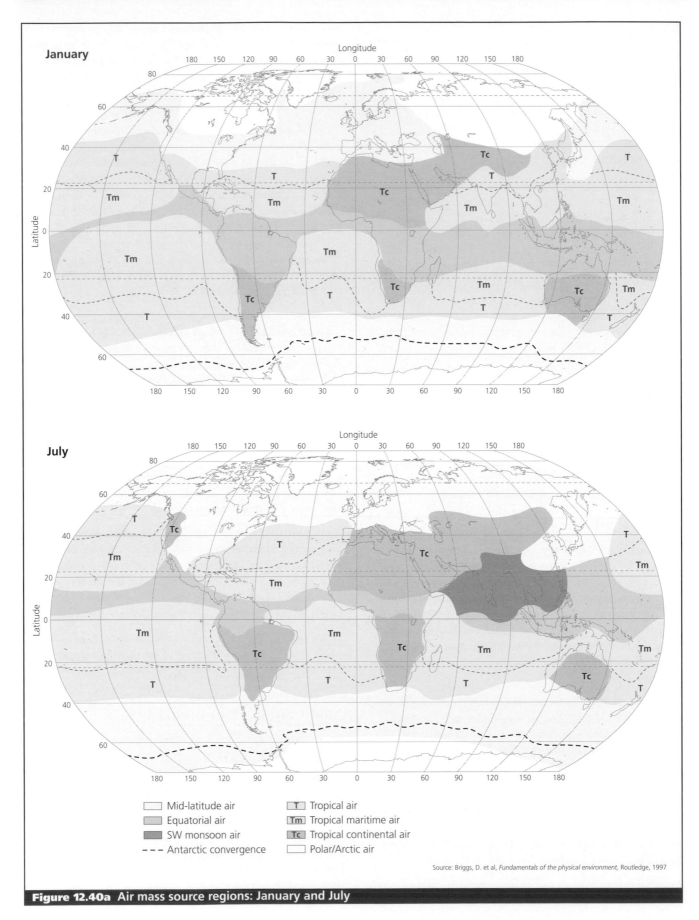

January

July

Mid-latitude air
Equatorial air
SW monsoon air
- - - Antarctic convergence

T Tropical air
Tm Tropical maritime air
Tc Tropical continental air
Polar/Arctic air

Source: Briggs, D. et al, *Fundamentals of the physical environment*, Routledge, 1997

Figure 12.40a Air mass source regions: January and July

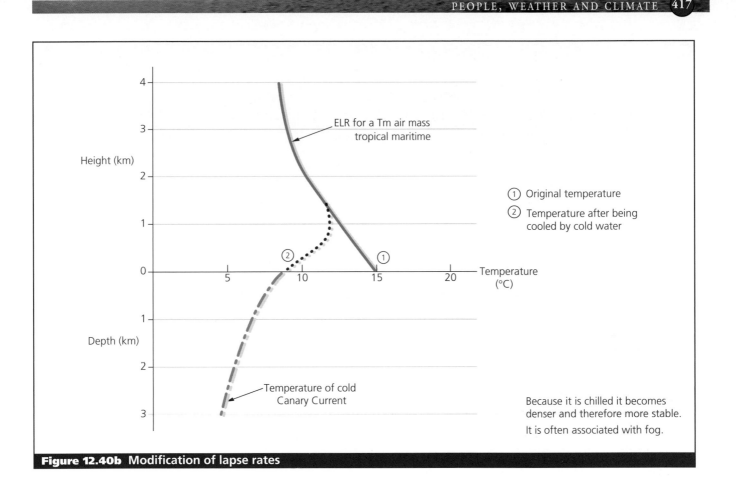

1 Original temperature

2 Temperature after being
cooled by cold water

Because it is chilled it becomes
denser and therefore more stable.
It is often associated with fog.

Figure 12.40b Modification of lapse rates

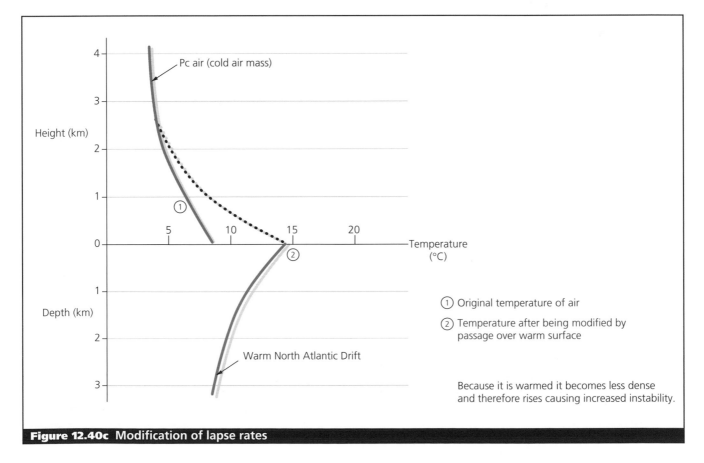

1 Original temperature of air

2 Temperature after being modified by
passage over warm surface

Because it is warmed it becomes less dense
and therefore rises causing increased instability.

Figure 12.40c Modification of lapse rates

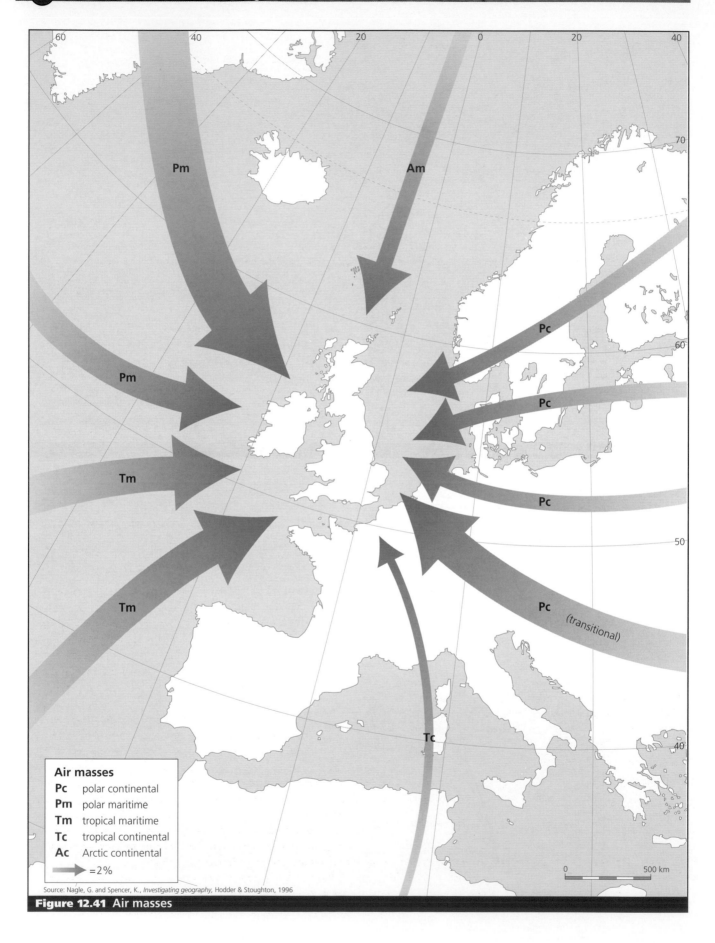

Air masses

Pc polar continental
Pm polar maritime
Tm tropical maritime
Tc tropical continental
Ac Arctic continental

━━▶ = 2%

Source: Nagle, G. and Spencer, K., *Investigating geography*, Hodder & Stoughton, 1996

Figure 12.41 Air masses

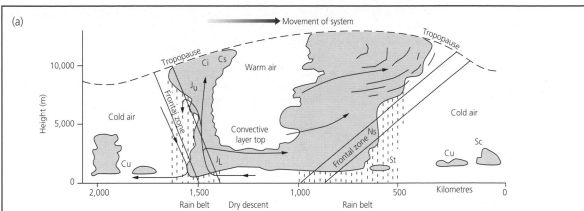

(a)

Cross-sectional model of a depression with anafronts, where the air is rising relative to each frontal surface. Note that an ana-warm-front may occur with a kata-cold-front and vice-versa. J_U and J_L show the locations of the upper and lower jet streams respectively.

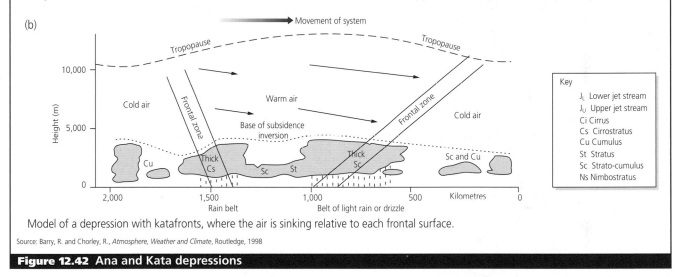

(b)

Model of a depression with katafronts, where the air is sinking relative to each frontal surface.

Source: Barry, R. and Chorley, R., *Atmosphere, Weather and Climate*, Routledge, 1998

Figure 12.42 Ana and Kata depressions

rain. Air masses which have been warmed are given the suffix 'w' and those which have been cooled are given the suffix 'k' (*kalt*).

Frontal weather

When two air masses meet they form a front. For example, when a Pm and a Tm converge the temperature differences between them may be over 10°C. This creates variations in density and allows the warmer air mass to rise over the cooler one. In any low-pressure system (depression or cyclone) there are a number of forces operating simultaneously:

■ the mixing of the two air masses

■ the Coriolis force

■ divergence of air aloft, in the upper regions of the troposphere.

The result of these forces is to drag air inwards to the centre of a low-pressure system. Warmer, lighter air invades the colder, denser air to form the warm sector, while warm air rises over the cold air at the warm front. Where the cold air pushes the

warm air up, a cold front is formed. The rising air is removed at altitude by the jet stream.

In general, the appearance of a warm front is heralded by high cirrus clouds. Gradually, the cloud thickens and the cloud base lowers. Altostratus clouds may produce some drizzle, while at the warm front nimbostratus clouds produce rain. A number of changes occur at the warm front. Winds reach a peak and gusts may reach 40 km per hour and change direction (e.g. from south to south west); temperatures suddenly rise (by as much as 10°C); pressure which had been falling (from 1010 mb to 990 mb) now remains constant. The cold front is marked by: a decrease in temperature (as much as 10°C); cumulonimbus clouds and heavy rain; increased wind speeds and gustiness and another change in wind direction; a gradual increase in pressure (up to 20 mb). After the cold front has passed, the clouds begin to break up, sunny periods are more frequent although there may be isolated scattered showers associated with unstable Pm air.

No two low-pressure systems are the same. The weather that is found in any depression depends on the air masses involved (Figure 12.42). The greater the temperature difference between the air masses involved the more severe the weather. Depressions are divided into **ana** and **kata** depressions depending upon the vigour of the uplift of warm air. The standard model of a depression was developed by Bjerknes in 1937. Where air masses of differing composition meet, an **anafront** is formed and this produces cloud systems of great height. By contrast, **katafronts** occur when the air

Rain bands

Rain bands are typically several hundred kilometres in length and 20 to 100 km wide. Classic descriptions of the pattern of rainfall in mid-latitude depression systems include the two principal rain belts running parallel to the SCF and the SWF (Figure 12.44).

There are two main problems with the Bergeron–Findeisen process. First, the speed of raindrop formation cannot be explained by this process because particles of the threshold value for rapid growth are not produced fast enough to match observed speeds of formation for significant quantities of rainfall. Second, the ice crystals which turn into raindrops and fall appear to outnumber ice nuclei (those particles around which ice crystals can form) by several orders of magnitude.

Recent research: depressions and the conveyor belt model

The conveyor belt model refers to the meeting of broad flows of air likened to the movement of a conveyor belt (Figure 12.44). To the south of a low-pressure centre or a depression, a broad flow of warm air originates from a high-pressure area. This is the warm conveyor belt (WCB) which runs parallel to and ahead of the surface cold front (SCF), and on contacting cold air at the surface warm front (SWF) it is forced to rise and flows clockwise, anticyclonically, out of the system at high level. At the same time a broad flow of cold air, referred to as the cold conveyor belt (CCB), moves from a high-pressure region to the east or south east of the depression towards the centre of the low. Initially, it flows parallel to and in front of the SWF but on emerging from beneath the WCB it too starts to ascend flowing clockwise out of the system at high level. The third flow of air simultaneously moves in towards the low from behind the SCF; this is cold, dry, descending air from the upper troposphere (5 to 10 km altitude) which splits into two flows, the upper part above the SCF and WCB and the lower part forming a mass of cold air behind the SCF.

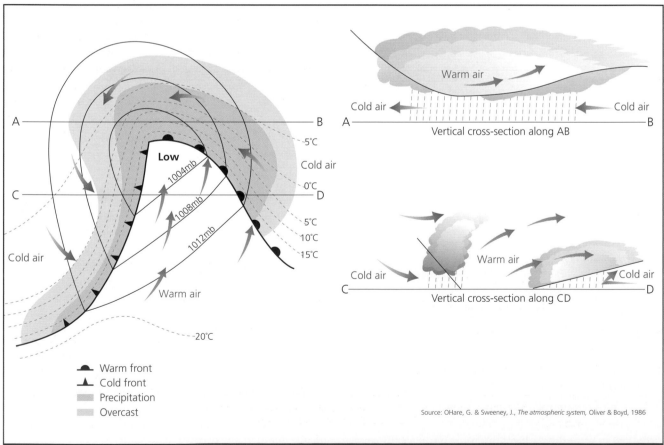

Source: OHare, G. & Sweeney, J., *The atmospheric system*, Oliver & Boyd, 1986

Figure 12.43 **Weather associated with a depression**

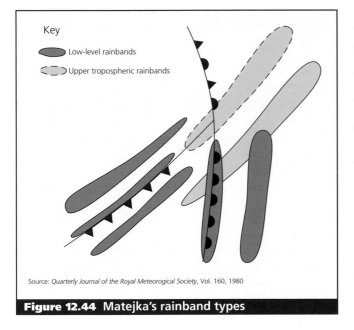

Key

Low-level rainbands

Upper tropospheric rainbands

Source: *Quarterly Journal of the Royal Meteorological Society*, Vol. 160, 1980

Figure 12.44 Matejka's rainband types

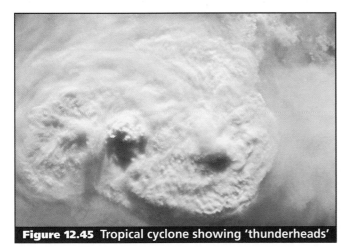

Figure 12.45 Tropical cyclone showing 'thunderheads'

masses are fairly similar in composition. The formation of precipitation is still largely explained in terms of the Bergeron–Findeisen process (1935) and the coalescence theory often working together simultaneously (see page 401).

Tropical cyclones

Tropical cyclones are intense low-pressure systems at low latitudes, generally about 650 km in diameter, which bring violent storms, high winds and sea surges to tropical and subtropical areas such as Bangladesh (Figure 12.45). They are also known as hurricanes and typhoons and affect a large proportion of the earth's surface (Figure 12.46). Unlike temperate depressions (also known as cyclones) tropical cyclones are not associated with fronts. Tropical cyclones last for about a week – the intense low pressure causes strong winds and raises sea level. Wind speeds of over 160 km per hr are common. Rainfall is intense – up to 2000 mm per day. In fact, one definition of a tropical cyclone is that it has wind speeds of 32 m per second or 63 knots per hour, and it develops in the tropics or subtropics. Tropical cyclones develop mostly in summer and in autumn and are large weather systems which include a ring of intense wind surrounding a calm central eye. The eye, typically 12 to 50 km wide, is cloudless with subsiding calm warm air. Around the eye winds rotate anticlockwise and updrafts are strong (Figure 12.47).

Plentiful supplies of moisture and temperatures above 27°C are required for tropical cyclones to develop. The updraft is fed by winds converging at ground level; although winds converge over a distance of up to 1000 km only about half that area is affected by rain and high wind speeds affect a belt of about 200 km. In the centre of the cyclone, air pressure is low, 950 mb or so. The lowest recorded pressure was 876 mb in the North West Pacific in 1975, thus there is a rapid decline of pressure as a cyclone approaches, up to 18 mb in 8 hours.

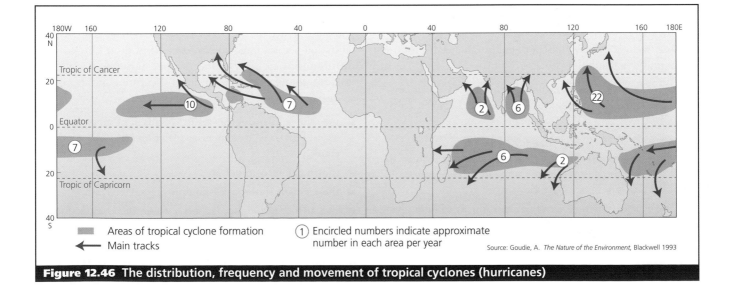

Areas of tropical cyclone formation

Main tracks

1 Encircled numbers indicate approximate number in each area per year

Source: Goudie, A. *The Nature of the Environment*, Blackwell 1993

Figure 12.46 The distribution, frequency and movement of tropical cyclones (hurricanes)

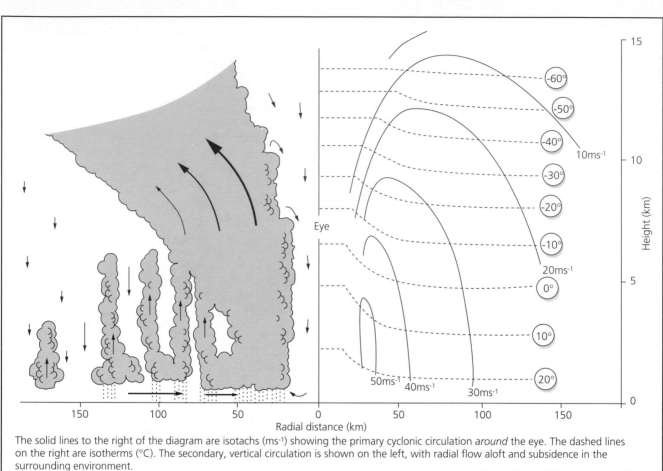

The solid lines to the right of the diagram are isotachs (ms⁻¹) showing the primary cyclonic circulation *around* the eye. The dashed lines on the right are isotherms (°C). The secondary, vertical circulation is shown on the left, with radial flow aloft and subsidence in the surrounding environment.

Source: Linacre, E. and Geerts, B., *Climates and Weather Explained*, Routledge, 1997

Figure 12.47 Radial cross-section of an idealised tropical cyclone

Formation of a tropical cyclone

A tropical cyclone has a life-cycle of about 10 days. Normally formation takes a few days while the core is still cool, one to two days while the core warms and pressure drops and a few days of more intensity, followed by a day or two while the tropical cyclone dies. A number of factors are needed for the formation of a tropical cyclone:

■ high sea surface temperatures (SST) of 27°C or more, hence tropical cyclones are found largely between 20°S and 30°N

■ generally SSTs are highest part of oceans

■ a significant Coriolis force is needed to deflect winds so that they rotate around a low pressure (thus cyclones occur beyond 5° of longitude)

■ over oceans moisture is needed as a supply of latent heat

■ the troposphere needs to be free of high-level winds of great strength (they effectively remove the lid of the cyclone)

■ easterly waves.

The mature stage

Cyclone tracks are difficult to predict. Nevertheless, in the northern hemisphere they move away from the equator, travel westwards and then rotate and accelerate polewards. Once the air rises it cools and on reaching saturation releases huge quantities of latent heat. This provides the storm with its energy. Once a storm moves overland it loses this source of energy. Cyclones decay for a number of reasons:

■ they move inland – this results in a lack of moisture or latent heat as well as increased friction reducing wind action

■ they move into colder areas

■ they remain stationary – cooling the sea beneath

■ they move into higher latitudes where the Coriolis force is increased – reducing the cyclonic spin relative to the ground

■ fast upper winds sheer off the top of a cyclone, thus uplift is reduced.

The Kandla hurricane

In June 1998 the Indian port of Kandla was devastated by a cyclone (Figure 12.48). Kandla is one of India's busiest ports and is a gateway to the north west. The official death toll was 1000 people, although local people believe it could be as high as 10 000. Only six port employees were known to have died; most of the dead were unregistered migrant labourers who worked for contractors in the port and the surrounding salt flats of the Gulf of Kutch. They lived in the shanty towns of Kandla surrounding the docks. Their improvised huts were no shelter for winds which were estimated to reach 150 km per hour, and waves which rose 2 m high over the land.

Thousands of people were unaccounted for, many were employed illegally beyond the reach of India's labour law and few companies had any records of their existence. The physical destruction was widespread, cranes were twisted beyond repair, unloading material was destroyed, chemical tanks were washed up in the town, fishing boats were dumped across the main access routes, the biggest salt works in Asia was ruined and the shanty towns around Kandla were destroyed without trace. In addition to the physical hazard, human factors intensified the problem. Although the cyclone had been tracked for three to four nights across the Arabian Sea by Indian scientists, no effort was made to warn port labourers and salt workers of the threat posed. Local politicians, officials and contractors have been criticised for allowing the growth of illegal shanty towns for the cheap, casual labour for the rapidly expanding port.

Moreover, there was little aid; immediately after the hazard state employers repainted Kandla's main highway while the relief organisation floundered. The hurricane is estimated to have caused over 1 billion Rupees (£15 million) damage to the port and £15 million to cargo stocks. Dozens of warehouses were wrecked, mountains of wheat and salt were soaked, containers carrying everything from cigarettes to cosmetics were damaged (Figure 12.48).

The tragedy could have severe consequences for the rest of the country. Kandla Port handled almost 40 million tonnes of traffic in 1997 and serves India's main route to the Middle East, the principal route for imported crude and petroleum products. Oil and petrol products from Kandla are taken from train and truck as far as Uttar Pradesh. Imports account for 90 per cent of Kandla's traffic. It also handles nearly 8 million tonnes of dry cargo each year. The entire north west of India depends on Kandla for its oil. The cargo jetty which handles agricultural products such as wheat, salt, onions, potatoes and soya, as well as containers was destroyed in the storm. In addition, so too were warehouses, storage tanks, container yards, dry docks, housing colonies, administrative buildings, power substations and road and rail links. The hazard at Kandla points not just to physical causes but also to human causes – a failure of government and of business ethics, and a basic disregard for the life of the poor.

Figure 12.48 Aftermath of the Kandla hurricane, June 1998

Flooding in Bangladesh
(see also Chapter 15, pages 513–4)

Bangladesh is among the world's most densely populated areas. Much of the country is a flat delta where the Ganges and Bramaphutra rivers drain into the Bay of Bengal, carrying 2 billion tonnes of fertile silt each year. Ordinarily the rivers flood annually in the monsoon period between June and September, inundating up to 25 per cent of the country and lining it with fertile silt. The river floods rarely cause deaths. It is the tropical cyclones in the Bay of Bengal that are largely responsible for the devastation that scourges Bangladesh. In 1970 up to 500 000 people died as a result of tropical surges, and in 1991 more than 140 000 died and over 10 million were made homeless.

The 1991 cyclone occurred on 29 April, the worst for nearly 30 years. However, it was not unexpected. It had been tracked from 25 April and scientists believed they had given ample warning.

Winds of 233 km per hour created 4.5 m waves which swept away whole communities. Some were lucky – on the island of Sanadia, 650 people climbed upon a 6-m-high cyclone shelter – and survived. But it would cost over $66m to provide shelters for all of Bangladesh's 'at risk' population. Only 10 per cent of the raised shelters have been built. Moreover, the coastal embankments built in the 1960s have been badly eroded over time and are in need of repair.

Tornadoes

A tornado is an intense storm with very high wind speeds (often over 400 km an hour in the funnel), capable of inflicting serious damage. They are relatively small in scale, often less than 500 m wide. Tornadoes are most frequent and destructive over the continental United States, this is due to the mixing of warm air from the Gulf of Mexico and cold air from the Arctic, the strong contrast in temperature causes vigorous uplift of the air.

Water spouts similar to funnels are found over the sea. Since the sea is cooler than the land, evaporation is less intense, thus water spouts are weaker than tornadoes.

Questions

1 Why were people in Bangladesh reluctant to evacuate the delta (supposing they had heard the warnings)?
2 **(a)** Why are disasters like this increasingly likely in the next few years?
   (b) Why do so many people die if a national disaster is so predictable?
   (c) What section of society (e.g. urban/rural, skilled, unskilled, etc.) are most vulnerable to flooding of the delta?
   In each part explain your answer fully.

World climates: a classification

The most widely used classification of climate is that of W. Köppen (Figure 12.50). His classification first appeared in 1900 and he made many modifications to it before his death in 1936. Although it has been refined since, it bears many resemblances to its early form.

Köppen classified climate with respect to two main criteria, temperature and seasonality of rainfall. Indeed, five of the six main climatic types are based on mean monthly temperature.

A Tropical rainy climate – coldest month greater than 18°C

B Dry (desert)

C Warm temperate rainy climate – coldest month –3°C to 18°C; warmest month greater than 10°C

D Cold boreal forest climate – coldest month –3°C or less; warmest month 10°C or more

E Tundra – warmest month 0 to 10°C

F Perpetual forest climate – warmest month less than 0°C.

The choice of the specific figures is as follows: 18°C is the critical winter temperature for tropical forests; 10°C is the poleward limit of forest growth; –3°C is generally associated with two to three weeks of snow annually.

There are subdivisions which relate to rainfall:

f – no dry season

m – monsoonal (i.e. short dry season and heavy rains in the rest of the year)

s – summer dry season

w – winter dry season.

For category B (deserts):

h – mean annual temperatures greater than 18°C

k – mean annual temperatures less than 18°C but warmest month above 18°C

k′ – mean annual temperatures less than 18°C and warmest month below 18°C.

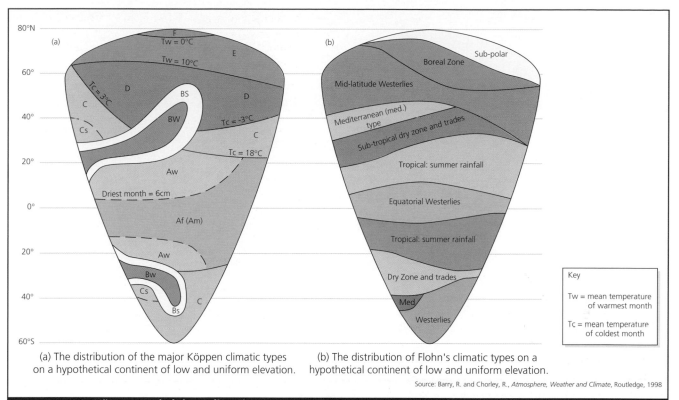

(a) The distribution of the major Köppen climatic types on a hypothetical continent of low and uniform elevation.

(b) The distribution of Flohn's climatic types on a hypothetical continent of low and uniform elevation.

Source: Barry, R. and Chorley, R., *Atmosphere, Weather and Climate*, Routledge, 1998

Figure 12.49 Köppen and Flohn's climatic types

European climate

Europe's complex and fragmented geography provides a variety of climatological and meteorological conditions. It contains a range of Köppen's climatic regimes. In general, there is a north–south variation, with southerly areas warmer than northern locations. In addition, there is an east–west factor, with places farther east drier and experiencing greater annual temperature ranges compared with maritime locations in the west. This gives rise to a fourfold division of European climates into: Mediterranean conditions in the south; temperate oceanic in the west; temperate continental in the east; boreal in the north. This simple pattern is further complicated by the presence of mountain ranges, proximity to the sea – in particular the North Atlantic Drift – and aspect.

The influence of the ocean is most marked in parts of Northern Europe. Areas beyond 45° N (Ireland, Britain and Scandinavia) experience positive temperature anomalies in winter. During summer, the ocean has a cooling effect on these places and they experience a negative temperature anomaly. By contrast,

continental areas such as Moscow are much hotter during summer but much colder during winter (Figure 12.51).

Europe's location between 36° N and 71° N means that there are considerable variations in the amount and intensity of insolation received from the sun. Annual sunshine varies from about 1000 hours in Iceland to over 3400 hours in Portugal and south east Spain.

Most of Europe is dominated by two great pressure systems – the Azores high-pressure system and the Icelandic low-pressure system. In addition, the Siberian high-pressure system influences temperatures during winter, while the Arctic high-pressure system and the South Asian low-pressure system may be influential during summer. Consequently, most of Europe is characterised by changeable conditions, although southern Europe is more stable during the summer because of the influence of tropical air masses.

These patterns of insolation and air circulation have an important bearing on air temperatures. During January isotherms

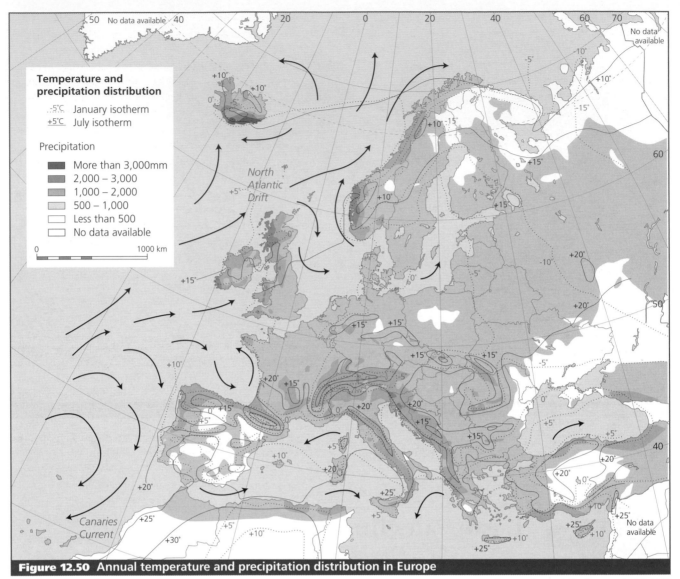

Figure 12.50 Annual temperature and precipitation distribution in Europe

Source: *Europe's Environment,* EEA 1995

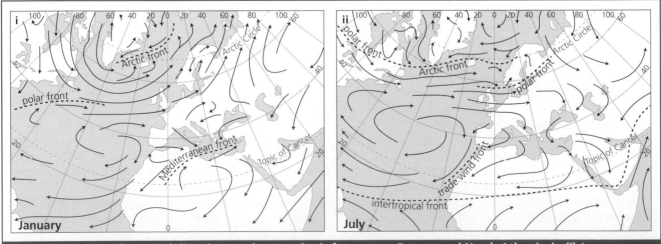

Figure 12.51 Prevailing wind directions and atmospheric fronts over Europe and North Atlantic, in (i) January and (ii) July

(lines of equal temperature) run from east to west. The 0°C isotherm divides the warmer south and west of Europe from the colder centre and north. The effect of ocean currents is most noticeable in the winter. By contrast, during the summer, the ocean has a cooling effect and there is increasing continentality towards the east. Temperature ranges vary from 8 to 10°C in Iceland to up to 28°C in parts of the CIS.

Rainfall levels are highest in western areas and over mountainous regions. This is because most of the rain-bearing winds come from the west, combined with the effect of relief on condensation and precipitation. Rainfall varies from between 1000 and 2000 mm in the western coastal areas of the British Isles (and over 4000 mm in Sprinkling Tarn in the Lake District) to below 500 mm in parts of Sweden, southern Spain, Greece and the Baltic States.

Southern Europe has a dry season (spring and summer) which lengthens eastwards and southwards. By contrast, the rest of Europe receives precipitation throughout the year, with western areas receiving a maximum in autumn and winter. Related to continentality, the proportion of summer rainfall (compared to mean annual rainfall) increases eastwards. In mountainous areas and the interior lowlands of Europe precipitation is most plentiful during spring.

These variations in climate may cause variations in type and amount of pollution. For example, in areas where precipitation is highest in winter, higher levels of pollutants are washed out of the atmosphere. By contrast, areas that are dry in winter may allow a build-up of pollutants in the atmosphere. During spring, when plants and animals are growing rapidly, there may be a sudden increase in the level of pollutants in the soil and the food chain.

Even throughout Britain there are significant regional differences. When averaged over three decades climate statistics for variables such as temperature, rainfall and sunshine smooth out the year-to-year fluctuations and give a good description of the climate experienced over a human lifetime. Britain's location means that it experiences the combined influences of the mid-latitude westerly winds and the North Atlantic Drift which comprises warm water from tropical regions. The British Isles are surrounded by this comparatively warm oceanic water, the temperature of which varies only slowly from month to month because of the high thermal inertia of the oceans. Oceanic climates such as Devon and Cornwall have annual fluctuations in temperature of less than 16°C, mild winters, autumn and winter maxima of precipitation and moderately warm summers; while sub-oceanic climates have an annual temperature fluctuation of between 16 and 25°C, mild to moderately cold winters, autumn to summer maximum of precipitation and moderately warm summers. For example, Gatwick Airport would fit this description.

1 Use Köppen's classification to identify the following climatic regions, and give a location example for each one: Af; Am; Bh; Bk; Cs; Ds.
2 Suggest which letters would identify Mediterranean climates, savanna climates, cold deserts and hot deserts.
3 Describe and account for the variety of climates in western Europe.

Local climates and microclimates

Small-scale variations in climate occur due to relatively small scale changes in surface albedo, vegetation, altitude, slope, aspect and moisture content. These cause variations in the climate between, for example, one side of a building and another, and around a garden or school.

Microclimate over bare soil

There are important variations in the microclimate caused by soil factors; for example, humus-rich (dark) soils absorb the heat more than light soils. Moist soils warm up more slowly than dry soils due to the specific heat capacity of water, hence soil temperature and moisture content varies between ridge and furrow in a ploughed field.

Air is a poor conductor of heat, meaning that soil that has a high proportion of air is a poor conductor of heat (e.g. sandy soils). Sandy soils may be hot by day at the surface but cool down rapidly with depth, and at night they become cold. By contrast soils with some moisture can transfer heat downwards. However, if there is too much water in the soil (over 20 per cent) it may take much longer to heat up the soil.

Radiation balance at night

Under clear conditions at night longwave radiation losses from the ground exceed the return of radiation from the atmosphere. By contrast, when conditions are cloudy, water vapour absorbs longwave radiation and returns much of it to the ground. Figure 12.52 shows a temperature profile on calm (high-pressure) and windy (low-pressure) days. On windy days air is mixed and so temperature variations are minimal. Under high-pressure conditions night-time temperatures are low and day-time temperatures warm. The factors promoting

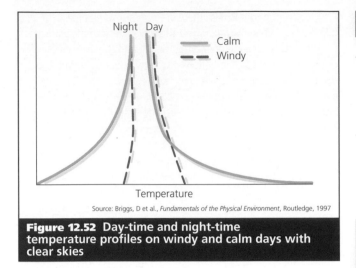

Figure 12.52 Day-time and night-time temperature profiles on windy and calm days with clear skies

Source: Briggs, D et al., *Fundamentals of the Physical Environment*, Routledge, 1997

Figure 12.53 Difference of relative humidity (%) between the inside and outside of a forest

Forest	January	April	July	October	Year
Deciduous broad-leaf	3.4	3.2	−0.8	1.1	2.2
Needle tree (conifer)	4.8	4.8	6.5	9.5	6.8
Japanese cedar	1.6	−1.1	1.5	0.5	0.8

Note: Positive values indicate that inside the forest is more humid.

Source: Briggs, D et al *Fundamentals of the physical environment*, Routledge 1997.

Figure 12.54 Sun flex in temperate rainforest, South Africa

maximum difference in day-time and night-time temperatures are:

- clear skies
- dry air
- lack of wind
- sandy soils
- snow-covered ground.

Woodland microclimates

Trees and forests can have a marked effect on climate; air movement is much less within a forest and temperatures are lower in summer compared with open land, also forests are more humid (less evaporation) than open land (Figure 12.53). Most of the incoming radiation is absorbed by the canopy layer, although some energy is reflected. However, the albedo varies between species (Figure 12.5). On average it is about 15 per cent and only a small proportion of the energy reaches the ground. The direct sunlight is known as sun flex (Figure 12.54), hence forests do not heat up as much by day, by night vegetation traps and returns much of the outgoing longwave radiation. The presence of water vapour also helps the forest to absorb longwave radiation by night.

There are important seasonal differences:

- deciduous forests lose their leaves in winter and there is much less absorption and interception then (Figure 12.55)
- large-leaved trees such as sycamore absorb more energy than small-leaved trees, such as birch and oak
- oak trees have a higher density of leaves than birch trees hence more light reaches the ground in a birch wood.

If a forest is layered there will be additional interception at each layer. In addition, the outgoing longwave radiation will be absorbed at each layer. In a tropical rainforest with as many as five layers, up to 99.9 per cent of the energy available is

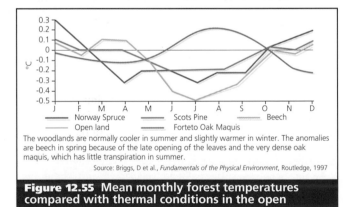

The woodlands are normally cooler in summer and slightly warmer in winter. The anomalies are beech in spring because of the late opening of the leaves and the very dense oak maquis, which has little transpiration in summer.

Source: Briggs, D et al., *Fundamentals of the Physical Environment*, Routledge, 1997

Figure 12.55 Mean monthly forest temperatures compared with thermal conditions in the open

absorbed by the trees and less than 0.1 per cent reaches ground level. Trees also affect wind flow. Vapour pressure is higher in a forest than in open land because of the presence of large amounts of moisture from the leaves and the low rates of evaporation due to cooler temperatures and low wind speeds.

Hedges have a similar, if less pronounced, effect on microclimate. A 2-m-high hedge could result in reduced wind speeds as much as 56 m beyond it, with the maximum

Figure 12.56 Effects of urbanisation on climate: average urban climatic differences expressed as a percentage* of rural conditions

Measure	Annual	Cold season	Warm season
Pollution	+500	+1000	+250
Solar radiation	−10	−15	−5
Temperature	+2	+3	+1
Humidity	−5	−2	−10
Visibility	−15	−20	−10
Fog	+10	+15	+5
Wind speed	−25	−20	−30
Cloudiness	+8	+5	+10
Rainfall	+5	0	+10
Thunderstorms	+15	+5	+30

*Note: Temperature is expressed as a difference only, not as a percentage.

Source: Briggs, D et al., *Fundamentals of the physical environment*, Routledge, 1997.

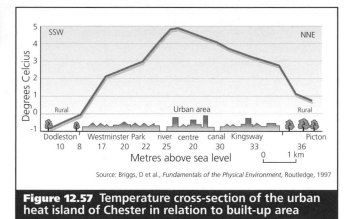

Source: Briggs, D et al., *Fundamentals of the Physical Environment*, Routledge, 1997

Figure 12.57 Temperature cross-section of the urban heat island of Chester in relation to built-up area

decrease – to 40 per cent of the original speed – occurring some 8 m beyond the hedge. This dramatic effect makes hedges extremely important in providing shelter for stock. The planting of long, thin blocks of trees as shelter belts has the same effect as hedges over even longer distances.

Hedges have a number of other microclimatic effects. Soil moisture content and the day-time air and soil temperatures can be increased by as much as 16 to 20 per cent in the lee of a hedge, with the effect reaching as far as around 10 times the height of the hedge. Evaporation can be significantly decreased at a distance of around 15 times the height of the hedge. A reduction in soil erosion also accompanies lower wind speeds.

Urban climates

Urban climates occur as a result of extra sources of heat released from industry, commercial and residential buildings as well as from vehicles. In addition, concrete, glass, bricks and tarmac all act differently from soil and vegetation. Some of these – notably dark bricks – absorb large quantities of heat and release them slowly by night. The release of pollutants helps to trap radiation in urban areas. Consequently, urban microclimates can be markedly different from rural microclimates (Figure 12.56).

Urban heat budgets differ from rural heat budgets. By day the major source of heat is solar energy in both urban and rural locations. However brick, concrete and stone have high heat capacities. In addition a kilometre of an urban area generally contains a greater surface area than a kilometre of countryside. Thus the large amount of surfaces in urban areas allows a greater area to be heated.

In urban areas there is relative lack of moisture due to:

- lack of vegetation
- high drainage density (sewers and drains) which remove water.

Little energy is used for evapotranspiration, thus more is available to heat the atmosphere; this is in addition to the artificial sources of heating such as industries, cars and people.

At night the ground radiates heat and cools. In urban areas the release of heat by buildings offsets the cooling process. In addition some industries, commercial activities and transport networks continue to release heat throughout the night (Figure 12.57).

The contrasts between urban and rural microclimates are greatest under calm high-pressure conditions. The typical heat profile of an urban heat island shows the maximum at the city centre, a plateau across the suburbs and a temperature cliff between the suburban and rural area. Small-scale variations within the urban heat island occur with the distribution of industries, open space, rivers, canals and so on.

The heat island is a feature which is delimited by isotherms (lines on a map joining places of equal temperature) normally in an urban area. This shows that the urban area is warmer than the surrounding rural area, especially by dawn during anticyclonic conditions. The heat-island effect is caused by at least five factors:

- **heat produced by human activity – low level of radiant heat which can equal 50 per cent of incoming energy in winter**
- **changes of energy balance – buildings have a high thermal capacity in comparison to rural areas, up to six times greater than agricultural land**
- **the effect on air flow – turbulence over a surface may be reduced overall although there may be funnelling effects of buildings**
- **there are fewer bodies of open water, therefore less evaporation and fewer plants, therefore less transpiration**
- **the composition of the atmosphere – the blanketing effect of smog, smoke or haze.**

Air flow over an urban area is disrupted, winds are slow and deflected over buildings. Large buildings can produce eddying (Figure 12.58).

The nature of urban climates is changing. With the decline

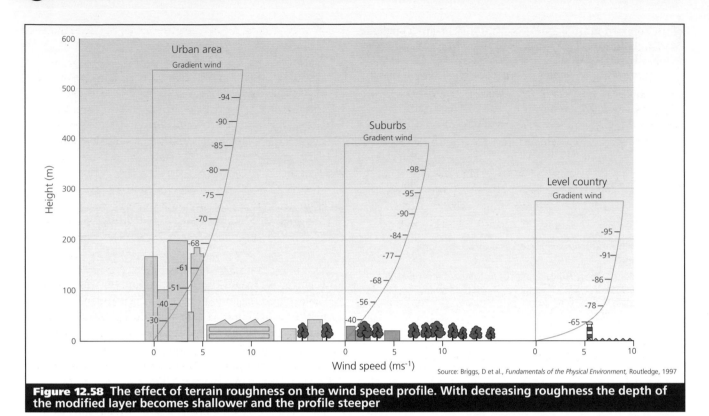

Figure 12.58 The effect of terrain roughness on the wind speed profile. With decreasing roughness the depth of the modified layer becomes shallower and the profile steeper

in coal as a source of energy there is less sulphur dioxide pollution hence less hygroscopic nuclei, hence less fog. However, the increase in cloud cover has occurred for a number of reasons:

- greater heating of the air (rising air leads to condensation)
- increase in pollutants, notably NOx, CO and CO_2
- frictional and turbulent air flow
- changes in moisture.

Valley breezes

Katabatic winds are winds which blow down a slope or valley at speeds of about 1 ms^{-1}. These typically occur by night as cold air drains down a mountain. During the day the heating of the valley floor causes air to rise, and the resulting upslope breezes are known as **anabatic winds** (Figure 12.59). (N.B. Remember the differences between anafronts, vigorously rising air, and katafronts characterised by subsiding air.)

Sea breezes

Sea breezes are formed by the differences in the specific heat capacity of land and sea. By day, under calm conditions, the land heats up quickly as it absorbs shortwave radiation. The ground, in turn, heats the air above it. By night, the land cools rapidly since there is little stored heat (the land is a poor conductor of heat and does not transport heat downwards efficiently).

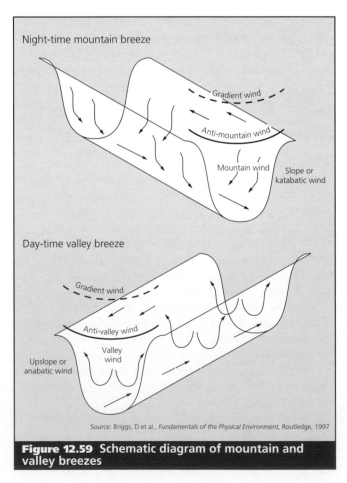

Figure 12.59 Schematic diagram of mountain and valley breezes

By contrast, incoming radiation can reach a depth of about 30 m in the sea, because water has a high specific heat capacity, thus it needs much energy to raise its temperature. In addition, tides and currents mix the heat over a large area, thus the sea gains heat slowly by day and releases it slowly by night. The contrast in temperature causes contrasts in pressure. By day, high pressure is over the sea (cooler) whereas low pressure is over the land (warm). Air blows from high pressure to low pressure as a sea breeze. By night, the land is cold (high pressure) whereas the sea is warm (low pressure). A land breeze blows from the land to the sea. Such convection cells can also be found over large lakes. Convection cells formed over the sea typically blow inland about 10 km and reach a height of 500 m or so.

Questions

1 Why are microclimates, such as urban heat islands, best observed during high pressure (anticyclonic) weather conditions?
2 Describe and explain the main characteristics of an urban climate.

Weather systems: impact on human activity

Experiencing the weather is probably many people's most direct and frequent experience of the physical environment. This is especially true for those who live in urban areas. The impact of weather on human activity ranges from the spectacular to the mundane. For example, the sinking of the *Titanic* occurred during a storm at night and might not have happened had there been better visibility and calmer seas. By contrast, the weather affects what we wear, how we feel and, in some cases, levels of health (Figures 12.60 and 12.63).

Biometeorology is the study of the effects of weather and climate on people, other animals and plants. In addition to the natural environment, it is possible to study the microenvironment of the home, school or office on people's well-being. There is a long history of writings on the impact of climatic systems on human activity (Figure 12.61).

An extreme view is that of **environmental determinism**. This states that if certain environmental conditions exist, the result can be predicted. According to Ellen Semple (1911) 'hot, moist equatorial climates encourage the growth of large forests which harbour abundant game and yield abundant fruits, they prolong the hunter gatherer stage of development and retard the advance to agriculture.'

Such an extreme view has been criticised on two main counts. First, similar environments do not always produce the same result. The Greek and Roman empires flourished in Mediterranean climates, but there have not been similar empires in other Mediterranean areas such as California, South Africa and south east Australia. Second, determinism fails to recognise the ways in which human activity can affect the environment.

However, rather than disregarding the influence of the environment entirely, the idea of **possibilism** was developed. This suggests that humans can act in a variety of ways in a given environment, but that some are more likely than others. This gives humans choice, and makes them active agents within the environment, but it also suggests that the environment sets limits within which human activity must take place.

It is not easy to measure the influence of the environment on human activity and, increasingly, most people have little direct interaction with the environment apart from through the medium of the weather. Nevertheless, many writers have attempted to define the influence of the environment on human activity. Aristotle believed that people from cold climates were brave but lacked thought, whereas those in warm areas were thoughtful but lacked spirit. Not surprisingly, most writers concluded that their own environment brought out the best in people. For example, Ellsworth Huntington and S. Markham concluded that temperate areas with frequent changes in weather, such as in western Europe, the north east United States and Japan, stimulate mental activity and leadership.

Nevertheless, there is evidence that climate and weather has an impact on a variety of features such as human comfort (Figure 12.62(a)), patterns of disease, crime and suicide. Figure 12.62(b) shows how environments vary in terms of their suitability for human activity.

An important influence of weather and climate on human activity is through the effects of hazards. Climatic hazards such as tornadoes, hurricanes, storms and droughts are dealt with elsewhere in this chapter. However, weather-related losses are large and increasing. Between 1950 and 1989 over 75 per cent of insured losses in the United States were due to weather disasters. But there are others, such as fog, poor driving conditions, wind chill and sunshine intensity which affect people.

Weather and climate have a direct impact on health and death rates. Death rates increase once a critical temperature has been reached. Mortality rates are higher too, in cloudy, damp, snowy places. Certain diseases have a seasonal pattern. Figure 12.63 shows the seasonal pattern of diseases in London and in a part of South Africa.

In addition, climate and weather have an important effect on economic activities, namely agriculture, the location of manufacturing industries and house building. The impact on

Figure 12.60 Applied meteorology: sectors and activities where climate has social, economic and environmental significance

Primary sector	General activities	Specific activities
Food	Agriculture	Land use, crop scheduling and operations, hazard control, productivity, livestock and irrigation, pests and diseases
	Fisheries	Management, operations, yield
Water abatement	Water disasters	Flood-, drought-, pollution-prevention
	Water resources	Engineering design, supply, operations
Health and community	Human biometeorology	Health, disease, morbidity and mortality
	Human comfort	Settlement design, heating and ventilation, clothing, acclimatisation
	Air pollution	Potential, dispersion, control
	Tourism and recreation	Sites, facilities, equipment marketing, sports activities
Energy conservation	Fossil fuels	Distribution, utilisation,
	Renewable resources	Solar-, wind-, water-power development
Industry and trade	Building and construction	Sites, design, performance, operations, safety
	Communications	Engineering design, construction
	Forestry	Regeneration, productivity, biological hazards, fire
	Transportation	Air, water and land facilities, scheduling, operations, safety
	Commerce	Plant operations, product design, storage of materials, sales planning, absenteeism, accidents
	Services	Finance, law, insurance, sales

Source: Goudie, A (ed.), *The encyclopaedic dictionary of physical geography*, Blackwell, 1994

This is the most temperate of countries. Cancer does not here drive you to take shade from its burning heat; nor does the cold of Capricorn send you rushing to the fire. You will seldom see snow here, and then it lasts only for a short time. But cold weather comes with all the winds here, not only from the west-north-west and north but equally from the east. Nevertheless, they are all moderate winds and none of them too strong. The grass is green in the fields in winter, just the same as in summer. Consequently, the meadows are not cut for fodder, nor do they even build stalls for their beasts. The country enjoys the freshness and mildness of spring almost all the year round.

The air is so healthy that there is no disease-bearing cloud, or pestilential vapour, or corrupting breeze. The island has little use for doctors. You will not find many sick men, except those that are actually at the point of death.

There is, however, such a plentiful supply of rain, such an ever-present overhanging of clouds and fog, that you will scarcely see even in summer three consecutive days of really fine weather.

Figure 12.61 The history and topography of Ireland by Gerald of Wales

farming systems is well known:

- plants require water to survive and grow – too much may cause soil erosion, too little may cause plants to die
- most plants require temperatures of over 6°C for successful germination of seeds; **accumulated temperature** is the total amount of heat required to produce optimum yield, for example wheat needs about 1300°C
- wind can increase evapotranspiration rates and erode soil
- cloud cover may reduce light intensity and delay harvesting.

Increasingly, climate is having an impact on manufacturing activity. In the United States, states with warmer climates, such as Arizona and New Mexico, have a cost advantage over colder states. This is because firms need to spend less on heating, as do workers. A large section of the aircraft industry has moved to the South West due to clearer skies (better flying conditions) and reduced heating costs in the hangars.

Weather also plays an important part in creative art. Dickens made effective use of weather to set the scene in his works, particularly in creating an image of London (Figure 12.64), while Constable's paintings are rich in atmospheric detail.

(a)

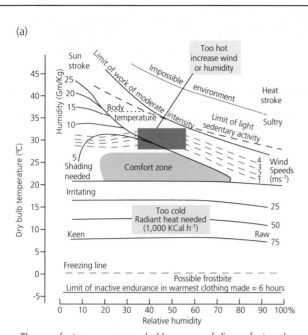

The comfort zone, surrounded by zones of discomfort and danger, within the range of climates experienced on the earth.

(b)

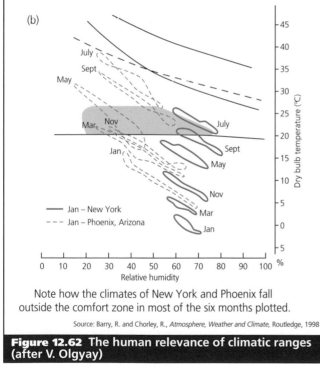

Note how the climates of New York and Phoenix fall outside the comfort zone in most of the six months plotted.

Source: Barry, R. and Chorley, R., *Atmosphere, Weather and Climate*, Routledge, 1998

Figure 12.62 The human relevance of climatic ranges (after V. Olgyay)

Finally, it is worth stating that climate influences people not only in the ways mentioned above, but in the very way it varies. These variations include long-term changes (such as global warming), seasonal changes (such as decreased temperatures in winter) and rapid, unexpected changes (such as the storm of 1987 in southern England). As a result there is a great deal of human interest in being able to predict the weather, and not being caught out.

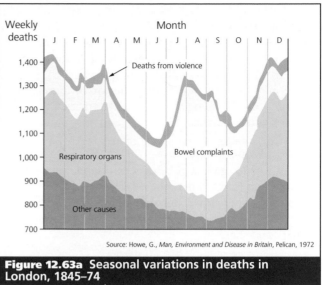

Source: Howe, G., *Man, Environment and Disease in Britain*, Pelican, 1972

Figure 12.63a Seasonal variations in deaths in London, 1845–74

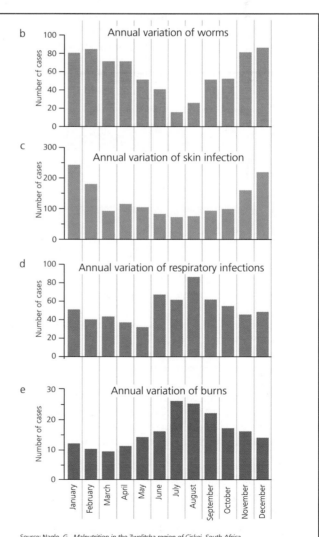

Source: Nagle, G., *Malnutrition in the Zwelitsha region of Ciskei, South Africa* (unpublished D. Phil Thesis, University of Oxford)

Figure 12.63b–e Seasonal variations in deaths in the Zwelitsha region of Ciskei, South Africa

Bleak House

Fog everywhere. Fog up the river, where it flows among the green aits and meadows; fog down the river, where it rolls defiled among the tiers of shipping, and the waterside pollution of a great (and dirty) city. Fog on the Essex marshes, fog on the Kentish heights.

Great Expectations

. . . those long reaches below Gravesend, between Kent and Essex, where the river is broad and solitary, where the water-side inhabitants are very few, and where lone public houses are scattered here and there . . .

Little Dorrit

It was a Sunday evening in London, gloomy close and stale . . . Melancholy streets in a penitential garb of soot, steeped the souls of the people who were condemned to look at them out of windows in dire despondency . . . Nothing to see but streets, streets, streets. Nothing to breathe but streets, streets, streets. Nothing to change the brooding mind or raise it up.

Figure 12.64 Dickens' use of weather and climate to re-create the East End atmosphere

Bibliography

References

Atmosphere, weather and climate by R. Barry and R. Chorley, Routledge, 1998.

Fundamentals of the Physical Environment by D. Briggs et al., Routledge, 1997.

Responding to the El Niño Southern Oscillation, by M. Golnaragh, and R. Kaul, *Environment*, 37, 1, 16–20, 38–44, 1995.

Climate Now by J. Gribbin, *New Scientist Inside Science* 44, 1991.

The Global Climate by J. Houghton (ed.), CUP, 1984.

Climates of the British Isles by M. Hulme and E. Barrow, Routledge, 1997.

Climate, history and the modern world by H. Lamb, Methuen, 1982.

Climates and Weather Explained by E. Linacre and B. Geerts, Routledge, 1997.

Atmospheric Effects of the Mount Pinatubo Eruption by M. P. McCormick et al, *Nature*, 1995, 373, 399–404.

Britain's changing environment by G. E. Nagle, Nelson, 1999.

The environment: principles and applications by C. Park, Routledge, 1997.

Questions

1 Study Figure 12.63 which shows seasonal variations in deaths in London and in a rural part of South Africa.
   (a) Describe the seasonal pattern of respiratory illnesses in London.
   (b) Describe seasonal variations in bowel (gastro-enteritis) complaints for London.
   (c) Describe the seasonal pattern of burns in South Africa. Suggest reasons for the patterns you have outlined above.
2 Using the extracts from Dickens (Figure 12.64), describe the image of the East Thames Corridor. How does Dickens use weather and climate to create an image?

13 ecosystems: processes *and systems*

The nature of ecosystems: structure and functioning

The structure of an ecosystem

Some ecosystems have distinct boundaries such as a pond or a tree trunk, whereas others do not, such as a desert. The zone where one ecosystem merges into another is called an **ecotone**. All ecosystems are open systems due to the flow of energy (sunlight) and matter (organisms, abiotic elements) across the ecosystem boundary (Figure 13.1). In addition, there are a number of basic components in all ecosystems. These include:

- **abiotic elements (the non-living environment)** such as water, nutrients and the atmosphere
- **biotic elements (the living environment)** such as **producers** or **autotrophs,** green plants that use energy, water and CO_2 to produce carbohydrates through photosynthesis
- **consumers** or **heterotrophs** that obtain their food by eating other plants or animals
- **decomposers** such as bacteria and fungi.

For example, in a small pond the abiotic elements include water, O, CO_2 and minerals. The autotrophs include minute phytoplankton, large rooted plants and floating plants, while the heterotrophs include zooplankton, which feed on phytoplankton, larger herbivores such as fish and ducks, carnivores such as game fish, and detritivores which live on the pond bed.

The **trophic structure** of an ecosystem refers to the organisation and pattern of feeding in an ecosystem. The **food chain** is the sequence of consumer levels. Normally they are depicted as linear sequences although in reality they are quite complex (Figure 13.2). There are two main types of food chain:

- **grazing in which plants are eaten live by herbivores**
- **detrital in which plants are eaten as dead material by detritivores.**

These vary in terms of importance. For example, in the ocean the grazing chain is especially important, whereas in a forest the detrital is more important.

Figure 13.1 Shotover – a managed deciduous woodland

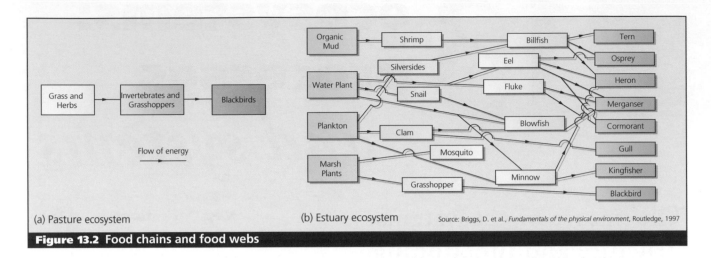

(a) Pasture ecosystem

(b) Estuary ecosystem

Source: Briggs, D. et al., *Fundamentals of the physical environment*, Routledge, 1997

Figure 13.2 Food chains and food webs

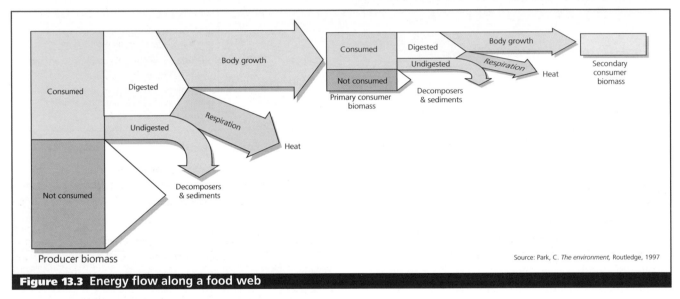

Source: Park, C. *The environment*, Routledge, 1997

Figure 13.3 Energy flow along a food web

In reality some animals, such as otters and foxes, will eat both animals and plants, live as well as decayed matter, and therefore cannot be put into one category. Therefore food webs are found rather than food chains. **Food webs** are very complex. Organisms which feed at the same level on the food chain are said to be at the same **trophic level**.

Energy flow and biomass

Sunlight energy fixed by green plants is passed through the ecosystem from one trophic level to the next. According to the First Law of Thermodynamics, energy cannot be created or destroyed, it can only be transformed from one sort to another such as from light to food energy. The Second Law states that no transfer of energy is 100 per cent efficient (Figure 13.3).

Just as energy is passed through the system it is stored at various layers. The storage of energy – the amount of the living matter present – is referred to as **biomass** or standing crop and is measured in terms of dry weight or ash weight or calorific value per unit area. The biomass at each trophic level

is an indication of the pattern of energy flow throughout the system. Biomass decreases at each trophic layer producing a trophic pyramid. The characteristic pyramidal shape of the trophic system is due to:

- **the large losses of energy between trophic levels**
- **large losses within each trophic layer, such as losses due to respiration and mobility.**

Productivity

Productivity refers to the rate of production of organic matter. There are two main types

- **primary productivity** at the autotroph level
- **secondary productivity** at the heterotroph level.

In addition, productivity can be divided into:

- **gross productivity** – the total amount of organic matter produced
- **net productivity** – the amount left after respiration.

Primary and gross productivity depend on light intensity and duration, and the efficiency of photosynthesis. The potential for gross primary productivity varies globally and is greatest at the Equator (Figure 13.4). By contrast, the efficiency of photosynthesis depends on many factors such as temperature, age of plants and nutrient availability.

Net primary productivity (NPP) depends on the rates of photosynthesis (producing carbohydrates) and respiration (using up carbohydrates). Of all light energy reaching the vegetation surface, only between 1 and 5 per cent (just enough to maintain life) is trapped as food energy. Natural systems are more productive than artificial ones.

Secondary production depends on conversion of plant substances to animal ones. The **ecological efficiency** is the efficiency of transfer of energy from one trophic level to another. For example, the transfer of energy from autotrophs to heterotrophs is only around 10 per cent efficient.

Nutrient cycles

The flow of energy is one-way (light energy to heat energy, stored and then lost) whereas nutrients are circulated and re-used frequently. The efficiency of nutrient cycling varies between ecosystems (Figure 13.5). All natural elements are capable of being absorbed by plants, as gases or soluble salts. Only oxygen, carbon, hydrogen and nitrogen are needed in large quantities (**macronutrients**). All others are **trace elements** or **micronutrients** needed only in small doses such as magnesium, sulphur, phosphorus. Nutrients are taken in by plants and built into new organic matter. When animals eat the plants they take up the nutrients, and eventually return them to the soil when they die and the carcass is broken down by the decomposers.

Nutrient cycles consist of a **reservoir pool** (large, slow-moving, non-biological components) and an **exchange pool** (smaller, more active components where nutrients are exchanged between biotic and abiotic elements). All nutrient cycles involve interaction between soil and the atmosphere and involve many food chains. Nevertheless, there is great variety between the cycles. Generally, gaseous cycles are more complete than sedimentary ones as the latter are more susceptible to disruption, especially by human interference.

Phosphorus cycle

The phosphorus cycle is an easily disrupted sedimentary cycle (Figure 13.6). Phosphorus is relatively rare but essential for growth. The exchange pool is the cycling between organisms, soil and shallow marine sediments, passed on via food chains and webs. It is returned by decomposition (either in the soil or in runoff to the sea). If it goes to the sea it is incorporated into marine sediments and lost from the exchange pool – except where upwelling currents may allow phosphorus to be

incorporated into marine food chains and to be returned to the land in the form of guano. This, however, is very localised, such as in Peru where it accounts for about 3 per cent of that which is lost from the land.

The depletion of phosphorus from the land is compensated for by the release of the element from phosphate rocks in the reservoir pool, by erosion and weathering. The reservoir pool is easily disrupted by the use of phosphate fertilisers in agriculture. Phosphate is taken from the rocks in the production of fertiliser, but rapidly lost from the exchange pool to marine deposits, because it is easily leached from the soil. This could lead to serious deficiencies in the future.

Nitrogen cycle

The nitrogen cycle is a gaseous cycle, and therefore easily disrupted. It is probably the most complete of all cycles (Figure 13.7). The atmosphere is the reservoir and the exchange pool operates between organisms and the soil. Nitrates are absorbed by plants and passed through the food chain. Ultimately, it is released as ammonia when organic matter is decomposed. Bacterial action changes ammonia to nitrates. These are either:

- **absorbed by plants, or**
- **lost from the exchange pool by leaching from the soils to shallow marine sediments or denitrifying bacteria breaking them down and releasing nitrogen into the atmosphere.**

Atmospheric nitrogen cannot be used directly by most plants. Thus it needs to be in the form of chemical nitrates first. The conversion of gaseous nitrogen to nitrates occurs by:

- **electrical action during thunderstorms, or**
- **conversion by electrical-fixing organisms (bacteria, algae and fungi) operating with leguminous plants. These are extremely important for maintaining soil fertility.**

Succession

Succession refers to the spatial and temporal changes in plant communities as they move towards a seral climax (Figure 12.8). Each **sere** or stage is an association or group of species, which alters the micro-environment and allows another group of species to dominate (Figure 13.10). The **climax community** is the group of species that are at a dynamic equilibrium with the prevailing environmental conditions. In the UK, under natural conditions, this would be oak woodland. On a global scale, climate is the most important factor in determining large ecosystems or **biomes** such as tropical rainforest, and temperate woodland (Figure 13.9). In some areas, however, vegetation distribution may be

Figure 13.4 Primary biological productivity of main ecosystem types (from Whittaker 1975)

Ecosystem type	Area (10⁶ km²)	LAI* (m² m⁻²)	Net primary productivity per unit area (gm⁻² year⁻¹) Normal range	Mean	World net primary production 10⁹ t year⁻¹	Biomass or standing crop kg m⁻² Normal range	Mean	World biomass (10⁹ t)
Tropical rainforest	17.0	6–16.6	1000–3500	2200	37.4	6–80	45	765
Tropical seasonal forest	7.5	6–10	1000–2500	1600	12.0	6–60	35	260
Temperate evergreen forest	5.0	5–14	600–2500	1300	6.5	6–200	35	175
Temperate deciduous forest	7.0	3–12	600–2500	1200	8.4	6–60	30	210
Boreal forest	12.0	7–15	400–2000	800	9.6	6–40	20	240
Woodland and shrubland	8.5	4.2	250–1200	700	6.0	2–20	6	50
Savanna	15.0	1–5	200–2000	900	13.5	0.2–15	4	64
Temperate grassland	9.0	5–16	200–1500	600	5.4	0.2–5	1.6	14
Tundra and alpine	8.0	0.5–1.3	10–400	140	1.1	0.1–3	0.6	5
Desert and semi-desert scrub	18.0		10–250	90	1.6	0.1–4	0.7	13
Extreme desert rock, sand and ice	24.0		0–10	3	0.07	0–0.2	0.02	0.5
Cultivated land	14.0		100–3500	650	9.1	0.4–12	1	14
Swamp and marsh	2.0	11–23	800–3500	2000	4.0	3–50	15	30
Lake and stream	2.0		100–1500	250	0.5	0–0.1	0.02	0.05
Total continental	149			773	115		12.3	1837
Open ocean	332.0		2–400	125	41.5	0–0.005	0.003	1.0
Upwelling zones	0.4		400–1000	500	0.2	0.005–0.1	0.02	0.008
Continental shelf	26.6		200–600	360	9.6	0.001–0.04	0.01	0.27
Algal beds and reefs	0.6		500–4000	2500	1.6	0.04–4	2	1.2
Estuaries	1.4		200–3500	1500	2.1	0.01–6	1	1.4
Total marine	361			152	55.0		0.01	3.9
Full total	510			333	170		3.6	1841

Units: km² = square kilometres; g = grams dry weight; t = tonne

*LAI = Leaf area index

Source: J. Tivy, *Biogeography – a study of plants in the ecosphere*, Longman, 1993

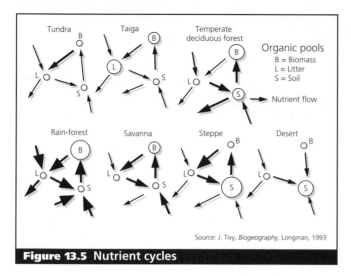

Source: J. Tivy, *Biogeography*, Longman, 1993

Figure 13.5 Nutrient cycles

determined by soils rather than by climate. This is known as **edaphic** control. For example, in savanna areas forests are found on clay soils, whereas grassland occupies sandy soils. On a local scale, within a climatic region, soils may affect plant groupings. The Isle of Purbeck illustrates this clearly (pages 443–4).

A **plagioclimax** refers to a plant community permanently influenced by human activity. It is prevented from reaching climatic climax by burning, grazing and so on. Britain's heathlands are a good example: deforestation, burning and grazing have replaced the original oak woodland.

Island biogeography

Islands are very important in biogeography. Their characteristics include:

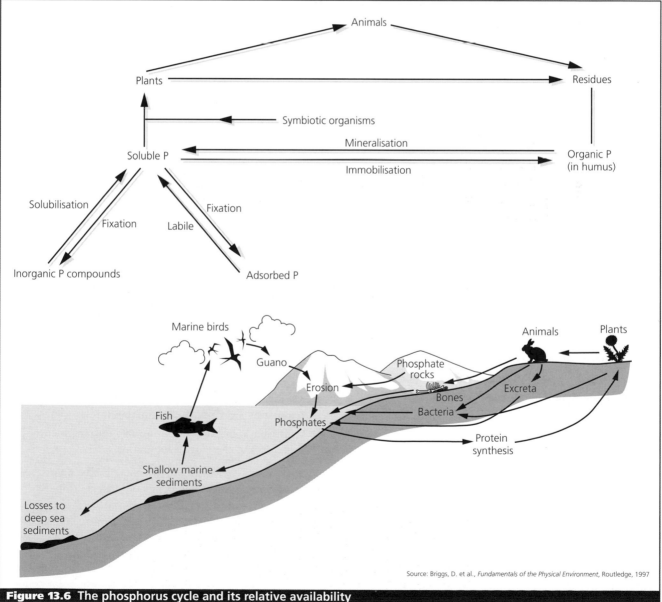

Source: Briggs, D. et al., *Fundamentals of the Physical Environment*, Routledge, 1997

Figure 13.6 The phosphorus cycle and its relative availability

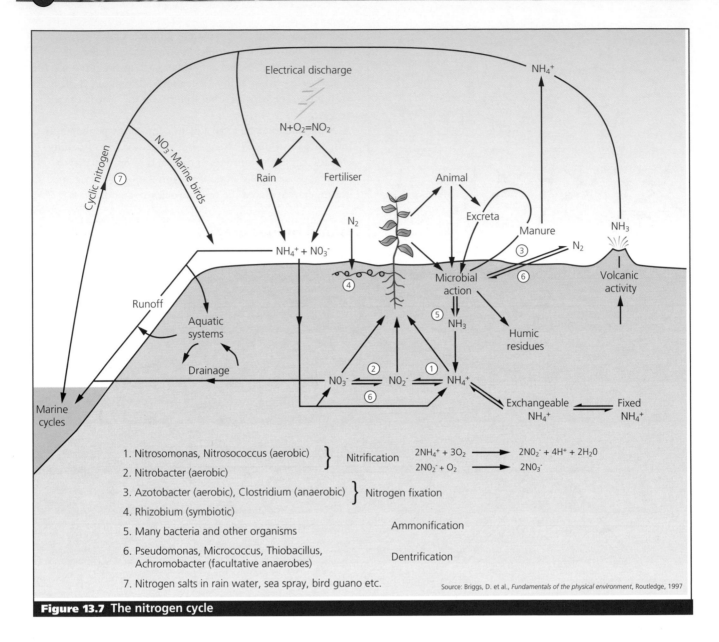

Figure 13.7 The nitrogen cycle

- a low species diversity compared to the continents
- decreasing diversity with distance from a continent
- larger islands contain more species
- islands are very susceptible to migrations, colonisation and extinctions
- human impact on island ecosystems is potentially great due to their fragile nature.

The theory of island biogeography suggests that the number of species on an island represents a balance or equilibrium between the process of immigration and extinction. The equilibrium number of species depends on the characteristics of the island, in particular its size, isolation from potential sources of colonists and the characteristics of the species themselves, in particular their dispersal abilities and population densities (Figure 13.11).

As habitats become fragmented they become more vulnerable:

- the reduction in total habitat area primarily affects population sizes and thus extinction rates
- redistribution of the remaining area into fragments affects dispersal and therefore immigration rates.

Temperate ecosystems are widely believed to be more resistant to the effects of habitat fragmentation than are tropical communities. Temperate species tend to occur in higher densities, are more widely distributed and have better dispersal powers than their tropical counterparts. However, it can be argued that one of the main reasons why habitat fragmentation is less severe in temperate areas is that most of the damage has already been done. Species whose extinction in Britain is related to the destruction of the original temperate

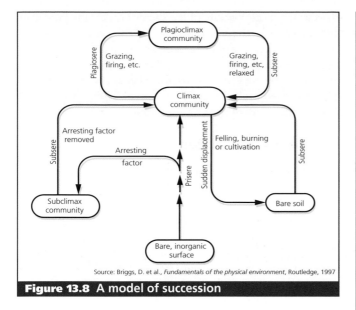

Source: Briggs, D. et al., *Fundamentals of the physical environment*, Routledge, 1997

Figure 13.8 A model of succession

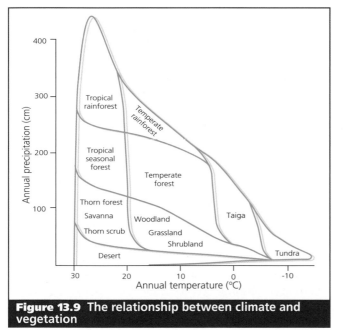

Figure 13.9 The relationship between climate and vegetation

Figure 13.10 Community changes through succession

Attribute	Early	Late
Organic matter	Small	Large
Nutrients	External	Internal
Nutrient cycles	Open	Closed
Role of detritus	Small	Large
Diversity	Low	High
Nutrient conservation	Poor	Good
Niches	Wide	Narrow
Size of organisms	Small	Large
Life-cycles	Simple	Complex
Growth form	r species	k species
Stability	Poor	Good

Source: Briggs, D. et al., *Fudamentals of the physical environment*, Routledge, 1997

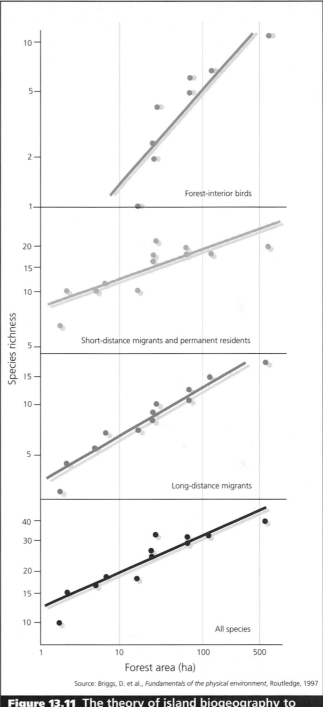

Source: Briggs, D. et al., *Fundamentals of the physical environment*, Routledge, 1997

Figure 13.11 The theory of island biogeography to explain species diversity

forest include the brown bear (extinct by the time of the Norman Conquest), the wild boar (18th century), wolf (18th century), goshawk (19th century) and capercaillie (18th century), although the last two species have now been reintroduced into new conifer plantations.

The species that survived the initial round of habitat fragmentation were the ones better able to withstand the human impact on the landscape. However, the problem is far from over. In Britain, the pressure on the land is so great that many of the semi-natural habitats which replace the original forest are themselves severely reduced and fragmented. Examples include lowland heaths, upland moors and calcareous grasslands.

Extinctions

The mechanisms of extinction include the size of the home range, the loss of habitat, heterogeneity, the effect of habitat surrounding, the number and size of fragments, and secondary extinctions. Even an apparently uniform habitat such as a forest or a grassland will contain many different habitats. Individual fragments may lack the full range of habitats found in the original block. Where habitats meet there may be increased predation by predators from one habitat into another. In addition there may be the transfer of parasites from one habitat to another and this may affect the survival of certain species.

The species most prone to current extinction are rare and local. Islands are particularly vulnerable. For example, since the European colonisation of the Pacific (1778), the Hawaiian Islands have lost 18 species of birds and 84 species of plants. Areas which face lots of extinctions are often characterised by large numbers of endemic species. For example, endemics constituted 90 per cent of Hawaiian plants, 100 per cent of Hawaiian land birds, about 70 per cent of Fynbos plants in South Africa, and 74 per cent in Australia.

Secondary extinction

A good example of secondary extinction is that of the large blue butterfly in Britain. To survive its larvae must develop within the nest of the red ant. The large blue butterfly almost became extinct when land development and reduced grazing by livestock eliminated the open areas it required. The remaining population vanished through a complex chain of events. An epidemic of myxamatosis in the mid-1950s reduced rabbit populations. As a result many of the sites became overgrown with scrub. The red ants were unable to survive in the overgrown areas and their decline meant the end of the large blue butterfly.

The colonisation of the Island of Surtsey

Surtsey (Iceland) was created in November 1963. It consists of lava, hardened ash (tephra), and sand and gravel beaches. It is a classic example of the colonisation of a new volcanic island. Surtsey shows clearly the processes and stages involved at the beginning of the succession. It involves different plant species creating conditions of greater protection, shelter and anchorage, where the next invading species can compete for the resources of light, water and nutrients better than the proceeding species.

Just six months after the eruption, bacteria, moulds and a single fly were collected from the island. Birds were seen flying above the island. A few parts of plants and plant seeds had been washed ashore. The spores of mosses (after 3 years), lichens (after 8 years) and ferns were transported by air. Groundsel and cotton grass also have very light seeds and were dispersed by air from Iceland. In addition nesting birds brought seeds in their excrement and on their bodies. The nests of these birds provide warm, fertile and sheltered areas for other organisms. Blue green algae are easily introduced and these are fed on by microzoa which are the pioneer consumers.

The environment is cool, rainy and windy, and the periodic drought on the island slows the succession process. As the tephra hardens, water retention increases and the potential for soil development increases. But if water cannot be held in the soil then plants will have great difficulty in establishing themselves. In the first stages of succession, there is high precipitation but little rain water accumulation.

The succession process occurs after dust and minerals are deposited on the newly developing soil. This enables successful colonisation. Mosses colonise the island. The mosses help with water retention and add organic matter to the soil. Pioneer lichens locate on higher ridges where it is drier. This helps to weather the lava further. The soil becomes deeper and higher plants invade.

In the most sheltered areas, a heath vegetation results with sedge, crowberry and low-growing willows. The natural climax vegetation of Iceland, birch woodland, will not be achieved on Surtsey because of the salt spray and the severe storms.

Most of the higher level species of fauna, namely herbivores and carnivores, are visitors, such as seals and gulls. At present there is insufficient biomass to fix the sun's energy to wholly support them. They rely on other sources off the island for much of their food. As in the case of most islands, the sea has a strong influence. Another excellent example of vegetation succession following a volcanic eruption is that of Krakatoa (Figure 13.12).

Figure 13.12 Primary succession on Krakatoa after the 1883 volcanic eruption

Year	Total number of plant species	Vegetation on the coast	Vegetation on lower slopes	Vegetation on upper slopes
1883		Volcanic eruption kills all life on the island		
1884		No life survives		
1886	26	9 species of flowering plant	Ferns and scattered flowering plants, blue green algae beneath them on the ash surface	
1897	64	Coastal woodland develops	Dense grasses	Dense grasses with shrubs interspersed
1908	115	Wider belt of woodland with more species, shrubs and coconut palms	Dense grasses up to 3 m high, woodland in the larger gullies	
1919			Scattered trees in grassland, single or in groups with shade species beneath. Thicket development in large gullies	
1928	214			
1934	271		Mixed woodland largely taken over from savanna	Woodland with smaller trees, fewer species taking over
early 1950s		Coastal woodland climax	Lowland rainforest climax	Submontane forest climax

Source: Park, C., *The environment*, Routledge, 1997

Vegetation and geology on the Isle of Purbeck

In some cases there is a very strong relationship between geology, soils and vegetation. For example, the Isle of Purbeck in southern Britain is a small area dominated by a mild, temperate climate. The climax vegetation should be oak woodland. Instead, there is a range of vegetation (and ecosystems) including heathlands, grasslands and forests, not to mention the coastal ecosystems.

The great variety of relief, drainage and geology on the Isle of Purbeck produces an equally varied range of habitats. Of Purbeck's 16 700 ha, about 75 per cent is under heath, woodlands and agriculture, while the rest is used for settlement, transport and industry. Human impact is apparent everywhere and the pressures of development are increasing annually.

Heathlands

Heath and moor are terms loosely applied to land covered in low evergreen shrubs. Moors, however, are treeless upland areas as in northern England, Scotland and Wales. There the decayed vegetation often forms a layer of acid peat. The term heath is usually applied to areas of sandy or gravelly soil, where instead of

the great depth of peat there is a thin layer of raw humus, sometimes only 2–3 cm deep. Much of the Purbeck heathland is found on podzolised sand and gravel soils with good drainage. Where clay occurs, the ground becomes waterlogged, especially in the valleys, and valley bogs develop. The term bog is often used to describe any waterlogged ground, but should strictly be applied to a wet acid peaty place where the principal plants are the bog mosses (sphagnum). These are well known for their capacity to hold large quantities of water.

Since 1960 only 400 ha of the original 30 000 ha of heathland in Dorset and Hampshire, west of the River Avon, still survive! There are many reasons for decline:

- agriculture 38%
- urban development 28%
- plantations 26%
- government uses 5%
- mineral works 2%
- golf courses 1%.

Thus there is little heathland left and that which remains is now designated as Sites of Special Scientific Interest (SSSI). These include Arne, and Studland and Harland moors. If it was not for human interference the heaths would have become forests, since pine trees and birches would colonise these areas if they were left to themselves.

Woodlands

Woodlands once covered 70 per cent of land in the British Isles, leaving all but mountain tops forested. Now this is only about 3 per cent. By contrast urban areas cover 16 per cent. In Purbeck wooded areas represent 12 per cent of the total area and consist of two main types:

- recent coniferous plantations on the acid soils
- natural deciduous copses and woods.

Geographically the two groups are separated by the limits of the chalk ridge that runs from Old Harry towards Warbarrow Bay.

The Forestry Commission started planting in 1924 but the Purbeck woodlands date from the 1950s. They are considered to be of poor quality with slow growth rates compared to other areas of Dorset. The policy of planting trees at 2-m intervals forces up young trees making plantations thick and impenetrable. They also cast a shade so dense that few plants other than fungi can survive between them. Land to the south of, and including, the chalk ridge has an alkaline soil on which deciduous woodland thrive. The most common management practice is that of coppicing – cutting a tree just above ground level and cropping the resulting growth at regular intervals. This produces shoots which are of roughly equal size. The shoots are then used as stakes for sheep hurdles, for fencing and for construction work in the quarries.

Woodlands are one of the richest environments to be found because of the amount of the vertical space they occupy. Trees are providers of shelter and protection for a host of different animal species and supply food for even larger numbers. There are now only a few areas, however, that support truly natural mature woodland.

Chalk and limestone downland

Downland describes all semi-natural grasslands occurring on soils derived from both chalk and limestone. Chalk downland in Purbeck is confined to the narrow ridge of hills running approximately westwards from Old Harry and Ballard Cliff on the north of Swanage Bay, through Corfe Castle to beyond Lulworth Cove and Durdle Door. In general the ridge exceeds 100 m rising to almost 200 m in places. The hills have a steep south-facing slope and unusually steep north-facing slope. Hence they form a hogsback rather than an escarpment. Farm machinery is limited to the flattened summit ridge. In addition, the soils on the slopes are too shallow and well drained to allow cultivation, whereas the soils on the ridge are frequently much deeper and more fertile. This reduces the pressure on the natural downland vegetation.

1 Figure 13.2 shows a simple food chain and a more complex food web. Explain why the food chain is vulnerable to disruption whereas the food web is more stable. Use information from the diagram to support your answer.

2 Figure 13.4 shows global variations in NPP.
Define NPP.
Identify the ecosystem with (a) the highest and (b) the lowest NNP/unit area.
Give reasons to explain why these two ecosystems should differ so much in terms of NPP/unit area.
Which ecosystem has the lowest mean biomass? Explain two contrasting reasons why the biomass is so low in this ecosystem.

3 Study Figure 13.8, a model of succession, and Figure 13.12, changes in species following the volcanic explosion of Krakatoa. Describe and explain the changes in vegetation succession on the island of Krakatoa.

4 What is meant by the term island biogeography? Explain why islands are fragile, and vulnerable to human activity.

Soil characteristics and processes

Soil is of crucial importance to human existence, as it is the growing medium for much of our food. Soils are also important geomorphologically as they are important for the flow and transfer of chemicals, water and energy in environmental systems. Most studies of soil have concentrated on form, but increasingly studies look at function and process. The interrelationship between form and process can be shown by the link between organic content of soils and nutrient cycling. For example, in rapidly cycling systems there is a relative lack of organic matter on the surface, but a larger concentration in the A horizon. By contrast, in cooler, wetter, less fertile conditions organic matter accumulates, producing organic acids which lead to the leaching of iron and aluminium, and the development of podzolic horizons.

Soil water

Soil water depends on a number of factors including texture, organic matter content and density (Figure 13.13). During winter, soil water increases and this is known as **field capacity**.

Figure 13.13 Storage capacity of soils (cm water/30 cm soil depth)

Soil texture	Field capacity	Wilting point	Available water
Sandy loam	5.6	2.8	2.8
Loam	8.4	4.3	4.1
Clay loam	9.9	5.3	4.6
Heavy clay	11.9	6.3	5.6

Source: Briggs, D. et al., *Fundamentals of the physical environment*, Routledge, 1997

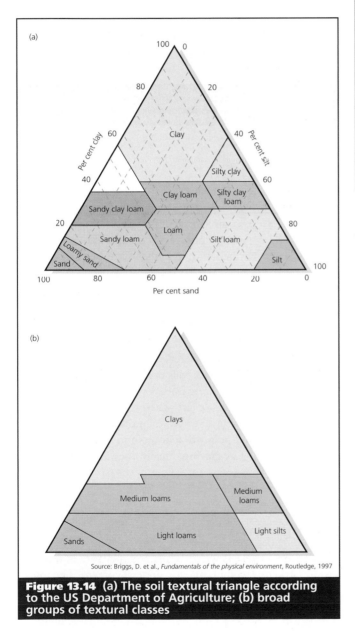

Source: Briggs, D. et al., *Fundamentals of the physical environment*, Routledge, 1997

Figure 13.14 (a) The soil textural triangle according to the US Department of Agriculture; (b) broad groups of textural classes

With free drainage, any excess water drains through the soil. Impeded drainage results in waterlogging. During spring, the loss of water by plant uptake and evaporation exceeds rainfall, and the soil begins to dry out. A **soil moisture deficit** (see page

Key Definitions

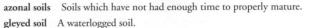

azonal soils Soils which have not had enough time to properly mature.

gleyed soil A waterlogged soil.

horizon A layer of soil which differs from other layers in terms of structure, texture, pH, colour.

humus Partially decomposed organic matter derived from the decay of dead plants and animals in soils.

intrazonal soils A classification stating that within a climatic zone soils vary with rock types.

parent material The rock and mineral regolith from which soil develops.

peat An unconsolidated deposit of plant remains with a carbon content of about 60 per cent.

regolith The irregular cover of loose rock debris that covers the earth.

rendzina A soil formed on chalk or limestone.

soil fertility The ability of a soil to provide the nutrients needed for plant growth.

soil horizons The distinguishable layers within a soil.

soil profile The succession of soil horizons between the surface and the underlying parent material.

zonal soils A classification which states that on a global scale soils are determined by climate.

450) develops which is measured as the amount of rainfall required to return the soil to field capacity.

Soil nutrients

Sources of the different nutrient elements and the rate of availability vary considerably. In the absence of fertilisers, nitrogen and sulphur are mainly derived from the breakdown of soil organic matter and inputs from acidic deposition. By contrast, elements such as phosphorus, potassium and calcium on the other hand are predominantly provided by the weathering of soil particles or parent material.

Soil structure

Soil texture refers to the size of soil particle (Figure 13.14) while soil structure refers to the shape of the particles (Figure 13.15). Silt soils are especially prone to compaction if ploughed when wet. In years of drought the shrinkage of some clays causes structural damage. Increasingly dry years may result in greater damage. Clayey soils are found predominantly in the south and east of England.

Soil fertility

Sources of the different nutrient elements and the rate of availability vary and involve complex interactions within the soil. In the absence of fertilisers nitrogen and sulphur are mainly derived from the breakdown of soil organic matter and inputs from acidic deposition.

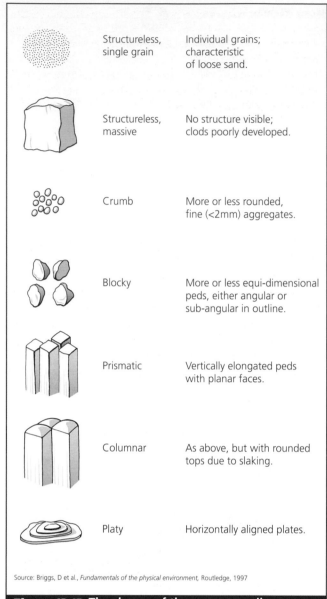

	Structureless, single grain	Individual grains; characteristic of loose sand.
	Structureless, massive	No structure visible; clods poorly developed.
	Crumb	More or less rounded, fine (<2mm) aggregates.
	Blocky	More or less equi-dimensional peds, either angular or sub-angular in outline.
	Prismatic	Vertically elongated peds with planar faces.
	Columnar	As above, but with rounded tops due to slaking.
	Platy	Horizontally aligned plates.

Source: Briggs, D et al., *Fundamentals of the physical environment*, Routledge, 1997

Figure 13.15 The shapes of the common soil structural units

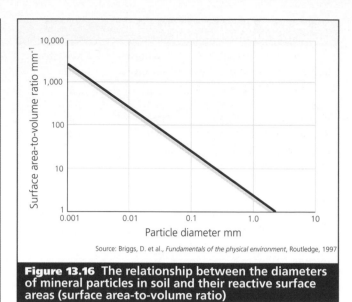

Source: Briggs, D. et al., *Fundamentals of the physical environment*, Routledge, 1997

Figure 13.16 The relationship between the diameters of mineral particles in soil and their reactive surface areas (surface area-to-volume ratio)

contrast, plants release hydrogen ions which tend to make the soil more acidic over time. Increasing acidity in soils is thought to be a contributory factor in forest decline in central Europe, although there is little clear evidence in the UK. Nutrients may be returned to the soil through litter decay, released through weathering or else added as fertilisers.

Soil colour

In some cases soil colour may reflect soil formation or parent material. For example, black soils indicate the presence of humus, and red soils indicate iron. A white crust in a semi-arid area indicates a saline crust, whereas in a humid environment, a white layer indicates heavy leaching. Grey-blue mottling (speckling) points to reduced iron compounds, poor drainage and therefore **gleying**. Finally, the C horizon, the lowest one, often takes on the colour of the parent rock, as it is largely weathered bedrock.

Soil horizons

Soil horizons are layers within a soil, and they vary in terms of texture, structure, colour, pH and mineral content. The top layer of vegetation is referred to as the Organic (*O*) horizon and consists of litter in various stages of decay. The mixed mineral-organic layer (*A* horizon) is generally a dark colour owing to the presence of organic matter. An *Ap* horizon is one that has been mixed by ploughing, *Ag* one that is waterlogged.

Leaching removes material from a horizon and makes the horizon lighter in colour. In a podzol, leaching is intense, and an ash-coloured *Ea* horizon is formed. By contrast, in a brown

Soft calcareous (lime-rich) rocks are generally quite fertile, as the rate of weathering is sufficient to make up for the loss of nutrients to plants or through leaching. These rocks, such as chalk, are often referred to as **base-rich** rocks. Some bases or nutrients are required in large doses. These are the **macro-nutrients** such as carbon and hydrogen and calcium (C, H and Ca). Others, by contrast, are only needed in small quantities. These are the **trace elements** such as iron, copper, magnesium and sodium (Fe, Cu, Mg and Na).

Clay and humus are the main areas of chemical exchange. Clay has a vast surface area in relation to its weight (Figure 13.16). Nutrients are recycled between the clay and the plants in a process known as **base exchange**. Bases are the positively charged ions, such as calcium, magnesium and potassium. By

O	Organic horizon
l	Undecomposed litter
f	partly decomposed (fermenting) litter
h	well-decomposed humus
A	Mixed mineral-organic horizon
h	humus
p	ploughed, as in a field or a garden
g	gleyed or waterlogged
E	Eluvial or leached horizon
a	strongly leached, ash-coloured horizon, as in a podzol
b	weakly bleached, light-brown horizon, as in a brown earth
B	Illuvial or deposited horizon
fe	iron deposited
t	clay deposited
h	humus deposited
C	Bedrock or parent material

Figure 13.17 Soil horizons

earth, leaching is less intense, and a light brown *Eb* horizon is found. The *B* horizon is the deposited or illuvial horizon, and contains material removed from the *E* horizon, such as iron (*fe*) humus (*h*) and clay (*t*).

At the base of the horizon is the parent material or bedrock. Sometimes labels are given to distinguish rock (*r*) from unconsolidated loose deposits (*u*).

Soil formation and development

Models of soil formation are simplifications (Figure 13.18). For example, many soil-formation models have suggested simple relationships between soil type and the soil-forming factors, especially climate (Figure 13.19) and bedrock (parent material). However, these are gross simplifications, since climate, for example, is not static but varies on a number of timescales (see pages 503–13). Similarly, the formation of deeply weathered tropical soils is often explained by their longevity (lack of Pleistocene disruptions such as glacial periods) as much as with

Key Definitions ③

calcification A concentration of calcium in the soil as a result of ineffective leaching, in areas of low rainfall.

cheluviation The removal of the iron and aluminium sesquioxides under the influence of chelating agents.

eluviation The removal of material down a soil through solution and suspension.

humification, **degradation** and **mineralisation** The process whereby organic matter is broken down and the nutrients are returned to the soil. The breakdown releases organic acids, chelating agents, which break down clay to silica and soluble iron and aluminium.

illuviation The redeposition of material in the lower horizons.

leaching The removal of soluble material in solution.

lessivage The removal in suspension of fine particles of clay.

podzolisation An intense form of leaching involving the removal of sesquioxides under acidic conditions.

salinisation The upward movement of soluble salts by capillary action, and their deposition in the surface horizons, forming a toxic crust.

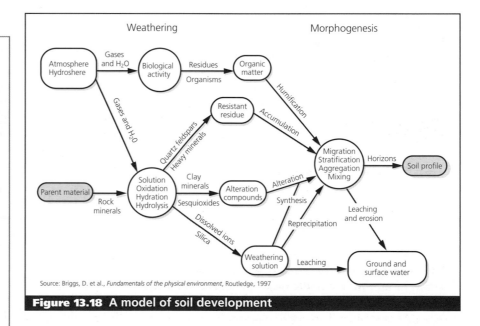

Source: Briggs, D. et al., *Fundamentals of the physical environment*, Routledge, 1997

Figure 13.18 A model of soil development

Figure 13.19 The relationship between soil type and climate regions in the British Isles

Climatic Region	Mean Annual Temperature °C	Mean Annual Rainfall (mm)	Soils
Warm/Dry	Greater than 8.3	Less than 1000	Leached brown soils
Cold/Dry	4.0–8.3	Less than 1000	Semi-podzols, podzols
Warm/Wet	Over 8.3	Over 1000	Acid brown soils
Cold/Wet	4.0–8.3	Over 1000	Peaty podzols, blanket peat
Very cold/Wet	Less than 4.0	Over 1000	Alpine humus soils

their current climate. By contrast, many UK soils have developed since the Pleistocene, and this is just as important as their location in the temperate climatic zone. True relationship between climate, soils and parent material can only exist if a state of equilibrium exists between the soils and climate. This is very rare in reality. For example, many of the soils in Britain are not yet fully adjusted to post-glacial conditions (the last 18 000 years). In addition, these soils have become increasingly modified by human activity, especially vegetation clearance which reduces the potency of the nutrient cycle and allows leaching to dominate. This favours podzolisation.

Factors affecting soil formation

There are many factors that affect soil development. These have been divided into:

■ **passive factors** such as soil material, topography and time, and

■ **active factors** such as climate and biological factors.

Soil classifications

The earliest classifications of soils were quite simple, such as Dokuchaev's division into zonal, intrazonal and azonal soils:

■ The **zonal** classification states that soils are determined by climatic factor. On a global scale a map of world climates (Figure 13.21) and a map of world soils bears a strong resemblance (Figure 13.22). Indeed, on a general scale this is the case, with brown earths in temperate climates, podzols in cool temperate climates and chernozems in continental climates.

■ The **intrazonal** classification states that within any climate belt soils vary with respect to local factors such as geology. Certainly this is the case with limestone and chalk which give rise to rendzina soils. A better example is the case of Purbeck where the geological sequence of limestone, clay, chalk, and fluvioglacial sands and gravels corresponds to rendzinas, brown earths or gleys, rendzinas and podzols respectively.

■ The **azonal** classification states that many soils are too young or immature and that there has not been sufficient time for them to develop the characteristics that would relate them to either bedrock or climate.

Other classifications are more complex, however. Figure 13.20 shows the Comprehensive Soil Classification System. The Northgate system, by contrast, is based on Australian soils, and divides soils into groups based on soil profile and textile, while the US Soil Survey's Seventh Approximation divides soils into ten groups which are then sub-divided into sub-orders and sub-groups. The Soil Survey of England and Wales designed in 1973 produces a series of regional accounts which describe the soils in particular parts of the country.

Figure 13.20 The Comprehensive Soil Classification System

Order	Main characteristics of typical soils
Alfisols	These soils develop in areas with 510–1270 mm of rain fall each year; most develop under forests; clay accumulates in the B horizon.
Andisols	These are volcanic soils, which are deep and have a light texture. They contain iron and aluminium compounds.
Aridisols	These are desert soils with little or no organic content but significant amounts of calcium. They are often affected by salinisation.
Entisols	These are soils with little or no horizon development, which are often found in recent flood plains, under recent volcanic ash and as wind-blown sand.
Histosols	These are organic soils, found in bogs, swamps and wetlands.
Inceptisols	These are young soils in which the horizons are starting to develop.
Mollisols	These soils form mainly under grassland. They are dark-coloured, with upper horizons rich in organic matter.
Oxisols	These are infertile, acidic, deeply weathered soils which contain clays of iron and aluminium oxides.
Spodosols	These are sandy soils which develop under forests, particularly coniferous forest. They are acidic and have accumulations of organic matter and iron and aluminium oxides in the B horizon.
Ultisols	These are acidic, deeply weathered tropical and subtropical soils with clay accumulations in the B horizon.
Vertisols	These are clay soils which expand when wet and crack when dry. They develop in climates with marked wet and dry seasons.

Source: Park, C., *The environment*, Routledge, 1997

Soils and climate

Climate influences soils in two main ways:

■ temperature affects the rate of chemical and biological reactions

■ precipitation effectiveness determines whether water moves up and down through the soil.

The rate of chemical weathering increases two to three times for every increase in temperature of 10°C. In cool climates bacterial action is relatively slow and a thick layer of decomposing vegetation often covers the ground. By contrast, in the humid tropics bacteria thrive and dead organic matter is broken down rapidly.

Precipitation effectiveness is the balance between precipitation and potential evapotranspiration. If precipitation exceeds potential evapotranspiration leaching occurs. Any soil

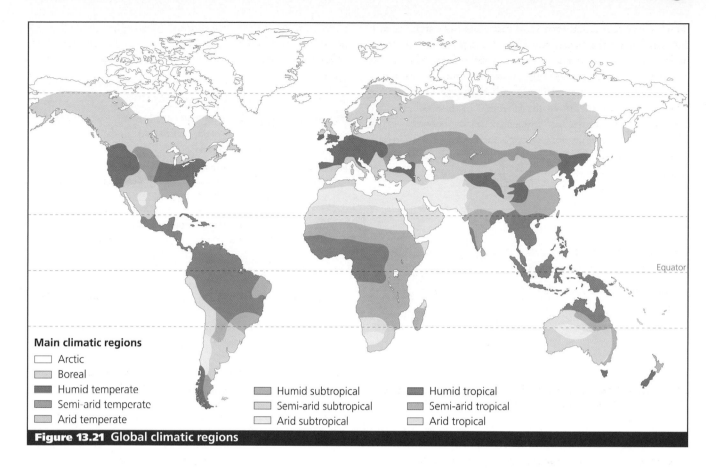

Main climatic regions

☐ Arctic
▨ Boreal
▨ Humid temperate
▨ Semi-arid temperate
▨ Arid temperate

▨ Humid subtropical
▨ Semi-arid subtropical
▨ Arid subtropical

▨ Humid tropical
▨ Semi-arid tropical
▨ Arid tropical

Figure 13.21 Global climatic regions

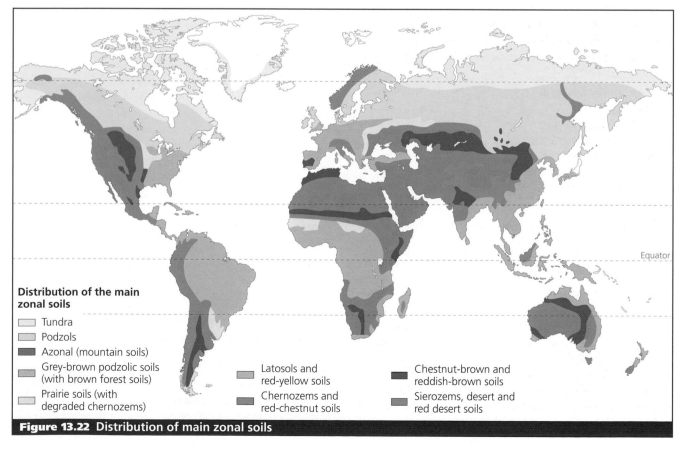

Distribution of the main zonal soils

▨ Tundra
▨ Podzols
▨ Azonal (mountain soils)
▨ Grey-brown podzolic soils (with brown forest soils)
▨ Prairie soils (with degraded chernozems)

▨ Latosols and red-yellow soils
▨ Chernozems and red-chestnut soils

▨ Chestnut-brown and reddish-brown soils
▨ Sierozems, desert and red desert soils

Figure 13.22 Distribution of main zonal soils

in which there is a net downward movement through the soil is known as a pedalfer. By contrast, if precipitation is less than potential evapotranspiration there is a soil water deficit. Water is drawn to the surface, bringing with it calcium carbonate. Such soils are known as pedocals and are typical of arid and semi-arid environments. In the USA east of the Rockies, pedalfers dominate the east whereas pedocals the west.

The soils of Britain are largely formed on deposits left by the last glacial period and have been through several climatic changes since then. It is probable many of them are not adjusted to post-glacial conditions. Soils in Britain have possibly gone through a number of stages following the post-glacial period:

- glacial deposits developed into immature skeletal soils, 10 000–5000 years before present (BP)
- during the early Flandarin period forest cover appeared, due to warmer and wetter conditions, and brown soils developed (5000–3000 BP)
- in the late Boreal and early Atlantic periods (2000–1500 BP) the brown soils developed in one of three directions:

  1 on coarse-textured materials podzolisation occurred;

  2 on fine-textured materials mature brown earth developed;

  3 some of the brown soils remained unchanged through to today.

Vegetation

Organic matter is a basic component of soil, although the influences of biotic factors range from microscopic creatures to man. Some influences may be visible, such as interception of precipitation by vegetation. Others are less visible, such as the release of humic acids by decaying vegetation. There is also a relationship between the type of vegetation and the type of soil (Figure 13.23). This is partly because certain types of vegetation require specific nutrients, such as grass in areas rich in calcium and magnesium.

Animals too have an effect on soils. In the top 30 cm of one hectare of soil there are on average twenty-five tonnes of soil organisms, that is ten tonnes of bacteria, ten tonnes of fungi, four tonnes of earthworms and one tonne of other soil organisms such as spring tails, mites, isopods, spiders, snails, mice etc. Earthworms alone can represent between 50–70 per cent of the total weight of animals in arable soils. In one hectare eighteen to forty tonnes of soil is ingested each day by earthworms and passed on to the surface – this represents a layer up to 5 mm deep. Man as an animal has obvious effects, ranging from liming, fertiliser application and mulching to mining, deforestation, agricultural practices and extraction for gardening purposes.

Topography

Soils can vary in their nature over quite small distances as any local soil survey will show. This reflects the range of climatic regions. However, on a very small scale, such as within a field, soils are largely affected by drainage and gradient, and position on a slope.

Slope angle is of great importance. Susceptibility to soil erosion increases with gradient. Steeper slopes are associated with thinner soils. Soils on hillsides tend to be better drained than those in valley bottoms which are subject to gleying.

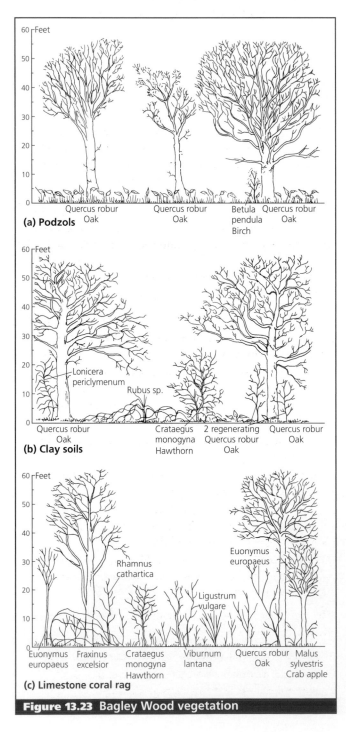

Figure 13.23 Bagley Wood vegetation

Aspect, the direction in which a slope faces, has an important bearing on soil formation as it affects the local climate or micro-climate.

The term *soil catena* refers to the sequence of different soils that varies with relief and drainage, though derived from the same bedrock (Figure 13.24). Such a sequence can be found when following a transect from a mountain or hill top to the valley bottom, reflecting changes in micro-climate, drainage and the position of the water table.

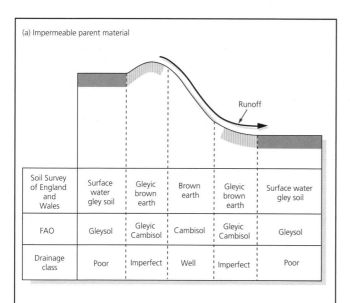

(a) Impermeable parent material

Runoff

Soil Survey of England and Wales	Surface water gley soil	Gleyic brown earth	Brown earth	Gleyic brown earth	Surface water gley soil
FAO	Gleysol	Gleyic Cambisol	Cambisol	Gleyic Cambisol	Gleysol
Drainage class	Poor	Imperfect	Well	Imperfect	Poor

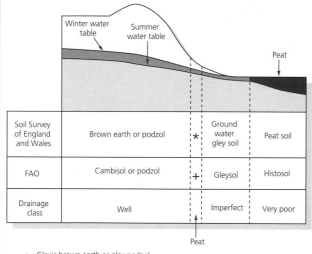

(b) Permeable parent material

Winter water table

Summer water table

Peat

Soil Survey of England and Wales	Brown earth or podzol	*	Ground water gley soil	Peat soil
FAO	Cambisol or podzol	+	Gleysol	Histosol
Drainage class	Well		Imperfect	Very poor

Peat

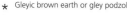

*   Gleyic brown earth or gley podzol

\+   Gleyic Cambisol or gleyic podzol

☐   Never waterlogged; unmottled

▨   Occasionally waterlogged; slight mottling

▧   Seasonally waterlogged; strong mottling

■   Permanently waterlogged; typically grey or blue-grey

Source: Briggs, D. et al., *Fundamentals of the physical environment*, Routledge, 1997

Figure 13.24 Effects of relief and hydrology on soils and drainage class

Time

Time is not a causative factor. It does not cause soils to change but allows processes to operate to a greater extent, therefore allowing soils to evolve. The amount of time required for soil formation varies from soil to soil. Coarse sandstones develop soils more quickly than granites or basalts and on glacial outwash a few hundred years may be enough for a soil to evolve. Phases of erosion and deposition keep some soils always in a state of evolution. Most mid-latitude soils are referred to as polycyclic, that is they undergo frequent changes as the major soil-forming processes change, in relation to changing inputs.

Soil-forming processes

Soils must be considered as open systems in a state of dynamic equilibrium, varying constantly as the factors and processes that influence them alter. All soils have processes in common but they vary in terms of the rates and types of processes. All soils show movement of water with soluble chemical elements, mixing of organic matter and so on. The weathering of bedrock gives the soil its C horizon, as well as its initial bases and nutrients (fertility), structure and texture (drainage).

The range of soil-forming processes is very large and includes:

- **chemical weathering** such as oxidation and reduction
- **physical weathering** such as hydration and freeze/thaw
- **leaching,** i.e. the downward movement of soluble chemical salts by water
- the **concentration of soluble salts** in the upper layers of the soil; this is the result of water being drawn through the soil by evaporation at the surface and the dissolved minerals in it being deposited
- the incorporation of decomposing organic matter from plants and animals
- the downward movement (translocation) of solid particles carried by water, especially clay
- gleying, i.e. the reduction of red or brown ferric compounds to blue or grey ferrous compounds and waterlogged anaerobic conditions
- biological disturbance of the soil by root penetration, the movement of soil animals, especially earthworms, and human cultivation.

The differences between soils are the results of differences in the relative importance of:

- the movement of water up or down through the soil
- the movement of soluble chemicals, e.g. iron or aluminium, up or down through the soil
- the mixing of organic matter in the soil.

Podzolisation

Podzolisation is a process widespread on acidic soils. Due to differential solubility, a situation develops in which the upper horizons of the soil become rich in silica, taking a characteristic ash-grey colour. Lower illuvial horizons become rich in sesquioxides, especially iron and aluminium. This may even cause an iron pan, a thin tough horizon of iron oxides. The cause of this translocation is the leaching of certain humic acids, called chelating agents. These are richest in heath plants and coniferous vegetation, and least frequent among grasses and deciduous vegetation growing in base rich conditions. Podzols are thus generally associated with coniferous or heathland vegetation.

Chelation is the process whereby the metallic cations (positively charged ions of iron, calcium, aluminium and sodium for example) in the thin layer of water that surrounds each soil particle are prevented from reacting with other soil constituents and are therefore free to be taken into solution by soil water. Water percolating downwards through the soil can therefore leach these minerals and deposit them elsewhere in the soil profile (Figure 13.25). The typical profile of a podzolised soil has a thick dark layer of organic matter, the pale grey leached or eluviated horizon in which the minerals have been removed, and layers, often coloured, where the minerals have been deposited in an illuviated horizon.

One fundamental distinction is between lateritic and podzolic weathering. In podzolic weathering organic acids mobilise iron and aluminium. These are leached from the upper horizons. The iron is redeposited further down the horizon due to changes in pH level, decay of organic substances and saturation of the organic acids with metal cations. By contrast, under tropical conditions the lack of these chelatory organic acids results in a lack of mobilisation of iron and aluminium. Silica is therefore more mobile giving rise to lateritic soils where iron is left as a residue towards the surface of the soil, giving a characteristic red soil.

Latosolisation

Latosolisation is the tropical equivalent of podzolisation. However, it produces very different results. Under sustained warm, wet conditions bacterial activity decomposes vegetation so quickly that chelation is rare. For example, in tropical forests in Costa Rica dead leaves decay with a half-life of 218 days in the dry season compared with only 32 days in the wet season. Chelation does not take place to such a great extent therefore, since the soil water is not acidic. In the relative absence of these humic acids, iron remain insoluble and so accumulates in the soil as red clays (hence they are sometimes known as tropical red soils) while silica (SiO_2) is washed down through leaching. Laterite is a hard layer within a tropical soil and is related to groundwater movement within the soil. This concentrates iron and aluminium oxides into a layer just above the water table.

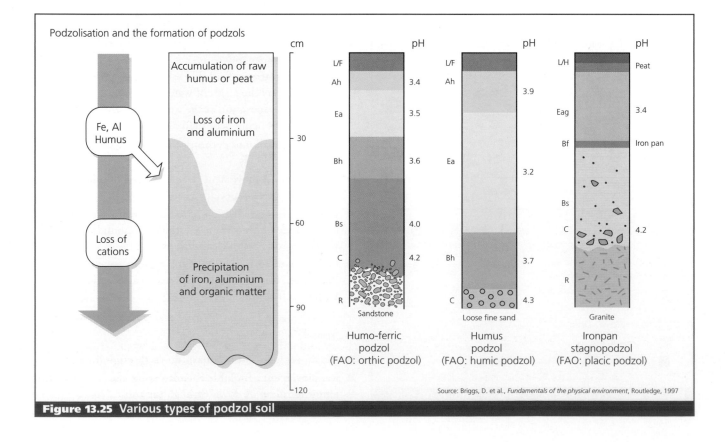

Podzolisation and the formation of podzols

Source: Briggs, D. et al., *Fundamentals of the physical environment*, Routledge, 1997

Figure 13.25 Various types of podzol soil

Calcification and salinisation

In arid and semi-arid environments potential evapotranspiration exceeds precipitation so the movement of soil solution is upwards through the soil (Figure 12.26). Calcium carbonates and other solutes remain in the soil as leaching is ineffective. This process is known as calcification. In grasslands, calcification is enhanced because grasses require calcium, draw it up from the lower layers and return it to the upper layers when they die down.

In extreme cases where potential evapotranspiration is intense, sodium or calcium may form a crust on the surface. This may be toxic to plant growth. Excessive sodium concentrations may occur due to capillary rise of water from a water table that is saline and close to the surface. Such a process is known as salinisation or alkalisation.

Organic changes

Plant litter is decomposed (humified) into a dark amorphous mass. It is also degraded gradually by fungi, algae, small insects, bacteria and worms. Under very wet conditions humification forms peat. Over a long timescale humus decomposes due to mineralisation, which releases nitrogenous compounds. Degradation, humification and mineralisation are not separable processes and always accompany each other. At the other end of the scale, human activity seriously alters soils.

Gleying

Gleying means waterlogged. Wet or waterlogged areas produce anaerobic (oxygen deficient) conditions, which favour the growth of specialised bacteria. These bacteria reduce ferric iron to the soluble ferrous (the process is known simply as reduction). Gley soils are characterised by a thick compact layer of sticky, structureless clay (Figure 13.27). Blue-grey blotches indicate the presence of reduced iron (red or brown suggests oxidised iron and is associated with periodic drying out of the soil). Gley soils are generally found within the water table or in areas of poor drainage.

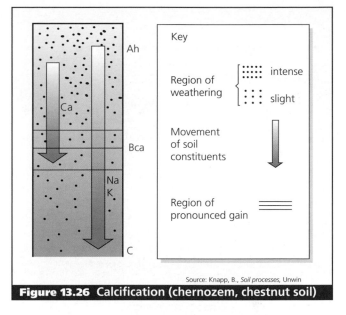

Source: Knapp, B., *Soil processes*, Unwin

Figure 13.26 Calcification (chernozem, chestnut soil)

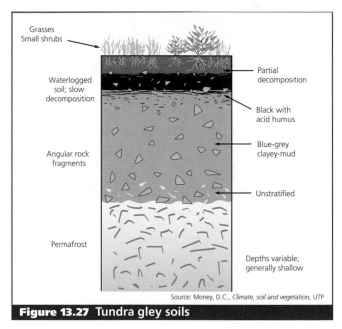

Source: Money, D.C., *Climate, soil and vegetation*, UTP

Figure 13.27 Tundra gley soils

Soil management

The main threats to soils include:

- soil erosion
- accumulation of pollutants
- organic matter loss and deteriorating soil structure and associated problems
- nitrate and phosphates in water resources
- organic contaminants in water resources
- acidification

- increasing urban areas, motorways and road building, and industrial development.

Soil erosion

The formation of 2.5 cm of soil may take anything up to 2500 years. A major difficulty in considering soil erosion has been measuring the rate at which it is occurring. About a third of arable land in England and Wales (20 500 sq km) has been identified as being at risk from wind or water erosion.

Research into the nature of erosion in one field at Albourne Farm, 10 km north west of Brighton, concluded that soil erosion was largely the result of farm management rather than

Soils and physical geography

Soils and hydrology

Soils to help to regulate the flow of water to bedrock and to streams. The movement of water in soils is complex. In well-structured soils water may flow down cracks and root channels. This may be an important contribution to rapid flow in the initial stages of storm hydrograph. Rapid throughflow may cause high discharge peaks similar to those which can be provided by overland flow. Such flow can also be important in the rapid transfer of nitrate fertiliser. Such bypassing is sometimes called **preferential flow** and when it flows down large pores it is termed **macropore flow**.

Soils and geomorphology

Soil acidity and water content have a major influence on the weathering of bedrock. More deeply weathered soils are found on older land surfaces whereas poorly developed profiles are found on younger surfaces, such as the soils of the New Forest area of Hampshire.

Water flow tends to increase downslope as water accumulates from upslope positions (Hortonian flow – see pages 247–50). Therefore, the transport of weathering products increase downslope. However, water increasingly becomes chemically saturated downslope as weathering products are removed. Hence the location of the greatest solutional erosion is downslope of the slope crest, where acidity combines with a degree of water movement but before chemical saturation occurs.

Soils and biogeography

The soil plant linkage is vital for the cycling of nutrients and energy. Most contemporary vegetation has been managed as a result of human activity. For example, upland grasslands, with podzolic soils are the result of deforestation in neolithic and historical times. If trees were present they would improve cycling and the flow of nutrients in the soil plant system.

Soils and agriculture

There is considerable concern about the loss of fertiliser nitrate from soils to drainage water. This represents a loss to the farmer as well as an increase in nitrate levels in groundwater and surface water. The nitrate increases the productivity of plants in the water systems. This is especially so when combined with phosphate derived from soils (by erosion) or from domestic sources (in sewage). This could lead to algal blooms whereby algae cover a water surface blocking off light to the lower parts of the water and leading to a loss of plant life at depth. Also, higher rates of nitrate can cause problems to human health, in particular the blue baby syndrome and stomach cancer. Nitrate is a greater problem than phosphate because it is more mobile in soil water. Up to a third of nitrates in fertilisers may be lost from the soil by leaching.

---

purely physical factors. The area studied was Grade 2 farmland with a fine loamy soil, brown earth. The field is over 330 metres long, with a gradient of 2.7° and a small stream at the base.

In 1979 the field was planted with strawberries, and within a year extensive erosion had occurred. Loss of soil occurred over the whole field, and the furrows between ridges of strawberries had been filled in. Channels had developed at the head of the field, and at the bottom of the field the crop had been buried by deposits up to 10 centimetres deep.

A number of factors increased the risk of erosion:

- **field size:** prior to 1962 this area had consisted of five fields, but by 1978 it was only one; the length of unbroken slope increased, therefore, from 90 metres to 335 metres

- **type of crop** meant that large areas and channels of soil were left exposed throughout the winter

- the land was worked **downslope** rather than around the contours

- the soils were highly **susceptible to erosion**, having a low clay and silt content (2–3 per cent), and with a tendency to form a crust or cap

- the farm manager suggested that a prime cause was the large number of **autumn storms** in 1979 – however, although August and December were particularly wet, the frequency of intense rainfall events (days with more than 7.7 millimetres) was below average.

The rates of erosion recorded at Albourne Farm were among the highest recorded in the United Kingdom (Figure 13.28). Over 200 m^{-3} of soil were removed from just 166 ha between July 1979 and March 1980. The surface lowering was about 12 millimetres with an annual removal rate of 241 tonnes per ha.

Methods of combating soil erosion include simple terraces, brushwood holding fences and gabions (stone-filled wire cages), and, probably the most effective, good land use management. This includes non-cultivation of steeper and more vulnerable slopes. In some areas, socially sensible plans are often those which involve low technology, easily maintained structures installed with little cost and with little political upheaval.

Nitrates in the soil

Nitrogen promotes leaf growth and nitrogen-based fertilisers are used by farmers to increase yields of arable crops. Their use has expanded enormously since World War II. Application of such fertiliser at an intensity of 100 kg per hectare can increase the farmer's income per ha by up to 50 per cent. There are three main types of fertiliser in use:

- ammonium nitrate ($NH_4 NO_3$)
- NPK fertilisers which are compounds of nitrogen (N), phosphorus (P) and potassium (K)
- nitrochalk $(Ca)(NO_3)$ and urea $(CO(NH_2)_2)$.

In the last 50 years inorganic fertiliser applications have increased by between 5 and 10 times to improve agricultural crop yields, and the area of grassland converted to arable use has increased. The risk of leaching of nitrate and pesticides into aquifers is greatest on shallow or sandy soils particularly where they overlie permeable substrates such as limestone and sandstone.

Pesticides and soil

The use of pesticides including insecticide, herbicide and fungicide is widespread and may increase yields by up to 100 per cent on arable farms. However there are a number of problems:

- destruction of non-targeted organisms
- killing of higher order animals
- the impact on humans through the presence of pesticide residue in food.

The importance of pesticides to soil scientists rests with an understanding of their persistence in the soil, i.e. how long the pesticides remain in the soil to contribute to each of the harmful side-effects.

Figure 13.28 Rainfall and soil erosion on a monitored site in the eastern South Downs, England, 1982–1991

Year	Total rainfall, 1 Sep.–1 Mar. (mm)	Total soil loss (cubic metres)
1982–3	724	1816
1983–4	560	27
1984–5	580	182
1985–6	453	541
1986–7	503	211
1987–8	739	13529
1988–9	324	2
1989–90	621	940
1990–91	469	1527
1991–2	298	112

Organic farming and soil

Organic farming involves a variety of farming methods such as crop rotation, mixed farming and the use of natural fertilisers. Organic farming has a number of impacts on soil. In artificial fertilisers there is a high concentration of essential nutrients. For example, nitrogen constitutes 15 per cent by weight of a typical NPK fertiliser but only 2 per cent of farmyard manure. In addition, the nutrients are more easily accessible to plants than those bound into the organic matter of FYM (farmyard manure). This accounts for higher crop productivity in artificial leaf fertilised soils. However, the nutrients from FYM are more easily retained in the soil because they are bound into complex organic compounds. This means that over a long period of time soils that are organically farmed retain higher levels of nitrogen and extractable potassium than do non-organic systems and similar amount of phosphorus (Figure 13.29).

The regular addition of organic matter in organic farming systems results in high levels of organic matter. The organic matter provides food for soil organisms and binds the soil particles together, thereby providing a good structure for plant growth. In addition the high numbers of soil organisms in organically farmed soils mean that aeration and mixing of nutrients are more effective. Soil structure and stability are of great importance to farmers. Organic soils are much more resistant to the impact of the farm machinery and livestock. These soils resist compaction (which causes waterlogging) and also resist breakdown into fine particles which are much more susceptible to wind or water erosion. However, the lower productivity of organic farms means that product prices are between 20–100% higher for most normal food products. Research has shown that only 24% of consumers are prepared to pay an extra 10% for products to ensure that they buy organic foods.

Organic farming also has some negative side-effects:

- it requires more land to produce the same quantity of food and therefore may be harmful to the conservation of wildlife
- organic waste can be a major pollutant of streams and rivers, especially during storage prior to use, such as in slurry lagoons. Disposal of sewage sludge on land has proved a significant source of heavy metal contamination in some soils.

Figure 13.29 Nutrient retention in two contrasting farm systems

	Organic farm	Non-organic farm
Total Nitrogen	1179	1066
Total Phosphorus	598	600
Extractable Potassium	1.2	0.7

(All figures are in milligrams per kilogram)

Questions

1 Identify the following horizons: Eb; Bt; Cca; Bg.
2 What abbreviations would you give for (i) a deposited horizon containing humus, (ii) a strongly leached horizon, (iii) a waterlogged organic horizon?
3 Study Figure 13.22. Describe how soil types vary with climate.
4 Explain two ways in which geology influences soil formation.
5 What is a soil catena?
6 Define the following terms: leaching, podzolisation, calcification.
7 Study Figure 13.25. Describe the process of podzolisation. How and why does it differ from (i) latosolisation and (ii) calcification?

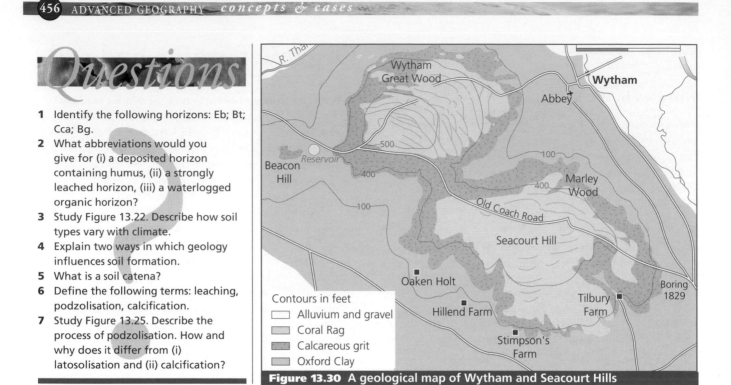

Figure 13.30 A geological map of Wytham and Seacourt Hills

Contours in feet
Alluvium and gravel
Coral Rag
Calcareous grit
Oxford Clay

Dynamic characteristics of ecosystems: deciduous woodlands and tropical rainforests – Wytham Woods

Wytham Woods, near Oxford, is one of the most intensively studied areas of woodland in the world. At least 500 scientific papers have been based largely or partly on findings or ideas generated by research there. Wytham has been monitored very closely for at least forty years and is one of eleven sites worldwide being used as an indicator of the effects of climatic change. The woods consist of 1000 acres of protected woodland located in a meander in the River Thames. It covers two low hills, formed of Jurassic Corallian limestone, which rise about 100 m above the river (Figure 13.30).

Enclosure Acts of the early nineteenth century led to large-scale planting of trees, especially beeches. Other areas were enclosed and gradually regenerated into woodland on their own. Today, however, the majority of the woodland is oak/ash forest with open areas of bracken. Nevertheless, in some areas large stands of sycamore are dominant, and there are a few areas where conifers dominate. The University Forestry Department extended the areas of woodland cover by planting up several areas of scrubland, mostly in the late 1940s and 1950s.

The main thrust of current management is to produce a closed canopy forest of native hardwoods, such as oak and beech, planting these in favour of the alien sycamore. At the same time, areas of grassland, small areas of conifer and areas where succession is occurring are being maintained to provide a wide range of habitats for teaching and research.

Soils and climate

The typical soil of the woodlands is the brown earth (Figure 13.31). These occur in warm temperate climate zones, such as the British Isles, where rainfall exceeds potential evapotranspiration, thereby allowing the downward movement of particles through the soil. Around Wytham, precipitation is about 750 mm, and potential evapotranspiration around 650 mm. Summer temperatures reach about 18°C, and winter temperatures 5–7°C. The main type of natural vegetation is temperate broad-leaved deciduous forest.

At the surface the annual shedding of leaves conserves nutrients and the humus that develops is a mildly acidic one called

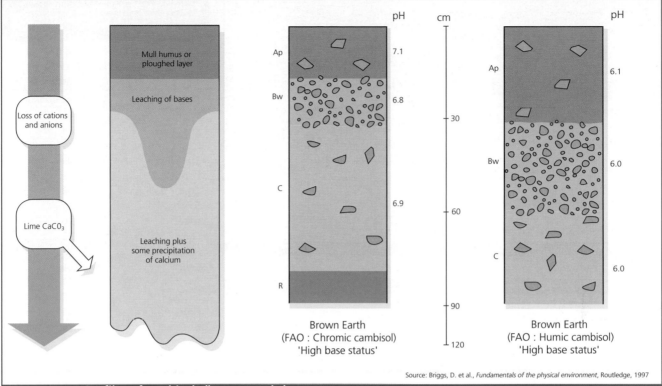

Source: Briggs, D. et al., *Fundamentals of the physical environment*, Routledge, 1997

Figure 13.31 Profiles of cambisols (brown earths)

mull, pH 5.5–6.5. The upper horizons are dark brown. The B horizon is light brown owing to the removal of clay and humus by eluviation, and iron and aluminium by leaching. This is not as marked as in the podzol and so the horizon is not as bleached. Instead it is light brown. Soil fauna flourish, consequently horizons are mixed. The soil is relatively fertile and may be up to 1 m thick.

The flora and fauna

Over 3800 species of animals have been recorded at Wytham. In addition, the flora is extensive and over 600 species of vascular plants have been identified. All five species of hairstreak butterflies are found; 34 species of butterfly and over 950 species of moths (450 macrolepidoptera, 500 microlepidoptera) have been recorded. On account of its very diverse ecology, Wytham has been designated a Site of Special Scientific Interest by the Nature Conservancy Council.

Predators and prey

There have been a number of long-term ecological studies in Wytham Wood. Many of these have examined the energy flow of the ecosystem (Figure 13.32) as well as productivity at successive trophic levels (Figure 13.33). One investigated the relationship between bank voles, wood mice and tawny owls. In years of high density of mice and voles, the owls breed well, most laying three (or even four) eggs. By contrast, when the rodents were scarce, the owls laid fewer eggs. In 1958, for example, when both mice

and voles fell to their lowest densities for 20 years, not a single one of the 31 pairs of owls in the wood attempted to breed.

Another study investigated the relationship between great tits, blue tits and caterpillars. It was thought that by taking many caterpillars the tits might reduce leaf damage and hence increase the growth rate of the trees. If so, increasing the density of tits, by putting up nesting boxes, might be beneficial to the forester. In years of high caterpillar numbers, a large individual oak tree might have half a million caterpillars. Each pair of tits, which has several oak trees in its territory, eat about 10 000 caterpillars during the whole of the nesting period, an insignificant proportion of the whole. Thus breeding success is markedly affected by the abundance of their food supply. However, neither the tits nor the owls had much effect on the numbers of their prey.

Another study of a predator and its prey carried out in Wytham was on the effect of sparrowhawks on the tit populations. The sparrowhawks hatch their young at about the time when the young tits are leaving the nest. The hawks feed heavily upon them. However, only those tits which have recently left the nest are easily caught by the hawks. Hawks which hatch their young later do not seem to be able to catch enough tits, nor can they find a good alternative prey.

Sparrowhawks became very rare in the late 1950s as a result of the widespread use of chemicals such as dieldrin and they ceased to breed in Wytham by 1960. However, after restrictions on the use of dieldrin, the sparrowhawks returned to the woods and some 6–8 pairs have been breeding in the wood since the mid-1970s.

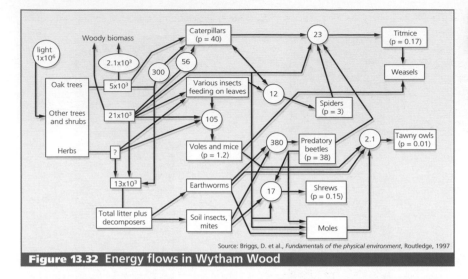

Figure 13.32 Energy flows in Wytham Wood

Figure 13.34 Insect species associated with common tree and shrub in Britain

Tree or shrub	Number of insect species
Oak	284
Willow	266
Birch	229
Hawthorn	149
Blackthorn	109
Poplar	97
Crab Apple	93
Scotch Pine	91
Alder	90
Elm	82
Hazel	73
Beech	64
Ash	41
Spruce	*37
Lime	31
Hornbeam	28
Rowan	28
Maple	26
Juniper	20
Larch	*17
Fir	*16
Sycamore	*15
Holly	7
Sweet Chestnut	*5
Horse Chestnut	*4
Yew	4
Walnut	*4
Holme Oak	*2
Plane	*1

* = introduced species

Figure 13.33 Productivity and energy values for Wytham Wood

Units	Ecological process		
	Biomass (kJ m^{-2})	Consumption (kJ m^{-2} year^{-1})	Primary and secondary production (kJ m^{-2} year^{-1})
All trees and shrubs			26×10^3
Oak trees	1×10^5		5×10^3
Total litter			13×10^3
Caterpillars	41	356	40
Predatory beetles	38	380	38
Spiders	0.5	12	3
Great and blue tits	0.02	23	0.17
Shrews	0.00075	17	0.15
Voles and mice	0.16	105	1.2
Tawny owls	0.01	2.1	0.01

Note: Where no values are given no information is available

Source: Briggs, D. et al., *Fundamentals of the physical environment*, Routledge, 1997

Change over time

During this century marked changes have occurred in Wytham resulting wholly from things that have happened outside the wood, such as the introduction of new species, new diseases and global warming. In the early part of the century, the introduced grey squirrel reached Wytham. These squirrels have a long-term effect on the wood as they strip the bark from the young beech trees. Few, if any, of the beeches planted in the 1950s survived their attacks. Along with the rest of southern Britain, Wytham lost all its elm trees during the 1970s from Dutch Elm disease. These were an important part of the surrounding hedgerows and field edges, and supported a wide range of insect species (Figure 13.34).

Another introduced mammal, the muntjak, appeared in Wytham in the 1970s and has since become quite common. The fallow deer has also become more abundant in recent years and, in places, the two species are having a noticeable effect on the

vegetation. In some years, such as 1998–9, the woods are closed to the public so that the herds of deer can be culled.

An introduced disease, *myxamatosis*, has also had a marked effect on Wytham as it has on many other areas. In the late 1950s it virtually wiped out the rabbit population and it took over thirty years before the rabbit population re-established itself. When the rabbits disappeared so too did the stoats, which are specialist rabbit predators. In addition much of the chalk grassland was colonised by invading birches that had formerly been kept in check by the rabbit. Much less expected was the predation of tit nests by weasels. This increased dramatically because either the weasels increased in the absence of stoats, or the weasels need baby rabbits while they themselves are breeding and, in the absence of rabbits, were forced to switch to hunting other prey, such as blue tits.

Global warming is also having an effect on the biogeography of Wytham Wood. For example, badgers have become thinner and the number of blue tits and butterflies had fallen by the mid-

1990s compared with earlier years. Scientists at Oxford University predict that by 2050 grasslands will become infested with weeds, common species of birds will become rarer and wetlands will dry up. Badgers have been badly hit in the one-thousand-acre wood. Cubs are unable to dig through the parched earth for worms and have been getting thinner than usual. Thin badgers are much less likely to survive to adulthood. The number of butterflies has fallen for several successive years. Species such as the speckled white

normally feed off ground vegetation but the dry soil has meant fewer plants. The dry weather has also hit birds. Caterpillars, the staple food of chicks have arrived too early in recent years and there has been a food shortage. The result is fewer blue tits and great tits. Streams and wetlands have also been drying up affecting the numbers of frogs, toads and water insects.

Soils and vegetation of the tropical rainforest

Equatorial soils

The soils of these areas are usually heavily leached and **ferralitic**, with accumulations of residual insoluble minerals containing iron, aluminium and manganese. The hot humid environment speeds up chemical weathering and decay of organic matter. This **biome** also covers ancient shield areas which have remained tectonically stable for a very long time and were unaffected by the Pleistocene glaciations. Not only are the soils well developed but they have been weathered for a long time and are therefore lacking in nutrients. Thus they are inherently infertile. More than 80 per cent of the soils have severe limitations of acidity, low nutrient status, shallowness or poor drainage. This is unusual given the richness of the vegetation that it supports. However the nutrients are mainly stored in the biomass due to the rapid leaching of nutrients from the A horizon. There is only a small store of nutrients in the litter or the soil itself (Figure 13.35).

The rate of litter fall is high – 11 t/ha/year, and there is humus turnover of 1 per cent a day. At 25–30°C the breakdown and supply of litter is roughly equal. The rapid rates of decomposition and the rapid leaching of nutrients from the rooting area has led to an unusual adaptation in this ecosystem. The main agents of decay are fungi in **mycorrhizal** relationships with the tree roots. Nutrients are passed directly from the litter to the trees by the fungi (living on the tree roots). This bypasses the soil storage stage when there is a strong chance that the nutrients will be lost from the nutrient cycle completely.

The rapid decay of litter gives a good plentiful of bases. Clay minerals break down rapidly and the silica element is carried into the lower layers. Iron and aluminium sesquioxides which are relatively insoluble remain in the upper layers, as they require acidic water to mobilise them. These leached red or red brown soils are termed **ferralitic** soils. Where it is wet the iron may be hydrated and yellow soils develop. Deep weathering is a feature of

these areas and the depth of the regolith may be up to 150 m deep. Where a parent material allows free drainage, and is poor in bases, such as a coarse sandstone, a tropical podzol will form.

These soils are not easy to manage. If they are ploughed severe soil erosion may occur. Vegetation interrupts the nutrient cycle. In the rainforest vegetation and soil are the major components in an almost closed nutrient cycle. The major store of plant nutrients is in the vegetation. The leaves and stems falling to the soil surface break down rapidly and nutrients are released during the processes of decomposition. These are almost immediately taken up by the plants. By contrast, the supply of nutrients from the underlying mineral soil is a small component. If the forest cover is removed, the bulk of the system's nutrient store is removed also. This leaves a well-weathered, heavily leached soil capable of supplying only low levels of nutrients.

Even when the forest is burnt the nutrients held in the plant biomass store are often lost. During burning there may be gaseous losses and afterwards rainfall may leach nutrients from the ash on the surface. In addition the soils have a low cation exchange capacity. Unless a plant cover is rapidly established, most of the

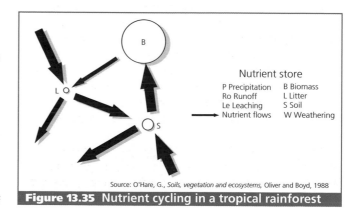

Nutrient store

P Precipitation   B Biomass
Ro Runoff   L Litter
Le Leaching   S Soil
→ Nutrient flows   W Weathering

Source: O'Hare, G., *Soils, vegetation and ecosystems*, Oliver and Boyd, 1988

Figure 13.35 Nutrient cycling in a tropical rainforest

nutrients released from the plant biomass during burning will be lost within a short time. Thus shifting cultivation can only take place for a few years before the overall fertility of the soil is reduced to such an extent that it is not worthwhile continuing cropping the plot. Indeed farmers try to replicate the rainforest environment by inter-cropping. This provides shelter for the soil and protects it from the direct attack of the intense rain (rain-splash erosion can otherwise be a serious problem). Compaction of the soil by heavy raindrops and the reduction of the infiltration capacity as a result will lead to overland flow and soil erosion even if there is only a slight slope.

Soils which are predominant in the region offer conditions only marginally suitable for most of these crops. They are often clayey textured, of low pH value, generally of less than medium fertility, and offering only restricted rooting depths.

Changes to rainforest soils

Tropical rainforests are disappearing at an alarming rate and 'green jungles' are being changed into 'red deserts'. The loss of rainforest is up to 200 000 km^{-2}/year. By AD 2000 it is possible that there will be no extensive tracts of primary tropical rainforest, but simply isolated refugia of a few tens or hundreds of square kilometres. The tropical rainforest is a unique natural resource with a tremendous diversity of flora and fauna, much of which has still to be scientifically identified and studied.

To those who live within or close to the rainforest, the forest is

a resource which they are eager to exploit. To many economically marginal households, the land presently occupied by forest is seen as a way of improving the quality of their life, and becoming self-sufficient in farming. Rainforests are areas of low population densities, and in some areas, relatively unexploited. However, in some cases new farmers have little experience of the tropical environment. Some are the urban poor, while others are farmers familiar with very different environments.

Figure 13.36 shows the incidence of different soil types in the tropics. Figure 13.37 contrasts a brown earth under deciduous woodland in southern England, such as Wytham Woods, with an **oxisol** (leached ferruginous soil) under tropical rainforest in Amazonas State, Brazil. The oxisol is deeper and more acidic

Figure 13.36 Distribution of main kinds of soil in the humid tropics

Soil type	Million ha
Acid, infertile soils	938
Moderately fertile, well-drained soils	223
Poorly drained soils	119
Very infertile sandy soils	104
Shallow soils	75
Total	1459

Source: Northcliff, S., 'The clearance of the tropical rainforest', *Teaching Geography*, April 1987, 110–13

Figure 13.37 A comparison of a brown earth soil under deciduous woodland in southern England and an oxisol under tropical rainforest in Amazonas, Brazil

Brown Earth Depth cm	% Organic Matter	% Sand	% Silt	% Clay	pH[1] (H₂0)	CEC[2] meq/ 100 g	BS[3] %
0–6	10.4	39	37	14	4.8	25	30
6–18	5.0	49	36	15	4.5	17	13
18–30	0.6	31	9	60	5.3	30	45
30–64	0.3	30	6	64	5.8	36	69
64–93	0.1	7	6	87	6.3	42	78
93–108	0.2	5	4	91	6.5	52	93

Oxisol Depth cm	% Organic Matter	% Sand	% Silt	% Clay	pH[1] (H₂0)	CEC[2] meq/ 100 g	BS[3] %
0–8	3.4	10	15	75	3.4	18	2
8–18	0.6	11	11	78	3.7	8	4
18–50	0.5	7	8	85	4.2	4	5
50–90	0.3	7	4	89	4.5	3	5
90–150	0.2	7	3	90	4.7	3	5
150–170	0.2	5	3	92	4.9	2	5

Notes:
1 pH determined in a 1 : 2.5 soil/water ratio
2 Cation exchange capacity expressed as milli-equivalents per 100 g of soil
3 Percentage base saturation (sum of base cations/CEC 100).

Source: Northcliff, S., 'The clearance of tropical rainforest', *Teaching Geography*, April 1987, 110–13

(lower pH) than the brown earth, but two other chemical properties are also very different. The oxisol first has a lower cation exchange capacity (CEC) and second a lower base saturation than the brown earth. The cation exchange capacity is a measure of the soil's capacity to absorb and exchange positively charged ions (cations) such as potassium, calcium, magnesium, hydrogen and aluminium. The base saturation measures the proportion of the exchangeable cations that are bases (i.e. not hydrogen and aluminium which are acidic). A low CEC and low base saturation mean that the soil has a poor reserve of nutrients readily available to plants and that it also has an undesirable balance between ions for plant growth. Thus it is infertile. In the Oxisol the only horizon with a substantial CEC is the surface horizon, due to the presence of organic matter. The brown earth has a much higher fertility than the oxisol.

Research near Manaus, Brazil, investigated changes in the soil's physical characteristics which resulted when rainforest was cleared, first using traditional slash and burn techniques and

Figure 13.38 Soil moisture content – comparisons between uncleared forest, burned and bulldozed sites, Amazonas, Brazil

Depth below final soil surface (cm)	Virgin forest % soil moisture	Burned content	Bulldozed
0–10	52.1	40.8	40.8
10–20	44.4	40.4	39.4
20–40	41.4	40.4	38.6

Source: Northcliff, S., 'The clearance of tropical rainforest', *Teaching Geography*, April 1987, 110–13

Figure 13.39 Crop response to forest clearance and different soil fertiliser applications, Vurimaguas, Peru

	Fertility level*	Slash and burn	Bulldozed	Bulldozed/ burned
		Yield tonnes per hectare		
Maize (grain yield)	0	0.1	0.0	0
	NPK	0.4	0.04	10
	NPKL	3.1	2.4	76
Soyabeans (grain yield)	0	0.7	0.2	24
	NPK	1.0	0.3	34
	NPKL	2.7	1.8	67
Cassava (fresh root yield)	0	15.4	6.4	42
	NPK	18.9	14.9	78
	NPKL	25.6	24.9	97

*Fertiliser applications
N – 50 kg nitrogen per hectare
P – 172 kg phosphorus per hectare
K – 40 kg potassium per hectare
L – 4 tonnes lime per hectare
Sites labelled 0 received none of the above fertiliser applications
Sites labelled NPK received applications of nitrogen, phosphorus and potassium
Sites labelled NPKL received all applications

second using a bulldozer. Several observations of soil characteristics were made, including changes in soil surface, dry bulk density, moisture content and infiltration rate.

On the site cleared by bulldozer the change in soil surface height ranged from 2–9 cm with an average of 5.7 cm. Thus much of the topsoil horizon was removed, leaving a denser subsurface horizon at or very close to the surface. The removal of the topsoil removes much of the soil organic matter, which is often the major store of plant nutrients within the soil.

There were increases in the soil dry bulk density resulting from the passage of heavy machinery over the surface, causing changes in infiltration rate (the rate at which water can enter the soil) from over 200 cm/hour under uncleared forest to 192 cm/hour at the slash and burn site to 39 cm/hour at the bulldozed site (Figure 13.38).

The moisture content of the 0–10 cm and 10–20 cm layers of both burned and bulldozed sites were similar, and were significantly lower than the uncleared forest site. These differences reflect the removal of the organic matter during clearance. The organic matter acts both as a store of moisture and as a natural mulch restricting moisture loss.

Crop yields were higher in burned plots (Figure 13.39) because of the nutrient content of the ash. The ash caused major changes in soil conditions. Soil acidity decreased and, compared with the bulldozed site, the organic matter was higher (although it was lower than that of the uncleared forest). The importance of ash to soil fertility and crop yield following clearance is substantial, especially in soils of low fertility.

Forest clearance in the tropics will continue in order to satisfy the demands of the growing population (see page 477). The priority therefore should be to slow down the rate of clearance. This can be done by making the most effective use of the cleared land and also by limiting the need for forest clearance to replace land cleared at an earlier stage. These aims can be achieved by:

■ increasing the productivity of land already cleared by selection of suitable crop and land management combinations;

■ minimising the damage which results from forest clearing methods by adopting methods of clearance and timing of clearance which produce the least detrimental effects;

■ restoring eroded or degraded land by the establishment of more appropriate land management systems.

Vegetation in tropical rainforests

There is also a wide variety of ecosystem types in the humid tropics (Figure 13.40). The tropical rainforest is the most diverse ecosystem or biome in the world, yet it is also the most fragile. This stems from the fact that conditions of temperature and humidity are so constant that species here specialise to a great extent. Their food sources are limited to only a few species. Thus when this biome is subjected to stress by human activity it often fails to return to its original state.

The net primary productivity (NPP) of this ecosystem is 2200 g/m²/yr. This means that the solar energy fixed by the green plants gives 2200 g of living matter per square metre every year. This compares to the NPP for savanna of 900 g/m²/yr, temperate deciduous forests of 1200 g/m²/yr and agricultural land of 650 g/m²/yr.

The hot, humid climate gives ideal conditions for plant growth and there are no real seasonal changes. Thus the plants are aseasonal and the trees shed their leaves throughout the year rather than in one season; the forest is turned evergreen as a result.

There is a great variety of plant species – in some parts of Brazil there are 300 tree species in an area of 2 km². The trees are taller and fast growing. The need for light means that only those trees that can grow rapidly and overshadow their competitors will succeed. Thus trees are notably tall and have long, thin trunks

with a crown of leaves at the top; they also have buttress roots to support their height.

There are broadly speaking three main layers of tiers of trees (Figure 13.41):

- **emergents** which extend up to 45–50 m
- a **closed canopy** 25–30 m high which cuts out most of the light from the rest of the vegetation and restricts their growth
- a limited **understorey** of trees, denser where the canopy is weaker; when the canopy is broken by trees falling, clearance or at rivers there is a much denser vegetation.

Trees are shallow rooted as they do not have problems getting water. Other layers include lianas and epiphytes, and the final

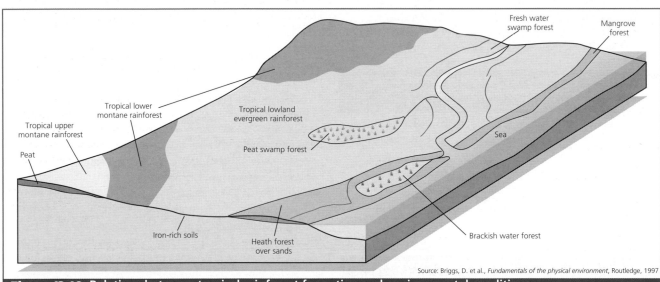

Source: Briggs, D. et al., *Fundamentals of the physical environment*, Routledge, 1997

Figure 13.40 **Relations between tropical rainforest formation and environmental conditions**

Nutrient cycling		Structure	Micro-habitat features
		Emergent species level	Exposed to full sunlight, wind and marked diurnal temperature change Animal life almost wholly birds and insects
		Canopy level cover almost continuous	Main habitat of forest animals
		Some 70 – 80% of incident light absorbed	Animals rarely descend to forest floor
		Many species bear fruit and flowers directly on trunk and branches	Most animals descend to forest floor for short periods
			Small diurnal changes, little wind, poor light, slow growth

Source: Briggs, D et al *Fundamentals of the Physical Environment*, Routledge 1997

Figure 13.41 **Vertical stratification of a tropical rainforest**

layer is an incomplete field layer limited by the lack of light. The floor of the rainforest is littered with decaying vegetation, rapidly decomposing in the hot, humid conditions. Tree species include the rubber tree, wild banana and cocoa; pollination is not normally by wind due to the species diversity, but by insects, birds and bats which have restricted food sources.

Rainforest supports a large number of epiphytes which are attached to the trees, many of these are adapted to a system on the small intake of nutrients. There are also parasites taking nutrients from the host plants as they may kill their hosts. Those flora living on dead material are called saprophytes, an important part of the decomposing unit. The fauna are as diverse as the flora.

Civil war and the Rwandan rainforest

In 1925 the Albert National Park, an area of lush tropical rainforest, was established by Belgian colonial authorities. In 1979 UNESCO declared the park, renamed Virunga National Park, as Africa's first national park heritage site, on account of its biodiversity. However, the park is being raped of its ecological treasures. Virunga has been plagued by problems for decades:

■ political and economic breakdown in Zaire has starved the park of funds

■ in the 1960s much of the big game was killed by poachers, rebels and government soldiers during the Civil War in the Congo

■ tourism in the park no longer exists, thereby reducing the park's revenue

■ poaching has halved the number of hippopotamus and buffalo in the area

■ villagers in the park have depleted the forest and over-fished the lake

■ the crisis in Rwanda has intensified pressures on the land.

The park is being looted by Rwandan refugees and Hutu soldiers from around the town of Goma in eastern Zaire. Up to 300 km² of forest was destroyed in under six months in 1994. Nearly 900 000 refugees live within or near Virunga and up to 40 000 enter the park daily removing about 800 tonnes of forest products, notably for food and fuel. Soldiers, too, are cutting wood to sell to the refugees. The rivers are being polluted by human and animal waste, medical products and the risk of disease transmission is very high. Once established it is almost impossible to move the refugee camps elsewhere and most of the refugees do not want to return to Rwanda as they fear for their safety.

1 Describe the main types of soil found under deciduous woodlands, such as Wytham Wood. How do you account for their formation?
2 Figure 13.32 and Figure 13.33 show energy flows and productivity in Wytham Wood. Describe the trophic structure of Wytham Wood. What are the top carnivores in Figure 13.32? What effects might changes in the populations of mice, voles and caterpillars have on the populations of owls and titmice. Explain your answer.
3 Study Figure 13.36 and state what proportion of tropical soils are fertile. Explain why tropical rainforests have some of the world's most luxuriant vegetation and yet some of the world's least fertile soils.
4 Compare and contrast the characteristics of a brown earth with those of a ferruginous soil (oxisol). Use Figure 13.37 to support your answer.
5 Using examples, examine the effects of human activities on tropical soils.

Global distribution of major ecosystems

Savanna ecosystems

Savannas are areas of tropical grasslands that can occur with or without trees and shrubs. All are characterised by a continuous cover of grasses although they vary considerably with respect to the other plant types present. Savannas cover about one-quarter of the world's land surface and are found between the tropical rainforests and the subtropical high-pressure belts that

produce the world's great deserts (Figure 13.42). The development and maintenance of savannas has occurred as a result of a variety of factors including climate, soils, geomorphology, fire and the grazing of human herds.

The climate that characterises savanna areas is a tropical wet-dry climate (Figure 13.43). However, there is great variation in the climate between savanna areas. The wet season occurs in summer: heavy convectional rain (monsoonal) replenishes the parched vegetation and soil. However, rainfall varies from as little as 500 mm to as much as 2000 mm, enough to support deciduous forest. However, all savanna areas have an annual drought, if not two dry seasons: these can vary from as little as one month to as much as eight months. It is on account of the dry season that grasses predominate. Temperatures remain high throughout the year ranging

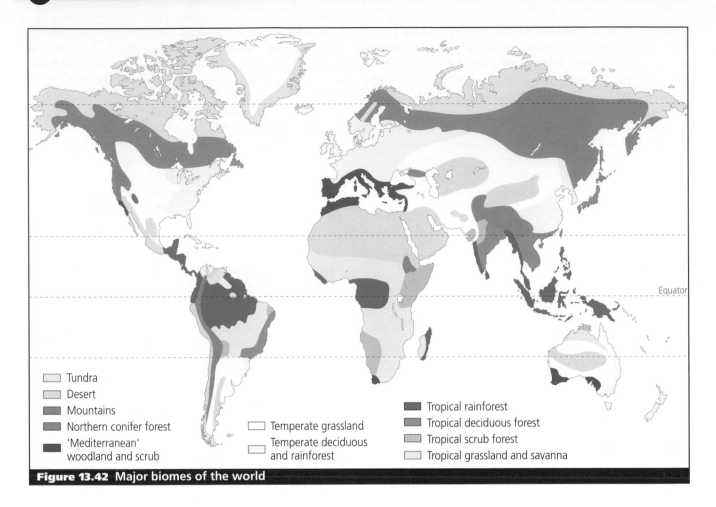

Figure 13.42 Major biomes of the world

Tundra
Desert
Mountains
Northern conifer forest
'Mediterranean' woodland and scrub
Temperate grassland
Temperate deciduous and rainforest
Tropical rainforest
Tropical deciduous forest
Tropical scrub forest
Tropical grassland and savanna

between 23 and 28°C. The high temperatures, causing high evapotranspiration rates, and seasonal nature of the rainfall cause a twofold division of the year into seasons – water surplus and water deficiency. This seasonal variation has a great effect on soil development (Figure 13.44).

The link between climate and soil could hardly be closer. Soils in the savanna are commonly leached ferralitic soils. These are similar to soils of the rainforest but not as intensely weathered, less leached and exhibit a marked seasonal pattern in soil process. During the wet season the excess of precipitation (P) over potential evapotranspiration (E) means that leaching of soluble minerals and small particles will take place down through the soil. These are deposited at considerable depth. By contrast, in the dry season E > P. Silica and iron compounds are carried up through the soil and precipitated close to the surface. However, geomorphology plays an important role too. Some areas, notably the base of slopes and river valleys, are enriched by clay, minerals and humus deposited there. By contrast plateaus, plains and the tops of slopes may be depleted of nutrients by erosion. The local variation in soil leads to variations in vegetation: this control by the soil is known as **edaphic** control (Figure 13.45). For example, on the thicker clay-based soils there is frequently woodland whereas on the leached sandy soils, with poor water

retention, grassland predominates. Savanna areas are frequently found on tectonically stable geological **shields**: these have therefore been weathered and are lacking in nutrients. Hence even the river valleys may not be as fertile as their temperate counterparts.

Savanna vegetation is a mosaic including grasses, trees and scrub. All, however, are **xerophytic** (adapted to drought), and therefore adapted to the savanna's dry season and **pyrophytic** (adapted to fire). Adaptations to drought include deep tap roots to reach the water table, partial or total loss of leaves and sunken stomata on the leaves to reduce moisture loss; those relating to fire include very thick barks and thick budding that can resist burning, the bulk of the biomass being below ground level and rapid regeneration after fire. The growth tissue in grasses is located at the base of the shoot close to the soil surface, unlike shrubs where growth occurs from the tips, hence burning, and even grazing, encourages the growth of grass relative to other plants.

The warm wet summers allow much photosynthesis and there is a large net primary productivity of 900 g/m²/year. This varies from about 1500 g/m²/year where it borders rainforest areas to only about 200 g/m²/year where it becomes savanna scrub. Similarly, the biomass varies considerably (depending on whether it is largely grass or wood) with an average of 4 kg/m. Typical species in Africa include the acacia, palm and baobab trees and elephant grass, which can grow to a height of over 5 m. Trees grow to a height of about 12 m and are characterised by flattened crowns and strong roots. By contrast Australian savannas are noted for eucalyptus trees and the Honduran savanna for pine trees.

The nutrient cycle also illustrates the relationship between climate, soils and vegetation. The store of nutrients in the

biomass is less than that in the rainforest because of the shorter growing season. Similarly, the store in the litter is small because of fire. Owing to fire many of the nutrients are stored in the soil thus they are not burnt and leached out of the system.

The role of fire, whether natural or man-made, is very important. It helps to maintain the savanna as a grass community, it mineralises the litter layer, kills off weeds,

Figure 13.43 Climatic conditions in the tropical rainforest (humid tropics) and the savanna (tropical wet-dry)

Month	TRF (Amazon)		Savanna (Nigeria)	
	Ppt	Temp. (°C)	Ppt	Temp. (°C)
Jan	262	26	0	23
Feb	196	27	2	24
Mar	254	26	13	27
Apr	269	26	64	28
May	305	26	150	27
June	234	26	180	25
July	223	25	216	24
Aug	183	26	302	23
Sep	132	27	269	24
Oct	175	27	74	25
Nov	183	27	2	24
Dec	264	26	0	23
Total	2677 mm		1272 mm	

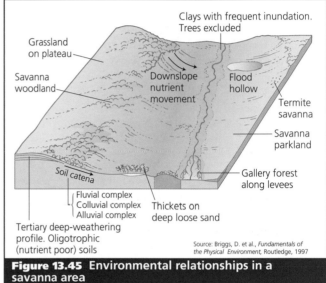

Source: Briggs, D. et al., *Fundamentals of the Physical Environment*, Routledge, 1997

Figure 13.45 Environmental relationships in a savanna area

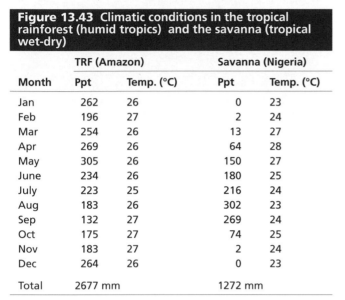

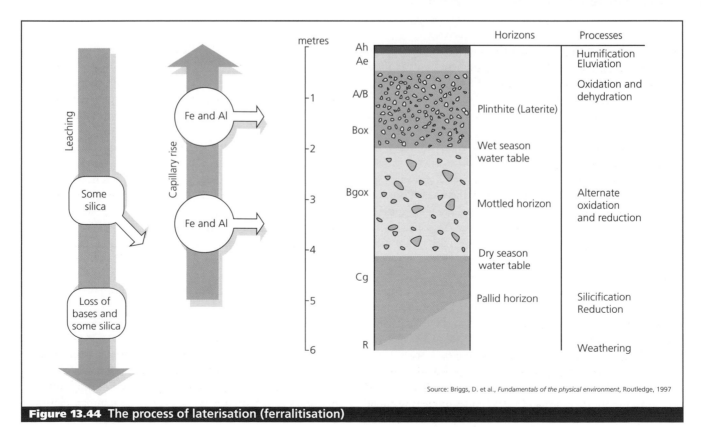

Source: Briggs, D. et al., *Fundamentals of the physical environment*, Routledge, 1997

Figure 13.44 The process of laterisation (ferralitisation)

competitors and diseases and prevents any trees from colonising relatively wet areas.

Other factors include the activities of animals. Notably, this includes locusts, which can decimate large areas of grassland with devastating speed, termites which aerate the soil and break down up to 30 kg of cellulose per ha each year. In some areas up to 600 termite hills per ha can be found, thus having a significant effect on the upper horizons on the soil.

The fauna associated with savannas is very diverse. The African savanna has the largest variety of grazers, over forty, including giraffe, zebra, gazelle, elephant and wildebeest. Selective grazing allows a great variety of herbivores: for example, the giraffe feeds off the tops of the trees, the rhinoceros the lower twigs (Figure 13.46) and gazelle the grass beneath the trees. These animals are largely migratory searching out water and fresh pastures as the dry season sets in. A variety of carnivores including lions, cheetahs and hyenas are also supported.

Figure 13.46 The rhino – a characteristic herbivore of a savanna ecosystem

Temperate grasslands

Temperate grasslands are found where rainfall is concentrated into one season in the year and is insufficient to support forest and woodlands. In addition, many areas of grassland or meadowland are related to geology, notably chalk and limestone, and some are man-made climax communities or **plagioclimax**. There are two main types of grassland (as well as also the meadowlands).

True temperate grasslands are found in continental interiors. On their arid margins they are called **steppes** and where they are moister they are termed **prairies**.

In North America, the soils of the temperate grasslands are transitional, ranging between **pedalfers** (where P > E and there is an overall movement of water down through the soil removing aluminium and iron from the upper soil horizons) and pedocals (where P < E and there is an upward movement of water in the soil depositing calcium in the A horizons). This occurs because precipitation decreases from east to west (Figure 13.48).

Chernozems are associated with continental temperate climates, such as the Steppes of Russia or the Great Plains of North America. Potential E > P, therefore there is an upward movement of water through the soil. Hence the soil is a pedocal. They are also referred to as black earths, owing to the accumulation of organic matter throughout the soil. The soil is alkaline and has a crumb structure (owing to the humus). Thus they are very good for agriculture. The thickly matted root system reduces the risk of soil erosion. The dominant process is the upward movement of water to the drying surface. Grasses also draw up calcium thus there is the accumulation of bases at the surface. Often there are no B or E horizons. Some leaching does occur, associated with snow melt in spring and periodic thunderstorms during the late summer.

There are two basic types of grass formation, **turf** forming grass such as wheat grass growing up to 60 cm, and **tufted** or

tussock grass such as feather grass, which grow in compact clumps in drier areas. In very cold winters the grass is dormant and growth begins when water is available from the spring snow-melt. The chinook (or 'snow eater') is a warm descending Fohn wind coming down the eastern slopes of the Rockies and is important as it raises temperatures rapidly for the beginning of the growing season and the germination of seeds.

The Pampas of Argentina is dominated by feather grass. Precipitation ranges from 500 mm in the west to 1250 mm in the north east, where the grassland gives way to deciduous forest. Evaporation is generally high and the soil is deep but lacking surface moisture. Shrubs and forest patches are found in wetter hollows.

The most extensive grasslands are found in continental interiors. The extent to which the grasslands represent a true climax vegetation system is debatable. Much temperate grassland has been destroyed by cultivation, the grazing of livestock, and the use of fire. In fact, some argue that temperate grassland would not exist without human activity, although in areas of 'natural' grassland, large herbivores such as buffalo would prevent the growth of tree seedlings.

The main soils associated with temperate grasslands include chernozems, chestnut soils and prairie soils. Chestnut soils are found in the driest areas while prairie soils where conditions are wetter. By far the most characteristic is the chernozem. These contain a high proportion of organic matter throughout their profile, and support some of the most important agricultural systems in the world.

Grasses decay quickly in the soil and soft plant cellulose is rapidly recycled. The pH of the soil is high, 7.0, and a thriving soil fauna mixes the soil. Due to the very cold temperatures in winter there is little decay of plant matter and few mineral nutrients are lost. There is a slight leaching following spring melt and due to convectional storms in the summer. However, the main process is the upward movement of soil water. The grasses draw nutrients (bases) from the soil and recycle them quickly. A black-brown A horizon develops, usually 25 cm deep. The colour reflects the high level of organic matter (8%–30%). Due to the large amount of organic matter in the soil, it has a crumb structure. Where conditions are wetter there is a greater removal of bases. This produces prairie soils. By contrast, where it is drier the lighter chestnut brown soils are found. These have a lower humus content due to a lower vegetation density, associated with higher temperatures, higher evapotranspiration rates and less precipitation.

Many grasslands are a plagioclimax, that is a man-made climax vegetation, as opposed to one controlled by climate. In many parts of Britain, such as western Scotland, areas which were once wooded are now covered by grassland. Regrowth of the trees is prevented by the grazing of sheep (eating young shoots) and the strong winds. Leached brown soils and podzols have been formed, with a low nutrient content, thereby preventing the recolonisation of trees. Grasses can also occur where soils are too wet for trees.

Coniferous forests or Taiga

Most coniferous forests (Figure 13.49) consist of a large number of a few species. Common species include pines, firs, and spruces. Trees are mostly in pure strands of one variety. Pines predominate in dry sandy soils, spruces on wetter soils. All trees become more stunted towards the poleward margin as the warm season decreases in length. The taiga is replaced polewards by the tundra. In coniferous forests there is little undergrowth. The layer of needle-shaped leaves decomposes very slowly to give a very acid podzol soil in which few plants will grow. Most trees have a conical shape, which reduces wind rocking and prevents extensive snow accumulation on the branches.

Typical climate is cold continental – over 3 months but less than 6 months with average temperatures over 6°C. Summer temperatures rise to just 10–15°C, but summers are very short and winters long and cold. Rainfall is concentrated in the short summer when it is most useful; precipitation is as snow in winter. 250 mm annual rainfall will support this type of forest.

The needle-shaped leaves reduce transpiration. The soil is often so cold that the tree cannot take in enough water to counteract transpiration loss which is increased by strong winds. The leaves are designed to conserve moisture.

Trees have to make the fullest use of the short summer for growth. Hence they are evergreen so the leaves are ready to begin work as soon as the temperature rises, without having to be grown as in the case of deciduous trees. Growth is, however, very slow. The summer is not long enough for flowers to be produced and pollinated and the seed dispersed in the same season (as in the case of the deciduous trees). Coniferous trees, therefore, are pollinated one season and the seed is dispersed the next.

The main soils are podzols. Podzols are perhaps the most distinct soil types. They are found under coniferous vegetation and heathlands. Climatically, they are associated with cool temperate regions. These areas have a low annual precipitation (500–800 mm), low winter temperatures (<0°C) and summer temperatures over 10°C. Rapid leaching occurs in spring as a result of snow-melt. Under heathlands, permeable sands and gravels allow the free movement of water downwards. Heather and coniferous vegetation release few bases (positive ions). Instead they release humic acids, called **chelating agents**. These allow iron and aluminium to be carried in solution (leached) down through the profile and deposited in the B horizon. Clay and humus may be carried in suspension by the percolating water (eluviation). This leads to the relative accumulation of silica in the upper horizons, giving the soil its characteristic bleached, ash-grey E horizon. The upper O and A horizons are black, owing to the presence of humus, in this case a very raw, acidic one called mor. The lower E horizon is also dark, reflecting the presence of deposited clay and humus. There may be an iron pan, a hard layer of deposited iron sesquioxides, creating an impermeable layer within the soil. The C horizon tends to take on the colour of the underlying bedrock. Podzols are very distinct soils because their acidic nature limits the presence of earthworms, one of the most important agents in mixing soil horizons.

Tundra ecosystems

Tundra ecosystems are found across large parts of the North America and Eurasian continents (Figure 13.47). It is difficult to delimit the tundra but in general it is found north of the 10°C isotherm for the warmest month and south of the 0°C isotherm. In addition, tundra areas are found at high altitude such as in the Alps and the Himalayas. In high-latitude tundra the low temperatures are offset by the prolonged sunshine in

Figure 13.47 Location of tundra ecosystems

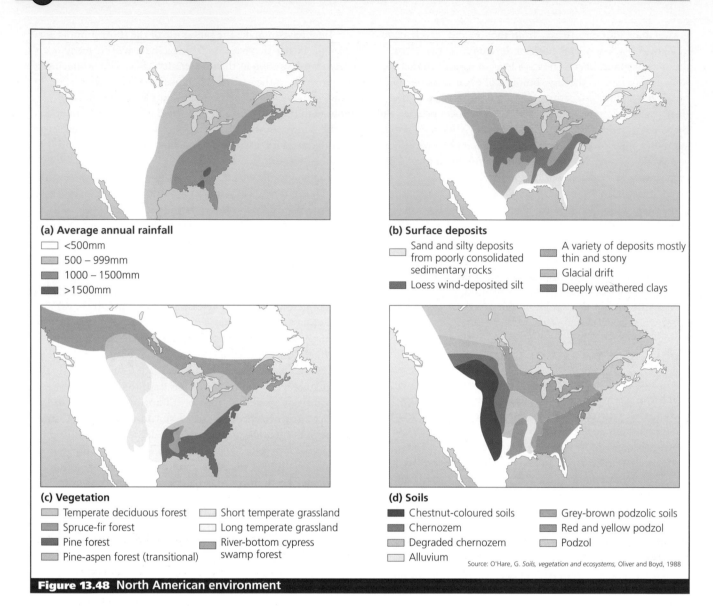

(a) Average annual rainfall
- [ ] <500mm
- 500 – 999mm
- 1000 – 1500mm
- >1500mm

(b) Surface deposits
- Sand and silty deposits from poorly consolidated sedimentary rocks
- Loess wind-deposited silt
- A variety of deposits mostly thin and stony
- Glacial drift
- Deeply weathered clays

(c) Vegetation
- Temperate deciduous forest
- Spruce-fir forest
- Pine forest
- Pine-aspen forest (transitional)
- Short temperate grassland
- Long temperate grassland
- River-bottom cypress swamp forest

(d) Soils
- Chestnut-coloured soils
- Chernozem
- Degraded chernozem
- Alluvium
- Grey-brown podzolic soils
- Red and yellow podzol
- Podzol

Source: O'Hare, G. *Soils, vegetation and ecosystems*, Oliver and Boyd, 1988

Figure 13.48 North American environment

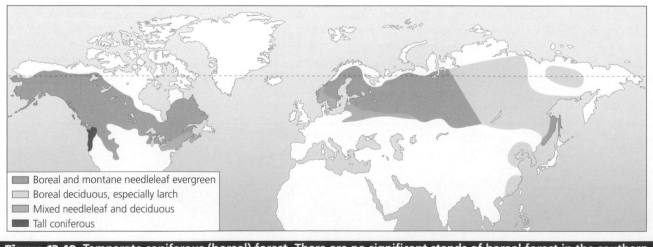

- Boreal and montane needleleaf evergreen
- Boreal deciduous, especially larch
- Mixed needleleaf and deciduous
- Tall coniferous

Figure 13.49 Temperate coniferous (boreal) forest. There are no significant stands of boreal forest in the southern hemisphere, due to the absence of land at an appropriate latitude

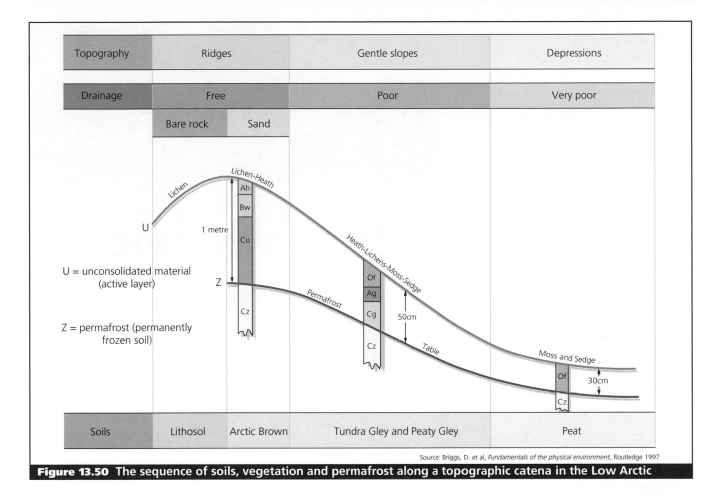

Topography	Ridges		Gentle slopes	Depressions
Drainage	Free		Poor	Very poor
	Bare rock	Sand		

U = unconsolidated material (active layer)

Z = permafrost (permanently frozen soil)

Soils	Lithosol	Arctic Brown	Tundra Gley and Peaty Gley	Peat

Source: Briggs, D. et al, *Fundamentals of the physical environment*, Routledge 1997

Figure 13.50 The sequence of soils, vegetation and permafrost along a topographic catena in the Low Arctic

summer. Snow remains on the ground until late spring or early summer and the resulting meltwaters cannot penetrate permafrost. This leads to waterlogging. Most rainfall occurs in summer. Average temperatures and precipitation are higher in maritime areas.

Permafrost (permanently frozen ground) dominates the tundra region. Waterlogging leads to the formation of an acid mor humus. Beneath the humus a gleyed horizon of clay is found. Here ferric compounds are reduced to ferrous ones as oxygen is lost. Due to low temperatures microorganism activity is low. Most tundra soils contain large numbers of angular rock fragments due to frost heave.

Not all tundra soils are waterlogged. Some are better drained and have developed horizons similar to a podzol (Figure 13.50). Parent material is important. For example, limestones provide material for soils which are not peat, and Arctic brown soils develop on better drained areas, especially when the bedrock is sandstone.

Low temperatures mean that mechanical weathering is limited and the decomposition of plant remains is extremely slow. This leads to the accumulation of organic matter at the surface. Upper horizons are acid but the lower ones are usually slightly acid or alkaline. Natural fertility is low and after 3–5 years cultivation heavy fertiliser application is required.

Manure must be partially decomposed before application due to the low temperatures.

Types of vegetation include hardy sedges and grasses (eriphorum or cotton grass) and tiny hygrophilous plants (water tolerant). Mosses such as sphagnum and lichens are most common. Small berry-bearing plants such as crowberry and bilberry are also common and there may be some trees such as dwarf willows and birches. Early summer flowering plants such as anenomes and saxifrage are favoured. Where the tundra is hummocky sedges are found in the hollows and the south-facing aspect is the most favoured. Alpine tundra is dominated by lichens, mosses and dwarf shrubs.

There are a number of stresses on the vegetation:

■ **winter is very cold and dark**

■ **winds are often very strong**

■ **summer is only 50–60 days without severe frosts**

■ **plants experience a physiological drought (water is there – as ice – but the plants cannot use it).**

Thus, productivity is low. NPP is only 0.14 kg/m²/year and the biomass is only 0.6 kg/m². Hence the tundra can support only low densities of species of fauna such as caribou and reindeer.

Questions

1 Describe and explain the relationship between climate, soils and vegetation in a savanna ecosystem.
2 Explain why tundra ecosystems have such low productivity.
3 How is vegetation adapted to survival in taiga forests?
4 Describe and explain the relationships between climate and soils in temperate grassland ecosystems.

Figure 13.51 Box Hill – a managed ecosystem

SPATIAL FOCUS

Box Hill – managing ecosystems and recreational pressure

Box Hill has been a favourite leisure area for Londoners since Victorian times. The rail link in 1849 gave easy access from London (Figure 13.53). Box Hill now attracts over one million visitors each year, mostly by car. It is popular for its views, geology and scenery, ecological diversity, wildlife, and, increasingly, educational visits.

In the early twentieth century, land taxes caused many landowners to sell their property. In 1912, 93 ha of Box Hill was offered for sale and the estate was purchased and given to the National Trust in 1913. The estate has expanded over the years and now covers over 485 ha. In 1971 the Countryside Commission designated the area as the first **Country Park**, followed by classification as a Grade 1 **Site of Special Scientific Interest** (part of the Mole Gap – Reigate Escarpment SSSI) from the Nature Conservancy Council. It is also part of the Surrey Hills **Area of Outstanding Natural Beauty** (AONB).

Surveys of the public using Box Hill reveal that they most value the open landscape and the wildlife. To maintain these a close control of the vegetation is essential:

■ through agricultural practices – on open downland winter grazing by sheep is allowed which thrive on the coarser grasses which present the problem

■ scrub which encroaches on to the dip slope is severely cut back

■ scrub creates a valuable habitat for certain species and it is maintained on the steeper scarp slopes

Key Definitions 4

Refugia zone A locality which has escaped drastic alteration following climatic change, in contrast to the surrounding region.

■ the woodland is managed to provide a mix of habitats.

The main soil found on chalk is a rendzina. Rendzina soils are found on a chalk or limestone bedrock. The upper horizon is black or brown, indicating a soil rich in organic matter as well as, in this case, calcium. This horizon is normally quite thin. Below this is the C horizon. At the top of the C horizon there may be angular fragments. These originate from a time when mechanical weathering was frequent on chalk and limestone, such as during a periglacial period. Beneath this is pure bedrock. If the rock contained many impurities, such as flint or chert on chalk or magnesium or iron on limestone, then these minerals could form the basis of B and E horizons.

Chalk soils occur on the escarpment and the sides of the valleys and support characteristic downland plants such as grassland and orchids. On alkaline chalky soils beech woodland is the climax vegetation. Where soil is shallower, often on the steeper slopes, yew is the alternative climax. By contrast, where there is a superficial covering of clay-with-flints, mixed woodland occurs. This variety provides a patchwork landscape of pockets of

Figure 13.52 Box Hill, a tourist 'honeypot' south of London

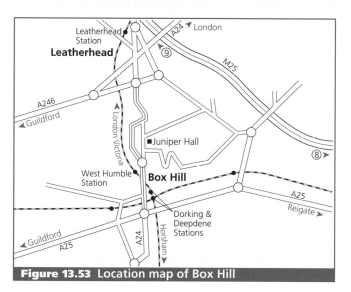

Figure 13.53 Location map of Box Hill

woodland and scrubland, with larger areas of grassland. Fallen trees are usually left to support fungi and insect life, which promote the recycling of nutrients within the woodland ecosystem, so assisting its maintenance in the long term.

Up until the end of the nineteenth century, sheep were grazed on the downland slopes by day and brought to the lower arable fields at night to manure them. Hence, nutrient levels on the downland were reduced, while those on the lower fields were increased. Because the downland was unimproved (i.e. unfertilised) only plants that are adapted to the thin, impoverished, fast-draining soils can survive. Otherwise the areas would be colonised by species needing high levels of nutrients, such as nitrates and phosphates. In addition, rabbits played an important part in maintaining the grass cover. However, in the 1950s, the rabbit population was decimated by myxamatosis, a disease carried by fleas. Since then encroachment by coarse grasses and scrub increased.

Chalk downland occupies about 120 ha at Box Hill. The main way of maintaining the chalk downland is through sheep grazing. Their grazing rotation is controlled by conditions such as season, climate and habitat needs. They are grazed the whole year round, except in the most extreme weather. Scrub and coarse grasses are a recurring problem, and grass burning in the 1970s led to a build-up of phosphates and hence tor grass took hold.

Typical grassland species include tor grass, yellow wort and orchids. Chalk downlands are also associated with butterflies, and Box Hill has a variety of species such as the common blue, chalk hill blue, and dark green fritillary species.

In addition to the chalk there is about 320 ha of woodland (Figure 13.51). Three important communities exist:

- The Whites – a natural river cliff and containing exceptionally dry soils tolerated by yew and box. The woodland is ancient (over 250 years old) and possibly primeval (to last ice age 10 000 years ago).

- Ash coombes – consisting of ash trees growing in the dry valleys.

- Plantations of larch, Scots pine, beech and oak found at Hill Top.

On chalky soils the climax vegetation is predominantly yew with beech and ash. By contrast, the clay-with-flints cap supports oak, hornbeam, birch and others. Typical woodland species include primrose, bluebell and foxglove. Animals found around Box Hill include roe deer, squirrel, badger, dormouse and sparrowhawks.

The woodlands of Box Hill need to be controlled and managed in order to maintain the diverse nature of the habitats that characterise Box Hill. The main management strategy is to promote native broad-leaved trees rather than coniferous trees. Natural regeneration is allowed to take place, as after the Great Storm of 1987. Coppicing of hazel, ash and sweet chestnut are common, and create areas of greater light intensity.

Management problems

Due to the large number of visitors and its easy accessibility, Box Hill has many problems. The policy of encouraging visitors may threaten and damage the very attractions people come to see. However, surveys have shown that up to 75 per cent of visitors stay within 400 m of their car. Thus it is possible to manage people and to zone land use, so that important ecological areas can be conserved.

Footpath erosion is less of a problem than in Victorian times, as fewer people walk up the hill (Figure 13.51). The busiest sections of the path are covered with hard-wearing limestone scalpings. The most serious erosion is caused by mountain bikes, especially on the steep slopes away from designated paths. The National Trust has attempted to manage the problem by developing interesting and challenging routes, which are clearly sign-posted. In addition, it has attempted to prevent irresponsible bikers by erecting barriers at strategic points in vulnerable areas. The Trust is also concerned at the loss of rare species by people uprooting or picking plants.

Dogs are another problem. They may foul footpaths, disturb nesting birds or worry sheep. Notices are clearly displayed reminding the public of the need to control their dogs in the interests of wildlife and other visitors. Vandalism and fires, either accidental or deliberate, are a regular threat, and the advent of snow brings casualties amongst hordes of skiers and tobogganists attracted by 'Surrey's Alp'.

Litter is a major problem at Box Hill. It is not just the rubbish that is discarded by visitors but fly-tipping, dumping of furniture and kitchen appliances, beds and carpets, toxic chemicals, and stolen cars. Pollution is another threat to the area. Cars are a major source of pollution, and the number of cars on the road is likely to increase.

Questions

1 For Box Hill, or another site that you have studied, identify the main conflicts of interest that need to be 'managed' and 'balanced'.
2 What are the geographic factors which intensify the pressures on this particular site?
3 How successful are the options that have been used to manage these conflicts?

Human activity and ecosystems

All ecosystems – whether the global ecosystem or a small-scale local one, are affected by human activities. In the most part these have had a negative impact on the ecosystem, although there are examples of positive impacts on ecosystems (see pages 291–2 on river restoration). Sometimes it is too late to redress the harm done. For example, people can lead to the destruction of sensitive ecosystems, such as coral reefs and rainforests, thus there is an urgent need for management.

Although 1.4 million species of animals and plants have been described there may be as many as five to thirty million species in total. However, the number of species is decreasing as the extinction rate increases. There have been five major extinction events during the geological timescale:

- **439 million years ago at the boundary of the Ordovician and Silurian periods**
- **375 Ma late in the Devonian period**
- **240 Ma at the boundary between the Permian and Triassic periods**
- **210 Ma in the Triassic period**
- **65 Ma at the boundary between the Cretaceous and Tertiary periods.**

The best known are the extinctions from the Cretaceous-Tertiary period when the dinosaurs died out and an estimated 70 per cent of the flora disappeared. This extinction is believed to have been caused by a series of meteorite impacts which caused huge volumes of very fine material to be injected into the upper atmosphere. This shaded the sun and absorbed the incoming solar radiation, thereby causing global cooling.

Homo sapiens have only been in existence for about the last 200 000 years yet their activities have resulted in the decline of huge numbers of species. Human activity has led to the extinction of many species of large land mammals (over 40 kg in weight). These became extinct shortly after the last glacial period, 10 000 years ago. More than 90 per cent of such animals became extinct in Australia, 80 per cent in South America, 73 per cent in North America and 29 per cent in Europe. Some of this was related to direct human impact, such as hunting, whereas much was indirect, through farming, habitat removal and modification. In addition, some extinctions may have been due to climatic change.

Human activity has not only caused extinctions, it has caused major changes in the structure and functioning of ecosystems. For example, agricultural and urban ecosystems are very much simpler than natural ones. Changes in vegetation have an impact on soil quality and cause disruptions in the nutrient cycle.

Degradation of a Caribbean coral reef

Coral reefs are renowned for their spectacular wildlife and beauty, as well as having considerable potential for fishing and tourism. However, many reefs around the world are increasingly vulnerable to overfishing and sedimentation. The latter is closely linked with human activities such as pollution, deforestation, reef mining and dredging.

Jamaica's coral reefs are amongst the most intensively studied in the world. Jamaica's population growth is extremely rapid (Figure 13.54). In 1870 it was less than 500 000 but doubled by 1925 and again by 1975. In the mid-1990s it reached 2.5 million. It is expected to reach 3 million by 2010. This has caused huge pressures on the land with most of the natural vegetation having been removed for agriculture and urban development.

Chronic overfishing is a major problem. By 1973 the number of fishing canoes off the north coast of the island was about 1800, about three times the sustainable level. As a result large predatory species such as sharks have disappeared, so too have turtles and manatees. Most of the species caught in traps are either small species or very young which means that the chances of the species reproducing is remote.

There are also natural threats to coral. In 1980 Hurricane Allen caused extensive damage to the Jamaican reefs. After the hurricane short-lived algal bloom occurred, due to nutrients washed off the land. In the absence of herbivorous fish the entire reef system of Jamaica has been changed (Figure 13.55). Many communities that survived Hurricane Allen were killed by the algal overgrowth. The decline in long-lived coral such as Montastrea is especially important because it is the most resistant to hurricanes. The scale of the damage is enormous. Surveys have shown that the proportion of coral along the coast has declined from 52 per cent to 3 per cent whereas the proportion of macro (large algae) has increased from 45 per cent to 92 per cent. As algae is able to recover faster than the coral, future hurricanes are likely to increase the proportion of algae since the filaments and holdfasts are able to regenerate quickly.

Changing upland ecosystems in the UK

There are two main types of peat bog in Britain: the blanket bogs of upland moors, and the raised lowland bogs that form large peat mounds in waterlogged river valleys. 'Blanket' bogs form in areas of high rainfall, usually in uplands (Figure 13.56). They literally blanket the landscape, whether on ridges, slopes or in hollows. While the highland bogs may have been created by early farmers cutting down trees and burning the grasses, lowland bogs formed naturally.

Raised bogs consist of plants, mostly sphagnum mosses, on top of a shallow mound of the compressed and waterlogged remains of dead plants. This peat, which has accumulated since the glaciers retreated 10 000 years ago, is sometimes tens of metres thick. Meagre supplies of nutrients and minerals come entirely from rain water, and the acidic conditions create unique ecosystems. Lowland raised bogs form in naturally

Key Definitions 5

piping The flow of water in naturally occurring pipes in the soil layer beneath the surface.

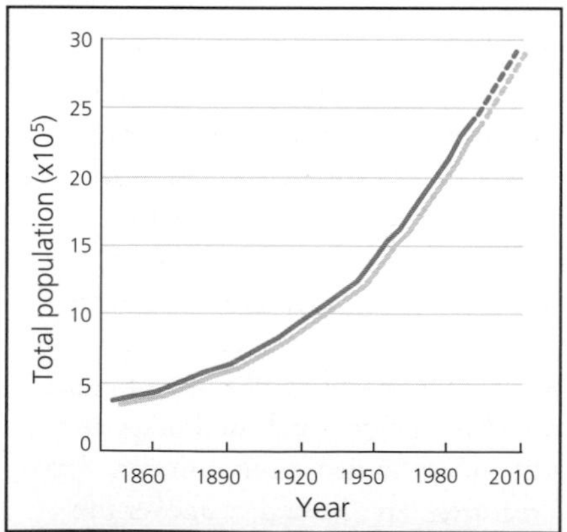

Figure 13.54 Population growth of Jamaica

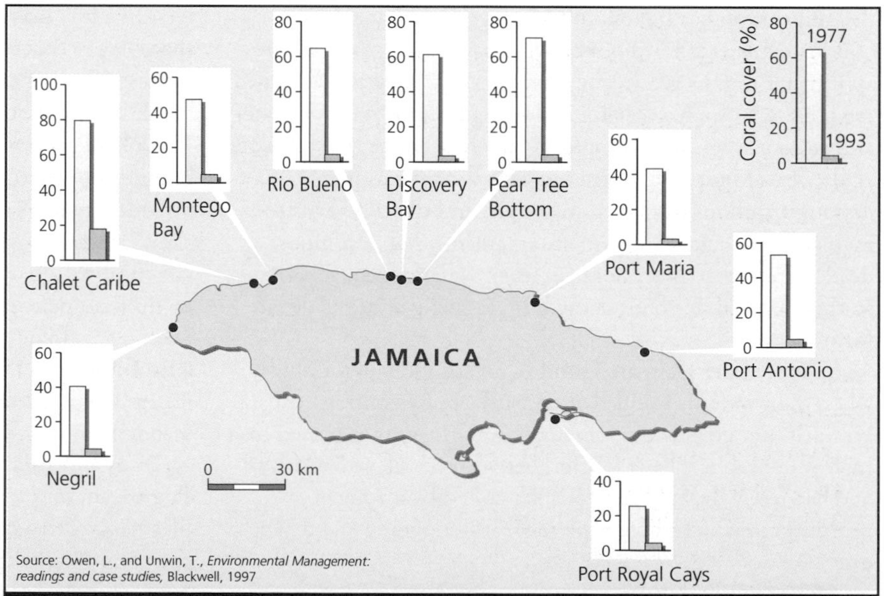

Source: Owen, L., and Unwin, T., *Environmental Management: readings and case studies*, Blackwell, 1997

Figure 13.55 Large-scale changes in community structure at fore-reef sites along >300 km of the Jamaican coastline, surveyed in the late 1970s (1977, tinted bars) and the early 1990s (1993, solid bars)

Figure 13.56 Upland moorland, The Begwyns, Wales

Figure 13.57 Lowland bog Stagmount, Co. Kerry, Ireland

waterlogged areas (Figure 13.57). The thin strip of living vegetation on the surface relies almost entirely on rain-fed nutrients. This means that sphagnum mosses, which grow in wet, acidic conditions, dominate the peatland.

A third type of wetland, lowland fens, contains areas which either did not develop into bog, or where the peat has already been stripped away. The Norfolk Broads, for example, are a result of the large-scale excavation of peat in the Middle Ages. Fens may be less acidic and relatively rich in plant nutrients, supporting vegetation such as sedges, reeds, willows and alders. Fen or sedge peat has a high mineral content.

Peat can only occur when the natural process of decomposition has halted. In waterlogged and anaerobic conditions soils tend to be acidic. This is especially so where sphagnum mosses grow. The mosses extract positively charged ions (cations) such as calcium and magnesium from soil water and in return release hydrogen ions, which make the soil more acidic. In addition, rain water is slightly acidic as it contains dissolved carbon dioxide from the air, and this also leads to increased soil acidity. The microorganisms that decompose dead plant material cannot operate in waterlogged, acidic soils, so this material does not decay but gradually accumulates to form peat.

Surface water gleys are found in areas of low permeability where rain water is ponded at the surface. By contrast, groundwater gleys occur where the waterlogging is caused by a high water table. The transition between the gleyed horizons and the freely drained horizons is marked by a zone of mottling, in which there is periodic waterlogging and drying out.

Moorlands and upland peat bogs are found in wet, highland areas in Ireland, Scotland and on high ground such as Dartmoor, the Brecon Beacons and the Pennines. By contrast, lowland peat is found in areas of impermeable rocks

such as the clays of the Somerset Levels and of Otmoor, near Oxford. Peat bogs have a limited diversity of plants but they are highly specialised, such as heather, cotton grass, purple moor grass. Other less dominant plants include sundews and bog asphodel. Over the last few decades peat bogs have been under threat and many have been seriously eroded.

Britain's heather-covered moors and blanket peat bogs are of international significance: 10 per cent of the world's peat bogs occur in Britain attracting a high proportion of the unique birds and plants inextricably linked with them.

The aspects common to all mountains and moorland are their bleakness and openness. Upland Britain lies north and west of a line from Humberside to Devon. Although more than 40 per cent of Wales is considered upland habitat, the highest, bleakest and most formidable peaks of the British Isles are those of the Scottish Highlands.

Upland vegetation includes a wide variety of plants, but bilberry, crowberry and heather are the most common and provide a major source of food for birds. In areas of steep slopes the soil is extremely thin and its fertility depends on the chemical nature of the underlying rock. Many mountains may be nutrient deficient as well as quite dry (if runoff is rapid). Such places frequently support different plants from the adjacent slopes. The long roots of the purple saxifrage anchor it firmly and penetrate deep into the cracks and fissures in search of water.

Birds and animals are adapted to moorland ecosystems. Ptarmigan, for example, rarely fly far, preferring a terrestrial lifestyle, making camouflage important at all times of year for protection against attacks from golden eagle and peregrine. Some animals have had to adapt to new environments. Red deer, originally forest creatures, have been driven over the years into wilder upland country, as human pressures on the lowlands have increased.

Managing heather moorlands

There are four stages in the growth of heather and each stage has specific characteristics (Figure 13.58):

- *The Pioneer Stage* – this accounts for the first 6–10 years. During this time the heather seedlings become established. The root system grows rapidly. The shoots are high in nutrients.
- *The Building Stage* – the heather increases in biomass until it completely covers the ground. The plants grow quickly and vigorously. This is the most valuable stage and lasts for about 6 or 7 years.
- *The Mature Stage* – during this stage the ratio of the less nutritious woody stems to the green shoots increases. The plants tend to become recumbent. The ground cover decreases as the old branches die.
- *The Degenerate Stage* – the old plants provide very poor grazing.

The objective of heather management is to keep as many plants in the most productive building stage by burning every 10–15 years. Small patches of heather (about 1 ha) are burnt each year. This still keeps enough heather in the area to provide cover and food for pairs of grouse. Burning destroys the old plants and the nutrients in the ashes are released for use by the new growth. It also stimulates the growth of new shoots. Perennating (overwintering) buds lie just beneath the surface protected from the effects of the fire. After the burn they grow into new plants. In a well-managed moor there will be little mature or degenerate heather.

A major problem in the rehabilitation of moorlands is to reproduce the hostile conditions, especially the very low nutrient levels, that allowed the original mosses to develop. If a bog is disrupted, even slightly, nutrients begin to run in from surrounding land or are leached from dying vegetation in the bog itself. Sensitive species, including long-leaved sundew and mud sedge, soon disappear. Cotton-grass and purple moor-grass may survive longer. Only if nutrient levels can be held down will the invaders depart and the most sensitive species revive.

Threats to upland ecosystems

Upland areas are vulnerable to a number of threats (Figure 13.59). In the Peak District, a third of all heather moorland has disappeared in the last 68 years, and more than 10 per cent in mid-Wales since 1973. One-third of Northumberland's upland SSSIs have been damaged or destroyed in the last 15 years. Populations of merlin, Britain's rarest falcon, have crashed over the last 15 years in Wales and Northumberland because it needs heather moorland to survive. It is declining in north and west Scotland and is virtually extinct in the Pennines and south west England.

Erosion of peat

Peat is eroded in a number of ways, especially by running water. The most important is water erosion. The initial stages of erosion involve the development of gullies. On the flatter slopes meandering gullies with islands of peat occur, whereas on the steeper slopes parallel and sub-parallel gullies are found. Most gullies are found where the precipitation is higher than 1400 mm per year. Thus peat erosion may be a result of increased rainfall as high rainfall would cause increased water flow and piping. Eventually this undermines the peat and the surface collapses.

When the vegetation cover is broken sheet erosion occurs, quickly removing the remaining peat. Water erosion is assisted by occasional bog burst. These occur after heavy storms when the peat becomes saturated and a sudden rapid outflow of water and peat occurs. These are well recorded in Ireland and Northern Ireland.

Figure 13.58 Some of the main changes during the four-phase Calluna vulgaris development cycle

Stage of development cycle	1 Pioneer	2 Building	3 Mature	4 Degenerate
Mean height (cm)	24.1	52.1	63.2	55.2
Mean age of individuals (years)	5.7	9.0	17.1	24.0
Biomass (g/m²)				
Calluna only	287.2	1507.6	1923.6	1043.2
Other dwarf shrubs and grasses	179.6	41.2	52.0	83.2
Total, all plants	889.2	1702.0	2305.2	1560.8
Net production of young Calluna shoots (g/m² in one year)	148.8	442.4	363.6	140.8
Light reaching soil surface (% of that in the open)	100.0	2.0	20.0	57.0

Threat – Problem

1 **Moorland improvement**   Some moorland areas have been turned into enclosed fields, by ploughing and draining the land, and adding fertilisers to improve the grass quality. Moorland loss was a problem on Exmoor in the 1960s and 1970s.

2 **Afforestation**   Many moorlands have been turned into forest, by being planted with coniferous trees, called plantation, such as in mid-Wales and parts of the Flow Country in Scotland.

3 **Erosion**   Moorlands can suffer from recreation. Soil erosion can be caused by walking boots, mountain bikes, skis, off-road vehicles and pony trekking. Several areas in National Parks have suffered including the Pennine Way.

4 **Overgrazing**   Too many grazing animals can cause soil erosion. Heathers are replaced by grasses. This also encourages bracken to develop. Bracken is poisonous to animals, and spreads quickly. It is difficult to get rid of, and it provides a habitat for ticks, which carry Lyme disease. Sheep numbers have doubled in England and Wales in the last 40 years. They are selective grazers and in winter heather is their main diet. If they crop heavily the heather becomes stunted and produces fewer new shoots and flowers poorly the following year. Progressive over-grazing destroys the heather altogether, coarse grasses replace it and radically alter the breeding habitat for grouse, golden plover and merlins.

5 **Acid rain**   Acid rain from cities has been damaging bog plants and sphagnum in the Pennines. When plants are damaged, the peat soils below can become exposed and eroded.

6 **Fire**   Accidental fires can get out of control.

7 **Flooding**   Some moorland areas have been lost, due to flooding by water-supply reservoirs, e.g. in the northern Pennines.

8 **The peat industry**

9 **Recreation, tourism and leisure**   Ski-lift developments in the Cairngorms have led to an outcry from environmentalists, because they fear an increase of people will cause serious erosion of the shallow delicate mountain soil. Most mountain flowers are endangered or threatened in Britain. The blue heath found only in Perthshire and Inverness and the Snowdon lily are being trampled out of existence by unwitting walkers.

Figure 13.59 The threats to upland ecosystems

The spread of bracken

Bracken covers large areas of upland Britain. It is the largest of the British ferns growing to a height of up to two metres when mature. It spreads by rhizomes in the soil and by spores which it produces in the autumn. It is predominantly a woodland species and never grows above the tree line. Bracken is seen as Britain's most prolific weed and the average rate of bracken encroachment is about 1 per cent per year.

This problem has been created by people. Bracken is not a pioneer coloniser of land but usually colonises land which has been deforested, over-burned, abandoned by farmers or where there is soil erosion. Invasion by the bracken is affecting the middle slopes in particular. Bracken completely dominates the areas it colonises, shading out other species and dominating the soil layer with its rhizomes. Useful grazing land is lost and passage to the upland grazing land for animals becomes more difficult. Bracken is also a likely cause of ill-health in animals and people. Diseases such as 'horse staggers' and tumours in cattle are more common in bracken-infested areas. It is also the habitat of the sheep tick which is a well-known pest in sheep-rearing areas. There is also some concern for human health in areas which get water from bracken-covered hillslopes as carcinogens (cancer-forming substances) have been identified in the water. The exact role played by the bracken is controversial as other factors such as rock type may be important.

By contrast, ecosystem management which has global impact is the destruction of the rainforest. But it is possible to manage the rainforest in an effective and sustainable way.

Putting a price on the rainforest

Tropical rainforest products have traditionally been divided into two main groups:

■ **timber resources** which include saw logs and pulp wood, and

■ **non-wood or minor forest products** such as edible fruits, oils, latex fibre and medicine.

Research suggests that the value of tropical rainforests for these other products is greater than for wood. Research on the forests near Mishana, 30 km south west of Iquitos in Peru, show that in a one-ha holding 275 species were found, 842 trees of over 10 cm diameter, 72 species of trees and 350 individual trees. Over 40 per cent of the trees provided an income. The forest produces fruit worth about $650 each year. In addition, rubber yields amount to $50/ha, fruit $400/ha and latex $22/ha. By contrast if the forest was used for fire wood it would provide $16/ha. Revenues for cattle pastures in Brazil are said to earn $148/ha/year.

Figure 13.60 A comparison between the milpa system and the new forms of agriculture

	Milpa system	Tobacco plantation or ranching
NPP	High, stable	Declining
Work (labour)	High	Higher and increasing
Inputs	Few (clearing & seeding)	Very high 2.5–3t fertiliser/ha/pa
Crops	Polyculture (244 species used)	Monoculture (risk of disease, poor yield, loss of demand and/or overproduction)
Yield (compared to inputs)	200 per cent	140 per cent if lucky
Reliability of farming system	Quite stable	High-risk operation
Economic organisation	Mainly subsistence	Commercial
Money	None/little	More
Carrying capacity (livestock)	Several families/4 ha	>1 family on a plantation (200 ha)
		Ranching: 1 ha of good land – 1 cow
		20 ha of poor land – 1 cow

Sustainable agroforestry

The Popoluca Indians of Santa Rosa, Mexico practise a form of agriculture that resembles shifting cultivation, known as the **milpa system**. This is a labour-intensive form of agriculture, using fallow. It is a diverse form of **polyculture** with over 200 species cultivated, including maize, beans, cucubits, papaya, squash, water melon, tomatoes, oregano, coffee and chili. The Popolucas have developed this system into a fine art which mimics the natural rainforest. The variety of a natural rainforest is repeated by variety of shifting cultivation. For example, lemon trees, peppervine and spearmint are **heliophytes**, light-seeking, and prefer open conditions not shade. Coffee, by contrast, is a **sciophyte**, and prefers shade while the mango tree requires damp conditions.

The close associations that are found in natural conditions are also seen in the Popolucas' farming system. For example, maize and beans go well together, as maize extracts nutrients from the soil whereas beans return them. Tree trunks and small trees are left because they are useful for many purposes such as returning nutrients to the soil and preventing soil erosion. They are also used as a source of material for housing, hunting spears, and for medicines.

As in a rainforest the crops are multi-layered, with tree, shrub and herb layers. This increases NPP/unit area, because photosynthesis is taking place on at least three levels, and soil erosion is reduced as no soil or space is left bare. Most plants are self-seeded and this reduces the cost of inputs. The Popolucas show a huge amount of ecological knowledge and management. In all, 244 species of plant are used in the farming system. Animals include chickens, pigs and turkeys. These are used as a source of food, for barter and exchange for money, and their waste is used as manure. Rivers and lakes are used for fishing and catching turtles. Thus it is not entirely a subsistence lifestyle since wood, fruit, turtles and other animals are traded for some seeds, mainly maize.

Pressures on the Popolucas

About 90 per cent of Mexico's rainforest has been cut down in recent decades, largely for new forms of agriculture. This is partly a response to Mexico's huge international debt and attempts by the government to increase agricultural exports and reduce its imports. The main new forms of farming are

- **cattle ranching** for export, and
- **plantations** or cash crops, such as tobacco.

However, these new methods are not necessarily suited to the physical and economic environment (Figure 13.60). Tobacco needs protection from too much sunlight and excess moisture and the soil needs to be very fertile. But, the cleared rainforest is frequently left bare and this leads to soil erosion and the loss of soil nutrients (Figure 13.61). Unlike the milpa system, the new systems are very labour intensive. Pineapple, sugar cane and tobacco plantations require large inputs of fertiliser and pesticides. Inputs are expensive and the costs are rising rapidly.

Ranching prevents the natural succession of vegetation, because of a lack of seed from nearby forests and the grazing effects of cattle. Grasses and a few legumes become dominant. One hectare of rainforest supports about 200 species of trees and up to 10 000 individual plants. By contrast, one hectare of rangeland supports just one cow and one or two types of grass. But it is profitable in the short term because land is available, and it is supported by the Mexican government.

Extensive **monoculture** is increasingly mechanised, and uses large inputs of fertiliser, pesticides and insecticides. However, it is very costly and there are problems of soil deterioration and micro-climatic change. Yet there is little pressure to improve efficiency because it is easy to clear new forest.

The Mexican rainforest can be described as a '**desert covered by trees**'. Under natural conditions it is very dynamic, but its **resilience** depends on the level of disturbance. Sustainable development of the rainforest requires the management and use of the natural structure and diversity, namely local species, local knowledge and skills rather than the type of farming developed elsewhere and then imported.

Marketing biodiversity

Destruction of the rainforest occurs because the environment is a resource. Because it is difficult for many countries to obtain much profit from the environment, they spend little money trying to protect it. Increasingly, however, developing countries need to assert sovereignty (ownership or rights) over their natural resources to control the extraction of resources by biotechnology and pharmaceutical companies for commercial development. Biotechnology, the science of recombining the genes of plants and organisms to derive improved plants, drugs and foods, has revolutionised ways in which natural resources are used in product development.

One of the first examples of a biodiversity agreement was between the presidents of Belize, Costa Rica, El Salvador, Guatemala, Honduras, Nicaragua and Panama. They signed an agreement in order to manage the foreign companies, especially biotechnology and pharmaceutical firms, that were using Central American natural resources to develop drugs. Until the agreement Central Americans received no share in the profits. The Madagascar periwinkle is a good example of the problem. The multi-million dollar cancer drug, Vincristine, was developed from the Madagascar periwinkle but Madagascar received no payment or share of royalties.

Natural resources are very valuable. For example, traditional medicines derived from natural resources provide health care for about 80 per cent of the populations in LEDCs. Drugs derived from natural resources include penicillin developed from a mould, taxol a cancer drug from yew tree bark, and the antibiotic streptomycin developed from a soil sample.

The extraction of natural resources for profit would appear to be at odds with the protection of biological diversity. This is especially true in LEDCs. The Merck-IMBio Agreement announced in 1991 was a research agreement under which Merck agreed to pay IMBio $1 million for all plant, insect and soil samples the Institute could collect in addition to a percentage of the royalties from any drugs that Merck developed from those samples. Under the agreement Merck received exclusive rights, or the right of first refusal, to evaluate the approximately 10 000 samples that IMBio agreed to supply to Merck. IMBio can enter into similar agreements with other companies but it must not supply the same species that it supplies to Merck. In addition to the $1m IMBio benefited from equipment donations worth $135 000. If IMBio receives 2 per cent of the royalties from sales of twenty products based on its samples they would receive more money than Costa Rica does from the sale of coffee and bananas, two of the prime exports.

More than one-quarter of Costa Rica's land is protected in some type of national park or preserve. Costa Rica contains over 12 000 plant species, 80 per cent of which have been described and more than 300 000 insect species, only 20 per cent of which have been described. Costa Rica contains between 5 and 7 per cent of the world's species and has more biodiversity/ha than any other country. This species diversity is due to diverse climates within Costa Rica. In addition, the country is mountainous, touches both the Atlantic and Pacific oceans and has ecosystems found in South America, the West Indies and tropical North America.

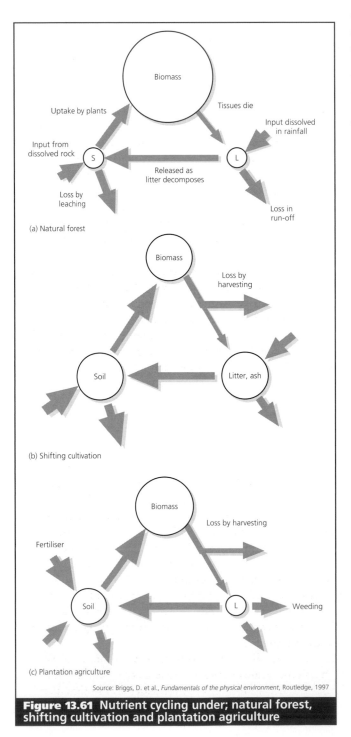

Source: Briggs, D. et al., *Fundamentals of the physical environment*, Routledge, 1997

Figure 13.61 Nutrient cycling under; natural forest, shifting cultivation and plantation agriculture

Figure 13.62 Soil requirements for ten crops grown widely in the tropics

Crop	Texture			Minimum rooting depth (m)	pH tolerance range	Nutrient requirement
	Fine	Medium	Coarse			
Maize		+		60–90	5.5–8.0	High
Banana		+	+	≥90	4.0–8.0	Medium/high
Cashew			+	≤90	5.5–7.0	Medium
Mango		+		≥90	5.5–7.5	High
Pineapple		+	+	30–60	5.0–6.0	Medium
Oil Palm		+	+	≥90	4.0–8.0	High
Soyabean		+	+	60–90	4.5–7.5	Medium
Cassava		+	+	≥90	5.5–6.5	Medium/low
Sugar Cane	+			≥90	4.5–8.5	High
Cocoa		+	+	≥90	4.5–8.0	Medium/high

Questions

1 Explain the variation over time in the biomass of the dwarf shrubs and grasses in a heather ecosystem.
2 Why is it important to manage heather and create a mosaic of different stages in its life-cycle?
3 What are the main pressures on Britain's moorlands and peatlands?
4 Why are moorlands and peatlands vulnerable to human activity?
5 Define the following terms: agroforestry, carrying capacity, and cash crops.
6 Compare the Popoluca's methods of farming and the natural tropical rainforest ecosystem. What lessons can be learnt from this?
7 Using the information in Figure 13.60 and Figure 13.62 describe and explain the differences between the traditional milpa system of the Popoluca Indians and the new methods and techniques of plantations and ranches.

The effects of agriculture on ecosystems

Agriculture alters natural ecosystems so that biomass, in the form of crops and livestock, is from the land and used for human or animal consumption. Production can be increased by the use of fertilisers, genetic developments, irrigation and mechanisation. At the same time crop losses to pests and weeds can be reduced by mechanical weeding, biological control and the use of pesticides, such as insecticides, fungicides and herbicides.

During the Second World War and the early years after, European agriculture failed to meet demand and increased food production became central to agricultural policy from the late 1940s. Farmers were encouraged to produce more food through a variety of mechanisms, such as price support, subsidies, and research and development. As a result, European agriculture met its food needs with increasing economic efficiency. However, there was an environmental cost.

There is no doubt that agriculture affects the environment. However, agriculture is also a victim of a degraded environment. Increased concentrations of sulphur dioxide and nitrogen dioxide in the atmosphere are harmful to plant growth. Tropospheric ozone, air pollution, and increased CO_2 levels can all reduce agricultural production. The effect on soils has been covered on pages 453–60.

Air pollution

Agriculture contributes to a variety of emissions to the atmosphere. This includes ammonia and methane in particular. About 90 per cent of European ammonia emissions (8–9 mt/year) come from livestock farming and the application of manure. In the UK cattle and sheep account for about one-quarter of total methane emissions (4.4 mt/year). These ammonia emissions damage terrestrial and aquatic ecosystems and are an economic loss of valuable nitrogen fertiliser as well. The problem is particularly severe in areas of intensive animal husbandry such as in parts of the Netherlands, Denmark and Belgium. The Netherlands and Denmark have specific programmes for reducing ammonia emissions from agriculture.

Use of fertiliser can contribute to gas nitrous oxide (N_2O) emissions. Denitrification by bacteria, especially in poorly drained soils, generates N_2O. Pesticides drift in the air and this can result in long-distance atmospheric transport of pesticides and pesticide residues in rain water.

Water quality

The main types of pollution from agricultural activities are from nitrates, pesticides, runoff of silage effluent, and slurry. Although the main source of phosphorus pollution is from sewage, animal manure is also an important source. Moreover, once phosphorus is in groundwater or soil, it is more difficult to remove than nitrates. Rising nitrate levels threaten the quality of drinking water. In addition, levels of nitrates and phosphates can lead to eutrophication of fresh and coastal waters.

The use of pesticides, especially herbicides, which are also used in non-agricultural activities such as on roads and railways, can lead to contamination of waterbodies and residues in drinking water supplies. Toxic pesticide residues can enter the food chain via groundwater and surface waters, the soil, the crop itself or through direct contact. Accidental spills and leaks of materials high in organic matter into waterbodies, such as slurry and silage effluent, can deprive aquatic organisms of oxygen and lead to serious loss of aquatic life. Erosion of agricultural soils and associated runoff can lead to sedimentation of waterbodies.

Habitat destruction

Many landscapes have been destroyed, in particular wetlands, peatlands and hedgerows. The channelisation of streams and small waterways running through agricultural land to improve land drainage has often been associated with a decrease in aquatic biodiversity in these waterways. Other landscapes have been altered by afforestation, tourism and recreation, infrastructural developments such as rural road networks, urban sprawl, and industrial development. All of these factors have played a role, but agricultural development has had the greatest influence on the reduction of biodiversity. The loss of natural habitats, combined with rising levels of toxic pesticide residues in the environment, has had significant effects on wildlife and biodiversity. Pesticides also have effects on **non-target species**.

The loss of visual amenities by changes in the rural landscape is also a matter of grave concern. For example, hedgerow removal, clearing of woods, realignment of watercourses, the disappearance of meadows and riparian forest along waterways, and the abandonment of terraces, make mechanised farming easier.

Agricultural policies

Some of the most important effects on the environment that can be linked to agricultural policy have resulted from price support systems for agricultural products. This was one of the main features of the Common Agricultural Policy (CAP). Most countries, especially those in Europe, have adopted relatively intensive policies to achieve greater and more efficient output from agriculture. These include:

- guaranteed prices regardless of the levels of output and demand for certain products such as dairy products, cereals, beef and wine
- financial support through subsidies and low-interest loans for investment in certain types of capital
- high import tariffs
- land reclamation and farm rationalisation
- support for farming in marginal areas (often with serious environmental consequences)
- an expansion of research services.

Policies using these measures were particularly effective among the countries of North West Europe, where agricultural production and labour productivity rose substantially from the 1960s. However, this success led to excess supply of some products and the creation of food mountains and wine and milk lakes.

The challenge therefore is to balance three different basic needs:

- the production of food and agricultural products
- the protection of the environment
- the maintenance of the socio-economic fabric of rural areas.

Specific measures designed to help farmers reduce impacts on the environment and to protect the rural landscape include financial compensation or assistance for:

- using less intensive farming methods, such as reducing the amounts of fertiliser and pesticide used or reducing the number of livestock grazed per hectare
- switching arable land to grasslands and meadows
- preserving farming areas/methods that maintain high-quality biotypes (hedges, mixed woodland/farmland) and biodiversity
- taking some agricultural land out of productive use and ensuring long-term 'set-aside' for other purposes such as wetlands
- afforestation
- organic farming.

Questions

1 In what ways have agricultural developments influenced ecosystems? Distinguish between positive and negative effects.
2 Briefly explain the impact of pesticides and fertilisers on ecosystems.
3 How does agriculture lead to a reduction in biodiversity?

Bibliography

References

Briggs, D. et al., *Fundamentals of the physical environment*, Routledge, 1997.

Briggs, D. and Courtney F., *Agriculture and Environment*, Longman, 1985.

Curtis, L et al., *Soils in the British Isles*, Longman, 1976.

Knapp, P., *Soil Processes*, Unwin.

Money, D. C., *Climate, soil and vegetation*, UTP.

O'Hare, G., Soils, *vegetation and ecosystems*, Oliver and Boyd, 1988.

Ollier, C., *Weathering*, Longman, 1984.

Owen, L., and Unwin, T., *Environmental management: readings and case studies*, Blackwell, 1997.

Park, C., *The environment*, Routledge, 1997.

Tivy, J., *Biogeography – a study of plants in the ecosphere*, Longman, 1993.

Trudgill, S., *Soil and Vegetation Systems*, OUP, 1977.

Trudgill, S., 'Soil Processes and their significance', in Clark, M., et al., *Horizons in physical geography*, Macmillan, 1987.

Vincent, P., *The Biogeography of the British Isles*, Routledge, 1991.

Internet

Ministry of Agriculture, Fisheries and Food
http://www.open.gov.uk/maff/maffhome.htm

Environment Agency
http://www.environment-agency.gov.uk/

14 pollution of the natural environment

Pollution: an overview

Pollution is defined as the contamination of the earth/atmosphere system to such an extent that normal environmental processes are adversely affected (Figure 14.1). Pollution can be natural, such as from volcanic eruptions, as well as human in origin. It can be deliberate or it may be accidental. It includes the release of substances which harm the sustainable quality of air, water and soil, and which reduce human quality of life. Polluted elements are disagreeable, noxious, toxic, harmful and/or objectionable. It is difficult to define the levels which constitute 'pollution' and much depends on the nature of the environment. For example, decomposition is much slower in cold environments thus oil slicks pose a greater threat in Arctic areas than tropical ones. Similarly, levels of air quality which do not threaten healthy adults may affect young children, the elderly or asthmatics.

The costs of pollution are widespread: death, decreased levels of health, declining water resources, reduced soil qualit, and poor air quality for example. These have a significant effect upon people's quality of life. Thus it is vital to control and manage pollution. To be managed successfully pollution must be treated at its source. However, unless point sources can be targeted, it may be impossible to deal with it effectively. There is no point merely treating symptoms, such as acidified lakes with lime, if the causes are not tackled, i.e. the emission of acid materials.

There has been mixed success in tackling pollution. The increase in vehicle exhausts and sewage waste are notable failures. By contrast, the reduction of detergent phosphates and CFCs have been effective in reducing pollution. For example, most synthetic cleaning products come from petrochemicals and many domestic cleaners contain bleaches and perfumes. However, detergents have led to many environmental problems. Early detergents did not break down rapidly in the environment, rather they built up in streams and sewage plants (foaming at the surface is characteristic). The production of biodegradable detergents in the mid-1960s reduced the problems, but an additional problem was the use of phosphates to soften hard water and to reduce its acidity. The phosphate-rich waste water accumulated in surface waters and groundwater leading to eutrophication of streams and lakes. The only way of avoiding this was the development of phosphate-free detergents.

Pollution and economic development

Pollution normally increases with population growth and with economic developement. Figure 14.2 shows a model of air

Figure 14.1 The ground around the Millennium Dome is rapidly becoming very polluted

Key Definitions ②

eutrophication A process whereby the oxygen in water becomes depleted as a result of the uncontrolled growth of plankton and algae.

hazardous wastes Wastes that pose a present or potential threat to humans or wildlife.

hydrosphere The totality of the earth's water, comprising oceans, lakes, streams, underground water and all snow and precipitation.

incineration The burning of refuse, often in a specially designed facility.

nonpoint sources Broad areas where pollutants originate and enter the natural environment.

point sources Discrete sources of contaminants that can be represented by single points on a map.

pollutants Materials that have harmful impacts and degrade the environment.

pollution Materials with harmful impacts on the natural environment, or the act of releasing such materials.

recycling The process of taking apart an old product and using the material it contains to make a new product.

salinisation Contamination of groundwater by salt water.

sanitary landfill A disposal site for waste in which a layer of soil isolates the waste from birds, insects and rodents and minimises the amount of precipitation that can infiltrate the refuse pile.

secure landfill A landfill that is specially designed and engineered to contain hazardous materials.

septic tank A holding tank designed to receive domestic sewage from a single household.

waste The residual materials and by-products that are generated by human use of the earth's resources and end up unwanted and unused.

wet deposition Materials transported in suspension in the air, which eventually settle out as precipitation.

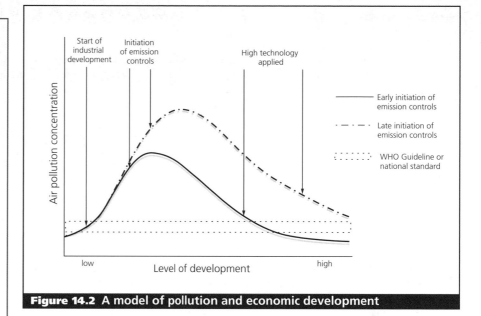

Figure 14.2 A model of pollution and economic development

Figure 14.3 Maquiladora developments – polluted drainage gulley in Mexico

quality and levels of economic development. Poor countries, such as Bangladesh, have weaker economies. Such countries favour industrialisation and the use of cheap, inefficient energy resources, such as lignite and low grade coal, as a source of energy. Hence investment in pollution control is minimal. By contrast, rich countries, such as the UK, which have gone through a process of deindustrialisation, have the capital and the technology to tackle air pollution.

Pollution is associated with development, in particular capitalist development. However pollution is not restricted to capitalist countries. The communist countries of the former Eastern Bloc seem to have large-scale pollution problems. In particular, the former East Germany has the highest sulphur dioxide emission rates per person in the world. And there is evidence that many multinationals are exporting (or developing) pollution in many NICs and developing countries. Many are related to the activities of multinational companies such as the Bhopal disaster in India (1984) and the impacts of maquiladora developments in Mexico (Figure 14.3). Pollution has often been regarded as 'the price of progress' or as the result of developments to improve the quality of life. However, the costs of the disregard for the environment are clear: the hole in the ozone, desertification, deforestation, dead seas and so on.

Managing pollution

It is easy to estimate the cost of controls but more difficult to assess (in monetary terms) the benefits of protecting the environment. Hence, it is difficult to develop any form of pollution control. In addition, it is complicated to assess the actual costs of pollution and to decide who should bear the costs. It is even more complicated to develop cross-frontier strategies when dealing with pollution. The 'ecological time-lag' means that pollution problems are often not recognised until it is too late to do anything about them, let alone decide on a course of remedial action.

There are a number of views and issues regarding pollution. For example, is pollution a necessary effect of growth and is it the price of progress? Are economic development and environmental management two opposing themes? Are they merely a battle between short-term profits and long-term costs? Pollution control measures and prevention strategies are often opposed on the basis of costs. But how do you cost fresh air, clean water and fertile soil, for instance?

Managing waste

Waste has increased in all developed countries. Major sources of waste include agricultural, industrial, municipal and mining activities. The type of waste varies by country, its type of activities and its stage of development. Waste is also changing in its composition. Increasingly, plastics and packaging materials form part of waste products (the impact of certain forms of packaging is discussed in Chapter 15, Global Environmental Change). In Europe, for example, most waste is disposed of in landfills (Figure 14.4). Without proper management, these can release pollutants into the soil and groundwater. In addition, CO_2, methane and other toxic gases may be produced in landfills.

There are a number of options to reduce and manage waste production. These include:

■ controlling pollutants (waste reduction or reduce emission; reuse, recover and recycle materials; treatment; landfill)

■ clean up contaminated sites

■ prevent waste movements.

Wastes should be minimised to such a level that natural resources and the environment are not threatened by their production and management. Ultimately, this requires changes in production and consumption patterns and modifications in people's lifestyles. For example, current levels of waste production in most European countries are unsustainable. To achieve sustainability requires minimising the use of resources and reducing their waste. This could be achieved through a variety of methods:

■ create **reduction targets** such as on the emissions of CO_2

■ design **waste management plans** which reuse, recycle and recover materials

■ develop improved **monitoring** of waste sites

■ establish a **comprehensive list** of contaminated sites

■ coordinate **waste management strategies** across international boundaries

■ establish **indices of environmental management** (Figure 14.5).

Figure 14.4 A major landfill site

The Index of Corporate Environmental Engagement includes whether a company has an environmental management system, publishes environmental targets, or a 'green' programme and whether it has a board member responsible for the environment. Companies that lacked such features were 'less likely to perform well' environmentally.

This helps explain why utilities, oil, gas, mining and chemical companies, which have the most to lose from environmental mishaps, tended to be in the top bands. Retailers, consumer goods, manufacturing and service companies, were scattered across the spectrum. The financial sector, however, tended to appear in the lower ranks.

Absolute scores (% of total points)	1st quintile 83-94 2nd quintile 69-82	3rd quintile 57-68 4th quintile 47-56	5th quintile 3-42

1st quintile	2nd quintile	3rd quintile	4th quintile	5th quintile
British Airways	Allied Domecq	Argos	Abbey National	Bass
BT	Asda Group	Bank of Scotland	Barclays	Burmah Castrol
Enterprise Oil	BAA	Blue Circle Industries	British Aerospace	Burton
ICI	BAT Industries	Boots	Cable & Wireless	Commercial Union
Marks and Spencer	BP	British Gas	Cadbury Schweppes	General Accident
National Power	British Steel	Courtaulds	Carlton Comms	Granada
National Westminster Bank	GEC	Glaxo Wellcome	Dixons	Great Universal Stores
RTZ Corporation	Grand Metropolitan	Guinness	Kingfisher	Land Securities
Safeway Stores	Hanson	National Grid	Ladbroke	Rank Organisation
Scottish Power	J Sainsbury	P&O Steam Navigation	Legal & General	Reuters Holdings
Shell Transport & Trading	Lasmo	Pilkington	Reckitt & Colman	Royal Bank of Scotland
SmithKline Beecham	PowerGen	Redland	RMC	Royal Sun Alliance
Thames Water	Severn Trent	Southern Electric	Rolls-Royce	Scottish & Newcastle
Unilever	Smith & Nephew	Tate & Lyle	United Utilities	Tesco
	Thorn EMI		3i Group	TI Group

Source: *Business in the Environment* 1996

Figure 14.5 Polluting industries marked by index

Contaminated sites in Denmark

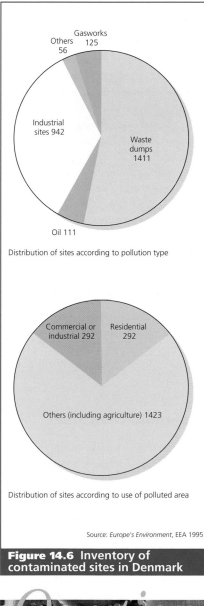

Gasworks 125

Others 56

Industrial sites 942

Waste dumps 1411

Oil 111

Distribution of sites according to pollution type

Commercial or industrial 292

Residential 292

Others (including agriculture) 1423

Distribution of sites according to use of polluted area

Source: *Europe's Environment*, EEA 1995

Figure 14.6 Inventory of contaminated sites in Denmark

There are about 11 000 contaminated sites in Denmark and by the mid-1990s over £75 million has been spent registering the sites (Figure 14.6), making them safe and beginning the clean-up operation. The total cost is likely to be over £2 billion. The majority of contaminated sites are former waste dump sites, and about 15 per cent are used for residential purposes (Figure 14.7). Leachates contain mainly organic substances, heavy metals, solvents, chlorinated organic solvents, oil, petrol, and other substances coming from tars.

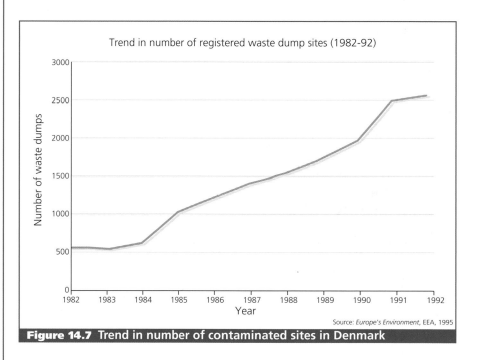

Trend in number of registered waste dump sites (1982-92)

Source: *Europe's Environment*, EEA, 1995

Figure 14.7 Trend in number of contaminated sites in Denmark

1 'Pollution is the price of progress.' Discuss, using examples to support your answer.
2 Using examples, describe how and why the nature of pollution differs between developed and developing countries.

Air pollution

Atmospheric pollution has been an important local issue for at least 2000 years, but has come to the fore as a global issue since the 1970s. The atmosphere has long been regarded as a dumping ground for gaseous and particulate waste. For example, in 1306 a Royal Proclamation banned people from using sea coal in London furnaces because of the impact it had on human health. However, it was not until the industrial revolution in the nineteenth century that air pollution intensified in dramatic fashion (Figure 14.8). Over the last century or so, land and water surfaces have been used on an increasing and unsustainable scale.

There were many attempts to deal with pollution. The Alkali Act of 1863 was the first attempt at a comprehensive clean air act, and the 1875 Public Health Act

Figure 14.8 Air pollution in the UK – associated with industrialisation

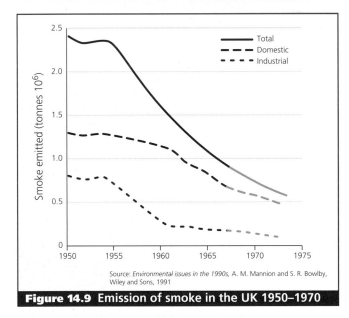

Source: *Environmental issues in the 1990s*, A. M. Mannion and S. R. Bowlby, Wiley and Sons, 1991

Figure 14.9 Emission of smoke in the UK 1950–1970

attempted to control the emissions of noxious gasses, smoke and dust from specified industries. In the twentieth century, however, air pollution continued to increase for a number of reasons:

- **population expansion**
- **industrial and technological growth**
- **increased standards of living**
- **greater manufacturing and energy consumption**
- **urbanisation concentrating people and manufacturing in close proximity.**

Air pollution has proved difficult to control, given the wide variety of sources and emissions. Industry is most readily subjected to control in the design and siting of plants. However, much of the cost is borne by the consumer. For example, in the acid deposition debate, coal-fired power stations are the main targets for reductions, whereas the

emissions of nitrogen oxides and sulphur oxides from vehicles continue unchecked. Moreover, much suspended particulate matter (smoke) is emitted from inefficient domestic burners and fires, and up to 90 per cent of sulphur dioxide comes from industrial and power stations.

Two of the pillars of pollution control in the UK are the 1956 and 1968 Clean Air Acts. Their impact is shown in Figure 14.9. The improvement in air quality took place despite an increase in population of 10 per cent, and an increase of energy consumption of almost 20 per cent. Coal was replaced by gas and electricity.

Motor vehicles account for about 35 per cent of total UK emissions (and about 60 per cent of US emissions). The main pollutants from vehicles include carbon monoxide (92 per cent of the total emitted), hydrocarbons (4.5 per cent), nitrous oxides (3 per cent) and sulphur oxides (0.5 per cent). Lead pollution is closely connected to emissions from car exhausts but also to coal burning and oil smelters. Each gallon of petrol contains about 2 g of lead. Of this between 0.5 g and 1 g becomes airborne in the form of stable lead halides and oxides. In 1970, car exhaust emissions of airborne lead in the UK were almost 10 000 tonnes, compared with 100 tonnes from coal burning. However, these were reduced by over 90% by the 1990s.

Sulphur is the major pollutant from the burning of coal and oil and more than two-thirds of sulphur dioxide emissions occur in the northern hemisphere. However, two-thirds of the global total come from natural sources such as sea spray and bacterial and organic processes. Similarly, over 80 per cent of carbon dioxide is produced naturally by animal respiration, the rest being produced by the burning of fossil fuels. Since the Industrial Revolution about 300×10^9 tonnes of the gas have been added to the atmosphere.

Air quality in developing countries

Poor air quality affects over half of the world's urban population, some 1.6 billion people. Each year several hundred thousand people die due to poor air quality, and many more suffer ill health. The problem is increasing due to:

- **increasing population growth in urban areas**
- **industrial development**
- **an increase in the number of vehicles worldwide.**

The world's population is growing by about 95 million people each year. This increases the demand for energy, transport and heating. As more people choose to live in urban areas they are increasing the levels of air pollutants in these areas.

In developing countries population growth is very rapid, and cities have less resources to cope than cities in developed countries. Overcrowding is widespread in many cities. In addition, in many developing countries indoor air pollution is high due to the burning of fuelwood and paraffin for cooking and heating. Up to 700 million people in the Developing World are at risk of high levels of indoor air pollution.

One of the major sources of air pollution is motor vehicles. At present, developing countries account for about 10 per cent of the world's motor vehicles and about 20 per cent of the world's cars. This proportion will increase greatly over forthcoming decades. In particular some countries, such as India and China, are expanding their car industries as a key part of their economic development. Cars and other vehicles in developing countries tend to be less fuel efficient and produce more pollution because they are older, poorly serviced and lacking in clean, environmentally friendly technology. In addition, roads are often in a poor state and this reduces the quality of vehicles quickly. In many cities there are limited funds to tackle urban air pollution since city planners have to balance the demands of the environment against the needs for housing, education, employment, health and so on. Environmental issues are rarely top of the agenda.

SPATIAL FOCUS

Air pollution in Beijing

Beijing, the capital of China, is sited between two rivers on the north-western border of the Greater North China Plain (Figure 14.10). Its population is about 11 million people and its population density about 27 600 people per square kilometre in the central area. Winters in Beijing are cold: the mean monthly temperature for January is 4.6°C, and minimum temperatures below −20°C are not uncommon. By contrast, summers are hot and humid: the mean monthly maximum is 26.1°C in July, and temperatures of over 40°C have been recorded. These temperature extremes, combined with the city's dependence on coal for heat and power, produce a large difference between Beijing's winter and summer air pollution levels – particularly levels of sulphur dioxide (SO_2) and suspended particulate matter (SPM) (Figure 14.11).

Beijing is a city full of potential sources of pollution. Over 5700 industrial enterprises operate in Beijing, including 24 power plants,

Figure 14.10 China

28 non-ferrous and 25 ferrous metal smelters, 18 coking plants, 194 chemical plants and 483 metal products factories. Coal accounts for 70 per cent of all energy used in Beijing. The city government has attempted to control industrial pollution by relocating certain industries, such as electroplating, away from the central area and new enterprises are actively discouraged from entering the city. However, the major iron and steel complex of Shijing, 24 km west of the city, has both blast and electric furnaces and remains a major source of industrial pollution.

Annual coal consumption in Beijing is 21 million tonnes. About 30 per cent of the coal is used in industry, 20 per cent for coking, 20 per cent for residential heating, 14 per cent for electricity generation and 16 per cent for other uses. Beijing coal has a fairly low sulphur content. Coal for domestic combustion is 0.3 per cent sulphur, and coal for small-scale industry and commercial establishments is from 0.5 to 1.0 per cent sulphur.

Since 1981, SPM and SO_2 measurements have been made daily at four stations covering central and suburban sites. Despite the coal's low sulphur content, SO_2 emissions exceeded 500 000 tonnes in 1985. This is an underestimation as it does not consider sources such as motor vehicles, heating boilers and commercial stoves. Since 1985, growing industrialisation has certainly caused increased emissions.

Industrial sources account for 87 per cent of SO_2 emissions. Of these, more than half come from just 24 power plants and 18 coking facilities. Household stoves account for 73 000 tonnes of SO_2 (13 per cent of the total), but their relative contribution is much higher in the cold winters.

Annual mean SO_2 concentrations remained relatively constant between 1985 and 1989. Monitoring stations in the city centre recorded levels twice as high as the the WHO annual mean guideline values of 40 to 60 pg/m³. By contrast, levels at the suburban stations met the WHO annual guidelines. Figure 13.11 shows the typical seasonal variation of SO_2. The highest SO_2 pollution – up to 250 µg/m³ – occurs between November and March, when large amounts of coal are burned for domestic heating. Despite nearby industrial sources, summer SO_2 levels are very low. Maximum hourly concentrations of SO_2 occur between 7:00 and 8:00 a.m. and between 6:30 and 8:00 p.m.

Levels of SPM also vary seasonally. Although Beijing is subject to severe dust fallout from dust storms coming from the western plains, these storms tend to be especially severe in the late winter and early spring. Yet, whereas natural sources account for 60 per cent of SPM emissions during summer, they account for only 40 per cent during winter. This is due to the vast amount of anthropogenic particulates emitted during the winter.

Anthropogenic SPM emissions have been estimated to be about 116 000 tonnes per year. However, this does not include emissions from motor vehicles, power plants or cooking. Industrial sources account for 59 per cent of anthropogenic SPM emissions. Heating boilers and household stoves account for 34 per cent of all SPM emissions, and are especially important during the winter. They have a disproportionate impact on human health because of to the low emission heights of chimneys and high emission

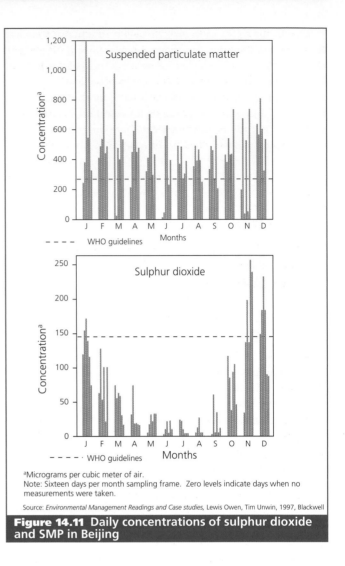

^aMicrograms per cubic meter of air.
Note: Sixteen days per month sampling frame. Zero levels indicate days when no measurements were taken.

Source: *Environmental Management Readings and Case studies*, Lewis Owen, Tim Unwin, 1997, Blackwell

Figure 14.11 Daily concentrations of sulphur dioxide and SMP in Beijing

densities (the local coal has a very high sulphur content, which leads to inefficient burning and dense SPM emissions).

Annual mean SPM levels exceed the WHO annual mean guideline of 60 to 90 µg/m³. Even without the wind-blown dust, the particulates from coal combustion alone would be above the WHO guideline value. Daily mean concentrations of SPMs are significantly higher during the winter. It is clear that the SPM pollution loads in winter represent a severe health risk for susceptible people, especially when combined with high SO_2 concentrations. However, because from 40 to 60 per cent of SPM is wind-blown dust, measures to control anthropogenic SPM emissions have only limited effects.

Due to the relatively low number of vehicles in Beijing, carbon monoxide (CO) should be a minor problem. However, indoor CO levels as high as 104 mg/m³ have been measured during cooking periods. The WHO guidelines for CO exposure are just 10 mg/m³ over 8 hours and 30 mg/m³ over any 1 hour.

Thus, many Beijing residents are exposed daily to high concentrations of SO_2, SPM and CO during the long, cold winters.

A specific pollution problem results from the many small

domestic combustion sources (Figure 14.12). Although the total amount of emissions from these small sources is relatively small, the sources contribute a high proportion of the SO_2, SPM and CO in the air because household stacks are low and pollutant dispersion is limited. For example, although household stoves contribute 13 per cent of total SO_2 emissions, these account for 38 per cent of the SO_2 concentrations.

In 1988, the Beijing Municipal Government passed regulations to implement the 1987 Air Pollution Prevention Act, which requires industries to monitor and report their own emissions. The Beijing government has also set stricter emission standards than the national standards.

Emission control programmes recently put into effect aim to:

- increase the supply of coal gas and natural gas for industrial use
- convert urban residential fuel from coal to liquefied petroleum gas and natural gas
- require residential sources still using coal to burn briquettes and shaped-coal to reduce emissions
- develop central heating plants to replace smaller boilers with a single large installation with emission controls
- modify existing boilers (where the location of industry makes central heating impractical) to reduce emissions by automatic feeding and ash removal (all boilers with a capacity greater than one tonne must install scrubbers)
- pave dirt roads and plant trees, flowers, and grass to reduce wind-blown dust.

Efforts to control Beijing's air pollution are limited by the huge capital investments necessary for control technologies. In spite of the use of environmental impact assessments for new projects, it is anticipated that emissions will continue to increase and that there will be difficulty in meeting air quality standards.

Figure 14.12 Air pollution in Beijing

Questions

1 When are the highest levels of SO_2 pollution in Beijing?
2 Suggest reasons to explain this pattern.
3 Briefly explain the daily pattern of pollution levels in a Beijing household.
4 How and why does pollution in Beijing differ from that of a UK city?

Pollution of the land

There is a wide variety of landscape pollution including rubbish dumps, spoil heaps and contaminated land. The annual production of domestic rubbish in the UK is over 300 kg per person, amounting to over 18×10^6 tonnes, in addition to 20×10^6 tonnes from commercial and industrial sources. The total volume of rubbish has increased by nearly 50 per cent since 1955. There are now more dustbins, bigger dustbins and more frequent collections. In addition, the dumping of over 700 000 cars annually is a major problem. Up to 90 per cent of all household rubbish is dumped in landfill sites. Most are controlled sites but many are uncontrolled.

Derelict land

Derelict land is land which has been so damaged by industrial or other development that it is incapable of beneficial use without treatment. This includes disused tips, worked-out mineral excavations and abandoned industrial installations. Other land may be contaminated as a result of leakages or through the dumping of waste on the site.

As with a number of geographical phenomena, there is a lack of adequate data regarding dereliction. There are two main reasons. First, many categories of derelict land are ignored by local authorities and therefore excluded from their returns to central government surveys. Second, some local authorities are unwilling to acknowledge the existence of derelict ground (perhaps because it has a poor image and negative political implications). For example, in the 1988 survey on derelict land, eight local authorities failed to respond to the government survey.

Derelict land occurs on former urban industrial, transportation and mineral extraction. Urban changes such as urban renewal and redevelopment may produce short-term dereliction whereas long-term dereliction is associated with many former mineral workings. Interest in dereliction began in the late 1940s, partly as an attempt to quantify the effect of wartime damage on Britain. The early surveys showed that dereliction was widespread. However, the causes were not entirely as expected. Although wartime damage was evident, so too was dereliction from mineral extractions, Victorian housing and industry, and some derelict buildings resulting from the 1930s economic slump. Following the Aberfan disaster of October 1966 geographers realised that contemporary processes were creating dereliction. Early estimates of the amount of derelict land in the UK varied from 60 000 – 100 000 ha with a further 1400 ha made derelict each year.

The 1988 Survey of Derelict Land recorded over 40 000 ha of derelict land in England (Figure 14.13). The most common forms of derelict land were disused spoil heaps (11 900 ha) and industrial dereliction (8500 ha) (Figure 14.14). Over three-quarters of derelict land was considered worth reclaiming, notably that in overcrowded, densely populated urban areas.

The major areas of dereliction were the urban-industrial complexes, although there were other important concentrations and causes such as china clay workings and copper mining in Cornwall and slate in North Wales. The amount of derelict land increased in Britain during the 1960s and 1970s. This was the result of many processes such as:

- **the decline of many traditional heavy industries such as engineering, shipbuilding, iron and steel production and coalmining**

- **changes in transport (the decline of railways and their associated works)**

- **an increase in construction (and an expansion in sand and gravel works).**

The total area of derelict land has declined since 1982 in all regions except Yorkshire and Humberside. The increasing awareness about derelict land, and the increasing pressure on land in and around cities led to a considerable amount of reclamation. Between 1982 and 1988 over 14 000 ha of derelict land were cleared. Of this, 63 per cent was used for sport, recreation, public open space, forestry and fishing, and 27 per cent for industry, housing and commerce (Figure 14.15). However, there are problems in trying to reclaim land. These include legal problems regarding ownership, lack of financial resources, and a lack of technical expertise. On top of this, certain land uses produce different types of derelict land. Railway property is often in the form of elongated strips, quarries exist as partly infilled holes, and military land may contain unexploded shells.

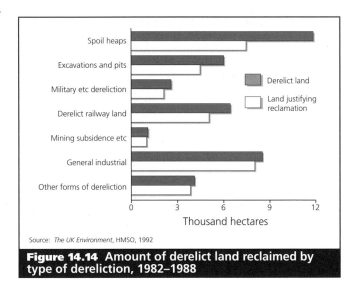

Source: *The UK Environment*, HMSO, 1992

Figure 14.14 Amount of derelict land reclaimed by type of dereliction, 1982–1988

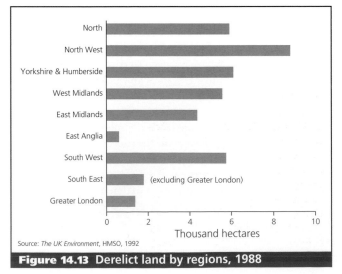

Source: *The UK Environment*, HMSO, 1992

Figure 14.13 Derelict land by regions, 1988

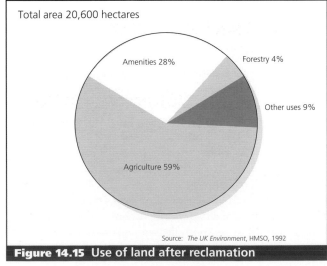

Total area 20,600 hectares

Amenities 28%
Forestry 4%
Other uses 9%
Agriculture 59%

Source: *The UK Environment*, HMSO, 1992

Figure 14.15 Use of land after reclamation

The most recent survey of derelict land (1990) reported that 49 000 ha of **urban land** in England was derelict. This may still represent an underestimation, as it is still up to Local Authorities and other public bodies to compile registers of derelict land.

The 1993 Derelict Land Survey (published in 1995) found that there were 39 600 ha of derelict land in England, of which over half were in urban areas. In all, 87 per cent of derelict land was considered worth saving. The 1993 figure represents a 2 per cent drop on the 1988 figure.

In Wales most dereliction and reclamation occurs in the south east. The Programme for the Valleys was an extensive programme of social, economic and urban regeneration covering an area of 2200 km². A second programme ran from 1993 to 1998. The area was seriously affected by the decline of the coal industry, with the number of coal miners falling from 270 000 in 1920 to 110 000 in 1945 and to just 400 in 1994. The steel industry has also lost jobs over the same period. The decline of both of these industries has caused a great deal of problems such as unemployment, poor quality housing and dereliction.

In Scotland, the major concentration of dereliction is around urban areas, notably Strathclyde (49 per cent) and Lothian (19 per cent) (Figure 14.16). There, long-term dereliction is common, i.e. nearly 60 per cent of the land has been derelict for over 10 years.

Contaminated land

Contaminated land is found in many former industrial conurbations. In addition, there are small pockets of contaminated land found throughout the country, related to the sites of gas works, scrap yards and waste disposal facilities. It is estimated that there may be as much as 100 000 ha of contaminated land in the UK (Figure 14.17).

The most common toxic soil pollutants include metallic elements and compounds, organic chemicals, oils and tars, pesticides, explosive and toxic gases, radioactive materials and asbestos. These substances commonly arise from the disposal of industrial and domestic waste products in landfill sites and uncontrolled dumps. For example, in the Netherlands 20 per cent of present and former industrial sites are contaminated, and in Germany it is between 10 per cent and 20 per cent. About £1.2 billion is spent each year trying to clean up contaminated sites. National estimates include DM 22 billion for Germany, HFL 3 billion for the Netherlands and DKR 400 for Denmark.

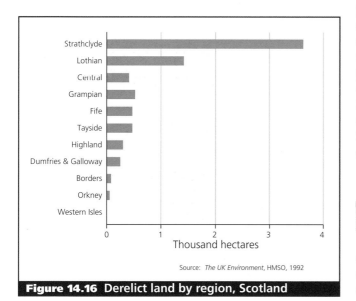

Source: *The UK Environment*, HMSO, 1992

Figure 14.16 Derelict land by region, Scotland

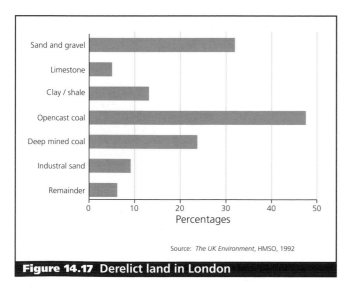

Source: *The UK Environment*, HMSO, 1992

Figure 14.17 Derelict land in London

Choose an appropriate method to map the distribution of derelict land in London using the information supplied in Figure 14.18a and b. Justify your choice of method and suggest reasons for the pattern of distribution mapped.

Figure14.18a Derelict land in London, 1993	
	Derelict land (ha)
Havering	386
Newham	243
Barking and Dagenham	220
Greenwich	219
Hillingdon	151
Hounslow	100
Ealing	49
Tower Hamlets	48
Bexley	41
Other boroughs	168
London	1625

Source: *Focus on London*, HMSO, 1997

The London boroughs

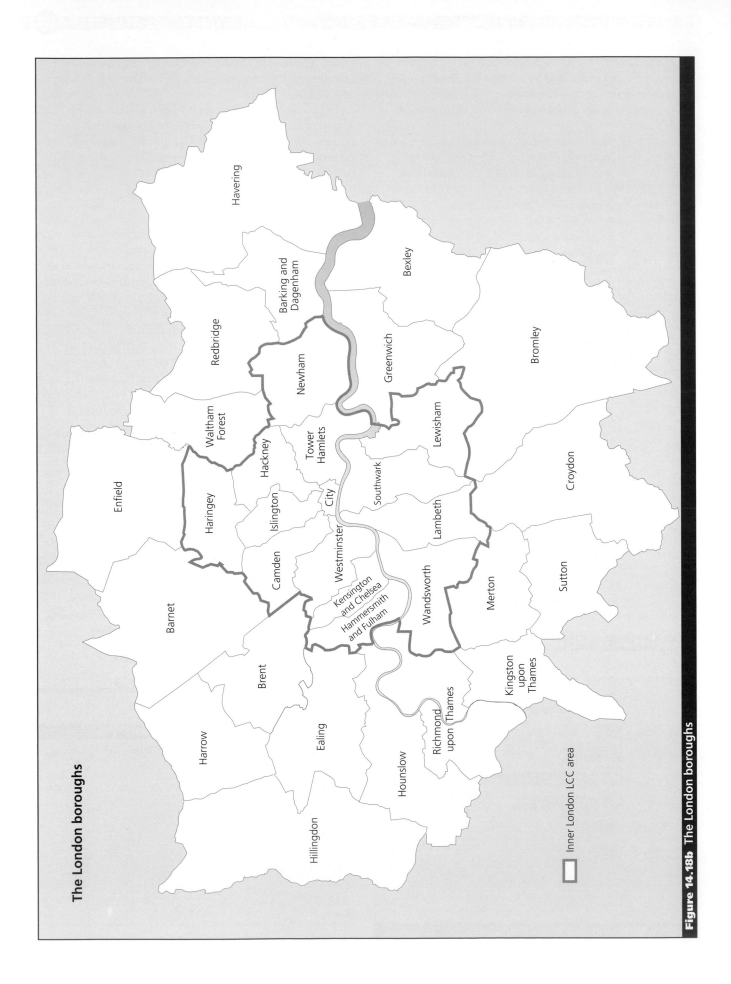

Havering

Barking and Dagenham

Redbridge

Bexley

Newham

Greenwich

Bromley

Waltham Forest

Lewisham

Hackney

Tower Hamlets

Southwark

Croydon

Enfield

Haringey

Islington

City

Lambeth

Westminster

Camden

Kensington and Chelsea

Hammersmith and Fulham

Wandsworth

Merton

Sutton

Barnet

Brent

Kingston upon Thames

Harrow

Ealing

Richmond upon Thames

Hounslow

Hillingdon

☐ Inner London LCC area

Figure 14.18b The London boroughs

Land issues in London

Restoration in practice – the Camley Street Nature Reserve

The area behind Kings Cross and St. Pancras stations in central London (Figure 14.19) contains a large amount of derelict land. It is also the scene of a bitter fight between developers and conservationists. On the one hand, the site contains a large amount of land in a prime position in London and is ripe for development (Figure 14.20). On the other hand, many of the buildings are a unique reminder of the conditions in Victorian London and contain some of the finest examples of tenement houses to be found in Britain. But the area is also important for another reason. It contains the Camley Street Nature Reserve, a beautiful ecosystem in the heart of London, which shows just what can be done with derelict land when the will is there.

In 1820 the Regent's Canal was opened. The area surrounding the canal was no more than a Victorian shanty town – the hovels that were built became known as Agar Town. The site of Camley Street Nature Reserve was part of Agar Town. By the middle of the nineteenth century land in the area was bought for the Great Northern Railway and Dickens referred to the 'notorious slums' in the region. In 1859 the first Underground Railway was opened and in 1864 the New Midland Railway started operating from the area. The Camley Street site was used as a coal depot and goods stations were later opened in the vicinity.

The area became derelict due to changes in British transport. In the nineteenth and early twentieth centuries the area prospered as the railways and storage depots increased in importance. Then, after the Second World War, as transport changed to roads rather than rail, the fate of the area was sealed. An area of 54 ha of rail land to the north of Kings Cross became derelict, along with former gas works and utilities. As railways, rail freight and coal all

declined in importance so the area became derelict. Due to the uncertainty which surrounds the future of the site (there are talks that this will become part of the Channel Tunnel Rail Link) there are no long-term plans for its development and the land has been given over to short-term activities such as car-parking, rock reconstitution (Figure 14.21) and nightclubs. These are commonly

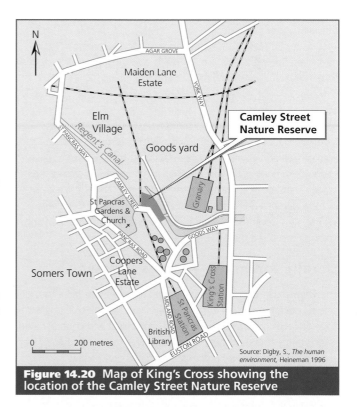

Source: Digby, S., *The human environment*, Heineman 1996

Figure 14.20 Map of King's Cross showing the location of the Camley Street Nature Reserve

Figure 14.19 King's Cross urban landscape

Figure 14.21 Rock reconstitution near St. Pancras

found in areas that lack development plans. Until the politicians and planners decide what to do with the site it will remain as one of the most important and potentially lucrative sites in London. And yet, even within the site, there is evidence of what can be achieved with a derelict site.

In 1981 the site was purchased by the Greater London Council (GLC) and used as a coach and lorry park. A survey of the wasteland plant community revealed that the site was comparable in species composition to the bombed sites during the war. By 1982 the GLC Planning Committee approved the layout and management of the site as an open space/ecological park. The area includes an ecological area, picnic area, field centre and footbridge over the region's canal to the towpath. The area of open water was increased and the range of aquatic habitat increased. However, in 1983 the site was occupied by travellers who left having fly-tipped the entire site. Clearance work had to take place and in 1985 the Camley Street Nature Reserve was officially opened.

Camley Street Nature Reserve is an ecologically important haven at a local level (Figure 14.22). It also provides much needed recreational facilities in an area of London which has a serious deficiency in open space and where dwellings have very limited access to gardens.

A recent report concluded that London is one of the most biodiverse cities in the world. A little under 20 per cent of the total area is covered by valuable wildlife habitat; this includes not just London's famous parks but its also less known lakes, woodlands, marshes and even suburban gardens. The top twenty wildlife sites include Hampstead Heath, Camley Street, Nunhead Cemetery, Wimbledon Common, Beddington Sewage Farm, Battersea Park, Epping Forest and the tidal Thames.

Dereliction in the Thames Gateway

The Thames Gateway (or East Thames Corridor) is an area that is often associated with dereliction. There is an image of the Thames Gateway which portrays it as remote, industrial and contaminated. It is certainly true that the Thames Gateway has a long history of industrial activity, including a wide range of potentially contaminative land uses, such as gas works, coke works, chemical manufacturing and refining, waste disposal sites and scrap metal stores. Up to 20 per cent of land which was outlined for development in a 1994 government survey in the Thames Gateway has accommodated such uses. In addition, railway engineering works and depots, heavy engineering works and power generation plants contaminate land. Housing is the most sensitive to contamination in the ground. About 10 per cent of land in the Thames Gateway with housing potential is contaminated.

Landfill sites also pose a threat (Figure 14.23). The main risk is that of landfill gas moving off-site over a long time period. At least 20 sites in the Thames Gateway are close to landfill sites. Of these four are producing gas and are close to open space/recreational land and housing sites. Current legislation states that new developments should not be within 250 m of a restored or currently operational landfill site. (As well as some land being

Figure 14.22 Camley Street Nature Reserve

One particular issue for landfills is the disposable nappy. Nappy waste is harmful, unnecessary and expensive. It costs £40m a year to dispose of an estimated 1 million tonnes of nappy waste, of which 75 per cent is urine and faeces. Most nappy wastage is taken to landfill sites where nappies can take an estimated 500 years to break down and add to the build-up of methane gas. Once councils have removed paper and glass and plastic from the equation they find that nappies account for 15 per cent of household waste.

Figure 14.23 Landfills and the disposable nappy crisis

derelict and contaminated some of the groundwater has been polluted. The Dartford and Gravesham areas, in particular, are located within the aquifer zone – see also Chapter 8.)

Nevertheless, the presence of contamination does not rule out development as there is a range of treatments available to restore contaminated land. In the UK the most common form of remedial measure is excavation and off-site disposal. This is becoming more difficult in the South East as sites become scarcer. It is still possible to develop derelict and contaminated land. Residential development has taken place at Thamesmead and Grays, and the Millennium Dome and associated developments are taking place on the Greenwich peninsula, a former gas works. But, there are significant cost implications. Treatment costs in the UK range from £100 000 to £350 000 per ha, but in exceptional cases it can be much higher. The actual costs in treating contaminated land in the Thames Gateway will depend upon the extent and nature of contamination, the level of clean-up required, the potential for the generation of landfill gas, the proposed after use, the implications for groundwater, and the availability of capital (money). With such costs it is likely that the cost of preparing the Thames Gateway for development will be £300 million to £350 million.

All change at the Great Western

The Great Western Designer Outlet Village (Figure 14.24) occupies the site of the former Great Western Railway works. Many of the old buildings of the works have been restored and incorporated into the shopping centre. Others now house the National Monuments Record Centre and Gallery. The original works included foundries for brass and iron, halls for the assembly of boilers and engines, painting shops and tool stores. The food store of the present Designer Outlet (Figure 14.25) incorporates part of Brunel's wagon works of the 1840s.

The Great Western Company was formed in 1835 to build a railway line between London and Bristol, a distance of 200 km with hilly ground towards the west. In 1840 steam engines needed an overhaul every 100 km and they had to be changed to cope with increases in gradient. A site of rough ground near a canal junction, close to the town of Swindon was chosen for a station and maintenance depot. Initially the station and depot were separate from Swindon but as the station expanded it eventually merged with the town. The depot was a great success. By 1845 it engaged in manufacturing and engineering. By 1900 Swindon had grown to 45 000, of whom 10 000 worked in the GWR.

The GWR peaked in the 1920s and after the Second World War the GWR declined. In 1948 the rail network was nationalised. Rationalisation and mechanisation reduced the importance of GWR as an employer. In 1960 the last steam engine was built and in 1986 engineering work finished on the site.

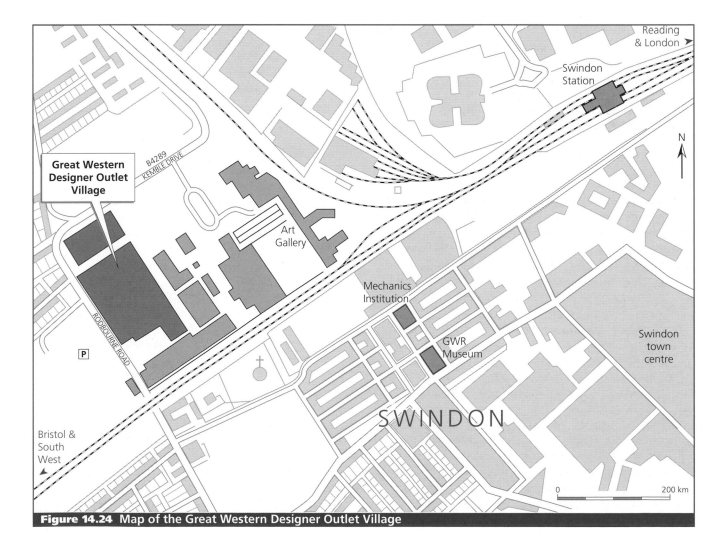

Figure 14.24 Map of the Great Western Designer Outlet Village

Transport has been a key to Swindon's changing success over time. The GWR was closely associated with Swindon's development and then the M4 was a key component. Swindon's accessibility made a good site for a wide range of activities such as car manufacturing (Honda), product distribution (W. H. Smith), computer services and corporate headquarters. In addition, modern transport patterns – the overwhelming dominance of the private car – has allowed the Great Western Designer Outlet Village to convert the derelict works into a thriving retail centre. Good accessibility to surrounding towns, such as Bristol, Reading, Cheltenham and Oxford, and large amounts of car parking, have helped the success of the centre. Buildings have been converted to house the National Monuments Record Centre, the Retail Village and a GWR heritage centre.

Figure 14.25 **The GWR redeveloped as a retail centre**

Mineral workings

Materials that are mined are normally classified in four groups:

- **metals such as iron ore and copper**
- **industrial minerals such as lime and soda ash**
- **construction materials such as sand and gravel**
- **energy minerals such as coal, oil and natural gas.**

Construction minerals are the largest product of the mining industry, being found and extracted in almost every single country. The amount of material extracted is immense. In the 1990s up to 20 billion tonnes of stone, sand and gravel were mined annually, and to build 1 km of motorway requires over 125 000 tonnes of crushed rock.

In the late 1980s 116 000 ha of land in England had permission for surface mineral extraction or disposal of mineral wastes (Figure 14.26). Permission for sand and gravel was the most extensive, accounting for 30 per cent of the area permitted for extraction. (Details about underground extraction and mining are less clear but are thought to amount to over 750 000 ha.)

Between 1982 and 1986 over 20 000 ha of land were reclaimed from mineral workings. The majority of this land (over 80 per cent) had conditions attached to their licence ensuring reclamation followed extraction. The main uses following reclamation are agriculture (59 per cent) and amenity (29 per cent) (Figure 14.15). Most of the land returned to agriculture came from three mineral types – sand, gravel and coal. On the other hand, disused mineral workings accounted for over half the derelict land recorded in England. Most of these sites were old sites whose licence had not included any provisions for reclamation.

The environmental impacts of mining are diverse (Figure 14.27). Habitat destruction is widespread, especially if opencast or strip mining is used. Disposal of waste rock and 'tailings' may destroy vast expanses of ecosystems. Copper mining is especially polluting – to produce 9 million tonnes of copper (world production levels in the 1990s) 990 million tonnes of waste rock are produced. Even the production of 1 tonne of china clay (kaolin) creates 1 tonne of mica, 2 tonnes of undecomposed rock and 6 tonnes of quartz sand. Smelting causes widespread deforestation. The Grande Carajas Project in Brazil removes up to 50 000 ha of tropical forest each year.

There is widespread pollution from many forms of mining. This results from the extraction, transport and processing of the raw material, and affects air, soil and water. Water is affected by heavy metal pollution, acid mine drainage, eutrophication and deoxygenation. Moreover, dust can be an important local problem. The use of mercury to separate fine gold particles from other minerals in river bed sediments led to contamination in many rivers. In Brazil up to 100 tonnes of mercury have been introduced into rivers by gold prospectors. Mercury is highly toxic and accumulates in the higher levels of the food chain, and can enter the human food chain.

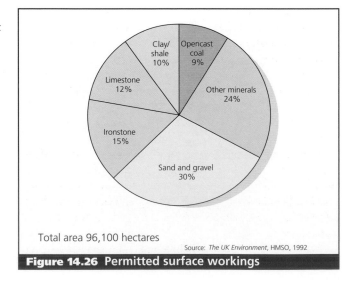

Total area 96,100 hectares

Source: *The UK Environment*, HMSO, 1992

Figure 14.26 **Permitted surface workings**

Key Definitions 3

opencast mining A form of extensive excavation in which the overlying material (overburden) is removed by machinery, revealing the seams or deposits below. In the United States it is referred to as strip mining.

spoil heaps Large unconsolidated mounds of waste materials extracted in the process of obtaining an ore.

tailings The impurities left behind after a mineral has been extracted from its ore.

Figure 14.27 Environmental problems associated with mining

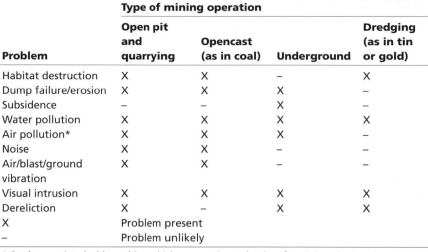

| Problem | Type of mining operation | | | |
	Open pit and quarrying	Opencast (as in coal)	Underground	Dredging (as in tin or gold)
Habitat destruction	X	X	–	X
Dump failure/erosion	X	X	X	–
Subsidence	–	–	X	–
Water pollution	X	X	X	X
Air pollution*	X	X	X	–
Noise	X	X	–	–
Air/blast/ground vibration	X	X	–	–
Visual intrusion	X	X	X	X
Dereliction	X	–	X	X

X   Problem present
–   Problem unlikely

* Can be associated with smelting which may not be at the site of ore/mineral extraction

Figure 14.28 The Cotswold Water Park

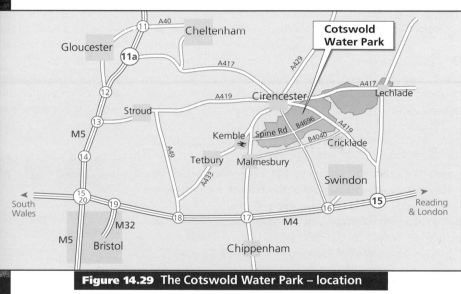

Figure 14.29 The Cotswold Water Park – location

Derelict land that results from extraction produces landforms of size, shape and origin. A major subdivision is between excavations and heaps. Heaps can be visually intrusive and have a large environmental impact. Heaps include those composed of blast furnace slag, fly-ash from power stations, as well as spoils of natural materials (overmatter) such as the white cones associated with china clay workings, oil shale wastes in Lothian, and colliery spoil heaps.

In England and Wales mineral planning authorities (MPA) are responsible for the regulation and control of mineral workings. MPAs include county councils, borough councils and National Park Authorities. New spoil heaps are now kept to a height of less than 15 m in an attempt to reduce their visual impact.

Damaged areas can be rehabilitated and managed. In many cases forward planning is the most useful method of cleaning.

Proper site surveys, replacement of topsoil after excavation and reseeding with original species helps to restore mined areas. Alternatively, spoil heaps can be stabilised with vegetation, reduced in height or landscaped. Waste materials can be used for landfill, as long as it is economic to transport it. Legislative controls, such as Environmental Impact Assessments, enable planners to work out the environmental costs of developments and to assess whether the benefits of any plan outweigh the costs. In many cases it is a matter of time. Many of the wetlands of lowland England result from flooded sand and gravel quarries. The pollution caused was temporary – but may have lasted decades. Similarly, the Norfolk Broads are an area of mediaeval peat cuttings.

Many former sand and gravel pits have been converted into recreational lakes for angling, water sports, and nature reserves. The Cotswolds Water Park is an excellent example (Figure 14.28). It is a complex of over 100 lakes offering an array of activities such as:

- two country parks each with picnic and barbecue areas, children's play areas and beach area
- three nature reserves
- walks, cycle routes and bridleways

- camping and caravanning, cabins, chalets, bed and breakfast
- corporate entertainment, conference facilities
- educational visits.

The CWP is a major employer and money earner in the area.

Opencast mining in West Virginia

America's second largest coal producer, Arch Coal, prepares to blast away mountaintops and dump the spoil in the valleys below. Eleven families once lived in Pigeonroost Hollow, West Virginia. Most families sold their homes rather than endure the dynamiting, noise and dust as the company prepares the land while waiting for a permit to start a strip-mining operation known as mountaintop removal.

Pigeonroost Hollow is a nature lover's paradise, with large butterflies, humming birds and trout in the brook. One local resident has filed a lawsuit against the state and federal governments for granting permits that allow companies to decapitate mountaintops and deposit tons of debris in the valleys. These huge waste disposal areas violate the Surface Mining Act and the Clean Water Act, so the permits should never have been issued.

Mountaintop removal – lopping 5000 m from the top of a mountain – involves little labour and gigantic £63 million machines called draglines wielding 53 cubic yard scoops. Once the trees are cut and the topsoil removed, the rock above the coal seams is blasted away. The debris is removed by trucks and draglines. Coal companies claim mountaintop removal is the least destructive and most efficient way to extract a vital resource. The land is then smoothed over, and grass and trees planted.

West Virginia, one of America's poorest states, possesses great beauty, rivers that are a whitewater rafter's dream and lush mountains. It is also blessed – and cursed – with coal. Coal has brought jobs, but the rapacity of coal companies has fermented conflict with the unions, notably the Battle of Blair Mountain in 1921 when 7000 workers fought 2000 government troops. West Virginia coal is prized as the southern mountains contain low sulphur coal which burns efficiently and produces less pollution than other coal. The 1990 Clean Air Act made West Virginia a favourite site with coal companies because the law fed demand for such coal.

Since 1995 West Virginia's division of environmental protection has permitted at least 38 new mountaintop removal mines covering 12 000 ha. Governor Cecil Underwood, a former coal

executive, previously appointed two coal executives in sequence as the state's environmental protection director!

Arch Coal wants to remove several mountaintops, extract coal and dump 150 million cubic yards of rock into five valley fills. When the work begins in earnest, Pigeonroost Hollow will become part of a 3100-acre strip-mine, the largest in the state's history. If the mining continues unabated, environmentalists predict that by 2020 half of the peaks of southern West Virginia will disappear.

Questions

1 Study Figure 14.27. Describe and account for the environmental problems associated with different types of mining.
2 Suggest reasons why there is so much dereliction in the Thames Gateway. What factors influence whether it will be cleaned up?
3 Using examples, show how former industrial land can be restored or reused.

Acidification

Sulphur dioxide (SO_2) and nitrogen oxides (NOx) are emitted from industrial complexes, vehicles and urban areas. Some of these oxides fall directly to the ground as **dry deposition** (dry particles, aerosols and gases) close to the source (Figure 14.30). By contrast, the longer the SO_2 and NOx remain in the air the greater the chance they will be oxidized forming sulphuric acid (H_2SO_4) and nitric acid (HNO_3). These acids dissolve in cloud droplets (rain, snow, mist, hail) and reach the ground as **wet deposition**. This can

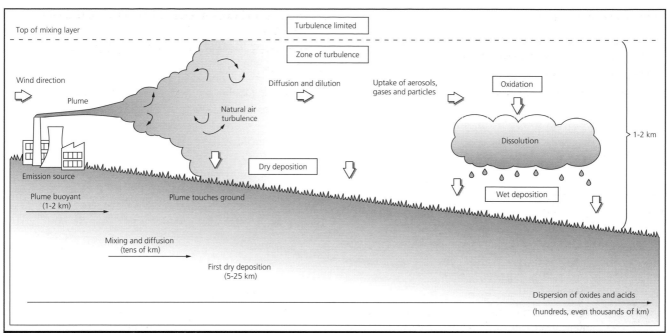

Figure 14.30 Dry and wet acid deposition

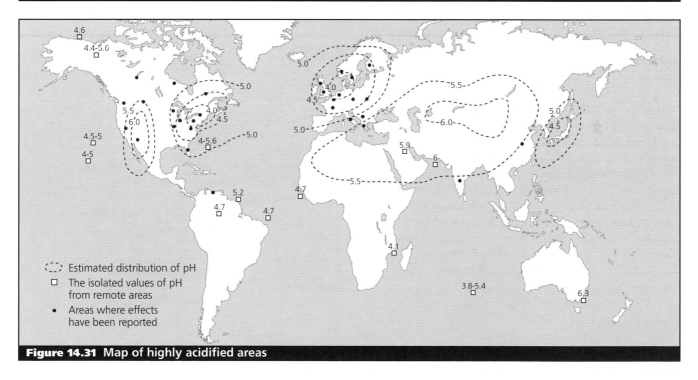

Figure 14.31 Map of highly acidified areas

be carried thousands of kilometres from the source. The dissolved acids consist of sulphate ions (SO_4^{2-}), nitrate ions (NO_3^-) and hydrogen ions (H^+). These ions form **acid rain**. In Britain 70 per cent of the acidity comes from sulphur, 30 per cent from nitrogen products.

The pH scale is logarithmic – this means that pH 6.0 is ten times more acid than pH 7.0. Natural rain water of pH 5.6 is about twenty-five times more acidic than distilled water (neutral water) of pH 7.0. Natural rain is acidic, largely due to the presence of carbon dioxide in the atmosphere. When

combined with rain water it forms a weak carbonic acid. Acid rain is frequently more than twenty times more acidic than natural rain water and rain over Scandinavia commonly has a pH of 4.2 – 4.3.

The direct effects of sulphur oxides and nitrogen oxides in the air include damage to human health, damage to plants and atmospheric corrosion. The worst hit areas include Sweden, Norway, eastern North America, Germany, Belgium, the Netherlands, Scotland, the former Yugoslavia, Austria and Denmark (Figure 14.31). The worst hit areas have a number of features in common:

- **industrialised belts**
- **downwind of dense concentration of fossil fuel power stations, smelters and large cities**
- **upland areas**
- **high rainfall**
- **they contain lots of forest, streams and lakes**
- **they have thin soils**

The future trends are likely to see increased sulphur emissions in NICs and developing countries such as China, South Africa, Brazil and Nigeria. These may lead to increased problems of acidification outside of Europe and North America where most of the problems are currently found.

Acid rain also creates acid surges and flushes especially after snow-melts and after droughts. A surge may also occur when dry deposits are flushed through a system, i.e. floods can cause acid surges. In addition, there are natural causes of acidification – bog moss secretes acid, heather increases acidity and conifer plantations acidify soils, so the increasing acidification might not necessarily be due to 'acid rain'.

The first effects of acid rain were noted in Scandinavian lakes in the 1960s. Over 18 000 lakes in Sweden are acidified, 4000 of which are seriously affected. Fish stocks in about 9000 Swedish lakes, mostly in the south and the centre of the country, are also badly affected. The most important health effect of acid water on human health is due to its ability to flush trace metals from soil and pipes. Some wells in Sweden have aluminium levels of up to 1.7 mg/l compared with the WHO safe limit of 0.2 mg/l. High levels of metal mercury in fish can cause serious health problems when eaten by people.

Trees and forests are severely affected by acid rain. Sulphur dioxide interferes with the process of photosynthesis. Coniferous trees seem to be most at risk from acid rain because they do not shed their needles at the end of the year. On a healthy conifer needles can be traced back for up to seven years but trees affected by acid rain often have needles

from only the last two or three years. If a tree loses over 65 per cent of its needles it will probably die.

Young trees in soils affected by acid rain often show abnormally rapid growth. This is because the nitrogen in the pollutants acts as a fertiliser. However, the root systems do not develop as well as in trees that have to collect their nutrients from a larger area and the trees are more easily blown over. Also, they are short of other vital nutrients and the wood can be very soft making the trees more prone to attacks from insects.

Damaged coniferous trees can be recognised because the extremities of the trees die, especially the crown which is most exposed. Needles drop and leave the tree looking very thin (Figure 14.32). Branches on some trees droop. In most cases acid rain does not kill the tree. It is one more pressure on the

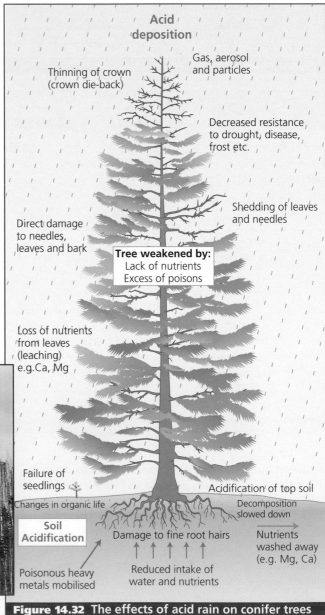

Figure 14.32 The effects of acid rain on conifer trees

tree which becomes stressed and more likely to suffer damage from insects, fungi, frost, wind and drought. Although deciduous trees generally do not suffer as much, research is showing that their growth is also affected.

Farming and forestry can also increase acidification. When plants grow they take up nutrients from the soil and it becomes more acid. When they die and rot back into the soil the nutrients are replaced and the soil becomes less acid. In farming and forestry the plants are harvested, not left to rot back into the soil which gradually becomes more acid. The removal of a whole tree including the branches and roots can be equivalent to the accumulation of 60 years of acid rain. Only taking the trunks reduces this to the equivalent of 20 years of acid rain.

Acidified lakes are characterised by:

- **an impoverished species structure**
- **visibility several times greater than normal**
- **white moss spreading across the bottom of the lake**
- **metals such as cadmium, copper, aluminium, zinc and lead becoming more soluble and are more easily available to plants and animals.**

It is the extreme pH values which cause most damage to plants and animals. Very often organisms are exposed to extremely low levels of pH during the most sensitive part of their life cycle. These short periods coincide with snow-melt and the accompanying acid surge. At these times the water also has a high metal content.

When plants absorb nutrients from the soil they release hydrogen ions, thereby acidifying the soil. However, decomposition of plants returns nutrients to the soil and offsets the acidification process. In arable areas plants are not left to rot on the land, they are removed for consumption. Hence a natural buffering mechanism is removed. In addition, use of nitrogenous fertilisers are acidifying.

The low pH of soil and the presence of metals may cause damage to root filaments (these are used by the tree to absorb nutrients). The tree loses vitality, growth is retarded, there is an inability to cope with stress (such as frost, drought and pests) and the tree becomes susceptible to injury. Needles turn brown and fall off, and finally whole branches snap away. In parts of Germany more than 50 per cent of spruce is dead or damaged.

Sulphur deposition damages plants and corrodes materials – these materials include steel, zinc, copper, nickel, aluminium, plastics, paper, leather, textiles, plaster, electrical contacts, sandstones and limestones (Figure 14.33). Acid rain corrodes metal and stonework making the maintenance of buildings more costly. The major threats are to older historic buildings. As the land becomes more acid, it is less suitable for growing crops and yields can be reduced. The crops themselves can be damaged, for example, pollen on maize affected by acid rain does not germinate so well and cannot fertilise the female plant. The effect on humans is to increase morbidity and mortality, especially vulnerable are the elderly, those with a heart problem and those with respiratory problems.

Some environments are able to neutralise the affects of acid rain. This is referred to as the buffering capacity. Chalk and limestone areas are very alkaline and can neutralise acids very effectively. The underlying rocks over much of Scandinavia, Scotland and northern Canada are granite. They are naturally acid and have a very low buffering capacity. It is in these areas that there is the worst damage from acid rain.

Acid waters can be neutralised by adding lime. This causes the aluminium ions to be fixed and precipitated to the lake bed; however this may poison species that live on the lake bed.

Since the 1960s sulphur concentrations in precipitation have remained fairly constant, although it is likely that dry deposition has increased (the more acid the air the more difficult it is for sulphur dioxide to become sulphuric acid).

Acidification is largely related to human activity but problems related to its effects on lakes, groundwater, soils and vegetation are diverse. There are environmental, social, economic, and medical implications. It is a 'post-industrial form of ruination, which pays little heed to international boundaries'. Many countries provide it and some, like Britain, export it. Nevertheless there are variations within these areas: some storms produce more acid rain depending on the source of the air mass movement in relation to the source of the oxides and the buffering capacity of the local environment.

Management: Prevention or cure?

Repairing the damage may include liming, however, this is not really sustainable. Prevention has a number of options:

- **burn less fossil fuel (this requires a government initiative in order to switch to nuclear or HEP)**
- **switch to low sulphur fuel (oil/gas plus high grade coal)**
- **remove sulphur before combustion (expensive – wash finely ground coal/chemical treatment)**
- **reduce sulphur oxides released on combustion (fluidised bed technology – FBT)**

Figure 14.33 Sulphur emissions in Europe and North America

Area	Sulphur emission combustion mt S / year	Industrial processes mt S / year	Total sulphur emissions mt S / year	Kg S per person
North West Europe	5.3	1.1	6.4	35
Southern Europe	5.0	2.0	7.0	30
Eastern Europe	5.3	1.0	6.3	57
USSR	9.8	2.5	12.3	47
North America	12.3	3.9	16.2	67

■ burn coal in presence of crushed limestone in order to reduce the acidification process

■ remove sulphur from waste gases after combustion (FGD).

Both fluidised bed technology and fluidised gas (FGD) are well developed and effective but they are very expensive.

Most nitrogen oxides (NOx) in the UK come from power stations (46 per cent) and vehicle exhausts (28 per cent). Emission from power stations can be reduced by FGD and use of different types of boiler; these reduce the amount of air present at combustion. Car exhausts can be reduced by different types of engine or exhaust, lower speed limits and more public transport.

Water pollution

As water is essential to life, people have always chosen to live close to it. However, human activities have polluted many waterways. Water pollution is a 'serious ecological disaster comparable in importance to the destruction of the tropical rainforests and desertification'. Fresh water sources, such as rivers, lakes, reservoirs and groundwater are in danger from pollution, runoff, toxic chemicals, soil erosion and invasion of exotic (non-indigenous) species (Figure 14.34).

Fresh water has many uses. These include

1 **Water uses**

■ **Lake Biwa in Japan supplies fourteen million people with drinking water.**

Questions

1 Define the term acidification.
2 What are the natural causes of acidification?
3 Which human activities lead to acidification?
4 Briefly outline the effects of acidification.
5 To what extent is it possible to manage acidification?

■ **Fresh water accounts for 70 per cent of the world's fresh water use, irrigation lands account for 18 per cent of crop land area but 38 per cent of the world's food supplies.**

■ **Hydro-electric power – in 1986 the Aswan Power Station supplied one-third of the electricity used in Egypt (in 1974 it was over 53 per cent) and provides power for a 200 000 tonne fertiliser plant.**

2 **Fisheries – in Africa fish account for 20 per cent of animal protein in the diet.**

3 **Tourism – lakes are important, e.g. the lakes of Killarney, Loch Ness, Kariba.**

4 **Biological diversity – in old lakes such as Tanganyka many of the species are endemic (80 out of 250). Since lakes are semi-closed systems fish have no means of escaping from the lake and therefore are vulnerable to ecosystem disturbances.**

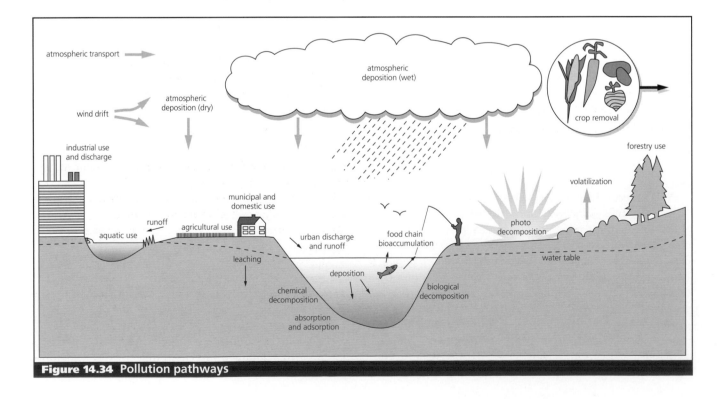

Figure 14.34 Pollution pathways

Water pollution is a major problem in many countries. It includes both physical, thermal and chemical changes. Thermal changes involve the accumulation of unwanted heat, for example from cooling water at power stations. For each kilowatt hour generated in a coal-fired power station two kilowatt hours must be dissipated by water used to cool the heat exchangers. This raises the water temperature by 5–8°C. Nuclear power stations increase the water temperature by over 10°C. The effects of adding heat to water are complex. Increases of about 2°C seriously affect fish and other aquatic life. The metabolic rate doubles with every increase of 10°C and this increases the demand for oxygen. However, at higher temperatures less oxygen is available. For example, dissolved oxygen decreases by over 17 per cent as water temperature rises from 20°C to 30°C. Hence, the effects of thermal pollution may appear invisible and innocuous.

Chemical pollution in water has many sources. These include domestic sewage, industrial effluent, acid drainage, toxic salts from mines, pesticides, pesticide fertilisers, and farm effluents (such as slurry and silage).

Like air pollution, there is a long history of legislation concerning water pollution. In the UK there are laws dating back as far as 1388 regarding the control of pollutants. For a long time, river pollution was considered the 'inevitable fate of development'. In the UK up until the 1970s pollution control was ineffective due to the decentralised administration of the water industry. There were over 1700 public and private companies! These were reorganised into 10 regional authorities in 1974.

Water uses and water quality

The world's fresh water resources are closely linked to human health:

- **25 000 people die every day because of poor water**
- **1700 million people lack clean water (1200 million lack proper sanitation)**
- **3 million people die of diarrhoea each year**
- **200 million people suffer from schistosomiasis each year.**

Increase of water pollution

There has been an increase in water pollution in the twentieth century for a number of reasons:

- **urbanisation, industrialisation and intensification of agriculture, especially when coupled with inadequate sewage collection or water treatment facilities**
- **deforestation for urban growth and agriculture**
- **the damming of rivers**

- **destruction of wetlands**
- **mining and industrial development**
- **agricultural development**
- **increased energy consumption.**

For example the world's agricultural production increased by 20 per cent between 1975 and 1984 and by over 40 per cent in less developed countries. Over-irrigation can flush nitrate water below the root zone into the groundwater zone. In addition energy consumption doubled between 1965 and 1984, resulting in increased emissions of SO_2 and NOx which has led to acid deposition.

Fresh water pollution

There is widespread pollution by sewage, nutrients, toxic metals, industrial and agricultural chemicals, but the most widespread is domestic sewage. Water pollution in many countries has intensified in the twentieth century as industrialisation and urbanisation have proceeded. Poor waste water treatment and an inadequate sanitation have resulted in an exponential increase in waste pollution.

There are six major problems facing the world's lakes and reservoirs (Figure 14.35) namely eutrophication, acidification, toxic contamination, decline of water levels, accelerated siltation and extermination of ecosystems, and biota.

Cooperation is required between producers of domestic water (high quality) and disposers of waste water (poor quality). Good management is required in the coordination and recycling of water too. However water pollution is increasing and to manage it effectively more understanding of the main pollutants is necessary.

The main pollutants

There is some evidence that developed countries have passed through a number of stages of water pollution. Figure 14.36 shows a model for the stages of water pollution. LDCs have experienced fewer stages but are expected to follow suit.

Pathogens

The most common form of water pollution is organic matter from domestic sewage, municipal waste and agro-industrial effluent. This organic matter includes faecal material, viruses, bacteria and other biological organisms. Water-borne infections include schistosomiasis, hepatitis A and gastroenteritis.

Most of these pathogens come from the sewage discarded directly into water but can also come from storm runoff, landfills and agricultural areas. In the United States 16 billion disposable nappies are dumped in landfill sites each year, a source of concentrated pathogens (see Figure 14.23). Water quality is often measured by the number of faecal coliform per one hundred millilitre of water. According to WHO coliforms in drinking water should not exceed 10 per 100 ml and faecal

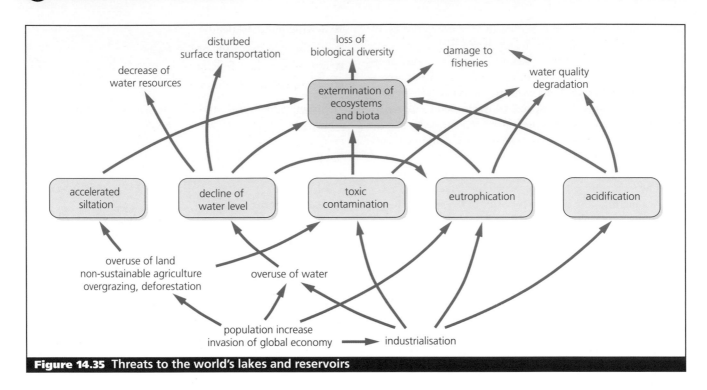

Figure 14.35 Threats to the world's lakes and reservoirs

coliforms should be zero. In parts of Asia, Central and South America high faecal coliforms correlate with high IMR (caused by gastro-enteritis). In the Yamuna river (Delhi) water flowing into the city contained 7500 faecal coliforms per 100 ml. By contrast water flowing out of the city contained 24 million faecal coliforms per 100 ml (Figure 14.37). This was a result of up to 200 million litres of raw sewage dumped into the river each day. (In Britain up to 25 per cent of beaches are contaminated by sewage.) The problem is most severe in areas of rapid population growth where the provision of water treatment facilities is much slower than urban expansion. This is most acute in developing countries. Nevertheless some developed countries have inadequate facilities. In Greece, for example, less than 2 per cent of the population is served by waste water treatment plants.

Organic matter

Organic matter contains a wide variety of carbon compounds, sources include domestic sewage and industrial effluents especially tanneries, paper mills and textile factories. Organic matter is broken down in water by aerobic microbes; this uses up oxygen from the surrounding water, thereby reducing the amount of water present in the stream. Large amounts of organic matter lead to severe reductions in oxygen levels causing a decline in biological diversity.

Nutrients and eutrophication

Large concentrations of nutrients such as inorganic matter and fertiliser can overload natural systems: many European rivers have extremely high levels of nitrogen and phosphorus, up to

fifty times the natural background levels. This overloading causes eutrophication (nutrient enrichment) which can cause algal blooms which in turn cause oxygen depletion and a decline in biological diversity. World fertiliser use is increasing rapidly, especially in developing countries and in areas where double or even triple cropping occurs. High levels of nutrient enrichment are also caused by seepage of water from septic tanks and pit latrines.

Up to 40 per cent of the world's lakes are eutrophic, small lakes are worst affected. One-third of Spain's eight hundred lakes are eutrophic, 25 per cent of major Chinese lakes are eutrophic and eutrophication is starting to occur in large waters (the Loire is heavily eutrophic) and coastal areas, e.g. Chesapeake Bay in the United States and Manila Bay in the Philippines.

Eutrophication

It is difficult to control eutrophication (Figure 14.38) because of the varied sources of the contaminants. In developing countries many cities have a limited or absent sewage system. In the UK a major problem occurs when nitrates from agricultural areas percolate into the groundwater. In east Suffolk, for example, over 40 per cent of wells have nitrate concentrations over 88 mg/l^{-1}, more than twice the safe limit. In parts of Nigeria, where nitrate concentrations have exceeded 90 mg/l^{-1} the death rate from gastric cancer is abnormally high.

In Dianchi Lake near Kunming City in the Yannan Province of China, blue green algae, micro cystis, have killed over 90 per cent of native water weed, fish and molluscs and destroyed the fish culture industry. Because water supplies

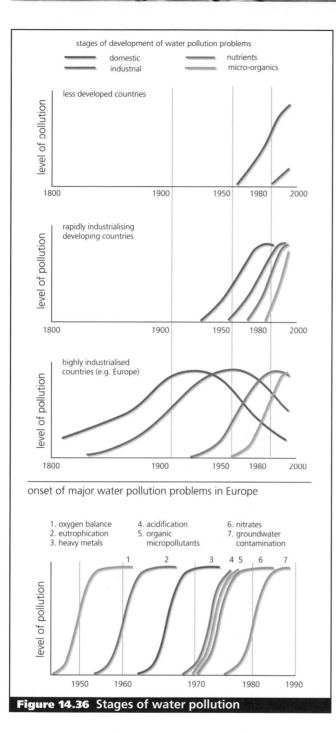

stages of development of water pollution problems

domestic   nutrients
industrial   micro-organics

onset of major water pollution problems in Europe

1. oxygen balance   4. acidification   6. nitrates
2. eutrophication   5. organic   7. groundwater
3. heavy metals   micropollutants   contamination

Figure 14.36 Stages of water pollution

Figure 14.37 Child eats a radish while his father washes clothes next to industrial waste foams: Yamuna River, Delhi

Figure 14.38 Global variations in eutrophication

Region	Percentage of lakes and reservoirs suffering eutrophication
Asia and the Pacific	54 per cent
Europe	53 per cent
Africa	28 per cent
North America	48 per cent
South America	41 per cent

- Asia and Pacific – 14 per cent of lakes and reservoirs suffer siltation
- Europe – 5 per cent
- Africa – 19 per cent
- North America – 13 per cent
- South America – 16 per cent.

Heavy metals

Heavy metals include cadmium, chromium, copper, lead, nickel and zinc. Estimates for the amount of heavy metals that have been mined and released to the atmosphere/biosphere are:

Cadmium	0.5 million tonnes
Chromium	310 million tonnes
Copper	310 million tonnes
Lead	240 million tonnes
Manganese	20 million tonnes
Mercury	20 million tonnes
Nickel	20 million tonnes
Zinc	250 million tonnes

have run short, lake water from Dianchi Lake has been used since 1992 to supply Kunming's 1.2 million residents. The city only opened its first sewage treatment plant in 1993, and this copes with only 10 per cent of the city's sewage.

Siltation

Siltation is caused by the over use or misuse of arable, grazing and forest lands. Of two hundred and fifteen lakes and reservoirs surveyed by the UNEP serious siltation was found to be widespread, for example:

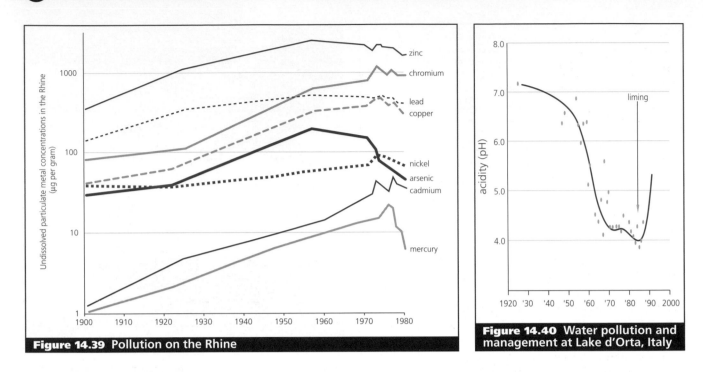

Pollution by heavy metals occurs in a number of ways:

■ **processing of ores and metals**
■ **industrial use of metal compounds**
■ **leeching from domestic and industrial waste dumps**
■ **mine tailings**
■ **contaminated bottom sediments**
■ **lead pipes.**

Heavy metals tend to affect water on a regional or local scale rather than global scale. However, it can affect areas downstream or downwind – for example the Rhine Basin supports forty million people and 20 per cent of the world's chemical industry. Until the 1970s the Rhine was severely polluted but levels have dropped significantly due to improvements in waste water treatment and replacement of certain metals in industrial processes (Figure 14.39). Nevertheless in the Ruhr catchment area about 55 per cent of heavy metals come from municipal and waste water.

Cadmium leached from mine tailings in Japan was absorbed by rice plants near the Jintsu river – the result was an increase in Itai-Itai disease during the 1950s and 1960s. Industrial waste water may become very saline, drainage from potash mines in Alsace has increased the salinity of the Rhine sevenfold since 1880; as a result Rhine water cannot be used for greenhouse cultivation as it is too salty.

Toxic chemicals

Contamination by oil occurs on a large scale on lakes where oil is extracted or transported, e.g. Lake Maracaibo in Venezuela which contains over five thousand oil wells. The lake has suffered from repeated spills during drilling, extraction and transportation and from oil-related industries on the shore.

In Lake d'Orta in Italy pollution has been linked to the development of a factory producing artificial silk (rayon). The factory deposited waste copper and untreated ammonium sulphate into the lake and the lake became seriously polluted (Figure 14.40). Only in the 1980s was a treatment plant established and the lake was treated by liming – the result has been a reversal in the acidification process.

Disruption of wetland ecosystems

Lakes are easily disrupted by the introduction of exotic species, for example the introduction of the zebra mussel in the Great Lakes ecosystem was only noticed in 1988. By 1990 the zebra mussel had bred from St Clare Lake to all five Great Lakes and by 1991 it had spread down the St Lawrence Seaway into the Mohawk and Hudson rivers and into the Illinois river via the Chicago Sanitary Canal. In affected areas dense colonies of zebra mussels clog the water intake systems of hydroelectric power stations, motor boats and waste supply systems. It is estimated that the mussels will cause up to $5000 million worth of damage to factories, ships, power plants, fisheries and water supplies by the year 2005. In Lake Victoria in East Africa serious ecological damage has occurred after the introduction of the carnivorous Nile perch and the tilapia fish, native species have become extremely rare and the haplochromine fishes are facing extinction.

Sustainable management of fresh water requires:

■ **control of non-point source pollution**
■ **control of water quality and quantity, and**
■ **reductions of erosion and salinisation.**

SPATIAL FOCUS SPATIAL

Doñana

During 1998 a flood of toxic sludge threatened one of Europe's most important wetlands, the Doñana National Park in Spain (Figure 14.41). Although the park was saved, land outside the park may have been contaminated with enough heavy metals to poison the entire region for years.

The disaster was caused by a breached dam at the open-pit mine at Los Frailes near Seville. In its first year, 1997, it produced 180 000 tonnes of zinc, lead, copper and silver from 4 million tonnes of ore. The waste water, crushed ore and chemicals left behind after the metals have been removed were dumped in a settling pond of another mine, abandoned in 1996 after almost 20 years of operation. An earth dam holds the effluent in place.

In April 1998 a 50-metre-wide breach in the dam released 4 million cubic metres of acidic water and silt down the Agrio river towards Doñana. Emergency bulldozing diverted the flood wave into the Guadalquivir river and into the Atlantic Ocean. Nevertheless, the flood waters still flooded 2000 hectares of land (Figure 14.42). These waters deposited most of their silt, as well as unknown quantities of cadmium, mercury, arsenic and other heavy metals. Once deposited, the metals are bound by soil particles and then they leak slowly into the groundwater, at a rate dependent upon rainfall levels and local acidity.

Runoff from contaminated land and groundwater flow could still reach the Doñana. Once there a catastrophe could occur. Metals would be taken up by plants at the base of the the food chain. Moreover, the flood water will damage Doñana without even reaching there. The flood critically damaged a protected region surrounding the park, a place used for nesting by birds that feed in Doñana. Migratory birds are also at risk. The disaster has angered local environmentalists, since in 1995 they launched a court case arguing that the dam holding back the settling pond was unsafe.

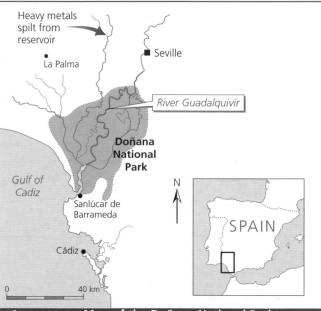

Figure 14.41 Map of the Doñana National Park

Figure 14.42 Scientists finding dead fish on the Guadalquivir River, Doñana National Park

Salinity

Salinity is caused by a combination of poor drainage and high evaporation rates leading to a concentration of salts in the soil. It is mostly associated with irrigation but can also be caused by over-pumping coastal aquifers (causing saline intrusion), use of salt on roads (to prevent icings), and as a result of mining (salt water is produced during oil production).

Irrigation accounts for almost 75 per cent of global water use (about 3300 km³/year). 270 million hectares of land are irrigated and up to 80 million hectares of irrigated land are affected by salinity – 30 million hectares severely so. The amount of land lost each year due to salinity is about 50 per cent that of new land brought into production.

Waterlogged soil is caused by unsuitable drainage (Figure 14.43). Some water may percolate down thereby raising the water table and bringing it to within a metre or so of the surface. Secondary salinisation refers to salts which are brought to the surface by ground water.

Salinity is a major problem in the Nile Valley, largely as a result of year round irrigation, poor drainage (the fine grained

Figure 14.43 Salinity and waterlogging

Countries with the largest areas of irrigated land severely affected by salinity

	total irrigated area (million ha)	(year)	area affected by salinity (million ha)	(year)
India	41.8	1986–88	12	1977
USA	18.1	1986–88	4	1985
Pakistan	15.9	1986–88	3.2[1]	1987
Iran	5.7	1986–88	1.2	1977
Iraq	2.0	1986–88	0.45[2]	1977
Egypt	2.6	1986–88	0.8[3]	1970

[1] 80 per cent of irrigated land is affected in the Punjab

[2] More than 50 per cent of the irrigated land in the Lower Rafidain Plain is affected

[3] Mostly in the north part of the Nile delta

alluvial soils do not allow easy drainage) and high evaporation rates. High evaporation causes a water shortage hence farmers irrigate more, this leads to secondary salinisation and to waterlogging.

More efficient techniques, e.g. trickle irrigation drip and sprinklers would help – open ditches and pumping from groundwater could reduce waterlogging by lowering shallow water tables.

Issues for future water quality assessment include:

- pollution from fossil fuels
- increasing strains and water supplies
- the impact of deforestation
- the impact of dams
- destruction of wetlands.

Questions

1 What are the characteristics of polluted water?
2 Figure 14.36 shows stages in water pollution. Compare how levels of pollution have varied between less developed countries, rapidly industrialising developing countries, and highly industrialised countries. How do you account for the differences you have noted?
3 Describe briefly the relationship between polluted water and health risk to humans.
4 Define the term salinisation. Suggest reasons why salinisation is increasingly a problem both in developed countries and developing countries.

Bibliography

References

Focus on London 1997, Government Statistical Service, HMSO, 1997.
The UK Environment, HMSO, 1992.
The East Thames Corridor, HMSO, 1993.
Urban regeneration, HMSO, 1995.
The changing geography of the United Kingdom by R. Johnston and V. Gardiner, Routledge, 1991.
The environment dictionary by D. Kemp, Routledge, 1998.
Environmental issues in the 1990s by A. Mannion and S. Bowlby, Wiley, 1992.
Acid Rain Transfrontier Air Pollution by C. Park, *Geography Review,* 1988.
Acidification SMA, Swedish Ministry of Agriculture, 2, 1, 20–24, 1983.
The Pollution of Lakes and Reservoirs, UNEP, 1994.
Freshwater Pollution, UNEP, 1991.
Air Pollution in the World's Mega Cities, *Environment,* 36, 2, 4–13,25–37, UNEP & WHO, 1994.

Internet

Envirolink
http://www.envirolink.org/
World Resources Institute
http://www.wri.org/wri/
CNN Earth pages
http://cnn.com/EARTH/
USGS National Water Resources
http://h2o.usgs.gov/

15 global environmental *change*

There is a long history of global environmental change. For example, the widespread use of **fire** has existed for about 500 000 years, while more localised use of stone tools has been dated to 2 million years ago at the Olduvai Gorge, East Africa. These, hand axes, chisels and hammers were made from stone and used to control the spread of natural vegetation. Although the impact of early hominids is likely to have been limited **spatially** because of their relatively low numbers and spatial concentrations, hominids may have been responsible for the extinction of up to 26 species of mammal. However, it is impossible to be sure and the extinctions may have been caused by climatic change.

Around 10 000 years ago, after the retreat of the Pleistocene ice sheets, humans advanced into most environments. **Agriculture** replaced hunting and gathering as the main source of food production, and only in North America, Australia and Siberia was agriculture limited. The impacts of agriculture on the environment were far reaching. Natural vegetation was replaced by cultivated species; energy flows were shortened and directed towards humans; nutrient cycles were broken and nutrients consumed by humans; productivity was reduced due partly to a lower biodiversity; soils became leached and acidified; important microclimatic changes took place too, such as changes to the albedo, evapotranspiration and wind speed. As human populations increased and agriculture developed, so the impact on the environment accelerated. What started as small-scale localised impacts eventually became global environmental change (Figure 15.1).

As technology increased so the human impact on the environment intensified. This is not just in agriculture but in energy consumption, manufacturing industry, transport and communications and so on. Almost all human activities have an impact on the environment. Many of these impacts are irreversible – such as the burning of fossil fuels or soil erosion (given the length of time it takes for soils to form), and some environments are especially vulnerable, such as tundra and low-lying islands. In some cases it would be wrong to portion all the blame on to humans – for example, there are natural reasons for desertification and global warming. Moreover, working out the relative contribution of natural and human causes is no easy task, and it is difficult to predict how these changes will develop, since it is possible for human actions to change.

Key Definitions

aerosols   Extremely fine particles or droplets that are carried in suspension; volcanic aerosols result from the reaction of volcanic gases with water vapour in the atmosphere whereas, increasingly, man-made aerosols are affecting the ozone layer.

carrying capacity   The maximum number of people an ecosystem can support, imposed by the limited resources of that ecosystem.

desertification   The spread of desert into non-desert areas.

drought   An extended period of exceptionally low precipitation.

exponential growth   The increase in a population by an accelerating rate over time.

glaciations   Periods during which the average surface temperature dropped by several degrees and stayed cool long enough for the polar ice sheets to grow larger; also referred to as glacial periods or ice ages.

greenhouse effect   The property of the earth's atmosphere by which long wavelength heat rays from the earth's surface are trapped or reflected back by the atmosphere.

ground-level ozone   Ozone that occurs in the lower part of the atmosphere, that is tropospheric ozone.

ozone hole   The phenomenon of stratospheric ozone depletion centred over the south polar region.

ozone layer   A zone in the stratosphere where ozone occurs in unusually high concentrations.

particulates   Pollutants that are carried in suspension in the air as extremely fine, solid particles.

Figure 15.1 The effect of fire on the rainforest environment

The greenhouse effect and global warming

The earth's atmosphere is vital for life and changes to it disrupt the natural balance of the earth's energy budget, both in terms of amount of radiation and type of radiation. There are a number of reasons why the earth's temperature changes, one of the most obvious reasons is a change in the output of energy from the sun. There is evidence of an 11-year solar cycle and longer periods of change such as the Milankovitch Cycle also occur. Slow variations in the earth's orbit affect the seasonal and latitudinal distribution of solar radiation and these are responsible for initiating the ice ages. On a shorter timescale, changes in atmospheric composition are linked with an increase in global temperature.

The earth's atmosphere raises temperatures on the planet by about 33°C. This effect can be illustrated by comparing temperatures on earth with those on the moon. The moon is an airless planet which is almost the same distance from the sun as the earth is. Average temperatures on the moon are about −18°C compared with about 15°C on earth.

Solar radiation is radiated mostly in the visible waveband between 0.4 and 0.7 micrometres (μm) (Figure 15.2). This radiation and shortwave infrared radiation passes through the atmosphere without being absorbed and although clouds may reflect some of it, most of it reaches the earth's surface and warms the land and the sea.

Water vapour in the atmosphere absorbs radiation in the 4 to 7 μm band and carbon dioxide absorbs radiation in the 13 to 19 μm band. Between 7 and 13 μm there is a 'window' through which more than 70 per cent of the radiation from the earth escapes into space. Roughly 7 per cent of solar energy is radiated at shorter wavelengths, below 0.5 μm; this is ultraviolet radiation and is important in maintaining a layer of ozone in the atmosphere. The infrared heat that is re-radiated from the earth warms the lower layer of the atmosphere (troposphere). In turn, air in the troposphere radiates heat back towards the ground and this is known as the **greenhouse effect**. Both the ground and the air above it are warmed by the greenhouse effect. As long as the amount of water vapour and carbon dioxide stay the same and the amount of solar energy remains the same the temperature of the earth should remain in equilibrium. However, human activities are upsetting the natural balance by increasing the amount of carbon dioxide in the atmosphere, as well as interfering with the other greenhouse gases (Figure 15.3).

There are a number of greenhouse gases, such as methane, ozone, nitrous oxides and chloroflourocarbons (CFCs) (Figure 15.4). These chiefly absorb infrared radiation in the 7 to 13 μm band where radiation has been able to escape freely. The best known are the CFCs and these are held to be responsible for the hole in the ozone layer over Antarctica. One molecule of CFC has the same greenhouse impact as 10 000 molecules of carbon dioxide. Emissions of CFCs used as aerosol propellants, solvents, refrigerants and foam-blowing

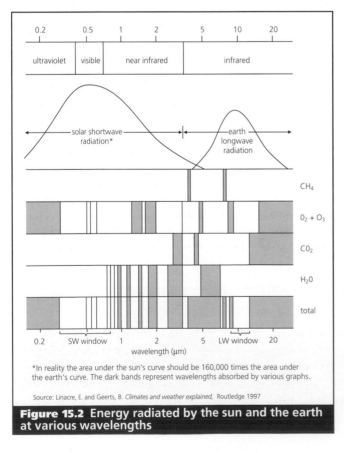

*In reality the area under the sun's curve should be 160,000 times the area under the earth's curve. The dark bands represent wavelengths absorbed by various graphs.

Source: Linacre, E. and Geerts, B. *Climates and weather explained*, Routledge 1997

Figure 15.2 Energy radiated by the sun and the earth at various wavelengths

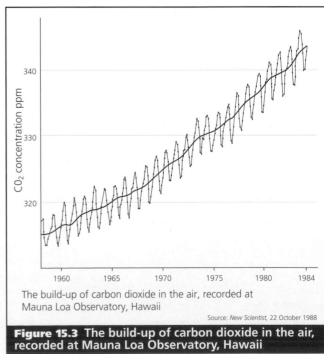

The build-up of carbon dioxide in the air, recorded at Mauna Loa Observatory, Hawaii

Source: *New Scientist*, 22 October 1988

Figure 15.3 The build-up of carbon dioxide in the air, recorded at Mauna Loa Observatory, Hawaii

agents are also well known. They were not present in the atmosphere before their invention in the 1930s. **Methane** is another greenhouse gas; at present it has an atmospheric concentration of about 1.7 parts per million (ppm) and is increasing at a rate of about 1.2 per cent per annum. This is largely due to the biological activity of bacteria in paddy fields and also due to the release of gas from oil and gas fields. Due to the increase of nitrogen-based fertilisers, the amount of **nitrous oxides** (NOx) is increasing from a concentration 0.3 ppm at an annual rate of 0.3 per cent. **Ozone** near the ground in the troposphere is increasing also as a result of human activities. By 2030 increases in these minor greenhouse gases will probably have the same impact as the doubling of carbon dioxide from 270 ppm to 540 ppm.

Since the industrial revolution the combustion of fossil fuels and deforestation have led to an increase of 26 per cent

in **carbon dioxide** concentration in the atmosphere. Accurate measurements of the levels of carbon dioxide in the atmosphere began in 1957 in Hawaii. The site chosen was far away from major sources of industrial pollution and shows a good representation of unpolluted atmosphere. The trend in carbon dioxide levels shows a clear annual pattern associated with seasonal changes in vegetation, especially over the northern hemisphere. In addition, by the 1970s there was a second trend, one of a long-term increase in carbon dioxide levels, superimposed upon the annual trends.

Studies of cores taken from ice packs in Antarctica and Greenland show that the level of carbon dioxide between 10 000 years ago and the mid-nineteenth century was stable at about 270 ppm. By 1957 the concentration of carbon dioxide in the atmosphere was 315 ppm and it has since risen to about 360 ppm. Most of the extra carbon dioxide has come from the burning of fossil fuels, especially coal, although some of the increase may be due to the disruption of the rainforests.

For every tonne of carbon burned, four tonnes of carbon dioxide are released. By the early 1980s, 5 gigatonnes (Gt) (1 Gt = 1000 million tonnes) of fuel were being burned every year. Roughly half the carbon dioxide produced is absorbed by natural sinks, such as vegetation and plankton.

Aerosols (small particles) in the atmosphere can also affect climate because they can reflect and absorb radiation. The most important natural changes result from explosive volcanic eruptions which affect concentrations in the lower stratosphere. Much of the evidence for the greenhouse effect has been taken from ice cores dating back 160 000 years. These show that the earth's temperature closely paralleled the amount of carbon dioxide and methane in the atmosphere. Calculations indicate that changes in these greenhouse gases were part, but not all, of the reason for the large (5 to 7°) global temperature swings between glacial and interglacial periods.

There are other factors which have the potential to affect climate – for example, a change in the **albedo** (reflectivity of the land brought about by desertification or deforestation) affects the amount of solar energy absorbed at the earth's surface. Similarly artificial aerosols made from sulphur emitted largely in fossil fuel combustion can modify clouds and this may act to lower the temperatures. Lastly, changes in ozone in the stratosphere due to CFCs may also influence climate.

Recent trends in greenhouse gas and aerosol concentrations

Over the decade 1980–9 the atmospheric abundance of carbon dioxide increased at an average rate of about 1.5 ppmv (0.4 per cent or 3.2 billion tonnes of carbon) per year as a result of human activities. This is equivalent to approximately 50 per cent of human emissions over the same period. The rate of increase of atmospheric abundance of methane declined in the 1980s slowing dramatically in 1991–2

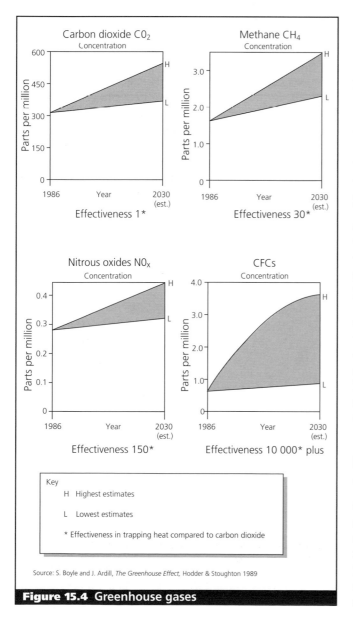

Source: S. Boyle and J. Ardill, *The Greenhouse Effect*, Hodder & Stoughton 1989

Figure 15.4 Greenhouse gases

Changes in greenhouse gases since preindustrial times

- The increasing levels of carbon dioxide since the preindustrial era from about 280 to 356 ppmv makes the largest individual contribution to greenhouse gas radiative forcing – 1.56 watts/m^{-2}.
- The increase of methane (CH_4) since preindustrial times (from 0.7 to 1.7 ppmv) contributes about 0.5 watts/m^{-2}.
- The increase in nitrous oxide since preindustrial times from about 275 to 310 ppbv[3] contributes about 0.1 watts/m^{-2}. The observed concentrations of halocarbons, including CFCs, have resulted in direct radiative forcing of about 0.3 watts/m^{-2}.

although with an increase in the growth rate from late 1993. The average trend between 1980–90 is about 13 ppbv (0.8 per cent or 37 million tonnes of methane) per year. By contrast, the atmospheric abundance of nitrous oxide increased at an average annual rate of about 0.75 ppbv (0.25 per cent or 3.7 million tonnes of nitrogen) per year. Similarly, the total amount of organic chlorine in the troposphere increased by only 1.6 per cent in 1992, about half the rate of increase (2.9 per cent) in 1989.

Stabilisation of greenhouse gas concentrations

If carbon dioxide emissions were maintained at 1995's level they would lead to a constant rate of increase in atmospheric concentration of carbon dioxide reaching about 500 ppmv, i.e. twice the preindustrial concentration, by the end of the twenty-first century. The stable level of carbon dioxide concentrations at values of up to 750 ppmw can be maintained only with emissions that eventually drop below 1990 levels.

Some effects of the rise in greenhouse gases

Researchers have considered the effect of a doubling of carbon dioxide from the base-line value of 270 ppm to 540 ppm. Such a rise would lead to:

- an increase of temperatures by about 2°C
- warming, likely to be greater at the poles rather than at the equator
- changes in prevailing winds
- changes in precipitation
- continental areas becoming drier
- sea level possibly rising by as much as 60 cm
- ice caps possibly changing in size (in fact, they may

increase due to more evaporation in lower latitudes and increased snow fall at higher latitudes).

Temperature

Global temperatures have been increasing over the twentieth century. However, other factors also affect global temperatures, such as changes in ocean circulation, solar output, volcanic eruptions and air pollution products such as aerosols. The global temperature change observed over the past 100 to 130 years of 0.45°C (+/− 0.15°C) is consistent with the expected increase in temperature estimated to result from greenhouse gases, taking into account the negative effect of ozone depletion and aerosols. Although the recent warming over Britain is probably a reflection of global changes, other fluctuations are known, in part, to be due to changes in atmospheric circulation, possibly related to changes in sea surface temperature.

Rainfall

There have been some long-term changes in the seasonal distribution of rainfall. Figure 15.5 provides evidence of a drying tendency in summer and an increase in rainfall in winter. Again, changes in atmospheric circulation are the likely direct causes of these changes but the reasons for the circulation variations are not known.

Sea level variations

Sea levels vary across a broad range of time and spatial scales for many reasons. These include:

- long-term changes in ocean base and volume from, for example, sea floor spreading or sedimentation
- medium-term changes in ocean mass from variations in groundwater, surface water or land-based ice
- short-term dynamic changes due to oceanographic (e.g. currents) or meteorological (e.g. atmospheric pressure) factors at the local or regional scale.

As a result of global warming, mean sea level may change for two reasons: expansion of the ocean due to higher sea temperatures and changes in land-based ice. The most recent projections suggest a rise of less than 1 m before the end of 2100.

Large-scale coastal movements can be important regionally. In parts of Scandinavia and Hudson Bay relative sea level is rising by about 1 m per century. Elsewhere, however, such as the east coast of North America and South East Britain, sea level is still rising due to land subsidence as a result of glacial isostatic change. In other areas it is a complex pattern, for example in the Mississippi Delta, relative sea level change is determined by the difference between the subsidence of the Delta, changes in sea level and growth of the Delta due to increased deposition as a result of river erosion. Rising sea levels are also threatening one of the most densely populated but poorest countries in the world, Bangladesh.

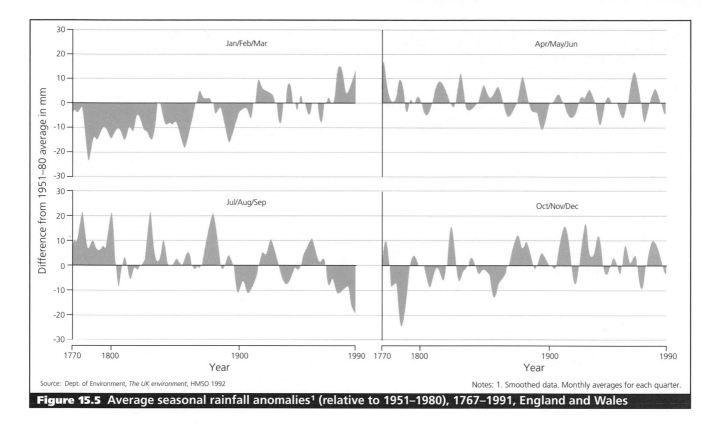

Source: Dept. of Environment, *The UK environment*, HMSO 1992

Notes: 1. Smoothed data. Monthly averages for each quarter.

Figure 15.5 Average seasonal rainfall anomalies[1] (relative to 1951–1980), 1767–1991, England and Wales

Bangladesh

Bangladesh is one of the least developed countries in the world. Less than one-third of the population is literate, the country has an average GNP of less than US $200 and there is a low per capita use of fossil fuels. The population, approximately 130 million in 1998, is growing at an annual rate of 2.2 per cent. Thus, Bangladesh contains about 2 per cent of the world's population. However, it contributes only about 0.06 per cent of the world's emission of carbon dioxide into the atmosphere. This densely populated low-lying country of about 144 000 km² consists largely of the delta of three of the world's principal rivers, the Ganges, the Bramaphutra and the Meghna. Bangladesh suffers recurrent climate-related disasters; floods in 1987–8 and the cyclone in July 1998 are good examples. For these reasons Bangladesh may be one of the countries least responsible for the causes of climatic change but is one of the countries which is most vulnerable to the effects of climatic change, especially sea level changes.

Sea level change has a number of effects other than sea levels rising: it includes adverse environmental effects such as salt-water intrusion into fresh water, groundwater, surface water, wetlands

and soils, erosion of beaches and cliffs, and inundation and flooding of farmland and homes (Figure 15.6).

The physical impacts on Bangladesh of sea level rise are difficult to predict: this is because the coastal system responds dynamically as sea levels rise. Huge quantities of sediment, about 1 billion to 2.5 billion tonnes per year are carried by the rivers, whose combined flood level can exceed 140 000 m² per second, into Bangladesh from the whole of the Himalaya drainage system including Nepal, China and India. About two-thirds of this sediment is deposited in the Bay of Bengal and over the long term causes land subsidence within the delta region. Consequently the delta is changing. As a result of this it is debatable whether residents would even notice a rise of 6 mm a year. Indeed if sedimentation rates keep pace with sea level rises the delta may remain little changed.

In Bangladesh it has often been said, but never proved, that deforestation in the head waters of the Ganges at Bramaphutra has affected runoff, sediment flow and deposition with consequent changes in coastline and flooding. The effects of this

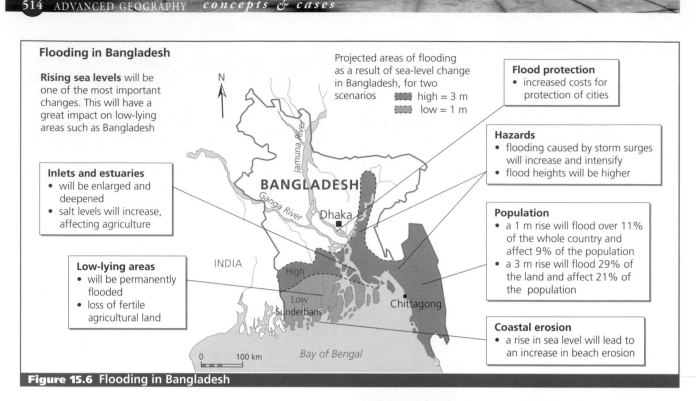

Flooding in Bangladesh

Rising sea levels will be one of the most important changes. This will have a great impact on low-lying areas such as Bangladesh

Projected areas of flooding as a result of sea-level change in Bangladesh, for two scenarios ▨▨▨ high = 3 m ▨▨▨ low = 1 m

Flood protection
• increased costs for protection of cities

Hazards
• flooding caused by storm surges will increase and intensify
• flood heights will be higher

Inlets and estuaries
• will be enlarged and deepened
• salt levels will increase, affecting agriculture

Population
• a 1 m rise will flood over 11% of the whole country and affect 9% of the population
• a 3 m rise will flood 29% of the land and affect 21% of the population

Low-lying areas
• will be permanently flooded
• loss of fertile agricultural land

Coastal erosion
• a rise in sea level will lead to an increase in beach erosion

BANGLADESH
Jamuna River
Ganga River
Dhaka
INDIA
High
Low
Sunderbans
Chittagong
Bay of Bengal
0   100 km
N

Figure 15.6 Flooding in Bangladesh

deforestation, however, may be minor compared to the effects that could occur due to interventions being considered under the flood action plan. The comprehensive plan includes major structures and extensive embankments. The main problem for Bangladesh is not a question of sea level rising, however; it is related to increased energy in the atmosphere. The biggest threat is the increase from storms, especially extreme events which cause major storm surges.

The analysis of the impact of global warming on Bangladesh highlights issues of global responsibility.

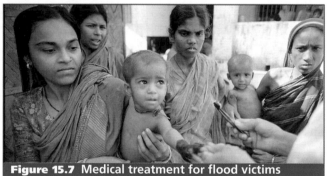

Figure 15.7 Medical treatment for flood victims

Climatic change impacts in the United Kingdom

Globally, by 2030, world surface air temperature will increase by between 0.7 to 2.0°C, with a mean estimate of 1.4°C. Summer temperature changes in the United Kingdom are considered to be comparable to the global mean value using the best model predictions available. However, winter temperature may warm faster than the global average. By 2030, winters in the United Kingdom will be 1.5 to 2.1°C warmer than today.

The mean global sea level could rise by 20 cm relative to today by the year 2030; this estimate can be applied broadly to the United Kingdom. There might be an increased frequency of storm events and coastal flooding. Areas particularly

vulnerable to changes in sea level, unless action is taken, include parts of the coasts of East Anglia, Lancashire and the Yorkshire/Lincolnshire area, the Essex mud-flats, the Somerset levels, the Sussex and Kent coasts and the Thames Estuary. The north Wales coast, the Clyde and Forth estuaries, and Belfast Lough would also be vulnerable (Figure 15.8).

The water content of soils is likely to decrease in response to increased evaporation. Such changes will have a major effect on the types of crops, trees and other land uses that soils in a particular area can support. The pattern of UK land use might change as a result. If summers are drier and warmer, many soils will shrink more than usual, which has important implications for structural stability. The areas most affected would be central, eastern and southern England where there are clayey soils of large shrink–swell potential.

Increases in the frequency of hot dry periods would lead to

decreases in water availability but increases in water demand. Groundwater provides about 20 per cent of the water supply to England and Wales.

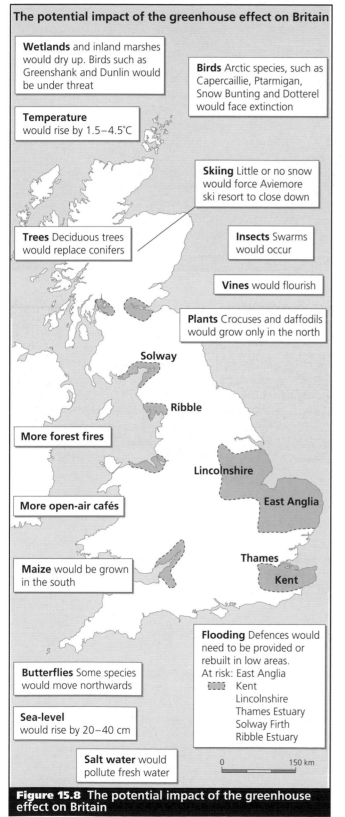

The potential impact of the greenhouse effect on Britain

Wetlands and inland marshes would dry up. Birds such as Greenshank and Dunlin would be under threat

Birds Arctic species, such as Capercaillie, Ptarmigan, Snow Bunting and Dotterel would face extinction

Temperature would rise by 1.5–4.5°C

Skiing Little or no snow would force Aviemore ski resort to close down

Trees Deciduous trees would replace conifers

Insects Swarms would occur

Vines would flourish

Plants Crocuses and daffodils would grow only in the north

Solway

Ribble

More forest fires

Lincolnshire

East Anglia

More open-air cafés

Thames

Kent

Maize would be grown in the south

Flooding Defences would need to be provided or rebuilt in low areas.
At risk: East Anglia
Kent
Lincolnshire
Thames Estuary
Solway Firth
Ribble Estuary

Butterflies Some species would move northwards

Sea-level would rise by 20–40 cm

Salt water would pollute fresh water

0   150 km

Figure 15.8 The potential impact of the greenhouse effect on Britain

Questions

1 Explain what is meant by the term 'the greenhouse effect'. Use a diagram to help you.
2 What are the main greenhouse gases? How do they vary in importance?
3 With the use of examples, compare the consequences of the greenhouse effect on a developed and a developing country. (See also Chapter 9 Coastal environments.)
4 What steps can be taken to manage the consequences of the greenhouse effect?
5 Who is responsible for the enhanced greenhouse effects and the prospective rise in sea level?
6 Who, therefore, should accept responsibility for the cost of reducing greenhouse gas emissions?
7 Who should pay for damages caused by sea level rise?

The ozone layer

The atmosphere of the earth consists of about 78.1 per cent nitrogen, 20.9 per cent oxygen, 0.96 per cent argon, 0.3 per cent carbon dioxide and 0.01 per cent helium and other gases. The amount of ozone in the atmosphere is a small (0.000062) but vital component. Ozone occurs when oxygen rising from the top of the troposphere reacts under the influence of sunlight. Most of this is created over the equator and the tropics since this is where solar radiation is strongest. However, winds within the stratosphere transport the ozone towards the polar regions where it tends to concentrate.

Ozone is constantly being produced and destroyed in the stratosphere in a natural dynamic balance. As well as being produced by sunlight it is also being destroyed by nitrogen oxides. However, human activities may tilt the balance one way or the other. There is now clear evidence that human activities have led to the creation of a hole in the ozone layer over Antarctica. Figure 15.9 shows that the mean total ozone over Halley Bay for Octobers from 1957 to 1985 matches closely the build-up of CFCs (particularly F11 and F12) in the southern hemisphere. It also highlights the reverse scale for CFCs.

The hole in the ozone layer over Antarctica was first discovered in 1982. It follows a clear seasonal pattern – each spring in Antarctica (between September and October) there is a huge reduction in the amount of ozone from the stratosphere. At the end of the long polar night, ozone is present in roughly the same quantities that were present in the 1960s and 1970s; as the summer develops the concentration of ozone recovers – so what causes the depletion in ozone during the spring? During winter in the southern hemisphere the air over Antarctica is cut off from the rest of the atmosphere by circumpolar winds – these winds block warm

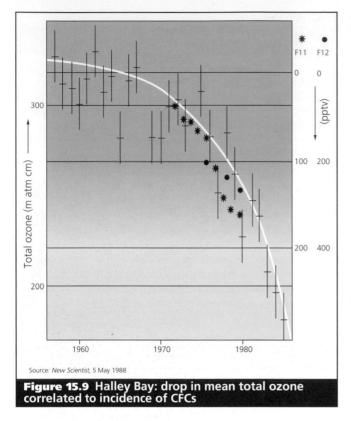

Source: *New Scientist*, 5 May 1988

Figure 15.9 Halley Bay: drop in mean total ozone correlated to incidence of CFCs

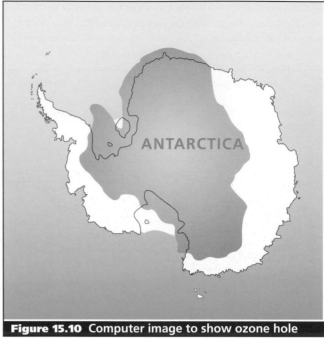

Figure 15.10 Computer image to show ozone hole

air from entering into Antarctica airspace. Hence the temperature over Antarctica becomes very cold, often as low as –90°C in the stratosphere. This allows the formation of clouds of ice particles. Chemical reactions take place on this ice which includes chlorine compounds, resulting from pollution by human activities. These reactions release chlorine atoms. Once the sun returns during the summer the chlorine releases atomic chlorine which destroys ozone in a further series of chemical reactions. Hence the hole in the ozone layer occurs rapidly in the spring. By summer, however, the ice clouds have evaporated and the chlorine has been converted to other compounds such as chlorine nitrate, until the following winter. The ozone hole fills in, although it returns each spring. The size of the hole is staggering (Figure 15.10). As early as 1987 it covered an area the size of continental United States and was as deep as Mount Everest. In addition to human activities, volcanic eruptions can also have an impact on the ozone layer.

The sources of chlorine atoms, CFCs, include materials used in refrigerators (for the working fluid in the pipes), air cooling systems, foamed plastic and aerosols. CFCs are particularly dangerous because they can be long-lived – over 100 years – and they spread throughout the atmosphere. In the case of Antarctica, the build-up of chlorine appears to have had little impact until it reached a critical threshold when only a small increase in chlorine led to a huge change in the ozone layer.

There are major implications of an increase in the size of the hole in the ozone layer. This is because ultraviolet

radiation would reach the ground in increased quantities. Some ultraviolet reaches the ground already – it is in the 290 to 320 waveband. This is known as UV-B, and can cause sunburn, skin cancer and eye problems such as cataracts. It is estimated that for every 1 per cent decrease in the concentration of ozone there will be a 5 per cent increase in the amount of skin cancers each year. Crops and animals have also been tested to see how they react to an increase in UV-B radiation – soyabean, for example, experiences a 25 per cent decline in yield when UV-B increases by 25 per cent, while cattle are affected by eye complaints including cancer of the eye.

Questions

1 Explain the meaning of the following terms: ozone, ozone layer, hole in the ozone layer.
2 What are the causes and consequences of the growth of the hole in the ozone layer?

Deforestation of the tropical rainforest

The environmental issues facing tropical areas are wide ranging. However, the one which has caught most public attention is that of deforestation of the rainforest (Figure 15.11). For example, satellite and television images of forest fires in South East Asia reinforced the view of environmental mismanagement (Figure 15.12). Nevertheless, deforestation is widespread (Figure 15.13) and its causes are varied. There is a large number of effects of deforestation including:

- **disruption to the circulation and storage of nutrients**
- **surface erosion and compaction of soils**

- sandification
- climatic change
- **increased flood levels and sediment content of rivers.**

However, there are wide variations in the scale of deforestation, its rate and its cause (Figure 15.14). First, a number of terms that need to be explained, and a few points need to be made about the data available regarding deforestation.

Scorched earth
Some recent large forest fires

Africa
Large fires have occurred in Rwanda, Tanzania, Congo and Senegal. Illegal settlers blamed.

Colombia
There were 7,000 forest fires in 1997.

Brazil
In three months in 1998 600,000 hectares of savanna burned, mostly to clear land for cattle. In 1997, 24,549 fires occurred in just 41 days.

Papua New Guinea
Careless land-clearance fires have destroyed vast tracts of grassland and rainforest. The worst drought for 50 years threatens famine.

Indonesia
In 1997 2 million hectares of forest and land were destroyed; smog made 50,000 Indonesians ill. Most fires were started deliberately by commercial interests. Now the forests are burning again.

Clearance rates
Percentage of the world's tropical forest cleared between 1960 and 1990.

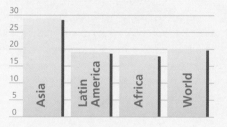

Asia | Latin America | Africa | World

How they start

Drought increases risk.

Drainage spells danger.

Climate change can cause drought.

Timber exploitation — forest fires are used to overcome laws about clearing timber for sale, or to create a source of damaged, and thus cheap, timber.

Selective logging can create artificially dry forests by opening up the canopy.

Lightning is the main natural cause of forest fire – 100 strikes to earth per second.

Land clearing is a major cause of fire. "Slash and burn" agriculture during dry and windy conditions can cause major fires.

Figure 15.11 The 1997 forest fires

Tropical forests include closed forests (those with a closed canopy) and open forests (savanna woodlands), in both humid areas (tropical moist forests or rainforests) and dry tropics (savanna woodland). It is, in fact, quite difficult to distinguish between these categories for they merge, so it is best to think of tropical forests as a mosaic which form some sort of four-fold division between wet/dry and closed/open.

Tropical moist forest includes two main types – tropical rainforest which has limited seasonality, and tropical moist deciduous forest (monsoon forest) which is found in areas which have a distinct dry season. In this section we concentrate on the tropical rainforest.

Deforestation is the temporary or permanent clearance of forest. It occurs when forest is replaced by another land use. This means that selective logging, for example, is not considered as deforestation, especially if there is some policy of replanting. By contrast, clear felling is considered to be an example of deforestation.

The most recent studies suggest that rates of deforestation are high, higher than previously estimated (Figure 15.15). In the 1990s the World Resources Institute calculated that up to 20.4 million ha of tropical forest, an area equivalent to one-third of the United Kingdom were being lost each year, nearly 80 per cent more than a similar estimate in the early 1980s. However, the rates are diverse spatially.

Many geographers question the accuracy of the data and draw attention to six factors that must be considered:

■ What is defined as forest?

■ What is defined as forest deforestation (e.g. does it include selective felling or just clear felling)?

■ How is the survey carried out (satellites, fieldwork, government estimates)?

■ Does the data refer only to commercially useful species or do they include all species?

■ Does the data for individual countries include all types of forest vegetation or just tropical rainforest?

Figure 15.12 The Indonesian fires of 1997 had local and global impact

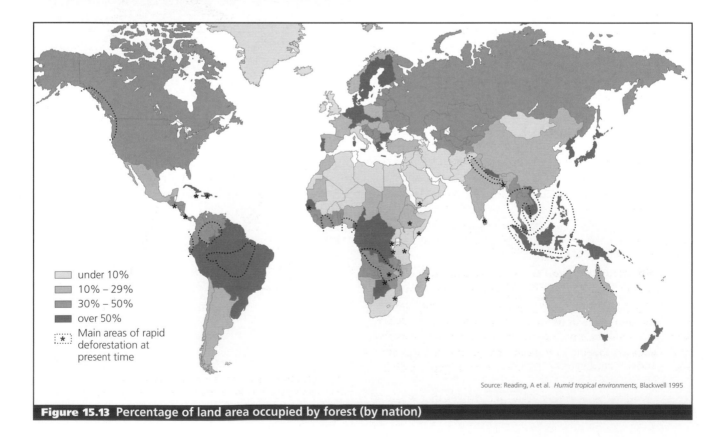

under 10%
10% – 29%
30% – 50%
over 50%
Main areas of rapid deforestation at present time

Source: Reading, A et al. *Humid tropical environments*, Blackwell 1995

Figure 15.13 Percentage of land area occupied by forest (by nation)

Figure 15.14 Deforestation rates for closed tropical forests

Country	Deforestation rates (10³/ha/year (%)) 1981–5	Recent
Tropical America		
Brazil	1480 (0.4)	8000 (2.2)
Costa Rica	65 (4.0)	124 (7.6)
Tropical Cameroon	80 (0.4)	100 (0.6)
Tropical Asia		
India	147 (0.3)	1500 (4.1)
Indonesia	600 (0.5)	900 (0.8)
Myanmar	105 (0.3)	677 (2.1)
Philippines	92 (1.0)	143 (1.5)
Thailand	379 (2.4)	397 (2.5)
Vietnam	65 (0.7)	173 (2.0)

(Source: Reading, A., et al., *Humid tropical environments*, Blackwell, 1995, Table 9.1)

Figure 15.15 Mean annual rates of deforestation, 1981–1985

Region	Undisturbed, productive, closed forest	Logged, productive, closed forest	All closed forests
Tropical America	0.29	2.80	0.64
Tropical Africa	0.19	2.41	0.61
Tropical Asia	0.39	2.14	0.60
All tropics	0.28	1.98	0.62

(Values are percentages of forest area in 1980)
(Source: Reading, A., et al., *Humid tropical environments*, Blackwell, 1995, Table 9.1)

■ **Do governments try to withhold information for strategic reasons?**

Deforestation disrupts the closed system of nutrient cycling within tropical rainforests which are found on some of the world's least fertile soils (Figure 15.16). Inorganic elements are released through burning and are quickly flushed out of the system by the high-intensity rains. Deforestation has been described as the 'pauperisation' of a region, as once the forest cover is removed so, too, are the region's riches. Once the vegetation is removed, nutrients are quickly removed from the system creating infertile conditions. For example, the carrying capacity of artificial pastures along a section of highway between Belem and Brasilia was between 0.9 and 1.0 head of cattle during the first year, but decreased to as little as 0.3 after just six years.

Soil erosion is also associated with deforestation. As a result of soil compaction, there is a decrease in infiltration and an increase in overland runoff and surface erosion. For example, in parts of Java sediment yields increased from 0.03 kg per m² under undisturbed forest to 0.08 kg per m² with an intact litter cover to 1.59 kg per m² with the removal of the surface cover. There are fears that deforestation could lead to a new 'Dust Bowl' in parts of Brazil.

Sandification is a process of selective erosion. Raindrop impact washes away the finer particles of clay and humus, leaving behind the coarser and heavier sand. Evidence of sandification dates back to the 1890s in Santarem, Rondonia. Here, as sandification progressed, the water-retaining capacity of the soil was reduced. This meant that young seedlings of trees found it almost impossible to grow, thereby preventing the regrowth of the forest.

As a result of the intense surface runoff and soil erosion, rivers have a higher flood peak and a shorter time-lag.

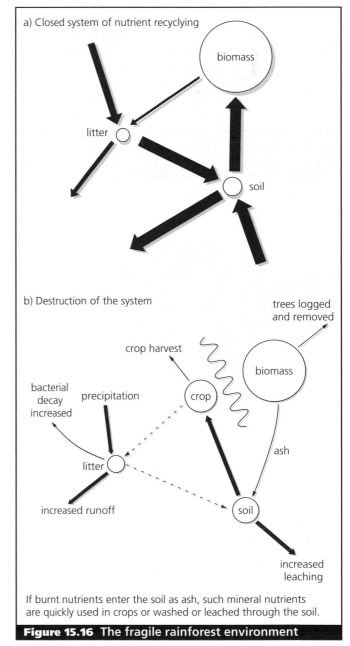

a) Closed system of nutrient recyclying

biomass
litter
soil

b) Destruction of the system

trees logged and removed
crop harvest
bacterial decay increased
precipitation
crop
biomass
litter
ash
increased runoff
soil
increased leaching

If burnt nutrients enter the soil as ash, such mineral nutrients are quickly used in crops or washed or leached through the soil.

Figure 15.16 The fragile rainforest environment

However, in the dry season river levels are lower, the rivers have greater turbidity (murkiness due to more sediment), an increased bedload and carry more silt and clay in suspension. The effects of deforestation vary with the methods used to clear the trees. Mechanical clearance, which cuts the trees above ground, has much less effect than bulldozer methods which uproot the trees and expose the soil. Compaction and rates of erosion are often highest along access routes where the soils are affected the most. In parts of Australia sediment loss increased twelve-fold along access routes. Almost 13 tonnes per ha per year of soil were removed and 190 m^3 per ha per month of runoff have been recorded following deforestation in Indonesia.

Other changes relate to climate. As deforestation progresses, there is a reduction of water that is re-evaporated from the vegetation, hence the recycling of water must diminish. Evapotranspiration rates from savanna grasslands are estimated to be only about one-third of that of the tropical rainforest. Thus, mean annual rainfall is reduced and the seasonality of rainfall increases. As rainfall is reduced in total it also becomes more variable. The new rainfall regime is one that is lower, more seasonal and more erratic than previously, and this has a detrimental effect on the regrowth of forest. The supply of water to vegetation is reduced for long periods of time and, as the groundwater levels in most rainforest areas are deep, it is difficult for shallow-rooted trees (as are many rainforest species) to obtain sufficient water.

It is widely claimed that deforestation has an important effect on global climate. Tropical rainforests are an important store of carbon. It is estimated that about 115 × 10^9 tonnes of carbon are retained in forest matter – this represents about 20 per cent of the carbon of the entire atmosphere's carbon dioxide. Conversion of rainforest to pasture results in a loss of about 80 per cent of the carbon content of the forest. Of the carbon lost, about half will disappear to the oceans. Hence, if the entire Amazon rainforest were burnt there would be an increase in the world's atmospheric carbon dioxide content of 8 per cent. Thus reports which claim that the rainforests account for 50 per cent of the oxygen production of the world are grossly exaggerated and are propaganda.

Climatically, deforestation causes changes in:

- heat balances
- water budgets
- aerodynamic roughness
- albedo
- energy balance transfer.

For example, the conversion of rainforest to savanna grassland reduces the albedo from 0.24 to 0.18 in the wet season and 0.14 in the dry season. However, if desertification follows deforestation the albedo rises to 0.28. This causes surface temperatures to decrease (due to increased reflection of solar radiation), a cooling of the atmosphere, increased anticyclonic (high pressure) subsidence, reduced convection and lower rainfall totals.

Deforestation leads to increased runoff, decreased soil moisture storage and increased soil dessication (dryness). Periodic dust storms increase the amount of dust in the atmosphere, which affects the regional energy balance. The increased dust veil may block solar radiation leading to a cooling of the area.

Of tremendous importance is the loss of biodiversity from the rainforest (see pages 476–8). Deforestation leads to irreversible reductions in biodiversity.

Causes of deforestation

Some commentators have compared the present-day destruction of the rainforest to the destruction of the Mediterranean woodlands during ancient Greek and Roman times, the loss of temperate deciduous woodland for agriculture, and the loss of the North American woodland in the nineteenth century.

It is difficult to generalise about the demographic and socio-economic characteristics of countries experiencing deforestation. The causes, however, can be summarised as:

- **conversion to agriculture**
- **commercial forestry**
- **shifting cultivation**
- **infrastructural developments (e.g. roads, towns)**
- **charcoal production for iron-ore smelting**
- **local demand for fodder and fuelwood exceeds supplies.**

These causes vary spatially. In Latin America, a large part of the deforestation is due to the conversion of land for agriculture, the use of charcoal (notably in Brazil) and for infrastructural developments. By contrast, in Africa the main pressures are for logging, shifting cultivation and for plantation development, whereas in Asia plantations, new agricultural land and logging are the dominant causes of deforestation.

Rates of deforestation

The most active areas of deforestation in Latin America are along the fringes of the Amazon Basin, in forest outliers (isolated patches of forest), along the main highways through the forest, and in parts of Central America, the Caribbean and north west South America. In Brazil, estimates for deforestation range from 1.7 million ha each year to 8 million ha a year. This may, in fact, reflect government initiatives in the late 1980s which reduced the tax credits for land clearance and increased attention to non-rainforest land. However, some of the error may be the result of estimates using satellite images. Some workers used the amount of smoke visible on satellite images as a surrogate for deforestation. Later estimates suggest an annual loss of about 4.8 million ha. As a result of government legislation the amount of destruction has been reduced in Brazil, but it has shifted the problem to other places such as the Bolivian rainforest.

There have been fewer studies of deforestation in Africa compared with Latin America. The main areas of rainforest are around the Zaire Basin, West and Central Africa, south and west Ghana, Cameroon and Equatorial Guinea. Most of

the destruction appears to be around West Africa and Madagascar. In Africa the main problem is the loss of savanna woodlands in East, West and Southern Africa. In Asia, Australasia and Oceania deforestation rates are increasing, mostly in a series of patches.

Comparing deforestation in Sierra Leone, Brazil and South East Asia

Sierra Leone

Sierra Leone has a long history of deforestation. Over the last 250 years the location and rate of deforestation has varied considerably. In the 1500s most of Sierra Leone was covered in rainforest, population densities were low and the impact of human activity was limited. Following European colonisation in the mid-sixteenth century, there were localised impacts, mostly the result of agricultural developments to support the scattered trading posts. Deforestation intensified in the nineteenth century as demand for timber for the British Navy, who were based in Freetown to control the slave trade, increased. Exploitation was rapid and by the 1860s there was a shortage of adequate timber supplies. At the same time, forest land was cleared and used for oil palm, one of the first cash crops in the region.

Development of cash crops expanded rapidly in the late nineteenth century. Following oil palm came cocoa, coffee and wild rubber. Much of the land converted was along the flanks of the railway line built at the end of the nineteenth century. Deforestation was so rapid that by 1913 forest reserves were created in order to safeguard Sierra Leone's rainforests (Figure 15.17). Nevertheless, forest clearance has continued throughout the twentieth century for agricultural land, timber extraction and diamond mining. In addition, mangrove swamps have given way to paddy fields.

The two main threats at present to Sierra Leone's forests are the conversion to agricultural land and the uncontrolled logging in the east of the country.

The Brazilian Amazon

Compared with Sierra Leone, deforestation in Brazil is a recent feature. Until the early twentieth century the main uses of the rainforest were for shifting cultivation and a small amount of rubber tapping. As rubber tapping used only 'natural' trees the impact was limited. The first major phase of deforestation occurred in the early twentieth century between Belem and Braganca with the establishment of 20 agricultural colonies to

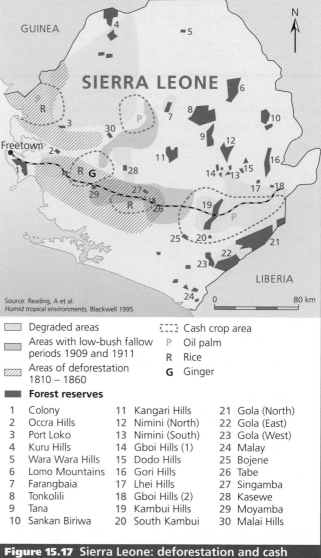

Source: Reading, A et al.
Humid tropical environments, Blackwell 1995

Degraded areas	Cash crop area
Areas with low-bush fallow periods 1909 and 1911	P Oil palm
	R Rice
Areas of deforestation 1810 – 1860	G Ginger
Forest reserves	

1 Colony	11 Kangari Hills	21 Gola (North)
2 Occra Hills	12 Nimini (North)	22 Gola (East)
3 Port Loko	13 Nimini (South)	23 Gola (West)
4 Kuru Hills	14 Gboi Hills (1)	24 Malay
5 Wara Wara Hills	15 Dodo Hills	25 Bojene
6 Lomo Mountains	16 Gori Hills	26 Tabe
7 Farangbaia	17 Lhei Hills	27 Singamba
8 Tonkolili	18 Gboi Hills (2)	28 Kasewe
9 Tana	19 Kambui Hills	29 Moyamba
10 Sankan Biriwa	20 South Kambui	30 Malai Hills

Figure 15.17 Sierra Leone: deforestation and cash croping, 1910–1911, and forest reserves created since 1911

grow food for the expanding city of Belem. These colonies were based upon slash and burn agriculture, and were characterised by rapidly falling levels of soil fertility once the natural vegetation had been removed, as well as rapid weed infestation. In order to produce more food, more forest was cleared for short-term cultivation. In addition, the completion of a rail link to Belem increased the demand for forest products for railway construction and for fuel.

Between the late 1920s and the mid-1950s the rate of deforestation declined. Large-scale activities such as the rubber plantations of Pirelli, Goodyear and Ford at Fordlandia and Belterra were established. Like their agricultural counterparts their success was limited by soil erosion and weed infestation.

However, rates of deforestation accelerated at an exponential rate from the 1960s onwards and are now among the highest in the world (Figure 15.18). There are five main causes of deforestation (Figure 15.19):

- agricultural colonisation by landless migrants and speculative developers along highways and agricultural growth areas

- conversion of the forest to cattle pastures especially in eastern and south eastern Para and northern Mato Grosso

- mining, for example the Greater Carajas Project in south-eastern Amazonia, which includes a 900 km railway and

extensive deforestation to provide charcoal to smelt the iron ore – another threat from mining are the small-scale informal gold mines, *garimpeiros*, causing localised deforestation and contaminated water supplies

- large-scale hydro-electric power schemes such as the Tucurui Dam on the Tocantins River

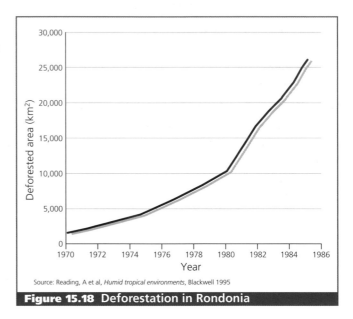

Source: Reading, A et al, *Humid tropical environments*, Blackwell 1995

Figure 15.18 Deforestation in Rondonia

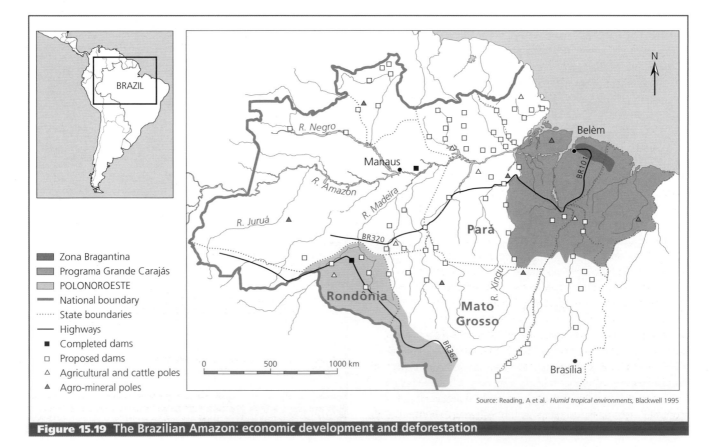

Source: Reading, A et al. *Humid tropical environments*, Blackwell 1995

Figure 15.19 The Brazilian Amazon: economic development and deforestation

- forestry taking place in Para, Amazonas and northern Mato Grosso.

Part of the exploitation has been planned by the Brazilian government as an attempt to promote economic development in the region, to attract migrants from other parts of the country and to thereby reduce the stress on Brazil's large cities and undeveloped regions.

Thus, deforestation in Brazil shows five main trends:

- it is a recent phenomenon

- it has been promoted partly by government policies (government policies to reduce deforestation, on the other hand, have had limited success)

- there are a wide range of causes of deforestation

- there are new areas of deforestation as well as the extension of previously deforested areas

- land speculation and the granting of land titles to those who 'occupy' parts of the rainforest is a major cause of deforestation.

Deforestation in Malaya and Borneo (Malaysia, Indonesia and Brunei)

There is a long history of deforestation in this region. Colonial powers initiated localised deforestation almost two centuries ago (similar to the case of Sierra Leone). One of the biggest changes was the replacement of natural forest by commercial plantations, and this occurred steadily during the nineteenth and twentieth centuries. Since the 1960s the main causes of deforestation have included farming, forestry and mining.

In Malaysia strip mining, which involves the removal of vegetation and topsoil to access the ore below, has been a major problem. Other areas where deforestation is particularly rapid include Borneo, due to shifting cultivation, logging and the extension of permanent cultivation.

The proportion of the world's timber originating from the region has increased (Figure 15.20). Forestry in this region has increased by 50 per cent more than in the rest of the tropical rainforests. This is due largely to their proximity to the main markets and their more efficient infrastructure enabling exploitation and export. In particular, logging is growing at an alarming rate in Borneo. Since the 1970s over half the world's hardwood exports have come from Borneo and since the mid-1980s there has been a significant increase in Borneo's exports of tropical hardwoods.

Deforestation in South East Asia would appear to be out of control. Cutting policies are abused, forestry inspections are inefficient and there is widespread illegal logging.

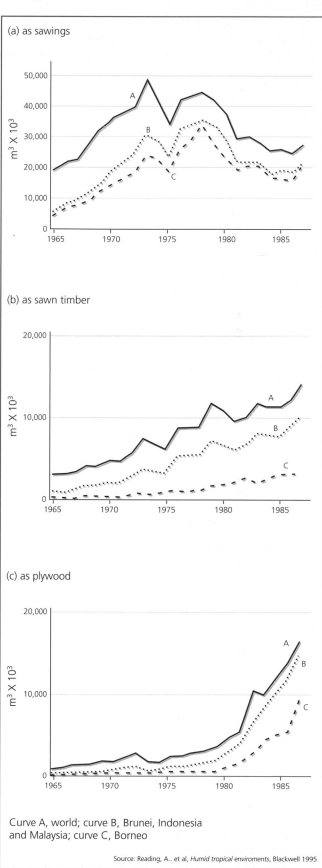

(a) as sawings

(b) as sawn timber

(c) as plywood

Curve A, world; curve B, Brunei, Indonesia and Malaysia; curve C, Borneo

Source: Reading, A.. et al, *Humid tropical enviroments*, Blackwell 1995

Figure 15.20 South East Asia: exports of non-coniferous tropical hardwoods

Figure 15.21 Forest land turned to desert by over grazing and deforestation, Burkina Faso

Desertification

There is a popular image of desertification in which sand dunes march and engulf towns in their wake (Figure 15.21). There is also an oversimplification that desertification is caused by a long-term decline in rainfall and aided by human activities such as overgrazing, burning and deforestation. Although there is some truth in these stereotypes, they can be inaccurate and misleading.

The term desertification was first used by the French geographer Aubreville in 1949 to describe the development of the world's deserts into semi-arid areas. However, popular use of the term came much later, following the 1977 United Nations Environment Programme World Conference on Desertification (UNCOD) and the droughts of 1968–74 and 1979–84 in the African Sahel. UNCOD defined desertification as a reduction 'in the biological productivity of the land . . . leading ultimately to desert-like conditions'. The definition has moved away from the 'spread of the desert' to a 'process of sustained land (soil and vegetation) degradation in arid, semi-arid and dry sub-humid areas, caused at least partly by man'. Some definitions go so far as to say that desertification is irreversible, and that it is caused only by human activity. Desertification suggests an irreversible conversion of non-desert to desert whereas degradation implies quite severe changes, but changes which can be reversed after a few rainy seasons and careful management. This is what appears to happen in reality. In addition, degradation implies the use of resources in a non-sustainable way. If agriculture is not sustainable, land degradation is taking place.

A number of geographers believe that desertification has been over emphasised, largely as a result of insufficient data and a lack of understanding regarding how societies adapt to drought and periods of food scarcity.

There are serious reservations regarding the quality of the data. The most frequently quoted statistics state that up to 20 million ha are desertified annually, 35 per cent of the earth's surface is threatened with desertification, and 20 per cent of the world's population lives in areas threatened with desertification. This was on the basis of a UNEP survey which asked respondents to differentiate between 'moderately desertified' and 'severely desertified'. The statistical reliability is extremely shaky. Indeed, the lack of reliable evidence has led to some geographers questioning whether desertification even exists! Nevertheless, recent estimates suggest that as many as 850 million people are directly affected by desertification, mostly in Africa, the Indian subcontinent and South America, and that about 65 million ha of once-productive farmland has been affected by desertification. It does not affect only developing countries – large parts of the United States, Australia, Mediterranean Europe and the CIS are affected, too (Figure 15.22).

The timing of surveys on desertification is important. Many are biased. For example, studies conducted during periods of drought will record low levels of biomass and soil moisture. Deserts are characterised by high variability in year-to-year levels of rainfall and biomass, so surveys which examine any two years are likely to be inaccurate.

The causes of desertification are varied and have a long history. They include salinisation and siltation of irrigation systems, colonisation by agricultural settlers, war, overgrazing, cultivation of marginal areas and deforestation. Locally there are other causes such as trampling, groundwater extraction, mining and urbanisation. Moreover, it is important to see desertification as a symptom, rather than the problem itself (i.e. what are the pressures which lead to desertification, overgrazing and so on). The root cause of degradation is likely to be found in the social, economic and political structures of society (Figure 15.23).

Natural causes of desertification – the decline of rainfall – is marked by a reduction in biodiversity, a decline in ground cover and an increase in the proportion of bare ground. Without a vegetation cover, the soil loses organic matter, its

Figure 15.22 UNEP estimates of types of dryland deemed susceptible to desertification, proportion affected and actual extent

	1977	1984	1992
Climatic zone susceptible to desertification	Arid, semi-arid and sub-humid	Arid, semi-arid and sub-humid	Arid, semi-arid and dry sub-humid
Total dryland area susceptible to desertification (million ha)	5281	4409	5172
Proportion of susceptible drylands affected by desertification (%)	75	79	70
Total of susceptible drylands affected by desertification (million ha)	3970	3475	3592

(Source Middleton, N., *The global casino*, Arnold, 1995)

Figure 15.23 Suggested causes of land degradation

Natural disasters	Degradation due to biogeophysical causes or 'acts of God'.
Population change	Degradation occurs when population growth exceeds environmental thresholds (neo-Malthusian) or decline causes collapse of adequate management.
Underdevelopment	Resources exploited to benefit world economy or developed countries leaving little profit to manage or restore degraded environments.
Internationalism	Taxation and other forces interfere with the market, triggering overexploitation.
Colonial legacies	Trade links, communications, rural–urban linkages, cash crops and other 'hangovers' from the past promote poor management of resource exploitation.
Inappropriate technology and advice	Promotion of wrong strategies and techniques which result in land degradation.
Ignorance	Linked to inappropriate technology and advice: a lack of knowledge leads to degradation.
Attitudes	People's or institutions' attitudes blamed for degradation.
War and civil unrest	Overuse of resources in national emergencies and concentrations of refugees leading to high population pressures in safe locations.

(Source: Middleton, N., *The global casino*, Arnold, 1995).

Factors that cause overgrazing include:

- **status** (wealth is widely measured by the number of animals that an individual or tribe owns)

- **food security** (having more animals would decrease the risk of starvation during drought)

- **food supply** (more animals are required for food supply as local populations continue to increase)

- **rise of export agriculture** (many of the animals are now exported and this has encouraged farmers in some dryland areas to switch from horticulture to cattle rearing)

- **veterinary care** (the number of animals that died because of diseases has declined sharply since about 1950 because of widespread vaccination and animal health programmes).

(Source: Park, C., *The environment: principles and applications*, Routledge, 1997)

Figure 15.24 Factors that promote overgrazing

soil structure and its water-retention capacity. This, in turn, makes the soil environment more hostile to plant survival and the process intensifies.

Overgrazing is one of the main causes of desertification in the world. Over 70 per cent of desertified lands are the result of overgrazing. As palatable species are removed, they are replaced by inedible ones. Although there is a decrease in productivity, there may in fact be an increase in biomass and vegetation cover, namely the unpalatable, inedible species. Trampling and compaction reduce soil structure and increase soil erosion. The reasons for overgrazing are varied and complex (Figure 15.24).

Overcultivation results from an intensification of farming. The results include a shorter fallow period, larger fields, greater use of machinery, deep ploughing, cultivation of steeper slopes and cultivation of marginal areas. Deforestation reduces the protective cover of vegetation on the soil and can lead to degradation. Around cities there is widespread deforestation. For example, there is said to be no tree within 90 km of Khartoum, Sudan and none within 80 km of Ouagadougou, Burkina Faso.

Salinisation is also a cause of desertification. Poorly managed irrigation schemes may result in rising water tables and the build-up of salts in the soil. As the salt tolerance of most cultivated plants is low, salinisation leads to a rapid decline in productivity. Up to half of the world's irrigated lands suffer from salinisation to some extent, and in Pakistan it is as high as 80 per cent of cropland. There 35 per cent of irrigated land is affected by salinisation and up to 40 000 ha of irrigated land are lost to salinisation each year.

It is possible that global warming will lead to an increase in land degradation in many regions. For example, in Mediterranean areas evapotranspiration rates may increase by as much as 200 mm pa and cereal-growing areas may become marginal due to warmer temperatures and less moisture. As a result, land degradation may spread.

Given the large areas affected by the rapid growth and spread of desertification, there is an increasing need to address it as a problem. This entails a broad mix of education, research, funding, training, publicity and increased awareness, monitoring and assessment. With such a wide variety of causes, it is hardly surprising that solutions are equally varied. Methods include:

- **dune stabilisation (by the planting of grasses and trees)**
- **increasing the water-retention capacity of soils (providing mulches on soils)**
- **reduction of salinisation in irrigated lands.**

Some solutions are 'natural' and require farmers to adapt to the natural environment. Adaptations to reduced biomass include:

- **increased mobility (the traditional way of dealing with insufficient amounts of rainfall and pasture)**
- **management of size and composition of herds**
- **exchange of livestock and livestock products**
- **increased use of drought-tolerant species**
- **mulching to preserve soil organic matter**
- **utilisation of wild species and tree crops (Figure 15.25).**

Figure 15.25 Native tree seedling planted in Brazil to begin land recovery programme

There is a major problem with desertification in north-west China. Various techniques are used including:

- **windbreaks to reduce wind erosion of bare soil**
- **irrigating with silt-laden river water to restore soil in badly eroded areas**
- **dune stabilisation using straw checkerboards and planted xerophytes (plants which can withstand prolonged water shortage)**
- **land enclosure to reduce wind erosion**
- **redistribution of material from palaeosols (soils from an environment of the past) to restore soils**
- **chemical treatment to restore soil fertility.**

(Source: Park, C., The *environment: principles and applications*, Routledge, 1997)

Figure 15.26 Combating desertification in China

SPATIAL FOCUS SPATIAL

Contrasting the causes of desertification

The Sahel

The Sahel is a semi-arid region stretching across Africa (Figure 15.27). It is bounded to the north by the Sahara desert and to the south by the savanna and wet tropics. It has experienced some of the world's worst droughts, famines and land degradation since the 1960s. Average annual rainfall is low and variable – between 100 mm and 200 mm a year with wide variations in annual totals.

Most of the rain occurs between June and September, and the natural vegetation is a mixture of xerophytic (drought-resistant) shrub and grass. Much of the agriculture is nomadic pastoralism.

Deserts expand and contract as rainfall changes over time and the Sahara is no exception. Climate has varied considerably over the Sahara and Sahel regions, and river deposits, relict soils, and cave art indicate that moisture levels were once much higher. In addition to long-term climatic change there are short-term,

...cadal changes and the droughts of the early 1970s, 1980s and 1990s may reflect some natural climatic fluctuation. The drought of 1968–74 was the worst for about 150 years in North Africa, and annual rainfall was below average throughout the period.

There are also important human activities which have led to widespread degradation. These include civil wars in Ethiopia, Eritrea and Somalia, population growth, and the sedenterisation of nomads. These interact in a number of ways to lead to vegetation decline and the removal of moisture from the soil and the local environment (Figure 15.28). Degradation continues in the Sahel. In the 1950s between 5 and 12 ha were needed to support each cow. By the 1980s stocking rates had risen to between 2 and 6 per ha, greatly exceeding the carrying capacity of the land. One of the main reasons why this increase could be supported was the drilling of wells to tap deep aquifers. Year-round continuous grazing prevented these areas from recovering. Consequently, some wet areas, such as central Niger, experienced increases in the amount of sheetwash, rill and gully erosion, partly as a result of increased compaction of the soil. By contrast, drier areas, such as Mali and Burkina Faso, experienced less erosion due to runoff, but relatively more due to wind.

The 1973–4 drought resulted in the deaths of about 100 000 people, mostly through starvation. Millions of cattle died, too. The process was repeated in the 1980s. Many deaths were due to the lack of drinking water, as well as the lack of food in the soil.

The United States

The United States experiences many of the features and processes associated with land degradation such as:

- increased dust storm frequency
- reactivation of sand dunes
- erosion of steep gullies
- falling groundwater
- ground subsidence
- waterlogging and salinisation
- overgrazing
- invasion of alien plants
- chemical contamination
- sedimentation in dams and reservoirs.

The most famous example is that of the Dust Bowl in the 1930s. This resulted from a combination of hot, dry years coinciding with a rapid colonisation by settler farmers in the region. These farmers had been attracted to the area by a succession of wetter years in the 1920s which had enabled higher levels of production. Degradation is still a major problem in the United States. Centre-pivot irrigation (Figure 15.29) has reduced groundwater levels in places such as the High Plains, while irrigation in the Central Valley of California has resulted in widespread salinisation. As a result of high salt levels, agricultural yields have been reduced in about 20 per cent of irrigated land. Shelterbelts and wind breaks have been removed to expand the cultivated areas; military training and urban growth have had more local impacts. Alien plants, such as the salt cedar, have colonised parts of the Rio Grande valley and use up almost 45 per cent of the total water available.

Ultimately, the rapid growth in population remains the fundamental cause of degradation in the United States. Degradation has followed human occupancy into dryland areas and has moved westwards over time.

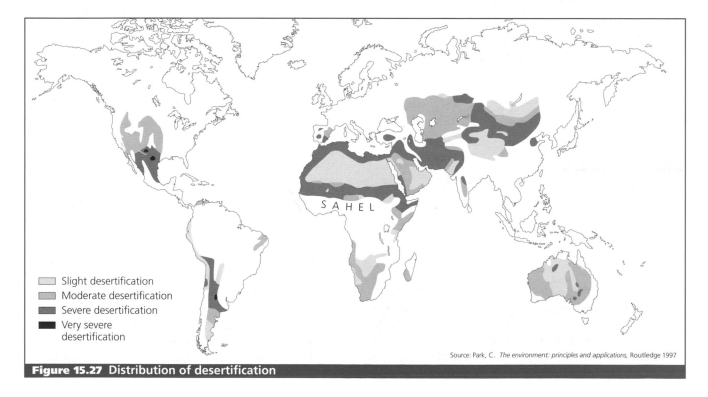

Slight desertification
Moderate desertification
Severe desertification
Very severe desertification

SAHEL

Source: Park, C. *The environment: principles and applications,* Routledge 1997

Figure 15.27 **Distribution of desertification**

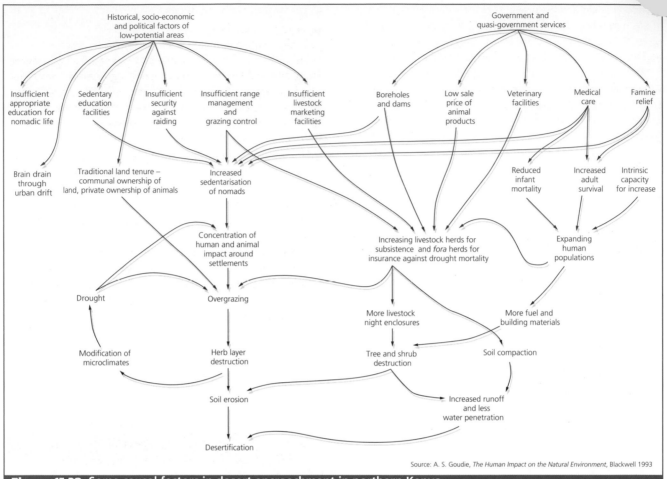

Source: A. S. Goudie, *The Human Impact on the Natural Environment*, Blackwell 1993

Figure 15.28 Some causal factors in desert encroachment in northern Kenya

Figure 15.29 Centre-pivot irrigation in Arizona

Pakistan

Irrigation has been practised in Pakistan since at least the eighth century. Much of the irrigation takes place on the Indus and along the Punjab rivers. The irrigation system is among one of the most complex in the world and provides Pakistan with most of its food and industrial crops, such as wheat, cotton, rice, oil seed, sugar cane and tobacco. Hence, the health of the irrigated area is essential to the health of the national economy.

Many of the drainage canals are in a poor state. Many are unlined and seepage is a major problem. Consequently, there has been a steady gradual rise in the water table (Figure 15.30) which has caused widespread waterlogging and salinisation (Figure 15.31). As noted earlier up to 40 000 ha of irrigated land are lost annually.

There have been attempts to rectify the problem. Two main methods are used: pumping water from aquifers (to reduce the water table) and vertical and horizontal drainage of saline water. These have met with some success. In parts of the Lower Indus Plain water tables have been reduced by as much as 7 m, and up to 45 per cent of saline soils have been reclaimed. However, the use of reclaimed land for agriculture only results in salinisation again.

Figure 15.30 Increase in level of water table in southern Punjab, Pakistan

Source: Mannion, A. and Boelby, S. *Enviromental issues in the1990's*, Wiley 1992

Tunisia

Land degradation in Tunisia has increased rapidly since Independence in 1958. In an attempt to control the fast-growing population and to provide more food, the government embarked on a programme of village construction, provision of schools and clinics and the construction of boreholes. The result was the settlement of many nomads in expanded villages and new villages.

The increase in population was reflected by an increase in the number of livestock. However, an important change was the decline of collective management of livestock and an increase in privately managed flocks. In addition, settlers kept their stocks close to the village, resulting in overgrazing and degradation around many villages.

Since Independence the composition of the flocks has changed. The proportion of goats to sheep has risen, as goats will browse on poorer quality pasture than sheep. During dry years surface litter might account for up to 90 per cent of a sheep's diet and over 60 per cent of a goat's diet.

Questions

1 Define the term desertification.
2 To what extent is desertification a problem of Developing World countries?
3 What can be done to manage desertification and its consequences?

Figure 15.31 Waterlogging and salinisation in Pakistan

Province	Waterlogged area (as percentage of area under irrigation)			Salinised area (as percentage of surveyed area)			
	Severe (0–1.5m)*	Moderate (1.5–3m)	Total	Slightly saline	Moderately saline	Highly saline	Total
Punjab	6.05	25.18	31.23	14.80	4.30	6.50	25.60
Sind	11.73	37.67	49.40	20.64	27.12	50.49	98.25
NWFP**	10.00	1.00	11.00	–	–	-	9.00
Baluchistan	–	–	–	–	–	-	6.88

* Values refer to depth of water table
** North West Frontier Province
Salinity (percentage soluble salts) levels
normal < 0.2 per cent
slight approx. 0.2 per cent
moderate 0.2–2.5 per cent
high > 2.5 per cent
(Source: Mannion, A., and Bowlby, S., *Environmental issues in the 1990s*, Wiley, 1992, table 15.5)

Sustainability

Sustainable development is development which 'meets the needs of the present without compromising the ability of future generations to meet their own needs' (Brundtland, 1987). It is a process by which human potential (standards of well-being) are improved and the environment (the resource base) is used and managed to supply humanity on a long-term basis. It implies social justice as well as long-term environmental sustainability. The definition suggests that humankind has degraded the planet and must make amends for future generations. The definition is somewhat difficult to comprehend, as it takes in economic issues, ecological concepts, sociological principles and moral rights. Indeed, some geographers have complained that too much attention has been devoted to the definition of sustainability and not enough detail to its practical implications.

The global economy depends on the natural environment as a source of resources, as a sink for emissions, as a provider of services (for example, a warm climate offers tourist potential). The capacity of natural systems to provide resources and to absorb increasing levels of pollution is the critical threshold to how far population can increase and the economy expand. One of the most widely used concepts in this regard is the carrying capacity. This is the maximum impact that an ecosystem can sustain. In population terms there is a qualitative element, too. It is the maximum population that can be sustained without a decline in standards of living. Acid rain, global warming, desertification and deforestation may reduce our standards of living. In order to be sustainable, the level and rate of resource exploitation should be no greater than the level and rate of natural regeneration of natural systems. However, as population increases so, too, does demand. As technology increases, the amount of resources exploited increases exponentially.

Moreover, with increasing trade and communications there is virtually no region which sustains itself purely with the resources from within its own boundaries. Most regions now depend upon the supply of resources from other regions, and the growth in world trade enables regions to exceed their carrying capacity by importing resources. A move towards sustainability would require difficult choices and some fundamental changes in attitudes, values and practices (Figure 15.32).

World crises

There are a number of interlinked crises that reduce efforts of achieving sustainability. These crises have a social, environmental and political slant. Currently about one-fifth of the world's 5.8 billion population lives in desperately poor conditions – these people are the global 'underclass', those whose lives are at the edge of existence and are continuously close to famine, disease, hunger and death. What is more, the gap between rich and poor is increasing (Figure 15.33). It is not just a question of GDP per head. Economic indicators fail to take into account the pollution and the depletion of natural resources. As developing countries provide many of the raw materials for economic development in the West, the Developing World is disadvantaged even more.

The environmental crises are a result of the limited amount of resources that the earth contains and the rate at which they are being destroyed (Figure 15.34). There is a social aspect to the destruction of resources: the 20 per cent of

---

Figure 15.33 Increasing inequalities between rich and poor

Ratio of income of richest 20 per cent of the population to the poorest 20 per cent of the population

1960	30:1
1970	32:1
1980	45:1
1989	59:1
1991	61:1

- Respect and care for the community of life.
- Improve the quality of human life.
- Conserve the earth's vitality and diversity.
- Minimise the depletion of non-renewable resources.
- Keep within the earth's carrying capacity.
- Change personal attitudes and practices.
- Enable communities to care for their own environments.
- Provide a national framework for integrating development and conservation.
- Create a global alliance.

(Source: Park, C., *The environment: principles and applications*, Routledge, 1997)

Figure 15.32 Principles of sustainable development

- 70 per cent of the world's drylands are degraded.
- Desertification costs $42 million a year.
- 39 per cent of NPP (net primary productivity) by plants on land is lost by people each year.
- The amount of farmland has fallen from 0.38 ha per person in 1970 to 0.28 in 1990, and at current rates will reach 0.15 in the year 2050.
- Fish catches in all of the world's 17 fisheries areas exceed sustainable limits.

Figure 15.34 Some of the world's environmental crises

the world's population that lives in developed countries consumes 80 per cent of the world's resources, whereas the 80 per cent of the population that lives in developing countries uses only 20 per cent of the resources. The world's environmental crises are growing rapidly, and cross international boundaries. For example, the transfer of radioactive waste and acid rain across western Europe and the build-up of greenhouse gases in the atmosphere cross international and terrestrial boundaries.

Political conflicts in the form of war, ethnic cleansing, refugee crises, trading blocs, trade wars and economic sanctions have become more widespread. These seriously hamper the prospects of achieving sustainable development.

The United Nations Conference on the Human Environment (Stockholm, 1972) was a turning point for a better understanding of human impact on the environment and, implicitly, sustainability. At the same time, the influential *Limits to Growth* model was produced which drew attention to shortages of natural resources, increases in pollution and the eventual collapse of human society some time around 2100.

More recently, environmental issues have come to the fore in the World Commission on Environment and Development through its publication *Our common future* (also known as the Brundtland Report) and at the Rio conference (United Nations conference on Environment and Development, 1982). Environmental problems are increasingly seen as being international in effect. Ozone depletion, acid rain, global warming and desertification affect scores of countries. They may even affect countries which are not causing any of the damage. One of the major outcomes of the Rio conference was the action plan for the 1990s and into the twenty-first century. This is commonly referred to as Agenda 21. This refers to detailed plans and strategies in all countries, from local governments up to national governments, aimed at achieving sustainable development. Strategies vary and include regulation (through legal and economic controls), management, co-operation, monitoring and assessment. A fundamental aim of the Rio conference was to replace environmentally damaging practices with sustainable and environmentally friendly forms of development (Figure 15.35).

Role of local Agenda 21

As a result of the Earth Summit national governments are obliged to formulate national plans or strategies for sustainable development – Agenda 21. It is **people** who engage in development, not governments, and therefore sustainable development is a local activity. Moreover, all people, however poor, have some ability, however constrained, of changing what they do in small ways. Managing and preserving the environment has a number of advantages (Figure 15.36).

Local authorities are beginning to translate the global sustainability agenda – Agenda 21– into local action. Just as global sustainability cannot exist without national sustainable policies, national Agenda 21 is incomplete without local Agenda 21 (Figure 15.37).

Sustainable development – development which meets the needs of the present without compromising the ability of future generations to meet their own needs.

Precautionary principle – this broadly demands that if an activity or substance carries a significant risk of environmental damage it should either not proceed or be used, or should be adopted at only the minimum essential level, and with maximum practical safeguards.

Polluter pays principle (PPP) – that polluters should pay the full costs of pollution-reduction measures decided upon by public authorities to ensure that the environment is in an acceptable state. More recently the PPP has been extended to accidental pollution.

Shared responsibility – the principle involves not so much a choice of action at one administrative level to the exclusion of others, but rather a mixing of actors and instruments at different administrative levels, enterprises or indeed the general public or consumers.

Environmental impact assessment (EIA) – the necessary preliminary practice of evaluating the risks posed by a certain project before granting permission for a development.

Best available technology (BAT) – signifies the latest or state-of-the-art techniques and technologies in the development of activities, processes and their methods of operation which minimise emissions to the environment.

Environmental quality standard (EQS) – the set of requirements which must be fulfilled at a given time by a given environment or particular part thereof.

Integrated pollution prevention and control (IPPC) – to provide for measures and procedures to prevent (wherever practicable) or to minimise emissions from industrial installations in order to achieve a high level of protection for the environment as a whole. The IPPC concept arose when it became clear that approaches to controlling emissions in one medium alone may encourage shifting the burden of pollution across other environmental media. This concept requires that emission limit values are set within the aim of not breaching EQS: only when EQSs or other relevant guidelines are missing can emission levels be based on BAT.

(Source: *Europe's environment*, EEA, 1995)

Figure 15.35 Concepts for environmental protection

- In Boston Harbour, retaining natural salt marshes saves up to $17 million each year in flood protection works.
- In Zimbabwe, the CAMPFIRE project, (Communal Areas Management For Indigenous REsources) has shown that cropping of wild species yields more than land converted to ranching.
- Agro-forestry uses a greater proportion of rainforest species without increasing the risks of environmental deterioration (e.g. the Poppalucan Indians in the Santa Rosa district of Mexico).
- Traditional herbalists provide primary healthcare to over 2 million people annually.
- Plant-derived drugs had a commercial value of over $43 billion in 1985.
- Simple genes derived from Ethiopian barley protects California's $160 million barley crop from the yellow dwarf virus.

Figure 15.36 Some benefits of biodiversity

The key issues that are now taken more seriously are:

- Inter-generational implications of patterns of resource use: how effectively do decisions about the use of natural resources preserve an environmental heritage or estate for the benefit of future generations?
- Equity concerns: who has access to resources? How fairly are available resources allocated between competing claimants?
- Time horizons: how much are resource allocation decisions orientated towards short-term economic gain or long-term environmental stability?

(Source: Park, C., *The environment: principles and applications*, Routledge, 1997, Box 1.14)

Figure 15.37 Issues within sustainable development

Questions

1 Define the following terms: sustainable development, precautionary principle, environmental impact assessment.
2 Using examples, explain what is meant by the term 'world crisis'.
3 What is Agenda 21? Find out what is being done in your area for Agenda 21. In what ways can your school or college adopt Agenda 21 policies?

Figure 15.38 The Japanese fish market – an example of unsustainable development

Bibliography

References

'Is desertification a myth?' by T. Binns, *Geography*, 75, 106–13, 1990.
The human impact reader, by A. Goudie, Blackwell, 1997.
'Rates of deforestation in the humid tropics: estimates and measures' by A. Grainger, *Geographical Journal* 159, 33–44, 1993.
Climate Change: The Intergovernmental Panel on Climate Change Scientific Assessment – Policy Makers Summary by J. Houghton et al, 1990.
Climatic Change, Radiative Forcing of Climate by J. Houghton et al, published by CUP, 1995.

Sustainable development by G. Nagle and K. Spencer, Hodder & Stoughton, 1997.
Humid tropical environments by A. Reading *et al*, Blackwell, 1995.
'The effects of deforestation in Amazonia' by H. Sioli, *Geographical Journal*, 151, 197–203, 1985.
'Future Sea Level Rise: Environmental and Sociopolitical Considerations', by Mintzer, I (ed.) in *Confronting Climatic Change: Risks Implication and Responses* by R. Warwick and A. Rahman, CUP, 1992.
Our common future by WCED, OUP, 1987 (also known as the Brundtland Report).

preparing *for exams*

Revision tips

1 First of all you need to know the exam format. If you do not have past papers already you can order some from the Exam Board. Ask your teacher for details of the Exam Board and the Syllabus number of your course. Write to the Board (the addresses are given below), attention of the publications department. Ask for the most recent papers. It is very useful to have a selection of past papers.

2 Study the past papers and familiarise yourself with the layout of the paper and the types of questions asked.

3 Work to a revision timetable – it is best if you have a timetable plotted and keep to it. This needs to take into account when your exams are in all other subjects.

4 Revise in short manageable chunks. Do not attempt to do all of a subject in one go, but take each topic in turn.

5 When you revise, use whichever method or methods you feel most happy with. These could include:
   - spider diagrams
   - pictures/sketches
   - highlighter pens
   - lists and rhymes
   - note cards
   - mnemonics (the first letter of words, e.g. CASH standing for corrosion, abrasion, solution and hydraulic impact, i.e. the types of erosion in a river or at the coast).

6 Have regular breaks. It is difficult to concentrate for more than forty minutes at a go. Keep your first break to fifteen minutes but, after the next forty minutes take a longer break.

7 Test yourself. This could be by writing answers to past questions, drawing sketch maps, learning facts and figures, identifying symbols on a map. Ask a teacher, parent or friend to assess you. If you ask a friend, the two of you are revising and helping each other work. This is very often the best method.

8 Reward yourself – lots of chocolate gives you lots of energy.

9 Do not work too late, get plenty of sleep and try to stay fresh.

Contact numbers

Assessment and Qualifications Alliance (AQA)
Stag Hill House, Guildford, Surrey GU2 5XJ

Edexcel House, 32 Russell Square, London WC1B 5DN

OCR Syndicate Buildings,
1 Hills Road, Cambridge CB1 2EU

Essay writing

There are many ways of answering an essay but first you must:

- examine closely the wording of the question, and
- plan your answer.

It is better to spend time thinking and planning, so that you do not waste time writing about irrelevant material. As a golden rule: more thought and planning guarantees higher grades.

Reading the question

Read the question carefully and underline the command words and the topic to be discussed. Interpretation is frequently more important than the recall of fact. If you do not answer the question you cannot get the marks. For example, questions stating 'With the use of examples …' may allocate one-third or half of the marks to the examples used.

Types of essay

There are three main types of essay – description, explanation and evaluation.

- **Descriptive** essays are the easiest and require factual recall.
- **Explanatory** essays require you to give reasons for a feature, pattern or process.
- **Evaluation** expects an opinion based on the evidence presented throughout the essay.

Writing an essay

Planning is essential. Quality is more important than length. One way of planning an essay is known as the **points-group-order** method. Write down a list of points that are relevant to the essay and then group them, and finally put them into order of importance. Other useful techniques for selecting and presenting information are mind maps and branching maps.

Writing the introduction is a key skill. Most examiners have a good idea of the grade a candidate will achieve after they have read the introduction! The introduction should:

■ define the terms
■ show the line of argument to be taken
■ list the main factors
■ state which examples and case studies will be used.

The introduction needs to be clear and full of impact, rather like the introduction in a newspaper article which catches your attention, shows the main line of argument, and has you wanting more.

The main body of the essay develops the argument(s). Each paragraph should have a key sentence or point and the rest of the paragraph explains and provides evidence. Paragraphs must be linked, and this is done in a variety of ways:

■ referring back to the point above
■ linking in a time-sequence
■ comparisons
■ contrasts.

The conclusion is more than just a summary. It may:

■ assess the changing nature of the topic
■ examine the changing importance of factors involved
■ draw out the uniqueness of the material used
■ look at the contrasts between developed countries and developing countries
■ look to the future
■ end with a question, for example 'Even if we can predict earthquakes and volcanoes can we stop people from living in hazardous areas?'.

Answering structured questions

The type of answer depends upon the type of question. For example the question may ask you to:

■ list
■ describe
■ explain
■ evaluate
■ compare
■ contrast.

For example, for a question such as '**State** three reasons why earthquakes occur' only a list of points is needed as in the example here.

Earthquakes occur as a result of:

■ plate movement
■ the construction of large dams and
■ the underground testing of nuclear weapons.

By contrast, a question which says '**Describe** the problems caused by earthquakes in an urban area that you have studied' looks for more **detail** and the use of **local information**. It is also asking for **full sentences**. An answer might read:

'The problems caused by earthquakes include primary hazards such as the loss of life and collapse of buildings and infrastructure as well as secondary hazards such as fire and contaminated water supplies. At Kobe in 1995 over 5000 people were killed, 30 000 injured and 750 000 made homeless. In addition, conditions were made worse by heavy rain and strong winds which made landslides a real possibility. Damp, unhygienic conditions helped spread disease, while fire, broken glass and broken water pipes delayed and hampered the rescue effort.'

Similarly, if the question is '**Explain** …' the answer requires **explanation** and **full sentences**. For example:

'The earthquake at Kobe was caused by the subduction of the Philippine plate underneath the Eurasian plate. The worst affected areas were those built upon loose, unconsolidated materials which liquefied when repeatedly shaken by the earth tremors.'

Questions which ask the candidate to '**evaluate**' require some assessment of the importance of the earthquake and its unique conditions. For example, the effects of the Kobe earthquake were made worse due to the fact that most people had little or no insurance cover, as the area was thought to be tectonically stable. It would also be possible to **compare** the problem of hazards in developed and developing countries.

Using case studies

Certain phrases used in exam questions tell you when to use case studies. Some of these are quite straightforward, for example 'Using an example from your studies …' or 'With reference to an area you have studied …' or 'For a named industry/city/region that you have studied …'. Even if you are not asked directly for case studies you should use them, as they support your answer with real-life examples.

Using case studies is essential for good grades in your exam. A case study is a detailed real example of something you have studied. For example, a flood, city, region or country. When you use case studies in an exam make sure you use:

- a real located example with a sketch map
- key facts and figures which support your views
- geographical terms as much as possible.

Do not write everything you know about the example. Select the information which fits in with the question being asked.

All exam boards expect you to learn about case studies within the UK plus a range from other parts of the world. A few syllabuses actually name the other countries (check with your teacher whether yours is one of these). Other syllabuses leave the choice to the teacher.

index

Acknowledgements

The Authors and Publishers would like to thank the following for their permission to use the following photographs.

1.2 The Natural History Museum, London; 1.5 M.R. Hill; 1.8 University Library, Cambridge; 1.13 Space Frontiers, Planet Earth Pictures; 1.17 Richard Powers, Life File; 1.18 Penny Tweedie, Colorific; 1.23 David Burnett, Colorific; 1.29 Alex Quesada/Matrix, Colorific; 1.33 John Greenlees; 1.37 James Aronovsky/Picture Group, Colorific; 1.40 Michael Yamashita, Colorific; 1.43 John Chaffey; 1.44 Jean-Claude Coutausse, Colorific; 2.6 Gary Braasch/Wheeler Pictures, Colorific; 2.11 Alex Williams/Planet Earth, Telegraph Colour Library; 2.19 Richard Dobson, Telegraph Colour Library; 2.23 Wayne Shakell, Life File; 2.28 Kieran Murray, Ecoscene; 2.29 Richard Powers, Life File; 2.34 Raghubir Singh, Colorific; 2.35 Small Planet Photography, Telegraph Colour Library; 2.36 Jim Pickerell, Colorific; 2.41 Stephen Simpson, Telegraph Colour Library; 2.42 Sally Morgan, Ecoscene; 2.48 Martin Jones, Ecoscene; 2.50 M. R. Hill; 2.53 Claus Meyer/Camara Tres, Colorific; 2.55 F.P.G.(c) A. Montes de Oca, Telegraph Colour Library; 2.56 John Chaffey; 3.24 Trackair aerial surveys; 4.1 Popperfoto; 4.2 Pictor International Ltd; 4.3 Mary Evans Picture Library; 4.5 Mary Evans Picture Library; 4.10 Maya Vidon/AFP Photo, Popperfoto; 4.24 Pictor International Ltd; 4.26 Scott Olson/Reuters, Popperfoto; 4.30 Pictor International Ltd; 4.33 Reed Saxon, Associated Press; 4.40b, 4.40c Pictor International Ltd; 4.47 Richard Lee Kaylin, Telegraph Colour Library; 4.49 Charles Bennett, Associated Press; 4.51 Charles Bennett, Associated Press; 4.55 Mark Edwards, Still Pictures; 4.59 David Levenson, Colorific; Graham Cross, Colorific; 4.65 Charlie Gray; 4.68 Popperfoto; 4.69 David Levenson, Colorific; 4.75 Charlie Gray; 4.76 Charlie Gray; 4.84 Popperfoto; 4.85 Popperfoto; 4.87 Charlie Gray; 4.88 Dylan Garcia, Still Pictures; 4.93 Edward Parker, Still Pictures; 5.10 Charlie Gray; 5.12 V.C.L., Telegraph Colour Library; 5.16 Thompson Studio Recording, Telegraph Colour Library; 5.17 Pictor International; 5.18 Sophie Molins, The Hutchison Library; 5.36 J Sims, Telegraph Colour Library; 5.37 Pictor International Ltd; 5.44 Bavaria - Bildagentur, Telegraph Colour Library; 5.46 Bavaria - Bildagentur, Telegraph Colour Library; 5.49 Yun Suk-bong/Reuters, Popperfoto; 5.50 Alberto Garcia/Christian Aid, Still Pictures; 5.57 Ford Motor Company; 5.61 Mercedes Benz; 5.63 Popperfoto; 5.64 David Hoffman, Still Pictures; 5.67 Alex Quesada/Matrix, Colorific; 5.71 courtesy of Meadowhall Shopping Centre; 5.72 Mark Edwards, Still Pictures; 6.13 Thomas Muscionico/Contact, Colorific; 6.15 Popperfoto; 6.19 Penny Tweedie, Colorific; 6.24 F.P.G. (c) Jim Mejuto, Telegraph Colour Library; 6.25 Leroy Woodson/Wheeler Pictures, Colorific; 6.37 M.R. Hill; 6.38 M.R. Hill; 7.3 J. Green/Poetical Sketches of Scarborough, Mary Evans Picture Library; 7.4 Popperfoto; 7.10 AFP/Mohammed Al-Sehiti, Popperfoto; 7.13 Pictor International Ltd; 7.15 Martyn Hayhow/Reuters, Popperfoto;

7.17 Pascal Rossignol/Reuters, Popperfoto, 7.18 M.R. Hill; 7.20 Crispin Rodwell/Reuters, Popperfoto, 7.21 Jonathan Scott, Planet Earth Pictures; 7.22 Masterfile, Telegraph Colour Library; 7.26 V.C.L., Telegraph Colour Library; 7.30 M.R. Hill; 7.31 F.P.G. (c) E. Garcia, Telegraph Colour Library; 7.32 Randa Bishop/Contact, Colorific; 7.35 Jeremy Hoare, Life File; 7.36 Sue Cunningham, SCP; 7.38 Bob Thomas, Popperfoto; 7.39 The Press Association Limited; 7.45 M. Gratton/Vision, Popperfoto; 8.8 M.R. Hill; 8.10 Gil Moti, Still Pictures; 8.20 Paul Ferraby, Ecoscene; 8.21 Mark Edwards, Still Pictures; 8.22 Gil Moti, Still Pictures; 8.24 Colin Monteath, Mountain Camera; 8.26 Rafiqur Rahman/Reuters, Popperfoto; 8.39 David Woodfall, NHPA; 8.59 John Greenlees; 9.1 John Chaffey; 9.13 John Greenlees; 9.16 John Farmar, Skyscan Photolibrary; 9.18 John Farmar, Skyscan Photolibrary; 9.24 Roger Wilmshurst, Frank Lane Picture Agency; 9.26 J. Sims, Telegraph Colour Library; 9.29 John Chaffey; 9.30 Jon Arnold, Telegraph Colour Library; 9.35 Maps reproduced from the Ordnance Survey mapping iwht the permission of the Controller of Her Majesty's Stationery Office © Crown Copyright; Licence Number 399450; 9.38 Hans Dieter Brandl, Frank Lane Picture Agency; 9.39 V.C.L, Telegraph Colour Library; 10.18 Curtis Martin, Telegraph Colour Library; 10.31 Shamil Zhumatov/Reuters, Popperfoto; 10.38 Associated Press; 10.41 Boccon-Gibod/Black Star, Colorific; 10.43 G Deichmann/ANA Press, Colorific; 11.3 C. Carvalho, Frank Lane Picture Agency; 11.9 John Chaffey; 11.11 John Chaffey; 11.13 John Cleare, Mountain Camera; 11.15 M.R. Hill; 11.17 John Greenlees; 11.19 John Chaffey; 11.20 John Chaffey; 11.26 Geoscience Features Picture Library; 11.28 John Greenlees; 11.31 John Greenlees; 11.34 North York Moors National Park; 11.36 Frank Lane Picture Agency; 11.43 Maps reproduced from the Ordnance Survey mapping the permission of the Controller of Her Majesty's Stationery Office © Crown Copyright; Licence Number 399450; 11.44 C.M. Dixon; 12.1 Rafiqur Rahman/Reuters, Popperfoto; 12.2 M.R. Hill; 12.14 AFP/Naeg, Popperfoto; 12.22 John Chaffey; 12.39 J.P. Fruchet, Telegraph Colour Libary; 12.45 Space Frontiers, Telegraph Colour Library; 12.48 Savita Kirloskar/Reuters, Popperfoto; 14.1 M.R. Hill; 14.3 Julio Etchart/Reportage, Still Pictures; 14.4 M.R. Hill; 14.8 Popperfoto; 14.10 David Money; 14.12 Rosemary Greenwood, Ecoscene; 14.22 Martin Jones, Ecoscene; 14.32 Clyde H. Smith, Still Pictures; 14.37 John McConnico, Associated Press; 14.42 Marcelo del Pozo/Reuters, Popperfoto; 15.1 V.C.L., Telegraph Colour Library; 15.7 Penny Tweedie, Colorific; 15.12 Supri/Reuters, Popperfoto; 15.21 Mark Edwards, Still Pictures; 15.25 Joel Creed, Ecoscene; 15.29 Chris Mattison, Frank Lane Picture Agency; All other photos Garrett Nagle.